Providing global models that are insta[...] useful to public policymakers, the b[...] shows how to apply the public administra[...] tion methods it describes. The models allow for quick translation of theoretical principles into workable strategies that bring results. A systems study is included of the strategic urban planning currently utilized in Paris, France.

Considering the major impact that the decisions of public administrators have on society today, this handbook is a must for all students and practitioners in the field. It stands alone as a volume of expert guidance on problems that are prevalent today in the public sector, as well as problems that will be more frequent in the future.

About the editor . . .

An international authority on the administration of large-scale organizations, **John W. Sutherland** is the author of five major books in the field, as well as of numerous scholarly papers. He has also served as a consultant to five national governments and many large multinational commercial enterprises. Currently chairman of the Department of Administrative Science at Southern Illinois University, Dr. Sutherland has held professorial positions at the University of British Columbia, UCLA, CUNY, and Rutgers University.

Management Handbook For Public Administrators

Management Handbook For Public Administrators

Editor:

John W. Sutherland
Chairman, Department of Administrative Sciences
Southern Illinois University
Carbondale, Illinois

Assistant Editor:

Augusto Legasto, Jr.
Department of Economics
Rutgers University
New Brunswick, New Jersey

 VAN NOSTRAND REINHOLD COMPANY
NEW YORK   CINCINNATI   ATLANTA   DALLAS   SAN FRANCISCO
LONDON   TORONTO   MELBOURNE

. . . the editor's effort in developing this volume is dedicated to the moment—and the memory—of Barry M. Richman, late Chairman of the Management faculty at U.C.L.A. That he will never see this work is a source of great sadness to me, for it owes so much to his inspiration and enthusiasm.

J.W.S.

Van Nostrand Reinhold Company Regional Offices:
New York   Cincinnati   Atlanta   Dallas   San Francisco

Van Nostrand Reinhold Company International Offices:
London   Toronto   Melbourne

Copyright © 1978 by Litton Educational Publishing, Inc.

Library of Congress Catalog Card Number: 78-1465
ISBN: 0-442-28073-4

Manufactured in the United States of America

Published by Van Nostrand Reinhold Company
135 West 50th Street, New York, N. Y. 10020

Published simultaneously in Canada by Van Nostrand Reinhold Ltd.

15 14 13 12 11 10 9 8 7 6 5 4 3 2 1

Library of Congress Cataloging in Publication Data

Main entry under title:

Management handbook for public administration.

 Includes index.
 1. Public administration—Addresses, essays, lectures. I. Sutherland, John W. II. Legasto, Augusto.
JK1351.M33   350   78-1465
ISBN 0-442-28073-4

And he gave it for his opinion, that whoever could make two ears of corn or two blades of grass to grow upon a spot of ground where only one grew before, would deserve better of mankind, and do more essential service to his country, than the whole race of politicians put together.

Jonathan Swift

Preface

The men and women who administer the range of public enterprises are the first-line servants of the public interest. They are the authors of our infrastructure, the husbanders of our communal resources, the producers of social goods, and the guardians of our collective health, welfare, security, and cultural integrity. On them devolve the most awesome analytical, organizational, and procedural challenges—and the most emphatic ethical and ideological constraints. The arena in which they must operate is fraught with complexity and confusion. Errors of judgment have the most profound and resonant consequences. In short, the public sector—at virtually all levels and in essentially all aspects— imposes the most significant and constant demands for administrative sophistication. The purpose of this handbook is to gather together as complete as possible a collection of suggestions as to how best to meet these demands.

This purpose can really be served only to the extent that public administration is lent a life and substance uniquely its own, and set somewhat apart from the dominating influences of political science and business studies under which it has so long labored. For public administration is something *different* from the reportage on the "realities" of political life and the peculiarities of political structure that so concern the traditional political scientist. It has normative and technical components that political science studies do not well comprehend. And public administration is something *more* than business administration, for the analytical and procedural demands that fall on the administrator in the public domain are usually far more complex than those faced by his commercial or industrial counterpart. It is the "different" and the "more" that mark the domain of inquiry of the essays in this inaugural edition of the handbook. What emerges, hopefully, is the first coherent presentation of public administration as a proper science. Because the field is still in its adolescence, there is more emphasis on concept, philosophy and imagination than on instruments or techniques. Yet the collective contributions in this volume bring great satisfaction to those of us who have been watching this young discipline exercise itself and grow toward genuine pragmatic significance.

With this end in mind, I asked the prospective authors *to define, within their respective realms of interest and expertise, those points that could be deemed minimally essential for successful, disciplined operations in the governmental, public and not-for-profit sectors.* The implicit suggestion was that, to the extent possible, they avoid treating subjects or raising arguments and issues that are dealt with elsewhere, in the existing literature of, for example, business administration, industrial engineering, economics, and political science. Finally, I asked the authors to give their individual subjects all the sophistication they deserved, and to refrain from making any assumptions about the background, interests, or sophistication of the potential readers of the handbook. This is an important point, for public administrators are not the placid, uninterested, and ill-schooled functionaries that many suggest. Indeed, the skills, talents, technical expertise, and intellectual stature of public administrators have undergone the most dramatic transformation over the last two decades. The stereotype of the self-satisfied, anti-intellectual, plodding civil servant is no longer tolerable. Thus, this editor makes no apology for the level of argument and discussion that the contributors have achieved. The papers contained in this volume will impose considerable challenge on the reader. The subjects treated here are not trivial; the instruments and procedures offered the public administrator are not mere expedients. Rather, the level of discussion merely reflects the magnitude of the analytical challenge that operations in the public sector impose. Thus, it is the set of realities the public administrator must deal with—not mere scholastic caprice—that has dictated the high level of sophistication of the contributions. To respond with less sophistication would be to abrogate the responsibilities the academic community owes its constituents.

Of the 150 and more essays that were proposed for consideration, only about 30 passed through all the various stages of evaluation and review to take their place in this volume. More contributions could, perhaps, have been included, but at the expense of the integrity of the volume itself. For the test of this *Handbook* must be the extent to which the reader captures the enthusiasm, energy, wit, and dedication of the individual authors—and the extent to which the insights, instruments, and procedures presented in these pages can be entered in the management calculus of the practicing public administrator. An equally critical test will be the extent to which the work we have done here accelerates evolution of public administration as a dignified academic discipline. Without question then, the rapidity with which both the art and science of public administration is carried beyond the horizons we have set here will be the surest sign of success for the authors and this editor.

JOHN W. SUTHERLAND

Contents

Management Handbook For Public Administrators

PART I

Components of a Public Administration Strategy

The five chapters that open our inquiry into public administration view the subject from the very broadest possible perspectives. Jacob Fried and Paul Molnar have developed an instrument that is widely considered to be the most "intelligent" tool for aligning an organization with the nature of the environment in which it exists and the mission it is to perform. Such an alignment is the first order of business for the senior executives of any public enterprise. In the second chapter, August Smith introduces us to the modern, system science concept of the way in which management functions should be organized and structured in complex enterprises; thus, he goes "beyond business administration" and into the kind of strategic considerations that are so vital to a proper theory of public administration. Peter Gomez deals with the development of a system-based, problem-solving methodology. Looking at management processes from the standpoint of the cybernetician, he develops a much-needed link between the world of advanced theory and the domain of practical managerial capability. Augusto Legasto then uses one of the dominant analytical instruments of our time—system dynamics—to show how the public executive might go about systematizing and rationalizing the highest-order functions of government: the management of the social and economic sectors. Finally, Michel Chevalier and Tom Burns offer us an insight into the complicated world of intergovernmental relations placing the issue of collective versus individual initiative into a disciplined, analytical framework.

1

Organizational Patterning Analysis: An Instrument for Structuring Complex Systems

Jacob Fried and Paul Molnar
Portland State University

INTRODUCTION

ˌModern industrial civilization is characterized by large, complex enterprise in every aspect of government: health services, education, *etc.* Unlike certain technological or scientific activities (though extremely complex, they are, nevertheless, highly rational, controllable, and predictable) many economic, social, and political behaviors of equal if not greater complexity are neither controllable nor predictable. What is becoming increasingly obvious in modern industrial society is that technological and scientific aspects of operations are merged with, and profoundly affected by, economic, social, or political circumstances. To "manage" the real world implies a need to orchestrate and balance a mixture of "open" and "closed" characteristics that are inevitably part of the structure of an enterprise. To treat the real world of complex affairs as reflecting clean-cut dichotomies of "closed" (predictable, *e.g.*, technological) *versus* "open" (unpredictable, *e.g.*, social) systems would ill serve the administrator and planner as practical models in many government and private corporations. The effective manager would, therefore, benefit from an instrument that could help him perceive what is going on in a complex field of interactions in which heterogeneous elements, such as men, machines, ideologies, and social institutions and conditions all combine to produce both intended and unintended results. When such a comprehensive grasp of the underlying dynamics of the complex situation is achieved, planning a course of action can take place under especially favorable conditions.

The search for effective planning and evaluating instruments has produced numerous models and techniques, such as Forrester's Systems Dynamics, the Critical-Path and PERT methods, and the Management-by-Objectives technique. Yet none of these approaches succeeds in producing a model and procedures that can both help the manager to choose an appropriate goal and to select an advantageous strategy for attaining that goal. Nor can any of these techniques evaluate the inherent organizational viability of a system. PERT and Critical-Path methods can only pinpoint bottlenecks that have already been embodied in a system's design. We find that systems dynamics fails to provide a theoretical framework for specifying what classes of data must be included or utilized as variables in order to model an enterprise. The Management-by-Objectives technique will permit a manager to determine how to achieve a specific chosen end in the best cost-effective manner, but it cannot determine whether achieving such an end will have favorable or unfavorable effects on a complex enterprise as a whole.

In sum, the techniques above are not associated with a *general* theory of organization, that alone would permit a comprehensive analysis of an enterprise as an ongoing process in which all elements that interact either contribute to or block the achievement of an effective overall pattern of organization. In addition, only a general theory of this sort will provide a common frame of reference for translating mixed categories of descriptive information into a single, interpretive overview of an ongoing, complex enterprise. For example, a manager today can be inundated with information supplied by engineers, economists, industrial psychologists, lawyers, *etc*. He cannot leave such information segregated in different compartments if he wants to form a comprehensive and coherent picture of the enterprise as a whole.

True, a manager cannot ignore the technical details of all the separate components of his operation and concern himself primarily with the economic success or failure of the "end product." If he did, a profitable outcome could mask serious operational dysfunctions—though only temporarily. We do assert, however, that a planless attempt to run down and identify this or that specific cause of difficulty in a complex enterprise—by assigning an array of individual experts to investigate each possible subsegment of the enterprise—will be quite futile. Such experts are of necessity narrow and parochial in their skills, and cannot supply an analysis based on interactions affecting the whole system. They may, indeed, identify certain real problems in specific areas, but attempts to rectify these difficulties can actually have adverse effects throughout the system unless there is the ability to analyze the effects of implementing recommended changes by an adequate model of the total field.

It is certainly not our intention to belittle or remove experts from planning or evaluating complex enterprises, but rather to suggest a better way to use their expertise. No manager could perform his function without the information and advice of knowledgeable experts and specialists, but he has to know *when* to use them, in what *context*, and how to interpret and evaluate their specific inputs. As we see it, the manager is the "middle man" who translates policy decisions about goals into operational procedures that produce objective and desirable results. Though policy-making is an essential feature of all complex enterprise, it must be linked to actual operations in a viable design. This is the manager's task. Though he may not be the source of policy, he must be able to understand the mutual interplay of policy and implementation and gauge their fit and viability.

We will suggest a model that we believe will permit a manager to create a *synoptic* picture of the field of interactions he must manage. This is accomplished by explicitly including political and managerial behaviors in the same frame of analysis as operational and technological procedures.

ORIGINS OF THE MODEL

Our model grew out of an exploration of the role of technology in culture change. We, as anthropologists, find that the resources of our discipline fall far short of supplying us with models that explain how technology and social organization affect one another in complex, modern society, even though there are heuristic models, especially in the field of culture ecology, that describe these relationships for simpler hunting, agricultural, or pastoral societies. Despite the limitations of current anthropological theory, we wish to preserve the holistic approach that is implied in the anthropological theory of culture. Critical for this presentation is the assumption that culture is a complex and heterogeneous system. Hence, analytic models designed to explore culture can be utilized to analyze many of its component subsystems. Thus, a related assumption is that industrial, military, medical, or other enterprises complex enough to display intertwining political, managerial, and technological behaviors will reflect processes typical of "culture" as a whole.

As anthropologists, we believe that technology, management, and politics cannot be treated as separate substantive entities at higher synthetic levels of analysis (this despite the convenience of doing so for various specialized technical reasons). We are convinced that an "additive" approach, rather than a dynamic, interactive frame of reference for modeling such interactions, will always fail to be effective in analyzing complex systems. The problems facing anthropologists, administrators, and managers of complex enterprises alike is the need to understand the process of change and adaptation via an *explicit theory*, rather than to expect mere masses of data to sort themselves into explanations.

The logical requirements for models that treat *processes* rather than mere events make it mandatory that we have a method for translating empirical or objective data into *abstract relational categories*. In other words, accumulating a lot of empirical data about some phenomenon does not inform us about how and why it is occurring. Whether those data concern industrial production statistics or cultural patterns of shearing sheep, the issue is the same for the model. Therefore, the first requirement of the model is that it must not be affected operationally by the nature of the subject matters utilized as data. It must be able to treat complex computer systems as easily as bow-and-arrow technologies. What is needed is a universal, generalized set of variables that is not specific or empirical in nature, but represents abstract, relational concepts. In addition, such variables must be inherently *quantifiable*, so that adequate comparisons within and between systems can be objectively accomplished. Only by creating data categories and variables that are abstract-relational in type—and quantifiable in character—is it possible to develop adequate models for analyzing complex situations with mixed data categories. Thereby we can hope to avoid designing a model that, though dynamically sophisticated in concept, is impractical in application because the data that the model requires are unspecifiable and, therefore, uncollectable (similarly, we avoid models where a great deal of information exists but no analytical procedures are specified.)

Practically speaking, mathematical techniques for manipulating data that are not grounded in a theory that specifies what data are needed—and macromodels that generate data without specifying the dynamics of interaction among them—are equally inadequate for managers. The model we present will specify and generate the relevant categories of data and will provide rules for analyzing their interaction.

THEORETICAL BASIS OF THE MODEL

To carry out any "managerial" activity in the real world, it is necessary to impose a pattern of organization on that activity such that a desired end is achieved. The major, initial issue, theoretically, is to define what we mean by "organization." This must be accomplished in a manner that permits defining its characteristics operationally so that this central concept can be applied in empirical situations. By defining "organization" as a *pattern of constraints imposed on a field of interacting elements*, we are able to translate any number of complex and heterogeneous sets of observed interactions into terms of a single, theoretically significant frame of reference. The actual nature, type, or category of entities involved in the interaction is irrelevant for determining the significance of their interaction. Only their attribute of *imposing constraint* on a resulting overall pattern of organization is relevant for analysis. What the model seeks to bring to light—by defining empirical behaviors as reflections of quantities of constraint—is an assessment of the degree to which an organizational condition is *viable*, given a desired set of objectives. Therefore, to use the model it is necessary to know not only how a manager is going to organize his resources for undertaking some set of tasks, but also what are the organizational requirements of the tasks themselves. Hence, the total model is a balanced relationship between generalized "task requisites" and "organizational responses" to the requisites, as carried out by the agencies that mobilize and utilize their resources in programs of action (Figure 1).

We intend to permit the measurement of adequacy of fit between goals and resources. Therefore, a basic requirement of the model is to utilize variables that measure, by quantitative scales, *degrees of constraint* that characterize "task requisites" and "organizational responses." The function of these variables is to translate empirical behaviors into the abstract-relational measures of constraint required by the model. Such abstract-relational measures of constraint permit the application in the model of certain "information theory" concepts, particularly those dealing with cybernetic processes. In this way, very complex empirical behaviors that are changeable in time and space can be perceived as conforming to patterns of change in organizational relationships. The critical issue, in practical terms, is determining what kinds of relationships are desirable or workable, given a specified set of objectives. The assumption is that *there are some genuine rules for responding to organizational problems, and if you violate them you fail to achieve goals.* It is assumed further that if the goals are beyond organizational resources, proceeding is futile. Also, if an organizational response cannot be coherently designed so that all the elements are doing what they are meant to do, there are many more or less adequate "suboptimal" postures the organization might obtain. In addition, the manager, by examining and measuring the inputs of various technological or administrative elements as specified by the variables of the model, can determine which sector of the operating entity is or is not making the proper level of required response. The model does not and cannot specify what should be done concretely in such

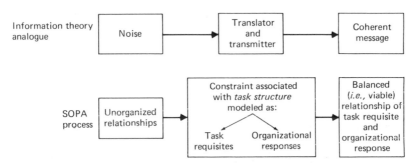

Figure 1. Social Organizational Patterning Analysis (SOPA) Model.

a case, but it does suggest the *direction* of change required to achieve an adequate response.

Given the importance of the concept of constraint to measure organizational conditions, more details about how we apply it in the model are indicated. Constraint is conceptualized as emerging from the interplay of three essential aspects of "action": a set of acting entities, a program of activity for entities to follow, and a setting embodying conditions necessary for the actions to take place. Translated into analytic constructs, these three aspects are termed *dimension*, *program*, and *boundary*. All the variables utilized in the model, therefore, are devised to describe and measure the constraint attributes of these three analytic constructs. There are measures of constraint for each of the variables that describe "task requisites" and others that concern "organizational response."

We derive the capacity of the variables to measure degrees of constraint from an assumption that the amount of constraint associated with a field of interacting entities is directly proportional to its degree of *complexity*. This, in turn, we derive from our assumption that organization *per se* implies that entities— by interacting—are imposing constraints on each other. The more complex the field of relationships and behaviors, the higher the constraint levels, and *vice versa*. Therefore, the three analytic aspects of organization we use to analyze social and technological behavior—dimension, program, and boundary—are described and measured by variables according to their degrees of complexity.

Each variable uses a triad of characteristics of complexity to measure constraint in an actual entity or pattern of behavior. In the detailed description of the model given in the next section, we will show what specific questions are asked of empirical entities and what conditions permit the coding of variables at descriptive levels of constraint in *a continuum from low to high* (see Table 2). Here we need state only that such questions are designed to tell us about properties of *heterogeneity*, *specialization*, *routinization*, and *interdependence* that the entities or behaviors display. The more marked the characteristics of heterogeneity, specialization, routinization, and interdependence, the higher the level of complexity assigned to an entity and its behaviors, and *vice versa*. This empirically derived coding of a level of complexity can now be utilized in the model as a level of constraint.

Analysis, as a set of operations in the model, implies the comparison of patterns of constraint within and between various sectors of the model, as shown in Figure 2. Imbalances exposed by variables coded at different levels of constraint are diagnostic of shifts occurring in a pattern of organization that can lead to dysfunction. In sum, the model operates on a matching/mismatching principle in order to begin the process of interpreting data.

With this knowledge of organizational processes, the manager can perceive in which direction change is occurring and can decide whether or not to reverse the

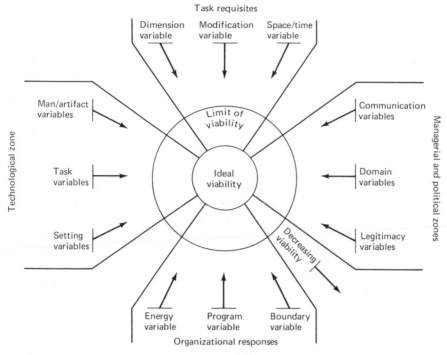

Figure 2. Dynamics of the SOPA model.

changes or to reorganize to make changes consistent with a new direction of responses. He now can conceptualize alternatives of reaction to change by manipulating the value of variables of the "task requisites" or the "organizational responses," separately or together. Clues given in the quantitative levels of imbalances among variables can help in assessing how radical or costly changes will be. The larger the quantitative gap in and between components of the model, the more radical the change required to attain a viable pattern.

TWO VERSIONS OF THE MODEL

There is a general version of the model that can be applied to evaluate, somewhat crudely, the degree to which "organizational responses" match "task requisites" in a viable or unviable format. It exposes the underlying dynamics of change by indicating whether levels of imbalance represent a growing ("amplificatory") or shrinking ("reductionist") trend within an existing pattern, or whether fundamental shifts are occurring that lead to an entirely new pattern of relationships ("transformational") for the system as a whole. This form of the model should be useful to managers at a policy level when they wish to determine in which general direction to plan operational procedures at a time enterprises are undergoing change. Only six variables are required for such "first-cut" analytic exercises: three for measuring constraint characteristics of "task requisites," and three for measuring those of "organizational responses" (Table 1).

The dynamics of the model operates by positing a feedback relationship among the variables of each half of the model and also between the two analytic categories. In brief, the model treats change and adaptation in complex systems as feedback systems, whereby one or another variable, for some reason or other, changes in character, ultimately forcing an accommodating reaction in other variables. In cases in which some variables increase or decrease in degree of constraint and fail to produce resonant changes in the others, we predict a growth of a condition of nonviability for the enterprise.

The way in which scaled values given to variables actually perform this function of indicating relative balance or imbalance in a system is best shown in the illustrative example we supply later.

In a planning or evaluative exercise, all factual data and information about the goals of an enterprise are translated into conditions of organizational constraint surrounding the carrying out of specific *tasks* through which goals are achieved. The variables of the "task requisite" category of the model tell us what questions to ask to code the variables:

1. *Dimensional variable:* What are the size, quantity, shape, and other conditions that characterize the desired end or product?
2. *Modification* (elaboration) *variable:* How much must be done to the elements, behaviors, raw materials, *etc.* before a finished product or end results?
3. *Space/time variable:* How many space and time conditions must be coordinated to bring all elements, behaviors, raw materials, *etc.* together?

The resources of any entity or agency that organizes an activity are evaluated by coding the constraint levels of the variables of the "organizational response" category of the model. These variables direct us to the information we need to accomplish this.

Table 1. Variables.

ORGANIZATIONAL RESPONSES	TASK REQUISITES
Energy	Dimension
Program	Modification
Boundary	Space/time

1. *Energy variable:* In what kinds of "packages"—men, tools, machines, *etc.*— are the units used in activities? In organizational terms what is important about "energy" is not an aspect of physics, but what treats of the organizational characteristics of the entities through which energy is channeled into activity. The quantity of energy involved is not a concern of the variable. Whether the channeling units are single, multiple, or heterogeneous in character has great organizational significance.
2. *Control variable:* What kinds of managing formats are available to program the activities of the available units that provide or channel energy?
3. *Boundary variable:* What are the limits of time and space within which the available programs are effective or can be applied?

The more detailed version of the model can be used to permit managers to assess in more detail their existing organizational capacities against future needs when specific innovations in technological or managerial activities are being contemplated. Or it can be utilized to diagnose the sources of dysfunctions in a current, complex situation. This form of the model is capable of indicating whether the problem areas are located in technological, managerial, or policy sectors of organization. These analytic and diagnostic capabilities stem from the ability of the model to distinguish between technological, managerial, and political zones of analysis, while permitting their interaction and impacts on each other to be modeled.

To solve the problem of how to include all the rich and heterogeneous data categories—treating engineering, economic, political, psychological, and sociological factors—in a single unified model, we assert that they all will fall into one of three basic zones of activity. Whenever activities concern manipulation of the physical universe by men, tools, or machines, they are to be modeled in a "technological zone." Whenever an activity is complex enough to require administrative manipulation of a series of activities to integrate or organize them, such behaviors are modeled in a "managerial zone." Finally, whenever "managerial" activities are complex enough to require an overall management, a "political zone" of activity emerges.

Each zone of the model utilizes the basic dimensional, program, and boundary analytic categories, but in more specific terms by using three different variables to describe and measure each of these analytic constructs. At least three points are required to describe a pattern of relationships. Thus, each zone is divided into three "components," representing the three basic analytic categories, measured by three variables. Hence, the operations of a complex enterprise can be modeled by measuring only 27 variables (Table 2).

To model the organizational characteristics of the "technological zone," we utilize three "components," each described and measured by three variables. These three "components," as noted earlier, represent the three analytic con-

Table 2. The 27 variables.

Technology

Man-artifact component
Locus of dominance variable
Complexity of assemblage variable
Phases of unit interaction variable

Task component
Serial characteristic variable
Operations-output variable
Output form variable

Setting component
Setting structure variable
Locus of input variable
Autonomy variable

Social organization

Communications component
Locus of authority variable
Number of channels of communication variable
Complexity of linkage component

Domain component
Size/quantity variable
Heterogeneity variable
Concentration variable

Legitimacy component
Boundary of authority variable
Social control variable
Locus of validation variable

---

structs that tell us about the characteristics of the action units themselves (the man/artifact component); the programs of action they engage in (the task component); and the setting conditions that surround action (the setting component).

The managerial and political zones both represent basic aspects of social organization, and are likewise analyzed by utilizing three "components" that tell us about the organizational characteristics of action units (the communications component), the programs of action they engage in (the domain component), and the requisite setting conditions for action of a "managerial" variety (the legitimacy component). Thus, they do not differ from the components of the technological zone as abstract-analytic constructs, but they do require differently designed variables to reflect the differences between behaviors of a direct technological nature and those that concern organizational procedures of a social or "managerial" nature.

As we explained in the discussion of the six-variable version of the model above, we assume there is a feedback relationship affecting the contributions or interventions of all three zones on each other, such that effective or viable programs of action are facilitated or blocked by the inputs made by all contributing and interacting elements. The ability to judge effective *versus* defective contributions of elements of a system depends on the capacity of our variables to tell us what levels of performance different input entities are achieving. The technological zone will tell us about how well-designed are the men-equipment-action configurations (programs) for given tasks. The managerial zone will tell us how well agencies are able to control and manage the resources allocated to a given undertaking. The political zone will tell us if the policy-making level does, indeed, have the means and resources to support its lower managerial echelons.

We can indicate only very generally here how the variables are designed to tell us about what is happening in each component of a zone. A more complete account is appended to this Chapter.

In the *technological zone*, the three variables of the "man/artifact component" tell us: 1) how open-ended or tightly organized the action units are as teams (men and machines); 2) how simple, complex, or numerous the action units are; and 3) how simple or multiphased the interactions are within and among action units.

The three variables of the "task component" tell us whether: 1) tasks are completed soon after initiation of action or after a series of actions over time; 2) whether outputs or results are achieved or occur at the immediate locale of operations or at some distant place; and 3) whether or not procedures are capable of being routinized.

The three variables of the "setting component" tell us whether: 1) inputs to operations can be relatively random or variable, as opposed to highly structured and controlled; 2) whether inputs come only from narrow, localized sources, or must be assembled from diverse places; and 3) whether a high degree of autonomy exists for action units because resources are few and simple, or whether a high degree of interdependence exists due to the complexity of inputs required for the task.

In the two zones of *social organization*, the three variables of the "communications component" tells us: 1) whether authority is shared and diffuse or concentrated in a single entity; 2) whether an agency has many or few channels of communication; and 3) whether single commands or a chain of linked commands directly manage an activity.

The "domain component" tells us: 1) whether the managerial agent or agency is small in scale and individualized, or represents complex, multiunit entities; 2) whether the managerial entity is composed of simple generalized units or heterogeneous, specialized ones; and 3) whether managerial activities are confined to a narrow sector of activity spatially, or extend to encompass distant units.

The "legitimacy component" tells us: 1) whether authority extends over a single area or a series of areas of jurisdiction and control; 2) whether a managerial entity has low or high coercive powers to ensure compliance of managed units; and 3) whether claims to authority have a temporary or personal nature, or an impersonal, technical, legal, or ideological nature.

In assigning levels of constraint to variables, we assumed that simple and homogeneous conditions and behaviors imply less constaint—in organizational terms—than complex and heterogeneous conditions and behaviors. We have devised a scale, where 1 is the lowest level and 10, the highest, to measure levels of constraint in each of the above variables, and we will illustrate how to apply the variables in analytic exercises in the next two sections.

We believe the model in its two forms offers the manager an enormously simplified and compressed interpretation of the dynamics of his organization. Instead of facing an awesome array of data presented in the specialized terminology of engineering, economic, or legal disciplines, the manager now has only a small number of significant variables to interpret, all in the context of a single frame of reference.

APPLYING THE MODEL: SIX-VARIABLE VERSION

The flow charts (Figures 3 and 4) represent in schematic form how a manager would move through various stages in order to analyze a given enterprise in the model. First we will illustrate the version of the model that deals with generalized responses to change. Here the six-variable version of the model is utilized. Such an exercise will yield a "rough and ready" product, but one of considerable use to managers when faced with the need to make decisions where data categories are hypothetical or highly qualitative in nature, or when actual empirical data and observation cannot be acquired to scale variables. For example, various experts' evaluations or estimates of future conditions can be used to code variables.

This generalized form of the model permits descriptive data not specifically or originally generated by applying our methods (see below) to be utilized.

1.0 *Problem selection.* Once the manager selects a target situation for analysis, that target must embody two features.

1.1 The analysis must consistently concern only those entities or interactions actually involved within a delimited frame or setting. Since complex operations can be analyzed at various levels, this level must be specified. The minimal unit of analysis can be a single operation of a larger complex of activities, provided that it concerns a total input-throughput-output cycle, and not some open-ended segment of a larger action. Or,

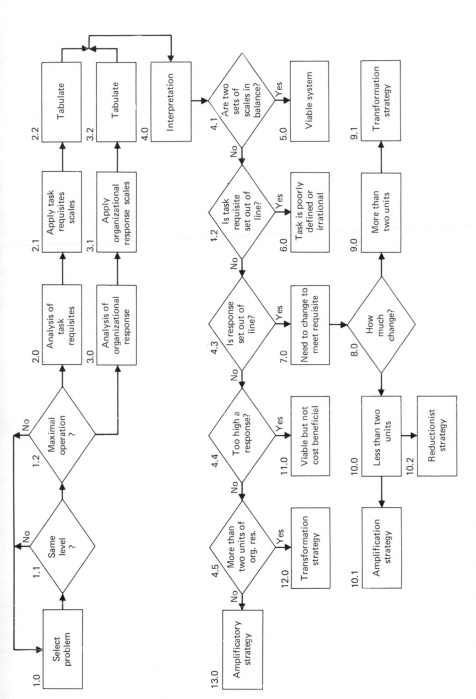

Figure 3. Six-variable version.

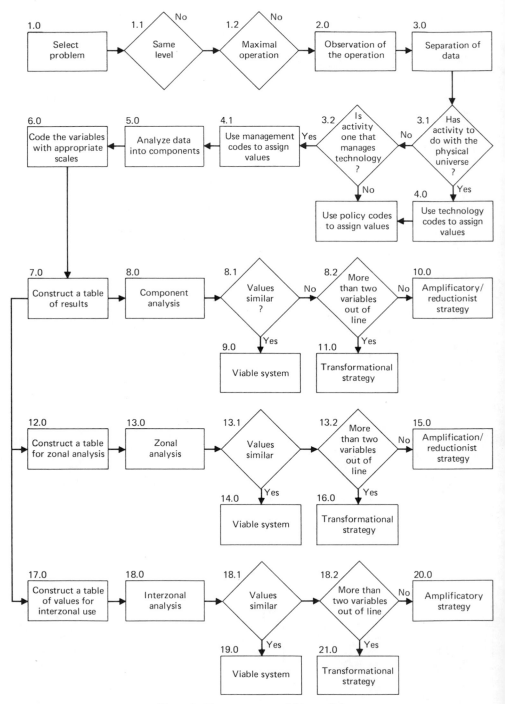

Figure 4. Twenty-seven-variable version.

it can concern the total, overall design of a set of linked operations and their ultimate products. In either case, one must not mix levels of analysis by mixing actors, actions, and settings from different contexts.

1.2   The second requirement is to choose, from all the involvements of the target set of actors and actions, the most complex or maximal tasks they confront or carry out. Scaled codings derived from analyzing these undertakings then represent the *maximal capacity* to respond available to that entity under those conditions. The assumption is that if the entity can respond effectively to such maximal demands, it can do so to lesser ones.

2.0   *Analysis of task requisites.* Having selected a set of operations for analysis, it is now necessary to conceptualize them in terms of the organization of a task or set of tasks through which goals are achieved. The "task," as a conceptual unit, is composed of three variables, each of which is scaled and whose codings describe its constraint characteristics as a pattern.

2.1   Utilizing the scales that measure each variable, determine a code value (low to high) for each variable.

2.2   Construct a table displaying these coded values for task requisites.

3.0   *Analysis of organizational response.* These organizational responses refer to the entities (workers, tools, machines, executives, *etc.*) who perform activities *via* certain programs in some setting or environment. The behaviors of these entities are delimited by three variables, and are measured by scales that define the pattern of levels of constraint for the organizational response section of the model.

3.1   Utilizing the scales that measure each variable, assign a value to each variable.

3.2   Construct a table displaying the coded values of organizational response.

4.0   *Interpretation of the significance of coded values for task requisites and organizational response.* The interpretation of the data given in the table of coded variables proceeds by asking the following five questions about the data.

4.1   Do the two sets of scales display similar values? If yes, proceed to 5.0; if no, go to 4.2.

4.2   Are discrepancies of levels found in the variables of task requisites? If yes, go to 6.0; if no, go to 4.3.

4.3   Are discrepancies in levels found in variables of the organizational responses? If yes, go to 7.0; if no, go to 4.4.

4.4   Do the variables of the organizational response display a uniform, but higher set of values than those found in the variables of task requisites? If yes, go to 11.0; if no, go to 4.5.

4.5   Do two or all three variables of organizational response display different levels? If yes, go to 12.0; if no, go to 13.0.

5.0   The codings of variables of the task requisite are equivalent to those of the organizational response. This organizational format is viable and cost-effective.

6.0 The scattered codings of the task requisites indicate a poorly designed or irrational task organization. No kind of effective organizational response is possible. The task should be abandoned or redefined.

7.0 The scattered codings of the variables of organizational response indicate a need to change the overall pattern of response. Such a level of response means that there is a failure to meet the requirements for behaviors specified by the task requisites.

8.0 Determine the number of variables that require changes in coded values, and what quantitative changes are required in order to achieve the desired level of response to meet task requisites.

9.0 If two or more variables require changes in coded values, then utilize a *"transformation strategy."*

9.1 A transformation strategy refers to a basic change in the overall pattern of organization (rather than an adjustment within an existing pattern of relationships). Changing two out of three elements will produce an entirely new pattern.

10.0 If only one variable requires a change in coded value, then utilize either an *amplificatory or reductionist strategy* for planning changes; that is, raise or lower constraint values in the variable.

10.1 An "amplificatory strategy" implies maintenance of the existing pattern of organization by raising the single anomalous level of constraint to conform to the levels of the other variables.

10.2 A "reductionist strategy" implies the maintenance of the existing pattern of organization by lowering the single anomalous level of constraint to conform to the levels of the other variables.

11.0 The coded levels of the organizational response are uniform, but consistently higher than those of the task requisite. This is a viable format, but not a cost-effective one. It is an example of redundancy or excess capacity, given the requirements of the task.

12.0 The preferred strategy is that of a "transformational" one (see 9.1 for definition).

13.0 The preferred strategy is either "amplificatory" or "reductionist" (see 10.1 and 10.2 for definition).

APPLYING THE MODEL: 27-VARIABLE VERSION

This is the more detailed, diagnostic version of the model, which is better suited to pinpoint sources of organizational difficulty in an ongoing enterprise where better empirical data are available.

The basic approach to applying this version of the model is the same as for the six-variable exercise. The purpose of this version, however, is *not* to evaluate goals, as embodied in the tasks, but to focus primarily on the organizational response sector of the model. This version seeks to determine if dysfunctions in organizational format exist, and where, specifically, they exist in various technological, managerial, or political aspects of organization.

1.0 *Select problem* (see item 1.0 in the six-variable version).

1.1 Specify level of analysis (see item 1.1 in the six-variable version).

1.2 Select appropriate maximal effort in the enterprise for analysis of organizational capacity (see item 1.2 in the six-variable version).

2.0 Observe directly, or as directed by an expert, the set of operations that make up the total input-throughput-output cycle.

3.0 Separate data for coding into three zones of analysis: technological, managerial, and political zones. To accomplish this respond to the following two questions.

3.1 Does the activity represent a direct operational set of procedures wherein men and materials are being manipulated, transformed, or both? If yes, go to 4.0; if no, go to 3.2.

3.2 Is the activity one in which behaviors concern control or management of the conditions surrounding production or operation? If yes, go to 4.1; if no, go to 4.2.

4.0 A *technological* sector of analysis is involved and the behaviors here are coded by scales measuring specialized technological variables of organization (see Table 2).

4.2 Where behaviors do not directly involve technological or managerial levels of analysis, but concern the articulation of a series of managerial tasks required to achieve an overall organizational goal, this refers to the *political* or policy zone of organization. Behaviors of this zone are coded, however, by the same scales and variables as those of the managerial zone because both represent a sector of social organization at two different levels of analysis.

5.0 Once the data are assembled according to the three zones, they are analyzed within the appropriate "components" that make up each zone.

6.0 Code the three variables of each "component" in each zone, utilizing the scales that measure the variables.

7.0 Construct a table displaying the results. The analysis of the data proceeds through three levels of comparison:
   1. the component level—a pattern of three variables (8.0),
   2. the zonal level—a pattern of three components (12.0), and
   3. the interzonal level—a pattern for all three zones (17.0).

8.0 *Component level of analysis:* to determine a coded value for each component, ask the following two questions.

8.1 Do the values assigned to the variables display similar values? If yes, go to 9.0; if no, go to 8.2.

8.2 Which of the three variables of the component displays discrepancies in value? If one is out of line with the other two variables, go to 10.0; if two or all three display different values go to 11.0.

9.0 The component does not indicate that the empirical entities or behaviors are organizationally nonviable. (A value for the component is assigned by averaging the values of all three variables.)

10.0 There is dysfunction in the organizational format, and the empirical entity whose behavior was used to code the variable is the source of dysfunction. The dysfunction can be overcome by assigning different behaviors to the entity representing an "amplificatory" or "reductionist" strategy (see items 9.1 and 10.1 in the six-variable version). A summative value is given to the component just as in the case where values were uniform.

11.0   A highly dysfunctional pattern exists where all three values of a component are dissimilar in value. All entities or conditions whose behaviors or effects are evaluated are implicated as contributing to an unviable format. A "transformation" strategy is needed to meet this condition (see item 9.1 in the six-variable version). Nevertheless, a summary coding is given the component in order to perform a zonal analysis.

12.0   Construct a table of all summed variables for all three components of each zone.

(13.0–   *Zonal level of analysis.*   Repeat the procedures described by items 8.0
17.0)   through 13.0 above, utilizing assigned values of components as data. Substitute the word *component* for "variable" in all these steps, and proceed as directed.

(18.0–   *Interzonal level of analysis.*   Repeat the procedures described by items
21.0)   8.0 through 13.0 above.   Substitute *zone* for *component*, as in step 13.0.

ILLUSTRATIVE EXAMPLE

Our selection of a complex enterprise to illustrate the model's capabilities was conditioned by the following requirements: 1) the managerial issues should involve both technological and policy interfaces; 2) the enterprise should represent a situation where changes are being contemplated; 3) the enterprise should, therefore, require a comparison of present operational format with some predicted set of future conditions to indicate what strategy of change would be most effective in planning. (The illustration we devised is entirely hypothetical, and is not meant to reflect actual research carried out by our methods.)

A police department of a medium-sized city (approximately 500,000 in population) can furnish a series of problems whose modeling meets these criteria. Among the various activities of a police department, an excellent issue for analysis is the patrol function.

First of all, a police-car-oriented patrolling strategy makes both the policeman and the public to a large extent dependent upon telephone and radio communications technology to initiate activity. By far the largest initial cause of police activity is a telephone call made by a citizen to the police department. These calls are received in a communications center at Police Headquarters where "decisions" are made as to which patrol car or cars are activated to respond.

A primary managerial function is located at the *precinct* level of the police department. The precinct manages the activities of a number of patrol units (cars) that patrol specific areas or districts of the city. Normally, the cars cruise on their routine patrol routes until they either observe some situation that requires their intervention, or, as is more likely, are sent to a specific address or location *via* a command from the radio dispatch system. These latter orders emanate from the headquarters communications center. There are, thus, certain technological aspects to the interface of the patrolman and the public. In addition, patrolman-public interfaces are mediated by precinct administrative personnel. The precinct administration level interface with the policy level can be studied *via* its relations with the central headquarters. The "policy level" refers specifically to the police chief and his administrative staff, who in turn, interface with the mayor, his assistants, and various organs of city government.

The issue for analysis can arise from, let us say, a political decision growing out of fiscal pressures to achieve a more economical police performance. It has been suggested by some "experts" that this can be accomplished by changing the format whereby police cars are dispatched to the scene of disturbances or crimes. The current situation is one in which all calls received from the public are given equal priority by the dispatching center. Cars are assigned in the order in which calls are received. The proposed change is designed to rationalize and improve the system of dispatching cars by assigning priorities to different classes of calls. In addition, not all public calls would lead to assigning a patrol car to the scene; other personnel could be assigned to render assistance to citizens.

This innovation could have profound effects on the precinct level of administration because controls over the behavior of the patrol cars will be more narrowly focused on decisions of a unit located in the central headquarters of the city whereas formerly there was a more balanced *sharing* of such decisions between the precinct's administrative personnel (captains, lieutenants, sergeants) and the central headquarters.

We will now utilize the model to illuminate the organizational issues that might surface under such changes and to predict potential dysfunctions or conflicts of interest that could arise if these administrative reforms were made. The 27-variable version of the model will be utilized to analyze the current situation, and then the projected changes in the system will be analyzed by the six-variable version.

We will assume that the procedures for applying the model have been carried out to the point where numerical values have been assigned to all 27 variables found in the three zones of the model that represent the organizational format of the present system. In this exercise we use a ten-point scale to measure levels of constraint in variables, 1 representing the lowest value, and 10 the highest. T_1 refers to the system before the innovation is introduced, and T_2, to the system after the innovation is introduced.

The analysis of the data summarized in Table 3 will permit us to carry out

Table 3. Component values.

TECHNOLOGICAL ZONE	T_1	T_2	MANAGERIAL ZONE	T_1	T_2	POLITICAL ZONE	T_1	T_2
Man-artifact component	5	3	Communications component	6	3	Communications component	8	9
Task component	5	3	Domain component	4	4	Domain component	8	8
Setting component	3	5	Legitimacy component	7	6	Legitimacy component	8	9

three analytical operations: 1) identify anomalies or inadequacies of organization in the current police patrol organization, and predict the effects of proposed changes in patrolling activity on a) the patrol car, b) the precinct, and c) the central headquarters; 2) interpret the effects of proposed changes in the interface between the three levels of organization in the police department; and 3) give some estimate of the magnitude of organizational change implied by the proposed innovation.

The values assigned to the components of the "technological zone" are utilized to interpret the behaviors of the patrol cars. The pattern of 5,5,3 is indicative of a somewhat open-ended situation (crime and disturbances are relatively diffuse phenomena) being met by police who have considerable leeway, behaviorally, in responding to such situations. The current response is an adequate one in that the patrol unit has more constraint ability than is called for in most situations. The proposed patrol response format we project will produce coded levels of 3,3,5 indicating a *reduction* in the capacity of the patrol car to respond to a somewhat more structured situation (the radio dispatch prioritized system), externally imposed, lowering responses based on the exercise of the patrol officer's judgment. The net effect on patrolmen, we suggest, will be to cause morale problems in that they will resent this loss of initiative. Routine, uneventful patrolling will be judged more boring than before, and the public will be dissatisfied with the lessening direct face-to-face contacts with police following a perceived crisis.

The managerial zone provides coded values of its components to analyze the precinct level of police organization. The coding pattern of the current situation of 6,4,7 indicates a locus of anomaly in the domain component, which measures the adaptive capacity of an organization to respond to situations. Obviously, today the precinct is responding to a very wide and variable set of demands for services, ranging from traffic misdemeanors to outright riots and violent crimes. The police department is organized along a somewhat rigid paramilitary model that is indeed effective in controlling "violent crime" against persons and property, but is not equally effective in providing various noncriminal-related services to the public, where civilian or professional agencies might prove more cost-effective and efficient. The proposed changes in prioritizing patrol cars' responses *via* a central communications center should indeed serve to segregate and specialize police responses by rerouting many social service and noncriminal requests for police action to other departments of the police force or to welfare agencies—both public and private, as well as to other departments of city government. The codings given to the future situation (3,4,6) reflect the reduction of precinct level "channels of communication" and "legitimacy." The net effect is predicted to decrease the responsibilities for responding to diverse situations from the precinct level and shift them to a higher administrative level in that the radio communications center is a headquarters function. That is, there is a shift in managerial function to a higher level, made possible by a new technological innovation. We predict that the precinct's administrative personnel will resent the consequent loss of power. What had formerly been a relatively more autonomous administrative unit has clearly lost ground.

The codings assigned to the components of the political zone indicate that currently, as expected, there is a high level of constraint available in this bureaucratic paramilitary organization (8,8,8). The policy implications of the proposed changes will have certain impacts as indicated (9,8,9) by the new codings. There is even greater concentration of functions directly associated with central headquarters. The somewhat lower domain component coding of 8 reflects the restriction of power of the police department imposed by the political restraints of city government. The policy decision is one representing a compromise between the city government's desire to reduce budgets and yet not offend the public's desire for police protection, and the police department's desire to avoid excessive involvements in noncriminal activities. Calls will be received for services that will not now automatically be responded to by the police themselves. Though there are real gains in this new arrangement for the central headquarters, these may well be perceived at lower echelons of the department as being achieved at their expense.

On the surface, the centralization of response by the police department in establishing a system of prioritizing responses to calls should have several benefits. It will free patrol cars from many purely service-oriented calls, and will permit a more effective concentrated response to criminal activities. The net effect is to increase the numbers of patrolmen available at any given moment without hiring new personnel. In this sense the proposed innovation is cost-effective. This appears to be a clear case of utilizing better technology to make human inputs more efficient. In fact, such technological innovations will make only one sector of police response more efficient, rather than the full range of police response. The public will not perceive telephone communications with the police as satisfying their desire for direct police presence regardless of how futile that presence may be. In addition, the police will, in fact, suffer from the lessening of contact with the public, which provides them with a "feel" for the district they patrol.

An overall inspection of Table 3 shows that the elements in the total system being modeled that exhibit change in values are numerous. This suggests that such an innovation has radical implications for the organizational pattern as a whole. It should prove to be a more difficult innovation to incorporate successfully within the existing organization than it at first appears. It is not merely a question of adding a new and improved communication function at central headquarters, but represents a fundamental change affecting other levels. The general strategy called for cannot be a modest "amplificatory" one in which some elements increase their powers while other elements lose some. Some major changes in management and operational police behaviors are involved that have "transformational" implications: that is, the real balance of power is being shifted in a more fundamental manner than is perhaps perceived, or even intended.

We have shown *via* our hypothetical exercise how the model, in the 27-variable form, might help a manager to analyze the specific implications of a change in one set of operational procedures of the police department, *i.e.*, the patrolling activity. A series of potential difficulties and dysfunctions was predicted to result from the proposed innovation. There is another level of analysis available, however, in which the patrol function is perceived as a single component of a larger range of police activities. Evaluating the impact of such a change throughout the entire police system, in terms of desirable or undesirable effects, may nevertheless lead to a decision to proceed with the innovation on the basis of indications that the entire system would, on the whole, benefit from the proposed change in procedure. The parameters of a single function of a complex agency cannot be used as a frame for viewing the entire system. That is, there are many other police activities besides the patrol function. Because approximately 75-80% of the manpower of a police department is involved in patrolling activities, and it is the most visible aspect of the police function for the public, does not mean that the efficiency of the entire department depends ultimately on the patrol function alone. Subsequent investigation procedures following crimes involving detectives, crime laboratories, data-retrieval systems, *etc.*, in fact are time consuming and expensive aspects of police procedures. Patrolling activity may initiate input procedures, but throughput and output procedures are located in other divisions. Therefore, a change in patrolling procedures may cause the dysfunctions we predict, but this change can have a positive effect, on balance, on the total police system. That is, only criminal behaviors on the part of the public affect these other divisions of the police department, whereas the patrolling officers spend 60-80% of their time serving public, noncrime-related requests for assistance or aid.

In this procedure the unit of analysis is the entire police department and its full range of functions. The focus of the analysis is on the impact of the change in communications-system procedure on the organizational response capabilities of the department in meeting its fundamental responsibilities of preventing crime and maintaining public order.

As in the explication of the 27-variable version, we will assume that the coding procedures for the six variables of the model have been carried out, and that values have been assigned for task requisites and organizational responses (Table 4).

The coded values of the variables of the task requisites sector of the model

Table 4. Variable loadings for total police department.

VARIABLE	TASK REQUISITE	ORGANIZATIONAL RESPONSE T_1	T_2	VARIABLE
Dimension	8	5	7	Energy
Modification	8	5	7	Program
Space/time	8	4	5	Boundary

indicate relatively high degrees of constraint that must be achieved in order for the social control function of the police department to be effective. Nevertheless, we note that the variables of the organizational response category do not achieve the optimal levels of constraint required to match the task requisites.

In analyzing organizational response we have two sets of values, T_1, to represent the preinnovation time period, and T_2, to represent the postinnovation time period. The innovation raises the constraint attributes of the police department in terms of its action units and the efficiency of their programs of use. Prioritizing policy responses, segregating simple service calls from serious criminal events, does increase the number of acting units (cars) available to respond to serious disturbances and crime without increasing numbers of personnel on patrol.

The central communications facility at headquarters does not increase in personnel and thereby cancel the savings in manpower because most new communications functions become automated. New technological capabilities thus permit the same manpower to handle the new communications requirements. The "program" variable indicates a rise in constraint characteristics associated with the new centralized dispatch system, which selects and matches cars with types of calls for service.

Therefore, the trend in "organizational response" is clearly in the required direction, since the task requisites are all too high for the existing response format. It is also clear, however, even with this innovation, which favorably affects action units and their programs, that there is a significant failure to achieve an overall optimal organizational response as evidenced in the much too low values assigned to the boundary variable. Raising the constraint level from 4 to 5, when the task requisites display a level of 8, is much too insufficient.

This, we believe, mirrors a basic difficulty in all democratic societies with reference to social control. Control procedures that could guarantee public order or permit crimes, once committed, to be ruthlessly investigated would be unacceptable in a constitutionally ordered democratic society. There must inevitably be a gap between organizational responses and task requisites in such situations.

In managerial and policy decision-making, however, the use of both the 6- and 27-variable versions of the model permits the evaluation of a set of alternatives in terms of immediate *versus* long range goals. The police department as a whole will benefit from this innovation because the pattern or response has improved from time T_1 to time T_2 as a result of the innovation. Yet, we still maintain that there will be a price to pay for instituting the new prioritizing system of responding to citizen requests for service, but these costs, as we have seen, need not be interpreted as being so high as to suggest that they overweigh results in general systemic improvements.

UTILIZING SOPA RESULTS TO GUIDE FOLLOW-UP ANALYSIS

A major use of the SOPA model is the guidance of the manager in selecting and using other techniques and approaches to solve managerial problems. Once SOPA has been used to identify the major dysfunctions and difficulties in either a current and operating or proposed and innovative set of procedures, then other specialized techniques designed to solve a particular type of dysfunction can be applied directly to the specific problem.

In the police example, three types of dysfunctions were identified and located: those that would directly affect the patrol function, due to the adoption of the prioritizing of messages at the communications center; those that would arise in the course of making technical and administrative adjustments during actual implementation of the new communications technology; and, finally, those that are unavoidable, structural characteristics of a policy department operating under the limitations of a constitutional order in a democratic society.

The types of dysfunctions we predict might occur if the suggested innovation in communications is adopted are: 1) a growing sense of boredom by the patrolman in his routine patrol activity resulting from a lessening of responses to public calls; 2) a growing frustration on the part of the public as a result of fewer contacts with police following perceived emergencies; and 3) an increased frustration on the part of the precinct's command structure as a result of a further shift of control over patrol activity to central headquarters. These major potential dysfunctions, resulting from the adoption of a technique to assign priorities to citizens' calls received at the communications center were, indeed, uncovered by applying the 27-variable version of the SOPA model. We do not claim that our model has the ability to offer specific practical *solutions* to these dysfunctions once they have been identified and located; that is within the scope of other techniques or experts.

The manager, faced with the identified dysfunctions noted above might well opt to use the services of an industrial psychologist or other "human factors" experts to assist in the reduction of boredom in the patrol task. Perhaps other arrangements, such as two-man cars rather than one-man patrols, would be possible with the savings offered by the prioritizing of messages. Two-man cars could at least offer the police officers some convivial conversation while on patrol. It is possible that different styles and varieties of patrolling tactics would also assist the patrolman in overcoming the boredom of a routine patrol. Such matters would have to be resolved by further research and testing procedures, but at least the manager would have sound justification for instituting such research and guiding its perspectives along the lines of the problems discovered by the SOPA procedure.

The decline in morale of the public, potentially a serious problem to the policy-makers—the civic leaders and command structure of the central headquarters of the police department—could possibly, for example, be combatted by a public relations campaign to emphasize the increased activity of the police against serious crime, and the tax savings resulting from the new procedure. Such a campaign, it could be argued, has a good chance to be successful since the "public" in a large city is essentially a heterogeneous and poorly structured entity, and, barring some counterorganizational effort by other political or special interest groups, would remain essentially ineffective in its opposition to the proposed change.

The more efficient use of precinct officers and administrative personnel raises yet other issues for analysis. The precinct is the major managerial unit in the preinnovation structure of the police department, and its partial loss of authority and decision-making power under the new set of arrangements presents serious problems for those responsible for instituting the innovation. The shift toward centralization, implied in the adoption of the prioritizing technique, may well signal the need to reconsider the whole precinct-central headquarters structure. An application of the Management-by-Objective (MBO) approach or perhaps a Task-Force approach, such as was utilized in the NASA program, might well be utilized to suggest new roles and managerial responsibilities for the precinct level in the chain of command within the police department. In any case, the redundancies of certain precinct responsibilities with those of central headquarters would have been only partially reduced through the adoption of the communications innovation. Other changes that produce equally valid, cost-beneficial changes may well result from applying the above techniques to the analysis of the precinct's function within the police department.

The second set of identified difficulties was seen to arise from the actual implementation of the innovation. A certain transition time will necessarily elapse before the new format of prioritizing is able to service the incoming calls effectively. It is clear that the whole procedure, once the policy decision has been made to adopt the innovation, needs careful structuring in phases in its implementation. It is exactly for such kinds of problems that instruments such as PERT and CPM have been designed. These two related techniques become even more effective with prior knowledge about the problems that are to be expected. Clearly these include matters that affect police department affairs and are beyond the narrow limits of the telecommunications network alone. PERT and CPM exercises can structure into their chains of logic these extratechnological factors and make the transition to the new system a much more effective and smoother operation.

Finally, there is a class of dysfunctions that has been identified through the application of the six-variable version of the model. These arise from ideological imperatives linked to preserving a democratic and constitutional order. Although such dysfunctions may be inherently insoluble in a free society, that recognition alone may provide a guide to political leaders and the public to be wary of changes that tend to infringe upon the freedoms of the citizen. The six-variable version offers a potential test for predicting impacts of proposed changes in an institution of social control—the police department. The boundary variables of the model interpret the degree to which these proposed changes potentially interfere with the constitutional liberties of citizens. If the proposed changes imply constraint levels that are too high, they can also imply a political danger to a democratic order. In this manner, SOPA can serve administrators of social control agencies and various legislative bodies that oversee their operations, identifying and checking a drift of bureaucratized agencies toward semitotalitarian controls.

APPENDIX: THE VARIABLES AND THEIR SCALES

Operational Definitions of the Variables of the Generalized Model

A. Variables of the Task Requisites Sector
   1. *Dimensional variable.* What are the size, quantity, shape, and other characteristics that condition the desired end or goal of the product?

Level	*Scale*
1–2	The activity or product concerns entities or conditions whose shape, size, and quantity permit it to be manipulated by the minimal basic single unit of energy available (in the form of a single human being).
3–4	The activity or product concerns entities whose size, quantity, and shape can be manipulated only by adding more action units of the same kind that do the *same* thing as the original units.
5–6	The activity concerns entities whose size, shape, quantity, *etc.* can be manipulated only by adding more units, each of which must perform *different* actions.

7–8   The activity or product concerns entities whose size, quantity, shape, *etc.* can be manipulated only by adding more units, each of which must perform different actions according to *schedule*.

9–10   The activities or products concern activities whose size, quantity, shape, *etc.*, can be manipulated only by diverse energy units performing different actions according to a strict and *fixed* schedule.

   2. *Modification variable.* How much must be done to the elements, behaviors, raw materials, *etc.* before a finished product or end results?

Level   *Scale*

1–2   What is used or acted upon requires no changes in form or content to be used immediately (in its "natural state").

3–4   What is used or acted upon requires some modification in form or content (from its natural status) but this is done by simple addition or subtraction (it remains recognizable).

5–6   What is used or acted upon must be modified in form or content by adding components of different form or content than it is normally associated with.

7–8   What is used or acted upon must be transformed into a condition totally unlike its "natural condition" in order for some limited feature of it to be used in a totally different context.

9–10   What is used or acted upon must not only be transformed from its natural condition, but must be a combination of many elements all of which are unlike their natural states.

   3. *Space-time variable.* How many space and time conditions must be coordinated to bring all elements, behaviors, raw materials, *etc.* together?

Level   *Scale*

1–2   Required inputs are all found in one narrowly limited place and are used *in situ.* Task can be performed at random intervals. Once started, task is completed soon after starting time.

3–4   Required inputs are all found in one place, but that place is extensive. Task must be performed within a fixed time interval once started, but completion time is still short.

5-6 Required inputs come from more than one place and must be trans-
ported from their source to be used. Task routine must be scheduled,
but not at fixed time intervals. Task completion is, therefore, more
removed from starting time.

7-8 Required inputs come from multiple places and must be assembled in
one place at a proper time according to a flexible schedule.

9-10 Required inputs come from multiple places and task completion must
be accomplished by a fixed and invariant schedule.

B. **Variables of the Organizational Response Sector**
  1. *Energy variable.* In what kinds of "packages" (men, machines, tools, *etc.*)
  are the units used in the activity?

Level   *Scale*

1-2 Energy is available in units composed of a single "individual" (minimal
empirical unit is the energy available to a human who acts alone).

3-4 Energy is available through action of multiple units of a single type aug-
mented by tools that extend the energy of men by simple mechanical
extenders, or by animal power.

5-6 Energy is available through the action of multiple units segregated into
units of different composition (either men in specialized roles, or animals, or machines) some components of which have more energy capacity than others.

7-8 Energy available through multiple units segregated into units of different composition and specialized roles in which some components (men,
animals, or machines) have more energy capacity than others, making
some components noninterchangeable with others.

9-10 Energy is available through action of multiple units (men, animals, or
machines) segregated into units of different composition and specialized
roles in which all units are noninterchangeable in action.

  2. *Program variable.* What kinds of managing formats are available to program the activities of available units that provide or channel energy?

Level   *Scale*

1-2 Where a single unit of energy working alone carrying out a single action
with close to immediate results, with strong, improvisational character-

istics, based upon inputs locally available with little or no modification . . . *control* takes the form of a single verbal signal and provides direction for immediate completion of activity; noncompliance brings no sanction; and authority is only advisory.

3-4   Where multiple units of energy are involved, where some inputs required must undergo a time lag to be made available, and some operations cannot be improvised, but follow a sequence . . . *control* takes the form of more than one verbal signal or order given to the acting entity; involves some time lag; some units may force others to relate to its actions; noncompliance brings a generalized social response based on "custom;" clear-cut authority is assigned for the duration of a specific activity only; authority over a series of activities may exist, but is only advisory.

5-6   Where multiple units of energy are involved and at least two units are of different types and operate sequentially; inputs cannot be used in their "natural" state; some of the operations will require alteration and ordering of behavior of participating units, while other components remain improvisational in their involvements; more than one unit is assigned roles that force some others to relate to its action . . . *control* takes the form of: authority validated by principles rooted in age, sex, or kinship; status is related to a permanent assignment of responsibility over the outcomes of tasks; noncompliance with orders brings a generalized negative social response when such authority is thwarted.

7-8   Where multiple heterogeneous units of energy are involved, operating sequentially in repetitive and cumulative actions; where heterogeneous inputs are not immediately available and must be modified and assembled; where operations require explicit orders that trigger other linked orders in a sequence . . . *control* takes the form of authority validated by principles other than age, sex, or kinship; is assigned on a permanent basis over a series of explicitly defined tasks or behaviors; noncompliance to orders brings punitive reaction by specialized agencies.

9-10   Where multiple heterogeneous units of energy are involved and must operate sequentially in an unalterable fixed sequence, with inputs that are heterogeneous, require much modification, and relocation to be utilized . . . *control* takes the form of permanent assignment of authority over all aspects of the full range of activities or tasks involved; in which the orders of such authority forces all components or elements to relate to its preset plan; coercion covers all areas of behavior, and is applied in a rigid manner by a specialized agency; authority is validated by abstract principles (law, justice, truth, efficiency) beyond age, sex, kinship, or ethnic status.

3. *Boundary variable.* What are the limits of time and space within which the available programs are effective and can be applied?

Level	*Scale*
1–2	Operations concern a single localized activity that can be completed immediately.
3–4	Operations concern two or more activities in a localized setting, but require a time period to complete.
5–6	Operations concern a series of activities spread in space, but these must be completed within a time period.
7–8	Operations concern a series of activities spread in space and located in different locations, but at some point all must be brought together at one time and place.
9–10	Operations concern a series of activities spread in space and in different locations, each of which is controlled according to a fixed time schedule and brought together at one time according to a fixed, nonvariant schedule.

Operational Definitions of Zonal Components and Their Variables

A. The Technological Zone
    1. *The man-artifact component.* What are the characteristics of the action units themselves?
        a. *The locus of dominance variable.* How open-ended or tightly organized are the action units (men, machines, *etc.*).

Level	*Scale*
1–3	Unit or units are multi-purposed, and can affect one another equally.
4–7	One or more of the interacting elements can force other elements to behave in relation to its action.
8–10	One or more of the interacting elements necessarily forces all other elements to behave in a preset pattern in relation to its action.

        b. *Complexity of assemblage variable.* How simple, complex or numerous are the interacting units?

Level	*Scale*
1-3	The action unit is a single entity.

4-7	The action unit is composed of a series of similar entities.

8-10	The action unit is composed of a series of specialized (noninterchangeable) entities.

    c. *Phases of unit interaction variable.* How simple or multiphased are the interactions among units?

Level	*Scale*
1-3	A single unit that does not require another one to carry out a single action.

4-7	Two or more units interact sequentially, but not necessarily in a single pattern.

8-10	Two or more units interact with repetitive sequential actions.

  2. *The task component.* What are the characteristics of the program of action wherein the action units engage?
    a. *Temporal characteristic variable.* Are tasks completed soon after the initiation of action, or completed after a series of actions over time?

Level	*Scale*
1-3	Task is completed immediately following a single action, and the task itself can be initiated at any time.

4-7	Tasks can be completed only *via* an extended time period, though the task can be scheduled at variable intervals.

8-10	Tasks can be completed only *via* a fixed and scheduled allocation of units of time for segments of tasks.

    b. *Operations-output relations variable.* Are results achieved at the immediate locale of operations or at some distant place, and are these results immediate or do they require development over time?

Level	*Scale*
1-3	Program of behavior is localized (completed where it is begun), and produces an immediate and complete result.

4–7   Programs of activity are spread in space, and task completion is a matter of cumulative "build-up."

8–10   Programs of activity are spread in space, and task completion is a matter of cumulative development with fixed time segments.

    c. *Throughput form variable.* Are procedures capable of routinization or standardization?

Level   *Scale*

1–3   An activity where all actions are variable and improvisational.

4–7   An activity where some operations or procedures require strict order, whereas other aspects remain improvisational.

8–10   An activity where *all* operational aspects require ordered procedures affecting all behaviors of all elements involved.

  3. *The setting component.* What is the nature of the setting conditions required for action units and programs to be effective?
    a. *Setting structure variable.* Are inputs to operations relatively random and variable, as opposed to highly structured and controlled; that is, how are inputs allowed into the arena of action?

Level   *Scale*

1–3   All inputs (resources, men, raw materials, *etc.*) to the field of operations are allowed to enter indiscriminately (randomly).

4–7   A distinct order is required for many of the inputs before they are allowed into the arena of action.

8–10   A distinct order is required for all of the inputs before they are allowed into the arena of action, where they are then combined into a complex program.

    b. *Locus of input variable.* Do inputs or elements in the field come from an immediate locale or must they be assembled from diverse places?

Level   *Scale*

1–3   Inputs or elements of an activity are all found in one narrowly defined place.

4-7   Inputs or elements of an activity are required from two or more places, but these places are variable and not specific.

8-10   Inputs or elements of an activity are required from a variety of specific, specialized places.

   c. *Autonomy variable.* Do action units and programs enjoy autonomy because resources are few, simple, and readily available, or is there a high degree of dependency upon multiple outside units?

Level	*Scale*

1-3   The activity can be initiated without the need for inputs other than those immediately available to the action units.

4-7   The activity requires resources or inputs that require some transaction with an external source of inputs or relationships.

8-10   The activity involves a whole series of resources all of which require transactions with external sources involving scheduled "deliveries."

B. Managerial and Political Zone
   1. *Communications component.* What are the organizational characteristics of "socially-based" action units?
      a. *Locus of authority variable.* Is authority shared or diffuse in character, or is it concentrated in some complex entity?

Level	*Scale*

1-3   No authority is exercised over or within the action units (an egalitarian orientation).

4-7   Authority is assigned to a specific entity for a limited series of tasks only.

8-10   Authority is vested exclusively in a single entity for the full range of activities, and extends over all members of the action units.

      b. *Channels of communications variable.* What is the relation of the number of channels of communications to numbers of units requiring organization?

Level	*Scale*
1–3	Communications occurs by face-to-face contacts within a single autonomous, homogeneous unit.
4–7	Communications between "levels" links two or more units that show some specialization and interdependence.
8–10	Communications flows through a series of levels linking nonautonomous units exhibiting specialization.

    c. *Complexity of linkage variable.* What is the nature of the messages or commands that manage an activity? Are they few and simple or linked messages and commands?

Level	*Scale*
1–3	A single order provides direction for the immediate completion of an activity.
4–7	The direction of an activity requires orders to two or more units, and these orders must be made at critical time periods.
8–10	The direction of an activity requires orders to numerous units, and must be made at a critical time period rigidly fixed by a schedule.

  2. *Instutitional domain component.* What are the programs of action in which managerial and political units engage?
    a. *Agency scale variable.* Is the managerial or political entity small in scale and individualized, or is it complex and large?

Level	*Scale*
1–3	The activity is managed by a single, small scale entity.
4–7	The activity to be managed requires that a series of persons be assigned to manage a set of activities.
8–10	An activity requires that a multiple series of sections, composed of multiple persons, be assigned to manage different aspects of a complex task.

    b. *Concentration variable.* Are managerial activities confined to a narrow sector of activity, locally based, or do these extend to encompass distant entities?

Level   *Scale*

1–3   The immediate presence of a managerial entity is required for an activity that is confined to a localized setting.

4–7   Orders are transmitted *via* an intermediary who directs a series of activities located in a number of places.

8–10   Orders are transmitted through levels of intermediaries to coordinate a series of activities, each located in a different place.

    c. *Heterogeneity variable.* Is the managerial entity composed of generalized units, or heterogeneous, specialized ones?

Level   *Scale*

1–3   A single unit without internal differentiation.

4–7   A complex unit, composed of multiple elements displaying some differentiated functions.

8–10   A linked series of specialized and internally differentiated units performing different aspects of a task.

   3. *Legitimacy variable.* What are the requisite setting conditions for effective managerial and political behaviors?
    a. *Boundary of authority variable.* Does authority extend over a single area of jurisdiction, or over a series of different areas of jurisdiction and control?

Level   *Scale*

1–3   Area of jurisdiction is limited to a single sphere of activity and that authority is only advisory.

4–7   The area of jurisdiction is over a limited and defined set of activities within a wider set of activities. Authority is "official" in nature.

8–10   The area of jurisdiction is total over the full range of activities, and authority is legally and strictly defined.

    b. *Social control variable.* Does the managerial or political entity have high or low coercive powers to ensure the compliance of the managed units?

Level	Scale
1–3	Noncompliance with managerial orders brings no formal sanctions (voluntary compliance).
4–7	Noncompliance with managerial orders brings some punitive reaction, not necessarily clearly defined or immediate.
8–10	Noncompliance with managerial orders brings strong and effective punitive reactions that are clearly defined and immediate.

    c. *Locus of validation variable.* Are claims to authority of an informal, personal nature, or of an impersonal, technical, legal, or ideological type?

Level	Scale
1–3	Legitimacy of authority is validated by voluntary evaluation of prestige or skill of an individual.
4–7	Legitimacy of authority is based upon identification representing some social or economic institution (technical or administrative criteria).
8–10	Legitimacy of authority is based upon an appeal to legal, ideological, or technological values that are held to validate specific institutions.

2

Organic Problem-Solving in Public Administration: A Systems Methodology

Peter Gomez
State University of New York

INTRODUCTION

Public administration can be characterized as the set of all managerial activities involved in implementing public policy. These activities normally take place in an environment of "organized complexity," sociotechnical systems that depict inherent complexities, uncertainties, and self-regulations, which make them a subject too complex to be approached analytically, but too organized to be tackled statistically [30, p. 19]. Therefore, *methodologies*, which take into account these characteristic features of sociotechnical systems, are needed to guide the public manager in his problem-solving activities. The development of these methodologies has to start from a new interpretation of the manager's role: he can no longer be seen as the "maker" or designer of events, but as a *catalyst* in the flow of all the processes that constitute public administration. His role is that of a controller, but in the very specific sense of *organic control*: use the inner dynamics of the system to perform those problem-solving activities that generate a desired behavior.

A methodology based on such a concept of organic control results when the framework and the tools of systems theory and cybernetics are combined with evolutionary procedures for tackling real-world problems to form an overall problem-solving strategy. While an *evolutionary approach* applies the *principles* of natural evolution to problem-solving in humanistic systems, ideas from the new sciences of *systems theory*, a framework characterizing features and problems invariant to broad classes of systems, and *cybernetics*, the science of effective organization [7, p. 425], specify the unique steps of the evolutionary trial-and-error process (for fundamentals of this approach, see [14]). The development of such a methodology has to start by answering the following questions. What are the needs, interests, and capabilities of managers? What do managers expect from such a methodology? Two aspects seem to be of overall importance in this context. First, the methodology should be of a form that allows the manager to use it *autonomously*. Problem-solving in sociotechnical systems is a permanent process; external consultants and specialists are available only in rare cases. In addition, the manager has to live with the solutions and recurring problems. Therefore, contrary to other systems methodologies (*e.g.*, the Rand approach [27] or the Lancaster approach [11]), the methodology to be presented here is tailored for an autonomous user confronted with any kind of management problem. The second important feature of this systems methodology is its *adaptability*. This means that the *same* methodology can easily be applied to both simple, day-to-day problems and complex, far-reaching problems without losing its power. This methodology is to be designed as a *hierarchical control mechanism* that selects, in every phase of the process, the reference frames and techniques appropriate to cope with the complexity of the corresponding problem.

We will now outline briefly the structure of such an adaptive systems methodology. After that, we will discuss in detail its stepwise procedure, some of its supporting techniques, and its practical application. As examples, we will use specific managerial problems in public administration.

SYSTEMS METHODOLOGY AS AN ADAPTIVE CONTROL MECHANISM

A methodology capable of tackling problems of varying kind, complexity, and duration, using the *same* fundamental procedure, has to be designed as a hierarchically structured mechanism that selects building blocks from a set of methodological steps, frameworks, and techniques to cope best with a specific problem. Such a mechanism is shown in Figure 1 (for this kind of modeling hierarchies, see [24, p. 78]).

A detailed description of this mechanism has been given elsewhere [15], and only its most important features will be summarized here. The adaptive systems methodology is characterized by four hierarchical levels, namely fundamental logic, phases of systems methodology, reference frames, and techniques; its structure and working mode can be illustrated as follows:

The methodology's overall degree of complexity is determined by the interplay of the fundamental logic of every problem-resolution process and the characteristics of the specific problem situation. As Popper [25, p. 242] has shown, the only possible way to acquire and modify knowledge, and, therefore, to solve problems, is by trial and error. This *evolutionary process* of blind variation and selective retention, in the terminology of Campbell [9, p. 418], consists of the following steps:

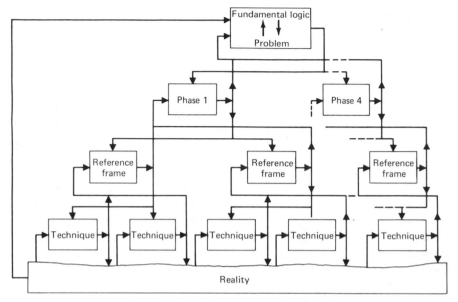

Figure 1. Adaptive systems methodology.

$$P_1 \longrightarrow TT \longrightarrow EE \longrightarrow P_2$$

The starting point is problems (P_1), whose solution is attempted by generating tentative theories (TT). These theories are critically tested for error elimination (EE), and this finally leads to new problems (P_2). Systems methodology refines these steps, according to the principles of systems theory and cybernetics, to specify different phases of the problem-solving process on the next lower hierarchical level of the control mechanism. Now the role of the interplay between fundamental logic and the specific problem situation as a selector of the problem-solving procedure can be interpreted: it determines 1) the individual phases of the problem-solving process necessary to cope with the specific situation, 2) the intensity of their elaboration, and 3) the sequence of performing these phases. This kind of structuring the interaction of the two highest hierarchical levels also leads to a meaningful use of the iterative procedure.

On the level of the *phases* of systems methodology, the general steps of the trial-and-error method are specified in the light of systemic and cybernetic principles. These phases, which will be discussed in detail in the following sections, form chunks within an overall procedure that specify actions to be taken by the problem-solver in different stages of the process. They can be grouped into the following categories: discovery and formulation of the problem; development of a control model of the problem situation; design of problem-solving strategies; and implementation and evolution of a monitoring system.

To every phase of systems methodology, a repertoire of *reference frames* is attached, to select from according to the complexity of particular problems. Reference frames incorporate specific perspectives of looking at a problem, as well as the corresponding programs and tools for tackling it. An example of such a reference frame is the General Systems Problem Solver [10], to be discussed later, which constitutes a framework for modeling problem situations from the point of view of their pattern of behavior and structure.

Finally, on the lowest hierarchical level, the *techniques* perform the job of gathering and processing the data necessary within the strategy of the reference frame. An example of a technique will be given later, in the form of the feedback diagram used to structure the process of problem formulation. Every reference frame disposes of a set of techniques whose use also depends on the characteristics of the problem.

The advantage of designing systems methodology as an adaptive controller is twofold. First, it allows the integration of a variety of reference frames and techniques as building blocks to cope with all kinds of problems. Second, and even more important, it enables tailoring the methodology to the specific characteristics of the problem situation and the problem-solver, *i.e.*, it gives the methodology a basic flexibility. How such a methodology could be realized will be shown in the following sections, starting with an outline of the underlying "philosophy" of systems methodology and its consequences for the development of the second hierarchical level, the *phases* of a systems methodology.

ORGANIC PROBLEM-SOLVING: FUNDAMENTAL TRAITS OF SYSTEMS METHODOLOGY

When facing a new methodology, any manager will first raise the questions: What can I get out of it? Which expectations about its possibilities are reasonable? Here at the outset, we should clarify one point: there is no *true* methodology that will certainly lead to a successful solution of any problem. There are methodologies, however, that come closer to this ideal state than others, because of their specific characteristics. Although the proof of the pudding is in the eating, observing some prerequisites will increase a methodology's chance of being successful. The most important prerequisite is its theoretical foundation [8, p. 132]. Systems methodology finds its theoretical basis in system theory, cybernetics, and evolutionary epistemology; therefore, some expectations concerning its problem-solving capabilities are justified, provided they do not lead to overestimating the methodology. It should be looked at simply as a mechanism for initiating search processes and for improving the problem-solving capabilities of managers, although its design as a hierarchical control mechanism makes it superior to linear methodologies.

Systems methodology, then, can be characterized as a procedure for organic problem-solving that *models* problem situations in the language of systems-thinking, and explores them, with the aid of cybernetics, seeking aspects of control relevant to the problem-solver. Possible solutions are designed according to a cybernetic model that reflects the problem-solver's potential to control the situation. These solutions are devised as constraints in order to influence the problem in a way that makes it behave according to the problem-solver's purpose.

The "philosophy" of systems methodology can be characterized by its way of modeling the problem situation and by its procedure of designing solutions to the problem.

Systems methodology aims at modeling the problem in light of the problem-solver's own potential to control the situation. No attempt is made to build up a perfect analytical model of the situation, because any such effort is necessarily doomed to failure due to the inherent complexity of the situation. The problem-solver must take the situation as a black box and concentrate on a few of its aspects, which he investigates with regard to his own possibilities of control. His referring actions are led by the following questions:

Which aspects of the problem situation have to be *monitored*, because they may indicate deviations from a desired behavior?
Which aspects are under my own control, and can be *manipulated* in order to change the behavior of the situation?
Which aspects are *outside* my own sphere of influence, but also determine the behavior of the situation?

The aspects found by answering these questions now have to be integrated into a *control model* of the situation that answers the following questions:

Which strategies have to be pursued regarding specific developments of the monitored aspects of the problem situation?
How can I anticipate the development of aspects outside my own sphere of influence in order to react prophylactically to specific deviations?
How can the realization of chosen strategies be tuned appropriately?

Within the model, these aspects specify a feedback, a feedforward, and a monitoring feedback, as will be shown later.

The procedure of *designing* problem solutions is largely determined by the above model of the problem-solver's control capabilities. This model also serves as an instrument for evaluating the success of problem-solving strategies. In order to find and maintain adequate solutions, the following questions have to be answered:

Which strategies for problem-solving are promising in light of the control model, and how can they be realized as constraints to the problem situation?
Which kind of realization allows an optimal use of the inner dynamics of the situation?
How can the success of this constraint-engineering be evaluated?
How can successful solutions be maintained and new problems be prevented?

This procedure for designing solutions meets the demand of the interpretation of the problem-solver's role as a *catalyst*, in which he sets constraints only in order to make use of the situation's inner dynamics for his own purposes.

This short description of the fundamental traits of systems methodology provides a framework for the detailed discussion of its individual phases and their logical sequence. The main objective of the following section, therefore, is to show the manager how to proceed by steps when tackling complex problems; an example from public administration will be integrated into the discussion to give the public manager a more concrete idea of the procedure.

THE PHASES OF SYSTEMS METHODOLOGY

Systems methodology involves four phases, each of which contains several substeps that specify a detailed procedure:

discovery and formulation of the problem,
development of a control model of the problem situation,
design of problem-solving strategies, and
implementation and evolution of a monitoring system.

Discovery and formulation of the problem

Problems in sociotechnical systems are first perceived as a vague feeling of irritation or of forthcoming difficulties. In most cases, they are hidden behind symptoms and have to be discovered and formulated before adequate solutions can be developed. Sociotechnical systems have no criteria to determine whether the stated problem actually is the "real" problem or whether proposed solutions are the real solutions sought. The only possible way to tackle these ill-structured problems in such complex systems is to develop *search procedures* that arrange the conditions in such a way as to increase one's chances of going deeper into the problematic area to gain more insight.

The most important search rule for discovering the problem can be formulated as follows: take the general nature of your problem for granted, and look at the perceived difficulties as *symptoms*. If a health service agency is confronted with an increasing number of diseases of a specific kind, it will consider it a symptom of an underlying problem, just as a doctor will normally diagnose the patient's fever as an indication of some kind of illness. The next step will be to establish a connection between observed symptoms and the problem looked for, which means localizing the symptoms within a wider context. This process can be facilitated by using techniques like the feedback diagram [23, p. 82] or the quantified flow chart [7, p. 433]. Figure 2 demonstrates the use of the feedback diagram as an aid to localize the above-mentioned problem of the health service

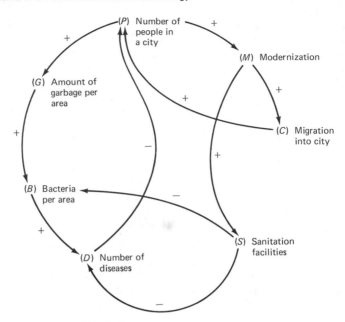

Figure 2. Feedback diagram.

agency.   This multi-loop model not only relates the symptom to several other aspects of the problem situation, but also indicates the mutual effect of their changes: the plus sign denotes an influence of the same polarity; the minus sign indicates an influence of opposite polarity.   As the example shows, an increase in the amount of garbage causes an increase of bacteria and of the number of diseases; but this leads to a decline in the number of people, which means less garbage, fewer bacteria, fewer diseases, and, therefore, more people in the future, *etc.*

The second technique proposed for localizing the symptom within a wider context originates from Beer [7, p. 433] : the quantified flow chart (Figure 3).   This iconic model of a dynamic situation represents the relevant quantities as boxes and their relations as arrows of different sizes.   The extension of the boxes is proportional to the capability—"what we *could* be doing with existing resources, under existing constraints, if we really worked at it" [6, p. 207]—of the quantities, and the shaded areas indicate the actual utilization of their capabilities. The size of the arrows varies in relation to the intensity of the connections.   This technique draws attention to bottlenecks (in our example, A), which could be the problem sought.

These techniques, lower-level building blocks in the control hierarchy of systems methodology (see Figure 1), allow the problem-solver a first structuring of his difficulties.   But how does he define the aspects relevant to the problem in

C_1

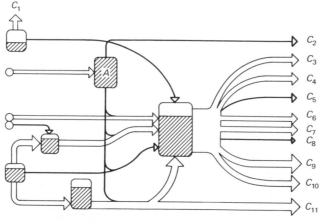

C_2

C_3

C_4

C_5

C_6

C_7

C_8

C_9

C_{10}

C_{11}

Figure 3. Quantified flow chart.

this context? Here, another search rule applies: look for changes in the extrinsic or intrinsic *constraints* in the environment of the symptom, changes that might define the real problem. In the above example, such a change in an *extrinsic* constraint might be the change in laws concerning migration into the city, whereas an *intrinsic* constraint might be removed by weather conditions favorable to the spread of bacteria.

The search rules and their supporting techniques should lead the problem-solver to a tentative formulation of his problem that can serve as a basis for the cybernetic modeling of the problem situation; this modeling will be attempted in the next phase of systems methodology.

Development of a control model of the problem situation

The problem formulated in the first phase now raises a question about the problem-generating *system*. The search for this system demands a fundamental understanding of the fact that systems are not something given in nature, but something defined by intelligence [5, p. 242]. The problem-solver will get an image of his problematic situation according to the perspective he takes; what is relevant in the specific context will be determined by his reference frame. Now the question arises: are there any perspectives or reference frames general enough to be applied usefully to any problem situation that managers of sociotechnical systems may face? This question elicits a positive answer in the form of the reference frames of systems theory and cybernetics. To be more specific, systems methodology is based on the theory that any modeling of sociotechnical systems should involve the following hierarchy of reference frames:

(General) systems theory,
Cybernetics,
Specific discipline, and
Situational knowledge.

These reference frames will now be discussed in some detail.

(General) systems theory

The concept of system nowadays is well established in most fields of science, and even in our daily environments the term "system" plays an important role; so we learn of computer systems, military systems, management information systems, *etc.* The system concept means different things to different people, however, and this is very often a source of confusion. Therefore, when talking about the reference frame of systems theory, the *general systems theory* as developed by Klir [20, 10] will be meant in the following pages. It can be characterized as a conceptual framework for scientific investigation and problem-solving in different fields, which is based on a taxonomy of systems, featuring the following epistemological levels [10, p. 4]:

> Dataless systems—a set of attributes (or variables) and their possible appearances (or states).
> Data systems—systems representing results of observation in the form of a protocol of state variation with respect to parameters.
> Behavioral systems—depicting invariants or patterns in data systems and, therefore, generating them.
> Structural systems—sets of constituent elements and their connections, which generate the above patterns.

In the modeling phase of systems methodology, this hierarchical sequence of levels has to be run through to get as much information as possible on the problem-generating system. First, the problem situation is characterized by a set of variables and their possible states. Second, a protocol of the sequences of system states relative to a parameter (usually time) is taken. Third, the pattern of systems behavior is deduced from the protocol, and finally, the structure generating this behavioral pattern has to be found. In the literature, there are several approaches for finding the pattern of systems behavior and for deducing the corresponding structure. In the following discussion, Ashby's and Conant's approach will be outlined briefly to demonstrate the fundamental principle [1, 2, 3, 12, 13].

In the first step of their method, the behavior of the system has to be recorded as a sequence of states of the systems variables. This record then is checked as to sufficiency of the sample size, which becomes a problem if the variables are not only investigated pairwise, as in Conant's procedure, but also in all their dependencies, as in Ashby's. Furthermore, at this point one has to determine if the inquiry should concentrate on *static* or *dynamic* relations, *i.e.*, if simultaneous or time-shifted dependencies are focused upon. Starting from the record of values of the system's variables, *frequency tables* are established for all variables individually and, following Conant, for all pairs of variables. For continuous variables, the problem of class formation has to be solved. The observed frequencies enable the computation of *entropies* for the individual variables, as well as for pairs of variables according to the formulas:

$$H(X_n) = -\sum_{i=1}^{M_n} p(x_i) \log_2 p(x_i)$$

$$H(X_m, X_n) = -\sum_{i=1}^{M_m} \sum_{j=1}^{M_n} p(x_i, x_j) \log_2 p(x_i, x_j)$$

These entropies enable the computation of transmissions between variables X_m and X_n according to

$$T(X_m : X_n) = H(X_m) + H(X_n) - H(X_m, X_n)$$

These transmissions are normalized and presented in tabular form, as the example from Conant, which models the dynamic relations between pairs of variables X_i, X_j' shows:

Table 1. Normalized transmissions.

	t_{ij}	X_1'	X_2'	X_3'	X_4'	X_5'
	X_1	0.098	0.013	0.690	0.161	0.073
	X_2	0.002	0.023	0.002	0.145	0.012
X_i	X_3	0.109	0.012	0.353	0.044	0.017
	X_4	0.002	0.413	0.002	0.009	0.021
	X_5	0.000	0.186	0.002	0.259	0.195

From Table 1, the most intensive pairwise relations can be deduced and condensed to the graphical representation shown in Figure 4. The size of the arrows —only the most important ones have been taken into account—is proportional to the intensity of the relation. Therefore, such subsystems as $S_1 = \{X_1, X_3\}$ and $S_2 = \{X_2, X_4, X_5\}$ can easily be deduced from the graphical representation. The structure within the subsystems also becomes visible, but with the restriction that the *kind* of relations cannot be determined.

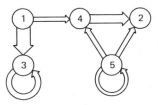

Figure 4. Graphical representation of transmissions [12, p. 552].

In a last step, Conant's method attempts, because of possible shortcomings of the pairwise inquiry, to falsify the structures found: the transmission *within* the subsystems is compared with the transmission between the subsystems.

Ashby's and Conant's approach has been further developed by Klir [18, 19], who also integrated it into a General Systems Problem Solver (GSPS). Cavallo and Klir [10] demonstrated the use of this sophisticated procedure in the form of a MINI-GSPS, which gives the manager direct access to the tools for finding the system's pattern of behavior and structure through an interactive computer device.

To come back to the representation of systems-methodology as a controller (Figure 1), general systems theory can be interpreted as *one* reference frame available in phase 2, and the MINI-GSPS and its programs would be the corresponding techniques. Another reference frame, cybernetics, will be discussed now.

Cybernetics

Cybernetics is, as Wiener originally wrote 30 years ago, "the science of communications and control in the animal and the machine" [31]. Pointing to the same laws of complex systems that are invariant not only to transformations of their fabric but also of their content, Beer redefined cybernetics as "the science of effective organization" [7, p. 425]. Effective organization is the key to successful problem-solving in any field, however. From the perspective of cybernetics, the problem-solver has to model his situation in light of possibilities for control; this implies a search for control mechanisms inherent in the problem situation. Therefore, the problem-solver needs reference frames in the form of *control mechanisms* to guide his search; three of them will now be discussed briefly.

The *servomechanism* or simple controller [24] realizes the fundamental cybernetic principle of a simple feedback, and, therefore, also forms the basic building block of every controller of higher order. His elaborated version can be represented as shown in Figure 5. If the problem-solver uses this mechanism to determine his possibilities of control, he has to ask the following questions, already cited earlier:

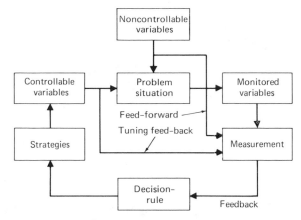

Figure 5. Servomechanism.

Monitored variables—which aspects of the problem situation have to be *monitored* because they may indicate deviations from a desired behavior?

Controllable variables—which aspects are under my own control, and can be *manipulated* in order to change the behavior of the situation?

Noncontrollable variables—which aspects are *outside* my own sphere of influence, but also determine the behavior of the situation?

Feedback—which *strategies* have to be pursued on specific developments of the monitored aspects?

Feedforward—how can I anticipate the development of aspects outside my own sphere of influence in order to react *prophylactically* to specific deviations?

Tuning feedback—how can the realization of chosen strategies be *tuned* appropriately?

The *adaptive* or *ultrastable controller* [1, p. 83] realizes the principle of double feedback, which allows an adaptation to disturbances not foreseen by its designer. To achieve this, the controller organizes a set of servomechanisms as building blocks and a selector (called an essential variable) to implement specific servomechanisms according to the development of the problem situation. The working mode of this controller (Figure 6) can be described as follows: a specific servomechanism is in action as long as its results correspond to the standards set by the essential variable. When this is no longer the case, a new servomechanism is selected to cope with the new developments. The overall objective is to hold the essential variable within it physiological limits.

The following questions have to be answered to specify the details of this control mechanism:

Servomechanisms—which simple control models have to be designed in order to cope best with possibly different developments of the problem situation?

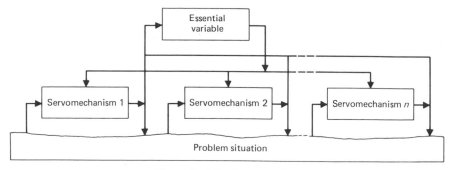

Figure 6. Adaptive controller.

Essential variables—which aspects of the problem situation indicate best the success or failure of the servomechanism in action?
Second feedback—when, and according to which criteria, are servomechanisms selected?

These two control mechanisms are the building blocks of the most sophisticated controller to be taken as a reference frame for depicting the cybernetic features of a sociotechnical system: the *organizational structure of any viable system*. A model of this structure has been developed by Beer [6], who used the human nervous system as a concrete case of viability to disclose the fundamental structure of any viable system. To be *viable*, a system must develop five basic funtions, which are characterized as systems 1 to 5 in Beer's organizational model:

1. Divisional control: controlling operations in organizational subunits;
2. Coordination of divisions: damping of oscillations, achievement of synergy;
3. Operations management: maintenance of internal stability, optimization of existing structures and processes;
4. Development management: integration of environmental information, planning of future strategies for the system; and
5. Policy function (top management): contemplation of possible futures, formulation and maintenance of overall policy of the system.

Without going into more details of the individual functions, Figure 7 will give some insights into the interplay of systems 1 to 5. To use this model for structuring the problem-solver's alternatives for controlling a specific situation, each system, 1 to 5, has to be interpreted as an adaptive controller, and the relevant questions outlined above have to be answered. For example, for system 5, the policy function, several servomechanisms, each projecting a possible future and developing an adequate policy, have to be designed and coordinated. Then, the links between the systems 1 to 5 have to be established according to the logic of Beer's model.

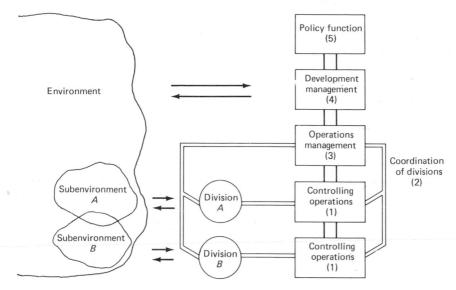

Figure 7. Organizational structure of viable systems.

To specify the details of this control mechanism, the following questions have to be answered:

Systems 1 to 5—how can the problem situation be interpreted in terms of the five basic functions of any viable system, and how can each function be characterized from the point of view of an adaptive controller?

Coordination—how should systems 1 to 5 be linked in order to get a functioning whole?

The choice of any of these control-mechanisms as reference frames has to depend on the complexity of the problem situation. Whereas in many day-to-day problems, the servomechanism may suffice entirely, the model of the viable system has to be chosen as a reference frame to guide the manager in reorganizations of his firm or agency. But, whichever controller is selected, an adequate perspective has to be used when applying it to real-world phenomena; this will be the topic of the next paragraph.

Specific discipline

The reference frames discussed above instruct the problem-solver to look, say, for controllable variables. But what is the real-world equivalent of this category of variables? The problem-solver obviously needs another reference frame to specify the *content* of these variables. Here, the perspectives of such disciplines as physics, medicine, history, *etc.* come into play. But which discipline should be applied in a specific problem situation, especially since they seem to overlap? Here, a technique developed under the name of *root definition* helps the problem-solver to make his choice.

Root definitions [28, p. 75] provide different views of the problem situation and, therefore, prevent the problem-solver from taking only one perspective when defining the problem-generating system. In addition, they give a more comprehensive picture of the situation, using the following eight categories to depict its main aspects: purpose, measure of performance, components, connectivity, wider systems environment, resources, decision-taking process, continuity [28, p. 79]. The systems of interest normally do not correspond to organizational groupings such as departments or sections; thus, a company seeking to reduce material costs may be characterized as "a materials-flow system" or "a temporary-storage-of-components system." A car, *e.g.*, could be defined as "a people-transporting system," but it could as well be seen as "a system for wearing out piston rings" or "a system that makes garages run at a profit" [4, p. 39]. Each perspective then leads to a discipline adequate for problem-solving: *e.g.*, in the car example, to traffic planning, mechanics, and business administration, respectively.

Smyth and Checkland [28, p. 81] illustrate the concept of root definition in the field of public administration by characterizing a community welfare center as "an institution encouraging and helping community action aimed at development of the community's own resources." This means that the center's role is interpreted as concerned with helping the community to develop its own resources, rather than doling out charitable benefits. But this perspective also implies the selection of a different discipline for solving the problem.

Once a specific discipline is chosen as a reference frame, the abstract cybernetic notions can be filled with content; in the car example, business administration tells the problem-solver to include "cost of manpower" as a noncontrollable variable. This leads us to the last reference frame of interest.

Situational knowledge

The discipline selected by the problem-solver according to his root definition allows a specification of the problem-generating system from a general perspective; it does not give the details of the situation, such as, *e.g.*, that the "manpower" mentioned above is, in fact, Bill Smith, the only employee of the garage. This situational knowledge, therefore, also has to be integrated in order to get a realistic image of the problem situation.

In Figure 8, the role of the hierarchy of reference frames is summarized, interpreting it as a filter to extract the problem-generating system out of the original problem situation. The selection of the set of reference frames necessary to determine the problem-generating system is the first step in the process of developing a control model of the problem situation. This process will now be described on

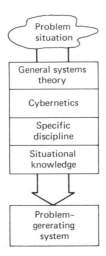

Figure 8. Hierarchy of reference frames.

two different levels, using a typical example from the field of public administration for illustration.

The two levels referred to are the management level and the processing level. Processing information for solving the immediate problem is only one aspect of tackling problems; its complement is the coordination and guidance of the people involved in the information processing. Systems methodology has to be applied on *both* levels to get satisfactory results. On the *management level*, the problem-solver coordinates the activities of his subordinates according to the principles of systems methodology; therefore his controllable variables, *e.g.*, are: motivating people, changing the composition of the team, giving professional advice, *etc.* On the *processing level*, the manager's subordinates use systems methodology to solve the immediate problem; therefore, their controllable variables might be: reducing costs, preparing a budget, developing checklists. The use of systems methodology on these different levels and their interaction is illustrated in Figure 9 [22, p. 310].

At time instant, t_1, the manager initiates, according to his control model, the search for solutions for a specific problem by delegating it to the processing level. Here, tentative solutions are developed and compared with the real problem situation; this process is symbolized by ⬦ . The result of this comparison is fed back to the manager, who evaluates it in the light of his criteria and (eventually changed) circumstances. This evaluation may lead to an intervention on the processing level by the manager, whether in the form of advice to change the control model, or a direct manipulation of the problem situation to provoke new solutions. These solutions have to be evaluated again, until a satisfactory decision is reached.

Now, we will illustrate the process of developing a control model on the pro-

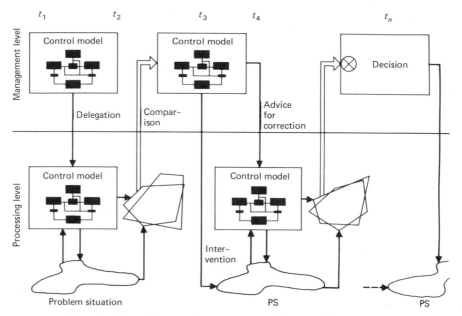

Figure 9. Interactive use of systems methodology on different levels.

cessing level; afterwards, an example characterizing the application of systems methodology on the management level will conclude these remarks on phase 2 of the methodology.

The *problem* given to a group of specialists by their manager might be formulated as follows: "Find the optimal form of organization for a specific public agency that especially helps avoid frictions with the demands of the given environment." To cope with such a complex topic, the problem-solvers will probably first select the organizational structure of the viable system as the cybernetics reference frame for modeling the problem situation. Then they will work out the details of systems 1 to 5 of the viable organization, interpreting them as adaptive controllers, and specifying the necessary servomechanisms. Special attention will be given to system 4, which is the function relating the agency to its environment. The process of specifying *one* servomechanism within system 4 could be represented as shown in Figure 10.

The specific discipline involved in modeling the public agency in its environment is the science of *public administration*. Its body of knowledge enables the problem-solver to characterize a typical environment of an agency and to specify possible interactions between agency and environment; for the above example, see [17, p. 34]. It is then the problem-solver's task to integrate his situational knowledge into this general image to get an adequate control model of the problem situation.

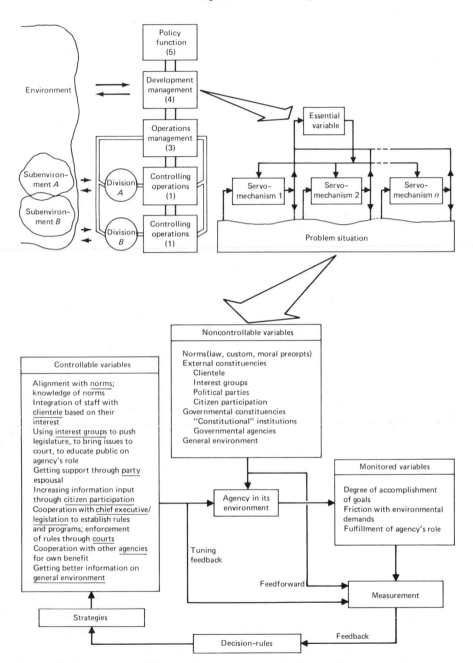

Figure 10. Cybernetic modeling on the processing level of the public agency in its environment.

Now the question arises: what specifically is meant by feedback, feedforward, and tuning feedback in the above control model? We now give some hints about their working mode with illustrations.

Feedback

The feedback mechanism links the monitored and the controllable variables by specifying strategies—in the form of manipulations of the controllable variables—to be set in action on critical developments of the monitored variables. Designing the feedback mechanism starts with setting up a *measuring device* for critical developments of the monitored variables; for example, it should be specified what the desirable levels of the indicators are and whether they have been achieved. Next, *decision-rules* have to be developed that link changes in the state of the system with actions to be taken. If, for example, a specific goal of the agency is not achieved, the decision-rule says to turn to the courts to enforce certain rules; for another goal, the decision-rule might be to increase cooperation with legislation. The aim of this design is to assign a *set* of actions to potential developments of the monitored variables *prior* to the rise of the actual problems. The development of good decision-rules is very much dependent on the *internal model* the problem-solver has of the interaction of the variables that constitute the system. If he is familiar with the pattern of interaction of the institutions of the chief executive, the legislature, and the courts, choosing a course of action to achieve a specific goal becomes much easier. If he has data about earlier court cases similar to his, he might even use the GSPS, described above, to find some structure that facilitates his decision about potential actions to be taken. Finally, different actions have to be combined to form powerful *strategies* for problem-solving, as for example, integrating campaigns of interest groups to push legislation with efforts to cooperate with legislators.

Feedforward

The feedforward mechanism serves to anticipate critical developments of the uncontrollable variables *before* they have an effect on the system. As the design of this mechanism is identical with the one of feedback, some brief examples will suffice to make the point. A change in party programs, new laws, and future economic developments normally can be anticipated, at least to a certain degree. If the problem-solver is prepared for these changes, he can take prophylactic actions to avoid critical states of his system. In the form of the feedforward, he establishes the necessary channels to get the relevant information, and he also develops courses of action for emergency cases.

Tuning feedback

This mechanism, finally, is responsible for a smooth implementation of the chosen strategies. Strategies can be implemented in a "big bang" mode. Normally, however, a more "diplomatic" procedure is recommendable to prevent oscillations of the system [for data on the bang-bang effect, see 26, p. 280]. A step-by-step, or incremental, procedure is often very promising, as for example: talks with the chief executive should precede taking a matter to court, through interest groups or by the agency itself. The tuning feedback consists of a set of decision-rules realizing such procedures, which can be put into action once specific strategies have been selected to cope with a problem.

Now, we turn our attention to the development of a possible control model to coordinate the activities of people involved in problem-solving on the processing level. According to a standard management dictum: "Management is getting things done through other people." In this sense, a control model on the *management level* has to specify all aspects concerned with guiding people to find the best solution to a problem on the processing level; on the simplest level, such a model could take the form shown in Figure 11.

As the logic of this control-model does not differ from the one used on the processing level, just a few remarks on its working mode will suffice. The *feedback* mechanism can be characterized by such decision-rules as: if there prove to be inconsistencies in the results of the search process, have them checked according to reference frames you provide for the processing level; or, if external information flows poorly, establish contacts with the relevant environment for your subordinates. The *feedforward* could, for example, involve setting up devices to detect tensions in the problem-solving group early and providing means to relieve them, before they disturb the output of the group. The *tuning feedback* might establish a procedure to delegate, step-by-step, more and more responsibilities to the processing level.

With this specification of the control model, the second phase of systems methodology reaches its final step. In the next phase, the strategies developed within the control model have to be adapted to the inner dynamics of the problem situation, and the best strategy for implementation has to be decided.

Design of problem-solving strategies

Given the control model and a repertoire of possible strategies for tackling the problem, the problem-solver now has to evaluate the feasibility of these strategies in the light of the specifics of the problem. Interpreting his role as that of a *catalyst*, he should be guided by the following rule: select, for realization, those

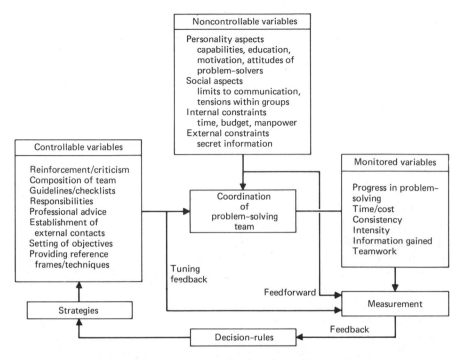

Figure 11. Cybernetic modeling of the coordination of a problem-solving team.

strategies that make the best use of the inner dynamics of the situation. This *organic* procedure, which could be characterized metaphorically as using the "entropic drift" of the system to fulfill the problem-solver's own purposes [5, p. 355], has to run through different steps, which will be discussed next.

In the first step, the strategies of the control model have to be compared with *former, similar attempts* to problem-solving in order to avoid the same failures or to reinforce successful strategies. Then the *objectives* of the problem-generating system have to be formulated as criteria for selecting strategies as solutions to the problem. In the third step, the strategies of the control model are *adapted* to the inner dynamics of the problem situation and integrated into a logical decision-space to test how well they attain the objectives. Finally, the strategies are *simulated*, and those to be implemented are chosen.

The *evaluation of former attempts* at problem-solving aims first at avoiding failures of the past, which might have been caused by an incomplete or erroneous control model. By comparing the new control model with these former models, such shortcomings as false categorization of systems variables, missing feedbacks, feedforwards, or tuning feedbacks might be detected, and this might shift attention to these specific aspects. Successful strategies from the past deserve special attention, too, and they should be evaluated first, because they might demonstrate how the inner dynamics of a problem situation were exploited.

The *formulation of objectives* of the problem-generating system is identical with determining the criteria for a successful solution of the orginal problem. Setting objectives in this context means specifying limits to the monitored or essential variables whose crossing initiates strategies to bring the variables back into their stable region. If the time an agency needs to implement a program has been identified as a variable to be monitored, specifying the objective means, *e.g.*, setting a limit of one year. If this objective is not met, strategies are initiated to get the job done as fast as possible; otherwise, the system is "stable" and the problem has been solved.

In this context, two problems arise. First, how can the objectives be ordered according to their priorities? Here, the control models provide a solution by their very organization: the hierarchical form of the adaptive controller, for example, leads to integrating objectives on different levels, creating the necessary subordination automatically. Second, how to proceed if the problem-solver does not intend to, or simply cannot, specify the objectives? In this case, he can let the system determine its stable state autonomously. Very often, it is practically impossible to anticipate the exact time of a project realistically, but as it develops, the circumstances define possible time horizons that the problem-solver can accept as his objectives.

After having set the criteria for evaluating the success of strategies, the *strategies* themselves now have to be *adapted* to the specifics of the problem. This demands that the problem-solver be especially aware of his role as *catalyst*. He can provide only the necessary conditions for a desired development, using the self-organizing forces of the problem situation in his favor. This self-organization mostly depicts some regularities he can take advantage of. Every situation is characterized by a pattern of its inner dynamics due to the existence of constraints. Constraints restrict the set of possible behaviors of a system, as laws of nature or rules of conduct exclude many potential states of natural or humanistic systems, respectively. In the context of the public agency, constraints exist in the form of norms, for example, be they laws or rules of democratic ethics or traditional administration [for a detailed discussion of such rules of conduct, see 21]. For the specification of his strategies, the problem-solver has to search for these constraints to get the best possible starting point for his actions.

To give a more concrete idea of the practical use of the inner dynamics of the problem situation, we will now discuss three fundamental principles: those of jiu-jitsu, recycling, and symbiosis [16]. The principle of jiu-jitsu says, in analogy to the old japanese sport, use the forces of your opponent to reach your own goals. In the present case, the problem represents the opponent, and its forces lie in its inner dynamics. Examples of the use of this principle are legion, especially instances of applying laws of nature as constraints: electricity is produced by water falling according to the law of gravity. Striking examples can be found in humanistic systems, too, as in the case of lowering speed limits on highways during the oil crisis; using this "entropic drift" was necessary to the success of such an undertaking.

The principle of *recycling* can be deduced from the existence of cycles in nature, economy, or business. Organic problem-solving means concentrating on those phases of the cycle where interventions meet least resistance or, in the optimal case, where the problem dissolves. A typical example, from biotechnics, is the microbes used to clean oil tankers on the high seas. The problem of environmental pollution is solved by artificially creating the next phase of the natural cycle, the bacteriological processing. Highly nourishing protein is a by-product. In business firms, characteristics of the life cycle of products may be used for better problem-solving, and in the public sector, the same may be true for the processing a motion until it becomes a law.

The *principle of symbiosis* propagates the living together of fundamentally different organisms for their mutual benefit, as is often practiced in nature. Applying this principle in industry leads to such solutions as pharmaceutical firms providing microbes for heavy industry in order to process metals without any other energy.

Having adapted the potential problem-solving strategies to the specifics of the problem situation, an administrator has to integrate them into a *logical decision phase* [6, p. 271]. The logical dimensions of this space are categories of strategies, and the number of strategies in each category determines its variety. For the example of the public agency, such a logical decision space could be characterized in Table 2. The number of possible states of the decision space in the table is 20 bits or 1,048,576; the decision process will have to reduce this variety to one state; *i.e.*, select *one* specific strategy from every category.

Table 2. Categories of strategies.

CATEGORIES OF STRATEGIES CONCERNING	NUMBER OF STRATEGIES	VARIETY IN BITS
Norms	4	2
Clientele	8	3
Interest groups	4	2
Political parties	4	2
Citizen participation	8	3
Constitutional institutions	8	3
Governmental agencies	4	2
General environment	8	3

To come to a good decision about the overall strategy requires finding dependencies between these strategies. This *structuring* of the logical decision space is necessary, because, *e.g.*, strategies involving political parties might collide with ones for citizen participation. Beer suggests specifying these dependencies in a logical formula, but this might take too long [2, p. 276]. Therefore, a statement about some fundamental dependencies often serves the purpose as well.

The *simulation* of the effect of potential problem-solving strategies is the last step before deciding finally which to implement. This simulation can be done in different ways: by thought experiments on the basis of the control model: by testing in reality; or by computer simulation. The logic of the control model enables the problem-solver to evaluate his strategies in the form of *thought experiments* led by the following question: how will the monitored or essential variables behave relative to the objective if specific strategies are implemented? Although this procedure is the least costly form of simulation, it has several shortcomings, the most severe being the demands made upon the human brain, which must observe the mutual interactions of different variables simultaneously. *Testing in reality* has the advantage that the system can, in a metaphorical sense, give the answers itself after an intervention. The problem-solver then bases his decision on empirical results, as is often done by businesses that use test markets to evaluate performance. The risks involved in such a procedure often outweigh its benefits. *Computer simulation* is the most sophisticated tool to evaluate performance, but its use heavily depends on the quality of the inner model at hand that specifies the intervariable relations of the system. If such a model has been developed—maybe as a result of the application of GSPS—it might be useful to apply a systems dynamics approach, such as Forrester's, to simulate strategies. Such a procedure can be recommended especially for very important problems with far-reaching effects.

As a result of the simulation, some strategies are judged to be more promising than others. These strategies now have to be evaluated, with respect to their variety-reducing effects within the logical decision space, by asking the following question: which other strategies are either *implied* or *excluded* by a decision for the promising strategies? Then, the optimal *sequence* of strategies has to be determined, namely, the one that reduces the variety of the decision-space fastest. An ideal sequence would have the form shown in Figure 12 [6, p. 281]. This ideal sequence of strategies constantly reduces the remaining possibilities of action by either implying other strategies or by excluding them. From this point of view, *decision-making* means reducing the originally enormous set of alternatives step by step, until only one or a few alternatives are left. This process normally will not run as smoothly as shown in Figure 12, but good decision-making will approach it.

The result of the third phase of systems methodology is a *decision* for a se-

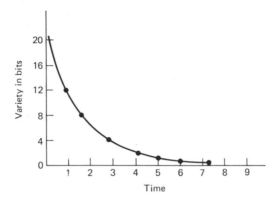

Figure 12. Ideal reduction of variety in logical decision-space.

quence of strategies to solve the problem. In the next phase, this sequence has to be implemented, and its success evaluated.

Implementation and evolution of a monitoring system

The realization of the strategies developed so far demands special attention and has to be custom tailored to the characteristics of the problem. In this context, it is most important that implementation not falsify the basic intentions of the strategies; this very often happens in humanistic systems when trying to avoid resistance of any kind or to dissolve conflicts within existing structures. Also, the intentions of the strategies should be made clear to the people concerned with implementation, in *their* language; otherwise, such fiascos occur as the failure to implement the PPBS in the executive branch of the US government [29, p. 48].

As implementation varies according to specifics of the problem situation, it is very difficult to provide a general rule for designing this process. One hint, based on the *recursive* working mode of systems methodology, can be given: formulate implementation itself as a *problem* and apply systems methodology to solve it. This procedure is especially recommended for very complex problems, where the specifics of implementation do not follow immediately from the structure of the strategies [11. p. 24].

The implementation of strategies finally has to be monitored. *Monitoring* consists not only of the immediate evaluation of the success of a strategy, but also of further observation of successful strategies. The *immediate evaluation* of the result of implementing a specific strategy is done with the aid of the control model. If the objectives set in phase 3 of systems methodology are not met, new strategies from the repertoire of the model have to be selected and implemented. This may require an *iteration*, a repeated running through of former phases of systems methodology, until the problem is solved. Here, the advantage of having developed an elaborate control model becomes obvious; the problem-solver is not dependent on the strategies chosen, he can go back to a repertoire of other strategies any time.

A *successful* solution should not lead the problem-solver to believe that he can file it and forget it; the problem situation has to be monitored permanently to prevent new problems. The design of such a *monitoring system* can consist of establishing warning signals at critical points of the former problem situation, but it is also possible to develop an integral monitoring system. Specifying singular *warning signals* can be done according to the logic of the control model. The limits of the monitored or essential variables (objectives) could be provided with a safe zone, similar to the red area of a car's tachometer, but this demands further observation of these variables. In addition, the feedforward feature should operate permanently to anticipate new disturbances. The design of an *integral monitoring system* has been demonstrated by Beer; his system allows the immediate discovery of significant changes in the situation—a prerequisite for initiating strategies in order to prevent new problems [5, p. 299; 7, p. 433].

Designing the monitoring system constitutes the last step of systems methodology. To summarize the foregoing discussion, its overall procedure will be presented again in the following section.

Table 3. Summary of systems methodology

PHASES	SUBSTEPS
1. Discovery and formulation of the problem	1. Deduction of the problem from symptoms
2. Development of a control model of the problem situation	2. Selection of the requisite control mechanism 3. Definition of the problem-generating system 4. Identification of the system's pattern of behavior and structure 5. Design of the control model
3. Design of the problem-solving strategies	6. Evaluation of former problem-solving attempts 7. Specification of objectives 8. Adaptation of strategies to dynamics of problem situation 9. Simulation of strategies 10. Decision for a sequence of strategies
4. Implementation and evolution of a monitoring system	11. Realization of strategies 12. Design of warning signals or integral monitoring systems

CONCLUSION: SYSTEMS METHODOLOGY SUMMARIZED

In Table 3, the phases of systems methodology and their substeps are summarized and integrated into an overall procedure. At the same time, the necessity for iteration is stressed when new information is needed or available. This iteration has to be interpreted in the sense of the organization of systems methodology as a hierarchical controller (see Figure 1); the arrows in that figure only indicate these relations.

NOTES AND REFERENCES

1. Ashby, W. R. "Information Flows within Co-ordinated Systems." In *Progress of Cybernetics*. Edited by J. Rose, vol. 1. London: 1970.
2. Ashby, W. R. *Design for a Brain*, 3rd ed. London: 1970.
3. Ashby, W. R. "Systems and Their Informational Measures." In *Trends in General Systems Theory*. Edited by G. Klir. London: 1972.
4. Beer St. *Cybernetics and Management*. London: 1959.
5. Beer St. *Decision and Control*. London: 1966.
6. Beer St. *Brain of the Firm*. London: 1972.
7. Beer St. *Platform for Change*. London: 1975.
8. Bunge, M. *Scientific Research II–The Search for Truth*. Berlin: 1967.
9. Campbell, D. T. "Evolutionary Epistemology." In *The Philosophy of Karl Popper*. Edited by P. A. Schilpp. La Salle, Ill.: 1974.
10. Cavallo R., and C. Klir. "A Conceptual Foundation for Systems Problem Solving." *International Journal of Systems Science* forthcoming.
11. Checkland, P. "Towards a Systems-based Methodology for Real-world Problem-solving." *Journal of Systems Engineering* 3(1972): 1.
12. Conant, R. "Detecting Subsystems of a Complex System." *IEEE Transactions on Systems, Man and Cybernetics*, September 1972, p. 550.
13. Conant, R. "Measuring the Strength of Intervariable Relations," *Kybernetes* (1973) 47.
14. Gomez, P., F. Malik, and K. H. Oeller. *Systemmethodik*, in German. Berne: 1975.
15. Gomez, P. "Systems-Methodology in Management: An Adaptive Procedure for Organic Problem-Solving." In *Applied General Systems Research: Recent Development and Trends*. Edited by G. Klir. New York: 1977.
16. Gomez, P. *The Cybernetic Design of Operations Management*, in German. Berne: forthcoming.
17. Gortner, H. F. *Administration in the Public Sector*. New York: 1977.
18. Klir, G. "On the Representation of Activity Arrays." *International Journal of General Systems* 2(1975): 149.
19. Klir, G. "Identification of Generative Structures in Empirical Data." *International Journal of General Systems* 3(1976): 89.
20. Klir, G. "General Systems Concepts." In *Cybernetics: A Sourcebook*, edited by R. Trappl. Washington D.C.: 1977.
21. Hayek, F. *Law, Legislation and Liberty*, vol. 1: *Rules and Order*. Chicago: 1973.
22. Malik, F., and P. Gomez. "An Evolutionary Approach to Corporate Decision Making." *Management-Zeitschrift Industrielle Organisation* 45(1976): 308.
23. Mayurama, M. "Mutual Causality in General Systems." In *Positive Feedback*. Edited by J. Milsum. Oxford: 1968.

24. Pask, G. "A Model for Concept Learning." In *Proceedings of the 10th International Congress on Electronics.* Rome: 1963.
25. Popper, K. R. *Objective Knowledge—An Evolutionary Approach.* London: 1972.
26. Powers, 1973 re bang-bang effect.
27. Quade, E., and W. Boucher. *Systems Analysis and Policy Planning—Applications in Defense.* New York: 1968.
28. Smyth, D and P. Checkland. "Using a Systems Approach: The Structure of Root-Definitions. *Journal of Applied Systems Analysis* 5(1976): 75.
29. Van Gunsteren, H. *The Quest for Control.* London: 1976.
30. Weinberg, G. *An Introduction to General Systems Thinking.* New York: 1975.
31. Wiener, N. *Cybernetics.* New York: 1948.

3

Systematizing Management Functions: A Staged Model for Public Administration

August William Smith
Texas A & M University

INTRODUCTION

In the modern era of space-age technology and systems, diverse methodologies exist for solving problems and making decisions. There are symbolic, syntactic, and semantic methodologies for describing how managers solve problems and how they make decisions. Then, there are less subjective and more systematic ways of structuring problems and illustrating sequential alternatives to their solutions, which are empirically tested, but not scientifically validated. In addition, there are different versions of the scientific method with its particular emphasis on controlled experimentation, laboratory testing, and control methodologies, usually defined within a particular discipline or set of related disciplines where the emphasis is on progressive development, improvement, and optimization of methods, results, or both. At present, these concerns are evident in the rise of the social sciences, decision and policy sciences, organizational and behavioral sciences, scientific management and management science, and even hybrid, interdisciplinary sciences, and "systems" science.

Systems Semantics or Antics

In particular, there is the semantic problem of defining "system." To some, "system" is a catchall concept used to illustrate ways of grouping phenomena. To others, the term simply means systematic or orderly ways of breaking down complex entities into component parts and sequential events or hierarchies. To academic researchers, it includes a scientific methodology for investigating the true nature of relationships between systems and their component parts. Often "scientists" focus attention on selected variables and attributes without considering the entire system or the scope of the entire problem. In this case, the analysis may be scientific, but not "systemic," which means pervasive enough to include all variables, attributes, and relationships that interact and affect the overall system, its various subsystems, or even its environment and other external systems relationships.

Toward Systemic Studies

The present trend is toward more completely systemic and pervasive studies of systems and environmental interactions. Often one derives a synergistic effect from bridging findings from separate disciplines and sciences with interdisciplinary, multidisciplinary, and interscientific approaches to problem-solving or decision-making. Unfortunately, when many individuals speak of pursuing a "systems approach" or involving "systems analysis," they mean only that they are being systematic (orderly) in their approach or procedure to identify relevant parts of the problem or "system," or else that they are being "scientific" in their approach by utilizing the scientific method to verify and validate "selected" relationships that may exist between particular parts of the problem or system. Often such "selected" relationships are biased by the researcher's own academic background and the scope of his educational and other prior experiences, usually in handling one specialized part of the overall problem, system, or decision process. For this very reason, truly interdisciplinary and integrative studies need to be undertaken by "teams" of operations researchers, management scientists, and systems scientists. Yet, even this does not guarantee that the resulting studies will be complete and truly systemic in scope. As a general rule, unless such studies include technical, economic, organizational, social, and human (or individual) variables, and specify some relationships among these variables and other existing external and environmental relationships as well, they will usually fail to be systemic and complete. Hence, there is always the need for further research to include more variables and relationships.

The concern to be systemic is often a matter of degree; some studies are more systemic than other studies. The trend toward more comprehensive and integrative simulation models and overall sensitivity analyses, as well as systems audits (as opposed to functional audits) indicates a definite move to more systemic methodologies in recent years.

Methodological Distinctions

In the search for more systems-oriented methodologies to guide problem-solving and decision-making, a distinction is emerging between indicators of system

Table 1. A typology of managerial and organizational concerns and issues.[a]

LEVEL-TYPE VALUES	DEFINITION	MANAGERIAL CONCERNS	ORGANIZATIONAL CONCERNS	NORMATIV BASIS AUTHORIT
Symbolic (Subjective)	Basic underlying reason for existing, survival	Manager as a spokesman and scalar person, symbolic leader	Pyramid organization, basic mission, operating identity	Tradition, mystery
Static (systematic)	Maintain order, stability, continuity, balance	Manager as a stabilizing force with standard supportive skills principles, and procedures	Operations levels, efficiency levels, standards department	Position, role, bureaucrati seniority
Scientific (specialties)	Search for progress, optimal methods and results	Manager as a specialized person trained in a particular discipline or set of disciplines	Staff and line specialists, study groups, department level	Expertise or interest, special training, license
Systemic (systems scope)	Integrative, interactive concern for overall external and internal relationships and effects	Manager as an interdisciplinary, systems-oriented, professional, resource person	Matrix organization, inter-disciplinary efforts/studies, systems departments, overall planning departments, division level, executive level	Individual recognition *via* extensiv credentials, membershi
Strategic (self-sufficiency)	Self-attainment, sufficiency essential to the ultimate survival, growth and inter-development of systems	Manager as an overall, organizational-development person, concerned with long-range, normative issues	Strategic planning departments, crucial contingency planning, corporate headquarters	Same as above, peer evaluation, individual approval

[a]This typology follows referents and categories partially noted by John W. Sutherland [21, pp. 284]. The sophistication of the methodologies increases as one reads down the table.

REDOMINANT ONTROL MODE D INSTRUMENT	BEHAVIORAL OBJECTIVE SOUGHT	COGNITIVE BASIS	ACCOUNTABILITY MEASURES
tualistic gma	Obedience, mechanistic	Observation, symbolic values, syntax	Cultural values, symbolic codes single-entry record-keeping
gorithmic, ocedural, ercive, tical	Programmable, predictive behavior	Stability, trial and error, closed systems, cybernetics	Operational productivity standards, double-entry record-keeping, breakeven analysis, payback methods
jective low-up, periments, ional ndards, nctional audits	Innovation, assiduity, diligent, rational behavior	Scientific management optimization, policy science, management science	Methods improvement, financial audits, operational audits, cost accounting
uristic, licy-making el, ulation, sitivity alysis tem-wide terfunctional) dits	Creativity, intuitive behavior, nonprogrammable, externally-directed behavior, "satisficing" behavior	Systems science, suboptimization systems design, systems architecture, synergy	Systems audits, budgeting systems, PPBS, zero-based budgeting, operating systems, productivity systems, environmental impact, cost-benefit analysis, cost-effectiveness, systems accountability
ategic nning vival, wth, velopment ues, f-regulation, ical codes, ial accountability	Self-sufficiency, interdirected behavior	System potential, systems regulation, self-regulation, metatheoretical level	Strategic planning studies, survival and development studies, human resource accounting, systems strategies, long-range resource development

size, scope, and "quantitative" precision in measurement, and indicators of system growth, interdevelopment, and "qualitative" attainments. There is also concern for attaining greater self-sufficiency and understanding strategic, long-run, normative issues related to systems and their ultimate survival or adaptability to changing conditions and contingencies.

With such a diversity of methodologies and approaches for solving problems and making decisions, managers are often confused, and operate in a "semantics jungle" of alternative ways to go about analyzing the situations they confront on the job. What one manager calls "systematic" another calls "a systems approach." While one emphasized the ultimate merits of undertaking an intensive "scientific analysis," another emphasizes undertaking a more extensive "systems analysis." Is it any wonder that the literature is so contradictory in explaining how to analyze problems and make decisions, or what to include and emphasize? Also, how can one compare results of studies that examine even the same variables and relationships, but differ in their underlying methodologies and degrees of precision? Yet, such comparisons are frequently made and become entrenched in the literature of many disciplines.

For this very reason, it is time to develop more meaningful guidelines and standards for defining what to include in particular types of research methodologies, and what degrees of rigor or precision to require in each type. Here, "research methodologies" refers to particular levels of sophistication in terms of the overall intensity (number of variables and degree of complexity) of the resulting analysis.

A Typology of Managerial and Organizational Methods

This article examines some ways to define and classify particular types of research methodologies, and makes some basic distinctions between the relative degrees of precision likely to be achieved from each methodology. (See Table 1.) The various research methodologies are presented as distinct, somewhat sequential, and hierarchical levels of study sophistication (intensity, extensiveness, and complexity) with increasing managerial, organizational, and social impact. In particular, an innovative overall framework, hierarchy, and taxonomy are presented to help managers simplify and standardize the various research methodologies and realize the importance of using appropriate methodologies to meet the scope of the problem or system being studied.

SYMBOLIC METHODS AND MANAGEMENT

The first classification involves symbolic methods and management. "Symbolic" is used to describe all underlying values and codes that are fundamental to any inquiry about a given problem or system. Cultures are built upon more symbolism than we can often imagine or acknowledge, without examining our closest held precepts about almost any subject, topic, or issue of importance. Symbols warrant separate study and analysis.

The manager often displays symbols in carrying out his functions, duties, and responsibilities. Certain rights, *i.e.*, rank has its privileges, RHIP, are quite symbolic and taken for granted. The manager often brings to the job certain preconceived ideas about the nature of people, workers in particular, often specified by symbolic codes of X and Y, indicating whether the manager considers workers to be inherently lazy or willing to work, respectively [14]. Also, the symbolic leader is one who stands out in the crowd, and appears to catch the attention of others because of certain traits or symbols acceptable to others, *i.e.*, bearing, charisma, strength, stamina, and so forth.

Cultural Symbolism

Cultures often emphasize different symbols that affect individuals, groups, organizations, and society at large, including the basic needs and rights of individuals and the symbols of status and role-playing in selected positions. Feelings, mores, and sentiments are also quite symbolic of group norms, variations, and behavior. To disregard such symbolism prevents understanding the logic of human and organizational behavior that explains why certain systems perform as they do in the real world.

Consider the case of Nicolo Machiavelli, whose *The Prince*, written in 1513, is a how-to-do-it book for rulers and aspiring leaders, based on political intrigue and discretions [15]. He stated ways to symbolize and show personal political strength, using force and deceit when necessary. Even today, Machiavellian tactics are symbolic of crafty, cunning policy and intentions, as well as unscrupulous actions, both in politics and in management.

Many principles of management are founded on symbolic meaning. The Unity-of-Command principle is symbolic of being able to serve only one master. Even the scalar principle of "chiefs and indians" is symbolic of the need to distinguish between leaders and followers, even in small undertakings. Also, the idea that management is universal is symbolic, but indicative, of what is needed to carry out an undertaking of any size that involves resources and people.

In cultures and social orders, languages identify enduring symbolic codes needed for verbal communication, subject to continuing evolution and modification as the symbols take on added or changed meanings over time. In any organization, symbolism and traditional values, including precedents and past actions, often affect present alternatives and future choices. Such values and actions provide stability, but also encourage stalemates. When tradition is unduly emphasized, *i.e.*, past actions become sacred and have emotional overtones, then undue resistance to change is likely to stifle innovative alternatives and reduce future options to the organization. For this reason symbolic values are important to consider and maintain, but only to some "reasonable" degree.

Limitations of Symbolic Management

The limitations of symbolic management are quite evident. They include stereo-typing tendencies and reliance on prior assumptions, which are forced into a new era and an altered basic situation. The symbolic leader is slow to accom-modate change—why take a chance on the new and unexpected? He tends to be parochial and subject to the whims of founders and other former leaders. He may walk in their footsteps. The "great-white-father" syndrome of organiza-tions, *i.e.*, Mao's teachings, symbolizing the Chinese, *etc.*, may be good or bad, but it must change to survive and adapt to a new era. Even symbolic leaders, such as kings, queens, and popes, with their vestiges of power, are adapting to changing situations and added management concerns in new eras of added com-plexity and uncertainty in the world. Symbolic leaders are relying on more specialists to keep them informed in a number of areas of special concern and needed analysis.

At best, symbolism is elementary, but necessary, to any complete understand-ing of management in different types of organizations and cultures. Yet, it is superficial in many respects, and indicates the need for more sophisticated methodologies for studying management. The following sections examine more sophisticated, static, scientific, systemic, and strategic methodologies, as they build upon symbolic forms of management.

STATIC METHODS AND MANAGEMENT

The second classification involves static methods and management. *Static* is used to describe stable, "tried-and-true" methods that become entrenched and endure unchanged. Some individuals view the manager as a stabilizing force with standardized supportive skills and a fixed set of principles and procedures to guide his actions. In fact, they often evaluate the manager based on how well he balances schedules, maintains standard priorities, *i.e.*, seniority, and stability and order at work, insures that basic safety and security provisions are being followed, and enforces work standards. In this regard, the manager is essen-tially a policeman and watchman who maintains the static continuity, stability, harmony, and balance in the planning, utilization, and control of resources in organizations.

In particular, static areas of concern are especially evident at the lower opera-tional and supervisory levels of organizations, where more precisely defined work standards and stable work loads and roles exist. The existence of "stan-dards and procedures departments," "work measurement" and "efficiency units," and "inspection stations" substantiates these concerns. Such organizational units exist primarily to handle routine matters, to detect exceptions in the quantity or quality of work, and to bring the exceptions back within acceptable standards or tolerance limits. The exception principle is a classic example of static management.

The static manager is one who attempts to find more suitable, orderly, and systematic methods of doing things, short of any comprehensive scientific methodology. At best, static methods are prescientific; yet, they provide a basis for empirical observation and data collection eventually needed to carry out any scientific inquiry. The static manager relies on general guidelines and principles, rather than scientific truths and findings. He considers the immediate facts without investigating the underlying causes or eventual impact. He attempts to segment and simplify often complex processes as a series of sequential events. He emphasizes the fact that problem-solving and decision-making are general processes of analysis.

Early Examples of Static Management

Perhaps some of the best examples of static management are found in the management principles developed by Henry Fayol, based on his empirical observations as an operations manager and top executive in the early 1900s. He stressed adherence to a number of static principles related to division of work, authority, discipline, unity of command, unity of direction, subordination of individual interests, remuneration, line of authority, order equity, stability of personnel tenure, initiative, and *esprit de corps* [9]. Fayol also believed that an administrative science applicable to all kinds of administration and organization, in both industry and government, would emerge out of concern for management principles. In Fayol's own lifetime, he personally witnessed the need to bridge segmented theories and principles, which varied symbolically from manager to manager, into a universal common set of stable principles that could be used to prepare future managers at all organizational levels everywhere.

The concern for static management is also noted in the twelve principles of efficiency developed by Harrington Emerson in 1912. His basic stabilizing principles include:

1. ideals—clearly defined goals
2. commonsense—practical views on everything
3. competent counsel—using knowledgeable people
4. discipline—including morale
5. the fair deal—all around treatment
6. reliable, immediate, adequate, and permanent records—cost-efficiency and comparisons
7. dispatching—scheduling and control

   8. standards and schedules—motion and time studies
   9. standardization conditions
  10. standardized operations
  11. standard practice instructions—uniform designs
  12. efficiency reward—incentive payments

Emerson stressed the overlapping nature of these principles, which he felt would insure orderly production and stable operations with time [12].

   The underlying basis for *laissez faire* economics is largely founded on a set of concepts that enhance static order and continued economic stability without external government intervention to achieve equilibrium in the economy. These concepts include the individual's right to private property and personal rewards, recourse and protection of contracts, with requisite justice and balanced, equal rights for all men before the law.

The Static Security of Bureaucracy

The essence of static management is characterized in Max Weber's model of bureaucracy, which is largely designed around maintaining static conditions and established roles, responses, and relationships. Weberian thoughts about bureaucracy involved six ideals, all of which are quite static ways to view organizations: a division of labor based upon functional specialization; a well-defined hierarchy of authority; a system of rules covering the rights and duties of positional incumbents; a system of procedures for dealing with work situations; impersonality of interpersonal relations; and promotion and selection or employment based upon technical competence [10]. Weber strongly emphasizes organizational "checks and balances," such as those that exist in the U.S. Government's separation of powers between the legislative, executive, and judicial branches. These internal checks help perpetuate organizational functions even at the expense of considerable duplication, "featherbedding," reduced productivity, and other internal inefficiencies.

   The bureaucratic ideal postulated by Weber provided a model for some nineteenth-century organizations, but it does not explain all operational demands or confines or controls of modern business organizations [21, p. 290]. Instead, bureaucracy has come to provide a general model for viewing structurally segmented and functionally differentiated organizations that have some potential for coercion at their disposal. Consider the religious orders of the church, and even ranks within orders; military rank in the various services; and standardized governmental and civil service levels and general scales (GS) rankings to permit comparability and movement between agencies of government. The regimentation of bureaucractic organizations is reinforced through uniforms, badges, medals, and other evidence of position or power or ability to take charge and exercise control over particular elements of the organization. These reinforcements are well-defined in advance, and every member understands the order of rank and power, and the exact line of succession in case of any unforeseen emergency situation or contingency.

Reinforcements for informal controls are also evident in the *esprit de corps* and the injection of strong ideological and affective sentiments, which are often perpetuated in traditions and standard practices that individuals may not want to change or improve upon. In some instances, *esprit de corps* can exist more strongly with one's basic work unit in the field than with regional and other parent units, and conflict and divided loyalties may result. For this reason, controls instigated around traditions and appeals to *esprit de corps* are at best static and subject to change, just as an individual's motivation and morale may change periodically.

Static Systems

Static systems depend upon fixed positions, roles, and duties that are elaborated in job descriptions and specifications. Individuals fill one particular position on the organization chart, and are expected to fulfill a particular role in carrying out that position. For the most part, a certain type of behavior is expected and reinforced by rewards. Certain algorithms and procedures are emphasized for nearly every aspect of work assignments. Policy and procedure manuals cover almost every conceivable situation in detail. Little, if anything, is left to chance. The emphasis is primarily on the means to achieve ends, and not upon ends *per se*. Because nonequifinal results may be achieved even when individuals follow the same exact procedures, it is evident that static procedures alone do not insure adequate control over work performance, outputs, or even desired end results and objectives. Yet, algorithms and defined procedures do provide a way to identify individual tactics for handling particular types of more routine problems and decisions with fairly predictive behavior.

Sutherland notes that static organizations often exhibit a high degree of coercive-algorithmic logic in dealing with individuals, and also a "symbiont ecological posture" [21, p. 292]. To be viewed in the symbiont role, a particular system or organization must be performing some function that is deemed useful to the broader system of which it is a part. As such, these systems perform critical functions necessary to maintain the integrity of the larger system itself. These functions can often be reduced to a set of programmatic, algorithmic processes distributed over several component parts that may be triggered by a particular external stimulus or event. Examples include organizations geared to national defense, mass education, domestic order, and administration of other national functions.

Such symbiont systems are quite static, as opposed to dynamic, in their interactions with the environment, and are often limited, and even somewhat stalemated, in their options for variability in behavior and performance. These systems are essentially systematized, with standardized ways of handling basic and recurring events to insure operational continuity and organizational stability, and predictive human behavior in dealing with such events.

Steady-State Systems

Static also applies to the steady-state-system concepts of von Bertalanffy [23] and Katz and Kahn [11, p. 23]. Katz and Kahn note that systems exist to maintain some constancy in energy exchange essential to the survival of open systems that are in a steady state. Steady state does not imply lack of motion or constant equilibrium; it simply means that, in the various exchanges with the environment, the internal character of the system and the relations between its parts remain the same. Furthermore, such systems can be stationary and structured the same through time with, usually, the same input-output relationship. As a result, this system is easier to work with and evaluate because of its predictive and deterministic nature. Hence, this explains why researchers often study organizations from a steady-state perspective.

Static and steady-state systems are often confused with cybernetic systems. Originally cybernetic systems were limited to explaining control practices in closed-loop systems, without environmental interaction. Today, cybernetics is applied and extended to all types of interactions involving communication, coordination, and control in machines, animals, humans, and social organizations. As organized entities become more complex and interrelated, cybernetic considerations become important to understanding their performance. The basic notion of cybernetics is to stabilize parameters in the face of uncertain or changing conditions. This stabilization is made possible by the existence of mechanisms—physical, human, or otherwise—that can detect changes occurring in the milieu, assimilate them, and dictate compensatory actions.

In a similar way, attention has focused on servomechanisms for detecting and maintaining certain types of rather standardized systems controls. Often these controls affect a particular process, algorithmic sequence, or organizational check point or decision point. They rely on sensors (visual, thermal, statistical, auditory, etc.) to capture values and compare them to preestablished standards and tolerance limits [21, pp. 316-317]. Such mechanisms can be installed only when such standards and tolerance limits are definable and predetermined. In some cases, static controls are being extended and refined because of technological advances and breakthroughs.

Standard Practices and Accountability

In terms of standard managerial practices, many commonplace activities and widely used methods of analysis are static because they provide limited accountability measures at only one point. For example, double-entry bookkeeping and record-keeping is a static but useful, standardized way to be sure that debits and credits balance at any given time. Similarly, break-even analysis provides a way to compare total revenues and total costs over a particular period of time or at a particular level of productive capacity. Pay-back methods and various depreciation and amortization methods provide rather static bases upon which to account for the use of physical resources that actually operate in a more dynamic and changing environment. Yet, such static methods provide a surrogate way to analyze resources that is acceptable and useful. Concern in recent years for productivity measurements, in light of declining and inconsistent productivity levels, will likely lead to new productivity standards based on a set of typical, average or "stabilized" (and hence static) assumptions. While such methods do serve a real purpose in ongoing operational analysis, they are by no means a substitute for more intensive scientific inquiry or more extensive systemic analysis.

SCIENTIFIC METHODS AND MANAGEMENT

The third classification involves scientific methods and management. *Scientific* implies the use of systematized knowledge derived from direct observation and study; it connotes progressive development and improvement over time, as opposed to satisfaction with what has worked well in the past; it involves the continual search for "truth" and better ways of doing things, not being satisfied with results to date; and it attempts to discover the best, and optimize both methods and procedures, and efficiency (better outputs per unit inputs) and effectiveness (better uses and values derived).

The concern for science in management emphasizes special functional skills needed to solve problems and make decisions relevant to particular resources. For example, the advent of personnel managers, facilities managers, and so forth indicates the importance of full-time functional specialists trained in particular disciplines and areas of management. In an age of specialization, new concerns emerge and prompt further specialization. Even since the days of Frederick Taylor's concept of functional foremen, specialists have been a part of scientific management; that is, Taylor stressed the use of specialists who could study and perfect particular aspects of the job and could keep individual workers trained in the better methods to achieve improved performance and productivity.

The original scientific management movement and the movements for management science and systems science in more recent decades highlight a continuing concern to develop a true science of management. The maturity and development of any science is gauged by the scope of its developing body of knowledge and by the overall degree of internal consistency in that body of knowledge [18, pp. 74–81]. In fact, the scientific method evolves as a process fabricated out of symbolization, description, explanation, and theorizing. To what extent has a true science of management evolved or progressed since the scientific management era of Frederick Taylor in the early 1900s?

Scientific Management Origins

A classic management work, Frederick Taylor's *Scientific Management*, essentially marked the beginning of a new scientific era in management thinking. In his testimony before Congress, Taylor noted that scientific management involved a mental revolution on the part of workmen and the foreman, superintendent, and owners. Only through continued scientific improvements and breakthroughs could society maintain both higher wages for labor and higher profits for owners at the same time.

At about this same time, similar concerns for scientific management appeared in other countries. Other management books in the early 1900s included Henri Fayol's *Administracion Industrielle et Generale* in France in 1916, Karol Adamiecki's *Harmonizacja Pracy (Harmonization of Labor)* in Poland, Frederick Taylor's *Shop Management* in the U.S., and Oliver Sheldon's *The Philosophy of Management* in England in 1923. The emergence of concepts of scientific management around the world suggests a definite chronological relationship between the development of the industrial and economic climates of the countries and cultures where it evolved [16, p. 870]. Clearly the world was ready for scientific management.

At first, the scientific inquiries in management-related areas focused on the physical aspects of work and job design, but eventually they extended to social and human factors that also affected work performance significantly. What began as industrial engineering and economic studies came to include sociological, psychological, and even anthropological dimensions. In turn, further specialization and extension of these disciplines led to hybrid integrative disciplines such as social psychology and econometrics, and the need for interdisciplinary and multidimensional methods for analyzing work relationships and explaining how they affect human and organizational performance.

Also in recent years, Herbert Simon's *The New Science of Management Decision* identified the importance of utilizing modern tools in scientific analysis, most notably in data processing, operations research, and computer science. He examined how these tools have altered the overall practice of management and how managers carry out specific functions and activities [19, p. 1].

Scientific Divisiveness

For purposes of study and analysis, science is often partitioned, parochial, pedogogical, and even polarized. This is especially evident in the social, behavioral, and administrative sciences where two distinct cultures (and numerous subcultures) exist between the behavioral sciences and the analytical sciences, and between academicians and practitioners of these sciences. As a result, policy-makers and decision-makers often find competing paradigms emphasizing certain aspects of a given overall problem, while holding constant (or avoiding) other relevant aspects of the problem. Even in individual disciplines, multiple schools of thought and approaches to problem-solving often exist.

In the midst of scientific divisiveness, how can one concentrate on overall problems as wholes and interrelate findings from several disciplines that bear on the problem? Consider the mechanical engineer who wants to consider the social, economic, behavioral, and political problems involved in designing cars best suited to consumer needs. In so doing, he separates himself from the traditional literature and typical mechanical and deterministic approaches used by his fellow engineers on the design team. Thus, he operates under a different analytical modality—an organic approach versus a mechanistic approach to problem-solving. The future of modern science and "technocracy" depends upon finding ways to bridge different analytical modalities, and developing measurement devices in the organic modality comparable to those in the mechanistic modality [21, pp. 18–20].

The Scientific-Technocratic Model

Although the bureaucratic modality may adequately meet the demands made on particular organizations, such as military combat units and traditional manufacturing plants, it is not as well suited to explaining less programmable, and less highly structured situations, such as those faced by social workers, service operators, school teachers, and others, where creativity, imagination, and judgment are vital ingredients in carrying out official duties. For this reason, the scientific-technocratic model recognizes the value of skills related to carrying out official duties, but also individualized, creative skills that come from careful study and specialized work experiences.

Functional specialization and high differentiation are hallmarks of the scientific-technocratic model, whereby any attempt to explain mission, position, purpose, and other organizational properties needs first to consider the types and extensiveness of technologies involved in that organization. In fact, this functional specialization is pushed down to lower levels of the organization and provides a necessary interface between the various technical environments carrying out their operational duties. In high-technology organizations, there is often a greater premium on decentralization, innovative ideas, and individualized reporting than in low-technology organizations.

In the scientific-technocratic organization, the normative basis for authority usually depends on one's expertise, special training, licenses, and special interest in a particular performance area. The work setting is competitive, as each person attempts to extend his expertise and influence to additional parts of the organization. This internal competition among employees for jobs, rewards, status, recognition, and so forth is often based on individual merit and motivation, rather than group merit and motivation evident in the bureaucratic model. The emphasis is more on personally demostrated ability as the way to achieve and advance, *i.e.*, get the starting position on an athletic team, get the first promotion ahead of peers, win more rapid career advancement, *etc.*

From a joint socioeconomic perspective, members of the scientific-technocratic organization tend to exist in a "nuclearized, individualized world, with very little expectation of, or opportunity to realize, social benefits within their work confines" [21, p. 296]. The stress on rationalistic or materialistic rewards outweighs social benefits derived on the job. Wages often become a substitute for the lack of social amenities and rewards, and, as a result, an almost constant, acrimonious bargaining occurs between workers and management. At higher levels of the organization, executives and white collar workers may also lose interest in social status benefits (such as a key to the executive washroom, or executive dining room) and concentrate on strictly materialistic instruments.

Strictly rationalistic instruments (such as money and carpets on the office floor) tend to induce employee mobility rather than loyalty. Whereas bureaucratic organizations stress worker continuity and seniority, the scientific model leads to greater turnover even among highly trained and needed specialists, and there is less emphasis on job security. One exception may be public universities and similar organizations where tenure is rather widely practiced to insure creative expression and academic freedom and other vested rights for staying with the organization.

Controls in the scientific-technocratic organization often depend upon placing the right man in the right job and position. This is not always easy to achieve, since the organization constantly changes, innovates, and adjusts to new developments, and there is continual displacement and mobility of personnel, and hiring and firing of entire work units when creating or disbanding certain technical projects and research ventures.

Some cognitive aspects of the scientific-technocratic model include: 1) emphasis on planning accompanied by the prediction of such probable future environmental states as markets; 2) translation of broad plans into successively more detailed ones, with operational criteria derived directly from desired performance levels; 3) concentration on the calculus of satisfactory performance determined *via* an audit process; and 4) residence of the entire system in a "rationalized" setting, where every possible event is numericalized and/or objectified, and where affective or subjective factors are not supposed (normatively) to intrude [21, p. 298].

These cognitive aspects are largely manifest in recent concerns and developments in optimization theory and decision theory involving multicriteria, and in the rise of policy science and management science methods that attempt to go beyond algorithmic approaches to include stochastic (probabilistic, risk) methods. Often the concern is to determine alternative ways of achieving equifinal results through greater internal efficiency, more intensive analysis, and optimization methods.

Scientific Accountability Measures

Managers involved in the scientific mode tend to stress functional evaluations and audits, *i.e.*, financial audits, operational audits, personnel audits, *etc.*, and reporting information and collecting data by specialized, operational units. Staff specialists often review and compare operating units, and evaluate performance in terms of "scientifically determined" norms or pretested levels of output. Often emphasis is given to a particular rate-of-return by profit-and-loss centers, or to a production or market quota for a particular worker or salesman. With end results predetermined, the emphasis is on auditing as the primary control mechanism. Ideally, actual results are compared against the original goals of quotas, and variations are subject to more intensive analysis and explanation. This is the case in cost accounting, which attempts to find the "true" nature of existing cost relationships in as close to real-time as is possible. Also, this is the case in quality control, where the intensity of sampling inspection of items increases when statistical norms, scientifically determined in advance, are exceeded.

Another aspect of the scientific mode involves continual improvement of methods and the search for internal efficiencies involving every resource type. For example, the search for better selection, and most cost-effective hiring, training, and career-development methods exists in manpower planning and the personnel area. Similarly, the search for better and most cost-effective materials-handling, equipment utilization, production scheduling, and inventory control exists in the production planning and control area. Science is a never-ending search for more and better results and means to achieve those results at both the macroorganizational level and the microindividual level. Yet, scientific precision in one area of concern is not to be confused with broader, overall "systemic" concern and understanding.

SYSTEMIC METHODS AND MANAGEMENT

The fourth classification involves systemic methods and management. *Systemic* means affecting the body as a whole, such as systemic effects of the entire human body, involving the respiratory, circulatory, digestive, mental, and other systems that form an integral part of the human and resulting states. From managerial and organizational viewpoints, both individual and organizational systems or social bodies, *i.e.*, word units and informal social groups, involve purposeful systems and systemic concerns. This means understanding: 1) the overall parameters of the various subsystems, component parts, and elements that encompass a given system, in terms of its overall size, scope, and boundary limitations; 2) the various types and levels of relationships that exist between these subsystems, component parts, and elements, which exchange energy, information, *etc.*, and; 3) the repercussions of external environmental factors on the various subsystems, component parts, and elements or the system as a whole, *i.e.*, exogenous variables and other externalities. Unless one investigates and understands something at all three of these levels, the investigation is not completely systemic, but only quasi-systemic in relative degrees.

Many past studies that advocate systems thinking, the systems approach, and even detailed systems-analysis methods fail to meet the criteria for being truly systemic. In fact, there is considerable diversity in the use of system terms, and considerable abuse rising out of their overextended use during the past several decades. Individuals with almost any background who take a systematic view of a problem consider themselves systems analysts, and offer their services to organizations as such. Few standards, if any, exist for evaluating the work of systems analysts.

Interdisciplinary Methods and Professionalism

The modern systems age spans almost every conceivable aspect of management and problem-solving. There are physical and human systems, communication and data processing and information systems, "industrial dynamics," "urban dynamics," and even "world dynamics" systems, ecological and environmental systems, production and service systems, planning and control systems, manpower-planning and personnel systems, performance and productivity systems, and even human motivation systems. Hence, it is no wonder that the systems concept is overextended. Likewise, it is true that many systems studies fail to encompass all the criteria and variables inherent in a system necessary to be truly systemic and complete. Although such studies make use of scientific findings from several disciplines and areas relevant to a given system, they are more accurately labeled *interscience*, rather than *systems science* or *systemic analysis*.

Systemic analysis also bridges findings from a number of areas of science and several basic disciplines and includes technical, economic, organizational, social, and human parameters that bear on the overall problem or system being investigated. For this reason, a systemic analysis is both interdisciplinary and multidisciplinary in scope, measurement, and evaluation. It often suboptimizes, rather than optimizes any single parameter, as is often the case in scientific, hence more segmented, analyses.

Because of its wider concerns, the systemic approach represents a more complete professional approach to management practice. As Robert Doktor and Michael Moses confirm [4, p. 5]:

> very few people really manage well enough to be worthy of the title professional manager. At the heart of the performance of management is the concept of linking (together systems of) diverse disciplines and bringing this linkage to bear upon a specific problem. It is not enough to be multidisciplinary; one must be interdisciplinary. It is not enough to be theoretical; one must be applied.

This is what is meant by striving to be a systemic, professional manager aware of all relevant factors that affect work systems.

With increasing complexity in modern industrial societies has come the need for well-trained "systems planners" and professional intelligentsia who can manage overall systems and organizational divisions efficiently and effectively. These individuals often rely on a number of technical, functional specialists to supply them with needed information in certain areas of concern. Yet, it is the manager who must interrelate the various information sources and alternatives and come up with overall answers to problems and make the "right" decisions. Systems managers are often found at division and higher levels. They must be able to digest diverse reports and sources from a number of specialists and see the "big picture."

Such high-ranking managers, executives, and administrators may have come up through the ranks in various functional specialties and assignments, but now deal with general, overall issues. This is similar to the military officer who follows a particular functional career branch for many years and who suddenly is promoted to general officer and loses his allegiance to any one technical career branch; after all, he must be able to direct overall military campaigns at this point in his career. A similar analogy can be made in industry for those who rise to the general manager, or superintendent level. How can one properly convey this difference between the more general systems orientation and functional specialty orientations? More specifically, what added training is needed to become a systems manager?

Contributions of General Systems Theory

General Systems Theory offers some real possibilities for training future systems managers, executives, and administrators. One important contribution to the study of management is in the analysis and synthesis of "organized complexities." Ludwig von Bertalanffy, the pioneer of General Systems Theory, stressed that a distinction be made between "general systems" and the "systems approach" [23, pp. 18-19]. This distinction is further noted by Kenneth Boulding, in his differentiation between science and systems [2, p. 17]:

> Science, for all its successes, still has a very long way to go. General Systems Theory may at times be an embarrassment in pointing out how very far we still have to go, and in deflating excessive philosophical claims for overly simple systems. It also may be helpful, however, in pointing out to some extent where we have to go. The skeleton must come out of the closet before its dry bones can live.

The distinction between science and systems thinking is crucial. Whereas traditional science promotes more discrete and diverse thinking and segmented analysis, the systems approach promotes more continuous and integrative thinking and overall synthesis. It is often easier to break out parts of an overall problem and identify differences of opinion than it is to reconcile those parts and differences in an integrative and rational explanation, model, or framework.

A New Age of Synthesis

In a number of disciplines that underly the study of management, recent studies stress the need to extend scientific concerns and the "age of analysis" to more systemic concerns—a new "age of synthesis." For example, Katz and Kahn, in their study of organizational processes, have shifted from the traditional emphasis on individual psychology and interpersonal relations and analysis to systems constructs and synthesis needed [11, pp. 452-453]. The trace classical organization theory and principles from a set of segmented, static principles and a closed system to new concerns for integrative and dynamic open-system explanations of modern organizations.

In the field of sociology, Pitirim Sorokin, President of the American Sociological Association, has stated [20, p. 883]:

If sociology is going to grow as a basic science of sociocultural phenomena, it is bound to pass into a new synthesizing-generalizing phase. Empirical signs indicate that for several reasons this transition has already begun. Stipulating certain conditions, we can reasonably expect a synthesizing sociology, unifying into a rich, logically and empirically valid system all the sound parts of the existing analytical theories and integrating all the little and "middle range" uniformities of today's sociology.

In essence, Sorokin has distinguished between the pursuit of science in sociology, and the projection and importance of systems in sociology.

The systemic approach follows the logic expressed by Walter Buckley [3, p. xxiii] :

The systems approach to the study of man can be appreciated as an effort to restore meaning (in terms of intuitively grasped understanding of wholes) while adhering to the principles of disciplined generalizations and rigorous deduction. It is, in short, an attempt to make the study of man both scientific and meaningful.

This perspective indicates that the systems approach enhances the overall pursuit of science by focusing on larger, overall, and more integrated levels of inquiry, where results can be more meaningful in systems studies that focus on the problem level rather than on the individual scientist or specialty level.

The Gestalt-Systemic Model—Systocracy

Mary Parker Follett, a not widely publicized management pioneer, was ahead of her time in understanding social systems. In the areas of coordination and control, she reflected on Gestalt psychology and the importance of considering the total situation. She felt that the basis for control resided in self-regulating and self-directing individuals and groups who, themselves, identified common interests and controlled their own tasks to some extent. The manager did not control individuals or deal with personalities, but instead focused his attention on complex interrelationships and overall situations. This pioneering work is useful in understanding early concern for an overall Gestalt and systemic approach to management, long before the popular appeal of General Systems Theory.

In modern terms, the Gestalt-Systemic model involves a dynamic dimension involving heuristic and opportunistic approaches to problem-solving, rather than the algorithmic and deterministic approaches discussed earlier. At best, algorithmic solutions are static and fixed; heuristic solutions are dynamic and flexible to meet changing requirements and situations. Heuristic programming involves using intuition and insight to converge quickly on viable alternatives and opportunities without being committed to any one of them.

The indeterminate nature of heuristic approaches and overall systemic analysis often depends upon the insight and unique qualities of its practitioners—the extensiveness and proportions of their skills, aptitudes, and talents. Careful screening and selection of members who can work on one-of-a-kind problems and generate feasible options is needed by systems planners. While some specialized planning is evident in the scientific-technocratic model, more integrative and indeterminate planning is characterized by the Gestalt-Systemic model and approach. This systemic approach is relatively new and still undergoing refinement.

The full impact of heuristic techniques and heuristic problem-solving perhaps marks the transition to a second industrial revolution, where machines will be programmed to investigate alternative courses of action and develop policy implications thus relieving people of the need to work with extensive details subject to human error, slower processing speeds, and a more limited human attention span. (For example, a computer can undertake multiprocessing and multiprogramming at one time, but the human mind can process only one thing at a time, often with a limited recall and range of observation accuracy.) This contrasts with the logic of the algorithmic, process concerns of the first industrial revolution where machines were "programmed" to carry out specific physical aspects of work primarily, but also included some pattern recognition, duplication, and copying, *e.g.*, textile weavers. Just as machines have not taken over all aspects of man's physical work, they are not likely to take over all aspects of his mental work or management's decision processes. These processes justify systemic analyses.

The systemic model came about for several reasons: 1) the failure of bureaucratic agencies to deal effectively with Gestalt-like social, economic, behavioral, and political problems; 2) the gradual, but striking, shift from secondary to tertiary industry in the highly developed countries; 3) the demand for expert consulting and staff organizations to lend specialized assistance in the face of an increasingly complex technologized milieu in all sectors—political, social, and economic; and 4) the increasing emphasis lent educational or intellectual, as opposed to experiential, attributes in an environment increasingly characterized by unprecedented events that demand creative rather than iterative or precedented responses [21, p. 299].

In the professional world, both ends and means are important, but often misunderstood. In the think tank, the nonprofit research organization, the research-oriented university faculty, we readily recognize the critical nature of individual inputs. There is less emphasis on universal performance criteria and more emphasis on individual criteria. Controls are often self-imposed, because external controls often do not work, and lead to defections from the organization. There is greater loyalty to one's professional orientation than to the organization. Often the administrative positions are subordinated in status to the professional or creative positions; *i.e.*, the manager of a research project often is less prestigious and paid less than operational professionals on the project.

The ineffectiveness of traditional control instruments, externally or internally imposed, leaves only autoregulation as a continuing and appropriate control modality. This is often indirect and somewhat general, and it relies on the use of peer evaluations, or peer pressures, or the existence of codes of ethics or professional codes, to constrain behavior [21, p. 300]. In this systemic model, objective audits can be performed only by qualified professionals with specified qualifications. School accreditation teams and faculty evaluation teams often display considerable flexibility in evaluation criteria and actual measurement instruments. The analyses undertaken are largely heuristic, and are tailored to the individuals involved. With greater professional latitude and more internalized motivation, there is less emphasis on organizational latitude and more externalized motivation from the environment. Clearly, certain trade-offs exist between the professional and organizational dimensions of systems.

The general lack of structural constraints evident in many systems contributes to their uncontrollability in the traditional sense. Instead of group interaction and involved productive processes with special roles and control points, there is more emphasis on individuals working alone with informal, rather than formal, patterns of interaction that often change continually. Managers in this type of environment find that their primary roles involve providing the kind of climate or milieu that allows personnel to direct themselves, and buffering employees from bureaucratic pressures and excessive demands. These roles are widespread in an industrialized society in such diverse areas as medicine, law, higher education, art, industrial market research, and R&D labs. They exist at executive, administrator, top management, and board member levels of organizations, where the emphasis falls on externally directed behavior as it affects organizational mission and the development of strategies to meet external pressures and opportunities [21, p. 301].

In terms of cognitive emphasis, the systemic manager is concerned with suboptimization of overall parameters, rather than optimization of any one set of parameters. He tends to develop satisfactory levels of performance, rather than to set optimal levels; he may pursue several levels of performance goals, and view these goals as levels of achievement toward some overall, often idealistic, end. He "satisfices" in his behavior from several alternatives and levels of performance attainment; he sees his levels of performance as relative degrees of attainment, rather than absolute ends in themselves. He is also concerned with creative design, and makes sure that he has considered all viable, alternative ways of structuring a given problem or situation. He is likely to stress the artistic, perceptual qualities of systems architecture and equate them with the rationalistic, objectively measured quantities of system inputs and outputs.

Systems Simulation, Sensitivity, and "Equifinality"

Along with consciousness of modern systems has come greater concern to model, and thereby explain better, actual, real-world systems and processes. Simulation techniques and programs are often based on "models," surrogates, and other suitable substitutes when it is impossible to measure or study the actual system or where it is too costly. Simulation provides a way to: experiment and evaluate systems; learn more about the system and its parts and relationships; familiarize personnel with a system or set of conditions in utilizing a system; and demonstrate and validate a new approach, a possible new system, or improve an existing system. Models that capture the essence of reality found in the actual system are considered to have verisimilitude. For example, fashion models—persons—are often used to obtain needed feedback and to measure buyers' early reactions, to allow manufacturers time to project demands and sales for particular clothes before they actually produce and distribute them. Fashion models, as measures of appeal, have verisimilitude.

Systems models are also useful for analyzing complex variables and relationships and detecting their relative sensitivities. That is, if a minor shift in the input value of a given variable causes major shifts in output, then that variable is considered to be quite sensitive and worthy of more intensive analysis and observation.

Systems models and analysis also help managers realize that equal, final outputs may be caused in quite different ways, even given the identical original inputs into the system (the equifinality principle). In other words, concern for internal relationships is just as important as concern for inputs or outputs in a system. This is the opposite of the black box concept, which states that one can adequately explain a system by understanding only its inputs and outputs, without regard for what goes on within the system or the black box. Concern for internal relationships is especially important in the study of social systems and organizations, including individual work groups and managers in organizations.

Matrix Organization and Systems

Innovative approaches to organization, such as matrix organization, represent a systems-oriented view of the dynamic and often changing organizational relationships that characterize certain types of modern organizations. Primarily, these organizations have a number of distinct projects, programs, or products and organ-

Table 2. Matrix organization—an open system.

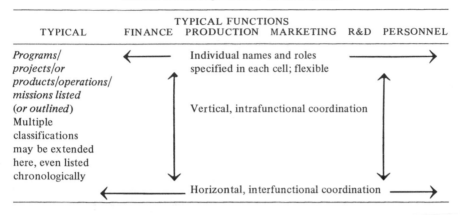

TYPICAL	TYPICAL FUNCTIONS				
	FINANCE	PRODUCTION	MARKETING	R&D	PERSONNEL

Programs/ projects/or products/operations/ missions listed (or outlined) Multiple classifications may be extended here, even listed chronologically

Individual names and roles specified in each cell; flexible

Vertical, intrafunctional coordination

Horizontal, interfunctional coordination

izational functions requiring separate identity, but also definite interface and even close coordination and joint accountability in some instances. In contrast with the pyramidal organization's fixed lines of authority and responsibility, the matrix organization permits more flexible lines of authority and responsibility, which may be shared between several individuals. Also, individuals may be assigned multiple roles and assignments; *i.e.*, fill several cells of the matrix. Individuals who fill more key coordinative roles may have more power in the organization than is explained by their relative position on the traditional organization chart. In this regard the matrix organization complements the traditional pyramid organization chart, and it allows for multiple modes of coordination as noted in Table 2. The flexibility of the matrix organization makes it especially useful in professional, technical and research organizations in both private firms and public institutions (it is applicable to universities and federal agencies, such as NASA for aeronautics and space, ERDA for energy, AEC for atomic energy, *etc.*). The matrix organization embodies systemic concerns for integrating technical and functional, organizational and individual roles and assignments in a flexible and highly adaptive framework useful for evaluating ongoing and changing programs, projects, and given missions and separate operations.

The Search for Overall Systemic Effectiveness

Warren Bennis notes that organizations are evolving from traditional bureaucracy and static concepts to "organic-adaptive systems" [1]. He also notes that we experience shortcomings in our view of organizational systems because we lack true scientific precision. If we are to achieve a truly scientific management, it will need to include the concept of organizational, or system, health. This re-

Table 3. Major variables in the study of organizational behavior [1, p. 37] .

	CRITERIA VARIABLES	
	ORGANIZATIONAL EFFICIENCY	SATISFACTION OR HEALTH
Technology (rationalized procedures)	Management science: systems research, operations research, decision processes, *etc.*	Human engineering
Human factors	Personnel psychology, training, and other personnel functions	Industrial, social psychology, and sociology

quires identifying effectiveness criteria covering the major variables and areas of study related to organizations and behavior. His framework is developed in Table 3. To be truly "systemic," studies should include technology and human factors and variables relevant to organizational efficiency and satisfaction or health, and should include interdisciplinary, behavioral, and analytical sciences if one is to understand the behavior and performance of individual workers, groups of workers, or entire organizations. Considering variables related to overall organizational performance or human resources separately or independently can lead to quite misleading results. The effectiveness of any organization is a function of some dimensions of organizational performance such as profit, cost, rates of productivity, or individual outputs, and also dimensions associated with human resources, such as morale, motivation, mental health, job commitment, cohesiveness, or attitudes toward the organization [12, pp. 237–268]. Relating dimensions of organizational performance with concerns of human resources is inherent in any overall model of systems effectiveness.

Systems Accountability Measures

Systemic accountability is highly dependent upon self-regulation and ethical and professional codes for evaluating actions and performance over time. Such accountability measures allow for more dynamic interpretation and flexibility than is possible with rigid, predetermined, and fixed measures of accountability noted in the static and scientific models. The manager often advocates systemwide evaluations and audits involving quantitative and qualitative measurements, rather than segmented functional audits, such as financial department audits, *etc.* Operational audits are considered important, as they relate to overall planning efforts at all levels of the organization, not just in individual departments and separate operating units.

Integrative budgeting approaches and systems are recommended, especially those that cover several time periods and allow continuing comparisons to be made between units. This is evident in the newer budgeting techniques such as the Planning-Programming-Budgeting Systems (PPBS) and zero-based budgeting systems, which have become popular since the 1960s. Such budgeting efforts are especially relevant to management decisions made in public institutions, although they have been used in private firms with some success.

New concerns for measurements of overall systems productivity have become more important in recent years because of declining productivity levels and new limits to growth. This is leading to extensive systems studies to develop more efficient and effective systems in terms of both physical and human productivity. Somewhat related to productivity measures are new concerns for more complete environmental impact statements and cost justifications before undertaking major research and development projects. Consider recent studies of the SST plane and nuclear power plants as examples of systems analysis.

Often linked to new budgeting techniques—and new concerns for more economical allocation and utilization of resources in an era of reduced growth and scarce resources—are greater cost-savings, cost-benefit and cost-effectiveness analyses used to decide which projects to undertake on the strategic-importance and order-of-projects priorities.

STRATEGIC METHODS AND MANAGEMENT

The fifth classification involves strategic methods and management. *Strategic* means identifying factors that are critical to long-range survival of all types of systems; in fact, it represents an extension of systemic concerns to their natural and ultimate limits, whether induced internally or externally. Strategic also implies grandiose concern for overall planning and managing over the long run. It involves "normative" issues, and identifying ultimate limits to growth and development. It is concerned with the role that specific types of organizations will play relative to society and posterity.

The strategic-oriented manager is concerned with self-sufficiency and self-attainment as essential to the ultimate survival, growth, and interdevelopment of systems. He is concerned with internal as well as external constraints to growth, and with both internal and external relationships that may delimit future options and possibilities for growth or survival.

The strategic manager is one who guides the overall destiny of the firm. He is the ultimate "steersman" or cybernetic force that directs and coordinates all types of communications and controls between and among organizational entities.   He is concerned with maintaining individual integrity and independent judgment, while also invoking greater efficiencies in internal and external processes and exchanges. He ultimately assumes the responsibility of overall organizational development and the career development of its members. He is likely to be an adviser to top management and high-level administrators and executives who manage the vital resources of the organization.

Strategic Planning and Planners

Evidence of this strategic concern can be noted in the rise of strategic planning departments and contingency planning departments that can react to volatile and changing situations and crises without delay. Most often these departments are part of the corporate headquarters staff, but they may be dispersed geographically and be located near potential hotspots. The strategic forces of the military and the State Department are examples, as are certain persons in the Central Intelligence Agency. Corporations continue to form corporate intelligence agencies and special joint industry associations—even interorganizational joint ventures, in some cases—to study and report on matters of strategic importance.

As in the case of systemic concerns, strategic concerns often involve the use of persons with exotic and unique talents who are given a high degree of personal discretion to carry out their studies. They are often given extended authority to intervene in actual ongoing operations and to check original data and information.   They have extended "functional" authority, which, in this case, may include authority sources, to examine and criticize efforts in virtually every functional area of the organization, depending upon the scope of the system under consideration.

Like systemic planners, strategic planners also impose self-regulation and self-controls in their work. Sometimes several strategic planners will divide up their areas of authority and responsibility, and interact when making crucial decisions that may have an ultimate or long-range effect. Sometimes these high-level superplanners work separately and independently of other organizational planners, though both report to top management, which ultimately makes the key decisions, usually after considerable deliberation and conferences with both types of planners. Then, the details may be worked out by a third type of planner, the operational-level planner, or tactician. In some instances numerous day-to-day operations and organizational concerns (ongoing tactics) relate to a particular strategy, and several strategies (by weighted priorities) relate to an overall objective. Hence, it is important not to confuse operational and organizational tactics with overall strategies and objectives.

Consider the case of Vietnam, which involved numerous tactics—military deployments, economic aid programs, *etc.*—related to a key strategy of the United

States to maintain the balance of power, military, economic, political, and social, in particular critical regions of the world. If one believes in the "domino theory" of aggression and power acquisition, a counterstrategy is necessary to insure the ultimate balance of power in the world, eventually limiting future growth of the United States and possibly threatening its very strategic survival in the long run. This is why the Pentagon Papers were so sensitive, even though they revealed only possible options. Yet, because they affected major policies, they could have been shared more directly and openly with the American public, if the issues were of strategic importance. In fact, some surmise that had the Pentagon Papers been shared openly, most Americans could perhaps have better understood and rationalized government actions in Vietnam and other faraway lands. Often this is the paradox: strategic issues may be deemed so critical that policy-makers and decisions-makers may not share them openly with individuals directly affected by them. This is true even in peacetime when revealing such issues might engender real conflicts. Yet, in time of war, some strategic issues may be shared because the action is already underway and already out in the open. Even so, the real strategic issues are still likely to be safeguarded, at least initially, during actual conflict.

Similar strategies exist among competitors in the marketplace, and even among religious orders and political parties that wish to perpetuate certain ideas and values they consider critical to their own long-range survival.

Strategy Development and Metatheoretical Systems

Strategy development often exists on the level of a metatheoretical system. An example is the rationale presented for free enterprise versus a communistic system. Each system is cognitively explained in terms of its ultimate potential for overall society and the individual. It often invokes and enforces self-regulations and system regulations to attain its desired results and objectives.

The strategic model is evident in the rapidly increasing concern for overall strategic planning studies and models by companies, churches, communities, countries, and worldwide organizations, such as the Club of Rome, NATO, etc. There is concern to identify the limits to growth from economic, political, cultural, and social standpoints, as well as productive, ecological, and environmental standpoints. There is also concern for a greater emphasis on protecting and accounting for human resources on a par with physical accountability measures, such as for equipment and similar resources. Such studies and models will likely increase in number and extent of predictive power in the next several decades, and there will likely be more cooperative efforts to share data and develop more truly systemic and strategic planning models for industrialized and developing nations and societies in the future.

The Strategic-Extended, Cybernetic Model

What some have previously labeled a "communications revolution" or an "information revolution" is more fundamentally a "cybernetic revolution" in reality. Because communications and information in many fields of study double every decade or so, the obvious results are mountains of data, larger data banks, data bases and retrieval systems, and larger and more extensive processing facilities. In this regard, it is becoming evident that there are limits to the manageable size of such systems, and that larger systems or superstructures do not always lead to greater efficiency, effectiveness, or cost-benefits. Yet, with added size and centralization, systems often become more vulnerable and require greater security precautions and controls, *i.e.*, access, processing, and output monitors, *etc.* In these systems, the real bottlenecks and limiting factors are often not hardware or software or support, but rather the managers and users of the system and what they hope to achieve with it. Often managers and users cannot agree on information priorities and needs or how best to obtain, structure, and refine information to meet their needs for decision-making. Often, there are real constraints to integrating data that cross organizational boundaries, thereby altering the information power base of units affected. For these and similar reasons, individuals often disguise their true feelings and meanings in communicating information that affect their organizational units. This provides the challenge for using cybernetics to help explain basic differences in communication, coordination, and control, and to find ways to reconcile such differences in both human and organizational social systems.

This cybernetic revolution will "require a total re-evaluation of many of society's closely held precepts." In addition [13]:

> Cybernetics will change the information availability of our culture. More information of more value will become available to more of the populace. It will be impossible for managerial philosophies of the future not to reflect this. Human values because of power of individuals will become more important in philosophy formulation. The power base will no longer rest with a sovereign or with the people. They will have the power to impose a humanistic orientation to the development of managerial philosophies.

The new era of systemic and cybernetic concerns is already challenging the more fixed and static foundations of traditional institutions and organizations, and is stressing the need for more dynamic and adaptive systems and methodologies for handling the increasing momentum of change in organizations.

For example, one political-systems scientist has examined the need for more immediate response and adaptability in the federal government [6]. Static principles, such as the separation of powers among the legislative, executive, and judicial branches of government and checks and balances among them, alone do not insure adequate, rapid, or complete responses and adaptability to meet crises and unexpected contingencies, such as Watergate. Though these static principles do help maintain systematic order and internal stability, due-process action is often slow and bureaucratic. From a cybernetic viewpoint, stability is achieved by separating the legislative, or decision-making, body from the executive, or effector, branch, and having an independent control element in the form of the Supreme Court. Yet, there is no separate receptor to provide immediate feedback to the political system at large. In this case, the receptor element exists only indirectly in the way public opinion judges the candidates, and infrequently influences whom the electorate chooses to be the decision-makers and effector of the system. As a result, the system often appears to go in separate directions, with divided intentions among leaders in the way they interpret public opinion or pressure groups. Ultimately this affects policy decisions and enforcement, diplomacy, and other external programs and relations, such as foreign assistance and military actions, and internal programs and relations, resource allocations, and national priorities. Note that in recent years, the receptor aspect of the system has increased through modern, mass communication and widespread public awareness of more and more aspects of the political system. This has even led to the formation of new citizens' lobby groups, like Common Cause, that represent attempts to keep the system in line with the more common issues of concern to the average citizen.

In the temporal-integral order that systems thinking provides, individuals are becoming more concerned about what has held true in the past by precedent, what is affecting decisions now in real time, and what is likely to be the future outcome or likelihood of knowing more about future alternatives and priorities. There are no easy rules for identifying key variables that will allow us to know and predict the exact impact of many social alternatives with any degree of accuracy or realistic assurance that they will occur as planned. For this reason, it is hard to effect social planning in a free society until we understand the decision and action, or effector, aspects of the system, and then observe public, or receptor, reactions and feedback.

In the final analysis, no matter how well any system is originally designed, the system that survives into another age meets the continuing challenges of its immediate environment. Although social Utopia does not exist, it reminds societies that they are far from perfect and subject to considerable improvement as dynamic, operational systems over time. Vital parts of the operating system, including underlying public, or receptor, values, such as social choice and social justice, that guide decision, and action, or effector, aspects of the system, including setting goals, values, objectives, and priorities, unfortunately, are presented only in generalized and somewhat idealistic forms—the Preamble to the Constitution, the Bill of Rights, *etc.*—which provide needed flexibility, but do not insure adequate or complete operational definition as to how they will be carried out.

Modern cybernetic concerns also help us better understand reasons for "cognitive dissonance," or internal conflicts, dysfunctionalism, or disunity, and entropy, or disorder, as they exist in large and complex organizations and other operational systems that usually operate in dynamic and changing environments. Traditional management principles often prove inadequate to help managers handle nonroutine situations, conflicts, crises, or contingencies. At best, such principles provide only general guidelines for action in rather typical circumstances and routine situations. Perhaps this explains why interdisciplinary operational research "teams" are often formed to handling pressing, overall organizational problems, and why cybernetic studies are on the increase in recent years.

The cybernetic approach to organization assumes full awareness of the virtue of effective, as well as efficient, managerial and interpersonal communications, which underly coordination and control efforts of any type. This is in contrast to the noncybernetic approach to organization, where goals are stressed in terms of rather standardized management objectives and behavioral practices, including individual participation. Participation with a purpose and purposeful behavior in communication underly cybernetic concerns. Ericson notes that cybernetic organizations are more adaptive to changing organizational outputs and measures of effectiveness, and exhibit greater potential for meeting human needs and values [8]. In particular, he suggests that cybernetically oriented organizations exhibit greater capacity to improve in a number of areas:

1. motivation of development
2. tolerance of ambiguity
3. participative problem-solving
4. search for "optimum instability" for a system
5. rationality
6. greater self-actualization *via* a "collegial" milieu
7. more freedom and autonomy
8. modification of organizational goals and values
9. reflection of social values through environmental viability
10. reflection of social values through environmental interactions
11. the potential for greater value-realization
12. meeting demands for different leadership styles
13. capacity to forecast challenges.

Cybernetics provides a way to achieve greater consonance in organizations and other dynamic systems.

Strategic Concerns and New Symbiotic Forms

Organizations are not only becoming larger and more complex systems that require more extensive systemic analysis, they are also becoming more concerned about strategic resources and future limits to growth both internally and externally. As a result, new hybrid organizations and mutations of organizations are occurring, and there is a new kind of interdependence between organizations that has never existed until now. It is not a matter of megalopolis; it is a strange case where each organization is using other organizations as agents for the accomplishment of its own tasks, functions, and roles. Peter Drucker devotes an entire chapter to the modern symbiosis of organizations, which highlights his new pluralism, or diversity of interests that guide modern organizations and planners today [5]. New coalitions between government, industry, labor, and other interests are becoming more and more evident. For example, Blue Cross and private insurance carriers are literally running Medicare for the government (perhaps this is to gain the benefits of better systems developed out of private competition, instead of the detriments of added government, bureaucracies *per se*). Even universities, formerly only citadels of learning, are becoming immersed in ways to become more "prolific breeders of new private businesses" [5, p. 180]. Scientific developments in university laboratories have become rich sources of spinoffs for new companies, enterprises, and organizations.

It is interesting that the lines between public and private are disappearing. Consider how business is moving into education. Large companies, such as IBM, GE, Westinghouse, Litton, RCA, and others, have extensive divisions actively involved in education. Litton even runs a community college to experiment with new learning techniques and tools. Such interactions are not only more complex to understand, but often lead to confused and diffused meaning as to what constitutes the underlying value structure of highly interdependent organizations. For example, how can one eliminate some of the obvious conflicts of interest or conflicts to mutual survival that are bound to exist? The question is not easy to answer. The pluralist structure of modern society cannot be ascertained by a new integrative theory. Any such new theory will require added insight into symbiotic and strategic relationships.

The Specification of Symbiotic and Strategic Organizations

A new book on management enterprise devotes one of its four sections to the roles of managers and leaders in bringing about symbiotic and strategic relationships among people, structures, and goals [17]. In analyzing these relationships those authors stress the fact that the organization exists for owners, policymakers, members of the organization, clients, and the public at large, where each group exhibits dissimilar origins, structural elements, developmental trends, ideological bases, internal or external environments, degrees of size and complexity, and so forth. They emphasize that organizations and society, as strategic systems, have four functional needs—goal selection, economic and productive functions, integration, and pattern maintenance. The priorities of these needs differ for various subsystems of society, however, and affect their structure. For example, governments are essentially goal-oriented; churches are oriented toward integration and pattern-maintenance; and economic institutions are adaptation-oriented [17, p. 17].

Based on their findings, one may conclude that governments should primarily focus attention on overall goals and values of a society and programs to carry them out; that churches should primarily communicate and integrate social goals with higher-ordered goals and values of a sect of society; that institutions of education and the family should primarily internalize and complement the various value systems; and that economic institutions should primarily adapt facilities and resources to facilitate the attainment of the various value systems. Yet, each type of organization cannot forget the other functions. For example, in a company, managers perform the task of goal selection, while the production department performs the task of adaptation, and so forth. Because all these subsystems and value systems coexist, the overall system of society is always unbalanced, and would likely go out of existence if it ever became totally balanced. Instead, the quality of society is measured in the way these subsystems provide for dynamic equilibrium and change in response to specific problems while attempting to meet overall goals.

In *Future Shock*, Alvin Toffler investigates new forms of organizations, and suggests that their modularism may be defined as the attempt to lend whole structures greater permanence at the cost of making their substructures less permanent [22]. He further suggests that this is a natural trend in contemporary, advanced societies; in fact, it presents an alternative future for bureaucratic structures, which will give way to more flexible structures in the coming "adhocracy." It is an interesting perspective on the future of modern organizations.

The Criticality of Strategic Planning

As one moves up the organization chart, the amount of relevant, factual, or objective data available to develop unambiguous, *i.e.*, deterministic, decision alternatives decreases as one moves from the operational, to managerial, to executive, and to strategic overall planning levels. This is evident in the various reporting and management information systems, and in communication, coordination, and control, or cybernetic systems that exist in the organization as well.

Often strategic planning involves considerable risk. For example, where several qualitatively different events have significant probabilities of occurrence (meeting a given criterion or not, or ultimately winning or losing, *etc.*), then stochastic alternatives and premises must be defined, tested, and refined over time until adequate results are achieved—if they can ever be achieved. In addition, strategic planning can involve indeterminate or unknown or unachievable solutions. In these instances, it is not even possible to assign probabilities of occurrence for particular system events or variables. This is often the case with "metarisk" problems, where we have no conceivable way of identifying states-of-the-world, or events, or variables, but must proceed to generate additional alternatives and contingencies because we can be sure only that something we have not yet thought of will eventually be the real event, and it may be too late to start planning for it after its occurrence.

Two factors are crucial in the strategic-extended cybernetic model, and worthy of special management concern now and in the future. First, managers need to examine the *normative* implications of strategic management—the process by which the organization becomes what its directors or goal-setters think it *should* be from among the universe of alternatives available. Selecting such alternatives should involve participative decision-making by those organizational and social groups most affected by the outcome of such social choices. That is, the decisions should not be left to bureaucrats or technocrats, but should involve direct interaction and feedback from society. Perhaps this will take the form of outside advisory boards that will interact directly with internal directors and board members in both public and private organizations.

Secondly, a *new technology* and *new techniques* must emerge in the strategic management-planning area. *Heuristic* procedures for evaluating policy-making alternatives will need refinement and more extensive utilization for documenting why certain alternatives are being undertaken and others are not justified. Perhaps this will arouse greater public awareness of social issues and choices, and lead to greater social accountability. Certain additional techniques in the areas of forecasting, premising, scanning, and futurology will also undergo added refinement and more widespread utilization in the future. Qualitative techniques, such as the Nominal Group and Delphi processes, will be used when quantitative, or historical data are not available or reliable.

NOTES AND REFERENCES

1. Bennis, Warren. *Beyond Bureaucracy*. New York: McGraw-Hill, 1973.
2. Boulding, Kenneth. "General Systems Theory—The Skeleton of Science." *General Systems Yearbook*, vol. 1, 1956.
3. Buckley, Walter. *Modern Systems Research for the Behavioral Scientist*. Chicago: Aldine Publishing, 1968.
4. Doktor, Robert, and Michael Moses. *Managerial Insights*. Englewood Cliffs, N.J.: Prentice-Hall, 1973.
5. Drucker, Peter. *The Age of Discontinuity: Guidelines to our Changing Society*, ch. 8. New York: Harper & Row, 1968.
6. Easton, D. "An Approach to the Analysis of Political Systems." *World Politics* 9 (1957): pp. 383–400.
7. Emerson, Harrington. "Twelve Principles of Efficiency." *The Engineering Magazine*. New York: 1912.

8. Ericson, Richard F. "Organizational Cybernetics and Human Values." *Academy of Management Journal*, March 1970. Reprinted in Jong S. Jun and William B. Storm. *Tomorrow's Organizations: Challenges and Strategies*, pt. 3. Glenview, Ill.: Scott, Foresman, 1973.
9. Fayol, Henri. *General and Industrial Management*. Translated by Constance Storrs. London: Pitman, 1949.
10. Hall, Richard H. "The Concept of Bureaucracy: An Empirical Assessment." *American Journal of Sociology* July 1963, p. 33.
11. Katz, Daniel, and Robert L. Kahn. *The Social Psychology of Organizations*. New York: John Wiley & Sons, 1966.
12. Katzell, R. S. "Industrial Psychology." In *Annual Review of Psychology*. Edited by P. R. Fronsworth. Palo Alto, Calif.: Annual Reviews, 1957.
13. Kurch, Samuel J. "A Study of Cybernetics, Power and Managerial Value Systems." *Academy of Management Proceedings*, Thirty-second Annual Meeting, 1972, pp. 246–248.
14. McGregor, Douglas. *The Human Side of Enterprise*. New York: McGraw-Hill, 1960.
15. Machiavelli, Nicolo. *The Prince*. Translated by Luigi Ricci. New York: New American Library, 1952.
16. Mee, John, F. "Scientific Management." In *The Encyclopedia of Management*. Edited by Carl Heyel. New York: Reinhold Publishing, 1963.
17. Mescon, Michael, William Hammond, Lloyd Byars, and Joseph Foerst. *The Management Enterprise*. New York: Macmillan, 1973. See especially section 2, pp. 59–116.
18. Miner, John B. *The Management Process: Theory, Research and Practice*. New York: Macmillan, 1973.
19. Simon, Herbert A. *The New Science of Management Decision*. New York: Harper & Row, 1960.
20. Sorokin, Pitirim A. "Sociology of Yesterday, Today and Tomorrow." *American Sociological Review*, December 1965.
21. Sutherland, John. *Systems: Analysis, Administration, and Architecture*. New York: Van Nostrand Reinhold, 1975.
22. Toffler, Alvin. *Future Shock*. New York: Random House, 1970.
23. von Bertalanffy, Ludwig. *General Systems Theory*. New York: George Braziller, 1969.

4

The Socioeconomic Functions of Government: A System Dynamics Approach

Augusto Legasto, Jr.
Rutgers University

INTRODUCTION

The pressing problems that confront present-day governments are of a different nature from those of the past. When, previously, the prevailing problems were of a material nature, *e.g.*, how to build roads and bridges or how to use fossil energy to reduce human toil, the solutions sought were of a purely technical nature. Today, at least in the developed countries, scientific technology has advanced so much that the resolution of the most urgent material problems has become a fairly straightforward process.

Neutralizing the most urgent material difficulties has served only to bring new types of difficulties to the fore: social, cultural, political, and spiritual. For example, the energy problem is a sociopoliticocultural problem as much as a technical one. At least in the short run, the major factor contributing to the recurring energy shortage in the United States is the standard of living to which most Americans have become accustomed. The average American consumed almost three times as much energy per annum from 1966 to 1974 as did the average western European.

Because today's problems are no longer either purely technical nor well-defined, the major analytical tools offered by management science and operations research (MS/OR) are no longer adequate. Until recently, with the exception of a few simulation models, these traditional tools permitted only oversimplified versions of reality that were discipline-bound or unidisciplinary, single-criterion, structurally static, short-term, and unaccustomed to qualitative contingencies. Reliance on the prevalent types of MS/OR models by governmental managers, such as planners and policy makers, would tend to exacerbate rather than eliminate the deficiencies of traditional governmental practices; these deficiencies include parochialism, myopia—*i.e.*, the failure to consider long-term consequences of a "beneficial" measure, management by the "squeakiest wheel" principle—which often results in a single-criterion model, analysis by fragmentation of a problem into several smaller problems, which in turn often results in severe suboptimization and reactive rather than anticipative management. The usual result is action that is too little, too late, or both.

Illustrations

1. The prevalence of *parochialism* is attested to by the popularity of pork barrel projects, in which the welfare of the state or province is placed above the welfare of the whole nation.

2. *Myopia* is experienced on two planes of the planning horizon: length and breadth. On the temporal plane, or length, for example, expressions of social rebellion may be controlled quickly by such strong-arm tactics as censorship and curfew. However, as long as the underlying socioeconomic causes of social unrest, *e.g.*, severe maldistribution of wealth, persist, the chances are that rebellious acts will eventually resurface and with greater violence.

As another example, procuring an unlimited supply of energy solves one problem, but creates an even graver one: how to manage the use of the energy such that the earth's thermal balance is not upset.

Model scope, the breadth of the planning horizon is also often limited. For example, pollution-control devices have been found to drain much of the car's power. The problem solved on one level aggravates another problem, *i.e.*, the energy problem, on a higher level. Failure to anticipate the consequences of the initial "solution" is testament to the manager's lack of appreciation of the power of feedback loops. The tendency to fragment a problem into "more tractable" subsystems further serves to encourage feedback-blindness.

As another example, the green revolution has greatly improved the yield of rice per hectare, though many in developing sectors of the world would rather not eat it. A purely technical solution ignored the behavioral implications of the changes effected.

These examples serve to demonstrate the deficiencies of traditional governmental practices. In order to overcome them, the governmental manager must be equipped with an analytical tool that systematically counteracts these deficiencies. The tool must be multidisciplinary and structurally dynamic. Specifically, this means that the tool must accommodate feedback loops, gross statements of ill-defined relationships, *e.g.*, of qualitative phenomena, long planning horizons, *i.e.*, over 20 years, lagged effects through time-delay functions, diverse sources of information (*i.e.*, there must be an attempt to tap any and every potential source), and active participation by the user in the formulation, validation, and analysis of the modeling process.

System dynamics (SD) has evolved into such a tool, having attained some limited maturity with the development of the *World Dynamics* model [9]. A brief description and critique of SD is presented below in this introduction. The subsequent text presents a scenario in which a tool such as system dynamics is made an integral part of the governmental control system, specifically to aid in the "thinking" process of the governmental manager.

System Dynamics

Broadly speaking, the SD approach is to identify the problem system's structure in terms of circular cause-and-effect relationships, formally construct a flow chart of these relationships, formulate a computer simulation model of this flow chart, and use the model as a basis for test runs to explore the impact of policy changes on system behavior—*i.e.*, for broad policy analysis. The model is basically an aggregate model of overall system behavior, rather than a detailed model of individual events and transactions.

The basic strategy of system dynamics is the identification of elementary feedback structures that are common to most complex systems. Each simple structure is studied in detail to provide insights into the behavior of more complex systems. These elementary structures are then used as the basic building blocks of more elaborate models. Modeling a real world system becomes an exercise in identifying the basic feedback structures capable of producing the real-world behavior of interest to the modeler.

The use of the simple feedback structures serves both educational and communication needs: it not only improves man's understanding of the complex system, its structure, and dynamic behavior, but also greatly facilitates communication across academic disciplines.

Feedback is the essence of complexity of organic systems. Through the feedback loop, information about past activities is fed back not only to the system "brain," but to numerous other ongoing activities. If the feedback loop is negative, the information carried stimulates goal-seeking activity; if positive, the information carried stimulates growth activity.

The first stage of SD model development is concerned with identifying the simple feedback loops that comprise a given problem system. Whereas this process of articulating the individual components of the simulation model is straightforward, though tedious at times, the process of projecting the net result of interaction among the various components is practically impossible without the aid of a simulation model and a computer.

The primary source of the articulation process is the modeler's mental model nourished by past experience, personal theories, and information provided by the literature, as well as other "experts," *i.e.*, academicians, managers, and other constituents of the problem system. The feedback loops are initially expressed as preliminary sketches of causal hypotheses. (Contrast this with the correlational type of hypotheses utilized in econometrics.) To facilitate communication, the sketches are given in the form of causal-loop diagrams describing, in gross fashion, the real-world variables deemed essential to the problem, the direction of, and the type of, each individual relationship. One such causal relationship exists between the variables, job availability (*JAV*) and migration (*MIG*):

The arrow indicates the direction and the plus sign, the type of feedback—*i.e.*, positive. In words, the causal diagram states that, *ceteris paribus*, a positive change in *JAV* generates a positive change in *MIG*. By contrast, in a "negative" relationship, a change in one variable produces a change in the opposite direction in the second variable.

Once all the essential variables and relationships have been identified, the second stage of SD model development can be initiated: the "level-rate" flow chart. Whereas the first SD stage is founded on the concept of feedback and an underlying theory of feedback dynamics, the second stage is built on the concept of integration. The specific form used by SD is the first-order difference equation. A fundamental principle of SD is that the dynamics of any system can be sufficiently represented by the integration process. The time behavior of an SD model is generated by integrating the difference equations used to represent the causal relations of the model.

To represent the integration process, two basic symbols or types of variables are used: a level and a rate (in the jargon of economists, these become a stock and a flow, respectively, and in that of businessmen, equity and income, respectively). The levels collectively describe the condition of the system at a point in time. They represent integrations or accumulations of system resources, *e.g.*, population levels. These, in turn, determine the rate variables. The rate variables are the activity or flow variables that determine how fast levels accumulate or diminish over time. The rate variable has four components: a set of ideal conditions (a goal), a set of observed conditions (the actual conditions perceived), a monitor that measures the discrepancy between ideal and observed conditions, and the action called for by the perceived discrepancy. In a positive feedback loop, "infinity" is the implicit ideal condition of the system.

The rate equation is thus treated as a policy statement. Many of the policies represented are involuntarily fixed, at least in the short run, *e.g.*, population birth rate. Some, which are of particular interest to the modeler, represent "intervention points" through which the modeler may attempt to manage and control system behavior, *e.g.*, the rate of governmental expenditure on public works. The rate equation is also given a second, but equally important role: to determine the dynamics of the system, such as delay in transit of a particular flow between two levels. This equation, in conjunction with an appropriate level equation, is used to depict the phenomena known as time lags or delayed reactions.

In this second stage of model formulation, every causal relationship identified in the causal-diagram stage is restated in greater detail and with much greater precision using the "level-rate" format. Each model parameter and variable is defined. The flow diagram is used to depict the interconnections between levels and rates. For example, the positive causal loop linking total population with net birth rate is transformed into a flow diagram linking the level variable, *POP* (population), to the rate variable, *NBR* (net birth rate), and back to *POP*. The population level at year *t* is the accumulation of the net births from year 0 to *t*. The net annual birth rate, expressed in people per year, depends on *POP* and a parameter to be called *NPBR*, "normal percentage annual birth rate" expressed in "fraction/year" units. In mathematical terms:

$$POP(t) = POP(t - 1) + NPBR \times POP(t - 1) \qquad (1)$$

To complete the description, an initial population level and an *NPBR* (parametric) value must be given.

The mathematical formulation of the flow diagram constitutes the third stage of model development. All level equations are represented as first-order difference equations, and the rate equations are represented by algebraic equations and table functions.

The third stage involves a more technical aspect of SD model development and, from the point of view of the governmental manager, may be relegated to a trained system dynamicist. The manager resumes his active role at the model validation, use, and implementation stages. Model use may be as simple as behavior generation of the base model to determine the long-run consequences of interaction among the model components; or it may be as sophisticated as analysis, evaluation, and comparison of alternative governmental policies or plans.

Although (according to the Forrester version) the system dynamics methodology is uniquely determined at every stage of model development, from problem definition through causal-loop diagrams to implementation, the character of SD derives mainly from the first three stages described above.

Beyond the first three stages, the system dynamics methodology is still striving to develop an identity of its own. Among these, the validation stage appears to be the most promising because of the qualitative nature of many model statements. The statistical tools useful for the validation of more traditional quantitative simulation models are unsuitable for validating qualitative behavior because of the lack of the necessary data. Model validity is also dependent on the "future behavior" of the model, although validity is not to be based on correspondence between a model-predicted and an observed system condition. Validation in SD is to be obtained by observing whether or not the model reproduces the behavior characteristics of the system such as stability, oscillation, growth, average period between peaks, general time relationships between changing variables, and tendency to alternate exogenous disturbances. (The reader who wishes to delve deeper into SD model formulation is referred to these works: 1) *Principles of Systems*, by J. W. Forrester, Wright-Allen Press, Cambridge, Mass., 1968; 2) *Dynamo II User's Manual*, by A. L. Pugh, MIT Press, Cambridge, Mass., 1973; 3) *Study Notes in System Dynamics*, by M. R. Goodman, Wright-Allen, Cambridge, Mass., 1974; and 4) *Urban Dynamics*, by J. W. Forrester, MIT Press, Cambridge, Mass., 1969.)

Critique of System Dynamics

The method of SD may appear to many to be simple and straightforward. The requirements are seemingly easy: the ability to identify model variables and parameters with direct counterparts in reality, and the ability to draw the arrows and signs depicting the interrelationships among variables and parameters. On reflection, however, it becomes clear that SD fails to provide a specific procedure to guide the user through the process of abstraction of data from managers and other problem system constituents. The problem-definition and model-formulation stages must be undertaken only with the help of a trained system dynamicist. Otherwise, the method is likely to be misused or even abused. The danger of abuse is further aggravated by the mechanical versatility of the DYNAMO computer simulation language, which greatly facilitates the modeling process: given the data and model, the DYNAMO compiler automatically checks the equations for logical consistency, "solves" the system of equations, and tabulates output data and graphically plots the behavior of specified variables.

This danger of abuse, however, is not a permanent flaw in SD methodology. The presence of a skilled system dynamicist in the research team is a sufficient antidote.

Serious flaws in the methodology do exist and ought to be brought to the user-manager's attention.

First, an explicit objective function is not an integral part of SD methodology. The specific criteria to be used in the analysis are not specified and are presumably left to individual judgment. Without this function, it would be extremely difficult to evaluate the effects of various manipulatory exercises performed on the base model. It would not be clear in which direction useful changes in the system should be made. It is not, for instance, universally true that the most stable system is the best one, *e.g.*, the most responsive. The results of manipulation are usually multidimensional. Therefore, a multiple-criteria, objective function would be needed to depict trade-offs between criteria.

Second, the model, being trend-oriented, is unable to represent stochastic events endogenously. For example, it is unable to represent the changing probability of incidences of social violence in response to changes in the socioeconomic environment.

Third, pitfalls exist in the interpretation of the effects of any model over long planning horizons. The cumulative effect of a change in, for example, a sensitive parameter may seem plausible in the short run, but may be totally unrealistic in the long run. This is partly due to a fourth flaw.

The model structure remains rigid over the entire simulation run. *New* reactions to undesirable behavior exhibited by some system variables are not accommodated. Although it is true that different assumptions can be made, and the model rerun with the new assumptions, the model structure remains static in the new run. In other words, adaptive and flexible responses to changing conditions are not built into the model to allow its structure to evolve, during the run, the way real-world systems do. A system dynamics model of a problem system is a theory about that problem. It is unreasonable to expect a single SD model, or any simulation model for that matter, to represent and anticipate the variety of structures that the modeled system may evolve in the future.

The following sections explore the central role that such synthetic models as system dynamics can fill in organizing the interface between a specific set of societal goal concerns and an array of policy alternatives.

DESIGN FOR RESPONSIVE POLICY FORMULATION

In a democratic system, the people-government linkage is best depicted as a feedback loop ferrying a constant flow of information and other entities. The people communicate their needs and desires to the government. On the one hand, the government's duty is to provide the means and opportunities to satisfy these needs and desires. The survivial of major governmental components hinges on the quality of performance of this duty. On the other hand, it is the government's responsibility to provide leadership toward the achievement of well-defined societal or supersystem goals, even if the needs and desires of certain individuals or interest groups are sacrificed.

These dual governmental concerns presume the existence of a sensory system that monitors the variety of information transmitted from the people, an analytical system that interprets the information and formulates responses and plans and policies, and, finally, an implemented capability to carry out the plans and policies.

Over the centuries, but especially in the last few decades, people and their dominant needs, values, and attitudes, have continuously undergone changes and persistently created unprecedented demands on the government. At least since the industrial revolution, however, the structural designs of these bureaucracies have hardly adapted to the changes. These structures have been designed to solve specific problems in the past, and they continue, by sheer weight and inertia, to perform essentially the same tasks until the time new crises force reevaluations and development of new tasks.

The people-to-government-to-people feedback system is apparently in need of an overhaul. The government is either unable or too slow to perceive shifts in attitudes and values and even slower, if able at all, to react to these changes. The perceptual handicaps are attributable to the lack of "variety" [1] and sensitivity of the sensory system. Specifically, government sensors are sensitive to economic, demographic, and political events and trends, but are ill-equipped to detect cultural, *i.e.*, sociological and psychological, conditions and shifts thereof [3, 13, 19, 22, 24]. Due to structural deficiencies, the government fails to sense the full range of needs expressed by people.

The feedback system is also handicapped by the crude and primitive tools of analysis employed in planning and policy-making activities, which often result in government by precedence, expediency, tradition and habits, incrementalism, parochialism, or advocacy, management by crises, and power struggles. The analytical tools fail to provide a systematic procedure to determine an appropriate balance among all competing factors that define a given problem.

A third source of impairment in the feedback loop is the implemental and coordinative arm of the governmental system. Given the defective sensory and analytical faculties of the system, one's expectation of useful and practicable plans and policies can only be extremely low.

Due to these deficiencies in the design of the governmental system, formal attempts to achieve system stability and directed growth are likely to encounter major structural difficulties.

GOVERNMENTAL BUREAUCRACY: THE CENTRAL MECHANISM IN THE FEEDBACK LOOP

The "Control" System

Every control system has a receptor system that performs sensory and perceptual processes. The sensory processes receive the raw or coded information while the perceptual processes decode, recognize, select, organize, and interpret the sensory data [29]. (For example, the division that monitors employment statistics is a component of the government's receptor system.) In their almost total reliance on well-defined and measurable phenomena, current governmental receptor systems have developed severe handicaps and blind spots especially with respect to ill-defined qualitative phenomena.

Second, a control system has an effector system that executes the commands originating from a "brain" or processing center. The effector system determines the timing and patterning of the indivdual activities comprising the tasks commanded by the "brain." Its primary responsibility is effective intercomponent coordination and implementation. A control system has a third component: a "brain," or central processing system, that intervenes between the receptor and effector systems. It is expected to set the supersystem's objectives, interpret the sensed data collected and processed by the receptor system, and command the effector system to perform certain tasks designed to close any existing gaps between supersystem objectives and sensed data. In other words, it performs these activities: goal-setting, control, computation, problem-resolution, decision- and policy-making. The executive branch and the GAO (in the U.S.) constitute two major parts of this "brain" system.

A Socioeconomic System Without a Control System

The simplest formulation of an uncontrolled socioeconomic system, *i.e.*, one without an effective government, is depicted in Figure 1. Disturbances are un-

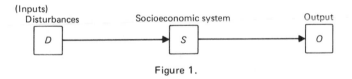

Figure 1.

expected and uncontrollable elements that apply entropic pressures on the socioeconomic system S (*i.e.*, they create undirected instability and consequently impair the socioeconomic organism). S is the socioeconomic organism and its immediate environment. Although in fact socioeconomic system elements exhibit a continuum of levels of manipulability, a dichotomous classification scheme suffices for our purposes: a set, M, of manipulable elements and not-M, of nonmanipulable elements. The set of outputs O consists of indicators or measurable representatives of *a priori* essential variables [1]. The "essence" of these variables is rooted in these organismic characteristics: survival and growth, or directed instability. Any variable related to survival or growth is defined to be an "essential output." These variables are assumed to exist prior to human perception. It is likely, therefore, that the set O is a strict subset of all "essential variables."

For convenience, we divide the states of O into two distinct sets: a set, $G-$ those that correspond to "good" states, *i.e.*, those reflective of organismic survival and/or growth—and not-G—those that correspond to "bad" states, *i.e.*, those reflective of undirected instability and death [1]. The states G are bounded by upper and lower tolerable limits. The set G suggests the existence of a set of standards or ideals against which system outputs, O, are assessed. In an uncontrollable system, however, these standards are rendered inoperative.

When no control system exists, the socioeconomic system S is more likely, as time unwinds, to exhibit output states of the not-G type. As the disturbances, D, operate unrestrainedly on S, the socioeconomic system will be powerless to counter the onset of chaos.

General Control System Designs

A control system, C, is to be designed to keep the system's, *i.e.*, S's, behavior, expressed in O (see Figure 1), within the tolerable limits of states G for any set of disturbance stimuli D. The first design (Figure 2a) depicts a control system whose effector component is directly coupled with the system D, thus enabling at least partial control by defusing or deflecting the dysfunctional subset of D stimuli away from S. Unfortunately, the current level of technology precludes adoption of this recourse.

A second design (Figure 2b) depicts an *anticipatory* control system. We contend that existing technology does provide us with concepts and tools for building at least a prototype of this design; it is to be accomplished mainly with the aid of systems theory, simulation modeling, multiple-criteria indicators, and the computer. This design situates the control system C between D and S: the sensor receives stimuli transmitted by D, and the effector is directed by the central processing unit to transmit coordinative signals to the socioeconomic system S. With predictive power, the control system anticipates significant dysfunctional disturbances, and manipulates the subset M of manipulable elements in S to counteract, or at least mitigate, their impact on S (and O). The control system's predictive power may derive from extranatural sources, as might be the basis for consistently perfect predictions, or from repetitive patterns exhibited by disturbances, as is more normally the case. A third design is presented as the most pervasive model of governmental control system designs (Figure 2c). This may appear to be a model of a car being steered ahead without the benefit of a front window. With total reliance on side and rear windows one's ability to stay on track depends on 1) disturbances: "unexpected" road curves, hazardous road conditions, adverse weather conditions, *etc.*, 2) the driver's ability to sense, per-

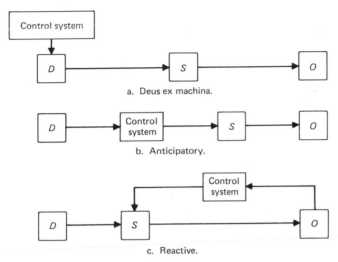

a. Deus ex machina.

b. Anticipatory.

c. Reactive.

Figure 2. Three control system designs.

ceive, interpret, analyze, decide, and react to both external disturbance stimuli and internal car conditions, and 3) the car's responsiveness to the driver's commands and its ability to react automatically, *i.e.*, independently of the driver, as when its wheels are confronted by the roadside curbs; each of its vital components must be in good working condition. The major disability of this design is its lack of anticipative power. Often remedies become operational only after crises have evolved to their full scope and force. Reaction is too little, too late.

And so it is with socioeconomic systems—in a limited sense. Just as previous experiences over the same track provide the driver with better information for steering more effectively, the history of societies provides governmental control systems with useful guidelines for managing socioeconomic systems.

Except for weather aberrations, road "disturbances" turn out to be static stimuli. Socioeconomic systems, however, are largely beset by dynamic stimuli.

As it is with the driver, a government's ability to keep the system "on track" depends on its ability to sense, perceive, interpret, analyze, decide, and react. Certain notable differences do exist, however: 1) the "track" is not as well defined for socioeconomic systems (this will eventually be referred to as the range of standards and goals preset for the system), 2) the complexity of the requisite sensory, central processing, and effector subsystems is of a totally different order from that required by the car-driver-track (CDT) system. This, for instance, subjects the government, or any bureaucracy for that matter, to critically long response times.

As it is with the CDT system, the ability of the system to stay "on track" depends on the system's responsiveness to government directions and manipulations and on it's own reactive capability to direct stimuli. Unlike the CDT system, however, the socioeconomic system offers no simple steering wheel. The effector system-socioeconomic system interface is of a totally different order of complexity. Secondly, unlike a car, a socioeconomic system has the pernicious or benevolent characteristic—depending on the circumstances—of possessing a seemingly independent will that possibly originates from inertia, a physical trait of large, dynamic systems, or from synergy, or from both.

The paradigm often adopted by present-day governments in determining the managerial responses to these dynamic socioeconomic stimuli has the following characteristics:

1. Reductionist. This rests on the assumption that reality can be fragmented and, once fragmented, analyzed and resynthesized without loss of meaning.
2. Culture- and value-insensitive. The spirit of the "scientific" approach cultivates the desire to formulate generalizable technical solutions that are valid regardless of cultural and social context. This has often resulted in the wholesale transfer of advanced technology to the less developed sectors without the requisite adjustments and adaptations to suit a peculiar context.
3. Short-run planning horizon. This characteristic is preoccupied with known options and short-term results. The system under usual study is represented as a rigid structure whose behavior is predominately determined by inertia.
4. Positivist. Planning and policy-making are based almost exclusively on extrapolative analysis. The extent of its anticipatory power is restricted to some single scenario predetermined by the model structure. The variety of future system behavior patterns is greatly underestimated, rendering the system constantly susceptible to surprises.
5. Elitist. The rationale of plans and policies is handed down from the top rather than extracted from the average citizen.
6. Unidisciplinary. This is reflective of the mode of development of the different scientific disciplines: physics, biology, economics, the social and political sciences, philosophy, theology, *etc.* To understand the diverse aspects of reality, traditional man has developed these alternative forms of systematic study systems, and to solve a problem he has relied on the experience and expertise in the "appropriate" discipline. The disciplines that dominate the rational activities of planning and goal-setting are the quantitatively-oriented social disciplines: economics and demography, particularly those subfields related to employment, mobility, and population growth. The rest of governmental activity is dominated by the political (rhetorical) process.

Grave doubts now exist about the efficacy of this classical paradigm in the perennial encounter between government and socioeconomic problems.

SOCIOECONOMIC DISTURBANCES

We classify socioeconomic disturbances, D, into two major categories: natural, including supernatural, and induced.   Natural and supernatural disturbances, such as earthquakes and hurricanes, are by nature random. Although certain organized efforts are being made to increase their predictability, the government relies more heavily on reactive plans, *e.g.*, disaster relief programs, than on anticipative plans, *e.g.*, requiring the construction of earthquake-resistant buildings. Induced disturbances are divided into two subcategories: random, such as outbreaks of war, terrorist acts, and technological breakthroughs, and systematic, for example, starvation, malnutrition, unemployment, inflation, and urban blight. Induced random disturbances are simply the natural consequence of systematic disturbances that have forced the socioeconomic system beyond certain critical thresholds of dysfunctional pressures. It is the rule, however, rather than the exception, that governmental bureaucracies treat these induced disturbances (economic problems are a notable exception) as though they were natural disasters. Government response is typically elicited at the critical stages of these disturbances: revolts are more apt to be put down violently than "nipped in the bud"; urban blight is countered with enormous infusions of brain and capital resources when the decline can no longer be reversed; malnutrition is likely to trigger the descent of medical armies and tons of highly nutritious shipments when too many children have already suffered irreversible damages.

THE SOCIOECONOMIC SYSTEM

A system is an assembly of related components each of which, in turn, is a system. With a socioeconomic system, the major components of interest are: 1) the environment, 2) a set of goals both immediate, *i.e.*, utilitarian, and normative, *i.e.*, ethical, 3) a set of inputs and resources, including disturbance stimuli, 4) outputs, a subset of which is monitored by measures of system performance, 5) a set of clients whose interests, and their priorities, are varied and often conflicting, 6) a control system, such as the governmental system, equipped with a sensor, an evaluator, and an effector. Attempts to develop systematic methods of inquiry into the management and control of this system presumes the existence of a system designer whose primary concern is to alter the system in such a way as to maximize the welfare of the system clients. A more operational statement of the basic purpose of government is provided: the maximization of opportunities for individuals, either by themselves or through interest groups, to fulfill as many levels of needs as possible from the purely physiological to the aesthetic and spiritual [17].

The socioeconomic system is primarily a homocentric system: its *raison d'etre* is the service of the human component. In the protodemocracy, the motivating forces are rooted in the needs, conscious and unconscious, short-term and long-term, and priorities of its clients. These needs [17], to survive, to attain security and stability, and to belong, insure the formation and maintenance of groups or communities. The existence of geographical, cultural, religious, logistical, economic, and other constraints inhibits the formation of a homogeneous world community, however. Rather, a variety of groups, differentiated by one or several of these constraints, is generated. Within itself, each homogeneous group shares values, attitudes, goals, and priorities. The stability associated with each group provides it with a recognizable and articulable (*e.g.*, in model form) property, *i.e.*, structure. A detailed illustration, which will also provide the background for a subsequent section, is developed below.

If we consider the problem of national development, not merely in the economic, but also in the social and political senses, the socioeconomic system of a developing country like the Philippines may, from one viewpoint, consist of four groupings distinct from one another along the rural versus urban and upper-income versus lower-income spectra. Each is a relatively homogeneous interest group of individuals in similar positions with respect to power, privilege, and prestige, as manifested and reinforced by the level of property, income, and education acquired. [2, 15].

The rural, lower class consists of the poor farm workers and migrant workers, the peasantry who typically own no land or property, serve as tenants of landowners, and generally have insufficient funds for both their subsistence and agricultural expenses. Perhaps because of their economic hardships, however, they have stronger family ties, a greater spirit of camaraderie—as demonstrated by the voluntary community assistance offered to someone erecting his house—a higher level of spiritual sensitivity, a deeper appreciation of interpersonal ties, such as friendship, a deeper reverence for nature and the environment, and a lower degree of attachment to material things than the people from the other three socioeconomic subgroupings. They bear what sociologists term the "subsistence outlook:" rural people, though they may express a longing for surplus, have a strong tradition of being contented with meeting each day's needs as they arise, with just "getting by" [11]. For example, men in a fishing town will often settle for "food for the day," when greater catches are possible. Another distinctive trait, the "leveling outlook," traditionally exerts a strong pressure to keep all members at the same level. Residents aid someone in need, but obstruct someone "getting ahead." Envy is prevalent and intense. One who wears different clothes or builds a larger house is likely to become the victim of gossip and the object of ridicule unless he proves continually that he does not think he is better than his neighbors. He must insist that his success is due to luck, and prove it by sharing his gains with others. Although the "subsistence outlook" and "leveling" act as deterrents to economic development, they may provide an environment more conducive to social development.

Almost a diametric opposite of the rural, lower class is the urban, upper class, which consists of 1) importers and exporters whose earnings are derived principally from exporting local raw materials and importing finished products from developed countries, 2) businessmen whose economic interests range from cottage industries and light manufacturing to "intermediate" industries highly dependent on imported raw materials, and 3) the so-called "petty bourgeoisie" characterized by relative self-sufficiency accruing either from ownership of a small amount of productive means, as in the instance of fishermen with their own motorized boats and fishing implements, or the possession of special training or skills, as for teachers and office clerks. By virtue of property ownership, savings, guaranteed income, access to education, leisure, and adequate health care, the urban, upper class enjoys economic security. This class, along with the rural, upper class, would place a high premium on industrialization and economic growth (GNP per capita), tend to resist governmental income-redistribution measures; oppose property-redistribution efforts, rank the importance of family, friends and the environment lower than the lower classes would, and place a high premium on "getting ahead" and achieving a comfortable, if not luxurious, style of living.

The rural, upper class consists of landlords, and rich and middle-income farmers who typically own land and earn at least enough to be comfortable. This class would hold attitudes toward economic growth and the redistribution of income and property like those of the urban, upper class's, but its view of socialization would be closer to the rural, lower class view.

The urban, lower class comprises industrial workers, the unemployed, and the underemployed. Economically, this group is closely identified with the rural, lower class but sociologically, with the urban, upper class. A breakdown of American society should reveal distinct interest-group counterparts, each with shared values, goals, needs, and priorities.

Such interest groups form the basic building blocks of socioeconomic systems. With each socioeconomic problem, or disturbance, is associated a subset of primary interest groups, who are directly and significantly affected, secondary ones, who are less affected, and so on. Distinguishing each group is a recognizable set of shared values, attitudes, goals, and priorities, which, over a short term, remain fairly stable, and form the bases for intragroup and intergroup interactions. As it is, within each group a pattern of intergroup relationships emerges and determines an articulable socioeconomic structure. This structure is, in turn, nurtured by an implicitly derived set of ultimate (super) system goals to which group (subsystem) goals are subordinated. Both these supersystem and subsystem goals constitute the motivational base of socioeconomic processes.

The short-run stability of this motivational base sets the stage for a simulation-model representation of the socioeconomic system. The modeling effort is aimed at capturing a snapshot portrayal of the existing socioeconomic structure. This portrayal, in turn, is to be utilized by the control system to design and evaluate alternative policies of socioeconomic system management. The validity of the time horizon chosen for this portrayal is carefully monitored.

Over the long run, the system structure is expected to evolve as changes occur in group values, goals, and the pattern of intergroup relationships (these change when new interest groups take on influential roles, as the environmental protection group did in the 1960s). The question of the possible role of government in the face of inevitable structural evolution then arises. Two extremes delineate the government's choices: 1) *laissez faire* evolution; and 2) "socialist" evolution. *Laissez faire* evolution will be founded on the belief that the "best" direction of system evolution can be established only when each individual, or interest group, is allowed to pursue what it thinks is in its best interest. Whereas in the economic sphere, compelling arguments exist in favor of the "free market" system, at least with respect to certain segments of the economy, the reasons are not quite as forceful *vis-à-vis* the socioeconomic sphere. For instance, evidence exists that *laissez faire* evolution abets rather than discourages economic and political inequality [2, 4, 15, 18]. "Socialist" evolution will be founded on the belief that the "best" direction of system evolution can be established only by formal design: what is best for the system in the long run has to be imposed upon each individual or interest group by a visible guiding hand.

THE PRIMARY DOMAIN OF THE CONTROL SYSTEM

Because random disturbances, both natural and induced, cannot be consistently anticipated with existing technology, and when anticipated, can rarely be prevented, system response is not deliberately formulated, but rather emerges as a patchwork of individual or interest-group reactions conditioned by custom, tradition, culture, and expedience.

The proper domain of governmental planning and policy-making consists of induced systematic disturbances. Unlike random disturbances, which precipitate problems of disorganized complexity [21], systematic disturbances create problem systems of organized complexity.

By definition, a problem of disorganized complexity [21] is one in which an "infinite" number of components is involved, each of which has an erratic or incomprehensible behavior. It follows then that the detailed pattern of problem behavior cannot be predicted consistently, although an average pattern may be discerned through statistical means. A problem of organized complexity, however, involves a sizable but finite number of components that are interrelated into an organic whole [21, 29]. The interrelation is complicated but orderly, and, hence, some patterns of problem behavior are predictable, *ceteris paribus*.

Table 1. A summary list of areas of national goals concern
and the corresponding principal indicators of goals output [26]

AREA OF GOALS CONCERN	PRINCIPAL INDICATORS OF GOALS OUTPUT
Freedom, justice, and harmony	Not yet defined
Health and safety	
Health	Mean life expectancy at birth
	Number of persons with chronic disabilities
Public safety	Violent crime rate
Education, skills, and income	
Basic schooling	Index of average achievement in language and mathematics, grade 12
Advanced learning	Percent of age group completing college
skills	Average earnings
	Number of persons outside mainstream of the labor force
Adequacy and continuity of income	Number of persons below present poverty standard
	Number of persons in near-poverty conditions
	Number of persons with permanent losses in levels of living over 30%
Human Habitat	
Homes	Proportion of persons living in inadequate housing
Neighborhoods	Proportion of persons living in satisfactory neighborhoods
Access	Index of cost of travel and transportation
Quality of environment	Percent of persons exposed to bothersome pollution
Recreation	Percent of persons regularly taking part in recreation
Finer Things	
Beauty of nature	Number of areas for preservation of beauty
Sciences	Number of scientists active in basic science
Arts	Number of active artists
Leisure	Average time free from work and chores
Economic base	GNP

The problem system has properties of its own, beyond those of its component parts, thus reflecting the emergence of a structure that is greater than the sum of its parts.

The problem of national development is of the organized type. Some disturbance stimuli associated with this problem include legislation designed to stimulate economic growth, educational curricula that implicitly reflect the values and attitudes of the ruling class, land reform, foreign-aid programs, multinational investments, radio commercials, and public works projects. Be the stimulus deliberate or spontaneous, each significantly influences the existing gap between the present and the idealized states of the socioeconomic system, one tugging to widen the gap, and another to narrow it.

In broad terms, the idealized state obtains when every individual knows the variety of human needs, has the freedom to choose the levels of needs in which to operate, and is confident that the opportunities to satisfy his minimum needs at the highest [17] levels chosen will be available.

Design of the sensory and implemental components of the control system is not to be considered explicitly in this paper, which focuses instead on the idealized design of the central processing unit. It is assumed, therefore, that idealized designs of the sensory and implemental components already exist. For instance, is is assumed that indicators of the goal concerns (see Table 1) expressed over the entire spectrum of human needs exist and are being monitored.

TOWARD THE DESIGN OF AN IDEALIZED "BRAIN"

A dilemma confronts the government when it tries to respond to the national development problem: first, maximization of a single goal concern can be achieved only at the expense of at least one other goal concern; and second, benefits can be rendered a particular interest group only at the expense of at least one other interest group. To illustrate: the high priority given economic development apparently favors the upper-income classes. Historically, the benefits produced by economic development have been enjoyed largely by the upper classes, although this does not imply that the fruits of economic development cannot be shared more equitably by the populace. By the same token, a high priority placed on the preservation of national traditions, customs, and culture would apparently favor the rural, agricultural classes of developing nations. Historically, modernization has been tantamount to the systematic dissociation from traditions, customs, and native culture, for much of these are regarded as deterrents to economic progress. The pursuit of a higher rate of economic growth is achieved at the expense of a relative loss in traditional, national identity, especially in the rural sectors.

Fortunately though, not all apparent dilemmas are bonafide. Moreover, incompatibility in one society may be mutual benefit in another. In many western societies, work is regarded as little more than a necessary evil. The psychological health of the individual has often been offered as a sacrificial lamb on the altar of expansion and economic progress. In a society like Japan's or Burma's, work is seen as serving three functions: to give the individual the opportunity to develop and use his skills and talents; to foster other-centeredness in him in an environment where he often has to work with others in common tasks; and to produce the goods and services required by the economy. In this context, the pursuit of a higher rate of economic growth can be extremely beneficial to the psychological health of the worker [23].

As one delves deeper into the nature of the national development problem, he becomes more convinced that the classical paradigm needs to be replaced by a new one with the following characteristics:

1. Synthetic. Because the problem itself is greater than the sum of its parts it ought to be tackled by means of a "holistic" tool.
2. Multidisciplinary. This element comes with the recognition that the problem transcends the economic boundaries artificially set by the more traditional development planners and modernizers.
3. Culture- and value-sensitive. With the acknowledgment of the vital roles played by noneconomic, or better, qualitative, factors, the notion of discovering purely technical and culture-independent solutions should be quickly dissipated. Moreover, the national system must not be treated as a homogeneous whole, but as a system of heterogeneous subsystems, mainly, interest groups. The interfaces of these subsystems generate many of the essential processes that codetermine the problem system.
4. Hypothetico-deductive and positivist. The hypothetico-deductive capability is needed to identify possible future patterns in the evolution of the system. The positivist capability is needed to articulate or project, usually with the aid of a computer, the socioeconomic system's behavior as a consequence of each structure alternately chosen from the set of hypothesized structures [14, 26]. The planning horizon should be a parameter rather than a "constant" of this paradigm. If a short horizon is elected, the hypothetico-deductive capability need not be exercised.
5. Democratic. With an idealized sensory system, the inputs provided by the average citizen *vis-à-vis* his needs should be a major factor in the design and implementation of government plans and policies.

MODELING UNDER THE PROPOSED PARADIGM

In the context of the national development problem, the classical paradigm may utilize one of the following vehicles: 1) an implicit or mental model that may be the product of either an individual mind (*e.g.*, a consultant-economist's or a political scientist's) or a group mind *via* the committee (face-to-face) approach, the Delphi (anonymous) method, or some other method; 2) an explicit model, *e.g.*, physical, graphical, and mathematical); or 3) a supernatural model, *e.g.*, astrological. Only the first two recourses will be evaluated.

The explicit model is believed to be potentially superior to the implicit model because of the following arguments:

1. The mind is better equipped to perceive interactions among factors related proximately in time or space, than to trace the long-run repercussions of an exogeneous change—*e.g.*, the implementation of a policy alternative—through an intricately structured system such as a socioeconomic system. In other words, the mind is better suited to provide the information needed to formulate an explicit model (*e.g.*, simulation) than to analyze the model's behavior. The unfolding, as well as the analysis of model behavior, is preferably performed on the computer.

2. Explicitness renders the model visible and accessible to the planner and policy maker. The explicit model exposes the assumptions made by an expert consultant, which, in turn, facilitates identifying internal contradictions and model assumptions to third parties.

   A major advantage accrues from making the expert's assumptions explicit: differences in the evaluation of a policy can be traced more reliably to differences in specific model assumptions. Therefore, rather than have the policy-maker choose from among several alternatives on the basis of subjective and parochial arguments, he can base his choice on more objective grounds, *e.g.*, on the plausibility or likelihood of occurrence of the events represented in the model assumption.

The same vehicles are available to the proposed paradigm. For reasons just given, the explicit model option is used unless the problem at hand is so severely ill structured as to defy attempts at formal representation. (In such a case, the extra abilities of the mind, *e.g.*, spiritual and extraperceptual, may offer the only recourse.) The explicit form helps the planner or policy maker to assess whether or not the model used by the consultant has the necessary characteristics of the proposed paradigm: synthetic, multidisciplinary, culture- and value-sensitive, hypothetico-deductive, and democratic.

Because of the sophisticated technology developing around the simulation approach (*e.g.*, system dynamics [9]), this explicit model is the preferred form of the proposed paradigm. While existing simulation exercises tend to focus on the quantifiable aspects of a problem—apparently because the model constant and parameter estimation processes and the validation and testing procedures are greatly simplified with the availability of useful data and statistical techniques—the proposed paradigm requires that the simulation model accommodate, as a matter of course, qualitative relationships. For this purpose, the simulation model is allowed, at the minimum, to contain gross statements of relevant "soft" relationships that merely indicate what factor is related to what and in which sequence. Only by permitting representation of "soft" and important phenomena can an adequate model of the national development, and, for that matter, any socioeconomic, problem be formulated.

The model is to utilize the most advanced information possible concerning the problem. Model precision and accuracy should increase as additional knowledge is acquired.

Model formulation and analysis are preferably carried out through group effort to increase the chances of achieving a synthetic, holistic viewpoint, multidisciplinarity, sensitivity to the national culture and to the subcultures that make it up, a hypothetico-deductive capability needed to create the various scenarios that may characterize the national system in the future, and a democratic model-formulation process.

This study has developed certain operational guidelines to aid the socioeconomic simulation modeling effort under the proposed paradigm. The guidelines are aimed primarily at the problem-definition and model-formulation phases of simulation modeling.

Problem-definition phase

With the problem of national development, definition begins by determining the scope of the problem. A model's scope lies on two planes, the horizontal and the vertical. On the horizontal plane, scope is set by choosing the number of discipline-bound subsystems to be represented in the model. For instance, a modeler may choose to build a purely economic model of the national system. His model would have a lesser scope than another that consists of an economic, a demographic, and a political module. On the vertical plane, scope is determined by the level of detail elected. For instance, a modeler may choose to build a homogeneous model of the national system basing it on a family with average income, rate of consumption, voting preferences, size, etc. The modeler may enlarge his vertical scope by increasing the variety of families, or interest groups, each type characterized by a unique set of average characteristics. The example developed earlier identified four interest groups: the upper-income agricultural, the upper-income industrial, the lower-income agricultural, and the lower-income industrial.

The statement of model purpose should enable the modeler to set an appropriate number of subsystems and level of detail. If, for example, the purpose is to study the effects of alternative rehabilitation programs on the criminal justice system, the subsystems required may include the political, the economic, the educational, and the technological. The level of detail may be set at the individual criminal level, by utilizing an average criminal's profile, or at the group level, whereby all criminals are grouped into homogeneous classes, such as the psychotic-killer class and the white-collar-felon class.

If the purpose of the study is to formulate national development programs, the subsystems required may include the economic, the social, the political, and the environmental.

Guideline No. 1: One must choose the simplest possible scope needed to accomplish the model purpose. This means choosing the *fewest* model subsystems and interest groups possible. Scope is preferably decided by group consensus, *e.g.*, *via* the Delphi technique [7, 26].

Model-formulation phase

Guideline No. 2: Enumerate the general needs of each interest group, *i.e.*, subgroup goals, in descending order of urgency, using Table 2 as a guide. Identify the goal concerns, *i.e.*, supersystem goals, implied by the more urgent needs of each group, using Table 3. If desired, a model objective function may be constructed to provide some overall indicator of the quality of system performance. For illustration purposes, suppose that the modeler's research uncovers these four goal concerns: economic base, adequacy and continuity of income, harmony, and justice. He constructs an objective function of a multiplicative or additive form. Since the multiplicative form is more commonly used [32], the following function is suggested:

$$\text{Indicator}(t,j) = GNP(t)^{W1,j} * DIST(t)^{W2,j} * HARMONY(t)^{W3,j} \qquad (1)$$

where t represents time period, W_{ij} represents relative value attached to the ith indicator component by the average individual from interest group j, $GNP(t)$ represents gross national product, and $DIST(t)$ represents both justice and adequacy and continuity of income. $DIST(t)$ could be measured in terms of the "GINI" ratio widely used to measure income distribution. $HARMONY(t)$ could be measured crudely by the divorce rate, the rate of filing of civil suits, the crime rate, or some other surrogate measure. The weight values are ideally set by a questionnaire-survey or, as a more practical though less reliable alternate, a "Delphi" group [7, 26].

Illustration

A set of plausible W_{ij} values (on a scale from -3 to $+3$) is given in Table 4 for the four interest groups identified in the "developing" socioeconomic system discussed in an earlier section. The *GNP* component is weighted positively across the four groups, the upper-income groups favoring it more heavily than the lower-income groups. Because of the relatively minor role played by the lower-income groups in the economy, the benefits from economic growth trickle down very slowly to these income groups. The lower, agricultural group shares these benefits the least because of its virtual nonparticipation in the cash economy.

Because a more equitable distribution of income would mean taking away

Table 2. Dalkey's list of components of an individual's quality of life [7].

CHARACTERISTIC	DESCRIPTION
Aesthetics	Aesthetic surroundings
Freedom	Freedom, lack of restraints, lack of compulsion
Pleasure	Pleasurable, satisfying, feeling of contentment; comfort, satisfying to the senses, warm; relaxation, easing recreation, leisure, rest; physical well-being, health, feeling good and "alive"; depression, sorrow, grief, tragedy (negative)
Meaningfulness	Evaluative, brings feedback; educational; meaningfulness
Newness	Innovative, creative; novelty, surprising, unanticipated, unexpected; new, unfamiliar; exciting, stimulating, arousing
Aggression	Aggression, interpersonal conflict, blowing off steam
Sexual fulfillment	Sexual fulfillment—sex life or love life
Security	Security, safety, not anxious or threatened
Dominance	Dominance, one-upsmanship, superiority, competition; control, directedness, under one's own power
Affection	Privacy, withdrawn from society *viz.*, personal intimacy, affection, friendship, closeness, tenderness; marital satisfaction
Fun	Humorous; playfulness, fun
Status	Social acceptance, belonging, recognition by peer group; accomplishment, achievement, meeting goals, success; self-esteem, ego satisfaction, pride, self-image; job satisfaction, job motivation, enjoyment of work; business esteem, job progress, success in work; material well-being, affluence, material comforts; status prestige, position, external image

some of the assets of the upper classes and giving them to the lower classes, the upper classes would value improvements in the distribution of income negatively, while the lower classes would value these improvements positively. Since most of the assets, especially landholdings, belong to the upper, agricultural group it stands to lose the most in a rearrangement and, therefore, is more opposed to this type of "improvement" than the upper, industrial group [2].

The *HARMONY* weights are based on the assumption that it is valued most in the poorer and more traditional areas because, for one, the lower-income groups depend, for their survival, on maintaining good interpersonal relationships. *HARMONY* is valued least, if at all, among the "most modern" groups.

Guideline No. 3: The goal concerns identified by the modeler provide the bases for establishing the content of each model subsystem in the same way that objective functions determine the relationships, *i.e.*, constraints, relevant to the problem system in mathematical programming models. For instance, if the objective is to maximize profit, each constraint selected must embody some process by which profit is significantly determined. For example, to generate the behavior of $DIST(t)$, the model needs to 1) subdivide the national system into distinct homogeneous units, 2) characterize each unit by the unique pattern of asset-accumulation or income-generation behavior of its human components, 3) monitor the aforementioned behavior for each unit, and 4) measure the disparities in yearly incomes or assets among the distinct units.

Modeling the processes that generate the average income of an interest group or the gross national product is a straightforward task in that both theoretical and empirical economics provide ample, sophisticated information to facilitate the formulation of the economic subsystem.

Modeling the processes that determine the behavior of $HARMONY(t)$, a highly qualitative concept, should also be a manageable task. Future guidelines will be provided to aid the modeler in formulating the qualitative relationships of the model.

Guideline No. 4: Organize each discipline-bound subsystem into a module. The model is thus constructed as a set of interrelated individual units called modules, linked together to form a more complete model. The following advantages accrue from this design:

1. It permits the independent development of a particular subsystem. Depending on the importance of a module *vis-à-vis* model purpose, or on the quality of the knowledge base of the relevant discipline, a particular module may be formulated with greater detail and precision than the others. The quality of module statements should reflect the quality of the referent knowledge base. Thus, the economic module is expected to utilize more precise and verifiable relationships than, say, the demographic module.
2. As new knowledge is acquired, the affected module may be revised with minimum changes effected elsewhere in the model.

3. Due to the discipline-bound expertise of most consultants hired by governments, the modular design permits optimal use of this resource. An effective interdisciplinary consultant or group may be employed to provide the relevant linkages at the subsystem interfaces. Such use of human resources prevents the user, *i.e.*, the government, from becoming overly dependent on a single expert, with the possible exception of the interdisciplinary consultant.

4. Assuming efficient utilization of the human resources, it is expected that much of the model revision efforts will center on the interfaces.

5. The modular design facilitates the validation and verification procedures of simulation efforts. Debugging and "hindsighting" tasks are simplified by the separability of model structure. A variety of validation procedures can also be accommodated. It is expected that the modules will differ in degree of quantitativeness. The more quantitative subsystems may be validated by means of systematic statistical procedures. The "softer" subsystems will have to be validated through other means, *e.g.*, subjective evaluation. The modular design permits the use of a variety of validation and verification procedures.

6. Finally, the modular design facilitates the presentation of the model to the user, not to mention documentation. "Flow-charting" becomes a simplified task, since each subsystem may be drawn independently. Using the subsystem charts as reference points, it becomes a simpler task to point out linkages between subsystems.

Increasing demand for socioeconomic models may justify the development of standardized modules for the economic, demographic, political, technological, and other subsystems. For a given problem, therefore, each new modeling effort will no longer be required to start from scratch.

Past efforts have generated models of the economic [5, 14, 31], employment [31], political [5], demographic [14, 31], and governmental [14] subsystems on which development of the standardized modules may be founded. (These references are by no means exhaustive.)

Guideline No. 5: The constants, parametric values, and input variable values of the quantitative relationships are derived through statistical means or by direct observation. Qualitative and semiqualitative (*e.g.*, between productivity and morale) relationships have to be formulated in a different manner, however, because they do not permit precise measurements on either the interval or the ratio scale [25]. Measurement is permitted on the ordinal scale, wherein numerals serve for both designation and statement of rank order or relative position. Social science research has centered around the development of correlational-regressional relationships, which are ordinal relationships. Aside from the social sciences, human judgment and intuition serve as the other primary sources of qualitative relationships.

In formulating qualitative relationships the minimum requirement is a statement of the factors interrelated and the direction of the relationship. The initial formulations may be given in the form of an ordinal function. Whereas the slope of the function at any given point, assuming continuousness, is itself an "interval" or a "ratio" numeral in "stronger" relationships, the slope obtains no more than an "ordinal" sense in ordinal functions.

In an ordinal function, the properties of interest are the sign of the slope (either positive or negative) and the relative, rather than the absolute, size of the slope. For pedagogical reasons, the ordinal function is stated in graphical form. The function is preferably formulated by a group rather than an individual, due to the exploratory nature of the effort [6].

The ordinal function is extensively used in system dynamics research [9]; the computer language commonly used by system dynamicists, DYNAMO [20], has a special provision for accepting graphical statements through the "TABLE" function.

The essence of the graphical statement can be captured by setting the following attributes:

1. The two variables whose *ceteris paribus* relationship is of interest. Selection of the independent variable sets the direction of the relationship. The independent variable is assigned the horizontal axis.
2. A reference point around which the whole statement pivots. This is the single, most important attribute to be set when formulating qualitative relationships. It provides a starting point for ordinal functions, a basis for rank ordering. In system dynamics, the (1, 1) point on the two-dimensional Cartesian coordinate system is invariably used as a reference point. To complete specification of this point a reference year is selected: the (ordinal) values of the variables on both the horizontal and vertical axes are arbitrarily set at 1 in the reference year.
3. Slope sign. (Assume that discontinuities may be replaced by smooth approximations.) A negative slope denotes an inverse relationship, and a positive slope, a direct one. (Slope is measured as the relative change in the dependent variable as a result of a unit change in a given value of the independent variable.)
4. Relative slope value. A decreasing slope value represents a weakening of the relationship, and an increasing slope, a strengthening.

The most common relationship will be of the "monotonic" type. An example is taken from *World Dynamics* [9] relating the independent variable, MSL (world material standard of living) to the variable BRMM (world birth-rate-from-material multiplier), which modifies birth rate in response to changes in the material standard of living. (See Figure 3.) MSL is intended to include the effect of medicine, public health, sanitation facilites, and all the amenities of industrialization.

If 1970 is selected as the reference year, a value of 1 for MSL signifies that the aggregate of material goods per capita is at the 1970 world wide average. BRMM

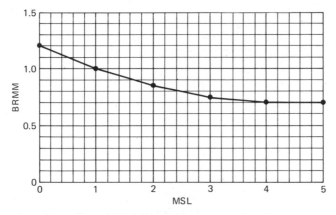

Figure 3. Birth-rate-from-material multiplier versus material standard of living.

Table 3. Mapping (Terleckyj's) goals concern onto Dalkey's quality of life components.

GOALS CONCERN	INDIVIDUAL'S QOL CHARACTERISTICS
Freedom, justice, and harmony	Freedom, security, affection, status, aggression, dominance
Health and safety	Pleasure, security
Education, skills, and income	Meaningfulness, newness, security, dominance, status
Human habitat	Pleasure, newness, sexual fulfillment, security, status
Finer things	Aesthetics, pleasure, meaningfulness, newness, sexual fulfillment, affection, fun
Economic base	Security, dominance, status

is arbitrarily assigned a value of 1 to neutralize the multiplier effect, *i.e.*, in any year when the 1970 MSL level is attained, the 1970 birth rate is applied to determine that year's gross gain in population.

Selection of the slope sign and relative change in slope value on either side of the unity point depends on the group's judgment of how MSL will cause the birth rate to change. It is surmised that determination of slope sign can be more readily achieved by group consensus than the setting of relative changes in slope values. If desired, the latter may be subjected to sensitivity analysis to test the impact of different "rates of change" in slope values. In experiences with socioeconomic modeling efforts to date, model behavior has seldom been sensitive to the assumed numerical values of the slope [10].

Additional Illustration

Let LUPMREM represent the multiplier that modifies the *potential* migration rate from lower to upper levels of income, in response to changes in governmental expenditures on education (EE). If 1970 is chosen as the reference year, the unity point fixes the 1970 expenditures for education against the 1970 potential migration rate.   To either side of the unity point the slope is nonnegative everywhere.   The slope decreases as EE is decreased.   At first the slope increases as EE is increased, but eventually it, too, declines. (See Figure 4.)

Some care must be exercised in setting the point at which the slope's "rate of change" changes, *i.e.*, when it goes from positive to negative, as well as in setting the point at which the slope sign changes, since, relative to the effects on model behavior of varying the slopes' numerical value, the impact of changes in slope sign and "rate of change" is expected to be of a larger order of magnitude.

Guideline No. 6: Ideologies, personal preferences, and biases should be kept to a minimum, if not eliminated. Wherever possible, statements of model relationships are to be observable or verifiable postulates, expressed in the most primitive form feasible.   This, for example, results in a preference for direct causal rather than correlational statements.

Thus, a phenomenon that appears to involve a necessary trade-off or dilemma from a correlational or ideological point of view may, upon disaggregation, turn out to be an orthogonal, or even a mutually reinforcing, relationship. For example, at an ideological level, economic growth and equitable distribution of wealth may appear to be mutually competitive, *i.e.*, more equitable distribution can be attained only at the expense of some economic growth. Disaggregation of the economic growth-wealth distribution linkage into a series of more primitive statements that intervene between the growth and distribution variables would tend to minimize the role of such subjective factors as ideology and prejudice and increase the role of such objective factors as probabilities in deciding the validity of a model statement. (This exercise of disaggregation may be useful in separating the spurious from the bona fide socioeconomic dilemmas.)

The specific series of intervening statements is expected to differ from one context to another.   Thus, the growth-distribution dilemma may be bona fide in some contexts, but spurious in others. For example, in systems where a strong positive relationship exists between the average rate of reinvestment by capital owners and the wealth or assets level, the dilemma is likely to be real.

Guideline No. 7: Once the model statements, both qualitative and quantitative, have been formulated in an initial form, specialists, *e.g.*, a system dynamicist and a computer programmer with expertise in large-scale simulations, are commissioned to complete the model specification and to aid in the implementation of the subsequent stages of the simulation project, *i.e.*, computer run, verification, validation, and policy/planning analysis.

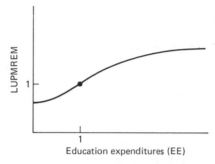

Figure 4. Potential-migration-rate-from-education multiplier versus education expenditures.

Table 4. Goal concerns weights by interest groups.

QOL COMPONENT I	UPPER, INDUSTRIAL	LOWER, INDUSTRIAL	UPPER, AGRICULTURAL	LOWER, AGRICULTURAL
		INTEREST GROUP J		
GNP	3	2	3	1
DIST	-2	3	-3	3
HAR	0	2	1	3

Guideline No. 8: In utilizing the model as a policy/planning aid, care must be exercised in preventing model misuse. The model can be used for purposes other than those intended only with extreme caution. For example, present simulation technology is not well equipped to produce predictive models. Simulation models of the type referred to in this study are intended mainly as tools for "broad policy analysis." This entails outlining the possible consequences of alternative actions available to the policy-maker or the planner. Its objective is not prediction but understanding.

Guideline No. 9: Assuming that the planning horizon is long, and that time, money, and other resources allow, the model's anticipative capability could be enhanced if the modeling effort accommodates alternative model formulations that reflect alternative routes of socioeconomic evolution, even if only informally. "Gaming" the alternative situations would be a more powerful, though expensive, recourse.

CONCLUSION

This study set out to develop a methodology for formulating plans or policies for socioeconomic systems. It focused on the development of the analytical capability of the control entity, *i.e.*, the government. The guidelines listed furnish the modeler and his client an operational procedure for modeling under a paradigm designed specifically to handle current and future socioeconomic problems that by their nature are systemic (hence, a synthetic model), nonconformist to the strict boundaries of traditional disciplines of the arts and sciences (hence, a multidisciplinary model), culture-based (hence, a contextual, rather than a general, orientation), value-centric (hence, the central role of goals), orderly and inertial in the short run, but evolutionary in the long run (hence, a positivist, hypothetico-deductive model), and people-centered (hence, a democratic orientation).

An improved analytical capability brings the control entity a step closer to providing satisfactory means and opportunities for people to fulfill their needs and desires, while providing leadership toward achieving societal goals with minimum sacrifice of the needs and desires of affected interest groups.

NOTES AND REFERENCES

1. Ashby, W. R. *An Introduction to Cybernetics.* London: University Paperbacks, 1964.
2. Baster, N. *Distribution of Income and Economic Growth: Concepts and Issues.* Geneva: UNRISD, 1970.
3. Bauer, Ray, ed. *Social Indicators.* Cambridge: MIT Press, 1966.
4. Boeke, J. H. *Economics and Economic Policy of Dual Societies.* New York: 1953.
5. Brunner, R., and G. Brewer. *Organized Complexity.* New York: Free Press, 1971.
6. Costello, T., and S. Zalkind. *Psychology in Administration.* Englewood Cliffs, N.J.: Prentice-Hall, 1963.
7. Dalkey, Norman. *Measurement and Analysis of the Quality of Life.* Santa Monica, Calif.: Rand Corp., 1970, #RM-6228-DOT.
8. Fayol, Henri. *General and Industrial Management.* New York: Pitman, 1949.
9. Forrester, Jay. *World Dynamics.* Cambridge, Mass.: Wright-Allen Press, 1971.
10. Forrester, Jay. "Educational Implications of Responses to System Dynamics Models." *Management Science* 1975.
11. Guthrie, G. *The Psychology of Modernization in the Rural Philippines.* Philippines: Ateneo University Press, 1970.
12. Koestler and Smithies, eds. *Beyond Reductionism: New Perspectives in the Life Sciences.* New York: Macmillan, 1969.
13. Lear, J. "Where Is Society Going? The Search for Landmarks." *Saturday Review* April 15, 1972, pp. 34–39.
14. Legasto, Augusto. "Socioeconomic Modeling: An Assessment of the Econometric, System Dynamic and Cross-Impact Paradigms." Working Paper No. RU-ECAL2, Rutgers College, 1976.
15. Lenski, G. *Power and Privilege: A Theory of Social Stratification.* New York: 1966.
16. March, J., and H. Simon, eds. *Organizations.* New York: John Wiley & Sons, 1958.
17. Maslow, A. "A Theory of Human Motivation." *Psychological Reviews* 50 (1943): 370–396.
18. Myrdal, Gunnar. *Asian Drama,* vol. 1. New York: Pantheon, 1968.
19. Nordhaus, W., and J. Tobin. "Is Growth Obsolete?" Cowles Foundation Discussion Paper No. 319, Yale University, 1971.
20. Pugh, A., III. *Dynamo II User's Manual.* Cambridge, Mass.: MIT Press, 1973.

21. Rapoport, A., and W. Horvath. "Thoughts on Organization Theory." *General Systems* 4 (1959): 87–91.
22. Reinhold, R. "Changes in Social Attitudes Monitored in Broad Surveys of the 'Quality of Life'." *New York Times*, August 20, 1973.
23. Schumacher, E. F. *Small is Beautiful*. New York: Harper & Row, 1973.
24. Sheldon, E., and W. Moore, eds. *Indicators of Social Change: Concepts and Measurements*. (New York: Russell Sage Foundation, 1968.
25. Stevens, S. "Measurement, Psychophysics, and Utility." In *Measurement: Definitions and Theories*. Edited by C. W. Churchman and R. Patoosh. New York: John Wiley & Sons, 1959.
26. Sutherland, J. *Systems: Analysis, Administration, and Architecture*. New York: Van Nostrand Reinhold, 1975.
27. Taylor, Frederick. *The Principles and Methods of Scientific Management*. New York: Harper & Row, 1911.
28. Terleckyj, Nestor. "Measuring Progress Towards Social Goals: Some Possibilities at National and Local Levels." *Management Science* 16.
29. Van Gigch, J. "A Model for Measuring the Information Processing Rates and Mental Load of Complex Activities." *Canadian Operational Research Society* 8:
30. Weber, Max. *The Theory of Social and Economic Organization*. Translated by A. Henderson and T. Parsons. New York: Oxford University Press, 1947.
31. Wery, R., G. Rodgers, and M. Hopkins. *BACHUE-2: Version-1 A Population and Employment Model for the Philippines*. Geneva International Labor Organization, 1974, WEP 2-21.
32. Zeleny, M., and J. Cochrane, eds. *Multiple Criteria Decision Making*. Columbia, S.C.: University of South Carolina Press, 1973.

5

The Public Management of Private Interest

Michel Chevalier
*York University and
Universite de Montreal*

and

Thomas Burns
University of Pennsylvania

INTRODUCTION

For those who would see them, the inadequacies of present institutions of public governance are everywhere apparent: in the growing imbalances between human communities and their physical environments, and in the growing disparity within and between them even within broader trends toward increasing material well-being. Part of the *problematique* with which we are concerned stems from the normative level: it can be resolved only through a further evolution of the public values guiding community decision-making at every level from local to global. But in part, these imbalances stem from institutional problems: the structures, processes, and techniques of public management can themselves constrain public action even when there is sufficient value consensus for concerted public action to occur. It is this latter problem with which this paper is primarily concerned.

*This paper is based on a background paper prepared for a federal government seminar in Ottawa, Canada, December 1-3, 1977, the third in a series sponsored jointly by the Canadian International Development Agency and the Canadian Department of the Environment on ecodevelopment concepts and strategies. We wish to acknowledge the important contributions that the seminar organizers, Charles A. Jeanneret-Grosjean and H. F. (Bob) Fletcher, and other members of CIDA and the DOE have made to our understanding of the range of opportunities and constraints confronting the innovative public manager, and of other practical issues raised by the rather speculative proposals contained herein.

The argument made here is somewhat speculative. It stems from the view that the present paradigm of public management is no longer an adequate basis for the design of the guidance systems needed for complex human communities to manage themselves and their environments. The theoretical underpinnings of the present paradigm, as well as the structures, processes, and techniques it supports, have evolved from earlier and often simpler conceptions of community well-being and development, and from more primitive conceptions of institutional regulation. Increases in the scale and complexity of public sector involvement in the affairs of communities and societies have not been matched by a similar evolution of institutional forms of regulation and control. This paper explores the conceptual and strategic bases for an essentially new form of public management of individual interest.

This paper has four sections that develop this general perspective. Section one fully describes an underlying dilemma of public management reflected in the inability of existing government institutions to reconcile fully individual and collective purposes. Section two proposes a conceptual reformulation of public sector management, based on a rethinking of the relations between individual and collective interest, and their relation to the contextual environment. Two complementary views of the individual are shown to be necessary as a basis for redesigning public management institutions, and this is argued to be a promising basis for constructing a new public management paradigm. Section three introduces a contrast between two management strategies—management by objective and management by interest. It suggests that they must be used together if the dilemma identified earlier is to be overcome. Section four relates these strategies to two contrasting patterns of public decision. One, a "regulated" pattern, is dependent on the build-up of specialized units and routinized control mechanisms to regulate relations among discrete entities within the overall community. The other, a "self-regulating" pattern, is dependent on a more diffused pattern of control and interactive decision-making among interdependent parts of the community. A new paradigm of public management will require a shift from a reliance on the former to the joint design of the latter.

A PUBLIC MANAGEMENT DILEMMA: THE RECONCILIATION OF INDIVIDUAL AND COLLECTIVE PURPOSES

Public management can be viewed as a process of reconciling individual and collective interests. Each kind of interest has a logic or calculus of its own. The calculus of individual decision operates according to a logic of maximization of particular interests. In the Western world, this calculus has long been the basis for the articulation and pursuit of collective purposes. Individual purposes are maximized within collectively established limits or constraints. Individual enterprise is universally present, but is legitimized to a greater or lesser extent according to the particular social, political, and economic values that may prevail in a given community.

The collectivity lives by virtue of its relation to its environment, both in a material and a sociocultural sense. Every community must maintain harmony (or equilibrium) with its environment if it is to endure over time. The calculus of collective decision thus operates according to a logic of survival and well-being in its environment.

In the postwar period, the Keynesian economic style of market management has had a dominant influence on the management of public affairs. But it has failed to resolve the growing conflict between the individual decision calculus and the collective decision calculus.[1]   The pursuit of individual goals has not been effectively harnessed in support of larger communities of interest. Individual interest has continued to flourish—in creation and invention, production and marketing, consumption and surfeit. Increasing knowledge in the theory of the human and natural sciences, in the practice of human organization, and in technology has escalated individual expectations and their achievement.

In terms of the logic of individual enterprise, such behavior is quite rational, and for the selected interests that have benefited, all is as it should be. But for other interests, those that are dependent or subservient, the rational course of events has not been so rewarding, regardless of whether their particular consumption profile rose or fell.

In terms of the logic of the collective interest, the postwar Keynesian approach has turned out to be much less rational. The social disparity within and between communities, which the escalation of individual expectation and achievement has brought or perpetuated, is well documented. This is also true for the growing imbalances between human communities and their physical environments.

There is a fundamental dysfunction here, which is not well understood in the management of public affairs. Increasing social dependency is seen to occur in settings of plenty in the consumption of goods and services. And it occurs also in settings of want. Increasing disequilibrium with the environment likewise occurs in both relatively prosperous and poor communities. Increasing social dependency leads to social unrest. And increasing environmental disequilibrium leads to decline in resource availability over time, leading in turn to increasing material disparity [2].

To continue to rely on patterns of public management that fail to reconcile individual and collective purposes is to continue to spread social dependence and the dissatisfaction and unrest that result from it. The narrow pursuit of individual purpose also weakens the community by undermining its environment. By providing an increasing flow of goods and services in such a way as to feed both material disparity and social disadvantage, the demand for material things can but rise faster and faster, fueled but never satisfied by rising and uneven resource consumption.

The failure of the postwar framework of public management to reconcile effectively individual and collective purposes within broadly acceptable democratic principles is only part of the present public management dilemma. The other has to do with changes in governing institutions themselves, those organizations with the legitimately vested responsibility for protecting and enhancing the community interest. As institutions of public management have expanded in scale and complexity over the past three decades, they, too, have failed to reconcile the purposes and interests of their individual parts with their own broader purpose. To an alarming degree, the broader purposes of government tend to be suborned by the pursuit of individual interests within it.

Particular interests are followed ostensibly for the public benefit, but not necessarily for the public benefit unless it coincides with the interest of specialized agencies, sectors, functions, programs, and the personal interests of those who manage them. There is no particular implication of malpractice here, only one of misapprehension. The public service organization tends to treat the extension of its particular function and sector as being synonomous with the public good, be it any broad function like economic policy, international cooperation, public expenditures control, consumer affairs, regional development, environmental protection, or any specified sector such as transportation or welfare or education. The public service executive, recognizing that his or her own career advancement is closely tied to the advancement and extension of a particular agency or unit, gives primary attention to the pursuit of its purposes. By extending the activities of a particular government unit within a particular field or sector, the public manager may or may not be serving the public interest. But there is a tendency for this to occur regardless of whether such expansion is warranted. This is often described as the process of bureaucratization. It is exacerbated by the frequent technocratic alliance of the administrator within a sector and other nongovernmental interests in that sector: a particular government unit joins with individual interests in its broader constituency of interests in ways permitting all parties to maximize their respective individual purposes. Such alliances of mutual self-interest are strengthened by the development of specialized scientific and technical knowledge, and by scientific and professional activities that further bind such special interests together.

The phenomenon of bureaucratization described here has been analyzed many times in theory, and in many governmental settings. There have been numerous attempts to control the shift or slide of public service organizations and executives toward further bureaucracy and toward the implicit or explicit alliance of individualistic interests in and out of government. A proliferation of techniques and mechanisms have been applied—from ever more stringent central planning processes, to integration of planning and budgeting, and lately to total yearly justification of activities by zero-based budgeting. But through it all, technocracy spreads and flourishes.[3]   Individual incentive and ingenuity tends to overcome such imposed constraints.

The conflict between individualistic and collective purpose continues and deepens in and out of government, as does the parallel conflict between the larger human community and its environment. The management of public affairs thereby fails to carry out its legitimized responsibility of pursuing the collective interest. The collective interest is only partially and sporadically heard in guiding the community's affairs, except, of course, in the eloquence of political discourse, and as a result of periodic confrontation by the more disaffected elements of the community.

This then is the basic dilemma in public management. Government is the only institution through which communities can articulate and pursue collective goals of social stability and environmental balance. But government also tends to drift toward the displacement of collective goals by individual ones, toward bureaucratization and increasing technocracy. Thus, the primary institutional regulator of the complex human communities is itself susceptible to the very weaknesses that it is responsible for controlling. This depends first on a deeper understanding of the relation between individual and collective purpose, and second on better methods of identifying collective goals and objectives and implementing them through new shared patterns of public and private decision-making.

A CONCEPTUAL REFORMULATION: INDIVIDUAL INTEREST, COLLECTIVE INTEREST, AND THE ENVIRONMENT

Getting around this dilemma would seem to require a rather basic pattern of reframing of the present perspective of public management and its application in the reconciliation of competing individual and community purposes. The overall pattern of public governance must evolve away from the present one of crude regulation of individualistic excess, imposed only as a constraining force when individual behavior threatens overall community stability. A viable new pattern of public management would seem to have to be based on a perspective of designed complementarity and mutual benefit among individual interests in the achievement of collective purposes. In order for that perspective to be broadly accepted, at least two kinds of perceptual shift would have to occur. Both of these could be fostered through a reconceptualization of the underlying theory of public management. The first has to do with the conception of the relations between individuals, collectivities, and their contextual environments; the second concerns the conception of the individual interest itself. Let us explore the nature of the required shift.

Every individual can be identified as being, on the one hand, a distinct entity, and on the other, a part of a community.[4] So the concept of human community contains three elements: the individual entity, the collectivity of entities that form a "whole" community, and finally the environment or context of that community. Various kinds and levels of human community can be distinguished, each displaying some degree of balance or equilibrium and a capability for self-regulation and change. At a global level, man-environment interactions may be perceived as holistic social and economic patterns of the activity, of people, groups, and organizations, of societies and nations. We often speak of particular communities like states or provinces, regions, cities, neighborhoods. To some extent, it is also possible to view social and economic groups, sectors of activities, metaorganizations like governments and large corporations, organizations and their elements, and even individual families and households as holistic communities, as systems of collective purpose.

Our point of departure in thinking about the management of human communities is the concept of resources. Resources are both social and material. Social resources are a distinguishing component of all social systems, and derive from knowledge and values expressed in patterns of symbolic communication. Material resources are a component of the physical world and derive from patterns of energetic interaction. All human resources are a combination of the symbolic and the energetic, reflecting the interplay of social and material resources in a range of expressions, from knowledge, culture, technology, values, and organizations, to the physical capabilities of the human being, singly and in the community. Development refers to the development of resources, both social and material.

The boundary between the community and its environment, and how it affects development, has to do with the balance between collective and individual purpose in a community. As was noted earlier, the relationship between collective and individual purpose is often considered with little regard for its context. This is true for the management of political, economic, and social affairs of a country, and also in the way the country exploits and maintains its material resource base. The context of environment of the country, in both the social and material sense, is often taken for granted, when in reality it is an integral and potentially volatile factor influencing the collective-individual relationship. It must be made part of the equation of public decision-making.

For that reason the governance of human communities must explicitly account for the dynamic relation between three types of community resource: individual, collective, and contextual. Individual resources are purposeful systems, systems that can articulate or choose ends and have means to pursue those ends. They can be a person, or a group of people who can agree to work together in informal organization, an organization, or a group of organizations. Collective resources are combinations of individual purposeful systems with a shared sense of community of purpose or interest: for example, a society, a country, a city, a neighborhood, a professional group, and so on. To some extent a collectivity or community can be defined as a purposeful system (although most often it is identified as "purposive," that is capable of choosing means but not ends) [5]. In that sense, the set of individual or operating purposeful systems that make it up are the operating expression of its purpose. It can then be treated as a purposeful system in operating as well as conceptual terms, one that can choose to maintain and extend itself in various ways.

Contextual or environmental resources are all resources (defined in some combination of social and material elements) outside the community. They may be in the form of existing individual or collective resources, or potential ones [6].

The distinction between the three resource types suggests two system boundaries —one between the individual and the collective, and the other between the collective and contextual. This is illustrated in Figure 1. Relationships between the three resource types take place at these boundaries, and the nature of boundary

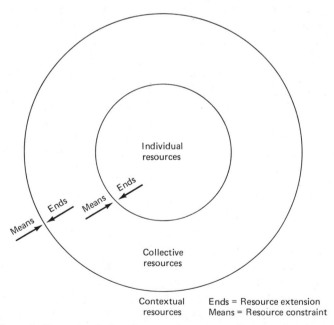

Figure 1. Dynamic relations between three types of community resource.

management governs the dynamic equilibrium between the three spaces. Continuous management of the two boundaries at all stages of decision-making is essential for continuing individual and community development.

At the first boundary, two forces are at play. The individual interests, as a purposeful subsystem, identifies its purpose from the resources it has now and from a combination of social and material resources it hopes to add to its present store. It wishes to extend or change its resource base. That is the first force of resource extension, which derives from individual ends.

The other (countervailing) force is one of resource constraint. It stems from the collectivity—all the other individual resources within the community. Some resources are available to all, some are more exclusive. These resources are the means by which individual ends can be met. Some part, then, of the collective resource space must be added to the individual resource space to meet the latter's purpose [7].

Generally, the individual will endeavor to find and apply resources within the collective space in pursuing its ends; or it will seek and apply them from the contextual space, in which case they become collective as well as individual resources. The means for the pursuit of individual ends, then, are in the collective resource space. The degree of availability of collective resources comprises the *constraint* on individual purpose.

At the second boundary, between collective and contextual resources, the same ends-and-means relationship occurs. The pursuit of collective ends is the extension of shared purposes by drawing on contextual resources. This is done in practice by individual interests as parts of the community. The availability of resources in the contextual environment is a constraint on collective purpose.

These two kinds of boundary relationship—in which collective resources constrain the pursuit of individual ends, and where contextual resources constrain the pursuit of collective ends—together offer a more satisfactory way of conceptualizing the overall dynamics of community development. They indicate how the reconciliation of individual and collective purposes affects and is constrained by the environment of any human community. This constitutes the first perspective shift suggested earlier.

The management of these two kinds of boundary relationship in conjunction with one another, rather than as separate concerns, depends on a further modification in the perspective that individual interests (including government interests) have of themselves in relation to the community and its environment. A perspective shift of this second kind would have profound impact on the present pattern of public management.

We have said that the individual interest is a purposeful system, which can choose both ends and means. The collectivity is only purposeful inasmuch as its individual parts combine to express community purpose. This requires a further distinction between the individual interest as a purposeful entity in itself, and as a part of a larger purposeful whole.

On one hand, the individual interest may regard itself as an entity, recognizing only one boundary—the boundary between its own resource space, and its environment. It is not concerned with the collective-contextual boundary, but seeks to maximize its resource space regardless of the collective or community interest. In the extreme, the individualistic entity tends either to disregard or single-mindedly exploit other interests in its environment in maximizing its own ends.

On the other hand, the individual interest may regard itself as a *part* of a community or collectivity. In doing so it implicitly recognizes two boundaries—that between itself and other parts of the community, and that between the community and its environment. It is a part, so it has individual characteristics. It is a part of some collectivity, so it reflects collective or community characteristics. And because it reflects the collective, it must also reflect the context in which that collectivity finds itself.

Every individual interest always reflects the qualities of both entity and part in some combination. It is the balance between these qualities of its individual members—between "individual as entity" and "individual as part"—that governs whether or not the development of a community is compatible with its environment. If *entity* is the primary perceptual element among individual interests in the community, there will tend to be incompatibility. If *part* is the primary perceptual element, there will tend to be compatibility.

The logic of the entity reinforces a pattern of individualistic development—an extension of individual resources without regard to equilibrium of the environment in either its social or material aspects. And the logic of the parts reinforces a pattern of collective development—an extension of individual resources with due regard for the community as an entity in its own right, one that must maintain stability with its environment.

We do not suggest that a complete perceptual shift to a logic of the parts would in itself be a satisfactory way of maintaining and extending a community over time. Nor do we suggest that a logic of "parts over entity" will guarantee stability between the community and its environment. Lack of information, poor judgment, the unpredictable immutability of extraneous forces at any point—any of these can bring turbulence or eclipse to a community. What we do suggest is that a combined logic of "parts over entity" is the best way of handling the unpredictable variety of challenge apt to face any community; such a combined logic would reflect aspects of independence, individuality, and innovation, and the potential for increasing variety as the individual marches to his own drummer, rather than to that of conformity with the community. But it could embody a new level of self-constraint on individualistic excess as reflected in aspects of dominance, exploitation, and centralization of power in the community.

The perceptual shift required must favor the positive side of individual interest in both of its aspects, as entity and as parts. The logic of the parts, however, must have precedence over the logic of the entity.

CONTRASTING APPROACHES TO PUBLIC DECISION: MANAGEMENT BY OBJECTIVE AND MANAGEMENT BY INTEREST

We have pointed to the need for a critical adjustment in the paradigm of public decision-making, and we have suggested the direction in which needed changes should occur. We now identify a promising starting point in making the transition —that is, through a modification and extension of two recognized management strategies, Management by Objectives (MBO) and Management by Interest (MBI). The assumption is that by changing the management procedures that have clearly helped to shape and maintain present institutional relationships in and out of government, larger pattern changes can be brought about to support greater compatibility between individual and collective decision-making and greater stability between human communities and their environments.

We have argued that the changes required must permit a more explicit identification and management of the boundary between a community and its contextual environment, to supplement a present preoccupation with the relations between individual and community purposes. This can be done through the use of concepts and methods that foster a perspective of holistic communities of interest, rather than as a discrete entity.

We begin this section by reviewing the MBO strategy, claimed by many of its proponents to be a means of coping with a variety of contemporary management problems. While not disputing its benefits, we argue that it is also likely to have a negative effect to the extent that it enforces the technocratic tendencies toward unconstrained growth and the pursuit of individual over collective purposes. We then introduce the strategy of MBI to show some of its potential advantages over MBO, as a means of managing multiple and competing interests in a collective decision process. Finally, we compare the main features of the two strategies, arguing that effective public management will depend on the discriminating use of both approaches, so as to constrain unnecessary bureaucratization and bring individual and collective purposes into closer alignment.

Limitations of Management by Objectives (MBO)

By MBO, we refer to the most current and most developed formulation of rational corporate planning theory, with somewhat more emphasis than previous approaches (PPBS, OPM) on involvement of organizational interests in the objective-setting process. As we shall see, it has much in common with earlier approaches—explicit definition of ends and means, setting of priorities, defining measures of performance, establishing evaluation procedures. But, like the others, it rests on several basic assumptions about the organization, its mission or task, and the environment in which that task must be performed. When this management approach is properly applied, with due regard for its limitations, it has undoubtedly been of great benefit. But often enough, it has been mis-applied, thereby bringing about a number of unintended and usually detrimental consequences [8].

The term Management by Objectives was popularized by Peter Drucker in 1954 [9]. Since that time it has been developed and formalized by several other management theorists [10]. The approach has, over the years, attracted both enthusiasts and detractors, and has been interpreted differently by those who have employed it. For some, it is an entire management system with potentially far-reaching effects on organizational control, efficiency, and produc-tion, as well as the structure of administrative responsibility, authority and decision-making, self-management and worker satisfaction, and overall problem-solving capabilities. For others more cautious in their assessment, it is a neutral instrument for dealing with certain managerial needs, generally at the operating level. Its important elements are: specificity in stating objectives; establishment of feasibility; short time frame, usually not more than one year; measurability of progress and results; definitive resource allocations in terms of operational plan, tracking, and evaluation; and reassessment and replanning of objectives [11].

Whether viewed as a management system, or an instrument or technique, the success or failure of MBO depends on many other organizational factors, and on the skill and judgment with which it is employed.

Despite a number of success stories, primarily in the private sector, MBO is viewed with some indifference or even hostility by many in the public sector, who see it as yet another example of procedure and technique being substituted for clear thinking and sound decisions. Examples of both good and bad exper-iences with MBO abound in the recent management literature. Rather than attempting to chronicle its successes or failures, we shall note some of the more negative consequences resulting from the misapplication of MBO and similar objective-based approaches in the public sector. Paradoxical as it may seem, these consequences are often most seriously negative in situations where MBO has been most "successfully" employed.

We have outlined elsewhere five main problems observed in connection with the use of MBO approaches. These include:

1. the distortion of public purposes to serve the purposes of organizational maintenance,

2. heightened resource competition among organizational parts,
3. a self-reinforcing pattern of program justification and personal reward,
4. subversion of lateral coordination across subunit boundaries, and
5. deterioration of service output [8].

Without elaborating on each of these problems, we wish only to suggest that a strict adherence to principles of Management by Objectives necessarily entails the distortion or neglect of other facets of organizational behavior critical to the overall effectiveness of the public sector organization in achieving the purposes for which it was created. Every good public manager knows that in order to "keep things running smoothly," something more than the careful pursuit of hierarchically-organized objectives is required. This additional aspect, the other side of management, as it were, is often implicit. We argue that it can be made more explicit, and that it has a logic of its own. By making it more explicit, we are able to learn about it and about how to employ it more effectively. This complementary management strategy is termed Management by Interest.

Applicability of Management by Interest

Management by Interest (MBI) differs from MBO primarily in its concern with the identification and management of the interests involved in a policy issue or decision, rather than the definition and pursuit of discrete objectives. MBI is a more flexible and incremental planning strategy, which aims to progressively link interests together into networks capable of planning and implementing actions moving toward solutions to complex problems.

The main elements of MBI—problem identification, identification of interests salient to the problem, and successive redefinition of both problem and interests until a working consensus on its solution is achieved—should be familiar to the public manager whose responsibilities include a significant amount of interaction with organizations other than his own. This liason person, the "boundary spanner," the expediter, the skilled negotiator, are all examples of management roles based primarily on the management of interests rather than objectives. In certain circumstances, MBI provides policy decisions. The singularity of overall purpose and differentiation of responsibility necessary for effective use of MBO simply do not exist.

One formulation of the MBI approach is termed "interest-based planning" [12]. The technique was first conceived as a way of engaging key urban interest groups in the design and execution of experiments and demonstration projects to complement existing municipal planning and administrative processes. The technique was later applied as a more general problem-solving approach in connection with a study of adaptation in the Federal Public Service [13].

The strategy of interest-based planning has five main stages:

1. *Identification of the problem.* The problem and its elements are defined in a preliminary way and both "calculable" and "incalculable" aspects of the problem are identified [14].
2. *Identification of interest groups salient to the problem.* The constituency of interests surrounding the problem is identified together with each interest's image or perspective of the problem.
3. *Successive definition of the problems and the constituency of interests.* The manager initiates a process of successive problem definition through interaction among the interest groups. The problem may be redefined in narrower, more operational terms when institutional or other constraints limit the means available for solving it. Or, the original problem definition may be expanded, and additional interests drawn into the process, to permit a more comprehensive solution to be sought. The manager may, during this process, introduce a variety of perspectives of the problem to open up new possibilities for its solution.
4. *Progressive linking of the interests of salient groups.* The manager seeks and encourages the development of common or complementary elements among the perceptions held by different interest groups. Linkages among the interests are built up around these elements, leading toward agreement as to how to respond to the problem or parts of the problem. The process may require further problem redefinition (Stage 3 on the previous page) and scanning for additional perspectives on the problem, to enhance the possibilities of a creative linking of interests above the level of simple trade-off.
5. *Achievement of a consensus among interest groups.* The progressive linkage of interest groups' perspectives of both problem and solution is guided by the manager toward some level of working consensus on how the problem is to be resolved. This will generally involve an interlocking set of decisions about how various resources are to be deployed in respect of the problem. The joint response can be one of commitment to a comprehensive solution for calculable problem, or to no solution, in which case a "disjointed incrementalist" approach is most likely to be followed [15].

The five stages are not discrete; in practice the stages may overlap and the sequence may change.

The significance of the technique is its flexibility, permitting it to be applied in a range of settings falling between two extremes among decision-making approaches—the comprehensive synoptic (or "rational") on the one hand, and the disjointed incremental ("muddling through") on the other. The strategy incorporates the problem-centered orientation of the incrementalist approach. It combines and balances the two orientations to achieve its purpose, which is the aggregation of commitments from larger constituencies of interests, in order to solve larger scale problems.

The applicability of the MBI-type approach to public decision-making is becoming increasingly evident. The inadequacy of objective-based approaches to planning, policy development, and program delivery is especially visible in a growing number of complex public policy areas of concern to multiple interests with conflicting and sometimes ill-defined objectives. MBI is a more open-ended approach. It provides the potential for more involvement of interest groups in the articulation and achievement of collective purposes through complementary individual decisions that meet individual ends as well. Though the MBI approach has not been (and perhaps cannot be) formalized to the same extent as approaches like MBO, it has nonetheless been applied in a wide range of complex decision situations. The experience gained from these applications has shaped an emerging body of management theory based on the principle of "planning by negotiation."

Comparing the Two Approaches

Table 1 contrasts the two approaches along six dimensions:

Table 1. Two management approaches.

MANAGEMENT BY OBJECTIVE	MANAGEMENT BY INTEREST
Decision-making within a structured hierarchy of responsibility and authority.	Decision-making within a flexible network of interpersonal and interorganizational linkages.
Integration achieved by vertical lines of communication and/or centralization of key decision-making.	Integration achieved by intensive communication and feedback through multiple network linkages.
Well suited to more clearly defined problems for which solutions are assumed to exist.	Well suited to "fuzzy," partially defined problems for which solutions must be invented.
Policies derived from comprehensive analysis and aimed at "optimal" solution.	Policies derived from partial analysis and aimed at "best possible" solution acceptable to interests involved.
Working relations determined by position in bureaucratic hierarchy.	Working relations determined by expertise and interest in problem to be solved.
Communications and feedback according to standardized procedures and defined measures of performance.	Communications and feedback in open, evolving pattern, with few defined measures of performance.

1. the organizational structures in which decisions are made,
2. the means by which integration of policies and actions is achieved,
3. the nature of problems to which the strategy is best suited,
4. the analytical basis for policy development,
5. the organizational basis for establishing and maintaining personal working relationships, and
6. communications patterns and evaluation procedures.

The two approaches are, of course, not mutually exclusive, but overlap one another in various ways. The contrasts indicated do help to differentiate the approaches in basic structural as well as stylistic terms, however.

Although the MBO strategy in itself falls far short of the panacea that some of its adherents would seem to have us believe it to be, it has undoubtedly contributed to improved public management. But we have argued that its misuse can produce a variety of unanticipated consequences.

MBI can, of course, also be misapplied with costly and frustrating consequences for all concerned. Inherent in it, however, is a potential for interdependent decision not present in MBO, which is increasingly required in public management. When used in parallel, MBO and MBI can effectively counterbalance one another. Achieving this balance will require more widespread recognition and acceptance of the legitimacy of MBI, and the design of management frameworks to assist in achieving a best fit between them.

FROM REGULATED TO SELF-REGULATING PATTERNS OF PUBLIC DECISION

In the second section we introduced a distinction between the underlying logic of the "individual as entity," and the logic of the "individual as part" of a collective whole. In the third section we suggested that MBO is a strategy most appropriate to the management of organizational units and functions that can be treated as entities, and MBI most appropriate to the management of interdependent parts, or part processes. Then we argued that the contrasting strategies of MBO and MBI complement one another, and that they can be used together.

In this section, we show how the strategies of MBO and MBI are integrated in two different patterns of public decision-making. One is the more established form of "regulated" decision-making, which stems from bureaucratic organizing principles; the other is the pattern of "self-regulating" decision, which stems from ecological (or systems cybernetic) organizing principles. A regulated decision pattern is marked by a high degree of functional specialization and routinization of activity and control among discrete, clearly bounded organizational entities. Responsibility for overall system guidance rests with specialized, central control agencies. A self-regulating decision pattern is marked by a high degree of functional overlap and flexibility in the allocation of responsibility.

System control is diffused throughout interdependent system parts, and regulation occurs as a result of interaction and negotiation among them [16]. MBO has primacy over and tends to constrain MBI in the former pattern, while the opposite is true in the latter pattern.

A Comparison of Two Patterns of Public Decision

In the realm of public governance, these two patterns differentiate two systems of decision-making, with different underlying logics and principles of organization. Each decision system has the same basic elements—government and nongovernmental organizational units of various kinds—but the systemic relations between them are different. The two types of decision system are hard to disentangle in practice, though a conceptual distinction between them has important practical consequences.

Let us examine more closely some differences in the logic underlying the regulated and self-regulating decision systems. These differences center on the relation between a particular government unit (a division, branch, service, department, agency, *etc.*) and a particular constituency of interest defined in relation to it. In the regulated decision sequence, the unit and its purposes are conceived as more of an entity (albeit one within a larger entity such as a level or jurisdiction of government). This conception guides the unit in defining its constituency of interest (usually in sectoral or functional terms) and its purposes are conceived quite differently, less as a discrete entity and more as an interdependent part of a holistic, encompassing collectivity with broader sets of purposes. The unit is part of a man-environment system, with a partial role to play in its governance. This distinction is most easily grasped by looking at how the unit behaves at four levels of decision-making as shown in Figure 2.

At the level of *goals*, in the regulated sequence the constituency of interest or client group is identified in terms of the partial concern that group might have for a predetermined range of services offered by the unit. In the self-regulating sequence, goal-setting explicitly subordinates its actual or potential functions to a statement of the overall interests and functions of the constituency.

At the level of *objectives* in the regulated sequence, the government unit specifies the feasibility of its goals, essentially in terms of resources allocated to it by more central agencies. This of course provokes competition for scarce resources between it and other government units, resulting in the pressure to escalate overall budgets to meet the pressures of demand from functionally distinct constituencies. In the self-regulating sequence the government unit's objectives specify the functions of the government unit in function of all the resources potentially available to the constituency. The pressure for the unit to develop and extend its exclusive pattern of functions and programs is lessened. Interdependence between functions is stimulated.

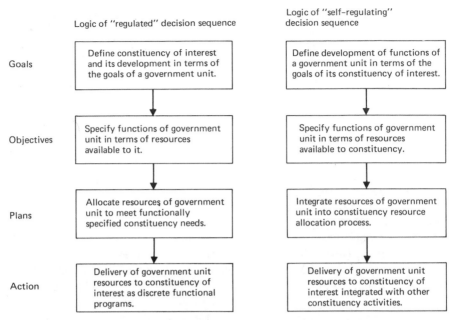

Figure 2. Two contrasting sequences of public decision.

At the level of *plans* in the regulated sequence, the government unit specifies the production and delivery of its functions or services. The unit endeavors to define and manage the boundary between its programs and the general pattern of activities of the constituency. The pressures of routinized central regulation in government require it to do so, in order to maintain and justify itself and the resources allocated to it. It must plan to spend to the limit of its budget, and to justify all this expenditure. In the self-regulating sequence the government unit's plans integrate the resources of the government unit into the overall activities of the constituency. Its own performance justification does not depend on fully allocated resources, because its interdependent approach to planning stimulates resource allocation from the most appropriate sources, not necessarily those under its control.

At the level of *action* in the regulated sequence, the government unit "delivers" its program or service to the constituency. That is the primary concern, and performance measures most often stem from it. In the self-regulating sequence, the government units actions are "successful" only to the extent they are integrated within the overall interests of the constituency as defined in its original goal statement. Performance assessment is done jointly with the constituency.

This initial comparative approximation of the two forms of public decision gives priority to MBO in the regulated and to MBI in the self-regulating. But both management strategies are present throughout all four stages in the decision sequence.

Of the two types of pattern just described, the regulated one predominates. Seldom do public managers operate in terms of the self-regulating sequence. Goals are usually not defined with reference to a constituency as a whole, except in polemic fashion. Rather, goals are usually those of entities—government units devoted to transportation, international cooperation, environmental control, and so on. We have suggested some of the impacts this has at other levels of the decision sequence; in the scope of objectives pursued, the nature of the planning process, and in the implementation of action programs.

There is little incentive for the decision-maker to do otherwise within the bureaucratic environment of big government. Survival depends on the manager giving primacy to his unit and its objectives and functions within the decision-making hierarchy. The regulated pattern of control is self-perpetuating. It fosters greater compartmentalization of function, thereby escalating the need for "heavy-handed" central policy direction and budget control. This self-perpetuating pattern can also be described as a synergetic relation between MBO and MBI. The modification of this pattern will depend on a reversal of this relationship, to shift from a "negative" to a "positive" synergy between them.

Synergies Between MBO and MBI

There is a negative synergy between MBO and MBI in a regulated decision system, to the extent that MBO leads toward centralization and routinization of command, and MBI tends to be employed only in peripheral organizational activities within well-established limits and guidelines. MBI is relegated to marginal decision-making, with little impact on key organizational and interorganizational decisions. To the extent that MBI impinges on more critical decisions it is often seen as subverting established purposes and procedures. It is controlled by tighter procedures and better central monitoring.

In a self-regulating decision system a positive synergy is possible between MBO and MBI. This occurs when MBO is used as a way of strengthening the decision-making process in areas where government units can function more or less autonomously in a decentralized pattern. MBI is employed as a means of managing interdependent decision-making in areas of mutual concern. In effect, the management of interdependent part processes through MBI becomes a prerequisite for the application of MBO to the independent decision-making of distinct organizational entities. Each supports the other, and MBO does not foster further centralization.

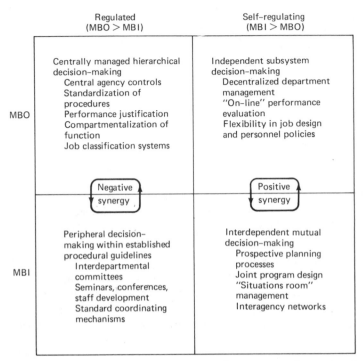

Figure 3. Synergetic relations between MBO and MBI strategies in regulated and self-regulating decision system's.

This argument is summarized in Figure 3, which also shows how certain organizational elements support these two kinds of synergy.

To sum up, the shift from a regulated to a self-regulating pattern will require a basic shift in decision-making procedures. We have characterized this shift as a reversal of priorities between MBO and MBI. At present the relation between these two management strategies, the manner in which MBO dominates and constrains MBI, perpetuates and strengthens the negative consequences of the regulated pattern. By increasing the legitimacy and respective influences of MBI over MBO, a shift toward a self-regulating pattern can be encouraged.

NOTES AND REFERENCES

1. Hirsch, Fred. *Social Limits to Growth.* Cambridge: Harvard University Press, 1976. Hirsch assesses the Keynesian framework of managed market economies since World War II.
2. A range of relations between patterns of increasing and decreasing resource use and patterns of increasing and decreasing social well-being are explored in M. Chavalier

and T. Burns, *A Field Concept of Public Management*. Report No. 14, Fisheries and Environment Canada, Office of the Science Advisor, 1976.

3. Some reasons why are discussed in Chevalier and Burns, *Public Management*, above.

4. In this regard, Angyal's conception of personality is an especially useful formulation of the relation between individual and environment. Angyal, Andras. *Foundation for a Science of Personality*. Cambridge: Harvard University Press, 1941 (revised, 1958).

5. On the distinction between purposeful and purposive systems, see Russell Ackoff, "Toward a System of System Concepts," *Management Science*, 1971.

6. To give an example of this distinction: individual interests in a country could seek or find mineral resources beyond or within its borders, and secure some form of ownership or access to them. The mineral resources, and the human knowledge and enterprise required to make use of them, would have changed from potential to actual resources in its contextual environment, to collective or community resources. They would be controlled or partially controlled by individual interests within that country or community.

7. One can conceive of a wholly self-sufficient individual purpose, in which case it is not in itself a matter of collective-individual reconciliation.

8. See Chevalier and Burns, *Public Management*.

9. Drucker, Peter. *The Practice of Management*. New York: Harper & Row, 1954.

10. Odiorne, George S. *Management by Objectives: A System of Managerial Leadership*. New York: Pitman, 1965. Humble, John. *Improving Business Results*.

11. Sherwood, Frank P., and William J. Page, Jr. "MBO and Public Management: Symposium on Management by Objectives in the Public Sector." *Public Administration Review* 36(1976): .

12. Chevalier, M. and J. Taylor. *The Dynamics of Adaptation in the Federal Public Service*. Ottawa: Information Canada, 1970. Conducted in 1966 for the Royal Commission on Bilingualism and Biculturalism, this study used a "strategy of interest-based planning." For a similar approach, see John Friedmann, *Retracking America: A Theory of Transactive Planning*, New York: Doubleday Anchor, 1973.

13. Chevalier and Taylor, *Dynamics of Adaptation*.

14. The use of the distinction between calculability and incalculability in the process of problem definition, as well as the relationship between the way a problem is framed and how it may be resolved are critical factors in the strategy.

15. Broybrooke, David, and C. E. Lindblom. *A Strategy of Decision*. New York: The Free Press, 1963.

16. This distinction is compatible with Emery and Trist's identification of two basic organizational design principles, one based on a "redundancy of parts" and specialized mechanisms of control, the other on "redundancy of function" among self-managing, semiautonomous parts. Emery, F. E., and E. L. Trist. *Toward a Social Ecology*. London: Plenum, 1972.

17. Emery, F. E. *Futures We Are In*. Leiden: Stenfert Kroese, 1977.

18. Jong, S. Jun., ed. "A Symposium: Management by Objectives in the Public Sector." *Public Administration Review* Jan.–Feb. 1976.

19. Michael, Donald. *On Learning to Plan and Planning to Learn*. San Francisco: Jossey-Bass, 1973.

20. Sachs, Ignacy. *Environment and Development: The National and International Contexts*. Ottawa: Publication CIDA/DOE, 1977.

PART II

Ideological and Ethical Considerations

The ideological and ethical constraints under which public administrators should labor have long been a matter of dispute, but have seldom been explored with any real discipline. To repair this neglect, Stephen Seadler, perhaps America's leading authority on ideological instruments, takes us through an elegant and dramatic survey of ideologics, and caps his work with a discussion of the way in which we might bring strict scientific analysis to the realm of values. In the second paper, Walter Weisskopf, one of the most important and articulate critics of modern value systems, lends the public administrator the benefit of his considerable insight into the shortcomings of our current social and economic perspectives; he argues eloquently for the reintroduction of ethical bases into the political calculus. We conclude this section with Edwin Boling's formidable inquiry into the problem of injecting ethical discipline into the public sector, and why such discipline is a necessity, rather than a luxury, for our modern age.

1

Ideologic Essentials of Public Administration

Stephen E. Seadler
Ideological Defense Center, New York

INTRODUCTION

The intent of this essay is to provide in very brief compass the basic elements of a new field that is essential not only to the viability of public administration, but to its continued existence. The proper recognition, development, and deployment of the principles and practices to be outlined here will not only greatly enhance the effectiveness of public administration in general, but may deter impending catastrophe and provide the essentials for a new era.

While the primary concern at hand is public administration in the United States, the present and rapidly increasing interdependence of all nations requires that the larger concern be public administration in all nations.

It will provide useful backdrop for what follows if the reader will pause to ruminate about world news, facts, analyses, indicators, etc., for, say, the past hundred years, make rough assessments of the domestic states and trends of affairs of nations in all regions of the globe, make similar assessments of international states and trends of affairs, and in so doing take into account a wide range of aspects of individual, community, national, and international life. This suggested review is not intended to imply to what degree public administrations are responsible for what aspects of life within their boundaries and beyond, but it does inherently assert that the mere premise of the existence of "public administration" implies *some* roles, hence responsibilities, and hence performance criteria, however minimal and varied they may be.

Central to this essay is the thesis that, underlying the set of all public administrative roles, there is a particular subset of elements common to all roles, which subset we can coalesce into a common factor. It is this common factor that we will elicit as our next step.

COMMONALITIES

In order to elicit the common factor, "comfact," among all public administrations, we need a working definition of such administrations. As is often, if not always, the case in the axiomatic development of a science, minimal definitions are preferred. Such is the case here. For our purposes, then, we have the following: *Public administration is the administration of public affairs of a political entity by whatever polity exists, including its agents, where "administration" potentially spans all functions from the highest-level policy- and goal-setting roles to the lowest-level operational details, the actual span varying from case to case, and where "public affairs" are whatever affairs of the society that its polity deems them to be.* With this full statement as background, we can provide a short definition as follows: *Public administration is the conduct of public affairs as defined and carried out by whatever polity exists.* In fact, this form can constitute the definition, and the prior form can serve as a concise elaboration or clarification. We will now proceed to probe into the meanings of the words involved, an exercise that provides the conceptual foundations for this new field.

"Polity" derives from the Latin *politia*, which carries the meanings of government, form of government, and commonwealth, which together convey the idea of a society organized for its government.

"Public" derives from the Latin *public(us)*, which means pertaining to or affecting a people, population, or community as a whole; that is, the idea of society is again the underlying concept.

In fact, to define "community" we are brought back to the concept of society, dictionary definitions having a common basis as follows: *a social group residing in a specific area and having a common government and culture.* Therefore, inasmuch as the concept of "society" underlies both polity and public, and is also fundamental to "social science," "sociology," "societal," and "socio-"—that is, inasmuch as the concept "society" is fundamental to all the matters with which we are dealing—our factor-extraction process comes to focus on that concept.

Dictionaries generally define "society" as an organized group of individuals associated together for various purposes, the list of which invariably includes "cultural." This, however, is intrinsically redundant because the other purposes are based on, and are aspects of, the society's culture.

At this juncture, then, we find "culture" to be the salient essence of "society," which is the foundation concept of both "public" and "polity," which are central concepts in the definition of "public administration," and we are thus led to *its* essence. The Latin root of "culture" is *cultur(a)*, and whether we proceed next in English or Latin the picture is the same: the stem "cult" (*cult*) plus a suffix of action or instrument "-ure" (*-ura*). Extracting the root of the stem "cult," we come to *cult(us)*, whose meanings include tilling and worship. This root, in turn, is derived from the past participle of *colere*, to cultivate, worship, or dwell.

The involvement of "cultivate" provides a significant lead, and we find that its Latin root also derives from *cult(us)*, as would obviously be expected. That is, the concepts "culture" and "cultivate" have the same root, *cult(us)*, a root signifying both worship and tilling. This becomes understandable and highly significant when we shed historical light on the matter: in particular, early man's close association of magic and religion with working the land to grow crops.

All of this leads us, finally, to converge on the English word "cult," and we find dictionaries defining it in sociological context as *a group having a sacred ideology and a set of rites with sacred symbols*. Such definitions, however, need updating and refining. We update them by recalling the ancient agricultural origins of the religious ("sacred") qualification and therefore removing it, and by broadening "rites" to "behaviors and customs." We refine the definition by correcting the simple addition of ideology, rites, and symbols, for these must be related and congruent. Furthermore, a group does more than simply "have" these components; they define, bind, and motivate the group.

Thus we arrive at an updated, refined concept of "cult" for contemporary sociological purposes as: *A group defined, bound, and motivated by an ideology and related sets of behaviors and customs together with unifying symbols*. The English stem "cult" now properly constitutes the basis for the construct "culture," which, in turn, constitutes the basis for the construct "society." Standing back a bit, we can now see the following conceptual organism: *The public and polity of public administration are based on an underlying society, the essence of which is its culture, at the core of which, and hence of all else, is ideology*.

Now, returning to our quest, we find that we have elicited a factor common to all public administrations: *ideology*. By having employed the concept of relatedness in defining cult, we have avoided the question of causality, that is, of whether ideologies determine behaviors and customs or *vice versa*, or whether they are interactively interdependent and, if so, which is predominant when. Instead, we leave matters at an irrefutable, minimal finding: ideologies are at the core of, and integral with, the cultural essence of societal behavior and structure, and, therefore, underlie and constitute a major common factor among all public administrations of society's affairs.

LOGOS

The preceding section found ideology to be a "major" factor common to all public administrations. In this section we will obtain a fix on *how* major it is.

We begin by remarking that the most remarkable feature of that finding is that it has to be made at all, inasmuch as it is so obvious. That men and societies are organized, guided, controlled, and motivated by systems of beliefs is at the foundation of our own Judaeo-Christian culture and of our democratic political system.

Among the Judaic founts of our culture are the Talmud and the Torah, the former being a collection of Jewish laws and tradition, and the latter being the Pentateuch, or first five books of the Old Testament. In some classifications the Torah is considered to be the entire body of Jewish law as contained primarily in the Old Testament and the Talmud. Whatever the case, the point here is the emphasis on law and tradition, where tradition encompasses rites, customs, and symbols—all-told the cult of culture—with powerful emphasis on "law," which together with the theology of the Pentateuch, comprise the ideological foundations of the Judaic culture—and ultimately of the Christian and Islamic cultures, which grew from it.

Among the Christian founts of our culture are the very concepts of *teachings*, *gospel*, and *message*—a new *testament*. The point is cogently set forth in the opening sentence of "The Gospel According to St. John":

> In the beginning was the Word, and the Word was with God, and the Word was God.

In the original Greek, "Word" is *Logos*, which means a thought or concept, or the expression of that thought. English dictionaries define "logos" as a philosophical term meaning the rational principle that governs and develops the universe, and give its Greek meanings as word, reason, speech, discourse, thought. The concept of *logos* was widely prevalent long before St. John. The idea of Idea as an essence of, or vital principle in, the universe has pervaded most religions and philosophic systems from antiquity to today.

In summary, then: thought, reason, discourse, in the sense of a body of thought, was recognized thousands of years ago to play a primary role in the affairs of mankind. So much so, that man projected this primacy out into the universe, and saw the universe governed and developed by Idea, because he saw his own society governed and developed by ideas.

The history of mankind is essentially the elaboration of this theme, and has become more intensely so with the advent of secular ideologies and the proliferation of religious, secular, and religiosecular ideologies.

PARAMOUNT OBJECTIVE

The most remarkable and serious deficiency of populist public administration is its total neglect of the most pervasive and powerful factor in the affairs that administrations seek to administer—the factor we have elicited, depicted, and assessed: ideology.

In one class of countries, however, the authoritarian, the situation is reversed:

there is intensive ideological involvement at all levels of administration. This statement becomes truer and more meaningful the more advanced the authoritarian country. The less developed the authoritarian country, the less developed the *indigenous* ideology, usually reducing to some variety of simple divine right. The primary purpose of the ideology is, of course, to legitimate the regime in the absence of popular legitimacy, and to bind and motivate its administrators and followers. In nonauthoritarian countries the pervasive primacy of ideology is just as great, but is less defined, less visible, more implicit, more tacit, more diffuse, more varied, and confusing.

In many countries, but especially in the United States, there is a special problem beyond mere nonrecognition of ideology: a counterforce, a cultural bias against explicit ideology and ideological considerations. This was strikingly depicted in the French motion picture that was shown in the U.S. under the title "Exhibition." The film purported to be the biography of a pornographic film star. In one scene in her apartment in which the producer interviews her, she responds fully regarding her sexual preferences and practices and the nature of her orgasm, but, when asked about her ideology, she declines firmly on the grounds that that is too personal a question!

In a very limited sense this has a healthy aspect, in that it offers poor soil for ideological extremes to take root in. But, in the larger perspective, ideological ignorance and neglect have produced public administrative and societal results marked by suboptimality, inefficiency, dysfunction—and peril—in proportion to the degree of ideological salience. This goes unrecognized because ideological salience itself goes unrecognized, or where recognized is ignored, or where not ignored is pronounced dead or otherwise dismissed.

These comments are borne of personal observations by the author over the thirty years that he has been seeking to promote ideological awareness *and operationality* in the business, academic, professional, and governmental communities in the United States and abroad. Thirty years ago the word ideology was to all intents and purposes absent from popular and informed discourse, management, and media, and from academe itself, save for such rarities as Karl Mannheim's 1929 classic *Ideology and Utopia* [1]. While immensely valuable, that work was typically a sociological-historical *study*, and one whose main thrust was not ideology, but rather, as specified in its subtitle, "An Introduction to the Sociology of Knowledge," the objective of which was given in the last sentence of the 1936 edition: ". . . to present the problem in as unified a form as possible in order to facilitate discussion." It certainly would have done so among the few so inclined, but it hardly widened the circle or affected public affairs, nor did it seek to, despite the fact that 1929-1936 saw the simultaneous rise of four virulent ideologies that spread hatred, death, and destruction over the entire planet: Bolshevism, Fascism, Nazism, and Tanakaism [2].

Our ideological neglect regarding Fascism and Nazism remains an example of official and professional ignorance and stupidity of such catastrophic proportions as to be almost undiscussable. William L Shirer devotes an entire chapter to it in *The Rise and Fall of the Third Reich* [3]. In his *Inside The Third Reich*, Albert Speer, Hitler's Minister of Armaments and War Production, and the only defendent at Nuremberg to admit his share of guilt in the crimes of the Third Reich, berates himself [4, p. 19]:

> Why did I not undertake a thorough, systematic investigation of, say, the value or worthlessness of the ideologies of *all* parties? Why did I not read the various party programs, or at least Hitler's *Mein Kampf* and Rosenberg's *Myth of the Twentieth Century*?
>
> For had I wanted to, I could have found out even then what Hitler really stood for and planned. Not to have worked that out for myself; not, given my education, to have read . . . not to have tried to see through the whole apparatus of mystification—*was already criminal. At this initial stage my guilt was as grave as, at the end, my work for Hitler. For being in a position to know and nevertheless shunning knowledge creates direct responsibility for the consequences—from the very beginning.* (Emphasis supplied in this paragraph.)

We will return to that last, extremely significant point, but for now, let us move on to the next historical period.

Under pressures of the Cold War, sporadic and isolated research was conducted on Soviet operational codes, statements, speeches, *etc.* For instance, Project Michelson, a project of the Behavioral Sciences Group at the U.S. Naval Ordnance Testing Station, China Lake, California, during 1963-1964, conducted factor analyses of content-analysis codings of U.S. and Soviet writings on stability, deterrence, and arms control. In the process some ideological-type variables were coded, but they were neither perceived nor treated as such *per se*, and were subsumed into factors dubbed Environmental, Perceptual, Behavioral, and Weapon System Characteristics in one study, and into concepts "that have weapon system correlates" in another.

By the 1970s the word "ideology" began to appear more and more frequently in the literate press, in professional journals, and in university course catalogues. In the press it now takes its place as simply another background characteristic of the event, with no operational significance. Similarly, in academe and government it is just another sociological item to mention, or, more rarely, to study, but in any event is certainly not something one *does* anything about.

One of the most remarkable examples of this is Henry A. Kissinger and his *American Foreign Policy/Expanded Edition* [5], which is exceptional for its ideological awareness and profusion of explicit and acute references to ideological salience in many aspects of world politics. Yet, curiously, his actual administration of foreign affairs evidenced no reification of that personal consciousness. Perhaps that was largely due to the unavailability of ideological levers, agencies, and staffs for immediate applications, especially when faced with monumental real-world crises and responsibilities—and, hence, his reverting to "operating within familiar procedures and concepts," which practice as a scholar he contemned, but foresaw [5, p. 94]:

> New administrations come to power convinced of the need for goals and for comprehensive concepts. Sooner, rather than later, they find themselves subjected to the pressures of the immediate and the particular. Part of the reason is the pragmatic, issue-oriented bias of decision-makers. But the fundamental reasons may be the pervasiveness of modern bureaucracy.

In any event, no matter what one's evaluation of the man and his administration of foreign affairs, we would do well to heed his vision, montaged as follows:

> In the years ahead, the most profound challenge to American policy will be philosophical [5, p. 79].... Side by side with the physical balance of power, there exists a psychological balance based on intangibles of value and belief. The presuppositions of the physical equilibrium have changed drastically; those of the psychological balance remain to be discovered [5, p. 85].... We require a new burst of creativity.... The contemporary unrest ... is proof of a profound dissatisfaction with the merely managerial ... qualities of the modern state [5, p. 96].... [A new administration] must found its claim not on pat technical answers to difficult issues; it must above all ask the right questions. It must recognize that, in the field of foreign policy, we will never be able to contribute to building a stable and creative world order unless we first form some conception of it [5, p. 97].

It is inherent in the process of addressing the "psychological balance" *via* ideology that "some conception" of "a stable and creative world order" will emerge, and it is the paramount objective of this essay to provide public administrators with such a conception and the means of achieving it.

These foreign affairs considerations apply *mutatis mutandis* to domestic affairs. There seems to be little chance, however, of introducing ideological operations into domestic affairs, into the administration of human rights, civil rights, equal opportunity, urban affairs, socioeconomics, crime prevention, juvenile delinquency, mental health, commerce, labor, etc., or to the diagnosis and treatment of myriad forms of social malaise, conflict, anomie, alienation, *etc.*, before such operations have been introduced into foreign affairs administration. Furthermore, it can be shown that many of those domestic problems are, in very large measure, consequences of ideological backwashes from international affairs, and interact with them.

Therefore, we shall focus on the most urgent, maximum payoff areas of public administration: international affairs and defense, and two major correlates of these, intelligence and arms control and disarmament.

IDEOLOGIC INQUIRY

The profound and pervasive primacy of ideology, together with the potential power derived by explicitly and formally dealing with it, plus the magnitude and complexity of the resultant subject, call for a special, new science to deal with it on both the theoretical and applied levels.

The word "ideology" is confusing, however, in that it represents both process and substance. Consequently, we shall use the term *ideologics* (ī'·dē·ō·lō'·gics) to denote the new science of the nature, structure, and dynamics of ideologies, of their roles in individual, societal, and international phenomena, and of methods for affecting those natures, dynamics, and roles. In classification, ideologics thus joins the family of behavioral and social sciences, along with cultural anthropology, economics, history, political science, psychology, sociology, psychiatry, linguistics, *etc.* In fact, ideologics intersects so extensively with, and is so fundamental to the other behavioral sciences, that it can be looked upon as a *basic* behavioral science [6].

Ideologic Predicates of War

The first step in approaching the problem of war is, of course, to formulate it, at the same time taking care not to overformulate it, which occurrence would unduly restrict the development of solutions. Considerably more breadth and depth in problem formulation are desirable than can be provided in this essay, but some feeling for the subject should be obtainable from even this brief account.

The word "feeling" was used deliberately. Although the mode of this essay and of the present state of the ideologic art are highly *cognitive*, and ideologies themselves are in varying degrees highly cognitive, it must be felt at the outset that the *affective* components of ideologics (*i.e.*, ideologies and the interrelated, interactive, individual, and societal behaviors) are as important as the cognitive components.

The reader may question why we focus on war rather than peace. The answer lies largely in a passage from Hobbes' *Leviathan*:

> For WARRE, consisteth not in Battel only, or the act of fighting; but in a tract of time, wherein the Will to contend by Battell is sufficiently known: and there the notion of Time, is to be considered in the nature of Warre, as it is in the nature of Weather. For as the nature of Foule weather, lyeth not in a Showre or two of rain, but in an inclination thereto of many dayes together: So the nature of Warre, consisteth not in actual fighting; but in the known disposition thereto during all the time there is no assurance to the contrary. All other time is PEACE.

The "inclination" and "disposition" to war are crystallized and manifested in its ideological foundations, which rationalize, legitimate, motivate, and unify "the Will to contend by Battell." This statement is merely a corollary to the primary role of ideology developed in the preceding sections of this essay.

The ideological foundations of war are ultimately rooted in the sheer desire for war, which is rooted in psychology, which is rooted in neurophysiology, which . . . let us stop there. For at that level we find an adequate, in fact vital, principle available: the principle of encephalization, which describes the fact that during the course of evolution the parts of our central nervous system that developed most are those nearest the head, and that, as the higher structures developed, older ones did not disappear. Hence structures and connections found, for instance in the shark, are still to be found in man. The higher and lower centers blend and contend in the dynamics of human psychology, and are reflected in such phenomena as the two-sidedness of the human coin: love and hate, construction and destruction. In behavior, the hate-and-destruction side expresses itself as a passion for violence, aggression, domination, and war.

Perhaps a measure of civilization is the importance and art of clothing savagery and naked plunder in the robes of higher purpose. For man is a moral being who must justify what he does [7]. It is characteristic of our times that every design for domination has needed a special ideology, and could not become a movement, or even a gang, until fused in the heat of passion with an ideology the provided unity, purpose, and justification. *In other words, ideological armaments have been found as essential as physical armaments.*

In the long view of anthropology and history this is nothing new. The progression, very roughly, is: primitive myth; divine right of emperors and kings; partially divine-partially secular right of nation-states; and now, ideological right of modern nations and international movements. The "right" concerning us here is the right to do what one wants in the way one wants. While some codes restrain, others grant license; while some codes extol peaceful means, others extol violence. The focus to follow is on ideologies that have at their cores code of violence and license with emphasis on promoting war. This is entirely different from fighting as a last resort, from the right to revolution, which is reserved and inherent in the United Nations Charter's recognition of the principle of self-determination, and in the concept of democracy and government by consent of the governed.

One of the earliest examples of ideological armaments is found in the Melian Conference during the Peloponnesian War. The Athenians sent an expeditionary force of 38 ships, 2700 soldiers, and 320 archers against the island of Melos, which had remained neutral in the war. The Athenians sought first to negotiate the island's surrender by explaining to the Melians the justice and purpose of their conquest by Athens: "You know as well as we do that the standard of justice depends on the quality of power to compel, and that in fact the strong do what they have the power to do and the weak accept what they have to accept. . . . Our opinion of the gods and our knowledge of men lead us to conclude that it is a general and necessary law of nature to rule wherever one can." The Melians did not debate the argument, but hoped to play the game and win by trusting to help from the gods and the Spartans. Help came from neither, and the Athenians put to death all men of military age and sold the women and children as slaves [8].

Even the incredibly ferocious Genghis Khan (Temujin) felt the ideological imperative, and employed revenge and the divine among his precepts. While not yet Khan, Temujin declared, "Heaven and Earth have strengthened my powers. I dedicate my forces to the service of almighty Heaven, and to our mother Earth. We have taken our vengeance on the Merkit, as men should. . . . Heaven and Earth have agreed together, that Temujin shall be the ruler of the people." In later years, after having become Khan, and being faced with authorizing an execution, he declared, "But I cannot kill him merely at his request, without proper justification; the oracle has not decreed that it should be so" [9].

The modern form of the problem can be considered to have begun in 1862, when Bismarck became Prime Minister of Prussia. At that time, Bismarck embarked on his program of "Blood and Iron" and a diplomatic career of deceit— aided, unified, motivated, and justified by a diffuse body of thought. From the philosophies of Kant, Fichte, and Hegel, and a profound sense of Christian mission, Bismarck and the Junkers developed the prototype of modern ideologies. It set forth the partially divine, partially secular right and duty of the German peoples to dominate the world by force and a special morality. This course was called for by natural, historic, and cosmic necessity, racial superiority, the dictates of the Absolute, and the "positive freedom" of the moral law of the "World Spirit," of which the German State was the instrument and highest expression, and into which the individual was to dissolve, freed from "private" moral restraints. It was a comprehensive theory of the individual, the state, violence, and morality. The head of the sage had joined with the arm of the soldier, and within nine years the Second Reich was created at Versailles, the greatest power on the Continent. Similar forces operated in the Kaiser's Germany.

The same pattern, and in fact the same lines of thought, were employed with variations and embellishments by Marx, Mussolini, and Hitler. The product was the same in each case: an ideology at whose core were a theory extolling violence and a theory setting up a new morality above and beyond the general principles accepted by the rest of the civilized world.

Mussolini wrote "Fascism" in 1928, wherein he set forth how "Fascism is not only a system of government, but also and above all a system of thought." The system of thought had its roots in, and was very similar to, the ideology of Bismarck's Second Reich, substituting a crude Social Darwinism in place of Germanism. "As a philosophy of life, Fascism adopted as a social creed the basically Darwinist doctrine of the survival of the fittest; hence it represented war as a necessary function in the life of a nation, and it considered peaceful and satisfied nations as decadent and doomed, fit victims for the appetite of young and dynamic nations [10]. For seven years the "system of thought" was ignored, and the first victim was Ethiopia.

The Japanese case was of the old school, the divine right of emperors, a combination of nationalism and religion. "The official cult [Shinto] became a powerful instrument in the hands of the militarists, who used it to glorify their policy of aggression" [10]. Their plans for world conquest were set forth in the Tanaka Memorial, which became known to the occidental world in 1931. "Its authenticity is open to question, though its contents in general agree with Tanaka's known views" [10]. All of this was ignored. Manchuria was first on his list, and it fell to the Kwantung Army three years later. Also on the list was the United States.

The case of the Third Reich was, like Italy, of the new school: a secular ideology of the Second Reich, to which were added the war-lust of Treitschke, the racism of de Gobineau and H. S. Chamberlain, and some distorted Nietzsche and Darwin. Genetics was distorted into geneticism and evolution was distorted into evolutionism (Social Darwinism) to give the concoction a scientific air, as befitted the times. The brew was published by Adolf Hitler in 1925 in *Mein Kampf*. For flavoring were added dashes of fierce old Icelandic legends that Wagner had already composed into what would later become the musical accompaniment of Nazism and its Third Reich. Below all—author, composer, book, Party, and Kultur drank deeply at their common ideological fountainhead: the virulent anti-Semitism launched by Martin Luther. Altogether it was a glorious movement, inexorably destined to stir the minds and hearts of Aryan men and women with love of Deutschland, Fuhrer, savagery, genocide . . . and war.

"Had the foreign statesmen of the world perused it carefully while there was still time," conjectures William L. Shirer in *The Rise and Fall of the Third Reich*, "both Germany and the world might have been saved from catastrophe." But, it too was ignored. For, Shirer exclaims with anguished exasperation, "his opponents inside and outside Germany were too busy, or too stupid to take much notice of it until it was too late" [11].

By 1933 the first phase was completed: the birth of the Third Reich. Five years later, unaware and unprepared, England and France handed over Czechoslovakia. A year after that the Wehrmacht plunged into Poland, and Europe was plunged into war. Two years later, with Japan's treacherous attack on a befuddled America, most of the world was enjoying the fruits of special, higher moralities, and reveling in the glory of man's highest function: war.

It was a war that had long been theorized, willed, planned, prepared, and threatened—explicitly, in published ideologies.

Although the resultant war against Fascism, the term now used generically, was won, and one might say that the United States government and its allies administered the problem successfully, in a larger sense it was neither won nor so administered. For extensive enclaves of Fascism exist throughout the world today, waiting for the right conditions for its renascence.

Religious Wars

Although the preceding historical overview alluded to religious components of ideological foundations of comtemporary war, religious wars themselves were omitted. That omission was designed to make separate provision for considering this oldest, bloodiest, most vicious class of wars, and the paramount problem that they represent today.

When one contemplates that most of mankind is still in the grip of primitive theologies—that implicitly and explicitly embody violent elements, that these theologies are becoming increasingly armed with the most advanced weapons of the thermonuclear age, that they have become pawns and proxies in Big Power Politics, that they have become terrorist factions, become allied with secular terrorist factions or become admixed into religiosecular terrorist ideologies, and that each of them claims divine origins, sanctions, and license, and demands faith against knowledge and reason—one must conclude that such religious and religiosecular ideologies constitute the most dangerous and intractable class of ideologies of violence.

Communist Ideology

The historical overview deferred consideration of Communism to this special section due to the magnitude of the subject and the immediate urgency of the problem it presents. During the 130 years since publication of Marx' and Engels' *Communist Manifesto*, an enormous body of written and spoken doctrine has been produced. Most of it does not concern us here, for we are concerned only with that aspect of it that directly relates to our problem formulation. That aspect is Marxism-Leninism, the official ideology of the Soviet Union. And within that we are concerned only with its *core* ideology of violence and licence. But that, too, involves such an enormous body of literature over the past ninety years that even an overview is not feasible, for greater breadth and depth are essential to proper recognition of the dimensions of the problem. Therefore, we will proceed to develop a "miniview" in two sections that we hope is sufficient to provide at least some sense of the rational (cognitive) and emotional (affective) components of Marxism-Leninism's *Core* that are salient to problem formulation and consequent ideologic operations. With these caveats and future elaboration in mind, we will nevertheless label the sections "overviews," and begin with the first one, on means.

Means and Dialectical Materialism

Soviet Communists call Marxism-Leninism their "theoretical treasure." In his speech to the twentieth Party Congress (Congress of the Communist Party of the Soviet Union (CPSU)), Nikita Khrushchev, author of the "post-Stalin" era, hailed "the invincible banner of Marxism-Leninism," "the all-conquering banner of Marxism-Leninism." In 1957 he declared, "The Party has fought and will continue to fight resolutely against every departure from Marxism-Leninism." In the same year, "The Fundamentals of Marxism-Leninism," a required course in all institutions of higher learning, was expanded into three courses, one of which was "Dialectical Materialism."

Dialectical Materialism is the world-view of communist societies, and provides the basic principles for communist life and communist relationships with the rest of the world. It was formulated by Marx and Engels, and thereby antedates Marxism-Leninism, and constitutes the core of Marxism *per se*, that is, Marxism without Leninism. The *Columbia Encyclopedia* describes it as "a method which is applicable to any problem of human thought, and in its fullest application has had a wider impact on the development of society than any other doctrine since the advent of Islam" [10].

The official *History of the Communist Party of the Soviet Union* reaffirmed that [12]:

> Marxism-Leninism is an integral and consistent *dialectical materialist* world outlook, and the theory of scientific Communism. It is the science of the laws of development of society, the science of the Socialist revolution and the dictatorship of the proletariat, the science of the building of Socialist and Communist society. From Marxist-Leninist theory the Party draws its strength and its confidence in the triumph of Communism. This theory enables the Party to ascertain the laws governing social life, to find the right orientation in any situation, to understand the inner connection of events and the trend of their development. It helps to find the answers to the basic questions posed by the revolutionary struggle and Communist construction [emphasis supplied].

"Dialectics" takes its name from the question-and-answer technique of logical argument (dialektiké) in Plato's *Dialogues*, but in Marxism it is a theory of violence. The most concise explanation of it is given in the 1951 edition of the *History*, and, briefly, here is its quintessence. Marx and Engels took the "rational kernel" of an early nineteenth-century philosophy (Hegel's), mixed it with the "inner kernel" of a later nineteenth-century philosophy (Feuerbach's), blended the mixture with their own interpretations of nineteenth-century physics and chemistry, and produced a "scientific world view" called "dialectical materialism."

"Dialectics" in Communist theory means that *the* method of change throughout nature is *not* continuous growth or evolution, but, rather, a process whereby unnoticed little changes in "quantity" *suddenly* develop into fundamental changes in "quality." That is, nature "leaps" from one state to another. "For example," the *History* quotes Engels, "in the case of water which is heated or cooled, boiling point and freezing point are the nodes at which, under normal pressure, the leap to a new aggregate state takes place, and where quantity is transformed into quality." As a further example, the *History* takes Engels' assertion that when a number of elements combine in different quantities they suddenly produce a body that is qualitatively different from what was there before: a leap from a change in quantity to a change in quality. Furthermore, declares dialectics, nature is composed of "opposites" and "contradictions" that "struggle" in a *dialectic* way, and in this manner and *only* this manner does the higher develop from the lower and the old give birth to the new.

Whereas Fascist and Nazi ideologies distorted evolution into evolutionism, and Herbert Spencer distorted it into Social Darwinism, Communist ideology distorts physics and chemistry to assert that evolution isn't evolution at all: go deep enough and you will find that evolution is actually a series of revolutions.

The History goes on to show how the USSR *applies* dialectics to "society and to the practical activities of the Party":

> If the passing of slow quantitative changes into rapid and abrupt qualitative changes is a law of development, then it is clear that [Communist aims] cannot be effected by slow changes, by reforms, but only by a qualitative change ... by revolution. Hence, in order not to err in policy one must be a revolutionary, not a reformist.

Hence, for example, tactics of subversion and disinformation call for destroying reformists in a target society. The "main enemy" according to Marxism is not the "capitalist," but the reformists, liberals, *etc.* —those who seek to sustain their social order by seeking reforms rather than seeking to smash the social order and build anew. "Capitalists," on the other hand, will indirectly contribute to the destruction of their society by such rigidity as will make it ripe for revolution.

This concept of violence encompasses all possible forms: large wars, small wars, assassination, mass deportations, secret police brutality, the Gulag Archipelago, incarceration in mental institutions, Berlin Walls, economic strangleholds, and so on through the catalogue of ancient and modern barbarities and modes of repression. These practical applications of dialectics to "society and the life of the Party" they call "Historical Materialism." It is within this ideological dynamic, then, that one must look for an understanding of Communist statements and activities. It has also become greatly enlarged by a vast repetoire of derivative Marxist-Leninist doctrine and applications, providing for great range and flexibility. Major examples are "peaceful coexistence," "detente," and arms control. Explications of these applications, however, are beyond the scope of this essay.

"Dialectics" is but one edge of a double-edged sword. Wielding this edge, however, runs into doubts, sensibilities, and values among the legions of leaders and followers required by a large movement. Millenia of human values, ethics, and ideals persist in the minds and hearts of real-life men and women, and could cripple a dialectical movement, were it not for "Materialism," the other edge of the sword. We have seen how Bismarckian, Fascist, Japanese, and Nazi ideologies recognized the need for special ethical codes that would give nation and individual the necessary license. Philosophical Materialism performs that function for Communism.

While not readily apparent, there is always a fundamental relationship between systems of ethics and beliefs about the nature of knowledge. In his monumental *History of European Morals* (1869), the brilliant Scottish historian W. E. H. Lecky wrote:

> It is obvious that this difference concerning the origin of our moral concep-
> tions forms part of the very much wider metaphysical question, whether our
> ideas are derived exclusively from sensation or whether they spring in part
> from the mind itself . . . and every influence that has affected the prevailing
> theory concerning the origin of ideas, has exercised a corresponding influence
> upon theories of ethics.

Our own theoretical foundations, which we have long lost sight of, were based on the composite theory, that is, that our ideas spring in part from sensation and in part from the mind itself. Our Founding Fathers drew heavily on the philoso-phy of John Locke, who developed these foundations at length in his *Essay Con-cerning Human Understanding* (1690). This theory of the mixed nature of knowledge—mental creation using sensed experience—is called "empiricism." Empiricism is in the middle between two extremes. At one extreme is "idealism" (rationalism), which says that all knowledge springs entirely from the mind alone. At the other extreme is "materialism," which says that all knowledge is comprised entirely of sensed experience.

Facist and Nazi ideologies were derived from "idealist" philosophies. Com-munist ideology claims to be based on "materialist" philosophies. The mate-rialist theory of knowledge as adapted by Marx and Engels is the basis of the materialism of "dialectical materialism." The theory was hotly defended against the implications of then contemporary physics and further developed by Lenin in his book *Materialism and Empirio-Criticism* (1909), which to this moment retains its status as one of the few most important works in all of Marxism-Leninism. It is science from a soap box, a vehement psuedoscientific diatribe, but nonetheless of incalculable consequence to the course of history, past, present, and future.

The most concise account of this brand of materialism is given in the 1951 edition of the official *History*. The philosophical materialism of Marx and Lenin, says the *History*, proves that the world is nothing but "matter in motion," moving in accordance with the "laws of movement of matter." These laws are "fully knowable," and our knowledge of them "is authentic knowledge having the validity of objective truth." In other words, valid knowledge consists *only* of direct "reflections" of material events through the senses onto the mind. No creative thought by the mind itself is involved, no "subjective" thoughts—only "direct reflections" of "objective reality." If this were not so, wrote Lenin, then "it is beyond dispute that humanity is entitled to create for itself in another sphere *no less* 'real concepts,' such as God, and so forth," and the Party would be hindered by "ethical encumbrances." In this way materialism cuts down the "and so forth" of mankind's ethics, values, and ideals. They are only figments of the imagination, and have no scientific basis; they are not authentic knowledge and lack the "validity of objective truth." As a guide to action, as "applied to the life of society," the *History* explains, materialism means that the Party should guide itself

> not on the dictates of reason, 'universal morals,' etc., but on the laws of development of society . . . not on abstract 'principles of human reason,' but on the conditions of the material life of society. . . .

In other words, whatever the given conditions indicate is most expedient for Soviet Russia to do, it may do, free from 'ethical encumbrances." If tactics, strategy, policy, or expediency call for any of many forms of violence and deceit, such a course is not only fully acceptable, but preferable and scientific, in accordance with "the laws of development," that is, dialectics and its applications, historical materialism, and philosophical materialism.

The reader will notice that this section has not presented the *goals* of Marxism-Leninism, either short- or long-term. That would require another lengthy synopsis, and is, therefore, beyond the scope of this essay. We have, however, noted the ideological weapons, or armaments, which are vital to the Soviet Union in reaching those goals, whatever they be, in that they provide the ideological foundations for the *means* with which it chooses to reach them. The reader can, nevertheless, with a little reflection see that these foundations also provide ideological armaments for the goals themselves, and that the ultimate goal very likely is world victory and domination by the Soviet Union.

Current Status

Assessment of the current status of Marxism-Leninism in the Soviet Union requires analyses of myriad official statements, speeches, editorials, articles, reports, broadcasts, *etc.*, including professional journals in the sciences and philosophy, and statements by leading Soviet academics, especially top members of the Soviet Academy of Sciences. For present purposes, however, a few examples and summaries will have to suffice, and we will begin at the top: Leonid I. Brezhnev, Marshall of the Soviet Union, Chairman of the USSR Defense Council, General Secretary of the CPSU Central Committee, and President of the Soviet Union.

In his book *Following Lenin's Course* [13], Brezhnev calls for advancing "Marxist-Leninist theory . . . to safeguard its principles and fundamental ideas," [13, p. 188], and repeats the famous dictum, "The great Lenin taught Communists that without revolutionary theory there can be no revolutionary movement . . . Marxism-Leninism has been and remains the ideological platform of the Communist Parties" [13, p. 216]. "Marxist-Leninists have always consistently fought deviations from our revolutionary teaching. . . . They have never retreated one iota from their scientific principles, nor will they ever do so" [13, p 217]. "The ideas and conclusions formulated in his [Lenin's] book, *Materialism and Empirio-Criticism*, have been brilliantly confirmed by the subsequent development of science" [13, p. 257]. "Marxism-Leninism is a coherent international teaching, it is a theory which belongs to all Communists and all revolutionaries, and serves them as a guide to action" [13, p. 261]. "Unexpected turns in the course of events are possible. For that reason Lenin's appeal that they be prepared for any change in the situation, for the use of any forms of struggle— peaceful and non-peaceful, legal and illegal—is particularly topical for Communists today. Armed with the all-conquering teaching of Marx, Engels and Lenin. . . ." [13, p. 299]. "The deeper the great ideas of Marxism-Leninism sink into the minds of the masses, the sooner will the revolution achieve new victories" [13, p. 304]. "The formation of a communist world outlook in the broad mass of the people and their education in the spirit of the ideals of Marxism-Leninism are the core of all the ideological and educational work by the Party" [13, p. 417]. "The Central Committee feels that it is necessary to intensify our entire ideological work. . . . We are living under conditions of unabating ideological war. . . ." [13, p. 425]. "Comrades, our Party is a party of scientific communism. It is steadfastly guided by Marxist-Leninist science. . . ." [13, p. 438]. "We have been and remain true to the basic principles of Marxism-Leninism and shall never make any concessions in questions of ideology" [13, p. 439].

The Soviet Union has repeatedly and explicitly excluded ideological warfare from "detente." That fact, and the Brezhnev quotes above, suggests that the Soviet core ideology, as overviewed briefly earlier, remains in full force and effect.

In February 1977, there appeared in *Kommunist* an article by Maj.-Gen. D. Volkonogov, "professor and Doctor of Philosophy," entitled "The Ideological Struggle in Conditions of Detente," in which he repeated Brezhnev's declaration in his keynote speech to the twenty-fifth Party Congress that "problems of ideological struggle are increasingly coming to the fore," and in which he (Volkonogov) urged, among much else, that Soviet servicemen be trained to take part in that struggle, as part of the social role of the armed forces in the modern world.

An editorial in *Kommunist* in December 1976 was entitled, "The 25th Party Congress Contribution to Marxist-Leninist Theory: THE COMMUNISTS' IDEOLOGICAL WEAPON."

In the long history of arrests, executions, dismissals, and changes at the top echelons of the Soviet state, including its Academy of Sciences, one position has remained steadfastly in the hands of one man: the position, Chief Ideologist; the man, Mikhail A. Suslov. When, in June 1977, Brezhnev became President of the Soviet Union, in addition to his other titles, the man who formally proposed him for the post was Suslov. The official photograph for the occasion of Brezhnev's actual election to the post by the Supreme Soviet showed three rows of three men each. In the first row were Brezhnev, to his right Prime Minister Kosygin, and to his right: Suslov.

ADMINISTRATIVE IMPLICATIONS

Of suns and worlds I've nothing to be quoted;
How men torment themselves, is all I've noted.
The little god o' the world sticks to the same old way,
And is as whimsical as on Creation's day.
Life somewhat better might content him,
But for the gleam of heavenly light which Thou has lent him:
He calls it Reason—thence his power's increased,
To be far beastlier than any beast.
                              —Mephistopheles to The Lord, in Goethe's *Faust*

As indicated earlier, this essay focuses on international affairs and defense, and two major correlates of these, intelligence and arms control and disarmament. These four areas have a substantial intersection, and it is in the area of their intersection that we will deal here. Nevertheless, the reader can well appreciate that if space limitation has been a severe constraint in formulating the importance, nature, and specifics of the ideological problem, then such limitation becomes almost prohibitive in formulating administrative principles and practices for administration and resolution of the problem. Worse yet, at this stage of history, any brief statements of such applications of ideologics subject it to varieties of incomprehension, incredulity, misunderstanding, and cavil. With that caveat in mind, we will nevertheless begin.

Any public administrator who has read this far and will still choose to ignore the ideologic dimensions of his responsibilities, courts guilt as surely as did Albert Speer, for means of basic ideological inquiry have long been available. They were first provided by the Covenant of the League of Nations, which constrained the High Contracting Parties to "open, just and honorable relations," and especially by Article 11, which dealt with "Any war or *threat* of war, or any circumstances whatever affecting international relations which *threatens* to disturb international peace or the good understanding between nations upon which peace depends" (emphasis supplied). The key point here is emergence of the concept of *threat* (to the peace) in an international document. The concept was inadequately conceived, however. The ideologic principle that emerges is to establish among nations the same everyday understanding of "threat" that exists among men, and apply it in international law, relations, treaties, and agreements in a manner analogous to its application in domestic law.

Assault

When a person threatens you with violence you are not obliged to wait for him to act; you can deal with the threat. Consider the Iowa Code, for instance. Chapter 76, "Security to Keep the Peace," provides for the arrest of any person who has *threatened* to commit any public offense punishable by law; Chapter 690.8, "Advising or Inciting Murder," provides up to twenty years imprisonment for advising, counseling, encouraging, advocating, or inciting murder, whether or not actually committed; and Chapter 694 provides imprisonment for assault, which is commonly understood to be the *threat* of injury by force "under such circumstances as create well-founded fear of imminent peril, coupled with apparent present ability to execute attempt, if not prevented." "Battery" in "assault and battery" is carrying out the threat.

In international affairs, a minimal concept of assault would correspond to a poised army and an ultimatum, or poised missiles and a demand. Such a crisis, however, is too late a point to await. Furthermore, given the conditions that a nation or movement has an official core ideology of violence and license, such a crisis is inevitable, as inevitable as the trajectory of a bullet given its initial conditions. Even if it were not inevitable, such ideologic cores—coupled with modern weapons—constitute a continuing state of international assault and a clear threat to the peace. In short, nations have been recognizing, waiting for and dealing with only extreme assault or actual *breaches* of the peace, rather than recognizing and dealing with the *threat*.

The United Nations

Ideologic applications of the concepts of threat and license are now provided for by the Charter of the United Nations, which provides means for dealing with ideologies of violence as "threats to the peace," and with ideologies of license that seriously violate the "principles," obligations," "purposes," "good faith," *etc.*, agreed upon by the community of nations comprising its membership. We also have at hand its principal judicial organ, the International Court of Justice at The Hague, to deal with ideologies of license. Its Statute includes a clause of great promise, for it lists as one of the major sources of international law "the general principles of law recognized by civilized nations." Arthur Larson, Director of the World Rule of Law Research Center at Duke University, has counseled us to "think of the vast treasures of legal principle to which this clause invites us. The clause tells us that if we look at the internal legal principles of the world's various systems and find a common thread of principle, that thread becomes elevated to the status of binding international law" [14].

All in all, a little creative reflection will unfold enormous possibilities of this ideologic dimension in deactivating ideological warheads of nationalist and transnationalist movements. No longer would ideologies of violence, hatred, and deceit be left to fester in dark corners until they erupt into catastrophe. They would be brought out into the open and subjected to the lights of world reason, principles, and law.

The ideologic principle of dealing directly with aggressive ideologic cores is profoundly expressed by the famed passage in the UNESCO Charter: "Since wars begin in the minds of men, it is in the minds of men that the defenses of peace must be constructed." Since the operative dynamic in the minds of men is ideology, the defenses of peace must include ideological defenses. Systems of measures constituting ideological defenses of peace constitute Ideological Defense Systems, or ID systems, for short. Such systems also have their counterpart in national defense.

Of particular cogency in implementing the foregoing is the UN Charter's Article 39: "The Security Council shall determine the existence of any *threat* to the peace, *breach* of the peace, or act of aggression and shall make recommendations. . . ."

Arms Control

These concepts subsequently appeared in an arms control context in the United States' proposed Treaty for General and Complete Disarmament in a Peaceful World (GCD), especially in: "Stage I, Sec. H.1. Obligations Concerning the Threat or Use of Force. The Parties to the Treaty would undertake obligations to refrain, in their international relations, from the *threat* or use of force of any type . . . contrary to the purposes and principles of the United Nations Charter" (emphasis supplied). The essential task, however, is to make progress toward GCD and "a peaceful world" while deeply entrapped in a warful world. For this, ideologics is essential, and must be started where we are: in the continuing process of futile arms control negotiations. To this end we have the following conceptual framework published by the US Arms Control and Disarmament Agency: "So the concept of 'arms control'—controlling, in the sense of calming, the military situation—was evolved. Arms control means measures, other than arms reduction itself, which lessen the risk of war. 'Arms control' is a twin to 'arms reduction'—*not* a substitute for it. Arms control measures are *not* intended to replace arms reductions but to accompany them" [15]. This concept, coupled with the many provisions in the Treaty whose language paralleled that of the UN Charter as noted above, all imbedded in an ideologic context, would have presented an enormous opportunity for achieving the Treaty's purposes. When one realized that the Treaty was delivered to the United Nations in 1961, one further realizes the cost of the lost opportunity. From these considerations the following principle emerges: Include ideological factors in arms control negotiations, agreements, and treaties.

The foregoing and other relevant concepts have since been formulated into the greatest single lode of ideologics-enabling provisions to date: the Final Act of the Conference on Security and Cooperation in Europe, concluded at Helsinki in August 1975, generally known as the Helsinki Accord, and signed by 35 nations, including Bulgaria, Czechoslovakia, the German Democratic Republic, Poland, the Soviet Union, and the United States.

One must also include ideological factors as primary elements in intelligence assessments and ideologics in the process of obtaining them. Currently such factors are ignored, subordinated, or buried under larger or other factor categories. Finally, the alert government will include ideological factors in arms control operations, inasmuch as they constitute weapons (armaments), threats to the peace, and explicit abrogations of agreements reached. Further, we must recognize that *ideological* arms control is a condition precedent, the *sine qua non*, of meaningful *physical* arms control. Similarly, when progress has been made to the point where negotiations toward disarmament can even be considered, recognize that ideological disarmament must be negotiated and achieved first, that it is the condition precedent, the *sine qua non*, of physical disarmament.

Ideological Defense

When confronted by a serious adversary in a protracted struggle, recognize that ideological defense systems must complement other defense systems, and do so on a massive scale. In this regard, work should begin now on the development of ID systems within the Defense Department and State Department. Such systems will inevitably and inherently constitute low-cost, low-casualty, high-impact, defense systems. The United States Army, due to its worldwide, ground-based nature and its large number of special and advanced schools and colleges, is an ideal service for such development and deployment. The Social Science Department of the United States Military Academy could prove to be an excellent training ground for the requisite officer corps. At the tactical and operational levels, we should develop and deploy ideological operations as a complement to psychological operations.

Clearly, ideologics is not a weapon for the maintenance of unjust and oppressive regimes against counterregime movements of the oppressed. On the contrary, ideologics offers a powerful weapon in the hands of the oppressed in their struggle against their oppressors. Because ideologics can collapse the essential ideological foundations of the oppressive regime, it offers the oppressed powerful and nonviolent revolutionary options. Furthermore, ideologic revolution insures that the victorious revolutionaries do not in their turn become oppressors. In fact, it can be shown upon fuller development that the inevitable consequence of applied ideologics is a just, peaceable, and democratic polity.

OPERATIONALIZING IDEOLOGICS

During the 1950s and 1960s this writer has, on numerous occasions, in meetings and by letters, radio broadcasts, articles, and papers, urged that the United States: 1) take Marxism-Leninism's core ideology before the United Nations as a threat to world peace; 2) promote development in UNESCO and elsewhere of committees to take up various issues related to that core, especially regarding its "scientific" validity, and to report and recommend thereon; and 3) take these and other ideological measures *via* various bilateral and multilateral approaches.

In the past he has also suggested through ambient Israeli contacts that Israel initiate ideological approaches to peace in cooperation with Arabic nations. In 1972 and 1974, he communicated similarly to Arabic parties, emphasizing UNESCO auspices, and suggesting the idea of ideological development. He also quoted a professor of Islamic thought at the Université Libanaise in Beirut, *viz.*, "You have to modernize your ideology as well as your technology." In the autumn of 1975 the Arab bloc turned the idea around, from a cooperative proceeding to an adversary proceeding, and initiated an historic event.

The United Nations

On October 15, 1975, the Third Committee (Social, Humanitarian, and Cultural) of the Thirtieth General Assembly of the United Nations agreed to receive a draft resolution under which the General Assembly would determine that Zionist ideology is a form of racism. On November 14, an Arab League statement contended that the resolution dealt with "a concrete phenomenon—a political ideology, a political machinery based on it and the policies of a government."

On November 18, the General Assembly adopted "Resolution 3379 (XXX). Elimination of all forms of racial discrimination," which, among other things: 1) reaffirmed that "any doctrine of racial differentiation or superiority is scientifically false, morally condemnable, socially unjust and dangerous"; 2) took note of a Declaration adopted at the Conference of Ministers for Foreign Affairs at Lima in August 1975 that "condemned zionism as a threat to world peace and security and called upon all countries to oppose this racist and imperialist ideology"; and 3) determined "that zionism is a form of racism and racial discrimination."

It must be made crystal clear to the reader that this section in no way implies agreement or disagreement with the substance of that resolution's references to, or determination regarding, Zionism. If the resolution is unjust, then that must not becloud recognition of its importance as a prototypical instrument for achieving justice and peace when the instrument itself is just. The importance of that resolution lies in its *nature*, which is characterized by its attacking the scientific validity, social consequences, and threat to world peace of an ideology, and by its incorporating findings in those regards by a conference or other body outside of the United Nations itself. Furthermore, the resolution constitutes the first, formal, explicit, international, ideological defense measure, and, as such, constitutes an event of world-historic importance.

On the other hand, even as a prototype, the resolution is fundamentally deficient in that it fails to cite chapter and verse of the ideology it condemns, or to attach a sufficiently authoritative companion document that does so, to substantiate its charges and determination. Therefore, it stands also as a prototype of simplistic name-calling political mischief, which feat can be accomplished by any bloc with enough votes, irrespective of the merit, substance, truth, and justice of the charges. Furthermore, such a proceeding can have no enduring significance other than to demean both its perpetrators and the institution that tolerates it. Ideologics and Ideological Defense are above all exercises in truth, reason, compassion, and justice, and can be of no enduring consequence without such essential integrity.

To the extent, then, that the resolution is properly prototypical, its immediate importance is greatly amplified by the fact that the Soviet Union and Soviet bloc countries fully supported and voted both for consideration of the draft resolution and adoption of the final version. Altogether, the proper nature of the event and its support by the Soviet Union constitute vital precedents for realizing the potential of the Helsinki Accord, to which we now turn.

The Helsinki Accord

The three large divisions of the Helsinki Accord have been dubbed "Baskets" by administrators dealing with it. We will limit consideration here to Baskets One and Three, and, within them, to the ideology of violence and license of Marxism-Leninism, which we will denote by the shorthand notation $и_i$, where i is a subscript to the Russian lower-case letter i, pronounced "ee." The notation is verbalized as either "Russ ee sub i," or "ideospace i"—reader's choice

[16]. Parenthetical page references are to the English-language version of the Accord [17].

Basket One. Basket One, "Questions Relating to Security in Europe," contains a preamble whose opening sentence reaffirms the objective of ensuring peace free from any *threat to* or attempt against the signatory nations. Part 1 then opens with section "(a) Declaration on Principles Guiding Relations between Participating States," which reaffirms common adherence to the purposes and principles of the United Nations. *Implementation:* Signatories should evaluate $\mathbf{u}_i$ against these provisions, make actionable recommendations, and act upon them.

Within 1(a) is a subsection "II. Refraining from the *threat* or use of force" (78, emphasis supplied). It includes the dictum that "No consideration may be invoked to serve to warrant resort to the *threat* or use of force in contravention of" the principles and purposes of the United Nations and the present Declaration. *Implementation:* Same as above.

Basket Three. Basket Three, "Co-operation in Humanitarian and Other Fields" (113), contains a mother lode of provisions for a wide range of ideological programs. Among them is section "3. Co-operation and Exchanges in the Field of Culture" (120), including, for instance, "(e) to seek new fields and forms of cultural co-operation" (121). *Implementation:* 1) Recognize that at the root of "culture" is ideology, as explicated in this essay. 2) Develop and undertake cultural programs that examine and debate the validity, consequences, and international acceptibility of $\mathbf{u}_i$.

Also within Basket Three is section "4. Co-operation and Exchanges in the Field of Education" (127), within which is section "(c) Science" (128), which is especially apposite for programs dealing with the self-proclaimed "scientific" validity of $\mathbf{u}_i$. Particularly relevant for such programs are the envisaged "Scientific Forum" (129) and the provision for developing "joint programmes" in an illustrative list of subject areas, including ". . . *the humanities and social sciences*, such as . . . philosophy . . . sociology . . . political and economic sciences; comparative studies on social, socio-economic and cultural phenomena which are of common interest to the participating States. . ." (129). *Implementation:* Develop and undertake ideologic programs to study the scientific validity and social, political, and peace consequences of $\mathbf{u}_i$, report and publish the proceedings and findings, and introduce appropriate resolutions in the United Nations, including recommendations for such sanctions and other action as may be appropriate in view of the findings.

To help move events along, some encapsulated ideologic cues for dealing with the scientific validily of ideologies are offered here. The scientific validity of an ideology can be attacked (in the sense of attacking a problem or task) along at least five dimensions:

Dimension 1 is the detailed, substantive attack in the domain(s) of the relevant science(s). For instance, in 1963, a member of the East German Academy of Sciences and I engaged in a good-natured, joshing debate by mail on whether there is anything in physical chemistry to substantiate Engel's derivation from physics and chemistry of his law that imperceptible small changes in quantity at some point generate a leap from a change in quantity to a change in quality, and that, therefore, to be scientifically correct one must be a revolutionary, not a reformist. The debate involved the nature of derivatives and integrals, processes at the triple point, partial pressures, coexistent phases, *etc.*, and we mentally used our kitchens as laboratories, boiling water on the stove, having our kids hold down and remove the lid, sealing and opening windows, raising and lowering the ceiling, *etc.*, as the debating points required [18].

Dimension 2 involves the nature of the sciences, most fundamentally physics, characterized: 1) as always limited, bounded, tentative, ongoing and controversial; and 2) as man-made fictions, highly creative, nonunique descriptions [19], with inherent indeterminacies and complementarities.

Dimension 3 involves the nature of mathematics, the Queen of Sciences, especially its unprovables, undecidables, and paradoxes. A classic example is the proof by Kurt Godel in 1931 that the axioms of elementary arithmetic are incomplete; hence there will always be "true" statements of arithmetic that cannot be proven from the axioms; hence, in principle, they are theoretically undecidable. In May 1977, Jeffery Paris, at the University of Manchester, further proved that some of the unsolved problems of arithmetic are really undecidable. Using sophisticated model theory and nonstandard analysis, he discovered an atypical model for which the axioms of arithmetic produced a false result, while in the ordinary model of arithmetic they produced a "true" result. It is now likely that many famous unsolved problems in arithmetic will be proven undecidable.

Dimension 4 involves the nature of models, especially socioeconomic models, that are always partial, very controversial, and highly subjective in structure and operation. Recently S. P. Chakravarty, Department of Economics, South Hampton University, demonstrated that even standard statistical techniques cannot provide a unique description of something as simple as the Beveridge wheat-price data, that mathematical models are expressions of subjective visions and personal prejudices, and concluded that the social sciences should involve ideological debate and focus on ideological and methodological biases in policy prescriptions [20].

Dimension 5 uses ideotopology to explicate the processes by which an ideology is fabricated, the structure and properties of the resultant fabrication, and thereby its sense, nonsense, and, in a word, validity [21]. This new methodology is in the early development stage; however, some idea of its nature and direction can be obtained from the following section.

Any ideology implicitly or explicitly involves one or more societal models, including axiological predicates, derivatives, and correlates. The Jeffersonian marketplace of ideas will be enhanced by ideologics in debating the benign forms. Malignant forms, however, such as ideologies with a Marxist-Leninist core, will find it impossible to sustain a claim of scientific validity when they are subjected to widespread and widely-publicized five-dimensional attacks. And when one is advocating so much as a single murder or oppression, the burden of proof weighs totally on the advocate; *a fortiori* for mass murder and oppression.

Although much more can be said regarding the ideologic implementation of the Helsinki Accord, especially regarding the content of the foregoing implementations, we must perforce break off here, and close this essay with an examination of ideologic analytics.

Ideologic Analytics

Mathematical and formal analytic methods are not *essential* to the establishment of ideologics in public administration, but they hold *promise* of powerful new methods and enhancements of casual syntactical approaches. The non-mathematical reader should, therefore, try to follow us a while, in order to gain at least an impression of the sorts of things that can be done, and thereby gain a deeper conceptual sense of operational ideologics. Our presentation of mathematical (analytic) ideologics will have to be restricted to highly compressed overviews. The presentation of *ideotopology* will have to be restricted to selected basic concepts and elementary formulations, but will, as a consequence, constitute core foundations of the field, albeit *sans* rigorous axiomatic development.

Adaptions of Extant Methodologies

Among the many possible ideologic adaptions of extant methodologies, two will be summarized here: ideologic cluster analysis and ideologic factor analysis.

Ideologic Cluster Analysis. Cluster analysis is a member of the class "multivariate statistical procedures for the behavioral sciences." In the ideologic application, its role is to delineate similarities between observations of sampled individuals i, and thereby mathematically to define population sets in ideological terms. "Individuals" can be entities such as companies, industries, unions, media, people, cities, and nations. The observations, or measurements, of these individuals for a number of characteristics provide a score for each individual on each characteristic, which scores together provide a "profile" of him (*it*). The measurements are obtained by means of a battery of m tests or a single test of m parts, each of which contains a set of measurements on a particular characteristic, or dimension. A "test" can be any of a wide range of instruments, such as survey-questionnaires, or content analyses of speeches, articles, and broadcasts. Out of a variety of possible cluster analytic objectives, ideologics then seeks to determine, without advance assignment of observations (individuals) to groups, what clusters (groups) of observations are "similar" with respect to their ideological profiles. Ultimately, the procedure develops a likelihood expression of the form

$$P_{ij} = P(H_j | X_i) = f(p_j, |D_j|, \chi_j^2)$$

for the probability of hypothesis H_j that individual i is a member of group j, where:

$j = 1, 2, \ldots, g$;

$i = 1, 2, \ldots, N$;

X_i = individual i's m-element deviation score vector;

p_j = individual i's probability of belonging (in terms of test scores) to group j, estimated from real-world relative frequencies of memberships in groups;

$|D_j|$ = an estimate of the dispersion of the population in sample group j; and

χ_j^2 = the "classification," derived from the usual chi square distribution, which determines the centour, *i.e.*, the hyperellipsoid representing a particular frequency, corresponding to group j.

This methodology enables us mathematically to define ideologies by defining memberships in them, and to define and measure distances within and between ideologies.

Ideologic Factor Analysis.   In cluster analysis, delineation of the m ideological characteristics of an ideological group, or ideology, is conceived and designed in advance, on the basis of expert knowledge of the ideologies involved. In some cases, however, it will be desirable to determine both the number and composition of ideological dimensions after having conducted exploratory research for that specific purpose. In such cases we have available a set of multivariate statistical techniques generically known as *factor anlaysis*.

Present limitations permit hardly more than mere mention of this complex and powerful methodology. In the ideologic adaptation the objective is to determine the fewest, simplist, and most meaningful ideological dimensions latent in a set of n measures X on a sample of N individuals i. The method of *principle components* within this genre of analysis is based on the simple model consisting of n linear equations of the form

$$z_j = a_{j1}F_1 + a_{j2}F_2 + \cdots + a_{jn}F_n = \Sigma a_{jp}F_p, \quad j, p = 1, 2, \ldots, n$$

which expresses each of the n observed variables in terms of n uncorrelated components, or factors F_p and their factor coefficients, or "loadings," a_{jp}. The procedures reduce the N-dimensional sample space to an n-dimensional test space in which the test scores (variable values) form a hyperellipsoid for which the procedures then compute the principle reference axes, or components, that uniquely define the factors F_p that the variables are measuring in common. These factors will, upon content-based expert interpretation, comprise the ideological "constructs," or dimensions, we are seeking, and will be given appropriate labels. In the event that the first set of derived principal component axes is not considered substantively satisfactory, in terms of ideological interpretation, they can be rotated, repeatedly, until a substantively satisfactory set is located.

Ideotopology

Whether we seek to define ideological groups or individual membership, as with cluster analysis, or to define ideological dimensions, as with factor analysis, we become involved with sets of ideological elements. These elements can be treated from another, very different perspective, that of topology. Although dictionaries tend to define mathematical topology as the study of properties of geometric forms that remain invariant under certain transformations, this is much too narrow a focus for our purposes.

In ideologics, topology should be viewed in its most fundamental nature: as any other branch of mathematics, topology is the study of collections of objects that possess structure. Sometimes this is phrased "a mathematical structure," but that causes us to miss an important point. Nothing inherently *possesses* a *mathematical* structure; things possess only *structure*; it is human beings who invent (create) mathematics and then *translate* structure into mathematical terms. In many cases we even *conceive* structure itself, and often do so in mathematical terms, where no structure was theretofore apparent, as, for example, Willard Gibbs did in his *creation* of statistical-mechanical thermodynamics. Similarly, Albert Einstein did not *find* that cosmic space *possessed* a Riemannian-geometric structure; he *gave* it that structure. Similarly, ideologics *provides* mathematical structure to ideology—using, not theoretical statistics or Riemannian geometry, but, rather, topology, thus giving rise to the field of *ideologic topology*, or more briefly, *ideotopology*. In providing mathematical structure to ideology, ideotopology makes use of one of the most fruitful concepts in all of modern mathematics, the concept of topological space, and thereby defines an *ideological space*, or *ideospace*, for short.

Webster's International Dictionary of the English Language, Second Edition, Unabridged, provides as its first definition of topology, "1. A mnemonic method based on the association of ideas with places." Such a concept also follows directly from the word's etymology: *topo- + -logy*. Application of mathematical topology to the study of the universe of ideas thus becomes a logical and inevitable development, and that development is ideotopology. Although derived from general topology, ideotopology at this stage is fundamentally different in that it develops not as a pure science, but as an applied science, and, furthermore, as a mission-oriented, applied science. Ultimately a rigorous formulation may evolve, and if so, its progression would then be similar to that of other branches of science, *e.g.*, probability theory evolving from games of chance. A further difference is that it does not start with raw experience and then creatively abstract and mathematize, but, rather, starts with already highly-developed, rigorous mathematics and then adapts the mathematics so as to achieve a predetermined operational goal: to develop real-world ways of dealing with ideologies and their implicit and explicit manifestations, especially in the realm of the intersection of international affairs, defense, intelligence, and arms control and disarmament. The motivation for choosing this route is the critically urgent need for operational ideologics—an urgency due to the serious deterioration of the free world's strategic position combined with the certainty of thermonuclear warfare given the trajectory of contemporary events. That need, in turn, calls for supplementing other principles and methods of ideologics with ideotopology, to which we now turn, albeit all-too-briefly.

Hierarchical Structure. The framework for ideotopology is provided by defining a universe of discourse U_Ω comprising the universe of knowledge discourse U_Θ and the universe of ideological discourse U_Φ, both in terms of a hierarchy of sets, as shown in Figure 1. The hierarchical structure is the same for both universes, although it is sketched only for U_Θ. At any level of the hierarchy in U_Θ, for instance, a class of sets is denoted by Θ, with primed subscripts, and a family (collection) of classes by $\mathcal{C}\Theta$, also with primed subscripts. In the other direc-

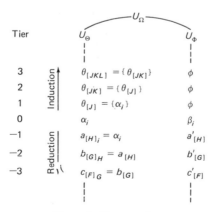

Figure 1. U_Ω overview.

tion, reduction of the set elements to successively lower-order components is also provided for, by an "archeoarchy" of more primitive elements, which are represented by lower-case Latin letters. For instances, at Tier -1, elements are represented by a_hs, a particular subset of the set that constitutes the element α_i at Tier 0. Set elements consist of words, groups of words (phrases), and parts of words, and symbols, definitions, concepts, equations, principles, constants, *etc.*, from the physical, biological, behavioral (social), and pure sciences. The hierarchy builds as follows. At Tier 1 we have sets $\theta_{[J]}$, where the generalized index set J comprises index sets $J_1, J_2, \ldots, J_j, \ldots, J_n$, where n is the number of θ sets in Tier 1. The elements of each θ set are selected elements α_i. Thus, we have

$$\theta_{[J]} : \theta_{[J_1]} = \{\alpha_i\}_{i \in J_1}; \theta_{[J_2]} = \{\alpha_i\}_{i \in J_2}; \ldots$$

where each J_j is an index set that specifies α_is at Tier 0, and, when in brackets, serves also as the identification "tag" for the set. Where, for instance, a set is composed of subsets and singleton elements, we have, for a hypothetical θ set number 7

$$\theta_{[7]} = \{\{\theta_j'\}, \{\alpha_i\}\}_{j,\, i \in J_7}$$

J_7 is thus a composite index set listing both *j*s and *i*s separately. Also, *j* is a composite number J_7/x, where the index set identifier is repeated so that a subset is completely tagged, *i.e.*, identified, and where x is the identification number of the specific *j*. All elements, subsets, and sets are catalogued in a master dictionary. Sets and subsets that are identical to each other or to others that appear elsewhere are asterisked and cross-referenced. When, subsequently, combinations of θ sets and/or their subsets, and/or elements are formed, a new, higher-order set is created and is located at the next tier, where it is tagged $\theta_{[JK]}$.

A set tag is simply a number or set of numbers the position of each of which indicates whether it is a J, K, or L, *etc.* However, a *sub*set tag must specify which of those it is. Thus, $\theta'_{J_7/19}$ indicates that this is subset number 19 of Tier 1 set number 7, the prime indicating a subset. Although the prime is redundant, inasmuch as the nature of the tagging indicates a subset, it is nevertheless used for quick clarity and handiness for computer sorting. Also, the subsubscripting of J is not essential, and we could just as well write $\theta'_{J7/19}$. However, the subsubscripting seems clearer, and it conforms with the generalized expressions that follow, a practice that makes it easier to translate back and forth between theory and application.

For instance, if a new set is formed from set $\theta_{[36]}$, subsets $\theta'_{J_7/19}$ and $\theta'_{J_{29}/32}$, and elements α_{67}, α_{321}, and α_{509}, the new set will be at Tier 2. If the next available J tag number at Tier 2 is, say, 752, and the next available K tag number at Tier 2 is 963, we have

$$\theta_{[752,963]} = \{\{\theta_{j_1}\}, \{\theta'_{j_2}\}, \{\alpha_i\}\}_{j_1,j_2,i\,\in\,J_{752}}$$

where

$$J_{752} = \{\,j_1 = 36;\, j_2 = J_7/19,\, J_{29}/32;\, i = 67,\, 321,\, 509\}$$

and $K = 963$ is simply the Tier-2, sequentially assigned identification number. At Tier 3 the K-position tag becomes the next available K tag number at that tier, and serves as the index-set identifier for the former Tier 2 sets, subsets, and singleton elements brought up to Tier 3 and incorporated into the new set. The J-position tag will change number and function for former Tier 1 sets, subsets, and singleton elements in similar fashion. The new L-position tag will simply be the Tier 3 sequentially-assigned identification number, and so on up the hierarchy. Subset number 27 of the above set would always remain $\theta'_{J_{752}K_{963}}/27$. Thus, the general expression for a Tier-3 θ set is

$$\theta_{[J_jK_kL_l]} = \{\{\theta_{j_1}\}, \{\theta'_{j_2}\}, \{\alpha_{i_1}\}, \{\theta_{k_1}\}, \{\theta'_{k_2}\}, \{\alpha_{i_2}\}\}_{\substack{j_1,j_2,i_1\,\in\,J_j \\ k_1,k_2,i_2\,\in\,K_k}}$$

By simple extension and simplification of notation, the general expression for a θ set at Tier n is

$$\theta_{[T_1,T_2,\ldots,T_n]} = \{\{\theta_{t_{1,1}}\}, \{\theta'_{t_{1,2}}\}, \{\alpha_i\}; \{\theta_{t_{2,1}}\}, \{\theta'_{t_{2,2}}\}, \{\alpha_i\};$$

$$\ldots;\, \{\theta_{t_{n-1,1}}\}, \{\theta'_{t_{n-1,2}}\}, \{\alpha_{i_{n-1}}\}\}_I$$

$$I = \{\{t_{1,1}, t_{1,2}, i_1 \in T_1\}, \{t_{2,1}, t_{2,2}, i_2 \in T_2\},$$

$$\ldots,\, \{t_{n-1,1}, t_{n-1,2}, i_{n-1} \in T_{n-1}\}\}$$

The $\{\ \}$ components (members) of the set $\theta_{[\ ]}$ expand out into sets, subsets, and elements that are specifically identified by the total index set I, whose component index sets T_1, T_2, etc. expand out into specific identifying tag sets $t_{1,1}$, $t_{1,2}$, etc.; that is, each $t_{1,1}$, $t_{1,2}$, etc., is an index set containing a set of tag numbers. Each tag number identifies a set, subset, or element in the master dictionary, where its composition is recorded. A member (set, subset, or element) retains the tag number of record that it was assigned when it first appeared in the system. When a subset is formed from a set where it did not appear as such before, it is assigned a tag number just as if it had existed and been tagged at the time that that parent set appeared. A member can appear at many different locations and will bear a different index j_n, or k_n, etc., at each location, but every index, except the is for αs and βs, expands into the aforementioned composite number, of which the first component is the member's original tag, as in the earlier example of $j = J_7/x$. The master dictionary catalogues each member together with all of the indexes it bears. Mathematically, it is the indexes that are processed, but the substantive meanings, evolution, and origins of the resultant structures are preserved by means of the dictionary.

This hierarchy-building system is intended to be an orderly way of identifying sets and their members, and ultimately topologies on them and the resultant spaces, especially for computer-based operations. The development that follows, below, is independent of the tagging scheme chosen, and is expressed in terms of simple indexes so that topological matters can be seen more clearly. In practice, temporary dummy indexes can be substituted for actual tags so as to facilitate mathematical procedures, and then translated back into tags after the procedures have been completed, a temporary computer "scratch pad" being used to store the temporary conversion table. These are straightforward matters for computer-based ideotopology research, development, and operations [22]. Two hierarchies, or universes, are provided in U_Ω because some sets have properties that distinguish them as *knowledge* sets, and are denoted by θ, while other sets in U_Ω have properties that distinguish them as *ideological sets*, *ideosets* for short, denoted by ϕ. Classes and families of ϕs are similarly denoted by Φ and $\mathcal{C}\Phi$, respectively, the latter with primed subscripts.

The choice of θ and ϕ as set symbols is substantive. Knowledge is based on theory, and traces back conceptually to the Greek concept *theōría*, whose first three letters are denoted by $\theta = theta$. Ideology is a branch of philosophy, which traces back to the Greek concept of *philosophia*, whose first three letters are denoted by $\phi = phi$. That there are distinctions between θ sets and ϕ sets is a principle of ideotopology, and explication of such distinctions is one of its objectives. Nevertheless, much of applied ideotopology can operate solely within U_Φ, with U_Θ involved only as reference, if at all. The choice of α to represent elements and of Ω as the subscript for the universe of discourse is also substantive, and comes from the expression "alpha and omega."

Functions. The collection of all functions f operating in U_Ω is represented by $\mathcal{F}(\Omega)$. Some generate θs and others operate among θs, and are, therefore, called *knowledge functions*, or *theta functions*. Their collection is denoted by $\mathcal{F}(\Theta)$. Other functions in U_Ω generate ϕs while others operate among ϕs, and are, therefore, called *ideological functions*, or *phi functions*. Their collection is denoted by $\mathcal{F}(\Phi)$. Note that $\mathcal{F}(\Phi)$ includes functions of two different types: $f: \theta_j \longrightarrow \phi_k$ and $f: \phi_j \longrightarrow \phi_k$. The $\mathcal{F}(\Theta)$ and $\mathcal{F}(\Phi)$ collections both include the basic set-building functions that generate θs and ϕs from αs, *i.e.*, of the type $f: \{\alpha_i\} \longrightarrow \theta_j$ and $f: \{\alpha_i\} \longrightarrow \phi_j$. In addition $\mathcal{F}(\Phi)$ includes functions of the type $f: \{\beta_i\} \longrightarrow \phi_j$ and $f: \{\{\alpha_i\}, \{\beta_j\}\} \longrightarrow \phi_k$, that is, functions that generate ideosets ϕ from ideological elements β_i solely and from knowledge elements α_i and ideological elements β_j jointly.

The concept of "function" here includes any mode, mapping, process, transformation, algorithm, *etc.*, that is appropriate to the specific instance or class of instances involved. In fact, a function in some cases may be only a black-box transform, that is, only the input and output are known, and the inside process is not. Such black-box functions can be classified into types and serve sufficiently, as in other branches of science and engineering.

Spaces. This brings us to consider classes of subsets of a given θ_i or ϕ_i. First let us recall that a class $\mathcal{T}$ of open subsets of a set X, called the underlying set, defines a *topology* on X iff (= if and only if) $\mathcal{T}$ satisfies four axioms: 1) X belongs to $\mathcal{T}$; 2) ϕ belongs to $\mathcal{T}$; 3) the intersection of any two sets in $\mathcal{T}$ belongs to $\mathcal{T}$; and 4) the union of any number of sets in $\mathcal{T}$ belongs to $\mathcal{T}$. The members of the topology $\mathcal{T}$ together with X, that is, the pair of objects $(X,\mathcal{T})$, comprise a *topological space*. For ideologic purposes it is sometimes advisable to add the concept of Hausdorff space, or "separated space," as a fifth axiom, *viz.*, 5) each pair of distinct elements $a,b \in X$ belong to disjoint sets; that is, there exist sets O_a and O_b such that $a \in O_a$, $b \in O_b$, and $O_a \cap O_b = \emptyset$.

Now, in ideotopology, a set θ together with a *knowledge topology* Υ on it defines a *knowledge space* (θ,Υ), which is represented by Γ; *i.e.*, $\Gamma = (\theta,\Upsilon)$. Similarly, an ideoset ϕ together with an ideotop on it defines an *ideological space*, or *ideospace*. (The ideosymbols are given below.) The formation of such spaces provides concise, parsimonious, and formal coherence to bodies of knowledge and ideologies, and makes available to ideologics the formalisms, principles and procedures of general topology for adaptation and conversion to applied ideologics. The generic term *ideotopology* includes *all* such work in U_Ω; that is, in and between knowledge spaces, as well as in and between ideospace and between knowledge spaces and ideospaces. Inasmuch, however, as the principle concern is with ideologies, special notation is provided for ideospaces. In order to avoid confusion with already heavily preempted English, German, and Greek letters, recourse is made to Russian letters, as follows.

An ideotop is represented by the lower-case Russian "l," that is, л, which appropriately, is composed of a T-like symbol on its left, similar to variants of "T" used in set theory and topology, and a sans serif "I" on its right joined together by means of a bar at the top. An ideospace is represented by the lower-case Russian "ee," that is, и, which, appropriately, comprises two English "Is", joined by means of a diagonal line. Thus, ideospace i defined by ideotop k on ideoset j is represented as $и_i = (\phi_j, л_k)$.

Substructures/Differentiation. We are now ready to employ the concept of *subspace* to define factions within an ideospace. Consider an ideospace $и = (\phi,л)$ and an ideo*sub*top $л_A$ that is the class of all intersections of л with an ideosubset A of ϕ. Then $л_A$ is called the *relative ideotop* on A, or the *relativization of* л to A, and $(A,л_A) = и_A$ is an *ideosubspace* of $и$. More specifically, $и_A$ represents a *faction space* within $и$, with A its *faction set* and $л_A$ its *faction top*.

Mathematically, it is said that, given A, π *induces* π_A on A, thus yielding the faction space $\mathbf{H}_A$. In other words, a faction set locates its faction space.

There can be a number of different faction spaces within a given ideospace, mathematically as well as ideologically, and it is possible for several of them to have identical faction tops, even though their faction sets are different, provided that the faction sets have identical classes of intersections with π. These different factions, then, are from the same parent ideospace and have a common core, the faction top. These characteristics are precisely, succinctly, formally, and graphically expressed by ideotopology. Altogether, the foregoing helps to reveal substantive relationships, nonrelationships, and insufficiencies, and provides bases for discussion and negotiation.

In a similar vein, a class $\mathcal{B}$ of subsets of a given topology $\mathcal{T}$ on a set X forms a *base*, or *basis*, for $\mathcal{T}$ iff: 1) X is the union of all members of $\mathcal{B}$, and 2a) every set $G \in \mathcal{T}$ is the union of members of $\mathcal{B}$, or, equivalently, 2b) for any $p \in G$ there exists a set $B \in \mathcal{B}$, such that $p \in B \subset G$. When subsets θ'_i of a particular $\mathcal{T}$ constitute a *knowledge base* $\mathcal{B}_\theta = \{\theta'_i\}$, we may say that the base comprises a pervasive foundation for the knowledge space, somewhat analogous to the common understanding of the basis for saying such-and-such. Similarly for an *ideobase* $\mathcal{B}_\phi = \{\phi'_i\}$ of ideotop π on ideospace (ϕ,π). Conversely, it is always possible to find a base for *some* $\mathcal{T}$ or π on their respective sets—that is, to find a base and then derive a topology for it. It is instructive and useful to determine what ideospaces are supported by what bases in a given ideoset ϕ_i. (We will return to bases later, after defining product space.)

On the other hand, in many cases we will want to partition a set X, and this is accomplished by changing property 2), above, to pairwise disjoint. That is, a class $\mathcal{P}$ of subsets of X is called a *partition* of X iff: 1) X is the union of members of $\mathcal{P}$, and 2) the intersection of any two sets in $\mathcal{P}$ is empty. In this way an ideoset ϕ_i can be partitioned into a class $\mathcal{P}_{\phi_i}$ of *ideoparts* $\hat{\phi}_{i,j}$; *i.e.*, $\mathcal{P}_{\phi_i} = \{\hat{\phi}_{i,j}\}_{j \in I}$. When properly crafted, ideoparts will reveal distinct substantive compositions of an ideology, thus facilitating discussion and negotiation. Now, within an ideoset ϕ_i consider any class $\mathcal{C}_{\phi_i}$ of ideosubsets $\phi'_{i,j}$, that is, $\mathcal{C}_{\phi_i} = \{\phi'_{i,j}\}_{j \in I}$. Consider also any particular ideosubset $\phi'_{i,k}$ that can be formed from the members of $\phi_{i,}$; that is, consider any $\phi'_{i,k} \subset \cup_j \phi_{i,j}$ where "member" can be an ideosubset $\{\alpha_l\}$ or just one element α_l, in either case written $\phi_{i,j}$. Then the class $\mathcal{C}$ is called a *cover*, or *covering*, of $\phi'_{i,k}$, or is said *to cover* $\phi'_{i,k}$, if $\phi'_{i,k} \subset \cup_j \{\phi'_{i,j}\}$, that is, if every element of $\phi'_{i,k}$ is an element of at least one ideosubset $\{\phi'_{i,j}\}$. This is analogous, in part, to the response "Yes, I'm covered ... in $\mathcal{C}$," to the query "Are you covered in saying $P(\{P_i\})$?", where P is a propositional statement made up of propositions $P_i \ni \forall P_i \subset \cup_j \{P_j\}$, $\{P_j\} = \mathcal{C}$, where $\mathcal{C}$ is substantively sufficient [23].

Be aware that we have been discussing *substantive* spaces, bases, partitions, and covers—not logic, statements, or propositions, which are the province of the functions, discussed earlier. This distinction is subtle and only partially true, but to the extent that it is true and comprehensible it should be borne in mind.

Construction/Integration. In the foregoing discussion of substructure, we have been working *within* a particular ideospace; in effect, differentiation in the ordinary, not calculus, sense. We could just as well, however, have been working *among* ideospaces, with a given ideospace (ϕ_i, π_i) considered as but one ideosubspace among others. This leads to the last procedure to be discussed here: construction of new, higher-level ideospaces from a collection of existing ideospaces. This is, in effect, integration in the ordinary, not calculus sense. To formalize this, however, is a bit more complex than for differentiation of substructures, and will require more explication, even in a summary outline. The procedure is called *product integration*, and we will begin its discussion by considering a class of ideosets $\Phi = \{\phi_i\}$ together with two principles that are useful in themselves, as well as serving as a bridge from differentiation to integration.

Consider a function $f \colon \{\phi_i\}_{i \in I}$ such that for every $i \in I$, $f(\phi_i) \in \phi_i$, that is, the image $f(\phi_i)$ in ϕ of an element α_i in ϕ_i is also an element in ϕ_i. Such a function in effect "chooses" an element α_i from each ideoset ϕ_i in the class of ideosets Φ and maps it into, or constructs, a new ideoset ϕ, and is called a *choice function*. The first principle, the Axiom of Choice, states that there exists a choice function for any nonempty class of nonempty sets [24]. The second principle, Zermelo's postulate, states that for any nonempty class of *disjoint* nonempty sets there exists a subset of their union such that the intersection of that subset and each original set consists of exactly one element [25].

The Axiom of Choice assures us that we can always find a function to select one member from each ideoset in Φ and map those members into a new or existing ideoset. Zermelo's postulate says the same thing another way, *i.e.*, given a class of disjoint ideosets, we can always find an ideosubset of their union such that the intersection of that ideosubset and the class of ideosets will consist of only one member from each ideoset in the class. (In general, "member" is synonymous with "element," but in order to avoid confusion with the basic elements α and β in situations where an element could also be a set or subset, we will use the term "member" or "point.") Although ideosets can include both α and β elements, predominantly β, we will for simplicity use only α when making general statements. Each principle implies the other, that is, they are equivalent, and together they start us on the road to ideointegration. Furthermore, the part of the equivalence proof that demonstrates that Zermelo's postulate implies the Axiom of Choice is particularly instructive. Again translating directly into ideo terms, we now let Φ be a class of any ideosets, which may or may not be disjoint, and set $\phi_i^* = \{\phi_i\} \times \{i\}$, where $i \in I$, and $\{i\}$ is a set consisting of a singleton member i. Then $\Phi^* = \{\phi_i^*\}$ is a disjoint class of ideosets, since $i \neq j$ implies $\phi_i \times \{i\} \neq \phi_j \times \{j\}$, even if $\phi_i = \phi_j$. For, in that case, each identical member-coordinate m_i would be paired with a different index-coordinate i or j, forming different members $(m_i, i) \neq (m_i, j)$. By Zermelo's postulate there exists an ideo-subset $\phi^{*'}$ of $\cup_i \phi_i^*$ such that $\phi_i^* \cap \phi^{*'}$ consists of exactly one member, $\{(m_i, i)\}$. Therefore, since $m_i \in \phi_i$, the function f on Φ defined by $f(\phi_i) = m_i$, where f consists of the foregoing steps and can be expressed by $f = \times \{i\} \cap (\phi^{*'} \subset (\cup_i(\{\phi_i\} \times \{i\})))$, is a choice function. In addition, the operator $\times \{i\}$ provides a handy way of tagging all members of a set for a variety of purposes.

Let us proceed a step further and recall that the cross (or Cartesian, or direct) product of a sequence of sets $A_1, A_2, \ldots, A_n$, written $A_1 \times A_2 \times \cdots \times A_n$, or $\Pi_i A_i$, is the set consisting of all ordered sequences (n-tuples) $\langle a_1, a_2, \ldots, a_n \rangle$ such that $a_1 \in A_1, a_2 \in A_2, \ldots, a_n \in A_n$, where the order of the elements in all n-tuples is the same, $viz.$, the order of the sets in the product. Then the cross-product of ideosets $\{\phi_i\}$, $i.e.$, $\phi = \Pi_i \phi_i$, is also the set of all choice functions defined on $\{\phi_i\}$. For, each choice function f_k defined on the class $\{\phi_i\}$ includes the order of the sets in it, and generates the unique n-tuple point

$$P_k = (f_k(\phi_1), f_k(\phi_2), \ldots, f_k(\phi_n)) = \langle \alpha_{k_1}, \alpha_{k_2}, \ldots, \alpha_{k_n} \rangle = \langle \alpha_i \rangle_{i \in I} \in \phi.$$

From either perspective, the result is the same: the *product ideoset* [26].

If there are n ideosets in $\{\phi_i\}$, and the product of the numbers of members in the ideosets is N, the product ideoset will consist of N members, each member being an n-tuple, that is, an n-element ordered subset. For example, if there are three ideosets composed of five, three, and two elements, respectively, their product ideoset will comprise 30 3-tuples, $i.e.$, 30 members of three elements each. In general, the N n-tuples in a product ideoset can be viewed as N n-member subsets of the new set, or as N points in n-dimensional space. We now have structure in the sense of a formal process for transferring elements or members from each set ϕ_i in the class Φ of sets $\{\phi_i\}$ to a new set ϕ, with the operational options of what sets to include in the class and in what order.

For integrating sets, only the product set is required, but for integrating spaces the product topology is also required. We need to define, then, an ideotop on the product set ϕ that may be regarded as the product of the ideotops on the factors ϕ_i of ϕ. To accomplish this, we will proceed from the fundamental perspectives of bases and projections.

Recall that when we touched on bases earlier, we specified the condition that a class $\mathcal{B}$ of subsets $\{\phi_j'\}$ of a *given* π must meet in order to constitute a base, or basis, $\mathcal{B}_\phi$, for π. The fact that $\mathcal{B} \subset \pi$ automatically informs us, via Axiom 3 for a topology, that for any $\phi_k', \phi_l' \in \mathcal{B}$, $\phi_k' \cap \phi_l' \in \pi$. To satisfy Axiom 4 for a topology based on $\mathcal{B}_\phi \subset \pi$, we have only to specify that every $\phi_j' \in \pi$ be the union of members of $\mathcal{B}_\phi$, as specifed earlier. However, when our concern is not whether a particular $\mathcal{B} \subset \pi$ is a base for the particular π, but is, instead, whether a particular

$\mathfrak{B} \subset \phi$ is a base for *some* π on the given ϕ, then we must specify that $\mathfrak{B} = \{\phi_j'\} \subset \phi$ meet the following two conditions: 1) $\phi = \cup_j \phi_j'$; and 2) For any ϕ_k', $\phi_l' \in \mathfrak{B}$, $\phi_k' \cap \phi_l'$ is the union of members of $\mathfrak{B}$. The first condition is necessary for every ideotop on ϕ. The second condition leads to the satisfaction of Axioms 3 and 4 for a topology. A little reflection will show that ϕ and $\emptyset$ inherently become members of $\mathfrak{B}$ and, hence, of π, thus satisfying Axioms 1 and 2 for a topology. Furthermore, given (ϕ, π), a class $\mathcal{S}_\phi$ of subsets of π is a *subbase* for π iff the class of intersections of members of $\mathcal{S}_\phi$ forms a base for π. And it can be shown that *any* class of subsets of ϕ is the subbase for a unique π on ϕ. That is, the intersections of members of any class of subsets of ϕ form a base for a unique π on ϕ. In this sense, any class of subsets of ϕ always *generates* a π on ϕ.

With this in the background, let us now reconsider the product ideoset $\Pi_i \phi_i$, this time as the set of all functions p defined by $p: I \longrightarrow \cup_i \phi_i$ such that $p(i) = p_i = \alpha_i \in \phi_i$. Then a point of the cross-product is $p = \langle \alpha_i \rangle$, as before. In this, $p(i) = p_i = \alpha_i$ is referred to as the *ith coordinate* of p. This leads us to define the *projection function* π_{i_0} from the product set ϕ to what is now called the *coordinate space* ϕ_{i_0}, which is the ideoset ϕ_i, $i = i_0$. The projection function π_{i_0}: $\phi \longrightarrow \phi_{i_0}$ is defined by $\pi_{i_0}(\langle \alpha_i \rangle) = \alpha_{i_0} \in \phi_{i_0}$, where α_{i_0} is referred to as the i_0*th coordinate* of the point p in the product set ϕ. That is, π_{i_0} is the i_0*th projection* of the point p in ϕ onto the i_0th coordinate space ϕ_{i_0}. The coordinate $\alpha_{i_0} \in \phi_{i_0}$ is also an element of some subset O_{i_0} of ϕ_{i_0}, i.e., $\alpha_{i_0} \in O_{i_0} \subset \phi_{i_0}$. It is these projections that will be used to define the ideotop π in th new ideospace μ.

We next define the *inverse projection function* π_i^{-1} from the coordinate space ϕ_{i_0} to the product space ϕ. (It might be helpful to note that this is directly analogous to inverse trigonometric functions, such as $\sin^{-1} a$, read "arc sine a," standing for the expression "an angle whose sine is a." Thus, if $y = \sin x$, then $x = \sin^{-1} y$.) Whereas $\pi_{i_0}(p) = \alpha_{i_0}$ gives the i_0th coordinate of a point p, $\pi_{i_0}^{-1}(\alpha_{i_0})$ gives the point or set of points whose i_0th coordinate is α_{i_0} and whose other coordinates are unrestricted or unspecified. Then $\pi_{j_0}^{-1}(O_{j_0})$ is the set of all points p in $\phi = \Pi_i \phi_i$ whose j_0th projection $\pi_{j_0}(p)$ is an element of $O_{j_0} \subset \phi_j$. This can be written

$$\pi_{j_0}^{-1}(O_{j_0}) = \prod_{i \neq j_0}^{n} \phi_i \times O_{j_0}$$

$$= \phi_1 \times \cdots \times \phi_{j_0 - 1} \times O_{j_0} \times \phi_{j_0 + 1} \times \cdots \times \phi_{j_n}.$$

Now, if $\{(\phi_j, \pi_j)\}$ be any collection of ideospaces $\{\mu_j\}$, and for each π_j there is a function $f_j: \phi \longrightarrow \pi_j$ defined on some arbitrary ϕ, then there is a subbase $\mathcal{S}_\phi$, called the *defining subbase*, which consists of the inverse image in ϕ of each O_{j_k} of every π_j in $\{\mu_j\}$. The ideotop π on ϕ generated by $\mathcal{S}_\phi$ is called the ideotop *induced* (or *generated*) by the functions f_j [27].

Accordingly, the class of subsets of the form $\pi_{j_0}^{-1}(O_{j_0})$ given above is the defining subbase for the product ideotop. Furthermore, since the class of intersections of the subbase members forms a base for a topology, we have:

the class of subsets of a product space of the form

$$\pi_{j_1}^{-1}(O_{j_1}) \cap \cdots \cap \pi_{j_m}^{-1}(O_{j_m}) = \Pi_i \{\pi_j\} \times O_{j_1} \times \cdots \times O_{j_m};$$
$$i \neq j_1, \ldots, j_m; \quad O_{j_m} \subset \pi_{j_m};$$

constitutes the general expression for a base. If a subset O_{j_k} from every π_j in the product is included on the left, then

$$\pi_{j_1}^{-1}(O_{j_1}) \cap \cdots \cap \pi_{j_n}^{-1}(O_{j_n}) = O_{j_1} \times \cdots \times O_{j_n}$$

is a basis set B_1, the class of which, $\{B_1\}$, constitutes the defining base $\mathcal{B}_\phi$ for the product ideotop π. The extension from $\mathcal{B}_\phi$ to π is then immediate, being simply the unions of all members B_1 of $\mathcal{B}$. The resultant product ideotop, together with the product ideoset obtained earlier, that is, the pair of objects (ϕ, π), comprises the product ideospace $\mathbf{и}$ of the collection of ideospaces $\{\mathbf{и}_j\} = \{\phi_j, \pi_j\}$ [28].

It is the inverse projections on the left of the above expression that are used in practice to obtain π. The right side of the expression shows that this definition can be considered to be a product of the original factors, which is what we sought at the outset of product integration. The product ideotop is not the only ideotop that can be formed on the product ideoset, but it is basic, handy, and possessed of valuable properties.

Specific ideotops and ideospaces are tagged for permanent identification in the master dictionary in a bracketed fashion similar to tagging θ and ϕ sets, but without the hierarchical structure. Two of the most important ideospaces are the Auschwitz space and the Magadan space, which we will denote here simply as $\mathbf{и}_{[A]}$ and $\mathbf{и}_{[M]}$, respectively. Substantial ideologic treatment of just these two ideospaces could have enormous impact on mankind's future.

Concluding Remarks

The family of ideotopological principles and processes described here, $viz.$, hierarchies, functions, spaces, differentiation, and integration, provide means whereby we can compose, vary, and select ideosets, compose and vary ideotops on them, develop ideospaces, subspaces, and faction spaces, and compute product ideospaces for combinations of those factors. As topology goes, these are elementary affairs, yet they provide a basic methodology for mathematically studying and dealing with the elusive but paramount world of ideologies. Discourse employing ideotopology approaches philosophers' ancient and continuing quest for "pure reason," and may come as close as we will ever get. When ideotopological discourse is combined with the new technology of computer-based teleconferencing (CBT), which spans global time and space, highly rational discourse, negotiation, and international relations will become a reality, and from that, a peaceful, progressive, and humane future may evolve. For, this new science is not a substitute for compassion, but, rather, is in its service [29] .

That such large-scale applications of ideotopology will be realized is highly probable, for education and training in its theory and practice have been kept well in mind during its development. Although this presentation may seem a bit involved upon first exposure, it would require little further explanation, some illustrations, and some worked-out examples to put basic ideotopology within reach of contemporary high school curricula, which already include some set theory.

While general topology primarily investigates the consequences of topological properties, which it axiomatically develops, ideotopology is not so oriented, and seeks merely to borrow the fewest and simplest elements of basic topology that will do the job. Actually, topology has so infiltrated nearly all of mathematics that it has become increasingly difficult to define or even characterize. The characterization perhaps most appropriate here is that topology is "a state of mind"—which makes ideotopology "a state of mind about ideologies." The full development and application of ideotopology does, however, require substantial maturity and background in epistemology, axiology, ideology, and philosophy, especially philosophy of mathematics and natural science. Much less than full application, though, will suffice for many real-world, practical affairs.

There is, of course, much more to ideotopology than has been presented here, but that, as well as demonstrations, will perforce have to await another occasion.

NOTES AND REFERENCES

1. Mannheim, Karl. *Ideology and Utopia/An Introduction to the Sociology of Knowledge.* New York: Harcourt, Brace & World, 1936.
2. The term "Tanakaism" is coined here to denote Japanese Imperial Ideology of World Conquest (a term also coined here) as exemplified in the Memorial Presented to the Emperor of Japan by Baron Tanaka in 1927. See Carl Crow. *Japan's Dream of World Empire: The Tanaka Memorial.* New York: Harper & Brothers, 1942.
3. Shirer, William L. *The Rise and Fall of the Third Reich.* New York: Simon and Schuster, 1960.
4. Speer, Albert. *Inside the Third Reich.* New York: Macmillan, 1970.
5. Kissinger, Henry A. *American Foreign Policy*, expanded edition. New York: W. W. Norton, 1974.
6. For those unfamiliar with classification of the sciences, they are all classified into three families: the physical sciences, the biological sciences, and the behavioral, or social, sciences.
7. This is partially explained by Dissonance Theory in contemporary psychology. While this theory has many facets and several paradigms, a relevant aspect can be summa-

rized as follows: When a person is induced to behave contrary to his beliefs, he experiences an uncomfortable state called dissonance. The degree of dissonance aroused depends on available justifications for his counterbelief behavior. The less the justification, the greater the dissonance. Ideologies serve to provide justifications and a new belief system, thereby bringing the new behavior into line with belief, and thus reducing or even eliminating dissonance.

8. From Thucydides. *The Peloponnesian War.* Translated by Rex Warner. London: Penguin Books, 1954.

9. From a Mongol chronicle, "The Secret History of the Mongols," written in 1240 at Genghis Khan's command, for use only by members of the ruling house. See Lister. R. P. *Genghis Khan.* New York: Stein and Day, 1969.

10. *The Columbia Encyclopedia*, 2nd ed. New York: Columbia University Press, 1950.

11. Shirer, *op. cit.*, ch. 4, "The Mind of Hitler and the Roots of the Third Reich."

12. *History of the Communist Party of the Soviet Union.* Moscow: Foreign Languages Publishing House, 1960.

13. Brezhnev, L. I. *Following Lenin's Course.* Moscow: Progress Publishers, 1972. This work is a collection of speeches and articles spanning the five-year period, 1967–1971.

14. Larson, Arthur. "The Role of Law in Building Peace." In *Preventing World War III: Some Proposals.* Edited by Quincy Wright, William M. Evan, and Morton Deutsch. New York: Simon and Schuster, 1962.

15. *Toward a World Without War/A Summary of United States Disarmament Efforts— Past and Present.* Publication 10, General Series 6, United States Arms Control and Disarmament Agency, Washington, 1962, p. 9.

16. The full notation is $\mathbf{n}_i = (\phi_j, \pi_k)$, where i refers to the ideospace comprising ideoset ϕ_j, j = Marxism-Leninism, with ideotopology π_k on ϕ_j, π is the Russian lower-case letter "el," and k = the core ideology in ϕ_j. Then $\mathbf{n}_i$ is the ideospace Marxism-Leninism core ideology. Insasmuch as only one ideospace is discussed in this section, we can represent it simply by $\mathbf{n}_i$, understanding all along what i refers to. See "Ideologic Analytics" for further explanation. Again, bear in mind that this mathematical approach is not essential; but it helps. In any event, while the use of $\mathbf{n}_i$ in the text links the text with the mathematical "Ideologic Analytics", its significance in the text can be accepted as simply shorthand notation similar to Gregg or any other.

17. *Conference On Security And Co-operation in Europe/Final Act/Helsinki 1975.* Department of State Publication 8826, General Foreign Policy Series 298, U.S. Department of State, Washington, D.C., 1975.

18. This correspondence was reproduced in part in Seadler, S. E. *Defenses of Peace.* Ft. Madison, Ia.: 1963, a privately published pamphlet. My invitation to a similar exchange of views by correspondence was accepted by Prof. V. S. Yemelyanov, former Chairman, State Committee on the Peaceful Uses of Atomic Energy, USSR, but never materialized, so I presume that it was blocked. Approaches such as those suggested in the discussion of Baskets One and Three could force such exchanges.

19. This point, together with its impact on theories of ethics, is made in the context of neurophysiology in Seadler, S. E. "Ragnar Granit and the Sense of Ideas." *American-Scandinavian Review* 44 No. 4. New York: American-Scandinavian Foundation, December 1956, which deals with Granit's research as Director of the Nobel Institute of Neurophysiology, Stockholm.

20. Chakravarty, S. P. "Econometric Models: Mathematical Expressions of Personal Prejudices?" *IEEE Transactions on Systems, Man, and Cybernetics* 7(1977): 462.

21. A brief scenario of a cooperative conflict-reducing application is narrated in Seadler, S. E. "Ideologics." In Sutherland, J. W. *Administrative Decision-Making: Extending the Bounds of Rationality*, Van Nostrand Reinhold, 1977.

22. The mathematics and methods of contemporary data base management systems (DBMS) in computer science are highly sophisticated, and in many aspects employ set-theoretic approaches. Many special applications of computers also employ topological approaches. When ideotopology moves from the stage of mathematical development to the stage of technological development, it will have available a very wide interface with extant and rapidly developing computer science and technology. The interaction between computer science and ideotopology may then result in some modifications of the mathematics set forth here, followed by synergistic, accelerating development of both fields.

23. Substantive sufficiency is an ideotopological property regarding which development work remains to be done.

24. Actually, the specification "nonempty" should be made in nearly all set and class statements in this section, but, in the interests of brevity and simplicity, this rigor has been omitted, except in stating axioms and postulates, where it seems unavoidable.

25. Bear in mind that the specification of a set or subset involves listing each distinct element or member only once, but with the element repeated in each multielement member in which it appears. The existence of a particular element more than once in a set, subset, or member does not alter the specification of that element only once in each such set, subset, or member.

26. Strictly speaking, each choice function f_k chooses one point α_k or m_k without inherent regard to order; it is we who provide the order. In set terms, however, $(a, b, c, d) = (c, b, d, a) = etc.$, unless we are interested in specifying, for instance, dominance order, which we are not here. Thus, although the cross-product convention produces ordered n-tuples, in choice function terms the order is irrelevant, and a given n-tuple is equal to any unordered member containing the same elements. Hence, the equivalence of the cross-product and the set of all choice functions.

27. The functions $f_j: \phi \longrightarrow \pi_j$ exist by virtue of the cross-product mechanics, are the projections π_{j_0}, and, therefore, are at least simple mappings, *i.e.*, in graphic terms, lines connecting a point p in ϕ with its coordinates. These projections and their inverses thus fall within at least one class of functions within the collection $\mathcal{F}(\Phi)$. Here again, ideotopology goes beyond general topology, for the f_j, as well as all other functions, are subject to criteria that bear on their *functional sufficiency*, and may become subjects of debate, pressure, and negotiation. Functional sufficiency is, however, closely related to the topological property of *connectedness*, especially *path-connectedness*. At this juncture the reader is merely advised of these considerations, for further discussion would take us far beyond the scope of this essay.

28. Additional notation to distinguish *product* ideosets, *product* ideotops, and *product* ideospaces is generally not needed, the context making matters clear enough. In situations where it *is* desirable to distinguish the product varieties, however, a simple degree mark, signifying the open subsets O involved in the process, suffices, and leaves the main symbol free for tagging and indexing. Thus, ϕ°, π°, and $\mathbf{n}^\circ$. Similarly for classes of these, *viz.*, Φ°, Π° and $\mathbf{H}^\circ$. And, of course, the same scheme holds for product knowledge sets, topologies, and spaces, and classes of these.

29. Our approaching "pure reason," however, is similar to a curve approaching an asymptote, especially one that is quite high above it. An asymptote is a limit, and like all

limits, is a mathematical fiction that is never reached, but is approached epsilon-close at the limit, which in the asymptote case is at another mathematical fiction, "infinity." Nevertheless, these idealizations are useful because, in specific instances, they have been designed to bear close and meaningful relationships with "reality" (another ancient and elusive quest). It is very important to realize these matters when seeking to approach "rational discourse," let alone "pure reason," and

> It is well worth a further moment to clarify this point for mathematical readers and to allay anxieties on the part of nonmathematical administrators of national and international destiny. In this writer's view, the concepts of "pure reason" and "value-free science" are illusions, and not encouraged by mathematicians or physicists who comprehend the highly creative nature of all knowledge, and, hence, the impact on science of human values, aesthetics, sensibilities, and metaphysical inclinations.

—which I have emphasized in "Ideologics," appendix to ch. 3, *q.v.*, for more on this vital point, in Sutherland, John W. *Societal Systems: Methodology, Modelling and Management.* New York: Elsevier North Holland, 1978. One of the remarkable features of ideotopology is that it allows for, and deals with, axiological elements and processes.

SYMBOLS IN IDEOTOPOLOGY

Indexing has been omitted except where essential

U_Ω The universe of discourse. The total, actual, real-world universe of discourse.

U_Θ Universe of knowledge discourse.

U_Φ Universe of ideological discourse.

$\mathcal{C}\Theta$ A family (collection) of knowledge classes.

$\mathcal{C}\Phi$ A family (collection) of ideological classes.

Θ A class of knowledge sets.

Φ A class of ideological sets.

θ A knowledge set.

ϕ An ideology set.

α An element of a θ.

β An element of a ϕ.

$a, b, ..$ Lower-order components of an α.

$a', b', ..$ Lower-order components of a β.

$\mathcal{F}(\Theta)$ A collection of knowledge functions.

$\mathcal{F}(\Phi)$ A collection of ideological functions.

f A function (mapping, process, transformation, algorithm). Its nature or type is indicated by its specification in specific instances, and referenced or catalogued by subscripted "tags."

X A set.

$\mathcal{T}$ A topology on X.

$(X,\mathfrak{I})$ A space.

Υ A knowledge topology.

Γ A knowledge space.

л   An ideological topology, or ideotop.

и   An ideological space, or ideospace.

A A subset of ϕ.

$л_A$ An ideosubtop: the relative ideotop on A.

$и_A$ The relative ideospace.

$\mathfrak{B}_\phi$ A base (for an ideotop: a class of subsets B of ϕ whose unions form the sets of an л.

$\mathfrak{S}_\phi$ A subbase (for an ideotop): a class of subsets S of ϕ whose intersections form a base $\mathfrak{B}_\phi$.

$\mathfrak{P}_\phi$ An ideopartition: a class of pairwise disjoint ideosets, or ideoparts, $\hat{\phi}_i$.

$\hat{\phi}$ An ideopart.

$\mathfrak{C}$ An ideocover: a class of ideosubsets ϕ' of ϕ that constitute a cover for a particular ϕ' in ϕ.

$\Pi_i \phi_i$ A product ideoset ϕ.

$\alpha(i)$ The ith coordinate of α. Also written α_i.

π A projection or projection function.

π^{-1} An inverse projection or inverse projection function.

O A subset of ϕ, especially one that is a member of an ideotop on ϕ and used in inverse projections to obtain the product ideotop.

O_{j_k} The kth subset of ideotop $л_j$ in the class of ideotops $\{л_j\}$.

$\pi_{j_k}^{-1}(O_{j_k})$ The j_kth inverse projection of O_{j_k}: the set of all points in the product ideoset whose j_kth projection is a member of $O_{j_k} \subset л_j$.

2

Symbolization and Values in Social and Economic Thought

Walter A. Weisskopf
Roosevelt University, Emeritus

To some extent, the social sciences have becoming willing and indiscriminate servants of decision and policy authorities in the public sector. In short, they have ceased to be prophets, and have become instruments of the political and military and social service systems. As such, much social science have become crassly instrumental, parochial, and purposive—and perilous as a source of information for public-policy-makers and governmental executives. The Handbook's editor believes some effort must be mounted to make the social sciences—insofar as they attempt to be of service to the public sector—aware of the dysfunctionality of disciplinary parochialism and the insidiousness of morally uninformed positions. To this end, I have asked Walter Weisskopf for a contribution he once read at a professional meeting that dealt with the implications of general system theory as an alternative methodology for the applied social sciences. What follows is the full text of that remarkable reading.   J.W.S.

INTRODUCTION

If I have contributed to the integration of the social sciences, I have done so by trying to uncover the hidden connections between economic thought and the human condition. I have not dealt with what nowadays is called economics, that is, with the techniques and models of economic, statistical, and econometric analysis, but with what might be called "economic philosophy"; the value-implications and presuppositions about human nature and about the human situation implicit in economic reasoning. I have approached economic philosophy within a historical and existential framework. Accordingly, I shall outline some

200

general principles of integration of thought and reality that I can distill from what I have done intuitively. I shall then exemplify these briefly by applying them to economics.

The actual practical cooperation among the social sciences taking place today, with the help of the general system theory, is productive because it permits the social sciences to break through the walls of professional and academic self-interests, which create, perhaps, more formidable obstacles to integration than the differences in methods and models. The enormous proliferation of the social sciences, the impossibility for a generally educated person to master them all, the specialized academic departmentalization, and the membership in a specialized discipline promote fragmentation. Individual and collective interests push toward differentiating one's profession from others. Even within the already fragmented traditional disciplines, there are strong tendencies toward further fragmentation.

This kind of organizational fragmentation reflects the marketplace. Each discipline tries to extend its share of the market for academic positions and publications just as monopolies and oligopolies do in business. Attempts at interdisciplinary cooperation are laudable, but sometimes they remind one of the collusion among firms to secure a larger corner of the intellectual market.

I shall have little to say here about the overall unity of the natural and social sciences. I shall confine myself to the social and behavioral sciences.

I am using the term "science" reluctantly because I do not want to create the impression that knowledge, even cognitive knowledge, is identical with "science." Knowledge is a universal human category, closely connected with consciousness; science is a historically limited form of knowledge that I confine to the Western sciences of the last 400 years. I would like to avoid the term "behavioral" (it was invented by a clever academic fund raiser who found politicians unable to distinguish between social science and socialism) because it seems to imply "behaviorism." For the sake of brevity, keeping these qualifications in mind, I shall talk about the human sciences, referring to all cognitive concern with human beings and with the structure of human existence. My discussion concerns the meaning and the problems of the integration of knowledge in the social and human disciplines that include the humanities, especially philosophy and history. I use the term "integration" advisedly when I talk about the general systems approach because, as will be shown, it is the broader, more inclusive concept.

THE EXPANSION OF DETERMINISTIC SYSTEMS

It is stating the obvious to say that the concept of a system was—explicitly or implicitly—used thousands of years before it became fashionable in engineering and computer technology, and long before Norbert Wiener developed cybernetics. It is as old as philosophy, theology, religion, and mythology. The first "systems" were developed by the cosmologies and cosmogonies that served as legitimations of the various Near-Eastern empires thousands of years ago. A system is "any set whatsoever of jointly considered variables, including the entire world or any lesser set" [1]. Thus, it is not the use of the system concept that distinguishes the sciences, but the *kind* of system they use. The relevant distinction was and is 1) between the number and kind of variables that were considered, 2) how the interaction between these variables was interpreted and what kind of interaction was dealt with, 3) whether the systems were open or closed, and 4) whether they aimed at a determinate solution and a deterministic view of reality. The systems used at first in the social sciences, especially in economics, were closed and deterministic. They were fashioned after the model of classical physics, mechanics, and astronomy. The skeleton of such a mechanistic model was always visible behind the richness of Adam Smith's description of the economy in the *Wealth of Nations*. His analysis of the workings of competition presents the movements of demand and supply toward an equilibrium price, a center of repose and continuance, analogous to the equilibrium of a physical mechanical system like a scale. Ricardo set the tone for the future mechanistic style of economics: in his model a few quantifiable variables, such as prices, wages, and profits and rents, vary either inversely or directly with each other, reaching an equilibrium under the restrictive impact of the law of diminishing returns.

The Malthusian population theory is of the same kind: three variables: the fertility of the earth, the fertility of the human female, and the subsistence wages maintain—through starvation, misery, and vice—an equilibrium between population and food supply. Alfred Marshall talks about economic equilibrium as a "balance of opposing forces" and compares it to the mechanical equilibrium of a stone hanging by an elastic string, or a number of balls resting against one another on a basin [2].

This physical, mechanistic-Newtonian model was never completely abandoned in economics, although Alfred Marshall, the founder of the neoclassical school whose teaching survived until today in all textbook economics, uses organismic comparisons in his equilibrium analysis.

Since the development of sociology and anthropology, integrational attempts consisted in expanding the number of variables of the system, adding some that were borrowed from the younger social sciences. Thus, in the attempts to interrelate sociology, psychology, and economics, the atomistic idea that random subjective preferences are the cause of all economic behavior was supplemented by taking into account the influence of social interrelations, internalized values, communal relations, and noneconomic motives. The epistemology underlying these attempts still implies that the universe, or at least the specific realm of the discipline under consideration, is wholly determinate, that it would be wholly closed, if only all the variables were known and included in the system. In such cases, interdisciplinary methods try to increase the number of endogenous variables taken into consideration. "An endogenous variable . . . is fully controlled by the other variables of the system" [1, p. 50] .

Interdisciplinary systems try to change variables that were previously considered exogenous into endogenous variables. "An exogenous variable . . . is not fully controlled by the other variables of the system" [1, p. 50]. The interdisciplinary endeavors of this kind imply that a scientific discipline must, in order to fulfill its alleged functions of explanation, prediction, and control, deal with a closed system. "In a closed system . . . all variables are endogenous. Its behavior is not subject to . . . influence emanating from variables outside the system" [1, p. 50]. This assumption has not been abandoned when new, previously exogenous variables are taken into consideration and included in the system, thus becoming endogenous. This has happened sometimes in economics when noneconomic factors were built into the system of economic thought. Marx, who was only partly an economist, and whose influence rests much more on his sociology and philosophy of history, was perhaps the first and most important thinker who thus expanded the realm of economics. Galbraith, Myrdal, Boulding, and Mishan are contempary examples of the same kind. Nevertheless, this form of interdisciplinary integration is not a new paradigm of knowledge. The basic idea is still that if enough variables are included in the system it will be closed, determinate, and able to serve as a basis for prediction.

GENERAL SYSTEMS THEORY

What is usually called a "General Systems Philosophy" is different from the integrative endeavors just described. The so-called systems approach developed during and since World War II, and centered around cybernetics and computerization. It abandoned the linear chain of causation as an explanatory device, and replaced it by the ideal of mutual, circular interdependence, most clearly seen in the idea of a "feedback." In the organic realm, there are entities whose behavior cannot be understood in terms of linear, cause-and-effective chains, but in terms of "multi-variable interactions, organization, hierarchic order, goal-directed processes and programs" [3]. This represented an abandonment of mechanistic thinking, whose paradigm was classical physics and mechanics, and a change to a new organismic paradigm taken from biology—a change that was important not merely for the natural sciences, but even more so for the social sciences. The term "general system theory" for the organismic paradigms has to be accepted because it is widely used; but it is imprecise insofar as a mechanistic interpretation is as much a "system" as an organismic one.

The step from a mechanistic to an organismic system in the life sciences and its application to the social disciplines represented a step toward differentiating our knowledge of reality. The new paradigm consists of a new concept of "wholeness —a holistic 'Gestalt,' together with the recognition of organization, of pattern and form, of an internal order. Wholeness, organization, dynamics—these general conceptions may be stated as characteristics of the modern as opposed to the mechanistic world view of physics" [4]. What is involved in holism is an abandonment of thinking in terms of unidirectional chains of cause and effect. Organismic thinking abandoned single-chain-of-causation thinking in which each preceding link is a cause and each succeeding link an effect; instead, it visualizes reality as a network of such chains where cause-and-effect relations are existing between *all* links of *all* the chains forming the network of reality. Every link is cause and effect at the same time. The units of an organismic-patterned system stand to each other in the relation of mutual circular interdependence. They are a general system in which every unit produces a feedback as a reaction to the influence of every other unit. This can be exemplified by the application of ecology to economics. The ecologists certainly have enlarged the scope of our economic and technological thinking by using the holistic approach. The essence of their criticism of technical measures, *e.g.*, of pest control, insecticides, *etc.*, is that "our single value approach conflicted with the complexity of the environment; we were concerned only with the detergents' commercial value as cleansing agent and ignored their effects on the environment as a whole" [5].

This and many similar examples of ecological reasoning are of enormous importance in economic and technological thought and practice. Yet, what is taking place epistemologically in this reasoning? A previously closed system, the market, is "opened" by a broader environmental viewpoint. Insecticides destroy not only the pests, but also the predators that kept the pest population low. This is not necessarily a new paradigm of sciences; it increases the number of variables and considers the feedback effects of human action. The cognitive horizon is enlarged, but it would be wrong to say "that the economy is changed from a closed system in which all the variables are endogenous into an 'open system' in which there are only exogenous variables" [1, p. 50]. The distinction between an open and closed system is a relative one, and is related to the division of labor between the sciences. Each of them deals with a segment of reality, thereby including some variables and excluding others. What and why some variables are considered endogenous and others exogenous is quite significant, and is often based on extrascientific considerations, such as style of life and perception, historical conditions, social goals, value judgments, *etc.* In the development of scientific thought from mechanistic and atomistic to organismic and holistic models, more and more variables were included and changed from exogenous to endogenous ones, without closing the system.

The ultimate question is what paradigm would be appropriate if the entire cosmos and the human position in it is taken into consideration? I submit that the entire universe is an "open system," but, furthermore, that it is essentially "indeterminate," indeterminateness being defined as partial "unknowability," or being a "mystery."

The approach of the ecologists to the economy and to technology is an example of enlarging the systems and transforming exogenous into endogenous variables; they are trying to enlarge the horizon of economics (and of economists). Ultimately, most of them, like all scientists, would maintain that the universe has a determinate order: an order that can be explained in terms of predictable laws or, at least, probabilities; that it is only our temporary ignorance and lack of knowledge of all relevant variables that prevent us from fully understanding it. Thus, the universe would be essentially a closed, knowable, and determinate general system. To this I propose the conviction that the universe, man, society, and history form an essentially open, partially unknowable, and indeterminate general system.

THE *CONDITIO HUMANA* IN THE COSMOS

It is part of the problem of integration that we have alienated ourselves from the spiritual experience and tradition of mankind that preceded the modern phase of Western history. It is my conviction that the integrative, general-system approach is, often unknowingly, an attempt to revive a prescientific, holistic worldview in order to escape the present fragmentation of life and thought. One can visualize the development of Western science of the last 200 years as a trend toward a cognitive reductionism in which one dimension after the other was peeled off reality until only the world perceived by the five senses and the mathematical skeleton of this world remained real. The integration movement and general-system thinking may be an unconscious attempt to regain the holistic view of mythological, religious, theological, philosophical systems of the premodern tradition. This is another way of saying that during the last 200 years all of reality was transformed into closed and determinate systems, and that it is our task to recognize reality as an essentially open and indeterminate system again.

If I am right, it is appropriate to refer to some thoughts of a modern metaphysician and philosopher of history whose thinking is deeply steeped in the Occidental tradition. In the first volume of his monumental *Order and History* Eric Voegelin describes the human situation in philosophical terms [6]:

> God and man, world and society form a primordial community of being. The community . . . is, and is not, a datum of human experience. It *is* a datum of experience insofar as it is known to man by virtue of his participation in the

mystery of his being. It is *not* a datum of experience insofar as it is not given in the manner of an object of the external world but is knowable only from the perspective of participation in it.

It is possible to translate Voeglin's metaphysical language into the language of general system theory. To him, man perceives the world as an open indeterminate system, not as a detached outside observer, but as a participant [6] .

> . . . man is not a self-contained spectator. He is an actor, playing a part in the drama of being . . . committed to play it without knowing what it is . . . the role of existence must be played in uncertainty of its meaning, as an adventure of decision on the edge of freedom and necessity.[11]

This situation has implications for the interpretation of human knowledge:

1. Ineluctably, the cosmos and the human condition are a *mystery* to man. The play and our role in it, that is the meaning and structure of the whole and of its parts, are unknown. There is a dimension of the unknown that, throughout the ages, has been pointed to in *symbolic, evocative*, language: the transcendental dimension, the depth-dimension of being, the ground of being, "the creative ground, the infinite and unconditional power of being [7] .

2. Human beings are not detached observers outside the open system of the cosmos. They are *participants*—and conscious of their participation. Their thinking, feeling, willing, and actions are part of the system, and stand in reciprocal interaction with other human and nonhuman elements of the system. The basic human situation is comparable to the Heisenberg principle, where subject and object, observer and observed are not independent of each other, but form a mutually encompassing system, *e.g.*, the century-long reductionism in the sciences and the fragmentation of life in modern Western society are mutually interrelated, and the integrative approach of which this meeting is a part, influences not only modern thought but the modern style of life as well.

   The reaction of human beings to the mystery of existence consisted in *symbolization.*

SYMBOLIZATION AND SOCIAL THOUGHT

Symbolization "is the attempt of making the essentially unknowable order of being intelligible as far as possible through the creation of symbols which interpret the unknown by analogy with the really, or supposedly, 'known'" [6, p. 5] . Symbolization has an *instrumental* integrative function: it serves the purpose of making the mystery comprehensible by giving it a name. A. H. Maslow has interpreted this function as satisfying a basic human "safety" need, a need for a "world philosophy that organized the universe and men into some sort of coherent meaningful whole" [8] . The integrative symbolization of the unknown concerns also the interpretation of *society* in its relation to a symbolic world order, which includes the interconnections between man, society, world, and the unknown. Society was interpreted either as a microcosm, as an analogue to the cosmos and its order, or as a *macrocosm*, as the symbolization of the social order by analogy to the human individual as a *macroanthropos* [6]. These paradigms of symbolization, illuminating the unknown and the mystery of human existence, are found already in the cosmogonies and cosmologies of the ancient Near-Eastern empire, which understood itself as a microcosm of the universe; and in Greek philosophy, where society was understood as a macro-anthropos after the cosmologically symbolized empires had broken down. These patterns are surreptiously used in the modern sciences, especially in economics. Since classical physics and mechanics, we have tried to interpret the human condition and society as macrocosms, in analogy to the planetary system. This is the approach against which holistic general system theory is directed. The organismic-system approach has used the paradigm of the macroanthropos. In both cases, we tried to fill the gap of the mystery that the sciences have left in our world view. This is an inevitable and legitimate procedure; the problem stems from a reductionist, scientistic method and not from the modern systems of symbolization of the unknown. We, as well as our ancestors, are confronted with the dimension of mystery and the unknown. In a process of progressive reductionism, we have discarded the ancient instruments of symbolization, such as myths and philosophy, and have replaced them by science. Therefore, we had to smuggle into science important elements of symbolization in order to make the essentially unknowable intelligible. Only in this way could we arrive at an idea of social order, which is indispensable for human existence in society. I shall call this the *symbolic function* of "science."

MAN AS PARTICIPANT-OBSERVER

The way this function is discharged is influenced by the position of man as *participant-observer*. Social reality, *e.g.*, the economy, cannot be understood as an object juxtaposed to a detached observing subject. The social sciences, including economics, are self-interpretations. That influence is the greater the more their ideas are accepted by other participants. Lord Keynes' dictum that most actions of politicians are derived from the ideas of some defunct economist is true in a literal, but also in a broader sense. Economics and the social system "is" what people—influenced by their historical experience and by social scientists and economists—believe it is; they will orient their economic system according to the beliefs of economists. Socioeconomic systems then are always "open" or "closed" only in thought; and they are not mere objects to be grasped cognitively, but they are changed by the cognition of the participant-observers. These aspects have to be included in any general system theory.

Voegelin's paradigm of metaphor of the actor who plays an unknown role in an unknown play applies not only to the general human situation, but especially to social and thought action. This was recognized in the *sociology of knowledge* and in the approach of the *Frankfort School* (Horkheimer, Adorno, Marcuse, Habermas). It was really started by Marx when he explained bourgeois economics as advocacy of the capitalist system; this was perhaps the most mischievous form in which thinking man was viewed, not as a detached observer, but as a participant. The sociology of knowledge, especially as developed by *Max Scheler and Karl Mannheim*, have enlarged this idea from the narrow interpretation of social thought as an expression of class interest to an expanded general system theory in which ideal and real factors in the historical position of the author were used to "explain" his ideas. This is a form of general system theory —preceding its origin in cybernetics and computer science—in which the historical conditions became an implicit part of explicit social thought. Social thought is dealing with these conditions by complementing the necessarily incomprehensible aspects of the situation through symbolization. To use again Voegelin's metaphor: the actor-participant of a social order who does not really know his role and the meaning of the play (of the social order) tries to develop ideas that make both the order and his role in it more comprehensible and meaningful.

FINITE FREEDOM

In the literal sense, however, an actor, the participant-observer, will have to exercise his finite freedom. "Scientific" social thought has wrestled unsuccessfully with the experience of freedom. In line with the mechanistic, deterministic tradition, the social sciences—even those that have progressed to the use of General System Theory—have tried to view every social subculture as a closed system, subject to deterministic necessity, general laws, and certainties of predictions. Social scientists believe that they have to be determinists. On moral grounds, however, Western social thought believes in the freedom and sovereignty of the individual. The dualism of deterministic necessity and moral freedom shows the tragic dilemma of science, which has not found a bridge between pure and practical reason. Science has reified its objects and treated human beings as things, a reflection of the industrial reification of work, where men become parts of machines or inefficient machines themselves. In a world of things necessity reigns, and freedom has no place.

A realistic analysis of the human condition requires what may come close to, but what is more than, a general systems approach. Man as a Gestalt, a whole, a centered unity, is free. He is free because his consciousness enables him to know that he is. Thus, he can put himself outside of the given actuality, grasp potentialities, remember the past, envision the future. Through transcending actuality, he can see the possibility of a "free" choice between alternatives. Every such choice is accompanied by the sacrifice of those alternatives that are not chosen; this is one way in which the burden of consciousness and freedom manifests itself: it is inevitably combined with renunciation and sacrifice. The greater the actual potentialities and the greater the horizon of consciousness of these potentialities, the more difficult is the choice between them and the greater the sacrifice.

This is one aspect of human freedom that makes it *conditioned* and *finite*. Man is a person, and as a person, a centered self, he is free; but this person is a bundle of physical, psychological, historical, social, economic, hereditary, and environmental conditions; this person is free to act and make choices *within the limits of these conditions that form the person*. A general systems approach will have to include both the freedom and the conditioning of this freedom (an all-important part of which consists in human aging and mortality).

In his finite freedom man needs guiding *norms* and *standards* for his choice and decision. The Biblical story of the Fall symbolizes the interrelation between consciousness and ethics. The serpent defined the essence of knowledge: *"eritis sicut deus scientes bonum et malum."* Consciousness requires knowledge of the distinction between good and bad. This is especially true of knowledge of society and of man. Ethics and morality are not mere epiphenomena of the physical and actual world; the normative dimension is an essential characteristic of human existence. The normative element rests on limited, conditioned freedom, transcendence of the given actual situation by consciousness, knowledge of alternatives (within the limits of freedom), the necessity of choice, and last, but not least, on the position of man as participant. *This is why the social and human sciences must contain normative elements.* When the participant-observer becomes conscious of actual social reality, he also becomes conscious of alternatives to this reality. This forces him to make value judgments. As a matter of fact, the enlargement of the horizon in the social sciences, the development from the mechanistic to the organismic paradigm, the very emergence of the general system concept—all this related to changes in values. Of course, the ecologists used "science" when they pointed to the interactions of populations and environments, but their very discoveries were made under the impact of value judgments about human ends: should profits be the ultimate goal? Are jobs more important than the pollution they cause? Should income be created regardless of its use? Are individual subjective preferences the ultimate judge of beneficiality or is there such a thing as the common good? What should be the time span that should be taken into consideration? The currently living population? One, two, three, or more generations? The existence of the species? Every economic and social question is an ethical question about ultimate and intermediate ends and about the moral appropriateness of means. Is not "triage" an ethical question? Technology, price controls, taxation, *etc.* are ultimately moral questions requiring normative answers to what should be in contrast to what is.

The social sciences are continuously challenged to give answers to these questions. Therefore, they must include the normative dimension.

To summarize: The social sciences, including economics, have to perform existential functions:

1. the harmonization of the world outlook of individual academic disciplines with the broader world outlook of the time;
2. the elimination of value conflicts between academic discipline and the values of the society;
3. the establishment of norms (values) for standards of behavior, for the determination of ends, for determining the relation between ends and means within specific fields of inquiry;
4. the legitimation and justification of academic disciplines as a part of society and of the world, by a unifying and harmonizing world-view and by investing the whole of society with a meaning that also assigns a meaningful role to the individual. All these functions are interrelated and form the integrative symbolism in the social sciences.

What I call symbolization or symbolism is often referred to as *ideology*, and Marxism is mostly used as an example. Karl Mannheim distinguished between ideology and utopia, and ascribed a conservative tendency to the former and a revolutionary one to the latter. The term ideology often implies a pejorative connotation I want to avoid. Ideological and utopian thinking provide meaning in a mysterious and helpless situation. They are not nonscientific elements that have to be eliminated to change the social disciplines into hard and pure science. They are part of cognition made necessary by the human condition.

This approach has very little to do with the Marxist economic interpretation of history, which considered only one factor as an influence on thought. To grasp the total of the human situation, one has to expand the world-view to arrive at the paradigm of Voegelin, which includes the unknown, mysterious aspects of openness, and a holistic theory of history and society. Symbolization (or ideology) constitutes a necessary complementation of that part of reality that can be verified by naturalistic, positivistic methods—by experiments and empirical observation. This complementation is clearly required by the openness, indeterminacy, mystery, and participatory role-acting in the *conditio humana*. But "it is not permissible to make the experimental method of verification the exclusive vehicle for verification. Verification can occur within the life-process itself" [9]. This is experiential, as distinct from experimental, verification. Verifications through experience of any kind are "truer to life, though less exact and definite than experimental ones. Verification by experience is based on life processes which have the character of totality, spontaneity, and individuality . . . by a participation in the life with which they deal. If this knowledge by participation is called *'intuition'* the cognitive approach to any life-process is intuitive" [9]. Thus, symbolization and ideology are "verified" by the intuitive participation of the observing social scientist or human being in the "general system" or the total reality he is researching, (re-search literally means searching for something that has been known before). Calling some social thought an ideolgy is not a derogation, but a characterization of an essential form of thought.

ECONOMICS AND SYMBOLIZATION

Economics lends itself very well to show the nonrational, philosophical, ideological and symbolic aspects of a social science. This is widely recognized by economists whether they want to preserve or attack the existing economic system of values and institutions. Most of those who discern ideological elements, do so in a critical mood; they declare economists either as lackeys of capitalism or as Marxist communists, all of these terms used in a pejorative sense to deny economics the dignity of a science. I propose to look at this situation differently. A social science cannot be purely "scientific" and positive. It must, for philosophical and existential reasons, perform some instrumental and existential functions. The ideological element is an essential characteristic of the human sciences, including economics.

E. S. Mason has clearly recognized the necessity that systems of economic thought (like all systems of thought concerned with human beings) have to perform a legitimizing, justifying ideological function: "It seems a fact that the institutional stability . . . of an economic system (is) heavily dependent on the existence of a *philosophy* or *ideology* justifying the system in a manner generally acceptable. . . . Classical economics in the form of a philosophy of natural liberty performed that function admirably for the 19th century capitalism." He concludes ". . . that the growth of 19th century capitalism depended largely on the general acceptance of reasoned justification of the system on moral as well as on political and economic grounds" [10].

In two books, I have analyzed the symbolic ideological and normative elements in the history of economic thought [11]. As an illustration for the preceding general propositions, I am summarizing in what follows some of the essential points of my analysis:

Economics was and is confronted with the ethical problem of legitimizing the ethos of acquisition, and with the problem of harmonizing the individual's striving for gain with the common good. In view of the scientific trends of the eighteenth and nineteenth centuries, this legitimizing and harmonizing function had to be performed in the form of a "scientific" system hiding the ethical content under the mantle of scientific analysis. I am turning first to the ethical question.

From the very beginning, economic and business ethics conflicted with Christian ethics. The latter are antichrematistic and other-worldly; the former are acquisitive, activistic, and directed at manipulation of the external world. Everything that business ethics considers to be a value is, more or less, a sin, hubris, and concupiscence in terms of Christian beliefs. Historically, the two conflicting value systems were synthesized in the "Protestant-Puritan, inner-directed, achievement-oriented value complex" (see Max Weber, Werner Sombart, David Riesman, David McClellan, or Talcott Parsons). Predestination, salvation, economic success, individualistic competition, the bourgeois virtues of hard work, thrift, and inner-worldly asceticism were harmonized in one unified value-attitude system. Economic success became mark and proof of religious salvation. In the nineteenth century, the value system was secularized and divorced from religion. Social Darwinism (Spencer, Sumner) made economic success the basis of self-respect and social status: a proof of one's worth and virtue. The success ethic became the predominant value system of Western free-enterprise, market society. This philosophy centered around a faith: faith in the harmony of individual economic self-interest, private property, and the common good. All three concepts and institutions were united by the idea that an individual has an exclusive property right over himself, owns himself. "The labor of his body and the work of his hands" (Locke) were considered to be emanations of the self-owned person and, therefore, his property. The value of his product was measured by the amount of his labor that he bestowed on it; and his income was commensurate with his labor-effort when he sold his products. Thus, prices and incomes are determined by merit and achievement. This moral underpinning was reinforced by the idea that individual gain promotes the common good because both are accomplished by an increase in production.

The individual was supposed to pursue gain in isolation, alone, without regard for, even in conflict with, others. This conflict, called competition, was considered to be a "socializing" force, however. Adam Smith's idea of natural harmony of interests implied that individual aggrandizement will lead to the common good. Thus, economic egoism was morally justified on *social* grounds (a point sometimes overlooked by modern libertarians to whom individual freedom from *all* restrictions seems to be an end in itself; thus, they proclaim themselves proudly as anarchists).

In the formulation of the classics, the ethical element, although already hidden, was still clearly visible. In neoclassical and marginalist thought (this developed in the second half of the nineteenth century, and is best exemplified by Alfred Marshall) the ethical content became more and more hidden; but not only that: it changed its content. From Marshall's time to the beginning of World War I, the ethical emphasis changed from impulse control, hard and systematic work, and preoccupation with the production of physical goods to psychological satisfaction of subjective, individual preferences. In Marshall's *Principles* (first edition, 1890) the Protestant ethos and utilitarian subjectivism are in conflict with each other. But more and more the ideal became subjective want satisfaction pursued with expedient "rationality" aiming at efficiency. The latter was defined in a formalistic way: a maximization of monetary and psychological gains, a maximum satisfaction of *individual* preferences. This subjective felicific calculus, originating with the Utilitarians, became more and more emptied of content, and was first refined by neoclassical and modern logistic model-building into a fine art of behavioral directives *more geometrico et mathematico*. Rational efficiency in the maximization of random, subjective, individual preferences, regardless of their social desirability, became moral imperatives not only in technology and business, but also in economic theory.

The framework for this line of reasoning was formed by what is today called static *equilibrium theory*. All economic forces and magnitudes—prices, wages, interest rates, incomes, and output of goods—were supposedly moving toward an equilibrium position that was defined in terms of a balance of forces. This was foreshadowed in classical thought, but elaborated by neoclassical, marginalist, and subsequent economics. It would take us too far to follow all the vagaries and vicissitudes of this concept. It is part of a mechanistic system. Already in Marshall's and increasingly in later thought, organismic and holistic elements were taken into the system, but until the 1930s the economy was interpreted in analogy to a clockwork moving toward a balance. The mover in this system was the profit motive. Equilibrium was reached when nobody who could influence a situation would have anything to gain from doing so. The equilibrium of the economy as a whole was interpreted as a situation in which total utility for all was maximized. The equilibrium concept was developed first for the single firm, then for an industry, and finally for the whole economy. It started with the individual firm and the individual consumer and ended with an interpretation of a society. The economy was—and still often is—viewed as a *macroanthropos* who can maximize his individual desires. This total equilibrium was supposed to lead to an optimum allocation of resources, brought about by a freely competitive market. It was originally assumed to lead—as in classical thought—to a harmony between individual and social goals. Thus, a mechanistic model was used for the ethical legitimation of the system, although the ethical aspects were hidden behind a screen of value neutrality.

This type of reasoning and its historical base was undermined by a series of socioeconomic events before and after World War I: 1) the growth of big business, monopolies, market power, cartels, *etc.*, in the Western economies, and the countervailing growth of governmental control and unionism; 2) the disruption of the free market system through World War I, the following abandonment of the gold standard, growing protectionism, the manipulation of monetary systems and domestic markets through central banking, tariffs, subsidies, regulation, *etc.*; and 3) the great depression of the 1930s, which undermined belief in the automatic, self-regenerating powers and beneficiality of the free market.

These events led to the disintegration, not of the free enterprise system as we understand it today (in distinction from socialism and communism) but of the nineteenth century free market, its theory, its ideology, and its ethical implications. These trends were reflected in economic theory. *Imperfect* and *monopolistic competition theory* tried to build market power into the neoclassical equilibrium model. Keynesianism abandoned the idea of the self-equilibrating free market and the macroanthropos image of the economy, and opened the system to include the previously exogenous factor of government manipulation on the aggregate level. Imperfect and monopolistic competition theory acknowledged what previous economic reasoning had denied: the existence of market power of large-scale business (oligopoly). The way this was done is a classic example of the amalgamation of theory and faith. A new factor—market power—was changed from an exogenous to an endogenous factor; but this was done in such a way that the basic theoretical and ideological structure of the system, especially its determinate and deterministic character was preserved. In great abbreviation, the following emerged [12]: it was assumed that a firm with market power is able to set the price it charges within the limits of a sliding scale (the famous declining-demand curve). Thus, an increase in the firm's price over the market price would not lead to a complete loss; the firm could still make profits at various prices higher than those of its competitors. Thus, such a firm could "administer" its prices and pursue all sorts of goals, such as a larger market share, smaller but stable long-run profits instead of short-run profit maximization, stability of operations through undisturbed relations with customers, labor force, suppliers, and stockholders and a favorable image in public opinion; it could even pursue political, social, humanitarian, and cultural goals. With such multiplicity of alternative goals, however, economics could not predict, or at least not construct, a final determinate equilibrium position of the firm, the industry, and the economy. The final result of this multiplicity of goals, actions, and reactions of oligopolistic firms with market power would be indeterminate. The economic universe of discourse would not yield a deterministic image. What is at stake here is that a determinate and deterministic system becomes (through the admission of a previously exogenous variable as an endogenous one) an indeterminate system. As *Robert Triffin* puts it: "No doubt there is a sense in which *the solution is always determinate: it all depends on the number of variables considered.* But it is clear that the variables that would have been considered to determine the solution might be of a different type from the ones generally used by pure economics of the equilibrium brand. Such considerations as financial backing, political influence, prestige, psychology, optimistic or pessimistic slant, enterprising or routine-like attitudes in business etc., may well play an overwhelming role in determining the solution" [13].

This passage shows clearly the problem not only of economics, but of any social science that tries to enlarge its horizon by including new, previously excluded variables: the solution may become indeterminate and the ingrained deterministic world-view of the science may be shaken. Triffin is wrong when he believes that the solution must, in the end, always be determinate if only a sufficient number of variables is taken into consideration. The universe is ultimately indeterminate; but he is right that the determinate solution of previous economic theory based on endogenous variables became invalid when new variables were taken into the system. Economic theory could not tolerate this opening, indeterminizing of the system. What imperfect and monopolistic competition theory did was to close the economic universe again; it eliminated the choice that market power gave to oligopolists and firms with market power by assuming that firms would not pursue any other goal but profit maximization at any point in time. Economic reasoning, in spite of its opening the door to noneconomic variables, closed it again by defining the equilibrium position (of firm and industry) merely by defining the equilibrium position (of firm and industry) merely in determinate terms of profit maximization. Technically, the firm is supposed to produce an output at which marginal cost equals marginal revenue; the actions of the firms were still defined in terms of the three traditional variables: revenue, cost, and output, excluding again all other noneconomic variables. Thus, the determinate character of the system was salvaged and with it also some remnant of its beneficial character. The recognition of a host of noneconomic variables, together with the unpredictable choices made by the executives of large corporations, resembled a Heisenbergian indeterminacy situation (the influence of the actors and the actual situation are inextricably intermixed). Clear-cut equilibrium of the firm, defined in terms of profit maximization, returned to a classical Newtonian image of the economic system.

The *Keynesian* system contained ethical and systemic innovations, conditioned by the historical changes in capitalism mentioned above. Ethically, it abandoned the idea of an autonomous, self-regulating market with its harmony of individual and common interests and the beneficiality of its total equilibrium. Crudely expressed, Keynes demonstrated that the whole economy can be in equilibrium with a substantial amount of unemployment. No automatic market forces will necessarily bring about a change toward full employment. Keynes' *General Theory* thus rang the death knell for the libertarian faith in the free market, which already had been undermined by the recognition of market power and oligopoly. He also undermined the Protestant ethic by putting in doubt the value of prudent consumption, thrift, and saving: Savings became the devil in his system, spending the angel. Nobody can earn a cent without somebody spending it, be it even government; just the opposite of Adam Smith's praise of parsimony and his condemnation of prodigality. President Eisenhower went on TV to exhort the people not to postpone the purchase of a car or other substantial expenditures in order to stimulate the lagging economy. The ideological function and ethical change is obvious, and Keynesian theory provided the "scientific" basis for it.

Keynes abandoned the macroanthropos paradigm of the economy, and founded what is called macroeconomics and the thinking in economic aggregates. Not any more is the model of the economy built up from the smallest units (firms, consumers) to large one (industries), and then to the mosaic of the economy as a whole. The theory of the firm and of the industry was largely left untouched by Keynes, so that present-day teaching of economics can superficially combine the neoclassical teachings of microeconomics (firm, industry) with Keynesian aggregative macroeconomics. The latter presented the economy as a whole, as a general system in which saving and spending are interdependent. The three sources of spending, consumers, businesses, and governments, receive what they spend from the same three sources in the form of incomes (wages, interest, rent, and taxes). The spending stream is reduced by the savings of all three groups; in order to increase it, these savings have to be mopped up and spent by any group, in the last resort by governments. (This is not a presentation of the ideas of the *General Theory* of Keynes but a crude version of the economy that emerged from it.)

It should be noted that this system also implied a change in economic goals: from the satisfaction of subjective wants to the creation of jobs (and income whose spending would again create jobs).

The Keynesian system is perhaps the closest approach to a general cybernetic feedback system found in *traditional* economics, although it still retains much of a mechanistic, "hydraulic" character. Its "generality" lies in its thinking in aggregates and in the mutual interdependence, the mutual feedback effect of saving and spending on each other. Its hydraulic mechanistic character lies in the naive "fountain" view of the economy: three faucets of spending can be turned off and on at will, and thus the economy can be fine-tuned and full employment guaranteed (with the help of monetary and fiscal policies).

The Keynesian philosophy was a child of the depression of the 1930s and, in the US, interrelated with the New Deal and its hostility toward corporate power. In view of the continuous discussion, not only among economists but throughout the nation and the world, about the respective roles of *government and business* in the economy, something should be said about its ideological and systemic meaning which has changed with the changing historical conditions. In the eighteenth century, in the formulation of Adam Smith, the attack against government restrictions of economic liberty was a revolutionary idea directed against the remnants of medieval regulation and mercantilistic policies. In the nineteenth century, the ravages of the free market, especially in the field of labor, required the exercise of governmental countervailing power, in the form of social legislation and policies. The free enterprise system could not have survived without governmental social protection [14]. In England and Europe, this countervailing power of the government rested on a relatively independent civil service bureaucracy and on the liberal and labor intelligentsia. In the US, this countervailing governmental power developed only late and slowly, and culminated in the New Deal. In this period, attack on government interference changed from an orginally revolutionary idea to an apologetics for business. Today much of the attack on government is a screen for big business. The government is largely under its influence; but it is convenient to blame it for the misfortunes and take the credit for the blessings of the economy.

Keynesian thought after World War II, embraced the ideology of *continuous economic growth*, which I prefer to call *growth-mania* or *GNP-fetishism*. This again reflects a shift in values of an ideological nature.

Neoclassical and marginalist thought—reflecting the individualistic subjectivism of the late nineteenth century—considered the maximization of total social utility as the *summum bonum* of the economy, brought about by the competitive free market. Partly under the impact of the Great Depression, this approach had to be abandoned; it was based purely on faith and ideology, especially because any measurement of total social utility, and intangible psychological magnitude, is impossible. The goals of the economy were, in theory and practice, changed from subjective, psychic satisfactions to goals of seemingly massive concreteness: an ever-increasing annual aggregate output (GNP or Gross National Product). Until 1970 the post-World War II period was dominated by the belief that, without any changes in the basic structure of the prevailing big business enterprise systems (combined with skillful governmental manipulation by monetary and fiscal policy and theory) depressions could be avoided, the business cycle eliminated, and *an affluent economy with full employment* achieved, which could guarantee infinite economic growth, *i.e.*, continuously rising standards of living.

But the belief in a *permanent economy* of abundance led to a questioning of our traditional economic values and goals. The ideal of unending economic growth, of forever increasing production and consumption, did not make sense once affluence is reached. Relative abundance has narrowed the gap between production and "needs" to such an extent that continuous growth appears as miserly greed and as an irrational compulsion to collect more and more, regardless of its usefulness. Affluence makes the *quantity* of acquisition and production less important, and the *quality* more important. This may force upon us the realization of a *hierarchy* and *balance* in the satisfaction of "lower" and "higher" needs related to different dimensions of human existence. More production of material goods and services conducive to comfort may be detrimental to the satisfaction of "higher," noneconomic needs such as love, friendship, silence, solitude, contemplation, aesthetic and religious experience, community, and environment. This poses serious problems in an economy seemingly dependent on continuous material growth and expansion.

The *affluent economy* raises once more the moral problem of distribution (social justice). It was pushed into the background in the free market eonomy, where inequality was supposed to be necessary to stimulate initiative. The problem was also neglected because of the mistaken assumption that the growth of the "cake" increases everybody's "slice" and makes superfluous any concern with a more equal (or more just) distribution. Our present socioeconomic system brings affluence to the majority, but tends to deprive certain racial, occupational and religious groups of its blessings. These stagnant pools of poverty remain outside the mainstream of economic life and do not benefit from mere aggregate growth. A moral question arises for the affluent majority, which has to overcome economic self-interest to provide for the poor minority. This is a unique situation in history because, in the past, the poor were always a large majority set against a small group of privileged people. The "war against poverty" is too recent to form convincing proof of a pervasive sense of moral obligation toward the poor minorities. Techniques to solve this problem have been developed: monetary and fiscal policies under the Full Employment Act, sliding scales of unemployment compensation, a guaranteed minimum income, or simply a guaranteed income for everybody. It is a moral and a political question whether these methods will be used in a democracy with majority rule.

The seemingly infinite expansion of the affluent society has become a myth, destined to justify the existing mixed economy dominated by the ruling alliance of the business, military, and political elite who manipulated the mass organizations of business, labor, and government. It served to "sell" the new collectivistic economic system to its participants by promising everyone increasing employment opportunities combined with rising incomes. GNP-fetishism was the ideology that replaced the faith in the free market, thus justifying the existing mixed economy with its monetary and fiscal instruments of manipulation wielded by a government allied with big business. This ideology fulfilled an important function of legitimation of the present system after the faith in the free market was badly shaken, the Chicago School and the opinions of the present administration notwithstanding.

This ideology in turn was undermined by the new growing natural and artificial *scarcities* and the *negative* effects of the affluent growth economy that were uncovered by the new ecological movement of the 1960s. Some economists replaced the term "goods" by the term "bads," and talked about the cancer of economic growth. The question of the *limits of growth* was brought to everybody's attention by the events of the 1970s, such as the oil embargo, the shortfall of harvests, the constant spread of malnutrition and starvation, and the shortage of industrial raw materials because of physical scarcity or cartel practices. Through one of the Hegelian ironies of history, the image of affluence and the image of ultimate scarcity moved economic thought and policy recommendations into the same direction. Affluence forced us to reexamine our life style and to shift emphasis from quantity to quality. It also revived the concern with distribution away from aggregate growth. The idea of the *limits of growth* (Club of Rome) and of the "spaceship earth" (Boulding) pointed in the same direction: if we cannot expand production indefinitely *what* we produce is more important than how much we produce; the emphasis shifts to quality, durability, and necessity. And if the total supply is limited, distribution becomes more important than production. For psychological and for ecological reasons a new paradigm of a so-called *steady state economy* (also called the *stationary state*) is in the process of being developed in economics [15]. This model shows all the traits of a general systems theory. It views the economy as an "ecosystem which contains the total stock of wealth and people as mutually dependent components. The ecosystem imports energy from outer space (sun) and exports waste heat to outer space. The stock of wealth consists of matter and energy. According to the second law of thermodynamics energy cannot be recycled, and matter only by using more energy (and matter). In order to preserve the stock of resources, the volume of production has to be kept as low as possible, and goods have to be as durable and long-lived as possible" [15, p. 18].

This new paradigm leads to a host of "ideological" consequences: a simpler standard of life, more equal distribution, more production of nonphysical goods: services and leisure. We have to move from a "cowboy economy" to a "spacemen economy" (Boulding). The goals must be protection, stability, and quality, instead of production, growth, and quantity [15, p. 20].

Because of the shift to services and leisure, noneconomic and less externalized life styles will have to develop, such as contemplation, meditation, communal activity; anything that does not use up matter and nonhuman energy. The idea of Consciousness III, developed by Charles Reich [16] is closely interrelated to the paradigm of a steady-state economy.

That this paradigm is again of a normative, visionary kind—a symbolization of faith and hope, and a way for individuals to become attuned to the new historical situation—can be of little doubt. The "steady-state" is as much an ideal as the "general system." General system thinking, and any new paradigm in economics and the social sciences will benefit if we have the strength to acknowledge "symbolization" as an essential aspect of thought. General system thinking will have to be enlarged again, taking into account the openness, the mystery of the universe, and the human needs for a unifying symbolism and a new hierarchy of values, a new ethos. Exogenous variables of a spiritual nature will have to become part of the calculus of public administration to make it receptive to a dimension of the human condition hitherto neglected in modern social thought.

NOTES AND REFERENCES

1. Schoeffler, Sidney. *The Failure of Economics: A Diagnostic Study*, p. 45. Cambridge: Harvard University Press, 1955.
2. Marshall, Alfred. *Principles of Economics*, 8th ed., p. 323. London: Macmillan, 1920.
3. von Bertalanffy, Ludwig. "General Systems Theory as Integrating Factor in Contempory Science and Philosophy." *Proceedings* of the 14th International Congress of Philosophy, Vienna, September, 1968, vol. 2, p. 336.
4. Bertalanffy. *Problems of Life*, p. 180. Quoted from F. W. Matson, *The Broken Image*. New York: George Braziller, 1964.
5. Commoner, Barry. "Frail Reeds in a Marsh World." *Natural History* 77(1969): 45, in a symposium, "The Unforeseen International Ecological Boomerang."
6. Voegelin, Eric. *Order and History*, vol. 1, p. 1. Baton Rouge, La.: Louisiana State University Press, 1956. Italics mine.
7. Tillich, Paul. *Systematic Theology*, vol. 2, p. 7. Chicago: University of Chicago Press, 1957.
8. Maslow, A. H. *Motivation and Personality*, p. 88. New York: Harper & Brothers, 1954.
9. Tillich. *Systematic Theology*, vol. 1, p. 102.
10. Mason, E. S. "The Apologetics of Managerialism." *Journal of Business* of the University of Chicago 30(1958).
11. Weisskopf, W. A. *The Psychology of Economics*. Chicago: University of Chicago Press, 1955. Reissued in Midway Reprints, 1975. Also *Alienation and Economics*. New York: E. P. Dutton, 1971. Reprinted by Dell Publishing, New York, 1973.
12. Weisskopf. *Alienation and Economics*. pp. 118 *ff*.
13. Triffin, Robert. *Monopolistic Competition and General Equilibrium Theory*, p. 77. Cambridge: Harvard University Press, 1940.
14. Polanyi, Karl. *The Great Transformation*. New York: Farrar & Reinhart, 1944.
15. *Toward a Steady Economy*. Edited by Herman A. Daly. San Francisco: W. H. Freeman, 1973.
16. Reich, Charles. *The Greening of America*, ch. 9. New York: Random House, 1970.

3

Organizational Ethics: Rules, Creativity, and Idealism

T. Edwin Boling
Wittenberg University

INTRODUCTION

The exposure of corruption in American government and the revelation that bribes were paid to foreign officials and businessmen are forcing new interest in an old subject—ethics! Faced with a "boom in ethics" [21], business and government are under general condemnation for what one writer has called *moral abhorrence* [61, p. 193]. Provoked by recent scandals, the present storm follows a gradual rise in moral anxiety produced by consumerism, environmentalism, and aversion to big organizations. This anxiety is represented by social movements that press for social responsibility; unequivocally, according to Max Ways, managers, *i.e.*, persons concerned mainly with carrying out prescribed organizational goals [43], are not prepared to deal with the situation.

From the business perspective, "social responsibility" is seen as a major concern for management and the public [16]. Society defines the quality of life, and business is expected to act as a corporate citizen toward the solution of general social problems. Ethics may be identified as a major subarea of the general focus upon social responsibility.

Management in the public sector has not escaped the pressure, especially in the area of ethics. Like business managers, government executives are expected to influence and to execute policies that generally improve the quality of life. Also, among public administrators as among businessmen, serious ethical problems have arisen due to conflicts of loyalty and involvement beyond the job. Individual judgments have become biased, and motivation for performance has been reduced [26].

The traditional rationale for public administrators, like that of business managers, is more efficient, economical management. Today, however, this traditional approach is being seriously pressured to include more emphasis on ethical concerns. Both the public administrator and the corporate executive, in the face of complicated ethical issues, are finding it necessary to expand their knowledge about social ethics [23].

ETHICS IN POLITICAL HISTORY

Corruption in politics is as old as bureaucratic governments. Hamer indicates that bribery was evident among officials, judges, and priests in the history of the ancient Egyptians, Babylonians, and Hebrews. He continues this historical review, stating [28, p. 382]:

> With the rise of Christianity and the Western tradition of thought that basic human nature was sinful and corrupt, the belief spread that any mortals with authority would seek to maximize their power and wealth. . . . Christian leaders . . . assumed that rulers would use their powers for self advancement, and this thought became an accepted doctrine under the absolute monarchies and pervasive papal power of the Middle Ages.

From the historical perspective, the American founding fathers were influenced to construct a government of checks and balances; corruption would be checked and controlled, if not eliminated. Dvorin and Simmons [19, p. 34] have characterized the ethical nature of this government and the ethical responsibility of those who administer it:

> Lacking indigenous values . . . the public bureaucracy acts as a mirror of values held dearly elsewhere . . . the first priority of public administration is . . . to begin developing an ethical framework based upon fundamental and irreducible values.

Some would question the priority given values and the ethical framework, yet decisions in the government of a free society cannot be separated from ethical considerations. The very principles upon which democracy rests demand that the development of an ethical framework should precede the exercise of power.

In the American society, belief that ethics should hold influence over power has been a generally accepted rule. Americans have tended to believe Plato's contention that a leader with the knowledge of "good" has immunity from corruption [28]. Yet, throughout our history we have witnessed a series of scandals involving the White House, the Congress, the courts, and governments at state and local levels. (Hamer's work explicates a number of these.) The ideology of ethics over power has been sorely tried.

Corruption is very much a recurring theme, forcing ethics to become a pressing theme of public interest. Various branches of government repeatedly investigate themselves and one another. Dealings by public officials and employees, often quite legal, become exciting newspaper copy. Committees for establishing and policing ethical codes are appointed.   Legislation demanding ethical practices is enacted *ad infinitum*.

In the face of such a history, each generation seems to view its scandals as the greatest. This assumption is borne out in the events of the present decade. Simmons and Dvorin [54] depict this view in a recent textbook where they call the 1970s a "decade of disillusionment." "Watergate" is described as a sordid, disheartening episode of political and moral corruption. The major crimes of the era are enumerated. A president threatened with impeachment was forced to resign, becoming the first president of the United States to be so disgraced. Key staff aides were prosecuted, convicted, and sentenced to lengthy prison terms. The Watergate litany of constitutional abuses extended into key agencies of government—Central Intelligence Agency, Federal Bureau of Investigation, Internal Revenue Service, *etc.* For Simmons and Dvorin, there is an obvious erosion of faith in the quality of public leadership and in the effectiveness of government. Therefore, those in public administration are forced to face a future of marked ideological unease.

Although the above authors speak of an erosion of faith, Presthus [47] states that attitude studies from the 1920s through the 1960s show public employment as rather unprestigious. These studies, as well as more recent ones [34], indicate a public skepticism regarding the honesty of government officials and employees.

The evidence of long-time skepticism and lack of trust in public personnel is quite strong, and certainly supports the contention of Rohr [48] that we would be unwise to focus too much attention upon the Watergate scandal as the major foundation for a call to transformation. Surely, in the light of historical evidence, such statements as the following, from Presthus, overemphasize [47, p. 239]: "Largely as a result of the Watergate scandal, there is an emerging concern in personnel administration with integrity." Actually, the concern is older than Watergate. One example of a slightly earlier concern is Executive Order 11222. Issued by President Johnson during the mid-1960s, this order prescribed standards of ethical conduct for all persons in government. The order states in part [30, p. 100]:

Employees (will) avoid any . . . action which might result in or create the appearance of

1. Using public office for private gain;
2. Giving preferential treatment to any organization or person;
3. Impeding Government efficiency or economy;
4. Losing complete independence or impartiality of action;
5. Making a Government decision outside official channels; or
6. Affecting adversely the confidence of the public in the integrity of the Government.

Obviously, the Watergate episode is clear evidence that the dictates of Executive Order 11222 proved less than effective. Why?

The answer to this question is the primary purpose of this essay. In pursuit of that purpose, a number of specific suggestions will be made toward explaining the present confusion about ethics. A system of thought based upon organization theory will be developed for clarifying the general confusion about ethics in public administration. Finally, illustrations and suggestions will be presented that may provide more effective and creative direction for ethical reform. Beyond the primary purpose outlined here, this essay will also propose a model for normative enrichment in organizations. The themes developed here will be used to construct a model that calls for a democratically determined clarification and enforcement of rules. The model also urges maintaining a creative quality in organizational life that will effect change toward high ideals.

Because of the continuous change of elected officials, stability in government often depends upon the work of career administrators whose influence upon those elected to office is inestimable. As with the practice of efficient, economical management, responsibility for ethical standards and moral practices also rests heavily upon the public career person. The public administrator needs ethical wisdom for himself, for his transient colleagues, and even for his elected masters [3]. The priority of this responsibility may be questioned, yet ethics in government has not been emphasized effectively, and career administrators have not been recognized for their roles in ethical leadership. Too often identified as a "servant," the public administrator is a leader. For this role, relative to ethics, one needs effective preparation.

Beyond informal training, how does one gain this preparation? Armstrong and Graham feel that undergraduate education should introduce persons to pragmatic ethical codes, that professional training should provide instruction in justifying ethical choices (both practically and rationally), and that the organizations for which people work should make ethics explicit.

In summary, a review of ethics in political history reveals that the "problem of ethics" is by no means new. It is neither peculiar to one government nor concentrated in one form of political system. Corrupt practices in social institutions are not confined to single generations; indeed, there is much evidence for questioning an evolutionary improvement in ethics. Not only is the violation of social ethics a problem, but social response to that violation is also a problem. Little or no movement away from corrupt practices marks a system that has not devised a way to deal with the problem of ethics effectively. To examine these assertions, we turn now to a review of how public administration establishes ethical behavior. First, since there is considerable confusion about what is meant by "ethics," we introduce that confusion. Later, we offer a clarification. Second, "ethical individualism" is presented as management's primary approach to ethical systems. This simplistic orientation is identified as the force behind ethical confusion.   Third, ethical legalism, often the excuse for less rigorous ethical programs, is presented as a questionable form of ethics. Finally, flowing from this review, we offer a critique of ethical inadequacy.

BASES FOR ETHICAL CONFUSION

The term "ethic" seems such a simple concept. Almost anyone recognizes the word. Most will quickly give some statement of what it means as a language symbol. Of course, the symbol stands for ideas that Boulding [14] feels are so simple that man arrived at many of them quite early in his history. Although man may have arrived at the knowledge of good and evil quite early, putting the knowledge to use has been most difficult, a fallacy not unrelated to the vague intellectual content of ethical concepts.

Conceptual Confusion

From a practical perspective, managers admit that the subject of ethics is "a difficult one." Ethics seems to be identified as both rules (law) and standards for behavior (ideals). Consequently, some will acclaim high ethical patterns when they meet the law, and feel no need to stretch toward an ideal.

Among academicians confusion may be even more paramount because of the diverse definitions of ethics. A cursory review of the literature demonstrates this intense diversity. Ethics is defined as rules of conduct [29], quality of human relationships [11], practical science [60], behavioral science [4], a branch of philosophic inquiry [37], criteria of judgment [14], normative standards of conduct [9], *etc*. One scholar even contends that ethics does not exist [62]. What at first thought seemed simple is actually quite complex, even complicated. Berkley illustrates this complexity in noting that ethics and values can conflict. Some values hold persons to be objects for manipulation and exploitation, while ethics views persons as entities to be respected. To confuse the situation even more, much of the literature does not distinguish between values and ethics at all.

Our purpose here is not to unravel the complexities of philosophical thought. Although an understanding of ideologies and their organizational contexts from the perspective of science is important, we are most interested here in developing practical knowledge, and will not, therefore, attempt an extensive investigation into political philosophy and humanistic psychology. Rather, in the limited space available, we will seek some clarification of conceptual meaning.

Charlesworth, in a volume of the *American Academy Annals* that contained several essays about ethics, supported conceptual clarification and the practical worth of ethics [15]:

Ethics is sometimes defined as the doctrine of moral principles, sometimes as the science of human conduct, and sometimes as moral philosophy. Sometimes it is categorized as one of the four classical divisions of general philosophy.... Unfortunately, the word "ethics" has been captured and prostituted by interest groups, but we must be sure to recognize that "guild" ethics are not ethics, but have been deliberately misnamed, like "Fair Trade" laws. And we must insist that in discussions of ethics the word "public" means the general and not the pertinent public.

Thus, Charlesworth leads us beyond the mere academic definition to the way ethics is used. Perhaps it is inevitable that what is defined so broadly and differently will also be applied diversely.

Ethical Individualism

An extreme individualistic, ethical orientation is an inadequate base for ethical behavior and ideals; yet, this is precisely the most common orientation in business and government.

Since the usual method for identifying moral or ethical data is an intuitive one, it is assumed that everyone knows what a moral judgment is [6]. Intuitive approaches have been found inadequate however, because the mere keeping of rules is made a basis for social life. Rules are often kept without understanding their purposes. Thus, with intuitiveness comes habitual action, and individuals are expected to "draw distinctions between right and wrong, good and bad, all the time, without being cognizant of the criteria we are employing" [6, p. 9].

The intuitive approach centers in an individual philosophy akin to that found in Judaeo-Christian and American civil religions. Fox [22] explains that there is a theistic perspective in management ethics that is based upon Biblical tradition and personal obligation to God. Even with an acknowledgment that managers fear a "Sunday-schoolish" orientation, a recent business article stressed moving the ethics-management balance back toward medieval thought where responsibility to society and God were given priority [1]. Although Fox focused on business, a similar approach is very prominent in the literature for public administrators and public service employees. Graham declares that the basis for the moral code of Western civilization is the Ten Commandments, and is, thereby, the basis for morality in American politics. He states that Christians inherited the Ten Commandments from the Hebrews and "each generation laboriously and painfully discovers the validity of this ancient revealed truth" [27, p. 61]. To a question about whether these commandments govern the conduct of public officials and others in public life, Graham responds:

All civilized men recognize that it must. The necessity is not challenged, and the reason is obvious. The code is the basis for group unity and stability, and the larger the group to be kept together as one, the more important it is that the code be observed by men in official position. . . . If officials are not faithful to the moral code, the law becomes unpredictable, justice loses its meaning, private interests replace the public interest in administration, uncertainty and resentment mount, the basis for loyalty fades, and disorder leads to chaos. . . . Without public servants of integrity, governments cannot be strong for long.

The emphasis is that a particular code, namely the Ten Commandments, contains the revelation of truth upon which individuals are to act.

Although the Ten Commandments are mostly individualistic, Graham [27, p. 63] asks rhetorically, "Does the moral code also govern group conduct?" Again he answers:

. . . if individuals can do through an organization what it is wrong for them to do as individuals, then the effectiveness of the moral code is destroyed and the unity of society is jeopardized. There can be no escape from the necessity of subjecting organized activities to the same moral restraints that are imposed upon individual efforts. The corporation, the trade association, the union, the farm organization, the party, and the government itself are all morally obligated—if the moral basis for the unity and stability of society is to be continued.

Coming even closer to Christianity, Graham contends that organizations and powerful persons have a universal obligation to yet a higher standard; he states [27, p. 64]:

Old Testament moral law . . . does not provide sufficient restraint or . . . guidance. . . . As discretion goes beyond the law, so must moral standards go beyond simple negations . . . men in authority must be imbued with a positive devotion to the welfare of their fellows which more nearly approaches the level of the great commandment—love the Lord and love one's neighbor as one's self. . . .

Golembiewski takes up the theistic theme, as opposed to positivistic determinism, from the organizational perspective, detailing that men can be free in organizations by the aid of a limited set of values derived from the Judaeo-Christian tradition. The idea that Christian ethics and the ethics of the market-place have to be independent, Golembiewski declares to be a "powerful folk myth" [24, p. 8]. The Judaeo-Christian ethic, by Golembiewski's estimation, will contribute to a high organizational yield and output, and will also satisfy members of the organization.

The theistic approach to organizational ethics is supported strongly by American civil religion, a secular religiosity expressed in a common set of beliefs, symbols, and rituals. Golembiewski identifies this phenomenon as a "quasi-religious spirit" [24, p. 39]. At the heart of this quasi-religious spirit is the idea that America is the promised land, dedicated to order, law, and justice, and destined to a divine mission. Common to this ideology is a trust in individualism that is demonstrated by a concern with personal integrity, individual achievement, *etc.* [51].

Civil religion does not identify God, the Bible, or the church as the source of ethical behavior. It does not reduce ethical behavior to a set of rules. Instead, ethical practices are supposed to arise out of individual characteristics shaped by commitment to religious, social, and philosophical issues. At the point of decision, one is to be guided by *his own* moral sense [49]. Much of civil religion is no doubt derived from Protestantism. For example, thrift, hard work, and sober living are shared by both the Protestant ethic and American civil religion.

Philosophically, ethical individualism views the person as the only unit of real worth; the group is the means whereby the individual expresses himself [53]. The individual is not dependent upon the group; in fact, the very notion of society as represented in law, custom, and tradition signifies a trait that is less important than individuals. This de-emphasis of the group and strong promotion of the individual contributes rather strongly to the idea that each person gains his worth by outdistancing others, *i.e.*, competitive success. Most often in Western culture this ideology has led to the identification of success with making money and the reduction of one's neighbors to the position of opponents [53]. Such an ethic, Golembiewski says, "sanctions competition by indiviuals for individual gain and unbridled competition at that" [24, p. 38].

Humanistic psychology has also made major contributions to ethical individualism [48]. The individual person is viewed as important over his career and his roles. Administrators, from this perspective, must rely upon an individual system of values—a personal sense of justice and fair play [51]. Presthus, confronting the notion of responsibility and public interest, concludes that in the end "we are in truth forced to rely upon officials themselves for responsible public administration" [47, p. 410]. In this same pattern, Appleby admonishes individual officials to have "moral purpose and strength" while guarding "social life, [and] carefully avoiding involvements" of a questionable nature [2, p. 220].

This same type of individualism continues to receive high marks in public administration today. In an award-winning manuscript (honored by the American Society of Public Administration), Wakefield assesses "where we are in terms of ethics and the public service" [59, p. 661]. She defines a system of values that reaches back to Judaeo-Christian tradition; the system rests on individual responsibility, the primary and ultimate source of public service ethics. Demands and external controls are only secondary supports for individual responsibility, the first line of defense against unethical behavior.

Wakefield contends that public administration has experienced a steady ethical decline in recent years. The decline parallels a number of institutional trends—change, specialization, and decentralization. Reliance upon external controls has fallen short of expectations; internal controls (*i.e.*, value systems) are advanced as the most opportune means for correcting the ethical situation.

Although it has been rather infrequent, ethical individualism has received some criticism for its inappropriate approach to ethics. In a cross-cultural study of personal value systems among managers, England [20] found that there was large individual differences in personal values. Some managers showed a pragmatic orientation (*e.g.*, do ideas work?), others were more ethical-moral (*e.g.*, is an idea right or wrong?), while still others were affective (*e.g.*, is an idea pleasant?). The managers were also found to be different by relationship to their organizations. Some were more strongly committed to the organization, and others had a greater concern for individual achievement or other personal goals. For example, Gouldner [25] identifies two kinds of individual roles among members of organizations: true professionals, who have little loyalty to the employing organization, a high commitment to skills, and an orientation to an external reference group; and nonprofessionals, who have a high degree of loyalty to the organization, a low commitment to skills, and an orientation to an internal reference group. England also found that personal value systems were rigid and tended not to change over time. Personal values influenced job performances; the most successful managers were those who favored achievement and interaction with others, while the least successful associated with a static, protected environment, and were rather passive in relation to the system around them. Reflecting the competitive, individualistic orientation, most of the managers held such values as ambition, ability, and skill. Trust, loyalty, and honor tended to be less important.

After a review of values in managerial decision-making, Walton [60, p. 125] made the following assessment of ethical individualism:

> . . . a personal ethic devised from traditional religious or moral codes is, of itself, too simplistic an approach to the problem of professional behavior in a large organization. Loftiness of purpose and purity of motive are insufficient bases on which to rest an ethical system totally adequate to midtwentieth century organizational realities.

The continuity of corrupt behavior in organizations, as represented in historical accounts, seems conclusive proof for the failure of ethical individualism. Whether advanced by religion, philosophy, or management theory, a dependence upon individual intuitiveness for moral action or ethical ideals seems designed for the continuance of corruption, confusion, and conflict.

The nature of organizations makes ethical individualism inadequate for complex organizations in a changing society. Organizations are interactive systems. The behavior of the whole cannot be derived by summing the individual parts. The presence of integrity within each individual in the organization does not mean that the organization will act with integrity. The organization's integrity must be determined and maintained as a separate ideal.

Beyond the fact that individuals cannot be summed into a total pattern is the simple reality of individual difference. Social indoctrination produces unique personalities as well as a variety of ethical orientations. In complex societies, as opposed to simple societies, the definition of right and wrong is quite diverse. It is because of this diversity that ethical individualism is an inadequate base for managerial ethics. Ethical individualism assumes that persons (whether employees, employers, or clients) have common religious beliefs and social values. Supposedly, this commonness leads to similar behavior, *etc*. In reality, religion, values, and subsequent behaviors can be quite diverse, especially for persons of different statuses and ethnic origins.

The complex nature of organizations and individual diversity demand that ethics be recognized as an organizational property. This is not to say that individuals do not have personal values, morals, or ethics. Rather, such a recognition may cause us to confront the conflicting demands of the individual and the organization in a new way, clarifying ethics for both.

Ethical Legalism

Although questionable as ethics per se, another inadequate base for managerial ethics is called "ethical legalism" [53]. This claim to ethical concern is represented by the well-worn phrase, "Our organization abides by the law," which by interpretation often means, "We are ethical." Compliance is identified with what is "right in this sense is a legal code. Ethical legalism reflects an inviolable or sacred view of law, which is taken literally, precisely, or as an allegiance to principle. Hence, the role of law in the management dimensions of human societies is to define the facts of social situations, to establish means for resolving contention and conflict, and to institute compromise toward a provisional solution of problems. In this manner, law sets rules for guiding specified behavior and applies sanctions for violations.

Laws cannot begin to prescribe all that moral conduct and ethical ideals should be for everyone in all situations. Indeed, morals and ethics serve as the leading edge of the law [36], often demanding behavior beyond that prescribed by law. It is possible for one to abide by the law in its fullest and to remain unethical or immoral. The question of ethics is not directed toward the social, cultural, and personal impact of having broken rules, which may be either moral or legal. In the strictest sense, ethical legalism falls short of being an ethical approach to behavior.

Summary

The above bases for ethical confusion contribute to the current diversity of moral opinion and ethical uncertainty in organizations. We lack a common "ethics" vocabulary; contributions to that vocabulary are sometimes incongruent. In practice, there are few well-defined concepts to fall back upon. Ethics in organizations is synonomous with indeterminancy and vagueness, an area to be avoided. It is small wonder that a participant in a recent executive development program should write in his evaluation of the program, "Too much time was given to ethics" (that time being 3 hours in a program which totaled more than 60 hours). This is not a phenomenon of practitioners alone. Sherwood [52] notes that courses that deal with ethics are hard to find and sparsely populated in most professional graduate education programs in public administration. The extreme amount of public attention now being given ethics in business and public service makes this lack of interest suspect. Certainly, the confusion about ethics indicates that *too little* time has been, and is being, given to ethics.

A SOCIAL-ORGANIZATION APPROACH TO ETHICS

The number, size, and power of organizations have increased drastically in the past few decades. Reflected in this growth are immensely more powerful national, state, and local governments that reach further into the lives of individuals. Even single departments within governments have multiplied and expanded into huge bureaucracies. Boulding identifies this phenomenon of expansion as an "organizational revolution," stating that in political, economic, and ethical thinking there is as much as a 100-year lag. Specifically, he says [14, p. 4]: "We are still . . . thinking in terms of a society in which organizations are rather small and weak, and in which the family is the dominant institution." Citing numerous economical, sociological, psychological, and political problems that need to be investigated, Boulding notes the importance of recognizing government as an organization not essentially different in structure and problems from other organizations. He also contends that ethics is a major component of organizations. In support of Boulding's emphasis upon expansion and the significance of ethics, Bernstein [12] identifies the expansion of governmental organization as a major factor in the problems of ethical conduct; Graham [26] contends that, because of the growing size and complexity of governments, ethical obligations will be difficult to maintain.

The Organizational Base

More than 25 years ago, Chester Barnard [5] expressed concern with the role of morality in the maintenance of organizations. Based upon a social-science approach to morality, Barnard saw the limitations of personal, Judaeo-Christian ethics and advocated the necessity of *organizational norms* of ethical quality. It was necessary for individual and organizational interests to coincide

Barnard's ideas, although projecting an organizational dimension, seem bound by ethical individualism. Strother's recent suggestion that we harken back to Barnard for theoretical implications toward ethical codes could well mean that organizational ethics would remain caught in the morass of contradiction and confusion [57].

Barnard's primary moral concern, both in practice and in theory, is *executive codes of conduct*, not *organizational norms* [45]. In spite of his emphasis upon cooperative systems, he sees codes of conduct in the last analysis as being created by moralistic executives (supermen) while workers (subordinates) cooperatively grant or accept this authority. Barnard's organizational ethics are no more than personal codes applicable to the collective through model leaders. Recent efforts toward establishing "association" codes [40] seem quite similar to Barnard's thesis. These codes do not cut across organizations; rather, professionals are models of behavior. Like Judaeo-Christian ideology, these codes call for moral leaders to be followed because of their "model" behavior. Thus, moral "rules" are made authoritative through the power of charasmatic leaders.

In contrast to Barnard and ethical individualism, a more appropriate organizational ethic is implied in the theory of Simon [55]. Simon recognizes that individuals have personal goals that do not always coincide with the goals of the organization. Individuals make decisions based upon personal standards, but organizations can control the standards and define the situations in which decisions are made. To shape behavior, the organization determines the "premises of decision-making." These premises are found in the vocabulary, the structure of communication, the rules or regulations, and the standard programs of the organization.

Individual choices take place in an environment of premises that are not determined accidentally; rather, the enviroment is planned and highly structured. Although individuals may modify the environment, modification is mostly an organizational matter, *e.g.*, organizations put individuals in psychological environments that force adaptation of decisions to organizational objectives. Through training and indoctrination, individuals are led to make decisions that comply with organizational goals. Simon concludes [55, p. 102]:

> ... the individual must in his decisions be subject to the influence of the organized group.... His decisions must not only be the product of his own

mental processes, but also reflect the broader considerations to which it is the function of the organized group to give effect.

Simon's theory of organization implies that decision-making will set the stage for, and give direction to, moral development, especially in societies of diverse, complex values. This theory rests in logical positivism with the organization as the empirical referent.

The people dimension of organizations, and more specifically their ethical behavior, is captured quite creatively in the works of social psychologists Piaget [46] and Kohlberg [32]. Simon insisted upon social psychological principles— that behavior persists on the basis of the internalization of rules and expectations placed in human minds by repositories of fundamental social values (*e.g.*, the family, church, and school). Beyond such primary influences, however, Simon's major concern was with the interpersonal mechanism of formal organizations. It is the social psychologists who give greater insight into individual development in social groups. Both "repositories of values" and "formal organizations" are mechanisms external to the individual, and are involved in the determination of individual behavior. The theories of Piaget and Kohlberg point out how groups affect morals and ethics.

Piaget theorizes that types of individual morality derive from the types of social structures in which persons are involved. In explanation, he holds that there are two models of morality. The first, *heteronomous* morality, is associated with children between four and eight years of age. The second, *autonomous*, is linked to children older than eight years. Heteronomous morality designates a moral code subject to adult authority. Norms are perceived as immutable facts, and immoral acts are defined as such in terms of adult sanctions. Hence, wrong is identified relative to adult punishment with regard to context or intention. The individual respects authority and his obedient attitude leads him to perceive moral values as absolute and universal and to accept the notion that justice is served by punishment.

Autonomous morality, on the other hand, identifies norms as artifacts of group agreements that are subject to change by the group. Norms are essentially instruments of cooperative action. Emphasis upon justice shifts from punishment to restitution, a matter of reciprocal rights and obligations. Hence, moral development is more than internalization of adult standards, it is also cognition in the social, peer context. Thus, autonomous moral judgments are internalized on the basis of *cooperative social relations*.

Although Piaget's subjects were children, it seems probable that his types of morality may also apply to adults in organizations. This probability is enhanced because socialization does not end with childhood; it is a lifelong process. On the one hand, some adults in organizations are heteronomous in moral action.

They yield to authority and fear punishment. Morality—or immorality—is defined relative to immutable rules; like children, obedience relates to being watched and being caught. On the other hand, some members or organizations may see rules as situational and subject to change by a peer group. Moral judgments aren't so rigid; specific rules aren't always internalized; rather, one develops a propensity for moral action based upon the ability to think and act autonomously.

Given the necessity for autonomous moral action in a world that increasingly depends upon "situation ethics," organizations may expect more effective moral decisions if they develop from cooperative social relations, or from what Kohlberg calls "social contract."

Kohlberg has pursued methods of inquiry similar to those of Piaget. Attempting to identify morals as separate from values, Kohlberg's primary concern has been with the study of *precepts for action*, or morality. In the context of one's environment, the acceptance of authority leads to a collective self-discipline. Morals are distinguished by the notion of obligation, and are represented by such terms as "ought" and "should," as opposed to value statements of preference. Although Kohlberg's methods are applicable to adults, like Piaget's, his studies have been conducted with children.

Problem situations are put to subjects who are asked to resolve a dilemma; from the resolution, Kohlberg identifies the individual's place relative to a stage of moral development, based upon six stages of developmental morality outlined by Kohlberg. Rules are first conceived as dependent upon external compulsions and punishments (stage 1); later, rules are instrumental to rewards (stage 2); then, rules are used for gaining social approval (stage 3); next, rules enable upholding an ideal order (stage 4); and finally, rules give way to articulation of collective principles (stages 5 and 6). Successively, these stages may be internalized by subjects.

Kohlberg's approach is significant because it attempts to differentiate morals and values and because of the stages of development. By this theory, individualistic morality evolves from one which is internalized from adults to one that is held on the basis of cooperative social relations in a peer group or other social system.

Cooperative social relations project organizations toward equity and democracy. This innovative departure from tradition has been suggested in the "new public administration" [38]. Beyond the workplace, which has tended to be autocratic and authoritarian, Americans have lived under a democratic system. At work, individuals are often frustrated with autocratic leaders, rules, *etc*. Opposing factions arise in both a formal and informal manner. Life in an organization depends upon synthesis, adjustment, compromise, and resolution. Along this range of techniques are mediational and democratic approaches [54]. For some time now, public and private organizations have been shifting toward mediational techniques, where decisions are made cooperatively; a few organizations are moving toward participative democracy, where there are restraints upon hierarchy and encouragement for maximum participation from all members.

Communal problem-solving does not require unanimity; consensus may be reached through majority rule where the majority requires those who dissent to conform. This is the essence of democracy. In the end, contractual association leads to the experience of yielding by democratic necessity to the will of the majority. In such an environment, individual worth is not demeaned, and group association is highly esteemed.

In the normative realm, traditional management views the rules of arbitration as sufficient for the control of subordinates. If law is an insufficient means from which to derive moral and ethical conduct, however, rules of arbitration are also inadequate. Therefore, organizations need new approaches to normative control. Such an approach is possible through the holistic notions of democracy. In fact, the experiments of participative democracy in some industrial organizations have proven quite successful in the normative area. Individuals from the entire organization have participated in establishing systems of values and rules; results from these experiments have shown uniformly high product quality, fewer absentees, and virtually no thefts or misuse of property.

In summary, organizations are cooperative social systems. Most organizations have certain moral and ethical expectations prescribed for their members, and management has largely depended upon individual integrity for achieving these expectations. In a changing world, organizations are part of an environment that demands corporate integrity. As individual and corporate integrity are not always synonomous and integrated, organizations are forced to give more attention to that part of their "premises of decision-making" that contains the rules, regulations, and standards for behavior. Since members or organizations may hold conflicting standards, each may need indoctrination into organizational expectations; hence, the need arises for each organization to put its members into psychological environments that force cognitive change and adaptation to the proper ethical objectives. To be sure, no organization can survive if it neglects this procedure relative to productivity. Greater attention to the moral and ethical principles will enhance primary goals.

At any rate, each organization sets its values, morals, and ethics, which may or may not be synonomous with those of other systems. To expect a person's "precepts of action" or morality to accord with the organization values and standards, and to have acceptable autonomous moral action, organizations must first clarify the normative dimension of their systems. It is toward this clarification that we now direct our attention.

The Need for Ethical Clarification

For the purpose of discussing, not to mention revising, an ethical system, we must differentiate between the moral and the ethical. Few persons writing about the ethics of organizations or management seem concerned about this conceptual difficulty. Perhaps a major reason for this lack of concern is the general neglect of ethics by social scientists. Those who have analyzed organizational behavior, developed methods of analysis, typologies, *etc.*, have not clarified that area of organizational life that is normative in character. So far, we have been satisfied with the use of ill-defined, or even undefined, concepts. Scholars and practitioners have followed a similar pattern in this lack of clarification.

Today we hear much about an "ethical" decline in business and government. Professional journals have published numerous practical articles on ethics. Academicians are proposing special programs for training students in ethics in professional schools. Commenting upon the necessity for this emphasis, Presthus states [47, p. 422] :

> . . . we cannot rely upon democratic values to insure that public officials are sensitive to the kinds of issues raised here. Instead, a self-consciously didactic process of education seems to be required. Here, hopefully, new thrust toward extended education and training for public officials will include the patent consideration of normative issues, under some such rubric as "ethics in administration."

Yet a cursory analysis of the present literature directed toward this problem leads to little more than confusion.

The pressure for "ethical" reform is heavy. Congress has adopted a code of ethics for itself and all federal employees [28]. Legislative bodies, committees, and special study groups have extensively studied ethics in the public sector, and have strongly recommended reform. Senator Paul H. Douglas directed a comprehensive study of ethics in government in the early 1950s, and the Association of the Bar of the City of New York conducted an extensive study of etnics in Congress around the turn of the present decade. In spite of recommendations, the problems have not gone away. In other positive action, organizations and professions have adopted "codes of ethics" [29] ; presidents have issued executive orders; proposals for reform have been outlined [29] ; educational programs have been developed and implemented [48] ; and centers for studying and teaching organizational ethics have been funded [8].

Even with such action, businessmen and public service executives are skeptical, and much of the skepticism occurs because codes of ethics are being interpreted as rules legislated to force conformity. What is the difference between new codes and old rules? To many, the new codes seem no more than what already exists.

Skepticism is fed by a lack of clear definition and procedure. We are all aware of an excessive number of rules and often attempt to ignore some of them. Obviously, setting up duplicate rules makes little sense. Establishing more rules and calling them "ethics" is further confusing because the study of ethics reveals that whatever ethics may be, it is not rules or regulatory codes. When bodies such as the Congress or official boards pass rules that stipulate what the behavior of organizational members *will be*, we have rules and not ethics.

Since no organization exists without rules, it seems that the major problem of organizational ethics is not a lack of rules; perhaps the problem is a lack of compliance with rules. Indeed, if a lack of compliance with rules is the problem, then it is a legal problem we face, not an ethical one. Actually, much of what has been called unethical is improperly lableled; it is in fact illegal behavior that by social prescription should carry a clearly defined punishment.

The problem is one of definition, but it certainly is not new, and it clearly remains unresolved. Resolution demands that an organization's normative structure should be separated into its various parts and examined in detail. Such a procedure for examining the morality of political units was suggested by Leys [35] more than 35 years ago. In writing about ethics and social policy, he noted the contention of some that one must go "beyond conscience" to establish political morality. Leys stated that conscience urges respect for "two sorts of values" —a) to respect and conserve good things that already exist, and b) to seek and honor ideals not yet realized [35; p. 273]. Hence, conscience learns to conserve what is valued and to be dissatisfied with the world as it is. Morality, then, is the upholding of values that already exist, while ethics imaginatively creates new values.

More recently, Barnsley, a sociologist, has demonstrated a similar concern for conceptual clarity. He alludes to the separation of much of the terminology that has been used interchangeably. In the context of what Barnsley calls an "ethical system," values are defined as "conceptions of the desirable" while rules of conduct are indentified as "basic elements of a moral code" [6, p. 52]. Others, without giving an obvious nod to conceptual clarification, have suggested that ethics is really beyond rules of conduct; ethics comprises creative ideals from which values, norms, and moral behavior receive stimulus for change [10].

ETHICS IN THE ORGANIZATIONAL MODEL

Social organizations are units of interaction; each unit is composed of specific elements in systemic relationship (see Figure 1). Although organizations do not exist without individual members, each organization exists as an entity separate from the individuals. Our primary concern in this paper is with ethics, but we must establish also the systemic relationship of ethics to other elements in the organization. Therefore, we will later define and clarify ethics as a part of

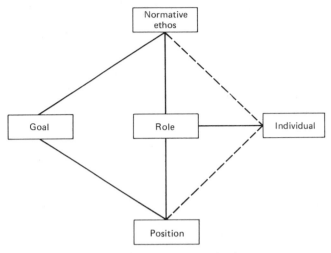

Figure 1. Elements of organization.

the organization's *normative ethos*. At this point, our purpose is to describe organizations in terms of their various elements.

Every organization has a *goal* or goals toward which it directs action and upon which its existence depends. For example, businesses must make a profit, and governments must raise the taxes necessary for governing. To achieve their goals, organizations establish *positions* and assign a specific function to each. Positions are the social locations required by an organization to achieve an objective. For example, a university has a president, vice-presidents, deans of colleges, departmental chairmen, faculty members, secretaries, and staff persons. Each position, or cluster of positions, is part of an integrated whole that has the purpose of educating students. Usually, *individuals* move into and out of the positions without drastic effect upon the organization's purpose or its survival. Each position carries certain prescribed *role* behaviors—expectations about appropriate behavior for a particular position. In a factory, positions and roles may be differentiated into several functions—production, sales, and distribution. An assembly-line worker has a role peculiar to that position, as have a manager of a regional warehouse and a salesman. Without a clarity of roles, confusion would reign and products would not be produced, stored, and sold. Yet, as all the roles depend upon one another, cooperative interaction is necessary for goal achievement.

As indicated by Figure 1, individuals are most directly related to the systemic processes of the organization at the point of filling a specific role or roles. In the strictest sense, organizational behavior means that individualism will yield to collectivism. Individuals cannot ignore others; one must know what others expect of him and he must know what to expect of others. Just as one could not play baseball without a knowledge of the positions and roles of those playing with him, so it is with efficient organization membership.

In order to secure individual behavior of a collective nature, organizations specify rules and ideals through a normative system—the *normative ethos*, or the guiding rules and ideals that characterize and pervade the organization. The orderly function of the organization toward its basic purposes depends upon compliance with these rules by the individuals who fill the positions and perform the roles. Even beyond the rules, there is usually also an imaginative quality of organization represented by idealistic standards. This is precisely the realm of ethics, and it is also an area of significant shortcoming in most organizational life.

The normative ethos is based upon *values* supported by *norms*, *morals*, and *ethics*. Quite often in the literature about organization behavior, these different concepts of the normative ethos are used interchangeably. This is a relationship between these concepts, but each does represent a distinct place in the normative ethos. An understanding of "organizational ethics" demands that we know the meaning of each concept and its contribution to the overall behavior of social groups. Such an understanding may also lead to the proper definition of ethical problems and to solutions for certain ill-defined practices.

Values are abstract standards that persist over time and identify what is right and proper for people in a society or group [31]. These standards provide a framework that influences individual behavior and affects social expectations, principally determining what is regarded as right, good, worthy, beautiful, etc. [39]. In relationship to other parts of the normative ethos, not all values are moral; there are also aesthetic values. The way people respond to social situations is often identified as a part of their values. Work, for example, is viewed as a positive value. Personal freedom and individual liberty are values.

Although values are abstract standards, we cannot escape the subjective aspects of value orientation; this is important to social reality because of objective results in the social order [9]. For example, society is more than an economic or psychological order; hence, builders do not erect housing developments without giving some thought to the availability of water, gas, and electricity, to recreational needs, and to the future population of the schools. Also, economic exploitation can destroy the unity of a society; so, in this realm it takes shared values to hold society together. In this sense, values are very much an "objective reality" [41, p. 21]. This is not to say that we can escape entirely the abstractness of values; in this quality they are often inconsistent and unreliable guides for thinking and action. Even in this dimension, however, values lead to the development of more rigorous standards—norms and morals—that regulate and determine behavior.

The regulations that guide conduct are called *norms*. Based upon group values —though not all agree with this basis [6] —the norms define what is acceptable or required in a situation. Norms are more than mere conceptions of right or wrong or valuations of what is desirable and what is not; they are institutionalized rules that are mediated to the individual through his particular group memberships. Norms are often internalized and taken for granted, thereby ordering the activities of persons in social groups, often as if by habit. Norms function in a broadly interpretive manner, making individual experiences meaningful in a social context. Norms provide a code by which to live—they guide our behavior. Overall, norms free individuals from the continuous reassessment of the meaning and significance of experiences and activities.

Some norms, called *folkways*, are quite simple; a violation carries only a slight sanction, such as embarrassment or verbal correction. Table manners and some standards of dress are representations of these rules. More serious norms, called *mores*, establish standards of stricter quality. Violation of group mores carries a more specific form of punishment, the most serious being that of expulsion from the group. Personal treatment of others—physically, sexually, and so forth —are examples of behavior controlled by mores. Sometimes mores are codified by legislative action and are made into legal standards; at this point the mores have become *laws*. The violation of a law carries a socially defined penalty that, theoretically, is equally applicable to each violator.

In relation to the normative ethos, norms are quite often moral rules, but this is not always the case, as in the rules of etiquette. Norms may also be inconsistent with values—prohibition was a law during the 1920s, was rejected as a social value, and eventually was repealed. Likewise, most organizations have rules that are inconsistent with personal values and sometimes even organizational values.

Whereas norms are group rules specifying what behavior ought to be, *morals* are personal judgments—relative to behavior—and morality is the behavior carried out under those judgments. Both judgments and behavior are based upon norms [17, 10]. One senses a "rightness" in conformity or compliance with norms and a "wrongness" in violation or noncompliance. In the struggle to set rationally acceptable justification for regulating behavior through moral judgment, persons may develop different views about what is moral or immoral. Beauchamp [7] identifies three different types of views: 1) arguments from the principles of individual liberty (judgments that attempt to make conduct illegal when others are not harmed are unacceptable); 2) arguments from the principle of democratic rule (judgments depend upon the weight of community sentiment, and supporters of this view believe society protects itself by legislating against immoral actions); and 3) arguments from the social necessity of morality (judgments are based upon legal enforcement, which is justified when order in society is challenged).

Moral judgments are made in compliance with the social constraints of orga-

nized communities or groups. Moral conduct requires rules and specific disposition of violations. In closing this brief discussion of morals as judgment and
behavior, it is only fair to note that nowhere is there an agreed upon interpretation of this concept [6].

The concept *ethics* represents the idealistic dimension of the normative ethos
and as such it extends beyond practice (as shown by moral conformity to
norms). Berkson writes (10, p. 238] :

> The ethical . . . derives from man's imaginative power, from his tendency to
> idealize, to envision perfection, to extend his selfhood in identification with
> humanity as a whole. Ethics is concerned with the quality of life . . . it sees
> the good as a form of beauty to be prized for its own sake. Both the moral
> and the ethical demand control and discipline . . . the ethical may also involve
> a struggle with the moral—with the conventionally approved and established
> positive law.

Ethics directs a rigorous examination of "what is" in terms of expected behavior
in the norms, as well as that reflected in morality. Out of this examination a
"what ought to be" ideal is generated, leading to change in the norms and morals
of groups and individuals. This interpretation was recently reflected by Hill
[29, p. 4] who contended that ethics "generate new patterns of behavior that
are ahead of and above the law." Others also see ethics from this idealistic
dimension. For example, Boulding, applying this orientation, views organizations as corruptible and forcing inconsistencies upon members. Despite this, he
contends that the ethical dimensions of organizational life should cause members
to be haunted by a vision of incorruptibility, and should set a direction of action
toward the less corruptible.

In summary, the components of the organization's normative ethos represent a hierarchy of specifications about what our actions should or should not
be. First, values are formed around specific ideals that are basic to social order;
second, norms and morals develop (often by the encoding of rules), ensuring
that values will be honored; third, beyond this specificity toward rules and
behavior are higher order principles that defy concreteness—ethics, or the
concerns directly related to social values that are in constant flux. From the
ethical concerns, new values arise and eventually new norms and moral behavior.
Hence, the normative ethos provides a dynamic process from which new standards are derived through ideals pushed toward reality.

PUBLIC ADMINISTRATION AND NORMATIVE ORGANIZATION

Concerning the normative ethos, we have spoken of organization in general; now
we turn specifically to public organization. By patterned activities, public
administration subsystems perform specific actions toward particular goals.

Most often these goals center in community problems and the actions needed to resolve the problems. The public administrator fills a position and performs a role in this *value-oriented* organization. His basic tasks probably include: 1) problem formulation, 2) identification of values, which in turn leads to the development of policy, and 3) implementation of programs, which are directed toward solving problems.

Public organization is normative by its very nature, and the public administration role is value-laden. Vickers [58] cites the articulation and analysis of values as one of the three basic elements in the administrative policy-making task. But can we say less for any organization? Simon [55] notes that all decision-making has a value component. Thus, management must relate to a normative ethos that functions integratively, aiding in the systemic relationships of adaptation, cooperation, and assimilation. The manager is a *valuer*, setting standards through knowledge, insight, and expertise.

Beyond the above community (or macrovalue) commitment, public administrators are also subject to specific organizational rules and particular professional codes [44, 50]. Simmons and Dvorin enumerate specific intraorganizational management concerns [54, p. 519]:

> Psychological transactions, social dynamics, the nature of due process, the problems involved in individual motivation, the structural formal and informal power arrangements, the nature of legitimate authority, the quality of formal and informal leadership and the nature of rule structure and relationships in an organization . . . decision making, organization task design and the utilization of energy and resources . . . selecting and supervision personnel.

These tasks represent in part what the administrator must be involved in if he expects his organization to be welded into a functioning whole. Increasingly, the tasks are being hedged by normative constraints, demanding that the public administrator's expertise include creative designs regarding organizational behavior.

In the foregoing pages, we have viewed organizations from the traditional perspective of Simon; yet, in the orientation of the "new public administration," we have suggested that the normative system should be based upon cooperative social relations. In this view we are advocating a democracy with strong humanitarian concern. Attention should be centered upon persons; values should be operative. Moral relevance in administrative power should be separated from operational needs, and techniques should be made subject to ethical ideals. This advocacy demands new organizational designs plus the application of innovation and experimentation. This approach, to a large extent, contrasts with the traditional, which has a bureaucratic ethic, places technology over values, is concerned with survival of the organization, and dehumanizes individuals.

In the following pages, we turn to a reform of the normative ethos of organizations. We do not propose total adherence to the "new public administration"; rather, in the sense of traditional organization theory, we propose to clarify rules and stipulate expectations for behavior and propose consequences for violations. Yet, in keeping with the ideas of the "new public administration," the normative ethos of the organization should receive major focus, and that ethos should be determined by participative democracy.

PROPOSAL FOR REFORM

Even with respect for law and dependence upon it, many people fear government. Therefore, in the American system, private enterprise, individual privacy and "self-regulation" have been sacred principles. Today, in the face of "ethical" probes, self-regulation—or the practice of allowing each organization to regulate its own normative action—is again a popular doctrine. Although this doctrine has not failed in every application, in far too many instances it has been found wanting.

Existing restrictions and procedures for enforcing moral and ethical conduct are seriously deficient. Conflicts of interest in business and government service often go unchecked. The values and norms of government seem insufficient to the integrity of the governing process. Out of this environment have come numerous proposals for reform, including proposed laws to require public financial disclosure, banning gratuities, divestiture of possible conflicting financial interests, postemployment restrictions, and establishing absolute measures of enforcement. Also, perhaps leading the way, are proposals for the adoption of *codes of ethics* [29].

All of these proposals are legalistic by design, except for codes of ethics, which, follow the self-regulation theme, and thereby have vast popularity, even among public administrators. Codes of ethics are intended to foster adherence to high ethical standards in some instances, but in others the intention is much more restrictive and legalistic. Sometimes imposed by leaders of the organization, codes may also be adopted by the vote of group members. Having the potential to sensitize members to moral and ethical issues, all too often these codes are inoperative and simply serve to make an organization look good to the general public.

Agreeing with the widespread skepticism toward codes of ethics, I feel that this procedure is inadequate on several counts. First, many persons consider codes as just another set of rules. Too many times, codes of ethics have been mere restatements of existing, but unenforced, rules. As such, a code is merely another official pronouncement with only the force of itself to secure its aims; indeed, codes of ethics claim no legal effect because they are not supposed to be regulations [42]. This assumption is often drawn by those who propose codes of ethics, but they also assign the codes the same function as regulations.

For example, in reference to a code of ethics, Monypenny speaks to implementation of an external standard with specific sanctions of enforcement, of devices for administrative control, *etc.* Scheiber, in a statement about the International City Managers' Association Code of Ethics [50], details the process for investigation of those who violate rules, the sanctioning process, and the probability for ultimate expulsion from the Association.

In explaining the establishment of a board of ethics and the adoption of a code of ethics for New York City officials and employees, Kreutzer points to the rigor of that code of ethics [33, p. 339]:

> Every councilmen, official and employee of the city is required to abide by the code of ethics, and violations of the conflict of interest laws [*sic*] are punishable by fine, suspension, expulsion or other disciplinary measures.

In fact, Kreutzer discusses the code of ethics and the laws relating to violations covered by the code without any differentiation.

In yet another instance, Smith [56] indicates that codes are enforced by one of two options: compulsion and persuasion. Compulsion is by regulation, sanction, *etc.* Since the maintenance of rigid discipline is recognized as quite difficult, Smith advocates the use of persuasion over compulsion, or seeking voluntary compliance through education.

In contrast to codes of ethics, Bolles [13] suggests that methods of corrective effectiveness in government agencies should be: 1) the use of vigor and clarity in setting goals of government policy, 2) a persistent inspection within agencies, and 3) swift legal action against acts of dishonesty. Sherwood [52] cites the ineffectiveness of codes of ethics with reference to the actors in the Watergate scandal. Here, the norms and traditions of the legal profession, as well as codes of ethics for governmental and public officials, had little or no influence in the control of behavior.

Our review of the state of ethics has indicated that the problem of ethics should center upon an analysis of an organization's normative ethos. In support of this idea, and in opposition to dependence upon codes of ethics, Sherwood gives the conclusions of a committee on professional standards of the American Society for Public Administration [52, p. 19]:

> ... higher standards lie not so much in demands for behavior (which tends to be characteristic of codes) as in organizational and societal processes that insist the individual consciously confront his values and take responsibility for consequent behavior.

From organization theory, we have learned that individual beliefs, values, and ideas can be superseded by the collective. Thus, from individuals in organizations, we expect contradictions of standards, meaning that organizations must assume the responsibility for normative direction. One cannot assume that individuals will automatically make choices that are in keeping with the values and norms of the collective. Therefore, a continuous process of socialization toward organizational expectations must be carried out. Eventually, the autonomous moral judgments of individuals will come to reflect the internalized values and norms that have been developed through cooperative social relationships.

If events such as Watergate have taught public administrators anything, they have taught us that "morality attaches to public office, not to the particular circumstances of appointment" [52, p. 13]. Sherwood concludes that value dimensions must be built into the thoughts, work, and acts of organizational life.

Organizations have not hesitated to train their members for productivity; they have however, left normative training to other means. In small, simple societies this may be sufficient, but in the societies of Boulding's organizational revolution it is not [14]. Problems in the normative realm have not remained simple; solutions have not kept pace with the revolution. Complex behavior in organizations forces dilemmas in personal morality, and too often individuals cannot escape being engulfed by the dilemmas.

Perhaps, as Boulding contends, organizations are corrupting; but they are also normative systems. Thus, each organization must seek harmony among its normative ethos, its goals, and its structures. Quite practically, Bernstein suggests a series of steps that organizations and agencies may take "to alert their officials and employees to ethical problems and dilemmas and to make them more sensitive to actual and potential problems that challenge their personal integrity and that of government as a whole" [12, p. 346]. He lists the following steps:

1. The conscientious employee should be able to turn to the legal officer of his agency or to some central office responsible to the chief executive to obtain reliable advice on ethical problems.
2. Agencies should develop imaginative orientation programs that help to develop better understanding of the importance of ethical standards and statutory and administrative restraints. They need to inform full-time and fully with codes of conduct and professional standards.
3. Another device is to request that each employee sign a statement that he has read the rules governing ethical conduct [sic] and understands them . . . each employee be required to report periodically any non-government employment . . . to reduce that incidence of conflicting interests and unprofessional conduct.
4. The head of an administrative agency should have authority, in carefully defined circumstances, to dismiss, suspend, or otherwise discipline an employee who has violated the statute or regulations.
5. Government and individual agencies should from time to time issue appropriate bulletins or handbooks, highlighting important problems and ways of solving them.

Although one may not agree with the above actions *in toto*, they do indicate the kind of positive action organizations and agencies should take toward normative reform. The most obvious qualities of these suggestions are their simplicity and systematic design.

Among the basic conditions of administrative responsibility are ambiguity and uncertainty. The good administrator develops insight into the cooperative processes for coping with a "temporary" society. He is not neutral; his commitment is to good management, which includes concern for values, morals, and ethical ideals. Beyond mere adherence to legalistic standards, an administrator is required to be a creative thinker, planning actions that will lift the values and the behavior of his agency or organization. From imaginative insight, he is aware of, and committed to, even more demanding ideals.

A MODEL FOR NORMATIVE ENRICHMENT

If the so-called problems of ethics are to be dealt with effectively, the normative ethos of an organization must be treated with the same respect and seriousness given to the other elements of the organization—goals, positions, and roles. Normative dimensions are as important as productivity. A program of normative enrichment ought to receive priority status, and should include an evaluation of overall conduct, clarification of rules, and programs of normative training. Toward this end, we propose a series of steps for a normative enrichment program.

The first step might be that of classifying the agency or organization into a particular type of environmental and normative orientation. From such a classification, decisions about change, reform, *etc.*, can be more adequately pursued. Although there may be other typologies, the following is given as an example. The model depicts diversity of organization types and normative patterns—stages of morality in the suggestion of Kohlberg. In this model, organizations are classified into six ideal types, which are listed below, with their characteristics.

1. Classical type. The emphasis of such an organization is totally upon efficiency and economy. Rules are stringent; right is what the authorities command. Obedience is sacred and punishment imminent.
2. Company (or agency) type. The primary focus is paternalism; in the human relations approach, employees' jobs and benefits receive excessive attention. Rules often yield to favoritism. Rewards are sought because of right behavior.
3. Consumer (or client) type. Greatest emphasis is given to the consumer's or the client's interests, tastes, rights, and so forth. Maintaining a good public image is paramount. The norms are viewed as situational, and conformity to the expectation of peers is a persistent pattern.
4. Cooperative type. Focus is on the organization and its survival. One's social investments are often directed toward the pursuit of some gain in

the organization.   The normative patterns are seen in a law-and-order dimension.   Right is one's duty; respect is owed to authority.

5. Civic type.   Such an organization attempts to be a citizen and is dedicated to corporate citizenship.   Social responsibility is accepted even beyond imposed obligations (laws, regulations, *etc.*).   Right action is defined in terms of individual rights as agreed upon by the group.

6. Creative type.   This type is engaged in advancing the quality of life.   Creative ideas are sought, encouraged, rewarded, and made a part of organizational practice.   The normative structure is less a matter of absolute rules and more a matter of conscience.   Moral behavior tends to be based upon decisions of conscience, which are made in the light of comprehensive, universal, and consistent principles of justice.

Public service agencies can probably be classified as any of the first four types, depending upon leadership and peer interaction.   Probably few agencies can match the characteristics suggested in the fifth and sixth types, although the ethical concern of public administrators may set these types as ideals, expecting thereby to forge significant social and organizational changes in the normative ethos.

The second phase of the normative-enrichment program may focus upon an analysis of norms, similar to that suggested by de la Porte [18].   By this procedure, a normative profile for the organization would be established.   Although this profile may be used for studying various factors, our concern here is only with determining a profile of the normative ethos.   What are the value commitments of members?   How well do members know organizational rules?   What are the most consistent patterns of rule violation?   To what extent is there an idealistic, creative spirit of value and moral concern?

De la Porte suggests that this evaluation should lead to cooperative action (*e.g.*, participative democracy) toward positive norms as goals, to determining a point of excellence for the organization, to establishing priorities for change, to developing a strategy for change, to implementing the strategy, to providing follow-through and to setting up a continuous process of evaluation.

De la Porte has listed a number of actual results from this procedure [18, p. 63]:

1. Quality defects in a manufacturing company were reduced by 55 percent.

2. The management committee of an international corporation found its decisions being made twice as fast (and just as accurately) with a tangible improvement in participant commitment.

3. Product breakage and pilferage in a retail chain was cut by 70 percent.

4. Average productivity of sales calls in a food service company was boosted by 60 percent.

5. A medium-size airline eradicated what it called the "bored ticket-puncher" mentality of its check-in hostesses.

6. Absenteeism in a manufacturing plant was halved, and turnover considerably reduced.

The third phase of normative enrichment could center on emphasizing the significance of rules (but try to avoid a police syndrome). Every organization has rules and must have them. The rules should be made public, and members of the organization should be informed of expectations for conformity. Two important principles are involved here; rules are made clear and they are enforced. Bolles speaks to the need for rule enforcement [13, p. 27] :

> The most effective corrective after the endowment of government with clear sense of purpose is swift punishment for public servants who are dishonest and unfair in the use of their powers. The congenitally unfair can be removed from the government payroll. The dishonest are usually guilty of a crime, an outrage against fundamental morality, such as bribe-taking.

Members of organizations tend to obey only those rules that they believe in, *i.e.*, rules that are legitimate in terms of their own values [9]. Thus, phase three in the normative enrichment program leads very appropriately into phase four, a definite program of training.

In the fourth step the organization recognizes and accepts the responsibility for socialization of its members. This program could begin with a presentation of basic American values. Williams [63] gives 15 themes around which most Americans organize the activities of their lives.

1. Achievement and success. Everyone ought to work and earn money. Without regard to social status, every person should be a high achiever.
2. Activity and work. Life should be disciplined and no one should fill a parasitic position. Hence, the lack of discipline and work among welfare recipients produces a negative stereotype.
3. Moral orientation. One is expected to view life in terms of right and wrong or good and bad.
4. Humanitarianism. Selfless concern is to be shown for others.
5. Efficiency and practicality. Technology should seek quick and easy solutions to the problems of daily life.
6. Progress. The future is viewed optimistically, and change for the better is inevitable.
7. Material comfort. A high standard of living is prized dearly.
8. Equality. Regardless of religion, race, creed, or nationality, all persons should have equal educational and occupational privileges.
9. Freedom. Individuals are to be free from restraints, and are to be free to act in accord with their desires.
10. External conformity. In spite of equality and freedom, most persons seek to tune their behavior to the expectations of those around them.
11. Science and secular rationality. Science solves problems and offers a rational philosophy for interpreting experiences.
12. Nationalism-patriotism. The nation and its symbols are highly revered; attackers, even of the symbols, are viewed as traitors.

13. Democracy. The government is best run by the principle of majority rule.
14. Individual personality. The individual has intrinsic worth apart from membership in a group.
15. Racism and group superiority. Persons should be assessed on the basis of personal characteristics and not racial or minority group origins.

Concerning these values, it should be determined to what extent members of an organization agree or disagree, conform or deviate, *etc.* Other questions of interest may be investigated. How does the organization or agency compare with these basic themes, *i.e.*, by its own value orientations? Can a more specific list of themes be devised for the organization or agency under investigation? To what degree do the rules of the organization reinforce values? From this analysis an organization may discover that there are rules that need rewriting, or that there is a need for developing new rules, or perhaps that there are old rules that should be discarded.

Having clarified rules and values, a program of motivation toward normative behavior should be inaugurated. Finally, the entire program should be conducted in a spirit of imaginative creativity where frank admission is made of the fact that we are engaged in a search for higher principles of behavior that will improve the quality of life.

CONCLUSION

The lack of clarification of an organization's normative ethos may have serious effect upon behavior in the organization and even beyond. In fact, this ill-defined aspect of organizational life seems central to the recurring confusion about *ethics.* Organizations have depended largely upon ethical individualism for social control, although the diversity of society jeopardized this method. Different cultures and even subcultures within a single culture have contradictory rules; in many social situations there are no specific rules. Even if one follows the general guidelines of a host culture, his actions may be contradictory and unacceptable in his parent culture's normative standards. Recent experiences of bribery among persons in multinational corporations are illustrative of this dilemma. Deviance from rules and expectations seems inevitable; yet, it is costly, embarrassing, and often even punishable under the law.

Given the above conditions, organizations must utilize normative controls more effectively. They must allot time and resources for normative evaluation and enrichment, as well as for technological efficiency. Generally, organizations expect that their members come morally and ethically predeveloped, *i.e.*, that they have already developed a "collective self-discipline" from the "repositories of values." To some degree, this assumption is certainly true, but we have a great deal of evidence to indicate that it is not totally so. Therefore, we look to the principles of social science for informative direction. Here we learn that one's socialization is never completed; it is an unending process. To assume that the earlier training by family, church, and school gives a moral capacity for organizational demands may be too much, at least for all persons and every situation. Since we do not make such assumptions about productivity, we should not make them about other dimensions of organizational life. Hence, even as persons are trained for technological know-how, they also need to be trained for normative behavior.

The *ethics problem* for organizations is essentially a problem with the *normative ethos*; it is futile to talk about ethics—the idealistic part of normative behavior—when abstract ideas, rules, and judgmental behavior are abused so flagrantly. Today's popular call for ethical reform demands that we first adhere to basic values and norms; then, perhaps through laborious normative practice, a desire for the higher principles will be born. Organizations should use their rules for the intended purposes, but beyond the rules, they should demonstrate concern for imaginative idealism. It is this imaginative process, this idealistic turn, this creative and innovative spirit that in reality comprises organizational ethics.

NOTES AND REFERENCES

1. "After Watergate: Putting Business Ethics in Perspective." *Business Week*, September 15, 1973, 178.
2. Appleby, Paul Henson. *Morality and Administration in Democratic Government*. Westport, Conn.: Greenwood Press, 1969.
3. Armstrong, DeWitt C., and George A. Graham. "Ethical Preparation for the Public Service: The 1970s." *The Bureaucrat* 4(1975): 5–23.
4. Bahm, Archie J. *Ethics as a Behavioral Science*. Springfield, Ill: Thomas, 1974.
5. Barnard, Chester. *Organization and Management*. Cambridge, Mass.: Harvard University Press, 1949.
6. Barnsley, John H. *The Social Reality of Ethics: The Comparative Analysis of Moral Codes*. London: Routledge & Kegan Paul, 1972. Barnsley disagrees with the tendency to present values as the primary dimension of moral codes; instead, he contends that general rules of conduct or specific prescriptions provide a more reliable and accessible means for understanding any particular moral code. Rules are more definite criteria.
7. Beauchamp, Tom L. *Ethics and Public Policy*. Englewood Cliffs, N.J.: Prentice-Hall, 1975.
8. Bentley College. *Business Ethics Report*. The First Annual Conference on Business Ethics, March 11–12, 1977.
9. Berkley, George E. *The Craft of Public Administration*. Boston: Allyn & Bacon, 1975. Berkley captures the subjective aspect of values by indicating that values involve deep emotional commitments to certain cognitive views of value objects; they stand behind rational social action, and are the engines of human activity, insofar as that activity is social.

10. Berkson, Isaac Baer. *Ethics, Politics and Education*. Eugene, Ore: University of Oregon, 1968.
11. Berlo, David K. "Morality or Ethics? Two Approaches to Organizational Control." *The Personnel Administrator* 20(1975): 16–19.
12. Bernstein, Marver H. "Ethics in Government: The Problems in Perspective." *National Civic Review* 61(1972): 341–347.
13. Bolles, Blair. "Correctives for Dishonest and Unfair Public Administrators." *American Academy Annals* 363(1966): 23–27.
14. Boulding, Kenneth. *The Organizational Revolution*. New York: Harper & Row, 1953.
15. Charlesworth, James C. "Foreword." *American Academy Annals* 363(1966): ix.
16. Davis, Keith, and Robert L. Blomstrom. *Business and Society: Environment and Responsibility*, 3rd ed. New York: McGraw-Hill, 1975.
17. Davitt, Thomas E. *The Ethics in the Situation*. New York: Appleton-Century-Crofts, 1970.
18. de la Porte, P. C. Andre. "Group Norms: Key to Building a Winning Team." *Personnel* 51(1974): 60–67.
19. Dvorin, Eugene P., and Robert H. Simmons. *From Amoral to Humane Bureaucracy*. San Francisco: Canfield Press, 1972.
20. England, George W. "Personal Value Systems of Managers—So What?" *The Personnel Administrator*. 20(1975): 20–23.
21. Flieger, Howard. "The Boom in Ethics." *U. S. News and World Report*, August 16, 1976, 72. This editorial characterizes the era as one of jolting moral scandals in public life and business. Its primary point is attention for a recent book of essays, which presses for greater focus on ethical issues.
22. Fox, Marvin. "The Theistic Bases of Ethics." In *Ethics in Business*. Edited by Robert Bartels. Pp. 85–88. Columbus: The Ohio State University Press, 1963.
23. Frederickson, H. George. "Toward a New Public Administration." In *Toward a New Public Administration*. Edited by Frank Marini. Pp. 309–331. Scranton, Pa.: Chandler Publishing, 1971.
24. Golembiewski, Robert. *Men, Management and Morality*. New York: McGraw-Hill, 1965.
25. Gouldner, Alvin W. "Cosmopolitans and Locals: Toward an Analysis of Latent Social Roles—I." *Administrative Science Quarterly*. 2(1957): 281–306.
26. Graham, George A. "Ethical Guidelines for Public Administrators: Observations on Rules of the Game." *Public Administration Review* 34(1974): 90–92.
27. Graham, George A. *Morality in American Politics*. New York: Random House, 1952.
28. Hamer, John. "Ethics in Government." *Editorial Research Reports* 1(1973): 375–381.
29. Hill, Ivan. *The Ethical Basis of Economic Freedom*. Chapel Hill, N.C.: American Viewpoint, Inc., 1976.
30. Huddleston, R. H. "Ethics and Politics, A View from 'Down in the Woodwork'." *The Bureaucrat* 4(1975): 99–103.
31. Kluckhohn, Clyde. *Culture and Behavior*. New York: The Free Press, 1962.
32. Kohlberg, Lawrence. "The Claims to Moral Adequacy of a Highest Stage of Moral Judgment." *The Journal of Philosophy* 70(1973): 630–646.
33. Kreutzer, Stanley S. "Protecting the Public Service: A National Ethics Commission." *National Civic Review* 64(1975): 339–342.
34. Lee, Robert D., Jr. "Watergate and the Image of the Federal Service Revisited." *Public Personnel Management* 3(1974): 111–114.
35. Leys, Wayne Albert R. *Ethics and Social Policy*. New York: Prentice-Hall, 1941.

36. Loevinger, Lee. "Social Responsibility in a Democratic Society: Government and Business Have the Same Public." *Vital Speeches of the Day* 39(1975): 388-396.
37. Luthans, Fred, and Richard M. Hodges. *Social Issues in Business*. New York: Macmillan, 1976.
38. Marini, Frank, ed. *Toward a New Public Administration: The Minnowbrook Perspective*. Scranton, Pa.: Chandler Publishing, 1971.
39. McMurray, Robert N. "Conflicts in Human Values." In *Public Administration*. Edited by Robert T. Golembiewski, Frank Gibson and Geoffry Y. Cornog. Pp. 314-327. Chicago: Rand McNally, 1966.
40. McNulty, Nancy G. "And Now, Professional Codes for the Practice of Management." *The Conference Board Record*, 12(1975): 21-24.
41. Means, Richard L. *The Ethical Imperative: The Crisis in American Values*. Garden City, N.Y.: Doubleday, 1969.
42. Monypenny, Phillip. "A Code of Ethics as a Means of Controlling Administrative Conduct." *Public Administration Review* 13(1953): 184-187.
43. Murray, Michael A. "Comparing Public and Private Management: An Exploratory Essay." *Public Administration Review* 35(1975): 364-371. Murray states that the term *management* is often used when referring to private business, and *administration*, to public organizations. He notes that this tendency is disappearing, however, and he argues that there are more similarities than differences between private and public managers. One example of an effort to identify differences may be found in Presthus [47]. Definitions of management and administration are essentially the same. For example, Berkley [9, p. 3] defines administration as a "process involving human beings jointly engaged in working toward common goals." Given the similarity of function, it is assumed throughout this paper that the managerial process in the private and public sectors produces similar ethical issues and problems.
44. Patriarche, John M. "Ethical Questions Which Administrators Face." *Public Management* (1975): 17-19.
45. Perrow, Charles. *Complex Organizations*. Glenview, Ill.: Scott, Foresman, 1972.
46. Piaget, Jean. *The Moral Judgment of the Child*. Glencoe, Ill.: The Free Press, 1951.
47. Presthus, Robert V. *Public Administration*. New York: Ronald Press, 1975.
48. Rohr, John A. "The Study of Ethics in the P.A. Curriculum." *Public Administration Review* 36(1976): 398-406.
49. Salisbury, Robert H. "Ethical Standards and the Business Community." In *Ethics and Standards in American Business*. Edited by Joseph Towle. Pp. 41-44. Boston: Houghton Mifflin, 1964.
50. Scheiber, Walter A. "The ICMA Code of Ethics." *Public Management* (June 1975), 15-16.
51. Schubert, Glendon A., Jr. "'The Public Interest' in Administrative Decision Making." In *Public Administration*. Edited by Robert T. Golembiewski *et al.* Pp. 392-411. Chicago: Rand McNally, 1966. Schubert states that being ethical in the public service is to develop integrity and loyalty toward democratic ideals.
52. Sherwood, Frank P. "Professional Ethics." *Public Management* (June 1975), 13-14.
53. Shirk, Evelyn. *The Ethical Dimension*. New York: Appleton-Century-Crofts, 1965.
54. Simmons, Robert H., and Eugene P. Dvorin. *Public Administration: Values, Policy and Change*. New York: Alfred Publishing, 1976.
55. Simon, Herbert A. *Administrative Behavior*. New York: The Free Press, 1976.
56. Smith, Robert H. "Make Your Code of Ethics Work Through a Program of Education." *Association Management* 28(1976): 44-48.

57. Strother, George. "The Moral Codes of Executives: A Watergate-Inspired Look at Barnard's Theory of Executive Responsibility." *The Academy of Management Review* 1(1976): 13–22.
58. Vickers, Geoffrey. *Values Systems and Social Process*. New York: Basic Books, 1968.
59. Wakefield, Susan. "Ethics and the Public Service: A Case for Individual Responsibility." *Public Administration Review* 36(1976): 661–666.
60. Walton, Clarence C. *Ethos and the Executives: Value in Managerial Decision Making*. Englewood Cliffs: N.J.: Prentice-Hall, 1969.
61. Ways, Max. "Business Faces Growing Pressures to Behave Better." *Fortune* (May 1974): 193–195.
62. Wheatley, Jon. "Ethics Does Not Exist." *Ethics* 84(1973–74): 62–69.
63. Williams, Robin. *American Society*, 3rd ed. New York: Knopf, 1970.

PART III

Information Gathering: Search, Research, and Solicitation

One of the ways in which the public sector differs most markedly from the commercial and industrial is the conduct of the information-gathering function. The search, research and solicitation processes become necessarily more complex when we move into the public arena. The four papers in this section make this clear indeed. Merrelyn and Fred Emery make a new contribution to the field of public administration by outlining a basic search process as it would have to be conducted by serious public-policy-makers. Following this, Frederick Rossini and Alan Porter give the reader some critical and well-researched advice on the management of the interdisciplinary teams that provide essential inputs to public enterprise. In the third paper, Richard Goodman and Anne Huff ask the public administrator to rethink fundamentally his or her approach to development of policy predicates, and to evolve and obey radically new procedural dictates. Maria Nowakowska, a renowned praxiologist, then uses the instruments of modern analytics (formal logic) to caution the reader about a little-understood process: the tendency for scientists and scientific sects to become overly enamored of their own worth, and, hence, to engage in monopolistic or exclusionary behavior. Thus, scientific inputs to public decision process are not always unadulterated and objective.

1

Searching: For New Directions, in New Ways . . . for New Times

Merrelyn and Fred Emery
The Australian National University

INTRODUCTION

This essay is designed to demystify the concept of search, to elucidate its internally consistent theoretical underpinnings, and to show its widespread utility as a solid model with predictive validity. That the search conference does what it is supposed to do is now beyond doubt; the rest of this document is partial evidence for that statement. That there are basic commonsensible rules to follow is also beyond doubt. That it is one of the few effective, replicable, and reliable means of coping with current social realities is similarly beyond question. That a comprehensive theory such as the one that produces the search conference has had the degrees of reality-testing that this process has had—and still survives as a viable and adaptive way of planning and organizing human affairs—is no small test.

WHY SEARCH?

Human beings can be as consciously aware of the past and the future as they are of the present, even though they may know the past, present, and future in different ways. They can also be as aware of changes in their environment as they are of changes in themselves. Another uniquely human characteristic is the capacity to seek wisdom by exploring the finite worlds of possibility.

The theoretical framework [1] within which the notion of search was originally conceived is a simple one (Figure 1). The circle represents an individual system, whether person or organization, whose nature and internal dynamics are designated L_{ij}. L represents a lawful relationship and L_{ij} means the lawful

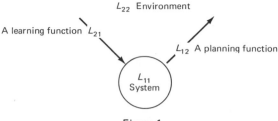

Figure 1.

ways in which the parts of a system relate to the whole and to each other. Outside the boundaries of this system, and underlying it, is the environment L_{22}. The system has transactions with, and affects, the environment (L_{12}) and, *vice versa*, is affected by it (L_{21}). Just as systems can be classified and described, so can social environments in the same sense of lawful relations between their parts and themselves as entities.

Five types of social environments have been specified. Only three of these will be treated here. They are:

Type II clustered, placid,
Type III disturbed, reactive,
Type IV turbulent.

A Brief Historical Survey of Environments

The work of archaeologists and anthropologists leaves no doubt that at earlier times man lived in a social enviroment that was essentially *placid* and yet suited to his purposeful nature [2]. Within this environment man could build forms of organizations that fulfilled basic human needs and enabled him to live in harmony with the physical environment (Figure 2).

The erosion of the value-laden and, implicitly, ideal-seeking behavior of this period can be documented in the Western world through the practical consequences of Christianity, with its caste and class system of domination and exploitation [3]. Man's growth from traditional forms of relationship and organization resulted finally in a full-fledged "disturbed reactive" environment, triggered in 1890–1900 by the technological breakthrough in the fields of energy generation and communications [4]. These allowed a rapid acceleration in the exploitation of natural resources and the growth in size and spatial extension of organizations that produced and supported the production of goods and services. The environment of this period was characterized by competition between growing and increasingly similar organizations whose similarity and standardization were achieved by building on the principle of redundant parts. By fragmenting jobs and specializing functions, these organizations used people

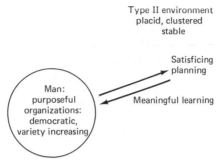

Figure 2.

as replaceable parts within a rigidly structured and mechanistic system—a bureaucracy. While the environment was competitive and exploitative, it was nevertheless stable and predictable; what instabilities there were, were cyclical and predictable. Bureaucracies then could continue to use the simple linear projection (Figure 3) as the basis of planning.

Bureaucracy as the Organizational Dinosaur

In the building of bureaucracies, which removed from men the opportunity for responsible decision-making about their own affairs, lay the flaw that ensured that the period of bureaucracy should be, in the West, a brief historical aberration. People are purposeful [5], not limited simply to adapting to the environment as given. The bureaucratic structure robbed men of the conditions under which they could fulfill basic human needs. It was inevitable for this reason that people would act in their own interests to undermine the bureaucracies and reassert the old values [6].

Together with the reaction to the unexpected consequences of the large-scale exploitation of the physical environment that disturbed long ecological chains

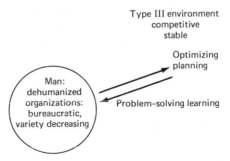

Figure 3.

and balances, this reassertion heralded a social environment characterized by rapid change and, most importantly, a high degree of relevant uncertainty. This *turbulent* social field was first noted as emergent in 1962 [7], entered into international consciousness in the period 1967–1969, and has now become an accepted and continuing phenomenon. Its future, too, is limited, as men continue to seek adaptive means of stabilizing and recentering such an uncomfortable environment [8]. The environment that will follow such an uncertain period is almost inevitably one of a placid, clustered stability, but one that will incorporate what has been advantageous to man in his most intense period of technological change and some of the recent awareness that have arisen as reactions to and from analyses of turbulence itself. These will become more obvious below, but the predominant good arising from awareness of turbulence has been the emphasis put upon the nature and enjoyment of the process of living. Man has a reawakened interest in the dynamics of his world (Figure 4) [9].

In the previous predictable environment, to have standard plans and standard designs for all organizations was good enough and effective enough. The historical uniqueness or character of an organization, or a community, was irrelevant in the face of a planning and decision-making process that focused only on the dimensions of effectiveness and relative value [10]. The race toward conformity suppressed awareness of the facts of character, style, and culture that embodied the values inherent in the historical development and situational characteristics of an organization. Without consideration of these facts, quantitative cost-benefit analysis seemed equally applicable to all human projects.

This bureaucratization of structure applied not only to the major institutions of our society, such as school, church, and family, nor only to large business and service concerns, but also to the multitude of processes involved in planning and running local community affairs, political machines and submachines, war, and leisure activities. "The cry of the urban crisis is really the echo of one which began with the Industrial Revolution" [11].

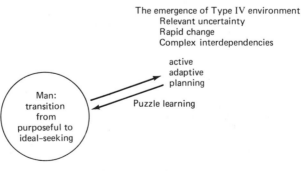

Figure 4.

There is a basic discontinuity between the nature of the bureaucratic form of organization and the current social field in which it attempts to function and plan. As interdependencies between parts of the environment grow, so do the unpredictabilities facing an organization. The simple linear projection and the optimizing mode using only technical and economic criteria, which lie at the base of much current planning, are doomed to failure in a turbulent social field. People are developing a new sense of the individuality and uniqueness of themselves and their organizations. This they continue to express regardless of decisions made for them on economic and technical grounds.

A choice in basic organizational design is so inevitable that there is no question but that men will make the choice even if they are not conscious of doing so. Man cannot hope actively to adapt to turbulence without restructuring his organizations along the lines of a design principle based on redundancy of the functions of individual parts, not redundancy of the parts themselves [12]. These will be referred to, respectively, as design principles 2 and 1. Bureaucracies are systems designed on principle 1.

Systems designed on the second principle will tend to be *variety-increasing*. To maintain and extend the multifunctionality of their members, they will seek to extend the range of their purposeful behaviors and increase the opportunities and support for ideal-seeking behaviors. That is, such systems will be organized on the assumption that they are best served by being instrumental to the potentially higher system capabilities of their individual members. This follows from the understanding that organizations function at one system level lower than their members. These capabilities include the functions of *learning* and *planning* to create a desirable ordering of human affairs through an understanding of the laws governing the environment in which they live. In times when individuals were functioning purposefully, it may have been sufficient for organizations to be merely goal-seeking; but it is clear that in times of turbulence, when individuals are becoming ideal-seeking, organizations must find ways of becoming purposeful.

Planning in a Turbulent Environment [13]

Planning implies some commitment to bring into being a state of affairs that does not currently exist and is not expected to occur naturally within the desired time. The planning we need now is the kind that will produce plans that will *probably* come to pass. It is not enough to have one of the optimizer's *feasible* plans. We need plans that will probably come to pass because the people involved in or served by their implementation want them to succeed. "There are no humanly 'neutral' acts of creation or invention" [14]. "The planners' own form of ostensible 'value-free,' 'scientific' methods have contributed to repression" [15].

The apparent dilemma in "modern" planning is *how does the expert make his contribution to planning without alienating people?* This has almost the makings of a paradox for social planners: the more knowledge the expert accumulates, the greater the gap in understanding between him and the people, and the less likely they are to go along with helping to implement his plans. Or to put it otherwise, the more we know the less we can do. In his own context Mao posed it as the problem of "red or expert."

We do not think we can suggest any way to resolve this dilemma unless we confront simultaneously another dilemma. Planning to produce a new state of affairs seems to presuppose that we know where we want to go, we know where we are now, we know what paths will take us from here to there, and we know what means we have for traversing those paths. For turbulent social environments this presumes an awful lot of knowledge. When the social setting and the human instruments of change are both changing, the knowledge we have today is increasingly less relevant. The dilemma is *how can we expect to improve our planning in the face of relatively decreasing knowledge?* Again we come close to a paradox: the more society changes, the more we need to be able to plan, but the less we have the knowledge with which to plan.

The common element in the two dilemmas is the notion of "expert knowledge." If we are to resolve these dilemmas we will have to ask whether what we understand to be "expert knowledge" is the kind of knowledge required for planning social changes in a changing society. We think there is room for doubt on at least three scores.

First, we think decision-makers mistake the nature of the situations for which they are seeking a planning solution. Even the optimizers seem to think they are engaged in problem-solving. They think they know the problem and simply have to search through existing knowledge in order to come up with a range of probable solutions, which they can then compare for probable effectiveness. Social planning has, however, come to be more like puzzle-solving then problem-solving. Each situation is so complex and unpredictable that one has to learn each unique set of steps that lead to a solution. In problem-solving it is typical to have the insightful "Eureka" experience when a solution suddenly becomes apparent, and after that it is just a matter of work to put the pieces together. In a puzzle one does not get this. The relation between the pieces is very much a matter of local determination. One can determine what is required for the piece to fit but, until that piece is found, one has very little idea of what is going to be required of the next pieces. Previous experience or training cannot enrich the repertoire of solutions: at best they may help a person "learn how to learn." This does not sound like our expert. The expert is usually chockablock full of knowledge about what solutions will solve a given class of problems.

Second, we think the experts in this field have tended to act on a faulty model of so-called rational decision-making. They theorize and write as if decision-making were explicable in terms of only two dimensions: Probable Efficiency of different paths and Relative Value of the outcomes. Another dimension is necessary. This other dimension is the Probability of Choice, and it reflects the *intrinsic* value of a course of action to the chooser (as distinct from its *extrinsic* or means-end value). This human dimension is reflected in the old folk wisdom of "better the devil you know," "furthest hills are greenest," "a bird in the hand. . . ." The persistent and pervasive role of these nonrational factors was unwittingly demonstrated in the "uncooperativeness" of humans in the 1960s rash of experimental studies of game playing and decision-making. Similarly, established organizations show their own style in their nonrational preference for ways of acting, particularly those that have had a special significance in their past, *e.g.*, Rolls-Royce and the "advanced technology" engine for the Lockheed 1011.

Third, we think planners have tended to assume that what we need to know are more and more facts, when what is actually needed is knowledge of values. This had come up very strongly with an earlier generation of "enlightened" operations researchers. Faced with the sorts of difficulties outlined above, they have sought for yet more knowledge—knowledge about people's motivations and how they can be manipulated to bring about predictable changes. We suggest that they are not about to get this knowledge from the social sciences (despite the pretensions of some social scientists), and that even if they did they would still be in a puzzle situation: the situational features to which the people respond would still be emerging in unpredictable ways, as planning and implementation continued. When people go from *A* to *B* in ways that can be determined only as they proceed, it becomes more important that they have a bit more knowledge about some of the paths. They must themselves be able to learn so that they can evaluate.

If one were to take these strictures seriously, then the role of the planners would be no longer that of the experts riding with the powers that be. Instead the planning functions would be seen to involve 1) conducting some search process whereby the main parties to the proposed change can clearly identify and agree about the ideals the change is supposed to serve and the kinds of paths most in character with them, and, hence, most valued; 2) designing a change process that will enable relevant learning to take place at rates appropriate to the demands of time. This appropriate period of time is that within which change must occur to avoid intolerable costs of not-changing and the time by which decisions need to be made if adequate resources are to be mobilized; 3) devising social mechanisms for participation, whereby the choice of paths will reflect the intrinsic value of these paths for those who will have to traverse them.

There are many considerations that lead us to regard identification of values as the first requirement for planning social change. Only ideals seem to have the necessary breadth and stretch in social space and time. Motivations, attitudes, and social objectives may well change as planning and implementation proceed, but human ideals do not appear to change as readily. This is not to say that the relative weightings of the ideals may not change, but even here we tend to have storm warnings well before the shifts become socially relevant (*e.g.*, the shifts in "the Protestant ethic" that have only now become broadly relevant, but which were heralded many years ago by the beat generation of Kerouac). Similarly, only ideals seem to have the breadth of influence to encompass the range of contesting interests that can be expected in an area ripe for planned change. Ideals do not ordinarily have the same urgency in human affairs as motivations, but what they lack in this respect may be more than compensated for if their identification displaces a zero-sum conflict with cooperative pursuit of common interests.

Ideals have the further advantage that they are not esoteric. Certainly social scientists can lay no claims to expertise in deciding these matters. If a planned change is supposed to serve certain ideals, then the layman can and will understand the criteria for judging the planning process before being confronted by the final and possibly irreversible outcome. The layman's judgment may not extend to a learned appraisal of why things are going wrong or what action should be taken, but at least he may sound the alarm in time for something useful to be done.

One special property of ideals needs to be noted because of the damage it does to the optimizer's claim to "planning excellence." The ideals that influence the behavior of people cannot be subsumed under a single ideal. Omnipotence, which is the one ideal that, if achieved, would permit the achievement of all other ideals, is only directly and single-mindedly pursued by infants and some sick, dependent people. Identification of the ideals involved in planned social change is almost certain to identify more than one noncomparable ideal, *e.g.*, homonomy, nurturance, humanity, and beauty. In such a context of multiple ideals, the skills of the optimizer cannot yield *the* plan, though his skills may still be utilized to solve tactical problems.

The other direction in which planning might change is toward designing ways of "learning to learn." Clearly this cannot be just a matter of pushing people in at the deep end. There must be some way of using accumulated experience and expertise to advantage. The current form of the search conference is a step in this direction.

In this mode of planning, the main cognitive searching shifts from searching for means to searching for ends. The search for means becomes less of a cognitive activity and more a matter of field experimentation. By such intervention one may get some sense of emerging possibilities and difficulties; for what resources are actually needed; what resources, including human commitments and innovations, can be generated in the process of change; what shifts in emphases or changes in duration are needed. In a situation of social change, this kind of intervention can give us information for the choice of paths that we cannot expect to get from the massive cross-sectional surveys favored by the engineers *cum* urban planners. These surveys give us little more than history. The two major limitations of surveys are:

1. that they are one-way communication. The questionnaire and choice of interview parameters predetermine a good deal of what is fed back. Attempts to reduce this predetermination by use of open-ended questions have largely gone by the board because of costs of coding and computer analysis;
2. that they do not indicate how people are interlocked in each others' affairs; what might happen to the views of individuals when they are confronted by others with their views and evidence.

In Freire's terms, surveys are a form of "culture invasion"—not action as cultural synthesis—as the former precludes the latter [16];

In contradistinction to surveys, the search conference provides opportunities for awareness of these interdependencies, and takes further advantage of them by asking the search community to tease out its own picture of the external environment. By exploring as a community the various causal strands that have become obvious, some idea is obtained of the changing texture of the social field in which change is planned.

Planning via the search mode must upset the traditional planner [17]. Where, he will ask, is the control that will ensure that each part of the plan is enacted in a way and at a time that will ensure optimal use of resources? Where are the objective, impartial decision rules (and protective departmentalization of *the* planning function) that will ensure that politically and personally motivated choices do not subvert the planned ends? These features are in fact absent, and their absence could be critical—to the optimizer's plans and planning. Our point is that in a rapidly changing society, the optimizing mode of planning for social change is about as adaptive as a pig in water—the harder the pig tries to swim the more it imperils itself. The optimizer tends to assume that he is preparing plans for a uninodal organization that will have the authority and power to command, through existing channels of coordination and control, that the plan be translated into reality. The new mode of planning assumes that there will be a multiplicity of nodes of power, and only a good measure of cooperation between them will produce change in the desired direction. Consequently, in this new mode, the planners create the basis for control that emerges from a shared sense of ideals and present requirements, and create channels of communication and initiation appropriate to the shared needs for coordination.

In a very real sense, the most important product of this style of active-adaptive planning is not the plan, but the *learning planning community*—experts and lay-men together [18]. The process creates the conditions for learning to learn; affirms the overriding significance of shared ideals, and reduces the need for planning as a separate, specialist, organizational activity. When new "matrix" formations seem necessary, or old forms need to be discarded, we can expect those people with potentially relevant *operational* responsibilities to come to-gether for a brief span of days and nights to search jointly for the implications of sensed changes in their shared environments. Thus, for instance, union leaders and leaders of productive enterprise will seek such opportunities to share their understanding of how the "rules of the game" are changing. They will not rele-gate this task to "research officers"; they will not risk waiting to infer it from changes in each other's tactics and strategies; they will not attempt to deal with such matters in committee. In committee it is necessary to stick with what is *significantly* probable, and trade from unchangeable corners. In "search," even the improbable must be considered as a possible key to the future. Existing bodies of data and current notions of what is relevant can be no substitute for a sense of what is coming over the horizon. The reason for this great openness is simply that today's *probabilities* are not a sure guide to the future, but the future is likely to emerge from some of the *possibilities* that now exist.

It is in this sense of being a compass that ideals do enter into and shape the organizations that men create [19]. By recognizing that organizations are in-deed created by men who are guided by ideals (whether consciously or not) and that once created these organizations affect the behavior of those who work within them, it becomes possible to begin the process of designing forms of social organization with explicit philosophies . . . forms that will produce adaptive behavior and a more stable environment. "Cultural synthesis serves the ends of organization; organization serves the ends of liberation" [20].

The strategy of search is based on the notion that it is in the design of their social organization that men can make the biggest impact upon environmental forces. We realize this is contrary to the Billy Graham strategy of going straight to the hearts of men, and that it is contrary to Jesuitical-psychoanalytical no-tions of controlling the cradle or the school. *We are suggesting that adults be the educators and that they educate themselves in the process of realizing their chosen organizational designs.* This takes us back to the question of what ideals we are pursuing. We suggest that the critical decisions about ideals for the future control of our turbulent environments are the decisions that go into choosing our basic organizational designs. If we spell out the possible choices in design, we can see what alternative ideals are involved and perhaps hazard a guess at which ideals will be pursued; *e.g.*, homonomy, nurturance, humanity, and beauty.

It is obvious that the central function of searching, the pursuit of ideals as guidelines for effective long-term planning decisions, is rooted in the reality of people coming together in groups.

The coming together in groups or organizations is the first step toward an adaptive process. We do not think that self-expression, "doing one's own thing," is an adaptive ideal unless it is concerned with expressing what is human, and concerned with inducing a human response. The philosophy of individualism has led straight into the trap of Pawley's *Private Future* [21]. Yet the most desirable alternative is *not* collectivism, conformity, or consensus.

We search for ways in which human groups can learn to create the conditions for that ideal-seeking behavior of individuals that *alone* has the potential of enabling us as groups to reduce the complexity and uncertainty of a turbulent social field.

In Summary

We search for three things:

1. Understanding of the social environment, which both constrains and provides opportunities for the emergence of individuals as ideal-seeking systems;
2. Learning situations within an active-adaptive planning task may be begun given the presence of such emergent individuals;
3. A form of management to initiate group-learning so that it avoids those forces that inhibit learning, and hence ensures that the capacity for future adaptive process and design is built into the search community itself.

HOW TO SEARCH

There are two forms of search: the search conference and the introductory "futures search."

The Search Conference [22]

This is neither a technique nor one part of a teaching package. A Search Conference is a planned and purposeful whole [23]. Its leading principle is to identify and support structures that best enable the collective learning processes of adaptive planning to occur [24]. It is not intended as a device whereby any particular plan or point of view may be pushed by an expert, nor is it yet so simple that those unskilled in the organization and management of dynamic open learning environments should be tempted to use it. Because it is designed to be open ended and to produce a self-generative learning community, it is demanding of staff resources and skills. It can create anxiety in staff who have not learned to cope with either group emotional forces or openness in a severely task-oriented situation, particularly those who are wedded to the concept of "expert." Similarly, the notion of openness to possibility as well as probability creates tension in participants, as most people abhor such a degree of openness, and behave irrationally when confronted with it [25]. They are not likely to put up with such a confrontation unless given ample time in which to search, freed from the compulsion to arrive at explicit decisions, and denied the escape into "urgent" demands of work and family.

It is this latter consideration that has led to the use of "social islands" as the venues for search conferences. The participants are brought together under conditions where they can form an isolated community for as long as seems necessary for them to do their searching. This temporary night-and-day community not only affirms that the overriding purposes must be important because such conditions are proved, but also provides psychological support to the individual. It represents a return to the older wisdom of the Persian tribes, reported by Heredotus, that no group decision reached in their night-time state of mind was binding unless reaffirmed in the harsh light of day, and *vice versa*.

Venues should be chosen to guarantee some degree of social island conditions for the participants and, internally, a maximum of freedom and comfort for face-to-face interaction, or for solitude when an individual feels that he needs it. To our knowledge, the first in the modern mode of consciously designed search conferences was held in 1959. It was designed to create a higher quality of human interaction and greater progress toward task, than was being achieved by committees, working parties, and the like. It was designed and managed by Fred Emery and Eric Trist, who over some three months, designed a face-to-face conference that would embody the implications of Bion's notions of group emotional processes, Selznick's concept of organizational character, and Asch's theory of shared psychological fields [28]. Since that time, many search conferences have been held—for corporate planning, community development, town planning, solving international conflicts, *etc.* Their diversity illustrates the versatility of the concept, but also suggests that the essential unifying feature of design and management is that individuals are enabled to move to a level of shared responsibility for their own affairs.

The Conference Design is the point from which a search conference succeeds or fails. A conference does not become a search conference because its organizers decide to label it as such, or because they wish it to engage in a search. Simply wishing does not make it come true. The design can be separated into structure and process.

Structure

Overall Structure. To appreciate the structure of a search conference is to appreciate the difference between planning and programming. We eschew any programming of the learning that will take place in such a conference. The plan, or overall structure is presented—and if accepted by participants as appropriate—is intended as a minimal set of signposts to enable them to get back on course or recycle when they so wish, and to help them assess their own progress.

The structure consists of a series of phases toward completion of the task, and will finally be determined by the requirements of the task as it progresses. It is impossible beforehand to time the phases of the task, and no restrictions are placed on the group returning to the work of earlier phases if it is felt that they need reworking. Figures 5 and 6 clarify the search structure with two real examples in a context of community planning. Although these diagrams illustrate the plan for the task, they do not reflect the erratic, recycling character of the natural learning process of a working group.

Figure 6, illustrating the plan for the search into the future of Canberra, presents through a different visual arrangement the same essential "homing in" on the purpose of the search from the widest and most open starting point. By leaving the constraints to the last minute, it is possible to ensure that the desired values are left explicit and not obscured (as they are when economic and technological constraints are the first and foremost consideration).

The starting point again was the reality of the future as it emerges today, and in Phase 1 the past has not come up for discussion.

In Phase 2 the past was explicitly focused upon, and its good and bad characteristics drawn out of the collective memory. In Phase 3 the work was oriented to the question of which of those features was it desirable to retain in the future

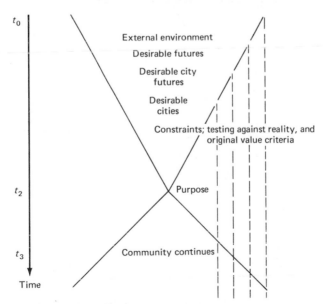

Figure 5. Overall structure of a search conference. An example from the planning of the community of Gungahlin.

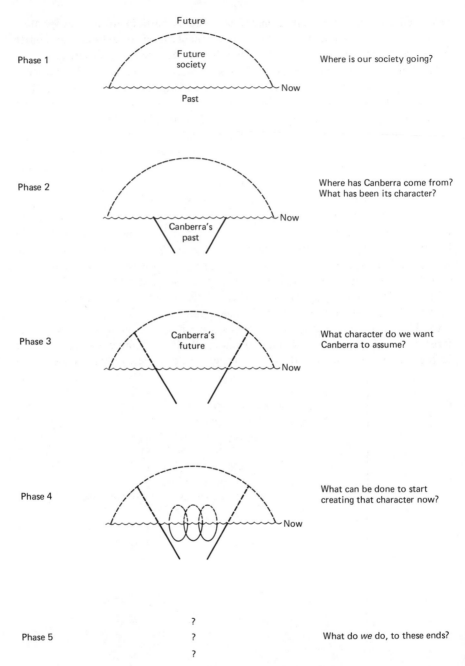

Figure 6. Plan for the search for Canberra's future.

development of Canberra. The diagram illustrates the continuity of the past into the future.

Phase 4 illustrates the coming into being of a new community (the search conference community) which has taken on the job of trying, through their own nature and mode of working, to further that character of the city that they have already agreed is the most desirable one.

The final Phase 5 was the session designed to make decisions about the most effective future course of action for the conference community.

The search for the future of Canberra illustrates another feature that is present in anything apart from a completely green-fields situation. In identifying the ideal goals that will be relevant to the planning process, the participants will need to build up a shared picture of where the system has come from, as well as of its likely futures. This applies equally strongly to an industrial or commercial organization as it does to a town or city.

Preparation for a Search Conference. Preparation should involve at least two phases. The first, ideally, consists of reading and thinking about the nature of the search conference in general. Following this, again ideally, there should be a meeting of all those to be involved in the conference to raise matters of concern and answer questions. Such a briefing session clarifies purposes, prevents crippling confusions and misunderstandings about process and method, and allows the work during the conference itself to flow more smoothly and efficiently.

Figure 6 (*continued*)

Phase 1. External environment, or futures we're in [27]. The task is to search out all the possible trends that are occurring in society by building a shared list of recent events; these will be technical, environmental, social, attitudinal, demographic, *etc.* [28].

Phase 2. Desirable futures. Having decided that all movements have been considered, the group constructs from this list a set of desirable futures, which will be based on an implicit or explicit list of agreed values. This will still be general insofar as it will not, at this stage, be saying "let us look at a set of desirable cities."

Phase 3. Desirable city futures. The set of generalized desirable futures will be translated into a set of desirable city pictures.

Phase 4. Constraints, testing against reality, and original value criteria. These city pictures will, in some way determined by the group, be reality-tested, but the process will involve going back to the original list of trends, directions, and agreed values for checking that the proposed desirable cities do actually meet the criteria. Some may be modified or discarded during this process.

Phase 5. Purpose: the present. The group slowly moves back from the future to the present as it considers implementation of the city designs. From consideration of the present circumstances of building materials, the lay of the land, and all necessary constraints, one or two of the desirable cities will emerge as the final outcome.

The first session. This is the critical session, as it is here that the ground rules are set for the common core of understandings needed to raise the probability of cooperation and learning [29].

The initial briefing about the total design and program for the whole search should make explicit the concept and structure of a search. It is desirable to do this, for the concept of a search itself is one of the tools that individuals and organizations may need to use again on other tasks in other areas of their lives. It particularly involves explaining why the approach to the task needs to be so circuitous. In situations where conflict and polarization about alternative solutions has occurred prior to the search, this explanation is particularly important if the second purpose is to be met.

In this first session, the search is for the embryos of social change, recent events that may provide clues about trends and directions in the social field. This attempt to understand what is happening in the L_{22} (the environment that functions independently of the actions or intentions of any individual system, person or organization) serves all the purposes of the search.

It does provide data on trends in society, and by taking the individuals participating in it out of their own narrow worlds, it begins to create a shared world.

This session is thus the first step toward community, in that individuals realize they are related to each other by way of shared context [30].

While this opening session is critical to the success of a search, it is physically and conceptually simple. All that is needed is plenty of large sheets of paper on the walls, a couple of felt pens, and an introduction along these lines:

. . . a very brief introduction to the nature of change and the environment, followed by an invitation to all present to contribute to our knowledge of the environment by throwing in the changes or events that they have noticed in the last few years. It is necessary to emphasize that while some changes may appear isolated or insignificant when they first happen, it is worthwhile noting them as possible forerunners of major trends. This first session is purely a recording one and not for discussion of whether a contribution is right, wrong, important, *etc.* This is a critical ground rule for this stage of the task. The introduction should make this clear, as a search involves looking at all the possibilities contained within the future One of the possibilities is that all people may learn that they have something to contribute to a shared task.

To make this first phase nonthreatening, it is necessary to avoid having high-powered, high-status staff giving a "proper" introduction. "The medium is the message" in this matter. No matter what the declared democratic, nondirective aims, people tend to get the message that, once again, someone is trying to shape them to some unrevealed end [31]. The instructions will seem inadequate, and we know that people will say at the end that "if only you had explained what you were about at the beginning we would have wasted less time." This is the wisdom of hindsight, however. More explicit direction would result in the group taking longer to come into existence and being more susceptible to antilearning modes. Inadequacy of instructions and explanations is easily remedied when a group is ready to get at its task.

A Futures Search might have been a hopeless procedure even 20 years ago. Such a search then might have been divisive. Just about everyone *would have seen the future* as more or less of the things they had at the time, *e.g.*, more years at school for everyone, less work for most because of automation, more cars and freeways, compulsory futuristic public transport. In recent years, when groups of people freely explore social futures, they display a high degree of convergence, and it is not about the 1984 of George Orwell. Groups converge in an understanding of a world that is self-directed toward the ideals of man.

The first session is, therefore, critical in bringing into being a group identity. The emphasis on extensive quantities of chart paper and wall space is for the same reasons of structure and process. Contrast can be made with the use of blackboards, epidiascopes, *etc.* Blackboards provide a constrained space for which individuals must compete. And the data recorded on blackboards are transient—sooner or later they must be wiped off and replaced. Rolls of chart paper help to confirm the message that there is time and space for all individuals to make their contribution to the shared record. While it is another aspect of the structure that indicates practical cooperation, it also conveys the fact that these contributions are the basic and long standing data that are needed. All individuals are shown to have a share in making the future.

When the list of changes is complete, it will contain contradictions and inconsistencies. It should remain in full view of participants for the next session, where it may be used in various ways for the whole period of the search, as a reminder that there is indeed a complex and shared reality.

Subsequent sessions. Whether the total group continues to work together throughout the conference or spends some time in subgroups is a question that can be decided only in terms of the requirements of each individual event. Generally, we feel that the longer the large group can continue functioning, the more effectively it is built up as a strong and continuing learning community.

Small groups can often provide a new stimulus to the process, however, and have been employed in a variety of ways to perform more specific functions. Among these we might list:

1. Working in parallel to verify the validity of any basic condensation of previous work, or to check whether the evaluative checklist schedule arrived at by the plenary group was coherent, consistent, and usable.
2. Working on different aspects of the total problem to explore proposals in greater detail than could be obtained in the time available to the large group.

3. Working on different sections of an organization to explore how best they be organized or restructured to meet the newly planned organizational purposes agreed upon by the total group.

These three examples are all of the type that would fit small group work into the final stage of the conference. It is usually not helpful to break into smaller groups immediately after the first session; any break should be delayed until the managers of the conference are convinced that the learning process of the first session is consolidated. The whole question is, however, one of judgment.

Internal Structure. A search conference is designed to bring into being learning, planning COMMUNITIES. While the critical relationship within the concept of overall structure is between participants and task, the internal structure revolves around the relationships between staff and participants. We have learned that the nature of staff-to-staff relationships must mirror precisely the nature of group or community relationships. That is, there must be a shared staff group responsibility for the conference as a whole. This is the staff-to-task relationship. Staff-to-participant relations must not be allowed to fall into a one-to-one pattern. The single fact that individual staff members become identified with individual groups of the community is often sufficient to account for various shortcomings in a conference.

Figure 7 illustrates the two divergent models, A and C. There is also an inter-

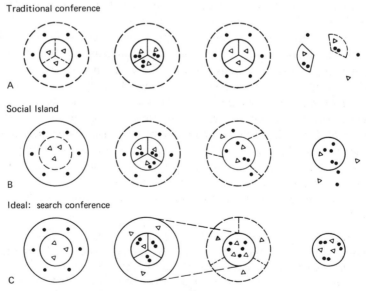

Figure 7. Internal structure of conferences over time.

mediate, less than ideal model, B. In the figure, we illustrate topologically the sequences of figure-to-ground relationships that operate in an effective community building search (C) or a traditional academic or leader and group building conference (A).

The models may be read as sequences in themselves or each may be compared at any point in time to provide an analysis of the effects of different initial and subsequent structures.

In the traditional conference, the initial conditions (t_0) involve the staff as figures against the ground of the task of community-building. It is staff input or action that provides the focus, data, and direction for subsequent process. Participants relate to or contribute to the task only indirectly. In the search conference t_0, while there must inevitably be some focus on staff because they have staff responsibilities, they seek to keep a low profile and allow the emphasis or figural properties to attach to the community task. Because staff have been briefed on their role, they act with group responsibility and without emphasis on individual specializations in their attempt to minimize the distance between themselves and participants as they continue to the first stage of the task.

At t_1 in the conventional structure, the conference breaks into groups with their own leaders or "facilitators," and the work of these groups continues to be figural not only against the background of the averred task of the community, but also against the other groups. The conference has failed to come together as a community itself by the final sessions (t_2), where the distinction between staff and participants remains as strong as at t_0, but with the added disadvantage that the boundaries between staff as individuals and with special areas and functions have been strengthened. Any end product of such a structure must evitably be an "and-summative aggregation" rather than an example of "productive thinking" [32]. Because the task of building a cohesive community was never the overall ambition the postconference possibilities must be as illustrated at t_3.

In distinction to A, Model C at t_1 continues with the staff as a group concerned with the figural properties of the community and acting accordingly (as a resource group to the participants, whose working group has the figural properties). By building in this dual-level message through structure, the final sessions (t_2) in this model show implicitly and explicity that learning about building communities is generated through the experience of building communities. Participants and staff as a new community have figural recognition as an instrumental condition only—internal scaffolding. These dynamics ensure that a community ensues into the postconference environment.

Model B represents a transitional or immature form of the search conference. While its structure at t_1 reverts to the predominance of group work over community generation, such factors as extreme social island conditions, accepting community responsibility for some domestic tasks, and the meaningfulness of the task, may be sufficient to reinstate the community as the dominant and continuing figure. It is obvious from the models that A is conducive to a competitive mode of interrelation, C to a cooperative or a community venture. Thus, the basic design fault in Model B is built in at t_1.

It can be seen that internal structure exerts a powerful and pervasive influence. Model A can produce tension and unease in a staff group that has come together with the best intentions of cooperation and with experience of having worked together before. It can prejudice any serious attempt at building cohesive communities, or producing constructive work during plenary sessions.

The traditional academic conference has a totally different purpose and ethic derived from the bureaucratic principle endemic in universities. Such conferences are not designed for a broad-based, responsible learning effort. They arose for the purpose of information-exchange from experts to the rest and, as such, are performance-oriented rather than task-oriented. Conferences that attempt to solve problems or puzzles, yet use a traditional academic format, inevitably result in inconsistencies, frustrations, and disappointment at the consequent inaction. The large international conferences, such as World Food, Law of the Sea, and the Women's Conference in Mexico, are good examples of these disappointments, despite the huge financial and human resources that were poured into their preparation and "staging."

We must appreciate that when the responsibility for a meaningful task is handed to a group, its members can cope effectively with the task and their own internal dynamics. There are resources hidden in groups that will be fully realized only under conditions of responsible and complete autonomy. The learning that occurs in leaderless, task-oriented groups can be fast and deep.

Staffs are usually chosen because they have greater experience and understanding of the task than participants. What then is the role of the staff group in Model C?

First, they must model the structure they know to be most effective in meeting the purpose of the conference. Second, their resources relevant to the content of the task have to be shared with participants in approriate ways at appropriate times.

In operational terms this means:

1. staffs function from the beginning as resources and managers, not as leaders in the traditional sense of content-oriented conferences;
2. small group work should not begin until this responsible learning mode has been fully established;
3. individual staff members must not, during small group work, allow themselves to become identified with a particular group or group product. It is

fine if staff members wander around the groups monitoring progress and then have their own group discussions at that time;

4. staffs manage report-back sessions, if any, as a group, and manage them in such a way that an integral community product emerges and furthers the mainstream of learning.

5. by not being drawn into the intricacies of any small group dynamics, staff members are left free to maintain a shared overview of the whole community and the progress toward the task. Therefore, any interventions they may make at this stage are likely to be task-effective and community-oriented.

Process: Managing Learning

A search conference comes into being in the first session when a face-to-face collection of people takes on its identity as a group *and* engages in group learning, but it has some all-important differences.

When a group is brought into existence it is then open to pervasive and strong emotional processes that are inimical to group learning [33]. The two very obvious ones are fight-flight and dependency. When a group switches into the fight-flight mode, the members are in no mood to learn from each other. Their concern is either with getting away from the subject matter or with winning and losing. When a group is in the dependent mode, the members feel no dependence for mutual edification. They feel they could only learn from the leader *cum* teacher *cum* expert. We note in passing that they usually do little to learn from the leader. They act as if his knowledge of whatever it is that they need to know is good enough. They do not have to learn, it is only a question of heeding the words and having faith.

To bring about a *group identity* that will subsequently support group learning it is necessary to:

1. create a nonthreatening situation where:
2. members can identify a framework of shared values and beliefs that is broad enough to encompass the areas of probable disagreement, and;
3. in the process allows individuals to give notice to others of their presence as individual persons.

There are many ways of bringing about group identity, but few of these groups are then capable of sustained group learning.

As discussed above, the first session is critical in both structure and process. For this reason, staff, in the first phase, should devote themselves to the task of recording, and to mobilizing the group to help an individual to express his idea to his own satisfaction for summary recording. This is the first chance that the group has had to prove to themselves that they can do a job together. Hence, the staff must be alert to when the search effort is sagging and requires stimulation. The stimulation should be such that it helps the people get onto a new unblocked path without specifying how they travel on that path.

For the *process of group formation*, the valuable things about the futures search are that:

1. staff are displayed in practice as just resource people,
2. responsibility for the work is clearly left with the participants, and
3. the task is such that the people are very likely to get a feeling of a successful *group* accomplishment.

The other task for the staff is that of controlling group emotions—lessening the time they spend in fight-flight or dependency. We know from practice that those processes can be deliberately influenced, but describing how is like explaining how one body-surfs. Demonstration is easy; explanation is difficult. Several things seem fairly sure:

1. The group, once it is in existence, must be forced, as far as it is possible, to dig into its own resources and not to turn to experts to answer questions of fact. As a corollary, it must be deterred from any logical evasions from questions of value and preference . . . deterred from expediencies of questions of fact or "further research." To do so is a sure way of moving into the dependent mode and rejecting its own responsibility. To say, as we have done above, that the group "must be forced" or "must be deterred", might suggest that the search conference is only a more sophisticated means of creating a dependent group. Just the opposite is true. When we recognize the natural forces in a group that act against any learning, group or individual, then it is encumbent on democratic "leadership" to oppose these group forces so that people are enabled to do their own learning.
2. The members of the group must be prevented, as far as possible, from making win-lose, zero-sum games out of issues on which they disagree. It is most unlikely that there is no solution from which they can both gain. Defining a broad framework of shared agreements in the first phase is only a rough solution. At that phase it is not possible to be sure whether it is an adequate framework. Hence, the staff must be ready to detect when it is necessary to go back for another look at the broader framework. This is made easier by the fact that the sheets of ideas from the first session are still hanging up around the walls. If this were not so, then the disputing parties would almost certainly interpret the past, of the last day or so, as proving that they were always in opposition! In particular this means that the staff should do nothing that might produce a fight-flight emotion in the group. Differences that exist should not be brought to confrontation until the group is able to find a nonzero-sum solution, a rationalization of mutual losses, or an "out" that leaves open some ways of starting again.

3. In discussing the role of the staff we have made no mention of what they get out of it. Clearly, they would have to be naturally motivated if they were to act along the lines we suggest. If it did not come naturally, then they would put across quite different messages. The abiding condition is that thus the staff itself get satisfaction out of manipulating the group through its various emotional phases.

4. The group must be allowed to work at its own pace and in its own style. When it is so allowed, one finds that the natural process is progression by fits and starts; exciting spurts of creativity as things seem to fall into place; plateaus when nothing much appears to be happening but reflection and reconsideration; phases of confusion when direction seems to be lost and where the group refuses to follow or take up any new direction suggested by its members, no matter how good they might think them ten minutes later; phases when the whole scene suddenly transforms itself into little noisy buzz groups of two or three neighbors. Furthermore, progression is in no way like the steady step-by-step progression through a prepared classroom lesson, or through the agenda of a formally chaired meeting. Instead, a learning group will be seen to go round in circles and quite happily go off at a tangent; matters are raised, half dealt with or apparently agreed, and then returned to later and worked over again.

   Even individual learning is much more like this than teachers are prepared to admit. If the staff acts on the classroom model, then the groups are likely to lose confidence in themselves as a learning group.

   There is not actually a great deal that the staff can do to influence the rate of learning. Its fundamental task is to bring the learning group into being, lessen the chances of it switching into the antilearning moods of fight-flight or dependency, and help re-cohere the learning group if it inadvertently gets destroyed. Paradoxically, the time the staff can most contribute to speed up the process is when the group is in its fastest moving phase of excited creativity. If the staff has bright ideas relevant to what the group is working on, they are likely to be accepted as a contribution because at that point many others of the group's own ideas will also be up in the air.

   When the group shows signs of getting onto a learning plateau, the staff can help if it can provide a clear and acceptable summary. Such a summary can be reassuring to the members of the group insofar as it shows they are making real progress. It may also aid them to digest what they have done.

   This is not to suggest that the staff has or ought to have some superior intellectual capacity for pulling things together. It is simply that as linesmen they are better placed to follow the whole game. They are not preoccupied with where to place the next shot.

5. Beyond this, the most important role of the staff is to maintain and display faith in the willingness of the learning group to work and its ability to do a good job. The job they do may turn out to be inadequate for the task they set out to do, but this is equally possible of any other human endeavor.

This faith can come only from actually observing the high commitment to work that is generated by learning groups, the extent to which they benefit themselves by resting phases, and the very high tempo of progress of which they are capable when the mood moves them. If the staff shows anxiety when the group is in a resting phase, it communicates a negative and harmful message to the group. If the staff shows agitation about whether there is enough time left to complete the work, it gives a similarly harmful message. Given enough of these messages a group will drop out of the learning mode by becoming defensive, withdrawing from the task, or, in effect, saying: ". . . you show us how to do it." If this happens and cannot be corrected, the group members will have no commitment to an end product, because it will not be felt to be theirs, and they can take no pride in it.

A slightly different role exists for the staff when, in the middle of an excited creative phase, the group dissolves into a noisy mass of buzz groups. This appears to be a flooding of the euphoric emotion the group experiences at seeing how good it is—"Isn't it great to be here." To an anxious staff it could easily appear to be a sudden switch to flight. In fact, it probably always has something of that in it: creativity has a disturbing resemblance to madness. In any case this euphoric group emotion, which has been described as the pairing phenomenon, seems to be very fragile compared with the other two basic group emotions. It is probably best for the staff not to let it go on beyond three to five minutes, so as to avoid a contagious spread of the fear-and-flight component, but rather to suggest a resting phase or introduce some quieting tangencies.

Sometimes a group will come back from such a pause with a renewed creative vigor. Nevertheless, the temptation for the staff is to try to bring them back to do just that, by calling them together to consider deeper implications of what they have just achieved, or to consider what meanings emerge if they summarize and pull together their achievements to date.

If this is misjudged, the flight component is very likely to turn into anger or even a fight against any such suggestion that they had meant that, or agreed to this. If the group is pulled together in the cautious resting mode, nothing more than a few minutes will be lost. It will quickly reassert its creativity when it is ready to do so.

The final phase has often been badly handled. Usually there is an expected group product on which the group will continue to work in other ways. Because the staff has been in an overviewing role, and has demonstrated this by its interventions to provide timely summaries, it too easily assumed that it has to be involved to ensure the best final report on what was done. The best and quickest end product may be nowhere near as satisfactory as a product that is due to the group's own efforts. If this is so, the end phase of a search conference should be so designed that the participants are thrown back on their own resources to so manage themselves that they decide what end product, if any, they need, how they are going to manage it, and what they are going to do with it [34].

Other Practical Matters

Selection of Participants. This is a matter for detailed discussion during the planning for a search conference; the only basic requirement is that the participants be among those people who have in the past shown leadership, in the sense of displaying an active concern about matters central to the search. Selection procedures and criteria will vary, depending for example on whether the planning to be done is for a large, formal organization or a residential community.

For corporate planning it is recommended that those persons in the organization with the highest operational responsibilities be included. This may seem unduly conservative. Yet, if the search process is to issue forth into a wide range of experimental interventions, it must have the sanction of the existing powers and the active support of those who control the operational units. If this support is not forthcoming, the matter is one for a power solution, not a planning solution. One further matter offsets the conservative bias. In a rapidly changing social setting, the greatest resistances to planned change are likely to arise from fear of change rather than from vested interests. Vested interests can be identified, calculated, and negotiated as part of the price of change. Fear of change cannot; hence, the great value of winning the hard core of professional leadership [35].

In the field of community planning, our experience with a search conference of citizens about Canberra's future may be helpful. There we sought a group of people that would: 1) adequately reflect how the population of Canberra, 185,000 people, would like to shape the future of the city; and 2) be a small enough group to engage in meaningful, face-to-face interaction about their views. That is, we wanted a microcosm of Canberra's population that would display not just differences in viewpoint and interests, but would show, through their interaction, how optimal solutions to these differences might be brought about. This meant that: 1) the selection of people had to be varied enough to reflect the probable range of *community* views, not the range of individual idiosyncratic opinion; 2) the selection had to be such as to avoid bias creeping in through factionalism, or persons being tied down to act as lobbyists for some outside interest group; and 3) the participants needed to be people who had evidenced some concern for the community beyond self-interest. It was *not* considered relevant that they be educated, literate, or articulate. We were confident that if they were concerned with the issue at hand they would find a tongue in the group setting.

Bias was deliberately sought 1) toward old people at all social levels who had spent most of their life in the region, and 2) toward young people who had grown up there. These low mobility groups tend to evince a greater identification with their cities, and to be more sensitive to the nuances of its character.

This raises the question of "representativeness." Representation, in the sense of designing and using "representative" systems of participation, is not part of search culture. That representative systems do not change actual conditions or provide new futures for the great mass of people has been documented [36]. Nor is there any place in a search conference for people who attend as representatives of a fixed interest or ideological position. This would only slow down or prohibit the process of search. All participants are briefed beforehand that they will attend and work just as themselves.

But it is in this sense that there is another aspect to representation. We have postulated a basic set of human ideals that appear to be part of the nature of man and, therefore, culture-free. One of the tasks of a search conference is to create the conditions within which these ideals can be formulated as practical and workable guidelines for decision-making. It is not too extreme to say that in these situations each participant is a representative of the human group. It has often caused surprise that each search group's product does embody the set of four ideals postulated [37].

The selection procedure in the Canberra search was by community referral, as at Geelong. A number of people scattered throughout the community, and as far as we know unconnected with each other, were asked if they knew someone other than themselves who would be sufficiently interested in community deveopement to give up a weekend to discuss Canberra's future. As it happened, some people were referred by more than one source. The validity of these referrals can be judged by the fact that of 38 approached only 3 did not agree to give up their weekend. Of these three, one was going to be overseas at the time and two had sickness in the family. Those who accepted agreed to come as individuals, not as representatives.

In all cases of planning selection procedures, it is essential to keep the total number of participants to 35, which is the upper limit to a workable learning community. A group smaller than 35 is preferable.

Duration and Scheduling. The length of a search conference can vary, but depends ultimately on the balance of size and complexity of job and the risk of cognitive overload in the participants. It is rarely necessary to extend a search beyond two days and nights. The designing of Gungahlin's future extended over five days, and left the overriding impression of immense energy and enthusiasm [38]. It is doubtful that this lengthy a period was necessary, however.

While the group of young people who designed Gungahlin showed resilience in the intense, continuous, creative mode, other experiences beyond the two-day-and-night limit have not been as happy in their long-term consequences. Also, although the planning of Gungahlin was a necessary first step in the diffusion of understanding of active, adaptive planning—as a detailed and reality-tested product was advantageous—subsequent community searches have not found it necessary to establish more than a consistent set of guidelines for development.

The scheduling of the conference usually has to conform to everyday considerations. The necessary main features are that:

1. the group has a chance to meet socially and informally over a dinner before they have a chance to get into confrontation about their differences;
2. they have a chance to reflect on the thought of what they are engaged in before they are committed, and to reflect on what they are producing before they shape up the final product; and
3. they have a minimum of two continuous days and nights, as implied above.

The need to "sleep" on things is not an old wives' tale. Time and again problems on which a learning group has been blocked have been resolved by a bit of dream-work.

The most facilitative schedule appears to be one where the conference begins in late afternoon or at dinner, and continues for two full days. The type of task required of the participants by the first session is not one that suits the average individual's morning activity. A shared, relaxed, and informal meal on the first night is also helpful in creating a supportive atmosphere for the further development of the learning community. Though these conditions do facilitate the task, they are peripheral to managing the learning process itself. Conferences, such as that at Geelong, have succeeded with suboptimal arrangements.

The Role of Observers. Others from an organization or sponsoring body, *etc.*, or who just want to see the search conference in action, often request admittance. Often such persons are present so that they can judge for themselves the meaning and validity of the sorts of statements that have been made about learning groups. To minimize switches into dependency or agression, it is better that observers be present throughout so long as the participants have no strong feelings against their presence, but that they should speak only when spoken to.

Usually by the time a conference is ready to break into small groups, these observers are freely admitted into the small-group structure to find their own level as contributors.

The Futures Search or Perspectives Session

There is an abbreviated form of search that serves as an excellent introduction to virtually any type of conference or meeting. It is usually conducted in the same way as the first session of a search conference. Opening a conference with such a session does *not*, however, justify calling the conference a "search conference." This has caused much confusion in the past. To reduce the confusion, we suggest that "Perspectives" is a more appropriate label for this introduction; it encompasses the past, as well as the future, and this is sometimes a relevant dimension of a task.

The usefulness of a perspective session as the introductory phase of a workshop or traditional conference is manifold:

1. Because of its power to bring into being a shared understanding of the social environment, it can clarify and give greater depth to the task of the remainder of the conference.
2. The experimental learning of the role of staff and participants can help overcome design faults and difficulties in other areas of the conference.
3. it serves as a backdrop and support to the efforts of individuals who strive to initiate adaptive changes in rigid and traditional programs.
4. It uncovers the alternatives that are possible in the future, and exposes the fact that there is a choice of alternative courses of action and consequence.

Depending on the time available for this contextual introduction, the session may be left completely open after production of the initial list. This allows individuals to reflect at leisure on the most probable futures emerging from their shared list. Alternatively, the conference may sort itself into smaller groups to explore to greater definition which will be the most probable future. This can be done in a variety of ways depending on the nature of the task itself. The conference may choose to divide itself into optimists and pessimists, who will later have to justify from the list their most probable scenarios, or it may simply form small groups to explore the most probable, or most desirable future.

However far toward closure this session is taken, it always provides a shared understanding of context and its nature. Design and redesign programs that have proceeded without benefit of this introduction have later encountered difficulties that can be traced to a lack of shared understanding of context [39].

Some Don'ts

These are not in any order of priority, but each will hinder the search process and its long-term consequences.

1. Don't try to prepare participants in advance of the first session. Some use a form of Delphi technique before the conference to alert people to the future. This is not only unnecessary, but actually precludes the process of search. Delphi is based on the probable, not the possible. It also elevates the isolated thinking of individuals and demotes the working through of

common ideals. There is no easy way to move from a Delphi to an appreciation of value trends.

2. Similarly, don't invite contributions or keynote addresses from people who are supposed to know. A search is designed to allow people to escape from traditional assumptions and best guesses. Nothing is more confining than either the "average" or the "considered expert" opinion. In fact, any event that is designed to focus the conference on the purpose of the task at the beginning will destroy the chances of a proper search, where the matter that is usually the background becomes the figure or focus. In other words, the environment or context of the task must come first.

3. Don't use simulations or game-playing techniques. Simulations directly conflict with the aim of a search, which is a concentrated exploration of reality. We have never found difficulty in getting people to look directly at the future, as they are already aware of the future in the present, either implicitly or explicitly. Simulations often provide the organizers with an escape from a threatening situation. One reason that a real search is such a unique event—and runs the risk of overload in both participants and managers—is its intense preoccupation with the hardest data of all—the fundamental reality of ideals and values. If these do not form the context within which the planning guidelines are arrived at, the guidelines or conclusions will be invalid.

4. Don't appoint a chairman. Search conferences may have managers or resource people, but the managers do not in any sense play the role of chairman. They must be experienced in the search process and capable of handling emotional phenomena in large learning groups.

5. Don't appoint rapporteurs. There is a difference between recorders and rapporteurs. The whole system of having rapporteurs taking notes and presenting *their* summaries at the end of a session again conflicts with the purpose and method of a search, where all data are recorded immediately on chart (or butchers) paper as a group product, obvious to all. This method of recording is advantageous in that:

   (a) the data are available for all to work on at any stage during the conference;

   (b) they may be summarized by the total membership when they decide it is necessary, or desirable;

   (c) it makes sure that all individual contributions are given equal weight, as all participants come as human beings, not as representatives;

   (d) it increases the potential of the conference as an experience of truly democratic process; and

   (e) it renders irrelevant any notions such as working to consensus or voting for majority views.

It is often difficult for some to believe in this particular dynamic before they have experienced it. Our society has not provided many situations where democracy can be effectively realized in practice. Representative systems of democracy have failed to accord high priority to common human ideals, and the main point in the above is that the participative democratic process must be entirely consistent with the purpose of the exercise if the end product is to be valid and reliable.

6. Don't allow the conference to be held on an everyday work site, such as somebody's office or conference room. First, as searching is not an everyday event, it needs to be taken out of the realm of everyday business. Second, the special conditions needed to guarantee a successful search include freedom from the telephones, routine decision-making, and responsibilities and interruptions. Searching is an intense single-minded activity, and the searching community needs well-defined boundaries between itself and the outside world.

7. Don't allow formal sessions to run overtime. This is to run an even greater risk of overstimulation of all involved. It also tends to break down an effective working relationship because responsibility for task completion can be seen to be drawn out and elastic. Nevertheless, a few drinks and an informal discussion in twos and threes after a formal session is a good way of airing and dissipating tension and anxieties, particularly before retiring for the evening.

8. Don't demand that uncommitted or hostile members attend as full participants. It is always possible to use the observer role if preliminary discussions have not been fully effective in conveying the nature and purpose of a search conference to a particular individual. Don't attempt to arrange a search conference unless there is a degree of commitment to it by most of the people who need to be there. This applies whether they be a group that spans the range of operational responsibilities included under the task of the conference or two or more parties to a dispute. It is obviously of little point to run, for example, an industrial relations search conference when twenty managers but only one unionist will attend.

9. Don't confuse a search conference with a T group or encounter group. The search conference is a highly specifically, task-oriented event in a way that other events that utilize small and large group dynamics are not.

10. Do not permit people who are without search conference experience to act as managers of either structure or process, except in a training role.

11. Do not anticipate having to mobilize or use massive resources of technical equipment, background information or audio-visual aids. Most of what is needed for a search conference already exists in the participants. Anything else that might come up during the process can either be coopted at the time or introduced later. Above all, do not allow the introduction of equipment as a substitute for face-to-face *communication*, regardless of arguments on economic or other grounds. There is no substitute for the close, all-sensory channel communication that takes place in a physically present human group. It is not possible to search through the medium of video-conferencing.

12. In preparation for, or execution of, a search conference, don't confuse decision-making in the bureaucratic sense with the conclusions and guidelines that arise from a search. A search group must have freedom from the compulsion to arrive at singular or hard-and-fast decisions. Otherwise the active adaptive planning of the group, with its core of understandings about the process of learning to learn and the creative evolution of structures, is going to be seriously inhibited. The process is not designed to realize a complete and finished solution for any problem or organization. Any attempt to produce this, as opposed to a set of guidelines, will result again in long term frustration and disillusion. The medium must be the message.

How Not to Search

A Comparision of the Search Conference with the Delphi Technique

Delphi	*Search*
This technique can be usefully applied only when specific possible future outcomes are precisely stated.	By contrast, the search conference starts by asking people to soften their *a priori* positions and suspend judgment about what specific outcomes will occur until something of a shared, overall picture has emerged.
This technique considers each issue in isolation. Special techniques of cross-impact analysis then have to be devised to get back to the realities of interdependence.	The search conference starts by exploring interdependencies and only then looks at what might happen to a specific issue in that context.
Delphi claims to get over the stifling effects of status in committees by the anonymity of the particular forecasts. Nevertheless, the deviant individual still confronts the majority forecast of anonymous experts. Will the people running the exercise think much of his claim to expertise and soundness? As the Asch experiments on independence and conformity would predict, the variance in predictions decreases markedly with each repetition. In a face-to-face situation, a deviant might	In a search conference, the ground rules insist that even the most improbable suggestions must be looked at. However outlandish something may seem, it must be given a chance to come into the overall picture if it is a possible happening. Not being anonymous, people can judge for themselves whether the critics of esoteric ideas are self-opinionated specialists; whether a view is promising, but the expounder needs help to develop it;or whether the questions they are asking themselves

be more inclined to hold out if he sees that someone he respects also shares his deviant view. He might also hold out if his explanation wins even some grudging approval from others.

To make sure that everyone puts the same interpretation on a question, the inevitable tendency is to place greatest weight on very specific and preferably technical matters.

Regarding relative attention to figure and ground, the Delphi technique focuses on figural properties, not the ground. The participants are required to focus upon specific events and make forecasts for those events, regardless of changes in the context.

are the wrong questions. They do not, as in Delphi, have to assume that everyone's judgment is as good as everyone else's. They do not have to assume that someone else's decision about the set of questions is unchallengeable.

Values and broad encompassing social processes are the main fare of search conferences, as they are the main features of social change.

In a search conference the participants are requested to do the opposite; to concentrate on identifying the broader context and its tendencies to change. Only within this defined context does the search proceed to examine figural properties of particular classes of events. It is not unusual to find in this process a restructuring or recentering of what was initially assumed to be an integral class of events.

Committees and their Workings

Characteristics	Consequences
Negotiation from positions of different interest	Striving for individual advantages
Limited, delegated authority, either to committee, or to the individual members	Constant looking over the shoulder to higher authorities
Rigid, detailed structuring to contain conflicts of interest	The structure itself becomes a major focus of committee work
Search for simple structure of its business to facilitate negotiation and resolution	Painstaking attempts to reassert the differences by splitting hairs and nit picking
Competition for allies and committee time to strengthen one's negotiating position	Concern with gaining psychological dominance; attempts to "fix the race" beforehand

The potential for joint search arises primarily from the universal, tacit, and compelling human assumptions, which constantly tend to shape the interactions between people and the psychological processes within people. The four major characteristics of these *ABX* situations, where *A-B* are people, and *X* is some set of objects or events, have been spelled out largely by the probing experiments of Solomon Asch. (They are discussed at length in *A Choice of Futures*, pp. 18-25, 163-165.)

What happens to the human assumptions about the *ABX* situation in committee working?

1. Does committee working confirm the existence of "an objectively ordered field open to all of the members"—"that things are what they appear to be?"

This is so far from being the case that astute observers always stress the need to identify "the hidden agendas." One cannot be sure what expressed disagreements really mean, whether the stated explanations correspond to the others' subjective perceptions. One cannot even be sure whether subjective disagreements are being hidden. The tendency will be to verbalize and obfuscate, not to focus, demonstrate, and clarify.

2. Does committee working confirm "the basic psychological similarity" of the members? Does it confirm that "the others are all decent, honest, intelligent people like myself"? To further one's own interests in committee, one must call into question the contributions of others who have conflicting interests. To defend one's own interest successfully, it is necessary to question the integrity of the other contenders, and the intelligence of one's potential allies. Contrast effects, not felt similarity, are what is generated in committee working.

3. Does committee working lead to the emergence of mutually shared psychological fields? Can each member learn to include the other as a potential action center in his perception of the situation? There can be little doubt that this will occur, as otherwise the committee work would breakdown completely, or drag on interminably (like the Panmunjon negotiations). A search conference seeks to realize the rich potential of face-to-face human interaction. This potential is not simply the ability to communicate. A model of face-to-face interaction that was based only on such things as modes, or channels, channel capacity, noise, and redundancy [40] would not reveal the potential to which we are referring (it might easily lead us to believe that the face-to-face situation could be closely approximated by conferencing *via* telephone or television).

The mutually shared fields will typically be asymmetrical, (as in superordinate-subordinate relations) as each seeks to better understand the hand held by the other while concealing his own.

4. Do individuals in committee working become more open, more "motivated to act on behalf of the other members, and to accept their contributions as psychologically equivalent to, and substitutable for, his own"? I think that we must conclude that the opposite is the case. The member is under pressure not

just to be close, cautious, and suspicious, but to develop a *persona* to deceive others actively. This will be so even with respect to his allies or clique.

The evidence is overwhelming that committee working contradicts three of the assumptions. As we have already pointed out, this sort of contradiction makes it highly likely that committees will spend most of their time in a state of fight-flight or dependency. Many might never even experience the pairing state.

Is there any indication whether fight-flight or dependency is especially favored? The dependency state inhibits learning and puts a wet blanket on constructive working. The fight-flight state disrupts and frustrates learning, and denies the spoils to the creator (his creative contributions are purloined by the more powerful with the silent connivance of the others). Still, in fight-flight *some* learning takes place, even though it is at a disheartening rate and level, and occurs in quite unpredictable fits and starts.

The good committee is probably one that spends most of its time in fight-flight, and the so-called good chairman is probably the person who can usually ensure this. (This is not to deny the value of a chairman who knows, or senses what cards the relevant members are holding, and, hence, knows what plays to facilitate and which to hinder.)

How could such an interpretation of committee working be true, and yet there be such continued, widespread use of committees? Surely people could not be so dense as to deny that there are real truths behind all of the cynical jokes about committee working?

We suggest that committee working is essential to the one-man, one-command structure of bureaucracies. It is "the continuation of war by other means," as Clausewitz said of politics—offensively and defensively. Committees are the preferred method of working when separate interests and territories have to negotiate their boundaries. Their primary function seems to be that of ritualized symbolic display of fight-flight tendencies, essentially the same function that has been studied in great depth in the lower orders of animals (Wynne Edwards, 1962) and man in some preindustrial societies (Heidner, *The Garden of War*).

The performances in the committee indicate what boundaries, if any, are threatened, and what additional ritualistic displays are required to intimidate others. In conditions of little change, little learning or creativity (of other than a tactical order) is required of committee working. Its function is very effectively performed by maintaining itself in fight-flight. In conditions of turbulence this is distinctively dysfunctional. It has been said of committee members and committees that "What is of most consequence at the social level is that one does not see facts in their proper context, or that one does not face them or that one violently stresses certain events at the expense of others, operations which produce misstructuring, or distortion in understanding and feeling" [41]. Such distortions in conditions of turbulence can only exacerbate the difficulties of evolving new joint responses and new forms of organization.

Traditional Conferences and Seminars

Basic Characteristics	*Consequences*
Confrontation of viewpoints to detect whether positions or paradigms existing are under challenge	Competitive striving for display; forms of arrogation build around "knowledge of"
Prior and rigid structuring of program of presentations, discussions, and topics, to lessen surprise attacks on dominant positions or paradigms	Readings from precirculated papers, already prepared to publication standards regardless of anticipated discussion
Matching of structure (time and alternative presentation) to existing statuses	Competition for time-slots and concentration on one new idea if in bottom slots; rambling in the very highest slots
Maximize apparent diversity of titles within topics (themes) to emphasize the continued fruitfulness of existing paradigms	One-upmanship in the form of hair splitting, *e.g.*, "agree wholeheartedly, but. . . ."

The basic group emotion induced by this setting is dependency, with only the occasional switch into fight-flight. It is these occasions that bring relief and delight to the participants, even though they may express shock at the manipulativeness. In the grip of dependency, the learning process is much as it is with viewing television—passive, unanalytical, and largely just conveying "knowledge of." In the fight-flight mode, the concern is with appearing to make "telling points," not with mutual understanding. To learn in this context it is necessary to follow the Bavarian Open University's rules for watching television.

Let us apply the same test to these classes of *ABX* situations.

1. Do the conference and seminar confront the participants with an open, objectively ordered world? They do not. Both in form and content, they emphasize that the world is tied into current paradigms. They further emphasize that these paradigms can be challenged only at great risk. The question-answer format has about it a marked asymmetry. The individual in the audience can hardly even make a dent in the armor of the speaker, if he is alone in his thoughts. The individual, as speaker, has practically no way of getting through to the audience if the latter is already ganged-up in defense of their shibboleths. Everything is weighted to preserve separate subjective worlds. The conference or seminar simply serves for their display, not for resolution of differences.

2. Do the conference and seminar affirm the basic psychological similarity of the participants? The best speaker is the one with the dominant interna-

tional reputation, the one who is above all others. Contrast between the levels of the speaker and the audience is sought, not similarity. The lecturer and the paper-giver themselves are motivated to display that they are above ordinary mortals in their understanding of the matter they are discussing. The unwillingness to accept that anything can be learned from the discussion of the paper is well confirmed by the frequency with which such papers have been submitted for publication even before presentation.

3. Is there an emergence of a mutually shared field? On the contrary, the whole exercise is about projecting an individual subjective world. The only response that is left open is to join or not to join.

4. Is there an increase in openness as such, as conferences and seminars proceed? No, the usual effect is divisiveness with each clique closing its mind to others.

A NOTE ON THE ROLE OF IDEOLOGY

There are two phenomena we frequently encounter in discussions of searching. First, there is the question asked of those of us who deal in the theory and practice of searching, "How can this process work when you are faced with people who have strong ideological positions and differences?" Secondly, there is the criticism that much of what is written in this essay, and performed in practice, is a function of our "ideology," or is "ideological." The question is usually serious, designed to elicit greater understanding of the process of searching. The latter, increasingly, seems to assume the status of a destructive, nondialogical criticism of the whole work. In brief, "ideology" and "ideological" appear to have become dirty words. Incidentally, "idealistic" also seems to have suffered the same fate.

These are interesting phenomena, and deserve a little attention. Let us begin to explore them by consulting the *Shorter Oxford English Dictionary*. Ideology is defined there as 1) the science of ideas; the study of the origin and the nature of ideas; 2) ideal or abstract speculation; visionary theorizing; 3) a system of ideas concerning phenomena, especially those of social life; the manner of thinking characteristic of a class or an individual.

Definition 1 would appear on the surface respectable and unable to cause the sort of problems and conflicts that are usually implied in the current popular use of "ideology." We shall come back to this point in our discussions of the ideology of "science."

Definition 2 implies quite clearly that humans have the ability to *imagine*, free of the constraints of empirical evidence or day-to-day living. The use of the word "ideal" gives the clue to one basis for condemnation, as the "idealist"—defined as "one who conceives or follows after ideals"—was first used depreciatingly as "not real or practical" in 1611 and as "visionary" in 1829.

Definition 3, a system of ideas, must apply to almost every human being who is capable of the power of thought, even though the system of ideas that guides behavior may not be thoroughly rational or made explicit. The use of the word "system" implies some coherence and internal consistency of ideas. Those who would claim to use "ideology" in this sense surely have an obligation to spell out what they see as their system of ideas, or the system of those to whom they apply the term.

It is obvious that there are common threads running through these three definitions. It is also obvious that whatever position is taken on the value implicit in these definitions, there can be no doubt that their usage acknowledges that having ideas, and seeking ideals, are basic human potentials, whether or not they are used. This is not a trivial statement. We put it to the reader that one of the reasons why all the words that derive from the concept of idea have recently become so powerful, either in their constructive or destructive application, is that we live in a period where there is little alternative other than to return to acknowledging the idea, the ideal, and the ideology as the real power source and direction-finder for human action. This has been dealt with at the outset of this essay.

The fact that "idea," "ideal," and "ideology" all stem from the same root has other implications for the term "ideology." When we examine what people say and do, however, it becomes more and more obvious that there are, and can be, only two basic ideologies. Any system of ideas, and any visionary speculation, is built on a system of values that has, as its core dimension, the position taken on human nature. There is really only a basic choice between a view of human nature as a holistic and purposeful entity, capable of imagining, creating, and destroying social products, and a view of people as necessarily dependent on the fabric of social institutions (designed by a higher class of humans?). Those who take the former view have also taken much pain to make their value system explicit and internally consistent [42]. It includes the apparent paradox that while people are capable of self-determination and purposeful planning, they may fully utilize these abilities only when they have a sense of being at one with others and the environment at large. It is this visionary experience of Unity, "at-oneness," that leads to the awareness of ideals or higher realisms" [43].

It is only as we begin to trace recent history that we come to see that we have all been caught up and trained in an ideology that was never really explicit. This ideology or metaphysic (definition 3), the philosophy put forward in the name of science, has been described as "bad, vicious, life-destroying" [44]. It has created the technocratic society "in which those who govern justify themselves by appeal to technical experts who, in turn, justify themselves by appeal to scientific forms of knowledge. And beyond the authority of science, there is no appeal." There are many good reasons why the ideology of science has remained implicit for as long as it has, but there can be no doubt that it is there, "simply invisible, having blended into the supposedly indisputable truth of the scientific world view" [45].

When we stop to examine the values that lie behind this scientific ideology with its emphasis on "objective truth," "rationality," *etc.*, we can begin to see why "ideology" is increasingly used, in the sense of not "real or practical," as an attempt to destroy a competitive ideology (definition 3). Science has determinedly used people as objects, and has denied them their ability to feel, value, and seek after ideals. It has elevated organizations and institutions and, above all, itself, over humanity at large. To reassert, then, the authority of people over the institution of science and its ethic, is a threat to the establishment of science and those who have been accorded by our many bureaucracies the right of dominance over others.

It is only to be expected then that there will be many who will react to this threat by claiming that such a human-oriented ideology is "unrealistic." But, as Roszak has said, "to postpone until 'later' consideration of the humanly essential in the name of 'being realistic' is to practice the kind of deadly practicality which now stands our civilization in peril of annihilation. It is to deliver us into the hands of dehumanized commissars, managers, and operations analysts—all of whom are professional experts at postponing the essential" [46]. As the antiscientific, human, ideal-seeking ideology gains ground, we can expect that the ideology of science will force its adherents into more extreme and uncompromising epithets, accelerating the process of double-think and new-speak [47].

The other sense in which definition 2 is evoked as destructive criticism of the ideal-seeking ideology is to claim that there is no empirical or objective evidence for the basic premise that people are purposeful and capable of ideal-seeking, or that there is no such evidence for the claimed results of processes such as searching. "Ideological," used critically in this sense of blind faith, springs either from a vast and honest ignorance or a malign attempt to destroy the reputations of those who hold with the new vision. Indeed, there is more evidence today for the justification of the ideal-seeking ideology than there is for the success of the ideology of science and bureaucracy. Goldsmith, himself a scientist, concludes that "on strictly empirical grounds one cannot avoid the conclusion that Science has been a failure" [48]. There are now many who have decided that only by fighting that ideology with conceptual and practical action, will we be able to restore human ideals to the center of the stage. Human creativity and ideals can be released from the straitjacket of the inhuman scientific ideology. Once released, they flourish, infecting others with the new spirit.

The technocratic society is also under threat from definition 1, as people increasingly query the honesty of science in discussing its own origins and evolution. Kuhn has pointed out that histories of science bear greater similarity to statements issued by the Ministry of Truth in *1984* than they do to genuine historical sequences [49]. In fact, it has not had an ideology per definition 1.

What happens when these two dominant ideologies meet each other head on? Is the search conference sufficiently powerful to achieve a successful outcome (in its own terms) with this situation? There is some evidence that it is. Subsequent to the initial publication of this essay, about 30 social scientists gathered as a search conference to explore the search conference both in theory and in experiential terms. It was, in hindsight, the clash of these two ideologies that caused the highly emotional and dynamic action that developed slowly over the three days. Some of the social scientists had great difficulty in working in the search mode. As a defense mechanism for this inability, they used, as criticism of the methodology, those labels that, in part, we have examined above. They could not accept a task that was explicitly subjective, projective, value-laden, underscored with effect, wide in scope, and deep in meaning—everything the scientific ideology had taught them to reject and repress. The fight that developed was so violent and traumatic as to shock them out of the dominant prevailing ideology into the alternative represented by the methodology of the search itself. The last day of this meeting, after the drama of the night before, was spent working as a constructive and cohesive community, concentrating on the most important tasks that lay ahead. Humanity had won. That disastrous event has had unexpected consequences. Much new action, designed along democratic, search lines, has been initiated by those participants. They have become one group of the new contagious viruses that threaten the health of the traditional scientific ideology [50].

We have implied that the word "ideology" is currently being used loosely, and as a powerful term of abuse. Many of the groups to whom "ideological" is applied, when analyzed, appear to be subsets or variations of the two major ideologies described above. People are often said to take ideological positions on issues that affect them, when in fact they are only arguing blindly, not systematically per definition 3, for the *status quo*. This is usually a nonconstructive approach that widens the gap between positions held, and postpones the time when the necessary area of cooperation is recognized and acted upon. In any situation where "ideological" is being used in this way, the only constructive move appears to be an effort to elicit and make clear to all, the coherent value system that lies behind the label, or the stand taken. All labels, such as "Marxist," "revolutionary," "conservative," "fascist," *etc.*, suffer from such use of "ideological," when, in fact, they could be seen as systems of ideas and beliefs.

We are not implying that the explicit definition of an ideology (definition 3) should be attacked head on. This would serve only to accentuate the fight situation, in most cases. The authors have been present on one occasion when a group of young "Marxists" very successfully stopped the work of a small group in a search conference by accepting an invitation to make their position clear. Because the dynamic in the group was already, through the labeling process, one of fight-flight, the "Marxists" could easily pursue their objective of prohibiting cooperative work by using as much time as possible and furthering, by this mechanism, the dissolute dynamic.

This is the only time we have seen such a position as that taken by these young Marxists succeed. More frequently, the dynamic of the search itself is sufficiently attractive to render such behavior ineffective. By beginning work with the task of building a shared context for the known, difficult issues, and by proceeding according to the ground rules for the first session, those who have strongly held beliefs about outcome and method have an opportunity to start exploring these as data in a way that does not invite conflict. In fact, more often than not, parties who originally perceived themselves as having very different ideologies find, by the time they come to decide on what is a desirable future, that their ideals are common, and that, on this level at least, there is no need to stand on defensive positions. Sometimes, there will still be argument about the means necessary to achieve these shared ideals. As the search conference is not designed to elicit a state of "consensus," there is room for a diversity of opinion about effective and ineffective means to the end. Because most people do sincerely appreciate the opportunities for cooperation and community learning that the search offers, this diversity is usually less than anticipated. Commonly desired ends, arrived at through a process that puts the sharing of ideologies (ideas and visions) to work in a constructive way, is a force for cohesion and further learning. Labeling is an infrequent phenomenon after people have had a chance to explore chosen values cooperatively.

The use of labels, whatever they be, is probably a direct result of the recent evolution in Western society. The process of dissociation, which has left individuals as separate and isolated entities and destroyed any sense of community, would encourage labeling. The dynamic of labeling appears to be one that both distances and makes familiar. By attaching a label to another, one has brought that other into one's sphere of control, particularly as there is usually no process whereby it is possible to verify that others mean the same by that label. At the same time, attaching a label, especially if it is intended to be a derogatory one, is a very easy device for creating a gap between the self and the labeled other. Labeling, then, is a mechanism for preserving the state of dissociation and isolation; a function and maintenance of lack of personal contact and knowledge. As labeling is one of the best known features of in-group/out-group phenomena, so it will be a common feature of a bureaucratically organized society. The degree to which individuals immediately label those with whom they come into contact could be a good index of how deeply dissociation has touched them.

It is not so difficult to understand why the search process, providing as it does for knowledge of others as people rather than as positions or objects, can overcome the use of labeling. We hope a time will come when such current labels as "ideological" can be done away with, except in their historical and accurate meanings.

NOTES AND REFERENCES

1. Not only this theoretical framework, but much of the following is to be found in F. E. Emery *et al. Futures We're In.* C.C.E., ANU, 1974. See particularly pp. 1–11 of the 1975 revised edition.

2. See also S. Boyden. "Universal Needs of Human Beings." In *Energy and How We Live.* Australian UNESCO Committee for Man and the Biosphere. Flinders University, 1973.

3. G. Rattray Taylor, *Sex in History*, Panther. Elizabeth Gould Davis, *The First Sex*, Penguin, 1973. Philip Slater, *Earthwalk*, 1974. Slater analyzes the nuclear family as a two-caste system, males and females, and a two-class system, children and adults.

4. A summary of the section "An Historical View of the Transition to Turbulence," pp. 15–26, of *Futures We're In.* This discussion is limited to the Western World. See also pp. 80–110, for "A Scenario for Asia and the West."

5. Ackoff, Russell L., and Fred E. Emery. *On Purposeful Systems.* Aldine-Atherton or Tavistock, 1972.

6. Cf. Christopher Caudwell. *Further Studies in a Dying Culture.* Oxford: The Bodley Head, 1949. "This power of men over men, exercised by a simple act of will and congealed in a property right is not freedom. . . . It is only a delusive short cut in which humanity was for a time lost."

7. It was published in 1965. Emery, F. E., and E. L. Trist. "The Causal Texture of Organizational Environment." *Human Relations* 18: 21–32.

8. Toffler, Alvin. *Future Shock.* Oxford: The Bodley Head, 1970. Toffler, Alvin. *The Ecospasm Report.* New York: Bantam Books, 1975. Bell, Daniel. *The Coming of Post Industrial Society.* Heinemann, 1974. What distinguishes this period of turbulence from previous ones is the high degree of relevant uncertainty that has been missed by authors such as the above. See *Futures We're In*, p. 37.

9. Compare William Irwin Thompson. *Passages About Earth*, p. 145. New York: Harper & Row, 1973: "Now the individual life span is long enough, and the cultural transformation short enough, that solitary man can become conscious of mankind in a way only the mystics knew before. We are the climactic generation of human cultural evolution." Compare also Freire. *The Pedagogy of the Oppressed*, p. 81. Penquin, 1972: "Intervention in reality—historical awareness itself—thus represents a step forward from *emergence*, and results from the conscientization of the situation."

10. Character or individuality is in the choice situation represented as the parameter called Probability of Choice. The first rigorous spelling out of a decision-making model that includes this dimension is, Russell L. Ackoff and Fred E. Emery. *On Purposeful Systems.* Tavistock, 1972. What the four parameters of choice could mean in the context of a community, has been spelled out in Fred and Merrelyn Emery, *A Choice of Futures—To Enlighten or Inform*, pp. 179–184, C.C.E., 1975.

11. Goodman, Robert. *After the Planners*, p. 66. Penquin, 1972.

12. Compare Richard Sennett, *The Uses of Disorder*, p. 81, Pelican, 1970. "That the functioning of the whole to its peak efficiency is the best means of life for the parts, holds in the design of machines, but how can it be justified in the affairs of men?"

13. Most of this discussion is taken straight from *Futures We're In*, pp. 40–64. See also A. D. Crombie. "Planning for Turbulent Social Fields," Ph.D. thesis. ANU, 1972.

For a further discussion of the function of ideals see Emery, Fred. *In Pursuit of Ideals*. C.C.E., ANU, 1976.

14. Sennett, p. 86. Sennett has a lot more to say about the responsibilities of planners in "a historical, unpredictable society, rather than in a dream world of harmony and predetermined order," which follows in most detail our own discussion below, but which is focused particularly on the city as the basis of reformation. See also the "Introduction to the British Edition" (John A. D. Palmer) of *After the Planners*, (as above) p. 49. "No just plan can be conceived or implemented without the consent and willing involvement of the people most affected." Palmer's introduction is an enlightened and well though-out picture of planning in a turbulent social field.

15. Goodman, *After the Planners*, p. 52.

16. Paulo Freire, *Pedagogy of the Oppressed*, pp. 146–148.

17. Cf. Richard Sennett, p. 18: "Professional planners of highways, of redevelopment housing, of inner-city renewal projects, have treated challenges from displaced communities or community groups as a threat to the value of their plans rather than as a natural part of the effort at social reconstruction. . . . What has really happened is that the planners have wanted to take the plan, the projection in advance, as more 'true' than the historical turns, the unforeseen movements in the real time of human lives."

18. Cf. Palmer in Goodman, *After the Planners*, p. 49 and p. 13, on planning as a "joint educational process."

19. Compare Freire, *Pedogogy of the Oppressed*, p. 148: "Instead of following predetermined plans, leaders and people, mutually identified, together create the guidelines of their action."

20. Freire, p. 150.

21. Pawley, Martin. *The Private Future*. London: Thames & Hudson, 1973.

22. This section is an amalgam of the Introduction to *Planning Our Town: Gungahlin*, by Merrelyn Emery, C.C.E., ANU, 1975, and our unpublished report to N.C.D.C., "A Search Conference of Canberra Citizens about Canberra's Future, C.C.E., ANU, 1975.

23. Cf. Palmer, p. 13, in Goodman, *After the Planners*. "The intervention for change must come from outside the system, and it too must be a planned intervention."

24. The work done in a search conference can be described as "the labour process, involving a social view of the necessities of the environment, a general consciousness in man of laws existing outside him in reality, involves also a social unity of response to these necessities, and this environment. The interaction produces a change, and as the change becomes more willed, it generates increasing consciousness, not only of the structure of reality, but also of one's own needs. The goal is a blend of what is possible and what is desirable, just as consciousness is a blend of what is response, and what is situation." Caudwell, *Further Studies in a Dying Culture*, p. 101.

25. This is one of the themes running through John Wyndam's novels, *e.g.*, *The Crysalids* and *The Day of the Triffids*.

26. Bion, W. R. *Experiences in Groups*. Tavistock, 1959. Selznick, Philip. *Leadership in Administration*. New York: Harper & Row, 1957. Asch, Solomon E. *Social Psychology*. Englewood-Cliffs, N.J.: Prentice-Hall, 1952.

27. The search conference is, in Freire's terms, "problem-posing education," and as such is "revolutionary futurity." "Hence it is prophetic (and, as such, hopeful)," p. 57. This may help to explain for some, why the book entitled *Futures We're In* takes an optimistic view of the future.

28. Compare Freire, p. 57: "since men do not exist apart from the world, apart from reality,

the movement must begin with the men-world relationship. Accordingly, the point of departure must always be with men in the 'here and now,' which constitutes the situation within which they are submerged, from which they emerge, and in which they intervene."

29. This may appear to raise a theoretical difficulty involving the nature of man and the possibilities of long-term cooperative societies. It does not. There is no evidence that when human beings are given the opportunity of working and living within a structure that permits and encourages cooperation, that they will do anything but cooperate with each other. In his analysis, *The Human Agenda*, p. x, New York: Bantam Books, 1968, Roderick Gorney concluded that "Cooperation is the law of life . . . the most deeply rooted theme running through the success of man." Robert Goodman states that "Any form of politics will ultimately fail if it is not consistent with people's most fundamental needs for cooperation, and a sense of love and joy in human experience—in essence, a humane existence" *(After the Planners* p. 216). His discussion reinforces awareness of the abnormality of a period of widespread bureaucracy in the history of man, and, taken together with the analysis of Sennett, makes clear that it is necessary to distinguish sharply between a pluralistic and diverse society based on cooperation, and one that is competitive. By working with small community groups or organizations in search conferences, we are building a pluralistic and diverse society, as one of the main features of this learning process is to redevelop awareness of character and uniqueness, as a shared and cooperative group is being established. It is only on the basis of shared understandings that mutual tolerance of individualities can be maintained. A search conference aims for cooperation, not conformity, nor fanaticism. Compare Freire, p. 16.

30. "Freedom appears, socially, when men . . . learn the necessities of their own nature and of external reality, and thus share a goal in common. Then the common goal and the nature of reality uniquely determine the only possible action without compulsion." Caudwell, *Further Studies in a Dying Culture*, p. 114.

31. Compare Freire, "A revolutionary leadership must accordingly practice *co-intentional* education" (p. 44). "In cultural synthesis, the actors who come from 'another world' to the world of people, do so not as invaders. They do not come to *teach,* or to *transmit,* or to *give* anything, but rather to learn, with the people, about the people's world" (p. 147).

Compare also Goodman, p. 221: "Instead of remaining the 'outside expert' . . . we can become participants in our own community's search for new family structures, or other changing patterns of association . . . in effect, we become a part of, rather than an expert for cultural change."

32. Terms from Max Wertheimer, *Productive Thinking*, New York: Harper & Brothers, 1945.

33. The following terms are taken from W. R. Bion, *Experiences in Groups*, Tavistock, 1959. We diverge from Bion's analysis in that we regard "pairing" as the creative working mode, not an inhibiting "group emotional" mode. Bion notes that in the "pairing" group there is a most unusual tolerance for people to get on with their discussions, the relation has bonds that have a libidinous character (p. 176), and the group is cemented with "messianic hope" as if it contained an unborn genius (p. 166). Nevertheless, he clearly suspects that psychotic anxieties of an oedipal type that may be triggered off in the "pairing" state. Carl Jung has also expressed deep uneasiness about this state.

We think, though, that the most important features of the pairing state coincide with the realization of the four universal tacit assumptions that underline human, face-to-face interaction:
1. the face-to-face situation takes on the character of an objectively ordered field open to the participants;
2. the mutual confrontations attest to their basic psychological similarity;
3. a mutually shared psychological field emerges; and
4. individuals become more open. (Asch, 1952. Fred Emery and Merrelyn Emery, *A Choice of Futures*, pp. 18–25, 1975.)

When these conditions are realized the predominant effect will be a fluctuation between joy and excitement, and the group members will be excited and enjoy the emerging genius of their own creativity. Too sustained an exposure to this effect can, of course, be finally distressing [Tomkins], but what is triggered then is a primal fear of information overload not oedipal love-hate anxieties.

Asch's statement of these conditions also gives us a detailed set of criteria for judging whether a group is in a pairing state. Furthermore, it gives us guidelines for detecting conditions that will lead to reassertion of the dependent or fight-flight states. Briefly, anything that contradicts these assumptions will heighten tension and increase the probability of a "flip-over," so called because that is what it is, making it even more important to detect what is building up before the change occurs.

The first condition is going to be contradicted if, for instance, anyone starts to suggest, however subtly, that only someone in his *unique position, e.g.*, a landlord, could really understand X or Y or whatever it is that the group is considering.

The second condition will be contradicted if anyone starts to suggest that in reality it is only he who could subsequently do anything about what is under discussion.

The third condition will be contradicted by anything anyone does to suggest that some other person is not part of *his* picture, when that other person believes he ought to be.

The fourth condition will be contradicted by any attempt by a group member to place himself at the center of the ongoing scene; who cannot accept that others can do the work of the group as well as he. It is also contradicted by someone withholding his contribution when the group is trying to elicit it. (Individual withholding has quite different connotations in the dependency and fight-flight states.) This latter may well be the earliest warning signal that the pairing state is becoming unstable. Openness emerges only as the first three conditions are realized. Closing down might start to take place as soon as the most sensitive (and open?) members sense danger.

Asch has suggested (pp. 604–605) that the way the group goes, to dependency or to fight-flight, might be determined by the character of those in the group who first signal danger (labile-hysterical personalities toward dependency, and rigid-compulsives toward fight-flight, Angyal).

Even if a challenge to openness in the group is the first detected sign of instability, this would not imply that this condition should be the focus of attempts to restore stability. Openness cannot be commanded or forced upon others. (Freire, on "The culture of invasion.") The task for the facilitators would be to be doubly alert to detecting which of the first three conditions is under challenge, and then work at restoring that condition. If this fails to stem the decline in openness, it is highly likely that the locus of emerging contradiction has been misidentified. By then it might, of course, be too late. One can expect, however, that a group that has had the creative excitement of the pairing state, will experience a quicker spontaneous recovery from the dependency of fight-flight.

34. Compare Freire, p. 129: "For development to occur it is necessary: firstly, that there be a moment of search and creativity having its seat of decision in the searcher; secondly, that this movement occur not only in space, but in the existential time of the conscious searcher."
35. From *Futures We're In*, as above.
36. Emery, F. E., and Einar Thorsrud. *Form and Content in Industrial Democracy*. Tavistock, 1969.
37. Sands, Angela. "The Search Conference at Guthega–a Year Later." *Planning Our Town: Gungahlin*, C.C.E., ANU.
38. Angela Sands, as above.
39. Postscript to Trevor William's *Democracy in Learning*, C.C.E., ANU, 1975.
40. Chopanis, *Scientific American*.
41. Asch, *Social Psychology*, p. 604.
42. See *On Purposeful Systems* and *In Pursuit of Ideals*, above, and references below, such as Watts, Schumacher, Roszak, *etc.*
43. Watts, Alan. *The Book: On the Taboo Against Knowing Who You Are*. New York: Pantheon Books, 1966. Deikman, Arthur J. "Deautomatization and the Mystic Experience." In *Altered States of Consciousness*. Edited by Charles T. Tart New York: John Wiley & Sons, 1969. Emery, Merrelyn. *The Search for the Barefoot Social Scientist*. C.C.E., forthcoming.
44. Schumacher, E. F. *Small is Beautiful*, pp. 74–75. Abacus, 1973.
45. Roszak, Theodore. *The Making of a Counter Culture*. London: Faber & Faber, 1968. See p. 7 and footnote, p. 56.
46. Roszak, p. 101.
47. Terms used in Orwell's *1984*.
48. Goldsmith, Edward. "Is Science a Religion?" *Ecologist* 5: 52.
49. Kuhn, Thomas S. *The Structure of Scientific Revolutions*, p. 213. Chicago: Phoenix Books, University of Chicago Press, 1962.
50. A fuller report of this event and an analysis of how the scientific ideology has affected social science can be found in *The Search for the Barefoot Social Scientist*, as above.

2

The Management of Interdisciplinary, Policy-related Research*

Frederick A. Rossini and Alan L. Porter
Georgia Institute of Technology

INTRODUCTION

Why Interdisciplinary Research?

In our individual and organizational roles we are often confronted by complex issues. Managers determining schedules must consider personnel and economic factors of their units in conjunction with a larger organizational picture. Administrators responsible for central city redevelopment programs must delicately weigh physical possibilities, institutional constraints, and social aspects. Societal policy-makers facing the propects of genetic engineering need to weigh biomedical potentials for good against those for disaster in a charged atmosphere of threatened human values. Across this gamut of issues, from the routine to the profound, decision-makers are required to balance disparate factors. The more complex of these problems demand the expertise of a variety of intellectual perspectives. It is in these instances, where the complexity extends beyond the ken of single individuals or disciplines, that interdisciplinary, policy-related research may be required.

The grouping of expertise from many disciplines can take place in two basic modes. In *multidisciplinary* research, experts from the relevant disciplines attack the issue, using the methods of their respective fields and focusing on the issues relevant to their particular disciplinary concerns. Economists address the economic aspects of a new highway, and civil engineers consider the roadway.

*This research was supported in part by the National Science Foundation, Grant ERS76-04474. The opinions expressed herein are those of the authors alone. The authors thank Patrick Kelly, Daryl E. Chubin, Stanley R. Carpenter, M. Andrew Lipscomb, and John Havick for their invaluable assistance on this project.

The outcome of this process is typically a collection of fragments connected by their concern with a common problem. In *interdisciplinary* research, the goal is an output that deals with the problem from diverse perspectives, but also interrelates the disciplinary components. For instance, an economist addressing the allocation of water resources in the western United States should incorporate expertise on land use patterns, agricultural politics, and statutory constraints to enable preparation of a sound and useful analysis. One can think of multidisciplinary research as a patchwork quilt and interdisciplinary research, ideally, as a seamless garment.

It is relatively easy to produce multidisciplinary research by simply commissioning a group of "experts" to work independently on a problem, and then integrating their reports editorially by putting the pieces into some reasonable order and writing an introduction and conclusion. Interdisciplinary research, however, involves complexities of a different magnitude. Not only should the disciplines contribute, but they should contribute together beyond the level of smooth writing and the consistent use of terms. The resultant analysis must amount to more than the sum of component disciplinary contributions.

From this simple introduction, one might surmise that interdisciplinary research is the way to go when faced with the need to understand a complex issue. This is not necessarily so. Many important problems and research questions that cut across disciplinary lines can be dealt with by a multidisciplinary approach that gives a collection of solutions to parts of the problem. This approach is quite workable where the problem can be decomposed into discrete parts that can be solved independently, and where the collection of solutions to the parts is essentially the solution to the whole. The problem of getting a human being to the moon and back was such a problem. This spectacular achievement required the joint effort of specialists in many scientific and technical disciplines. Once certain boundary conditions were specified, however, the discrete tasks could proceed independently. For example, one group could devise a propulsion system for a specified payload, while a different group addressed metallurgical problems caused by temperature stresses at the anticipated vehicle speeds.

It has been suggested that the same skills and organization could solve the problems of the cities [26], but, unlike the man-to-the-moon problem, the decompositions of major urban problems are not clear. NASA was handed its billions; a city must generate its own revenue and politic with federal and state governments for additional funds. Thus, where NASA could simply take its budget as a given (even though lobbying and negotiations took place, a fixed total appropriation appeared at some point), a city can alter its revenue by changing taxes. This affects the potential of the city to fund improvement programs, though, at the same time, it may alter the city's demographic composition—increased taxes may drive away mobile businesses and individuals. Beyond the funding concerns, urban renewal raises issues of community preferences, transportation requirements, land use, political power shifts, and the distribution of economic benefits and burdens. Not only the problem, but the possibility of solution, as well, cuts across disciplines in so jagged a fashion that decomposition for multidisciplinary analysis is an imprudent strategy. Such instances call for interdisciplinary analysis.

We therefore assert that complex real-world dilemmas often offer a poor fit for analysis by a single discipline. In those instances in which decomposition of the problem into isolated components amenable to disciplinary expertise is possible, we suggest multidisciplinary analysis. Only for those remaining policy issues, in which the interrelationship of realms of expertise is vital, do we recommend interdisciplinary analysis. It is to these situations that we now turn our attention.

Types of Interdisciplinary Research

Having indicated that "interdisciplinary" is used in a variety of ways, it appears proper for us to describe our perspective on it. Table 1 arrays several dimensions on which we hope to locate this discussion. With respect to the dimension labeled "perspective," we are concerned with providing information pertinent to making decisions to effect future courses of action. We are concerned with all of the three phases of decision processes: 1) intelligence, 2) design, and 3) choice, as categorized by Simon (31). With varying degrees of emphasis, we may focus upon information-gathering, analyzing options, or weighing alternative courses of action. An interdisciplinary study may restrict itself to providing information or it may range into policy recommendations and decision-making. In contrast, one could study past occurrences in an interdisciplinary manner, either out of general interest (to learn from analogous cases, *e.g.*, the workings of past societies) or with specific future actions in mind (*e.g.*, program evaluations).

The second dimension, "openness," flags the possibility that interdisciplinary policy research may be done differently, and with very different ends in mind. Studies done in-house need worry less about discretion, access to proprietary information, or fine-tuned editing. Limited dissemination may make contributions less edgy about the possible criticisms of their disciplinary peers. In contrast, studies performed externally pose extra problems in coordination and ascertaining that the research focuses on the sponsor's needs. Studies for wide dissemination may be politically sensitive. In combining questions of study preparation and dissemination, we hope to highlight the potential implications of both, and of their interactions.

Scope is particularly important in that it connotes the possible diversity among the analysts involved. This can extend over several respects—the com-

Table 1. Dimensions of interdisciplinary policy-related research.

Perspective:	action-oriented versus explanatory
Openness:	internal decision needs versus outside dissemination
Scope:	Wide-ranging versus tightly focused
Scale:	Large versus small

prehensiveness of factors involved, the related sophistication of the study (quantitative or qualitative, need for modeling), the range of disciplinary types included (*e.g.*, natural scientists, social scientists, engineers, lawyers, humanists), and the likelihood of differences in human values. Interaction is presumed to be more difficult, the greater the differences among participants.

Last, the scale of the enterprise is likely to color its character. Large-scale, long-term studies (those that cost over $100,000 and last over a year) may bring together unacquainted professionals for extended periods. This can be contrasted with short-term, small-scale studies, performed in-house, that do not interrupt the careers of their participants.

We are not concerned with basic scientific research, *e.g.*, into biochemistry. The "policy-related" in our title is a fair reflection of our thrust toward complex, wide-ranging issues that are likely to involve quite disparate personnel. Those concerned with day-to-day interdisciplinary situations dealing with more routine issues, less appropriately called research, will, therefore, have to extrapolate (cautiously!) from our findings. We focus upon interactions among professional researchers, not upon the interactions between such information providers and the information users, nor between professionals and concerned citizens (a potentially volatile situation, according to Arnstein [1]. Specifically, we draw primarily upon a study of a particular form of interdisciplinary, policy-related research: technology assessment (TA). TA can be characterized as typically:

action-oriented,
for outside dissemination, performed by outside contractors.
wide-ranging in scope, and
large-scale.

Technology Assessment (TA)

"Technology assessment may be defined as the systematic study of the effects on society that may occur when a technology is introduced, extended, or modified, with special emphasis on the impacts that are unintended, indirect, and delayed" [5]. This description of technology assessment has implicit within it both the potentials and the pitfalls of this new version of *policy analysis*. The potential payoffs are in the form of better information upon which to base decisions concerning technological developments. Insofar as TA can deliver an approximation of a "systematic study of the effects on society," decision-makers will be in a better position to select alternatives wisely, to avoid unintended side effects, and to generate additional indirect benefits. The pitfalls pertain primarily to the difficulties in accomplishing such a task. One must address the complexities of social systems, which are subject to a wide range of economic, political, and other influences, and which occasion a wide range of interactive economic, political, and other impacts. In such a milieu, technological and economic forecasting, upon which is based the assessment of prospective effects, is perilous indeed. In turn, the nascent arts of impact identification, analysis, and evaluation must overcome both methodological and political hurdles.

Technology assessment developed as a concept on "the Hill," in the face of growing recognition of the pervasive role of technology in our culture, and our too-frequent lack of understanding of the implications of technology-intensive decisions. Congressman Daddario, as head of the House Subcommittee on Science, Research, and Development, provided the entrepreneurship. Beginning in the late 1960s, he pushed for formation of a Congressional Office of Technology Assessment (OTA), which was approved in 1972 and is now active, with a staff of about 100, providing information to Congress. Concurrently, the institutionalization of the National Environmental Policy Act of 1969, with its famous (or infamous) Section 102c, which requires environmental impact statements, has boomed the notion of impact assessment into the American way of life.

In addition to those in government and industry practicing TA, or a limited version of it in the form of environmental impact assessment, two federal agencies have also spotlighted it. The OTA, just mentioned, and the National Science Foundation have undertaken assessments of such topics as: alternative work schedules, bioequivalence of drugs, integrated hog farming, metric conversion, mobile communications, and solar energy development. These studies have been performed by National Academy panels, consulting firms, and universities. In addition to this federally-sponsored activity, various industrial, state governmental, and international activities can also be identified. By and large, these do not pretend to the same large-scale effort (typically $150,000 and more) of these federal assessments, nor do they follow a uniform emphasis. Naturally, an industrial TA activity would be done with attention to the impacts of greatest corporate concern.

Performing a TA is a strenuous, interdisciplinary task. There are various schema to organize assessment activities, but the following appear to be essential elements [28, ch. 2]:

1. Defining and bounding the assessment focus (including the comprehensiveness and depth of coverage)
2. Describing the technology to be assessed (including a discussion of technological alternatives)
3. Forecasting the development of the technology (technology forecasting)
4. Describing the most important features of the context (social, economic, environmental) with which the technology interacts most closely
5. Forecasting the development of the technology's context
6. Identifying direct and, where possible, higher order consequences or impacts of the interaction between the technology and its context
7. Analyzing these consequences (economic, environmental, social, institutional, *etc.*) by various quantitative and qualitative techniques
8. Evaluating the impacts and integrating the findings
9. Identifying and analyzing the policy issues and options involved and possibly making recommendations
10. Communicating the results of the assessment.

Above all, the various elements need to be iterated—experience indicates that the process of assessment often leads to revision of the focus, new perspectives on the system, and new impacts to be considered.

The uses of a TA are a function of the particular needs that generated the study, the functioning of the sociotechnical system, and the decision-making process. Naturally, one would not expect a proprietary study by a firm to be handled in the same way as a public study. The following list conveys the general range of outcomes possible from a well-executed TA [2, p. 16]:

1. Modify the project;
2. Specify a program of environmental or social monitoring;
3. Stimulate research and development, particularly to deal with adverse effects on the technology;
4. Stimulate research to specify or define risks;
5. Develop latent benefits;
6. Identify regulatory and legal changes to promote or control the technology;
7. Define institutional arrangements appropriate to the technology;
8. Define intervention experiments to reduce negative consequences or enhance positive ones;
9. Delay the project or technology until some of above are completed;
10. Stop the technology;
11. Provide a reliable base of information to parties at interest.

In sum, this new form of policy analysis has gained wide visibility through federal government sponsorship of assessments and environmental impact statement requirements. In concept, the notion is as sensible as the adage "look before you leap." In practice, TA is an uncertain activity demanding broad-ranging, yet careful, analyses, but promising both immediate and long-range benefits in return.

Strategy For the Study and This Paper

This paper grew out of a study of the interdisciplinary processes that take place in TA. The study considered all of the 24 large-scale TAs sponsored by the National Science Foundation prior to our study. From a literature review and our personal impressions, we generated a number of preliminary hypotheses as to what affects the integration of TA. Because we did not have a strong conception of what was crucial, we adopted an exploratory approach. Dividing the group of 24 TAs in two, we interviewed participants in 12, using a focused interview technique [24, 25]. Following these interviews, we constructed a simple model of what influenced the "integration" (to be discussed shortly) of these interdisciplinary studies. This was then investigated through more structured questioning of participants in the remaining 12 TAs. The management and social-psychological domains proved easy to discuss with study participants. Epistemology (or the structure of knowledge), together with value differences, proved more difficult because there is no fixed vocabulary and the problems are not widely discussed; thus, the degree of specificity there was lower. The plan of the study was to link the process data gained in the interviews with information about the product as obtained from the evaluation of reports. The TA reports were read and evaluated by a panel of researchers as to their comprehensiveness, depth of analysis, and integration. The resultant model, substantiated by selected data from the interviews, is discussed in the next section.

From the interviews we abstracted four apparent mechanisms potentially useful in integrating disciplinary contributions. These were further explored through a series of small group experimental sessions. To date six sessions, involving two distinct groups of five professionals, were observed. Each of the groups addressed three separate, small-scale, interdisciplinary tasks, operating under different procedural instructions, in half-day sessions. A discussion of the different ways to attempt integration, based on these sessions and the interviews, appears in the third section.

In the last section, we offer some practical implications for the management of interdisciplinary research.

A MODEL OF THE FACTORS AFFECTING INTERDISCIPLINARY RESEARCH

Integration—The Key to Interdisciplinary Research

The central issue, as we see it, is to understand how the expertise held by disciplinary experts (*e.g.*, economists, social psychologists, chemists) can be drawn together to yield a richer, more valid, more complete interdisciplinary analysis. We address this *via* the concept of integration. We thus conceive of integration as bound up in the study *process* and reflected in the study *output*. We are therefore seeking to clarify what characteristics of a technology assessment influence the integration observable in the study products.

So far we have talked about interdisciplinary research as having an output in which the various disciplinary components are integrated or interrelated. In the most basic sense, this means that the terms and concepts used are consistent throughout the research, and that the relationships between the various parts of the analysis are editorially linked. But this could be done to a multidisciplinary product by a skilled technical editor. In addition there should be a common view of what the problem is and substantive linking of the various component analyses. For a study to be integrated, the analyses from different (disciplinary) perspectives are interrelated so that their outputs are substantive (not heuristic) inputs into the other analyses. Integrating fields by the use of "bridging" or interfield theories takes place only between intellectually close fields, for example in biology and chemistry [6]. A theory that will integrate "everything" is not a reasonable expectation.

There are some potential trade-offs involved in attempts to integrate. Everything else being equal, it is easier to integrate fewer components than many. In fact a single disciplinary research output is a perfect, but trivial, example of interdisciplinary integration. Hence, the degree of *comprehensiveness* of the study should be considered. Not surprisingly, a second potential tradeoff is with *depth of analysis*. All other things being equal, the shallower the analyses, the easier they should be to integrate. In the fully superficial case, the problem solution is a simple narrative without any significant depth. Here one has only the integration of the technical editor.

Each research project is different in that the requirements for output vary considerably. We have mentioned comprehensiveness, depth of analysis, and integration as important marks of output. Interdisciplinary projects can be classified along these dimensions. Table 2 indicates how this may be done and loosely names the various combinations.

Table 2. Possible categories of study products.

NAME	EXAMPLE	LEVEL OF INTEGRATION	LEVEL OF COM-PREHENSIVENESS	LEVEL OF DEPTH OF ANALYSIS
Broad inter-disciplinary research	Successful tech-nology assessment	High	High	High
Multi-disciplinary research	Multistage engineering project	Low	High	HIgh
Narrow inter-disciplinary research	Analysis of ecological im-pacts of proposed project	High	Low	High
Disciplinary analysis	Econometric modeling	Low	Low	High
Narrative	*Time* magazine	High	HIgh	Low
Anthology		Low	High	Low
One-liner		High	Low	Low
Crock		Low	Low	Low

A Basic Conceptualization

The extensive literature on research and development (for a useful bibliography, see [10 and 20; ch. 3]) is fragmented by disciplines and does not consider integration. The sparse literature on interdisciplinary (consisting almost exclusively of records of personal experience [34, 33, 7]), together with our experience, yielded three general categories of factors that are involved in the process of integrating interdisciplinary research. These categories of factors are [29]:

1. *Management*, embracing such concerns as congruence with the organizational context and leadership style of the research leader.
2. *Social-Psychological*, including factors such as patterns of interaction within the project group, motivation of participants, and relationships between the group and any consultants and subcontractors involved.
3. *Epistemological* (i.e. relating to the structures of the various types of knowledge involved in the study), concerning the character of knowledge in the various professional disciplines involved in the research and matters which cut across disciplines, such as relative importance of data and speculation. In addition, there is the problem of the diversity of values and interests which are involved in policy-related research.

Although this division is convenient for analytic purposes, clearly the factors do not always fit into one category. For example, consider study bounding (delimiting what is to be included). Bounding involves a management decision in the end, but this decision may be arrived at through group processes. Furthermore, the act of bounding a complex and ill-structured problem has epistemological overtones as one decides what is the most crucial information and what are appropriate methodologies for proceeding.

Using the three categories enables us to pinpoint some fairly obvious relationships that make it easier to understand and deal with the problem of integrating interdisciplinary research. Management decisions can facilitate the development of effective interaction by structuring group work, and they can influence the structuring of knowledge in the project. The most helpful organizational environment can be thwarted by ineffective group work and intellectual narrowness, however. Excellent group interaction potential can never achieve realization in a nonsupportive organizational context. One might usefully look at the three classes of factors as if they were three rings, concentric about integration (Figure 1). Effective management would be the first necessary condition; social-psychological factors, the second; and epistemological, the third—none being sufficient in the absence of the other two.

Figure 2, displays the ten factors upon which we focused as likely to be the essential determinants of integration. The model conveys a general progression in these influences from those factors established prior to the onset of the pro-

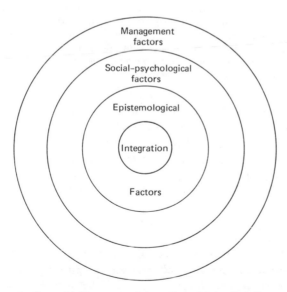

Figure. 1. General influences on integration of interdisciplinary studies.

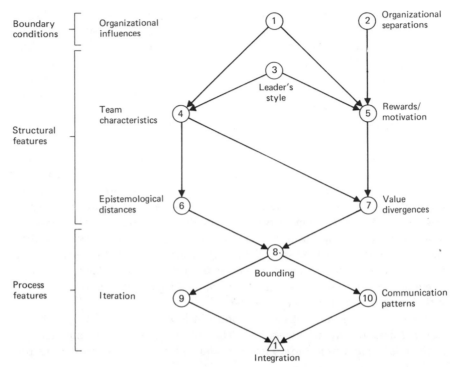

Figure 2. A model of the essential influences upon interdisciplinary integration.   This schematic figure attempts to show composite direct and indirect influence patterns; it does not distinguish every relationship. For instance, epistemological distances may directly affect communication patterns, but no direct linkage is displayed. (Incidentally, our attempts to fully represent all such important relationships were derided as "spaghetti and meatballs"—they simply were not informative.)

ject (the *boundary conditions*), through those that serve to structure the nature of the interdisciplinary interactions (the *structural features*), to characteristics of the interactions in the course of the research (the *process features*), and thence to the integration of the product. Note that each of the ten bears a strong kinship to management, social-psychological, or epistemological categories, but their ordering is based on perceived real-time relationships.

Boundary Conditions

We first consider the influence of the *organizational context* upon the research project. A central concern is to what extent the project is congruent with its organizational environment. Interdisciplinary, policy-related research encounters problems when performed in the context of the academic department where status, reward, and interest go to pure, displinary research [8]. The problem is less acute in programs or institutes in academic institutions. Here, too however, the focus may be on some specialized activity. Contract research organizations are not immune from this problem. Divisional barriers may put time constraints on key project personnel and make other researchers in the organization difficult to use on the project.

To summarize our observations on the 24 TAs, it appeared that small, relatively unstructured organizations were most supportive of interdisciplinary work. Meetings were reportedly more enjoyable and epistemological gaps less severe in less structured organizations. In our interviews, we specifically inquired about tensions between project needs and the larger organization. We found that TAs conducted under such tensions tended to be less well integrated.

Another factor, not included in the model (Figure 2), that acts as a boundary condition in the sense that it is a given, is the nature of the *topic under study*. We found that studies of more technical topics (*i.e.*, physical versus social issues; technology versus policy focus) resulted in less integrated reports. It may be reasonable to extrapolate this to say that matters requiring greater specific expertise will be more difficult to integrate fully.

Organizational separation (Influence No. 2 in the model) deals with such matters as the appropriate use of consultants and subcontractors to supplement the team's capability. Their use was relatively common on the projects we studied. Subcontractors were sometimes a problem, especially when the organizational structure and goals of the subcontractor significantly differed from those of the performing organization. Likewise, physical distance can create problems by limiting interaction. Subcontractors' work is often poorly integrated into the study as a whole, and, as a result, is often most appropriate when it can be used as a discrete contribution. Consultants, too, present problems. Though one can often engage senior and well-known individuals as consultants, it is not common for such individuals to produce major, substantive output. Their most effective contribution is often their insights and critique of the work of others.

It seems intuitively likely that integration will be made more difficult by physical or ideological separations. Our data on the 24 TAs have little to say in this regard, however. Studies using subcontractors and consultants heavily exhibited no particular handicap in integration.

Structural Features

We now shift attention to certain attributes that are more changeable than the boundary conditions, but still relatively fixed for a given study. These include the characteristics of the interdisciplinary team and its leader, the motivating influences upon their styles of seeking knowledge, and their inherent values.

A most important factor to consider in project management is the style of the leader. Hill notes three *leadership styles* commonly addressed in the literature [17, p. 11] :

(1) nondirective, permissive, a *laissez faire*, accommodative or abdicative style where the leader relinguishes any influence in setting group goals to the group;
(2) *democratic*, a participatory, group-centered subordinate-centered, employee-centered, human-relations-oriented style where the supervisor allows and encourages a mutual relationship with subordinates;
(3) autocratic, *authoritarian*, boss-centered, task-centered, production-centered, close and punitive style where the supervisor allows his subordinates little or no influence in the setting up of work procedures, while primarily concentrating on achieving task goals.

We dealt with management style in these terms. A *laissez faire* project leader would be characterized by letting the project group set objectives and procedures, lacking adequate control over project personnel, and weakly supporting the project team. The democratic, or facilitating, leader would be characterized by shared decision-making among leader and team on project objectives and procedures, adequate control over project personnel, and support for project participants. The authoritarian leader would be characterized by personally making decisions about project objectives and procedures, strong control over project personnel, and selective support of project personnel.

In an interdisciplinary research project, the leader invariably lacks the full range of required skills, necessitating the use of an interdisciplinary team. This implies that the leader defer to the expertise within the team to some extent. At the same time, the leader bears ultimate responsibility for the finished project, and hence needs to take steps to assure that the project is integrated. Thus, it appears reasonable that the democratic, facilitating leader is most effective at achieving integration (and hence most appropriate for interdisciplinary research projects).

While our data were limited to 24 cases, it is intriguing to relate the disciplinary training of the leader to success in integration. We anticipated that leaders who themselves had eclectic backgrounds (*i.e.*, multiple fields of training or major interests in areas such as systems, planning, or technology assessment) would be most effective integrators, but the evidence did not support this. Social scientists and economists tended to do best; the eclectic leaders did poorly; and engineers and scientists were in between.

Team characteristics encompass a variety of issues. The selection of personnel for interdisciplinary research is a significant problem. We considered the importance of disciplinary expertise and interpersonal skills as criteria, although they often seemed to be moderated by the individual's availability in the organization at the time the study was taking place. Such other matters as the existence of mixed backgrounds in individuals, and prior experience with each other and with interdisciplinary research, seemed likely predictors of integration success, but the data did not show such relationships. Most surprisingly, the presence of a substantial proportion of the team with mixed/eclectic backgrounds even correlated negatively with product integration. Our results for team members, as for project leaders, do not support "internalizing" the interdisciplinary function in single individuals. This point merits further study.

Some general thoughts about effective participants in TAs come from Professor Samuel Estep of the University of Michigan Law School (private communication, 1977). A participant in a TA, he said, should be intelligent in the culture of academic life. Common sense helps, and the participant should be open-minded with intellectual curiosity. A stable ego can take attacks on one's ideas without interpreting them as personal attacks. One's own value assumptions can be questioned. Internal organization and self-discipline are complemented by a hard-nosed result-orientation. The would-be interdisciplinary participants must not be afraid to ask simple or stupid questions, and must never be intimidated by abstruse terminology or easily snowed. Being able to get along with other people, they should accept responsibility for mistakes and learn from them. In addition to Estep's list of positive qualifications, some characteristics to avoid are intellectual narrowness, inflexibility, and inability to complete assigned tasks on time.

A related area, which is not often considered, is team stability. Because interdisciplinary research requires team interaction, personnel changes in the middle of a project would seem costly in the loss of continuity through personnel changes, most importantly changes of project leadership. Personnel turnovers were costly and created problems in accomplishing integration in some of the TAs. Nevertheless, we did not find any general relationship of this sort in the 24 TAs.

We now consider the *motivations* of the participants and the rewards available to them. Rewards feed in from the boundary conditions, as established by the larger organization. Our present focus is on the congruity between the motivation of the participants for their participation and the range of rewards the project leadership can provide, given the purpose of the study. Motives that bode well for integration include interest in interdisciplinary research, hope of interdisciplinary publications, and interest in the substantive topic of the study. Desire for disciplinary publication does not fit well with the character of interdisciplinary research. Anecdotal, not statistical, findings from the review of the TAs supported this hypothesis, as faculty members battled entrenched disciplinary reward structures to participate in certain TAs.

Both *epistemological gaps* and *differences in human values* can impinge upon interdisciplinary efforts. Epistemological differences relate to different cognitive frameworks for structuring the world and determining what in it is problematic.

These are typically identified with intellectual disciplines. Values involve different judgments of what is good, proper, or appropriate—both in methodological and social senses. Methodological values refer to choices of appropriate procedures for knowing about things and, thus, are very close to the various disciplinary structures of knowledge just mentioned. Social values could include differences in belief as to the appropriateness of population control and the importance of sex differences in the formulation of social policy, for instance.

Statisical analyses of our interviews turned up an unexpected finding. It appears that the comprehensiveness, depth, and integration of interdisciplinary assessments increase with diversity on the study team. Indeed, the greater the disciplinary range on the team, the less the tendency for significant epistemological differences to arise. Of course, epistemological differences need not follow disciplinary lines. Modes of inquiry [4] and basic thinking styles [22] can vary quite independent of academic training. Culture is a potent influence. Intradisciplinary differences (*e.g.*, humanistic versus behavioral psychology) can be particularly sharp. We are just beginning to think about such issues with respect to research and management.

As we explored the experiences of participants in the TAs, four common gaps in the type of knowledge structure emerged. We discuss these now, based on an earlier treatment [29], in order to give a flavor of the type of problems that may be encountered in interdisciplinary research.

These epistemological problem areas are:

1. Relying solely on data in hand versus speculating about the future beyond the current data.
2. Doing social impact assessment—how should or can it be done?
3. Relating economics to other disciplines and modes of analysis.
4. Using techniques designed specially for technology assessment.

We now offer an elaboration of each of these problems.

The problem of *data versus speculation* occurs when researchers involved in a technology assessment or other future-oriented study rely exclusively on a data-based methodology, which allows only observation and experiment on real systems to provide significant information. For them, prediction of the future is dependent on validated theory. Otherwise, the researcher is left only with data relating to the present and past. Speculation or conjecture not based on data or theory is not seen as valid. It is simply unscientific.

A general pattern emerged from our interviews of more willingness to speculate in areas where, it was believed, sound knowledge did not exist. It was often felt that there was no point in gathering data when common sense, possibly coupled with some expert opinion, was perfectly adequate. In these cases the need for additional data to form an adequate basis for speculation about the future became a matter of controversy. A specific example of such a controversy will be articulated in the subsequent section on the problem of social impact analysis. Further, the interviews revealed that there was more willingness to speculate in areas where the individual doing the speculating was not an expert, rather than in those where he or she was. This was especially the case in assessing social consequences.

Social impact assessment presented a somewhat different problem. It was universally perceived as necessary in TA, yet no one claimed that there was a foolproof way of doing it, and no one was fully satisfied with the way it had been done. Some claimed that social impact assessment could not be done, or at least could not be done beyond the level of simple common sense, and then with limited reliability. One respondent compared social impact assessment to dreaming. In part, such sentiments arose from an often expressed preference for "hard" engineering or scientific approaches. Social science was seen as "soft," and hence wishy-washy and undesirable. The "hard" science-oriented researchers seem to go two different ways at this point. Some abandon hope of anything like a systematic analysis of the area, but, realizing that the area is extremely important in a TA, they turn to a common sense discussion of social impacts in ordinary language. Others turn to quasi-quantitative techniques, developed to organize and anaylze opinion, speculation, and other "soft" forms of information into output with the form and quantitative precision associated with "hard" methodology. In neither case is anything like complete satisfaction expressed in the research output.

In a number of cases the TA teams contained no senior social scientist. This was generally perceived by team members as a significant deficiency. In a number of instances when TA teams did contain social scientists, the social scientists felt that the project team leader—a hard scientist or engineer by training—was deprecating social science and its methodologies, while treating the social scientist participant unprofessionally. Sometimes whether the social scientists should conduct surveys of elites as input to the social impact assessment (SIA) component of the TA was at issue. Rejection of such surveys as useless or irrelevant to the study signaled to the social scientists the deprecation of their discipline.

This problem did not exist in cases where a social scientist or policy analyst was the team leader, nor did it exist when the team leader allowed the social scientists to follow their methodological bent. Interestingly, physical scientists and engineers in general felt far more confident doing social impact assessment (such as they perceived could be done) than social scientists felt in considering future technologies.

A point that indicates the strong coupling between social-psychological factors and epistemology is the "pecking order" of prestige among the academic disciplines. The social scientists are at the bottom of the "academic totem pole." As they are often considered to offer little firm knowledge, their results are judged less significant than those of physical scientists. Since group consensus within the social science disciplines is not as strong as that within the physical sciences, more methodological uncertainty is expressed. This combination of factors has operated in a number of projects to alienate social scientists and cause friction on the project team, leading to output fragmentation.

Economics stood out as a discipline with a view of the world that frustrated many of the other TA participants. One recurrent comment dealt with the jargon of economists and their difficulty in translating it into language intelligible to noneconomists. Though all disciplines have their own terminology, terminological problems with economists seemed to stand out in their universality and perceived importance. Yet, it is universally conceded that economics is an extremely important discipline for TA, since changes in technological systems invariably have economic consequences.

Beyond the problem of jargon, there are other substantial problems in interaction with economists. Economists are wedded to building and using complex mathematical models that appear to have little validity or utility. One project leader wished that his team's economists could find the middle ground between highly complex models and relatively trivial extrapolations.

According to a common perception, economists require data that are not only unavailable, but unobtainable, as input for their complex models. This combination of esoteric models and data demands led to frustration by other team members in a number of cases.

Another significant problem with economists appears to be their inability to extend their analysis from costs measured in money flows to costs associated with social and other factors. Some TA participants wondered at the value of the economists' work, given their disregard of and for these broader considerations. More than most, economists seemed to feel their work was a self-sufficient reflection of reality, with little need for the analytical contributions of other disciplines.

The problem of the use of *"TA techniques"* refers to the question of the validity and utility of the collection of techniques for generating and processing information about the future. These techniques include Delphi surveys, cross-impact matrices, relevance trees, and so on [15, 16]. The avowed purpose of these devices is to make quantitative, precise, and systematic what is qualitative and imprecise.

There are three reactions to these techniques. First, they may be ignored. This was the most common view among our respondents. For these respondents, the techniques do nothing significant; they simply recast what is already known. If anything, they give a false impression of quantification and precision to what remains qualitative and imprecise. Another reaction is to use some of the techniques sparingly as a device for organizing thought. Thus, cross-impact matrices are seen as devices for focusing further impact analysis. No claim is made that the "guesstimates" that went into filling the matrix have been transformed into anything more than that. The final reaction, which was the least common among our respondents, is approbation of the techniques because they make the study quantitative and precise. For some practitioners with a hard science and technology background, the ability to be quantitative gives the study worth—a methodological value bias. Others of similar backgrounds are completely unimpressed, however.

Process Features

We now turn to two factors, bounding and iteration, that involve the study process itself. Typically, policy-related research does not offer well-structured problems. *Bounding* is necessary to delimit the problem, and focus the team's effort. In trying to bound a complex problem one is caught between two extremes. One is effecting an early and decisive closure that allows the team to proceed, but is impervious to later changes in perception of the problem. The other is holding on to a total openness almost to the end and allowing differences about the research to remain unresolved. It seems desirable to walk the middle course: fixing most of the main features of the study early, and allowing for some uncertainties that can be resolved as the research proceeds.

Considering the 24 TAs, several measures of bounding corroborated its importance. Integration, comprehensiveness, and depth of analysis were all served by satisfactory bounding.

Iteration is simply redoing the research one or more times. Its purpose, in the case of an interdisciplinary research project, it to allow the initially discrete analyses to affect one another substantively, so that results gained in one area of expertise may be used substantively in another area of expertise. In addition to this integrative function, it has the additional function of smoothing and better organizing a final product for communication with the user.

Probably more than any other factor, iteration appeared to contribute to a better integrated product. We note that the iteration involves more than editorial redrafting. Unfortunately, many studies run short of funds, time, or both. Scheduling to allow iteration of results, with implies critical review and revision, can be recommended for interdisciplinary studies.

Communication patterns within the project group are the final factor we address. In this case management decisions affect what the group actually does. Communication patterns may vary through different phases of the project, as the character of team activity changes. Two basic communication patterns within a core team merit attention: all-channel, shown in Figure 3 for a team of five;

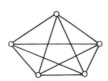
Figure 3. All-channel communication.

Figure 4. The wheel.

and wheel (spokes), shown in Figure 4 for a team of five. Intermediate configurations are possible and, indeed, common.

In the classic literature on small groups, Bavelas [3] and Guetzkow and Simon [13] have found the wheel the most effective communication arrangement for communicating simple factual information and performing simple tasks. As the complexity of the tasks increases, the all-channel configuration becomes more appropriate. The additional complexity of the all-channel pattern over the wheel increases quickly as the number of participants increases. For N participants, the number of links in the wheel is $(N - 1)$, and in the all-channel it is $(N/2)(N - 1)$ or $(N/2)$ (number in the wheel). Maintaining these additional links requires time and effort that would replace individual research effort. The trade-offs involved are different in each situation. To maintain a core team of reasonably small size, one may consider support arrangements for core team members that decrease the number of links in contrast to a large all-channel system. Some possibilities are illustrated in Figure 5. True interdisciplinarity seems to require something more than the wheel, but the unwieldiness of the all-channel system with larger groups leads to complications as well. If an all-channel system is used, the strength of the channels should probably be unequal. Figure 6 shows the communication pattern drawn by the principle investigator of a successful TA. It is all-channel with links of varying strength.

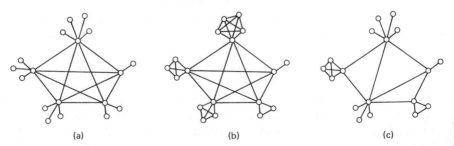

(a)   (b)   (c)

Figure 5. Possible combination communication profiles for project groups: (a), all-channel with wheels; (b), all-channel with all-channels; (c), combination.

Strength of channel

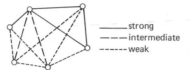

Figure 6. A communication profile in one successful study.

In a statistical sense, we found support for the all-channel pattern in fostering integration. It also seemed to be more enjoyable for the participants, leading to more frequent informal and formal interactions. (Nevertheless, there was no evidence of a relationship between project meetings and product integration, *per se*.)

In the last section we will offer pragmatic conclusions based, in part, on our study of this set of factors affecting integration.

FOUR APPROACHES TO INTEGRATION

In team research, and especially in interdisciplinary research because of the need for integration, the actual development of knowledge involves social-psychological as well as cognitive elements. There are two philosophical perspectives from which to approach the development of knowledge. Kuhn [19] stresses the group process by which consensus takes place, while Lakatos [21] emphasizes the internal "logic" of the process. We found it necessary to consider the social and cognitive aspects to be very closely linked and interactive. In so doing, we were able to identify four social-cognitive frameworks in which the actual integration of knowledge may take place. There are:

1. common group learning,
2. modeling,
3. negotiation among experts, and
4. integration by a leader.

As we present them, they are ideal types. Individual frameworks are rarely, if ever, used exclusively in a single study. Combinations are possible. In some cases no attempt at integration is made. This discussion draws upon the small group experiments, mentioned earlier, and the discussions with participants in the 24 technology assessments. We believe that these four approaches have general applicability to the problem of drawing together disparate pieces of knowledge.

Common Group Learning

The framework we refer to as common group learning was developed and used for TA by Don Kash and his coworkers in the Science and Public Policy Program of the University of Oklahoma [18, 35]. The key to this approach is that the research output reflects the common intellectual property of the entire research group. In the end there are no experts in any particular part of the research; the group is the expert.

Typically the process begins when the group first makes a preliminary bounding of the problem. If necessary, technical experts are brought in to educate the group on the subject of the study. Then the problem is divided into areas based on the expertise and interest of the members of the group, and individual analyses are prepared. The group reconvenes and criticizes each of the individual products in group sessions. The pieces are then rewritten, almost always by a *different* individual—often by someone who is not an expert in the area. At the same time the group's productions are criticized by outsiders who are either experts in some phase of the subject matter or parties at interest to it. This procedure is iterated until the group and its leader feel that the work is finished. Naturally, the needs of outside sponsors and project schedules drive the group to complete its work at a particular time. Figure 7(a) illustrates common group learning schematically.

Because the status of expert belongs to the group as a whole, the project output is taken from the portion of the knowledge of each team member that is common to all, *i.e.*, the intersection of the individual's knowledge. This property has the effect of limiting the technical sophistication of the terminology used in the study, as it must be familiar to each member of the group. Likewise, this approach limits the use of complex theories and sophisticated models in the study. Hence, it tends toward a lower depth of analysis. Locating experts from specific disciplines for the project is not a high priority in this framework. Kash and the Oklahoma group emphasize policy analysis in their technology assessments. A policy focus seems to be more appropriate for such a strategy than a highly technical focus. This approach also means that, in principle, any member of the group could represent the group in activities relating to the research.

In our preliminary experiments, we noted that groups tended to prefer this mode, whatever their instructions were, constituting themselves as interactive panels and relying on their collective wisdom. Education and training typically do not equip professionals for solving complex and ill-structured problems. Thus, it would appear that in the case of short-term interactions, professionals prefer to rely upon a common group learning strategy, possibly because of lower personal risk.

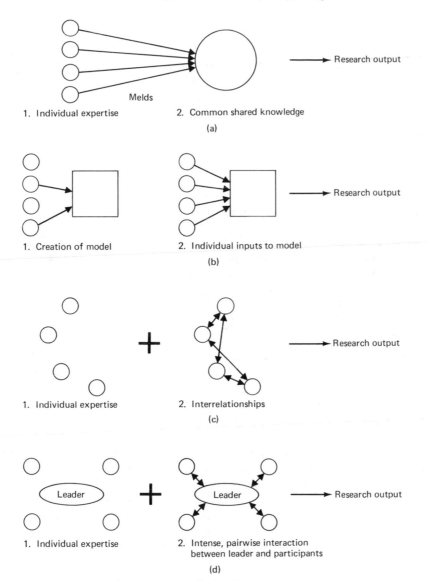

Figure 7. Approaches to knowledge integration: (a), common group learning; (b), modeling; (c), negotiation among experts; (d), integration by leader.

Modeling

Another commonly used framework for integrating the assessments we studied was modeling. Described loosely, a model is a simplified representation of part of the world. A model is supposed to contain the most important relationships of a part of the world so that its essential workings may be studied. In addition to abstract structure, most models require data. Thus, a model of world resource depletion needs some data on what resources exist and how fast they are being used in order to project the world's resources in, say, the year 2000.

A variety of model forms exist. For instance, there are physical models, conceptual models, and mathematical models. Many of the latter can be programmed onto computers. Models of various levels of processes exist from models of the entire world [23] to models of basic physical processes and chemical reactions.

Most commonly encountered in TAs were computerized models—a finding we believe to be typical of policy-oriented research. These dealt largely with socioeconomic relationships for which quantitative data could, at least in principle, be obtained. The models typically emphasized economic features. They usually were not based explicitly on a particular theory, but tended to relate to calculating the costs of various systems under different conditions [14, 9]. This "common sense" approach took advantage of data that were available or could be estimated. Models addressing relationships among persons and institutions tended to take the form of influence diagrams. Relationships were represented by drawing boxes to depict elements and connecting these by directional linkages. Modeling is schematically illustrated in Figure 7(b).

This description illustrates some properties of models that affect their use as integrative frameworks. Models tend to narrow the focus of interest. Even models of the entire world look at it as a world with only a small number of factors involved. These factors are related in such a way that data can be obtained to substantiate the workings of the model. Thus, a model can link various forms of data from diverse sources. This favors the inclusion of "quantitative" technical, economic, and (some) environmental parameters to the exclusion of many "qualitative" social, institutional, and psychological factors. Typically, the "softer" considerations, including policy, will lie outside the model proper. In summary, models narrow the research focus both by excluding nonessential relationships, which is desirable, and by excluding relevent aspects of the world that do not fit within their framework, which is not desirable. They favor empirical (data-based) analysis, which is good, but sometimes go to questionable lengths to invent the needed data. Thus, they may be subject to the old criticism of "garbage in, garbage out."

Under instructions to model, our experimental interdisciplinary groups were primarily interested in relationships and only secondarily in data. The groups favored conceptual models because of their simplicity of development in the short time available. They were confronted by one of the common problems of modeling—what levels of aggregation to adopt. In attempting to handle this problem, the groups fell back to their most comfortable mode of operation— common group learning.

Negotiation Among Experts

Unlike common group learning and modeling, negotiation among experts was not the dominant framework for integration in any of the TAs we studied. From our interviews with participants, we found that this strategy appeared in a limited way in a number of studies. In the ideal case, negotiation among experts is a process where, after bounding, the study is divided among the members of the project team on the basis of their individual expertise. This division typically would reflect their disciplinary backgrounds. Individual analyses would, in turn, reflect this expertise, incorporating any complex and esoteric theories and approaches that seem germane. The integration of the various analyses would then take place by a process of negotiation.

The subject of the negotiation can be considered as the boundary region between analyses as their contents substantively affect each other's conclusions. Effective integration requires the initial analyses to be redone to reflect substantively the inclusion of the findings of the other expert analyses. For example, an economic analysis must be effectively linked to the institutional analysis if it is to be realistic and useful. In negotiation among experts, depth and expertise are preserved. There is no question of nonexperts redoing an analysis. Figure 7(c) illustrates negotiation among experts schematically.

Petrie [27] claimed that knowledge of the meanings of important terms and the observational categories of the other disciplines involved was essential for successful interdisciplinary work. This ideal offers an effective starting point for the process of negotiation. But this starting point can, in addition to serving in negotiation among disciplines, also be used for negotiation among different value-laden perspectives. These would represent the different parties and interests affected by the technology (or policy) being assessed. Negotiations among this sort of "expertise" approximate the integration of adversary technology assessments, a concept discussed by Green [12] and Arnstein and Christakis [2]. An adversary TA is an aggregate of assessments made from the different value perspectives concerned with the subject matter.

When we attempted to give our experimental groups instructions to divide their problem on the basis of expertise and to negotiate the integration of its solution from the expert positions, they generally resisted the instructions. One group divided by having each of its members represent a different general party-at-interest, rather than a disciplinary perspective. Another group nearly had to be forced to split up. It insisted on using the dimension of parties-at-interest to integrate its members' disciplinary perspectives.

Integration By A Leader

Integration by a leader is another ideal type. It involves a communication pattern based on the wheel, in which the problem is divided on the basis of team members' expertise. The leader functions as the sole integrator, and interacts individually with each member of the team to understand and assimilate that member's contribution. The members *do not* interact among themselves. The leader-integrator develops the interrelationships between the component analyses. See Figure 7(d) for a schematic representation.

When the wheel integration framework was used in the TAs we studied, the leader gave assignments and collected them. The weakness of this procedure is the enormous demands it places on the leader-integrator. Does such a superhuman being exist? or are the routine demands of leadership such that they prevent any leader from playing such an active role? The level of interdisciplinary integration that resulted in those TAs using this mode was not as satisfactory as that obtained under other modes of integration. This approach may be better suited to simpler problems.

In the group experiments where the leader had to interact with the group collectively, the leader abdicated an aggressive intellectual role and concentrated on orchestrating the contributions of the others. When these same individuals were assigned a nonleadership position, they became intellectually aggressive and made substantive contributions. From this, we might speculate that the role of interdisciplinary team leader involves high personal risk. The task of taking on professionals in their own areas of expertise is difficult. Consequently, the leader attempting to integrate individual contributions of experts may tend to play down integration in favor of mild editorial revision. The result may lean more to the multidisciplinary than the interdisciplinary. From the perspective of the leader of an interdisciplinary venture, the other three integration strategies may be more comfortable. Common group learning places the burden of confronting an expert upon the whole group. Use of a model may depersonalize confrontation in favor of forcing individuals to meet the information demands of the model (possibly a computer program). Negotiation among experts suggests confrontation at the boundary between regions of expertise where more equal conditions may exist.

Discussion

The actual context of knowledge integration in interdisciplinary research is both cognitive and social. Ignoring the situation where a single individual, "the ideal polymath," [32] performs the entire research, it seems that the social and cognitive factors are closely linked because of the necessity of some group process. It is this closeness that we try to reflect in the explication of the four frameworks discussed. These frameworks are not mutually exclusive in that only one can be used in a particular project. Indeed, elements of more than one occurred on many of the projects we studied.

As we have gone through the four frameworks and noted their principal properties, it is apparent that their strengths lie in different areas. Common group learning fits well when the group lacks overwhelming expertise in the subject to be studied, and when the output required does not need to reflect esoteric analyses. This mode favors a relatively untechnical vocabulary and a policy-making focus (as contrasted with the provision of technical information).

Modeling works best with a problem emphasizing highly technical, or potentially quantifiable, content. Problems with high social and values content are not good candidates for this mode. Modeling requires the existence of modeling capability within the team, and is enhanced by the existence of prior modeling efforts in the area under study. Subtleties and nuances are generally not captured well by models.

Negotiation among experts might be beneficially attempted when the team possesses substantive expertise that can be immediately applied to the problem and where a realistic division of labor on the basis of discipline can be made. It requires that the experts be sufficiently self-conscious to realize that there are many ways of looking at complex problems, that these ways are potentially complementary, and that their analyses should be subject to revision to reflect this. Such an approach seeks to preserve expertise and depth while attempting integration. It requires conscientious effort and strong leadership to enable it to transcend multidisciplinarity.

In integration by a leader, the participants are subordinate to the leader. In a sense they are research assistants gathering the material which the leader will use to produce a final synthesis. This mode asks a question as much as it offers a solution—can one person integrate a large project? Our limited observations show no case where this was successfully accomplished. Those cases where the wheel communication pattern dominated, with the leader at the hub, were typically not highly integrated.

The parameters of a study should help provide guidance to how the group should try to integrate its work. The next and final section provides more specific guidance on the question of integrating interdisciplinary research.

PRAGMATIC CONCLUSIONS

In this concluding section we discuss some practical guidelines for organizing and structuring interdisciplinary research. After commenting on the analysis of the factors affecting integration in the second section, and the frameworks for integration discussed in the third section, we use the dimensions of Table 1 to focus our considerations on specific types of interdisciplinary studies. Because the focus of our research has been on TA, some care should be taken when using these results to understand analogous cases. Both the factors affecting integration and the approaches to integration are general enough, however, to apply to other types of policy-related, interdisciplinary research.

We begin our general observations by noting the desirability of the project leader's being a facilitator, rather than an authoritarian or passive laissez faire leader. In interdisciplinary research, the individual team members make specialized contributions that need to be interrelated. By allowing the participants a measure of responsibility, without relinquishing the power of effecting needed closure, the leader allows the participants to use their professional judgments while assuring that their efforts are part of an integrated whole. If the leader relinquishes control, he or she risks allowing the efforts of the individual participants to be defocused, thus increasing the odds of a fragmented project. By taking an excessively authoritarian stance, the leader risks the dissatisfaction of the team members and resentment of unprofessional treatment, which may lower the quality of their performances.

Effective bounding of the study is crucial in policy-related research. Few policy questions have closely defined bounds. They tend to be bounded by social relevance rather than by some well-cast theoretical structure. Premature and excessively narrow bounding is to be avoided, as is delayed bounding of the main features of the problem. An example of unfortunate study bounds is the TA on the automobile [11], which reduced its considerations to pollution caused by automobiles. The study ignored the cost of energy, which proved to be so salient when the energy crisis struck during the final months of the study. This vitiated some of the study's central conclusions about the control of automotive pollution.

Iteration requires expending time and resources, but it brings the individual contributions, and the whole, under the repeated scrutiny of the team so it can discover, analyze, and incorporate potential interrelationships into the body of the study. If the study is involved in gathering primary data or assembling data from secondary sources, this should be done as early as possible to allow the data to be a part of the iterative process. Iteration is a most essential requisite of integration.

It is important to establish a communication pattern within the group that facilitates the use of all necessary channels between group members. At the same time, it should be noted that unnecessary communication consumes time that could better be used for substantive research. (Of course if integration by leader is attempted, that strategy would dictate a wheel pattern.) We might call this recommended communication pattern "any channel."

Table 3 summarizes both the general observations and those for specific types of research projects as categorized in Table 1. We use the dimensions of Table 1 to suggest strategies for integrating various types of interdisciplinary studies. The first dimension in Table 1 contrasts an action-oriented perspective with an explanatory perspective. The action-oriented perspective would seem to require a greater direct involvement of parties-at-interest and emphasis on the values involved relative to an explanatory perspective. The latter would tend toward enhanced emphasis on explanation from disciplinary or intellectual perspectives. The explanatory emphasis would suggest greater depth. Thus, in choosing approaches to integration, negotiation among experts or modeling would be preferred in cases where the subject matter is sufficiently orderly. Values are poor subjects for modeling, and, hence, heavy emphasis on values precludes modeling.

Table 3. Procedural suggestions and observations.

I. FOR ALL STUDIES

Facilitating, democratic leadership appears most effective

The study should be bounded, but not prematurely

Sufficient time and resources for a number of iterations of the study should be provided

Consider an all-channel communication pattern, rather than the wheel

II. FOR SPECIFIC TYPES OF STUDIES (DIMENSIONED AS IN TABLE 1)

A. Perspective

Action-oriented	*Explanatory*
Various perspectives of the parties at interest require attention	Greater emphasis can be placed on disciplinary or intellectual perspectives
Common group learning is an appropriate approach to integration	Modeling (where appropriate) and negotiation among experts are prime approaches to integration

B. Openness

Internal use	*External use*
Sponsor's interest and focus should influence team characteristics and study bounding	In general a broader range of team capabilities and study boundaries are necessary than in the internal case

C. Scope

Wide-ranging	*Tightly focused*
A wide range of intellectual capabilities is required on the team	Study is correspondingly less complex than in the wide-ranging case
Broad study boundaries are necessary	
Epistemological gaps and value divergencies are likely to arise	
Iteration is especially important	
Common group learning and negotiation among experts are the most promising approaches to integration	Modeling may be useful for integration if the study is technical

D. Scale

Large	*Small*
With increasing project magnitude, comes larger teams; added complexity of bounding, increased difficulty in iteration, and more complex communications patterns	
With respect to integration, modeling might be useful for a large, narrow study; integration by leader seems extraordinarily difficult; and common group learning becomes unwieldy as the number of team members increases	In approaching integration, negotiation among experts is unlikely to be useful in brief studies; integration by leader is possible, and panel studies may be useful

---

For action-oriented studies, common group learning, at whatever depth time and resources allow, is the first choice. Integration by a leader is an alternative where the composition and location of the team, the leader's character, and the available resources indicate it (Table 3).

The second dimension for consideration is the openness of use of the study. We contrast cases that will be used only by a sponsor and studies that will be disseminated externally. In the former case, the characteristics of the team and the study's bounding can reflect the sponsor's interests as closely as convenient. For example, an agency with predominantly nontechnical personnel cannot easily assimilate a highly technical study and should probably avoid obtaining one. In the case of studies for external dissemination, consideration of the uses to which the study may be put needs to inform the makeup of the study team and the bounding of the study. In general, a study for external dissemination would seem to require greater scope, both in team capability and problem bounding, than an internal study. In addition, more care may be required in the quality of analysis in order to withstand external scrutiny. A similar situation obtains, however, when the study is used to shed light on a divergence of views within the sponsoring agency. Almost any approach to integration is usable in the internal case, though negotiation among experts appears the least likely as it is the most complex. In the external case, the approach depends on other study characteristics.

Study scope is the third dimension to be considered. Wide-ranging studies obviously require a greater diversity of intellectual capabilities on the study team than do tightly focused studies. An analogous argument holds for setting the study boundaries. It is especially important in wide-ranging studies that the leader operate in the democratic, facilitating mode. Wide-ranging studies consider a greater variety of intellectual and values perspectives than do tightly focused studies, thereby leading to a greater possibility of epistemological gaps and value divergences. In this case it is useful to assume that there will be problems. On a few occasions, TA team leaders did not think they had any difficulty in integrating their studies and ended up producing poorly integrated reports. The broader the study, the more attention must be given to iteration in order to relate the pieces. Common group learning and negotiation among experts appear to offer the best approaches to integrating a wide-ranging study. Effective models are typically restricted in scope, and broad models often lack specific content. An exceptional leader would be required to integrate a truly broad study. Instances of TAs that we reconstructed as containing attempts at integration by the leader, without the leader being conscious of the full range of demands of his role, did not fare well as integrated documents. The leaders seemed to choke on the pieces. Tightly focused studies put less burden on integration so that any appropriate approach can be followed. In technical studies, modeling may be very useful.

The final dimension we will consider is scale. Large-scale studies place more demands on the leader and require larger numbers of participants. Because of the scale, bounding is more complex, iteration more difficult, and the maintenance of good communications within the project team more critical than for small studies. Integration by leader would seem a poor mode for integrating a large study unless that study was at the same time very narrow in focus. A large, but relatively narrow study might make use of modeling. Common group learning becomes more difficult as the number of participants approaches ten. There were no core teams larger than eight in our study of TAs. In a small study, however, integration by leader is a possible choice. Panel studies of limited depth may be used in small, short-term efforts. If the time frame of a study is short, negotiation among experts is a poor candidate. Table 3 summarizes these observations.

We hope that this discussion provides insight into the factors involved in managing interdisciplinary, policy-related research. Applying the management strategies discussed requires a great deal of insight, not only with respect to the various considerations we have raised, but to those we have not. And we have no bounds to place on those—only some confidence that the factors emphasized here are likely to be important in almost all interdisciplinary efforts.

NOTES AND REFERENCES

1. Arnstein, S. R. "A Working Model for Public Participation." *Public Administration Review* 35(1975): 70–73.
2. Arnstein, S. R., and A. Christakis. *Perspectives on Technology Assessment.* Jerusalem: Science and Technology Publishers, 1975.
3. Bavelas, A. "Communications Patterns of Task Oriented Groups." *Journal of the Acoustical Society of America* 22(1950): 725–730.
4. Churchman, C. W. *The Design of Inquiring Systems.* New York: Basic Books, 1971.
5. Coates, J. F. "Technology Assessment: The Benefits ... the Costs ... the Consequences." *The Futurist* 5(1971): 225–231.
6. Darden, L., and N. Maull. "Interfield Theories." *Philosophy of Science* 44(1977): 43–66.
7. DeWachter, M. "Interdisciplinary Teamwork." *Journal of Medical Ethics* 2(1976): 52–57.
8. Dressel, P. L., *et al. The Confidence Crisis.* San Francisco, Jossey-Bass, 1970.
9. Enzer, S. *Some Impacts of No Fault Automobile Insurance—A Technology Assessment.* Menlo Park, Calif.: Institute for the Future, Report R30, 1974.
10. Glueck, W. F., and C. D. Thorp. *The Management of Scientific Research.* Columbia, Mo.: Research Center, School of Business and Public Administration, 1971.
11. Grad, F. P., *et al. The Automobile.* Norman, Okla.: Universtiy of Oklahoma Press, 1975.
12. Green, H. P. "The Adversary Process in Technology Assessment." *Technology and Society* 5(1970): 163–167.
13. Guetzkow, H., and H. R. Simon. "The Impact of Certain Communication Nets upon Organization and Performance in Task Oriented Groups." *Management Science* 1(1955): 233–250.
14. Harvey, D. R., and W. R. Menchen. *A Technology Assessment of the Transition to Advanced Automotive Propulsion Systems.* Columbia, Md.: Hittman Associates, HIT 541, 1974.
15. Hetman, F. *Society and the Assessment of Technology.* Paris: Organization for Economic Co-operation and Development (OECD), 1973.
16. Hencley, S., and J. R. Yates. *Futures in Education: Methodologies.* Berkeley, Calif.: McCutchan Publishing, 1974.
17. Hill, S. C. "A Natural Experiment on the Influence of Leadership Behavioral Patterns on Scientific Productivity." *IEEE Transactions on Engineering Management* EM-17(1970): 10–20.
18. Kash, D. E. "Observations on Interdisciplinary Studies and Government Roles." In *Adapting Science to Social Needs.* Edited by Scribner and Cholk, pp. 147–167. Washington, D.C.: American Association for the Advancement of Science, 1977.
19. Kuhn, T. S. *The Structure of Scientific Revolutions*, 2nd ed. Chicago: University of Chicago Press, 1970.

20. Kelly, P., *et al. Technological Innovation: A Critical Review of Current Knowledge*. San Francisco Press, 1977.
21. Lakatos, I. "Falsification and the Methodology of Scientific Research Programmes." In *Criticism and the Growth of Knowledge*. Edited by Lakatos and Musgrove, pp. 91–196. Cambridge: Cambridge University Press.
22. Maruyama, M. "Paradigmatology and Its Application to Cross-Disciplinary, Cross-Professional, and Cross-Cultural Communication." *Cybernetica* (1974): 136–156, 237–281.
23. Meadows, D. H., *et al. The Limits to Growth*. Washington, D.C.: Potomac Associates, 1971.
24. Merton, R. K. *The Focused Interview*. New York: The Free Press, 1956.
25. Mitroff, I. I. *The Subjective Side of Science*. New York: American Elsevier, 1974.
26. Nelson, R. "Intellectualizing about the Moon-Ghetto Metaphor: A Study of the Current Malaise of Rational Analysis of Social Problems." *Policy Sciences* 5(1974): 375–414.
27. Petrie, H. D. "Do You See What I See? The Epistemology of Interdisciplinary Inquiry." *Journal of Aesthetic Education* (July 1976): 9–15.
28. Porter, A. L., F. A. Rossini, S. R. Carpenter, and R. W. Larson. *A Guidebook for Technology Assessment and Impact Analysis*. New York: Elsevier North Holland, forthcoming.
29. Rossini, F. A. "Epistemological Problems in Technology Assessment." *The General Systems Paradigm: Science of Change and Change of Science*. Edited by White, pp. 455–462. Washington, D.C.: Society for General Systems Research, 1977.
30. Rossini, F. A., *et al.* "The Epistemology of Interdisciplinary Research: The Case of Technology Assessment." In *The General Systems Paradigm: Science of Change and Change of Science*. Edited by White, pp. 451–498. Washington, D.C.: Society for General Systems Research, 1977.
31. Simon, H. R. *The New Science of Management Decision*. New York: Harper & Row, 1960.
32. Taylor, J. B. "Building an Interdisciplinary Team." In *Perspectives on Technology Assessment*. Edited by Arnstein and Christakis, pp. 45–60. Jerusalem: Science and Technology Publishers, 1975.
33. Walsh, W. B., *et al.* "Developing an Interface Between Engineering and the Social Sciences." *American Psychologist* November 1975, 1067–1071.
34. Weingart, J. M. "Transdisciplinary Science–Some Recent Experience with Solar Energy Conversion Research." American Association for the Advancement of Science Annual Meeting, Denver, Colo., 1977.
35. White, I. L. "Interdisciplinarity." In *Perspectives on Technology Assessment*. Edited by Arnstein and Christakis, pp. 87–96. Jerusalem: Science and Technology Publishers, 1975.

3

Enriching Policy Premises for An Ambiguous World*

Richard Alan Goodman and Anne Sigismund Huff
University of California, Los Angeles

INTRODUCTION

The world is complicated and our responses to it are complicated, but we tend to proceed as if this complicated reality were not so. For instance, the applied researcher, seeking to aid the policy-making process, attempts to reduce the context for decision and action to a finite set of variables that sufficiently describes the world and ideally allows the construction and manipulation of a formal analytic model. This action is taken because, in the applied sciences, the basis for explanation and ultimately for action in the world is taken to be a workable theory. Inherent in the concept of theory is the necessary and desirable simplification of relationships in a form that can be objectively validated by a specifiable data set.

As a result, in policy analysis and policy formulation, we are more comfortable dealing with the simplification than with the reality. Yet life remains without the models' elegance. Instead it is experienced as *exceedingly complex*, charac-

*The thinking behind this paper was first formulated in a year-long series of discussion seminars held with two graduate students—George Obonyi, now at the University of Ottawa, and Michael Lawless. The output of that joint effort was a paper by the four of us entitled, "An Alternative World-View for Policy Analysis and Policy Making (or Beyond Systems Theory)," published in the *Proceedings* of the Southeastern Society for General Systems Research, Baton Rouge, Louisiana, April 1977. The first and third subsections of this paper are revised from the *Proceedings* paper. We appreciate and acknowledge the input of these two colleagues. George Obonyi also made helpful comments on later drafts of the paper, and allowed us to adapt his ideas on sequential acceptance of alternatives. Finally, we also appreciate helpful comments made by James R. Jackson and James Dyer.

334

terized by *ever-changing pressures*, and *frequently surprising*. It is this existential sense that leads to our discomfort with most of the prescriptive outlines for the policy process.

In the search for alternatives, we thought that if there were a way to conceptualize a policy situation that preserved greater richness while allowing the observer to grasp it in a useful way, we might expect great improvement in our problem appreciations, in Vickers' sense [16]. Further, and more important, we felt that this richness, ordinarily lost, contains elements that might change the substance of analysis and of resulting action.

This paper offers a means of expanding understanding of the world within which policy is formulated. It is aimed at both the policy-maker and the policy analyst. We feel that the ideas presented give the policy-maker more options for the design of the policy process. They also give the policy analyst a considerably different framework within which to embed the wide range of techniques and approaches now available.

THE IMPLICATIONS OF VIEWING THE WORLD AS AMBIGUOUS

The great disparity between the world as projected by a model and the world as we experience it has led us to attempt a basic reconceptualization. Thus, we are starting with a fundamentally different assumption about the nature of the world and about the nature of how we can understand the world. We continually face situations that resemble the old story of the blind men and the elephant. Each person, using his own data and his own perceptions of the world, describes a situation quite differently. We argue here, that in terms of the story, there is no omniscient observer what can see the whole elephant. Nor is it reasonable to expect that different observers will come to share one composite image that can be identified as an elephant. More strongly, there is, in fact, no well-defined elephant to be discovered.

Somehow, we need a view of the world that accepts and works with this ambiguity of experience, this difficulty of making sense of the world and of sharing that sense with others. We are basing our work upon a definition of the world as *ambiguous* [2], as "open to various interpretations, having several possible meanings . . . equivocal . . . lacking clearness or definiteness; obscure; indistinct," according to the *Random House Dictionary of the English Language*. This definition of the world has many implications for action-taking and policy-making. Let us begin by detailing four important concepts.

1. *The "external environment," as the world of experience, and the "internal environment," as the individual's world of reflection, are intertwined.* Judgments of fact that arise from experiencing the external environment and judgments of value that arise from reflection are interrelated. Thus, facts become

invested with values as they are perceived by various participants. There is no way to "see" the world independent of these personal and value-tinged meanings.

2. *The meaning of events and entities is impossible to prespecify.* "What is" is a function of both the context and the observer. Any formulation of an "overall design" and positive identification of its "component parts" is, therefore, relativistic with respect to time and to the specific reflecting minds. If one cannot operate in the world as if there is a unique, absolute reality, then reflection and action in the real world no longer depend on the construction of an objective theory that describes or predicts "the truth out there." Decisions and actions are based on experiences of reality, and are not related to a prior specification of the exact nature of the external environment.

3. *The coexistence of multiple appreciations results in simultaneous alternative truths.* A set of perceivers, each with his own image of the world, data sources, and valuations, may hold not only different but incompatible appreciations of the same phenomenon, none of which can be called the best. One implication is that to accept the perspective of some outside "expert"—who ostensibly "has the accurate model"—is invalid, because no single reality exists that can be inferred by any method—*e.g.*, the scientific method—known to the "expert."

4. *Shared experience suggests that causal relationships themselves sometimes change in unpredictable ways.* The preceding implications of ambiguity have to do with the uniqueness of individual experience. To the extent that shared meaning is possible, however, there is also some indication that the world itself exhibits ambiguity. In the physical sciences elementary behavior of matter is not always predictable. In the social sciences, similar thoughts are beginning to prevail. In addition to being ambiguous, we might say that the world characteristically "lacks distinctive form" or is "amorphous."

PUBLIC POLICY IN AN AMBIGUOUS WORLD

An ambiguous world-view appears to be useful in a broad range of situations. In the public arena, a fundamental feature of the ambiguity of experience is political. An ambiguous world-view of policy-making in the public sector might include the following:

1. Interest groups affect problem formulation and resolution. As special interests are accommodated, policy tends to expand and become more complex.
2. Values are paramount. Each constituency is formed specifically around a set of core issues and an ideological approach to action with respect to these issues. In general, these values are grounded in common experience.
3. Common higher order goals among interest groups, or mutually acceptable incentive systems, are often not readily apparent.

4. Key considerations often emerge during the process of hearings, legislation, and rule-making, rather than being known *a priori*. These considerations are not easily quantifiable or comparable.
5. Further complexity arises from the increasing scope of intended government action.

It is apparent to us that these characteristics fit well into the definition of ambiguity. Policy-making in public settings, in our view, is a *collective* activity that involves a search for widely tolerated solutions that are ideally effective (they adequately meet the needs of the relevant parties) and stable (they have sufficient consensus that implementation is not immediately threatened by waxing and waning of power). These conditions are most likely to be met when participants come to recognize, in addition to their local interests, some wider common experience as well.

Communication plays a key role in developing common vocabularies of interest. One of the most important roles of the policy process is helping reach "agreement" on how a situation can be usefully regarded. In our view, this is not likely to be achieved through some highly simplified representation of a complex political environment. The more thorough the process initiated by the policy-maker, even to the point of including contradictory statements, the more likely that world-views will emerge with enough commonality for consensual action. The rest of this paper develops an expanded version of the policy process that relies heavily on the idea that initial development of broad understanding is essential to policy-making under conditions of ambiguity.

GUIDELINES FOR ACTION

The implications of an ambiguous world-view become most apparent when action is desired. An example, which many have experienced, is the frustration of trying to complete some project that is suddenly resolved, not by direct effort, but by coming to a radical new way of conceptualizing the project. The new conceptualization then suggests appropriate action. We have suggested above that such examples support the notions that internal and external "reality" are intertwined, that "meanings" are not stable, and that multiple, contradictory meanings can be, and are, constructed. Satisfying action might, therefore, be expected when the individual has some skill in manipulating internal as well as external reality, in changing the meaning applied to problem situations, and even in being comfortable with adopting new meanings that are incommensurate with immediately previous world-views.

The need for such skills is magnified when *groups* of individuals attempt to coordinate actions to produce more desirable conditions for each of the participants. This situation is often noted in business organizations, but is particularly relevant in the public arena. Most interesting and important problems require some adjustment and coordination among public agencies that have an independent charter and relate to a specific constituency. The "public interest" and public interest groups compound the need for complicated coordination. Thus, skill in dealing with symptoms as they might be interpreted under a variety of world-views, seems particularly necessary in public policy formation and action-taking. As a preliminary orientation to such action, we suggest that the following guidelines are among those that are compatible with an ambiguous world-view.

1. *Greater recognition of individual values and perspectives in decision-making.* It is not just that decisions are only as "good" or "useful" as the individual making them; decisions cannot be separated from the unique world-view of the individual making them. Thus, policy-makers have a responsibility to broaden their appreciation of possible interpretations before conceptually isolating the situation by defining "problems."

2. *Flexibility in interpretation and assigning value.* In ambiguous settings the ability to see the world in different ways at different times, and even to change opinions about outcomes that are valued, is highly adaptive. To the extent that those in a policy-making situation adopt this flexibility themselves and act in ways to encourage other actors to adopt similar flexibility, mutually satisfying action is likelier.

3. *Alternative "futures" rather than specific goals.* It is difficult to define invariant boundaries for solutions, since it may be that a desirable action that is dominant in some limited problem formation will not remain so once the boundary is changed. The apparent boundary of a problem will often lose its relevance because of constantly changing patterns of events and influences. Because of these ambiguities in the development of experience, goal-setting is a less precise part of action-taking than is generally assumed. Specific goal targets used in formal analysis might be replaced by less definite and broader views of possible futures, as approximated by the concept of scenarios. The "aim" of action, then, becomes constellations of events and not single-valued specifics. In many cases, goals are better described as directions or thrusts than as desired end states.

4. *Temporary planning processes.* If relations among events in the world are ambiguous, we should recognize the rationality and wisdom of action-taking efforts that grow and wane. That is, we should consciously design our actions to have a limited duration and expect to discontinue the actions and the organizational units needed to execute the actions. All aspects of the "situation" (participants, structures, goals, *etc.*) are likely to have a limited life span and conform to life-cycle phenomena of growth, stability, and decay. In general, the implication is to allow for new forms in the future that will be more closely related to experiences at that future time.

5. *A new importance for "energy."* Once events are recognized as difficult to control, energy—commitment or willingness to expend effort, whatever the result of its intended use—becomes important in making decisions and in affecting outcomes [2]. Actors with energy are likely to have some effect on others' experiences. They are an important part of the situation facing policy-makers. Policy-makers, in turn, must recognize the convergence between decision-making and action in planning their own work.

6. *Tolerance for ambiguity in the timing of action.* An essential characteristic of an ambiguous world-view is the occurrence of breaks in causal understanding. Working from "islands" of rationality, the decision-maker is partially released from the search for critical interventions. Hindsight may still suggest missed opportunities for action in an ambiguous world. Nevertheless, the decision-maker need be less concerned with finding the one correct moment for action in an environment where outcomes are not always clearly linked to causes, and more concerned with responding to a range or set of dimensions over periods of time.

A THREE-THRUST APPROACH TO UNDERSTANDING AN AMBIGUOUS WORLD

At this point, these guidelines do not indicate specific methodologies, although an ambiguous world-view is radically different from the single-perspective views underlying most policy methodology. New techniques and planning processes are called for. Ambiguity implies that appropriate techniques must be more intuitive, holistic, multidisciplinary, and multiappreciative. Policy formulation must be more open to value influences throughout the process, and must allow for discontinuities in problem understanding and proposed remedial action. *These are more than "complications" of traditional approaches; they suggest a new direction in the practice of policy-making.*

We have suggested that the world is both ambiguous and amorphous. As a practical result, the policy-making process that fits the world must also have elements of ambiguity and changing form. Yet policy-making is an attempt to make specific changes. The tension between the demands of the situation for changing appreciation and the demands of participants for creating a specific state pulls the sensitive policy-maker through an iterative and somewhat contradictory cycle.

Three activities can be described in this process: shared learning, diagnostic intervention, and formal analysis. Figure 1 suggests a view of "synthetic understanding" and an interlacing of the three perspectives. Each part of the process works "with" and "against" the others to contribute to a broad world-view from which policy can be formulated.

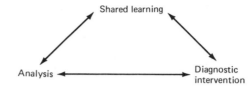

Figure 1. Synthetic understanding of the policy situation.

Shared Learning

If the world cannot be described in one way, the policy-maker *must* seek multiple appreciations. Although there are inherent limitations in any one person's ability to encompass the understanding of others, a major task is to push the understanding of the world to the broadest possible view. In order that the recommendations that flow from this new understanding fit the situation, the process also *must* promote shared learning and synthesis of understanding among participants affected by policy.

This calls for much more than the passive collection of clients' opinions about the problem, which conventional wisdom discounts as symptomatic. The task is to create a setting in which each person learns about the world along with other participants, so that all emerge with strengthened and broadened worldviews. The envisioned process calls for:

1. Each party attempting to understand his own and others' feelings, values, perceptions of fact, and models of the world.
2. The synthesis of these inputs into new appreciations of the policy-making situations, which is consensual where possible, but does not neglect incompatible understanding.
3. Fitting the resultant world-views, which will still be divergent, into the "solution" or action-taking phase.

This is participative policy-making in the fullest sense. The job begins with the notion that *appropriate* understandings of the world reside in the participants. In practice, this part of the policy-making process is difficult and time-consuming. Participants in a given situation tend to be wedded to specific interpretations of the situation, even when an ambiguous and amorphous world has moved away from validating those interpretations. The total set of relevant actors, particularly in public organizations, may be so large that their involvement is impractical. Conflicts between individuals who are involved may cause those responsible for policy-making to despair of achieving shared world-views. Dominant individuals may inhibit shared learning of all participants.

These problems are exacerbated by the view that the ambiguity of the situation itself will quickly reduce the usefulness of whatever shared synthesis might emerge by changing, once again, the understandings of participants and the context for action. Further, participants are often anxious that *some* action be taken. These are the conditions that suggest the need for the second perspective of the process we envision.

Diagnostic Intervention

Richer understanding of a problem situation often follows attempts to change the nature of that situation. The implication is an increased willingness to act— with an orientation toward acting and *learning* rather than acting and *solving*. Action or "experiments" on the situation are suggested, but in a way radically different from scientific inquiry. The objective is not to test a hypothesis about a situation presumed to be stable, but to discover the nature of the situation as it currently exists and to explore the range of possibilities for future change.

In the shared-learning phase work begins with the belief that appropriate un- derstanding of the situation resides in the participants. The diagnostic-action perspective begins with the belief that knowledge of appropriate action also resides in the participants. Of course, this knowledge is obscured on both counts — or the time-consuming and expensive process would never have been initiated.

In an attempt to clarify appropriate policy, diagnostic intervention involves the following process:

1. focus on one or more especially ambiguous or conflictually interpreted as- pects of the problem situation;
2. select an action alternative. This alternative may reflect broadly shared rec- ommendations from participants, or may be chosen to illuminate differences;
3. implement the action; and
4. evaluate the outcome by using a shared-learning perspective of the results from each of the participants.

Although the action-diagnostic process is also highly participative, it is distinct from the understanding phase in that it focuses on clarifying specific aspects of the problem that shared perceptions have not been able to resolve satisfactorily. And, it works from participants' feelings for appropriate action, rather than from their verbalized perceptions of the state of the world and cause and effect in that world. In fact, it is expected that similar actions will be recommended from very divergent beliefs about their effect. Conversely, participants with similar statements of the situation may recommend disparate interventions.

Diagnostic intervention is an experiment involving the understanding of par- ticipants. Action is taken in an attempt to create an environment that heightens the understanding and sharing of desirable actions to be codified as policy. Diagnostic intervention is aimed at provoking new communication between participants so that policy-making can proceed. It will also, of course, trans- form the reality of the situation itself. The policy-maker with an ambiguous world-view is more comfortable with this likelihood, given the belief that the world is constantly changing at any rate, and that there is little pressure to await the perfect time for formal policy-inspired action.

Formal Analysis

The synthesizing process we have been discussing has formal analysis as a third perspective. Table 1 is one summary of the many techniques available to this aspect of the process. Policy-makers will continue to use such techniques as an aid to understanding complex situations. We suggest, however, that complex situations will be more amenable to formal analysis as their nature is revealed through shared learning and diagnostic action.

A review of these techniques, most of which are assumed to be familiar to the reader, also indicates that many of them include the capability of indicating various definitions of the situation and also suggest some possible outcomes of action. This overlap between the three parts of the process we describe for developing understanding of policy situations is characteristic, and not necessarily to be avoided.

The generic questions being asked at this point are: What is a good set of descriptors, quantitative or qualitative, of the situation? What values *do* these descriptors have for participants. What other values might participants be encouraged to hold? What in the nature of possible actions should be specially attended to? These questions can be explored using a wide range of individual techniques. Some of these questions can be approached by basically quantitative methods—demographics, input/output analysis, simulation, systems analysis. They can also be approached by descriptive techniques—hearings, case studies, field visits, broad discussions, scenario writing, *etc.* Intuitive and creative techniques—analogy, guided fantasy, word association, role playing, visual mapping, semantic differential, paliestrics, and so on—may also be useful.

Each of the indicated approaches has a strength and a weakness. Basically, the source of both strengths and weaknesses lies in the underlying world-view about what are data and what is cause and effect. The quantitative techniques have little facility for measuring values and manipulating them. They do allow for the coordination of massive amounts of data into information for policy appreciation. They also allow for experimental manipulation of very complex situations (albeit in drastically simplified forms), the primary value of which may be to reveal concerns of relevant parties. When the process needs enriched descriptions of the situation, the descriptive approaches allow for anecdotal commentary and judgments that may not have occurred to policy-makers. This richness should provide insights that have subtle but powerful leverage upon the success or failure of a policy approach. Unfortunately, the descriptive approaches make

Table 1. Some techniques for policy analysis [5] .

STUDY TECHNIQUES	1 STRUCTURING THE PROBLEM	2 THE SYSTEMS ALTERNATIVES	3 POSSIBLE IMPACTS	4 EVALUATING IMPACTS	5 IDENTIFYING DECISION-MAKERS	6 IDENTIFYING POSSIBLE ACTION OPTIONS FOR DECISION-MAKERS	7 PARTIES AT INTEREST	8 MACROSYSTEMS ALTERNATIVES	9 EXOGENOUS VARIABLES, STATE OF SOCIETY	10 CONCLUSIONS AND RECOMMENDATIONS	11 PARTICIPATION OF PARTIES-AT-INTEREST	12 PRESENTATION OF RESULTS
Historical surveys	●	●	●		●	●	●	●		●		
Input/output	●			●			●					●
Compilation of prior work	●	●	●	●	●		●	●	●	●		
Cost-benefit	●			●			●					●
Systems analysis	●		●	●			●		●			
Risk-benefit	●						●					●
Systems engineering	●	●	●	●				●				
Simulation	●	●	●	●			●		●		●	●
Expert panels, workshops	●	●	●	●	●		●	●	●		●	●
Modeling	●	●	●	●			●		●		●	●
Hearings	●	●		●	●		●	●	●	●	●	●
Interpretive structural modeling	●				●		●			●	●	●
Field or on-site investigation	●		●	●			●			●		
Signed digraph	●		●	●	●	●						●
Trend extrapolation and analysis			●	●								
Physical models			●	●								●
Delphi	●	●	●	●	●	●	●	●	●		●	
Scenarios/games	●	●	●	●	●	●	●	●	●	●	●	●
Cross impact	●	●	●	●		●			●		●	
Moot courts			●	●	●		●			●	●	●
Checklists	●	●	●		●	●	●					●
Telecommunication participation			●	●	●		●		●	●	●	●
Morphological analysis	●	●						●				
Syncons			●	●	●	●	●	●	●		●	●
Historical analogy	●		●	●	●	●	●		●	●		
Survey techniques				●					●	●		●
Decision/relevance tree	●	●	●	●	●		●					●
Ballots				●				●		●	●	●
Fault tree	●		●	●								●
Decision theory				●		●				●		●
Scaling				●					●	●		●
Brainstorming	●	●	●		●	●	●	●	●	●	●	
Graphics				●							●	●
Judgment theory				●		●				●		
Dynamic modeling	●	●	●	●					●	●		●
KSLM	●	●	●	●				●	●	●	●	●

data manipulation difficult and even make it difficult to share exactly what any given individual has learned from the process. The use of the third, intuitive techniques is based on the observation that some knowledge held by individuals cannot be elicited easily by direct methods. Creative, nondirected, "irrational" techniques may, in fact, make the greatest contribution to an understanding of the ambiguity of complicated, intractable policy situations.

A SIMPLIFIED MODEL OF THE POLICY PROCESS

How does the decision-maker decide whether or not to proceed under the assumption of ambiguity and invoke a process similar to the three-thrust one we have described? An ambiguous world-view leads to procedures that are likely to be costly, and the decision to evoke them should not be entered into lightly. Aside from the cost factor, the overuse of the process will probably dull its edge and lead to *pro forma* execution, rather than the deep investment required.

Stimulus

We recommend that the ambiguous world-view be adopted under the following conditions:

1. familiar policy techniques have not yielded satisfactory results,
2. the situation is likely to have a long-run impact on the decision unit,
3. current or future conditions relate to major goals,
4. there is an opportunity to make a significant change,
5. the environment is consuming a disproportionate share of organizational resources,
6. successful implementation appears to require widespread support.

The word "stimulus" thus has a double meaning. In the first place, most organizational activities respond to some specific condition. One traditional way of identifying these triggering mechanisms is the vocabulary of organizational opportunities and threats. The second sense of the word stimulus is more specific to the process for policy-making under ambiguity as developed here. The policy-maker is stimulated to attempt the more difficult open-ended search for understanding only when more traditional methods do not yield (or are not predicted to yield) satisfactory results, *and* when the situation is important enough to warrant this more difficult approach to understanding.

These conditions suggest the criteria whereby the policy-maker can assess the "importance" of situations that might be more fully understood by an ambiguous world-view. For instance, when an issue is slippery and hard to put a handle on, it is generally too narrowly explored or too complex for the policy-maker to grasp. The unevaluative listening mode characteristic of shared learning would tend to counteract this problem and would result in an improved problem statement and more intellectual/intuitive resources. Similarly, a policy that has a definite long term impact, or relates to major goals, is likely to preempt future action alternatives. A good understanding of present policy and future options is critical in such a situation. This would seem to call for a wider "testing" of approaches before policy formulation than might otherwise be taken.

The situation in which the environment is using too many resources is one that usually develops over time and suddenly becomes experientially pressing. A regulation changes (affirmative action), a resource becomes constrained (10% less water), a judicial decision is rendered (extension of product liability). Suddenly it feels as if the environment is requiring an overwhelming portion of available resources directing attention from more central missions. This situation often calls for a deep and thorough reevaluation of purpose and decisions that affect organization structure and allocation of resources. Here again the deeper, more thorough processes triggered by an ambiguous world-view would seem particularly valuable. Finally, when widespread cooperation is necessary for a policy to be successful, then a widespread appreciation of the concerns and values of policy-makers and participants is essential for successful implementation.

Identification of relevant parties

The relevant parties in a policy situation are either organized externally (the Chamber of Commerce, The Select Committee of Clergy, the AFL-CIO Trade Union Council, the Property Owners Association, *etc.*), or are functional units of the policy body (The Department of Sanitation and Flood Control, the Probation Department, the Chief of Police, *etc.*). The formal relationship of these entities to the policy process is often open to interpretation by the decision-maker. External "independent" entities most often provide information to policy-makers through an advisory structure. Functional entities are normally subordinated in a hierarchical structure, and tend to provide technical, analytic support in the policy process.

In general, these uses of relevant actors undervalue the capabilities and knowledge of those involved in a policy situation. They also tend to underestimate the stake these actors have in policy outcomes. Denied an active voice in policy formulation, relevant actors become critical factors in policy implementation, as policy-makers are discovering more and more frequently. The confrontation of the policy-maker with relevant parties who have had little role in policy process also tends to solidify prematurely the positions of those involved, making it more difficult for additional data to change either the world-view or the outcomes desired by participants.

Early identification of many relevant parties can be accomplished by examining the impact of current conditions on those in the environment, and by projecting the impact of possible action alternatives. This crude guideline to relevance leaves the policy process with three other issues before beginning the synthetic understanding phase—membership, competence, and relationship.

The question of membership can be stated as two ends of a continuum. At one end, the formal leadership of each relevant entity nominates participants in the policy process. These participants tend to represent the organizational "party line" and to be well briefed about the issues. Being political appointees, they also may tend to negotiate for the views of their constituency and to be somewhat inflexible in accepting alternatives. A converse strategy for choosing representatives would be the use of a sampling approach to select lay members from each entity or constituency. The information available to the process from such a selection would probably be somewhat closer to the feelings of the membership involved, but would suffer from a lack of briefing on critical issues. Rank-and-file participants are also likely to experience initial difficulty in dealing with the process *per se*, but are likely to learn more from it and may, perhaps, exhibit somewhat more overall creativity or diversity in their inputs.

These two strategic choices for determining representatives of relevant entities raise the issue of competence. Many representatives will be unfamiliar with the policy process and the constraints and opportunities facing the policy-maker. They may also be deficient in techniques for formal analysis or group problem-solving processes. Thus, the first stages of perspective building will often necessarily be aimed at enriching the competencies of those involved. This can be accomplished by altering techniques of the policy process, by clustering members with various strengths and weaknesses, by formal training sessions, and so on.

The question of advisory input or more participative involvement in policy decisions is exacerbated by the "start-up costs" of developing familiarity or "competencies" in representatives. If the potential impact of representatives is small—neither the organization nor the individual participant is as willing to become involved in the extended process we describe. Further, the process of involvement, and increased understanding, may increase participant demands to be able to influence final decisions. We outline a participative process despite these problems because of a deep conviction that understanding and implementing decisions in difficult situations *depends* upon broad multiplicative world-views. This necessity is independent of a philosophical belief in democratic forms.

A final problem that must be considered involves the difficulty of large groups. The parties relevant to complicated policy decisions are often too numerous for direct interaction. This problem will necessitate a creative approach to the group process, which might entail overlapping small groups or Delphi-like procedures for larger groups that cannot meet face to face because of locations and schedules.

The Three-Thrust Development of Perspective

Once the policy-maker has been stimulated to action, and some notion of relevant parties has been developed, the three-thrust process of understanding we have described becomes important. As developed in the preceding section, this process involves three separate modes.

1. *Shared learning.* Under an ambiguous world-view, shared learning is directed at developing the multiple appreciations of the situation held by relevant parties. The intention of this stage is not necessarily to achieve agreement among these participants about the nature of the situation, but to achieve as broad an appreciation as possible in the minds of the participants who will ultimately be involved in the resulting policy.

2. *Formal analysis.* One likely result of the shared learning perspective is the identification of certain ideas or tasks amenable to more detailed exploration using adaptations of current analytic approaches. The results of the application of these techniques become input to the learning process we have outlined. The exchange of ideas and values would be expected to gain in clarity from the use of analytic expression. Thus, individuals with skills and values compatible with particular technical approaches would be encouraged to explore the implications of their concern using those technical skills. This use of technical analysis is in contrast, however, to the more common practice of accepting a specific analytic style or technique as the arbiter of the policy process. In our view, technical skills should add enrichment to the policy process rather than constrain it.

3. *Diagnostic action.* The foregoing approaches to the policy problem will often fall short of providing the information necessary for decision. Another modality is available: the action-oriented experiment. Diagnostic action can be taken to discover more about the nature of the situation. Or, if an uncertainty exists about the effects of a particular action alternative, one may safely use diagnostic action to discover some implications of implementation. The diagnostic intervention should be reversible, if possible. The situation of the action should have all the flavor of a protected experiment with prenegotiation about how to return to the status quo (or, at least, to cease the experiment) after a reasonable length of time. The project should have all the characteristics of action research to assure that it is properly measured. It might be a feasibility study, a demonstration project, or even a full-scale implementation. The key difference here is the attention paid to taking the action in order to learn more about the situation.

The action program ensuing in this phase yields, as an output, data for later action. The approach taken to this diagnosis must be formative as well as summative [6]. That is, it must look for new dimensions and issues, as well as measure expected results on preconceived scales. Thus, the data gathered should be intuitive and qualitative as well as quantitative.

Policy Articulation, Implementation, Evaluation

These three thrusts are alternatively pursued in our version until we feel that further synthesis and understanding would be only marginally improved by continuing the process. At this point, the more familiar process of articulating policy begins. Ideas and insights are codified into guidelines, and the details of implementation are worked out. A formal evaluation approach is developed, and the policy is promulgated. The actual workings of this policy are monitored and evaluation is then used to tune the policy or to recognize the need to start all over again. Most of the early evaluative work will be focused on adjusting various facets of the program such that it approximates the intent of the policy. Only much later would it be expected that the evaluation would point to an extensive new policy. When this happens, however, the very failure of readjustments suggests the need for extensive perspective building (of the type described above) before policy reformulation is attempted again.

A SUMMARY STATEMENT OF THE PROCESS

Figure 2 represents the mix of tasks that make up the policy process over time. This mix is shown as an overlapped set because the process is neither a linear nor a simple iterative one. The various parts of the process blend into each other and blur the boundaries between stages. The policy process begins with a stimulus for action. This may be a pressure that builds over time and finally reaches a threshold of consciousness, or it may be one or more dramatic events (Supreme Court decision, urban riot, drought, *etc.*). As the stimulus grows stronger, relevant actors emerge or are sought out in the first steps of dealing with the issue. After the relevant parties are identified, the process enters the three-thrust perspective building phase designed to increase understanding of an ambiguous world. Shared learning approaches are used to derive a broad world-view that includes areas of disagreement. Diagnostic intervention is attempted to clarify or resolve questions that arise from the world-view. Formal analysis is undertaken to explicate issues that are amenable to available techniques. These three modes of inquiry react with each other, sometimes dominating the process and then again as mutually supportive approaches. At some point new insights do not appear to merit the resources consumed by another iteration.

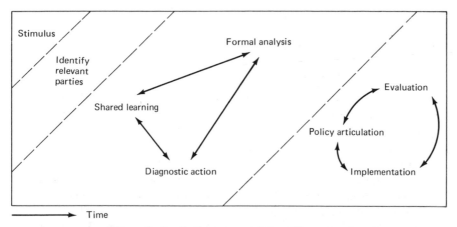

Figure 2. Synthesis as a part of the policy process.

Then the more formal tasks of policy articulation, implementation, and evaluation become the major focus of the process.

The figure as a whole is "loosely" drawn to indicate the poor demarcation between stages of the process. This is a key aspect of policy-making under conditions of ambiguity, and is a primary distinction of each part of the model described. For instance, major shocks in the environment (a new administration, an oil embargo, lack of refunding) may cause ongoing efforts to be abandoned and stimulate new iterations of the process as a whole. Similar perturbations may occur when an excluded group demonstrates its relevance and must be included in an effort to create useful perspectives. Or, new understanding generated internally by the development of policy itself may lead to a discontinuous jump in the action that next seems appropriate. (We have the likelihood of such discontinuities in mind throughout our discussion.)

FOUR EXAMPLES OF PERSPECTIVE-BUILDING TECHNIQUES

We now turn to the more specific procedures that we find consistent with an ambiguous world-view and with the notions of the policy process just developed. The discussion of procedures is made more difficult by our view that *flexibility in method is as essential as flexibility in perception* when operating under conditions of ambiguity. "What to do" must fit the specific situation—as it develops. The process, using the reiterative ideas of building understanding just presented, is likely to use several different approaches to fit each "cycle."

We have already suggested six guidelines for choosing these approaches:

1. seek individual perspectives,

2. encourage flexible attitudes,
3. focus on alternative futures versus specific goals,
4. make planning processes adaptive,
5. pinpoint "energy," and
6. allow ambiguity in timing.

Though the guidelines suggest desirable characteristics, it is difficult to find one course of action that simultaneously gives attention to each. An additional impetus for the use of different approaches at different times is the necessity of focusing efforts on one or two of these ideals at any one time.

Iterative attempts at understanding and multiple guidelines for action do more than encourage the use of varied "techniques" or procedures in the policy process. They also encourage the decision-maker to *adapt* and *develop* new ways of acting that fit the unique situation. This section of the paper discusses four techniques for analysis under conditions of ambiguity as examples of how the individual guidelines we propose might be met. Our intention is to show illustrative courses of action that respond to a specific situation. In response to other situations, the policy-maker is expected to adapt or develop other techniques. The section following these examples gives additional guidance for this devlopment.

Example 1: Reciprocal Scenarios

Objective. This course of action is designed to encourage a small group of individuals to explicate to each other—and the decision-maker—the values that are most important to them. The series of scenarios produced cast these values in terms of desired outcomes, and the process encourages all participants, including the decision maker, to understand the experiential quality of the individual point of view.

Illustrative Situation. The prison board meets to discuss the possibility of holding an art show outside the prison, allowing the inmates personally to manage the exhibition and sale of their work. The meeting includes individuals from the guard force, the prison industries staff, and the psychological staff. The warden, responsible for making a decision on the feasibility and character of the show, is concerned that this issue appears to continue well-entrenched differences between individuals.

Participants. Three individuals with strongly held and apparently incompatible views are asked to interact. All participants have agreed to consider the session more as an exploration of mutual ground for future policy than as an arena for negotiation of policy.

Setting.   The meeting place is provided with a blackboard, or large sheets of paper. Summary statements of all steps in the exercise are recorded so that they can be viewed by all at the meeting.

Procedure.
1. Each of the participants describes in turn, 1) the ideal outcome of policy from his perspective; 2) dysfunctional outcomes that give him greatest concern.
2. A possible course of action that best assures desired outcomes and guards against undesired outcomes is generated for each individal by one of the other two participants. Scenarios are generated by a "lagged" assignment so that no one describes a scenario for the person who has already developed one for him (*i.e.*, *A* describes a scenario of action that fits *B*'s initial description; *B* describes a scenario for *C*, and *C* describes one for *A*).
3. Each participant indicates what he likes best about the scenario designed to meet his interests and what aspects appeal to him least.
4. The individual who initially generated each scenario then alters it until the recipient agrees that the general perspective fits his interests.
5. In the last synthetic phase of the exercise, the group as a whole identifies common elements in the initial descriptions of interest and in the amended scenarios. This common ground may become a starting point for generating action alternatives in another session.

Rationale.   The exercise is designed to elicit detailed information about individual interests in an atmosphere free from threat, negotiation, or interaction among participants with potentially conflicting interests. The procedure outlined is also intended to give participants experience in generating and considering a range of alternatives before considering actual policy alternatives.

The exercise begins with positive possibilities for the individual in the situation being considered. This positive tone is characteristic of the exercise as a whole, which is designed to create information about desired action and change. The listing in step 1 is done quickly (participants are reminded that additional information can be added in step 4), and comments by other participants are discouraged. Clarification is expected as a result of subsequent steps in the interaction.

The round-robin format of the second step is designed to avoid negotiation or argument. This step is also carried out quickly. The intention is: 1) to make sure that each participant's interests are "heard," 2) to generate a broad range of action alternatives, and 3) to encourage all participants to identify with the process of designing policy.

Steps 3 and 4 allow interaction between the scenario designer and its "recipi-

ent." This process is likely to indicate new priorities or dimensions of importance to the recipient, and encourages the designer to be responsive to another's
desires, at least in design. Too much detail is not encouraged. The final scenario
should represent the essential aspects of a positive strategy rather than details
of implementation.

Interaction should not be undertaken until the policy-maker is committed to
considering some action. In addition, it should be undertaken only among
participants who are perceived by the policy-maker as having a "right" to understand the reasoning behind policy decisions. (Note that the situation used as
illustration does not necessarily involve inmates.)

Follow-up. If common elements can be discovered in the ideal scenarios generated, these become an obvious nucleus for generating policy. The interaction
is also likely to highlight areas of greatest disagreement, which can then become the subject of attention as well. It is critical that the policy-maker indicate beforehand the procedures that will be used (including the prerogatives of
the decision-maker) to act upon areas of agreement and disagreement revealed
through interaction.

Example 2: Sampling Constituents

Objective. The impetus for this course of action is the large number and disparity of participants in a policy situation. The analyst cannot share the perceptions of all those affected by policy, but believes it is important to understand
as diverse a set of perspectives as possible. In particular, the following procedure
is designed to elicit the insight of those who have *not* been chosen as representatives of larger constituencies. The information-seeking procedure described is
designed to seek the initial understanding of participants, and then "develop"
these views through interaction with others who have different experiences in
the situation.

Illustrative Situation. A very large industrial organization is considering a new
policy regarding unionization of middle management. It wishes to *consult* widely
with the staff, rather than deal in negotiation at early stages in the process.

Participants. Ten to 12 individuals can be accommodated in each iteration of
this "exercise," which follows the general logic of the nominal group process [4].
The choice of participants may vary. Groups might be deliberately composed
of "representatives" and members of unrepresented constituencies. They might
include individuals who will be affected only indirectly. "Extreme" positions
might be included [15].

Setting.   The meeting place is comfortable and, ideally, removed from the workplace. Large sheets of paper are available so that ideas recorded can be seen by all participants; they have sufficient room for the voting procedures to be described below.

Procedure.
   Part 1.

1. Participants are asked to list on a small piece of paper, individually and silently, elements that are important in the situation given.
2. These ideas are then collected in a round-robin format, one idea from each person at a time. The pace is meant to be rapid; questions can be asked only for clarification. Ideas are recorded in the words of the participant on the large sheets of paper at the front of the room.
3. After all ideas are collected, and no one has additional ideas suggested by the list, a structural discussion is held. Each individual is asked in turn to speak briefly "for" one description that he or she finds to be most descriptive of the situation, and to speak "against" one that is felt to be least descriptive.
4. After two or more rounds of discussion, participants are asked to "vote" for descriptors. Votes are recorded by colored stickers. Participants simultaneously file in front of the list at the front of the room placing stickers (approximately ten per individual) by the items that they feel best describe the nature of the policy situation.

   Part 2.

5. The analyst chooses one or two of the elements that many participants consider intrinsic to the situation. Participants are asked to consider silently possible actions to deal with these aspects of the situation.
6. Listing, discussion, and voting among ideas for action then proceed according to the procedure outlined above under steps 2, 3, and 4.

   Part 3.

7. Participants are asked to consider a series of possible policy decisions that have been identified before the exercise. Each person is asked to estimate likely outcomes for themselves and other selected actors in the situation. This information can be collected in a questionaire, or by following the normal group procedures discussed above for a third round.

Rationale.   The general rationale for this exercise is that those involved in the day-to-day aspects of an organization, or other interactive situation, have important information that is not readily accessible to policy makers (though the participants may not, in turn, have full information about constraints and options for action on a larger scale). This exercise uses a version of the nominal group technique to elicit that information. The group format encourages a wide consideration of options, with evaluation limited to sequential comments and democratic "voting."

The first part of the exercise asks for information about the nature of the situation itself. This provides a basis for the remainder of the exercise and may be analyzed separately from the results generated subsequently. The second part of the exercise focuses on participants' suggestions for possible courses of action. It is anticipated that a varied group of participants, with knowledge of the situation that the decision-maker does not hold first-hand, is likely to suggest new ways of thinking about action alternatives. The first part of the exercise, which reveals aspects of the situation that are most widely shared, as well as the diversity of understanding, is expected to provide a more realistic background for the generation of action alternatives that participants removed from policy-making may not have initially held.

The third part of the exercise elicits participants' knowledge about cause-and-effect relationships at their point of contact with the policy situation. This information may help the decision-maker anticipate real or imagined effects of policy decisions.

Follow-up. Courtesy would suggest that, at the least, participants in this exercise be informed of the course of policy decisions on the issues they have discussed. This exercise is also likely to reveal areas of concern, and individuals holding that concern may become "energized" by prospective policy decisions. These concerns may even be heightened by the interaction just described, and should be considered for follow-up action.

Example 3: Sequential Testing of Options [13]

Objective. The motivation for this procedure is the need to understand individual experience and values in terms of specific policy alternatives. The procedure described identifies action alternatives that are perceived by various interested parties to be advantageous, tolerable, or undesired.

Illustrative situation. An umbrella organization for 20 health-related private organizations is considering centralized fund raising and accounting procedures. Coordinated services appear likely to decrease costs to the individual organizations, but also run counter to many established traditions and procedures. A wide variety of possibilities exists for the nature and timing of coordination. Many of these have been discussed among the membership without any clear consensus emerging.

Participants. Primary decision-makers in each of the relevant units are involved in this information-seeking procedure.

Procedure.
1. The analyst subdivides the policy question into areas of potential action.

2. For each area an "exhaustive pool" of possible action alternatives is generated. These actions are described in terms of the implementation steps involved. The analyst may also decide to describe apparent effects, in both numerical and qualitative ways, or may choose to leave the diagnosis of impact up to each participant. A specific attempt is made to vary the time horizon of implementation efforts and the "scope" of effect.

3. Each item in the pool is then described to a participant (or group of participants representing the same "entity"). The participant considers each item singly and "votes" on the desirability of the option from his point of view. Votes can be either yes and no or scalar.

4. This procedure, repeated for each participant, generates a set of choices that can be anlayzed to yield a set of widely acceptable alternatives. If the set is small or unacceptable to decision-makers, further analysis may group relevant parties usefully on the basis of preferred types of alternatives, or group alternatives to indicate areas of agreement and disagreement among relevant parties.

Rationale. The key rationale for this approach is the idea that arguments among relevant parties in a decision situation proceed with respect to both philosophy and specific action alternatives. The exercise forces participants to express values in terms of action preferences rather than abstract argument. The second rationale is that responses to alternative policy may rest only on one part of a combination of actions. Areas of agreement and disagreement may be more closely specified by disaggregating policy alternatives into smaller parts. The approach described does not guarantee a viable policy as a direct result. It does provide a methodology for looking at the implications of nonaligned value systems.

Follow-up. It may be highly desirable to devise a means for participants to communicate with each other at some points in the process described. At any rate it will probably be desirable to agree that the indications of preference are not binding. Special interaction on options in disagreement may provide rationales for acceptance or rejection that other members find compelling. This interaction may also, by focusing on the implications of specific action alternatives, allow the emergence of a more widely shared sense of purpose and desired outcome.

Example 4: Reconstructive Planning

Objective.   The articulation of this planning perspective is motivated by the desire to respond appropriately to organizational structures and senses of purpose that appear to wax and wane over time.

Illustrative Situation.   A university department has tried a variety of mechanisms to support closer faculty-student interaction. Each idea appears to work for a time, but then fails to catch student or faculty interest and falls into disuse.

Participants.   The mode of planning to be described is particularly useful when the participants in a policy-making situation vary over time, and autonomy of action is characteristic of at least some of them.

Setting.   Similarly, this procedure is appropriate to settings that regularly provide for a variety of "connections" between participants.

Procedure.
1. No action is taken until participant interest is high enough to initiate action.
2. The decision-maker (facilitator) encourages participants to specify, as clearly as possible, specific goals and procedures for achieving those goals while energy and interest are high. It is desirable that interaction create a strong "vision" of shared purpose, and a shared vocabulary to use in implementing that vision.
3. The decision maker-facilitator encourages rapid implementation of procedures while participant interest is high.
4. If interest "cools," the facilitator tries evoking the "common vision" developed earlier. If this is not effective, active efforts to end the implementation are taken.
5. If and when the interest of system members again coalesces around similar issues, *new* goals and procedures are developed.

Rationale.   Underlying this way of acting is the notion that individuals vary in the commonality of their interests and the energy to develop them. Specific goals are seen as useful to define the commonality of interest and to motivate action. They are not seen as states that are very often achieved. Rather than cling to goals that no longer express the consensus of a group of interacting individuals, new goals are formulated. Interaction is conceptualized as a process of reconstructing and using a series of strong goal statements without the anticipation of their actual achievement. The role of the decision maker-facilitator is to respond to the situation at hand by encouraging, maintaining, and finally diffusing group activities.

DEVELOPING OTHER TECHNIQUES

These four activities are illustrative of approaches that may be helpful in an ambiguous world. Each focuses on a few of the guidelines to policy-making presented in the second section of the paper, as outlined in Table 2. The techniques are presented in the hope that they will suggest other ways of approaching situations that face the policy-maker. As an aid to the generation of other techniques, each of the six guidelines to action under conditions of ambiguity is presented again in somewhat greater detail, using the four techniques as a source of examples.

Seek individual perspectives

Although it is easy to agree with this guideline in principle, it is often difficult to carry out. Alternative perspectives can obscure an already complex situation. The solicitation of opinion may increase participants' stakes in the policy outcome. Interactive techniques may increase animosity among conflict interests.

The first three techniques offer some alternatives for seeking the unique insights of relevant parties, while controlling some of the risks inherent in this process. All three techniques are structured to give each participant "equal time" to state important aspects of a shared situation from his own perspective. The reciprocal scenario and sampling constituents techniques encourage other participants to "hear" this information, since it is used in later aspects of the

Table 2. Comparison of illustrative techniques.

GUIDELINE	TECHNIQUE RECIPROCAL SCENARIOS	SAMPLING CONSTITUENTS	SEQUENTIAL TESTING OF OPTIONS	RECONSTRUCTIVE PLANNING
1. Seek individual perspectives	X^1	X^1	X^1	
2. Encourage flexible attitudes	X	X		
3. Focus on alternative futures vs. specific goals			X	
4. Make planning processes adaptive	X			X^1
5. Pinpoint "energy"		X^1	X	X
6. Allow ambiguity in timing				X^1

X^1 = primary emphasis.

exercise.   Interaction is designed to encourage each participant to clarify and prioritize his interests, while minimizing what could heighten conflict.

In general, it might be suggested that policy-makers should take care not to promise specific response to the desires of participants revealed in information-gathering exercises such as the three just mentioned. The first two have the additional advantage of simultaneously collecting the (often incompatible) perspectives of other participants and underscoring for all those involved the diversity with which policy-makers must cope.

Finally, each of these techniques shares the desirable characteristic of minimizing the analysts' involvement in defining relevant avenues for data-gathering. The value of techniques that attempt to gain information about the unique perspective of others at this early stage of analysis will most often be proportional to the latitude built into the technique for the respondent to structure the *type* of information presented, as well as to provide the information itself.

Encourage flexible attitudes

The attempt to understand an ambiguous situation involves activities that may, of themselves, impact on the situation facing policy-makers. In an effort to encourage flexibility among participants who will almost inevitably have to accommodate themselves to nonoptimal outcomes, it is desirable that even the understanding stage of the process promote the ability to see situations from various perspectives. Two of the techniques developed stand out in this respect. The reciprocal scenarios exercise, although it encourages the generation of individual ideals, also provides for the reciprocal generation of those ideals. The request to think in terms of another's perspective can provide a powerful expansion of perspective. In addition, the recipient of an ideal scenario must, in turn, think of another's ideal.

Part of the logic of the sampling-constituents approach is also compatible with this guideline. The procedure disassociates individuals from their own ideas by discouraging discussion until a large pool of possible ideas is generated. The request that each individual speak for and against one of the descriptors in the "pool" tends to reassociate the individual with other ideas from the group as a whole. The visible voting procedures of this approach also clarify shared and unique aspects of experience.

Focus on Alternative Futures rather than Specific Goals

The thinking behind this guideline is that specific states are very hard to achieve purposefully under conditions of ambiguity. It makes sense, then, to begin at the outset with looser ideas about the desired goal of the policy process. Two of the techniques outlined focus on this guideline. The sequential testing of options is founded on the idea that many different actions are possible responses to a specific situation, and, moreover, these can be sequenced in many ways. The reconstructive planning notion may appear to violate these guidelines. Although specific goals are outlined in this technique, it is assumed that they will become "obsolete" before being realized, and that new targets will be developed.

Make Planning Processes Adaptive

This guideline, like the one on flexible perspectives, assumes that the methods of analysis themselves contribute to the nature of the policy situation. The reciprocal senarios technique responds to this guideline by developing possible alternatives that are almost certain to be incompatible, and thus not achievable as first stated. The technique promotes the notion that many different planning alternatives are possible, and likely to be considered before a more stable policy is formulated. The reconstructive planning notion pursues this idea in a more temporal form. This technique operates under the assumption that, through time, different planning perspectives will be developed and then deliberately abandoned.

Pinpoint "Energy"

In complex situations, actors with energy are often able to have some affect on the policy process because of the many possible avenues for action. In ambiguous situations, the sources of energy that may thus shape anticipated outcomes are often not apparent. The sampling-constituents technique offers one way of at least testing for "energy." The technique assumes that representative group arrangements are likely to reflect past issues and sentiments. New policy is likely to generate somewhat different opinions among the constituencies involved in the situation. The technique provides an opportunity for increasing information and early interaction on issues that are likely to be critical in the future. Similarly, the reconstructive planning idea is triggered and extinguished by energy among participants.

Allow Ambiguity in Timing

This guideline suggests that the response to ambiguous situations must itself contain some ambiguity to best match conditions in the environment. The reconstructive planning technique focuses specifically on this guideline with its emphasis on ending and beginning collaboration efforts at intervals specified only by the ongoing sense of the situation.

CONCLUSION: THE EXPANDED ROLE OF POLICY ANALYSTS AND POLICY-MAKERS

We have argued from an initial premise that the world is open to various and changing interpretation. Yet, policy analysts have been under the impression over the last several decades that they can fixedly describe the world, and their continued employment indicates they have some success in convincing others of their ability. For problems limited in time and scope, the stable and simplified world-view used by most policy analysts is a tolerable basis for policy-making and leads to useful outcomes. As the issues expand in importance, however, this world-view cannot accommodate the complexity and ambiguity of experience. Despite good will, policy and planning are too rarely implemented and even more rarely effective. Policy analysis has not faced this crisis in ability. Tools that have value in limited situations have been expanded beyond their limits. Lack of result is justified with the platitude that "there are no easy answers to difficult problems."

We believe it is necessary to go back to basic ideas of the nature of the world, and the possibility for analysis, to strike out in new directions. The enriched process we have outlined is undeniably difficult and time-consuming. It is in itself ambiguous in form. There will be fewer guidelines to the policy process even as experience with this perspective increases the methodologies available. We are not willing to argue that the process outlined will always be "worth it." We do feel that something similar in form to the above proposal is critical in those policy-making situations that are complex and difficult to structure. It will be useful, in short, for those situations in which policy-makers are genuinely perplexed and sufficiently concerned to spend resources for proper analysis.

It may seem that the process we have outlined blurs the line between the policy analyst and the policy-maker. The more traditional view of analysis focuses on defining the nature of problem situations and recommending policy alternatives. The introduction of diagnostic intervention may seem to step into the realm of the policy-maker. The difference between these two roles, in our view, remains distinct. The analyst is a short-term participant in any given policy situation, although it is important in the process outlined that the participation is real. The policy-maker is embedded in the situation with ongoing responsibilities for decision-making, including the decision to bring in the analyst. The value of the analyst lies in the ability to organize new perceptions of problems in a relatively short period of time.

It may also sound as if an ambiguous world-view requires the analyst, and even the policy-maker, to be merely a moderator of other people's perception and understandings. This is not the case. In our view, the analyst is still characterized by the skill of being able to recognize patterns and explanations that those closer to the situation have not been able to identify. The analyst must also balance the process of moving between expansive attempts to understand the nature of the world and focusing attempts to understand specific aspects of that world through action. The policy-maker, in turn, is still characterized by the responsibility (and, ideally, the power) to choose among options and move on toward implementation and evaluation, despite the knowledge that any "solution" will itself be temporary and eventually resubmitted to the process of analysis.

NOTES AND REFERENCES

1. Archibald, K. A. "Three Views of the Expert's Role in Policy-Making: Systems Analysis, Incrementalism and the Clinical Approach." Santa Monica, Calif.: Rand, 1970.
2. Cohen, M. D., and J. G. March. *Leadership and Ambiguity*. New York: McGraw-Hill, 1974.
3. Cyert, R. M., and J. G. March. *A Behavioral Theory of the Firm*. Englewood Cliffs, N.J.: Prentice-Hall, 1963.
4. Delbecq, A. L., A. H. Van de Ven, and D. Gustafson. *Group Techniques for Program Planning*. Glenview, Ill.: Scott, Foresman, 1975.
5. Dobrov, G. M. "The Dynamics and Management of Technological Development as an Object for Applied Analysis." Laxenburg, Autria: International Institute for Applied Systems Analysis, 1977.
6. Foster, M. "Evaluation Without Objectives." *Educational Technology* 1973.
7. Leavitt, H. J. "Beyond the Analytic Manager." *California Management Review* 17(1975).
8. Maruyama, M. "Paradigms and Communication." *Technological Forecasting and Social Change* 6(1974): 3–32.
9. Mason, R. O. "A Dialectical Approach to Strategic Planning." *Management Science* 16(April 1969).
10. McWhinney, W. "Paedogenic Designing: A Chapter in a Theory of Change." Human Systems Development Study Center Working Paper #74-9. Graduate School of Management, UCLA, November 1974.
11. Mitroff, Ian I., and L. V. Blankenship. "On the Methodology of the Holistic Experiment: An Approach to the Conceptualization of Large-Scale Social Experiments." *Technological Forecasting and Social Change* 4(1973): 339–353.
12. Moch, M. K., and L. R. Pondy. "The Structure of Chaos: Organized Anarchy as a Response to Ambiguity." Review of James G. March and John P. Olsen, *Ambiguity and Choice in Organizations. Administration Science Quarterly* 351–362.
13. Obonyi, G. Untitled dissertation. Graduate School of Management, UCLA, 1977.
14. Polanyi, M. *The Tacit Dimension*. Garden City, N.Y.: Doubleday, 1966.
15. Pondy, L., and M. L. Olson. "Theories of Extreme Cases." Unpublished paper presented at the American Psychological Association Symposium, Toward a Reconceptualization of Research and Method, San Francisco, August 1977.
16. Vickers, G. *The Art of Judgment*. New York: Basic Books, 1965.
17. Weick, K. E. "Educational Organizations as Loosely Coupled Systems." *Administrative Science Quarterly* 21(1976): 1–19.

4

Monopolization and Exclusion in the Scientific Community: An Alert for Public Executives

Maria Nowakowska
Institute of Philosophy and Sociology,
Polish Academy of Sciences

INTRODUCTION

The complex issues dealt with by public policy-makers demand that they make constant and aggressive use of information developed by—or contracted from— the scientific community. Unfortunately, certain behavioral dynamics operating within the scientific community itself require public policy-makers to be both cautious and discriminating, as well as aggressive, for instances of monopolistic behavior operate in the domain of academic and professional science, suggesting that, on occasion, scientific inputs may be biased or otherwise less than objective. The purpose of this essay is a formal analysis of the mechanisms governing the evolution of a group of persons involved in a power struggle, all seeking control over some scarce commodity. Given the orientation of this handbook, the "group" on which we shall concentrate and around which we shall generate our theoretical inquiries will be the scientific community. As we shall see, certain intragroup dynamics of a competitive order may operate to dilute the relevance of the opinions and data that the scientific community offers to executives of the public interest.

For simplicity of presentation, the considerations will be given for the special case of a scientific community; it will be clear, however, that the formal model is of a general character, and may describe the evolution of any group of persons fighting for power.

This essay is an extension and refinement of an earlier paper [2]. The basic intuitive notions underlying the system—in the case of a scientific community—

may be summarized as follows: the scientific community is inherently unstable because the growth of the individual scientific authority of its members will eventually make any fixed assignment of scientists to positions unacceptable. This causes an increasing tendency toward change; the forces opposing it tend to create monopolies, trying to get control over the distribution of some scientific goods. This inevitably leads to alienation of some group of scientists and results in a tendency to form countermonopolies.

The above mechanism may be formalized in a relatively simple way, and the formalism allows us to put forward several hypotheses about some of the finer details of the development process of the community. The formalism will be developed gradually, beginning with the simplest concepts, which will later be refined.

BASIC STRUCTURE

Let us first restrict the considerations to a fixed moment t. One of the principal elements of the description of the state of a scientific community is specifying who occupies which position.

To put it formally, let S denote the set of all scientists under consideration, and let P denote the set of all positions.

The concept of "position," being, in some sense, a primitive notion of the system, should be interpreted in such a way that one position can be occupied by only one scientist. Thus, for example, if there are n scientific institutes under consideration, then there are also n positions of directors, a certain number of positions of deputy-directors, so and so many positions of heads of departments, assistants, *etc.* Next, each scientific journal gives one position to the editor-in-chief and several positions to members of editorial boards; the same applies to scientific committees, scientific councils, university chairs, elected bodies in scientific societies, *etc.*

Formally, the distribution (or assignment of occupancy function) of positions among scientists can be described by a function

$$\varphi : P \longrightarrow S$$

which assigns to each position the scientist who occupies it. The symbol

$$\varphi(p) = s$$

means that scientist s occupies position p (function φ is well defined because of the assumption that one position can be occupied by one scientist only).

It is important to note that φ means any occupation function, not necessarily the one that actually takes place at time t. In other words, if Φ denotes the class of all functions φ that map P into S, then at any moment t the actually existing assignment is one particular function, say φ_t, from Φ.

Here the elements φ of Φ may be partial functions, *i.e.*, some positions in P may be left vacant (no element of S is assigned to them). Also, the function φ need not exhaust the whole set S: there may be some elements in S that are not in the range of φ (*i.e.*, there may be some scientists without positions).

It is important to mention that φ need not be one-to-one, that is, the same scientist may occupy two or more different positions.

The sets

$$P_\varphi = \{p \in P : \varphi(p) = s \text{ for some } s \in S\}$$

$$S_\varphi = \{s \in S : \varphi(p) = s \text{ for some } p \in P\}$$

represent respectively the class of all occupied positions, and the class of all scientists who hold at least one position (under the occupancy function φ).

The basic type of set considered in the sequel will be

$$\varphi^{-1}(s) = \{p \in P : \varphi(p) = s\}$$

that is, the set of all positions occupied by the scientist s under the hypothetical assignment φ. In this notation, $\varphi_t^{-1}(s)$ is the set of all positions held by s under the assignment that actually takes place at t.

ADMISSIBILITY

The next aspect to be taken into account is that not every occupancy function is admissible. The admissibility or inadmissibility of occupancy function is related to various requirements, either specified by laws, statuses of scientific organizations, *etc.*, by some unwritten traditions, or simply by common sense or common consent. To explain the nature of these requirements, it is best to give some examples of admissible or inadmissible occupancy functions.

Thus, a function that assigns the position of a director of an institute to a graduate student may well be formally inadmissible (regardless of how the remaining positions are distributed among scientists), if a law specifies that the direction must have a Ph.D. Another regulation might, for instance, require that the director of an institute must also preside over its scientific council; hence any occupancy function that assigns different persons to these two positions is inadmissible. Such a function would also be inadmissible, if no such formal regulation exists, but there is a long-established tradition in some institution that the director presides over its scientific council. Finally, though it may not be written specifically, an assignment that gives the position of editor-in-chief of a journal in, say, nuclear physics to a linguist might not be admissible, *etc.*

As may be seen from these examples, the admissibility of the total assignment of scientists to all positions is related to admissibilities of "elementary" assignments of one position to one scientist. Moreover, it ought to be clear that admissibility is not a binary concept, but rather a fuzzy one; hence to every occupancy function there should correspond a number between 0 and 1, representing the degree to which this function is admissible.

The "elementary admissibility, of a scientist s to the position p, is also a fuzzy concept; moreover, this admissibility changes in time. Consequently, with every scientist s and every position p, we may associate a function

$$g_{s,p}(t)$$

with values between 0 and 1, representing the degree of admissibility of s for p at time t. The condition $g_{s,p}(t) = 1$ means that at time t, the scientist s is a completely admissible candidate for p; if $g_{s,p}(t) = 0$, he is totally unacceptable, while the intermediate values represent the partial degrees of admissibility.

Treated as a function of p, $g_{s,p}(t)$ is the membership function in the fuzzy set of positions admissible for s at time t; treated as a function of s, it is the membership function in the fuzzy set of candidates admissible for the position p.

The function $g_{s,p}(t)$ is, as usual in the theory of fuzzy sets, evaluated subjectively. This does not constitute any serious obstacle because we will subsequently use only the following qualitative postulate.

Postulate 1. For any $p \in P$ and $s \in S$, the function $g_{s,p}(t)$ satisfies the relation: for $t_1 < t_2 < t_3$

$$g_{s,p}(t_1) > g_{s,p}(t_2) \Rightarrow g_{s,p}(t_2) \geqslant g_{s,p}(t_3). \tag{1}$$

This postulate asserts that $g_{s,p}(t)$ has, in a sense, a single peak: if it ever begins to decrease, it cannot increase again. Thus, the three main types of behavior of this function within an interval may be represented schematically in Figure 1 as "Increase," "Hump," and "Decrease." Naturally, the function $g_{s,p}(t)$ may have jumps, and also periods of constancy, so that in particular cases, the pictures may look as in Figure 2.

The justification of Postulate 1 is as follows: imagine that at time t the scientist s is not qualified for the position p; then the value of admissibility function is

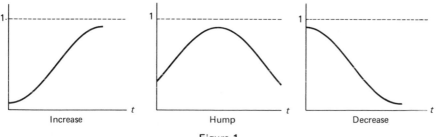

| Increase | Hump | Decrease |

Figure 1.

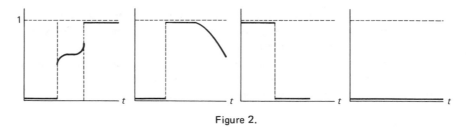

Figure 2.

0. As his scientific authority increases, he may become more eligible for the position p, and $g_{s,p}(t)$ increases; in particular, the jumps may occur at such moments as his Ph.D., *etc.* As the time goes on, however, he may start being less and less acceptable for the position p, simply because he may be overqualified for it. The jumps downwards may occur at times such as his retirement, *etc.*, where he may become totally unacceptable for a given position. Figure 3 shows a hypothetical change of head of a laboratory and director.

Naturally, in some cases, the admissibility decreases all the time (*e.g.*, for the position of junior assistant, beginning from the time of graduation from the university); it may also continuously increase (*e.g.*, for the position of honorary president of a scientific society, where for a long time the admissibility stays at 0, and then may move upward). Finally, for some cases, the admissibility may be constant throughout, for instance, identically equal to 0 (*e.g.*, if the scientist s is a linguist, and p denotes the position of, say, director of a nuclear research institute).

Now, the admissibility of an occupancy function φ, at time t, will be determined by the "weakest link" principle, specified by the following postulate.

Postulate 2. The admissibility $a_\varphi(t)$ of an occupancy function φ at time t equals

$$a_\varphi(t) = \min \{g_{s,p}(t) : \varphi(p) = s\}. \tag{2}$$

Thus, to determine $a_\varphi(t)$, one considers all positions p, and admissibilities

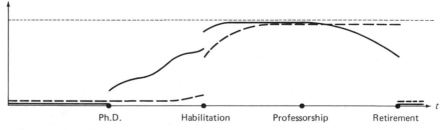

Figure 3. Admissibility for the position of head of laboratory (solid line), and for the position of director (broken line).

$g_{s,p}(t)$ of persons assigned to these positions under φ; the minimal of these admissibilities is, by definition, the admissibility of the whole occupancy function.

From Postulates 1 and 2 follows:

Theorem 1. The function $a_\varphi(t)$ satisfies the same relation as each $g_{s,p}(t)$, that is, for all $t_1 < t_2 < t_3$,

$$a_\varphi(t_1) > a_\varphi(t_2) \Rightarrow a_\varphi(t_2) \geqslant a_\varphi(t_3). \tag{3}$$

For the proof, assume that the premise in Eq. (3) holds for some $t_1 < t_2$, and let s_0, p_0 be the pair with $\varphi(p_0) = s_0$ for which the minimum is attained at t_2. We then have

$$g_{s_0,p_0}(t_2) = a_\varphi(t_2) < a_\varphi(t_1) \leqslant g_{s_0,p_0}(t_1).$$

Thus, $g_{s_0,p_0}(t)$ decreases between t_1 and t_2, and by Postulate 1, we must have

$$g_{s_0,p_0}(t_2) \geqslant g_{s_0,p_0}(t_3) \geqslant a_\varphi(t_3)$$

which completes the proof.

The situation is perhaps best illustrated with the following greatly oversimplified example. Imaging that $S = \{s_1, s_2, s_3\}$ and $P = \{p_1, p_2, p_3, p_4\}$; let φ be the assignment

$$p_1 \longrightarrow s_1$$
$$p_2 \longrightarrow s_2$$
$$p_3 \longrightarrow s_3$$
$$p_4 \nearrow$$

so that scientists s_1 and s_2 hold positions p_1 and p_2, respectively, while s_3 holds the remaining positions p_3 and p_4.

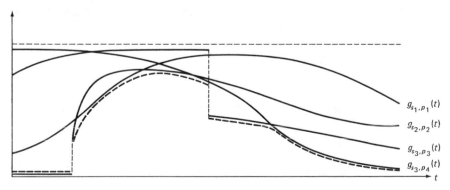

$$g_{s_1,p_1}(t)$$
$$g_{s_2,p_2}(t)$$
$$g_{s_3,p_3}(t)$$
$$g_{s_3,p_4}(t)$$

Figure 4. Dotted line is admissibility $a_\varphi(t)$.

Figure 4 shows the functions $g_{s_1,p_1}(t)$, $g_{s_2,p_2}(t)$, $g_{s_3,p_3}(t)$, $g_{s_3,p_4}(t)$, and their minimum $a_\varphi(t)$.

Theorem 1 asserts, therefore, that admissibility of any occupancy function has the same "single-peakedness" property as the admissibility functions $g_{s,p}(t)$ for individual scientists and positions: in any given time interval $a_\varphi t$ can be only one of the three, as depicted in Figure 1.

PREFERENCES

We shall now consider another important feature of the system, so far unexplored; namely, the fact that various positions in P have different "values."

The discussion of the nature of these values will be postponed till the following sections. At this moment, it is sufficient to rely only on the intuition according to which the differences in values of various positions p are related to the fact that each of them gives at least partial access to some scientific goods, either directly, or by providing control over some other goods (such as distribution of research finances, fellowships, rights of publications, refereeing, *etc.*).

The overall effect of differences in values of positions of P is that the scientists are not indifferent with respect to various occupancy functions. Firstly, the basis for judgment (of a given occupancy function φ) for the scientist s is the set $\varphi^{-1}(s)$ of positions to which he would be assigned under φ. Secondly, given two occupancy functions φ_1 and φ_2 with $\varphi_1^{-1}(s) = \varphi_2^{-1}(s)$, that is, occupancy functions under which he would have the same positions, the scientist s need not be indifferent about them: he may judge them according to the positions occupied in φ_1 and φ_2 by his friends, enemies, superiors, subordinates, *etc.*

Admittedly, when a possible change of occupancy function is discussed (say, in a nominating committee), the discussion usually concerns some alternative functions φ_1, φ_2, $\cdots$, which differ very little from one another: the differences are only in the positions under discussion, the remaining positions are not taken into consideration (they are assumed to be equal to those under the "present" function φ_t). Nevertheless, it will be convenient to postulate formally that to each scientist s there corresponds a preference relation $\geqslant_s$ over the class of all functions φ. The symbol

$$\varphi_1 \geqslant_s \varphi_2$$

will mean that scientist s prefers weakly (*i.e.*, he prefers or is indifferent) φ_1 to φ_2. The relation $\geqslant_s$ will be assumed connected and transitive for every s, *i.e.*, we have the following postulate.

Postulate 3. For every $s \in S$ and all occupancy functions $\varphi_1, \varphi_2, \varphi_3$,

$$either \quad \varphi_1 \geqslant_s \varphi_2 \quad or \quad \varphi_2 \geqslant_s \varphi_1 \quad (or\ both); \qquad (4)$$

$$if \ \varphi_1 \geqslant_s \varphi_2 \ and \ \varphi_2 \geqslant_s \varphi_3, \ then \ \varphi_1 \geqslant_s \varphi_3. \tag{5}$$

In the usual way, the strict preference $>_s$ and indifference $\sim_s$ are defined as:

$$\varphi_1 >_s \varphi_2 \ if \ \varphi_1 \geqslant_s \varphi_2 \ and \ not \ \varphi_2 \geqslant_s \varphi_1; \tag{6}$$

$$\varphi_1 \sim_s \varphi_2 \ if \ \varphi_1 \geqslant_s \varphi_2 \ and \ \varphi_2 \geqslant_s \varphi_1. \tag{7}$$

From Definitions (4) and (5) it follows that $\sim_s$ is an equivalence, and that $>_s$ is a strict order in the class of equivalence classes of $\sim_s$.

The system of relations $\{\geqslant_s, s \in S\}$ now allows introducing some concepts to the group structure of the set S of scientists. At the beginning, let us introduce the following two definitions, which will be basic in the considerations below.

Definition 1. The scientist s_1 will be called in *preferential concorde* with s_2, to be denoted by $s_1 -\text{::} s_2$, if

$$\varphi >_{s_1} \varphi' \Rightarrow \varphi >_{s_2} \varphi'. \tag{8}$$

Definition 2. The preferences of s_1 and s_2 will be called *orthogonal*, to be denoted by $s_1 \perp s_2$, if

$$\varphi \not\sim_{s_1} \varphi' \Rightarrow \varphi \sim_{s_2} \varphi'. \tag{9}$$

Intuitively, preferential concorde of s_1 with respect to s_2 means that the preferences of s_2 are the same as those of s_1, except that in a case when s_1 is indifferent toward some occupancy funtions, s_2 may have strict preferences between them.

In terms of motives of supporting, one can say that in this case s_2 will be inclined to support the tendencies of s_1 to change the existing occupancy toward a new, preferred occupancy function, since these changes are also preferred by him. On the other hand, s_1 will not be inclined to block the tendencies of s_2; he will either support them, or be indifferent to them (observe that the relation of preferential concordance $-\text{::}$ is not symmetric with respect to s_1 and s_2). The relation $\perp$ of orthogonality (obviously symmetric with respect to s_1 and s_2) means that s_1 and s_2 have no motive either to support or to block one another: both are indifferent to any changes toward occupancy functions preferred by the other.

With the provisions discussed below, one can hypothesize that any group of scientists supporting one another will consist of individuals who are either in the relation of preferential concordance, or will have orthogonal preferences. Thus, the relation structure

$$S, -\text{::}, \perp$$

could be called a *prestructure of coalitions* in S: any coalition system that violates the relations $-\text{::}$ and $\perp$ *i.e.*, that contains a coalition with two or more individuals connected neither by $-::$ nor by $\perp$ is likely to be unstable. Indeed, if s_1 and s_2 are neither in relation $-::$ nor in relation $\perp$, then there exist two occupancy functions such that their preferences toward these two functions are both strict and opposed. In such cases, the interests of s_1 and s_2 do not agree, and they would tend to break away from any coalition that contains both of them.

The provision mentioned above concerns the validity of this hypothesis: for the tendency to break away from a coalition containing both s_1 and s_2, it is necessary that the occupancy functions on which their preferences strictly differ are sufficiently highly admissible, so that they constitute a real possibility.

This necessitates some weakening of the definitions of relations $-::$ and $\perp$, by restricting the implications (8) and (9) to subsets of Φ, which consist of occupancy functions with sufficiently high admissibility. Formally, one can define the relations $-::_r$ and $\perp_r$ by requirements:

$$s_1 -::_r s_2 \quad \text{if for all} \quad \varphi, \varphi' \quad \text{such that} \; a_\varphi(t) \geqslant r,$$

$$a_{\varphi'}(t) \geqslant r_\varphi >_{s_1 \varphi'} \Rightarrow \varphi >_{s_2} \varphi' \tag{10}$$

and similarly,

$$s_1 \perp_r s_2 \quad \text{if for all} \quad \varphi, \varphi' \quad \text{such that} \; a_\varphi(t) \geqslant r,$$

$$a_{\varphi'}(t) \geqslant r_\varphi \sim_{s_1 \varphi'} \Rightarrow \varphi \sim_{s_2} \varphi'. \tag{11}$$

It follows at once that as r increases, the relations $-::_r$ and $\perp_r$ become weaker (more pairs become related); that is, if $r < r'$, then

$$s_1 -::_r s_2 \Rightarrow s_1 -::_{r'} s_2,$$

$$s_1 \perp_r s_2 \Rightarrow s_1 \perp_{r'} s_2.$$

Since the values of admissibility $a_\varphi(t)$ and $a_{\varphi'}(t)$ change in time, both relations $-::_r$ and $\perp_r$ are time-dependent. This may account for the fact that a coalition structure satisfying the stability condition at time t need not satisfy it at a later time t'.

POWER

In order to be able to express the hypotheses concerning the mechanisms underlying the evolution of a scientific community, one more concept is needed, namely that of power. Power will be connected with a set of positions occupied by one scientist, and will be expressed as the force this scientist can exert toward the change from the existing function φ_t to a new function φ, or against such a change.

If at some moment t the existing occupancy function is φ_t, then the set of positions occupied by s is $\varphi_t^{-1}(s)$. Suppose now that a change is contemplated, which will replace φ_t by some other function φ. Obviously, s will support this change if $\varphi_t <_s \varphi$ and will oppose it, if $\varphi <_s \varphi_t$. If $\varphi_t \sim_s \varphi$, he may support it, oppose it, or remain neutral in any efforts to replace φ_t by φ.

If the scientist occupies the positions $\varphi_t^{-1}(s)$ under φ_t, his power (speaking qualitatively) is derived from various sources: first, he may occupy positions that give him the right of making certain types of decisions that influence the fate of others in some specific way. Being head of a department, a director, a member of an editorial committee, a committee that distributes funds or fellowships, *etc.*, can serve as an example. The power may also lie in the ability to exert tacit or direct pressure on others by being in position of "transaction" (called "co-positions" in [2]) of some kind. As an example, one can take the process of refereeing someone's Ph.D. dissertation. Barring the extreme cases of very good and very bad dissertations, the middle cases might sometimes offer the possibility of pressure on the supervisor of the given Ph.D. One could argue that the set of such informal or semiformal ties in a scientific community is extremely important for the prediction of the actual development in a given concrete situation. For the description in terms of the general laws, one can only rely on the fact that certain positions in P offer more chance of entering into such bargaining positions, and hence, should be assigned higher power.

For the considerations below, it will be sufficient to present the situation in terms of two summary indices, denoted by

$$f_s(\varphi_t \longrightarrow \varphi)$$

and

$$f_s(\varphi_t \parallel \varphi)$$

to be interpreted as follows. The value $f_s(\varphi_t \longrightarrow \varphi)$ is the total pressure that s can exert *toward* the change from φ_t to φ. The second value, $f_s(\varphi_t \parallel \varphi)$, is the *resistance* s can offer against the change from φ_t to a new occupancy function φ.

The following two postulates about the forces $f_s(\varphi_t \longrightarrow \varphi)$ and $f_s(\varphi_t \parallel \varphi)$ will be utilized in the subsequent considerations.

Postulate 4. The forces $f_s(\varphi_t \longrightarrow \varphi)$ and $f_s(\varphi_t \parallel \varphi)$ are additive, that is, the total force of a group of scientists for or against a given change equals the sum of their individual forces.

Postulate 5. The forces $f_s(\varphi_t \longrightarrow \varphi)$ and $f_s(\varphi_t \parallel \varphi)$ depend on the positions occupied by s under φ_t and tend to decrease or increase in time together with the admissibility of s for the positions he occupies under φ_t.

This postulate means that when s is occupying some positions such that he is becoming more and more admissible for them, his force will tend to increase, but when he is becoming less admissible for these positions, his force will tend to decrease.

STABILITY AND MONOPOLIZATION

We are now in a position to begin formulating the hypotheses that describe the mechanisms underlying the evolution of the scientific community. It is, perhaps, worthwhile to recapitulate the concepts introduced so far, which will serve as ingredients of further definitions and hypotheses.

The logically independent concepts, which may, therefore, serve in some sense as "primitives" of the system, are:

the class Φ of all occupancy functions $\varphi : P \longrightarrow S$;
the functions $g_{s,p}(t)$, which describe the changes of admissibility of scientist s for the position p;
the preferences $\geqslant_s$ of scientists in the class Φ,
the forces $f_s(\varphi_t \longrightarrow \varphi)$ and $f_s(\varphi_t \parallel \varphi)$ that a scientist s, under assignment φ_t, can exert toward and against the change from φ_t to φ.

The most essential among the concepts defined in terms of the above are:

the set $\varphi^{-1}(s)$ of all positions occupied by s under the function φ;
the function $a_\varphi(t)$, describing the dynamic changes of admissibility of the occupancy function φ;
the relations $-\mathbin{:}\mathbin{:}$ and $\perp$, or preferential concordance and othogonality between the scientists.

Assume now that at the time t, when the occupancy function is φ_t, a change of φt into a new function φ is being contemplated. The function φ may represent some radical changes in the whole community, or may mean a "local" change, say a nomination of a scientist to a certain position (so that, in the latter case, $\varphi_t(p) = \varphi(p)$ for all positions except a limited number of positons p). With respect to the change from φ_t to φ, all scientists will divide into three categories:

1. the set $A^+(\varphi_t, \varphi)$ of those s for whom $\varphi >_s \varphi_t$ (favoring the change);
2. the set $A^-(\varphi_t, \varphi)$ of those s for whom $\varphi_t >_s \varphi$ (opposing the change); and
3. the set $A^0(\varphi_t, \varphi)$ of those s for whom $\varphi_t \sim_s \varphi$ (indifferent with respect to change).

We can now formulate the following postulate.

Postulate 6. The change from φ_t to φ does not occur if

$$\sum_{s \in A^-} f_s(\varphi_t \parallel \varphi) > \sum_{s \in A^+ \cup A^0} f_s(\varphi_t \longrightarrow \varphi) \tag{12}$$

where for simplicity $A^+ = A^+(\varphi_t, \varphi)$, $A^0 = A^0(\varphi_t, \varphi)$, etc.

In other words, the change to φ will not occur if the total force against it is greater than the total force that could possibly be gathered for it (*i.e.*, the force of those who are for the change, plus the supporting force of those who are indifferent to it).

This allows us to characterize the conditions for stability of the function φ_t: it is stable if there are not enough forces to replace it by any other function φ. Formally, we phrase it as follows.

Definition 3. The occupancy function φ_t is *stable*, if the condition (12) holds for any φ.

It is important to observe that the lack of stability of the existing occupancy function φ_t does not imply that it will be changed. Indeed, Postulate 5 specifies only when an occupancy function will not be replaced by another one. If φ_t is not stable, then there is one or more alternatives such that the total forces that *could* support the change exceed the resistance. It does not imply, however, that there actually are forces strong enough to support one alternative over φ_t, since the forces for a change may split among several alternatives, and moreover, the persons indifferent to the change may not join the persons supporting the change.

The definition of stability above did not utilize the concept of admissibility of φ_t and φ. Generally, one could expect that under "normal" circumstances, if there exists φ such that $a_\varphi(t) > a_{\varphi_t}(t)$, then φ_t cannot be stable at the moment t: if there exists at least one assignment that is more admissible than φ_t, then the forces that block φ ought to be smaller than the forces favoring the change.

The above is a condition of "fairness" or "social justice," and its violation may in some cases signify the existence of a "blocking monopoly." In terms of formal definitions, it may be summarized as follows.

Definition 4. The structure of a scientific community is *fair*, if whenever φ_t is stable then $a_{\varphi_t}(t) \geqslant a_\varphi(t)$ for every φ.

A partial converse to the above definition is the following. Equivalently, S is fair if a socially unfair φ cannot be stable, or if there exists a φ that is socially better than φ_t, then φ_t is not stable.

Since by the theorem on "single-peakedness" of a_φ, the admissibility of the "present" arrangement φ_t will begin to decrease after some time, the scientific community faces the following dilemma:

to ensure fairness, one must make frequent changes;
to ensure stability, one must sacrifice fairness.

A partial converse to Definition 4 follows.

Definition 5. The set

$$U \subset A^-(\varphi_t, \varphi)$$

is a φ-blocking monopoly, if the following conditions are satisfied:

1. $a_\varphi(t) > a_{\varphi_t}(t)$;

2. $\displaystyle\sum_{s \in U} f_s(\varphi_t \parallel \varphi) > \sum_{s \in A^+ \cup A^0} f_s(\varphi_t \longrightarrow \varphi)$ where, as before, $A^+ = A^+(\varphi_t, \varphi)$,

$A^0 = A^0(\varphi_t, \varphi)$.

Thus, a φ-blocking monopoly is a set of scientists who can successfully block the change from φ_t to a more admissible occupancy function φ.

The definition of a blocking monopoly is relative to the new occupancy φ. Generalizing the above definition leads to the following.

Definition 6. A set U is a Q-*blocking* monopoly, if $U \subset A^-(\varphi_t, \varphi)$ for all $\varphi \in Q$, and for any $\varphi \in Q$ such that $a_\varphi(t) > a_{\varphi_t}(t)$ we have

$$\sum_{s \in U} f_s(\varphi_t \parallel \varphi) > \sum_{s \in A^+(\varphi_t, \varphi) \cup A^0(\varphi_t, \varphi)} f_s(\varphi_t \longrightarrow \varphi).$$

Thus, a Q-blocking monopoly is such that it may successfully block any occupancy function from Q that is more admissible than φ_t.

In a similar way, one can now define the concept of an enforcing monopoly: it is a group of scientists who are jointly strong enough to enforce an arrangement φ, which is less admissible than φ_t. Formally, we have the following.

Definition 7. The set $U \subset A^+(\varphi_t, \varphi)$ is a φ-*enforcing* monopoly, if

1. $a_\varphi(t) < a_{\varphi_t}(t)$

2. $\displaystyle\sum_{s \in U} f_s(\varphi_t \longrightarrow \varphi) > \sum_{s \in A^- \cup A^0} f_s(\varphi_t \parallel \varphi)$

and U is a Q-enforcing monopoly, if $U \subset A^+(\varphi_t, \varphi)$ for all $\varphi \in Q$, and whenever $\varphi \in Q$ is such that $a_\varphi(t) < a_{\varphi_t}(t)$, then the condition (2) above holds.

Needless to say, a group U may be a blocking monopoly with respect to some set Q, and an enforcing monopoly with respect to some other set Q'.

HYPOTHESES ABOUT MONOPOLIES

From the definitions above one can obtain some consequences about the strategies of monopolies. The considerations will concern both types of monopolies, *i.e.*, both blocking and enforcing.

It is perhaps valuable to observe that the concept of a monopoly need not necessarily carry negative connotations. Indeed, though a monopoly is, by definition, blocking some arrangements that are more admissible than the existing one, or enforcing some that are less admissible, such an event need not be bad. The crucial point is whether the blocked or enforced arrangement will be increasing or decreasing in admissibility.

As an example, imagine that the present arrangement φ_t is declining, or about to begin declining in admissibility, and a new arrangement φ is enforced by some group. Suppose that *at time t*, the new arrangement is less admissible than φ_t. By definition, such a group forms a monopoly—at first an enforcing one, and then perhaps a blocking one, in order to defend a new arrangement φ against further changes.

It may well happen that the admissibility of the new arrangement φ will increase in time (such as in the case of nomination to a high position someone young and without adequate scientific authority, but whose authority is rapidly growing).

In such cases the monopoly cannot be assessed negatively. The negative assessment is justified only if the enforced or defended arrangement is not only worse than the replaced or alternative one, but is also becoming less and less admissible —so to speak, a monopoly can be judged negatively it it creates a social injustice, or scientific unfairness, which is getting worse.

Suppose now that Q is the class of arrangements in which the monopoly U is interested (say, to block). If one looks at the conditions for U to be a Q-blocking monopoly, one can see that there are several ways that will enhance the preservation of the conditions under which elements of Q are blocked.

One way is by allowing φ_t with possibly high admissibility, so that there may be fewer φ in Q that are more admissible than φ_t. This leads to the following.

Hypothesis 1. A monopoly interested in avoiding an arrangement from Q will attempt to support the "fair" changes, that is, changes toward more admissible arrangements, as long as the new arrangements are not in Q.

In other words, members of the monopoly will try to appear fair in matters that do not concern the interests of the monopoly.

Another way of preserving the monopoly condition is to preserve the defining inequality for the forces. This, in turn can be achieved in the following ways:

1. increasing the number of summands on the left-hand side (coopting new members to the monopoly);
2. decreasing the number of summands on the right-hand side (winning the neutrals to the monopoly's side);
3. increasing the individual terms on the left-hand side (increasing the individual powers of monopoly members); and
4. decreasing the individual terms on the right-hand side (decreasing the individual powers of the opponents).

Next, the character of the set Q and the stability of the monopoly may be combined as follows.

Hypothesis 2. A monopoly will be more stable, if the set Q it is blocking is small and of minor importance for a large number of scientists.

As an example, one can use here a monopoly formed from the editorial committee of some narrowly specialized scientific journal.

When one also considers the internal structure of the monopoly, induced by the relation of preferential concordance $-::$, and the individual powers of the members of the monopoly, one can distinguish two extreme types:

1. a monopoly U that has one member s_0 with high powers $f_{s_0}(\varphi_t \longrightarrow \varphi)$ or $f_{s_0}(\varphi_t \parallel \varphi)$, and such that $s-::s_0$ for $s \in U$, but not necessarily $s-::s'$ for other members of U.
2. a monopoly U with $s-::s'$ for all $s, s' \in U$, and such that $f_s(\varphi_t \longrightarrow \varphi)$ and $f_s(\varphi_t \parallel \varphi)$ are small for all $s \in U$.

The first type is exemplified by a "school," consisting of a powerful professor and those he favors. Here the relational structure with respect to preferential concordance $-::$ is "starlike," with s_0 (professor) occupying the center.

The second case is exemplified by, say, a group of members of a professional society, large enough to block some decisions in voting in general assembly, yet where each member has little power of his own.

In both cases one can expect some kind of stability of blocking, despite the fact that the group as such may not be too stable. In each case, the monopolizing group may fluctuate, some members of the monopoly leaving it, and some others joining. How long the assignments from Q will remain blocked depends here on the power of the central figure in case (1), and on the size of fluctuations of the joint power in case (2).

Next, one could try to formulate some other conjectures about the monopolies, not derived directly from the formal definitions.

Given a present arrangement φ_t, the scientist s has positions $\varphi_t^{-1}(s)$, and he would or would not join the monopoly depending on the rewards he expects from joining it.

One obvious reward may lie in the possibility of blocking those assignments φ that offer him positions worse than those he has at present, or in enforcing such arrangements that offer him better positions. The rewards, however, need not involve positions, but also other types of "goods," such as invitations for lectures, research funds, publication rights, or simply recognition of one's work.

Generally, when a person considers the possibility of entering a monopoly, he takes into account such factors as his position and expected duration of this position, expected duration of the monopoly, and the costs and profits from membership.

Hypothesis 3. If a person expects that the monopoly will not survive long, he will join it only if the rewards greatly exceed the cost.

Hypothesis 4. Every scientist has his subjectively optimal expected length of membership in a monopoly, depending on how long he expects to hold his present position. When his position changes, he will try to join a higher monopoly, *i.e.*, a monopoly whose leaders have higher positions.

It is clear that the interests of members of a monopoly coincide, at least to the extent that they all prefer the existing φ_t to elements of Q in case of a blocking monopoly, or conversely, for an enforcing monopoly. However, beyond that, the preferences (interests) of members of the monopoly may differ to some greater or lesser extent. In connection with this, one may hypothesize further.

Hypothesis 5. The fewer conflicts of interest between members of the monopoly, the stronger the monopoly.

Finally, comparing the expected and actual rewards, one may also hypothesize.

Hypothesis 6. The more often members of the monopoly receive at least the reward they expected, the more stable the monopoly is.

Hypothesis 7. The more often the waiting time for the reward exceeds the expected waiting time, the less stable the monopoly becomes.

PERSONAL EQUILIBRIUM AND ALIENATION

It is now possible to describe in terms of the suggested system the concepts of personal equilibrium and the type and degree of alienation [1; 3].

Consider, therefore, the actual arrangement φ_t and a fixed scientist s, whose set of positons under φ_t is $\varphi_t^{-1}(s)$. Let $p_1, p_2, \cdots$ be the positions in $\varphi_t^{-1}(s)$, and consider the functions $g_{s,p_i}(t)$ for positions $p_1, p_2, \cdots$.

According to Postulate 1, each of these functions, at the moment t, is either still in its increase period (possible period of constancy) or is already in its period of decrease.

One can now define the phenomena of internal disequilibrium, external disequilibrium, and alienation. Speaking first qualitatively, the internal disequilibrium is characterized by the fact that some of the values of the functions $g_{s,p_i}(t)$ are low and some are high. If this property is true at the moment t, but is going to diminish some time in the future, the disequilibrium may be called *apparent*;

otherwise, it may be called real. Next, *potential* internal disequilibrium may be characterized by the requirement that all values of $g_{s,p_i}(t)$ are close at the moment t, but some of these functions are going to decline, and some will increase, so that there will be an internal disequilibrium at some time in the future.

Schematically, for the case of two positions only, the above types of internal disequilibria may be characterized as in Figure 5.

The above concepts are evident enough that repeating them as formal definitions seems unnecessary.

Now, an *external* disequilibrium occurs if—again, speaking qualitatively—at least one of the values $g_{s,p}(t)$ is low and declining, while there exists another φ, more admissible than φ_t, and preferred to φ_t by s, in which s would have higher positions. Finally, *alienation* occurs, if there is an internal disequilibrium, and the function φ satisfying the above conditions is blocked by some monopoly.

To put it formally, we may state the following.

Definition 8. The occupancy function φ_t leads to *external disequilibrium* for s, if the following conditions are met: there exists φ such that

1. there exist $p \in \varphi_t^{-1}(s)$, $p' \in \varphi^{-1}(s)$ *with* $g_{s,p'}(t) > g_{s,p}(t)$; the latter function decreases;
2. $\varphi >_s \varphi_t$
3. $a_\varphi(t) > a_{\varphi_t}(t)$.

Definition 9. The occupancy function φ_t leads to *alienation* of s, if in addition to conditions 1, 2, and 3 above, we have

4. the assignment φ is blocked.

The intuitive justification of the necessity of all four conditions for alienation is the following.

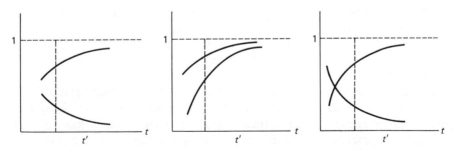

Figure 5. Internal disequilibrium at time t': real, left; apparent, middle; and potential, right.

For simplicity, imagine that the present assignment φ_t gives only one position to s, that is $\varphi_t^{-1}(s)$ consists of only one position p.

Imagine now that an alternative occupancy function exists, which assigns to s another position p'.

For the external disequilibrium, condition (1) states that under alternative assignment φ, scientist s would occupy a more appropriate position.

This condition alone does not guarantee either disequilibrium, or alienation: a further prerequisite is that s must prefer the new assignment φ to the present assignment φ_t (condition 2). Indeed, some persons could be empolyed more adequately than they are employed, but if they do not want the new positions, there is no reason to suppose that they feel alienated.

These two conditions, $i.e.$, 1 and 2, in turn, are still insufficient for disequilibrium: the alternative occupancy function φ must not only be more appropriate and preferred by s, it must also be more acceptable "socially," $i.e.$, it must not lead to lowering the admissibility of positions of others. This is stated in condition 3.

Altogether, s is in an external disequilibrium, if there is an alternative assignment that is at the same time fairer than the existing one and both more appropriate and preferable to s.

Blocking such an assignment (condition 4) leads to alienation of s with respect to the φ-blocking monopoly.

One can now see that the measure of the degree of alienation must contain the components corresponding to conditions 1-4, which may be referred to as

1. individual injustice component,
2. preference-blocking component,
3. social unfairness component, and
4. strength of monopoly component.

If 1 is violated, that is, the difference $g_{s,p'}(t) - g_{s,p}(t)$ is large, the scientist s will feel highly alienated, because the blocked alternative φ is such that he would be in a highly more appropriate position than at the present assignment φ_t.

If 2 is violated, that is, the blocked alternative is "very much" prefered to the present φ_t, the scientist s will feel highly alienated because he is deprived of the highly desired goods.

If 3 is violated, that is, the difference $a_\varphi(t) - a_{\varphi_t}(t)$ is large, then s will be highly alienated because the new alternative φ, which is being blocked, is not only better for him, but would also be much more acceptable socially.

Finally, if 4 is highly satisfied, that is, the blocking monopoly is very strong, then s will feel highly alienated because he has more feeling of "powerlessness."

Any adequate measure of the degree of alienation should therefore, combine in an appropriate way the components 1-4 for all alternatives blocked by some monopoly U.

HYPOTHESES ABOUT ALIENATION, MONOPOLIZATION, AND STATUS DISEQUILIBRIUM

Let us observe first that the concepts of internal and external status disequilibrium, as defined above, are closely related to the concepts of status disequilibrium of Randall and Strasser [3]. According to them, a necessary condition for status disequilibrium is status multidimensionality, with the existence of separate rankings in each dimension. Disequilibrium occurs if the ranks do not "match."

In the case under consideration, when the situation is restricted to science, the dimensions of status correspond to various positions occupied under φ_t by the same person (in the case of internal disequilibrium), and also admissibilities of various positions in alternative assignments φ (in case of external disequilibrium).

It is worth mentioning that the terms "internal" and "external" as used here do not carry any psychological connotations: an internal disequilibrium is such that it is defined only in terms of the existing assignment φ_t, without reference to what "could be," while an external disequilibrium calls for comparison of the actual and the potential assignments.

The main mechanisms conjectured by Randall and Strasser are formulated as a hypothesis that a person will try

1. to maximize the highest rank, and
2. to equalize all ranks by increasing the "lagging" ones.

To see how these mechanisms carry over to the present case, let us proceed systematically, and consider first an internal disequilibrium (regardless of the possible existence of external disequilibrium or alienation).

Thus, we consider only the positions *held*, without relating them to those that could be held, and suppose that the person in question holds two positions.

Apparent internal disequilibrium

Clearly, one can distinguish here three basic types, as depicted in Figure 6.

Hypothesis 8. An increasing apparent internal disequilibrium for scientists occurs most often in the early stages of the career, when they are somewhat prematurely advanced.

Hypothesis 9. A decreasing apparent internal disequilibrium for scientists occurs most often in the late stages of the career, or when ill or disabled.

Hypothesis 10. A mixed internal disequilibrium for scientists occurs most often in the early stages of the career, when they are "selectively alienated," *i.e.*, kept in positions they have outgrown.

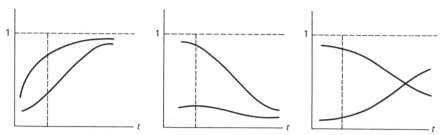

Figure 6. Apparent internal disequilibrium at time t': increasing, left; decreasing, middle, and mixed right.

Clearly, the apparent internal disequilibrium does not present too much of a problem for a person, and there is no reason to assume that a person would display any tendency to reduce it: the situation will "equalize" in the course of time within some finite time horizon.

Real and potential internal disequilibrium

This is typified in Figure 7, where the disequilibrium tends to become more and more severe. Now one can further hypothesize.

Hypothesis 11. In case of a real (potential) internal disequilibrium, a person will try to reduce (prevent) it by advancing in position, even prematurely (moving from an "upper branch" to a lower curve), or sometimes even resigning from some positions, if they are "unbecoming" (resigning from a position represented by a "lower branch").

External status disequilibrium

Let us now consider a more interesting case, namely, one of external status disequilibrium, possibly combined with alienation. Here a necessary (but by no

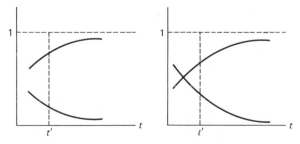

Figure 7. Internal disequilibrium at time t': real, left; and potential, right.

means sufficient) condition is the existence of an alternative φ, which offers persons s more admissible positions. For simplicity, let φ_t and φ give the person s one position only. For an external disequilibrium, the picture must be such that the admissibility of the position held (solid line) lies below that for the position under alternative φ (dotted line); see Figure 8.

For an external status disequilibrium, the picture must be not only such as in Figure 8, but the new assignment must also be preferred by s, and socially be fairer than φ_t. If it is blocked, there is also alienation.

Though the configuration in Figure 8 alone does not suffice for disequilibrium or alienation, one can hypothesize about the types of configurations that are likeliest to be associated with disequilibrium and alienation.

Hypothesis 12. External disequilibrium and alienation are more likely to be associated with cases when the two curves of admissibility diverge than when they converge (they diverge if what s holds at present becomes less and less admissible, while what he could have becomes more and more admissible).

Of course, the remarks concerning the measure of alienation can be translated into hypotheses, such as that (in the above case) suggesting that the greater the difference between the two curves, the higher the alienation, *etc.* Such hypotheses, being rather tautological, will be omitted here.

One can, however, state the following hypotheses relating the levels of positions and levels of alienation.

Hypothesis 13. The substitution of positions or goods leading to a decrease of alienation is easier (for the monopoly) to achieve for those on lower positions. More precisely: the same degree of de-alienation is achieved by smaller advancement from a lower position than from a higher position.

Hypothesis 14. The substitution of preferences (change of preference for some

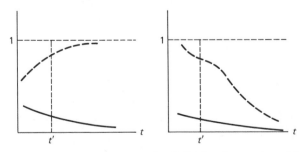

Figure 8. External disequilibrium at time t'.   Solid line is actual $g_{s,p}(t)$; broken line is potential $g_{s,p}(t)$.

positions or goals, achieved by means such as sociotherapy, *etc.*) that lead to the same level of de-alienation is easier to achieve for those in lower positions than for those in higher positions.

Hypothesis 15. It is easier to introduce new rules of admissibility that would lead to the same level of de-alienation for those in lower positions, as for those in higher positions.

Hypothesis 16. An increase of strength of the monopoly leads to a greater increase of alienation for those in higher positions that for those in lower positions.

The above hypotheses correspond respectively to the conditions 1-4 for alienation.

Let us now look at the situation from the point of view of a monopoly that alienates a group of persons. Such a monopoly is, generally, interested in preventing the appearance of a countermonopoly.

The hypothesis may be formulated as follows.

Hypothesis 17. The appearance of a countermonopoly in the group of alienated persons is *less* likely, if

1. the variance of the degree of alienation among those alienated is large;
2. the group structure, among those induced by the relation $-::$, is loose (*i.e.*, there are few connections altogether, and no subgroups strongly connected).

The intuitive justification of point 2 requires no comment. As for 1, the hypothesis asserts that the more "homogeneous" with respect to their levels of alienation the group of alienated persons is, the likelier it is that they will form a countermonopoly.

We also state.

Hypothesis 18. Each person perceives the distribution of levels of alienation in his reference group. The more skewed to the right this distribution is (*i.e.*, the more highly alienated the persons), the more probable that a person will have a greater tolerance for alienation.

Hypothesis 19. The larger the group of alienated persons is, and the greater the density of relations $-::$ of preferential concordance, the greater the chance of an appearance of transient coalitions, formed in order to enforce some partial goals against the monopoly's blocking.

Hypothesis 20. The greater the chance of joining the monopoly is, the shorter the average duration of transient coalitions from Hypothesis 19 will be.

The above hypotheses concerned the appearance of countermonopolies, and the strategies of a monopoly to preserve its existence. Finally, one can formulate some hypotheses about the individual reactions of persons who are alienated.

Generally, one may categorize such reactions into two broad categories: fight and withdrawal. The first can take on such forms as protests and complaints to higher authorities, letters to editors, *etc.*; the reactions of withdrawal may range from change of work, and illness to suicide.

One could expect that some relations exist between time of reaction, its type, the degree of alienation, and the person's position.

Hypothesis 21. The time of reaction of an alienated person tends to be shorter, if

1. any of the alienation components is high;
2. the admissibility of the present position is rapidly decreasing;
3. a person belongs to the group related by preferential concordance, who are as alienated as he; and
4. a person is on a higher position.

Hypothesis 22. Given that a reaction occurs, it is more likely to be of withdrawal, if

1. the person is in a lower position; and
2. the alienation concerns more "intangible" goods, such as recoginition of one's work, *etc.*

The reaction is more likely to be of the fighting type, if

1. the person is in a higher position; and
2. the alienation concerns more "tangible" goods, such as reserach grants, travel funds, *etc.*

Generally, is is obvious that a person will join a monopoly if the prospective profits, in the form of a share in the monopolized goods, *etc.*, are sufficiently high; in choosing between several monopolies, he will select the one he judges to be best, in the sense of its strength, prospective horizon of existence, and goods it provides.

When a person is in a monopoly, he receives some goods, and the chances of being satisfied increase. In such case, he will later try to join another monopoly. These considerations suggest that the distribution of the duration times of participation in a monopoly has the following "aging" property.

Hypothesis 23. The longer a person belongs to a monopoly, the greater are the chances that he will leave it to join another. Formally, if $f(x)$ is the probability that the duration of membership in a monopoly will be exactly x, and $F(x)$ is the probability that this duration will be less than x, then $f(x)/(1 - F(x))$ is an increasing function of x.

Here $f(x)/(1 - F(x))$ is the conditional probability that a person will belong to the monopoly for exactly x, given that he belongs to it for x or more. In other words, this quantity represents the "defection rate" for those who are in the monopoly for at least x.

NOTES AND REFERENCES

1. Jaroszewski, T. M. Alienacja. Warszawa: PWN, 1965. In Polish. A Marxian view of alienation.
2. Nowakowska, M. "Alienation and Monopolization in Science: a Formal Approach." In *Die Idee der Emtfremdung in der Sozialwissenschaften*. Edited by M. Brenner and H. Strasser. Dordrecht, Netherlands: D. Reidel, forthcoming.
3. Randall, S. C., and H. Strasser. "On the Theory of Status Disequilibrium. Some Causes and Consequences Reconsidered," preprint. Vienna, Austria: Institute for Advanced Studies, 1975.

PART IV

Planning and Policy Formulation

The techniques of planning and policy formulation appropriate to the public sector are, again, different from those that we would expect to find operating in industry and commerce. For example, as Eric Trist so clearly shows, effectiveness in the public sector demands the full exploitation of the potential of adaptive planning, which, in its own right, implies major changes in the way we organize public enterprise. Gregory Daneke and Alan Steiss then take us through a survey of the systems-analytical instruments available to the public planner and policy-maker, and again serve to set the problems of public administration into a category all their own. David Carhart then explores, in a wide-ranging essay, the legitimacy of the public policy-maker's reliance on the "global models" that have so completely captured the attention of so many management scientists and consultants. Hasan Ozbekhan then shows the reader how modern planning technology was put to work in an urban setting (Paris), presenting a paradigm that most public planners will find to be both critical and compelling. Finally, Andrew Sage and David Rajala bring an engineer's eye to the problems of developing a responsive and disciplined structure to the planning, decision, and policy-formulation process, and establish a new linkage between the functions of policy-making and decision-making for public enterprise.

1

Developing an Adaptive Planning Capability in Public Enterprise and Government Agencies

Eric L. Trist
University of Pennsylvania

THE INDIVIDUAL AND THE ORGANIZATION

The development of managers and the organizations they manage are correlated processes. One cannot take place without the other. By saying that they are correlative, we mean that they each have distinctive properties but that they are interdependent. Classical organization theory looked at the organization too much as a thing in itself, whose inhabitants could be scarcely more than ciphers or "organization men." Classical personality theory looked at the individual too much as if he could be separated from his social relations and memberships. A more modern approach would recognize that it is fundamental to the dilemma of the human condition that man needs the organizations he builds, yet is frustrated by them—he is "a group animal continuously at war with his own groupishness" [7].

However cooperative he may be in any particular organization to which he belongs, he is also "recalcitrant" to it [61] because it satisfies only some of his needs. He is in a relation of only "part includedness" to it. He belongs to many others and to his own unique personal life cycle. The individual brings an element of instability, as he does to life, into any organization. Furthermore, the social aggregate formed by all the members or their main subgroups creates an informal organization alongside the formal one, which is always to some extent at odds with it. This simultaneously creates the danger of subversion and the possibility of innovation. The balance between individual and organization is always to some extent precarious. To maintain a reasonable balance requires continual managerial effort. The work of "integrating the individual with the organization" [4] is never done.

Moreover, it requires more work than it used to, since the large, complex organizations that characterize the modern world make enormous demands on their members, especially their managers. In order to function well they require *commitment*. This means that the individual has to be willing to have a great deal of himself included in his organizational life. Commitment cannot be obtained by coercion. It can only be given. This gift is made only when the objectives and modes of behavior of the organization match his own goals and values. Otherwise he is alienated, and alienated members do not perform up to the level of their capacity.

DEVELOPMENT

Much past work has made the mistake of regarding the characteristics of either managers or the organization as relatively fixed. They are not, nor do we know what the upper limits of learning and development are for organizations or people. This did not matter too much when organizations, especially public ones, were quasi-stable "bureaucracies" in slowly changing environments. Now government agencies and public enterprises, as much as organizations in the private sector, have innovative and developmental as well as regulative tasks. Like them, they exist in rapidly changing environments. Therefore, their personnel and their organizations have to be considered in terms of *transbureaucratic models* [5]. This means that both must develop rather than merely maintain the steady state.

As regards the individual, it was assumed until recently that a man finished his education, went to work, learned a skill or profession, and practiced it for the rest of his life or, joining one organization, stayed there quasi-permanently in one line of work. Now we think rather in terms of further education being undertaken after work has commenced—of "lifelong learning," of the serial rather than the single career. This has come about because the increasing obsolescence of much existing knowledge is an inherent part of the "knowledge explosion."

It also used to be commonly thought that the individual did not develop significantly in character and personality once he had reached adulthood. Now we think rather of personal growth continuing throughout life [42, 22]. More and more people are coming explicitly to adopt for themselves goals both of lifelong learning and lifelong personal development. Increasingly, they are seeking careers that will enable them to pursue these goals in the organizations to which they belong.

As employment opportunities are now so much wider, it has become relatively easy to shift from one organization to another when frustration and disappointment are encountered. Many of the best managers, actual and potential, hold these values. They quickly leave organizations that restrict their opportunities. These organizations lose their stock of talent, which, once run down, is hard to replace, while those offering wider scope—to the many rather then just the few —gain the most precious of all resources.

As regards the bureaucratic model, its value has been that it established standards of integrity, fairness, and professional competence. These have been effective in combating corruption, favoritism, and amateurism. These values have to be established where they do not exist, and maintained where they have been established. The civil services of certain Western countries provide examples. Nevertheless, the recent reforms in the British Civil Service consequent on the Fulton Report [25] indicate the need for change in such bodies. There is danger that developing countries will follow outdated models. The experiences of public enterprises in a number of such countries have shown the negative effects of political interference, but old style civil service conceptions are not the antidote.

There is a growing consensus that large organizations, whether government agencies, public, or private enterprises, and whether in developing or developed countries, have so much in common in the contemporary world environment that they can be regarded as members of a common set from the viewpoint of management and organizational development. This may be said without prejudice to the importance of differences that inevitably arise from differences in purpose and function, stage of development, or cultural setting.

The bureaucratic model tended to make government agencies and public and private enterprises into closed corporations with internally developed elites drawn from privileged sections of the society passing out of the most prestigious establishments of higher education. The transbureaucratic model requires open corporations with an import and export of personnel at all levels, drawn from a much broader social base, yet preserving the level of competence and increasing its variety.

The bureaucratic model provided stability. But it was static. Its capability for adaptation to change was low. The transbureaucratic model is designed to produce adaptability. Its difficulty is to maintain stability while responding to change. Some recent attempts to solve this problem will now be examined, for unless organizations can learn to develop, as well as simply to expand, they will neither meet the realities of the environmental situation nor provide contexts for personal growth.

GOING BEYOND BUREAUCRACY

The kind of formal organization that became the dominant organizational form in Western societies in the nineteenth century, whether in the public or the private sector, has been called by sociologists a bureaucracy [80]. A bureaucracy operates by the existence of rules, division of labor, the hierarchical organization of offices, the choice of technically trained officials, the separation of ownership from management, the adherence of rights to offices and not to incumbents, and the recording in writing of administrative acts, decisions, and rules.

Such organizations represented a great gain in capability for their purposes over what Weber called patrimonial organizations, which had characterized the preindustrial era and persisted rather maladaptively into industrial societies. But as technology developed, bureaucratic organizations reached a size, a complexity of hierarchies, and a degree of fractionation of their work that made them overly mechanistic. Work-study and O & M whatever their merits, produced a stifling degree of detailed control. As technology developed still further in terms of the second industrial revolution based on information technology, rather than simply the energy technology on which the first was based, a level of complexity and a rate of change came into existence that could not be coped with by the bureaucratic model. Burns and Stalker [11], through their studies of the electronics industry in Scotland, came to contrast the bureaucratic or mechanistic with what they called the *organismic* pattern of organization. The following account of their work and of related attempts to formulate transbureaucratic models is taken from Hutton [31], whose short book *Thinking about Organizations* is one of the best introductions to recent organizational theory.

In a mechanistic system we have an arrangement that tends to conform to the ideas of classical management, with clear job specifications, clear hierarchies, people higher up resolving conflicts between those lower down, and the assumption that both power and knowledge exist at the top ("all communications to be addressed to the manager"). The emphasis is upon effective performance of prescribed tasks, with the job of integration and cohesion left to superiors. In the organismic form of organization, emphasis is on the way in which tasks contribute to the whole and upon the development of patterns of control and communication which increase the effectiveness with which people can get the information and sanction they require. There is greater tendency to value expert power—a matrix form of organization would be organismic. It is important to note that Burns and Stalker do not say as Weber did of bureaucracy that the mechanistic form is good, neither do they say, as many people have subsequently assumed that they say, that the mechanistic form is bad. What they do say is that it is adapted to stable conditions. By the same token, they do not say that the organismic form of organization is good, only that it is what works under conditions of rapid change. It is the expression of the development of flexible operations to handle the changing requirements of subenvironments. The two forms of organization are seen as the ends of a continuum along which enterprises will be located, but the characteristics which Burns and Stalker use to define each are not abstract dimensions or measures; they are statements of ongoing actual processes across a wide part of the culture and working climate. . . . Argyris's "mix model" (1964) picks up and echoes the mechanistic-organismic continuum with a particular emphasis upon the appreciation of the whole and the inter-relationship of the parts as against emphasis on the parts. He argues that effectiveness of the enterprise will increase insofaras its core activities, of adapting to the external environment, achieving objectives and maintaining the internal system, approximate to the "right hand" end of the continua in the mix model.

Argyris identifies four stages of progress from a traditional bureaucratic classical management type of structure to the most un-hierarchical form of organization.

Structure I, the pyramidal structure, would, he suggests, be appropriate where rapid decisions are made, for instance in emergency situations; where the decisions are not critical and are covered by a previously established consensus; where the decisions do not affect the existing distribution of power, controls and information; where there are simply too many people to get together; or where people are apathetic and non-involved or antagonistic to the enterprise and want to remain so.

Structure II, the modified form of pyramidal structure, is where Argyris would locate Likert's work. Likert's (1967) continua from the System 1 to the System 4 form of ogranization relate to leadership processes, the assumptions and values held about people and the decision and control processes operating and performance and training standards. They do relate to ways of doing things and insofaras they affect structure it is in the emphasis on group decision-taking and group supervision which exists in System 4. It is true that Likert's work implicitly assumes the existence of a hierarchy, and deals with the way in which a manager deals with his subordinates as one group and also belongs to a group consisting of his colleagues with their superiority. To Argyris, this is a modification of the pyramidal structure, which is only one stage in the direction of Argyris's extreme. He suggests that this form of structure is appropriate for decisions which are not routine but still do not upset power, information and control, where time is available to include managers but not everybody and where decisions cannot be completely delegated but participation is desired to decrease resistance to change.

Structure III, power according to functional contribution, is one where the distribution of controls, power and the right to information is much more evenly spread through the network. "The individual is given power as a function of his potential contribution to the problem." This is the kind of system under which project assignments develop and may be given to the command of somebody more junior in career stage or hierarchy than some of the members of the team, which does happen. I know of a firm of consulting engineers where a project may very well be given to a young engineer with high expertise and competence for the job in hand and where, for this job, he may have under his "command" a director of the company. It is clear that command under these conditions is not the kind of command that goes along with assumptions of hierarchical position. Argyris, in his book mentions a firm of his acquaintance where the same thing happens. We could almost be writing about the same firm, but we are not. Apart from this kind of project assignment, Argyris suggests that the decisions requiring this kind of structure would be those concerned with new product development or the solution of departmental problems or long range policy planning. It is interesting to note that these are examples of integrative devices such as those studied by Lawrence and Lorsch (1967). They found that the factors which were associated with the effectiveness of integrative sub-systems included an emphasis on the performance of the total system with a more equal distribution of power, which echo what Argyris is talking about.

Structure IV, power according to inevitable organizational responsibilities, is one in which each individual has equal power and responsibility and may not relinquish it. Argyris suggests that there are situations where this may be appropriate, for instance for decisions in which maximum individual productivity and feelings of responsibility and commitment are desired, or these would be decisions which significantly affect the distribution of power, control and information and decisions which define the rules under which these various structures would be used.

This last type of structure is more common in certain subsystems of organizations than in total organizations. Autonomous work groups at one end and boards of management at the other would be examples. Excess complexity at any level tends to produce group decision structures. Collegiate type bodies are frequent in many contexts when guiding values have to be chosen and the rules of the game formulated or changed. Reference back to the ultimate constituency is common on such occasions in representative bodies. In fast-changing environments where the novel and the emergent have increasingly to be encountered, problems of value change and making new ground rules arise with a frequency quite uncharacteristic of a more slowly moving environment.

These trends are indicative of a world process. They are not confined to any one country, developed or underdeveloped, whatever the variations in context. In developing managers and organizations in the last third of the present century, we must think in terms of developing competencies in both relevant to the emerging world of the second industrial revolution rather than to the more sedate world to which the Weberian model was adapted.

PARTICIPATION AND LEARNING IN THE ORGANIZATIONAL CONTEXT

An organization cannot develop itself or its members unless opportunities for organizational learning are built into all its activities at all levels. This depends on how far superior-subordinate relations are conducted in a "democratic" rather than an "authoritarian" spirit and the extent to which and the manner in which planning, implementation, and review of operations are systematically carried out in a climate of openness and trust that permits maximum "search" and maximum criticism.

Development of the requisite competences means building opportunities for participation and learning into all areas of the organization's life for all members. Participation and learning go hand in hand. One learns best by taking an active part in acquiring a new piece of knowledge, or indeed any additional resource or needed capability. Modern educational methods are based on this principle, which has been established by extensive research as regards the individual. But it is also true at the social level. Though more recent, research in social psychology and sociology may be said now to have established it here too.

The more bureaucratic and mechanistic the organization the less the degree of participation and learning. The boundaries of what one can do and is required to know are prescribed; to cross them is proscribed. The more organismic and adaptive the organization the greater the degree of participation and learning. Boundaries are permeable and every extension of individual competence is used to strengthen the organization's capability. Entirely mistaken is the view that the presence of participation and learning represents an intrusion into organizational life of humanistic values out of touch with organizational realities. They represent system characteristics whose presence or absence defines opposite organizational modalities. Their presence in a high degree is a required condition of success in any organization that must adapt to a high degree of complexity and change. These are the conditions that allow relevant innovation to take place.

A costly error is to suppose that participation and learning can be reserved for the higher echelons—top and upper-middle management. They must extend not only to middle management and supervision, but to the rank and file. As they are system characteristics they need to pervade the organization as a whole. Their absence at any one level impairs their effectiveness at others. This does not mean that everyone has to be party to all decisions or to know everything. It does mean that people must actively develop their own domain and join in the regulation of its affairs with those of neighboring domains. Organizational democracy begins in the individual's own workplace, whatever and wherever this may be. If it is not present here it does not matter to him if it is present somewhere else. Organizational democracy is not rooted in systems of formal representation, though joint councils and committees have their proper place, but in the way in which concrete tasks are carried out. To cope with task complexity requires what James Thompson [68] has called *pooled interdependence*; to adapt to frequent task change requires what Warren Bennis [5] has called *temporary systems*. Such organizational strategies require organizational democracy. A very great deal has been learned about all this in the last few years through the Norwegian Industrial Democracy Project [19]. A review of this and related fields has been given elsewhere [73].

Though the variation in cultural idiom may be great, the requirements outlined are universal for organizational adaptation to a rapidly changing environment. The nineteenth century cannot be repeated in developing countries in the last third of the twentieth. A fallacy is to suppose that large scale organizations in these countries must, initially at least, be regimentally constructed in the bureaucratic mode that is beginning to decline in the advanced countries. Evidence is mounting that the preindustrial traditions of many developing countries enable transbureaucratic styles to be learned more quickly than in some advanced countries where a great deal of unlearning has first to take place. Among other studies, this was demonstrated in a highly successful change project carried out by a colleague of the writer's in the Indian textile industry [55].

MANAGEMENT, SELECTION, TRAINING, AND DEVELOPMENT

It is for organizations with the characteristics outlined that schemes of management selection and development on the one hand, and organization development on the other are required. Such programs need external as well as internal resources, and international as well as national participation. The wider aspects have become important since the organizations concerned belong increasingly to a world system. The investment in these activities will need to be considerable in terms of the management time and attention required. Management and organization development are as important as any other aspect of organizational life. Unless this is appreciated by top management and known to be so appreciated throughout the organization, any technical schemes adopted will be of little consequence.

There is need to make use of the *widest possible pool of resources* as regards manpower. Therefore, the greatest openness must be maintained between agencies and enterprises, not only within the public sector, but between it and the private sector—in recruitment, promotion, transfer, and career planning. This entails transferable pensions and any other devices that will increase mobility. A narrow competitive strategy of locking people up in particular organizations will not pay off. Hoarding talent, especially when resources are scarce, is the best way to prevent a general stock pile of talent from growing. Developing countries would do well to keep a national inventory of managers, scientists, technicians, and specialists of all kinds and regularly to survey their deployment. The development of plans for optimizing their utilization as a total population merits priority consideration. The planned deployment of talent on the basis of a national register was carried out with great thoroughness in countries such as Britain during World War II (people such as Lord Snow taking a considerable part in it.) The kind of effort that was made to *mobilize* human resources in advanced countries under conditions of emergency needs to be repeated in appropriate forms in developing countries on a long-term basis. If the first problem of all is the primary production of trained talent—through upgrading the educational system—the next is one of resource mobilization rather than of allocation. Nevertheless, candidate supply, initial selection, subsequent selection, training, promotion, deployment, *etc.* are all parts of a total process that needs planning as such. Intimate and sustained collaboration is required at all stages between the government, public and private agencies, and enterprises and educational institutions.

Selection procedures depend on the balance of supply and demand. Where supply is short candidates have to be searched out. The extensiveness and resourcefulness of the search process become the main feature of the operation, which must remain heavily constrained if no data bank of the type described above exists even at a rudimentary level. Moreover, people remain ignorant of possible career openings unless provided with information. Apart from the type of information that remains on paper, much may be gained from having potential recruits visit and even spend trial periods at the kinds of organization in which their careers may be launched. The wider and the deeper the explorations and inspections made the better. The process is two-way between potential recruits and potential employers, and there should be no strings attached. Again it needs to be developed comprehensively with the participation of all relevant authorities.

Selection methods themselves are of two types—"squeezing procedures" and "creaming procedures." The first are concerned with finding all those who can satisfy a minimum standard. They are rejection procedures, the object being to keep out the unsuitable. This is difficult when criteria are unclear and qualities hard to judge. They are, nevertheless, worth considerable trouble, as the presence of grossly unsuitable people in organizations even for trial periods is disturbing and costly. Probationary arrangements can, however, rarely be dispensed with.

Creaming procedures have to contend with intangible problems such as "guessing" potential. This is complicated by the awkward fact that the qualities required in initial jobs are often different from those required for subsequent and more senior appointments. From the beginning, therefore, one must look at the person as a whole.

While management recruits need a high level of formal education and proven intellectual ability, *character and personality* are no less important and count most in the end. Modern group-selection procedures can help here, creating situations that give extended scope for the exercise of intuitive judgment by the decision-makers. Where group procedures are inappropriate, the findings of several individual appraisals can be systematically reviewed by the decision-makers in concert. The most senior personnel must be involved in these decisions, but more than one generation must be included among selectors. The competence of judges increases very remarkably through repeated sharing of such experiences. This represents an instance of organizational learning with a multiplier effect, for not only are the core values of the organization clarified through such encounters, but the improved judgment is used by the managers involved in the many other personnel decisions they have to make. A deepened understanding of human character becomes embodied in the culture of the organization. Simplistic stereotypes are not so easily tolerated.

Internal appraisal procedures need to be equally systematic and thorough. The group of judges should include a man's immediate manager, his manager once removed, any specialist comanagers, and a representative of the personnel division. Appraisals must separate present competence and *future potential*. The existence of frequent doubt about future potential requires frank acceptance. A good deal of experience has also been gained in recent years of involving the "appraised" individual in the appraisal process. A man makes his own self-appraisal, which becomes the basis of a discussion with his superior [45]. Feedback is most valuable when it is two-way. Dissonnant perceptions of an individual are frequent in groups of judges and at different periods. The gradual resolution of these is a valuable learning experience for all concerned. An individual needs to know how he is being assessed and what his prospects are. The all too common traditions of secrecy through which people are kept in the dark about their standing and their future are not compatible with the open but confrontational climates required in complex organizations seeking to adapt to a rapid change and to maximize for this purpose the use of the talent available to them.

All the managers of the enterprise or agency should be reviewed at suitable intervals, annually, biannually, *etc.* as the case may be, so that cumulative records can be built up, stored in central personnel files, and used in making appointments from the total pool of resources available. A personnel division would not force a manager to take someone he did not want, but would enable him to make his choice from a wider field of candidates and take into account the longer range needs of the organization and the man's own career prospects, as well as his own immediate needs to have a particular job filled. In this way knowledge of people is not locked up in one department. As more and better and self-correcting information is acquired, it can become the basis of concern-wide career planning. This enables the stock of talent to be brought on rapidly and distributed according to strategically envisaged priorities. It is too scarce to be lost or misplaced.

Every manager is the on-the-job trainer of his subordinates. This has to be legitimated as being of *equal importance* to his operational duties in the organization's value system. If training is going to be taken seriously, managers need to be trained to train their subordinates. The quality of the transactions between superior and subordinate is the basic element in management development [36; 37].

The requirement of continuous learning for all staff has to be built into the practices and *budgets* of the organization. Otherwise obsolescence is the penalty. This is neither an optional nor a marginal cost, but a necessary and central one. It is to be regarded as part of the capital investment budget—*investment in the future human resources* of the enterprise. Human resources are increasingly recognized as the most scarce and critical of all resources for which competition is the most ruthless, within and between countries. Bold action here is imperative to reduce brain-drain.

In addition to continuous on-the-job training, regular internal and external courses of many varieties are required. These concern both the technical and human and organizational side of the enterprise. The organizational and human implications of technical matters should be included in courses about them. Internal courses are more particularistic, external courses more universal. They have complementary functions.

These courses must be phased in with a manager's career phase and related to the type of decision he will be concerned with in his next role. They are, therefore, best related to role changes—to points of transition. These create stresses and challenges that give opportunities for learning. Very few organizations make use of the wide variety of possibilities now available. These emergent learning "technologies" need to be made widely known.

Major career development points may be characterized as representing passage from specialist management 1) to the coordination of specialisms; and 2) to the relating of wide activity domains to the external environment—general management in the fullest sense. It is desirable, whenever feasible, for a man to spend a period outside his organization in relation to such changes. These periods may consist of transfers or external courses.

Transfers may be to other organizations similar to the given organization or to contrasting organizations. External courses may be custom built for the needs of members of several similar organizations or may consist of general educational experiences. Both are necessary. Experiences in other countries and international bodies should be included, as well as experiences in the man's own country, both for transfers and courses. Periods of time away can vary according to purpose: one month, three months, six months, nine months. The findings of studies of "postexperience" courses are that, for significant change to take place, the periods away have to be from three to nine months. Periods for technical education can be shorter than for attitudinal and emotional learning.

Investments in opportunities for attitudinal and emotional learning for key personnel are critical for an organization's *capacity for self-renewal.* A period away of six to nine months is of cardinal importance at midcareer. This provides an opportunity for self-review, and can lead to the type of personal growth necessary in men who will be able to meet the demand of higher management roles between the ages of 35 and 45. There is evidence that another period away after these ages can also be beneficial and such a period is being sought at the present time by top executives in large industrial organizations and in the civil service of several countries. Such periods are akin to sabbatical years in the university world. If people are to go on being creative they cannot be worn out. A great variety of psychological and sociological approaches to the handling of these periods is now available [52; 62].

In many developing countries the initial preparation of management entrants is inadequate. Special methods and investments are necessary to remedy this. Greater economies are possible if resources are reserved to be spent on those shown to have a greater likelihood of proving suitable after thorough initial selection and trial on first jobs. This means recruiting more people, for some will always be training. But this, in turn, increases the "stock" of future managers— a prime need of developing countries.

DEVELOPING THE ORGANIZATION'S CLIMATE, CULTURE, AND INNOVATIVE CAPABILITY

The focus so far has been on the development of the individual manager. The complementary focus is that of the development of the organization itself. The large literature that has grown up in this field in the last twenty years centers on organizational change, not unnaturally, since it is the advent of a more rapid change in the environment that has given rise to the need for organizational change at a pace and scale not previously known. Can the capacity for organizational change be systematically improved, and can organizational change itself by systematically planned? The classic book of readings that surveys the present state of the art for the manager as well as the social scientist is *The Planning of Change* [6].

The modern tendency is to treat the organization as a *learning community* as well as an operational entity, and to assert that in order to function well as the second it must recognize the need to become the first. This means that the organization at all levels has to take time out, frequently, to observe what has been happening to it and to learn from this experience. It has to build this approach into the way it goes about its daily operation. This is what is meant by creating an organizational climate of a learning community.

Attention centered at first on the small face-to-face group, its interpersonal relations and dynamics as a group. A new field was opened up by the invention of the Laboratory Method of human relations training, which included the introduction of unstructured training groups (T groups) in which the members examine what goes on in the group and their relations with each other in the "here" and "how," usually with someone present in a consultant or training role. The field with special reference to organizational settings has been reviewed in *Personal and Organizational Change through Group Methods* [58]. T groups have now been conducted in most countries of the world.

The method is not suitable in its original form for use inside organizations without modification unless in special circumstances. But its existence has drawn attention to the importance of relations in the small group, especially of superior and subordinates, in organizational life. Much is now acknowledged about interpersonal conflict, difficulties over authority and leadership, "hidden agendas," resistance to change, and the anxiety that impending change produces that was not accepted in the norms of organizational life two decades ago. This has convinced a very large number of people that a more open organizational climate is both necessary and possible in organizations moving into the post-bureaucratic era.

More recently attempts have been made to use more structured derivatives of the T-group approach systematically to improve change capability throughout entire organizations. The best known of these is the Managerial Grid [8]. This is based on a concept of managerial styles as mixes of concern with "production" and "people" (the managerial grid). A high concern with both, called the "9, 9" style is regarded as optimum, and the objective of an organizational change program is defined as a systematic attempt to induce an overall change in management behavior in this direction throughout the enterprise. There are six phases:

1. off-site training in "diagonal slice" groups with an emphasis on structured exercises, rather than unstructured settings, to avoid too high a level of initial anxiety;
2. off-site team training based on "family" groups;
3. on-site intergroup training to achieve better integration between functional groups;
4. discussions with various managerial groups to set goals for the total organization;
5. consultant help in implementing the consequential changes;
6. their consolidation, and withdrawal of the consulting team.

The overall program takes a minimum of four years. First attempts have been made to evaluate its application and some positive evidence has been adduced for its effectiveness both in terms of "intervening" and "outcome" variables. It has the limitations of any "packaged deal."

Another method, developed at the University of Michigan, concerns the method of the systematic feedback of survey data for group discussion in "organizational families," developed by Floyd Mann [41]. Data of this kind were fed back to each organizational family beginning with the top in a large company; each level had discretion to consider the implications of the findings for itself; but each level reported the outcome of its meetings up the line. Repeats were made in some parts of the company, with others omitted as control groups, at intervals that allowed for consequent actions and changes in climate to be realized. Results consistently favored the experimental groups. This research, which lasted some four years, demonstrated the effectiveness of a method that can become self-administering and provide a basis for continuous organizational learning. It has had wide application [66].

A large variety of methods have now been developed for improving group relations, conflict resolution, communication, and dealing with intercultural problems. These have been tried out with considerable success in some developing countries and are described in a *Handbook of Staff Development and Human Relations Training* [46]. This documents material developed for use in Africa.

In much of this work attention has been given too exclusively to top management. The lower echelons cannot be left out else there is a serious split, which impairs operational capability. A special task concerns "unprogramming" older personnel, especially in middle management, who have got stuck in obsolete practices and beliefs. A rigid, outmoded, and despairing middle management belt is one of the severest obstacles to the achievement of change. Here group psychological methods can be used with advantage.

Currently, research concerned with organizational development is advancing into new types of analysis of the policy-making process, of the relation of the organization to the environment, and of the planning process.

The instrumental aspect of decision-making has been overemphasized, the "appreciative" aspect being neglected and poorly understood. The balance has been redressed by Sir Geoffrey Vickers in *The Art of Judgment: A Study of Policy Making* [78].

When interest centered on the internal workings of the organization it was treated as a "closed system" shut off from its environment. With the rapid change rate, however, organizational effectiveness depends, crucially, on ability to meet and to anticipate environmental change. The openness of the internal climate has to be paralleled by openness of the organization to the environment. One is needed for the other. Types of environmental context have been analyzed by Emery and Trist [17]. The relevance of a contextual orientation to administrative problems and organizational learning is emphasized in *Appraising Administrative Capability for Development* [76].

The increasing change rate and the uncertainty this creates has led to a new emphasis on planning. Ideas of comprehensive planning and extreme forms of "disjointed incrementation" have given way to new concepts of adaptive planning [1]. Recognition of planning as a continuous process has made the acquisition of a future orientation essential to any organization that expects to survive.

ACTION RESEARCH

What this may mean begins to become clear as soon as we look at planning as a collaborative undertaking between those of many kinds concerned with social action and those, also of many kinds, concerned with planning. In such a concept, the process is more important than the plan, the learning that takes place more critical than the results obtained. Each fresh step, in conjunction with environmental factors, provides the starting point for the next. There is no finality. The need is to develop a capability, not a product. This strengthening capability has to be brought into existence simultaneously at the individual, organizational, and societal levels.

But such a capability cannot be acquired except by those who are willing to look into what they are doing and to regard this as experimental, rather than proven beforehand or incapable of investigation. People with such an experimental attitude will expect that what they set out to do will contain error and require modification; and they will regard it as incumbent upon them to make explicit any implicit assumptions and hypotheses they are making.

This is the core of the "action research mentality," which, in conjunction with "adaptive planning," constitutes a modality that must prevail as a social value and a social methodology if we are to attain one of the more desirable, rather than one of the more undesirable, of the futures that may by open to us.

To make myself intelligible, I must first of all state my general position in the philosophy of science, which is that of a contextualist, following C. S. Pepper [48]. Like Ackoff and Emery [2], I think of outcomes as being "coproduced" by systems and their environments, rather than resulting from linear causal chains. Like Angyal [3], I think of organic life as occurring in the "biosphere"— the universe composed by the organism and its environment taken together—and of social life as taking place in the "sociosphere" [9; 10]. Only for analytical purposes may one separate system and environment [74].

Let me next refer to certain ideas introduced by my colleague Fred Emery and me concerning *The Causal Texture of Organizational Environments* [17]. We have suggested that any set of events in social behavior (at any level) requires explanation not only in terms of the internal interdependencies of the target system, or of the transactional interdependencies of its task environment, but also in terms of the interdependencies of its contextual environment. When the contextual environment remains placid (stable), it may for most purposes of social analysis and social policy be neglected, but as it becomes more dynamic it must be increasingly taken into account. For events in the context now begin to penetrate the transactional field. If the first industrial revolution, based on mechanization, has produced a prevailing "disturbed-reactive" context, now the second industrial revolution, based on information, is producing what we have called a "turbulent field." In a turbulent field it is as if the "ground" itself is in motion, not merely a number of "figures."

This state of affairs has been described by several writers in different terms. Schon [59] refers to loss of the stable state, Ozbekhan [47] to irrationality in the whole, Vickers [78; 79] to transcendence of the limits of the regulable. The turbulence results from the effects, direct and indirect, or accelerating technological change. This has vastly increased the levels of uncertainty, complexity, and interdependence in the world process, however unevenly this may be proceeding within and between countries. It has produced the "future shock" that Toffler [69] has made a byword. It has also produced "past shock," if one takes into account the influence, especially on the young, of writers concerned with "unprogramming" the minds of their readers (with the aid of space age hindsights) from our accustomed view of historical, biological, and cosmological evolution (*cf.* Velikovsky [77] ; Thompson [67]).

How far the human species can adapt successfully to the conditions of a turbulent environment is an open question, not that we are without means of establishing some degree of control over it. Nevertheless, the continued salience of these conditions is strengthening maladaptive social defenses of superficiality, segmentation, and dissociation [18], while increasing stress overload [60] and the degrees of alienation and violence [33] .

Currently prevailing coping mechanisms cannot meet the demands of emergent social processes under these conditions. By currently prevailing coping mechanisms, I refer to a variety of faltering adaptive postures: achievement orientation, bureaucratic organization, fragmented social policies, instrumental problem-solving, keeping the priorities on competition—the list is too long to go on with. These postures have worked well enough (at the "satisficing" level) in the societies that have arisen in the wake of the first industrial revolution, but they will not enable mankind to realize a postindustrial order.

Useless for the purpose of establishing any viable future is simple regression to small preindustrial societies. Equally useless is to let things happen as they may: to take the passive role. Vickers [79] has noted that we have reached the end of "free fall," Crozier [16] that we can no longer depend on the smooth functioning of "auto-regulative processes" in the macroenvironment (whether as regards the market place or population growth). Reference projections, as constructed by futurologists, make the assumption of nonintervention. In consequence they yield disaster scenarios. One of these, the *Limits to Growth* [43] , seems to have given an unusually large number of people a considerable fright. Let us not forget that despair can, as psychoanalysis has shown, function as a resistance and a defense as well as being a direct and overwhelming affect. Under present circumstances it can enable too many for too long to hang on to the more familiar and less difficult passive role.

But if the passive role is no longer available there is no alternative to taking the active role. To take the active role means to intervene. Intervention entails planning.

ADAPTIVE PLANNING

Planning on a large scale has emerged in Western societies since World War II in response to the increased complexity and faster change rate experienced. The results have been disappointing, and disillusionment is frequently expressed about planning at the present time. But if nonplanning is of no avail and planning is also of no avail, the ensuing double bind begins to seem hopeless. Before concluding that it is, we would do well to consider another possibility: that it is the kinds of planning so far essayed that have been found wanting and that a transformation of the planning process might offer a way out.

During the fifties, and to some extent during the sixties, planning efforts were guided by comprehensive planning. This assumed that the whole system could move forward in step and be maintained in balance, that all future system states were knowable and could be predicted and controlled. It proceeded, therefore, in terms of blueprints and forecasts. But emerging open-ended social reality refused to do what it was told. Vast miscalculations were made in urban development, in schemes for health and social services, in prescriptions for ailing economies and in formulae for getting the developing countries to the point of take-off. Similar miscalculations have been made in designing complex industrial organizations, schools, prisons, *etc.*

When comprehensive planning was seen not to work, its opposite was tried in the form of disjointed incrementalism. Particularly as developed by Hirschman and Lindblom [30], this assumed that growth requires imbalance. This alternative worked admirably in fields such as weapons design in which innovations in one subsystem, being pushed to the limit, had the consequence of forcing innovations in others, that may not otherwise have taken place. In such fields, however, the value-base has already been selected, the general direction set, the overall mission defined. In fields where these conditions are not satisfied, disjointed incrementalism has turned out to be no better than "muddling through." Degenerating into nonplanning, it has landed us back in the double bind. Disjointed incrementalism would hold up in such fields only if it could be shown that the resolution of conflicts between parts would take care of the whole when no overriding value direction has been established at this level. Unfortunately, in all major fields of social planning and organizational design, the determination of a value direction is the fundamental problem that we must face.

Though opposite in important respects, comprehensive planning and disjointed incrementalism are similar in that both assume that what McWhnney [40] has termed "domain selection" has already taken place: *i.e.*, that what we should do can be taken as given, or left to chance (for these statements are equivalent in that each asserts that domain selection is "no problem"). For this reason, comprehensive planning and disjointed incrementalism are both forms of instrumentalism. In developing his concept of "appreciation," Vickers [78] has shown the danger of overemphasizing the instrumental aspect of policy-making. The appreciative aspect that melds together judgments of value and of fact, to allow domain selection, is the more critical and has been neglected.

The transformed planning theory that can more effectively replace comprehensive planning and disjointed incrementalism emphasizes appreciation (in Vickers' sense) rather than instrumentalism. It is becoming known as adaptive planning. Writers such as Friedman [23], Michaels [44], Friend and Jessop [24], Ackoff [1], Jantsch [32], and Ozbekhan [47] all in their own way exemplify this direction of thought, as do Emery, my close collaborator from Tavistock days, and I. Adaptive planning is concerned with the creation of adaptive social organizations capable of continuous learning. It asserts the primacy of the normative level and of the proactive posture, and the necessity for multiple interest group engagement if implementation is to be achieved. It looks forward to the establishment of a "negotiated order" (*cf.* Strauss [64]) with repeated feedback for evaluation and self-correction.

An elucidation of what this set of terms might mean is best begun by referring to the concept of a "design principle" as developed by Emery. The values that govern men's lives are embodied in their organizations. These may be built either on the redundancy of parts, which expresses the machine principle, or the redundancy of functions, which expresses the life principle. The machine principle proceeds by the elaboration of external controls, the life principle by the elaboration of internal controls. Each additional control contains its own error. A system that debases its primary parts and compensates by building up serried ranks of external controls contains more error than a system that enhances its primary parts by building in internal controls that make them self-regulating. For then the number of external controls becomes far fewer, and the error in the total system is reduced. This makes a system based on maximizing the self-regulation of the primary parts better able to cope with rising levels of environmental uncertainty, complexity, and interdependence than a system based on maximizing external regulation. Its adaptability and flexibility, and, therefore, its survival value, are far greater, as is its capacity to learn.

The primary parts in social systems are people. The basic issue, therefore, is whether our designs enhance or debase the quality of human life.

The social systems created by men differ in a fundamental respect from systems that are simply biological; though a biological system as a whole may exhibit purpose, its component organs do not, whereas the component organs of a social system are men who are themselves purposeful systems (Ackoff and Emery [2]). Given their capacity to think abstractly as well as concretely, men in making societies, create metapurposes (called by Ackoff and Emery ideals). Indeed these authors think man can be distinguished from other species in respect of his being an "ideal-seeking system."

There are, therefore, sound reasons in general systems theory for assigning primacy to the normative level. The implications for planning, considered as a "system of human action," have been clarified by Ozbekhan [47] in his distinction between results and consequences. Results are immediate outcomes of specific courses of action. Consequences are more distant outcomes, which include effects that may appear in wider social systems often only after considerable periods of time. Many of these effects are unintended. The first task of the planner is to envision as far as he can the field of possible consequences of contemplated courses of action. This may be a difficult technical task, but only by undertaking it can we determine what ought to be done. The normative decision consists in selecting a set of intended and desirable consequences. This now creates the problems of strategic choice and thence of securing appropriate operational outcomes. The sequence is from what ought to be done to what can be done to what will be done, as summarized in Figure 1A. Then this must be carried out, evaluated and corrected in the spirit, and by the evolving methods of action research—else no learning takes place.

The paradox is that by being normative we become experimental, reaching the action research mentality rather than arresting ourselves in dogma or flying by the seat of our pants.

The normative approach involves taking the proactive posture as conceived by Russell L. Ackoff and summarized in Figure 1B. Reactive planning is concerned with putting right a state of affairs that has already gone wrong. It involves the wait-and-see attitude, the satisficing level of aspiration, and the use of feasibility as a basic criterion. It proceeds in terms of the art of the possible.

More technically ambitious is preactive planning, which involves forward programming with the aid of instrumental technologies (PERT, PPBS and cost-benefit analysis would be examples). It reflects the "predict and prepare" attitude and attempts to optimize in terms of a quantitative criterion. While allowing for contingencies it does not envisage systemic change. It proceeds in terms of the art of the calculable.

Proactive planning opens up a very different world, being based on the "make it happen" attitude. This means taking the active role to bring about a "willed future" chosen as a desirable path from the analysis of fields of consequences. Entailed is the building up of adaptive flexibility in the face of environmental

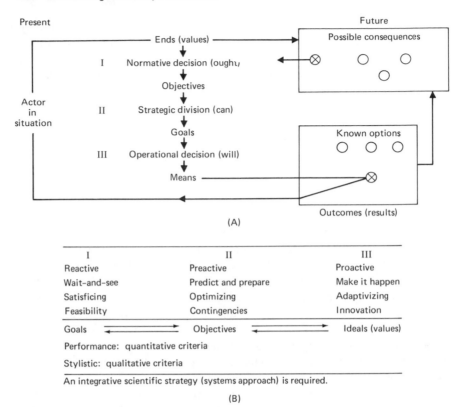

Figure 1. A, planning levels (adapted from Ozbekhan). B, planning postures (adapted from Ackoff).

uncertainty. Proactive planning involves innovation because systemic change is postulated as required. But as the outcome is uncertain (is incalculable), it must proceed in terms of action research.

Ackoff also distinguishes between performance and stylistic objectives. Performance objectives are solely concerned with efficiency. By contrast, stylistic objectives are idiomatic and qualitative. They express preferences that embody value judgments. Stylistic objectives are concerned with effectiveness in terms of preserving or developing a wholeness that is valued by those concerned. Wholeness is particular, not general. It has an aesthetic quality that counters depersonalization.

Stylistic preferences embody the ultimate ends that govern normative choices. Ackoff defines ideals as ends that can be approached but never reached—hence their compelling, sustaining power. Objectives can be reached but not in the period planned for, whereas goals can, and should, be reached in the period planned for.

It was noted earlier that reference projections model the future on the assumption that no interventions will take place. Their use is to identify areas requiring intervention. In fast-changing, complex, turbulent environments, a number of these areas have disaster potential. Reactive planning would be too late, preactive planning too slight to cope with disturbances on such a scale. Only proactive planning has a chance of anticipating and preventing them.

But how are large numbers of people to become able to learn to make these critical choices and to follow through their implications in appropriate courses of action? The experts known as planners are advisers only. The plans that count—those that will be implemented—must be evolved by those directly concerned. In relation to this aspect of the planning process Michel Chevalier's theory of interest-group planning [12] has particular relevance. Interest-group planning involves progressively knitting together the multiple interest groups concerned in social action programs by involving them in the identification and selection of objectives and goals and in the execution and evaluation of what was attempted. Adaptive planning is democratic, for without participation that learning cannot occur that will allow resistance to change to be overcome.

The presence of a participatory factor means that the tempo of adaptive planning will be slow. It will be too slow to meet effectively the challenges arising from rapidly moving dysfunctional processes in turbulent macroenvironments —unless means can be found that will accelerate the learning process. Several studies suggest that there is a line of hope. As long as organizations feel no need to attempt more than forward or projective planning, which is largely programming involving the use of predict-and-prepare instrumentalities, they are content and able to go it alone. When, however, they begin to feel a need to venture into futures or prospective planning, and begin to take the proactive posture, they find that they encounter metaproblems ("messes" in Ackoff's terminology), rather than simply problems. Metaproblems they cannot solve by going it alone. This wider form of *problematique* commonly affects a number of organizations so that collaborative relations must be established. These collaborative relations entail assembling what Chevalier refers to as "a caste of organizational characters." The assembly of such castes can be promoted as a conscious planning strategy.

The assembly and progressive linkage of castes of organizational characters lends support to a hypothesis put forward by Emery and me: that in turbulent fields dissimilar organizations tend to become positively correlated. When problems transform themselves into metaproblems one has to contend with them subjectively and objectively at the same time, for they exist in oneself as well as in the others with whom one has to deal. This supplies a basis for cooperation that would not otherwise exist. Not that the basis of cooperation is likely to be total, covering all the interests of all the parties; it is more likely to be partial. Systems theory would suggest that the common areas are likely to be among the most embracing—those that relate the caste as a whole to still wider groups in the transactional and contextual environments. In this way win-lose situations may be avoided and win-win situations identified within which give-and-take can take place on proximate issues. One of the principal tasks of adaptive planning becomes that of improving the simultaneous management of relations of cooperation and competition in sets of organizations. These dilemmas pose problems of "organizational ecology" [21]. They give scope for new kinds of process intervention in interorganizational relations, conceived of as social matrices and social networks.

Another principle aim of adaptive planning is to reduce the disturbance emanating from environomental sources by increasing the variety in respondent systems. This is an application of Ashby's law (1960) of requisite variety. An organism or organization cannot meet increasing variety in its environment unless it increases the range of its response repertoire. This requirement imparts to adaptive planning an inherently innovative as well as an inherently democratic character.

The value of being variety-increasing also supplies a criterion for the critical evaluation of policies and programs. An example of a variety-increasing program in the mental health field is a family clinic being pioneered in South Philadelphia. Not only is the clinic staffed by paramedicals, with the psychiatrist and other M.D.s as resource personnel, but the aim is to improve the capability of each family to develop its own health plan. The clientele will become less dependent on, but more skillful in using, scarce professional resources. The professionals must be willing to deprofessionalize so that laymen may become more professional. This is one meaning of deschooling a society, and illustrates in a practical from what is entailed in the creation of a continuous learning system. This project has been explicitly undertaken as action research.

To be variety-increasing is to follow the design principle of the redundancy of functions. Adaptive planning is, therefore, antibureaucratic, for bureaucracies are variety-reducing. Based on the redundancy of parts, they grow by the elaboration of external rather than internal controls, accumulating in so doing a degree of error that makes them unadaptable to the complex, fast-changing environments now emerging. To transform bureaucracies into learning systems constitutes still another of the principal tasks of adaptive planning.

OPERATIONAL IMPLICATIONS

A clue as to how this transformation might be effected is afforded by the experience with autonomous work groups that has been accumulating over the last 25 years, first in manufacturing and later in administrative organizations, and in the public as well as in the private sector.   The ability of autonomous work groups to regulate their activities more effectively than when these are carried out under close supervision, and by so doing to afford a higher quality of work life to their members, was first demostrated in Britain [70]. This led to the formulation of the sociotechnical concept concerned with what has become known as the joint optimization of social and technical systems.

The wider importance of this theory, however, was not recognized until the Norwegian Industrial Democracy project, as a combined operation in action research and adaptive planning [19], got under way during the sixties (with the support of the Norwegian Confederations of Employers and Labour and later of the Government).   In the last five years the process has spread into Sweden, with Saab-Scania and Volvo abandoning the assembly line.   Now in the seventies, the seriousness of work-alienation has become generally recognized and in all industrial countries planned attempts are being made (though still for the most part on a small scale) to introduce more democracy into the workplace.

The value change involved is fundamental, entailing a complete shift in design principle from the redundancy of parts to the redundancy of functions. Such a fundamental change cannot be confined to one subsystem of an organization. The larger system either negates it or is transformed by it.   The sustaining of such transformations requires the working out of a new organizational philosophy, as in the Tavistock project with Shell's refineries in Britain [29].   This must make explicit the relevant implications of the value change in terms acceptable to and understandable by all concerned—at all levels, including the trade unions.   It must also show how individual and organizational purposes may be reconciled, and how these purposes relate to wider societal changes.   The more bureaucratic controls are reduced, the more does it become evident that shared values are decisive in holding the members of an organization together under the conditions of turbulent fields.

The articulation of these principles makes it more likely that new organizations will be designed in the new idiom.   In fact, quite a number of industrial plants and a few nonindustrial organizations that make systematic use of them have already been brought into being.   In a number of them the users, both managers and workers, have collaborated with the designers in evolving the plan as well as implementing it.   Moreover, these organizations have commenced operations aware that design will always remain unfinished.   For not only will improvements be made as experience is gained, but alterations, sometimes radical, will be necessary as unforeseen circumstances are encountered. These organizations are continuous learning systems that continuously use adaptive planning and "research" what they are doing.

One or two of these organizations have now been in existence long enough for there to be some evidence that experience of greater participation in the workplace has induced greater participation in the family and in community activities. Just as one key subsystem of an organization cannot sustain significant change unless corresponding changes take place in others, so significant change cannot be sustained in one part of the life space of the individual without congruent change occurring elsewhere. Systematic use may be made of this interdependence in adaptive planning. Moreover, the change-originating area may lie within any class of organizations and be correlated with any sector of the life space: education, as in the rise and rapid spread of student participation; the family, as in the advent of the dual-career family [53]; psychiatry, as in the extent to which the model of the therapeutic community has influenced parts of society scarcely aware that therapeutic communities exit.

One key strategy for accelerating the learning process is to bring together in temporary assemblies more frequently those concerned with steering congruent change processes in different social sectors. A multiplier effect may so be obtained.

In his recently proposed STEM model, Chevalier [13] has extended the sociotechnical concept from operating organizations to the regulation of the urban field by considering the relation of physical to social planning. De Greene [26] has proposed a general sociotechnical treatment of all societal domains.

SOCIAL AGGREGATIONS

The perspective of our analysis so far has been that of people as members of structured role sets (organizations). The complementary perspective is that of people as members of social aggregates, whether of their society as a whole or segregable parts of it. The social individual exists as much as the social actor (even if sociology neglects the one and pyschology the other). Churchman and Emery [15] refer to populations as the duals of organizations. Following Lewin, they suggest that such statistical aggregates have the properties of power fields. If the structure of an organization composes a social figure, its members, as an aggregate, make a social ground. The connections between ground and ground are more fluid than between figure and figure. For the social individual as "culture carrier," as Edward Sapir noted long ago [57], takes with him wherever he goes all the part-inclusions of himself that pertain to his various organizational roles.

It is my hypothesis that in complex turbulent environments the power fields exerted by social aggregates become stronger than under simpler and more stable conditions. Though the contrary is more usually affirmed, people are no longer so bound by social structures as they used to be. Cats have improved their knack of getting out of bags. The high priest, the professional, the patent office, and even the Official Secrets Act cannot contain them with their accustomed aplomb. When leaks occur they are apt to travel rather rapidly and quite far (as certain disclosures recently made in the United States may serve to illustrate). The social ground, however, is a conductor of matters more substantial than leaks—life styles and new values, for example. Schon [59] comments on the extent to which the contemporary youth movement has spread round the world without needing to establish any formal structure. McLuhan's contribution [38; 39] is to have understood these phenomena earlier and more deeply than academic social scientists. The media made available by the technologies of the second industrial revolution are indeed turning the world into a global village—in the sense that they are establishing a common ground in the contextual environment.

Our training has made us figure-focused, disabling us from perceiving the ground. Should we not turn our gaze away from the hills and, as ideal-seeking systems, learn to look downward? In my hypothesis the most important change forces operating at present are working in the social ground rather than in the institutional figures we have erected upon it. These figures will undergo adaptive change as they learn to resettle themselves on the ground that is changing beneath them. For this ground constitutes their value-base.

Adaptive planners must learn to work with the ground forces. But who are the adaptive planners? They certainly include the leaders of many of the grass-roots movements at present afoot. With these, institutionally based change-agents must, if they are to succeed, become "engaged," or "directively correlated" —to use the concept introduced by Sommerhoff [63]. An example is Ackoff's work [1] with the black community neighboring the University of Pennsylvania, one of the longest sustained and most successful action research and adaptive planning enterprises currently proceeding in the United States. The prototype evolved has already been reproduced in several other cities. It has involved the choice of a smaller unit than that used by community planners who have based themselves on a whole urban system.

In *Est, the Steerman's Handbook*, Clarke Stevens [65], a social critic from California, puts certain aspects of this whole matter in a way I have found particularly useful. Having defined the "establishment" as the population block whose thinking has remained exclusively linear, he refers to what he calls "neo-primitives" as a population block whose thinking has become exclusively nonlinear. Contrasted with both are the Est people who are able to think simultaneously in the linear and nonlinear modes. These are the "novelty detectors."

Ravenswaaij [54], the Dutch social psychiatrist, uses this term to draw a parallel between a connector in the brain, which has this function, and the innovating individual. In such people a form of consciousness is building up that may allow the future to be shaped in ways compatible with survival.

Est consciousness is not confined to the members of countercultures, most of whom are neoprimitives. It may exist in anyone, in any role, in any institutional setting, in any age group, though it is more common among those generations on the younger side of their midlife crisis. Positive resolution of the midlife crisis (in the sense of Erickson and Jung) increases the likelihood, as I would see it, of older people being able to keep "out front" in their value position. A vanguard of the older is necessary as well as a vanguard of the younger, their experience being complementary. Intergenerational coalitions are, I believe, beginning to form at the present time on such issues as the ecological, population, and energy crises—the broadest themes whose scope enables conflicting subgroups to unite.

The word consciousness is used to indicate that a person cannot deny what he has come to see, perception having a "demand character" more compelling than that of belief alone. The Est person cannot help but behave along the line of his insight, wherever he is and whatever he is doing. It is his behavior that makes him a steersman, and thus able to act as a natural learning center, and to create more room for the future in any role space he happens to occupy.

Est people tend to recognize each other. Being widely dispersed throughout the social aggregate, the networks they form extend continuously. Their latent capability to introduce learning into social structures is considerable. We must learn to walk through walls—a strategy of change that befits an electronic age.

In connection with castes of organizational characters, further mention must be made of the importance of "shared parts" as a means of adapting to turbulent environments. If the metaproblems encountered in the "prospective" tend to induce cooperation, this cooperation, as was noted, is likely to be less than total among the organizations concerned. Which parts can best go with which becomes the critical issue for adaptive planning and action research jointly to establish.

Some organizations have begun to make considerable headway with this problem. For example, in fields such as the multinational corporation [49; 50], the resources required are often too great for even relatively large firms to go it alone. Volvo and Peugeot are building a joint engine plant in France while continuing to produce their own passenger models. Complex clusters of multiply linked parts are appearing with bewildering rapidity among medium-sized enterprises. Nor is this process confined to industry. Recently a medical colleague of mine persuaded three hospitals in a small American town each to supply one major service on behalf of all while retaining their independence in other respects. Even a number of universities in the United States, some quite celebrated, are exploring interdependent arrangements, recognizing that no one can excel in all departments and that some pooling will be beneficial from both an educational and an economic viewpoint. The British and the French are collaborating to develop the Channel Region, the Danes and the Swedes to develop the Sound. The countries of the Andean Pact have begun to allocate key activities on a regional basis, and have developed an investment code likely to become a model for other regional groupings in the Third World. The OPEC-prompted emergence of a new Islamic identity may permit cooperation among countries hitherto in disarray. In Cairo there is already an Arab World Bank. In London an East West Bank. Europe has pooled research in high energy physics in Bern. The US and the USSR have begun to share resources in fusion research.

INTERDEPENDENCY AND THE PLURALISTIC PERSPECTIVE

What is new in all these instances is the acceptance of interdependence as a cardinal value and the consequent attempt to replace competitive with cooperative relations. By such means a negotiated order may be established first in some areas and then in others. The establishment of a negotiated order is essential for the social regulation of a turbulent environment. To find ways of bringing it into being is a central task for adaptive planning; and it requires action research, of the most concrete kind, with multiple pilots. The program inaugurated by the National Quality-of-Work Center in the United States to establish 20 demonstration projects in work-quality, each jointly "owned" by management and union in key industries across the country, may serve to illustrate. They are being independently evaluated.

The establishment of a negotiated order will entail a process with which *not* many of us, I suspect, have yet become comfortable—namely some surrender of sovereignty—psychosocially and sociopolitically. Nurtured as we have been in a tradition of individualism, the cultivation of interdependence will entail us in new learnings: at the level of the individual the discovery of the self rather than the pursuit of the ego—the process Jung has called centroversion; at the societal level acceptance of the fact that the nation-state and its physical boundaries are less sacred than the cultural configuration in which man's core identities are molded. Without a core identity of their own, firmly established in such a mold, people cannot confidently relate to others with core identities also firmly established in other molds. They lack the security to tolerate pluralism, which, if necessary in the present, is likely to be even more necessary in the future.

Along with surrender of sovereignty goes surrender of power. To acquire power, whether at the individual, corporate, or national levels, has been the strategy of choice for survival in the societies of the first industrial revolution— the era now drawing to a close. To continue the power game (balanced or unbalanced) into the world being brought into being by the second industrial revolution is a strategy of suicide. The levels of complexity and uncertainty are too great for the necessary control to be obtained. The greater interdependence of the parts of the environment requires a greater interdependence among the actors—compelling some surrender of power. But the criteria for deciding who should have what, and how much constitutes a fair share, have scarcely been worked out by any western society. On their being worked out depends the feasibility of establishing a negotiated order. Severe conflicts may be expected, which it will be a task of adaptive planning to diminish.

A related but neglected issue that planners and their clients must face in attempting to regulate better the transition from industrialism to postindustrialism is the *confusion* that abounds in contemporary western societies over the relations of welfare and development.* I will offer a systems treatment that may serve the interests of clarification.

1. Welfare, or well-being (to continue to function well), refers to states of a system under conditions that maintain the steady state. Its opposite, illfare or ill-being (to be dysfunctional), refers to states of a system under conditions that do not permit the steady state to be maintained. Welfare is concerned with the "statics" of adaptation—with stability (not to be confused with stagnation, which is a state of illfare) and with the regulation and maintenance of stability.

2. Development or progression (to continue to advance), refers to processes by which a system reaches higher order steady states of a more adaptive nature. Its opposite, deterioration or retrogression (to go back), refers to processes by which the system returns to states of a lower order (stagnant or unstable), which are maladaptive. Development is concerned with the "dynamics" of adaptation—with positive change leading to the establishment of widened and preferred orders (not to be confused with negative change, which leads to disorder). Development involves discovery and innovation. It is concerned with the regulation and maintenance of growth.

Let us first consider development as a function of welfare. This state expresses the relation that obtains under conditions of the more placid environments, where the maintenance of stability is the principal requirement for adaptation. It is typified by preindustrial societies, particularly in their earlier and simpler forms:

a. Welfare is maintained by autoregulative processes operating through the kinship system, which plays the role of a "leading," or pivotal, part.

b. Development measures are required to maintain established states of welfare when autoregulative mechanisms can no longer cope in the face of

*These ideas were originally developed for the Conference on Welfare and Development, Canadian Center for Community Studies, Ottawa, 1967, and are further elaborated in [21].

internal and external threats. Development processes under these conditions are not autoregulative, but involve taking the active role. Modes of intervention in these societies are characterized by coercive methods, illustrated in the rise of autocratic regimes with bureaucracies and regular armies.

Let us next consider welfare as a function of development. This state expresses the relation that obtains as the environment becomes more dynamic, when internally generated growth (resulting from technological change) is now the principle requirement for adaptation. This state is typified by industrial societies.

    a. Development is maintained by autoregulative processes operating through the market system, where enterprises now play the role of the leading part.

    b. The welfare of increasingly numerous classes of people and segments of society is no longer autoregulative. The maintenance of their welfare requires taking an active role. Modes of intervention in industrial societies cannot remain solely coercive if disturbances of a revolutionary type are to be offset. Legislative reform based on "democracy by consent" (Clegg, 1960) makes its appearance.

SOME POLICY IMPLICATIONS

Finally, let us consider welfare and development as interdependent functions. This state expresses the relation that obtains as turbulent conditions become salient in the transition to the postindustrial society. Adaptation now depends on the socioecological regulation of the interdependencies in all their dimensions of the innumerable subsystems that characterize large societies undergoing rapid but uneven change.

    a. The welfare of subsystems now inherently involves their development; otherwise the accelerating change rate soon renders them obsolescent— when they fall into states of illfare.

    b. Subsystem interdependence also increases so that states of illfare in a relatively few subsystems (especially if their position is crucial) can produce widespread dysfunction in larger systems. The development of particular subsystems is dependent on the welfare of other subsystems to a greater extent than when the degree of societal interdependence is less.

    c. Unevenness in a change rate widens the range of outcomes, so that social segmentation increases. The number of groups perceiving themselves, or being perceived, in subthreshold states becomes greater as the expectations that set the thresholds rise and as the sense of "relative deprivation" grows.

    d. The effects of these contradictory trends are magnified by an increase in the number, diversity, and size of subsystems, which raises the overall level of complexity.

    e. This, in turn, raises the level of uncertainty. It now becomes less possible for a given subsystem to remain directively correlated with a relatively closed set (*e.g.*, for agriculture to live in the "rural world"). Each member of the immediate set to which a subsystem belongs tends to be linked with a growing and changing number of other sets that cannot be completely identified. These sets tend to be related to each other in different ways, and often belong to different "universes." It, therefore, becomes harder to predict if, or for how long, a particular subsystem will continue to develop, or remain in a state of welfare.

The metaproblems created in this situation pass the limit within which auto-regulative processes can adaptively operate with respect to either welfare or development, so that an active role becomes required, *i.e.*, adaptive planning becomes mandatory. Such planning must base itself on the premise that the best development is the one that promotes welfare and the best welfare the one that promotes development. The one has become transeconomic, the other trans-social in a world where economic and social costs can no longer be separated. Neither can be neglected at the expense of the other.

This statement has many implications. One entails opting for production for durability as a new *economic* value, along with improvement of the quality of work life as a new *social* value. To give up producing for obsolescence will do as much as anything to slow economic growth in an acceptable way. To give up designing jobs simply as instruments for extrinsic satisfaction and transform them into means of intrinsic satisfaction will do as much as anything to restrain insatiable wage demands in a way that will make inflation control acceptable (not forgetting also the regulation of prices and profits).

I would be wrong to conclude this paper without referring to the role of planning in the developing countries. It is already apparent that their pattern of development cannot follow ours, and that, unless they find a different model, we will be drawn into their suffering, since the world as a whole has become interdependent. Therefore, the concept of development styles, introduced by Ignacy Sachs [56] seems to me to have much to commend it. He begins with the *consumption* rather than production pattern; in relation to this he considers the *resource* base, the *energy level* and its preferred modalities, and, in relation to all of these, *innovative* rather than transferred technologies that might best improve their situation. Is there not something that we in the advanced countries can learn from this approach?

As a final thought let me draw your attention to the importance of small advanced countries as laboratories for social innovation. Because they have small and well-educated populations and distinctive traditions, they can often pioneer changes more difficult to manage in large heterogeneous countries. I got to thinking this way through being involved in projects in Scandinavia. Countries such as Australia and Canada, though they have large land masses, have relatively small populations and traditions of the kind described and, therefore, belong in my category of small advanced countries.   At any rate I have found myself able to perceive certain relationships and processes when I have been working in Canada that I have not been able to see when in the United States or even in Britain—in the thralls as it is of coming to terms with the larger European Economic Community.   For example, the connections between emerging cultural values, organizations, philosophies, and strategies of social ecology, which are developed in *Towards a Social Ecology* are the result of work I did there.   They are central to my thinking about planning under conditions of uncertainty.   One of the suggestions they contain is that we should build our institutions in ways that use more of the understanding of the human service professions and less of the formulas of the engineering professions, and embody the redundancy of functions rather than the redundancy of parts.

These requirements are all concerned with improving the quality of life—in the world as a whole.   For me this is the overriding value that must guide the normative choices on which the planning process and its associated change strategies must depend.   And I don't see how we can test the appropriateness or measure the effectiveness of the operations we then engage in unless we subject them to action research whether of the more implicit or the more explicit kind.   Let us be content with modest observation under some conditions, but demand rigorous analysis under others.

Ideally, everyman will become his own change-agent and his own researcher. Moreover, he need not lose out on living by so doing.   The split between thought and being, research and action belongs to our minds, not to existence.   Action research and adaptive planning, in interpenetrating each other, are beginning to create a new modality that will hold them together.

NOTES AND REFERENCES

1. Ackoff, R. L. *A Concept of Corporate Planning*. New York: Wiley, 1969.
2. Ackoff, R. L., and F. E. Emery. *On Purposeful Systems*. Chicago: Aldine Press, 1972.
3. Angyal, A. *Foundations for a Sciecne of Personality*. Cambridge: Harvard University Press, 141. Reissued 1958.
4. Argyris, C. *Integrating the Individual and the Organization*. New York: Wiley, 1964.
5. Bennis, W. G., and P. E. Slater. *The Temporary Society*. New York: Harper & Row, 1968.
6. Bennis, W. G., K. D. Benne, and R. Chin eds. *The Planning of Change*. New York: Holt, Rinehart and Winston, 1969.
7. Bion, W. R. *Experience in Groups*. London: Tavistock Publications, 1961.
8. Blake, R. R., and J. S. Mouton. *The Managerial Grid*. Houston, Texas: Gulf, 1964.
9. Boulding, K. *The Image: Knowledge in Life and Society*. Ann Arbor: University of Michigan Press, 1956.
10. Boulding, K. "Conflict Management as a Learning Process." In *Conflict in Society*. Edited by A. de Reuck. London: Churchill, 1966.

11. Burns, T., and G. Stalker. *The Management of Innovation.* London: Tavistock Publications, 1961.
12. Chevalier, M. "Interest Group Planning," Ph.D. thesis, University of Pennsylvania, 1968.
13. Chevalier, M. Unpublished manuscript, Université de Montreal, 1973.
14. Churchman, C. W., *et al. Experiments on Inquiring Systems.* Berkeley: Social Sciences Group, Space Sciences Laboratory, University of California, 1967.
15. Churchman, C. W., and F. E. Emery. "On Various Approaches to the Study of Organizations. In *Operational Research and the Social Sciences.* Edited by J. R. Lawrence. London: Tavistock Publications, 1966.
16. Crozier, M. *The Bureaucratic Phenomenon.* London: Tavistock Publications; Chicago: University of Chicago Press, 1964.
17. Emery, F. E., and E. L. Trist. "The Causal Texture of Organizational Environments." *Hum. relat.* 18: 21–32.
18. Emery, F. E. "The Next Thirty Years: Concepts, Methods and Anticipations." *Hum. relat.* 20: 199–237.
19. Emery, F. E., and E. Thorsrud. *Form and Content in Industrial Democracy.* London: Tavistock Publications, 1969 (Norwegian edition, Oslo University Press, 1964).
20. Emery, F. E., ed. *Systems Thinking.* London: Penguin, 1969.
21. Emery, F. E., and E. L. Trist. *Towards a Social Ecology.* New York: Plenum Press, 1972.
22. Erickson, E. H. *Identity: Youth and Crisis.* London: Faber & Faber, 1968.
23. Friedman, J. *Retracking America.* New York: Doubleday, 1973.
24. Friend, J., and N. Jessop. *Local Government: A Strategy for Choice.* London: Tavistock Publications, 1969.
25. Fulton, Lord (Chairman). *The Civil Service,* vol. 1: *Report of the Committee.* London: Her Majesty's Stationery Office, Command 3638, 1968.
26. Greene de, K. B. *Socio-Technical Systems.* Englewood Cliffs, N.J.: 1973.
27. Gross, M. B. "The State of the Nation." In *Social Indicators.* Edited by R. Bauer. Cambridge: MIT Press; London: Tavistock Publications, 1966.
28. Gross, B. M., ed. *Action Under Planning.* New York: McGraw-Hill, 1966.
29. Hill, C. P. *Towards a New Philosophy of Management.* London: Gower Press, 1971.
30. Hirschman and Lindblom. *In Systems Thinking.* Edited by Emery. Harmondsworth: Penguin Books, 1969.
31. Hutton, G. *Thinking about Organization.* Bath: Bath University Press, 1969.
32. Jantsch, E. *Technological Planning and Social Futures.* New York: Halsted Press (Wiley), 1973.
33. Laing, R. D. *The Politics of Experience.* London: Penguin Books, 1961.
34. Lawrence, P. R., and J. W. Lorsch. *Organization and Environment.* Division of Research, Graduate School of Business Administration, Harvard University, Cambridge, 1967.
35. Likert, R. *The Human Organization: Its Management and Value.* New York: McGraw-Hill, 1967.
36. McGregor, D. *The Human Side of Enterprise.* New York: McGraw-Hill, 1960.
37. McGregor, D. *The Professional Manager.* New York: McGraw-Hill, 1969.
38. McLuhan, M. *Understanding Media.* New York: McGraw-Hill; London: Routledge & Kegan Paul, 1964.
39. McLuhan, M. and N. Barrington. *Take To-day—The Executive as Drop-out.* New York: Harcourt Brace, 1972.

40. McWhinney, W. "Organizational Form, Decision Modalities and the Environment." *Hum. relat.* 21: 269–281.
41. Mann, F. *Studying and Creating Change: A Means to Understanding Social Organization.* Industrial Relations Research Association, Publication No. 17, 1957.
42. Maslow, A. H. *Toward a Psychology of Being.* Princeton, N.J.: Van Nostrand, 1962.
43. Meadows, I., *et al. The Limits to Growth.* Cambridge, MIT Press, 1971.
44. Michaels, D. *Learning to Plan—Planning to Learn.* San Francisco: Jossey-Bass, 1973.
45. Murray, H. *An Approach to Appraisal.* Tavistock Institute of Human Relations, Doc. T. 63, 1963.
46. Nylen, D., *et al. Handbook of Staff Development and Human Relations Training.* N.T.L., N.E.A., 1201 Sixteenth St., N.W., Washington, D.C., 1967.
47. Ozbekhan, H. "Planning and Human Action." In *Hierarchically Organized Systems in Theory and Practice.* Edited by Paul A. Weiss. New York: Hafner, 1971.
48. Pepper, S. C. *World Hypotheses.* Berkeley, University of California Press, 1961.
49. Perlmutter, H. V. "L'entreprise Internationale—Trois Conceptions." *Revue economique et sociale* 2(1965): 1–14.
50. Perlmutter, H. V. *Some Management Problems in Spaceship Earth: the Mega Firm and the Global Industrial Estate.* In Managing Complex Organizations. Edited by W. P. Scott and P. P. le Breton. Seattle: University of Washington Press, 1969.
51. Perlmutter, H. V. *Toward a Theory and Practice of Social Architecture.* London: Tavistock Publications, 1965.
52. Rapoport, R. N. *Mid-Career Development.* London: Tavistock Publications, 1970.
53. Rapoport, R., and R. N. Rapoport. *The Dual Career Family.* Harmondsworth: Penguin Books, 1970.
54. Ravenswaaij, I. Paper presented to Strategies for Change Conference WFMH, Amsterdam, 1972.
55. Rice, A. K. *Productivity and Social Organization: The Ahmedabad Experiment.* London: Tavistock Publications, 1958.
56. Sachs, I. *La Decouverte du Tiers Monde.* Paris: Flammarion, 1971.
57. Sapir, E. International Seminar on the Impact of Culture on Personality. Yale University, 1932.
58. Schein, E. H. and W. G. Bennis eds. *Personal and Organizational Change Through Group Methods: The Laboratory Approach.* New York: Wiley, 1965.
59. Schon, D. A. *Beyond the Stable State.* London: Temple Smith; New York: Basic Books, 1971.
60. Selye, H. "The Stress Syndrome." In *Stress and Psychiatric Disorder.* Edited by Tanner. Oxford: Blackwell, 1958.
61. Selznick, P. *Leadership in Administration.* Illinois: Roe Peterson, 1957.
62. Sofer, C. *Men in Mid Career.* Cambridge: Cambridge University Press, 1970.
63. Sommerhoff, G. "The Abstract Characteristics of Living Systems." In *Systems Thinking.* Edited by F. E. Emery. Harmondsworth, Middlesex: Penguin Books, 1969.
64. Strauss, A., *et al.* "The Hospital and Its Negotiated Order." In *The Hospital in Modern Society.* Edited by E. Friedson. New York: The Free Press, 1964.
65. Stevens, C. *Est—the Steerman's Handbook.* New York: Bantam Books, 1970.
66. Tannenbaum, A. S. *Personnel Survey Methods in Appraising Administrative Capability for Development.* New York: United Nations, 1969.
67. Thompson, A. G. *The Edge of History.* New York: Hafner, 1972.
68. Thompson, J. D. *Organizations in Action.* New York: McGraw-Hill, 1967.
69. Toffler, A. *Future Shock.* New York: Random House, 1970.

70. Trist, E. L., and K. Bamforth. "Some Social and Psychological Consequences of the Longwall Method of Coal-Getting. *Hum. Relat.* 5(1970): 2.
71. Trist, E. L. "Science Policy: The Organization and Financing of Research." Section 3 in *Main Trends in the Social and Human Sciences*, pp. 693–811. Paris: Mouton/ UNESCO, 1970.
72. Trist, E. L. "The Professional Facilitation of Planned Change in Organizations." Review paper, *Proceedings*, International Association of Applied Psychology XVIth International Congress, 1968.
73. Trist, E. L. "A Socio-Technical Critique of Scientific Management." *Proceedings*, Edinburgh Conference on the Impact of Science and Technology, 1970.
74. Trist, E. L. "Organisation et Systeme," *Revue Francaise de Sociologie*: numero special.
75. Trist, E. L., G. W. Higgin, H. Murray, and A. B. Pollock. *Organizational Choice: Capabilities of Groups at the Coal Face under Changing Technologies*. London: Tavistock Publications, 1963.
76. United Nations. "Appraising Administrative Capability for Development." Prepared by Interplan, United Nations, New York, 1969.
77. Velikovsky, I. *Worlds in Collision*. New York: Dell Press, 1950.
78. Vickers, Sir Geoffrey. *The Art of Judgment*. London: Chapman & Hall; New York: Basic Books, 1965.
79. Vickers, Sir Geoffrey. *Value Systems and Social Process*. London: Tavistock Publications; New York: Basic Books, 1968.
80. Weber, M. *The Theory of Social and Economic Organization*. New York: Free Press, 1947.

2

Planning and Policy Analysis for Public Administrators*

Gregory A. Daneke and Alan Walter Steiss
Virginia Polytechnic Institute

INTRODUCTION

Considerable pressure has developed in recent years for more systematic techniques (or "systems" approaches) to resolve the many complex problems and issues confronting government and the constituent publics served by government. This emphasis can be seen in public sector applications of such management science techniques as systems analysis and operations research, in the advent of program budgeting, in the development and refinement of techniques of cost-benefit and cost-effectiveness analysis, in the growing attention to more systematic approaches to policy analysis and evaluation, and in the quest for a science of policy-making.

A Working Definition of Public Policy Analysis

Although many have tried to define public policy analysis as an emerging field of practical inquiry, concensus among these definitions is very rare. This lack of a definitive statement might be explained as follows:

1. The concern for public policy is a fairly recent phenomenon.

*This essay was generated from the overview materials that accompany the Urban Management Curriculum Package completed for the National Technical Development Service through a grant from the Department of Housing and Urban Development. The authors would like to acknowledge the assistance of the other members of the Policy Analysis Team: John Dickey, Harvey Goldstein, Leo Herbert, Elaine Morley, John Ross, Douglas Smith, Robert Stuart, Richard Yearwood, and Richard Zody. Errors, omissions, and painful elaborations of the obvious are, of course, the sole responsibility of the authors.

2. Unique academic disciplines and groups of practitioners have developed highly disparate approaches to the subject.
3. The inquiries of individual research are unavoidably colored by personal preconceptions, as are the collective formulations of various disciplines.
4. Many writers, when dealing with public policy, prefer to use other terms— such as decision, judgment, or choice—without making clear distinctions as to the similarities and differences implicit in these terms.

For example, Thomas Dye, political scientist, has described public policy analysis as the purely descriptive study of "whatever governments choose to do or not to do" [1]. Roy Burke and James Heany, engineers, suggest that it is the investigation of, and involvement in "a series of incremental steps reflecting mutual adjustments among competing interests . . . that attempt to move away from bads rather than toward goods" [2]. Carl Friedrich, political theorist, implies that policy analysis is both the descriptive and prescriptive inquiry directed at "a proposed course of action of a person, group, or government within a given environment providing obstacles and opportunities which the policy was proposed to utilize and overcome in an effort to reach a goal or realize an objective or a purpose" [3].

While the debate continues over the exact content, context, and configuration of policy analysis, it appears that a new professional dimension is gathering momentum. Arnold Meltsner, editor of the journal *Policy Analysis*, suggests the practitioner orientation has become a dominant theme and that it is significantly different from the earlier attempts at scientific investigation [4]. As a professional pursuit it has emerged as a multidisciplinary approach to problem-solving, integrally concerned with the development and execution of policy, as well as its assessment.

Along these lines of thought, and for the purposes of this discussion, the following terms take on their rather stipulative definitions [5]:

1. *Value*—an element of a shared symbolic system (referred to as a value system), acquired through social learning, which serves as a guide for selection from among perceived alternatives of orientation.
2. *Goals*—an articulation of values, formulated in light of identified issues and problems, toward the attainment of which policies and decisions are directed.
3. *Decision*—an intellectual assertion (judgment) as to appropriate ends, or appropriate means to achieve some ends, arrived at after careful consideration and deliberation of alternatives, and conditioned by an articulated policy or set of policies.
4. *Policy*—a) a broad guide to present and future decision, selected in light of given conditions from a number of alternatives; b) the actual decision or set of decisions designed to carry out the chosen course of actions; and c) a projected program consisting of desired objectives (goals) and the means of achieving them.

5. *Program*—a clear statement of action commitments or activities derived from a policy.
6. *Public Policy Analysis*—a systematic process involving the delineation of pertinent problems and issues, the clarification of goals and objectives relevant to these problems, the identification and comparison of available alternative courses of action (often requiring the design and synthesis of new alternatives), and the determination of at least satisfactory (optimum, if possible) means (resources) necessary to attain the desired goals and objectives. Although the policy analysis process may be descriptive or prescriptive, its basic aim is to develop guidelines to assist public policy-makers in the exercise of their judgmental responsibilities regarding action commitments.

A Systematic Approach

Based upon the above list of definitions, this discussion will be concerned primarily with a description of a basic set of tools and strategies applicable to the practical pursuit of policy. Quite obviously, it cannot hope to do justice to the broad array of mechanisms that fall under the rubric of professional policy analysis. It is merely designed to provide a general overview and introduction to this burgeoning enterprise. In this context, the list of devices enumerated in Table 1 will be discussed in summary fashion. These tools and strategies can be categorized into three functional modes. These modes are not entirely mutually

Table 1. A systematic policy process.

FUNCTIONAL MODES	TOOLS AND STRATEGIES
Discovering goals and objectives and generating alternatives	1) Strategic planning 2) Issue paper techniques 3) Long-range forecasting 4) Management by objectives
Financial planning and analysis and the commitment of resources	5) Cost-benefit effectiveness and analysis 6) Performance and program budgeting 7) Capital facilities planning and debt administration
Implementing and evaluating policies and programs	8) Implementation procedures 9) Productivity assessment 10) Performance auditing

exclusive; rather, they represent a continuing and interrelated process of policy development.

This package of tools and strategies is by no means exhaustive. The purpose here is to provide a very basic set of methodologies, a starter set if you will. These techniques cannot resolve every policy dilemma or address every policy issue. No set of techniques provides a panacea for every problem. Policy analysis in general and systematic analysis in particular are delimited by a number of forces ranging from the complexity of social phenomena to the resiliency of political tradition. Thus, it is the larger purpose of this discussion to explore both the constraints and opportunities associated with systematic policy analysis and to leave the reader with an appreciation of its utility and limitations.

DISCOVERING GOALS, FORMULATING OBJECTIVES, AND GENERATING ALTERNATIVES

The initial stage of the policy process is largely one of articulating goals. It is, therefore, a highly qualitative realm. This does not imply armchair analysis or guesswork, rather it is a blend of professional judgment and systematic planning. This realm is where policy practitioners experience the greatest difficulties, but it is also an area of great promise in terms of analytical development. As Kenneth Kraemer has pointed out: "the greatest potential benefit of policy analysis is in just those areas where the problems are the most complex, the costs and risks the highest, the uncertainties the greatest, and the results most likely to be seen only over an extended period of time" [6].

These processes of discovering goals and formulating objectives may be more readily visualized in contrast to the more simplistic applications of quantitative techniques such as operations research and queueing theory. With these mathematical devices, the purpose is to increase efficiency in situations where it is clear what efficiency means. E. S. Quade, for example, describes several case studies in which the policy problem is readily operational (*e.g.*, involving the allocation of resources) such as modeling the routes and schedules of fire engines [7]. There are many other public policy situations, however, where such analytical techniques can only assist in the solution of subproblems or minor components of larger complex problems. Such situations normally involve more than the efficient application of resources among some clearly defined set of alternatives. These more complex problems are not "solvable" in the same sense as efficiency problems in which some "pay-off" function can be maximized in a clear expression of what is to be accomplished. Under these more complex situations, the difficulty often lies in determining what ought to be done (*i.e.*, planning), as well as in how to do it (*i.e.*, management). In these situations it is not altogether clear what "more efficient" really means, and many aspects of the problem may elude quantification.

The devices to be discussed in this section are expressly designed to cope with the challenge of reducing uncertainties in those realms of highest uncertainty and to lend greater objectivity to highly subjective judgments. In this regard, these mechanisms attempt to replace political guesswork with more rigorous approximations of societal demands. In addition, these devices are designed to develop task orientations and establish action commitments within those organizations that must meet these demands.

Strategic Planning

Public officials at all levels of government frequently are criticized for short-sighted decisions and policies. Elected officials are accused of looking forward only as far as the next election and placing narrow, parochial interests above the general public welfare. Administrators may be accused of looking backwards —of being unwilling to adopt new approaches to problem-solving that have not been tested through long-standing practices and procedures. To some extent, such criticisms may be justified, although even the political novice or the administrative neophyte recognizes that his stay in office will be short if he does not take some positive action in the public interest. Such action is the primary objective of strategic planning.

Strategic planning, like many policy processes, has its origins in military history. In the context of military decision-making, the concept implies a comprehensive preparedness sufficient to meet any and all eventualities; strategic planning also implies a synoptic and long-range vision as compared with tactical judgments involving short-range action commitments.

The notion of strategic planning has also become integral to business and industry. In the corporate sphere it suggests anticipating future market conditions. The vital role of long-range corporate planning appears to be an outgrowth of the following trends [8] :

1. The lead time required for production development and organization building.
2. The rapidity of change and the geometric increase in market uncertainty.
3. The increasing size and complexity of organization.

Military planners have to outwit "the enemy," and corporate moguls must outfox the competition or the consumer. Though this type of terminology is rarely applied to local government policy, nevertheless, analogous processes often are apparent. The public manager must anticipate and prevail against the forces that threaten the desires of his agency or community. The planning effort must both define and protect the manager's milieu in much the same way as corporations guard their profit margins and generals defend a nation-state.

To begin to visualize how the concept of strategic planning might be applied to public management, it may be useful to delineate those local government activities that qualify as strategic planning processes:

1. *Infrastructure Improvements:* Strategic planning is often called for in the process of developing long-term investments in capital intensive facilities such as sewers, water supply and treatment projects, and transportation networks.
2. *Capital Improvements:* Strategic planning is particularly useful in the development of public improvements such as parks, fire and police equipment, and schools facilities.
3. *Finance and Debt Administration:* Revenue policies involving assessment, taxing, pensions, and grant requirements qualify as realms of effective strategic planning.
4. *Organizational Development:* Strategic changes in the structure and function of organizations may require careful advanced planning.
5. *Policy Redefinition:* The recognition of policy in response to citizen demands is certainly an area of strategic planning.
6. *Dealing with Natural Disasters:* Unforeseen or potential disasters such as earthquakes, floods, *etc.* demand contingency plans.
7. *Economic or Technological Crises:* Rapid inflation, depression, unemployment, fuel shortages, *etc.* also require the ability to make strategic adjustments.
8. *Major Administrative Innovations:* The introduction or interface of programs budgets, computer systems, and other management techniques may also involve serious advance planning.
9. *Persistent Social Problems:* Comprehensive reassessments of perpetual social dilemmas such as crime, welfare, aging, and drug abuse involve strategic plans.
10. *Special or Unusual Events:* Parades and sports events, as well as civil unrest, often demand special contingency plans similar to strategic planning.

Strategic planning is both a process for discovering societal goals and for translating these goals into action commitments. It has three essential aims:

1. identification and clarification of long-term needs in the context of a short-range planning process;
2. design of plans and policies that reduce the impact of unintended social consequences (spill-over effects); and
3. creation of integrated approaches that tend to maximize social satisfaction while minimizing costs, waste, inefficiencies, and time delays.

Strategic planning is a generic concept implying a vast array of more particular techniques, including survey research, attitudinal studies, public awareness and involvement programs, long-range forecasting, scenario generation and simulations, diagnosis of trends, formulation of effectiveness measures, and so forth.

An overall characteristic of strategic planning is that of *comprehensiveness*;

an attempt is made to integrate and coordinate the operations of all identifiable (relevant) variables and alternatives in the process. This comprehensiveness seeks to eliminate piecemeal planning and to allow prediction and correction of perceived problems, both in the present and the future. Furthermore, this comprehensiveness includes elements of theoretical and practical planning.

Catanese and Steiss, in their "hybrid" of systems analysis and comprehensive planning, which they call "systemic planning," identify the following steps in the process of strategic planning [9] .

1. definition and clarification of current and future problems and interrelationships among these problems;
2. prediction of future conditions arising from identifiable problems;
3. identification of parameters, boundary conditions, or constraints that determine the range of possible solutions to the totality of problems;
4. determination of goals and objectives at varying levels—a) maximal and minimal levels, b) optimal levels, and c) normative or Utopian levels;
5. definition and analysis of subsystems—a) breakdown of the system into its component parts (subsystems), so that subsystem analysis can proceed in parallel, and b) identification of particular problems and needs associated with each subsystem;
6. formulation of alternatives;
7. evaluation of qualitative and quantitative cost-effectiveness of each alternative;
8. simulation of the alternative in the projected environment of the urban system in order to test overall performance, as well as to determine possible by-products and spill-over effects;
9. determination of the implementation sequence for each feasible alternative based on the critical dimensions of certain defined subsystem requirements and on the definiteness of subsystem specifications;
10. recommendation of a) minimal, b) optimal, and c) normative alternatives;
11. feedback from political and public interests to determine necessary modifications in suggested alternatives;
12. selection of alternative course of action and initiation of action programs to bring about the desired conditions;
13. development of predictive capacity within the system to identify changing conditions that might necessitate modifications in the selected course of action.

A less ambitious picture of strategic planning might focus on the following ingredients: 1) basic research and analysis (data collection and inventory studies, including a determination of a "planning horizon" and the levels of population to be served); 2) diagnosis of trends and needs and the consequent formulation of effectiveness measuures; 3) forecasts of alternative futures based on specific trends; 4) statements of goals and objectives as definitions of the desired state of the system; 5) formulation, analysis, and evaluation of alternative courses of action; and 6) the formulation of policies that govern the acquisition, use, and disposition of public resources.

The Elements of Strategic Planning

The procedures of strategic planning, as defined here, carry over into the implementation and evaluation stages of the policy process in order ensure continuous feedback with regard to societal preferences. The procedures, in essence, are designed to hold up the unfolding of present programs to the mirror of future needs.

In planning for future growth and development, it is appropriate to define a *planning horizon* (the farthest point in the future that can be anticipated based upon development trends). This horizon designation can provide the basis for a series of policy statements to guide long-range future growth and development toward a desired state of the system. As time passes and the planning horizon draws nearer, it becomes possible to anticipate points in the future. Just as with the natural horizon, as the initial "target" is approached, the planning horizon continues to recede, making adjustments in long-range goals and objectives and the policies designed for their achievement both necessary and possible. Therefore, the horizon concept provides a dynamic approach to strategic planning; the horizon can be changed, revised, or dismissed as the body of knowledge on which it is based is enlarged.

The *formulation of policy statements* to guide future growth and development must be based on research, measurement, and data collection. Relevant data would include diverse indices drawn from demographics, citizen surveys, public awareness meetings, professional assessments, and so forth. These data provide a basis for an approximation of the type of community or organizational development that may occur (and should occur). The data set, of course, will depend upon the types of policy problems under consideration.

The *development of goals* is a very murky area, but it is crucial to the definition of more specific objectives and the evaluation of needs. The formulation of goals should involve a high level of public input. Once goals and objectives are defined and agreement established, alternative policies must be designed to meet them.

Goals can be formulated by two methods. An *inductive approach* arrives at goals through extensive surveys of public opinions, attitudes, and objectives. Through a *deductive approach*, the task becomes one of forming tentative goal sets and effectiveness measures and testing them in the context of a specific population, thus allowing new factors to emerge. Though goals should be representative of the attitudes and aspirations of the specific community or population, the strategic planning model provides for the establishment of more normative goals based on identifiable trends in the society at large.

Forecasting is a vital step in the strategic planning process. Regular forecasts of trends and changes in population, physical characteristics of the community, and resource allocations are essential for the development of long- and short-range plans. An annual estimate of current conditions will aid in the assessment of expected changes. Forecasting enables the planner to project future needs and to design programs to meet these needs. Several basic forecasts can be made:

1. changes in environmental factors,
2. changes in financial conditions,
3. demographic trends,
4. macro trends,
5. structural changes, and
6. alternations in land uses.

These forecasts, based on applied and technical studies, should attempt to carry forward most of the key variables, and thereby assist planners and managers in the development of appropriate programs. By predicting future needs and desired conditions, resources can be allocated more effectively and many problems can be anticipated and thus ameliorated.

The development of policies and programs should also include the *assignment of priorities* to the various objectives to assist in the allocation of limited resources. Priorities may be formulated in terms of:

1. public demand and support,
2. programmatic feasibility,
3. certainty of attainment (risk threshold),
4. funding sources,
5. relative linkage to, and support provided other objectives, and
6. level of information available.

In the final phase of the strategic planning process, system inputs are considered, weighted, and evaluated to produce an output (policy or program recommendation). *Policies and programs* should cover the entire range of actions required by the identified goal sets and should be structured according to social needs and organizational objectives. Policies must address such basic questions as:

1. What is to be accomplished (objectives)?
2. How it is to be accomplished (means)?
3. Where it is to be accomplished (locus)?
4. Given limited resources, what is to be accomplished first (priorities)?
5. What are appropriate measures of accomplishment (standards for evaluation and control)?

This culminative phase involves the *selection of the best policy statement* based upon feasibility, program consequences, financial considerations, and the needs and requirements of the community or population. This is the actual "decision" stage of strategic planning, and all previous stages have been the buildup to make the decisions easier and more logical (as well as less risky and uncertain).

Strategic Planning and Adaptive Planning

Another unique element of strategic planning is the continuous feedback and reassessment activities. In a somewhat parallel context, various authors have referred to this subprocess as "adaptive planning" or "contingency planning." Friedmann makes an important distinction between developmental and adaptive planning [10]:

> The former (developmental planning) is concerned with achieving a high rate of cumulative-investment for a given area by activating unused resource capabilities; the latter (adaptive planning) is interested chiefly in qualitative adaptations to the changing interplay of economic forces within the area. To put it another way, adaptive planning generally takes place in response to externally induced development.

Adaptive planning is based on the contemporary characteristics of urban development and the high degree of interregional dependency that governs current decision-making. As a consequence, planners and managers must be in a position to formulate responses to exogenous forces, taking advantage of newly developed resource capabilities or other opportunities and constraints. The contingency approach, on the other hand, is aimed at creating conditions whereby the effects of unforeseen crises can be deflected or absorbed at minimum cost or inconvenience. The field of engineering has followed this strategy for years by introducing large safety factors into designs to reduce to a tolerable level the likelihood of materials failure. The engineer may also offer a cost-reliability trade-off, *i.e.*, the relative costs of designing a facility to meet different contingency levels.

Contingency and adaptive planning, taken in the abstract, share a basic problem —they seek to avoid the worst, while providing relatively little guidance as to how to achieve the best. As a subprocess in strategic planning, this shortcoming is at least partially circumvented since one of the major objectives of the strategic planning process is to gain agreement as to what the "best" is or should be.

Strategic Planning Versus Traditional Planning

The difference between strategic planning and the more traditional approaches to planning might be summarized as follows:

1. Strategic planning strives to reduce rather than extol intuitive judgments and to place such judgments on a more objective and professional basis.

2. Strategic planning seeks to establish guidance mechanisms based on an aggregation of social goals and objectives, rather than relying on linear extrapolations of past and current trends in the physical environment.
3. Strategic planning provides a basis for adjustment between long-range goals and short-range needs, rather than maintaining the invariability of forecasted future.

In essence, strategic planning establishes a frame of reference with which to test policies and programs, allowing for continual experimentation and refinement, rather than blind commitment to what is often self-fulfilling growth policy. Strategic planning offers the basis for a *thesis* as well as a *synthesis*.

Issue Paper Techniques: Identifying the Boundaries of Policy Problems

As has been suggested, the decision process quite often is laced with intuitive, professional judgments. This element of intuition does not imply that such judgments are ill-founded. Nevertheless, such judgments often place a cloak of mystery over the intervening logic between the factual characteristics of a problem and the formulation of alternative courses of action to resolve that problem. The techniques embodied by the *issue paper* are vital not only to the clarification of policy problems, but also in the removal of this cloak. Thus an issue paper may provide a substantial aid to the many educated laymen, as well as the professional analyst or administrator, who may take part in the policy-formulation process.

As originally conceived, the purpose of an issue paper was to explore a problem in sufficient depth to provide decision-makers with a fairly complete idea of its dimensions and the possible scope of its solution. On the basis of this initial exploration, decision-makers could then determine further courses of action and commitments, including the development of more definitive studies leading to specific policy and program recommendations. In practice, however, the issue paper has evolved as a formal, systematic assessment of all that is currently known about a particular problem or issue based on data that are readily available. Thus, an issue paper serves as a first-phase study, the objective of which is to establish *boundary conditions* in order to lay a foundation for more extensive policy and program analyses as may be indicated by this problem perspectus.

An issue paper attempts to identify the real problem or problem set, to isolate the fundamental objectives involved, to suggest appropriate measures of effectiveness and alternative courses of action, and to identify the population subgroups currently affected or likely to be impacted by the problems. Government agencies and private organizations concerned with various aspects of the issue are identified, and resources currently available and those that can readily be applied to the problem are listed. An issue paper stops short, however, of the actual investigation and evaluation of the impacts of the various alternatives.

Originally developed in conjunction with the techniques of Planning-Program-ming-Budgeting Systems, the issue paper has received widespread application in a broad range of public problem-solving situations.

An issue paper seeks specific answers to such critical questions as:

1. What is the magnitude of the problem, how widespread is it currently, and how important is it likely to be in the foreseeable future?
2. What public goals and objectives are associated with the identified problems, and what are their impact on these objectives?
3. What measures of effectiveness and efficiency can be developed to monitor progress toward the resolution of the problem and the attainment of the associated goals and objectives?
4. What specific activities relevant to the problem are currently being under-taken by government, and what alternative programs or activities should be considered for meeting the problem?

To be reasonably certain that no aspect of the problem is overlooked, it is appro-priate to work through a standard format in fairly systematic fashion, even though all the required data and information may not be available, accurate, or dependable. In addition to assisting in the further articulation of the prob-lem and the identification of related problems, by-products, and spill-over ef-fects, such a standard format can help to provide an appropriate management perspective.

Major Elements of an Issue Paper

The major elements of a standard issue paper are outlined and discussed below. Since the original format for the issue paper was designed primarily for use with program budgeting, application to other problem situations may not require all sections. In some cases, it also may be desirable to add categories such as an accounting of the political constraints associated with a particular policy issue or problem.

1. *The background and sources of the problem.* This section should offer a clear and concise description of the problem, issue, or situation for which further analysis is proposed; identify the origins of the problem; specify the particular manifest symptoms; and, to the extent possible, suggest some of the root causes. Since it is important to distinguish between symptoms and causes in order to identify the real problem, basic cause-and-effect rela-tionships should be clarified to the extent that they are known.
2. *Why the "problem" is a problem.* This section explains why the situation warrants the assignment of analytical resources at this time and the possible consequences if the problem is permitted to continue unabated. Such a statement serves to justify the expenditure of public funds for analysis.
3. *The groups or institutions toward which corrective action is directed.* Of-

ten in the formulation of a program or decision to eliminate a problem, the exact "who" or "what" that is to serve as the target is ambiguous. Thus, it is necessary to spell out the specific population, if it is other than the general public, and to provide general characteristics, such as age group, race, income class, special needs, and geographical location. For example, if a health program were being considered, the target group might be those with a particular illness or those who were in a high-risk category. It is also important to distinguish between those persons who are actually in the target group and the impacted population to be included if certain alternatives are undertaken.

4. *The affected publics.* The question of who gets the benefits and who pays the costs is central to the resolution of most public policy problems and issues. Therefore, it is important that these groups are clearly delineated (to the extent possible, it would be desirable to have quantitative estimates and projections of the numbers in the various beneficiary and target groups) so as to alert decision-makers of these existing and potential "clientele groups."

5. *Current programs and policies related to the problem.* The issue paper should provide a list of specific activities currently underway that affect (or potentially could affect) the problem. Such programs should be identified, and to the extent possible without inordinate effort, related program costs and their impacts on the target and beneficiary groups should be estimated. Indications of the number currently being served by these programs and projections are helpful. It is important to make the list as complete as possible—federal, state, city, and county, as well as private sector programs should be identified. Any new efforts to achieve the same or similar objectives should obviously be integrated and coordinated with those of all other agencies having effect on the problem or issue.

6. *Clarification of goals and objectives.* It is important to identify the goals and objectives associated with a particular issue or problem clearly, carefully, and precisely. Imprecise or incomplete statements of objectives may result in misconceived measures of effectiveness, incorrect and ineffectual specifications of alternatives, and misdirected investments of resources that can do little to alleviate the problem. It is important to look beyond the immediate problem situation to call attention to longer range goals and any possible spill-overs to other public programs. In this connection, the data base developed through the procedures of strategic planning may be applicable to the identification of societal goals.

7. *Designation of effectiveness measures.* Effectiveness measures involve a scoring technique for determining the state of a given system (organization, community, state, *etc.*) at a given point in time. They are indicators that measure direct and indirect impacts of specific resources in the pursuit of certain goals and objectives. Under this approach, goals are defined by: 1) level of current performance, 2) the impact of current resources on performance, and 3) a comparison with desired levels of performance.

8. *Identification of a framework of analysis.* This section explores the methodological approaches to be applied if the issue paper leads to a full-scale analysis. The analytical framework also defines the basic conceptual assumptions as well as the types of methods to be utilized. At this stage, of course, the methodology can only be discussed in very tentative terms. It is important, however, to establish this framework and to test its efficacy against what is known about the problem in order to determine if extensive new data will be required to operationalize the selected approach.

9. *Generation of alternatives.* In this stage of the issue paper, an attempt should be made to generate the broadest possible range of alternatives, even though some of them may seem impractical, costly, technically infeasible, or highly unorthodox. Later, when the full-scale analysis is underway, many of these alternatives may be rejected. At the outset, however, it is important to take a wide-open, free-wheeling, unconstrained look at all of the possibilities. While it is probably adequate to focus primarily on the "pure" or distinct alternatives, where it seems obvious, the possibility of mixed solutions or combinations and permutations arising from the basic alternatives should also be discussed.

10. *Setting forth recommendations.* Examples of the types of recommendations to be set forth in an issue paper include: 1) to undertake a full-scale study, 2) to continue the analysis, but on a low-priority basis, or 3) to terminate any further analysis since the problem is below some threshold of concern. Occasionally, sufficient information may come to light during the development of the issue paper to provide the basis for decisive conclusions regarding one of the alternatives. In such cases, the preliminary design to initiate the study has, in fact, become the study.

Actual issue papers may involve additional or compound stages and indices as necessary. In some instances, it will be deemed appropriate for the policy analyst to comment upon the political conditions and the arena through which the policy should seek passage. In other situations, the analyst may wish to specify the organizational setting most conducive to successful implementation.

A final item of concern with respect to an issue paper is the appendix. Since a primary purpose of an issue paper is to produce a document that is concise and clear enough to be read in its entirety by decision-makers, it may be appropriate to include much of the technical materials in an appendix. Such an appendix (or appendices) might include extensive authoritative references, footnotes, tables, charts, raw data, computer print-outs, extensive calculations, special exhibits, and any other items that might be helpful to the analysts in verifying the informational content of the issue paper.

In sum, then, an issue paper is a formalized and elaborated form of "brain storming," that serves as the hub of the professional discussion of policy problems. It channels that discussion in the direction of more systematic thinking, as well as providing greater visibility for ultimate policy decisions [11] .

Long-Range Forecasting and the Projection of Alternative Futures

In both of the policy-planning mechanisms discussed thus far, the processes of forecasting or projecting served as a prominant feature. Techniques for predicting the future, more often than not, are viewed by the layperson as tantamount to soothsaying. This view is somewhat justified in reference to past experiences in which futures were predicted on little more than hunches. An even more distressing situation is where forecasting was used (or misused) as an instrument in the hands of community growth agents (*e.g.*, developers, businessmen, and real estate owners).

Despite these abuses of forecasting, society is more dependent on their use than ever before. As Alvin Toffler points out in his epic, *Future Shock*, the vast majority of technological innovation has taken place in the reader's lifetime. This decade is fast becoming known as the "Age of Uncertainty." For a whole variety of economic, environmental, and political reasons, it is more difficult to feel confident in a smooth transition into the future. Planning ahead for 10 to 15 years, which often is required for extensive (and capital intensive) public works projects, seems to be an increasingly hazardous task, and many local officials complain that they cannot even predict revenues and expenditures a month ahead of time, much less 10 to 15 years.

Part of the forecast problem has to do with the techniques available.

In the past it had been a relatively easy task simply to extrapolate from historical trends. If revenues went up 5% a year for the past ten years, then they would probably go up another 5% next year and every year thereafter. But the energy crisis disturbed this complacency by bringing out a set of rather uncommon factors that had not had a significant impact on past events. No one gave much thought, for example, to the price of gasoline as a factor in highway revenues until it took a quantum jump in 1974. Then local officials quickly realized that many of their desired highway and transit projects could not be funded, at least until sometime in the future, because of state and federal revenue shortfalls.

The types of techniques to be discussed here under the heading of long-range forecasting, or what has often been labeled "technological forecasting," are expressly designed to achieve reduction of uncertainty with regard to unique or perhaps even cataclysmic events. Making forecasts, even on a very short-term basis, is a difficult pasttime. While these techniques certainly cannot be viewed as dispelling all or even a large part of the mystery enshrouding the future, they do have their benefits. The primary advantage is that the experience and intuition of a group of people with a broad range of expertise can be employed to identify the unique events that otherwise might not be considered. Another advantage lies in the use of mathematics to help trace these experienced forecasts to their logical ends. In these ways, technological forecasting derives the best benefits from two worlds—the intuition of experienced practitioners and the rigor of mathematical deduction. The result is a much more informed view of the future (and its uncertainties) than might otherwise be available.

The term "technological forecasting" has now become somewhat of a misnomer. It comes from a history of applications, to a great extent in the military, in which researchers were trying to track the evolution of various technologies (weapons systems) and use their findings to forecast future developments. Yet the techniques associated with technological forecasting have a much wider applicability and currently are being employed in a very broad spectrum of economic, social, environmental, and political contexts. They also are being utilized to supplement an array of statistical estimation tools that traditionally have been used by, say, economists, to help make predictions [12].

Some of the techniques described below are as old as mankind, but most were developed within the last 5 to 15 years and have only recently been applied to policy problems. Thus, while there has been a considerable number of successful military and private sector trials, there have been relatively few public or civil applications.

The most common tools in long-range forecasting include the following techniques:

1. *Regression:* a statistical technique for determining straight line relationships between a pair (or more) of variables.
2. *S-Curves:* relationships that form an S-curve over time; that is, when growth trends are slow initially, then rapid, then taper off quickly as some limit is reached.
3. *"Genius" Forecasting:* that done by an individual with some expertise without interaction with any other people.
4. *Committee Forecasting:* that done typically by a structured group of people.
5. *Analogy:* prediction in which characteristics or events similar to that in some known entity are assumed to hold for the unknown entity.
6. *Delphi:* a structured committee in which feedback is anonymous and statistical.
7. *Gaming:* competitive actions between groups to generate simulated future outcomes.
8. *Morphological Analysis:* a search for unique forms or combinations of characteristics or events that may evolve.
9. *Relevance Trees:* a hierarchy of goals and functions indicating the most productive (relevant) parts for future developments.
10. *Probe:* a "critical path" arrangement of future events showing which ones are needed for a particular event to occur.
11. *Cross Impact:* a process for taking into account simultaneously the strength and direction of interaction expected between events.

The range of problem areas to which these techniques can be applied is broad, and for some techniques it is not even necessary to have "hard" data as input. The techniques can be employed for both short- and long-term horizons for helping to make forecasts of factors such as population, employment, revenues, expenditures, racial tensions, public attitudes toward particular issues, and the like. Of course, the techniques also can be utilized for forecasting technological developments in such areas as solid waste disposal, transportation equipment, and energy generation. The usefulness of such forecasts naturally will vary with the item being considered, but generally will be of higher quality for technical rather than social factors. Moreover, social forecasts experience disparate performance with regard to internal elements such as cost, time, and knowledge of participants (Table 2).

Nevertheless, as social indicators (quality of life and social well-being) are refined, along with unique social forecasting techniques, perhaps commensurate or at least approximate quality will eventually be achieved. At present even minor reductions in the level of uncertainty augur well for continuing policy applications.

Management By Objectives: The Translation of Societal Goals into Organizational Objectives

Arriving at approximations of societal goals and objectives and achieving socio-political consensus regarding their pursuit are *not* guarantees that complex public organizations will be able to carry out these plans and programs. Organizations often develop implicit, if not explicit, goals and objectives of their own. A primary organization goal is survival, and surviving may not be directly dependent upon fulfilling the broad mandate or specific policy missions given to the organization. Also individuals within organizations have a panoply of personal goals that may be quite divergent from the goals of the organization. Several management techniques have been developed to bring about action commitments within complex organizations and to make them harmonious with those demands arising in the broader decision environment. One general title given to these tools and techniques in *Management By Objectives* (MBO).

MBO has been recognized as valuable tool in the private sector for over 50 years. It has been only in recent years, marked by the rapid growth of the public sector, that MBO has been explored by public organizations. While not strictly an alternative to Planning-Programming-Budgeting Systems (PPBS), it has been in the wake of PPBS that MBO has gained attention and application at the federal level. Interest at the state and local levels of government has quickly followed.

MBO is a relatively simplistic approach that attempts to provide a framework for identifying, integrating, monitoring, and evaluating individual and organiza-

Table 2. A rough comparison of forecasting techniques.

TECHNIQUE	ACCURACY	"QUALITY OF IDEAS"	COST	TIME TO COMPLETION	DATA REQUIRE-MENTS	INDIVIDUAL KNOWLEDGE NEEDED	GROUP KNOWLEDGE NEEDED	PARTIC-IPANTS' BENEFITS
				FEATURES				
Regression	High if past factors operative	Very low	Low	Very low	Fairly high	High	NA	None
Gompertz	High if past factors operative	Very low	Low	Very low	Medium	Very high	NA	None
"Genius"	Varied	Medium	Medium	Low	Very low	Very high	NA	None
Committee	Varied	Medium	Medium	Medium low	Low	Medium	High	Fairly high
Analogy	Medium	Fairly high	Medium	Medium	Fairly high	Medium	NA	None
Delphi	Medium	Fairly high	Very High	High	Low	Fairly high	High	Fairly high
Gaming	Fairly high	Fairly high	High	Medium	Medium	Fairly high	High	High
Morpholog-ical analysis	Medium	Medium	Low	Low	Fairly low	Very high	NA	None
Relevance tree	Varied	Fairly high	Medium	Medium	Fairly high	Very high	NA	None
Probe	Medium if factors "discrete"	Low	Medium	Medium	High	Very high	NA	None
Cross impact	High if factors "discrete"	Medium	Very high	High	Fairly high	Very high	NA	None

tional objectives. It requires that these objectives be operationalized in empirical if not quantitative terms. Such verification is significant in the public sector where objectives are frequently and deliberately obscured in order to achieve political consensus, or where objectives often must undergo significant redefinition when made operational.

As suggested, the most essential feature of MBO is the integration of individual (personnel) goals with broader organizational missions. In the MBO cycle, personnel become aware of not only *what* they do but also *why* they do it. They learn what the organization is trying to accomplish, what are their individual performance targets, and what has been their progress toward these targets. It is theorized that such increased awareness will improve motivation and deepen commitment toward efficient work performance. A vital element of MBO is the encouragement of innovative decisions within the parameters of organizational goals.

As systematic analysis becomes increasingly utilized at all levels of government, it has been recognized that a "... major difficulty in evaluating the accomplishment of goals stems from the inadequate information and communication for setting program objectives" [13]. MBO attacks this problem at several points. Initially, open communication is fostered. Superior and subordinate identify, discuss, and evaluate individual objectives and relate these to the broader context of the program or organizational objectives. Milestone charts can be used as a technique for subsequent performance evaluation. This technique is buttressed by explicit definitions and careful measurement in order to span from the process of objective formulation to the evaluation of performance, and subsequently to the realization or reassessment of objectives.

The Objectives of MBO

In general, MBO strives to develop the following mechanisms:

1. A clear and concise statement of organizational goals and objectives in relation to societal goals, and a working out of accommodations between conflicting objectives.
2. An open atmosphere in which administrators are encouraged to make innovative contributions to the realization of organizational goals.
3. A specification of tasks and responsibilities of individuals in reference to organizational goals.
4. A set of standards by which individual and programmatic decisions can be evaluated in terms of their goals achievement.
5. The provision of systematic reassessments and continued innovation in the pursuit or organizational goals.

Along these lines, MBO is integrally linked to external decision demands through increased information flow and higher levels of organizational visibility.

Frank Sherwood and William Page suggest that MBO has the ". . . potential for reassuring legislators and the polity that government units actually are committed to specifying objectives and reporting progress toward them" [14] .

In addition, MBO in the public sector attempts to harness the reform zeal of movements such as the New Professionalism and the New Public Administration. Under the rubric of MBO, individual administrators are given incentives to express their concern that the organization meet broader societal goals. Individuals are also granted greater reasonsibility over their particular area of expertise.

MBO increases not only self-control or autonomy but also accountability. Whereas the individual has virtual self-control in producing his expected results, the manager has a better defined overview of job responsibilities and thus, can better hold certain areas or individuals accountable for failures and successes. While in one sense MBO advocates a certain *laissez faire* approach to management, it also provides the necessary feedback mechanism so that managers can quickly identify and adjust problem areas. Flexibility and adaptability to change are salient features of MBO.

To be most successful, MBO entails ". . . that the way in which a manager relates to his employees must change from a highly structured or 'bureaucratic' form of managing to a more unstructured and more democratic form of managing" [15] . Certainly, this approach will be more natural to some managers than to others according to personalities and their personal theories of management.

When MBO is introduced it should be in a nonthreatening fashion. Care must also be taken so that managers really do understand what MBO is, its merits, and shortcomings. To the extent possible, experience should be obtained in MBO prior to implementation. Administrators must be able to anticipate problems in the initial phases of MBO if it is not to cause frustration and be discarded prematurely. Knowledge of concepts and techniques may not be sufficient; skill and savvy may be necessary. Various organizations and programs will have their own unique characteristics to which the administrator must be sensitive in introducing MBO. Moreover, commitments of top-level administrators are essential to the effective implementation and operation of MBO. Correctly applied, MBO can be an effective instrument of both responsible and responsive administration.

FINANCIAL ADMINISTRATION AND ANALYSIS

At the core of any administrative enterprise is the management of the dollars and cents (in the federal bureaucracy, the billions and millions). Yet, with regard to this crucial process, there is a great deal of difference between private sector and public sector financial administration. The distinctions are myriad—the most essential perhaps is the lack of a "profit motive" in the public sector.

While public organizations, particularly those of local government, are subject to severe budgetary constraints, they are seldom motivated by the bottom line of a balance sheet. Moreover, achievement in the public sector is rarely realized in financial terms. Nonetheless, the performance expectations placed upon public organizations are often just as rigorous as any leveled by the stockholders or trustees of a private corporation.

The focus of this section is on some of the analytical measures designed to meet the expectations of efficiency, fiscal integrity, and program effectiveness. This focus will include a discussion of the techniques of *cost-benefit and cost-effectiveness analysis*, procedures for the application of *performance/program budgeting*, and consideration of the responsibilities for *capital facilities planning and debt administration*.

Cost-Benefit/Cost-Effectiveness

Cost-benefit analysis is a methodology for coping with the age-old problem of allocating scarce resources. In theory, the problem is quite simple; it is difficult only in practice. In theory, one merely must decide what is wanted (specification of ends), measure these wants (quantification of benefits sought), and then apply the limited means to achieve the greatest possible value of the identified wants (maximize benefits). In contemporary society, the means become public budgets, and, therefore, the problem is one of maximizing benefits (once specified and quantified) for any given set of fiscal inputs (*i.e.*, specified and quantified costs).

Cost-benefit analysis is not a new technique born of modern computer technology and systems-thinking. In a rudimentary sense cost-benefit thinking was manifest when mankind first decided to compare the positive and negative aspects of any decision. Cost-benefit analysis in a form roughly analogous to current practice was first initiated in 1902 (Rivers and Harbors Act) for the assessment of water resource projects; it was formalized in 1936 as a result of the National Flood Control Act. Here the federal government accepted the responsibility of undertaking flood control measures whenever and wherever the "benefits to whomsoever they may accrue are in excess of the cost" [16]. In 1950, the subcommittee on Cost and Benefits of the Inter-Agency River Basin Committee published its "shoppers guide" to project benefits, better known as the "Greenbook." The Greenbook also outlined acceptable principles and procedures for determining benefit-cost ratios. While these procedures were more or less adhered to, the determination of benefits and designation of favorable ratios were often highly politicized, particularly in the water resource area [17].

With the injections of systems analysis into the federal programs of the 1960s, cost-benefit took on a much more analytical and less political coloration. Roland McKean and others redefined cost-benefit in the terminology of systems. McKean describes the components of cost-benefit analysis as follows [18] :

1. Definition of program objectives, i.e., what achievements need to be made in order to yield the desired benefits?
2. Identification of alternative courses of action (policies and programs) to achieve stated objectives.
3. Estimation of costs associated with each alternative.
4. Construction of mathematical models to assist in the estimation of benefits and costs and the subsequent choice between alternative policies, programs, or systems.
5. Development of a *criterion of preferredness* or *social discount rate* to assist in the selection of the "best" alternative.

In recent years, concurrent with the development of program budgeting, more systematic analyses of benefits and costs associated with public programs have become an increasingly important part of the budget-makers' responsibilities. Though it may be assumed that governments have always considered both the benefits and costs associated with various programs requiring the allocation of limited fiscal resources, these examinations often have been haphazard with little systematic effort to quantify benefits or to include all costs and benefits. Too often, the public decision-making process has been dominated by a "money first" approach, whereby only a certain amount of revenue is available and, therefore, expenditures are confined to this amount. At other times, an "absolute needs" approach is manifest in which a given set of expenditures is deemed so essential that it must be undertaken irrespective of the costs [19]. Due partly to the increasing scope of governmental activities, however, there has been a significant increase in emphasis on various cost-benefit forms of analysis.

As suggested, cost-benefit is quite simple at the skeletal level, it is the fleshing-out of the process that often involves highly complex analyses. The "Green-book" describes the process as comprised of the following discrete steps [20] :

1. Establishment of need;
2. Estimation of each of the project's benefits and costs in standardized units, allowing a meaningful comparison of alternative projects;
3. Establishment of the scope of the project development; and
4. Development of the most economical means of realizing project purposes.

Each of these subprocesses may entail elaborate assessments, based to a large degree upon professional evaluative judgments. Moreover, there are many situations that require supplemental criteria, such as "environmental costs" [21] and "social equity" [22], to augment pure budget costs and mechanistic efficiency.

Cost-effectiveness is similar to cost-benefit in nearly every detail, except that cost-effectiveness involves "a comparison of alternative courses of action in terms of costs and their effectiveness in attaining some specific objectives" [23]. Cost-effectiveness analysis was originally developed for military expenditures; *e.g.*, "bang for buck" considerations. The level of performance was expressed in terms of minimum acceptable standards. This rationale was easily transferred to social programs for which the benefits were difficult to calculate in monetary terms. Cost-effectiveness analysis thus involves discovering the procedures that achieve social objectives for the least cost. Noticeably, the establishment of these fixed objectives may depend upon the mechanisms mentioned previously under the heading of strategic planning.

Two of the major advantages of cost-effectiveness over cost-benefit analysis are that: 1) the goals and objectives must be explicitly articulated, and 2) all degrees of quality of information on "benefits" are allowable in the analysis. Thus, the analyst does not have to compress all "benefits" into a single number expressed in dollar terms. Rather, the analysis focuses on effectiveness considered in terms of a number of dimensions.

The principal utility of cost-benefit/effectiveness analysis is that it provides a better understanding of the implications of embarking upon alternative courses of action. These approaches force the analyst to examine the structure of the costs, constraints, and benefits of each alternative. If one attempts to go beyond this in the analytic process, *i.e.*, to let the result of the analysis make the decision, then there may be some problems. Although cost-benefit analysis is a scientific approach to evaluating alternatives, it is not an exact scientific tool, nor is it value-free. Nevertheless, given appropriate inputs, it is capable of highly useful results [24]. Moreover, while it is primarily a mechanism of efficiency, it can be used with various social programming techniques to produce effective policies.

Performance/Program Budgeting

At the hub of this discussion of policy and program analysis is the concept of performance/program budgeting. This concept combines and extends fiscal planning and control elements from the management orientation of performance budgeting and the planning orientation of program budgeting (or PPBS). In addition, it adopts the elements of accountability and personnel control from more traditional budgeting approaches (line item or objects of expenditure budgets). This dual or mixed approach is being discussed with increasing frequency in conjunction with such concepts as zero-base budgeting, mission budgeting, and performance auditing. Moreover, cost-benefit and cost-effectiveness analyses often are applicable under performance/program budgeting in support of efforts to develop more cost-effective public policies.

Performance/program budgeting is oriented to a strengthening of the role of strategic planning in the budget process. The primary objective of performance/ program budgeting is to secure more rational bases for decision-making. This greater rationality is accomplished by providing the following elements: 1) increased efficiency through the analysis of data on the costs and benefits of proposed public objectives, and 2) increased effectiveness through measurements of output (performance) to facilitate a continual review of public activities. As a policy device, performance/program budgeting departs from more basic models of efficiency in which objectives are fixed and quantities of inputs and outputs are adjusted to secure an optimal relationship. In performance/program budgeting, policy and program objectives may be considered as variables. Analysis is thus aimed at creating new objectives.

Performance/program budgeting focuses on aggregates of expenditures, *i.e.*, broad program classifications that may cut across established lines of responsibility. Detailed itemizations of expenditure categories are brought into play as they may contribute to the analysis of the total system. These fiscal details may also have potential impact on marginal trade-offs among competing objectives. In performance/program budgeting, the emphasis is on comprehensiveness and on the grouping of data into categories that facilitate comparisons among alternative mixes of public expenditures.

Object-of-expenditure classifications, as found in traditional line-item budgets, offer two distinct advantages not possessed by other types of budget systems: 1) *accountability*—a pattern of accounts that can be controlled and audited: and 2) *information for personnel management*—personnel requirements are closely linked with other budgetary requirements, and the control of positions can be used to control the budget. These administrative features of a line-item budget (used for the documentation and accounting of both monies and personnel) are retained in the performance/program budget model, thus providing a "dual system" for policy formulation and administration.

Performance Budgeting as a Tool of Management

The notion of performance budgeting grew out of the redefinition of budgeting as a management process in the thirties and forties. The terminology *performance budgeting* first was used by the Hoover Commission in recommending the adoption of improved budgetary techniques by the federal government [25].

Performance budgeting has a strong management orientation; its principal objective is to assist administrators in their assessment of the *work-efficiency* of operating units. It seeks this objective by: 1) casting budget categories in functional terms, and 2) providing work-cost measurements to facilitate the more efficient performance of prescribed activities. Generally, its methods are particularistic, with the reduction of work-cost data into discrete, measurable units. Performance budgeting derives much of its conceptual and technical basis from *cost accounting*. The budget is envisioned as a work program. As Mosher has stated: "... the central idea of the performance budget ... is that the budget process be focused upon programs and functions—that is, accomplishments to be achieved, work to be done" [26].

While the traditional performance budget shifted attention from fiscal inputs to performance outputs, the emphasis of this approach is on efficiency—on the allocation of scarce resources among competing claims on a least-cost basis. Questions of efficiency, however, are generally defined and answered in fiscal or economic terms, with minimum consideration of priorities or relative worth. This shortcoming may be observed in the continual efforts of public agencies to achieve economies without decreasing services or outputs. The focus is the elimination of waste: with fixed resources, of producing more of *A* without decreasing the production of *B*. By pretending that technical analyses—analyses that focus on efficiency—are sufficient for political decisions, decision-makers may lose the very information necessary to determine effectiveness.

Program or Mission Budgeting

Recognition of these shortcomings has led to the development of budgetary techniques and concepts that are also output-oriented, but that consider the *impact of resources* as well as the resources themselves. These techniques make a clear distinction between efficiency and effectiveness in an attempt to supplant financial-type controls in favor of unambiguous and nonpecuniary accounting techniques to measure the output in terms of effectiveness in achieving public goals and objectives.

Program or mission budgeting represents one such organized approach to the measurement of effectiveness. Generally speaking, a program budget has the following five major elements [27]:

1. identification of goals and objectives;
2. program structuring;
3. extended time horizon;
4. program analysis; and
5. program up-dating procedures.

Identification of goals and objectives, of course, is the essence of strategic planning, as discussed previously. Strategic planning can mean the difference between success and failure in the delivery of vital public services. Unfortunately, the concepts of strategic planning are the least developed among the various modes of public planning. Goals and objectives must be translated into a time schedule for achievement, and specific resource requirements must be identified. The achievement "time-line" and resource requirements (personnel, materials and supplies, equipment, *etc.*) form the basis for determining fiscal commitments—the fundamental inputs of the budget process.

A second major component of program budgeting involves the *structuring and analysis* of public agency activities *in programmatic terms*. A program is defined as a group of interdependent, closely related services or activities that possess or contribute to a common objective or set of allied objectives. In PPBS, programs were to be structured "across-the-board," *i.e.*, without concern for the variety of agencies that might be involved in the process of implementation. While across-the-board program structures may be an ideal to strive toward, many public agencies cannot make a meaningful transition to such a format in the short time span envisioned under PPBS. Therefore, such comprehensive structuring is viewed as a long-range rather than an immediately realizable objective of performance/program budgeting. A significant effort must first be launched in the development of management information. The interdependencies of various agency activities can be examined and the goals of government structured in a more comprehensive manner.

The *extended time horizon* envisioned in the formulation of a program budget is necessary to establish a long-range process that might be able to circumvent the "crisis programming" mentality of many public activities. This longer time horizon serves to guide the total activities of government in a more coherent and comprehensive fashion. The *multiyear program plan* is needed to indicate the proposed outputs of public facilities and services according to the objectives outlined in the strategic planning stage. The magnitude of each program is determined through this phase of the budgetary process. The *multiyear financial plan* serves to project costs for each program as outlined by the decisions made in program planning. Cost estimates, outlined in varying levels of detail according to the time span covered, should be matched with estimates of revenue sources required to support the proposed programs. Only through such an examination is it possible to determine the adequacy of current sources of revenue in light of future demands.

Program analysis is the cornerstone of performance/program budgeting. Through a systematic analysis of alternatives, programs are selected for multiyear plans. Although program analysis may take several forms, stated simply, it involves the reduction of complex problems into their component parts so that each can be studied in greater detail, followed by a synthesis of these parts back into the whole. The analytical task in program analysis involves the use of existing resources or the generation of additional resources to create new means-ends patterns. In general, this task involves:

1. identification of questions relevant to the inquiry;
2. operationalization of vaguely stated objectives;
3. elimination of imprecise factors;

4. ascertainment of quantifiable variables;
5. specification of assumptions;
6. selection of models and other tools of analysis;
7. specification of alternatives; and
8. selection of "best" or "optimal" course of action or program.

Through *program updating* procedures, program analysis techniques are applied to determine needed modifications and improvements once programs are implemented. Regular and systematic collection of performance measures in a *management information and program evaluation system* (MIPES) can provide public officials and managers with periodic reports. Such feedback provides managers with the mechanisms for program control and evaluation, *e.g.*, cost-effectiveness ratios.

The performance/program budget model incorporates these five basic elements and utilizes the concept of activity classifications to gather all the expenditure data needed by a public manager to administer a unit or "cluster" of activities. These activity classifications are defined in end-product terms so as to orient their analysis more directly to the mission and purpose. By using unit cost components as the building blocks for the budget, these data can be "cross-walked" from the programmatic format to the more traditional control format.

Performance/program budgeting holds the potential of providing a more meaningful interface between long-range planning and decision-making and the day-to-day operations of government. As such, it is essential that public management personnel become fully involved in the further development and refinement of the concepts and techniques underlying this budgetary approach.

Capital Facilities Planning

Not all aspects of the budgetary process involve exotic calculations or nebulous societal goals. Yet, even the more workaday budgetary concerns can be highly perplexing. This problem is certainly evident in the planning of capital facilities and the administration of the debt resulting from efforts to finance construction.

Capital facilities planning encompasses those activities of government that attempt to provide public improvements for a community in a timely and orderly manner. These improvements must be evaluated and scheduled by comparing anticipated needs with the estimated capacity of the community to support and finance these facilities and associated service programs. The problem of allocating resources for public inprovements is complicated by the uncertainty of future conditions. It cannot be assumed that conditions in the community will remain static during the life of a public facility and, therefore, capital facilities planning must be considered as a function of changing public requirements and facility capacity. Improper scheduling for the construction of public improvements may not only impede the growth of a community, it may inhibit the delivery of adequate levels of public services.

Thus, a major objective of capital facilities planning is to provide decision-makers with data on future needs and resources of the community. This information should be sufficiently reliable to justify decisions involving long-term and relatively large commitments of public resources. This emphasis on meeting growth demands does not imply the "self-fulfilling policy" mode mentioned earlier, for it is usually in situations of service crisis that communities are panicked into uneconomical investments and overdevelopment. Comprehensive capital facilities planning can avert these crises and, thus, facilitate a more realistic and rational pattern of community growth.

The major problem confronting capital facilities planning is the tendency to separate decisions regarding needed public improvements from the rest of public sector requirements and programs. Public improvements support operating programs and are a critical factor to be considered in program planning and scheduling. Ideally, commitments for capital facilities should be an integral part of the program budget. Moak and Hillhouse point out that: "Any less comprehensive view of these processes invites the construction of projects as ends in themselves, rather than as elements of the entire process of providing governmental services" [28]. The following model of capital facilities planning attempts to develop a comprehensive planning perspective [29].

Strategic Planning. Once again, strategic planning provides the basic groundwork for the development of policy. In this instance, emphasis is placed upon population estimates, economic forecasts, social preferences, and other projections of community development and social expectations. This long-range planning framework must include a financial plan that reflects the public service and facility needs of the community beyond the limits of the traditional annual budget. The following elements should be considered in the formulation of this long-range financial plan:

1. External factors influencing public programs, including anticipated shifts in significant demographic characteristics, projected changes in economic activities, social trends, scientific and technological changes, *etc.*;
2. Total public service needs and demands (assumptions, standards, and criteria used to quantify and project needs and demands should be identified);
3. An evaluation of the present and future roles of various levels of government and private enterprise within designated functional areas; and
4. Interagency allocation of responsibilities in terms of total public needs and demands, including recommendations regarding the elimination of significant areas of overlap through formal coordination or realignment of responsibilities.

Population Forecasting. The demand for public improvements is a function of growth; in effective capital facilities planning it is necessary to identify the elements of the population in which this growth is occurring. The population should be disaggregated as much as possible to anticipate the types of public improvements future populations will need. For example, an aging population will require specialized health facilities and housing. Not only age, but income levels, household size, racial composition, and any attribute of the future population that can be reliably forecast provides information that is useful to decision-makers. Identifying and forecasting the population of the community by age cohorts offers a good basis from which to develop population projections. These forecasts are not merely linear extrapolations, for many factors may cause a leveling or even a decline in population as particular demographic configurations reach their peak. Assumptions are vital components of these projections and estimates. Based on factors that can be expected to affect the trends identified, assumptions improve the validity and reliability of forecasts by considering the factors of change in a community. As assumptions are re-examined in light of more refined data, adjustments can be made in calculations.

Economic Projections. Information concerning economic conditions of the community is critical to the development of an effective capital facilities plan. Economic forecasts are a factor in calculating population projections, since assumptions concerning population growth or decline are correlated with the expected economic activity of an area. For example, if a locality is experiencing rapid industrial growth, it will likely produce a wave of worker immigration. The age and socioeconomic characteristics of these new groups should be forecast. Capital facilities planning then translates these projections and forecasts into community needs for physical facilities. If the industrial growth of an area is expected to attract young workers and their families, this will result in increased demands for educational services and schools as well as public improvements to support these services. Conversely, if the municipality is not responsive to these demands, it will result in negative feedback on the growth and economic activity of an area. Information concerning future economic conditions is essential in determining the financial capacity of a community to absorb capital expenditures. Economic indicators, such as employment data, cost of living indices, information regarding disposable income, building activity data, bank deposits, *etc.*, can be built into trend analyses and used with assumptions to suggest the future capacity [30].

Program and Financial Planning. It is important to evaluate and schedule public improvements in harmony with the scheduling of public service programs. Without such coordination, inefficient use of resources may result. Moreover, public improvements provided prior to their need represent resource commitments that could be used more effectively for other projects. Efficiency demands that program planning and capital facilities planning be coordinated in their mutual objective of delivering public sector services. Capital facilities, as an integral subset of community financial administration, are dependent upon careful financial planning. Financial planning by local governments has been complicated by the "fiscal crisis"—the imbalance between the rates of increase in revenues and expenditures of local governments. Demands for services and facilities increase and change as a function of growth and socioeconomic characteristics of the population. Revenues tend to increase at a slower rate, creating an ever-widening fiscal gap. This inelasticity of local government revenues is attributable, in part, to the tax structure, which forces local governments to rely heavily upon property taxes. Present pressures have proven property taxes to be inflexible and unresponsive in meeting increasing demands.

Revenue and Expenditure Analysis. When local governments are struggling to "break even," it is difficult to impress decision-makers with the necessity of planning ahead. While information gathered through various projections and estimates can give credibility to the arguments for the future needs of the community, the fiscal squeeze can severely delimit alternatives available to local government for financing not only capital facilities, but also operating programs. Tools such as revenue and expenditure analysis have been applied to foster a comprehensive financial planning process sensitive to this plight.

Revenue analysis disaggregates the sources of revenue into appropriate categories, with the analysis of each category including not only the estimate of dollar receipts, but also the percentage of the total revenues that each category represents. Based upon these disaggregated figures, trends in absolute and relative increases and declines can be calculated for each category. Such analysis provides a more accurate picture of the current financial situation and contributes to the accuracy of forecasts and projections.

Expenditure analysis also requires disaggregation of data into major expenditure categories. Data from past fiscal years provide a basis for the calculation of rates of increase or decrease, and subsequently, for the computation of multipliers appropriate to each expenditure category. Future levels of expenditures can be derived from these multipliers, which also can be adjusted for changes in population characteristics, inflation rates, and so forth.

Broadly defined, policy or program implementation is concerned with deciding in advance the goals and objectives to be sought, what should be done, who will do what, and how various activities will be accomplished. In addition to deciding what should be done and organizing physical and fiscal resources into a cohesive unit, implementation is concerned with the motivation of men and woman in such a way as to achieve the stated policy or program objectives. Thus, implementation is a *process of coordination* and, at times, manipulation of political, physical, fiscal, and human resources. Such concerns require that attention be given to multiple actions over an extended period of time. In this respect, the program manager must have timely answers to questions that arise during the implementation process. In order to maintain control, the manager must develop a dynamic system for planning, scheduling, delivering, monitoring, and evaluating program operations—one that produces the best possible initial operations plan and, while at the same time, allows for reaction to changing conditions.

The implementation process can be broken down into five basic states:

1. clarification of programmatic goals and objectives;
2. task delineation;
3. organizing, planning, and scheduling;
4. delegation of responsibility; and
5. follow-up evaluation.

These processes are discussed in greater detail below.

Clarification of Programmatic Goals and Objectives. A distinction should be made between *strategic planning* and *operations planning*, the latter being an integral part of the processes of policy or program implementation. As suggested earlier, strategic planning involves the selection of overall goals and objectives and the development of strategies (including policies and guidelines) for achieving those objectives. Operations planning is concerned with *tactics of performance* and the use of resources to achieve the overall objectives that are integral parts of strategic plans. Effective and comprehensive strategic planning may mean the difference between success and failure in the delivery of vital public services. Effective and efficient operations planning means the difference between "on time" and "late." The first step in operations planning involves the translation of broad goals and objectives into more specific programmatic targets. In this process, issue paper techniques and MBO procedures can provide useful mechanisms for defining the problems of implementation in terms of task orientation.

Task Delineation. Duplication of effort, confusion, backtracking, and delays can only be avoided by dividing the policy or program implementation task into specific, clear-cut, logical details, sequential steps, and by analyzing the methods, time requirements, and cost of each step. Persons concerned with the same activity should be grouped together, and all activities should be arranged so that each is a step toward the overall completion of the task. Having broken tasks down to subunits, the crux of delineation is efficient reassembly. Methods drawn from management science, such as the Critical Path Method (CPM) and

Program Evaluation and Review Techniques (PERT)—forms of network analysis —can be highly useful in this reconstruction. CPM arrays the time elements of a program or project for "minimum slack" or slippage, and can indicate the sequences in which subtasks should be initiated. PERT provides even more sophisticated methods for assessing time and cost requirements of complex tasks requiring the effective coordination of highly interrelated activities [31].

Organizing, Planning, and Scheduling.   Providing the data for PERT and CPM is carried out through a variety of simultaneous processes. *Organizing* refers to the structuring of critical time and resource questions.   Out of this organization process emerges the operations plan that serves to define the proper sequence of activities to be performed.   The operations plan goes beyond organization by attempting to assign priorities, and focuses on the utilization of resources and the location of funding.   It is at this point that *scheduling* begins to be integrated into the planning process.   Scheduling is largely concerned with the allocation of resources, based upon programmatic objectives, and the determination of the calendar dates of resource utilization.

Debt Administration.   Financial planning is essential in anticipating the capacity of a locality to absorb the debt impacts incurred in the financing of capital facilities.   Where shortfalls of revenue can be foreseen, changes in financial policies must be considered: taxes raised, expenditure curtailed, new revenue sources sought.   Since the life span of public improvements usually ranges from 15 to 20 years, debt financing is consistent with the *benefit principle* of public finance. Persons who will use the facility in future years (receive the benefits) should also bear a portion of the burden of payment.   Jurisdictions must be cautious, however, so that the term of debt does not exceed the useful life of the facility. Determining the type of bonds, term of their maturity, and other optional features is, therefore, an important part of capital facilities planning and debt administration.   The interest to be paid on municipal bonds must be an integral consideration in determining appropriate debt forms, since interest payments increase the total cost of the facility as the maturity period lengthens.   Debt should be incurred only within the financial and administrative capacity of the municipality.

In the final analysis, the theory of capital facilities planning still exceeds the practices of most local governments.   However, the outlook for the increased utilization of these planning mechanisms is encouraging.   Improvements in budget techniques among localities have promoted the utilization of capital budgeting, programming, and planning.   Also, the "fiscal crisis" informed decisions to produce the most efficient and effective projects and programs.   Mistakes or misjudgments are expensive.   As techniques and skills improve, so do the potential contributions of capital facilities planning to local governments. Capital facilities planning cannot solve all the problems of municipalities, but it can be a valuable tool in providing the community with the best possible government services. Together with strategic, program, and financial planning, capital facilities planning provides mechanisms and processes by which communities can anticipate future needs and react appropriately.

IMPLEMENTATION AND EVALUATION

This final section is a mixed bag of devices designed to facilitate implementation and evaluation processes. Some have suggested that implementation is where analysis leaves off and administration (in the pure sense) begins. As this discussion will illuminate, such an artificial distinction is useless and may be dysfunctional to effective public management. Implementation strategies at once direct and account for resource allocations. Likewise, evaluation, assessment, or accounting is integrally linked to prerequisite management decisions. Clear implementation and evaluation strategies are vital to coherent policy development. While occurring toward the end of the policy process, they should be spelled out at the onset and should be implicit in the initial formulation of objectives (*i.e.*, within the strategic planning process). It should be evident that in the process of deciding what one is going to do, it would be well to establish guidelines for how it should be done, and criteria that would indicate if and how well it had been done.

The four devices selected as indicative of this vast realm of management and measurement strategies are:

1. general program implementation strategies;
2. policy evaluation and sunset laws;
3. performance auditing; and
4. productivity assessment.

These devices are, of course, not totally representative of the wide array of available mechanisms. They are, however, congruent with the analytical and budgetary processes discussed above, and thus provide a degree of closure.

General Program Implementation

Pressman and Wildavsky, in the title of their study, *Implementation: How Great Expectations in Washington Are Dashed in Oakland*, convey a portion of the frustration involved in policy or program implementation. Getting things to work properly is often a patchwork arrangement at best—much like the Rube Goldberg mechanisms portrayed in their text. While even meticulous analysis cannot circumvent all the "foul ups," it can reduce the level of ineffectual activity and resulting wasted time and resources.

Delegation of Responsibility. Whenever possible, the program manager should try to avoid doing everything himself. To a large extent, the amount of cooperation that the manager will receive from staff will depend on how much he or she is willing to let them specify their own tasks. The manager must avoid the hazards of "overplanning" the tasks of others, and must be willing to use the concept of program control known as *management by exception*. This control concept is based on three premises:

1. management is vitally concerned with coping with change;
2. the future can never be predicted exactly; consequently, estimates will always differ from reality; and
3. it is important to respond to a given situation as soon as possible.

These premises define dynamic control and further illustrate exceptions by not defining them; that is, exceptions are the deviations or difference between what is anticipated (or what is scheduled to happen) and what actually does happen. *Dynamic control*, then, is responding with corrective action within an appropriate time to make such action useful and meaningful. The timeliness of corrective action can be increased if staff members are involved in the programming of their specific tasks and given responsibility for monitoring the effectiveness of their own activities.

Follow-up Procedures. Before beginning policy or program implementation, the manager should have a definite plan for checking to see that activities are properly, effectively, and efficiently being accomplished. Follow-up efforts will allow the administrator to determine if implementation is behind schedule and, if it is, to determine why and how to correct the situation. In addition to aiding the manager in corrective actions, follow-up procedures should allow the decision-maker to evaluate the overall implementation. Follow-up activities should be forward-looking in the sense that they attempt to assure that policy or program objectives will be achieved—that the implementation process is being carried out as planned, and that the public is being well served.

The policy development and implementation processes are continuous. Thus, the role of the manager is both political and administrative. The managerial role involves activities of supervision and control of policies or programs, and initially the manager should find out as much as possible about the activities that will be involved in the process (including sociopolitical ramifications). Experts, private groups, and others must be consulted so as to obtain both information and advice. Implicit in the consultation stage are the bargaining and maneuvering activities that take place so as to resolve or at least limit conflicts resulting from differing values and priorities. Program managers have, of course, the cumulative results of previous strategic analyses to aid them in this process of readjustment.

In general, the realm of program implementation is probably the weakest link in the chain of systematic analysis. This need not be the case. Careful operational planning can strengthen this enterprise and thereby strengthen the entire policy process.

Policy Evaluation as the Isolation of Ineffective Programs

Practitioners from the private or business sector often are quite baffled by the fact that in most cases public administrators are largely unaware of the impact and import of their involvement in policy development. James Anderson suggests some of the following reasons why this might be the case [32]:

1. the uncertainty of goals with regard to public programs;
2. the problems of confirming causality;
3. the diffuse impacts of public policies;
4. the problems of data acquisition; and
5. the resistance of public officials to formal evaluations.

Despite these obstacles, there seems to be an ever increasing emphasis on policy evaluation. Through such mechanisms as "Sunset Laws" [33], federal and particularly state managers are being asked to provide elaborate justifications of their programs. Failure to do so may signal the demise of those programs or cause them to "self destruct." Gerald Kopel explains that "the term 'Sunset' implies a fading out of bureaucracy, but it could as aptly have been called 'High Noon,' a confrontation between the legislature and the legislature's creatures" [34]. Bruce Adams of Common Cause outlines the following ingredients of a Sunset process [34, p. 139]:

1. Programs and agencies should automatically terminate at a certain date unless affirmatively re-created by law.
2. Termination should be periodic (*e.g.*, every seven or nine years) in order to institutionalize the program review process.
3. Like all significant innovations, the Sunset mechanism should be phased in gradually.
4. Programs and agencies in the same policy area should be reviewed simultaneously in order to encourage coordination, consolidation, and responsible pruning.
5. Existing entities (*e.g.*, budget and planning offices and legislative auditors) should undertake the preliminary program evaluation work, but their evaluation capacities must be strengthened.
6. The sunset proposal should establish general criteria to guide the program evaluation process.
7. Substantive preliminary work must be packaged in manageable decision-

making reports for policy-makers to use in the exercise of their professional judgment.

8. Substantial legislative committee reorganization is a prerequisite to meaningful Sunset review.

9. Safeguards must be built into Sunset laws to guard against arbitrary termination.

10. Public participation is an essential part of the Sunset process.

In short, Sunset and other evaluative processes attempt to differentiate between effective and ineffective programs, policies, and, in some cases, entire agencies. The primary focus of evaluation is on existing programs (through feedback on current and previous activities), although it may be used in an experimental or demonstration mode, as when pilot programs are mounted before the implementation of full-scale programs to determine whether such programs are likely to fulfill their objectives.

Basic Methods of Program Evaluation

The focal point of policy evaluation is the development of measures and methodologies of comparison. Harry Hatry and his colleagues at the Urban Institute have summarized some of the basic methods of comparison as follows [35] :

1. *Before vs. After Program Comparison*—Compares program results from the same jurisdiction measured at two points in time: immediately before the program was implemented and at some appropriate time after implementation.

2. *Time Trend Projections of Pre- and Postprogram Data*—Compares actual postprogram data to estimated data projected from a number of time periods prior to the program.

3. *With and Without Comparisons*—Compares data from jurisdictions (or population segments) where the program is operating with data from other jurisdictions (or population segments) where the program is not operating.

4. *Controlled Experimentation*—Compares preselected, similar groups, some of whom are served and some of whom are not (or are served in different ways or with different levels of services). The critical aspect is that the comparison groups are preassigned before the program implementation so that they are as similar as possible except for the program treatment.

5. *Comparisons of Planned vs. Actual Performance*—Compares actual, postprogram data to targets set in prior years—either before program implementation or at any period since implementation.

The controlled experiment is generally regarded as the most sophisticated of evaluation strategies, but also the most difficult to carry out. In the absence of experimental conditions, statistical manipulations can induce the so-called Quasi-Experimental Design, but these approaches have had limited applications thus far [36].

Many evaluation strategies are considerably less exotic than new statistical techniques. The basic goal is the same, however, that of isolating ineffective programs. For the most part, they are designed to strengthen the evaluative capability inherent in existing policy procedures such as auditing. Yet in addition, these devices represent a step beyond the traditional postaudit inquiry. As E. S. Quade explains [37]:

> The conventional post-audit tended to be backward-looking; it attempted to place blame. It contributed to improvement only in the sense that it served a deterrent function. . . . An evaluation, on the other hand, should be primarily forward-looking and it should help management to decide what to do next.

Performance Auditing

Auditing is a process for monitoring the flow of dollars and cents. The *traditional financial audit* involves an examination of the accounting records of governmental units and the underlying systems of data processing and internal control. The objective is to verify that all financial transactions have been properly handled and recorded in compliance with legal restrictions so that statements produced from those records accurately reflect the financial condition. The financial audit ordinarily will involve examining the source documents, records, and procedures relating to all financial transactions. For example, in examining the property tax revenues of a city, the auditor will use a number of interlocking checks to confirm that property tax revenues, collections, receivables, and related allowances are accurately and fairly presented. Similar devices covering other types of transactions and related balance sheet items enable the auditor to form an opinion of the statement as a whole.

Despite seemingly clear-cut requirements of the independent audit, there often is confusion in the establishment of appropriate financial organizations within local government. This confusion stems from a failure to distinguish between the two kinds of audit necessary to monitor financial operations. One is the current audit performed by the controller or other designated official within the department of finance and often called the *preaudit*, since it is made prior to the payment of all claims. This audit, which extends to a daily check of all revenues and receipts of a community, serves as the basis for the entries in the controller's accounts and is the only valid and proper method of accounting control. The independent audit, often called the *postaudit*, is performed after transactions have been completed and the necessary accounting entries made.

Although the financial audit checks the correctness of the records and the legal propriety of the transactions, questions of the value of the activities and the efficiency of their operations are left unanswered. These questions have led to the development of *performance auditing*, also known in some quarters as operational or management auditing. In addition to a financial audit, a performance audit includes a review of management policies and administration. As its purpose is to identify opportunities to reduce costs, increase efficiency, and improve program effectiveness, it thereby serves to extend and improve management control.

A major factor in the increasing prevalence of performance auditing has been the growth of professionalism in governmental administration and the resulting increase in emphasis on quantitative and qualitative analysis. Moreover, with growing public awareness of the impact of the government sector, managers are called upon more often to report and justify their administration of public resources.

The rise of the grant-in-aid and the demands of the grantors of funds for evidence that the monies are being spent both honestly and wisely gives additional impetus to performance auditing. The so-called "Yellow Book," issued in 1972 by the US General Accounting Office points to the direction for governmental auditing by emphasizing that a complete audit should cover three elements: financial compliance, economy and efficiency, and programs results [38]. These will be described below.

Financial Compliance. Very similar to traditional audit requirements, this aspect of performance auditing reviews total operations to see that they are properly conducted and that financial reports are fairly represented. Moreover, it maintains the application of specific legal stipulations and management regulations.

Economy and Efficiency. This set of criteria seeks to determine whether a given government entity is using its resources (personnel, property, space, *etc.*) in an economical and efficient manner. In addition, this test strives to discover the causes of inefficiencies in management information systems, administrative procedures, or organizational structure.

Program Results. This final element has, perhaps, the most far-reaching implication. Here the auditor is concerned whether desired results and benefits are being achieved, given the level of expenditures. An assessment is also made as to whether the agency or government entity has considered other alternatives that may be more cost-effective.

These elements of cost-effectiveness are, of course, hampered by the same constraints discussed earlier in reference to cost-benefit/cost-effectiveness analysis. Moreover, the question of achieving meaningful performance measured for highly nebulous and intangible social programs remains germane. Nevertheless, acceptable standards of performance auditing are very likely to emerge in the wake of the federal decision to apply the test to local grant-in-aid programs.

Productivity Assessment

The final item picks up where the previous discussion left off; *i.e.*, with the question of performance measures. While productivity is a very different concept from performance, the "bang for bucks" analogy still applies. Stated briefly, productivity in the public sector is "the efficiency with which resources are consumed in the effective delivery of public services" [39]. This definition includes elements of quality as well as quantity. Nevertheless, it is too general to be directly applied in a practical manner. In more usable terms, productivity measurement may be said to involve the relationship of outputs (preferably *final* outputs) and inputs, usually expressed as a ratio.

The major difficulty in implementing productivity programs is measurement. As noted above, both input and output measures are required to determine productivity. Input measurement does not present a significant problem. Measuring public sector output is exceedingly difficult however. One reason for this difficulty is that government agencies are generally engaged in performing various types of services, which are highly intangible, *e.g.*, welfare activities. The lack of physical outputs is less problematic in the case of private sector services because productivity can be estimated by use of prices associated with these services, *e.g.*, in terms of dollars worth of output per man hour. Since public services are generally provided without direct charge, this method of productivity measurement generally is not applicable.

This measurement problem has led to the establishment of two distinct classes of output:

1. *Activity Measured.* This output is the consequence of a direct service activity, such as *police patrols.*
2. *Result Measured.* This output is an indirect manifestation assumed to be causally connected to the direct output, such as *crime rate.*

Direct outputs are more easily quantifiable, but often fail to account for the quality expectations of those public services.

The simplist type of productivity measurement is to allow input or output measures to serve as surrogates for productivity, as with output/input ratios. Improvements in management techniques and/or money-saving measures taken by government agencies have also been used as indicators of increased productivity, primarily in the context of New York City's productivity program. With the exception of output/input ratios, the above measures are not really satisfactory indicators of productivity. They have come into use, however, in response to the need for proxy measures in cases where difficulties in measuring outputs and/or inputs have proved insurmountable.

An alternative approach to estimating productivity, which does not require output measurement, has also been devised. This approach utilizes changes in expenditure data, which are divided into three components: cost, workload, and a third residual factor reflecting changes in quality and productivity [40]. The distinct advantages to this approach are the availability of expenditure information and the ability to devise proxy measures for cost and workload.

Implementation of productivity programs poses another set of problems, which might be summarized as follows [41]:

1. *Organization Type and Level.* Implementation of productivity may need to be considered on a city-wide as well as agency-wide basis. It may even be advisable to establish a separate agency to oversee productivity.
2. *Costs of Implementing Productivity.* The costs to be considered in implementing productivity measures are both monetary and the disruptive effects upon agencies.
3. *Administrative Resistance.* As suggested earlier in the general discussion of policy evaluation, agencies may simply not want to be evaluated. Thus, they will make conscious efforts to undermine such a program.

Growing fiscal difficulties, particularly in local governments, suggest a need to discover methods for reducing expenditures without reducing public services. Productivity improvement in the provision of public services is one way of achieving this goal. While not a simple process to invoke, its promise seems to warrant the effort.

SUMMARY AND CONCLUSIONS

This brief overview of a few selected techniques cannot hope to provide more than a glimpse of their actual content. Nevertheless, it is hoped that sufficient information was provided to display the extensive utility of these devices.

For summary purposes, it may be suggested that the processes for developing public policies include seven basic stages, as follows:

1. Assessment of needs and screening of public demands and wants.
2. Identification and clarification of public problems and issues.
3. Definition of problem constraints arising from the decisions environment, identification of the problem parameters that define feasible solution sets, and clarification of organizational (system) objectives and expectations.
4. Formulation, analysis, and evaluation of policy alternatives and related courses of action.
5. Definition of a "best" or optimal policy and the modification of this policy to gain acceptance.
6. Conversion of policy into a series of action-oriented decisions leading to policy/program implementation.
7. Monitoring of performance and evaluation of policy/program impacts.

The various concepts and techniques covered above have application to these

Table 3. Application of module techniques to the states of the policy development process.

Policy/program analysis and evaluation techniques	Stages of the policy development process
Strategic planning	Assessment of needs and screening of demands
Issue papers	Problem identification and definition
Managment by Objectives	Environmental constraints, problem parameters, and systems expectations
Long-range forecasting	Formulation and evaluation of alternatives
Cost-benefit and cost-effectiveness	Definition of a "best" policy and determination of an acceptable policy
Performance/Program Budgeting	Conversion to action
Productivity assessment	Feedback and evaluation
Performance audit	
Program implementation	

seven basic stages of the public policy formulation process, as illustrated in Table 3. It is essential to note that the lengths of the lines in this diagram represent a sequential development, rather than an accounting of all the residual parameters.

The ability of policy-makers and policy analysts to assess the overall needs of a community and to screen public demands to determine priority action requirements is highly dependent upon the structural configuration of the policy system. A well-developed structure—one in which there are extensive couplings among critical components—will be highly sensitive to public needs, wants, and demands. A less well-constructed system may fail to provide the necessary awareness of unsettled situations and, subsequently, their accompanying problems. Thus, this stage in the policy-formulation process can be likened to an early warning device—the system is alerted to the possible impingement of some policy-demanding situation, and can be readied to take appropriate action to remedy the attendant problems and issues. In this connection, the techniques of strategic planning provide the policy analyst with a substantial set of mechanisms for increased sensitivity to pending policy or decision requirements.

Attempts to discover the relevant facts about a problematic situation and to define and delimit the nature of the problem (its environmental constraints, parameters, and the expectations of public organizations that will be called upon to implement action programs to resolve identified problems) can also be facilitated by the mechanisms of strategic planning, aided by issue papers, techniques, and the framework provided by management by objectives procedures. Long-range-forecasting techniques also have applications in this and in the previous stage of the process.

A statement of the policy problem and an identification of the conditions the solution must meet, plus a sufficiency of relevant facts, may then be used to suggest relevant policy alternatives—the fourth stage in the process. Most public policy decisions involve stochastic situations, and therefore, activities in this stage of the process evidence "seek-and-find" or "trial-and-error" behavior characteristics. This search process can be organized and assisted by the analytical framework of performance/program budgeting and the techniques of cost-benefit and cost-effectiveness analysis.

In the fifth stage, available policy alternatives are tested in an effort to arrive at a "best" or maximal solution. Here again, the organizational framework of performance/program budgeting, the longer range perspectives provided by capital facilities planning, and the analytical procedures of cost-benefit and cost-effectiveness approaches can assist immeasurably in the search for a "best" solution. This policy solution must then be modified to take account of adjustments and compromises necessary to effectuate the chosen courses of action in light of the resources available and the expectations of the system. Out of this stage of the process emerges an optimal policy, given the political realities of the situation.

In the sixth stage, policy is converted into action by making specific assignments of responsibilities. This assignment, in turn, may require adjustments in the structural configuration of the system based on an assessment of the productivity of various components within the organizational units that will implement the action programs. In fact, the structural configuration of the system may be altered at any time during the course of the policy development process. This alteration often is necessary to achieve an acceptable policy decision (one that is capable of implementation).

Feedback occurs, intentionally or unintentionally, at many stages in the process. Much of this feedback is internal to the process, resulting in a recycling of a given stage in order to achieve further refinements and modifications. Information monitoring and reporting are particularly important, however, after a policy decision has been reached in order to provide continuous testing or expectations against actual events. Even the best policy decision has a high probability of being wrong, and even the most effective policies eventually become obsolete. Failure to provide for adequate feedback is one of the primary reasons for persisting in a course of action long after it has ceased to be appropriate or rational. As Drucker has observed, unless decision-makers build their feedback around direct exposure to reality, their decisions may result in a sterile dogmatism [42].

A basic aspect of the policy development process is the creation of a predictive capacity to identify changing conditions that might necessitate modifications in the selected courses of action. In this context, the techniques and procedures of performance auditing, productivity assessment, performance/program budgeting, and program implementation can provide significant assistance in the evaluation of performance and policy impacts. Evaluative controls should be developed for a given policy by:

1. defining what constitutes a significant change for each variable and relationship that serve components in the policy decision,
2. establishing procedures for detecting the occurrence of such changes, and
3. specifying the tolerable range within which a policy can be modified and beyond which new solutions must be sought.

Although the preceding model is presented in seven distinct stages, it would be misleading to assume that policy problems are so obliging as to permit an easy, logical sequence of attention. As Joseph Cooper has observed [43]:

(Problems) conceal their true nature so that halfway down the path of a decision you may find that you must retrace your steps for a new beginning. Or you may have alternatives for decision presented to you which, in your belief, are not the only or the best possible courses. This, too, will send you back to the beginning.

Policy alternatives usually are not created by moving in orderly sequences from the first to last stage. It is not uncommon for a new alternative to occur while data about the problem are still being collected. Moreover, in a complex situation, different phases of the process may develop at different rates. For example, the stage of alternatives may be reached for one aspect or subsidiary problem of a complex problem situation while other parts of the same problem are still in the stage of definition and analysis. Nevertheless, it is necessary to approach the task of public policy formulation in an orderly fashion in order to adequately analyze the problems and issues and to uncover meaningful and useful insights as to their resolution. The concepts and techniques outlined in the discussion may provide the policy analyst, the program manager, and the policy-maker with major components of more effective, efficient, and responsive policy decisions.

Throughout this discussion, references have been made to the integral interrelationships between these analytical processes; as this connecting thread has been more or less readily apparent, only a cursory reexamination is needed here. Basically, the entire process might be described as a systematic redirecting of resources to a constantly evolving set of societal priorities. Initially, this entails aiding decision-makers and the public in the articulation of goals and objectives and their translation into programmatic alternatives. In turn, alternatives are assessed and narrowed to specific action commitments. These commitments are then interfaced with budgetary and evaluative techniques in order to determine the following items:

1. what level of effectiveness will meet societal expectations;
2. how said effectiveness will be assessed; and
3. what procedures will create the most efficient pursuit of said effectiveness.

Concurrent analyses attempt to predict and reduce the impact of sociopolitical and organizational constraints upon systematic development. The resulting procedures schedule, coordinate, and motivate administrative process. Meanwhile, general effectiveness is being calculated with regard to task and subtask effectiveness. As results are produced impacts are assessed, both in terms of internal criteria and external feedback. In short, this is a "cybernetic" approach. Each element in this process draws upon the methodological and informational contribution of the previous stage, spreading its impact throughout.

This interdependency does not imply that each device is unable to stand on its own merits. Individually they constitute a substantial enhancement of the level of analytical capability, collectively they constitute a vast improvement of the entire administrative policy process. Whether one chooses to use all or merely some of these analytical tools, they are likely to produce a noticeable departure from the "seat of the pants" policies and programs of the past. The authors hope this discussion has provided the path for such a departure.

GLOSSARY

Accounting: a system of controls and reporting mechanism regarding the use of money and property with a view to prior determination that expenditures are in accordance with law, local ordinances, and any rules and regulations governing these matters; a system by which public officials and employees can be held accountable for the money and other government property for which they are custodians or managers.

Affected Publics: Those individuals impacted by a policy who may or may not be interested in participating.

Auditing: the process of examining documents, records, reports, and systems of internal control, accounting and financial procedures, and other evidence to ascertain whether accounts present fairly the financial position and results of financial operations of the constituent funds and balanced account groups of the governmental unit; procedures to ascertain the stewardship of public officials who handle and are responsible for financial resources of a governmental unit.

Bond: an interest-bearing certificate of debt representing the obligation of a public body to repay a certain sum—usually issued in $1,000 units—on a specific date, with interest at a fixed rate to maturity.

Budget: a document that expresses the anticipated revenues and expenditures of government for a specified period of time; a plan for allocating scarce resources among competing public needs and wants; a budget is future-oriented in that it expresses anticipated actions as distinguished from an accounting balance sheet that indicates actual revenues and expenditures.

Capital Budget: a plan for the expenditure of public funds for capital purposes, showing as income the revenues, special assessments, free surplus, and down payment appropriations to be applied to the cost of a capital project or projects, expenses of issuance or obligations, engineering supervision, contracts, and any other related expenses.

Capital Improvements: acquisition, construction, replacement of, or major repairs to public facilities with a relatively long useful life.

Capital Improvements Program: a comprehensive schedule for staging the construction or acquisition of capital improvements and the allocation of costs by sources of revenue, in accordance with a system of priorities, usually covering a period of five to six years.

Citizen Participation: the continuing interaction and information exchange *within* the planning period of a public program, or the development period of a public policy.

(CPM) Critical Path Method: an operations research device for determining the path of least resistance and the proper scheduling of interacting processes. Most effectively used in the space program to insure that different components would be available when needed.

Effectiveness Measures: attempts to estimate the success of a particular program or output in reaching desired objectives such as changes in social states, *i.e.,* higher college admittance scores, *etc.*

Efficiency Measures: measures concerned with the manner in which resources are combined into final products, *i.e.,* production involving minimal waste, expense, or effort.

Externalities: spill-over effects; consequences of an action that affect parties not directly involved in that action, *e.g.,* air pollution.

General Systems: a basic theory that holds that social and physical phenomena are reducible to a common set of principles and axioms, and that natural systems and their maintenance functions provide a model for social systems.

Line-Item Budget: a budget format in which funding requests are supported by detailed objects of expenditures—tabulations of the myriad items required to operate a governmental unit, such as salaries and wages, rent, office supplies, equipment, travel, and other such inputs—developed during the era of fiscal controls when annual balancing of the budget was considered a fundamental principle of sound fiscal policy.

Management By Objectives: management techniques that strive to make agency objectives more explicit through the identification of conflicting objectives (both vertical and horizontal); greater opportunity for participative management through a cyclical goal-setting process; and the introduction of performance feedback and measurements of accomplishment.

Management Planning: the process by which steps are taken to assure that public resources are used effectively and efficiently in the accomplishment of public objectives; it involves: 1) the programming of approved goals into specific projects, programs, and activities, 2) the design of organizational units to carry out approved programs and plans, and 3) the staffing of these units and the procurement of necessary resources.

Management Science: the application of mathematical and related approaches involving a "systems" perspective to the solution of relatively large-scale social or management problems; management science includes such areas as operations research, systems analysis, information theory, management cybernetics, cost-benefit and cost-effectiveness analysis, gaming and simulation, and so forth.

MOR (Mangement by Objectives and Results): "MOR is further refinement of the MBO process, incorporating a closed-loop approach to insure that results achieved do in fact resemble the objectives that were set. . . . Management defines in advance the results to be achieved and the action plans required for their achievement. Implicit in this management approach is a plan for overcoming obstacles and for establishing priorities when crises do occur (as they will)."

The New Public Administration: a reemphasis of moral and philosophical concepts within public administration initiated after the turbulence of the 1960s. It is concerned with human values within and without public organizations.

Operating Budget: the annual budget adopted by a municipality or school district each year, showing an itemized list of proposed operating expenditures, revenues, or other available funds by source.

Operations Control: control and reporting procedures, such as position controls, requisition and purchasing procedures, restrictions on fund transfers, post-audits, the purpose of which is to secure compliance with policies made by central authorities.

Operations Planning (or Scheduling): the process of assuring that specific tasks are carried out efficiently and effectively; in its more advanced forms, operations planning involves the application of such management tools as PERT (program evaluation and review technique) and CPM (critical path method).

Operations Research: a series of analytical techniques designed to optimize the performance of a system through the application of scientific methods and problem-solving tools to provide those in control of the system with optimum solutions to the problems.

Performance Administration: the process of deciding, in advance, what an organization will do in the future, who will do it, and how it will be done, as well as the management and improvement of ongoing operations and activities.

Performance Auditing: procedures that extend the traditional audit of financial operations for fidelity, legality, and accuracy to encompass the degree of achievement of management objectives in terms of economy and efficiency and in terms of program results (effectiveness).

Performance Budgeting: a budgetary approach that focuses attention upon the general character and relative importance of the work to be done or the services to be rendered, rather than upon things to be acquired, such as personal services, supplies, equipment, and so on; the principal objective of performance budgeting is to assist administrators in their assessment of the work-efficiency of operating units.

(PERT) Performance Evaluation and Review Technique: A scheduling and assessment process that combines operations research techniques with a management Delphi to plot an implementation strategy with minimum slack and maximum efficiency.

Policy: 1) a broad guide to present and future decisions selected in light of given conditions from a number of alternative courses of action; 2) the actual decision or set of decisions designed to carry out this chosen course of action; and 3) a projected program consisting of desired objectives (goals) and the means of achieving them.

Policy Analysis: a systematic process, involving the delineation of pertinent problems and issues, the clarification of goals and objectives relevant to these problems, the identification and comparison of available alternative courses of action (often requiring the design and synthesis of new alternatives), and the determination of the optimal means (resources) necessary to attain the desired goals and objectives.

Policy Evaluation: procedures for the assessment of the effectiveness of ongoing programs in achieving public objectives that rely on the principles of research design to distinguish a program's effect from those of other forces working in the situation; it aims at program improvement through policy modification (as contrasted to the formulation of new policy).

(PPBS) Planning-Programming-Budgeting-Scheduling System: a budgetary format whereby budgetary requests are presented in terms of program "packages" rather than in the traditional line-item format; a conscious effort is made in PPBS to state end objectives, seek a wider range of alternatives over a longer time horizon, and link program and financial plans.

Productivity Bargaining: formation of collective bargaining agreements that include changes in work rules *etc.*, designed to achieve increased productivity in exchange for benefits to employees.

Program Budgeting: a budgetary approach that is built around five major components: 1) identification of major public goals and objectives in programmatic terms; 2) the structuring and analysis of public activities in programmatic terms; 3) extended time horizon and multiyear program and financial plans; 4) systematic analysis of alternatives; and 5) program monitoring and updating procedures.

Quality-of-Life/Social Well-Being: a diverse set of indicators that attempt to account for the various intangible yet significant social aspects of policy, *e.g.*, one's general welfare beyond monetary or economic security.

Queueing Theory: mathematical techniques often used for determining delivery times and sequencing based upon several factors, including: 1) demand frequency; 2) resource allocation; and 3) service productivity.

Strategic Planning: the process of identifying public goals and objectives, determining needed changes in these objectives, and deciding on the resources to be used to attain these objectives.

"Sunset" Legislation: a requirement that every agency or commission regularly justify its budget and its existence (and documents its achievements) to the legislative body that authorized it, or "self-destruct."

Systems Analysis: a systematic examination and comparison of alternative courses of action to achieve specified objectives for some future time period, which involves a critical examination of the cost and utility of each alternative over an extended time horizon and recognized explicitly the numerous interactions among the key variables in the problem situation; systems analysis focuses most often on research and development and investment-type decision problems.

Zero-Base Budgeting (or *ab initio* budgeting): a budgetary approach that stresses the necessity for each department or agency to defend annually the level of every activity, and even the existence of the department or agency.

NOTES AND REFERENCES

1. Dye, Thomas R. *Understanding Public Policy*. Englewood Cliffs, N.J.: Prentice-Hall, 1972, p. 18.
2. Burke, Roy, III, and James P. Heaney. *Collective Decision Making in Water Resource Planning*. Lexington, Mass.: D. C. Heath, 1975, p. 139.
3. Friedrich, Carl J. *Man and His Government*. New York: McGraw-Hill, 1963, p. 79.
4. Metsner, Arnold J. "Bureaucratic Policy Analysis." *Policy Analysis* 1(1975): 115–132.
5. The perspective upon policy analysis exemplified by these definitions is developed in Alan Walter Steiss and Gregory A. Daneke, *Performance Administration*, Lexington, Mass.: D. C. Heath, 1977.
6. Kraemer, Kenneth. *Policy Analysis in Local Government*. Washington, D. C.: International City Management Association, 1973, p. 25; also note that Kraemer has a useful matrix of policy problems in which he differentiates between "Operational Problems," "Programming Problems," and "Development Problems." Developmental Problems require "intuitive judgment," and "qualitative modeling." Compare this perspective with that of E. S. Quade, "What Sort of Problem? What Sort of Analysis," in *Analysis for Public Decisions* New York: American Elsevier, 1975, pp. 13-31.
7. Quade, E. S. In *Analysis for Public Decisions*, p. 15–16.
8. Webber, Ross A. *Management: Basic Elements of Managing Organizations*. Homewood, Ill.: Richard D. Irwin, 1975, chapter 12.
9. Catanese, Anthony J., and Alan Walter Steiss. *Systemic Planning: Theory and Application*. Lexington, Mass.: D. C. Heath, 1970, p. 35.
10. Friedmann, John. "Regional Development in a Post-Industrial Society." *Journal of the American Institute of Planners*, 30(May 1964).
11. For a parallel, yet more elaborate discussion of issue papers, see E. S. Quade, *Analysis for Public Decisions*, New York: American Elsevier, 1975, pp. 68-74.
12. Dickey, John W., Thomas Watts, and John P. Ross. *Methodology for Urban and Regional Studies*. New York: McGraw-Hill, 1977.
13. Havens, Harry S. "MBO and Program Evaluation, Or Whatever Happened to PPBS." *Public Administration Review* (January/February, 1976): 5.
14. Sherwood, Frank P. and Willaim J. Page. "MBO and Public Management." *Public Administration Review* (January/February 1976): 11.
15. Varney, Glenn H. *Management By Objectives*. Chicago: 1971, p. 45.
16. Quoted in Lawrence G. Hines, *Environmental Issues*, New York: W. W. Norton, 1973, p. 111.

17. Maass, Arthur. *Muddy Waters*. Cambridge: Harvard University Press, 1951. Ferejohn, John A. *Pork Barrel Politics*. Standford: Stanford University Press, 1974.
18. McKean, Roland N. *Public Spending*. New York: McGraw-Hill, 1968, pp. 136–138.
19. Due, John F., and Ann Friedlaender. *Government Finance–Economics of the Public Sector*. Homeville, Ill.: Richard D. Irwin, 1973, p. 62.
20. Report of the Inter-Agency River Basin Committee. *Proposed Practices for Economics Analysis of River Basin Projects*. Washington, D. C.: Government Printing Office, 1950, p. 13.
21. For a general discussion of the problem of basing environmental decisions on cost-benefit alone see Gregory A. Daneke, "Life-Quality Management and the Changing Nature of Resource Development," paper presented at the Conference of the American Society for Public Administration, Atlanta Georgia, 1977; also note Orris C. Herfindahl and Allen V. Kneese, "Measuring Social and Economic Change: The Cost and Benefits of Environmental Pollution," in *The Measurement of Economic and Social Performance*, edited by Milton Moss, New York: Columbia University Press, 1973.
22. For an overview of the prospects and problems of cost-benefit/effective see Ronald W. Johnson and John M. Pierce, "The Economic Evaluation of Policy Impacts: Cost-Benefit and Cost-Effectiveness Analysis," in *Methodologies for Analyzing Public Policies*, edited by Frank P. Scioli, Jr. and Thomas J. Cook, Lexington, Mass.: D. C. Heath, 1975; for an elaborate discussion of social equity and cost-benefit, see E. J. Mishan, *Cost-Benefit Analysis*, New York: Praeger, 1976, pp. 382–415; also note David Berry and Gene Steiker, "The Concept of Justice in Regional Planning," *Journal of the American Institute of Planners* (November 1974).
23. Thomas A. Goldman, ed. *Cost-Effectiveness Analysis*. Washington, D.C.: Operations Research Council, 1967, p. 2.
24. King, Barry G. "Cost-Effectiveness Analysis: Implications for Accountants." In *Public Budgeting and Finance*. Edited by Robert T. Golembiewski and Jack Rabin. 2nd ed. Itasca, Ill.: Peacock Publishers, 1975.
25. U. S. Commission on Organization of the Executive Branch of the Government. *Budgeting and Accounting*. Washington, D.C.: Government Printing Office, 1949, p. 8.
26. Mosher, Frederick C. *Program Budgeting*. Chicago: Public Administration Service, 1954, p. 79.
27. These concepts are drawn from Alan Walter Steiss, *Public Budgeting and Management*, Lexington, Mass.: D. C. Heath, 1972, ch. 7.
28. Moak, Lennox L, and Albert M. Hillhouse. *Concepts and Practices in Local Government Finance*. Chicago: Municipal Finance Officers Association, 1975, p. 98.
29. Many of these ideas are drawn from Alan Walter Steiss, *Local Government Finance: Capital Facilities Planning and Debt Administration*, Lexington, Mass.: D. C. Heath, 1975.
30. Ferguson, Don E. "Determining Capacity for Capital Expenditures." *Municipal Finance* (August 1967).
31. For a simple and nontechnical explanation of PERT and CPM see: Nicholas Henry, *Public Administration and Public Affairs*, Englewood Cliffs, N.J.: Prentice-Hall, 1975, pp. 337–343.
32. Anderson, James E. *Public Policy-Making*. New York: Praeger, 1975, pp. 138–142.
33. For a detailed discussion of the implication of "Sunset" see Benjamin Shimberg, "The Sunset Approach." Address before the Western Regional Council of State Governments, Salt Lake City, July 23, 1976.
34. Kopel, Gerald H. "Sunset in the West." *State Government* (Summer 1976): 135.

35. Hatry, Harry P., Richard E. Winnie, and Donald M. Fish. *Practical Program Evaluation for State and Local Government*. Washington, D.C.: The Urban Institute, 1973, pp. 39–40.
36. Wilson, L. A. "Statistical Techniques for the Analysis of Public Policies as Time Series Quasi Experiments." In *Methodologies for Analyzing Public Policies*. Edited by Frank P. Scioli and Thomas J. Cook. Lexington, Mass.: D. C. Heath, 1975, pp. 105–112.
37. Quade, E. S. *Analysis for Public Decisions*. New York: American Elsevier, 1975, p. 225.
38. US General Accounting Office, Comptroller General of the United States. *Standards for Audit of Governmental Organizations, Programs, Activities, and Functions*. Washington, D.C.: Government Printing Office, 1972.
39. Hayward, Nancy S. "The Productivity Challenge." *Public Administration Review* 35(1976): 544.
40. Ross, John P., and Jesse Burkhead. *Productivity in the Local Government Sector*. Lexington, Mass.: D. C. Heath, 1974.
41. For a discussion of union resistance to productivity measures in New York see Raymond D. Horton, "Productivity and Productivity Bargaining in Government," *Public Administration Review* 35(1976): 407–414.
42. Drucker, Peter F. "The Effective Decision." *Harvard Business Review* 45(1967): 95.
43. Cooper, Joseph D. *The Art of Decision-Making*. Garden City, N.Y.: Doubleday, 1961, pp. 15–16.

3

Global Models: Their Usefulness to Public Policy-Makers

David H. Carhart
The George Washington University

INTRODUCTION

Since 1971, several attempts have been made to model the complexity of the world's interactions. The formulators of these models have then obtained predictions and attempted to get high government officials to use these forecasts in their decision-making processes. Most notable are the models developed under the sponsorship of the Club of Rome; nevertheless, these and other efforts have not drawn the desired response in terms of governmental action.

This essay will deal with several different facets of this problem, and will begin with a general background that outlines the problem faced by the administrators. This problem is basically twofold: 1) what are the current pressures being put on administrators by increasing global systems, and 2) what should be the decision-making style of the policy-maker so that interaction with the modeler is facilitated?

In addition, the leaders of today are faced with the headache of classifying and evaluating varying types of models. A bilevel taxonomy has been provided that classifies models first by their type (subdivided using methodological criteria), and then by the type of decision for which they were developed.

This paper will analyze only three of these models in detail: Jay Forrester's World Dynamics models, as presented in *World Dynamics* [1] and *The Limits to Growth*, [2] Mesarovic and Pestel's Scenario Analysis, as presented in *Mankind at the Turning Point*, [3] and the qualitative dialogue coordinated by Jan Tinbergen, presented as *RIO: Reshaping the International Order* [4]. The major reason I have selected these three for special analysis is their potential impact on government operations. It is entirely possible that other models are better representations of the global interactions, but the public policy-making process has not yet had time to digest the claims made.

It would appear that public response has been most extensive with respect to the World Dynamics models; yet the complexity of the models hinders a good understanding of the promises and pitfalls they contain. Thus, little *action* has been taken. I would, therefore, like to present a step-by-step formulation of a smaller, two-sector model with the goal of increasing the administrator's understanding of the modeling process.

Finally, I will attempt to provide qualitative answers to some of the critical issues facing policy-makers in the area of global modeling.

THE PROBLEMS FACED BY ADMINISTRATORS

General Global Conditions

Recently, the various governments of the world have faced many interrelated problems. The United States exemplifies this, with its recent history of postwar recession, inflationary spiral, sagging production, and high prices. Unemployment was high, the availability of energy was in doubt, the poor and elderly faced severe monetary difficulties, "crime" was on the rise, and, in general, the victims of the dysfunctional economy of both the US and the world were crying out to their respective governments to do something. Governmental action just for the sake of governmental action was of no help, however [5], and what help was offered was intended only to address part of the problem. This partitioning effect, taken by individual governments, was not able to cope with increased pollution, a widening gap between the "have" and "have-not" nations, continued pressure from an increasing population, tense political undertones, and various natural adversities such as drought.

The administrators of the world (if such people really exist) thus faced the problem of formulating a strategy for the future, simultaneously allowing for the ramifications of continued growth. But this implies many separate, yet related complexities: What are the available resources? What levels of pollution are tolerable? What levels are desirable? How much economic growth is possible? Are there feasible solutions? What are the choices before us? Should we use global models at all? If so, who should formulate them? Who should evaluate them? And so forth . . . CAN WE, OR SHOULD WE, LIMIT GROWTH?

Figure 1 depicts the dilemma all policy-makers share. Alvin Toffler states the case very succinctly [7]

If we do not learn from history, we shall be compelled to relive it. True. But if we do not change the future, we shall be compelled to endure it. And that could be worse.

Figure 1. Public policy-makers hard at work [6]. Reprinted with permission of William Hersey and © Yale Alumni Publications, Inc., 1973.

Mankind is about to collide with the future [8], and from this *fact* has grown an awareness represented by the "futurists" in all countries. Whether they are organizations, institutionalized programs, individual workers, or governments, their main activity is the study of the future. And this increase has led to another of the administrator's problems: given that he or she wants to get reelected, how does one deal with these groups?, How strong are they?, *etc.*

In summary, the major political powers of the world are being asked to solve a set of crises the dimensions of which are unmatched in human history. They have turned, and are turning, to the quantitative analysts for assistance, and the plethora of global models that have appeared is a function of the money that has suddenly become available. These analysts have predominantly used computer-based mathematical models that take a *very* macro view of the situation; the prime distinguishing characteristics seem to be the time horizon selected and the criteria for establishing the world's sectors, *e.g.*, geographic verses economic.

Varying Administrative Styles

Before the administrator can decide upon the appropriateness of a given global model, he must first decide on the "correct" policy-making mechanics in which he is going to engage. In the literature on social policy-making there are several dozen specific and unique decision models offered by various theorists as a means for explaining this "correct" procedure; a quick overview of these might include the comprehensive rationalist view, the incremental (disjointed) view, the mixed-scanning view, classical democracy, democratic elitism, public choice models (several of these appear), collective action models, optimal models, autocratic processes, *etc.* The list continues, and the administrator is faced with four very difficult questions: 1) How do I know that I have selected the right model to use for deciding problems of this importance; 2) Am I using the right theoretical perspective for my perceived reality of the policy situation; 3) Can I justify the assumptions I have made in my model selection; and 4) what decision-making style is appropriate for dealing with the quantitative analyst.

Presented below is a short analysis of four of these models and their impacts on both the world situation and on the global analyst attempting to model the situation.

Yehezkel Dror's Optimal Model. Yehezkel Dror has made many useful distinctions about the way we think and deal with policy-making knowledge. He distinguished between knowledge that pertains to a given policy decision and knowledge that is relative to the theory and practice of policy-making. He recommends that for an informed policy decision, the needed empirical data be gathered and analyzed. On the other hand, "policy-making knowledge" is knowledge about how to make policy. It is one step removed from discrete policy issues and deals with metapolicy, or how one should change the decision rules so the policy about making policies can be set [9].

While Dror does use qualitative as well as quantitative data, he bases his model on both rationality and what he calls extrarationality, or the playing of hunches. But to do so, he relies solely on *economic* rationality in the spirit of Adam Smith, with a built-in feedback mechanism. Dror then incorporates the above two concepts when he labels policy issue knowledge and policy-making knowledge as "policy knowledge" and includes a broad definition of policy science. Without addressing the issue of "policy knowledge," it becomes apparent that the quantitative analyst who is dealing with a Drorian policy-maker can hope to effect change only when some critical mass is reached in terms of the acceptance of his model. More specifically, the analyst is expected to have not only *all* the data (both qualitative and quantitative) at his command, but that rare insight to "play the right hunch." Although this model is adopted by others, *e.g.*, Laszlo takes this approach in his *Strategy for the Future* [10], it is very hard to defend against other social analysts.

The Rational Model. The decision models of comprehensive rationality require the policy-maker and the analyst to search out all possible solutions, define all possible goals, assess all possible values and interests, objectively rank these, and then apply some criterion to select the "optimal" goal or value, and initiate the process by which these ends may be achieved. It requires that the values be clarified, and that some sort of hierarchical arrangement of the alternative pay-offs be established using the "correct" normative criteria. Again, the analyst working for such a policy-making system is faced with a tremendous burden. It is obviously impossible to know ALL the alternative feasible solutions, and difficult to resolve the "correct" normative criteria to be used. Historically, two have been used almost exclusively: EFFICIENCY and UTILITY MAXIMI-ZATION. Even if a single-valued criterion function can be established, however, and a hierarchical decision rule implemented, a major problem still exists. As Lindblom notes, the rational method ". . . assumes intellectual capacities and sources of information that men simply do not possess" [11]. This may be coupled with an epistemological assumption: that man has the capacity for pure rational thought and action. This dual overextension of man's faculties allows one to formulate the following list of potential pitfalls that the analyst must be made aware of [12]:

1. rationality is not the same thing as central decision making;
2. it is hard to reach agreement about values;
3. perfect information is seldom available so that *all* alternatives may be considered;
4. the model is not realistic (at least, it is not consistent with current policy-making processes in Western societies);
5. many policy changes end up being remedial in an attempt to maintain an equilibrial state; and
6. an elitist hierarchy must be established.

The Incremental Model. Lindblom describes a more realistic "rational" policy-making process in which only incremental departures are taken from the *status quo*. It avoids a comprehensive study of all alternatives, and concentrates on the relationship between the means and the ends. A great deal of the value in what is obtained may be attributed to the ease with which it is obtained. Thus, consensus or compromise is required among the decision-makers in order to reach a binding decision. In this process, some outcomes, some alternatives, and some affected values are neglected, and a succession of comparisons that are made reduces the reliance on theory that the rational model requires (this is why Lindblom calls this the Successive Limited Comparison Method [11].

Amitai Etzioni elaborates on this procedure, noting that the strategy to be applied is to investigate only those alternatives that differ to an incremental degree. Claiming that omission is better than confusion, it is thus better to investigate all *relevant* choices, not all choices. This procedure will not solve the problem, but will provide a method for deliberate exploration [13]. Thus, public policy problems are not solved by attempting to understand them, and sufficient agreement for the selection of alternatives just *does not exist.*

An analyst working for the US Government or other bureaucracy that follows an incremental approach is faced with the problem of identifying only the "relevant" choices and then making subsequent decisions. But how does one effect a degree of change other than incremental? One does not! To a global modeler, this would be extremely frustrating, for one cannot ever hope to see a major implementation of the model developed. The analyst must agree with the policy-maker's assumptions, the major one being that the governing body is pluralist. In addition, the incremental approach assumes a normative criterion in the society being governed, that of utilitarianism. If this is the case, then the major values of this model would include its utility (sub)maximization, its stability, its realism, and its agreement. But accepting these assumptions forces the analyst to ignore, the rational approach, strategic planning, contingency plans, and the question of equity [12]. Even worse, the analyst is forced to ignore overdue innovation needs, and thus can operate only in a society that is faced with a *lack* of major problems. Clearly, this is not the case, and is one of the reasons that little, if any, implementation of this global modeler's efforts is likely to be undertaken by the US Government in the near future.

The Mixed-Scanning Model. Given that the incremental model may not make the right decision at the right time, and that a string of wrong decisions is virtually impossible to reverse, Etzioni has offered a "mixed-scanning" model in an attempt to take the best features of both incrementalism and comprehensive rationality. In an effort to avoid the disjointed and conservative nature of incrementalism and the unrealistic and costly requirement of full search and total knowledge requirements of comprehensive rationality, Etzioni's model is a calculated combination of the two, in which the number of decisions made in the incremental mode is *very* much greater than the number made in the rational (fundamental) mode [12]. With this system, the basic alternatives are investigated as contextual decisions, and in this respect, the model assumes a middle-of-the-road stance, or a metapolitical *satisficing* role. Thus, the major decisions will be investigated individually, and the day-to-day operations will continue to be uninterrupted by major conflicts in policy formulation and orientation [13, p. 283]. So, mixed-scanning is less exacting than rationalism, not as constricting as incrementalism, and implies that the scanning procedure should be done at different levels. These different levels arise when one performs the fragmentation of the data before implementation, and now decision-making can be evaluated as follows [13, ch. 12] :

1. if incremental strategies are used, one cannot rank the values (ordinally)
2. if the rational model is used, then *all* alternatives must be evaluated
3. if the mixed-scanning process is used, then one may deal with the degree of success of the primary goal *and* note the effect on the secondary goals.

The major normative criteria (values) that the mixed-scanning model implies are responsiveness and equity [12]. Clearly, Etzioni wishes to maximize these by retaining the fact that all alternatives cannot be handled, but that a reasonable attempt should be made.

Operation of the Quantitative Analysts. One may summarize from the above descriptions of potential bureaucratic climates as follows: It is extremely difficult for a global modeler ever to implement his work on a full scale. For this reason, the major efforts have been concentrated in the private sectors, and one of the major sponsors of such research has been the Club of Rome [14]. Grants awarded by this group are usually given to academic endeavors, and it has been in academia where many of the current models have been developed.

Once funding has been obtained, the analysts usually form into interdisciplinary teams and use a systemic approach to the problem. By far the most common of these approaches has been the utilization of large scale, computer-based mathematical models that are used to simulate future conditions so that, for example, long-term forecasts or assessments of policy alternatives can be obtained.

Because few administrators are experts in the quantitative techniques employed, a recommendation may be made for the policy-maker who has need of a model and an analyst: 1) be willing to accept what has been done elsewhere, or 2) engage your own modeler and operate in a decision-making mode that provides an atmosphere conducive to large-scale modeling efforts. It is my opinion that the best of these processes for the global modeler to operate in is the mixed-scanning process. The analyst has no desire to involve himself with the day-to-day operation of a given governmental operation, but rather is concerned with the major problems that require major policy decisions. Unfortunately, this climate does not dominate the federal scene of most governments (with the possible exception of the Kremlin, *etc.*) and again, the quantitative work performed has little chance of ever being implemented.

A TAXONOMIC FRAMEWORK FOR LARGE-SCALE MODELS

Because so many models of the world or sectors of the world have been constructed recently (see Appendix A for a partial listing), the administrator faces the enormous problem of model selection and evaluation. Different policy-makers use different classification schemes to help with their decisions, and often base these upon methodological criteria. I propose that a taxonomy that first uses the model type, *i.e.*, form of expression of the model, and then subdivides along methodological lines is more useful. To complete the framework, a summary of the types of decisions for which the models were developed is also presented.

Taxonomy of Model Types

Using the form of expression to clarify the basic model types, the analyst can identify four: descriptive, physical, symbolic, and procedural.

Descriptive models are cheap, easy to formulate and common; the methods of prediction used are usually internal, however, and thus communication is often difficult. Physical models overcome this problem, both for the technical analyst and for the nontechnical administrator, but suffer from high costs and an inability to represent information processing. Symbolic models are mathematical in orientation and deductive in operation; their cost is also low. Simulation models are by far the most common form of procedural models, and most large-scale global efforts employ this technique. Such models do not lend themselves to solution by standard computational techniques, and the overall size and complexity of the problems require high-speed computer help [15].

Table 1 elaborates on the models, and includes some evaluation for the policy-maker [15, p. 10].

To classify the models further, as a function of the techniques employed, requires that only symbolic and procedural (simulation) models be discussed. Descriptive models do not follow specific techniques, and physical models range from simple floor diagrams to complicated aircraft wind tunnels [15, p. 10].

Table 1. Evaluation of model types.

|)DEL | METHOD OF PREDICTION | METHOD OF OPTIMIZING | COST | EASE OF COMMUNICATION | | LIMITATIONS |
				TECHNICAL	NONTECH.	
crip-	Judgment	?	Low	Poor	Poor, but often appears good	Cannot repeat the prediction process
sical	Physical manipulation	Search	High	Good	Good	Cannot represent the information processes
nbolic	Mathematical/ Numerical	Mathematical	Low	Good	Poor	Needs previously developed mathematical structure
ce-al	Simulation	Search	High	Fair	Good	General properties not easily deduced from the model

Symbolic models can be exemplified by linear and statistical economics and operations research artifices; procedural models by land-use analysis and systems dynamics. Thus, an elaboration of the original taxonomy may take the following form [16]:

I. Descriptive
II. Physical
III. Symbolic
    A. Linear Economics
       1. Input-Output Analysis (Leontief)
       2. Linear Programming (Dantzig)
       3. Game Theory (von Neumann)
    B. Operations Research
       1. Probabilistic Methods (Morse, Blackett)
         a. Monte Carlo Simulation
         b. Decision Trees
       2. Algebraic Methods (Dantzig, Kantorovich, Koopmans)
    C. Statistical Economics
       1. Econometric Modeling (Tinbergen, Klein)
       2. Microanalysis (Orcutt)
IV. Procedural/Simulation
    A. Land-use Analysis (Lowry)
    B. Systems Dynamics (Forrester)
    C. Scenario Analysis (Mesarovic, Pestel)

Briefly, these individual techniques are discussed below [16, pp. 87-127; 15, pp. 25-27]:

Input-Output Analysis. First developed by Wassily W. Leontief and formally present in 1936, I/O analysis identifies an economic sector by its industries and activities, with each requiring the production output of another as the inputs for its own production process. The analyst must be willing to accept the simplifying assumption that the ratios of inputs to outputs across an entire industry are constant. This further requires the assumption of negligible technological progress and other outside effects.

Should these assumptions be valid, then fixed production coefficients may be determined for each industry and arranged in a square matrix called the input/output matrix. This provides a structural representation of the economic sector under study, and clearly demonstrates the interactions among the interdependent industries and activities. I/O analysis has been severely criticized, however, because of the requirement of a "stagnant" economy, and in 1953 the Eisenhower administration cancelled the publications of the official I/O tables that the Bureau of Labor Statistics had published the previous year.

Linear Programming.   Linear Programming (LP) goes beyond I/O analysis in that it does not restrict itself to only one industry at a time, but rather deals with any number of feasible solutions or combinations of activity levels. Although it does assume linearity, it helps the policy-maker choose from a set of alternatives by evaluating each feasible one by a criterion or objective function, which usually measures these "payoffs" in monetary terms. The purpose of LP is to optimize, *i.e.*, to choose the *best* alternative, and one of the best known techniques to do this is the simplex method developed by George Dantzig in 1947. Owing to the size of the problems that can be addressed by LP, the high-speed computer has proved to be an invaluable aid.

Linear Programming models are quite common, and even though most policy-makers will agree that the "real world" is not linear, making a linear approximation is often so close that the gain in the ease of computation more than offsets the errors introduced by the assumption.

Game Theory.   When Oskar Morgenstern and John von Neumann first publicized their ideas of game theory in 1953, they were making an analogy between parlor games of skill and chance and the real conflict situations in economic and political life.   Thus, they correctly identify that there are a number of participants with incompatible objectives, and that the problem faced by each is to formulate his or her plans so that an optimal result is obtained.   These plans must include the probable actions of the opponents, and its was von Neumann's achievement to show that each participant can act so as to guarantee himself at least a certain minimum payoff.   Once the other players realize this, this payoff becomes the actual gain.   Thus, the game is determinate and zero-sum (what one player wins the other player loses).   Unfortunately, the results, though they appeal to a quantitative analyst, have not been used by policy-makers because the political environment is seldom a true zero-sum.

Probabilistic Methods of Operations Research.   Probability is the core of many of the operations research (OR) techniques, *e.g.*, queueing theory, Bayesian analysis, portfolio analysis, inventory models, reliability theory, search models, *etc.*, but often leads to extreme complexity when attempting to represent structural interdependencies such as those typically found in global models.   One technique that can handle such complexity is *Monte Carlo Simulation*.   This probability sampling technique was originally developed by von Neumann and Stanislaw Ulam in the 1940s, and has since been extended and applied to social systems.   Monte Carlo Simulation uses probability distributions to represent the elements of the system under study and random sampling techniques to infer interactions. Thus, different decision strategies may be evaluated by exercising the simulation many times and looking at the likely results.   Such a method has been widely used by policy-makers, and military operations employ it extensively.

Decision Theory. Decision theory provides an overall view of the possible consequences of a decision, and incorporates three basic variables: 1) the probability of each of the possible consequences of a decision; 2) the cost of each possible action by the decision-maker; and 3) the "payoff" that would be obtained should that action be chosen and the appropriate set of events actually effected. Thus, the technique employs a Bayesian approach and does provide an evaluation of alternatives. It can also help determine the value of additional information about a situation. In cases where the payoffs are measured linearly, this comparison becomes simple, and thus the technique is widely utilized. Nevertheless, it assumes that the future can be identified by the appropriate series of events and that the consequences of actions can be determined, which means that all the required data can either be attained or estimated. When social events are being considered, however, the payoffs may not be linear, and other measures, often subjective, are needed. For this reason, decision theory and utility theory (in an economic sense) are closely linked.

Algebraic Methods of Operations Research. There are many other techniques of OR that do not employ probability theory. These are often given the generic title of algebraic methods or, more commonly, mathematical programming. Linear programming has already been discussed, and nonlinear programming, geometric programming, quadratic programming, and dynamic programming are also useful methods. In addition, network theory and graph theory make significant contributions, most notably via PERT (Program Evaluation Review Technique) or CPM (Critical Path Method). These are techniques that force the policy-maker to consider each major event and activity that is associated with a given objective and to estimate either the time required (PERT) or the cost required (CPM). Once these have been calculated, a network can be constructed showing which events are critical and which are not—this allows for the transfer of resources from those that do not lie on the critical path. Recently, a combination of the two has been developed; it follows the same general technique, but incorporates both measurement schemes: PERT-COST.

Econometric Modeling. When one thinks of econometrics, one thinks of statistical economics, for econometrics makes such heavy use of empirical data that some method of quantitative analysis is needed—thus, the use of statistics. Most econometric models are sets of simultaneous equations that form a very gross model of an economy. For example:

$$Y = C + I$$

$$C = a + bY + cC_{-1} + e$$

where:

Y = national income,
C = total consumption,
I = total investment,
a, b, c = appropriate constants,
C_{-1} = total consumption in the previous time period, and
e = random error term.

Such models, albeit far more complex than the two equations above, provide the policy-maker with a predictive model that includes both the endogenous and the exogenous variables in the national economy.

Microanalysis. Econometric models such as those of Tinbergen and Klein are models of major sectors of the economy, and are aggregative, or macro models. Microanalysis deals with that portion of the economy that is more common to the individual: individual families, individual firms, banks, insurance companies, labor unions, local governments, *etc.* One of the originators of this technique was Guy H. Orcutt, who noted that this analysis was compatible with the analysis of distributional effects. This means that microanalysis can represent decision units by microeconomic relations called operating characteristics; these update the status of the variables in the model. Because these characteristics are usually probabilistic in nature, *e.g.*, the marriage of an individal within a certain time period, the use of probability distributions is justified, and microanalysis is often moved forward in time by a Monte Carlo Simulation.

Land-use Analysis. Land-use analysis is a cousin of microanalysis, and was developed in 1960–1963 by Ira S. Lowry. He tried to build an operational model understandable to laymen, one dealing with land-use patterns in a major city. This city was broken into separate zones. In each, a simple iterative scheme to allocate employment and residential activities was applied. Once these allocations were coupled with the known population density limitations, the model could infer the total amount of employment necessary to serve the residential population in each zone.

Lowry acknowledged that his was a crude model, but it paved the way for further developments such as the Time-Oriented Metropolitan Model (TOMM), the Bay Area Simulation Study (BASS), and the Cornell Land Use Game (CLUG). Such developments have been responsible for the active federal support of these modeling efforts, and it appears likely that this support will continue.

System Dynamics. Systems dynamics is a relative newcomer to the modeling scheme, although the original methodology was set forth by Jay Forrester in 1961. All the dynamics models take a long-term time horizon, and provide a framework within which the internal operations of a system can be observed. A major assumption for the analyst is thus the closed boundary, for all relevant activities must take place within this region.

Forrester measured these activities in two ways: 1) levels, where a number represents the state of some part of the system; and 2) rates, which define the amount by which a level will change in the next time interval. Although complex, these models do provide an orderly and coherent structure that has been applied to some of the world's most complex problems.

Scenario Analysis.   Scenario analysis as utilized by Mesarovic and Pestel is very similar in scope to the system dynamics models, but takes more of a regional approach. Here, the critical variables are specified by "local experts," and then these are used as inputs for large-scale computer simulation runs. (Note: much more detail about both the system dynamics models and scenario analysis is presented in the individual analyses of the Forrester model and the Mesarovic and Pestel model later in this essay.)

Use of the Models

The ability to classify a model is only the prelude to being able to utilize that model; what is needed to complete a taxonomic framework is the knowledge of which types of model to use in different decision situations. Table 2 provides such a general summary [15, pp. 12 and 17]. Of course, Table 2 represents only a small fraction of the total number of possible situations that the policy-maker faces. I hope, however, that such a listing does provide the administrator with some degree of "model sense" concerning their usefulness, their usability, and their use [17].

THE CLUB OF ROME REPORTS

Jay Forrester's World Models

Forrester first presented his World Dynamics Model in *World Dynamics* in 1971 [1]. Called World 2, this model was subsequently refined, and it evolved into the guiding approach in *The Limits to Growth* [2], where it was called the World 3 model. Both of these models share certain general features [18]:

1. the description of the world as a closed system with no external influences (The "Spaceship Earth" concept);
2. the specific choice of the major variables:
   a. population
   b. capital investment
   c. geographic space
   d. natural resources

Table 2. Summary of the types of decisions for which models have been developed.

DECISION	POSSIBLE SITUATION	MODELS THAT COULD BE USED
How much service capacity and how organized; priority rules	Queueing, waiting for service	Queueing, sequencing, simulation
Timing of maintenance and repair	Facilities that wear out	Replacement theory, reliability theory
Amount and timing of orders	Items stored for future use	Inventory, simulation
How much of each resource to allocate to each activity	Allocation of resources to activities; appropriate funds for subsidy programs such as agriculture, housing, and food	Linear programming, nonlinear programming, goal programming, mathematical programming
Price constraints, market regulations, subsidy levels, *etc.*	Marketplace distribution of goods, money, and services	Econometrics, Input/Output analysis, industrial dynamics, simulation, Markov techniques
Amount to spend on information acquisition	Determine whether to obtain more information before a decision (by survey or by experiment)	Decision trees, Bayesian analysis
Strategy to employ	Competition for limited resources	Game theory
Establishment of incentives, constraints, or regulations	Impose (or remove) a limit on the price that can be charged, *e.g.*, natural gas at a wellhead	Statistical econometrics, Input/Output analysis
Approval and initiation of programs or projects	Pass legislation for a health insurance subsidy to people	Simulation
Forecast overall trends to pinpoint problems and to suggest possible solutions	Forecast pollution levels in region, global modeling	Simulation, scenario analysis

    e. pollution
    f. food production
3. interactions and feedback processes of the subsystems;
4. the use of world averages for all parameters;
5. the amount of detail (the number of relationships specified); and
6. the nonprobabilistic nature of the predictions.

Consistent with the choice of the major variables are the required input parameters [2]:

1. birth rate,
2. death rate,
3. resource usage,
4. pollution generation,
5. food consumption, and
6. capital investment [19].

One may note that these are quantifiable and measureable, with the exception of pollution. At no time is a clear definition of just what constitutes pollution presented.

The use of these input variables in the model results in the following output variables [2]:

1. population level,
2. capital investment level,
3. pollution level,
4. natural resources available, and
5. quality of life, in satisfaction units.

Clearly, the last variable is subject to many interpretations, and was explicitly omitted from the World 3 model (it had been included in World 2). Nevertheless, careful analysis finds that this concept was used in an *implicit* fashion in several of the functional relationships in World 3.

To obtain these outputs from the specified inputs, Forrester established five corresponding critical subsystems. These subsystems will be discussed in turn, and, after each, certain problems facing either the analyst or the policy-maker will be raised. One should note that energy does not receive the same level of attention, and does *not* appear as one of the critical subsystems.

Nonrenewable Resources Subsystem

Meadows *et al.* assume that the world has a 250-year supply of minerals, and that the capital costs of locating, extracting, processing, and distributing the natural resources will rise as the resources are depleted. They also assume that the expansion of technology will not be sufficient to counteract this trend as the fraction of resources remaining approaches zero. Thus, they address their efforts to the location of the natural deposits in the earth, and to a determination of the extent to which these resources can be exploited [18, pp. 33-42].

The analyst here immediately questions the data sources—are the locations and extents of the deposits to be determined solely from historic data? And what about the inducement to dig out the resources—does one have to assume fixed economically available resources? A policy-maker might ask: Besides the economic limits on mining, are there social limits? If so, what are they?

Population Subsystem

In *Limits*, the population subsystem is used primarily to generate numbers for the other subsystems' calculations, and, thus, the only major assumptions are that the fertility and mortality rates are separate, independent entities. The key questions addressed are simply, the levels of food supply and health services to be chosen and the distribution of these [18, pp. 43-55].

Again, the analyst is faced with the question of knowledge. Does Forrester have real-world knowledge of the population dynamics? Does he know the extent to which population growth is determined by matters of a policy nature as well as a physical nature? Policy-makers are already concerned with not only the mechanical questions concerning population, but also with the ethical and cultural ones.

Agricultural Subsystem

The agricultural and food production subsystem as presented concentrates primarily on food production on land. Inexplicably, the oceans as a source of food are ignored. Thus, it is concluded that food is produced from arable land only (to distinguish from deserts, *etc.*), and that food production increases when the fertility or quantity of arable land is increased. It is correctly noted that the amount of land is finite, and that it can erode, or disappear entirely if built upon.

The regenerative capacity of land is measured in decades, and air pollution will lower the yield both now and during the period of decades. A feedback effect occurs when the land is heavily used, for this generates increased pollution, which in turn decreases the fertility of the land.

Based on this description, the possible yields and costs of land development are the considerations of the Meadows group. As an analyst, I would again question the weak empirical data base, and would also wonder about possible technological innovation. As a policy-maker, I would surmise that political and economic constraints would be the binding constraints, not the physical production constraints that concern the authors [18, pp. 56-65].

Capital and Industrial Output Subsystem

With the advantage of knowledge about the current economic situation, I must severely question the description of the Capital Investment Subsystem. In this description, the average life of industrial capital is 14 years, and the industrial capital/output ratio is constant. In the model, however, diminishing returns will not affect investment (!) and the economic values for the entire World 3 model are constant (!!).

The last two claims are subject to heavy criticism, because this assumption of inflexible relationships and constants *forces* the typical modes of behavior of the model to overshoot and collapse. The model has excluded the possibility of adaptive, flexible response to changing circumstances. Yet we know such changes do occur: for example, the money invested in research and education is directly for generating such responses [18, pp. 66-79].

Pollution Subsystem

Persistent pollution is the result of continued industrial and agricultural activity, and there is a time delay between the emission of the pollutant and the effects it has. This is easily substantiated by fact, and one need look no further than the heavy use of DDT; outlawed some 20 years ago, its effects are still appearing now. Further, the time required to absorb pollution increases as the pollution increases.

The assumptions stated above appear reasonable, but one assumption made leads to catastrophe: the accumlated percentage of pollution is a function of both the current emission and the previous cumulative total. The inability of the model to do anything with pollution except aggregate it precludes any result except total collapse (given a long enough time horizon). The only question to be answered is: When will this collapse occur?

In addition to this obvious flaw, the analyst is again faced with a very weak data base, one that does not include methods for predicting the effects of pollution. Further, exactly what constitutes a pollutant is never given. While the aggregation procedure is still relatively unknown, I would not be willing to accept the implication that pollutants have long-term effects over wide ranges, for this would seem to be a function of many things, among others:

1. physical and chemical properties of the pollutant,
2. concentration,
3. duration of exposure to the environment,
4. locus and mode of uptake into the environment,
5. environmental conditions at the time, and
6. nature of the pollutant.

Furthermore, the effects are still not yet established as the end result of functional realtionships, and whatever these may be, the total aggregation in the model ignors the local concentrations of most pollutants, thus giving rise to the "Global Asphyxiation" prediction [18, pp. 80-89]. In addition, the impact of religion, individual values, and ethics in these policy decisions are again ignored.

Energy

As stated previously, the attention given to energy does not seem to be adequate. (Of course, one must remember the 1971 publishing date.) The Meadows group simply assumes that abundant supplies of energy are necessary for economic growth, and that these resources are finite. In addition, the demand for these energy resources grows exponentially.

But how can one predict the availability of energy—especially with so many programs to develop energy still in their infancy. Do we know what the actual limits to finite supplies are? Are they really finite? (Obviously yes, but if solar power is harnessed efficiently, it might be considered infinite for practical purposes.) And what about technological innovation? Here, more than in the other areas, will a major breakthrough cause the model to be invalid [18, pp. 90-106]?

The political implications are again ignored. For example, the Middle East has the oil, the US and the USSR have the coal, and the US, France, Canada, and Australia have the cereal grains. Should trade-offs be made? What about the have-nots? Should international cartels in the spirit of OPEC be formed? The model does not attempt even to address such questions.

The Model as a Whole

The above subsystems are then synthesized into an integrated whole using a four-step procedure [2, pp. 90-91]:

1. the causal relationships are listed and the feedback loops traced;
2. the relationships are quantified;
3. the simultaneous operation of the relationships over time are calculated; and
4. the effect of different policies on the model are tested.

This interactive result may be seen in Figures 2 and 3. In the first, the World 2 model is presented as a formal flow diagram in the systems dynamics style. Figure 3 is a representation of the World 3 model as used in *Limits*, and one may note both the similarity of this model to World 2 and also the increased level of complexity.

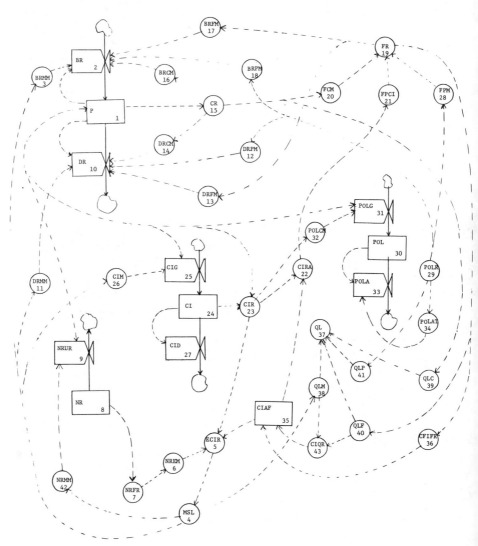

Figure 2. The World 2 model [18, pp. 16–17].

1	P	Population
2	BR	Birth Rate
3	BRMM	Birth Rate from Material Multiplier
4	MSL	Material Standard of Living
5	ECIR	Effective Capital Investment Ratio
6	NREM	Natural Resource Extration Multiplier
7	NRFR	Natural Resources Fraction Remaining
8	NR	Natural Resources
9	NRUR	Natural Resources Usage Rate
10	DR	Death Rate
11	DRMM	Death Rate from Material Multiplier
12	DRPM	Death Rate from Population Multiplier
13	DRFM	Death Rate from Food Multiplier
14	DRCM	Death Rate from Crowding Multiplier
15	CR	Crowding Ratio
16	BRCM	Birth Rate from Crowding Multiplier
17	BRFM	Birth Rate from Food Multiplier
18	BRPM	Birth Rate from Pollution Multiplier
19	FR	Food Ratio
20	FCM	Food from Crowding Multiplier
21	FPCI	Food Potential from Capital Investment
22	CIRA	Capital Investment Ratio in Agriculture
23	CIR	Capital Investment Ratio
24	CI	Capital Investment
25	CIG	Capital Investment Generation
26	CIM	Capital Investment Multiplier
27	CID	Capital Investment Discard
28	FPM	Food from Pollution Multiplier
29	POLR	Pollution Ratio
30	POL	Pollution
31	POLG	Pollution Generation
32	POLCM	Pollution from Capital Multiplier
33	POLA	Pollution Absorption
34	POLAT	Pollution Absorption Time
35	CIAF	Capital Investment in Agriculture Fraction
36	CFIFR	Capital Fraction Indicated by Food Ratio
37	QL	Quality of Life
38	QLM	Quality of Life from Material
39	QLC	Quality of Life from Crowding
40	QLF	Quality of Life from Food
41	QLP	Quality of Life from Pollution
42	NRMM	Natural Resource from Material Multiplier
43	CIQR	Capital Investment from Quality Ratio

The rectangles represent measureable levels, the valves represent rates that influence the levels, and the circles represent auxiliary variables that influence the rate equations. Solid arrows represent the movement of physical quantities, broken arrows represent causal relationships, and clouds represent external sources or sinks.

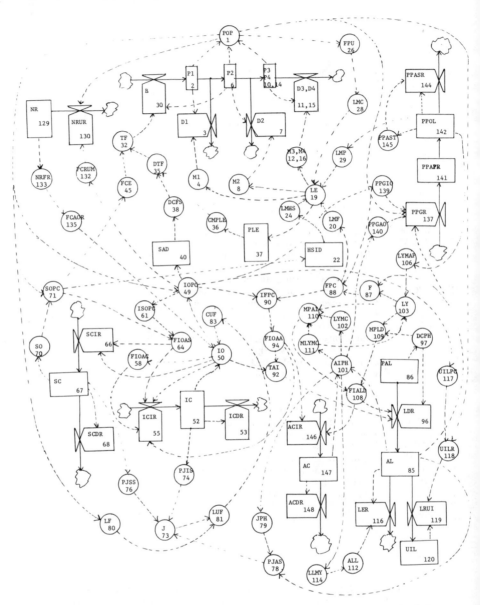

Figure 3. The World 3 model as presented in *Limits to Growth* [2, pp. 102-103].

1	POP	Population
2	P1	Population, Ages 0–15
3	D1	Deaths, Ages 0–15
4	M1	Mortality, Ages 0–15
6	P2	Population, Ages 16–45
7	D2	Deaths, Ages 16–45
8	M2	Mortality, Ages 16–45
10	P3	Population, Ages 45–64
11	D3	Deaths, Ages 45–64
12	M3	Mortality, Ages 45–64
14	P4	Population, Ages 64+
15	D4	Deaths, Ages 64+
16	M4	Mortality, Ages 64+
19	LE	Life Expectancy
20	LMF	Lifetime Multiplier from Food
22	HSID	Health Services Impact Delay
24	LMHS	Lifetime Multiplier from Health Services
26	FPU	Fraction of Population Urban
28	LMC	Lifetime Multiplier from Crowding
29	LMP	Lifetime Multiplier from Persistent Pollution
30	B	Births per year
32	TF	Total Fertility
35	DTF	Desired Total Fertility
36	CMPLE	Perceived Lifetime Expectancy Multiplier
37	PLE	Perceived Life Expectancy
38	DCFS	Desired Completed Family Size
40	SAD	Social Adjustment Delay
45	FCE	Fertility Control Effectiveness
49	IOPC	Industrial Output per Capita
50	IO	Industrial Output
52	IC	Industrial Capital
53	ICDR	Industrial Capital Depreciation Rate
55	ICIR	Industrial Capital Investment Rate
58	FIOAC	Fraction of Industrial Output Allocated to Consumption
61	ISOPC	Industrial Service Output per Capita
64	FIOAS	Fraction of Industrial Output Allocated to Services
66	SCIR	Service Capital Investment Rate
67	SC	Service Capital
68	SCDR	Service Capital Depreciation Rate
70	SO	Service Output
71	SOPC	Service Output per Capital
73	J	Jobs
74	PJIS	Potential Jobs in the Industrial Sector
76	PJSS	Potential Jobs in the Service Sector
78	PJAS	Potential Jobs in the Agricultural Sector
79	JPH	Jobs per Hectare
80	LF	Labor Force
81	LUF	Unemployed Fraction
83	CUF	Capital Utilization Fraction
85	AL	Arable Land
86	PAL	Potentially Arable Land
87	F	Food
88	FPC	Food per Capita

90	IFPC	Indicated Food per Capita
92	TAI	Total Agricultural Investment
94	FIOAA	Fraction of Industrial Output Allocated to Agriculture
96	LDR	Land Development Rate
97	DCPH	Development Cost per Hectare
101	AIPH	Agricultural Inputs per Hectare
102	LYMC	Marginal Land Yield from Capital
103	LY	Land Yield
106	LYMAP	Land Yield Multiplier from Pollution
108	FIALD	Fraction Input Allocated to Land Development
109	MPLD	Marginal Productivity of Land Development
110	MPAI	Marginal Productivity of Agricultural Inputs
111	MLYMC	Land Yield Multiplier from Capital
112	ALL	Average Life of Land
114	LLMY	Land Lifetime Multiplier from Capital
116	LER	Land Erosion Rate
117	UILPC	Urban-Industrial Land per Capita
118	UILR	Urban-Industrial Land Required
119	LRUI	Land Removal for Urban-Industrial Use
120	UIL	Urban-Industrial Land
129	NR	Non-renewable Resources
130	NRUR	Non-renewable Resources Usage Rate
132	PCRUM	Per Capita Resource Usage Multiplier
133	NRFR	Non-renewable Resources Fraction Remaining
135	FCAOR	Fraction of Capital Allocated to Obtaining Resources
137	PPGR	Persistent Pollution Generation Rate
139	PPGIO	Persistent Pollution Generated by Industrial Output
140	PPGAO	Persistent Pollution Generated by Agricultural Output
141	PPAPR	Persistent Pollution Appearance Delay
142	PPOL	Persistent Pollution
144	PPASR	Persistent Pollution Assimilation Rate
145	PPAST	Persistent Pollution Assimilation Time
146	ACIR	Agricultural Capital Investment Rate
147	AC	Agricultural Capital
148	ACDR	Agricultural Capital Depreciation Rate

Note: The World Model as presented in *Limits* is actually a simplification. A more complete version of the world model may be found in: *Dynamics of Growth in a Finite World*, Dennis L. Meadows, et. al., Wright-Allen Press, Inc., 1974, p 490–491.

But the rates themselves are determined from other levels in the system. For example:

$$DR_{jk} = (DRN)(DRMM_k)(DRFM_k)(DRPM_k)(DRCM_k)$$

where:

DRN = death rate normal (based on 1970 standard, DRN = 1),
$DRMM_k$ = death rate from material multiplier at time k,
$DRFM_k$ = death rate from food multiplier at time k,
$DRPM_k$ = death rate from pollution multiplier at time k, and
$DRCM_k$ = death rate from crowding multiplier at time k.

To handle the introduction of nonlinear relationships without resorting to the explicit algebraic form, Meadows *et al.* extensively use look-up tables, which were originally derived in the background efforts for the World Dynamics model of 1971.

Continuing with the above example, one may find the death rate from material multiplier ($DRMM$) as a function of the Material Standard of Living by utilizing such a table, as shown in Figure 6. The method of calculation is to "integrate" the first difference equations between an initial and each subsequent time period and use a computer simulation to plot these accumulations versus time. Still, a major problem in modeling dynamic systems is that of instability, which operates with negative feedback loops in the model. A further problem arises when one attempts to ascertain the data to be used—national figures collectively are not always correct, and, as will be shown, small errors can make a significant difference. In addition, how does one extrapolate beyond the range of the data given?

The World 2 model is a five-sector model, with 7 rates and 28 auxiliary variables. The World 3 model is fancier (see Figures 2 and 3 for comparison), and has been documented in *Dynamics of Growth in a Finite World* [21]. Here, the computer runs may be inspected, and one becomes aware that the basis for all calculations is the aforementioned difference equations. An example of the derivation of the equations is given below, and the functional relationships f_{14} and f_{15} again require the use of look-up tables, which also use background data from the original World Dynamics model.

One interesting observation may be made from analysis of the final, combined POL_k equations: that the pollution at time k will almost certainly be larger than at some previous time j. As noted previously, the aggregation of pollution can lead only to collapse; *e.g.*, the death rate increases due to respiratory ailments.

Example of the Difference Equations Used in the Calculations

$$POL_k = POL_j + (DT)(POLG_{jk} - POLA_{jk})$$

$$POLG_{jk} = (P_j)(POLCM_j)$$

$$POLA_{jk} = POL_j/POLAT_j$$

$$POLCM_j = f_{14}(CIR_j)$$

$$POLAT_j = f_{15}(POLR_j)$$

$$CIR_j = CI_j/P_j$$

$$POLR_j = POL_j/POLS$$

where:

POL_k = pollution units per person per year at time k
POL_j = same, at time j
$POLG_{jk}$ = pollution generation in the interval from j to k
$POLA_{jk}$ = pollution absorption between j and k
DT = the time interval between j and k
P_j = the population at time j
$POLCM_j$ = pollution from capital multiplier at time j
$POLAT_j$ = pollution absorption time at time j
CIR_j = capital investment ratio at time j
$POLR_j$ = pollution ratio at time j
CI_j = capital investment at time j
$POLS$ = pollution standard

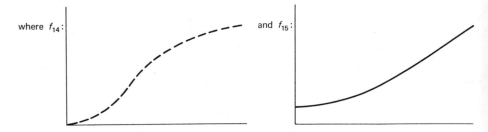

where f_{14}:   and f_{15}:

It is this complexity that is often confusing; therefore, the major interactions and feedbacks of the subsystems have been summarized and presented in a more intelligible fashion in Figure 4. Such an oversimplified schematic highlights some of the obvious shortcomings of the model. For example, the following additions, among others, could easily be made:

1. culture,
2. remove the assumption of the homogeneity of the world,
3. add the possibility of technological innovation,

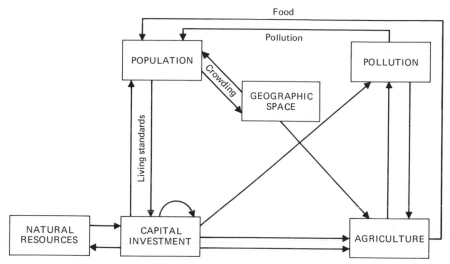

Figure 4. Simplified World 3 model showing the major interactions and feedbacks of the subsystems [18, p. 26].

4. politics,
5. energy,
6. ethics/values, and
7. religion.

Some of these omissions are specifically addressed by the Meadows group. For example, politics is omitted because of its "unquantifiability." This argument seems a little specious when one considers their treatment of pollution, and in fact, politics really is included implicitly in their computer runs, with the underlying assumption that the political climates will never change. This omission in the early simulation runs could be forgiven (?), but should definitely have been included in the runs of the equilibrium state. Here, population and industrial rate parameters are again held constant, and the possibility of a parameter that could interact and make short-run adjustments is ignored.

A more theoretical criticism is economic: Nowhere has a pricing mechanism been effectively incorporated into the model. If anything, it is avoided: "By making simple extrapolations of the demand growth curves, we have attempted to estimate, roughly, how much longer growth of each of these factors might continue at its present rate of increase" [2]. As shortages begin to develop, prices will rise and the marginal uses of the resources will be cut back, substitutes will appear, and technology will begin to devise more efficient uses of the resource. The critical aspect is that of demand—they have assumed and abstracted away from supply [20].

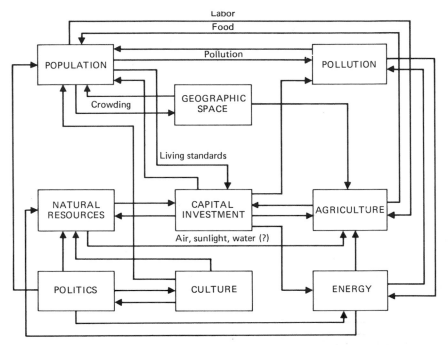

Figure 5. Simplified World 3 model as "corrected" by the addition of politics, culture, and energy.

Further criticisms are easily made: the inability to deal with money, the incorrect conceptualization of "capital," the "freezing of the system" and the requirement of a low investment rate when wealth is being redistributed, and the oversimplification of the entire economic situation are but a few.

It is not difficult to make the model more realistic with the addition of several new subsystems and several more feedback loops. A few of these have been added, and the updated model appears in Figure 5. Again, one must realize that even this version of the model is extremely simplified, and that many more feedbacks and interactions could be added to make the final result more realistic.

Construction of the Equations and Functional Relationships

Specific construction of the equations is based on the rates at which the physically measurable quantities are influenced and the values caused to change over time. This procedure is used throughout the model (see Figure 6) and can best be explained by the use of an example [18, pp. 29–30]:

$$P_k = P_j + (DT)(BR_{jk} - DR_{jk})$$

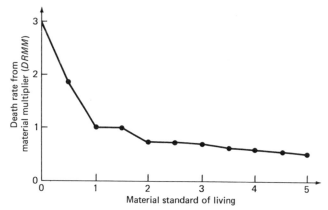

Figure 6. Relationships between *DRMM* and the Material Standard of Living. Actually used in the model as a look-up table programmed into the computer [1, p. 40].

where

P_k = population at time k,
P_j = population at time j,
DT = length of intervening period jk,
BR = birth rate during jk, and
DR = death rate during jk.

Combining these:

$$POL_k = POL_j + (DT)\ P_j f_{14}\ \frac{CI_j}{P_j}\ -\ \frac{POL_j}{f_{15}(POL_j/POLS)}$$

So the pollution at time k may be expressed as a function of pollution, population, and capital investment at time j. But as stated, this is nothing more than a difference equation.

Geneal Problems with the Model as a Whole

Probably the major cause for alarm on the part of the policy-maker is the lack of many interactions and feedbacks. It would be preferable to know such relationships in the areas of 1) economics, 2) technology, 3) social interactions, 4) politics, and 5) culture. The analyst is alarmed because of the possible systematic bias of numerical values used in many of the relationships, and the inadequate data base (not the fault of the Meadows group). Given this limited data, however, certain additional problems arise from exercising the model to test its validity.

The model is "zeroed" over the 1900–1970 range; if it is to be an accurate predictor, however, then it should work in reverse. Running the model back-

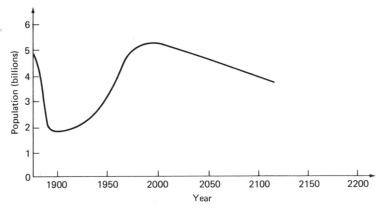

Figure 7. Results of running the World Dynamics model beyond the original time interval.

ward, even if one assumes changes in the input constants, will result in a dramatic decline in population around 1880. Similar problems are encountered if the model is run *far* in either direction. Figure 7 demonstrates the point [18, p. 113]. Figure 7 is based on the 1970 standards and has merely been extended in time. It is known, however, that there was not a significant decline in population in 1875-1880 (the population was not high enough to fall that far), and it is doubtful if the cyclical effect shown for the future is realistic.

Further exercises lend credence to the suggestion that the model should have included technological, economic, and social feedback mechanisms. For example, if one allows for only a small, incremental improvement in technology, one gets results as in Figure 8 [18, pp. 113-114].

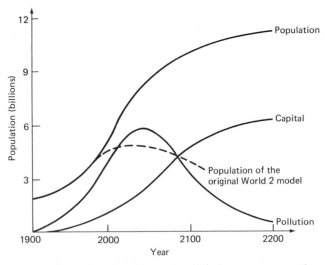

Figure 8. World 2 model with a technological progress assumption.

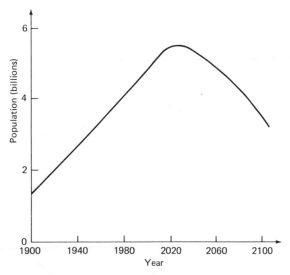

Figure 9. World 2 model with pollution restricted to the region of emission.

A strong criticism against the model made earlier was the error introduced by the use of world averages, especially in pollution considerations. Changing from the average to a restricted level of pollution one obtains Figure 9 [18, p. 121].

Further errors may be introduced by ignoring the dynamic aspects of the situation, by introducing rounding errors [22], and by using arbitrary (?) starting points. The lack of an empirical data base to validate the functional relationships allows one to question the assumptions, and if these are changed, then *very* different results may be obtained. Figure 10 is a reproduction of the basic model with the "standard" catastrophe occurring around the year 2100. This is obtained by entering the 1970 values for all six input parameters: birth rate, death rate, natural resources usage rate, pollution rate, food coefficient (units per capita), and capital investment. (This is observable in more detail as the first exercise in Appendix B.)

The standard graph in Figure 10 may now be used for comparison with the four subsequent graphs (Figures 11, 12, 13, and 14), and one easily notes the differences that result from a change in the assumptions [18, pp. 127-129]. Figures 11 through 14 would seem to indicate the instability of the model, which is not what the authors claimed, for they made a clear statement concerning the lack of sensitivity of the model to changes in the input parameters. This is certainly not the case, however, and if one changes the resource, pollution, agricultural, and capital distribution assumptions simultaneously, he obtains results like those in Figure 15 [18, p. 130]. As Cole, *et al.* conclude [18, p. 131], ". . . even on the basis of the World 3 Model and even with a very high

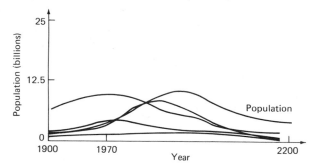

Figure 10. World 3 "standard" run to facilitate comparison with following graphs.

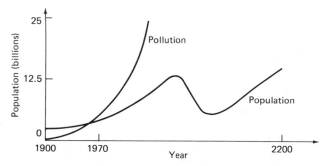

Figure 11. World 3 with changed resource costs.

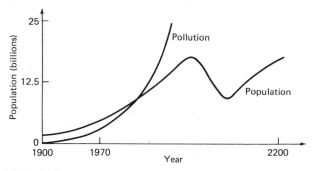

Figure 12. World 3 with changed resource and industrial pollution assumptions.

population figure, continued growth, at least for the next two centuries, will not inevitably stop at an early date because of physical limits." (Note: it is quite easy to change the results of the model by changing the values of the input parameters, as has been done above. Appendix B contains more detailed instructions concerning these variables, as well as selected runs to demonstrate the results of further changes.)

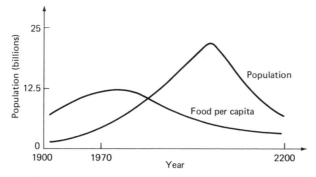

Figure 13. World 3 with changed resource and pollution assumptions.

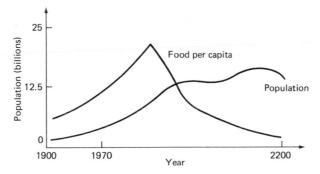

Figure 14. World 3 with changed resource, pollution, and agricultural assumptions.

The other major problem, the inability to obtain reliable figures, means that any analysis based on these figures must include realistic social control mechanisms to balance the various growth rates. Part of this problem is clearly the difficulty in quantifying all the data for ease of computation; and in the measurement aspects, a common rubric does not exist, especially for the "quality of life."

Conclusions

The general claims of *Limits* include: 1) given a) exponential patterns of exponential growth; b) limited resources; and c) long adaptive delays; 2) then a) growth stops; b) much sooner than expected; c) delays cause overshoot and collapse; and d) obvious actions either delay the outcome only slightly or make matters worse. Specifically, a Malthusian catastrophe will occur sometime in the next 50 to 100 years owing to increases in pollution, population increases greater than corresponding increases in food supply, *etc.* This is forced by the assump-

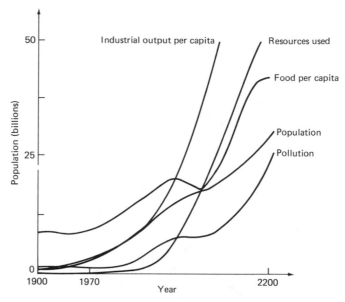

Figure 15. World 3 with changed resource, pollution, agricultural, and capital distribution assumptions.

tions inherent in the model. I would, therefore, agree with the conclusions of Cole [23]:

1. The results are sensitive to the inclusion of small rates of technological change and resource discovery—it therefore seems likely that some factors have been omitted from the original model.
2. World 3 is more satisfactory than World 2, for Meadows made an attempt to gather empirical, useful information, whereas Forrester had no empirical information.
3. The "mental model" one chooses to use when modeling the world is ultimately a function of one's values, interests, aspirations, etc.
4. All calculations are hindered by the lack of an adequate data base.
5. The model is neither totally objective nor totally apolitical, and the modelers should not pretend that it is.
6. Can the policy-maker resolve the conflicting, fuzzy goals without data in a useful form?
7. What about TIME? Is not the world dynamic?
8. World Dynamics and Limits to Growth have suffered a lot of criticism and received a lot of praise, but for what I consider to be the wrong reasons. I must give credit to anyone who attempts to model the world, and this model does provide an excellent beginning for future research. Nor does World 3 try to predict the future; it merely suggests the consequences of

continuing current trends. I must look to other possible models, however, when I realize that the entire model is based on a series of first difference equations, and these are somewhat arbitrarily generated.

Implementation

The implementation of this model has been virtually nonexistent, although it has created a great deal of discussion and controversy. Perhaps the major benefit of this model has been the increased awareness of the interrelatedness of the world's problems. For effective action to be taken, however, the action-taker must possess enormous resources. Thus, the federal government is the logical choice. Yet, as noted, little action has been taken.

One may speculate as to the reasons why this herioc effort has not been utilized, and postulate that 1) the policy makers do not possess the quantitative background required, 2) the models are overly complex, and, thus, unrealistic, or 3) analyses of the models refute their warnings. An example of the latter would be Walton J. Francis' article [24]. There Francis argues that no radical action is required, because the Meadow's group's assumptions were erroneous. But, if *Limits* is right, then we should not ignore this warning. On the other hand, if wrong, the cost of premature and perhaps incorrect action could also be catastrophic.

The complexity of the model (see no. 2 above) has the added effect of lending rigor due to the elaborate and hypothetical calculations, and the model does agree with our intuition that time is short. This complexity masks the questionable usefulness of the results, however, for all the model really tells the administrator is that infinite material consumption in a finite world is impossible even when coupled with the assumption of "unlimited" energy [8, p. 122].

Fortunately, subsequent models have dealt with many of the difficulties noted in the Forrester model.

Mesarovic and Pestel: Mankind at the Turning Point

The model presented in *Mankind* is also a simulation mode, again using a large-scale computer to perform the mathematics of the simulation. The scenario analysis technique employed by Mesarovic and Pestel is better than the World 3 model presented by Meadows *et al.* for several reasons, which are discussed below.

One of the questionable assumptions of the Forrester model was the homogeneity of the world. Mesarovic and Pestel avoid this by dividing the world into ten socioeconomic regions [3, p. 40]:

1. North America
2. Western Europe
3. Japan

4. Australia, South Africa, and the rest of the market-economy-developed world
5. Eastern Europe, including the USSR
6. Latin America
7. North Africa and the Middle East
8. Tropical Africa
9. South and Southeast Asia
10. China

A second major failing of the World 3 model was its very weak data base. In *Mankind*, the authors claim the use of much better data, for they state that the world's governments are becoming more and more uneasy about the world situation, and are much more receptive to central information collection agencies such as the United Nations. Unfortunately, the analyst does not have access to this data, for while the politicians may be more receptive to the idea, the actual transfer and centralization of data have been less than what *Mankind* would lead one to believe.

The authors claim that they have been able to learn from Forrester's mistakes, but one must note that the input and output variables used are very much the same. Nevertheless, the major advantage of the scenario analysis technique is that it allows for:

1. politics
2. war
3. culture
4. technological innovation
5. price and cost controls
6. redistribution of the wealth of the world
7. dynamic character of the world

Again, the quantitative analyst must use caution, for many of the inputs that allow for the inclusion of these factors come from local "experts," and hence, are likely to be quite value-laden.

Problems Addressed by the Model

Mesarovic and Pestel establish three critical problems that they feel are the basis for the current situation: 1) the gap between man and nature is widening, 2) the gap between the have and have-not nations is widening, and 3) there is a widening military and ideological polarization taking place in the world [3, pp. ix-xi]. In addition, there are six subproblems that are directly related to these three major problems; they are 1) the industrial world is guilty of tremendous waste, 2) delay is costly [25], 3) mankind does not have the luxury of dealing with one crisis at a time, 4) there is a 20-year time lag between implementation and actual results [26], 5) the exponential population growth is placing too much demand on the food production capabilities, and 6) we need to develop other energy resources besides oil, which we will not do as long as petroleum energy is cheap.

Approach of the Model

The model begins with a breakdown of the world into the ten socioeconomic regions specified previously. Within each region, six major areas are considered:

1. individual
2. sociopolitical
3. population
4. economics
5. agrotechnology
6. ecology

These areas are given very broad definitions, and are used to establish the scenario. Once this has been established, a stratified approach is used, with the following five strata [3, pp. 41-43]:

1. environmental stratum—geophysical states in physical environment;
2. technology stratum—all human activities with a matter-energy transfer;
3. demoeconomic stratum—accounting for goods and services;
4. group stratum—system of institutional and societal processes, and the
5. individual stratum—man's inner world, his biological makeup.

Thus, the approach can be envisioned as a partitioning process—first into regions, then into the major areas of consideration, then into the strata.

The quantitative analyst at this point is cognizant of the subjective aspects that are consistent with the use of the scenario analysis technique. At least five such aspects are identifiable:

1. uncertainty in dealing with *all* possible conditions;
2. the sequence of possible events and sociopolitical choices are undefined (note: Mesarovic and Pestel define a scenario as just such a sequence);
3. subjective probabilities are required;
4. both objective and subjective data are applied in the model; and
5. the ability to change and adapt is incorporated in the model, but is left to the discretion of the modeler of that particular scenario.

To try to reduce the subjective domain, Mesarovic and Pestel have assumed that both the individual and the group assumed a purpose and did not operate in a strict trial-error mode. They have also assumed that all future inputs and parameters will be specified over the entire time period.

This final assumption is quite extensive, for there are 10 regions X 6 major considerations X 5 strata = 300 interdependencies for which all subrelations

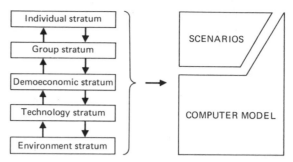

Figure 16. Computerization of the world system model.

must also be specified. Clearly, this is where the computer enters the technique, and one is able to obtain different degrees of resolution for different interdependent evaluations. For example, for a nonagricultural sector, one might apply the Cobb-Douglas function [16].

As a basic model, one might therefore obtain a schematic such as that in Figure 16 [3, p. 42]. Here, the strata for a given scenario within a given region are specified, and the computer model containing the cause-effect linkages is applied to the specified parameters in the scenario. Naturally, the computer cannot contain all the relationships and processes, and must also incorporate a decision-making model as part of its internal programming. This refinement of the model and corresponding elaboration result in the version in Figure 17 [3, p. 50]. As presented, the decision-making model is the key to the entire simulation; it is useful, therefore, to elaborate further on this operation. The establishment of the norms is done exclusively by "expert opinion," and is considered to

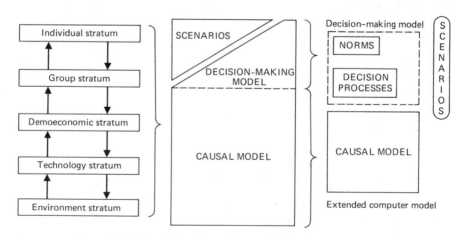

Figure 17. Extended version of the world system computer model.

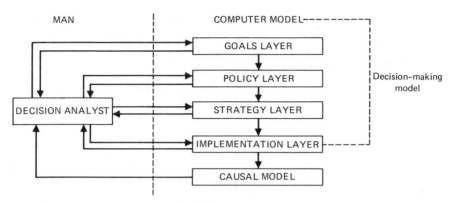

Figure 18. Refinement of the decision-making model.

be data that are available for a given scenario. The decision processes that form the linkage between the norms and the causal part of the computer model must be further subdivided, however. This is again portrayed schematically in Figure 18 [3, p. 51]. The major function of the decision analyst in this model is to arrive at a set of inputs that is necessary for a computer run. This is accomplished by making an appropriate set of choices, sequentially, on each of the layers in the model. Again, one notes the requirement of subjectivity on the part of the analyst.

Conclusions

A major concern of the two authors is the availability of cheap energy via petroleum. They feel that the price of oil should be raised about 50%. This would force the development of other energy sources while the oil is still available. Concurrent with this, a global redistribution of wealth must take place, with the "haves" providing capital to the "have-nots" so that each region eventually becomes economically balanced. This is not the same as economically self-sufficient, for each region has certain local advantages, but after the wealth transfer, this balance, once attained, needs to be maintained. (Note: the authors observe that while this is transpiring, a temporary food distribution must accompany the wealth redistribution until the balance is attained, and this requires a change in the eating habits of the industrial world.)

The above is not to imply a stagnation on the part of the overdeveloped world. Both the overdeveloped and the underdeveloped must concurrently grow. To accomplish this, the overdeveloped world must consume less, while the underdeveloped world must begin to practice some form of population control. Both authors believe that the developed nations can survive longer with their standard of living than the lesser developed countries (LDCs) can. Thus, aid to the LDCs will be more effective if started *now*. The balance can be obtained as self-sufficiency is reached; for example, in an LDC, the cost of energy will drop because of improved transportation and distribution systems.

In summary, the new global ethic must be enacted now—delay is not only costly, but fatal. This point is remade when one compares the *Mankind* report with the *Limits* report.

Comparison of the Forrester and the Mesarovic and Pestel Models [3, p. 55]

The models as developed by Jay Forrester lead one to accept three basic theses:

1. The world can be viewed as one system.
2. The system will collapse some time in the middle of the twenty-first century if present trends continue.
3. To prevent collapse, economic growth must be slowed immediately, leading to equilibrium in a relatively short period of time.

These may be compared with the Mesarovic and Pestel theses:

1. The world can be viewed only in reference to the prevailing differences in culture, tradition, and economic development; *i.e.*, as a system of interacting regions—a homogeneous view of such a system is misleading.
2. Rather than collapse of the world system as such, catastrophes or collapses on a regional level could occur, possibly long before the middle of the next century, although in different regions, for different reasons, and at different times. Since the world is a system, such catastrophes will be felt profoundly throughout.
3. The solution to such catastrophes of the world system is possible only in the global context and by appropriate global actions. If the framework for such joint action is not developed, none of the regions will be able to avoid the consequence. For each region, its turn will come in due time.
4. Such a global solution could be implemented only through a balanced, differentiated growth, which is analogous to organic growth rather than undifferentiated growth. It is irrefutable that the second type of growth is cancerous and would ultimately be fatal.
5. The delays in divising such global strategies are not only detrimental or costly, but DEADLY. It is in this sense that we truly need a strategy for survival.

Implementation

The chances that the *Mankind* model will be implemented are very slight—the economic problems of global redistribution of wealth, while oil costs 50% more, will not be supported by politicians trying to get reelected. There is a chance, however—the world is still awaiting the outcome of the Geneva Conference on just this issue.

Further hindering the chances for implementation is the lack of data. Although some empirical, qualitative data do exist; *e.g.*, China has eliminated famine by meeting 80% of its fertilizer requirements with organic matter and sewage (at a high cost of hydroelectric and fossil fuel energy), Mesarovic and Pestel lack the quantitative data for validation [27].

A far greater difficulty will be changing the world's cultural values. A recent Gallup poll of the world noted that in India, where overpopulation is one of the primary causes of starvation, more than one-half of the people still want larger familier [28]. Political action is necessary, but cultural values are slow to change and we don't have the time to wait.

Jan Tinbergen: RIO: Reshaping the International Order

Tinbergen's report to the Club of Rome is a rarity in that it presents a qualitative dialogue rather than a quantitative model. The report was generated to address the following question [4, preface]:

> What new international order should be recommended to the world's statesmen and social groups so as to meet, to the extent practically and realistically possible, the urgent needs of today's population and the probable needs of future generations?

This issue is critical to policy-makers, and the prose style of the twenty-one authors makes comprehension relatively simple. As Tinbergen himself notes, however [4, preface]:

> Given the complexity of the subject, the *RIO* project could only realistically aim at attempting to make a model contribution to the growing dialogue on the new international order.

In this it has succeeded; it does attempt to delineate a step-by-step procedure for politicians of the international community. The entire orientation of Tinbergen *et al.* is to help construct a more equitable international order based on knowledge currently available. (Here, the more quantitatively oriented analyst notes that this translates into an assumption of little or no technological innovation.)

Problems Specifically Addressed

As stated, the macro problem is to create a new international order from the current state of world disorder; this is subdivided into micro problem areas, which are addressed individually:

1. the armaments race,
2. population,
3. food,
4. human settlements,

5. the human environment,
6. the international monetary system,
7. natural resources and energy,
8. science and technology; transnational enterprises,
9. ocean management,
10. outer space,
11. international institutions, and
12. planetary interdependencies.

These are highlighted by discussions of current activities dealing with these problems, *e.g.*, some of the recommendations of the UN sixth and seventh special sessions.

Approach

After identifying the current problem areas of the world, the authors commence construction of the mechanics to help the policy-maker get to Utopia. The first step is an unconstrained, prescriptive list of what should be developed at both the national and international levels. The basic argument centers around social and economic equity. Several of the RIO authors contend that the best approach for such equity would be [4, p. 63] :

> . . . *humanistic socialism*, since it would aim at equalizing opportunities within and among nations and be founded on universal human values.

Unfortunately, they attempt neither to define explicitly what the universal values are, nor to clarify how one would obtain acceptance of these values even if they could be agreed upon by all mankind. Only such generalities such as "needs should be satisfied" and "poverty should be eradicated" are offered, and these, although they provide little room for debate, do not provide the policy-maker with much more than "apple pie and motherhood" statements [29].

Much more useful is the development of strategies for the industrialized nation. Public policy-makers must be prepared to [4, p. 84] :

1. move from a growth philosophy to an overall welfare concept;
2. establish controls on technological development—the social costs must be carefully monitored;
3. promote the economical use of available resources, with more emphasis on quality rather than on quantity;
4. curtail the armaments race; and
5. reinterpret the concept of national sovereignty.

It is this last recommendation that probably will create the most resistance, for the acceptance of the concept of functional rather than national sovereignty with an ultimate aim at decentralized planetary sovereignty would seem to have a basic change in human emotional makeup as a precondition.

The second major step in the Tinbergen approach is to reduce the differential between the rich and the poor. Tinbergen *et al.* agree with the Mesarovic and Pestel concern that the rich are getting richer and the poor are getting poorer and that current attempts to mediate the situation only widen the gap. Thus, they similarly conclude that the time for action is *now*. They go further, however, and set as a necessary target an annual growth rate for the world of 5%! It is admitted that this is largely dependent upon the Third World expanding its manufacturing capacity; nevertheless, as a policy-maker attempting to establish *equitable* international orders, continued growth at 5% in the industrialized countries seems a bit unrealistic. Although this is clearly intended to be a general figure, I am again struck by the "apple pie and motherhood" context for this statement.

Step three in the *RIO* approach returns to generalities. While I agree that the industrial nation states control the balance of power, and that adjustment, compromise, and reform are needed, simply to make such a statement provides little help for the policy-maker. Fortunately, a more detailed analysis of the legal aspects of the new international order and the need for a framework treaty is presented [4, pp. 114-117]:

1. all states shall facilitate access to technology and scientific information;
2. all states have the obligation to expand and liberalize international trade;
3. ocean space and the atmosphere beyond precise limits of national jurisdiction are the common heritage of all mankind;
4. developed countries must ensure positive net flows to LDCs of resources;
5. no state shall be totally dependent on others for food;
6. all states shall use energy rationally;
7. all states will use a single international currency;
8. all states shall accept the evolution of a world organization with the necessary power to plan, to make decisions, and to enforce them.

The *RIO* authors seem to feel that really specific guidance should not be given, (perhaps because it is not likely that there is *one* correct way to attack such reforms); both the analyst and the administrator must have other inputs, however, especially when dealing with such adjustments as No. 7 and No. 8 above. Therefore, individual proposals for change are given, but again, are presented only from a qualitative standpoint.

Conclusions

The major endeavor of the authors is to specify proposals for change. Table 3 summarizes these recommendations.

Two major trends are observable in these proposals: 1) a large number of new international agencies are recommended to oversee the development of the new orders, and 2) a great deal of early assistance is provided to the Third World

Table 3. Proposals for change from RIO: Reshaping the
International Order [4, pp. 126–175]

WITH RESPECT TO	MEDIUM-RANGE PROPOSALS	LONG-RANGE PROPOSALS
International monetary order	Phase out of national currencies; official intervention in exchange markets; better adjustment policies	Worldwide agreement on international reserve unit; regional currency mergers
Income redistribution	Concessional resource transfer target of 0.7% of GNP by 1980 and 1.0% thereafter; increased element of automaticity; channeled through multilateral institutions; increase in role of Third World countries; orderly renegotiation of past concessions	World treasury
Food production	Enhance self-sufficiency of Third World countries; adequate stockpiling; agreements on prices and production schemes; reduced food wastage in industrialized countries; development of rural communities; expansion of research efforts; create world monitoring system	Large-scale projects designed to improve irrigation and flood prevention; emergency stocks; alleviation of population pressure on food supplies
Industrialization, trade, and the international division of labor	More multilaterality in trade relations; reduction of import impediments; implement UNCTAD program on commodities; transform UNCTAD into world trade and development organization; increase negotiating power of Third World countries	Full employment policy by all governments

countries. This is consistent with the necessity to achieve a balance between population growth and food production, and one is tempted to agree with many or all of the ideas proffered. Two points of caution still exist for the policy-maker, however: 1) who oversees and coordinates all the new agencies? The problems are so interrelated in nature that with such agencies I can envision "jurisdictional" disputes, the result of which would be the nonsolution of the original problem; and 2) the entire set of proposals would work only with enforcement by the world organizations functioning in a truly democratic man-

Table 3. Proposals for change from RIO: Reshaping the
International Order [4, pp. 126–175] (continued)

WITH RESPECT TO	MEDIUM-RANGE PROPOSALS	LONG-RANGE PROPOSALS
Energy, ores, and minerals	Formation of producer's associations in primary commodities; examine present markets and prices for advantages for Third World countries; create a world agency for mineral resources; intensify research; implement energy-saving measures	Maintenance of remunerative price to producers; avoidance of heavy price fluctuations; recycle larger proportion of nonrenewable resources; switch to solar radiation and the use of hydrogen to meet energy needs
Scientific research and technological development	Subsidize technology transfer to Third World countries; organize centralized pool of technological know-how; reduce "brain-drain" from Third World countries	Concentrate on human welfare problems, rather than military matters; create world technological development authority with its own bank
Transnational enterprises	Agree on level of disclosure of transnationals; compliance of transnationals of host nation's development plan; more uniform tax structures; formulation of code of conduct	Establish intra-, or supranational authority; international trade unions
Human environment	Quantify wastefulness of present patterns of resource use; create national agencies with responsibilities for global resource management; experiment with life-size ecodevelopment plans; define the regime of the "international commons"	Continuous formulation and voluntary coordination of national resource, environmental, and locational policies

ner [4, p. 185]. If truly democratic, then a significant transfer of power from *both* superpowers (although more notably the Kremlin) will be required.

Implementation

The radical and sweeping changes that the *RIO* authors recommended would appear to meet the original objective: to add to the growing dialogue on this issue. More realistically, it would not appear that the world can change as outlined. The discourse does offer several advantages over the previous models,

Table 3. Proposals for change from RIO: Reshaping the
International Order [4, pp. 126–175] (*continued*)

WITH RESPECT TO	MEDIUM-RANGE PROPOSALS	LONG-RANGE PROPOSALS
Arms reduction	Exert pressure on super-powers to redirect military expenditures; achieve a treaty on a comprehensive nuclear test ban; ban chemical weapons; regulate the arms trade; reinforce the UN peace force; review the need for a world disarmament agency	Recognize that cultural diversity is desirable and not dangerous
Ocean management	Strengthen regional cooperation and organization; establish regional institutes; enhance participation of developing landlocked states; enforce UNCTAD Code of Conduct for liner conferences; extension of concepts of zones of peace, *e.g.*, Mediterranean; clarify the law of the sea; coordinate development of marine resources with land-based resources	Preservation of the marine environment; harmonize ocean apace uses; active sharing of benefits; international public enterprises; international tax on ocean use; cooperative international services, *e.g.*, ice patrols; effective compulsory and binding dispute settlement system

however, in that it accounts for cultural differences, uses only existing knowledge, recognizes the need for a single international currency, *etc.* Its overall usefulness to policy-makers is limited by the tendency of the authors to issue "apple pie and motherhood" statements not supported by sufficient detail. On the other hand, some specifics are offered; should the policy-maker wish to adopt the philosophy of "humanistic socialism," then many recommendations, *e.g.*, ocean management, are full of promise.

FORMULATION OF A SMALLER, TWO-SECTOR MODEL [30]

As noted above, the large, complex models are seldom implemented, and although many reasons exist for this, one of the primary causes of this nonuse is a lack of understanding on the part of the administrator. I would, therefore, like to develop a smaller, two-sector model in the spirit of the larger models, and do so in a step-by-step manner so that a better feeling for the modeling process can be obtained.

The model is designed to approximate the world's population and food imbalances. In that food per capita is critical to the continued existence of mankind at its current level, an explanation of several of the major factors contributing to changes in this level should be useful to public policy-makers. What is proposed is that food per capita is a function of the birth rate, the death rate, the labor force available, and the food produced per worker. More formally, and including time, the variables are defined as:

$P(t)$ = population at time t,
$F_s(t)$ = food supply at time t,
$W(t)$ = labor force available in the interval $(t, t + 1)$,
$W_f(t)$ = fraction of the labor force available to produce food over the interval $(t, t + 1)$,
$BR(t)$ = birth rate over the interval $(t, t + 1)$,
$DR(t)$ = death rate over the interval $(t, t + 1)$,
$F_p(t)$ = food produced per worker over the interval $(t, t + 1)$,
$F_c(t)$ = food per capita at time t

$$= \frac{F_s(t)}{P(t)}$$

It has been assumed that the rate of consumption of food per capita is constant, and although this is not literally true, I feel that this assumption does not invalidate the model or the modeling process.

Having identified the variables, it is now necessary to specify the functional relationships between the four independent ones (birth rate, death rate, fraction of labor force available for food production, and the food produced per worker) and the variable of interest (food per capita). To start, postulate the existence of four such functions:

$$BR(t) = g_1[F_c(t)]$$

$$DR(t) = g_2[F_c(t)]$$

$$W_f(t) = g_3[F_c(t)]$$

$$F_p(t) = g_4[F_c(t)]$$

Now the shape of these functions must be ascertained from a *qualitative* standpoint. Thus, the relationship between the food per capita and the birth rate (g_1) might take the general form:

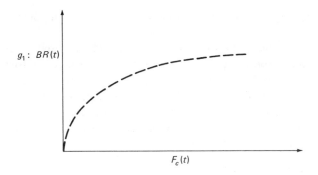

which implies that as the food per capita rises, the birth rate rises to a point, then levels off as other variables begin to have an impact. Quantitatively, this could be approximated by the general form:

$$BR(t) = \beta_1 - e^{-\alpha_1[F_c(t)]}$$

Similarly, the other relationships may be obtained:

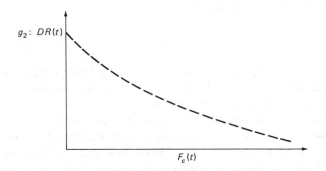

which follows logically from the fact that as the food per capita increases, the death rate will decrease, and is of the general form:

$$DR(t) = (1 - \beta_2) + \beta_2 e^{-\alpha_2[F_c(t)]}$$

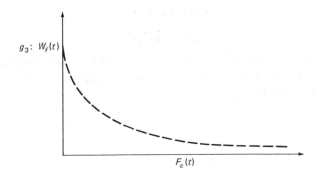

This shows the drop-off in the fraction of the population available to produce as the food per capita increases. It general form will be similar to g_2:

$$W_f(t) = (1 - \beta_3) + \beta e^{-\alpha_3 [F_c(t)]}$$

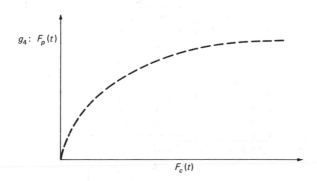

Here, the productivity per worker reaches a plateau (perhaps a function of man's physical capacities) as the food per capita rises. Its general form is like g_1:

$$F_p(t) = \beta_4 - e^{-\alpha_4 [F_c(t)]}$$

To verify these functional relationships will require empirical data; once satisfactory values are obtained for the parameters, however, the model can be made to work as follows:

$$W(t) = W_f(t) \cdot P(t)$$

The labor force available to produce food is the appropriate fraction of the total labor force.

$$F_s(t + 1) = F_p(t) \cdot W(t)$$

The food supply available at time $t + 1$ is the product of the productivity per worker times the number of workers.

$$P(t + 1) = P(t) \cdot [1 + BR(t) - DR(t)]$$

The population at time $t + 1$ is the population at time t times the change in population, which is the additions due to births minus those lost to death.] Schematically, these driving relationships may be coupled with the input variables as shown in Figure 19 [31].

At this point, the reader has probably noticed that this model has a good deal of the "flavor" of the Forrester model, and this continues when one ascertains the net effect of the above relationships [32]:

$$F_s(t + 1) = g_3[F_s(t)/P(t)] \cdot g_4[F_s(t)/P(t)] \cdot P(t)$$

$$P(t + 1) = [1 + g_1[F_s(t)/P(t)] - g_2[F_s(t)/P(t)] \cdot P(t)$$

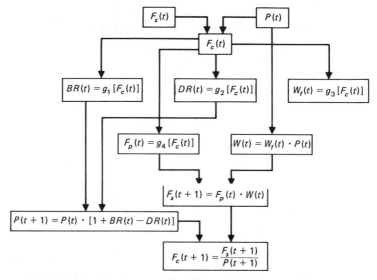

Figure 19. Schematic representation of the two-sector model.

So $P(t + 1) = [1 + g_1[F_c(t)] - g_2[F_c(t)] \cdot P(t)$

$$F_c(t + 1) = \frac{g_3[F_c(t)] \cdot g_4[F_c(t)]}{1 + g_1[F_c(t)] - g_2[F_c(t)]}$$

For simplicity of notation, let use define:

$$Q_1 = 1 + g_1 - g_2 \quad \text{and} \quad Q_2 = g_3 \cdot g_4$$

Thus,

$$P(t + 1) = Q_1[F_c(t)] \cdot P(t)$$

$$F_c(t + 1) = Q_2[F_c(t)]/Q_1[F_c(t)]$$

Similarly,

$$P(t + 2) = Q_1[F_c(t + 1)] \cdot P(t + 1)$$

$$= Q_1 \left[\frac{Q_2[F_c(t)]}{Q_1[F_c(t)]} \right] \cdot Q_1[F_c(t)] \cdot P(t)$$

and so forth. At this point, a complete model has been constructed that would allow one to predict the population for a future time interval.

Truthfully, I do not know if a model this simple is actually applicable—what I do hope is that the public policy-maker can follow the logic here and that he can begin to appreciate what the model can do for him.

CONCLUSIONS FOR THE POLICY-MAKER

Some policy-makers, such as Walton J. Francis, might be inclined to conclude that the global models are relatively worthless on account of some of the major criticisms that have been identified [27, pp. 363 and 397]:

1. The models are extremely aggregated, and only a single, global average is used for the model's parameters;
2. The models assume a Malthusian condition that the inventory of natural resources can never be increased;
3. The Forrester and Meadows models do not allow for capital investment expenditures to reduce pollution;
4. Energy is not dealt with explicitly;
5. The Mesarovic and Pestel model is complex, and empirical data so scarce, that it is hard to validate the model properly;
6. From a mathematical standpoint, the MIT models are merely coupled sets of ordinary difference equations.

Others may be added to this list:

7. The world's "goals" are fuzzy and conflicting;
8. Time as a relevant variable is virtually ignored [33];
9. All models are ultimately a function of the assumptions of the modeler.

To accept this viewpoint is dangerous, however, for today's crises will not wait. This immediacy has been observed by scholars from Thoreau ("What good is a house if you haven't got a planet to put it on?") to Vajk [27, p. 397]:

> The questions . . . must be investigated. For if a stable equilibrium is not possible, then we must either find ways to sustain growth indefinitely, or we must find ways to radically alter the structure to remove all destabilizing couplings, or we must accept collapse back to subsistence farming. This last option is unacceptable to virtually everyone; the second option requires more time than seems to be available.

Nevertheless, the policy-maker faces the immensely difficult task of attempting to ascertain which is the best policy when considering problems with such global import. The first question that he should ask himself is: Should global modeling be done at all?

A case may be constructed both for and against this issue. Because it is vital that overpollution, overpopulation, mass starvation, and increasing energy costs be attacked from a worldwide standpoint, an affirmative answer could be given to the above question. Yet, one may counter with the argument that since global models are discussed and then put "on the shelf," why should we invest the time, effort, and money in the first place? My analysis for the public official is that in spite of the "incremental" [34] usage, *the insights to be gained and the potential for increased global interactions and awareness more than offset the cost of the modeling* [35].

Once the politician has decided that the model is worthwhile, what should be the balance between science and politics on the part of the practitioner? Historically, the scientist has felt that the politician did not understand anything quantitative, and the politician has felt that as long as he had the scientist, he did not need a strong background in the quantitative fields. This is changing as the complexity of the problems increases. Now, more than ever, the politician must be quantitatively oriented. I am not suggesting that he be a member of a "tech staff," but I do feel that, when dealing with problems of this magnitude, quantitative methods may provide the needed fairness. For example, I cannot envision addressing the problem of the redistribution of wealth without using quantitative techniques.

Now let us assume that politicians do have this background. The question arises of how the global models should be evaluated, and who should evaluate them. The "who" part of the question is perhaps the easier, for the logical evaluators remain in academic settings. The "how" question lies unanswered. To my knowledge, there does not exist the single-valued-criterion-function so cherished by optimization theory that can be applied to global models. Thus, human lives, economics, elitist strategies, *etc.* could all be used in some form to determine which model is best. The best conclusion to be drawn from this is to let the evaluators analyze the model and then use their recommendations. For example, I believe that a choice between the Forrester model and the Mesarovic and Pestel model is not difficult once both are carefully analyzed. The implications of implementation are something else, however, and the politician must deal with them very carefully.

A subsidiary question to the how/who question above is: Who should do the modeling? How should the effort be organized [36]? This has been answered previously, and I will continue to plead for the modeling to stay in the hands of the private sector, and not fall into the public sector, whether it be a democracy or a dictatorship. But this leads to yet another question: How to create a framework for carrying on this kind of work? Should a favorable climate be encouraged? Again, speaking only for the Western societies, the "marketplace" of the private sector will determine the framework, and in my opinion, it will remain favorable for some time.

If all has gone well, the public policy-maker has allowed the private sector to construct and analyze the models, but it is the decision of the policy-maker to decide on the workability of these models. He must determine (presumably in coordination with his quantitative staff) if the models reflect the right relationships, if the numbers seem reasonable, and if they are understandable to others who will be involved in applying the model. This is a function that the global modeler should leave to the politician, for the balance between science and politics should be designed to allow each to take advantage of the other's expertise.

In conclusion, let me remind both the scientist and the public policy-maker of a quote from Paul Ehrlich, which summarizes the urgency of the current situation [37] :

> It is the top of the ninth. Man, at bat, has been hitting Nature very hard. However, it is important to remember, that *Nature bats last!*

APPENDIX A: MODELS OF THE WORLD OR SECTORS OF THE WORLD NOT ANALYZED IN THE TEXT

The following list is broken into two categories: those that present a single complete model in detail, and those that synopsize the modeling efforts of others. The public administrator may find the second group more useful; the analyst is more likely to be interested in the first.

The references below are not presented in any order beyond alphabetic, and are far from constituting a complete list of such efforts.

Individual Models

Beek, W. J., *et al. Work for the Future.* The Hague, Netherlands: Stichting Maatschappij en Onderneming, 1973.

Burnett, Robert, and Paul, Dionne. "GLOBE 6: A Multiregion Interactive World Simulation." *Simulation* (June 1973: 193. Burnett and Dionne originally developed GLOBE 5; this was later refined and published as GLOBE 6.

Forrester, Jay W. "National Model for Understanding Social and Economic Change." Unpublished.

Forrester, Jay W. *Industrial Dynamics.* Cambridge, Mass.: The MIT Press, 1961.

Forrester, Jay W. *Urban Dynamics.* Cambridge, Mass.: The MIT Press, 1969.

Glickman, Norman J. *Econometric Analysis of Regional Systems; Explorations in Model Building and Policy Analysis.* New York: Academic Press, 1977.

Kaya and Deiters, in *Activity of the Japan Work Team of the Club of Rome,* Japan Techno-Economics Society, June 1972, began work on a model that incorporates the effect of income distributions around the world. They intended to extend the work to examine the effect of localized natural resource shortages in greater detail using a model in which similar growth patterns are classified separately.

Oerlemans, T. W., Tellings, M. M. J., and H. de Vries. "World Dynamics: Social Feedback May Give Hope for the Future," *Nature* 238: 251–255.

Pestel, Eduard. "Multilevel Regionalized World Modeling Project: Motivation, Objectives, and Conceptual Foundation." Delivered at the International Institute for Applied Systems Analysis, Vienna, April 1974, p. 12.

Rockwell, William F. Jr. "Proposal for an Integrated Social and Economic Analysis of the United States Leading to a National Socioeconomic Model System." North American Rockwell Corporation, November 20, 1970.

State of Oregon. *Energy and State Government: A Decision-Making System Designed to Integrate Social, Economic, and Environmental Processes*, July 1, 1973.

Tuerpe, D. R. *A Two-Sector World Model.* University of California, Lawrence Livermore Laboratory Reprint, UCRL-75500, Livermore, California, December 1974.

Woodrow Wilson International Center for Scholars. "A Proposal for Developing a Capability at the National Level for Strategic Policy Assessments." August 9, 1973.

Discussions of Models

Beltrami, Edward J. *Models for Public Systems Analysis.* New York: Academic Press, 1977.

Chatterji, M. *Space Location and Regional Development.* New York: Academic Press, 1977.

Cole, H. D. S. "World Models, Their Progress and Applicability." *Future* 6(Jan. 1974): 201–218.

Dixon, L. C. W., and G. P. Szego, eds. *Towards Global Optimization.* Amsterdam: North-Holland, 1975.

Gass, Saul I., and Roger L. Sisson, eds. *A Guide to Models in Governmental Planning and Operations.* Potomac, Md.: Sauger Books, 1975.

Gray, Elizabeth, David Dodson Gray, and William F. Martin. *Growth and Its Implications for the Future.* Branford, Conn.: The Dinosaur Press, 1975.

Greenberger, Martin, Matthew A. Crenson, and Brian L. Crissey. *Models in the Policy Process; Public Decision Making in the Computer Era*, New York: Russel Sage Foundation, 1976.

Helly, Walter. *Urban Systems Models.* New York: Academic Press, 1975.

Kneese, Allen V., *et al.* "Perspective." In *Economics and the Environment: A Materials Balance Approach.* Baltimore: The Johns Hopkins Press, 1970.

APPENDIX B: SELECTED EXERCISES OF THE FORRESTOR MODEL [39]

DO YOU NEED INSTRUCTIONS (YES OR NO) ? YES

WORLD MODEL IS A HYPOTHETICAL DESCRIPTION OF THE WORLD
'SYSTEM'.   WRITTEN BY JAY FORRESTER OF MIT AND DESCRIBED IN
HIS BOOK 'WORLD DYNAMICS' (IN THE LIBRARY UNDER HD82.F63),
IT MATHEMATICALLY PORTRAYS THE RELATIONS AMONG POPULATION,
FOOD PRODUCTION, CAPITAL INVESTMENT, POLLUTION, NATURAL RE-
SOURCES, AND 'QUALITY OF LIFE'.   IN THE BASIC VERSION, THE
USER ENTERS CERTAIN ASSUMPTIONS ABOUT CURRENT RATES OF BIRTH,
DEATH, ETC., AND THEN VIEWS THE OUTPUT WHICH CORRESPONDS TO
THE 'LEVELS' OF FUNDAMENTAL VARIABLES OVER TIME.   TO UNDER-
STAND THIS, YOU SHOULD FIRST READ FORRESTER'S BOOK.

----->INPUT ASSUMPTIONS:

   (1) BR: THIS EQUALS THE 'BRN1' (BIRTH RATE-NORMAL, YEAR 1)
        IN FORRESTER'S MODEL. IT IS EXPRESSED IN FRACTIONS/
        YEAR, AND GIVES A MEASURE OF BIRTH RATE IN 1970.
        TO LEAVE THIS UNCHANGED (I.E., NO ABRUPT INCREASE
        OR DECREASE IN THE BIRTH IN 1970), INPUT A '1'; TO
        RAISE OR LOWER IT, INPUT SOME NUMBER HIGHER OR LOWER
        THAN 1: 1.7, OR .25. FOR EXAMPLE, IF A RADICAL BIRTH
        CONTROL PROGRAM INTRODUCED IN 1970, REDUCED THE BIRTH
        RATE BY 75%, INPUT A '.25' FOR BR.

   (2) DR: THIS EQUALS THE 'DRN1' (DEATH RATE-NORMAL, YEAR 1)
        AND CORRESPONDS TO THE BIRTH RATE, ABOVE. TO LEAVE
        1970'S VALUE UNCHANGED, INPUT A '1'; OTHERWISE, YOU
        MAY ELECT TO RAISE OR LOWER THIS FRACTIONALLY.

   (3) NR: THIS EQUALS THE 'NRUN1' (NATURAL RESOURCE USAGE RATE-
        NORMAL, YEAR 1) IN NATURAL RESOURCE UNITS/PERSON/
        YEAR. AGAIN, THE NORMAL VAULE FOR 1970 IS '1'; A RADI-
        CAL INCREASE IN THE USE OF NATURAL RESOURCES MIGHT
        BE APPROXIMATED BY AN NR OF '2' (A 100% INCREASE).

   (4) POL: 'POLN1' (POLLUTION-NORMAL, YEAR 1) IN POLLUTION UNITS/
        PERSON/YEAR. 1970'S 'NORMAL' VALUE IS '1', AND IN-
        CREASES OR DECREASES IN 'POL' REFLECT YOUR POLICY
        CHANGES IN THE RATE OF POLLUTION GENERATION.

   (5) FC: 'FC1' (FOOD COEFFICIENT, YEAR 1) WHICH IS DIMENSION-
        LESS. THIS MEASURES THE 'FOOD RATIO' (UNITS PER CAPITA)
        IN 1970, AND IS '1' UNLESS YOU MAKE POLICY ASSUMP-
        TIONS ABOUT THE AVAILABILITY OF FOOD BY INCREASING OR
        DECREASING THIS.

   (6) CI: CIGN1' (CAPITAL INVESTMENT GENERATION-NORMAL, YEAR
        1), WHICH FOR 1970 IS USUALLY '1', MEASURES THE RATE
        OF CAPITAL INVESTMENT GENERATION IN CAPITAL UNITS/
        PERSON/YEAR.

  ----->OUTPUT VARIABLES:

   (1) P: POPULATION LEVEL, BILLIONS OF PEOPLE
   (2) C: CAPITAL INVESTMENT LEVEL, CAPITAL UNITS
   (3) W: POLLUTION LEVEL, UNITS OF POLLUTION
   (4) N: NATURAL RESOURCES, IN UNITS
   (5) Q: QUALITY OF LIFE, IN SATISFACTION UNITS

----->USING THE MODEL:

(A) FOR A FIRST TRY, ASSUME NOTHING CHANGES IN 1970 (ALL
    6 COEFFICIENTS=1) AND SEE THE RESULTS.
(B) NOTE THE DISASTROUS RESULTS (PRIMARILY DUE TO NATURAL RESOURCE
    DEPLETION). TO REMOVE NATURAL RESOURCED AS A CONSTRAINT,
    ARBITRARILY REDUCE 'NR' (NR USAGE RATE) IN 1970 TO '.25'
(C) NOTE CATASTROPHIC RESULTS (DUE TO THE LACK OF AN 'NR' CONSTRAINT
    ON INDUSTRIALIZATION, THUS CAUSING EXTRAORDINARY POLLUTION).
    NOW REMOVE POLLUTION AS A CONSTRAINT (ALONG WITH NR) BY
    MAKING BOTH NR AND POL EQUAL TO, SAY, .25.
(D) CONTINUE TRYING TO AVOID CATASTROPHE

    ----->HELP FOR HELP, READ FORRESTER.

```
BR,DR ? 1,1
NR,POL ? 1,1
FC,CI ? 1,1
```

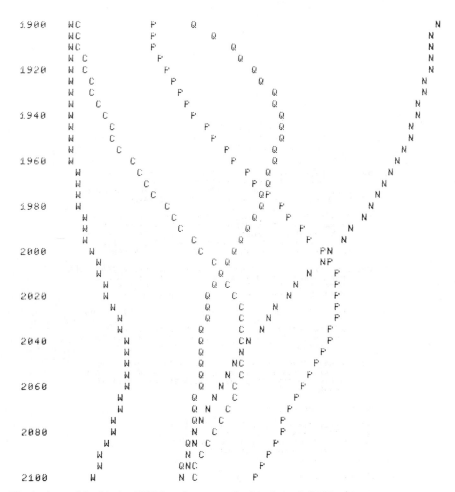

```
1900    WC                  P       Q                                          N
        WC                  P           Q                                      N
        WC                  P               Q                                  N
        W C                   P              Q                                 N
1920    W C                    P               Q                               N
        W   C                    P               Q                             N
        W    C                     P                 Q                         N
        W     C                     P                Q                         N
1940    W      C                     P                 Q                       N
        W        C                      P               Q                      N
        W        C                       P              Q                      N
        W          C                      P            Q                      N
1960    W            C                      P          Q                     N
         W             C                      P Q                         N
         W               C                     P Q                      N
         W                C                     QP                   N
1980     W                  C                    Q   P            N
          W                  C                    Q.    P       N
          W                    C                    Q       P      N
          W                    C        Q         P     N
2000       W                    C       Q                 PN
           W                           C Q                NP
           W                            Q            N    P
            W                           Q C         N     P
2020        W                           Q    C      N     P
             W                          Q      C  N       P
              W                         Q      C N        P
              W                        Q       C N        P
2040          W                        Q       CN        P
              W                        Q      N        P
              W                        Q      NC       P
              W                        Q     N C      P
2060          W                        Q   N C      P
             W                         Q  N   C       P
             W                         Q N  C      P
            W                          QN  C      P
2080        W                          N  C      P
           W                           QN C    P
          W                            N C    P
          W                            QNC    P
2100      W                            N C    P
```

The basic model with the 1970-based rates continuing through 2100.

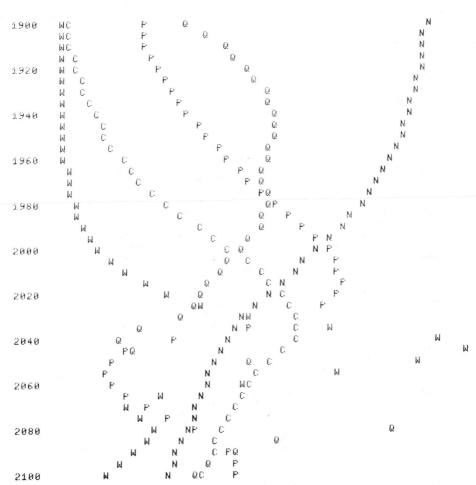

A 20% increase in capital investment.

```
BR, DR ? 1, 1
NR, POL ? 1, 1
FC, CI ? 1, 1. 5
```

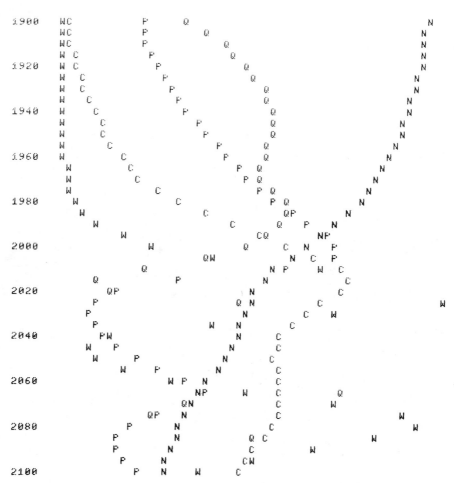

A 50% increase in capital investment. Note that the quality of life dramatically increases around 2080–2100.

```
BR,DR  ?  1,1
NR,POL ?  1,.75
FC,CI  ?  1,1


1900   WC              P        Q                                                    N
       WC              P           Q                                                 N
       WC              P              Q                                              N
       W  C           P                Q                                            N
1920   W  C            P                  Q                                        N
       W   C            P                  Q                                      N
       W   C             P                   Q                                   N
       W    C            P                   Q                                  N
1940   W     C          P                     Q                                N
       W      C              P                 Q                              N
       W      C               P                Q                             N
       W       C               P               Q                           N
1960   W          C              P             Q                           N
        W          C                P  Q                              N
        W           C                 P Q                           N
        W            C                   Q                        N
1980    W             C                  Q  P                   N
        W             C                  Q      P            N
        W              C                Q        P        N
        W              C              Q            P    N
2000   W               C            Q           PN
        W                 C  Q              NP
        W                  QC            N      P
         W                 Q C          N        P
2020   W                 Q      C      N          P
        W                 Q       C  N            P
        W               Q         C  N            P
        W               Q          C  N          P
2040    W               Q            N           P
        W               Q             N          P
        W               Q             NC        P
        W               Q           N C        P
2060   W                Q         N  C       P
         W               Q      N    C      P
         W               Q    N    C       P
         W                Q N    C        P
2080    W                Q  N   C       P
         W                Q  N C       P
       W                 QN    C      P
        W                 Q  N C     P
2100   W                 QN  C      P
```

A 25% decrease in pollution. Note that this changes the model very little.

```
BR, DR  ?  1, 1
NR, POL  ?  .25, 1
FC, CI  ?  1, 1
```

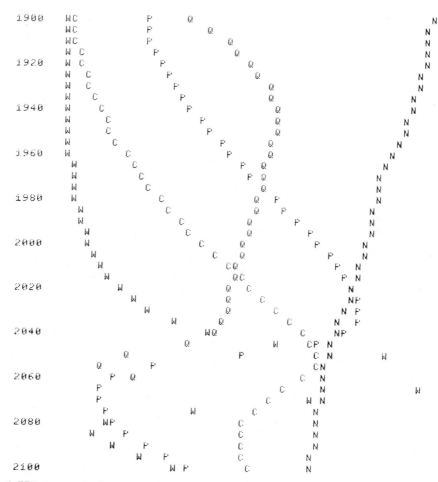

A 75% decrease in the rate of usage of natural resources.

```
BR,DR  ?  1,1
NR,POL ?  1,.9
FC,CI  ?  1,1.2
```

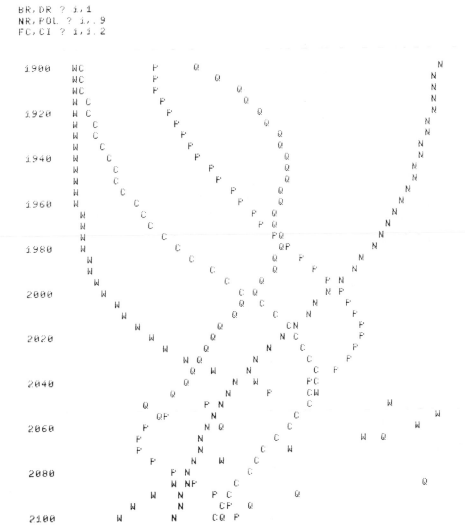

A 20% increase in capital investment with a corresponding decrease of 10% in pollution.
Note that this still leads to collapse, but after 2060 the population begins to rise.

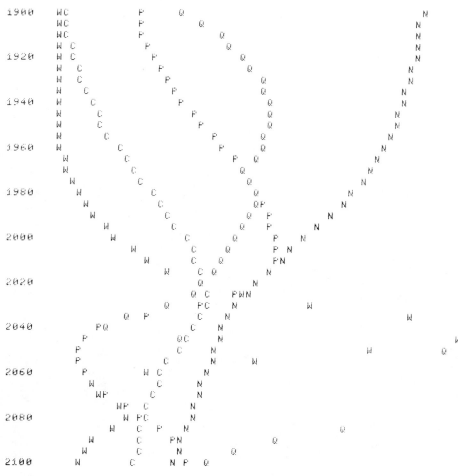

A 10% increase in the death rate, a 30% increase in the rate of usage of natural resources, a 60% increase in pollution, and a 5% decrease in the rate of food consumption. Note the very high quality of life between 2040 and 2080 (off the graph), but that in 2080–2100 a very fast "catastrophe" occurs.

```
BR, DR ? .5,.8
NR, POL ? 1.25,1.2
FC, CI ? 1,1.1
```

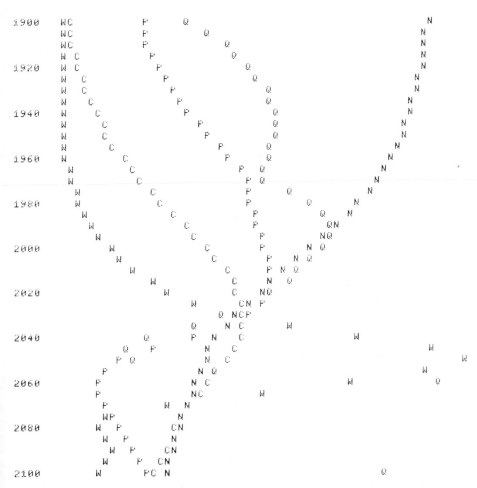

A 50% decrease in the birth rate, a 20% decrease in the death rate, a 25% increase in the rate of usage of natural resources, a 20% increase in the pollution level, a 10% increase in the level of capital investment.

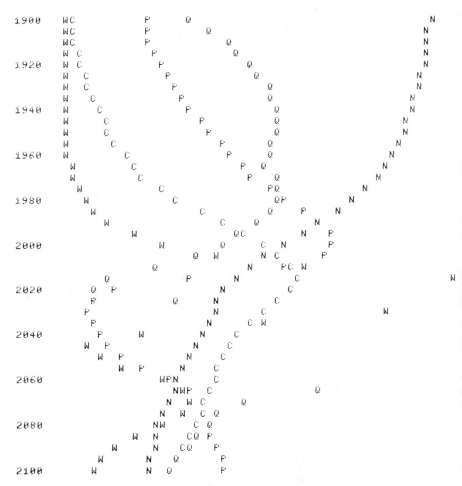

A 50% increase in the rate of usage of natural resources, a 20% increase in the pollution level, a 10% increase in the rate of food consumption, and a 40% increase in the rate of capital investment. Note that this leads to an overall collapse of a more "gentle" nature.

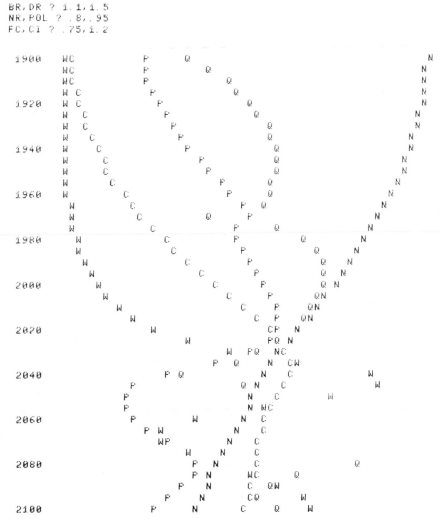

```
BR, DR ? 1.1, 1.5
NR, POL ? .8, .95
FC, CI ? .75, 1.2
```

A 10% increase in the birth rate, a 50% increase in the death rate, a 20% decrease in the rate of usage of natural resources, a 5% decrease in the pollution level, a 25% decrease in the rate of food consumption, and a 20% increase in the rate of capital investment. Note that the model now provides fluctuating results.

```
BR, DR  ?  1, 1
NR, POL  ?  .5, .5
FC, CI  ?  .9, 1.2


1900      WC              P        Q                                              N
          WC              P          Q                                            N
          WC              P             Q                                         N
          W C              P             Q                                        N
1920      W C               P               Q                                     N
          W  C                P               Q                                    N
          W  C                 P                Q                                  N
          W   C                P                 Q                               N
1940      W    C                P                  Q                             N
          W     C                 P                 Q                           N
          W     C                  P                Q                          N
          W      C                  P              Q                          N
1960      W       C                  P            Q                          N
           W        C                   P   Q                              N
           W         C                    QP                              N
           W          C                    PQ                             N
1980       W           C                    Q                            N
            W            C                   Q  P                      N
            W             C                  Q    P                    N
            W              C                 Q      P                 N
2000        W               C                Q        P      N
             W                C            CQ              PN
             W                    Q  C              N P
              W                        Q          C         N      P
2020          W                         Q              CN          P
               W                         Q              N C           P
                W                         Q              N   C           P
                 W                         Q              N      C        P
2040              W                         Q              N         C      P
                   W                         Q                N         C   P
                    W                         Q                N          CP
                     W                         Q                  N         PC
2060                  W                         Q                 N        P  C
                       W                 Q          N                    P     C
                        W                Q         N                    P        C
                         W               Q       N                     P         C
2080                      W              Q     N                     P           C
                           W             Q   N                     P             C
                            W            Q   N                   P               C
                            W            Q N                    F                C
2100                        W            Q N                  P                  C
```

A 50% decrease in the rate of usage of natural resources, a 50% decrease in the pollution level, a 10% decrease in the rate of food consumption, and a 20% increase in the rate of capital investment. Note that the model is relatively stable around 2100.

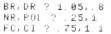

```
BR,DR ? 1.05,.8
NR,POL ? .25,1
FC,CI ? .75,1.1
```

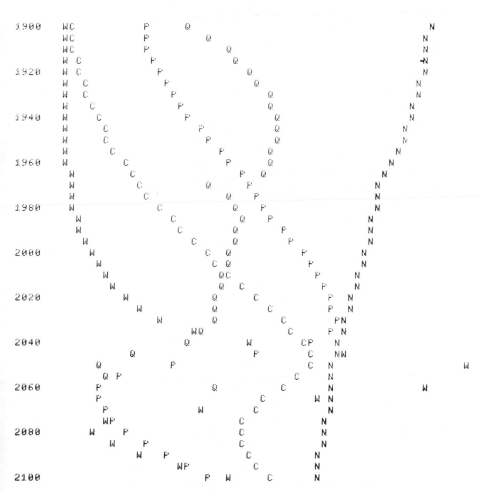

A 5% increase in the birth rate, a 20% decrease in the death rate, a 75% decrease in the rate of usage of natural resources, a 25% decrease in the rate of food consumption, and a 10% increase in the rate of capital investment. Note that by 2080–2100, conditions seem relatively favorable except for the increase in the pollution level.

NOTES AND REFERENCES

1. Forrester, Jay W. *World Dynamics*. Cambridge, Mass.: Wright-Allen Press, 1971.
2. Meadows, Donella H., Dennis L. Meadows, Jørgen Randers, and William W. Behrens, III. *The Limits to Growth*. New York: Universe Books, 1972.
3. Mesarovic, Mihajlo, and Eduard Pestel. *Mankind at the Turning Point*. New York: Dutton, 1974.
4. Tinbergen, Jan, coordinator. *RIO: Reshaping the International Order*. New York: Dutton, 1976.
5. Greenberger, Martin, Matthew A. Crenson, and Brian L. Crissey. *Models in the Policy Process*. New York: Russell Sage Foundation, 1976, p. xiii.
6. Adapted from the *Yale Alumni Magazine* and reprinted in Elizabeth Gray, David Dodson Gray, and William F. Martin, *Growth and Its Implications for the Future*, Cambridge, Mass.: The Dinosaur Press, 1975, p. 131.
7. Toffler, Alvin, ed. *The Futurists*. New York: Random House, 1972, p. 3.
8. Toffler expands upon this idea in *Future Shock*, New York, Bantam Books, 1970.
9. Dror, Yehezkel. *Public Policymaking Reexamined*. Scranton, Pa.: Chandler Publishing, 1968, p. 8.
10. Laszlo, Ervin. *A Strategy for the Future; The Systems Approach to World Order*. New York: Braziller, 1974.
11. Lindblom, Charles E. "The Science of Muddling Through." *Public Administration Review*, 19(1959): 80.
12. Harmon, Michael. "Administrative Policy Formulation in the Public Interest." *Public Administration Review* (Sept.–Oct. 1969): 483–491.
13. Etzoni, Amitai. *The Active Society*. New York: The Free Press, 1968.
14. A group of 100 leaders of industry, government, military, and business that first gathered in Rome to discuss problems of global scale. Quite international in scope and membership, these individuals seek to understand the crises in our present-day socioeconomic systems and to devise strategies to avert the crises. Giving credit where credit is due, both the Meadows report and the Mesarovic and Pestel report were funded by the Volkswagen Foundation, and other fund-granting institutions, such as the Ford Foundation, are quite active in their support.
15. Gass, Saul I., and Roger L. Sisson. *A Guide to Models in Governmental Planning and Operations*. Potomac, Md.: Sauger Books, 1975, pp. 9–11.
16. Greenberger, Martin, Matthew A. Crenson, and Brian L. Crissey. *Models in the Policy Process, Public Decision Making in the Computer Era*. New York: Russell Sage Foundation, 1976, pp. 86–87.
17. Adapted from a discussion of modeling with William W. Hardgrave in March 1975: Models must be useful, usable, and used. If a model fails these criteria, then it fails as a model.
18. Cole, H. D. S., Christopher Freeman, Marie Jahoda, and K. L. R. Pavitt. *Models of Doom, a Critique of the Limits to Growth*. New York: Universe Books, 1973, p. 25.
19. The list of variables used as inputs is very similar to a list formulated by Ricardo and Smith, two classical economists. It is impossible to discern if a link between these two and Forrester exists, however.
20. Gose, Donald. Unpublished manuscript. The George Washington University, 1976, p. 3.
21. Meadows, Dennis L., William W. Behrens III, Donella H. Meadows, Roger F. Naill, Jørgen Randers, and Erich K. O. Zahn, *Dynamics of Growth in a Finite World*. Cambridge, Mass.: Wright-Allen Press, 1974.

22. Several possible sources exist for these errors. Two of them are: 1) the approximations used in the relationships; and 2) the use of the Euler approximations in the calculations.

23. Conclusions 1 through 5 are taken from Cole [18, pp. 132–134].

24. Francis, Walton H. "A Report on Measurement and the Quality of Life and the Implications for Government Action of the *Limits to Growth*." Washington D.C.: US Department of Health, Education and Welfare, 1973.

25. The authors provide a most dramatic presentation of the "cost" of delay when they calculate that if Latin America were to wait until 1990 to institute "Planned Parenthood" instead of doing so in 1975, and the population trends do not change during that interval, then the total number of deaths due to starvation that would be incurred by waiting would be 500,000,000. (And this number is generated with the assumption that the rest of the world mobilizes to try to help.)

26. This is highlighted by the authors by the use of age distributions within a given population. For example, in Mexico, if zero population growth were attained today, the high percentage of young individuals would place increasing demands on food as they grew up and consumed more per capita.

27. Vajk, J. Peter. "The Impact of Space Colonization on World Dynamics." *Technological Forecasting and Social Change* 9(1976): 387.

28. Gallup, George. "What Mankind Thinks about Itself." *Readers Digest* (Oct. 1976): 132–136.

29. Adapted from "TOPPIX," the Chicago Tribune, 1977.

30. The basis for this model was originally proposed by Dr. William W. Hardgrave, The George Washington University. It remains as a working document, and is not for reproduction or redistribution without explicit written permission.

31. The reader is strongly urged to trace these connections for himself to verify that his intuition and the model are in agreement.

32. I am aware that this model does have some of the "flavor" of the Forrester model; the two models are *not* the same, however, and careful examination will reveal the simplifying assumptions inherent in the two-sector model.

33. Meadows *et al.* have responded to some of these criticisms: "Any long-term model that is being used to aid the policy-making process must therefore be constantly updated to incorporate surprising discoveries . . . and to assess how they may change the options for human society." From Meadows *et al.*, "A Response to Sussex," in [18].

34. Incremental as in the spirit of Lindblom; see [11].

35. Naturally, the administrator will want to verify this for himself with economic, social, and cultural data; nevertheless, I am confident that careful investigation by policy-makers will lead to exactly this conclusion.

36. The basis for the formulation of these questions is a series of discussions that were part of the annual convention of the Operations Research Society of America in Chicago in 1975.

37. Ehrlich, Paul. "Eco-Catastrophe." In *The Futurists*. Edited by Alvin Toffler. New York: Random House, 1972, p. 26.

38. These runs were performed on the PDP 11/40 owned by the School of Government and Business Administration, The George Washington University.

4

The Future of Paris: A Systems Study in Strategic Urban Planning*

Hasan Ozbekhan
University of Pennsylvania

INTRODUCTION

Early in 1971 the French Government asked me to undertake a study on the future of Paris—a future expected to unfold amid the dramatic changes forecast for the last three decades of the twentieth century. In this chapter I hope to describe as succinctly as I am able how my colleagues from the Wharton School at the University of Pennsylvania and I conducted the work [1].

It is impossible to relate all, or even most of, the intricate detailing that had to be wrought from the situation in order to come up with the analyses and conclusions that the sponsors expected. I shall, therefore, limit myself to describing those aspects of the work that I believe to be conceptually the most interesting.

I should note at the outset that what was done in no way resembles the typical urban or typical strategic planning study. It turned out to be something else, something whose nature is most closely suggested by the relatively new expression "systems thinking." It is this difference that I shall try to emphasize, especially in terms of the study's methodological underpinnings. For it is in the methodology developed as part of the research that I find the synthesizing principle that might enable me to deal with the subject without getting mired in details. But first, let me outline the background of the project and its working organization.

*This chapter appears here with the concurrence of the Royal Society, London, England.

BACKGROUND

Desire for change, feelings that something needs to be done, and decisions taken often arise from rather vague perceptions and assessments of a situation. This state of initial awareness, which does not yet involve any real understanding, is what I call "the disquiet."

It was, I believe, the upheavals of 1968 that induced a number of Frenchman (many in positions of authority) to realize that despite a remarkable recovery from the wounds of World War II, profound dissonances continued to exist within their country. This feeling soon grew into a diffuse but massive disquiet that led the French Government to attempt to investigate the main forces that were shaping their polity's development.

In the main, these studies tended to indicate that Paris, as a city, is an urbanizing region, and is the locus of important events operated as a powerful force in French life. Whatever happened in Paris seemed to radiate and resonate throughout France; in one way or another it affected the entire country. Every piece of research suggested that the future development of France, what France would stand for, desired to become, or aimed to achieve, greatly depended on how Paris evolved. Yet, and this came as something of a surprise, Paris was found to be suffering from administrative neglect. It had been virtually taken for granted; that is, ignored in may subtle ways. It had, for instance, escaped the jurisdiction, and hence, the attention, of D.A.T.A.R. (*Délégation à l'aménagement du territoire et à l'action régionale*), which had done such imaginative and useful work in territorial management for the rest of France. Paris had been allowed to grow unplanned or, still worse, according to a general, somewhat confused, monothematic plan inspired by what the French called "economic rationality," which seemed to ignore all the other functions, roles, and activities that go into the making of great cities.

These conditions, which the events of May had crystallized, now led the French authorities, as well as the intelligentsia, to focus their attention on Paris in an effort to understand the problems besetting the capital. And, by 1970, this large-scale soul searching had brought to light a number of discrete issues. What the press dubbed *la rogne de Paris* (an expression whose meaning comes alive if one remembers that *rogne* is translated as "mange" in this context) can be reduced to the following points:

Urban deterioration, visible in the city's physical degradation ("Paris contains the best nineteenth century and worst twentieth century architecture in the world"), but also affecting the city's cultural life and social make-up—its overall *style* along with everything this implies for the quality of experience that had formerly made Paris so special;

Loss of a sense of "role," especially in the political arena *vis-à-vis* the expanding EEC (the United Kingdom was soon to join it, and this seemed to make the French nervous); the enhanced importance of Brussels where international organizations had moved, thanks to one of President de Gaulle's least comprehensible decisions; the growing competition from cities such as Amsterdam, Rotterdam, Frankfort, Zurich, Geneva, Milan, and now London within a new and still mysterious European order;

Lack of a sense of the future, attributable to a myopia regarding the functions of Paris and their relation to such events as the unmistakable evolution of advanced industrial economies into what had already been called "The Postindustrial Society"—a society grounded on a "Global Industrial System" in which the Third World must fully participate;

Lack of a concept of what Paris "ought" to be, a lack of vision and purpose concerning the city's identity, or what the French preferred to call its "vocation," in a changing world and also within the context of France itself; for Paris was seen as pursuing its haphazard course at vast cost to the country as a whole, disequilibrating the economic balance by acting as a "suction pump" that concentrated a constantly growing share of economic activity and decision-making authority within its already unmanageable confines.

These and many other similar issues were sensed, but not articulated in detail; nor was it yet grasped that they might be symptoms of deeper dysfunctions that, being interactive, fed upon each other and thus gained momentum at an alarming rate.

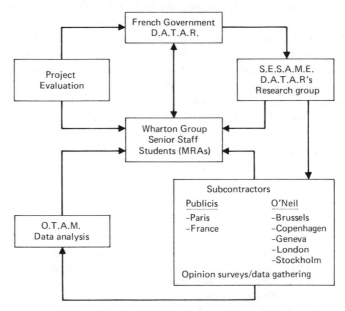

Figure 1. Organization of project.

Such a possibility was not seriously considered because, at the time, traditional, incrementalist approaches were still believed adequate to cope with the kind of policy issues I have just noted. It must also be admitted, however, that some agencies of the French Government, notably D.A.T.A.R., were beginning to realize that the situation might warrant experimentation with some of the new ideas that had originated in those reaches of systems thinking that have since come to be known as Planning Theory, and which the French called *"Prospective."*

It was at this point, and because of D.A.T.A.R.'s desire to explore new avenues, that the Wharton Group was invited to undertake what is now referred to as the "Paris Project."

From the start, the work to be done was viewed as a long-range planning study of the action research type. Activities were organized with the aim of achieving the widest possible participation by French authorities and by selected constituencies representing a broad spectrum of opinion. To save space I am giving a simple outline of this organization in Figure 1.

PARIS: DESIGN OF A FUTURE

The study's initial and guiding precept was that a methodology had to be invented that could cope with an extremely complex and unbounded subject, for we already knew "Paris" included levels and dimensions of reality that greatly transcended its usual meaning. Construction of this methodology was considered to be an integral part of the research.

Methodological formalism was abandoned in favor of more flexible, heuristic approaches. These, and the substantive issues they permitted us to deal with, can best be expounded with reference to a general planning process that I developed in the late 1960s, which now became central to our work. Certain aspects of this type of planning—it has since been named "Interactive Normative Planning"—should be explained at this point. First, the principles from which its fundamental conception was derived, postulate that:

- planning is a "holistic," as against an "incrementalist" approach to the solution of interlinked, nonsegregatable sets of complex problems;
- in planning what is meant by *solution* is the "design" of some new situation that represents an outcome that is more valued than the present situation;
- planning always involves "experimentation" in the design of outcomes and in the selection of means to achieve such outcomes;
- planning is a decision-making, hence a "voluntaristic," process;
- planning is aimed at the formulation of "policy"—that is, the determination of *interventions* that will be made in a situation so as to change that situation into a more preferable one.

The operational meanings of these principles will become evident as we pro-

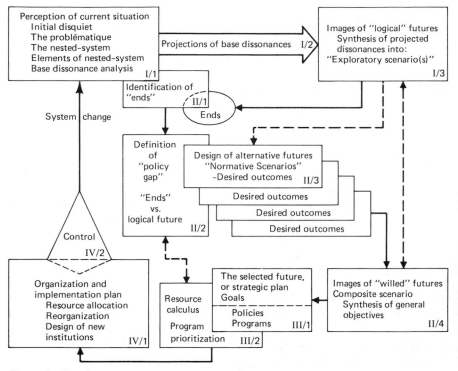

Figure 2. The planning process. Shaded areas indicate the steps covered in the Paris Project.

ceed. For the moment let me add only that the main techniques used in this kind of planning are system-analytic models and scenarios of different kinds.

The paradigm of the process as a whole is given in Figure 2, where the various *phases* involved are indicated by Roman numerals: I. The Reference Projection; II. The Normative Plan; III. The Strategic Plan; IV. The Organizational and Implementation Plan. It is in terms of these phases and of their component *steps* (indicated by Arabic numerals) that I shall now try to describe how the Paris Project evolved.

Phase I: The Reference Projection

Basically, what is termed Reference Projection is an attempt to structure the highly confused, overlapping, blurred sets of problems that trigger an initial disquiet—something I shall henceforth call the *problématique*—into a model capable of suggesting causal linkages among them [2].

To build such a model it is necessary to visualize the *problématique* in all its relevant dimensions, namely as pertaining to a nested-system. The latter can be conceived as consisting of three concentric environments: the "internal environment" of the core-system (Paris in this case); a larger surrounding "transactional environment"; and a still larger embedding "contextual environment" [3]. The main criterion for determining the boundaries of these environments is the degree of intersensitivity and synergy among the events generated by each and radiated throughout the entire nested-system. Once such environments are determined, it becomes necessary to identify and name their major functional and structural components. The detailing such analyses involve is extensive in the case of the internal environment, somewhat less so for the transactional, and merely indicative for the contextual. The most important among the elements identified in the Paris Project are shown in Figure 3.

After the nested-system has been mapped in this fashion, the most intensive interactions among the elements must be found and investigated in some depth. In doing this we relied on the information at hand, which, among other things, repeatedly pointed to the fact that "throughout France, but especially in Paris, economic forces were the driving forces, while political forces played a restraining role." The operational significance of this belief, which seemed to be universally shared, should, if one succeeded in investigating it fully, permit us to penetrate the *problématique*. Such investigation required that a dissonance analysis be made to study the pattern of interactions existing between the political and the economic subsystems. (The ensuing discussion will be easier to follow if repeated reference is made to Figure 3.) This initial analysis disclosed a number of provocative points that can be highlighted as follows:

- In the economic subsystem, the ECO 2 Sig sector displayed the highest rate of growth and the most marked tendency to concentrate in Paris;
- Its dynamism was at the source of certain major problems since it caused the displacement of ECO 2 RP, competition for residential and office space in the better districts, inflationary increases in rents, heightened traffic congestion, *etc.*
- The increasing power of ECO 2 Sig appeared rooted in an informal but formidably effective coalition it had created with HCS (the higher strata of the political subsystem). This coalition seemed quite natural, not only because of ECO 2 Sig's need to influence government policy while benefiting from government support, but also because of the total commonality between the two groups' social background, attitudes, outlook, and interests—both chiefly comprising individuals with SU 1 and PU 1 backgrounds, and both sharing strong (p) attitudes;
- So far so good, except that by 1970 this ruling coalition was becoming strained over two major policy issues: 1) ECO 2 Sig needed and favored foreign investments, whereas the government distrusted them; and 2) disagreements concerning the attitudes and products of the educational subsystem, which need further comment:
  The educational subsystem in France is an arm of the government and be-

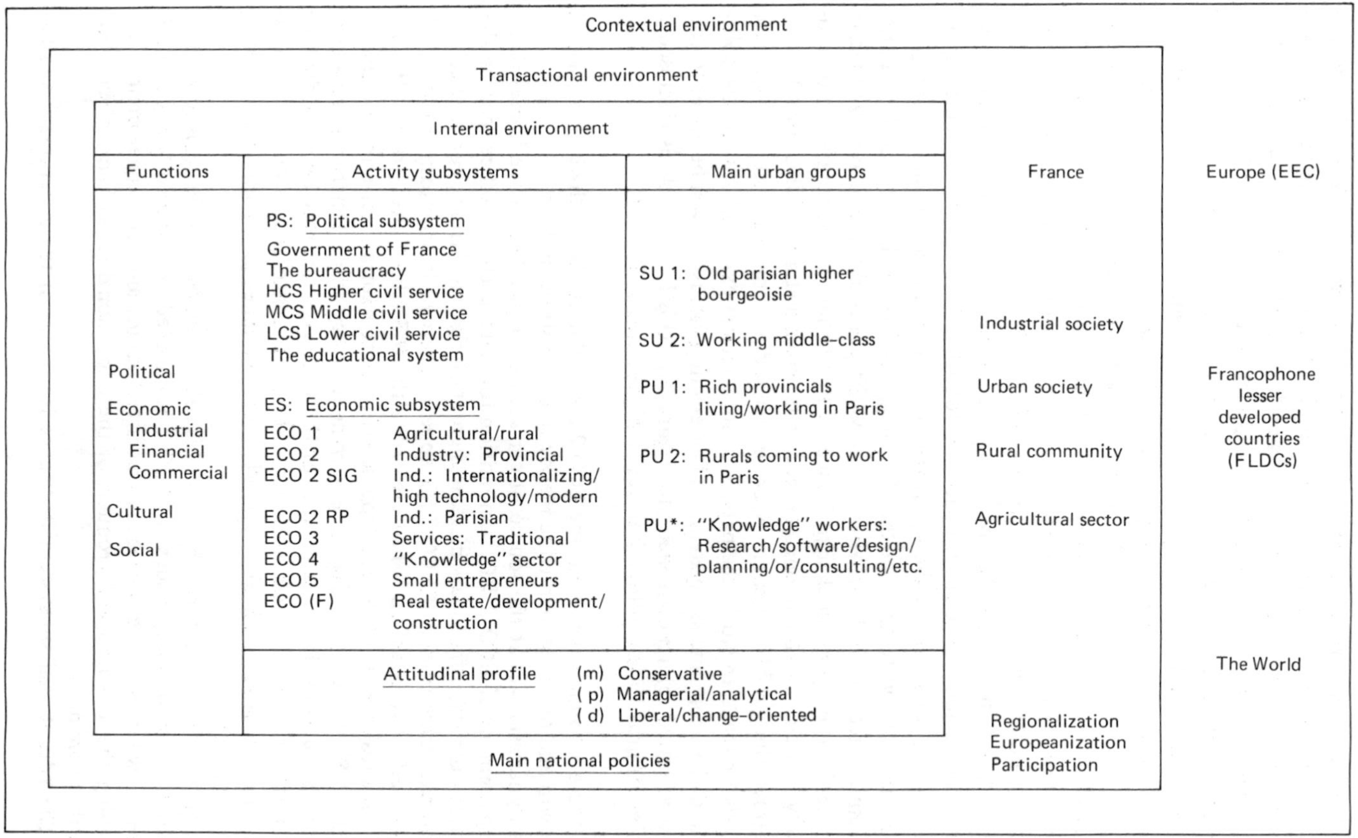

Contextual environment

Transactional environment

Internal environment

Functions	Activity subsystems	Main urban groups	France	Europe (EEC)

Political	PS: Political subsystem
	  Government of France
	  The bureaucracy
	  HCS Higher civil service
	  MCS Middle civil service
	  LCS Lower civil service
	  The educational system			

		SU 1: Old parisian higher bourgeoisie	Industrial society	
		SU 2: Working middle-class	Urban society	
Economic Industrial Financial Commercial	ES: Economic subsystem ECO 1 Agricultural/rural ECO 2 Industry: Provincial ECO 2 SIG Ind.: Internationalizing/high technology/modern	PU 1: Rich provincials living/working in Paris	Rural community	Francophone lesser developed countries (FLDCs)
	ECO 2 RP Ind.: Parisian	PU 2: Rurals coming to work in Paris	Agricultural sector	
Cultural	ECO 3 Services: Traditional ECO 4 "Knowledge" sector	PU*: "Knowledge" workers: Research/software/design/ planning/or/consulting/etc.		
Social	ECO 5 Small entrepreneurs ECO (F) Real estate/development/ construction			

	Attitudinal profile (m) Conservative
	                (p) Managerial/analytical
	                (d) Liberal/change-oriented
			Regionalization
			Europeanization
			Participation
				The World

	Main national policies			

Figure 3. The Nested-System and its Component Elements.

longs to the Civil Service. With a few notable exceptions in the *Grandes Ecoles*, it suffers from virulent traditionalism in its world view, pedagogy, and organization. It upholds deeply entrenched (m) attitudes and seeks to imbue students with the same inertial conservatism, which makes it almost impossible for it to produce ECO 4 types of "knowledge" workers in the quantities ECO 2 Sig needs in ever greater numbers. ECO 2 Sig's disenchantment with the educational system (a very powerful sector of the political subsystem) was difficult to remedy because the student riots of 1968 had hardened all sectors of opinion, and the political subsystem tended to side with the educational, especially that people in ECO 4 fields of activities were known to be infected by (d) attitudes, and, thus, to favor change.
Because of all this, ECO 2 Sig had, by the early 1970s, begun to reevaluate its position and its commitments, and HCS reacted by doing the same. These realignments generated tensions as ECO 2 Sig's acquired momentum was increasingly hedged in and controlled by the now heightened inertia of the political sector.

Thus, our first probe of the Paris *problématique* revealed that an old equilibrium that had characterized the situation until about 1968 was now losing stability and coherence due to factors such as:

- Economic overconcentration in and around Paris (with enormous costs to the rest of France);
- The increasingly international needs and outlook of ECO 2 Sig;
- The rapid rise of an important change-oriented activity group (ECO 4);
- The dependence of ECO 2 Sig on ECO 4;
- The inability of the educational subsystem to satisfy the needs of ECO 2 Sig, and the hardening of its (m) type attitudes, especially at the higher levels of the Civil Service;
- A growing cohesion of outlook among groups sharing (d) type attitudes;
- The emerging possibility of new coalitions between (p) and (d) type attitudes;
- The general neglect of most other economic activity groups (except for ECO F, which always appeared to work in conjunction with ECO 2 Sig).

The first and last of these factors made the supposition unavoidable that such events unfolding in Paris must also create serious dissonances throughout France among the main components of the Transactional Environment identified as "Industrial Society," "Urban Society," "Rural Community," and "Agricultural Sector." This inference proved justified when the dissonance analysis was extended to the country seen as a whole. To do this we introduced another set of elements; namely, the principal current "Policies" of the French Government —"Regionalization," "Europeanization," and "Participation," which had been identified as important components of the Transactional Environment. Whether and how these policies reconfigured the dissonance map was a fundamental issue to be probed in depth. I should mention here that, later, the map was expanded to include the Contextual Environment; however, the analysis in that instance was relatively cursory, because at that particular stage there was no need to go beyond what was happening in France. The format of the entire map, reduced into a Base Dissonance Matrix, is outlined in Figure 4.

The findings at this point informed us, among other things, that France's industrial pattern was being rapidly altered by eastward migration toward Paris and the "dynamic regions" [4]; that this was, in some areas, weakening the texture of the Urban Society, whereas in others it was creating infrastructural havoc and confusions that would lead to new disruptive *problématiques*; that the Rural Community had become an archaic institution in the nation's makeup and had no visible chance of surviving to the end of the century; and, finally, that the Agricultural Sector's structure, which traditionally had been one of small land-holdings, was well on its way to becoming one of conglomerate units, owned by corporate entities and operated commercially along integrative agri-business lines. Of course, these major, wrenching changes were occuring haphazardly, without benefit of any planning, and as the result of the supposed free play of economic forces. These occurrences were also felt to be consequences of what was happening in Paris. Furthermore, it was implicitly evident that the policy of Regionalization (on which a great many hopes were riding) would not arrest these trends; that the policy of Europeanization would help only the large corporations in Paris; and that there did not exist anything that might be called a policy of Participation.

The full set of findings from the Base Dissonance Analysis provided a compli-

Nested system functions	1970		
	Political	Economic	Sociocultural
S = IE Internal Environment Politcal subsystem Economic subsystem Urban groups			
TE Transactional Environment Industrial society Urban society Rural community Agricultural sector			
CE Contextual Environment Europe (EEC) Francophone LDCs The world			

Figure 4. Base dissonance matrix.

Nested-system Policies	1970												1970 – 85												1985 – 2000											
	Regionalization				Europeanization				Participation				Regionalization				Europeanization				Participation				Regionalization				Europeanization				Participation			
Functional impacts	P	E	C	S	P	E	C	S	P	E	C	S	P	E	C	S	P	E	C	S	P	E	C	S	P	E	C	S	P	E	C	S	P	E	C	S
IE PARIS	1.1												1.2												1.3											
Political S-system																																				
Educational S-system																																				
City government																																				
Economic S-system																																				
Urban Groups																																				
TE FRANCE	2.1												2.2												2.3											
Industrial society																																				
Urban society																																				
Rural community																																				
Agricultural sector																																				
CE EUROPE (EEC)	3.1												3.2												3.3											
Francophone LDCs																																				
The world																																				

Figure 5.   Projective dissonance matrix.

cated, loosely structured, yet fairly orderly snapshot of the current situation in Paris and its environments. The next step was to enlarge this picture by projecting it into a thirty-year time horizon through extending the matrix. The format of this extension is outlined in Figure 5.

This figure contains three separate matrices of three levels each. From left to right we have: a replication of the 1970 Base Dissonance Matrix for the periods 1970-1985 and 1985-2000. In Frames 1.1, 1.2, 1.3, 2.1, and 3.1, the elements whose interactions have already been identified are kept unaltered. On the other hand, Frames 2.2 through 3.3 are seen as dynamic, and are studied in terms of the changes or trends that are most likely to occur in them under the impact of *un*changed current policies. This procedure yields new and very different distributions of (future) dissonances within the transactional and contextual environments.

When the cross-impact effects of these trends are analyzed, a series of new *intense dissonances* come to light. These represent dysfunctions that will grow within the internal and transactional environments if no corrective interventions are made in the interim—that is, if no *new* "Policies" are formulated and acted on during the period 1970-2000.

It is by organizing these intense dissonances into the description of a situation that, in the last step of the Reference Projection, one constructs the kind of scenario I call "The Image of the 'Logical' Future."

Since this scenario describes what might be expected to happen if things are let alone and the system is allowed to evolve without new interventions, the future it depicts is entirely unreal, aside from being wholly disastrous. Nevertheless, as I noted earlier, it serves to enlarge the original picture of the current situation and reveals the *problématique's* latent structure—something that had not been visible to the naked eye.

It is not necessary here to dwell on the content of the three "images" of the Logical Future that were built—one, for each of the three policies being considered. Suffice it to say that every one of them fully confirmed the catastrophic potentialities hidden in the current situation—potentialities that somewhat earlier D.A.T.A.R. had sensed while investigating where Regionalization might lead, and published in a monograph that the French public had immediately named *le scénario de l'inacceptable*.

Phase II: The Normative Plan

Once the structuring of the current *problématique* has been completed, it becomes necessary to concern oneself with the *design* of those future states of the system that are deemed to be good, hence "desirable." The design of such future states requires, first, that concerted decisions be made defining what is desirable; and secondly, that concerted actions be defined to realize the decisions. It is in the Normative Planning phase of the process that one addresses the question of desirable futures. This is done by visualizing two types of future states for the system: 1) the "Ends," which the actors involved are able to conceive in the form of ideals to be constantly approximated but never completely achieved; and 2) "Objectives," which are the most valued future states that one can derive from such ends, and which, while fully attainable, remain beyond the specified planning horizon (Ackoff) [5].

The formulation of ends presents rather formidable difficulties, since ends reflect the *value system* of those participating in the planning work, and that of the society they represent.

The method for eliciting these values has since been refined by Ackoff in his work on the process of idealization, idealized design, and idealized scenario construction. In 1971, however, when we had to figure out the value-base from which to proceed, the scenario approach was still too cumbersome and time-consuming. We chose to rely primarily on interviews and the interpretation of the survey data being generated by the French subcontractors (Figure 1). After much work a consensus was reached regarding the values that were generally held about Paris. These could be reduced to the twin notions of *primacy* and *uniqueness*—both being, in the French mind, historical properties of Paris as an "ideal city." Having determined what the French thought Paris "ought" to be, it became necessary to ask "What form should *primacy* and *uniqueness* take?" Or, "What ends, within what context, do 'primacy' and 'uniqueness' name?"

It is these questions that led us to qualify the meaning of primacy and uniqueness by using the expressions, "Privileged Crossroads" and "Mediating Center." (Unfortunately, the wealth of meanings these expressions connote in French is lost in translation.) And it became possible to conclude the "Ends-setting" step with the statement:

> To satisfy the values of "primacy" and "uniqueness," Paris must become a *privileged crossroads* and a *mediating center* within environments whose evolution will be relevant to, and legitimatize, this vision of the city's future.

The environmental evolution mentioned in the statement referred to: 1) the emergence of a European Community of Nations that would give a political dimension to the European Economic Community; 2) the development through industrialization of the Third World; 3) the transformation of the present Advanced Industrial Countries into a Postindustrial Society; and 4) the advent of a Global Industrial System, institutionalized within a new World Economic Order.

When these elaborations of the ends are set against the findings obtained in the Reference Projection, a "gap" comes into view that must first be filled in by the objectives, and ultimately, by the goals. The gap itself defines the gulf between current reality and the future state that the present value-system dictates. The steps needed to fill it, namely, how to get from here to there, are suggested in Table 1.

This table is divided into five frames. The main elements of the *problématique* are listed in Frame A, the values that have been elicited in Frame E, and the ends hitherto identified in Frame D. What remains to be filled in are first the objectives (Frame C), then, in the next phase of the process, the goals (Frame B). If all this can be done in a logically consistent manner, then, as we shall see, the chart can be read from left to right and reveal what needs to be done to close the gap. For the moment we shall be concerned only with the formulation of objectives—that is with the steps to be taken to fill Frame C.

The definition of objectives begins with what in Figure 2 (above) I called "Design of Alternative Futures," and the main instrument used in such design is the Normative Scenario.

The Normative Scenario proposes a future state of a system configured in accordance with the "context-related assumptions" that have been stipulated in the process of Ends-Setting. Then the system—in this case Paris in terms of its current *problématique*—is introduced into these macroviews and redesigned (changed, altered, and manipulated) in ways that render it capable of maximally approaching its "Ends," while minimizing, or possibly eliminating, the dysfunctions in its present situation. Thus, such scenarios are constructed around a set of variable relationships among assumed future configurations of the transactional and contextual environments and the idealized image of a currently dysfunctional internal environment. They are "normative" in the sense that while the external environments are based on assumptions, the shape and behavior of the internal environment are prescribed.

In the case of Paris, most of the needed elements having already been identified and detailed, it was not difficult to choose two major scenario *themes*. The first rested on the "privileged crossroads" idea, namely: "How should Paris be redesigned so that it may become a 'privileged crossroads' within a context defined by a European Community of Nations, a Global Industrial Society, and a Postindustrial Society, which are assumed to have come into being during the period considered?" The second rested on the idea of "mediating center": "How should Paris be redesigned so that it may play the role of 'mediating center' in a context where the development of the Third World needs to be facilitated and accelerated in such a way that the diseconomies and environmental costs that inhere to known industrial modes of life, are avoided—or at least minimized."

In terms of new functions and roles, the first scenario led to a visualization of Paris as a Multinational City; the second, as a Global City where *grands desseins*

Table 1. Value-base, ends, and the present policy gap.

A CURRENT PROFILE OF PARIS	B GOALS	C OBJECTIVES	D ENDS	E VALUES
National capital				"Primacy"
"Nationalistic" city				
Elitist center				
Conservative center				
Authoritarian admin.				
Nonself governing				
Costly to France				
"Suction pump" effect			"Privileged crossroads"	
Reliance on "economic rationality"	The present "policy gap"			
Growth through industrialization alone				
ECO 2 Sig dominated			"Mediating center"	
Weak in financial functions				
Deteriorating environment				
Francophone LDC-oriented				
Culturally "ethnocentric				"Uniqueness"
City of diminishing creativity in all functions				

Table 2. Objectives derived from ends to change current profile into that of "global city."

CURRENT PROFILE OF PARIS	GOALS	OBJECTIVES	ENDS	VALUES
National capital "Nationalistic" city Elitist center Conservative center Authoritarian admin. Nonself governing Costly to France "Suction pump" effect Reliance on "economic rationality" Growth through industrialization alone ECO 2 Sig dominated Weak in financial functions Deteriorating environment Francophone LDC-oriented Culturally "ethnocentric City of diminishing creativity in all functions		"Political regiocentricity" "Economic geocentricity" "Urban rationality" "Postindustrialism" "Cultural policentrism"	"Privileged crossroads" "Mediating center"	"Primacy" "Uniqueness"

of world import could once again be generated and carried out [6]. These scenarios yielded a considerable number of outcomes, or future-state descriptions. In the next step, *i.e.*, the construction of the "Composite Scenario," they were combined, evaluated, and synthesized to produce the "Image of the Willed Future" from which the "Objectives" to be attained are distilled.

The objectives that the very complex and lengthy "Composite Scenario" yielded can, for brevity's sake, be paraphrased as shown in Table 2.

Phase III: The Strategic Plan

The Strategic Plan corresponds to what Ackoff has called "Means Planning," that is, the identification and organization of the means needed to pursue the Objectives. In my terminology "means" refers to "Goals," "Policies," and "Programs."

Goals are defined as desired outcomes of action attainable within the time horizon of a plan. They are derived from objectives or, to be more precise, the meanings of the objectives are exploded into goals. Policies (*new* policies) are then extracted from the goals. Programs are the elaboration of these policies into specific, scheduled, and organized activities. Goals translate objectives into guidelines for action, while policies reorder such statements in the light of strategic choices, and programs pattern the action within a framework of priorities dictated by both synergies and resource limitations.

It is, of course, to define goals and derive new policies from them that any planning is undertaken in the first place. Therefore, this phase of the work will be discussed in greater detail than the previous ones.

The goals that were derived from the general objectives are shown in Figure 6. I shall, in the following pages, reorganize the goal-sets in terms of functional relationships and discuss some of the relevant action recommendations that were made in the strategic plan.

Goals Related to Political Functions

These goals are among the most critical and significant ones. They were primarily aimed at making Paris independent of the rest of France, and at preparing

GOALS	PRIMARY FUNCTION	SECONDARY FUNCTION
1. Self-government	P (olitical)	
2. Open-city Status	P	E (conomic)
3. Denationalization	P	
4. Capital of ECN	P	
(8. Seat of multinational authorities)	E	P

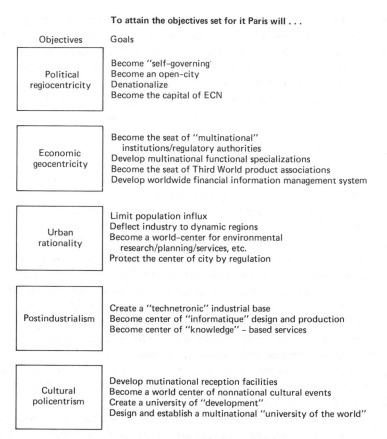

To attain the objectives set for it Paris will . . .

Objectives	Goals
Political regiocentricity	Become "self-governing" Become an open-city Denationalize Become the capital of ECN
Economic geocentricity	Become the seat of "multinational" institutions/regulatory authorities Develop multinational functional specializations Become the seat of Third World product associations Develop worldwide financial information management system
Urban rationality	Limit population influx Deflect industry to dynamic regions Become a world-center for environmental research/planning/services, etc. Protect the center of city by regulation
Postindustrialism	Create a "technetronic" industrial base Become center of "informatique" design and production Become center of "knowledge" – based services
Cultural policentrism	Develop mutinational reception facilities Become a world center of nonnational cultural events Create a university of "development" Design and establish a multinational "university of the world"

Figure 6. Goals derived from objectives.

the city for the role of Europe's capital should the expected evolution of the European Economic Community into a European Community of Nations take place.

The reasoning, in the first instance, arose from the fact that among all French cities Paris was the only one that did not have its own government, a situation that has recently been corrected. It was administered by national government appointees—a situation felt to be increasingly intolerable by most Parisians, and one of the major causes of current tensions and an important element of the *problématique*. Nor, as we found out while constructing the Alternative Futures Scenarios, could Paris hope to become a "privileged crossroads" and a "mediating center" under this form of governance. It could not become an "open city" with the multinational status that economic change demanded and the study envisioned for it. Certainly, it could not aspire to become the capital of a new Europe. For this last, it not only needed to undergo all the changes just suggested but also to "denationalize." This meant Paris could no longer remain the administrative capital of France. The *national* part of the government would have to move to some other city, and Paris would have to find a new regiocentric, political, and geocentric economic identity of its own.

These views, which might appear radical or "far out," as American parlance would put it, were reduced to specific recommendations and accepted in their entirety by the sponsoring authorities. Recent developments in French policy regarding the institutional redesign of Paris would indicate that the implementation of the recommended steps is being pursued according to the schedules that were proposed.

Goals Related to Economic Functions

GOALS	PRIMARY FUNCTION	SECONDARY FUNCTION
(2. Open-city status)	P	E
5. Seat of LDC product associations	E	
6. Center of GISC's specializing in:		
Transnational marketing		
Information systems	E	
Financial planning		
Organization planning & development		
OR activities		
7. Deconcentration of industry through deflection to dynamic regions	E	
8. Seat of multinational authorities	E	P
(9. Limit Parisian population through deflection)	E	S(ocial)
10. Center for environmental research —Planning/Services, *etc.*	E	
13. Specialization in "software" (*informatique*)	E	E
14. Industrial base: technetronic industries	E	E
15. Center for new worldwide financial functions	E	
16. Center for "knowledge"-based services	E	S
17. Center for multinational "reception" facilities	E	C(ultural)
(18. Seat of University of development)	C	E
(20. City of "knowledge" workers)	C	E

These goals represent the largest subset, as could have been expected, given the economically weighted nature of the initial situation. In discussing so large a set it might be helpful to group the goals.

In order of importance the first grouping would consist of those goals aimed at changing the *economic profile of Paris* into one more consonant with the political outcomes we have just considered. Such a group would contain goals 7, 9, 13, 14, 16, 20, 10, and 15.

The first two (7 and 9) are tightly interconnected in that they aim to alter the trend towards industrial concentration in and around Paris and to stabilize the region's population at a viable level (12 million for the region by the 1980s).

"Deconcentration" turned out to be a complex phenomenon. First of all, it is not basically a Parisian problem, because "concentration" in and around Paris is the result of the economic organization and dynamics of the country as a whole. This situation is portrayed in Figure 7, which shows a France divided by a straight line going roughly from Le Havre to Marseilles. All viable economic activity tends to move to the eastern side of the line—toward several of the main urban centers but especially Paris—whereas the western part of the country is rapidly becoming in the words of the French, themselves, *"le désert français."* Such a pattern of development creates a dual issue: saving Paris through deconcentration, and reclaiming the west, which in the main has deliberately resisted large-scale industrialization. To attack this twin problem we had, among other things, to take a closer look at those eastern regions where industrial growth was proceeding apace, and where much of the overflow from Paris would have to be absorbed.

Our analysis led first to a reconceptualization of the western regions and to a further detailing of the idea of "microzones" through the designing of supporting economic activities. The work indicated that new industries based on local traditions (*i.e.*, mariculture, tourism, *etc.*) plus the natural growth of the existing economic base would revive the western regions and increase their drawing power.

On the other hand, a review of the centers of attraction in the eastern half of the country (excluding Paris for the moment) proved of striking interest. Here, not only surprising concentrations of industries and workers were noticeable, but the patterns of such concentrations revealed that the existing government policy of Regionalization was not quite relevant to the events that were actually shaping the area. Most importantly: conurbanization around metropolitan centers such as Lille, Metz, Nancy, Lyon, St.-Etienne was occurring at a rapid rate; and, as viable industrial structures, the "dynamic regions" developing around these cities were not exclusively French, but *transnational* in character. We realized that the emergent metropolitan agglomerations were new combinations of industrial centers, embedded in new regional configurations, which are detailed in Figure 8.

Clearly the expansion of these emergent transnational regions would have a major influence on what happened in Paris—and *vice versa*. Their potential for growth was carefully studied and recommendations for the deliberate fostering of the development of these industrial "catchment areas" were made. That

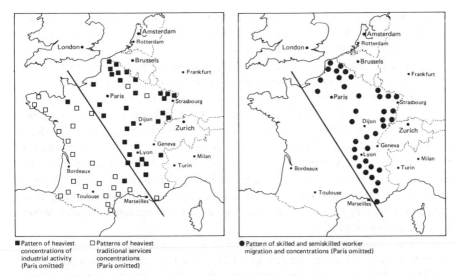

Figure 7. Economic concentration patterns.

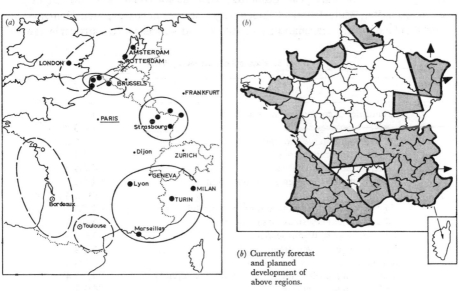

(b) Currently forecast
and planned
development of
above regions.

(a) —, Dynamic
'transnational'
regions; – – –,
proposed southwestern,
western and
northern development
patterns.

Figure 8. New regional concepts.

the French authorities are following up on these recommendations can be seen from a recent D.A.T.A.R. map delineating the main areas in which, as a policy, directed-development is being contemplated (Figure 8).

Given these possibilities of "decongesting" Paris through deconcentration and deflection, most of the remaining goals related to economic functions were attempts to define the new, desired economic profile of the city. As could be expected, in the new profile (Table 3) traditional industrial activities are almost entirely replaced by ECO 4 types of activities (technetronic industry, software design and production, "knowledge"-based services, environmental services, *etc.*). This postindustrial emphasis should not be considered as resulting only from the encouraged migration of ECO 2 Sig and ECO 2 RP activities to the "dynamic regions"; it is the outcome of conscious policies seeking to alter the population makeup of the city so as to encourage greater, more creative synergies between the (d) and (p) attitudes.

Such a change is needed for political as well as economic reasons, as can be surmised from the next grouping of goals; those (2, 6, 8, 17) having to do with "multinationalization" of the city, and thus related to the vision of Paris as the capital of the European Community of Nations and as a "Global City." Such a capital, aside from its "open city" status, needs a population mix of worldwide outlook, transnational contacts, and the ability to deliver what we

Table 3. Expected activities profile.

ACTIVITIES	TYPE
Traditional commerce and trade	ECO 3
"New" services	ECO 3
"New" commerce and trade	ECO 5
Technetronic industries	ECO 4
"Knowledge" industries	ECO 4
"Informatique" design and production	ECO 4
Consulting	ECO 4
Environment enhancing and protecting industries	ECO 4
Environmental-systems design services	ECO 4
Urban-systems design services	ECO 4
Research and development	ECO 4
Multinational reception services	ECO 4
Multinational health delivery systems and services	ECO 4
Multinational eduction	ECO 4
Multinational recreation facilities and services	ECO 4
Construction/area development/area renovation	ECO F
Maintenance services	ECO 3

Main acitvity   ECO 4 & F
Supporting activity   ECO 3 & 5

labeled "multinational services"—health care delivery systems, worldwide financial information management systems, reception facilities, education, *etc.*, all of a multinational character. On these points the economic goals have strong synergies with those related to Cultural Functions.

One aspect of multinationalization is also directly linked to the Third World and the city's prospective role as "mediating center." Goals 5, 16, and 18 were formulated to strengthen this link.

Goals Related to Cultural Functions

Two of these goals (11 and 12) reflect the concern of Parisians over the erosion of the city's physical beauty and architectural harmony. Since, by the time the

GOALS	PRIMARY FUNCTION	SECONDARY FUNCTION
11. New construction in center of city will be regulated	C	
12. Private traffic will be eliminated from center of city		
(17. Multinational reception facilities will be created)	E	C
18. A university of development will be established	C	P
19. A world university will be established	C	
21. Center of nonnational cultural events	C	

project started, new districts such as Rueuil and La Défense were already being developed as business areas, it was decided that high-rises would continue to be built in them. The real problem was the older parts of central Paris—the Marais, the Bastille-République area, the Fifth and Seventh Arrondissements. In these and the Halles vigorous *assainissment* and reclamation were needed, given the deterioration of buildings and the high value of the land they stood on. Despite the high cost of restoration and pressures from financial interests to exploit the land more profitably by constructing skyscrapers, recommendations against this move were accepted, and no new high-rise construction in these central areas of Paris has taken place since then. A major consideration in this decision was how to preserve the old districts without turning Paris into a *monument* or a museum. Current opinion is that this can be done if residential and commercial activities are kept functioning in these areas even after reclamation work has been completed.

Two of the most exciting ideas to surface among cultural function related goals were: the University of Development, and the University of the World.

Table 4. Proposed indicative schedule of evolution.

CURRENT PROFILE OF PARIS	1970	1980	1990	2000	OUTCOMES AS DEFINED BY OBJECTIVES
National capital			Capital of ECN		Denationalization
"Nationalistic" city			Denationalization		Multinationalization
Elitist center			Capital of France moved		Decongestion
Conservative center			to other city		Change of economic
Authoritarian admin.			New social structure with		structure
Nonself governing		Open-city	more (d) and (p) attitudes		Change of cultural
Costly to France					outlook
"Suction pump" effect		Self-government			Change of Social Organi-
Reliance on economic rationality		Technetronic ind. base	*Informatique* design & production		zation and relationships
Growth through indus- trialization alone		Population limit and deflection			Arising from:
ECO 2 Sig dominated		Change of economic			Political regiocentricity
Weak in financial functions		activities mix, and increase			Economic geocentricity
Deteriorating environment		in postindustrial services			Urban rationality
Francophone LDC-oriented		Multinational functional services			Postindustrial evolution
Culturally "ethnocentric"		Development of transnational regions			Cultural policenterism
City of diminishing creativity in all functions	Regulate city's center	Multination- alization Environment research/ planning/services	Development of worldwide financial information management system		Should create the desired global city
		University of development			
	LDC product associations		University of the world		
		World center for non- national cultural events			
		Change city's social structure			

The former was conceived to support the *"Centre Mediateur"* concept, and would be exclusively directed at facilitating the socioeconomic development of the Third World. A special curriculum for this institution was outlined, and it contains interesting innovations in this long-neglected field. The second, more ambitious, idea was to create at some later date a university that would be multinational in every sense—curriculum content, faculty, and student body. The University of the World is envisaged as one of the central nodes of a global educational network whose detailed design is expected to be undertaken sometime toward the end of the 1970s.

Goals Related to Social Functions

No specific goals relating to the social functions of Paris were derived. This was based on the reasoning that if the preceeding sets of goals were to some degree attained over the course of the next 30 years, their very realization would, of itself, create the social structures and the human and group relationships that were natural and necessary to make them viable. Almost all the stipulated goals were taken (in fact known) to possess social dimensions, and it was agreed that Social Functions should be left to mature within the frame of the other outcomes.

Final Organization of Goals within the Planning Period

The ordering of the goals in terms of an "Indicative Schedule" completed the Strategic Planning phase of the work, inasmuch as the Wharton Group had not been asked to formulate new policies or propose specific programs. The Indicative Schedule that marked the penultimate stage of our activities is given in Table 4.

CONCLUDING STEPS

One final activity had not been anticipated at the beginning. Our sponsors desired to find out whether the idea of Paris as a Global City, and the steps that must be taken to make it one, had validity in the opinion of the various constituents that had been introduced into the overall design. The Wharton Group was asked to address this question, as such an investigation fit the principle of "Participation" we had established from the start. Under the circumstances this had to be done as an *ex post* procedure, and involved a number of persons who had not worked on the project—who did not even know of its existence.

To satisfy this request it was decided to design a modified Delphi survey, which would be run from Philadelphia. We determined to select four panels of respondents as follows:

Panel I: A sample composed of the heads of large French industries (ECO 2 Sig, ECO 2 RP and ECO 2).

Panel II: A sample of French opinion leaders:
  eminent political personalities,
  higher civil servants,
  labor leaders,
  student leaders,
  eminent intellectuals, writers, and journalists,
  eminent artists, and
  university professors and administrators.

Panel III: A sample composed of heads of non-French multinational corporations:
  European,
  North American, and
  Japanese.

Panel IV: A sample composed of Third World personalities:
  members of governments,
  heads of planning agencies,
  heads of development agencies,
  higher civil servants, and
  university personnel.

Members of Panels I and II were chosen by French authorities; those of Panels III and IV by the Wharton Group. The number of respondents totalled some 70 persons. The questionnaires prepared were lengthy and detailed, describing the origin and unfolding of the project and explaining how the various "Goals" had been derived. Answers were requested pertaining to the validity of the premises, of the reasoning, and of the conclusions. It was asked whether the goals were acceptable to the respondent and if he felt them to be feasible—that is, substantively and in terms of the proposed Indicative Schedule.

A Delphi survey is difficult at best and, when conducted over long distances, it is terribly cumbersome. It can as a distinct surprise, therefore, that a consensus began to emerge as early as the third iteration, and finally became stable at a cumulative range of between 76 and 87%.

The Delphi was probably the most time-consuming portion of the Paris Project, but its outcome was both enlightening and encouraging.

Inasmuch as all the details cannot be reported here, let me finish by citing two points: one that came out through what seemed to be unanimous agreement; and another concerning French policies that our analysis of the responses caused me to reach.

Almost unanimously the participants believed that the notion of Global City as conceived in the Project, was not only a valid idea but that it reflected a general evolution of worldwide trends that made it inevitable. They felt Paris would undoubtedly emerge as such a city by the year 2000; however, it would not do so alone. New York, Sao Paulo, and Singapore would follow the same development and end up functioning as similar Global Cities. This opinion, I believe, makes great sense and should stimulate studies of the role of Global Cities within the evolving world order.

The second point had to do with the three national policies—Regionalization, Europeanization, Participation—that the French Government had defined at the outset as the basic guidelines for national action. As I was studying the responses to the Delphi questionnaires, I sensed that the meaning originally given to these policies had now changed as a result of our work on the Project. And the changes were interesting in that they were enlarging ones. What had been meant by Europeanization now appeared to have become the Globalization of Paris; what had been understood by Regionalization now seemed to imply the Europeanization of France; and the narrow meaning given originally to Participation seemed to have become akin to the process Ackoff has since called "humanization"—something that suggests realms of social, but especially cultural, consonance among peoples. All this led me to think that the work done had perhaps given us an inkling of what we really mean when we say that, under certain circumstances, the system reorganizes itself at a higher level.

NOTES AND REFERENCES

1. The main study team, which came to be known as the "Wharton Group," included Professors R. L. Ackoff, H. V. Perlmutter, E. L. Trist, and M. Chevalier (the last from the University of York and Montreal) with me acting as Principal Investigator. A number of students also contributed greatly to the project.
2. I had first used *problématique* in 1969 when writing the basic prospectus of the Club of Rome. The French noun became part of our terminology, as English has no word that corresponds to it exactly. Ackoff uses "mess" to describe the same thing. Although it is colorful and expressive, I don't find his term totally apt. In French, *problématique* has been employed to refer to a synthesis of the questions that a particular philosopher addresses—*e.g.*, "*La problématique cartésiene.*" Recently the meaning of the word has been enlarged to encompass any set of ill-structured, ill-defined, or poorly delimited problems.
3. The terms "transactional" and "contextual" environments, as descriptions of a system's "external environment" were suggested by Professor Eric L. Trist.
4. These will be discussed later in the text.
5. "Goals" are also desired future states, and they are defined as being attainable *within* the planning horizon. I agree with this further formulation of Ackoff's. In the planning process that I am describing, however, goals are seen as the "outcomes" of particular actions. Therefore, they are assumed to belong in the Strategic Planning phase, which will be discussed later.
6. The "Multinational Scenario," as it has come to be known, was written by Professor H. V. Perlmutter, and "A Distinctive International Role for Paris" by Professor Michel Chevalier.

5

On the Role of Structure in Policy Analysis and Decision-Making*

Andrew P. Sage and David W. Rajala
University of Virginia

INTRODUCTION

This paper considers, within a systems engineering framework, the role that structure can take in facilitating the analysis of decisions and policies. The role of various structural models, such as interaction matrices, intent structures, and DELTA charts in the development of structures suitable for decision and policy analysis are discussed. In particular, methods and algorithms, based principally upon the use of interpretive structural modeling, are given for determining decision tree structure, the structuring of information for uncertainty resolution, and the structuring of preferences. In addition, sufficient development of decision analysis models from fundamental principles is presented in order to clarify the use and the ultimate potential of interpretive structural modeling in decision-aiding methodologies. Finally the decision criteria of expected utility maximization are examined, and procedures for assessing utilities and encoding uncertainty are given. Employing these procedures within a systems-engineering framework greatly enhances the ability of a decision-maker to make quality decisions concerning multiattributed problems in the face of uncertainty, where the environment is dynamic and complex, and where decisions have long-term implications involving substantial commitments of resources.

*Research leading to the development of this chapter was supported by the National Science Foundation under Grants ENG 76-20291 and AER 77-16865.

A DECISION-MAKING FRAMEWORK FOR SYSTEMS ENGINEERING

The Need for Systems Engineering

The existence of complex, large-scale societal problems such as those involving energy and other resource depletions, environmental pollution, and inadequate health care, as well as the ubiquitous economic problems, make technological approaches to problem amelioration or resolution appealing. But there is strong historical evidence of obtaining unsatisfactory results from many applications of technology to societal and sociotechnological problems. One reason for this is that technology has often been applied to problems only at the level of symptoms, and has not been addressed to solving fundamental problems leading to the original difficulty. Lack of understanding of the structure of the underlying system contributes to inadequate approaches to problem resolution, which so often involves the "tech-fix" symptomatic solution. Also, attempts to produce a solution for one critical problem may well be to the detriment of, or at the expense of, a crisis in another problem area, due perhaps to tightly coupled feedback interactions.

To apply technology to large-scale problem areas successfully, issues must be addressed at three levels [1] :

symptoms   institutions   values

Approaching problems at the level of institutions, as well as at the level of symptoms, would permit the design of new institutions to make full and effective use of new technology. In addition, there is a need to deal with problems at the level of values, to explore the significance of values and to identify those in conflict with one another. Approaches to problem resolution at these three levels enables complex problems to receive a comprehensive examination that should impart greater understanding concerning these complexities as well as enhance solution efforts.

To accomplish effective problem resolution, we need a means of identifying successfully and considering fully all relevant problem definition elements, long-term implications, uncertain or imperfect understanding of key elements, and any other pertinent linkages and relationships between the problem definition elements. Further, we require a means of identifying and utilizing complex preferences; developing alternative policy proposals or solution approaches; and providing guidelines for making good choices or decisions among policy alternatives. This must all occur within the dynamic, uncertain, complex environment of the real world.

It is suggested that systems engineering possesses the above characteristics. A functional definition of systems engineering that suffices here is: systems engineering is an appropriate combination of the mathematical theory of systems and behavioral theory in a setting appropriate for the resolution of real-world problems.

A purpose of systems engineering is to develop policies and decision options for management, direction, and regulation activities relative to planning, development, production, and operation of total systems to satisfy specified objectives based upon needs. Throughout a systems study it is important to maintain the proper relationship between sponsor, client, and researcher or various maladies may and generally will result [2].

Systems Engineering Methodology

An open set of procedures that provides the means for solving problems has become known as a methodology. Words, mathematics, and graphics are elements of systems engineering methodology and communication, and they are used to form various tools of systems engineering such as operations research. The combination of a set of tools, a set of proposed activities, and a set of relations among the tools and activities constitutes a methodology. The Hall activity matrix [3] is selected here as a guide to the development of a structural basis for decomposing problems in decision and policy analysis into a set of elements to facilitate efficacious analysis of them.

A comprehensive three-dimensional framework, or morphology, for systems engineering was published by Arthur D. Hall in 1969, [3] representing an extension of his earlier pioneering study [4] of systems engineering methodology. Figure 1 is an adaptation of Hall's representation of the three major dimensions, time, logic, and knowledge, of systems engineering.

The time dimension includes the coarse phases that are characteristic of systems efforts. It begins with the *program planning* phase of systems engineering in which programs or policies to be pursued are defined, analyzed, and selected. Specific projects to be carried out are the result of efforts in the *project planning* phase. Implementation of projects necessary to develop the system is made together with production plans in *system development*. In the *production* phase the total system is produced, and plans are made for its installation. Installation of the system occurs and operational plans are completed in the *installation* phase. In the *operation* phase the system serves its intended use. The systems effort concludes with the *retirement* phase in which the system is withdrawn from use and is modified or replaced by a new system.

The logic dimension deals with the steps that are carried out in each of the systems engineering phases. The *problem definition* step of Hall's activity matrix for systems engineering is aimed at developing a descriptive scenario of the existing situation through a presentation of sufficient history and data to indicate the

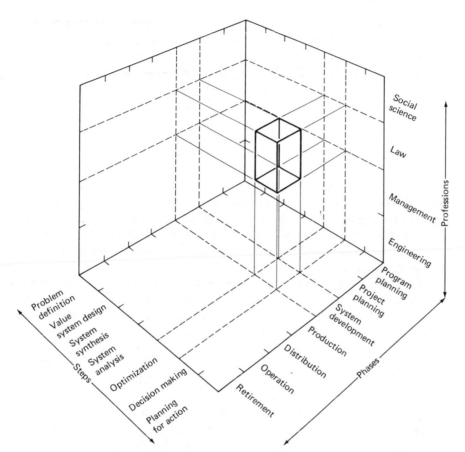

Figure 1. Morphological box for systems engineering.

evolution of the problem. Clarifying, developing, and defining objectives of problem resolution occurs in the *value system design* step. Values must be well articulated because choice among competing alternatives is dependent upon values expressed. The *systems synthesis* step involves conceptualization of potential policies, activities, controls, or whole systems for the attainment of objectives. Insights into interrelationships, behavior, and effects of proposed policies, activities, controls, or systems in terms of need satisfaction and objective attainment is obtained through *systems analysis* (and modeling). The principal objective of this step is to create a process with which to produce information concerning consequences of proposed policies, activities, or controls. Although a model is only a substitute for reality, it is descriptive enough of system elements—variables either under or not under direct control of the decision-maker—

under consideration to approximate system behavior in response to changes in policies or controls, all things in the environment remaining relatively unchanged. A model must depend on the problem definition elements as well as the value system and the purpose behind its construction and utilization. It may be deterministic, probabilistic, or some combination of the two. It is important to verify and validate the model, for a poor model of the system can lead to the creation of possiblities of catastrophic consequences by selecting dominated policies, activities, or controls [5]. Strategies and particular policy components are selected such that each trial policy is the best possible in terms of values represented in objectives in the *optimization* step. *Decision-making* involves a choice among policies, activities, controls, or systems; that is to say, an action event takes place as opposed to the forming of an intention to do something. In *planning for action* the previous steps are prepared for efficient transition into the next phase of a systems engineering effort. DELTA charts [6] are effective structural models suggested for use in this step. Proceeding through these steps is generally an iterative process.

The knowledge dimension refers to specialized knowledge from the various professions and disciplines. It is the two-dimensional representation of this morphological box consisting of the phases and steps of systems engineering that is known as the Hall activity matrix. Hill and Warfield [7] published a definitive study of the program planning phase of Hall's activity matrix in 1972. Their efforts led to an examination of the steps of this phase as a connected or unified set. In addition they provided a further refinement of the problem definition, value system design, and system synthesis steps.

The problem definition step was structured into a number of elements. Key parts of the problem definition step include identification of needs, constraints, alterables (both subject and not subject to the decision-maker's control), societal sectors, and determination of the interactions among these elements. Comprehensive problem definition must also include an appropriate problem title, a descriptive scenario of the problem, an understanding of the professions and disciplines relevant to the problem, an assessment of scope, an identification of those to be involved in problem-solving, partitioning of the problem into relevant elements, and isolation of subjective elements of the problem. Determination of needs for a given problem may be obtained through utilization of brainstorming, brainwriting, Delphi, [8] or normative group approaches. The graphical tools of self- and cross-interaction matrices are used to portray linkages or relationships between the problem definition elements of needs, constraints, alterables, societal sectors, and the interactions among these.

Value system design is concerned with defining objectives, objectives measures for objective achievement, ordering objectives into a hierarchical structure, and determining the interaction of objectives and objectives measures with each other and with the needs, alterables, and constraints associated with problem definition.

A sound development of value system design is crucial. Complete and accurate specification of objectives and priorities based upon needs identified during problem definition provide the basis for a quantitative assessment of preferences. Objectives are defined as desired levels of attributes of outcomes of decisions. Priorities are the basis for establishing trade-off rates. Preferences are quantitative representations of values. One important aspect of the value system that influences the selection of decisions under an expectation criterion is risk preference level. Establishment of risk preference levels is in every sense a policy decision and so it must be examined carefully. Another important aspect is that of time preference and time preference levels, for these also amount to a policy decision. The development of a hierarchical structure of objectives will be discussed in detail in the next section, for this has a significant role in structuring of preferences for decision-making. The graphical tools of self- and cross-interaction matrices are used to portray interactions between objectives and their measures and needs, alterables, and constraints. Other structural models useful in this step include subordination matrices and intent structures [8;9].

System synthesis involves identification of policies, activities, controls, or complete systems, that is to say a set of alternatives, activities measures, and interactions between proposed activities and activities measures, as well as interaction between activities measures and objectives measures, between activities and constraints, and between activities and objectives. Alternatives are generated that are perceived to lead to attainment of objectives. Activities measures are necessary to measure the degree of accomplishment of proposed activities. Self- and cross-interaction matrices can be used to display these interactions. Figure 2 illustrates graphically the program planning linkages for these three steps of problem definition, value system design, and system synthesis.

A fundamental idea behind the development of this systems engineering framework is that sufficient labor should be expended to structure a problem adequately to insure that decision and policy analysis efforts are addressing the right question at the right time within a well articulated value system and within reasonableness constraints imposed by the economic size and impact scope of the problem under consideration.

It is quite unfortunate, however, that the problem definition, value system design, and system synthesis steps are often understudied and underdeveloped relative to other steps of the systems engineering framework. We hope the linkage of structural aspects of these steps with structural elements of the decision analysis efforts described here will assist in ameliorating this problem by demonstrating the need for critical attention to these steps. It should be noted that it is not suggested here that systems engineering contains sufficient constructs to cope successfully with all of the many challenges inherent in problem definition, value system design, and system synthesis. Nevertheless, much of value can be obtained from even a partial development and understanding of

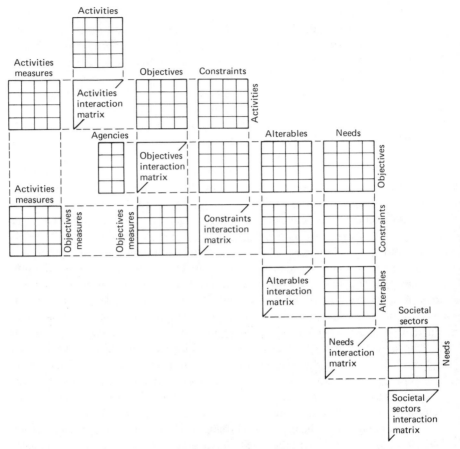

Figure 2. Program planning linkages.

the elements in these important steps and their interactions. We conjecture that significant outscoping to determine relevant problem elements and inscoping to determine structural relationships between them will greatly enhance our abilities to communicate and to comprehend complex issues.

Structural Models for Decision Analysis

Our effort in this section is divided into four parts. The first part gives an overview of the structural concepts of decision analysis. Next, decision analysis models and related quantitative information for these models are given. Since the structure of decision analysis models lends itself to graphic representation in tree form, the role of interpretive structural modeling, a concept originated by Warfield [9], is discussed and applied to the determination of decision tree structures. The penultimate subsection considers probability encoding and the structuring of information for probability resolution through the use of inference structures. Our last part considers structuring of preferences. Axioms of utility theory are presented, risk preference is considered, and decomposition principles, based on independence properties of attributes to obtain various functional forms of multiattribute utility functions, are developed. This section is concluded with the development of a hierarchical structure of objectives, that is, a single sink digraph tree, by means of interpretive structural modeling [8, 10].

Decision Analysis Concepts

Decision analysis, whose foundations have been examined by Howard [11] and Raiffa [12], is a technology for assisting decision-makers to make better decisions, principally by structuring the relationships between the various considerations that enter any decision. Numerous attempts have been made to characterize the structure of the decision-making activity, some of which are examined in detail by Eilon [13]. Generally, a decision problem is decomposed into well-defined components, such as alternatives, events with outcomes characterized by uncertainty, and preferences that reflect values. Information provided by the decision-maker about the consequences of a decision can be represented through formal decision tree models to show structural relations, and can be used to assist in quantifying uncertainties in the form of probability distributions. Other sources of information, such as experts [14], may also be utilized. Preferences are quantified and attitude to risk is accounted for based upon objectives and priorities established in the value system design step. The logical decision, based on a specified choice criterion, may then be derived for implementation into the decision-making process. Sensitivity analysis may be utilized to test the robustness of the indicated result to probability estimation errors. The value of obtaining additional information can also be established and compared with its cost.

A primary advantage of structuring the decision-making process is that attention can be directed to the different elements while still preserving their interrelationships. The intended result is to enable quality decisions to be made, as differentiated from obtaining a quality outcome, which is something that cannot be guaranteed either by the decision-making step of systems engineering or by systems engineering.

Structuring the Decision Tree

In constructing a formal decision model, it may be desirable to begin by relating the alternatives, called decision variables, and outcomes, called state variables, to each other by utilizing a deterministic relationship among these elements. Uncertainty about the outcomes of a decision can then be encoded through probability assignments on the state variables. Next a value can be assigned to each outcome through the evaluation of a value function. This value function is dependent on the decision selected and the outcome occurring. Risk preference is expressed through a utility function, which contains measures over the value function and associated risks.

The simplest decision analysis model is the static model. Here the decision-maker makes a decision based only upon prior experience and with the expectation of no additional information. The five components of this model are, in vector form:

1. An admissible set D of decision vectors $d = (d_1, \ldots, d_m)$ from which a single d must be selected. That is, D must be a set consisting of all choices available to the decision-maker, no two being identical.
2. A set X of relevant state vectors $x = (x_1, \ldots, x)$ consisting of all possible outcomes, no two being identical, and of which one and only one can occur.
3. A conditional probability distribution $F(x_1, \ldots, x_n)$, dependent upon the decision-maker's prior experience and encoded to express likelihood of occurrence of the states. Depending on the content of the problem, F may or may not be independent of D.
4. A value function $v(x, d) \in V$ describing the worth of each pair (x, d), $x \in X, d \in D$, as evaluated by the decision-maker.
5. A utility function $u(v(x, d)) \in U$ on the value function expressing the decision-maker's risk preference. For convenience this may be written $u(x, d)$.

The problem statement is if $u(x, d)$ and $F(x)$ are determined in accordance with appropriate sets of conditions for every $d \in D$, then the optimal alternative is the d that maximizes expected utility, computed by

$$d^* = \underset{d}{\text{Max}}\, E(u(x, d)) = \underset{d}{\text{Max}} \sum_{x_1} \cdots \sum_{x_n} f(x)u(x, d)$$

if $f(\cdot)$ is a probability mass function, and

$$= \underset{d}{\text{Max}} \int_{x_1} \cdots \int_{x_n} f(x)u(x, d)\, dx_1 \cdots dx_n$$

then $f(\cdot)$ is a probability density function. These appropriate sets of conditions are the axioms of utility theory and of probability theory, which we shall state later. This model may be portrayed in tree form as shown in Figure 3, where (a) shows the general form and (b) shows a tree for a two-decision, two-state problem.

When a decision-maker anticipates the opportunity to obtain information, $z \in Z$ related to the state X, it is possible and perhaps, depending on the cost of information acquisition, desirable to make some parts of the decision strategy dependent upon that information. If a decision to acquire information is con-

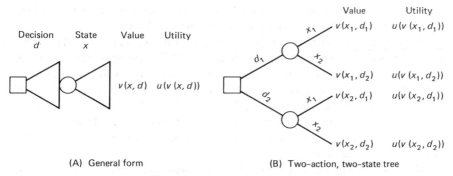

(A) General form   (B) Two-action, two-state tree

Figure 3. Statis decision model.

sidered prior to the selection of $d \in D$, then the problem is to select the sequence of decisions that maximizes expected utility. The expected utility of a decision d after information z becomes available is computed by:

$$E(u(x,d(z))) = \sum_z \sum_x f(x|z)g(z)u(x,d(z))$$

or

$$= \int_z \int_x f(x|z)g(z)u(x,d(z))\, dx\, dz$$

where z is a state variable, $g(z)$ is appropriately either the probability mass or density function for observing a particular z, and $f(x|z)$ is, where appropriate, a conditional mass or conditional density function. $g(z)$ is related to the revised distribution on $X, f(x|z)$, by Bayes rule, where

$$f(x|z) = \frac{h(z|x)f(x)}{g(z)}$$

The expected utility maximizing decision with information is denoted

$$d^*(z) = \underset{d(z)}{\text{Max}}\, E(u(x,d(z)))$$

If information z is available from an analysis or by acquisition, then the expected value of the information, denoted EVI, is just the difference between the expected value-maximizing decision with information and the expected value-maximizing decision without information. Thus

$$EVI = E(v(x,d^*(z))) - E(v(x,d^*))$$

where $d^*(z)$, denotes the intention to select the appropriate d^* after z is available. This quantity enables a decision to be made regarding whether to acquire information by comparing it against the cost of acquisition. The expected value of perfect information is computed by taking the difference between the sum (or integral) of the product of the maximum attainable value for each state and its probability and the maximum expected value with information. This quantity may be used as a guide to establish how much it is worth to eliminate all uncertainty. In a similar manner these quantities, the expected value of information and expected value of perfect information, may be determined for utility.

The decision model described above is conveniently portrayed by a tree structure. Two methods of developing the decision tree structure, both of them iterative, are presented here.

The first method, undoubtedly the most common approach in current use, accomplishes tree construction on an *ad hoc* basis. Quite simply, the alternatives and states are delineated and related based upon information in the decision-maker's mind. A tree structure is obtained, although several iterations may perhaps be required. A substantial amount of structural understanding of the problem is required of the decision-maker. A computer-aided approach to conversational elicitation of the decision tree structure is given in [5].

When structural understanding of the problem does not clearly exist in the decision-maker's mind, such as may occur with complex decision problems, Warfield's interpretive structural modeling approach [8; 9] may transform a mental model into something better defined. The process of interpretive structural modeling, through the systematic, iterative application of graph theoretic concepts, associates a binary matrix with a graphical representation of a directed network, a special case being the single source digraph tree [8; 9], which is the structure characteristic of a decision tree. Two elements fundamental to the process of structural modeling are an element set and a contextual relation.

The element set is identified and defined within a situational context. For the tree structuring problem, the element set consists of decision and state variables. The decision variables (or alternatives) are obtained from the problem definition and system synthesis steps. The state variables are obtained from the problem definition step. Desirable properties that a set of state variables should have are given by Keeney and Raiffa [16], and include:

1. completeness, in the sense that the variables are sufficient to indicate the degree of satisfaction of the overall objectives covering all important aspects of the problem;
2. operational, in the sense that the variables should be meaningfully used in the analysis;
3. decomposable, so that the evaluation process can be facilitated by breaking it down into parts;
4. nonredundant, so that any double counting possibilities are eliminated;
5. minimal, to keep dimensions as small as possible for practical purposes.

The contextual relation is selected as a possible statement of relationship among the elements that is contextually significant for the purposes of the inquiry. Relations to be utilized must be transitive. Some possible relations of use include: precedes, is followed by, and occurs after.

The next step in the process is to create the reachability matrix Q. The set of n elements to be structured is denoted by $P = \{p_i\}$. P is used as both the vertical and horizontal index set for the reachability matrix. A pairwise comparison of the elements is made to determine if p_i is contextually related to p_j (denoted $p_i R p_j$), if $p_j R p_i$, or both, or neither. If $p_i R p_j$, then assign $Q_{ij} = 1$. If p_i not− R p_j, then $Q_{ij} = 0$. By convention $Q_{ii} = 1$. The reachability matrix may be filled up by answering the n^2 questions. However, since the contextual relation R is selected to be transitive, a partitioning approach for constructing a reachability matrix can be utilized to substantially reduce the number of questions answered.

To do this, consider an element $p_i \in P$. The following are possible:

1. There may exist a set of elements $L(p_i)$ to which p_i will be subordinate. This is called the lift set of p_i. The reachability set of $p_i R(p_i)$, contains $L(p_i)$ and p_i.
2. There may exist a set of elements $D(p_i)$, called the drop set of p_i, which are subordinate to p_i. The antecedent set of $p_i R(p_i)$, contains $D(p_i)$ and p_i. Elements in $L(p_i)$ cannot be in $D(p_i)$.
3. There may exist a set of elements $V(p_i)$, called the vacancy set of p_i, such that p_i is not subordinate to any element in it and no element in the set is subordinate to p_i. Thus, it can contain no elements of $L(p_i)$ or $D(p_i)$.

If an element in $L(p_i)$ is subordinate to p_i, then feedback exists. This is a distinguishing feature of interpretive structural modeling. It means, however, that the tree structure is not available. Attempts can be made, if desired, to alter the element set so that a tree structure may alternately emerge. But to continue with the interpretive structural modeling process, it is convenient to partition the lift set as follows:

4. A subset $NF(p_i)$ of $L(p_i)$ may exist to which p_i will be subordinate but which will have no element subordinate to p_i. This is called the nonfeedback lift set.
5. A subset $F(p_i)$ of $L(p_i)$ may exist to which p_i will be subordinate and whose elements will be subordinate to p_i. This set is called the feedback set of p_i, and is not permitted in a simple subordination matrix for a single source digraph tree.

The various element sets described above of the reachability matrix are determined by specifying the existence of the contextual relation between elements p_i and p_j, $j = 1, \ldots, n$, $j \neq i$, filling in the responses on the reachability matrix, and examining the result. Figure 4 shows the determination of the various sets of the reachability matrix by partitioning.

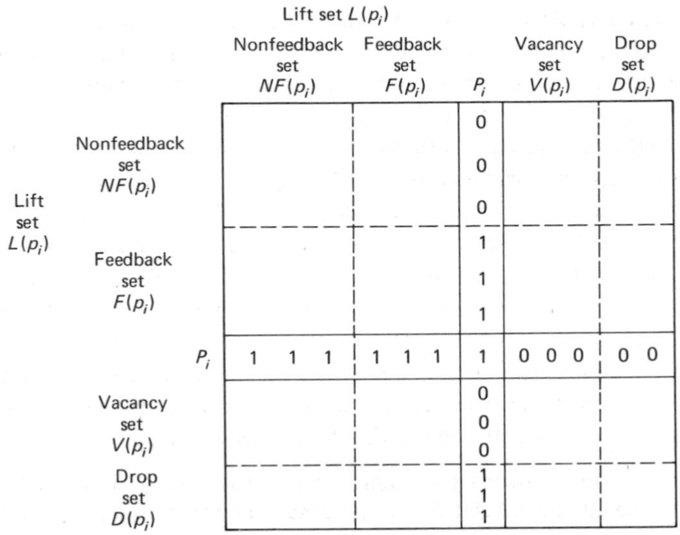

Figure 4. Determination of critical sets by partitioning.

A major advantage of the partitioning approach is that transitivity* permits inferences on many entries to the reachability matrix as either 0 or 1. The inferred entries are:

1. The lift set $L(p_i)$ cannot be subordinate to either the drop set $D(p_i)$ or the vacancy set $V(p_i)$. Thus, entries of $Q_{LV}(p_i)$, which are elements Q_{jk} where j spans all elements in $L(p_i)$ and k spans all elements in $V(p_i)$ and $Q_{LD}(p_i)$ must be 0.
2. The vacancy set $V(p_i)$ cannot be subordinate to the drop set $D(p_i)$. Thus, $Q_{VD}(p_i)$ must be all 0.
3. The drop set is subordinate to the lift set, so $Q_{DL}(p_i)$ must be 1.

For a general structure, no additional inferences can be made. For a single-source digraph tree, it is required that $Q_{DV}(p_i) = 0$.

The total number of entries filled in the reachability matrix by inference depends on the careful selection of an initial p_i to partition about. But after partitioning, obtaining responses about the partitioned element, and drawing transitive inferences, it is still necessary to determine $Q_{LL}(p_i)$, $Q_{VV}(p_i)$, and $Q_{DD}(p_i)$, which are reduced order reachability matrices. The partitioning approach may be used to fill these matrices, or direct questioning can now be utilized. The matrix $Q_{VL}(p_i)$ is a cross-interaction matrix, which must be determined by direct questioning. Figure 5 displays element entries of the reachabil-

*Elements x, y, and z are transitive if XRY and YRZ implies XRZ.

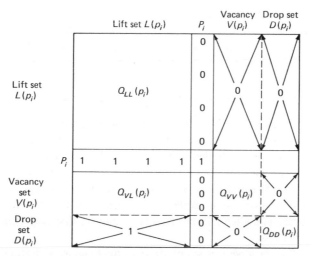

Figure 5. Element entries determined by partitioning and inference using the special requirements of a single-sink digraph tree.

ity matrix determined by partitioning and inference under the requirements of a single-source digraph tree.

A simple procedure, perhaps the simplest, to extract the interpretive structural model from the reachability matrix for a single-source digraph tree is row elimination [8; 10] . This is accomplished as follows:

1. Partition the reachability matrix into levels.
2. Change all main diagonal entries from 1 to 0.
3. Eliminate the first row in the partitioned matrix since it contains all zeros. This will be the source element in the digraph tree.
4. Eliminate all columns containing all zeros. These correspond to the last elements in the digraph tree.
5. Find a regular row (that is, a row containing a single one). This will show a subordination relation, say i subordinate to j.
6. Form a new column vector for the jth column C_j^* by multiplying the old jth column vector C_j by the complement of the ith column vector C_i, written $C_j^* = C_j \bar{C}_i$. Replace C_j with C_j^*. If there is no ith column, $C_j^* = C_j$.
7. Delete the ith row.
8. Delete all rows and columns filled with zeros.
9. Add to the evolving structure the index i showing its heirarchical relation.
10. Return to Step 4. Continue the process until a single row remains. From the last row the hierarchical structure is shown.

An advantage of the use of interpretive structural modeling here is that an exact specification of causal relationships between variables and the direction of the relationship is obtained. Nothing is specified about the quantitative relationships between the elements in the structure at this point. This deterministic relationship can readily be altered to account for particular alternatives and out-comes at this point by just discretizing, say, each variable where there will be uncertainty as to its realization.

Probability Encoding and Structuring Information for Probability Resolution

In the systems analysis step of systems engineering, questions occur regarding whether uncertainty relative to a particular state variable should be encoded, or whether it should be modeled in further detail. If encoding is accomplished, the assigned probability distribution reflects the decision-maker's state of knowledge (or information) about a given quantity or event. The process of extracting and quantifying individual judgment about uncertain quantities is called probability encoding. Extensive discussions on this subject may be found in [17; 18; and 19].

Because of the iterative nature of proceeding through the steps of the Hall activity matrix, it is generally more practical to utilize crude models initially and through successive iterations of the steps provide greater refinement, stop-ping when the costs of additional refinements fail to provide sufficient improve-ment in information.

Our intention here is to review briefly guidelines for encoding of probability distributions on state variables. Within the context of the encoding problem, however, attention will be focused on the structuring of information on the uncertain quantities.

The personal probabilities under consideration here are required to adhere to some fundamental probability laws. For this purpose, let X be a sample space containing all possible outcomes x, assume $P(x)$ is defined, when $P(x)$ is referred to as the probability of x, and that $P(x)$ satisfies

1. $0 \leqslant P(x) \leqslant 1$
2. $P(X) = 1$
3. for any sequence $x^1, x^2, \ldots$, of outcomes that are mutually exclusive, that $x^n x^m = \phi$ when $n \neq m$, then

$$P \bigcup_{n=1}^{\infty} x^n = \sum_{n=1}^{\infty} P(x^n)$$

4. for $P(x^j) > 0$,

$$P(x^i | x^j) = \frac{P(x^i x^j)}{P(x^j)}.$$

Several principles to follow to enhance the process of defining and structuring an uncertain variable for encoding have been presented by Spetzler and Staël von

Holstein [17]. These are:

- only uncertain quantities important to the decision should be selected;
- the quantity under consideration should be a well-defined state variable, *i.e.*, a variable not within the control of the decision-maker;
- the quantity should be structured carefully, being conditional upon other quantities if the decision-maker decomposes the uncertain quantity in that manner;
- the quantity should be defined accurately;
- the quantity should be described using a scale meaningful to the decision-maker.

There are several methods commonly used for eliciting subjective probability distributions. Indirect response techniques require the decision-maker to provide comparisons of the probabilities with various reference items, such as shaded areas or probability wheels, intervals, or likelihood ratios. Direct response techniques require direct numerical assignments, as in the assignment of fractiles, verbal encoding, and graphical portrayal of quantities.

Often a decision-maker claims to have no knowledge regarding an uncertain outcome of a state variable when questioned. But actually this is the beginning of the process of structuring knowledge about uncertainties. The "no knowledge" claim may be encoded into a uniform probability distribution by giving each outcome equal likelihood. After all, the decision-maker is claiming that any of the outcomes may occur. Upon further introspection, the decision-maker may realize that certain outcomes are more likely. In the event that the decision-maker is unable to express a particular probability distribution on the state variable, it is possible to work with incomplete information on the distribution when it is of one of the following types:

1. null measure, where a uniform distribution is a good approximation;
2. ordinal measure, where rank order of likelihoods of outcomes is available from the decision-maker;
3. sets of inequalities, where the relative likelihood of one set of outcomes compared with another set is available;
4. bounded interval measures, where each outcome of a state variable has an upper and lower probability of occurrence.

Methods for generating point estimates for a distribution with this information and the sensitivity of decisions under these conditions have been considered by Fishburn [20].

Typically the decision-maker's assessment of uncertainty on a state variable is subject to biases (cognitive and motivational), which are produced in a manner dependent upon the individual's intuitive assessment procedure, or mode of judgment. Further discussions on bias may be found in [17; 18].

After an initial iteration through the steps of the Hall activity matrix, it may be determined that additional information relative to resolving uncertainty over a state variable may be economically beneficial. The usual mechanism for incorporating this information into the analysis is Bayes rule, which we have previously discussed.

Often, however, as a result of decomposing a state variable and conditioning the new quantities appropriately, there may be information available from several sources, such as experts, models, data collection efforts, and tests. It is desirable, as in the encoding process, to carefully relate this new information to the probabilistic information already encoded on key state variables. A structural model relating the new variables to those from prior analysis may be developed to display the inferences to be made.

An *ad hoc* approach to the development of a structure for making inferences requires the decision-maker to define and relate the variables to each other based upon a conceived structure in the individual's mind.

In situations where the structural relationships among these state variables are not well understood, the interpretive structural modeling approach as described above may be utilized. This is considered further in [21]. Additional considerations in structuring information for inference analysis appears in [22].

Both approaches should yield the same structure if the relationships are correctly identified. The bottom level elements, assuming the structure is portrayed as a hierarchy, are new state variables supplying probabilistic information to the previous state variables, for which a subjective probability distribution already has been encoded. All state variables at any level are assumed to be independent or should be so developed by refinement and redefinition of terms. Conditional probability assignments are made for all variables not on the top level, with the resulting structure called a deductive hierarchical inference structure. To develop an inductive hierarchical inference structure, two types of inferences need to be made: 1) relating a conditional probability vector of an element to an element two levels higher, and 2) coalescing several conditional probability vectors in the element on which they are conditioned. For 1), define

$$X_1 = \{x_1^i\}\, i = 1, \cdots, n_1, \ X_2 = \{x_2^j\}\, j = 1, \cdots, n_2, \ X_3 = \{x_3\}$$

such that a path from the lowest to highest element in the structure is $X_3 \longrightarrow X_2 \longrightarrow X_1$. Then

$$P(X_3 | X_1) = \sum_{k=1}^{n_2} P(x_2^k) P(X_2^k | X_1)$$

For 2), if elements $X_2, \ldots, X_p, X_1 = \{x_1^i\}\, i = 1, \ldots, n$ are such that $X_2, \ldots, X_p$ coalesce into X_1, then

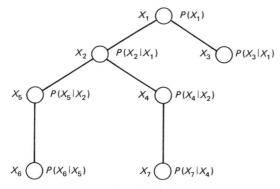

Figure 6. Example of an inference structure.

$$P(X_2, \cdots, X_p | X_1) = \prod_{j=2}^{P} P(X_j | X_1)$$

Using these and then applying Bayes rule, the posterior distribution on the top level elements is obtained. A sensitivity analysis of the posteriors to changes in the conditional distributions would enable the robustness of the result to be examined. An example of an inference structure in which both types of inference must be made, showing variables $X_1, \ldots, X_7$ and then associated probability distributions is illustrated in Figure 6.

Structuring Preferences

In choosing among alternatives using the decision analysis approach, some means of indicating the decision-maker's preferences among possible outcomes and resultant consequences is required. This is because the preferred course of action depends on the probabilities of the possible outcomes and preferences for consequences. The analysis of the alternatives requires quantification of the decsion-maker's preferences. A utility function makes it possible to incorporate these concepts into a formal analysis. The utility concept has been in existence for some time [23], but it was von Neumann and Morgenstern [24] who developed a set of axioms that established a cardinal utility function on an interval scale that suggested the possibility of consistently evaluating alternative decisions in an uncertain situation. Before discussing utility theory, it is useful to define a lottery. The existence of $X = \{X_1, \ldots, X_r\}$ is assumed. A lottery is a chance mechanism that results in an outcome with consequence X_1 with probability P_1, an outcome with consequence X_2 with probability $P_2, \ldots$, and an outcome with consequence X_r with probability P_r: where

$$P = \left\{ P_i \middle| P_i \geqslant 0 \quad_i \text{and} \sum_{i=1}^{r} P_i = 1 \right\}$$

The lottery is denoted

$$L = [P_1 X_1, P_2 X_2, \cdots, P_r X_r]$$

and is illustrated in Figure 7.

In order to establish a utility theory, it is common to make several asumptions. The approach of Luce and Raiffa [25] is presented here.

Axiom 1. Orderability. Any two consequences may be ordered according to a preference or indifference relation, which is read X_i is preferred or indifferent to X_j, such that $X_i \gtrsim X_j$. This relation is also transitive so that if $X_i \gtrsim X_j$ and $X_j \gtrsim X_k$, then $X_i \gtrsim X_k$. It is assumed without loss of generality that the consequences are ordered and indexed such that $X_1 \gtrsim X_2 \gtrsim \ldots \gtrsim X_r$ and that for at least one pair of consequences, $X_i \gtrsim X_j$.

Axiom 2. Decomposability. The preference ordering for the consequences is not affected by the way in which the lottery is resolved. A compound lottery may be reduced to a simple lottery by the usual rules of probability.

Axiom 3. Continuity. Each consequence X_i is indifferent to some lottery involving only the most preferred and least preferred consequences, X_1 and X_r, respectively. That is to say, for some probability Q_i, there exists a lottery such that

$$X_i \sim [Q_i X_1, \quad Q X_2, \cdots, Q X_{r-1}, \quad (1 - Q_i) X_r]$$

This lottery is denoted by $\tilde{X}_i$. The consequence X_i is sometimes called the certainty equivalent of $\tilde{X}_i$.

Axiom 4. Substitutability. In any lottery, the lottery $\tilde{X}_i$ may be substituted for the consequence X_i without altering the preference for that lottery. Thus

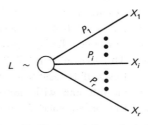

Figure 7. Representation of a lottery.

$$[P_1X_1, \cdots, P_iX_i, \cdots, P_rX_r] \sim [P_1X_1, \cdots, P_i\widetilde{X}_i, \cdots, P_rX_r]$$

Axiom 5. Transitivity. The preference relation and indifference relation among lotteries are transitive. Thus $\widetilde{X}_i$ can be substituted for X_i for all i, and have

$$[P_1X_1, \cdots, P_rX_r] \sim [P_1\widetilde{X}_1, \cdots, P_r\widetilde{X}_r]$$

Since each $\widetilde{X}_i$ is a lottery in terms of Q_i, X_1, and X_r, Axiom 2 can be applied to reduce the lottery to

$$L = [P_1X_1, P_2X_2, \cdots, P_rX_r] \sim [QX_1, (1 - Q)X_r]$$

where

$$Q = P_1Q_1 + P_2Q_2 + \cdots + P_nQ_n$$

Axiom 6. Monotonicity. For any two lotteries $L = [P_1X_1, (1 - P)X_r]$ and $L' = [P'X_1, (1 - P')X_r]$, $L \gtrsim L'$ if and only if $P \geqslant P'$. If X is a set of consequences and $>$ is a binary preference relation, then we require a utility function $u: X \longrightarrow R[0, 1]$ such that for all $X_iX_j \in X$,

$$X_i > X_j \text{ if and only if } u(X_i) > u(X_j)$$

Defining $u(X_i) = Q_i$, the axioms give such a function where $Q_1 = 1$ and $Q_r = 0$. Axiom 5 gives the utility of the lottery

$$u(L) = \sum_{i=1}^{r} P_iQ_i$$

which is unique up to a linear transformation.

If the consequences of the lottery are described by $X = \{X_1, \ldots, X_r\}$, utilities can be measured by assigning the Q_i to lotteries of the type $[Q_iX_1, (1 - Q_i)X_r]$ that are indifferent to the consequence X_i. If the consequences are $X \in [X_1, X_r]$ (*i.e.*, continuous over the interval), utilities can be assessed as above or the decision-maker can determine what consequence $X_{0.5}$ is indifferent to a lottery $[0.5X_1, 0.5X_r]$ where X_1 and X_r are as before. This process could be continued for other probabilities to obtain a utility curve representing the decision-maker's risk preferences. If the utility curve is a straight line, the decision-maker has an expected value risk preference; if the utility curve is convex, then the decision-maker is risk-seeking; and if the utility curve is concave, that is, if

$$u[E(\widetilde{X})] > E[u(\widetilde{X})]$$

then the decision-maker is risk-averse. To see this, consider a lottery that yields consequence X_1 with probability P_1 and consequence X_r with probability $P_r = (1 - P_1)$, $0 < P_1 < 1$. Then for risk-averse utility functions

$$u[P_1X_1 + (1 - P_1)X_r] > P_1U(X_1) + (1 - P_1)U(X_r)0 < P_1 < 1$$

which is the definition of strict concavity.

It is interesting to consider decision-maker acceptance of the axioms and their implications as well as the existence questions of utility functions. These have been examined elsewhere by Alchian [26] and Roberts [27], which should be referred to for discussions on these issues.

Until this point it was assumed that the utility of each outcome could be indicated by considering lotteries involving some single attribute of the outcome. In dealing with complex problems, assessments of this utility for use in analyzing alternative decisions generally requires consideration of more than a single attribute of each outcome. That is to say, consideration is given to an n-tuple or vector of attributes, $x = [x_1, \ldots, x_r]$, where x_k is one index of a consequence measured by the kth attribute. The utility of the consequence must then be some function of the n-tuple

$$U[x] = U[x_1, \cdots, x_n]$$

The purpose of the remainder of this section is to examine methods of assessing vector-valued preferences through the use of any structure existing among the attributes. Due to the extreme difficulty in assessing and comparing vector-valued quantities, a useful means of doing this is through decomposition of the complex decision problem into a number of relatively simple smaller decision problems. In these subproblems with fewer attributes it is generally easier to assess and quantify the decision-maker's preferences and to obtain well-defined probability distributions. Decomposition principles form the basis for systematic assessment of multidimensional utility functions. Fundamental to this approach is the utilization of trade-off analysis among the many, perhaps uncommensurable, attributes, thus enabling a single overall performance index to be established.

The decomposition principles depend primarily upon the existence of independence conditions among the attributes. A survey of the development of independence conditions in multiattribute utility theory is given in [28], but the decomposition approach followed here is due to Keeney [29; 30; 31].

Again define the state (or consequence) space $X = X_1 \times X_2 \times \ldots \times X_n$ to be a finite dimensional Euclidean space, with a particular consequence denoted by $x = (x_1, \ldots, x_n)$, where x_i is a realization of attribute X_i. Define

$$X_{\bar{i}} = X_1 \times \cdots \times X_{i-1} \times X_{i+1} \times \cdots \times X_n$$

and

$$X_{\bar{i}\bar{j}} = X_1 \times \cdots \times X_{i-1} \times X_{i+1} \times \cdots \times X_{j-1} \times X_{j+1} \times \cdots \times X_n.$$

Definition. $X_i \times X_j$ is preferentially independent of $X_{\overline{ij}}$, for fixed $x_{\overline{ij}}$, the decision-maker's preference order for consequences $(x_i, x_j, x_{\overline{ij}})$ are independent of value of $x_{\overline{ij}}$.

Definition. X_i is utility independent of $X_{\overline{i}}$ if, for fixed $x_{\overline{i}}$, the decision-maker's preference order for all lotteries defined over X_i is independent of the value of $x_{\overline{i}}$.

The existence of these independence conditions in a problem enables the assessment problem to be simplified to a number of smaller problems. This is stated in the following result [31].

Theorem. Let $X = X_i \times \ldots \times X_n$ be a finite dimensional Euclidean space, with $n \geqslant 3$. If, for some X_i, $X_i \times X_j$ is preferentially independent of $X_{\overline{ij}}$ for all $i \neq j$, and X_i is utility-independent of $X_{\overline{i}}$, then either

$$u(x) = \sum_{i=1}^{n} k_i u_i(x_i)$$

$$1 + ku(x) = \prod_{i=1}^{n} [1 + kk_i u_i(x_i)]$$

where $u(\ )$ and the $u_i(\ )$ are utility functions satisfying axioms 1-6, the k_i are scaling constants with $0 < k_i < 1$, and $k > -1, k \neq 0$ is a scaling constant.

Thus the multiattribute decision problem can now be decomposed into one involving assessment of a utility function for each attribute and scaling constants provided, of course, that the independence conditions are satisfied. The functional form of the multiattribute utility function is either linear additive or multiplicative in each attribute, and through algebraic manipulation the multiplicative form can be rewritten in quasi-additive form (additivity among terms where some forms consist of products of utilities). The actual assessment process will be discussed in the next section, but it should be clear that with the careful identification of objectives and priorities in the value system design step, the quantification of preferences is greatly simplified.

There are, of course, other forms in which multiattribute utility functions are expressed, but these are the most frequently occurring forms. Huber [32] gives a survey of field and fieldlike research studies concerned with the development and use of multiattribute utility models. The above independence conditions and results have been generalized and extended, leading to greater flexibility in application of multiattribute utility theory, and are discussed in [28].

In the value system design step a list of objectives and objectives measures was developed. A meaningful way to illustrate the relationship between objectives is through the use of a hierarchical structural model. The concern for the decision analyst is, however, to relate the achievement of objectives to the consequences of alternatives under consideration. For this reason, hard thinking is required to generate a list of elements containing general objectives as well as subobjectives that clarify meaning and completely account for all characteristics of the higher objectives. By developing a hierarchical structure from which attributes for the analysis can be obtained, the difficulty in identifying a multiattribute utility function to indicate effects of alternative decisions is eased, providing that a tree structure is obtained. A multiattribute utility model could be constructed from elements on a relatively high level of aggregation in the hierarchy or from the lower level elements if a more detailed analysis is warranted or is convenient. Keeney and Raiffa [16] discuss development of the hierarchy from an *ad hoc* perspective, but they give inconclusive, though helpful, guidelines on how to relate it to the problem. An interpretive structural modeling approach is considered in [10] and [33]. Here the objectives can be related through a contextual relationship concerning one of the independence conditions, thus eliminating the need to apply them all after constructing the hierarchy. The procedure for doing this is documented in [10] and is similar to that described in the creation of a single-source digraph tree. The advantage of this approach is that the structure is developed systematically, although it may not necessarily be any better (or different) than the result obtained from the *ad hoc* approach.

One additional factor must be considered while dealing with structuring of preferences, and that is time. Many attributes have a time value associated with them, and care should be given to see it is appropriately incorporated.

Evaluating Alternative Decisions

In order to select the decision that maximizes expected utility, a means of assessing the decomposed multiattribute utility function needs to be given. The single attribute utility functions (on a discrete or continuous scale involving objective or subjective quantities) may be assessed using the procedures described in the previous section under the topic of structuring preferences. The scaling constants are assessed by first ranking the attributes in order of importance and next establishing their actual value by assessing specific trade-offs between attributes. A measurement is obtained from the trade-offs on how much the decision-maker is willing to give up on one attribute to gain a specific amount on another with all other attributes held at a fixed level. This trade-off analysis serves to validate preferential independence empirically. The penultimate step in assessing the scaling constants involves determining a probability p such that an alternative with the most important attribute at its best level and all other attributes at their worst levels is indifferent with another alternative yielding all attributes at their best levels with probability p and all attributes at their worst levels with probability $(1 - p)$.

The final step involves sequentially computing the values of the scaling constants from the information obtained and applying the theorem of the last section. The scaling constant of the most important attribute, note, takes on the value p since $u(x) = 1$ when all attributes are at their best levels and $u(x) = 0$ when all are at their worst levels. The other constants follow. Specification of the multiattribute utility function in multiplicative form is complete with the assessment of the constant k. Assessing the scaling constants for the additive form requires only that the k_i be determined. Another method for assessing the multiattributed utility function is given in [34]. Reviews of methods of estimating additive utilities are given by Fishburn [35] and Huber [32].

Prior to terminating the decision analysis, it is useful to conduct a sensitivity analysis to determine the robustness of the alternative or strategy for maximizing expected utility. Three aspects of the problem that may be considered for a sensitivity analysis are: 1) scaling constants, 2) consequences, and 3) probability estimation. The scaling constants may be varied over a range that preserves their rank order to determine the effect of their perturbations on the expected utility-maximizing alternative or strategy. Consequences not precisely understood may be varied to account for uncertainty in their description. A sensitivity analysis of decisions to probability estimation errors can be conducted by varying the probabilities some desired amounts, but there is an approach taking advantage of some structural properties of decisions over the state space.

Information may be thought of as being complete enough to generate point estimates for the probabilities, or there may be incomplete knowledge on the distributions such that information may be nonexistent, ordinal, a set of inequalities on the probabilities, or bounded interval measures on the probabilities. An appealing approach provides the decision-maker with information on how much the initial probability estimates must be perturbed in order to change the expected utility-maximizing alternative. An algorithm providing this minimum distance solution for a static, single-attribute decision analysis problem with no information other than an initial estimate of the probability distribution over the states is due originally to Fishburn, Murphy, and Isaacs [36]. As a result of applying the algorithm, structured decision policies are obtained.

To pose the main problem, let p_j be the decision-maker's subjective probability estimate for state x_j, and let $u(x_j, d_i)$ denote the decision-maker's utility for the consequence resulting from the selection of decision alternative d_i and the realization of x_j. Define P_i to be the probability distribution for which alternative i maximizes expected utility, and denote it by

$$P_i = \left\{ p_j | p_j \geqslant 0 \quad j, \sum_{j=1}^{n} p_j = 1, \right.$$

$$\left. \text{and } \sum_{j=1}^{n} p_j u(x_j, d_i) > \sum_{j=1}^{n} p_j u(x_i, d_k) \text{ for all } k \neq i \right\}.$$

Suppose for definiteness that an estimate $\hat{p}_j$ for all j is such that

$$\sum_{j=1}^{n} p_j u(x_j, d_0) > \sum_{j=1}^{n} p_j u(x_j, d_i) \quad i = 1, \cdots, m$$

Then the main problem can be written as:
   Find $p_1, \ldots, p_n$ to

$$\min \sum_{j-1}^{n} (p_j - \hat{p}_j)^2$$

subject to

$$\sum_{j=1}^{n} p_j u(x_j, d_i) = \sum_{j=1}^{n} p_j u(x_j, d_0) \text{ for some } i > 0$$

$$\sum_{j=1}^{n} p_j = 1$$

$$p_j \geqslant 0 \quad j = 1, \cdots, n$$

Because of the difficulty in implementing the first constraint, a way to solve the main problem more conveniently is to decompose it into a number of smaller subproblems, one for each alternative. Then if a solution exists to the subproblem, it can easily be shown that the distance-minimizing solution of all subproblems is a solution to the main problem.

   The outline of the algorithm is defined in the following steps.

Step 1. Initialize. Set $n' = n$, $k = \{1, \ldots, n\}$, $s_j = \hat{p}_j$ for each $j \in k$.

Step 2. Compute $H, \bar{u}, M$, and p_j' for each $j \in k$ where

$$H = - \sum_{j \in k} s_j (u(x_j, d_i) - u(x_j, d_0))$$

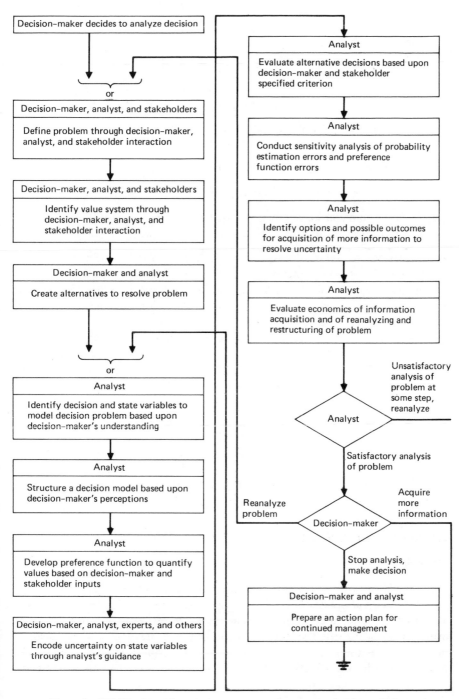

Figure 8. DELTA chart of steps to structure and analyze a decision problem.

$$\bar{u} = \frac{1}{n'} \sum_{j \in k} (u(x_j, d_i) - u(x_j, d_0))$$

$$M = \sum_{j \in k} (u(x_j, d_i) - u(x_j, d_0) - \bar{u})^2$$

$$p_j' = s_j + H(u(x_j, d_i) - u(x_j, d_0) - \bar{u})/M \text{ for each } j \in k.$$

If $p_j' \geqslant 0$ for all $j \in k$, the obtained distribution is the solution to the ith subproblem. If $p_j' < 0$ for at least one j, go to Step 3.

Step 3. For each $j \in k$ for which $p_j' < 0$, compute

$$a_j = s_j/(s_j - p_j') \quad (0 \leqslant a_j < 1)$$

and let a_r = minimum a_j. Set $p_r = 0$, replace k with $k - \{r\}$, replace n' with $n' - 1$, and replace s_j with $a_r p_j' + (1 - a_r)s_j$ for each $j \in k$.

It is necessary to iterate through the algorithm until all p_j have nonnegative values with the resulting distribution the solution to the subproblem. Multiparametric sensitivity analysis for the multiattribute decision problem may be conveniently conducted through a brute force simulation involving simultaneous variation of the probability distributions. Sensitivity of decisions to prior probability estimation errors and cost function perturbation in dynamic decision analysis problems (those employing Bayes Rule to incorporate new information into the prior distribution) is considered in [37]. Modeling errors and associated catastrophic losses due to these errors are discussed by Edwards [5].

To illustrate the process of structuring problems for decision and policy analysis, a DELTA chart is given in Figure 8. This DELTA chart shows sequentially the steps involved and their interrelationships. It is especially important to note the roles of the three principal actors; the systems engineer or analyst, the decision-maker, and the problem stakeholders, in this diagram. It is of course possible, but unlikely, that a particular problem situation model is such that one person or one group will play all three of these roles.

EXAMPLE AND CONCLUSIONS

Example

An example of how to structure a decision problem for public administrators to indicate potential applications of systems engineering methodology is helpful. The problem selected concerns the long-term role of livestock production, and in particular beef cattle production, in the United States food supply. Aspects motivating attention to this problem include the rapidly growing demand for food worldwide, the affects on the technology and resource base of increased food production, the continuing lack of adequate nutrition in some people's diet, and volatility in food prices. Factors affecting world food supply and demand have been the subject of study in a recent issue of *Science* [38] , and some national food problems have been discussed in an issue of the *American Journal of Agricultural Economics* [39] . The beef cattle industry is just one segment of the food industry, but its problems must be dealt with in the context of problems of the entire food industry.

Causes of the recently occurring (1972–1975) shortages and volatile prices of agricultural commodities have not been agreed upon. Proposed reasons for the appearance of these symptoms vary from the occurrence of unusual short-term transitory factors to growing fundamental changes in the world food supply-and-demand situation. But at least through the present, there appears to have been sufficient capability to satisfy demand, if only the problem of distribution could be overcome [40] .

Although the United States has remained a net food exporter through the shortages, it has not escaped the effects of the worldwide crisis. The livestock production industry, whose food products have a principal role in the diet of United States consumers, has been particularly subject to adverse effects of the food crisis. In addition, data indicate [41] that with present technology the world has neither the fossil energy resources nor available land resources to feed the present world population an average United States consumer's diet. Because of these pressures coming to bear on agricultural resources, there is a need for establishing the role of beef cattle production in a national food policy. Expeditious efforts are a necessity, since a less efficient allocation of resources by producers occurs when flexibility to possible changes in the rules under which they operate must be maintained. The consequence of delay translates to higher food prices for consumers and also risks forcing producers with a small profit margin, who must increase flexibility, out of the industry.

Problem Definition

The first step in applying systems engineering methodology to structure this problem for development and evaluation of policy decisions is problem definition. This step was structured into twelve parts in the above discussion, and these must all be considered. The key parts, identification of needs, constraints, alterables, societal sectors, and determination of interaction among these elements, will be considered here to illustrate the process.

Identification of Needs. Needs can be characterized as either a lack of something required, desired, or useful, or a condition that requires relief or supply. Needs for this problem would appear to include:

N1 the opportunity to obtain a balanced, nutritional diet,
N2 the opportunity to pursue profitable operations on beef cattle production,
N3 the opportunity to consume agricultural commodities according to personal preferences,
N4 adequate supply of food in the marketplace,
N5 adequate supply of beef in the marketplace,
N6 competition for sales among beef cattle producers,
N7 adequate distribution facilities to bring cut beef to the market,
N8 a balanced and nutritious diet for children,
N9 the opportunity to control the amount of government intervention into private sector concerns, and
N10 the existence of factors that compose a livestock market.

A self-interaction matrix for these needs is displayed in Figure 9.

Identification of Alterables. Alterables are those items pertaining to needs that can undergo change, and are either controllable or uncontrollable. Controllable alterables may be set to achieve or affect an outcome; uncontrollable alterables cannot be influenced, and uncertainty on what outcome is realized from them exists. Both types are of use in developing a decision model. Alterables for this problem include:

A1 tax structure,
A2 weather,
A3 personal tastes and preferences for food items,
A4 land allocation among various uses,
A5 crop production,

1	0	1	1	0	1	1	0	0	N1 – Diet opportunity
1	0	0	0	0	1	0	1		N2 – Profit opportunity
1	0	0	1	0	1	1			N3 – Personal taste satisfaction
1	1	0	1	0	1				N4 – Supply of food
1	0	0	1	0					N5 – Supply of beef
1	0	0	0						N6 – Marketplace competition
1	0	1							N7 – Beef distribution facilities
0	1								N8 – Children's diet
0									N9 – Control of government
									N10 – Livestock market existence

1 Interaction exists
0 No interaction exists

Figure 9. Needs self-interaction matrix for beef cattle production problem.

A6 production factors (land, labor, capital, technology) or inputs needed to produce beef,

A7 market efficiency,

A8 the number of persons at risk of malnutrition,

A9 physiological requirements of persons,

A10 trade regulations,

A11 processing and manfacturing capabilities of food products,

A12 distribution programs of food for the poor in the US,

A13 distribution programs of food for the rest of the world,

A14 government programs to influence consumption,

A15 redistributing income to the underprivileged to increase their operating budget,

A16 government interventions to affect price structures,

A17 market influence on technology used by producers, and

A18 nutritional level of person's diet.

Identification of Constraints. Constraints establish restrictions under which needs are to be satisfied and over which controllable alterables can be varied. Constraints for this problem would appear to include:

C1 existing government structure,

C2 sites suitable of beef cattle production,

C3 available government funding to address this problem and satisfy needs,

C4 time—such that activities are pursued before market forces affect the environment in which the beef cattle industry operates, and

C5 currently existing facilities supporting beef cattle production and cattle numbers from which to begin.

Societal Sectors. Societal sectors could be partitioned into the following groups:

consumers,
beef cattle producers,
government,
other industries involved with bringing beef cattle to the consumer.

Value System Design

Value system design, the second step in applying systems engineering methodology, is concerned with defining objectives and objectives measures, determining their interactions, and ordering objectives into a hierarchical structure.

Objectives. Objectives are identified such that their achievement provides satisfaction of needs under the constraints imposed and within the range of the alterables. Objectives for this problem would appear to include:

O1   to have an adequate food supply at reasonable prices to domestic consumers,

O2   to have an adequate beef supply at reasonable prices to domestic consumers,

O3   to provide a diet to all children that meets certain nutritional standards,

O4   to have the beef cattle industry producing efficiently,

O5   to provide equal opportunity in entrepreneurial endeavors to all,

O6   to maintain competition in the marketplace,

O7   to provide a degree of income protection to beef cattle producers from declining prices due to oversupply,

O8   to regulate extreme price fluctuations and attendant stocks to consumers and producers,

O9   to assist in international famine relief,

O10 to provide food assistance to domestic consumers who cannot afford an adequate diet,

O11 to provide the opportunity for adults to have a diet that meets certain nutritional standards,

O12 to maintain freedom of the individual,

O13 to develop more efficient food production means, and

O14 to prefer benefits sooner to later.

Objectives Measures. Attainment of the objectives is measured by these quantities. There does not have to be a one-to-one correspondence between objectives and objectives measures. Some objectives measures for the above objectives are:

OM1 average percentage of budget allocated to food expenditures by consumers,

OM2 percentage of children whose diet meets certain nutritional standards,

OM3 percentage of adults obtaining food assistance,

OM4 percentage of adults receiving adequate food assistance,

OM5 number of beef cattle producers forced out of business due to fluctuating prices, and

OM6 dollars of food assistance provided to other nations.

Systems Synthesis

The system synthesis step is concerned with creating alternative activities for attainment of each objective and determining the degree of accomplishment of the activities. Activities might include adjusting controllable alterables to levels maximizing achievment of objectives.

Activities. Activities for establishing the role of beef cattle in the national food supply based upon needs and objectives would include:

AC1   establishing and implementing government programs to influence consumption,

AC2   establishing and implementing government programs to alter production factors,

AC3   revising tax laws,

AC4   educating the public on sound nutritional habits,

AC5   teaching the producer efficient usage of production factors in beef cattle production,

AC6   doing more research on the subject,

AC7   doing nothing,

AC8   government intervening to affect price structures,

AC9   promoting reduced consumption of food, and

AC10 establishing a food assistance program to aid other nations in famine relief.

Activities Measures.   Activities measures might include:

AM1   amount of dollars spent on government programs to influence consumption,

AM2   amount of dollars spent on government programs to alter production factors,

AM3   amount of tax incentives,

AM4   amount of dollars spent on international food assistance program, and

AM5   number of malnutrition cases reported to health officials.

The problem definition, value system design, and interactions of the elements developed in the above three steps may be portrayed graphically using self- and cross-interaction matrices, as we previously considered under unified program planning. If binary interactions are used, the cross-interaction matrices of activities measures versus objectives measures, constraints versus activities, alterables versus objectives, needs versus objectives, and needs versus constraints can be determined by Boolean algebra. The remainder must be filled in by direct assessment. Not everything, however, is contained in these matrices because it must be assured that: 1) every objective can be potentially accomplished by at least one activity, 2) each need must be fulfilled by attaining one objective, and 3) the constraints of the problem cannot be violated by an activity achieving a need-satisfying objective.

A single decision model may be constructed to illustrate the procedure for evaluating alternative activities. This is not intended to provide a comprehensive analysis of the decision problem, but is intended to display the linkage between the decision and the structuring efforts of the first three steps of systems engineering methodology.

Producers require three conditions to be satisfied to adopt new technology: 1) the technology must be invented, 2) they must know how to use it efficiently, and 3) incentives must exist to use it efficiently. Prior knowledge indicates that the second condition may not be satisfied for beef cattle producers, so consideration is to be given to the decision of educating them. It is a decision that the public sector (government) cannot avoid. The producers must either be taught the efficient use of production factors or they must be left to learn on their own. Questions concerning the right of the government to intervene in private sector affairs must, of course, be addressed.

Thus the activities or decisions to be considered here are: activity 5 (AC5)—teaching the beef cattle producer efficient usage of production factors—and activity 7 (AC7)—doing nothing. The consequence of taking either of these actions is determined by the effects realized after the program is implemented. The effects can be expressed by uncontrollable alterable 17 (A17), which, for a preliminary analysis, may be partitioned into three states to approximate the outcome:

X^1: the beneficial effects. The average effect is a reduction in input and operating costs, thus providing the producers with the opportunity to maintain attractive profit levels and also yielding opportunities for nutritional gain to consumers. Additionally it is anticipated that market forces will enable savings to be passed on to consumers, at least partially.

X^2: the null effects. There is no relative change in beef cattle production costs and no net change in nutritional status of the consumer.

X^3: the detrimental effects. The average effect is to increase the total price of factor inputs, possibly reducing profitability, and thus forcing marginally profitable producers out of the industry. In the short run, at least, the nutritional status of the consumer will be hurt and in the long run the health of the beef cattle industry will be damaged.

This uncertainty on the outcome of the decision may be conveniently modeled by a decision tree. A decision tree for this problem appears in Figure 10.

A probability distribution based upon the decision-maker's current knowledge is to be encoded on state variable A17, with the probabilities denoted $P(X^i)$, such that the sum of the $P(X^i)$ is one. If the decision-maker is unable to provide sufficient information on the distribution, alternate sources for encoding may be used. These include agricultural enconomists, nutritional experts, other individuals knowledgeable of the subject matter, or statistical data. They can either be used in lieu of the decision-maker in the encoding process, or with the decision-maker by using hierarchical inference structures of other methods of incorporating expert opinion.

There are, typically, a number of factors affecting the probability distribution over the possible effects of the decision. It is useful to identify these factors explicitly when encoding. One example of such a factor for this problem is the degree to which current methods of beef production are entrenched in the

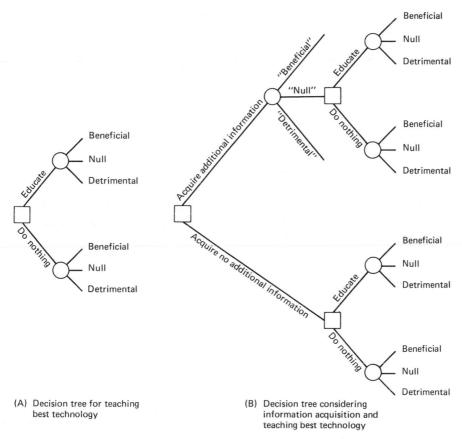

Figure 10. Decision trees for beef cattle production problem.

producer's behavior. If current methods are firmly embedded, it may be difficult to affect change. The distribution should reflect the impact important
factors may have on the outcome.

The value of an outcome is measured by the degree to which objectives specified in the value system design are satisfied. It is required that the set of objectives against which outcomes are evaluated must be complete in the sense of
considering all goals, and must not state the same goal more than once. Each
objective may be thought of as an attribute by which outcomes can be evaluated.
If preferential and utility independence conditions apply, a multiattribute
utility function may be used. This requires a joint probability distribution to
be assessed for attributes having more than one possible outcome. But we have
chosen here not to decompose the problem—rather we have considered only
the total effects of taking a decision. Some of the effects are readily measurable

in monetary terms, while others, such as subjective effects, are not. The net effects for each outcome can be obtained by first estimating the decision-maker's willingness to pay to acquire or avoid a certain effect on all items not already convertible to monetary terms and then summing the value of all the items considered.

With probabilities encoded and benefits measured for each alternative and related outcomes, the decision giving maximum expected value is to be selected. A sensitivity analysis should be conducted, the expected value of additional information should be computed, and a decision should accordingly be made on whether to proceed through another iteration of the steps of systems engineering methodology or to expand the decision model in order to acquire additional information.

The decision to acquire additional information must be considered prior to making a choice on whether or not to teach producers. This decision is activity 6 (AC6)—doing more research on the subject. A distribution on the outcome, which in this case is the same as the outcome to decision AC5 (including the level of discretization to discriminate between effects), is encoded, with probabilities denoted $P(Z^i)$, $i = 1, 2, 3$. The information gained from doing more research is used to update the assessment of the prior probabilities $P(X^i)$ by Bayes rule, where

$$P(X^i|Z^j) = \frac{P(Z^j|X^i)P(X^i)}{\sum_{i=1}^{3} P(Z^j|X^i)P(X^i)}$$

The optimal strategy after doing more research for Z^j obtained, $j = 1, 2, 3$ is

$$\text{If } E(v(X, A5(Z^j))) > E(v(X, A7(Z^j))), \text{ select A5}$$

$$\text{If } E(v(X, A7(Z^j))) > E(v(X, A5(Z^j))), \text{ select A7}$$

The expected value prior to doing additional research is

$$E(v(X, d^*(Z))) = E(v(X, d^*(Z^1)))P(Z^1) + E(v(X, d^*(Z^2)))P(Z^2)$$
$$+ E(v(X, d^*(Z^3)))P(Z^3)$$

where $d^*(Z)$ denotes the intention to select the appropriate maximum expected value decision d^* (either AC5 or AC7) after information Z is obtained. So to evaluate the decision to acquire additional information, the expected value of information is to be compared with the cost of requiring it. Figure 10b shows the decision tree when information acquisition is also considered. Information acquisition and iterating through the steps of systems engineering methodology should stop when the expected gain from additional information no longer exceeds its cost.

Concluding Remarks

The approach taken here has been to examine decision-making and policy analysis problems within a systems engineering framework. The structure of systems engineering methodology was developed, and structural models that had a role in systems methodology were discussed. The role of problem definition, value system design, and system synthesis as they relate to resolving the decision- or policy-making problem was emphasized.

As a preliminary to developing structural models for decisions analysis, the fundamental concepts of decision analysis were developed. The role and use of structure in aiding in the application of decision analysis was discussed. In particular, interpretive structural modeling procedures for developing decision-tree structure, structuring of uncertainty for probability resolution, and structuring of preferences were presented. Also structure associated with optimal decisions was utilized to display sensitivity analytic procedures for aiding in evaluating alternatives. These techniques and our approach here suggest and document the considerable potential structuring and decomposition principles have in assisting decision-makers improve the overall quality of their choices.

NOTES AND REFERENCES

1. Chen, K., M. Ghausi, and A. P. Sage. "Social Systems Engineering: An Introduction." *Special Issue on Social Systems Engineering, IEEE Proceedings* 63(1975): 340–343.
2. Sage, A. P., ed. *Systems Engineering: Methodology and Applications.* New York: IEEE Press, 1977.
3. Hall, A. D. "A Three Dimensional Morphology of Systems Engineering." *IEEE G-SSC Transactions* 5(1969): 156–160.
4. Hall, A. D. *A Methodology For Systems Engineering.* Princeton: Van Nostrand, 1962.
5. Edwards, W. "Error in Decision Analysis." SSRI Research Report 75-4, University of Southern California, April 1975.
6. Warfield, J. N., and J. D. Hill. "The DELTA Chart: A Method for R&D Project Portrayal." *IEEE Transactions on Engineering Management* EM-18(1971): 132–139.
7. Hill, J. D., and J. N. Warfield. "Unified Program Planning." *IEEE Transactions on Systems, Man and Cybernetics.* 2(1972): 610–621.
8. Sage, A. P. *Methodology for Large-Scale Systems.* New York: McGraw-Hill, 1977.
9. Warfield, J. N. *Societal Systems: Planning, Policy, and Complexity.* New York: Wiley, 1976.
10. Sage, A. P. "On Interpretive Structural Models for Single Sink Digraph Trees." *Proceedings 1977 International Conference on Cybernetics and Society.* Washington, D.C., Sept. 1977.
11. Howard, R. A. "The Foundations of Decision Analysis." *IEEE Transactions on Systems, Science, and Cybernetics* SSC-4(1968): 211–219.
12. Raiffa, H. *Decision Analysis: Introductory Lectures on Choices Under Uncertainty.* Reading, Mass.: Addison-Wesley, 1968.
13. Eilon, S. "What Is A Decision?" *Management Science* 16(1969): B-172–B-189.
14. Morris, P. A. "Decision Analysis Expert Use." *Management Science* 20(1974): 1233–1241.

15. Leal, A., and J. Pearl. "An Interactive Computer Program for Conversational Elicitation of Decision Structures." *IEEE Transactions on Systems, Man and Cybernetics.* SMC-7(1977): 368-376.
16. Keeney, R. L., and H. Raiffa. *Decisions With Multiple Objectives: Preferences and Value Tradeoffs.* New York: Wiley, 1976.
17. Spetzler, C. S., and C. S. Staël von Holstein. "Probability Encoding in Decision Analysis." *Management Science* 22(1975): 340-358.
18. Tverskey, A., and D. Kahneman. "Judgment Under Uncertainty: Heuristics and Biases." *Science* 185(1974): 1124-1131.
19. Winkler, R. L. "The Consensus of Subjective Probability Distributions." *Management Science* 15(1968): B61-B75.
20. Fishburn, P. C. "Analysis of Decisions with Incomplete Knowledge of Probabilities." *Operations Research* 13(1965): 217-237.
21. Sage, A. P., and D. W. Rajala. "On Structural Relationships in Decision Analysis." *Proceedings 7th Annual Pittsburgh Conference on Modeling and Simulation*, Pittsburgh, Pa., April 1976.
22. Rajala, D. W., and A. P. Sage. "Hierarchical Inference Structures in Decision Analysis." *Proceedings 1976 International Conference on Cybernetics and Society.* Washington, D.C., Nov. 1976.
23. Stigler, G. J. "The Development of Utility Theory." *Journal of Political Economy.* 68: 307-327, 373-396. (Reprinted in A. N. Page, ed. *Utility Theory: A Book of Readings.* New York: Wiley, 1968, pp. 269-296.
24. von Neumann, J., and O. Morgenstern. *Theory of Games and Economic Behavior.* New York: Wiley, 1944.
25. Luce, R. D., and H. Raiffa. *Games and Decisions: Introduction and Critical Survey*, New York: Wiley, 1957.
26. Alchian, A. A. "The Meaning of Utility Measurement." *American Economic Review* 43(1953): 26-50.
27. Roberts, F. S. "What if Utility Functions Do Not Exist?" *Theory and Decision* 3(1972): 126-139.
28. Farquhar, P. H. "A Survey of Multiattribute Utility Theory and Applications." In *Multiple Criteria Decision Making.* Edited by M. K. Starr and M. Zeleny. New York: North Holland Publishing Co., 1977.
29. Keeney, R. L. "Utility Independence and Preferences for Multi-Attributed Consequences." *Operations Research* 19(1971): 875-893.
30. Keeney, R. L. "Utility Functions for Multi-Attributed Consequences." *Management Science* 18(1972): 276-287.
31. Keeney, R. L. "Multiplicative Utility Functions." *Operations Research* 22(1974): 22-34.
32. Huber, G. P. "Multi-Attribute Utility Models: A Review of Field and Field-like Studies." *Management Science* 20(1974): 1393-1402.
33. Sage, A. P., and D. W. Rajala. "On the Use of Structure in Determination of Multi-Attribute Utility Functions." *Proceedings 7th Annual Pittsburgh Conference on Modeling and Simulation*, Pittsburgh, Pa., April 1976.
34. Keeney, R. L. "An Illustrated Procedure for Assessing Multiattributed Utility Functions." *Sloan Management Review* 14(1972): 37-50.
35. Fishburn, P. C. "Methods of Estimating Additive Utilities." *Management Science* 13(1967): 435-453.
36. Fishburn, P. C., A. H. Murphy, and H. H. Isaacs. "Sensitivity of Decisions to Proba-

bility Estimation Errors: A Reexamination." *Operations Research* 16(1968): 254–267.

37. Pierce, D. A., and J. L. Folks. "Sensitivity of Bayes Procedures to the Prior Distribution." *Operations Research* 17(1969): 344–350.

38. *Science*, special issue on food 188(May 9, 1975).

39. *American Journal of Agricultural Economics* 58(May 1976).

40. Wittwer, S. H. "Food Production: Technology and the Resource Base." *Science* 188(May 9, 1975): 579–584.

41. Pimentel, D., *et al.* "Energy and land constraints in Food Protein Production." *Science* 190(Nov. 21, 1975): 754–761.

PART V

Control and Accountability

If there is to be accelerated infusion of management science technology into public administrative practices, the tactical problems of operations and control would be a prime area. In an incisive study, Anatol Rapoport delineates the proper domain of business-oriented normative models of decision theory, specifying not only their major limitations but also adjustments that are needed to make decision theory better adapted to its environment. Essentially, the limitations are rooted in the fuzziness of significant aspects of societal problems and exacerbated by the conflicting interests addressing the administrators. For these reasons, the tasks of measuring productivity, analyzing effectiveness and efficiency, and operationalizing accountability in public administration are severely ill-structured. Curtis McLaughlin develops comprehensive guidelines designed to enable the administrator "to compete effectively for available resources." James Knickman directs his attention to a specific criterion for determining a public program's effectiveness: cost/benefit. The pervasiveness of value judgments in public, in contrast to business, enterprises is acknowledged in his development of a modified cost-benefit criterion. John Sutherland then moves us to the accountability-decision interface. In his contribution, he develops a scheme that operationalizes the function of accountability within a rationalized budget allocation process. Finally, Stephen Brown, Lonnie Ostrom, and John Schlacter present a new slant on marketing technology as it might be applied in the public sector, and link their analysis to the use of PPB (Planning-Programming-Budgeting) mechanisms as major sources of discipline within the ill-structured domain of social service systems.

I

Has Decision Theory a Future?

Anatol Rapoport
University of Toronto

As it stands, the question sounds bizarre. So let me first indicate a context in which it might be sensible. We say something has a *future* if we expect it to continue to exist and, perhaps, more than just exist—to prosper. A biological species prospers if it is numerous or widespread. An institution prospers if it is firmly entrenched in the social fabric. A theory prospers if it occupies the attention of many investigators in the field to which it applies, above all if it becomes an integrative focal point of that field.

Such are the overt manifestations of "prosperity." Opposite manifestations are even more cleary discernible. Species and institutions become moribund and eventually extinct. So do theories; phrenology, the phlogiston theory of combustion, the Lamarckian theory of evolution, and the homunculus theory in embryology are examples.

It is indicative of how deeply we have internalized the biological theory of evolution that we tend to associate "prosperity" with viability, and viability with adaptation to environment. It is tempting to think of extinction not only of biological species, but also of institutions and cultures as results of insufficient adaptation—and of the extinction of theories as well. So we might pose the question of what it means for a theory to be "well-adapted." If we can answer it, perhaps we can assess the degree of adaptation of decision theory and extrapolate it into the future.

It is tempting to think of the degree of adaptation of a theory in terms of its correspondence to observation. Indeed, if one thinks of a theory as a collection of hypotheses, and of hypotheses as verifiable assertions, this concept of adaptation corresponds to the conventional conception of the scientific method with its cycle of observations, generalizations, formulations of hypotheses, and empirical tests. A theory, however, is not just a collection of hypotheses. It is also a repertoire of concepts. Moreover, only in textbooks does the viability of a theory stand in direct relation to the verification of observations predicted by it. A theory does not exist in the way a biological species exists, incorporated in bodies of living organisms. A theory exists in the minds of people. It exists as long as people believe in it. It goes without saying that people's beliefs are not determined exclusively by what is observed, certainly not ordinary beliefs, which could also be regarded as "theories", even in the sphere of science.

For the purpose of this discussion, let us distinguish three types of theories, all in the context of science. The first kind, which could be called *predictive* theories, are those most generally associated with the product of scientific activity. The assertion in the form "If so ... , then so" is the paradigm of discourse. Empirical evidence constitutes the last court of appeal for the truth of a predictive theory.

Another kind of theory, which could be called the *normative*, is concerned not with actual observations or predictions of observations that are expected on the basis of an actual state of affairs, but rather with what *would* be observed under certain highly idealized conditions. For instance, the kinetic theory of a perfect gas, in which the molecules of a gas are assumed to be perfectly elastic spheres, is a normative theory. The theory of the pendulum, in which the pendulum is pictured as a mass point supported by a weightless rod of zero thickness, is a normative theory. In reality, neither a mass point pendulum nor a perfect gas exists. The power of normative theories in the physical sciences stems from the circumstance that physical systems that approximate the idealized models do exist or can be designed and make possible a translation of normative physical theories into predictive ones.

On the other hand, if we are willing to accord the status of theory to what we have defined as normative theory, than a theory can be completely divorced from observable states of affairs. For instance, we may have a theory of planetary motion where the law of gravitation is an inverse fifth-power law instead of the inverse square law, even if nothing even remotely resembling such systems exists in nature. In principle, in fact, all mathematical theories are quite independent of observations. Empirical verification is neither necessary nor admissible in mathematical theories.

Usually the term "normative theory" is used in a sense somewhat different from that just mentioned, but it nevertheless related to it. A normative theory is, as a rule, conceived as one that is concerned with optimization. Optimization is clearly related to idealization, since optima refer not to how things are but to how things *ought* to be. Optimization, however, carries an additional connotation of value. Thus, normative theories oriented toward optimization are value-oriented. Decision theory is most often regarded as a normative theory in this sense. It deals with singling out choices among alternative courses of action, which a "rational" actor *ought* to make if he wishes to bring the outcomes of his choices as close as possible to some specified optimum. Clearly, if a "rational actor" is an idealization—seldom if ever encountered in real life—then decision theory conceived in this manner is a normative theory in the broader sense we defined.

In this discussion we shall be concerned also with a third type of theory that could be called the *structural*. Unlike a predictive theory, a structural theory makes few, if any, predictions. Unlike a normative—prescriptive theory, it is not concerned with optimization. Its principal task is to formulate concepts in terms of which some portion of reality can be better "understood." In what follows, we will spell out just what we mean by "understanding" in the context of a structural theory. First we will offer some examples of such a theory.

There are scientific disciplines that are developed in an almost purely descriptive mode (*e.g.*, geography). Geography deals with watersheds, mountain chains, plains, types of climate, and so on. One could insist that the study of geography leads to verifiable predictions, for instance predictions of where you will find yourself if you travel an indicated distance in an indicated direction. Actually the "theory" underlying such predictions amounts to no more than a belief that geographical features are stable. These predictions are not in the same class with those of theoretical physical science where eclipses of the sun are predicted decades in advance, or the existence of chemical elements not yet discovered is deduced. The "theory" underlying geography resides in the concepts with which the geographer works, features of the earth's surface that are central in a systematic discussion of the earth's surface.

The same can be said of the descriptive (taxonomic) branch of biology and of structural linguistics. Systems of classification and concepts generated by these systems are the core of these descriptive-structural theories. They are called "structural" because the descriptions are made with the view of revealing the relatedness of the parts to each other and to the whole of some aspect of reality. Before a theory can become predictive, that is, formulated in the "If so . . . , then so" paradigm, one must know what to put into the "if so" part, namely what to pay attention to. A structural theory "points" to the structurally significant aspects of some portion of reality.

In assessing the possible future of decision theory, we shall be examining it in the normative and in the structural aspects. We shall not be concerned with predictive aspects. Hence, we shall not even raise the question of how people actually make decisions under specified conditions, which is the sort of question a predictive theory can be expected to answer. We shall pose the question of how a "rational" actor *ought* to make decisions under certain conditions, which is the concern of a normative theory. This question will lead to certain difficulties.

Then we shall turn to the structural aspects of decision theory for the light it can shed on the source of these difficulties.

We spoke of viability or "prosperity" of something—be it a biological species, an institution, a language, an art form, or a theory—as depending on the degree to which it is adapted to its environment. This notion stems, obviously, from biology, where the nature of adaptation to environment is clear. Also the connection between adaptation and viability is clear. A species is viable as long as sufficient numbers of its members survive to reproduction age. The nature of adaptation and of its relation to viability is less clear in some of the other contexts we have mentioned.

Take languages, which bear a striking resemblance to biological species in that they fall into hierarchically organized taxonomic categories, evolve, split into "subspecies" and become extinct. Clearly a language remains viable as long as there are people who speak it. People are replaced by succeeding generations, but the viability of a language does not altogether depend on generational continuity. On the one hand, descendants of a language group may abandon the language. On the other hand, a language may be adopted by people genetically unrelated to the original speakers. On what factors besides generational continuity does a language depend?

Or take an institution: proponents of the structural direction in sociology maintain that an institution continues to exist as long as it performs some function in preserving the "structure" of a society. But this view ignores the dynamics of structure. There is some truth in the idea that every type of social structure contains the seeds of its own destruction; and it may very well be that the continued existence of some institutions accelerates rather than delays the dissolution of the social structure in which they are embedded. On what, then, besides a function of "preserving structure" does the viability of an institution depend?

I raise these questions in order to forestall the facile but sterile answer to the question of whether decision theory has a future; namely, "Yes, if it continues to fulfill some need." The answer is little more than a tautology. It merely raises other more interesting but more difficult questions: what sort of needs, and, above all, whose needs? These are the questions that are relevant to all inquiries about viability. Why are railroads practically extinct as passenger carriers in North America but not in Europe? Why did slavery persist in the United States long after it became extinct in Europe? Why is mathematics becoming ever richer, so that one cannot point to any "golden age" in its past where achievements seem to have been greater than in the present? Why is this not true of some art forms or some genres of literature? On the other hand, certain special branches or methods of mathematics seem to have gone through spurts of rapid development and then become relatively quiescent, *e.g.*, synthetic geometry from Euclid to Appollonius, the method of quaternions developed by Hamilton, class field theory in algebra.

In recent decades there has been a rapid expansion of formal decision theory grounded in mathematics. Has it reached its peak? What has instigated the expansion? If it arose in response to "needs", what needs are these and whose? To what extent have they been satisfied or will continue to be satisfied or will one day be satisfied? And if certain of these needs are satisfied, will this spell the decline of decision theory or will new needs be raised as a consequence? These are the questions generated by the question we have raised: does decision theory have a future?

As has been said, it is most natural to regard decision theory as a normative theory where the central question is how "rational" actors ought to make decisions in certain types of situations. The development of any theory starts with definitions of key terms, in this case "rational" actor and "decision", and with some classificatory scheme, in this case a taxonomy of situations in which decisions are made.

Easiest to define is "decision". In all approaches to formal decision theory, a decision is identified with a choice among available actions. An acceptable definition of a "rational" actor might be that he takes into account the consequences of his decisions. The definition is all right as far as it goes, but it does not go far enough. What does it mean "to take into account"? Intuitively, we might interpret this as being guided by the desirability of consequences rather than by the immediate attractiveness of the actions taken. Desirability is related to values. Thus, we are led to posit the actor's values with regard to consequences, and this leads to a whole host of questions with which formal decision theory is concerned. Attempts to answer these questions lead to a taxonomy of decision situations.

The simplest decision situation is one where a single actor is faced with a finite set of actions (or choices), each of which leads with certainty to a clearly defined consequence. In this situation, if the actor can order the consequences on a scale of preference, his decision problem is solved. He chooses the action that leads to the most preferred consequence. Or somewhat more generally, if he does not know in advance which of the envisaged consequences will actually occur, he chooses a *strategy*—that is, a choice for every conceivable situation. For instance, if Action 1 is feasible, I choose it because it leads to the preferred Outcome 1; if Action 1 turns out to be unfeasible, I shall choose Action 2, which leads to the next most preferred Outcome 2; and so on.

Normative decision theory has nothing further to say about this situation. It does not raise the question of whether Outcome 1 ought to be the most preferred, nor even the question of whether Action 1 in fact results with certainty in Outcome 1. The first question concerns a theory of values, not decision theory. The second question concerns the degree to which the actor is *informed*, not the degree to which he is rational. He is rational to the extent that he optimizes what he *believes* to be the consequences of his actions. Therefore, this model of the decision situation is a trivial one.

Decision models become interesting when the actor does not know with certainty what the consequences of his actions will be. This state of ignorance, however, is not enough to specify the model. Certain assumptions must be added, and categories of decision situations depend on the nature of these assumptions.

The best known class of models are those that deal with decision *under risk*. The simplest of these models are representable by a matrix in which rows are the available actions, columns are so-called "states of nature", and the entry in each cell represents the actor's utility for the outcome that is determined by the conjunction of his action and a state of nature. It is further assumed that a probability distribution is "given" on the states of nature. The "rational" decision in this case can be defined as the action that maximizes expected utility.

This model and its ramifications have both practical and theoretical spinoffs, and it is these that must be examined as potential determinants of future developments of decision theory and of its viability. Let us look at the practical spinoffs first. This means, we will first bypass the theoretical questions raised by the model, such as how an actor's utilities for the outcomes are operationally defined and how probabilities can be assessed of "the states of nature" when it is impossible to conceive them as recurrent. We will return to these questions when we discuss the theoretical spinoffs. Let us then assume that the probabilities of the states of nature have been unambiguously defined and that the actor's utilities have been precisely determined, and also that the actor accepts the principle of maximization of expected utility as the principle of rational decision. If all these suppositions are granted, then the problem of decision under risk is in principle solved in the general case—a substantial contribution of decision theory.

What if the suppositions are not granted? The question sounds like a corresponding one regarding a predictive theory: what if the underlying assumptions of the theory are false? However, the two questions only sound alike. Their fundamental contents are quite different. In the context of a predictive theory we are concerned with the *objective* truth of the underlying assumptions. They are either true or false or, better said, they approximate more or less some actual state of affairs or else fall wide of the mark. In the context of a normative theory we are not dealing with suppositions concerning an "actual state of affairs". We did not pose the question whether the suppositions are true. We posed the question of whether the suppositions are *granted*. If they are, the model not only solves the problem of decision under risk already formulated but, which is even more important, suggests formulating decision problems in this format. If the suppositions are not granted, the decision problem is not even formulated, let alone solved. But granting or not granting suppositions is a matter of choice because the suppositions, as we said, refer not to supposed states of affairs, but rather to suggested ways of formulating decision problems. Therefore, our attention turns to the sort of situations in which it is easy (or difficult) to grant the suppositions and to the kind of people who are inclined or disinclined to grant them. The categories of situations and people are of course related because certain kinds of people often find themselves in certain kinds of situations.

The contexts in which it is easiest to accept the decision under risk (also called a "game against nature") are those where utilities are directly related to some precisely measurable commodity, like money, and where the probabilities of states of nature can be estimated from frequencies of occurrence. Situations of this sort are common in the business world. In fact, textbook exercises in management science are typically problems of optimization identified with maximizing profits or minimizing costs, many of which are closely related to decision under risk *e.g.*, portfolio management, insurance, *etc.*

Once the paradigm is accepted, complications can be introduced. For instance, the probabilities of the states of nature can be conceived in Bayesian terms, where estimates are compounded of prior and posterior distributions. The latter are modifications of the former *via* examinations of new data. Since the generation of new data usually costs money, one can define the utility of information so gained since the posterior distribution can increase subjectively expected utility gain compared to that generated by the prior distribution. In fact, the introduction of Bayesian statistics into decision theory has opened up several paths of technical development, and with them new areas of application, particularly in management science and in operations research.

Then what about the situations where the paradigm is less easy to accept, when, for instance, the outcomes of decisions are associated with intangibles rather than with precisely measurable commodities? Here it must be noted that "precisely measurable commodities" need not be money. They may be amounts of energy or time, or numbers of patients cured, or human lives saved or destroyed—anything that can be unambiguously measured. The "intangible" enters when it is difficult to assess utilities associated with these numbers, and especially when it is necessary to trade off some quantities against others. Take traffic control. It is quite probable that the recent substantial reduction in fatalities, injuries, and collisions in Ontario is related to the reduction of legal speed limits. The frequency of these calamities could be further substantially reduced (and also much energy saved) if the legal speed limit were further reduced, say to 35 miles per hour on highways. That such measures are not likely to be undertaken attests to the large likelihood that there would be public resistance to them. Somewhere, then, there is a break-even point in the trade-off of human lives, injuries and property damage, and time spent in going from place to place.

Even when payoffs are comparable, there are problems. When a new drug or vaccine is introduced, lives saved must be weighed against lives lost through idiosyncratic allergies, adulterated samples, misuse, and so on. In general, simply taking the algebraic difference to calculate "expected gain" will not do. Suppose a 100% effective vaccine against leukemia is discovered, which, however, has a mortality effect of its own. Then let the probability of dying from it be one-half the probability of succumbing to leukemia. I doubt very much that this drug would be readily accepted. The point is that dying from a "natural cause" has in the minds of most people a very different disutility from that of dying at the hands of a nurse who administers the vaccine. The difference is entirely psychological. Without the vaccine one does not *know* what one should have done to avoid succumbing to the dread disease. With the vaccine one knows only too well: had I not had my child vaccinated, the child would have lived. It is not a logical argument because we have assumed that the *a priori* probability of the child's death was greater for the unvaccinated than for the vaccinated child, but that is not the way ordinary people associate utilities of decision with probabilities.

We see, then, that formal decision theory in the context of decisions under risk generates problems. Systematic approaches to such problems constitute the theoretical spinoffs of decision theory in this context. For instance, it is not enough to take for granted that outcomes of decisions have utilities. One must also specify how such utilities are to be operationally defined— that is, indicate procedures for measuring them. Such procedures were indicated in the second edition of von Neumann's and Morgenstern's *Theory of Games and Economic Behavior* [1], the force of which is that it is possible *in principle* to determine the utility of any event on an interval scale. "In principle" means that certain axioms must be satisfied by the patterns of the actor's choices in risky situations. Whether they are actually satisfied is an empirical question. Thus lines of empirical investigations are suggested—spinoffs from the theoretical spinoffs of decision theory.

Next, even if the axiomatic foundation of utility theory is sound in specific situations, problems arise, because the operational definition of utility as given by von Neumann and Morgenstern fixes utility on a scale no stronger than the interval scale. This means that utilities of different people for the same outcome cannot be compared. As we shall see, this limitation is not essential in many areas of decision theory, particularly in the theory of the two-person, constant-sum game. In other areas, however, the limitation is "destructive." It renders meaningless certain concepts of equity, social welfare, and social justice, and so undercuts the foundations of a possible normative social science. That these foundations are shaky goes without saying; but it ought to be an open question of whether they should be for that reason altogether demolished or whether attempts should be made to strengthen them. Such questions can also be regarded as theoretical spinoffs of decision theory and its ramifications.

Attempts to develop decision theory by systematically attacking the above-mentioned problems could be regarded as attempts to make decision theory better adapted to its environment, by which I mean, of course, the social environment, the sum total of people's thoughts and attitudes toward values and decisions. Actually, an opposite tendency is also discernible: attempts to adapt the social environment to *existing* decision theory. If the theory demands the assignment of utilities and probabilities to events envisaged, the tendency is to *make* such assignments without much regard to problems of consistency or psychological meaningfulness so as to get on with the task of decision-making. This is not to say that the actual decision-makers, men of affairs, rulers, and such, regularly resort to formal decision theory. (We said at the outset that we would not be concerned with how people *actually* make decisions, which is the concern of a predictive theory.) But to the extent that activities surrounded by an aura of "scientific procedures," *i.e.*, surveys, tabulations, data processing, preferably on computers, and so on, enjoy prestige—and they do in technocratically oriented societies—the presuppositions of formal decision theory tend to assume a sort of "reality" in the minds of decision-makers in those societies. It is recognized tacitly, at times explicitly, that cost-benefit analysis is applicable to all important decisions. And of course, to the extent that the policies, habits of thought, and outlooks of the ruling elites are rejected by noncomformist or dissident sectors of society, opposite trends gain momentum. Then any sort of attempt to arrive at decisions on the basis of some kind of objective analysis of options and consequences meets with determined resistance.

So far we have examined only the most elementary area of formal decision theory, the so-called game against nature involving a single actor in an uncertain environment. We have presented the barest outlines of the formal theory, and have treated its practical, theoretical, and social spinoffs. The same can be done in two other contexts, namely the theory of games and the theory of social choice.

A game can be regarded as an extension of a decision problem to the situation where several actors make their choices simultaneously. A particular set of choices determines an outcome that, in general, has different utilities for different actors, now called players. In the simplest case, there are exactly two players and their preferences for the outcomes are exactly reversed. Thus, their "interests" are in total conflict. Examples of such games are so-called two person, zero-sum games in which the sum of the utilities or "payoffs" to the two players in every outcome is zero. The fundamental theorem of game theory states that in every such game where each player has a finite number of choices, there is available to each player an "optimal strategy" that may be one of the available alternatives or a probabilistic mixture of these alternatives. The strategy is optimal in the sense that playing against a player who chooses *his* optimal strategy, a player cannot do better than choose his own optimal strategy. That is to say, the optimal strategy guarantees a minimum payoff (or expected payoff) to each player. Since an increase of one player's payoff in a zero-sum game means a decrease of the other's, it follows that the pair of optimal strategies reflects a sort of "balance of power" of the players. Finally, it should be noted that if there are several optimal strategies, the choice of any of them by each player results in the minimum guaranteed payoff to each. Therefore, a prescription can be made to a "rational" player, *i.e.*, one who is concerned only with the maximization of his own payoff and one who supposes that his opponent does the same—namely, "Choose one of the optimal strategies." We have, then, a clearly prescriptive theory. Let us see to what sort of environment it is adapted.

Decision-making in conflict situations is the principal occupation of many professions in societies that are both technocratically and competitively oriented. The manager of a firm in a competitive environment, the career politician depending on the votes of a constituency for the continuation of his career, the attorney representing the interests of his clients, the specialist in public relations, the promoter, and finally the military strategist are all immersed in strategic conflicts on a day-to-day basis. They are constantly faced with the question of how to choose among a set of available courses of actions in the knowledge that others are faced with the same problem, that the outcomes will depend on the strategic choices of all concerned, and that the utilities of these outcomes are different for different actors.

Clearly from the point of view of these professionals, a theory of decision in conflict situations applicable in practice would be an extremely valuable addition to their repertoire of skills. It is hardly surprising that the appearance of the mathematical theory of games on the intellectual horizon stirred up a flurry of interest in military and business circles. It appeared as if decision theory (viewed as a normative theory in the sense of providing methods of optimizing choices of action) had been extended to conflict situations and so should serve as a foundation of a sophisticated science of strategy. The generous support given by the US military establishment—directly and through its think tanks—to research in the theory of games speaks eloquently for sanguine expectations in this regard.

It turned out, however, that the range of applicability of game theory as a science of strategy, *i.e.*, a methodology for optimizing strategic choices, was very narrowly circumscribed. This finding, be it noted, was not merely a consequence of recognizing wide disparities between idealized game models of conflict situations and reality. It was rather a consequence of purely structural analysis of conflicts beyond the level of two-person, zero-sum games. The difficulty of extending the methodology of choice optimization to these contexts is related not merely to the complexities, the fluidity, or ambiguity of real life conflicts. It is primarily a *logical* difficulty related to the ambivalence of "rational choice" in conflicts beyond the level of two-person, zero-sum games.

This can be seen when we attempt to extend the concept of a "solution" of a game from a two-person, zero-sum game to the two-person, nonzero-sum noncooperative game—that is, one in which the two players must choose their strategies independently. The crucial feature of two-person, zero-sum games is that their solutions are "equilibrium pairs", that is, pairs of strategies such that each is "best" against the other. In this way, in choosing a strategy that is one of an equilibrium pair, a player guarantees himself a certain minimum payoff. Since each player can do this, and since the goal of assuring a minimum for oneself in a zero-sum game means keeping the other's payoff from exceeding a certain maximum, the equilibrium pair represents a sort of balance of power between the two players.

Two-person, nonconstant-sum games also have equilibrium pairs, and accordingly they are singled out as "solutions" of such games. There is, however, a crucial difference between equilibria of constant-sum and nonconstant-sum games. The former are always interchangeable and equivalent, but the latter are, in general, not. Equilibria are equivalent if the payoffs to a player in all of them are the same. They are interchangeable if, whenever each player chooses a strategy that is a member of an equilibrium pair, the outcome is always an equilibrium. Therefore, in a two-person constant-sum game, where all equilibria are equivalent and interchangeable, it is always possible to prescribe an optimal choice of strategy independently to each player: choose a strategy that is a member of an equilibrium pair—any such pair. Because in a nonconstant-sum game the equilibria are not necessarily interchangeable, such a prescription cannot be made. For it may happen that each player chooses a strategy that is a member of an equilibrium pair, but the outcome is not an equilibrium.

There have been attempts to get around this difficulty by Harsanyi, who has proposed a method of choosing from all the equilibria of a nonconstant-sum game a particular one (or one of a class of equivalent equilibria) as "the" solution [2]. To effect this solution, the players must coordinate their strategy choices either explicitly or implicitly, in that each assumes that the other, being rational", can "solve the game" and so come to a decision in his choice of strategy. The outcome, then, is the equilibrium singled out as "the" solution.

Note, however, that in assuming such coordination, we have introduced a new element into conflict—namely a form of cooperation between the conflicting parties. At this point, however, a perplexing question arises. If the players must *cooperate* to reach a "rational solution" of a nonconstant-sum game, why can they not cooperate in order to effect a solution that they both would prefer to all the equilibria? The point is that equilibria are not, in general, Pareto-optimal. This means that there exist other outcomes that are *not* equilibria. Such outcomes are preferred by both (or all) players to the several equilibrium outcomes. There is an answer to this question. Equilibrium outcomes are "self-enforcing" in the sense that if a player knows (or is convinced) that other players have chosen strategies that are members of equilibrium pairs (or n-tuples in n-person games), then shifting from *his* equilibrium strategy can only impair his outcome. Outcomes that are not equilibria are not self-enforcing in this sense. To effect them, the players must make an *enforceable* agreement. Games in which such agreements can be made are called cooperative games.

The theory of cooperative games, two-person and n-person, is now an extensively developed sector of game theory. Note, however, that the problematics of this theory are far removed from the fundamental problem originally posed in the mathematical theory of games, namely that of optimizing one's strategic choice in a conflict situation. In the theory of the cooperative game, *collective* rationality of the players is assumed, which means that the solutions that come under consideration are generally Pareto-optimal solutions, not equilibria. In the context of a normative theory this means that the solution, say, the final apportionment of payoffs, is recommended to the entire set of players, not to each player individually. It is no longer a matter of finding "optimal strategies". It is rather a problem of *resolving* the conflict situations. Considerations of power—*e.g.*, the player's bargaining positions—are often taken into account in these solutions, explicitly or implicitly, along with certain equity principles. In this context, therefore, game theory becomes not a theory of strategic conflict, but rather a theory of conflict resolution.

In this role, game theory loses its attractiveness for the professional decision-maker. Evidence for this can be found by perusing books and proceedings of symposia organized in recent years by the US military on applications of game theory. The applications, almost without exception, are confined to those involving two-person, zero-sum games—that is, to contexts where game theory can serve as a theory of optimizing strategic choices.

Although many of these applications are textbook examples of tactical problems (therefore drastic simplifications of actual military situations that have at most heuristic value), some of the applications may well be relevant to real problems of concern to the military. I am referring to so-called differential games where strategies are functions of time rather than elements of a finite set. Games of pursuit and evasion are among the best known examples.

Consider a "game" between an Intercontinental Ballistic Missile and an Antiballistic Missile. The "aim" of the former is to explode as closely as possible to the intended target. The "aim" of the latter is to intercept the ICBM as far away from the target as possible. Hence this "conflict" can be modeled as a two-person, constant-sum game in which the payoffs can be quantified in terms of the distance from the target at which the ICBM is incapacitated. The "strategies" in this game are programs built into the devices, where the inputs are data concerning the "opponent's" parameters of motion (position, velocity, acceleration, *etc.*), and the outputs are control functions related to one's own parameters (that is, a pursuit course for the ABM and an evasion course for the ICBM). Stochastic variables can be incorporated into these strategies, corresponding to mixed strategies. The mathematical problems involved can be formidably complex, and methods of dealing with them would depend on advancing the theory of the two-person, constant-sum game far beyond its original formulation in terms of matrix games where each player has an arbitrarily large but finite (or at least discrete) set of strategies.

Here, then, is at least one context in which game theory—and, by implication decision theory, of which game theory is a branch—can be said to have a "bright future" in the sense suggested above of viability and "prosperity" rooted in a continued demand for solutions of concretely posed problems.

This prognosis, however, brings out forcefully the dependence of the "future" of a theory on its adaptation to a particular social environment. The examination of this dependence raises the fundamental question concerning the social stratum or sector whose needs the theory and its application serves. In the example cited this sector is clearly identified: it is the technologically oriented defense community comprising not only the military establishments themselves, but also their industrial and scientific entourage. To this sector the growing might and sophistication of lethal technology appear as continued sources of challenge and expansion of opportunities: in short, as "progress". Consider the following prognosis by General William C. Westmoreland [3] :

> On the battlefield of the future, enemy forces will be located, tracked, and targeted almost instantaneously through the use of data links, computer-assisted intelligence evaluation, and automatic fire control. With first-round-kill probabilities approaching certainty, and with surveillance devices that can continually track the enemy, the need for large forces to fix the opposition physically will be less important. . . .
> Hundreds of years were required to achieve the mobility of the armored division. A little over two decades later we had the airmobile division. With cooperative effort, no more than 10 years should separate us from the automated battlefield.

The general thinks mainly in terms of hardware, but analogous prognoses of progress in "software" can be easily appended to his rosy vision of the future.

Design of "software", with due consideration of the fundamental fact of life that the opponent's intelligence and competence are comparable with one's own (sometimes forgotten by military professionals), brings in perforce applications of the theory of games.

There is no question, therefore, that the theory of games considered as a methodology of optimization of strategic choices has at present a fertile soil in which to grow and prosper. Developed in directions where applications to automated warfare suggest themselves, it can admirably serve the professional and psychological needs of the defense community. What about the rest of us? What do the rest of us have to gain from growing sophistication of automated warfare, especially in view of the fact that this sophistication keeps growing *everywhere*, not just in the establishment that is supposed to "protect"us?

I recall a science fiction fantasy about some extragalactic civilization where wars are fought on computers. For instance, a computer printout may say, "1,237,630 of your citizens have just been annihilated". The rules of the "game" require that this outcome must be actually carried out. However, the cost of carrying it out is greatly reduced. It is not necessary to manufacture and deliver the lethal weapons. The annihilation can be done cheaply and humanely at home. Thereupon, the next strategic choice is fed into the computers to be processed and converted into an outcome. I doubt whether it is necessary to belabor the point that a game of chess has one meaning for the players and quite another to the pieces. The future of chess would become problematic if the pieces had a voice in the matter.

Our first conclusion concerning the future of game theory is, thus, the following: Conceived as a theory of strategic optimization (as it was originally formulated) the theory of games has a rich future in the one area where it can be applied in that way, namely in the area of the two-person, constant-sum game. But his future depends crucially on the continued existence of professions and institutions concerned with the planning and conduct of conflicts of complete opposition, primarily the military establishments. The growing sophistication of the theory in not likely to confer any advantages on any one side since developments of a theory cannot be kept secret. Thus, sophisticated developments can be said only to contribute to the continued prosperity and self-esteem of the global military establishment. To those of us who consider themselves to be enemies of the global "defense community", this is not a bright prospect. We hope eventually that this parasitic community—a constant threat to the viability of the human race—can be dismantled, so that the only source of nourishment for strategic decision theory will be intellectual curiosity and esthetic gratification, not "practical applications".

Turning to the theory of cooperative games, we see its application potential in an entirely new light. As we have seen, in that garb game theory is no longer a theory of strategic choice, but rather a theory of conflict resolution. The fact that collective rationality can play no part in conflicts of complete opposition is central in the theories of cooperative games. Its applications, therefore, do not depend on the nourishment that it can provide to professions concerned with strategic conflict. A prognosis of a bright future for this sector of decision theory would be a comforting thought to those concerned with continually widening the areas of human cooperation and developing imaginative methods of conflict resolution.

Unfortunately mixed-motive conflicts of the sort that lend themselves to cooperative solutions are not easy to model "realistically" in terms of cooperative games. In general, the outcomes of these conflicts are not of the sort to which numerical utilities can be readily assigned. Moreover, the proposed solutions—not generally being equilibria either in the sense of strategic choice or in the sense of coalitional stability—are not "self-enforcing". Thus, even if utilities could be unambiguously assigned, the implementation of the solutions would require *a priori* agreements by the parties concerned to abide by the outcomes. In short, conflict resolution is possible only when the utilities to the participants of the various outcomes can be specified with sufficient precision, and *only* when the participants are already committed to whatever resolution of conflict emerges from the analysis.

Situations where such commitments exist do occur in civilized societies. Recourse to arbitration, to adjudication by courts, *etc.*, is institutionalized in many areas of social conflict. In fact, no society, civilized or not, could exist without some commitments of this sort. One could even conceive of a "measure of civilization" of a society by the extent to which its members are committed to the resolution of conflicts according to principles internalized by almost every one as "just". It is conceivable that some such principles might be suggested by the theories of cooperative games and ways of applying them could be worked out in specific contexts. An interesting experiment on consensus formation based on concepts suggested by the theory of cooperative games was recently performed under the auspices of the US National Aeronautics and Space Administration. The decision to be arrived at was a choice of trajectories for two unmanned spacecraft to be sent to Jupiter and Saturn in the summer of 1977. The conflicting interests were those of ten different science teams, each interested in different data and, therefore, favoring different trajectories. The problems that arose in designing and performing that experiment were highly instructive to anyone concerned with ways of applying formal methods of conflict resolution in concrete situations.

In summary, the range of applications of multiobjective decision theory, which is methodologically intimately related to the theory of the cooperative n-person game, and the future of this sector of decision theory depend on the extent to which methods of conflict resolution developed in the theory are socially accepted. The rapid growth of the volume and sophistication of research in this area (including the theory of consensus formation) justifies a certain degree of cautious optimism on this score.

In my opinion, the future of decision theory depends not so much on its role as a normative theory—that is, on concrete applications to specific instances of conflict resolution—but rather on its role as a structural theory. Formal decision theory reveals at the very outset the structure of a decision problem and so focuses on the key concepts in terms of which this structure is described. These concepts—for example, dominating strategy, expected utility, the equilibrium of a game, Pareto-optimality, and so on—are not all intuitively clear. A precise understanding comes only after formal, logically rigorous analysis. In the course of such analysis the problem is often seen in an entirely new light. It is in this way that a structural theory fosters understanding, while not necessarily promising increased potentials of prediction and control. This function of theory is all too often lost sight of in technologically oriented societies. The blessings of science are identified with power, not with wisdom.

If the wisdom-conferring potential of decision theory as a structural theory comes to be accepted, then the viability and prosperity of decision theory can be assured for a protracted future.

The theory of social choice is an excellent example of decision theory in its structural role. The origins of that theory go back to the eighteenth century, to the researches of Condorcet and Borda on the structure of democratic decisions. The mathematical theory of voting does not purport to predict how people will vote. Originally it was concerned with the justification of different voting schemes, and so took on an aspect of a normative theory. However, the recent publication of Arrow's Impossibility Theorem has stimulated the flowering of the formal theory of social choice. The conclusion of this theorem, namely that *no* voting scheme could satisfy the few seemingly minimal and innocuous requirements of democratic procedure, raised a host of questions about the structure of collective decisions and stimulated research on conditions under which the axioms of democratic social choice *could* be satisfied. Subsequent investigations revealed the deep structural connection between the assumption that interpersonal comparison of utilities is impossible and the difficulties of defining (let alone implementing) a social welfare function. Moreover, the incomparability of interpersonal utilities turns out, upon examination, to be an *ideological* assumption rooted in the metaphysical underpinnings of classical market economics and perhaps in those of Hobbsian social philosophy. These are rich *philosophical* spinoffs of modern decision theory, analogous to the mathematical spinoffs of interesting new problems and even of new areas of mathematical research. Both of these spinoffs, the philosophical and the mathematical, yield intellectual rather than "practical" dividends, as practical dividends are understood in power-oriented societies. They nourish intellectual vigor and confer perispicacity and wisdom rather than predictive capacity (usually the power of control). Thus, the viability and prosperity of decision theory as a science serving the human race as a whole, rather than power-oriented institutions, depend crucially on whether the acquirement of wisdom atrophies or flourishes as a fundamental and universal human value.

NOTES AND REFERENCES

1. von Neumann, J., and O. Morgenstern. *Theory of Games and Economic Behavior.* Princeton: Princeton University Press, 1947.
2. Harsanyi, J. C. "Rationality Postulates for Bargaining Solutions in Cooperative and Non-cooperative Games." *Management Science* 9(1962): 141–153.
3. Cited in Dickson, P. *Think Tanks.* New York: Atheneum, 1971, p. 169.

2

Productivity and Effectiveness in Government

Curtis P. McLaughlin
University of North Carolina

INTRODUCTION

In a society with an expanding population, inflation, unemployment, and dwindling resources, the public administrator must be able to compete effectively for the available resources. This implies getting a stable or increased share of people's incomes to meet human needs. To do this the administrator must have a reputation for efficiency and effectiveness. He or she must be increasingly productive under these circumstances and must deliver the goods and services as soon as possible where, when, and how the public desires. Anything less than this reduces the quantity and quality currently provided and loses the credibility that is the basis for getting funds in the future.

Cordtz claims that this interest is new, at least in urban government [8]. He observes that federal programs often involve direct payments or services to some entitled group and are easier to discern than municipal activity. Also, the real estate property tax with its single payment as opposed to the less visible income tax withholding irks urban dwellers more, especially when they see the quality of life deteriorating. Furthermore, income tax increases accompany perceived income rises, but rising real estate values are not visible to the owner until the property is sold. Then there is the fact that many cities have reached the limit of their borrowing power, while the federal debt is underwritten by the central bank and by the printing press. So the public administrator, especially at the local and county level, is under the gun to produce or else.

626

Terms

Productivity is a measure of the efficiency of an organization, *i.e.*, its ability to transform resources into a set of products or services of a given quality. Productivity as a concept has gotten a bad name through the unwillingness of "efficiency experts" to deal with the problems of mix and levels of service.

> We believe productivity estimates based . . . solely [on] immediate products such as "tons of garbage collected," "gallons of sewage treated," "number of examinations given," can be uninformative or even grossly misleading [15, p.3].

As government expenditures have risen and social problems have seemed to stay with us, many people have felt that productivity has been decreasing, and government administrators have come to dread the word. It leaves them feeling that they must do more and more with less and less. This is not necessarily true when the concepts of productivity and effectiveness are used together.

Productivity of a System

Figure 1 illustrates the generic system producing a service. A system must be analyzed at each of the stages in the figure. At the input stage an administrator must evaluate the availability of resources. Productivity is generally defined as the relationship between inputs and outputs. Inputs are measured as labor, material, and capital, and outputs are units of work done and products and services provided.

Indices of productivity are units of output per unit of input. Holzer [17] points out that productivity improvements can be induced by four basic situations.

1. Increased outputs with constant inputs (what most organizations strive for).
2. Constant outputs with reduced inputs (what people generally mean when they talk about efficiency).
3. Increased outputs with decreased inputs (rare case).

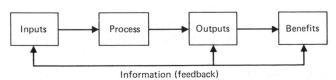

Figure 1. The productive system.

4. Both increase but output increases faster than inputs (often the least painful way to increase productivity).

There is a tendency to measure the productivity of public organizations in terms of output per dollar of input, but that is a very unstable and misleading measure in an inflationary economy. It is more useful for management purposes to use output per labor hour or per equipment hour or per kilowatt.

Effectiveness refers to the degree to which the organization performs its intended mission. It includes the qualitative impacts of the program as well as the measurable output, and it implies the degree to which the consumer is satisfied with the intangible attributes of the process and output. An effective program with adequate inputs will contribute to a set of benefits for a society. But it is important to remember that major benefits to clients may be the results of a number of programs. For example, a desired benefit for the public may be "safety in the streets." This may occur, but if it does, it will not be achieved solely through more patrols, or through education, or through employment, or through housing. Many actions of a society combine to produce the desired outcomes, so it becomes extremely hard to attribute benefits to one or more programs. Though programs are most often justified by benefits eventually, managers are in quicksand when they try to use benefit/cost ratios as a program's justification.

Benefit/cost ratios involve extremely difficult problems such as blending individual preferences for benefits into a single valuation, measuring intangible properties and tangible ones at once, and comparing and evaluating present benefits against future ones. Therefore, most analysts have retreated to the previously prepared position of *cost-effectiveness analysis.* Cost-effectiveness finesses the question of maximizing benefits given a cost constraint. It says, given a politically determined set of outcomes, determine the least-cost way of providing these outcomes. It implies choosing a *process* most capable of producing a set of outcomes of the desired quantity and quality.

Clearly this attempt to finesse the measurement of effectiveness by the analysts does not relieve the public administrator of the responsibility for making choices about what form of effectiveness to use, with or without the input of elected representatives or the body politic. Thus, while there may be other much longer sections of this book focused on evaluation, we will pause briefly to look at some terms and concepts in this field also.

Evaluation of Effectiveness

Two tasks are often confused when it comes to checking up on the productivity and effectiveness of a program—monitoring and evaluation. Monitoring refers to the data-gathering task, the recording of who, what, where, and for how much. It provides the feedback that will *then* be used for evaluation and further planning.

Suchman suggests the following set of criteria for analyzing the effectiveness of programs [32] :

Effort,
Impact,
Adequacy of performance,
Cost-effectiveness, and
Process.

Much more elaborate schema exist [29; 31; 15], but they all seem closely related.

Effort is a criterion that asks whether or not, given the validity of a specific approach, the quantity of activity (often measured as inputs) is adequate to service the anticipated need or demand. This is a weak criterion because it assumes that the service delivery approach is adequate. It also does not differentiate between need and demand. The demand for a service may be very different from those who would presumably benefit from it, *e.g.*, the number of riders on a bus system may be very different from those who could use it economically *or* the number that would have to ride it to clear up undesirable traffic congestion.

An *impact* criterion is the measure of how well the program accomplishes its outcome objectives. In the bus system example, impact would be what the program has done to reduce fuel consumption or to alleviate congestion. It is a stronger criterion than effort. Yet it begs the question of whether the impact was worth achieving or whether it was achieved efficiently and with the least undesirable consequences.

Evaluation must also deal with the *adequacy of performance* of the delivery unit. This relates to whether or not the impact was sufficient to meet the need. In a solid-waste-collection system we can measure the effort and then the impact in tons of garbage collected, but may still not know whether the area is dirty or clean. The introduction of an index of cleanliness would provide adequacy of performance measure.

Cost-effectiveness has been mentioned above, but we repeat Suchman's warning that this is often subverted into a *cost-efficiency* measure.

Process refers to the way the program delivers its services, collecting data on why the program performed as it did. Too often the evaluator spends much time on the other measures and reports to the administrator in terms of effort, impact, adequacy of performance, and cost-effectiveness. But the administrator then asks, "what do I change to improve this performance"?

Grubb [13] reports:

Perhaps the major constraint on evaluation is that programs are conducted by organizations. Indeed, organization and evaluation may be antithetical. Organizations usually stand for stability, the status quo; evaluation seeks change. Organizations inculcate loyalty and commitment, evaluation is scrutiny and skepticism. Being evaluated, particularly with the prospect that the judgment of that evaluation will be disseminated to a large audience, is a threatening experience.

The public administrator needs a specific strategy for overcoming that constraint, if he or she is to establish a reputation for productivity and effectiveness. In a later portion of this paper we discuss such a strategy and a way of developing it.

Fuzziness in Complaints

The public administrator has to be especially wary of jumping to conclusions when the public complains. He or she has to accept the fact that a broad complaint has to be narrowed down to a specific area. Take, for example, the complaint that *the cost of health care is too high*. Figure 2 illustrates the possibilities behind such a complaint. The complainer may mean that too many people are going into hospitals (input), or that too many things are done for a patient (process), or that the bills are too high for an outpatient visit (output), or that for all we spend we do not really live any longer (benefits). He or she may also mean that for all we spend in money and time, we ought to get better services (cost-effectiveness). In analyzing what the consumer's complaint is, the public administrator must try to identify the type of evaluation that is implied before responding. Unfortunately the public can be pretty fuzzy.

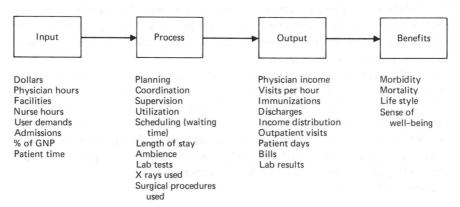

Figure 2. Meanings of "why costs are too high."

Political Rationality, Accountability, and Centralized Control

Not only must the public administrator operate his or her system to be productive and effective, he or she must do so in a manner that is *politically rational*, a way that takes into account the political realities. For example, the literature on public administration emphasizes the importance of clear goals. Yet most public programs are the result of unstable conditions that come together as the result of a political understanding, often one achieved at the expense of raising the goals to a high enough level of abstraction that all parties can agree. The net result is vague goals and a program that might lose its support if the administrator tried to get all parties to agree on concrete, operational goals. So you may have to be prepared to live with vague goals and the potential for lost efficiency that they imply.

An example is a community development project. Some see it as a way to improve property values and expand the tax base. Others see it as a way to provide local jobs. Still others see it as a means to improve their living space when they can afford no more taxes or assessments. Clearly, any attempt to make these groups decide exactly how the project will be designed is likely to please one group at the high risk of losing one or two of the others. If the program needs the support of all these, it would be better to accept fuzzy goals.

When public officials are faced with ambiguous (fuzzy) situations, they tend to *centralize* control [9]. The cardinal sin is to fail to appear fully in touch with what is going on in one's organization. Therefore, in the absence of clear goals to illustrate performance, the emphasis is on knowledgeability. So all information and power is brought together under one wing.

Services must be delivered on a decentralized basis, however, spread out over the countryside where the people are. Unlike goods, services cannot be inventoried and shipped out on demand. The user participates in the timing and conduct of the process, which must be *timely*, *accessible*, and *equitably distributed*. So centralization does not work in the long run.

Thus, we have a system of centralized decision and decentralized delivery mediated by sets of *guidelines*, *standards*, and *procedures*. In addition, the notion of *accountability* is introduced. As local managers turn to multiple funding sources to cope with complex local needs, they find themselves facing multiple accountability requirements and conflicting guidelines. One agency requires that a particular project be cost-effective, another that it provide training and employment for the hard-core unemployed. Perhaps another project must provide health care to a population, a certain portion of which is medically indigent, while another guideline requires it be economically self-supporting. The gyrations that one must go through to meet these conflicting demands of funders produce a process that looks neither efficient nor effective to the local populace, but may be politically rational.

PRODUCTIVITY MEASUREMENT

There are a number of methods of measuring productivity, especially labor productivity. But today, governments are moving increasingly into the field of human services, providing health services, welfare services, care and education for the dependent (Title XX), *etc.* It is not just the efficiency and effectiveness of the local government subsystem that is to be measured. Such services are delivered through a complex network of multiple local public and private agencies, which deal with various subsets of the multiple needs of disadvantaged families. Economic support and food stamps may come from one agency, job counseling and vocational training from another, remedial education from another, health care from another, mental health care from another, *etc.* To look at any one agency and say how well a case is managed is likely to generate an inaccurate measurement. Attempting to measure anything in a field full of intangibles is often risky.

Methods of Measuring Productivity

A number of methods have been applied to measuring productivity in the public sector. The most extensive studies of these are in the report of the Joint Economic Committee, US Congress [38], and Ross and Burkhead [27]. The approaches can be classified as:

1. the cost data approach,
2. the workload approach,
3. the industrial engineering approach, and
4. the econometric approach.

Cost Data

Hatry and Fisk [15] report that the cost data approach is the measure most used by local governments. It involves making sure that the budget is broken down by program and by type of service. For it to be useful, the organization must have a relatively sophisticated cost accounting system and a program budget. Though a weak productivity measure, cost data is a necessary forerunner to a good productivity measurement system.

The managerial question then becomes: we spent so much this past year, can we do it for less next year? If so, we have improved productivity. It is an input measure relatively understandable to elected officials and to the public. It can be distorted by inflation and by changing service demands. Usually the major item in a budget is labor and everyone usually knows what percentage of wage increase the workers have received, so that an increase of that amount in the salary line item usually is accepted as an adjustment even before productivity performance is assessed.

But, if there is a workload change, a cost data approach begins to break down. The school superintendent who presents the same or a slightly smaller elementary school budget after the recent decline in birth rates hardly ought to be a hero. And where subdivisions or new industrial plants are added to a town, the ability to hold a program's budget growth at or below the inflation rate represents improved productivity, but how much no one knows. Furthermore, cost data say nothing about changes in effectiveness.

Workload Measurement

Once the cost system is established, including allocation of maintenance and overheads to the service delivery system, the next step is to measure the units of workload produced. Workload units might be gallons of water treated, pupil days, crimes investigated, fire calls answered, acres of park land maintained, *etc.* Dividing these by program cost or by man-days gives a productivity measure.

The town or state can monitor its performance by looking at the trend in productivity, often through the use of trend charts updated monthly, and by exchanging data with other providers to compare performances. The motivation for improvement then becomes one of competition against one's past performance or of bettering that of the other jurisdiction.

Workload productivity figures do not take into account effectiveness. Crimes investigated do not necessarily imply crimes solved. While we might be interested in the cost per fire call, we might be even more interested in response times, fire damage losses and injuries, and loss of life experienced. But any system that goes into a comparison of political units also has to be able to report local factors used in interpreting local quality and quantity claims. For example, in comparing local fire departments we need to know something about local construction, weather, and population densities.

Such data often are expensive to collect, but are useful for studies about how to improve services. For example, a study of where best to locate the next fire station would use much of the same data, plus additional data on travel times and location of high-risk structures such as schools. Table 1 shows such a list, prepared by Hatry and Fisk for the National Commission of Productivity. Table 2 shows their suggested way of presenting workload data to include adjustments for quality and inflation. The difficulty with using such indices is that it may be impossible or at least difficult to get agreement on, and acceptance of, quality indices. It is possible that the cost of setting up the system would exceed the value of the information produced.

Table 1. Illustrative set of workload measures, quality factors, and local condition factors that should be considered in productivity measurement[a].

SELECTED SERVICE FUNCTIONS[b]	ILLUSTRATIVE "WORKLOAD" MEASURES[c]	ILLUSTRATIVE QUALITY FACTORS i.e., MEASURES OF CITIZEN IMPACT, THAT SHOULD BE CONSIDERED IN INTERPRETING PRODUCTIVITY	ILLUSTRATIVE LOCAL CONDITION FACTORS THAT SHOULD BE CONSIDERED IN INTERPRETING PRODUCTIVITY[d]
Solid waste collection	Tons of solid waste collected	Visual appearance of streets "Curb" or "backdoor" collection Fire/health hazard conditions from solid waste accumulation Service delays	Frequency of collection Private vs. public collection Local weather conditions Composition of the solid waste (including the residential-commercial-industrial mix; type of waste, etc.)
Liquid waste treatment (sewage)	Gallons of sewage treated	Quality level of effluent, e.g., "BOD" removed and remaining after treatment Water quality level resulting where dumped	Initial quality of waterway into which the sewage effluent is released Community liquid waste generation characteristics
Law enforcement (police)	No. of surveillance-hours No. of calls No. of crimes investigated	Reduction in crime and victimization rates Crime clearance rates, preferably including court disposition Response times Citizens feeling of security	Percent of low income families in population Public attitude towards certain crimes
Law enforcement (courts)	No. of cases resolved	No. of convictions/No. of plea-bargain reduced sentences Correctness of disposition Delay time until resolution	Number and types of cases
Health and hospital	No. of patient-days	Reduced number and severity of illnesses Conditions of patients after treatment Duration of treatment and "pleasantness" of care	Availability and price of health care Basic community health conditions

Function	Workload measure[c]	Effectiveness measures	Factors affecting[d]
Water treatment	Gallons of water treated	Water quality indices such as for hardness and taste; Amount of impurities removed; Accessibility of low-income groups to care	Basic quality of water supply source
Recreation[b]	Acres of recreational activities; Attendence figures	Participation rates; Accessibility to recreational opportunities; Variety of opportunities available; Crowdedness indices; Citizens' perceptions of adequacy of recreational opportunities	Amount of recreation provided by the private sector; No. of individuals without access to automobiles; and the available public transit system; Topographical and climatic characteristics; Time available to citizens for recreation activities
Street maintenance	Square yards of repairs made	Smoothness/"bumpiness" of streets; Safety; Travel time; Community disruption: amount and duration; Dust and noise during repairs	Density of traffic; Density of population along roadway; Location of residences, homes, shopping areas, recreational opportunities, *etc.*
Fire Control	Fire calls; Number of inspections	Fire damage; Injuries and lives lost	Local weather conditions; Type of construction; Density of population
Primary and secondary education	Pupil-days; Number of pupils	Achievement test scores and grade levels; Continuation/drop-out rates	Socioeconomic characteristics of pupils and neighborhood; Basic intelligence of pupils; Number of pupils

[a]More extensive lists of workload measures and quality factors (often called measures of effectiveness or evaluation criteria) can be found in the bibliography of Hatry and Fisk [15].

[b]Numerous subfunctions each with its own submeasures could also be identified. Care should be taken, however, to avoid going into excessive, unuseful detail.

[c]Dividing these by total dollar cost or by total man-days yields workload-based productivity measures.

[d]Such local conditions as population size and local price levels are relevant to all service functions.

Table 2. Illustrative productivity measurement presentation:
solid waste collection example

	1970	1971	CHANGE
Data			
Tons of solid waste collected	90,000	100,000	+10,000
Average street cleanliness rating	2.9	2.6	−0.3
Percent of survey population express-			
ing satisfaction with collection	85%	80%	−5
Cost (unadjusted)	$1,200,000	$1,500,000	+$300,000
Costs (1970 dollars)	$1,200,000	$1,300,000	+$100,000
Productivity measures			
Workload per dollar (unadjusted	75 tons per	67 tons per	−11%
dollars)	thousand $	thousand $	
Workload productivity (1970	75 tons per	77 tons per	+3%
dollars)	thousand $	thousand $	
Output index: $\dfrac{(1) \times (2) \times (3)}{(4)}$			
(unadjusted dollars)	0.185	0.139	−25%
Productivity index: $\dfrac{(1) \times (2) \times (3)}{(5)}$			
(1970 dollars)	0.185	0.160	−14%

Industrial Engineering Standards

The cost data and workload approaches are comparative rather than normative. They show how well we have been doing and whether the results have been getting better or worse, but they fail to deal with the question of how well we could do or ought to be doing. Perhaps people are leaning on their shovels only 40% of the time instead of half the time.

Technical experts trained in industrial engineering have been employed by industrial organizations and governments to study jobs and to determine how long a normal worker working at a normal pace under normal conditions should take. Then the managerial question becomes one of whether or not the workers or system of workers are achieving that productivity level, and if not, why not.

The primary productivity payoff of the industrial engineer frequently comes more from the study of the method of doing the job than from the introduction and enforcement of the resulting standards. All too often the way the worker goes about doing his or her task is ill-defined, varies from supervisor to supervisor, and takes little account of principles of motion economy or consideration of labor-saving investments. The first thing the industrial engineer does is set up the ideal method considering worker capability, organization of materials and supplies, and possible uses of available equipment. Once he is reasonably sure that he has the best method, he goes ahead and trains a worker to use that method and watches how fast he can be expected to go using that method.

Note that, while the standards being developed are for the workers, they do involve some consideration of the use of capital equipment and changed staffing patterns, something that the literature often overlooks. In fact the development of a standard method using present equipment is the first step in performing an evaluation of whether or not new capital investments could be economically justifiable. All too often new equipment evaluations look good solely because the present equipment is being used inefficiently. If we were using our present equipment in the best manner possible, these glowing productivity estimates from the suppliers might not seem so attractive so often.

The industrial engineer may use one of four approaches to establish the standard: 1) time study; 2) work sampling; 3) predetermined standards; and 4) standard data. *Time study* is an approach used in industry, but there have been legal constraints on its use in the federal government stemming from concerns about job security. An engineer or engineering technician trains the worker to do the job by the prescribed method. Once that worker reaches a normal pace on the task, a stopwatch or movie camera is used to time each distinct element of the task. Once the task has been timed a sufficient number of times, the times are averaged. Then the observer adjusts the times according to the pace of the worker—above or below the normal pace for this organization. To this adjusted time the observer than adds standard allowances for unavoidable delays and personal or rest time.

The Joint Federal Productivity Project reports that [39] :

> The standard developed using time study techniques is generally considered a valid and reliable standard. The job content and the standard time are specifically defined, and because the method, quality, working conditions, and operator performance are standardized, it is possible to identify deviations from standard and to assign a cause for the deviation.

These are some caveats to this approach. Each organization has to develop its own concept of what a normal pace is. It varies from industry to industry and place to place, and you can expect to have to spend a great deal of time and effort getting management, employees, and engineers to agree on the definition of normal and standard allowances. Secondly, time study is used most effectively for highly repetitive tasks. Many government tasks are repetitive, but not in quite the same way as jobs that produce goods. The garbage collector lifts cans over and over, the letter carrier fills boxes over and over; yet each location is somewhat different. The number of cans and letters differs from day to day, the distance walked varies from location to location and carrier route to carrier route. Time standards may be subject to dispute from the workforce on a number of grounds, which is why standard data, often based on time studies, are often more acceptable.

Many government organizations use *work sampling* instead of time study. Again the activities being done in a department are broken down into elemental activities, and a careful selection is made of which observed activities are work and which are nonwork. A period is designated for the study, and the units of output for the period are measured. During the test period a trained observer visits the department at randomly selected intervals and observes which activities are taking place. Enough visits must be made to produce a statistically valid sample, and the observer must still rate the performance level of the workers being observed.

Let us take the hypothetical case of the drafting department of a state highway department. The observer has noted the following frequency of activities:

Drawing	685 observations
Doing calculations, using tables and catalogues	215 observations
Arranging workplace, sharpening pencils	70 observations
Talking with supervisor or engineers	130 observations
Looking out window, talking to other draftsmen	183 observations
In cafeteria, restrooms, at water cooler	217 observations
	1500 observations

Assuming that the last two classifications are nonwork, we can see that the draftsmen worked 73.3% of the time. The study covered 4 weeks during which the workers put in 400 man-hours and produced 600 drawings. The observer reported that the draftsmen worked at an average 105% of normal pace when he observed the first four items. The standard allowance for this organization is 15% of the total time worked. So the observer would set a standard for the drafting department as follows:

Our draftsmen worked 1100 observations out of 1500 in 400 hours to produce 600 drawings, so the actual working time per drawing was

$$\frac{1100 \text{ working observations}}{1500 \text{ observations}} \times \frac{400 \text{ hours}}{600 \text{ drawings}} = 0.489 \text{ working hours/drawing}$$

But they worked at 105% so the slower normal time would be 0.489 × 1.05 = 0.513. The standard also has to include a 15% allowance so the standard would be 0.513/1 – 0.15 or 0.604 hours per drawing. Note that while the workers were faster when they worked, they took more time off than was allowed; hence the standard was less than the observed 0.667 hours/drawing.

The supervisor adopting such a standard would still have to be ready to hear arguments such as whether or not looking out the window was creative time and work-related. What is interesting about work sampling is that it can be applied to a wider range of tasks like drafting and still be used to set some standard workload measures. It is far less obtrusive than the stop watch and generally is less threatening to the individuals being observed.

Predetermined time standards are a highly developed system for determining values for minute job elements from prepared tables, rather than using a stop-watch. The methods break tasks down into five motions of the hand and body and set a time value, synthesized from the predetermined standards, for each motion. Using these standards requires training in, and access to, someone's system. This makes it a costly procedure to install and one that is applicable to high-volume tasks. In government it would be most applicable to such high-volume clerical jobs as processing insurance claims or loan applications.

Many organizations develop their own *standard data* for tasks or parts of tasks. These would be like the predetermined time standards in principle, but generally the elements are not nearly as short and complex in definition. Simple curves or charts may be used to estimate time. For example, the amount of garbage that a crew ought to be able to load could be related to the number of residences serviced and the number of curb miles involved, plus a standard time for trips to the landfill to unload. From these elements and others, one might then decide on what the output ought to be once allowances are included.

These form methods are considered more objective than historical workload patterns, but they still are subject to the criticism that they ought to take into account quality and local conditions just as historical workload measures should. Here is where the public administrator must take care in introducing industrial engineering specialists into the organization. They must be made to understand the service philosophy that you wish them to adopt and apply. At the same time you should be willing to ask them to do studies to illustrate the impact of alternative service levels on productivity and cost. In some areas it may turn out that a major increase in quality will result from a very slight additional investment, whereas in other programs a very slight alteration of service downward will yield a major improvement.

Standards do not necessarily have to be developed internally. Sometimes they can be acquired from outside experts, from other governmental units, or from trade associations. This is far more economical but it may yield results that are not adaptable to local conditions, and it does not induce the pride of local authorship, which often speeds local acceptance.

The industrial engineer may deal with *staffing patterns* either indirectly, through the development of standards, or directly through *ad hoc* studies: *e.g.*, whether or not a garbage truck operates more effectively with one driver and two loaders or one driver-loader and one loader; or whether public safety officers can substitute for a certain number of police officers and fireman. Sometimes this involves the design and administration of planned experiments and then their thorough evaluation.

The Econometric Approach

The public administrator is likely to put much of his or her energy into the types of productivity analyses already cited when undertaking special studies concerning the adoption of a new piece of equipment or a new technology. But there are those broader questions about "efficiency for what, effectiveness for whom, or should the service be provided in the first place"? These kinds of questions are often the concern of economists. Economists also are concerned with the output of the public sector as a whole, with whether it is motivated to invest sufficient capital, whether the increased wage rates in the private sector are spilling over into the public sector and making them relatively more expensive, and what special incentives or procedural unblockings might encourage greater productivity.

Ross and Burkhead have published an extensive review of existing studies, and report that the "cost, workload, quality-productivity approach" [27, p. 125] still provides the operational framework for measuring local government productivity changes. They cite the New York City effort as far ahead of most others, and claim that tying productivity to collective bargaining was the key to that success story. "In the process they have made both sides more aware of what can be done to improve efficiency of public service delivery. The results of New York City's efforts are impressive. Note that this approach is different from that of the federal government and from the other 'academic' studies that have been reviewed in this chapter" [27, p. 92].

The New York City image has tarnished considerably since this was written. The administration was not able to keep to productivity bargaining and the team that produced these results did not survive a change in administration. Still, that does not necessarily mean that the approach was inappropriate. Horton suggests that the reported productivity bargaining agreements were illusory and work rule changes not effectively implemented [16].

> And given the inherent uncertainty of outcomes in bilateral bargaining processes, the possibility exists that managerial expectations concerning appropriate outcomes will not be realized at all. The degree of managerial risk in productivity bargaining appears high, particularly in governments where preexisting legal or power relationships dictate that productivity bargaining occur, whether formally or informally.

Monitoring Productivity and Effectiveness

Once measures of productivity are identified, it becomes a relatively simple task to monitor the results. A reporting system collects inputs and outputs for display to the administrator, the supervisors involved and the workers. One can then use this to monitor and to identify when to follow up.

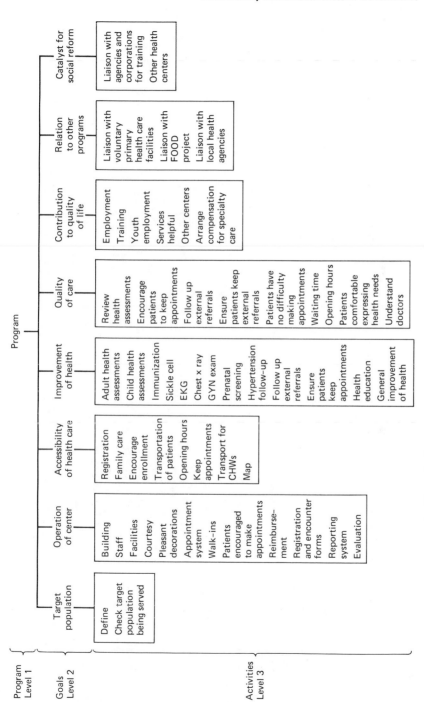

Figure 3. Goals and activities in a primary care organization.

Table 3. Activities, targets, measures, and weights (goal V: deliver high quality health care; goal weight = 5).

ACTIVITY	ASSESSMENT REGIME					
	TARGET	OUTCOME MEASURE	WEIGHT	OUTCOME	ACHIEVEMENT	EFFECTIVENESS
Establish a routine series of tests and examinations for a complete health assessment	September 1971	$x = \begin{cases} 0.4 \text{ if no} \\ 0.6 \text{ if yes} \end{cases}$ Achievement $= x$	4	Yes	0.60	1.00
Encourage patients to keep appointments	65% of appointments should be kept	$\left[\dfrac{\text{Proportion of appointments that are kept January–June 1972}}{}\right] \times \dfrac{12}{13}$	2	61%	0.56	0.93
Establish mechanisms to facilitate follow-up of patients referred to other institutions	Mechanisms established by March 1972	$x = \begin{cases} 0.4 \text{ if no} \\ 0.6 \text{ if yes} \end{cases}$ Achievement $= x$	3	Yes	0.6	1.00
Ensure that patients referred to other institutions appear for a consultation	50% of externally referred patients appear for a consultation at the institution to which they are referred and notification of results sent to center	$\left[\text{Proportion of externally referred appointments kept about which center notified}\right] \times \dfrac{6}{5}$	3	161 appointments. Notifications received for 60 i.e., 37.3%	0.45	0.75
Ensure that patients have no difficulty making an appointment at the center.	85% of a sample of patients answer negatively to the question: "Have you every had any difficulty making an appointment at this center"?	$\left[\text{Proportion of a sample of patients who answer negatively}\right] \times \dfrac{12}{17}$	2	97%	0.68	1.14

Monitoring effectiveness requires much more extensive attention to specific measures and their weightings. Here you have to turn to evaluation technology to get some approaches for quantifying the unquantifiable. These must be tailored to the individual characteristics of a program. One approach is a weighted vector of goals for attributes of process and outputs. Continuing with the example of health cited in Figure 2, we can use the approach suggested by Dennis Gillings of the University of North Carolina for a community health center. He first developed the levels of goals and activities for each program (Figure 3), and then, for each goal, he developed a set of weights and for each activity, a measure of achievement and a weight, as illustrated in Table 3. The scales were designed so that 60% achievement was considered effective. With the weights, it would then be theoretically possible to produce a single figure giving a weighted average measure of effectiveness for each set of activities under a goal. If the five goals under quality of care were the only ones (there were actually nine), then the effectiveness for that would be

$$\frac{(4 \times 1.00) + (2 \times 0.93) + (3 \times 1.00) + (3 \times 0.75) + (2 \times 1.14)}{4 + 2 + 3 + 3 + 2} = \frac{13.39}{14} = 0.96$$

This may prove to be a much more complex monitoring system than you would choose to develop, but it illustrates a direction in which to move in wrestling with the display of process and outcome performance.

Having A Strategy

One key element in delivering an effective and efficient program is having a long-range plan. Here the word *plan* does not necessarily imply a concrete, detailed set of steps, but rather a framework within which the pragmatic administrator can respond to events—a strategy. The process of public administration is likely to remain incremental, despite program budgeting, zero-based budgets, management-by-objectives, *etc.* But the key question is "Incremental toward what?"

There has to be a set of goals for each program, something to reach for as opportunities arise. They may change as the community expresses new wants, as funding sources change, or as new technology is introduced, but these goals must be there. Otherwise the program, after a sequence of incremental changes, may end up where you never intended it to be in the first place [14; 26]. This is true even in the face of the uncertainty of the appropriations process. But this uncertainty cannot be used as an excuse for avoiding strategic planning and long-range budget projections by funding sources and by program uses. Without these the administrator is in no position to make decisions about growth, personnel development, the funding sources to cultivate, capital investment for productivity, mix of services and activities, service level performance measures, and marketing strategy.

Life is Too Short

The argument can be made that the tenure of administrators is too short for long-range plans [6]. This shortness of tenure, given impetus by the election cycle at all levels, can also be used to argue for having a strategy.

If one's useful life is likely to be limited, then almost every decision must serve multiple purposes. The technical term for this is synergy, the attribute that the whole is more effective than the sum of the parts. Actions taken for one program need to support the ends of others as well, if progress is to be rapid.

The Strategic Planning Process

Figure 4 illustrates the strategic planning function and its components. This process can be started at any number of places. Most organizations talk about goals

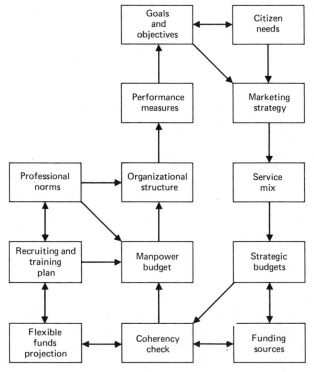

Figure 4. Formulating long-range strategy.

and objectives as the starting point, but with many it is really the budget process where they start [24]. Key external information inputs are expressions of citizen needs, legislative intent as to goals and objectives, norms and expectations of professional groups, and the values and capacities of funding sources (taxpayers, legislative bodies, elected officials, federal and state agencies, and foundations).

The loop illustrated in Figure 4 is not intended to be definitive. Alternative sequences can be expressed. For example, the organizational structure might determine the manpower budget instead, although that is, to my view, a passive approach to management.

The most unusual step is the coherency check. It emphasizes the necessity for an overview of the steps taken to see whether or not the whole operation makes sense. Given the set of inputs cited above, there is no reason to assume that the resulting whole will, of necessity, make sense. Otherwise the programs of a government can look like a camel, an animal meant to be a horse, but designed by a coalition.

If the funding sources have not provided funds in the appropriate forms (line items or program budgets), it is up to the administrator to apply funds from flexible fund sources or to arrange a reallocation of local revenues. Provisions for access to flexible funds, for example, allow the whole to make more sense in the long run.

This process can be used in a rough or in a detailed way. The administrator can go through the process once in his head or can institute a detailed system with mission statements, plans and objectives, performance measures, user and taxpayer surveys, employee attitude studies, *etc.*

Most of the information for this process will have to be developed specifically for it. Such plans are made at irregular intervals and the analysis usually has to be developed specifically for the task [3].

A single external (environmental) event may affect several stages of the process at once. For example, unionization of the sanitation force is clearly likely to increase the need for funds and, in more conservative communities, may alienate the taxpayers. But nonwage bargaining may also affect the manpower plan by affecting staffing patterns, hours of work, and service mix. The optimal schedule might be for the most workers on Monday, but collective bargaining might yield a uniform work week that, with the normal pattern of absenteesim, might produce a lower than normal manpower availability. Unionization of professionals produces demands for higher skill levels in the professional workforce and, hence, change the recruiting and training plan as well.

Legislation can often be a major environmental change. For example, the trend to force the school systems to do a fully comprehensive job in educating the retarded and the handicapped (special education) has imposed new professional norms, added new constituencies, set up new goals and objectives, and made some new funds available.

Goals and Objectives—MBO, Zero-based budgeting

Drucker has suggested a set of basic steps to go along with this cycle [11]. He urges the administrator to

1. Define the "business" that the agency is in and what it ought to be after considering a number of alternative definitions.
2. From this definition derive a clear set of goals and priorities.
3. Plan your efforts by setting priorities for concentrating on targets, standards of performance for each target, and setting deadlines and for actually getting on with the work.
4. Define and promulgate the measures of performance.
5. Provide for an audit of the results to see where the program was satisfactory and where it should be revised. This process should include a mechanism for "sloughing off" unproductive activities. MacLeod reports one technique used by a community mental health center for sloughing off services that its staff and its constituency did not strongly support [23].

Future Issues in Productivity

The public administrator remains the key to productivity—more than legislation, guidelines, budgets, site visits, and audits. He or she must mediate the array of funds coming from multiple sources with:

1. the standards that professionals bring,
2. the federal and state guidelines and standards,
3. the wills of local governing bodies, and
4. the perceived needs of clients and taxpayers.

The future will see an increase in the human services provided directly and indirectly under public sponsorship. The key to productivity in this area will be the ability to coordinate a network of services involving government agencies, private nonprofit organizations, and for-profit contractors. This will involve the allocation of tasks, coordination and evaluation of results and the development of control and incentive systems that produce efficient and effective behaviors. The skills of the industrial engineer and the bureaucrat will be less important, and those of the behaviorist and political scientist will emerge as critical skills for management.

First and foremost will be the ability to develop a coherent concept of the system being managed. This topic has been discussed in the preceeding section. A subsidiary skill will be a sense of which attributes of the system control capacity and productivity. Few public administrators seem comfortable in thinking of their agencies in terms of capacities, flows, bottlenecks, and constraints. This approach has not been adequately articulated. For example, the government of a developing country is attempting to speed up its development program by training multipurpose workers to assist with family planning, health, and nutrition. It wants to know how much can be expected in each area and what allocation of time is appropriate. An evaluation of agencies for the blind determines that the continued emphasis on vocational rehabilitation results in more and more services for fewer and fewer people as the pool becomes less one of veterans and incubator-damaged babies and increasingly one of the aged and those having multiple birth defects.

Another choice involves the community mental health center that has had deinstitutionalization as its goal. This involves setting up a local network of group homes, day care facilities (sheltered workshop or outpatient care or both), and an extended medication program. To do this there are many, many relationships to manage.

> The center acquires a variety of inputs (staff, supplies, etc.); it exports a variety of outputs (community members with enhanced job skills, research reports, etc.); and it maintains relationships with a number of groups and organizations (community groups, professional societies, family service agencies, health delivery organizations, etc.). The CMHC must create multiple boundary role structures for the management of these relationships . . . the primary task of organizational management, namely, regulating the linkages between organization and community. . . .
>
> The center needs active ties with other health agencies, private practitioner networks, referral sources and therapeutic sources of all kinds. Beyond these, it has to develop working relationships with numerous other groups and institutions: schools, courts, employment resources, welfare agencies, government programs, and groups representing various ethnic, religious, class, and other sectors of the community. The ES (entry system) requires input ratio into such interaction because these center-environment transactions may serve to increase the potential applicant pool or may be utilized as referral sources for the center [20].

This kind of management will require a hefty set of skills in building and maintaining coalitions, acquiring resources of the right type and amount, setting up incentive systems, managing groups, and resolving conflicts.

Coalition skills

Once the process has been characterized it must be presented in goal packages that meet the needs of each constituency. Shapiro emphasizes that, for each group, attention must be given to price, product, promotion, and place [30]. Goals do not have to be vague to maintain a coalition. Different constituencies focus on limited sets of product and service attributes. They may be willing to accept some negative ones, as long as their positive needs are met. Marketing is not getting people to take something they do not need. Kotler has outlined an extensive array of uses of marketing technology to achieve desirable social ends [18].

Once there is a commitment to more concrete goals, the effective manager will have to deal with developing and implementing subunit goals. Levinson states [21] that adequate attention to individual and group personal goals benefits the manager: the use of "many additional frames of reference in both horizontal and vertical goal setting, he would need no longer to see himself under appraisal (attack, judgment) as an isolated individual against the system". Levinson cites special skills needed for:

leadership,
defining a transcendent purpose for the organization,
group management,
conflict resolution, and
teaching others skills of administration, group management, and conflict resolution.

Resource Acquisition Effectiveness

The key here is to spend a sufficient amount of energy to generate the slack or flexible resources mentioned in the section on strategy. These funds are regarded as organizational slack and are available as side payments to key individuals, perhaps as a reward to them for sticking it out with their agencies during trying times.

Resource acquisition effectiveness often involves the inclusion of the funders in the coalition. One national organization related to educating the developmentally disabled was heavily dependent upon one bureau of the federal government. The staff became somewhat resentful of the "interference" of the federal employees who were located nearby, and they brought up the issue with the bureau director. He agreed to more of a hands-off policy, but the organization soon experienced much more difficulty in getting consultancies approved and in getting permission to move grant funds from one line item to another.

Setting Up Incentive Systems

The public administrator giving out funds must also seek to have his or her domain include the agency in the coalitions of the contractors or grantees. One of the key decisions is whether or not to bargain hard for the price and quantity of services procured from and exported to the network. Benson provides a useful way of seeing how these bargaining behaviors involve territories, domains, professional ideologies, positive evaluations (back-scratching), and work coordination [5].

The critical question is how much resources to offer to induce the delivery of services and maintenance of the coalition and still be accountable and give the impression of being interested in productivity and effectiveness. The place to start is with an effort to stay current with the rapidly developing literature on the political economy of organizations.

Group Management

There is a vast and growing amount of knowledge and literature on managing diverse groups. Here again the best defense is staying current. Certainly there will be key areas, such as:

psychological contracting,
managing boundary roles and interactions,
uses of rewards and incentives, and
team-building

Any manager is evaluated by at least three criteria: 1) ability to meet short-run performance criteria; 2) ability to develop subordinates; and 3) ability to develop viable work groups [6].

The individuals entering the organization either as clients or as professionals need to have clear understandings of where they are, what is expected of them, and what they can expect from the organization. Kotter points out that [19]:

1. The initial match of expectations is a critical determinant of satisfaction, turnover, and productivity.
2. "Matching" is critical in both directions. Giving more seems to be almost as bad as giving less than was expected.
3. The individual should be encouraged to express these expectations and the case should be followed to see whether they can be met by an efficient and effective organization. If not, then the organization must either change its expectations or its policy of personnel selection.

Adams reports the fact that those people who handle the boundary relationships between organizations and their environment are under considerable stress [1]. They represent the organization to the outside world and interpret the outside world to the organization. They are responsible for maintaining its image and for much of the bargaining for resources in and services out. Because it is necessary to see both sides to be an effective bargaining agent, their loyalty becomes suspect to both sides. If they are to be effective they must have considerable attention, strong emotional support, and a clear reward system. They, perhaps more than any other employees, need to know the organization's current strategies and plans.

Public administrators have often had to rely on idealism, honor, and professional values to maintain the quality and quantity of public services. But when the service sector of society is at least half of its output, the mystique is hard to maintain, and the labor pool cannot be particularly select. In the private sector, especially in medicine, we have used monetary rewards, allowing the professional who works harder to achieve a much larger income. The fallacy of such an incentive system is that it will guarantee more productivity out of increased individual effort. On the contrary, services require the effort of many individuals —clients, professionals, administrators, paraprofessionals, and support employees. Therefore, the efficient and effective service delivery system has to be run by a team. Despite professionalism and states, the public administrator has to build in a suitable fit for both individual and group needs.

One action/research team that has been working for a number of years has determined that the process of building teams requires careful attention to [36]:

goals and mission statements,
role expectations that break down status barriers,
conscious decision-making processes for the group,
communication and leadership training for all members,
explicit and implicit group norms, and
conflict management.

Service delivery tasks are much more complex and variable than industrial ones [33]. Therefore, it is risky to stay with old, simplistic definitions of competency and jobs. Many tasks can be managed only in a team context.

Conflict Management

In a complex environment, situational conflict is always high. Short budget cycle and the funding uncertainties increase the tension. Thus, effective organizations must learn to accept, tolerate, and perhaps even relish high situational conflict levels. Many governmental organizations become so attuned to this that they adopt a "crisis mode" of problem-solving [35]. The key to productivity is to tolerate the situational conflict while holding interpersonal conflict at a minimum. It is the interpersonal conflict that drains away the creative energies of the organization. This is one reason why the role of the administrator in interpreting the environment, coalitions, strategy, and plans is key. If the employees do not have a good map of the situational territory, they cannot be blamed for interpreting the conflicts they experience as interpersonal rather than situational. And if such misinterpretations go unchecked, productivity suffers markedly. Only in this manner can the public administrator lead individuals and task force groups to develop objectives and performance measures to fit the situation and their personal, professional, and group needs under the pressures of accountability, professionalism, and regulation.

There is much that can still be done with the traditional, engineering-oriented notion of productivity in public services. Better performance measures are needed, as are better techniques of resource allocation where complex, multiple criteria are used. Administrators need better methods of forecasting the demand for services and for scheduling the workforce to meet it. Technological and labor substitution possibilities have barely been scratched, often due to the inflexibility of the budget process.

Still, when we consider these industrially developed techniques, we have to temper our enthusiasm with the reality that services must be decentralized. They must serve small numbers of varied human beings. Therefore, modern mathematically based approaches often fail and the low volume makes the costs of change hard to recover. Thus, the public administrator's job is likely to remain one of facilitating team-building and, on a larger scale, local service networks. More and more it will be at the level of effective managing at local networks that the productivity war will be won or lost.

PRODUCTIVITY, ACCOUNTABILITY, AND SMALL SIZE

There is, finally a dilemma: the organization that delivers services in a community would ideally be small; yet much of the technology of measuring productivity and, thus, facilitating accountability is not very adaptable to small organizations working in dispersed geographical areas. The reason for this is primarily cost-related. The costs of a study or a technique or an analyst can be spread over fewer clients or units of service or units of population. So the need is for approaches that have a low cost per unit.

Accountability is too often confused with accounting. Clearly one of its major aspects is the fiduciary responsibility of the public administrator. But it goes much further into being able to demonstrate to the constituencies of an organization that it has been responsive to their goals and needs and exercised a good stewardship of their resources.

Accountability technology is only one of many types of technology affecting services. Berg lists a number of problems [4]. A working list for public administration includes:

1. Small size of units,
2. Ownership and control dispersed,
3. Lack of a market measure of value,
4. Separation of technology provider and consumer,
5. Time horizon for decision-making, and
6. Supply of skills and funding available.

The small organization cannot afford heavy investments for evaluation or for the staff to meet accountability requirements (especially the new ones); local funding sources are not used to paying for the requisite manpower and skills. The cost of most accountability requirements do not vary much with the number of units of service provided. They are fixed costs primarily; their cost per unit relates inversely with the volume produced and, therefore, a small unit is affected more heavily than a larger one.

One example is that of a state that asks organizations soliciting funds from the public to have two people present when the mail containing donations from the public is opened. Their reasoning is clear. This prevents the possibility that one key employee could divert the donations. For small organizations with an office staff of one, or two, however, this constitutes a major hardship.

Smaller organizations may have ownership of their own domain, but not control of their own destiny. They cannot influence the accountability requirements imposed by their funding agencies, especially the state and federal governments, and often they lack leadership to set standards for the industry, if these bureaucracies are passive or conflicted.

Under most circumstances, when the private sector wishes to show its accountability to the public, it points out that the public can choose to purchase its products in the marketplace or not. In that sense the consumer is sovereign. But in the case of the public organization, we have no such measure of how the public values the services rendered, and the smaller organization lacks the wherewithal to launch extensive studies of what the public wants or values. Thus, they operate with a relatively limited knowledge about their consumers. There is a frequently made claim that they are more responsive to their markets because they are "closer" and hence more knowledgeable, which may not be true.

One big problem in expressing accountability for the technological and economic behavior of public organizations is their lack of sufficient resources to innovate. The investment in technological development can be made only by the individual or firm that hopes to sell the services or goods to a large number of small units and recover the development costs much more easily. Thus, expertise in accountability and evaluation tends to be centered in a few large organizations, such as the federal governments, some state governments, some universities, and consulting organizations. The latter especially can provide services to a large number of potential clients. These services can be delivered as applied technology or as technological transfer (training), but there are a number of problems when the consumer and the providers of technology come from separate backgrounds. The provider will develop what is most attractive to those who are ready to buy and tend to ignore those who have to be persuaded. The consumer of this technology is widely dispersed, harder to reach, and may have insufficient input and, hence, may lack commitment to the approach. There tends to be a poor match of available technology to the needs of the small consumer and a very slow rate of adoption by the consumer. This could be especially critical in an activity as threatening as accountability.

The pace of decision-making in public administration tends to be fast [6], often too fast considering the complexity of the problems being faced. This accountability technology must give fast results, if it is to give useful information at the next critical juncture—budget review, election, change of senior administrator. The choice of time-horizons (time of evaluations) for accountability can vastly affect the technology to be used. Differing time horizons are often behind apparent differences of opinion among evaluators. This focus on the short-term accountability measure (*e.g.*, for political reasons) often puts consumers at odds with social planners, who usually focus on long-term effects. But the providers of technology tend to favor the short approach, too, because it matches the consumers' felt needs and provides a quicker return on investment.

There also is the obvious and important problem of a shortage of personnel and funds to develop accountability technology, especially for small agencies. It is all too easy to say that the people just are not there. It may be true in many cases, but often that is an argument people fall back on all too easily, as an excuse for not developing skills that, though rigorous, are simple. An example is cost accounting. The field of accounting is wrapped in a mystique: about professionalism and technical rules and high levels of training; yet the elementary aspects are ridiculously simple and should be known by any public administrator who expects to be taken seriously by his or her peers or subordinates.

Having noted the problems of personnel and funding, we now proceed first to an assessment of the approaches that might be used and then to the question of what might be done to overcome these problems.

Stages of Accountability

Table 4 shows four stages in the process of producing public goods and services—inputs, processes, outputs, and benefits. We have earlier argued that a public administrator should concern himself not with some of these but with all four. Therefore, he or she should plan to be accountable for performance at all four stages.

For each constituency that the public administrator is accountable to, there are a few basic questions that he or she must be prepared to answer [29]:

1. Am I dealing with the current problems that this constituency would like me to address using values consistent with theirs?
2. Is my program for this constituency based on sound hypotheses about the problem and effective solutions to it?
3. Given these hypotheses, am I using cost-effective methods to implement the chosen alternative?
4. In implementing these methods am I fully utilizing the resources available to me in terms of resource allocations, control of costs, time, and effort versus accomplishment in quantity and quality?

Table 4. The stages of accountability.

TYPE OF ACCOUNTABILITY	STAGE			
	INPUTS	PROCESS	OUTPUTS	BENEFITS
To board—				
By coherency check:	Sufficiency of resources	Resource utilization *cost-effective methods* Manpower plan	Sound hypotheses about *impacts sought* Goal statements	Relatedness to current problem
To other constituencies—				
By constituency through:	*Program budget* Cost accounting system	Conformity to: program *goals and plans* Service values of constituency	*Goal statements* *Service statistics* *Performance budget* Service ambience	*Client surveys* Special studies
To the Payers—				
By financial audit:	Fund accounting	*Audit reports* Manpower records	Cost accounting system	Special analyses
By management audit:	*Standards* *Level of effort* Certification	Site visit *Manpower plan* Accrediation	*Performance budget* Effort allocation	Client surveys
To professionals—				
By technical audit:	*Service standards* Line-item budget	Site visit *Standards review* Comparative analysis	*Peer review* Comparative outcomes	Special studies
By coherency check:	Sufficiency of resources	Resource utilization Cost effective methods Manpower	Sound hypotheses *about impacts sought* Goal statements	Relatedness to current problems

5. Have I acquired sufficient resources that, if used efficiently and effectively, will meet the needs of the constituency in terms of quantity and quality?

One type of constituency is the governing board of the agency and professional peers who will ask these same kinds of questions in the coherency check mentioned earlier. The question of coherency asks whether, once you have dealt with the needs of each constituency, you can answer the same questions for the organization as a whole. Is there a single philosophy that governs its approach to problems and to its set of constituencies?

This coherency check has been placed first in Table 4 under the stages of accountability to the governing board and last for the peer group—an alpha and omega for accountability in the small organization. Although unsophisticated, it does require wisdom and insight. A good example of a coherency check is the PASS (Program Analysis of Service Systems) evaluation system developed by Wolfensberger for institutions dealing with the retarded and other developmentally disabled under a philosophy of normalization of treatment and life style [37].

Each specific constituency will need to be assured that it's interests and goals have been attended to efficiently and effectively. Thus, it becomes necessary for the agency to provide data on the budget and cost report. Much of this can be prepared by using the standard reporting procedures required by the conventional financial audit used to establish fiduciary accountability under any system —whether or not specific constituencies request it. At the *process* stage, the public administrator must be prepared to argue or demonstrate that the program has been developed in accordance with the program's goals and its prior plan and how the services will be delivered in a manner consistent with the values of the constituency. One way of doing this is to take steps to sell the staff on the values attached to the delivery process. To get staff conformity is a continuing process, and the administrator should take the credit for it (or the blame) [28]. This is why service ambience is listed as an accountability measure under output.

Accountability at the *output* stage naturally starts with a goal statement, preferably one expressed in terms of service levels—levels of quantity and quality of services to be provided a client group. With this the agency can then compare planned versus actual services in quantity and quality and then compare both against the budget. Also, the quality can be evaluated by looking at the ambience provided the client as expressed through professional and user assessments.

The *benefits* stage for constituents is a more nebulous stage, because it is clear that benefits in the public sector can be the product of multiple programs involving multiple agencies and jurisdictions. Nevertheless, it is still possible for local agencies operating on a small scale to consider client studies or special analyses of perceived benefits. These are best accomplished through cooperative arrangements with other agencies having similar values and client interests.

In olden days accountability related primarily to the use of public funds. The idea was not one of effectiveness, but rather of a fiduciary responsibility for the use of public funds. This is still true to a large extent. This often tends to be a biased affair. The auditor has a vested interest in finding something wrong to prove the need for continued audits. There is little reward in reporting that everything is all right, but in recent years a more positive orientation has emerged, *i.e.*, toward problem-solving. This is best exemplified by the Government Accounting Office (GAO), which, as an arm of the congress, is now involved in evaluation as opposed to technical nit-picking. The orientation of such organizations now allows for the identification of substantive, rather than technical, areas of accountability. So, taken in proper perspective, the financial audit still represents a major opportunity for generating and assessing useful data about the organization and how it allocates and utilizes its critical resources. This process requires that the organization appropriately account for the funds received for specific programs and goals and relate this to the manpower efforts expended on behalf of these programs. These data are critical for internal transfers of funds among programs and for the crucial interchanges between the organization and its political-economic-environmental network of organizations and agencies [34; 2]. The first step in financial accountability is fund accounting, which in its extreme form involves accounting for money "in several separate pots, each of which is called a fund. Each fund has its own set of accounts, that are self-balancing, and each fund is therefore a separate entity, almost as if it were a separate business. The purpose of this device is to insure that the organization uses the resources made available to each fund only for the purposes designated for that fund" [3, p. 104]. But, as Anthony and Herzlinger point out, this approach is not important to the management process. If anything, it substantially reduces managerial flexibility and coherency. Yet the administrator must be prepared to show that funds allocated for a purpose were applied to that purpose. Inasmuch as most public organizations are very labor-intensive, they rely heavily on manpower-utilitzation reports to justify the basis for charges to funds and programs. Thus, while the administrator and the professionals may be very aware of the imprecision and arbitrariness of time reports, considerable attention should be given to how they look. In a number of organizations, the skillful manipulation of time allocations on the employees' weekly or monthly sheets is a key to meeting mutual inconsistencies in requirements of coherency and accountability.

These same time records then become the basis for cost accounting for services delivered and for future performance budgets for constituencies and funders. In a cost accounting system the costs incurred are allocated according to an agreed set of game rules to the services being provided. The objective is to retrieve the full cost, including overheads (space, insurance, administrators). There are a number of procedures for this, though, unfortunately, they vary with funding agencies. The administrator or an associate must be familiar with these differences or the organization can be left with certain costs unfunded. In the hospital industry, it has been necessary for the institutions to go to court to protect their interests against the conflicting accountability and payment rules of third-party payers.

Clearly there is a dilemma here for the administrator. Time records are often set up to reflect the funding of the positions rather than the duties performed by the employees in the current time period. This meets the minimal needs for accountability to the funding source and allows for greater flexibility in actual manpower allocation. But the use of these same time records for cost accounting purposes yield biased cost accounting data for management decision-making. The only way out of this seems to be two separate estimates of time allocation. The time sheets for accountability purposes and the use of special *ad hoc*, but more accurate, estimates of time allocations for costing for managerial decisions. Small organizations have to use their limited personnel in multiple roles, and cannot afford to be bound completely by funding sources. Larger, more bureaucratized organizations handling larger volumes of work can afford the slack manpower that such compartmentalization induces.

In a small organization it is best to link the fund accounting requirements as closely as possible with program budgets. This will reduce the accounting costs and also give the most flexibility within programs.

Just as the public accountant has the responsibility to audit the financial transactions of an organization, procedures can be developed to audit the management process as well. The management literature is full of rules to follow in assessing management performance. In the public sector the most widely cited are those of Drucker [10; 11]. He calls for a discipline that exhibits a clear definition of "what our business is and what it would be," clear goals and objectives, priorities for concentrating on selected targets with measures of performance attached, feedback and use of results for self-control, an audit of objectives and results, and a mechanism for "sloughing off" obsolete or unproductive activities.

Marvin Bower also sets up some criteria for the manager (administrator) that include Drucker's norms and add [7] :

developing an organizational philosophy—"the way we do things around here,"
planning the organizational structure,
providing personnel,
providing facilities,
providing capital, and
activating people—commanding and motivating.

He suggests as a philosophy:

1. high ethical standards,
2. decision-making based on facts,
3. people judged on the basis of performance,
4. heavy emphasis on adjustment to the environment, and
5. administration carried out with a sense of urgency.

The last items of both of these lists imply to Bowers an individual leader who works with zest; sees time as the scarcest commodity in his or her life; is decisive; seeks out and faces up to problems, especially difficult personnel problems; and focuses all at once on short-run performance, and the development of people *and* the building of viable work groups.

More specific standards may also exist. For example, those developed for voluntary health, welfare, and recreation organizations by the National Budget and Consultation Committee [22] set "standards" dealing with governance, personnel policies, budget, planning, interorganizational relations, education programs, financial and management accounting, public reporting, and evaluation. Clearly a management audit would take into account such standards and evaluate the level of effort being maintained by the staff and leadership.

Another way of being accountable for the *inputs* is by providing personnel who are certified as being appropriate and qualified by professional organizations. This implies the acceptance of someone else's standards rather than developing one's own.

With respect to *process*, a relatively efficient method of presenting evidence about one's quality of management is to convene a team of experts for a "site visit"—an expert review of programs, policies, and practices. The team can be managerial, technical, or both. This tends to be a very superficial process, but it also can be a very effective review. The key is that the visitors are allowed to fan out through the organization, talk to a number of people individually, and then come back and compare notes. The report of such a group can be a self-serving document or it can be a surprisingly useful analysis of process, identifying strong points *and* suggesting where operations can be improved.

A similar process is used often to review an organization for accreditation by a professional body, where one exists. This process usually involves a set of standards and a review by a visiting team of experts. It also tends to mix the technical and the administrative. Accreditation teams tend to emphasize the technical in their rhetoric and then to report on and weight most heavily the procedural side of administration, because that is more concrete. Where an organization provides an intangible professional service, accreditation and certification carry considerable weight as proxies for more direct accountability measures.

The management audit must emphasize the area of manpower development. That is the future lifeblood of the organization. It also provides evidence that the administrator is giving due attention to the critical resource—critical by the amount of money consumed and critical to the quality of the services delivered.

The management audit also would look at performance budgets and the effort allocated to various program components. It might or might not choose to look at client attitudes toward the service-delivery system depending on the resources made available and the issues that were apparent during the planning stages and the interviews of staff and board during a site visit.

The technical audit is closely intertwined with the management audit. Here the same or different people would review the standards of service that had been established and the specific items to be used in the programs as expressed by a line-item budget. A site visit is also useful here, as is a review of how well service standards are being met. These standards and the performance against them can be compared to the performance of similar organizations both in terms of the process used and the impacts achieved.

To demonstrate effectiveness it may be necessary to have a group of professionals from outside the organization observe the results achieved on paper and in interviews with selected staff and users. They can then suggest where the organization stands in terms of its effectiveness and efficiency. Because services are so intangible, the administrator who does not undertake to have reports from outside evaluators is opening up the organization to injury by any dissatisfied subset of users, unless this evaluation is performed and then made available to those to whom he or she is publicly accountable.

Peer evaluations and site visits need not be costly. In many fields professionals tend to do this as mutual favors to each other and as a professional responsibility, and still accept the federal government standard of $100–$150 per day plus travel and *per diem*. The important thing is to provide for adequate staff support including a good briefing, preferably by an outsider who knows the organization well, and ample, qualified clerical and editorial assistance in completing and circulating the report. In areas where this is routinely done, the start-up costs are low for the participants who know what to look for, especially if one or more has participated in this routine in prior years and can provide continuity.

It should be clear that the working definition of accountability used here is very like that of evaluation. The dictionary definition of accountability stresses terms like *answerable, liable,* and *responsible*. It implies that the public administrator should show that he can answer whether or not he has behaved responsibly and done the best with what he has. Administrators have to be prepared to demonstrate just that, within the limits of technology and resources available to them. In some cases the responses may be detailed, as with the accounting system, or as simple as "Yes, sir, we did consider that question in developing our program and we have allocated adequate resources to meet that goal." Evaluations may be necessary by regulation in some fields, but the concept of accountability necessitates them today even where the regulations do not.

Improving Accountability Technology

This discussion started with reference to why small organizations have difficulty with the technology of accountability. The first reason comes not from size, but from the fact that small organizations have relatively little experience with accountability and evaluation. Only recently have accountability demands been great and focus been on anything but the larger, more sophisticated organizations. The first rule when encountering these new demands is to remember that they are simpler than you think and constitute what a competent administrator ought to be concerned about anyway. The question is how not to be swept overboard by documentation requirements. Remember that it is much cheaper to generate documentation as part of the planning and evaluation process than to do it well after the fact to meet accountability requirements.

The key to improved technology and reduced bureaucracy for accountability is for small units to band together into local working groups and into a professional association. The former will provide manpower on a reciprocal basis for management audits, technical audits, and coherency checks. The latter can work toward an industry-wide set of standards, procedures, and evaluation protocols. In many cases any such relatively solid group can receive assistance from funding agencies to develop these and train personnel regionally to use them. These funding agencies are hard pressed by their own accountability pressures, and are all too pleased to be able to show their constituencies that they are doing something concrete in this area.

Also, such an industry or agency-representative organization can lobby for more reasonable standards and documentation requirements in the accountability area. In essence this is an attempt to improve the interface between technology-provider and technology-user. Very often the experts who develop accountability requirements are enamored of their own techniques and want to see them applied most fully. The administrator must push to see that they are used only to the extent that the added benefits outweigh the extended costs. But their more politically sensitive supervisors usually lend a sympathetic ear to suggestions about how to make the guidelines and regulations more workable.

The key element here is to get in early, to get maximum agency input into the process of formulating guidelines and standards from the beginning. It is very much like the process of bidding on a request-for-proposal (RFP). The one who has the best chance is the one who worked with the government to develop the specifications. The same is true with accountability requirements. Early collaborators are respected for their input and insight. Latecomers are suspect as self-serving. And those who have experienced trouble meeting the initial accountability requirements are often seen as candidates for punitive responses. Only if their leaders respond to the process of setting accountability requirements as a group can they avoid the dilemma quoted by Berg: "American society has not yet learned how to rapidly update its control mechanism to better reconcile technical advance and quantifiable aspects of progress with other facets of the good and safe life. To an alarming extent, society is not even aware of the problem" [25, p. 148].

NOTES AND REFERENCES

1. Adams, J. Stacy. "The Structure and Dynamics in Organizational Boundary Roles." In *Handbook of Industrial and Organizational Psychology*. Edited by M. D. Dunnette. Chicago: Rand-McNally, 1976, pp. 1175–1199.
2. Aldrich, Howard. "Resource Dependence and Interorganizational Relations: Local Employment Service Offices and Social Sector Organizations." *Administration and Society* 7(1976): 419–463.
3. Anthony, Robert N., and Regina E. Herzlinger. *Management Control in Nonprofit Organizations*. Homewood, Ill.: Richard D. Irwin, 1975.
4. Berg, Sanford V. "Determinants of Technological Change in the Service Industries." *Technological Forecasting and Social Change* 5(1973): 407–426.
5. Benson, J. Kenneth. "The Interorganizational Network as a Political Economy." *Administrative Science Quarterly* 20(1975): 229–249.
6. Bower, Joseph L. "Effective Public Management." *Harvard Business Review* 55(1977): 131–140.
7. Bower, Marvin. *Will to Manage.* New York: McGraw-Hill, 1966.
8. Cordtz, Dan. "City Hall Discovers Productivity." *Fortune* October, 1971.
9. Downs, Anthony. *Inside Bureaucracy.* Boston: Little, Brown, 1967.
10. Drucker, Peter F. "Managing the Public Sector Insititution." *The Public Interest* 33(1973): 43–60.
11. Drucker, Peter F. *Management.* New York: Harper and Row, 1974.
12. Gillings, Dennis. "Evaluation: A Methodology for Determining the Effectiveness of a Social Program in Terms of Goal Fulfillment." Department of Biostatistics, School of Public Health, University of North Carolina at Chapel Hill. Reproduced in part in Anthony and Herzlinger, pp. 145–148.
13. Grubb, Charles T. *Program Evaluation and Local Administration.* University of North Carolina at Chapel Hill, Institute for Social Services Planning, School of Social Work, 1977.
14. Halberstam, David. *The Best and the Brightest.* New York: Random House, 1972.
15. Hatry, Harry P. and Donald M. Fisk. "Improving Productivity and Productivity Measurement in Local Governments." Washington, D.C.: The National Commission on Productivity, 1971.
16. Horton, R. D. "Productivity and Productivity Bargaining in Government: A Critical Analysis." *Public Administration Review* 36(1976): 412.
17. Holzer, Marc, ed. *Productivity in Public Organizations.* Port Washington, N.Y.: Kennikat Press, 1976.
18. Kotler, Philip. *Marketing for Nonprofit Organizations.* Englewood Cliffs, N.J.: Prentice-Hall, 1975.
19. Kotter, J. P. "The Psychological Contract: Managing the Joining-Up Process." *California Management Review* 15(1973): 91–99.
20. Levinson, D. J., and B. M. Astrachan. "Organizational Boundaries: Entry Into the Mental Health Center." *Administration in Mental Health* (1974): 3–12.

21. Levinson, Harry. "Management by Whose Objectives." *Harvard Business Review* (1970): 124–133.
22. Lippincott, E., and E. Aannestad. "Management of Voluntary Welfare Services." *Harvard Business Review* (1964): 87–98.
23. Macleod, Roderick K. "Program Budgeting Works in Nonprofit Institutions." *Harvard Business Review* (1971): 59–69.
24. McLaughlin, Curtis P. "Strategic Planning and Control in Small Health Organizations." *Health Care Management Review* 1(1976): 45-53.
25. Nelson, R. R., M. J. Peck, and E. K. Kalachek. *Technology, Economic Growth and Public Policy.* Washington, D.C.: The Brookings Institution, 1967.
26. Pressman, Jeffrey L., and Aaron B. Wildavsky. *Implementation.* Berkeley: University of California Press, 1973.
27. Ross, J. P., and J. Burkhead. *Productivity in the Local Government Sector.* Lexington, Mass.: Lexington Books, 1974.
28. Sasser, W. E., and S. P. Arbeit. "Selling Jobs in the Service Sector." *Business Horizons* (June 1976): 61-65.
29. Schaefer, Morris. *Evaluation/Decision Making in Health Planning and Administration.* HADM Monograph Series Number 3. Chapel Hill, N.C.: Department of Health Administration, School of Public Health, 1973, pp. 84-101.
30. Shapiro, Benson P. "Marketing for Nonprofit Organizations." *Harvard Business Review* (1973): 123-132.
31. Schulberg, B. C., A. Sheldon, and F. Baker, eds. *Program Evaluation in the Health Fields.* New York: Behavioral Publications, 1969.
32. Suchman, Edward A. *Evaluative Research: Principles and Practices in Public Service and Social Programs.* New York: Russell Sage Foundation, 1967.
33. Van de Van, A. H. and A. L. Delbecq. "A Task Contingent Model of Work Unit Structure." *Administrative Science Quarterly* 19(1974): 183-197.
34. Wamsley, G. L., and M. N. Zald. "The Political Economy of Public Organizations." *Public Administration Review* (1973): 62-73.
35. Weinberg, Martha W. *Managing the State.* Cambridge, Mass.: MIT Press, 1977.
36. Wise, H., R. Beckhard, I. Rubin, and A. L. Kyte. *Making Health Teams Work.* Cambridge, Mass.: Ballinger, 1974.
37. Wolfensberger, W., *et al. Normalization: The Principle of Normalization in Human Services.* Toronto: National Institute on Mental Retardation, 1972.
38. Joint Economic Committee, US Congress, *Measuring and Enhancing Productivity in the Federal Sector.* 92nd Congress, 2nd Session, 1972.
39. Joint Federal Productivity Project. *Guidelines for Evaluating Work Measurement Systems in the Federal Government.* 1972.

3

Conceptual and Technical Considerations in Cost-Benefit Analysis

James R. Knickman
New York University

INTRODUCTION

Definition

Cost-benefit analysis is a strategy for determining how best to allocate scarce resources for the provision of public goods. Public goods include all the activities, services, and social programs that are sponsored by governments [1]. Since it is not possible to operate all conceivable government programs with scarce resources, it is necessary to compare and evaluate proposed alternative programs and to develop criteria for determining which programs should be undertaken and which not.

In cost-benefit analysis, the basis for a recommendation that a program should be implemented is the common sense idea that the value of a program's benefits to society should exceed its costs. Benefits of a government program are defined as any valued end result of the program. A benefit might be a physical output or commodity, a service, or an intangible factor such as security, scenic beauty, or social justice. The value of any benefit, or end result, is considered to be the amount of money individuals in society would be willing to pay for the benefit. Costs would include the value of foregone benefits, because using a given amount of resources on one government program precludes benefits from other projects that were not implemented.

Although the basic idea of cost-benefit analysis is simple, a series of conceptual and technical issues must be understood in order to use this technique properly for evaluating alternative programs.

The conceptual issues focus on the precise definition of the criteria used to rank-order public programs by their social values. It is first necessary to justify the use of hypothetical willingness to pay as a measure of a program's value to an individual [2]. Secondly, a criterion must be specified and justified for choosing between two programs when some people prefer one program and other people prefer a second program. This case of conflicting preferences is common for government programs, since many programs have at least some opponents.

The technical issues in cost-benefit analysis focus on specifying the exact end results of a public program and on measuring individuals' willingness to pay for these end results. The specification of end results, or the enumeration of benefits, is not always straightforward, for public programs often have probabilistic results. They affect the likelihood that some social goal will be achieved, rather than absolutely assuring that the goal will be achieved. Once a program's benefits are enumerated, a cost-benefit analysis must determine individuals' willingness to pay for the benefits. The measurement of individuals' willingness to pay for a public program must be done indirectly because individuals do not usually pay directly for public programs. The method used to measure willingness to pay varies from study to study. But, in general, cost-benefit studies attempt to measure a public good's value by identifying a market price of a comparable good or service that is produced by a firm and sold in the marketplace. This market price is often a good measure of individual's willingness to pay for a public output.

Applications

Cost-benefit analysis can be used in many different contexts. In principle, it can be used as a guide for distributing society's resources to alternative public projects, with the explicit goal of maximizing the social value of all goods and services produced in society. In this sense, cost-benefit analysis is a guide to a central planner for optimal resource allocation.

In a more limited context, however, cost-benefit analysis can be used to make simple choices between any two proposed activities or strategies for achieving a social goal [3]. The cost-benefit analyst attempts to decide which alternative use of resources will best improve the well-being of individuals in society given existing institutional arrangements, the existing distribution of private resources, and existing public programs. This use of cost-benefit analysis ignores the question of whether the *status quo* plus one new program is better or worse than radical changes in the *status quo*.

The history of the development of cost-benefit analysis indicates that it has been used primarily to choose from among a limited set of alternative uses of economic resources [4]. The first systematic use of the ideas incorporated in cost-benefit analysis was in the evaluation of American water-resource development projects in the 1930s [5]. The Flood Control Act of 1936 mandated that all proposed water-resource projects meet the criteria that "the benefits to whomsoever they may accrue (be) in excess of the estimated costs" [6]. Cost-benefit techniques were also used in the 1930s to evaluate highway construction projects in Oregon [7].

During World War II, the ideas of cost-benefit analysis were employed by the United States government to guide decisions regarding allocation of resources [8]. After the war, other applications of cost-benefit analysis were studied. Applications were developed for cost-benefit analysis in the areas of transportation, health, recreation, education, manpower training, and urban renewal, among others. In the late sixties, the federal government initiated a budgeting process termed PPBS: the Planning, Programming, and Budgeting System. PPBS called for "Special Studies" by all agencies to justify program plans. These Special Studies were to "review in terms of costs and benefits the effectiveness of prior efforts, compare alternative mixes of programs, (and) balance increments in costs against increments in effectiveness at various program levels" [9]. Partly due to the tremendous time needed to evaluate all public programs every year, PPBS was substantially changed in 1971 so that only new programs would be evaluated in terms of benefits and costs.

A separate strand of cost-benefit research is concerned with public investment analysis in developing nations. Both the United Nations and the Organization for Economic Cooperation and Development (OECD) have published guidelines for making public investment decisions in developing areas of the world [10], *i.e.*, for evaluating alternative strategies for making major investments in a local economy. This is a case in which cost-benefit analysis determines optimal resource allocations for achieving long-term social goals, rather than allocations that marginally improve the *status quo*.

In the following sections, the conceptual basis for cost-benefit analysis is outlined, and a series of technical issues related to the measurement of benefits and costs in program evaluation is discussed. The principle aim of this essay is to explore three basic aspects of cost benefit analysis:

1. the concept of valuation;
2. the delineation of what should and should not be considered a benefit or cost of public programs; and
3. techniques for measuring the value of a program's benefits in terms of willingness to pay.

The discussion attempts to show that cost-benefit analysis is best considered a foundation for evaluating alternative programs, rather than a well defined set of specific procedures.

THE CONCEPTUAL FRAMEWORK OF COST-BENEFIT ANALYSIS

The Two Components of Program Evaluation

Two separate components of any program evaluation should be distinguished. The first step in evaluating a public program is to measure what the program does; the outputs or effects of a government program must be identified and measured.

In the private sector, the identification of outputs is usually straightforward. The produced commodity must be identifiable in order to be sold at an established price. Thus, food, clothing, automobiles, newspapers, and gasoline are all commodities that can readily be traded from a producer to a consumer.

Sometimes, public sector outputs also are easy to identify. For example, publicly constructed dams supply electricity and irrigation water, two outputs that are easy to measure. Similarly, sanitation services involve the collection of trash, a service that can be measured in terms of barrels collected per day.

Often, however, public outputs are not so easy to identify. For instance, the government-sponsored Head Start program provided preschool learning activities for disadvantaged children, but the principle output the program was expected to produce was greater achievement in school for the program participants. To measure this output, it is necessary to understand and identify the relationship between preschool activities and future educational achievement. Similarly, job counseling programs are designed to make it easier for unemployed individuals to find jobs. To identity this output it is necessary to determine the relationship between job counseling and job attainment.

The problem in identifying the outputs of public programs of this nature is that the programs do not always affect every person in the same way. Some people who receive job counseling may get jobs and others may not. Also some people who do not receive job counseling will get jobs and other people who received job counseling would have found jobs even without the counseling. Thus, the program has probabilistic effects; the program, if successful, increases the likelihood that a person will find a job. The relationship between the program and the desired goal of the program is not completely deterministic because numerous other factors partially determine whether or not the goal is attained. In situations where the public program is not the only cause of some social goal, it is necessary to determine statistically whether or not the program has a positive effect on the attainment of the goal.

A rich literature on evaluating public programs in terms of their "effectiveness" or outputs is available [11]. In general, the methods of experimental design, quasi-experimental design, or multivariate analysis are used to compare what happens when the public program is in operation to what happens when the program is not in operation.

In numerous cases, evaluations of the social effectiveness of programs have indicated that the programs have no measured effects on the goals they are designed to achieve. For instance, some studies of Head Start have shown that the program does not significantly increase school achievement scores. Similarly, some manpower training programs have been shown to have no effect on future earnings capacities of participants.

In cases where a program has been shown to have no positive effects on the achievement of some social goal, it is easy to decide that the program should be abandoned or changed. By any reasonable criterion, a program with no positive effects will be judged not worth the effort to run.

If a program is shown to have a positive effect on the attainment of some social goal, however, a second type of evaluation is necessary in order to judge whether or not this positive effect is worth the money it costs to run the program. Since economic resources are finite in supply, not every activity that has a positive effect can be undertaken. It is this second step of the evaluation process that distinguishes cost-benefit analysis. Rather than focusing exclusively on measuring the effect of a program on a social goal, cost-benefit analysis uses an established and consistent set of criteria for determining whether the value of the benefits due to a program exceed the value of the resources needed to run the program.

In this paper, attention is focused on this valuation aspect of cost-benefit analysis. The methods used in cost-benefit analysis for determining the "effectiveness" of a public program are synonymous with the methodologies developed throughout the field of program evaluation. The valuation of a program's effects, however, is distinctive to the cost-benefit framework.

The Criterion for Judging the Social Value of Public Programs

The criterion used in cost-benefit analysis to judge whether or not a public project should be undertaken can be stated simply: If the amount of money each and every person in society would be willing to pay for the project is aggregated, and if the sum then exceeds the total economic costs of the project, the project should be undertaken. Economic costs of a project are defined as the value of all real resources that are used to produce the project.

The justification for this "benefits greater than costs" criteria for judging public projects is based on the view that the goal of government activity is to produce goods and services that are of value to individuals in society. This social goal is sometimes termed the aggregate consumption goal: government should attempt to maximize the dollar value of all goods and services in society.

The Pareto Principle As a Basis for Resource Allocation Decisions

The aggregate consumption goal is an efficiency goal. It can be defended on the basis of the Pareto principle, which is a key normative assumption of welfare economics [12]. The Pareto principle judges any allocation of resources in society to be inefficient if those resources could be reallocated so that some people are made better off, but no one is made worse off due to the reallocation. "Well-offness" is defined in terms of the dollar value individuals place on the set of goods and services they have under any given allocation of resources.

The decision criterion of cost-benefit analysis, however, differs in one important way from the Pareto principle. Whereas the Pareto principle would suggest that a project be undertaken, i.e., that resources be reallocated, if some people are made better off by the project and no one is made worse off, the actual criterion used in cost-benefit analysis requires only that the sum of the benefits across all individuals be greater than the sum of the costs across all individuals in order to justify the project. Thus, the cost-benefit criterion justifies the existence of some programs that cause some people in society to be worse off than they would be in the absence of these programs.

This cost-benefit criterion is sometimes termed the "Potential Pareto Principle" because any project that is judged to be socially desirable by this principle could potentially be justified by the Pareto principle if those who are made better off by a project would be required to compensate those who are made worse off [13]. The compensation would have to be enough that the losers would be indifferent between not having the project done and having the project done with compensation. Thus, instead of requiring that those who benefit from a project compensate those who do not benefit, the potential Pareto criterion requires only that the size of the gains and the size of the losses associated with a program be such that compensations could potentially be made.

The value judgment involved with the potential Pareto criterion is more controversial than that of the Pareto criterion. The potential Pareto criterion assumes that from a social viewpoint a dollar's worth of benefits (measured in terms of willingness to pay) to one person just offsets a dollar's worth of costs to another person. Similarly, the criterion assumes that a dollar's worth of benefits has the same social value no matter who is the recipient of the benefits. In this sense, the cost-benefit criterion is distributionally neutral; it ignores the question of who benefits and focuses exclusively on determining the aggregate quantity of benefits.

The principal justification for the potential Pareto criterion is that compensations or income redistributions that are judged desirable or equitable can be made through the taxation system. Thus, if a particular program helps one group of people, but has a detrimental effect on another group of people, rather than not undertaking the program, it might be sensible to initiate the program and to give a tax break to the group of people made worse off due to the program. Often, however, compensations will not be considered necessary because individuals who are hurt by some programs are helped by others. Also, those who oppose a project may be judged to deserve the cost imposed by the project. Consider, for example, an antipollution law that results in a net cost to an industrial firm due to expenditures the firm must make to reduce pollution. It is unlikely that most individuals in society will think the firm should be compensated for its net losses resulting from the antipollution law.

In some cases, it is costly to use the tax system to make compensations that are judged to be fair. Direct transfers in the form of tax reductions can affect the work incentive of individuals and the investment incentive of firms. By affecting various economic incentives, direct transfers through the tax system can thus have unintended and undesirable effects on resource allocation.

Whenever the tax system is not useful for making desired compensations, constraints can be set on the project choice process so that only projects that have "socially acceptable" distributions of benefits and costs among individuals are considered. Decision-makers must decide which distributions are "socially acceptable." Along these lines, I. M. D. Little [14] suggests that the potential Pareto criterion be used for evaluating public projects, but that projects judged desirable by this criterion be adopted only if they result in "a good distribution of wealth." He says that decision-makers must decide on the definition of "a good distribution of wealth."

Similarities and Dissimilarities of Private and Public Investment Criteria

It is helpful to understand the relationship between the investment criteria used in the private sector and those in the public sector, which are outlined in the text. In many ways, the two criteria are directly analogous. A private sector firm will produce an output whenever the potential revenues from the sale of the output exceed or just equal the estimated production costs. Revenues are determined by the market price, and the market price represents each purchaser's minimum willingness to pay for the output.

If each purchaser's minimum willingness to pay (*i.e.*, the market price) is aggregated, this sum will always exceed the total cost to the producer. Thus, private sector goods are produced if and only if aggregate value, measured by willingness to pay, exceeds total supply costs.

The key difference between the results of decisions in the private sector relative to the public sector is that, in the case of the private sector for any given commodity, no one suffers a loss due to costs that exceed benefits. If an individual does not judge the value of a given commodity to be worth its costs, he or she is free to not purchase it. Thus, reallocations in the private sector are made on the basis of the Pareto principle rather than the potential Pareto principle. The reason individual choices are mostly not possible in the public sector is related to the joint consumption properties of most public goods.

The Willingness-to-Pay Provision

It is important to understand the link between willingness to pay and the value of any given commodity. The use of willingness to pay as a measure of value is based on reasoning developed in microeconomics. If a person is willing to pay $10 for a newly available commodity, this willingness must imply that the individual considers himself better off by spending the $10 on the new commodity than on any other available commodity. This leads economists to state that the person values the commodity more than any other commodity that costs $10. Similarly, it follows that if willingness to pay is $12 for one item and $10 for a second item, then the first item is more valued than the second item.

By valuing a public project in terms of willingness to pay, cost-benefit analysis measures the outputs of all alternative projects in a single, comparable unit: the dollar value of the project. This common unit of measurement allows for the comparison of the value of diverse types of outputs and diverse types of costs. It should be emphasized that dollar value is not the only value index that could conceivably be devised for comparing benefits and costs of alternative public projects. Neverthless, since willingness to pay in terms of dollars is explicitly revealed in the marketplace for many goods and services, the dollar value index is a convenient base for comparing alternative projects.

It is helpful to keep in mind that the dollar value of a commodity is a relative, rather than an absolute, measure of value. The use of willingness to pay as a measure of value is restricted to comparisons; dollar value is not helpful for understanding anything about the inherent or absolute value of a commodity or a state of the world. Fortunately public decision-making always involves the choice between two alternatives; *i.e.*, undertaking one program rather than a second, or using resources for a public project rather than leaving resources in the private sector to produce private goods and services.

Willingness to pay should be distinguished from what the person considers a fair price. If, for example, an unregulated monopolist charges a price that exceeds cost of supply, a person may consider the price to be unfair. Despite his or her feeling about the unfairness of the price, the person might still be willing to pay the price set by the monopolist because he or she values the commodity and cannot obtain it elsewhere.

The Treatment of Nonefficiency Goals

A possible criticism of the cost-benefit approach to valuing public programs is that the potential Pareto criterion emphasizes the aggregate goal of public activity to the exclusion of other legitimate social goals. For instance, in addition to projects that increase the value of aggregate consumption, the United Nations [15] lists the following activities as legitimate concerns of governments in developing nations: 1) redistributing income, 2) lowering unemployment rates, 3) increasing the economic growth rate, 4) decreasing reliance on outside governments, and 5) the supply of "merit wants" [16].

Some research in recent years has addressed the question of how best to incorportate nonefficiency goals into the cost-benefit framework. One area of agreement among people who have thought about the problem is that a value judgment must be made concerning society's willingness to forego aggregate consumption in order to achieve other goals. The role of making explicit value judgments belongs to a decision-maker, however, rather than to an analyst.

Some researchers take the view that cost-benefit analysis should be concerned only with the evaluation of proposed projects in terms of the projects' aggregate consumption effects. This view holds that the analysis of a project's effects on other goals should be done independently, and that cost-benefit analysis should be considered only one part of an evaluation and just one input into the decision-making process.

In practice, one evaluator is usually responsible for assessing all aspects of a proposed project. In this case, a complete evaluation should include an analysis of the net impact of the project on the value of aggregate consumption (*i.e.*, a statement of the benefits and costs related to the goods and services produced by the project) and a listing of the project's effects on nonefficiency goals that are relevant to the decision process.

Some research has been directed at aggregating into one measure both the social value of the goods and services produced by a project and the social value of other program effects. In principle, this aggregation can be done if decision-makers specify society's willingness to pay for any given nonefficiency goal. For instance, if a decision-maker states that society is willing to give up $1000 worth of goods and services to increase the level of employment by one person, then a cost-benefit analysis can quantitatively compare two programs that have varying effects on aggregate consumption and varying effects on employment. Consider, for example, two alternative public programs: program A results in an increase of $80,000 in the value of aggregate consumption along with an increase in total employment of 100 people; program B adds $120,000 to aggregate consumption and adds 50 people to the work force. Given the judgment that a unit increase in the employment level has a social value of $1000, the cost-benefit analysis can conclude that the total value of program A is $180,000 while the total value of program B is just $170,000.

To achieve this integration of efficiency and nonefficiency goals, however, an explicit statement of society's willingness to pay for nonefficiency social goals is essential. Often, decision-makers are unable or unwilling to articulate such an explicit value judgment. In this case, the effects of a project on various nonefficiency goals can be listed in the cost-benefit analysis only in nonvalue terms. A value judgment relating efficiency goals to nonefficiency goals must be made outside of the evaluation framework.

TECHNICAL ASPECTS OF COST-BENEFIT ANALYSIS

Enumerating Benefits

In conducting a cost-benefit analysis of a public project, it is essential to measure intended and unintended benefits, tangible and intangible benefits, benefits from extra outputs and benefits from saved inputs. In general, benefits of a public project are defined as any outputs, aspects, or effects of a public project that are of economic value to individuals in society [17]. Economic value is defined as the money that individuals would be willing to give up to ensure that a project is undertaken.

Intended and Unintended Benefits

In most instances, public projects have multiple effects. Although the program may be designed with the purpose of achieving just one goal, an evaluation of a program should consider all of the outputs or effects of the program [18]. For instance a preschool program may be developed to help children prepare for grade school classroom work. But, besides this effect on the children, the program may also allow an extra parent time to take a job. Both effects of the program must be considered in computing the total benefits of the preschool program. Analogously, a cancer-screening program has the intended benefit of identifying individuals with early stages of cancer, but examinations may also diagnose other health problems. Although this latter benefit may be unintended, it is of real value to society, or some members of society, and thus should be included as a benefit of the program.

One task of cost-benefit analysis is to identify all of the end results of a public program. Good intuition and a thorough knowledge of the environment affected by a given public project are necessary for the analyst to be capable of predicting what the intended and unintended effects of a project will be. Often, it is helpful to run a small-scale demonstration or experiment to study the likely effects of a public project. Recently, demonstration projects and experimental programs have been used to study a number of potential public programs including income support programs, public housing projects, public employment projects, and national health insurance plans.

Intangibles

Many cost-benefit analyses are criticized because they consider only tangible or easy to measure effects of public programs and ignore intangible considerations such as a public project's effects on natural scenery, clean air, quietude, self-esteem, or self-reliance.

The definition of an intangible in cost-benefit analysis is any end result (a benefit or a cost) of a public project that is not readily measured in quantitative terms. It is important that intangibles be such that individuals are willing to pay for them. Otherwise, intangibles have no economic value and should be excluded as benefits in cost-benefit analyses. However, if individuals would be willing to pay more money for a project that provides some given set of tangible benefits along with some intangible effects than for a second project that results in the same set of tangible benefits but no intangible effects, then these intangibles should be measured as benefits.

At the present time, methods for identifying and measuring intangibles and for determining their economic value are not well developed. When an intangible cannot be quantitatively measured, a cost-benefit analysis can describe only qualitatively the expected impact of a project on the intangible. The decision-maker will have to make a value judgment concerning the proper trade-offs between the economic value of tangible benefits and intangible benefits that result from public programs.

The method of accounting for intangible benefits and costs in a cost-benefit analysis is identical to the procedure suggested for integrating the consideration of nonefficiency goals into cost-benefit studies. In fact, there is no practical distinction between an intangible and a nonefficiency effect of a public program. Both are aspects of a program that cannot be quantitatively measured or valued in money terms in a manner comparable to other benefits and costs of a program.

Note that few things in life are inherently unmeasurable. A major task of research in cost-benefit analysis is to develop quantitative measures for difficult to measure effects of public policy. Concerning this, Haveman and Weisbrod make the following point

> In the historical process of developing measures, variables that were not measured at one point later came to be measured, and measures were constantly improved over the course of time. This is surely also the case for the benefits and costs relevant to economic analysis.

Saved Resources

In some instances, the principle benefit of a public project is that it reduces the costs of producing some output or service. For instance, a public sewer system makes it unnecessary for individual homeowners to purchase septic tanks or other means of waste disposal. In this case, each homeowner's willingness to pay for the public sewer system, assuming it produces the same quality of service, is the cost of the septic tank. The homeowner who does not have to buy a septic tank can use the saved resources to purchase other goods and services he or she values. A cost-benefit analysis would recommend the construction of a sewer system if the costs of the public system were less than the total costs of installing privately owned septic tanks.

Cases where public projects are aimed at reducing the use of private resources needed to supply some good or service are numerous. Expenditures on health screening programs are aimed at saving resources needed to treat illness; expenditures on highways are aimed at reducing travel time, which is a resource that can be used to produce additional work or additional leisure; expenditures on public transportation are aimed at saving resources needed to purchase and operate private transportation. It is important, therefore, to identify resources that are freed due to the goods or services supplied by a public project. The value of these saved resources should be counted as benefits caused by the public project.

Transfers

It is important to count as benefits only aspects of a program that add value to the aggregate goods and services in society. In particular, care should be taken to avoid counting as benefits any transfers of money from one individual to another. Transfers do not add value to aggregate consumption in society, because for every dollar's worth of benefits transferred to one person another person loses a dollar's worth of benefits. Thus, from a social perspective, the benefits and costs of a dollar's transfer just cancel each other.

Although income transfers are of no value from a cost-benefit perspective, it is clear that individuals in society do value at least some redistribution of income. The government, however, must justify transfers on the basis of a nonefficiency goal. Transfers do not add value to the amount of aggregate consumption in society and, therefore, cannot be justified on efficiency grounds.

Transfers can be found in many guises in government programs. One frequent transfer occurs when a public program changes market prices. Consider, for example, an antitrust law that results in lower consumer prices. For those consumers who were paying the higher price before the law, the decrease in price results in a transfer equal to the price change. The transfer is paid by the former monopolist to the consumer in the form of a lower price and, thus, the value of the goods and services in society has not changed due to this transfer. For every extra dollar of income that consumers save as a result of the law, the producer loses a dollar [19].

Public projects often affect existing market prices. For example, a new convention center will increase both the demand and the market price for local hotel rooms. For those who used the hotel rooms before the convention center opened, the higher rent is just a transfer from them to the owners of the hotel.

In underdeveloped nations, large-scale industrial development projects often bid up the price of inputs needed for the projects. The price of steel and the price of labor throughout a nation may increase due to a large public project. These changes in price will result in income transfers from the old users of steel and labor to those who sell steel or supply labor.

Secondary Effects

Besides the outputs that are directly produced by a public project, a project may have indirect or secondary effects on outputs in a society. A secondary effect is defined as any change in the outputs of the private sector that is a response to a new public project. For example, a convention center may spur the opening of a new hotel or a new retail store.

Secondary benefits should be counted as benefits only if they represent real increases in the supply of goods and services to society. Often these secondary effects represent only transfers of activity from one location to another or from one support service to another. Consider the case of a new hotel adjacent to a convention center. If the hotel market is competitive, the new hotel will just earn enough to cover capital costs, operating costs, and a market return on capital investment. The return on capital investment is the only net benefit due to the hotel and this return on investment could have been earned in numerous other private investment projects that would have been available whether or not the convention center had been built. For this reason, it is not proper to count the net benefit from the new hotel as a benefit caused by the convention center.

Secondary effects represent real benefits only when there are unused resources in society. For example, in a time of recession, unused capital stocks, *i.e.*, machinery and plants, and idle labor may be available in society. In this case, the secondary effects that are stimulated by a public project can be achieved at no (or little) real social cost because the inputs used to produce the secondary effects would not produce anything else in the absence of the public project. The opportunity costs of such secondary effects are, thus, zero.

Secondary effects may also be considered benefits if a decision-maker is concerned not with societywide benefits and cost, but with benefits and costs in a restricted area or for a restricted set of people. Local decision-makers may often find this limited perspective most appropriate as a guide for project choice. For example, local decision-makers may wish only to consider the benefits and costs that affect citizens who live in their community. Thus, in deciding whether or not to undertake an activity that will promote new business in the community, local decision-makers may consider new taxes paid by the business a benefit, but may ignore the cost of lost taxes borne by the locality from which the business moved.

Although the framework of cost-benefit analysis is perfectly appropriate for guiding choices based on this nonsocietal perspective, some projects will be recommended by this application of cost-benefit analysis that will result in net benefits to a local community, but will have total social costs in excess of social benefits. This result is not a flaw in the cost-benefit framework but rather a function of the institutional structure of public decision-making [20].

Measuring the Value of a Public Project's Outputs

Once all of a project's benefits have been enumerated by a cost-benefit study, measures of individuals' willingness to pay must be developed for each of the end results of a project. This part of the cost-benefit analysis is often the most difficult step to accomplish. The task of finding measures for willingness to pay calls for insightfulness and a thorough knowledge of the policy environment on the part of the cost-benefit analyst. Perhaps the best approach to becoming skilled at developing willingness-to-pay measures is to read numerous case studies of cost-benefit analyses. Looking at case studies acquaints one with the diverse approaches that have been used in the past to measure the economic value of government projects [21]. Although appropriate measures of willingness to pay vary from project to project, some general considerations can be outlined as a guide to developing measures for specific evaluations.

As explained above, the reason for determining individuals' willingness to pay for public outputs is to be able to compare the dollar value individuals place on one public output versus another or on a public output versus a privately produced output. The principal problem in constructing willingness-to-pay measures is that, in most cases, individuals do not have to pay directly for public outputs. Everybody derives the benefits of police and fire protection, local roads, street lights, court systems, and national defense, independent of how much tax they pay. The process of allocating public goods is distinctly different from the allocation procedure used in the private sector where a person obtains a commodity if and only if he or she pays the cost, *i.e.*, the price, of producing the commodity. The act of buying a commodity at a set price in the private sector explicitly reveals that the purchaser's marginal willingness to pay for the commodity is equal to the commodity's market price [22].

The aim of the cost-benefit analyst in constructing willingness-to-pay measures for public goods is to construct value measures that are directly analogous to prices in the private sector. In fact, a willingness-to-pay measure for a public good is often termed a shadow price, which is defined as the price that would exist if a public good could be produced and sold in the market place [23].

Three types of shadow prices are used in many cost-benefit studies: 1) existing market prices for a public output; 2) the price of privately produced commodities that can be considered substitutes for a public output, and 3) the value of increased productivity caused by a public project. Other methods can also be found for measuring shadow prices, but these three methods are the most common means of valuing the outcomes and outputs of public policies. Each of the three types of shadow prices are discussed in turn in the next sections [24].

The Use of Existing Market Prices

The easiest type of public output to value is an output that is already bought and sold in the private market. The existing market price is the proper willingness-to-pay measure for this type of output. There would be no reason for an individual to pay a price higher than the existing market price for any readily available output. Consider, for example, publicly produced electric power. If privately produced electric power were available at the price of $40 per month, a person would not be willing to pay more than this amount for the publicly provided electricity. By the same reasoning, a person who purchases privately produced electricity is obviously willing to pay at least $40 per month for electricity because this is the amount he currently pays. The fact that the person would not pay more and does not pay less allows the inference that willingness to pay for public electricity is equal to the market price of electricity [25].

In order to use existing price as the measure of willingness to pay, it is usually necessary that the people who will be provided the publicly produced commodity are already purchasing some of the commodity in the private market. If people are not currently purchasing a readily available commodity, then their willingness to pay must be less than the price of the commodity. Consider, for example, a proposal for a public day care center in a locality. If a private day care center exists in the locality and charges $80 per week for its service, this market price information does not reflect the willingness to pay of families that choose not to send their children to the existing day care center. The $80 per week price would overestimate the value of a day care center to current nonusers. It is necessary, therefore, to use some other type of shadow price to measure the value of day care to those currently not using existing facilities.

Inferring nonusers' willingness to pay from users' willingness to pay occurs in a slightly different context when a good or service exists in one location but not in another. Often it is assumed that the potential value of the service to people in an area that has not had the service provided in the past would be equal to the price paid by the people in an area where the service is provided.

Whether or not this assumption is valid depends on the precise reasons why a service is provided in one area but not in another. If the reason for lack of supply in one region is related to the fact that people in this region have different needs or preferences concerning the service relative to the people in the area where the service is provided, then willingness to pay is likely to differ between regions. If, on the other hand, a service is not supplied in a region because the supply costs have been too high due to region-specific factors, then the existing price in the region that has had the service supplied in the past is likely to be a good measure of willingness to pay in the other region.

One further potential problem in using the observed price of a service in one area (or for one group of individuals) to measure the economic value of a service in another area (or for another group of individuals) is that some individuals in either area may be willing to pay more for the service than the market price. It is necessary to measure this consumers' surplus (*i.e.*, the difference between price and willingness to pay) when computing the total value of the service [26].

The Price of Substitutes as Measures of Public Output Values

When the type of output produced by a public project is not bought or sold anywhere in the marketplace, a commonly used measure for inferring the value of a publicly provided good or service is the price of a close substitute. For example, the willingness to pay for proposed public day care may be estimated by the costs of currently available baby-sitting; the willingness to pay for subway service could be estimated by the cost of bus service; and the willingness to pay for public refuse collection could be measured by the cost of having the refuse collected by private firms. In each case, if individuals had to pay for the proposed public service, they would not be willing to pay more than the current price charged for private provision of a substitute service.

When using the price of a substitute as a value measure for a proposed public service, it is important to make sure that the quality of the public service is the same as that of the substitute. For instance, a day care center may provide a more stimulating environment than a baby-sitter (or *vice versa*), and the subway service may be quicker than the bus service. Whenever quality differences exist, the price of the substitute should be adjusted to reflect them.

The Value of Increased Productivity Due to Public Projects

The output of some public projects has the effect of increasing productivity in the economy. In these cases, the value of the public output can be measured as the value of the extra goods and services resulting from the increased productivity. Manpower training programs, expenditures on public education, research and development projects, expenditures on health care, and highway construction projects all result in increased productivity in some sector of the economy.

In each case the value of the increased productivity can be measured as the increased earnings or cost savings in that part of the economy. Thus, the value of manpower training is reflected in, and can be measured by, the increased income earned by trained workers. Similarly, one value of new highways is the reduction in transportation costs due to time savings. For example, if a new highway reduces travel time between two cities by one hour and in each year 10,000 truck shipments are made between the cities, then the annual dollar savings for trucking companies due to the highway would be 10,000 times the hourly wage rate of truck drivers.

Level of Precision

In many cases, shadow prices are not measured precisely. As is made clear in the above discussion, there is a great deal of room for error in computing hypothetical willingness to pay in the absence of actual market transactions. This imprecision does not necessarily negate the usefulness of cost-benefit analysis. In many cases, estimated shadow prices are good indicators, if not precise indicators, of the value of public projects.

A rough estimate of a project's benefits is more useful than no estimate to decision-makers as long as the magnitude and direction of the estimate's likely error is clearly communicated. The problems of imprecise shadow prices should be interpreted as evidence that more methodological research needs to be done in cost-benefit analysis. Better measurement of the economic value of public program impacts will expand the reliability, accuracy, and, therefore, usefulness of cost-benefit analyses.

Cost Effectiveness Analysis and Unvalued Benefits

In situations where methods for measuring the value of a public project have not been developed, it is often useful to apply a less data-intensive evaluation technique called cost-effectiveness analysis. Cost-effectiveness analysis compares the costs of alternative strategies for achieving a given goal.

Whereas cost-benefit analysis attempts to guide decision-makers in determining what goals should be pursued, cost-effectiveness analysis offers no judgment as to the desirability of alternative goals. Cost-benefit analysis can be viewed as having two parts: first, the most efficient means of accomplishing each possible social goal is determined, and second, the goals that are actually worth pursuing are singled out. Cost-effectiveness analysis then is half of a cost-benefit analysis; the second step is circumvented in cost-effectiveness studies. Goals must be decided on outside the evaluative context.

The cost-effectiveness approach has been used in many areas of government activity where it is taken for granted that the activity is of value to individuals in society. National defense, public education, preservation of natural resources, and maintenance of public roads are all areas of policy where it would be difficult to measure the value of the public activity, but where alternative approaches exist for achieving the objectives of each activity. Cost-effectiveness analysis can compare these alternatives on the basis of their varying costs and then make judgments concerning the relative efficiency of each approach in reaching the stated goal.

The cost-effectiveness approach is very useful at the agency or department level of government. In a practical sense, many agencies are set up to solve a single type of social problem or to produce a given type of service. The agency personnel are often interested in how to achieve the agency's mission as efficiently as possible, rather than in justifying its mission in terms of benefits and costs.

Measuring Costs

Both cost-benefit and cost-effectiveness analyses require that the costs of alternative public programs be computed. In general, to determine a project's costs it is necessary to determine what goods and services are sacrificed by society due to the public project. The economic or opportunity cost of a project is the value of the foregone goods and services due to the project.

In a practical sense, what must be sacrificed due to a public project is somewhat determined by political and institutional constraints. If the total public budget is a fixed dollar amount that is determined outside the cost-benefit framework, then the real costs of undertaking one project are the foregone benefits of another public project that cannot be undertaken. For example, if a high school principal is assigned a fixed budget which he has freedom to spend as he wishes, then the costs of a special reading program will be a decrease in expenditures for some other activity that could have been conducted with the money used for the reading program. If this money were to have been used on an expanded athletic program, for example, then the opportunity cost of the reading program would be the foregone value of the extra athletic expenditures. In cases like this, the problems of measuring costs are the same as the problems of measuring the value of benefits.

It is important that costs be measured as the value of the next best alternative use of the resources. If extra athletic expenditures are more valued than extra expenditures on textbooks, it is incorrect to use the value of additional textbooks, rather than the value of additional athletic programs, as the cost of the reading program.

The foregone activity used to measure opportunity costs also must be a feasible activity. It would not make sense, therefore, to compute the value of an equally priced music program as a measure of the cost of the reading program if the school board does not allow money to be used for the former. Although the money for the reading program could technically be used to produce the music services, this alternative is not feasible because of the school board's constraints.

When the size of the public budget is not fixed, and a possible alternative use of resources is available in the private sector, opportunity costs often are computed as the market value of the resources needed to run the program. In a competitive market, the prices of these resources reflect the marginal cost of producing them. The marginal cost of any commodity is the amount a producer must pay to supply the commodity.

Existing market prices are not accurate measures of an input's social cost, however, whenever market prices differ from the total marginal costs of the input's production. Market price must be adjusted upwards, for instance, to reflect the social cost of an input whenever the production process involves external costs that are not borne by the producer. The value of these external costs to individuals in society must be computed and added to the market price of the input to obtain an accurate measure of the input's total value.

Existing prices may also misrepresent the value of an input when an unregulated monopolist sets a price that exceeds marginal cost. Since a monopolist's costs are the true measure for the value of the resources needed to produce the public project's input, these costs should be used to measure the project's opportunity cost. The difference between market price and costs is a transfer from the purchaser of the monopolist's product to the monopolist. This transfer does not represent an actual social cost.

One ongoing debate in cost-benefit analysis concerns the correct method for valuing the use of labor in public projects when there is unemployment in the economy [27]. If the project uses labor but results in the employment of formerly unemployed individuals, then the real cost of the labor may be zero. Often a project hires workers who would be employed even in the absence of the public project. Nevertheless, some unemployed workers might fill the jobs that the new public employees held in the past. Thus, public projects could have direct or indirect effects on unemployment. A thorough understanding of the labor market is necessary in order to determine correctly how much labor a public project diverts from the private sector and how much labor is directly or indirectly obtained from the pool of unemployed workers.

When computing costs of a project it is important to distinguish between economic costs and accounting costs. Certain expenditures made by the government to run a project are not real economic costs, but rather are transfer payments. For instance, if a project hires unemployed workers, the budget cost for this labor is positive but, as discussed above, the economic costs are zero. The money paid to the new workers is a transfer as far as society as a whole is concerned. The money paid to the new workers is a benefit from the perspective of the new workers, but a cost from the perspective of other taxpayers. The difference between the benefit and cost of transfers is zero and, therefore, transfers are best ignored in cost-benefit studies.

The Social Rate of Discount

One important and somewhat unresolved consideration in cost-benefit analysis is the proper valuation of benefits and costs that occur in the future. The important question is whether or not a dollar's worth of benefits or costs occurring in the future is worth a dollar's worth of current benefits or costs.

In general, individuals seem to value present consumption more than future consumption. The empirical validation of this presumption is the existence of a market interest rate that transforms \$1 worth of savings to $\$1 \cdot (1 + i)$ worth of savings in one year from the present. (The letter i in the formula represents the value of the market interest rate.)   Similarly, in order to borrow $\$1/(1 + i)$ in the present, an individual must agree to pay back \$1 in one year. The fact that people borrow and lend money at positive interest rates implies that they place more value on present consumption than on future consumption. For instance, those who borrow money are "willing to pay" a price of $\$1 \cdot i$ in order to obtain \$1 in a current period instead of in a future period.

One possible reason for this time preference is the fact that, in general, income rises over time. If the marginal satisfaction from the consumption of goods purchased with a person's last dollar of income decreases as his income increases, then an individual will be willing to pay a premium to transfer some income from the future to the present as long as he thinks his income will be higher in the future than it is in the present.

Uncertainty of survival is another possible explanation of preferences for present consumption relative to future consumption. The slight probability that a person will not be alive next period to consume anything may cause him to discount the value of future consumption.   The United Nations' Department of Social Affairs has computed the appropriate discount factors individuals would apply to future consumption based on actual relative frequencies of mortality at various ages.   In the United States, the discount factors vary from .04% for a person between 5 and 9 years of age to 7.45% for an 80- to 84-year old person. In India, the rates vary from 1.1% to 10.55% [28].

If individuals do value future consumption less than current consumption, then cost-benefit analyses should discount the value of future benefits by some fraction in order to make the value of future benefits comparable to the value of

present benefits.   An unresolved issue, however, is what to use as a social discount rate.   The existing market interest rate is one possibility because the interest rate does measure people's marginal willingness to pay for transfers of
consumption between periods.

The interest rate, however, is determined not only by borrowers' willingness to
pay for funds but also by the rate of return on capital investment, government
monetary policies, and uncertainty about a borrower's future ability to repay
a loan [29].   It is the interaction of factors like these that determine observed
interest rates.   For various reasons, many analysts think that an interest rate that
results from the interaction of these factors is not an appropriate measure of
the discount rate that should be applied in valuing intertemporal benefits and
costs of public programs.

One shortcoming of the observed interest rate is that it does not reflect the
value to society of economic growth that is aided by deferred consumption.
Any given individual considers the effect that his small savings would have on
the benefits he would derive from economic growth to be negligible and, therefore, each individual is likely to ignore this consideration when making intertemporal consumption decisions.   Still, economic growth that is aided by the
sum of many small investments does confer benefits that are shared by everybody, and this benefit should be reflected in a social discount rate.

Some researchers also consider the interest rate an inappropriate measure for
valuing future benefits and costs because they think individuals' observed preferences for current consumption relative to future consumption are somewhat
nonrational.   These preferences are considered more a result of impatience or
necessity than of rational planning or systematic thinking about the trade-off.
Some researchers argue that time preferences can be thought about systematically only if lifetime resources can be estimated with some degree of certainty
[30].   Since this estimation is not possible for many people, their observed behavior may reflect something other than a thoroughly considered valuation of
future consumption relative to current consumption.   Consider, for example,
a poor family with not enough money to eat or live comfortably.   Such a family's borrowing in times of need is not likely to reflect a well-thought-out value
structure concerning present and future consumption.   Their borrowing, however, will affect the observed interest rate.

These criticisms of market interest rates suggest that the social discount rate
should be lower than market interest rates.   The appropriate rate, however, must
be determined by a value judgment.   Only a decision-maker can specify society's
relative preferences for present and future consumption.

It is often useful to compute the present value of benefits and costs of alternative public programs using various plausible social discount rates.   One possible
result from this type of comparison, which is termed a sensitivity analysis, is that
one program might always have larger net benefits than other programs.   This

result would indicate that the one program is the best alternative no matter what social discount rate is specified. When the order of alternative programs does vary with the choice of a discount rate, the decision maker can use the results of a sensitivity analysis as an indication of which program is most valued in each range of the discount rate.

CONCLUSION: A REEMPHASIS OF SOME IMPORTANT POINTS

This paper has introduced the conceptual framework of cost-benefit analysis and has outlined some of the principle technical problems that occur while doing cost-benefit studies. As a summary, the following five points should be reemphasized.

1. A cost-benefit study must have two parts: the end results of any given public program must be enumerated, and then the value of these end results must be compared with the value of the resources used to produce the results. The first part might be called "effectiveness" analysis and the second component can be termed "efficiency" analysis.
2. The valuation of goods and services resulting from a public program is based on individuals' willingness to pay for the goods and services. If the value of a program's end results aggregated across all individuals in society exceeds the value of the resources used to run the program, then cost-benefit analysis suggests that the program is socially desirable. This investment criterion is termed the potential Pareto criterion and it ensures that a public program is undertaken only if the program increases the aggregate value of society's goods and services.
3. A series of important value judgments must be made in conducting a cost-benefit analysis. Trade-offs must be established for comparing efficiency or aggregate consumption effects of public programs and nonefficiency effects of public programs. For example, a value judgment must be made to decide whether or not society is willing to undertake some programs that have costs that exceed aggregate consumption benefits, but that redistribute income in socially desirable ways. A value judgment also must be made in comparing intangible effects of programs to tangible effects. It is not possible to determine analytically a shadow price for an intangible benefit or cost; a value judgment must establish society's willingness to pay for an intangible benefit or to avoid an intangible cost. The social discount rate also must be established by a value judgment. Existing interest rates suggest a range for the social discount rate, but to determine a precise discount rate analytically is not possible. All of these value judgments must be made by a decision-maker, rather than a researcher or analyst. The fact that value judgments must be made in order to complete a cost-benefit analysis makes clear that the evaluation process cannot be an exclusively technical undertaking. Technical aspects of a cost-benefit analysis are important and aid the social choice process, but technical analysis cannot

provide value-free recommendations about program choice. It is essential that a cost-benefit study clearly state the nature and source of any value judgments that are implicit in the criteria used to compute the value of a program's benefits and costs.

4. A cost-benefit study can be done only when both the benefits and costs associated with a program can be measured and valued. If prices or shadow prices cannot be found or constructed for a program's benefits and costs, then the cost-benefit framework is inappropriate as an evaluation technique. If costs of alternative programs that have the same basic benefits can be computed and if the social desirability of the benefits is independently determined, cost-effectiveness analysis may be a useful evaluation tool. Cost-effectiveness analysis compares the cost of alternative methods of achieving a social goal.

5. Research in cost-benefit analysis should be directed at developing more accurate measures of willingness to pay for different types of public goods. Techniques for valuing intangibles and for valuing public goods that have no close substitute in the private market must be developed in order to expand the usefulness of cost-benefit analysis. In principle, the cost-benefit framework can be used to evaluate any type of public activity; in fact, however, the current absence of willingness-to-pay measures for many types of public goods hinders the application of cost-benefit analysis in many areas of government activity.

NOTES AND REFERENCES

1. We use the term public goods to mean any activities undertaken by the government. At times, economists reserve this term to describe goods that are communally consumed, such as roads and public safety. Governments sometimes provide goods and services that are not communally consumed, such as electricity and water. For a discussion of alternative definitions of public goods, see J. G. Head, "Public Goods and Public Policy," *Public Finance* (1962).

2. Willingness to pay is hypothetical in the case of public goods whenever individuals do not have to pay money directly in order to obtain the public good. In most cases, individuals pay indirectly, through the tax system, rather than directly.

3. Cost-benefit analysis is also used to determine the optimal scale of a program. That is, for any given program, cost-benefit analysis can suggest what support level is such that additional support would not be worth the effort.

4. Two good histories of the development of cost-benefit analysis are included in Leonard Merewitz and Stephen Sosnick, *The Budget's New Clothes*, Chicago: Markham, 1971; and Stephen Margolin, *Public Investment Criteria*, Cambridge Mass.: MIT Press, 1968.

5. Eckstein, Otto. *Water Resource Development*. Cambridge, Mass.: Harvard University Press, 1958. Eckstein summarizes and discusses early work in cost-benefit analysis.

6. 49 Stat. 1570. Quoted in Stephen Margolin, *Public Investment Criteria*, Cambridge, Mass.: MIT Press, 1968.

7. McCullough, C. B., and John Beakey. *The Economics of Highway Planning*. Salem, Ore.: Oregon State Highway Commission, 1937.

8. Some of this military work is summarized in Charles Hitch and Roland McKean, *The Economics of Defense in the Nuclear Age*, Cambridge, Mass.: Harvard University Press, 1960.
9. US Bureau of the Budget. "Bulletin No. 68-2." July 18, 1967. Quoted in Fremont Lyden and Ernest Miller, *Planning Programming, Budgeting*, Chicago: Markham, 1972.
10. The UN guidelines are described in 15, below. The OECD suggestions are contained in I. M. D. Little and J. A. Mirrlees, *A Manual of Industrial Project Analysis in Developing Countries*, Paris: Organization for Economic Cooperation and Development, 1969. Other good references on cost-benefit analysis in developing nations are: United Nations Industrial Development Organization, *Evaluation of Industrial Projects*, New York: United Nations, 1968; Stephen Marglin, *Public Investment Criteria*, cited above; and Lyn Squire and Herman von der Tak, *Economic Analysis of Projects*, Washington, D.C.: World Bank, 1975.
11. Quade, E. S. *Analysis for Public Decisions.* New York: American Elsevier, 1975. Rossi, Peter, and Walter Williams. *Evaluating Social Programs.* New York: Seminar Press, 1972. Campbell, D. J., and J. C. Stanley. *Experimental and Quasi-Experimental Designs for Research.* Chicago: Rand McNally, 1966. These works discuss analytical methods for measuring the effects of public programs.
12. The Pareto principle derives its name from Vilfredo Pareto, who first suggested the idea about 75 years ago. For a discussion of welfare economics, see Peter Bohm, *Social Efficiency*, London: Macmillan, 1973; E. J. Mishan, *Welfare Economics: An Assessment*, Amsterdam: North Holland, 1969; or J. de V. Graaff, *Theoretical Welfare Economics*, London: Cambridge University Press, 1971.
13. The term "Potential Pareto Principle" is used by Mishan, *Economics for Social Decisions*, New York: Praeger, 1972. The cost-benefit criterion for judging public projects is also termed the "Kaldor-Hicks criterion," after the originators of the idea. See Merewitz and Sosnick, *The Budget's New Clothes*, for a discussion of Kaldor's work and Hicks' work. The sources for the seminal work, itself, are N. Kaldor, "Welfare Propositions of Economics and Interpersonal Comparisons of Utility," *Economic Journal* 49(1939); and J. R. Hicks, "The Foundations of Welfare Economics," *Economic Journal* 49(1939).
14. Little, I. M. D. *A Critique of Welfare Economics.* London: Oxford University Press, 1960.
15. United Nations Industrial Development Organization. *Guidelines for Project Evaluation*. New York: United Nations, 1972.
16. A "merit want" is defined as a benefit whose value is not recognized by individuals in society at a given point in time, but whose value would become apparent in the future. Public education, health care, and industrial investment projects in developing nations are all programs that might include "merit want" benefits.
17. Some people distinguish between a negative benefit, which would be an output or effect of a project that is negatively valued by some individuals, and a cost, which is the resources that must be given up to do a project. These people would enumerate negative benefits under a discussion of a program's benefits in a cost-benefit study. Other people consider any aspect of a project that is negatively valued to be a cost of a program and, thus, enumerate negatively valued effects when discussing program costs. Either approach is acceptable and results in the same benefit-minus-cost figure; the important points are that negatively valued effects should be included somewhere in the analysis and that they should not be counted under both benefits and costs.

18. Unintended effects are not always unexpected. As used here, the term *unintended effects* refers to side effects or any impacts of a public policy that are not the prime reason for considering the policy.

19. The law may have the additional effect of expanding the output produced by the monopolist if more people are willing to purchase the monopolist's output after the price is lowered. This extra output will add value to aggregate consumption in society because the new purchasers will have a willingness to pay that is slightly higher than the extra cost of producing the output.

20. Deciding which secondary effects are transfers of activities from one endeavor to another and which are real benefits attributable to a public project is often a very difficult judgment to make. Eckstein notes that: "An important choice [must be made] in the selection of the chain of effects which should be pursued, both on the benefit and on the cost sides. The proper circumscription of the analysis is one of the critical points in the economics of public expenditures." Eckstein, Otto. "A Survey of the Criteria of Public Expenditure Criteria." In *Public Finances: Needs, Sources, and Utilization*. Princeton: Princeton University Press, 1961.

21. Dorfman, Robert, ed. *Measuring Benefits of Governmental Investments*. Washington, D.C.: Brookings Institution, 1965. Layard, Richard, ed. *Cost-Benefit Analysis*. Baltimore: Penguin, 1972. Niskanan, William, *et al.*, eds. *Benefit-Cost and Policy Analysis 1972*. Chicago: Aldine, 1973. Zeckhauser, Richard, *et al. Benefit-Cost and Policy Analysis 1974*. Chicago: Aldine, 1975.

22. If a consumer purchases more than one unit of a commodity (*e.g.*, five pounds of meat per week or ten shirts per year), it is possible that his willingness to pay for initial units is greater than his willingness to pay for the marginal item (*i.e.*, the last item purchased). If he or she pays a set price for each unit, then for the initial items, he or she derives consumers' surplus, which is defined as the difference between willingness to pay and price. In a competitive market, price equals the willingness to pay for the last item bought.

  In the case of a service or a commodity that is purchased as a single unit, some individuals who purchase the commodity or service would have been willing to pay more for it, while others would not have purchased the commodity or service had the price been higher. The market price measures the willingness to pay of this latter group only. Individuals in the former group derive consumers' surplus from the purchase.

23. When a commodity's production results in external benefits, a properly constructed shadow price should reflect the value of these externalities. External benefits, which are benefits a person enjoys whether or not he or she pays for a given commodity, are not reflected in market prices, but should be accounted for in a shadow price that is used to quantify the value of a public program. Even though a producer cannot extract revenue from external benefits caused by a production process, these unpriced benefits are real social benefits and must be included in a cost-benefit analysis. Similarly, when a production process causes external costs which are costs that are not paid for by the producer, these external costs should be reflected in a shadow price used to quantify the costs of a public program.

24. The obvious question might be asked: why not just ask a person how much he would be willing to pay for a public output? This would be a legitimate procedure if the person quizzed was sure to answer accurately and honestly. In practice, individuals have a difficult time answering survey questions about willingness to pay. What they say they are willing to pay and then what they actually pay or refuse to pay when con-

fronted with a real situation are very often different amounts. The problem would be compounded if individuals were aware that the interviewer was planning to use the answers to value a public project. The individual might overstate his willingness to pay if he wanted the program to be undertaken and if his taxes were unaffected by the answer. The opposite might occur if his taxes were affected by his answer.

25. When a public project has a scale large enough to alter market prices, these changes in market prices should be considered in valuing the benefits. Market price will change if a public project substantially adds to the existing supply of a commodity and if the total demand for the commodity varies with the commodity's price. See Mishan, *Economics for Social Decisions*, for a discussion of how to measure benefits properly when a project alters the market price for an output produced by the project.

26. The measurement of consumers' surplus usually necessitates an estimation of the demand curve for the service. Applied consumption analysis is an area of economics that studies methods of estimating the shape of demand curves. See Louis Phlips, *Applied Consumption Analysis*, Amsterdam: North Holland, 1974, for a discussion of these methods.

27. For a detailed discussion of this issue, see Robert Haveman and John Krutilla, *Unemployment, Idle Capacity, and the Evaluation of Public Expenditures*, Washington, D.C.: Resources for the Future, 1968.

28. The United Nations' figures are quoted in Eckstein, *Water Resource Development*. Note that the figures refer to mortality rates in the early 1950s.

29. The fact that an interest rate reflects uncertainty about a borrower's ability to repay the loan results in multiple interest rates that are applied to different types of individuals and different types of loans, depending on the risk involved in each specific case. The existence of numerous market interest rates complicates the application of these rates in cost-benefit studies.

30. See 15, above, for a detailed presentation of this argument.

4

Accountability in
Public Enterprise

John W. Sutherland
Southern Illinois University

INTRODUCTION

One finds the origin of accountability concepts in the principles and procedures of capital budgeting, a process that has been carried to considerable sophistication in the commercial sector. Capital budgeting, however, implies that we are able to generate relatively precise relationships between inputs and outputs, such that one can talk meaningfully about the "profit impact" of some proposed investment. In the public or not-for-profit sector, these neat relationships seldom emerge, and capital budgeting technology cannot be employed in the same way as it is among business enterprises. There are several reasons for this:

1. There is the problem that the outputs (products) around which most public enterprise centers simply do not lend themselves to precise, objective, and quantitative formulation. In many cases, the public system has no clearcut definition of the product it produces (*e.g.*, is the output of a university the number of graduates it produces, the quality of the graduates, or a complex combination of the two; or should output be thought of in terms of positive impact on the surrounding community? What about the proper output target for a community hospital or a local welfare agency?). In short, the lack of definability of numericalized outputs prevents many public enterprises from adopting, in any meaningful way, the kind of cost-effectiveness calculus that is available to firms producing a highly structured, easily defined, "countable" output.

2. While a majority of decisions undertaken within the private sector may legitimately involve alternatives with clearly specified outcomes (being matters mainly of precisely defined or even numericalized quantities), many decisions that must be made by public administrators, operating even at the lower levels of the enterprise, involve "value" issues and have distinct policy and sociopolitical implications. Most managers within the private sector—

except for those operating at the highest levels—are shielded from such considerations by the 'umbrella of certainty' under which they operate. Thus, they may behave as if the system or phenomena with which they deal are effectively deterministic, whereas virtually all problems emerging within the confines of public enterprise may involve elements of uncertainty that are largely "external" to the normal business decision-maker.

3. Because public enterprise so often deals with issues involving the public welfare, the common good, the dignity of human beings, or other such elusive criteria, the public manager must treat the consumer of his product as a "client" *per se*, with all the ambiguity and ethical responsibility that that entails. On the other hand, the business manager is largely freed from any fiduciary responsibility toward the consumer (and in many cases, the link between the operating manager and the consumer may be a long and indirect one). In short, the business decision-maker more or less legitimately can consider only the welfare of his own firm, whereas the public manager (for admittedly political as well as philosophical reasons) must have a bifold calculus, which involves client as well as organizational welfare [1].

4. The performance of the decision-making manager in the private sector is most often audited on objective bases, with the specific criteria generally known to the manager beforehand (and often a result of a bargaining process between the manager and his superior). In such a context, the decision-maker can approach his function in terms of its probable impact on his overall performance audit (*e.g.*, as a profit center). But in the public sector, the manager (at virtually all levels) often has his performance—and, therefore, his career and personal welfare—judged on the basis of subjective criteria, some of which may not even be known to him beforehand, some of which may be tacit rather than explicit. In fact, many real performance criteria in the public sector run contrary to policy statements and, therefore, cannot even be articulated after the fact (*e.g.*, as with the auditor of the United States Navy who found significant cost overruns—which was his job—but who was fired for reporting them). Thus, the path the public administrator follows is tortuous and perilous; often by doing the job formally assigned him, he can run afoul of "latent" criteria or of the irrational components so prevalent among bureaucracies. Small wonder, then, that there is the tendency among many officers of public enterprise to make as few decisions as possible. For, in the ill-structured, subjective, *ad hoc* public arena, a positive action may often correctly be perceived as carrying more potential for unpleasant surprises than for adulation or reward. And in this predilection, the officer of public enterprise joins a majority of his counterparts in private industry.

The defense offered by the public administrator may thus be summarized as follows: the basic unamenability of public enterprise to objective accountability criteria means that the public administrator can be *legitimately* freed from the objective (if reflective) criteria under which the performance of his commercial counterpart is assessed. And if he is legitimately freed from objective performance criteria, on what basis can his performance really be audited? The answer many public administrators would have us accept might be phrased like this: "Well, if there are no objective criteria by which my performance can be legitimately judged, then my performance really cannot be judged at all!"

THE PROGRAM BUDGETING ALTERNATIVE

The program budgeting technology—building on the capital budgeting base—was introduced to take cognizance of these arguments. The program budgeting logic attempts to equip each investment alternative with a cost-benefit (or cost-effectiveness) estimate, which is fundamentally a surrogate for the profit-impact estimates that commercial organizations attach to their investment or project alternatives. In general abbreviation, a more or less sophisticated program budgeting process would involve the following procedures:

1. First, the various missions (functions) that the organization is to serve must be specified. As a general rule, missions should be specified in such a way that they become cross-correlated; that is, like the teaching, research, and external service functions of the prototypical university we shall be using as a case study later in this essay, they are mutually reinforcing (or related positively).
2. The strategic decision-makers will presumably have set generic utility indices on the several functions, as will our university executives. These strategic weightings may or may not be known to the lower-level unit managers.
3. Given these functional specifications, each unit manager, department head, program director, *etc.* is asked to submit activity specifications for the coming period, suggesting what he wants his unit to do. As a general rule, the activity proposals (program statements) should meet the following criteria:

    a. They should correlate to one or more of the strategic missions of the organization.
    b. They should express performance criteria with respect to effectiveness (or utility).
    c. They should not be identified exclusively with any specific operating unit (that is, they should presume no organizational structure *per se*).
    d. They should carry a projected cost-effectiveness index, showing the different levels of output (effect) associated with different resource levels, *e.g.*, a specification of the expected functional relationship between inputs and outputs [2].
4. The various activity proposals are all collected and then arrayed across the various missions, giving the *a priori* (or gross) benefit configuration for the organization, such as shown in Figure 1. The actual activity aggregates submitted by the array of unit managers must then be compared against the

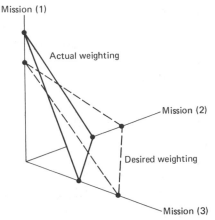

Figure 1. Benefit configurations.

desired mission weightings developed by the strategic higher-level decision-makers (presumably as the output of their impact programming analysis). In the figure, we see that the subordinate decision-makers gave more weight to mission 1 than was desired and less to missions 2 and 3. The more serious the deviation between tactical and strategic benefit configurations, the more radical must be the revision of the program (activity) schedule.

5. The disparity between actual and desired weightings will, of course, be resolved through the resource allocation process. That is, the budget configuration—representing the proportional allocation of resources to the several mission areas—will be isomorphic with respect to the desired configuration, not the actual. However, when the desired and actual are very far apart—and relations between strategic and tactical decision-makers are not amicable—then the adjustment to the desired mission orientations may be made gradually, perhaps over several iterations of the program-budgeting process.

6. To arrive at the budget configuration, we do the following:

   a. We eliminate all redundant program or activity specifications, so that we have a set of mutually exclusive alternatives.
   b. We then rank each of the proposed activities (programs) according to their apparent cost-effectiveness or cost-benefit ratios, within the several mission categories.
   c. Where an activity (program) purports to support more than one mission, it is ranked according to its distributed effect (that is, according to aggregate cost-effectiveness). At any rate, any given activity will appear in the program array only once.

7. At this point, we will have an ordered array of programs pertaining to each of the n-functional areas, as in Figure 2. Now, we will have previously par-

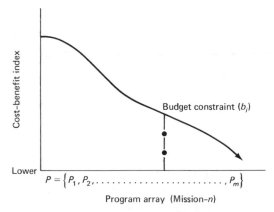

Figure 2. Ordered program array.

titioned the aggretate resources (or aggregated budget) into segments reflecting the expected utility of the various mission areas (functions).   These represent the *ceiling* investment levels for each functional area:

$$B = \sum_{i=1}^{n} b_i,$$

where

$$\frac{b_i}{B} = T(U_i), \ \Sigma U_i = 1.0.$$

8. The procedure is then to allocate resources, up to the ceiling b_i, according to the resource demands of the ordered programs.   Resources associated with mission 1 are thus dedicated initially to the most apparently favorable investments in terms of some return function (cost-effectiveness).   When the budget ceiling is reached, the programs that remain unfunded are simply not implemented.   When this has been done for all missions (functional areas), then the ostensible objective of the program-budgeting process has been met.   That is, the probabilistically most favorable allocation of resources has been achieved.

Under a scheme such as that just described, accountability technology becomes thoroughly intermingled with (or coextensive with) the range of normal decision science procedures.   The implications of this conjunction are interesting, and must be elaborated.   What follows, then, is an effort to describe how the combined accountability-decision logics might be set to work within the framework of a particular type of public enterprise–a university.

OPERATIONALIZING THE ACCOUNTABILITY-DECISION LOGICS

Initially, there is the problem of establishing an operational (actionable) goal for a public enterprise, one that permits the program budgeting and accountability logic to be put to work. This would mean that the grandiloquent, rhetorical goals that public enterprises tend to set for themselves must be replaced by something more pedestrian. We shall operate here with the following:

> a social service agency (of which a university is a specific case) should operate to *maximize unallocated per capita resources*, up to the point where diminishing marginal returns set in [3].

We can readily see why this is the case. Let us consider the ratio x/y, where x is the funding level of the organization (the resource base) and y is the population the organization serves (*e.g.*, the number of students in a university, patients in a hospital, welfare clients in an urban service program). The result of this raito, z, gives us the *per capita* expenditure level. When we consider that service (utility) is positively correlated with *per capita* expenditure levels, the three things that can happen to the x/y ratio at the initiation of any new operating period would have the following implications:

1. $\dfrac{x_t}{y_t} > \dfrac{x_{t+1}}{y_{t+1}}$ indicates an erosion in the *per capita* service level and, hence, a dilution of the imputed effectiveness of the organization;

2. $\dfrac{x_t}{y_t} = \dfrac{x_{t+1}}{y_{t+1}}$ indicates a proportional change in the ratio, which signifies no change in the organization's service posture;

3. $\dfrac{x_t}{y_t} < \dfrac{x_{t+1}}{y_{t+1}}$ indicates a proportional increase in the *potential* level of service the organization is able to deliver.

In the first case, the aggregate support level has declined relative to the population to be serviced; this means less for everybody, assuming that services are distributed across the population symmetrically. In the second case, *per capita* service levels need not be affected. And in the third case, the resource base has increased at a faster rate than the client population (or the client population has decreased more rapidly than the resource base). In either case, the organization is left with a more favorable *per capita* situation.

The relationship between *per capita* resources (z) and organizational effectiveness should be clear. Subject to the conditions of diminishing returns to scale, a higher z assumes that the organization can make a relatively greater contribution to its clients' welfare. For example, it can have more books or laboratory equipment for its students, and more drugs, physicians, nurses, or janitors per patient; it can give its welfare clients higher payment, more food stamps, or more counseling. Presumably, the *more* services an organization offers its clientele, the more effective it is. In short, a university with a lower faculty-student ratio, a relatively large library, and more laboratory equipment per user may be presumed to do a more effective job than a competitor with fewer services to offer each student. We must qualify this, of course, and suggest that this would demand that the services per student be rationally structured and distributed; we will introduce this qualification in a moment. Even so, when the organization's executives increase the *per capita* expenditure level, they increase the *potential* effectiveness of their organization. Therefore, in the service sector, it is possible to measure the potential *utility* of an organization (and hence the unqualified *performance* of its executives or operating officers) by looking at the time-dependent changes in the x/y ratio. In almost any case, an executive may be said to have failed his organization (although not necessarily the community at large) when the x/y ratio is allowed to fall, even if it reflects increased efficiency at the operations level [4]. From the parochial perspective we are adopting here, "more is always better," although we will later qualify this considerably.

What about the restrictions on the use to which an incremental increase in z may be put? Generally, we would have to consider two possibilities: 1) the funds are *categorical*, granted only to perform specific functions, and 2) the funds are *unallocated*, and may be spent at the discretion of the organization's executives. Now, categorical funds are to be used in a specific way: to educate American Indians over the age of 40; to give maternity benefits to welfare mothers; to build a statue on the campus in memory of an alumnus; to add modern French lithographs to the community art museum; and so on. Of course, the categories are virtually limitless. A *priori* dedicated inputs may, therefore, vary considerably in their impact on the effectiveness level of the organization. As a rule, they should always be accepted. They automatically carry a *zero opportunity cost*, for they are not available for any other purpose from the standpoint of the receiving organization. They may represent relatively idle investments, but they do not cost the organization anything. Thus, categorical increases in the funding base may or may not advance effectiveness, but in no case might they be expected to reduce it.

Unallocated funds are the most promising because they are potentially available to be invested in zero-opportunity-cost investments without *a priori* restriction. The executives would now be expected to search throughout the entire organization for the best uses for the funds, so that the most productive investment could be made. Thus, unallocated overhead funds or resources should enable the organization's executives to directly increase its effectiveness level. In the context of rationality, these funds should be used to maximize the incremental utility-resource ratio. But, to the extent that the organization's executives lack either wit or integrity, the incremental increase in z may be used poorly.   In fact, it may be used to feather the executives' own nests—new carpeting, larger expense accounts, new office buildings—in much the same way that overhead could be employed in commercial enterprise.   And what often happens in the service sector—perhaps even more frequently than in commercial or industrial enterprises—is that incremental increases in overhead merely expand the administrative structure at the expense of directly productive service functions.   Thus, either ignorance on the part of the executives or the lack of an adequate accountability mechanism can act to deteriorate the productivity of any funding increases.

Such a point is gratuitous.   But the question of accountability as a control on organizational quality is central to our interests.   At this point, we must investigate the relationship between organizational effectiveness and efficiency. For, as is clear, the net effectiveness associated with any x/y ratio will depend upon the rationality of the resource allocations made internally.   Thus, the *per capita* expenditure level is the strategic parameter for us in the service sector, but tactical considerations now force us to look at the productivity of x.   In short, we must ask about the extent to which the *potential* of any x/y ratio is actually realized.

We know that potential benefits will increase as the x/y ratio increases (Figure 3a).   But when we consider tactical efficiency, we also know that there will be a range of benefits (b_is) associated with any given x/y level, as in Figure 3b). Particularly, the x/y captured by an organization's executives sets the potential benefit level (the "ceiling" effectiveness or utility index) for the organization; however, the quality of the tactical decisions will determine the actual benefit levels associated with any given x/y, with the expectation that the b_is might

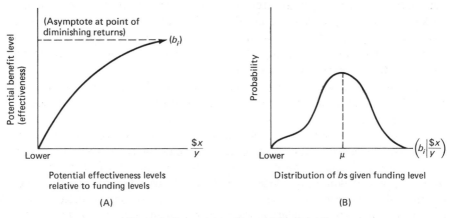

Figure 3. Potential and actual benefit levels.

be distributed more or less normally across any set of competitive service organizations (*e.g.*, any set of hospitals or colleges in a region).

Clearly, the attribute working in Figure 3b is *decision rationality*. Specifically, more sophisticated decision-makers are expected to obtain results consistently in the more favorable segment of the distribution of b_is. To make this clearer, and to show how accountability and decision rationality may reinforce each other within the confines of a service organization, we turn to our example.

Recall that we will be working with some prototypical university, given a goal formulation directing the organization to "maximize unallocated *per capita* resources." Given such a goal, the first step is to identify the various sources of inputs (*e.g.*, funding bases). A typical university may have a mix such as that in Table 1.

The input sources in the table are more or less obvious in their implications. Formula budgets pertain mainly to public-supported or sectarian (*e.g.*, religious) institutions of some kind, where inputs are generated on a *per capita* basis, with the *per capita* funding base sometimes unrelated to actual costs. Contract funds, such as those made available by governments, foundations, private agencies, and corporations, are tied to some output; that is, they exact some performance from the university. In some cases, however, some latitude may be associated with the expenditures; hence, the bracketed check mark in the Unallocated column. For example, the funds may be for free (or pure) research, for curriculum development, or some sort of subject-free innovation in instructional methodology. In other instances, the contract inputs may be disposed of at the

Table 1. Funding partitions (input sources).

SOURCES	PER CAPITA	CATEGORICAL	UNALLOCATED
Formula budgets (*F*) (from an external agency—state, community, church, *etc.*)	X	–	–
Contract funds (*C*) (for either directed or free research, program development, *etc.*)	–	X	[X]
Student tuition (*S*) including fees and profits on internal operations—cafeteria, bookstores, *etc.*)	–	–	X
Alumni donations and bequests (*D*) (including proceeds from any endowments, *etc.*)	–	X	[X]
Public fees (*P*) (admission to athletic contests, concerts, special lectures, *etc.*)	–	–	X

discretion of the university itself, in which case they are *a priori* unallocated. Student sources provide both tuition and fees (which again may be unrelated to actual costs) and also offer a potential for profit on internal services such as cafeteria, dormitory, and book fees. There are generally no external constraints on the disposition of tuition and fees, and so forth. Alumni donations and other bequests are usually categorical, but not always. In some cases, a bequest may carry no constraints as to its uses and, hence, may be spent at the direction of university officials. Finally, fees charged for university-sponsored events are usually available for free allocation.

These various inputs eventually find their way into the support of the several *functions* performed by the normal university. Table 2 identifies three major functions, with notes on their basic outputs. Inputs devoted to functions go directly into the development of the resource base of a university, perhaps consisting of:

1. faculty (for teaching, research, *etc.*),
2. administrative and staff positions (management, secretarial, *etc.*),
3. infrastructure (plant, equipment, facilities, *etc.*), and
4. student support (fellowships, grants, scholarships, *etc.*).

The actual outputs (or products) of a university thus ultimately depend on how the preceding resources are distributed across the major functions, and on the quality of the resources (*e.g.*, the amenities of plant or grounds; the prestige or teaching effectiveness of faculty). In the simplest sense, then, the decision structure of our prototypical university might look something like Figure 4. Particularly, it is the general responsibility of the university's directors (its board of governors, regents, or trustees) to determine the *mission* that the institution is to carry out. This implies responsibility for developing what we will

Table 2. Function and output relationships.

FUNCTION	FIRST-ORDER OUTPUTS
Teaching	Structure of education offerings, curricula, degree structure, degrees and certifications granted, *etc.*
Research	Advances to subject knowledge attributable to studies by faculty (and sometimes, students)
External services	Accessible as the events (athletic or cultural, *etc.*) sponsored by the university; as the products associated with any contracted projects (*e.g.*, government studies, corporation consulting projects); as the schedule of services offered by faculty, staff, or students to any external agency (*e.g.*, addresses to the Rotary Club, journalistic efforts, consultation to civic governments, activities on academic associations)

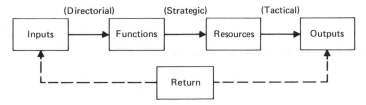

Figure 4. Transformation functions.

call a functional configuration for the organization. In the present case, three generic configurations, as illustrated in Figure 5, concern us.

Now, these various configurations may either be imposed on the university exogenously, or they may represent a deliberate choice on the part of the institutional executives. For example, a decision to emphasize teaching may, in some instances, be taken by default. If the institution has an unfavorable resource ratio (a low x/y), then it will have to employ virtually all its resources in the direct education function; this is typical of many local or community colleges, especially those with open enrollment. Such a school is not likely to be big in football, nor will it fund many concerts or have a well-developed research capability. Some institutions will have to emphasize research however. For example, they may be categorically endowed to do research (*e.g.*, Rockefeller University), or they may have a mandate for graduate education, with its implied research support, (*e.g.*, as with a state university as opposed to a state college). Finally, some institutions must attend to external services, especially those that depend largely on alumni endowments; therefore, athletic programs at the Univeristy of Southern California and Notre Dame demand considerable emphasis.

Any of these configurations, in the absence of such exogenous imperatives, may be deliberately invoked. A school may emphasize teaching in an effort to

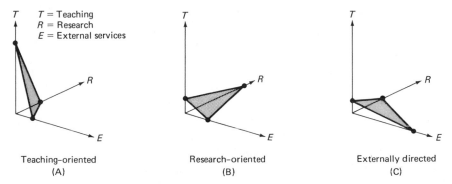

Figure 5. Functional configurations.

minimize the student-faculty ratio and therefore gain a reputation as "humanistic" (and perhaps become a school of "social significance" as well). A university might seek to develop and emphasize a research capability because of market conditions (e.g., there may be a great demand for graduate education in the region that is not met by other institutions). Finally, a school may seek to amplify its external services, again perhaps because of local market conditions or because the university is the *only* source of cultural or athletic interest in a region.

At any rate, the basic functional configuration simply sets gross constraints on the use of whatever resources are available to the university (to the extent that they are unallocated). For example, teaching implies the maintenance of faculty, construction or maintenance of an educational plant, and certain administrative functions (e.g., the registrar's office, academic record-keeping, dormitory management); it may also imply the dedication of some inputs to support student-teachers. On the other hand, a strong external services dimension would imply certain other resource loadings. For example, an athletic program would probably raise the demand for coaches, uniforms, equipment, a ticket office, a press relations officer, student scholarships, and the construction of spectator facilities. A research orientation might imply the need for a high-level faculty, many graduate assistants, expensive and sophisticated laboratory facilities, and a strong grants administration and research support office. The strategic allocation decision thus always involves the determination of a dedication of blocks of resources to potentially competitive functions, within whatever normative constraints are provided by the board. For, in most cases, a faculty position employed in one functional area (one mission domain) leaves it unavailable for other uses; a dollar used to support classroom education is a dollar lost to the football team or the physics laboratory. Therefore, strategic resource allocation is of critical importance in the service organization, and is the counterpart of the major product or service decisions made in commercial enterprise (e.g., determinations of what businesses we are in).

These aggregate (strategic) allocations may be made either casually or with significant scientific discipline. A casual approach is simply to take existing aggregate allocations and expand or contract them according to increases or decreases in total resource availabilities for the coming period (e.g., the inertial budgeting scheme). Or, resource allocations may be subject to political or axiological criteria (e.g., a member of the board may be very fond of football and *a priori* ill-disposed toward biogenetic research; or the president may be a mediocre scholar and, for subjective reasons, may act against the interests of fundamental research). Obviously, there are no limits to the irrational procedures by which allocations to basic missions may be made. But there are distinct limitations on the proper scientific approach to basic mission loadings (strategic allocation decisions). Rational allocations would first of all demand calculation of the direction and then the magnitudes of the relationships between the several functions (missions) and the resource-providers (input sources), perhaps as follows:

$$UI = f(F, C, S, D, P)$$

$$G = (UI_{t+1} - UI_t)$$

$$G = (\Delta f[F, C, S, D, P] = f[T, R, E])$$

where

    UI = unallocated income as a function of the several input sources,
    G = the incremental change in UI as a function of the several missions (teaching, research, external service),
    F = formula budget,
    C = contract research funds,
    S = student fees, tuitions, *etc.*,
    D = donations, bequests, *etc.*, and
    P = public fees (for events, publications, *etc.*).

The general function for our purposes is thus

$$MAX[G] = f(I_{i[t+n]}|E_{j[t]})$$

where

    I = the set of all input sources for the next and all subsequent periods, and
    E = the set of all missions (functional areas) for the current period.

Were we interested simply in maximizing the resource base, without regard to unallocated funds, then the decision-makers would simply replace G with X, the undifferentiated resource base.

Now, we have to assign each functional area (or mission) a utility index that reflects its expected *leverage* on unallocated inputs. This utility function U is the operator that relates the functional loadings to inputs:

$$[I]U_j[E]$$

where

    U_1 = teaching function,
    U_2 = research function,
    U_3 = external service function, and
    $\Sigma U_j = 1.0$.

We are thus searching for a master relationship to be evaluated, which for the present context is

$$EV(G) = (W_{i,1}U_1 + W_{i,2}U_2 + W_{i,3}U_3)$$

where

$W_{i,j}$ = resources devoted to the jth function,

and

$i = 1$ implies faculty,
$i = 2$ implies staff (administrative) support,
$i = 3$ implies infrastructure (*pro rata*), and
$i = 4$ implies student support (scholarships, fellowships, *etc.*).

We can see, then, that one possible strategy is to allocate resources to the several functions proportional to their utilities (that is, their expected leverage on input sources):

$$\frac{W_j}{W} = \frac{U_j}{1}.$$

Our real problem at the strategic analysis stage is thus to get reasonably reliable estimates of the U_js, as these are the direct determinants of our actual allocations and, hence, the basis for the actual ($G = f[W_j]$) that eventually emerges. As a matter of practice, the calculation of utility values in the context of the service organization is an enormously demanding task. But we know something about the components of the appropriate utility index. Specifically, we will have to be concerned with three dimensions: direction of influence, order of effect and magnitude.

The direction of influence simply refers to the qualitative relationship between an input and a function—*e.g.*, does an incremental increase in the loading of a function (for instance, an increase in teaching effectiveness or level of education) yield a positive (*P*), negative (*N*), or indeterminate (*I*) effect on the input source? Order of effect reflects the fact that some impacts may be *lagged* through time (*e.g.*, some effects are immediate, others take time to develop and operate through intermediate functions). Finally, magnitude measures the strength of the impact of a functional area on an input source—the "rate of return," as it were.

In any strategic allocation problem, it is useful to develop a master matrix, with a "cell" assigned to each of the possible critical relationships. For the problem at hand, we have a matrix like that in Table 3.

The entry in column *a* for each input source and functional pair specifies the expected direction of relationship, while the column *b* entries reflect our expectations about order of effect. In practice, these two dimensions are highly inter-

Table 3. Dimensions of a strategic allocation analysis.

	INPUT SOURCES														
	FORMULA BUDGET (F)			CONTRACT FUNDING (C)			STUDENT INPUTS (S)			DONATIONS, BEQUESTS (D)			PUBLIC FEES (P)		
FUNCTION/MISSION	a	b	c	a	b	c	a	b	c	a	b	c	a	b	c
Teaching (T)	I	2	$m_{1,1}$	P	(3)	$m_{1,2}$	P	(1)	$m_{1,3}$	I	3	$m_{1,4}$	P	4	$m_{1,5}$
Research (R)	I	3	$m_{2,1}$	P	(1)	$m_{2,2}$	P	2	$m_{2,3}$	P	4	$m_{2,4}$	P	4	$m_{2,5}$
External service (E)	I	3	$m_{3,1}$	P	4	$m_{3,2}$	P	2	$m_{3,3}$	P	2	$m_{3,4}$	P	(1)	$m_{3,5}$

dependent. Therefore, to suggest something of our logic in these assignments, we will elaborate on the implications of the increase in teaching effectiveness (T).

1. Cell (1, 3):* The increase in teaching effectiveness (or level of educational service) is expected to have an immediate and positive impact on S; particularly, it is expected to lead to greater enrollment demand and to subsequently higher tuition and student fees in the next period.
2. Cell (1, 1): Presuming a positive effect of T on S in the first period, the impact of T on F in the second period is *a priori* indeterminate. The impact is delayed and indeterminate because we do not know whether the increase in funding from student sources (following an increase in T) will cause the funding authorities to adjust downward the *per capita* formula budgeting rate, to compensate for the increase in S. That is $[T, F] = I$ because $[F, S] = I$. To eliminate this indeterminacy, we would have to try to get a commitment from the funding authorities that would guarantee the formula budget rate over some range of increases in S.
3. Cell (1, 3): Here we presume that an increase in T led to an increase in S in the first period, with some portion of ΔS being available to hire new faculty with research ambitions; these then permit us to exert leverage on contract research funds in the third period (via cell 2, 2).
4. Cell (1, 4): Given an increase in S responding to a prior increase in T, we have an indeterminacy in the third period with respect to $[T, D]$. For example, there is a possibility that alumni and others will lessen their donations and bequests as student enrollment grows. Their intentions would have to be evaluated very carefully to eliminate the redundancy, and we would of course have to develop a magnitudinal measure, $m_{1,4}$, given that there was a possibility of a negative donation level in response to an increase in S. The general expectation is that $[T, D] = P$, assuming that the growth in student population may be expected to develop new donors at a faster rate than old donors are alienated, *etc.*

*For example, Cell (1, 3) would be the element at the conjunction of the first row and the third column, and so on.

5. Cell $(1, 5)$: We assume, here, that the ultimate impact of an increase in T on P is positive, but significantly lagged. Our logic is this: assuming that an increase in S accompanies an increase in T in the first period, we have some unallocated resources to invest based on S. We may elect to invest these, for example, in the development of an athletic program in the second period. This would imply hiring a coaching staff, purchasing equipment, and starting recruitment. A team may thus be fielded in the fourth period (or perhaps even the third), and a claim laid to fees for attendance at the games, television royalties, and so on.

We emerge with a strategic trajectory for each of the rows of the master matrix. The first row might be diagramed as in Figure 6. The various segments of the network each carry a probability index (in brackets) and a directional operator (in parentheses). At the point where we are concerned about the relationship between $[F, S]$, we enter a *stochastic node*. This suggests that there is some probability $(1 - p)$ that F may be reduced to negate the increase in S. If this occurs, then we do not have the unallocated inputs to devote to increasing the research capability (to generate $\Delta R \xrightarrow{(+)} \Delta C$) or to developing the external service dimension (implying $\Delta E \xrightarrow{(+)} \Delta P$). Given this stochastic node (assuming that it cannot be *a priori* eliminated), we have two possible utility calculations to consider:

$$U_T \equiv (\Delta G | \Delta T) = c_1 | (F, S) = P$$
$$= c_2 | (F, S) = N.$$

Of course, the condition where $(F, S) = N$ is tantamount to a punishment for success, which perhaps is not an unusual condition in the public sector. But generally, we can see that when missions are properly defined so that they are all correlated positively and are mutually reinforcing, then we can improve any one of the functions and eventually be able to improve them all. Thus, where

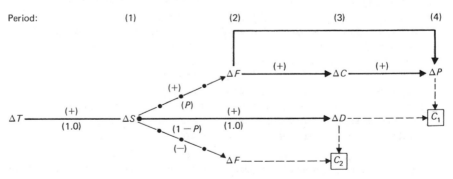

Figure 6. Strategic network diagram.

unallocated resources are available for rational investment, and where organizational missions are properly defined, our service organization becomes comprehensible as a *positively reflexive system* (one that can move secularly along an upward spiral in terms of potential effectiveness over some considerable range of inputs). Consider Figure 7. We can readily see that the development of these strategic networks to evaluate the impact of major missions can consume considerable time and resources. But there are often some tricks to reduce the scope of the strategic analysis process. Such a trick is available here when we recall the dictate that the service organization should act, at the strategic level, to $MAX(\$x/y)$. Consider that the fundamental utility of any mission will be measured with respect to this objective, so we get the following:

$$U_j = p_1F + p_2C + p_3S + p_4D + p_5P|\Delta W_{j(t)}.$$

The coefficients (the p_is) reflect the proportion of the increases in any of the inputs that are expected to be unallocated. Now, we may simplify our strategic analysis by recognizing that

$$p_1 \longrightarrow 0$$
$$p_2 \longrightarrow 0$$
$$p_5 \longrightarrow 1,$$

yielding a simplified utility formulation,

$$U_j = p_3S + p_4D + P|\Delta W_{j(t)}.$$

The logic behind this simplification is direct. The formula-budgeting input

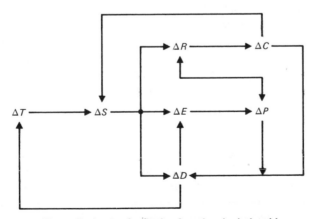

Figure 7. Array of reflexive functional relationships.

source tends to be fully allocated on the basis of real costs of educating a student (plus some fixed and usually minimal overhead contribution). If F were the only funding source available to the university, then x and y could increase (or decrease) only proportionally, and the strategic allocation problem would thus be moot. In short, the proportion of inputs from a formula (*per capita*) budgeting system that are unallocated goes to zero. So, as a rule, do inputs for the contract research function, for the C is predicated on the real costs of performing the research called for by the contracting authority (again with a minimal overhead loading). Therefore, p_2 also approaches zero. Funds drawn from external services (P) will, on the other hand, be totally unallocated, so that p_5 approaches unity and thus disappears. There may be some sort of internal contract that specifies that a certain portion of public fees (for example, from a football game) would revert to the athletic department, in which case we would have to compute p_5. But when such internal protocol is not in force, then the totality of public fees may generally be considered allocable at the discretion of the organizational authorities themselves.

IMPLICATIONS FOR RESOURCE ALLOCATION

The simplification of the basic calculation function becomes extremely important when we move into the constant-sum game, where an increase in resources devoted to one function (mission) implies a reduction in the resources available for the other missions. In such a case, an evaluation of the *cross-impact* conditions is required. A strategic network would have to be developed for each of the mission areas (*e.g.*, development of a network for R and E, in addition to the T network already illustrated). The analytical requirement is that cross-impact conditions be evaluated by *superimposing* the several networks (mathematically or logically), and searching for the optimum trade-off point or neighborhood— the point where the marginal product of funds allocated among competing functions is maximized. Although this task may sound onerous, many econometricians and system analysts are well-equipped to undertake it. The general technology would be a simulation program that can evaluate the "staged" redistribution of resources, so that we attempt to converge on the optimum through several different periods rather than make dramatic, one-shot redistributions. At any rate, when we have to work in a constant-sum-game context [5], we are looking for the *net* utility for any function (the effect that is adjusted for the detrimental consequences of decreasing the loadings on other missions). The simplified utility formulation just developed helps us here, for our simulations will have to operate on three factors instead of the original five. Thus, the policy that asks service organizations to emphasize return in terms of unallocated resources has some analytical advantages directly at the strategic level.

The basic allocative strategy, however, is the same, irrespective of the method of calculating utilities (*e.g.*, with or without cross-impact calculations). Suppose, for example, that we have an unallocated increment, ΔX. This increment will be distributed across several missions: $\Delta X = \Sigma X_j$. The formula for determining the actual allocations is thus:

$$X_j = U_j(\Delta X).$$

When we translate this funding increment into specific resources, we get the formulation we suggested earlier,

$$W_j = U_j(\Delta W).$$

It is worthwhile to note the obvious corollary: the strategy for *reducing* resource allocations in the face of a net decrease in the funding base. Expanding on the logic just developed, it is clear that reductions should be allocated with respect to the *reciprocals* of the utility indexes, as follows:

1. $(X_t - X_{t+1}) = Y, \quad Y > 0$

2. $Y = \Sigma Y_j$

3. $Y_j = + \dfrac{1}{U_j}(Y), \quad \dfrac{1}{U_j} = 1.0.$

We have yet to mention an obvious qualification to what we have done with respect to utilities. In many cases, we will not be able to develop specific numerical utility values (at least not without engaging in a possibly elaborate and certainly extended "learning" exercise). Therefore, in practice, we may have to content ourselves with a *ranking scheme*, in which we are satisfied that, for example, the utility for one mission is significantly greater than that for some other. That is, our utilities now become "ordinal numbers," which merely reflect comparative positions in a continuum of rankings.

We now move on to discuss the tactical allocation decisions within a service organization (and here there is a strong correspondence with the allocation process as it would be conducted in the prototypical commercial or profit-oriented organization). We know at this point that the allocation of resources according to mission utilities—determined on the basis of their relative leverage on unallocated inputs—leads to: $MAX(G) \equiv MAX(\$x/y)$. But at this point, our strategic allocations were really based on an expectation operator: $EV(G)$. Assuming that our strategic allocation decisions were properly (rationally) developed, $EV(G)$ becomes an *imputed optimum*, and the extent to which actual input leverage (actual G) approaches the imputed optimum depends on the rationality with which the tactical decision-makers allocate resources *within* the missions defined at the strategic levels (and subject to the utility constraints developed there).

Therefore, the major performance index for the tactical decision-makers is

$$\frac{G}{EV(G)}.$$

Consistent with the outline of the program budgeting logic presented earlier, the tactical decision-makers can use the facilities of the accountability system to try to converge on a favorable G. That is, allocations at the tactical level—within missions or functional sectors—become subject to some *a posteriori*, empirical discipline, *given* an adequate accountability system. For the case at hand, allocations should be made to individual units (or programs) on the basis of their *demonstrated marginal productivity* [6]. Therefore, the tactical allocation process becomes coextensive with the accountability system.

As in nearly all accountability situations, we are concerned with two dimensions, *quality* and *quantity*. Obviously, the best of all possible worlds is where each unit of the organization does a large amount of high-quality work. However, it is common to think of quantity and quality as competitive targets, as in Figure 8. Both the curves in the figure reflect this trade-off condition. Yet, curve I_1 is clearly superior to curve I_2. There is still a competitive relationship between quantity and quality, but it is softer (less elastic) for the former curve. Thus, under curve I_1, given any particular quantity of output, the associated quality is higher than on curve I_2. For any given level of resources (*e.g.*, a budget ceiling), the unit associated with curve I_1 will deliver a greater level of productivity than a unit associated with the curve I_2. Thus, the curves become intelligible as *productivity functions* (when we consider productivity as a given quantity of services delivered at some specific level of quality). So, the unit associated with curve I_1—because it makes more efficient use of *whatever* resources are allocated to it—becomes the preferred recipient of any incremental

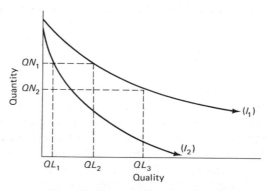

Figure 8. The tactical trade-off model.

resources, up to the point where it can be demonstrated that diminishing marginal returns set in.   (Because productivity functions are comparable only within some specific *range* of input values, it is very important that all cost-benefit projections for proposed programs be put in the form of a proper production function and not merely posed as tabular data.)

Within the context of our university example, we have a tautological issue at hand. When we ask how one unit might achieve a more favorable productivity curve than another, the answer that emerges is straightforward: because it has higher-quality resources to begin with. That is, a "better" teacher is one who can realize greater educational effectiveness in a larger class than can a "poorer" teacher; a "better" researcher turns out more work at any given level of quality than a "poorer" researcher.   Thus, the major factor determining the overall output structure for any university, and hence the value for the guiding function $G/EV(G)$, is the *quality* of the resources employed in the various units. The tactical accountability problem becomes the maintenance of the highest-quality personnel (and perhaps, equipment) base across all units. In this respect, the allocative decisions made in service organizations may sometimes reflect different criteria than those made by industrial firms. With the latter, increases in the quality of resources are generally accompanied by proportional increases in the cost of resources, which therefore permits a whole family of trade-offs. In service organizations, because of the difficulty of precisely measuring utility contributions, the relationship between quality and cost may be less elastic.

But service organizations often face a problem that is not present to the same extent within commercial and industrial enterprise. Particularly, many employees of service agencies tend to gain a form of tenure, which insulates them from recrimination for all but the most heinous activities (*e.g.*, moral turpitude, embezzlement).   A considerable portion of a university's personnel thus might be relatively immune from the effects of accountability. To this extent, as in the civil service in general, tenure may be an institutionalized detriment to organizational effieiency and effectiveness.   Of course, the essential argument for tenure is that it protects employees from managerial caprice. We hope to show that a proper accountability system can do the same thing, without concretizing suboptimality.   But to the extent that tenure exists, the university or general service organization should be prepared to pay more attention to selection and appointment of personnel. Once an individual is appointed, or granted tenure, he is difficult to remove or control. Therefore, the proper accountability system should also serve as a guide for the selection decisions of a service organization. That is, individuals seeking an appointment should be subject to the same accountability criteria as those seeking promotion or tenure, and so on. In summary, every unit as a whole—every department, every college, every division—and every individual seeking membership, promotion, or tenure should be required to demonstrate their probable contribution to the major missions of the university. Resource allocations would then be directed to those individuals and units that, among all alternatives, exhibit the highest productivity indexes.

For our purposes, the productivity indexes may take the form of utility values, perhaps computed according to a master function such as the following:

1. $u_{i,j} = \Sigma a_{n,i,j} U_n$

   where

   $n = 1$ = teaching function,
   $n = 2$ = research function, and
   $n = 3$ = external service function.

2. $MAX(u_{i,j})$ is the objective function.

3. $W_{i,j}/u_{i,j}$ or ($\$_{i,j}/u_{i,j}$) is the cost-benefit function (where w or $\$$ indicate resources allocated to the jth unit of the ith collectivity)

   where

   i indicates a collective unit,
   ($i = 1$ = department,
   $i = 2$ = division,
   $i = 3$ = college, and
   $i = 4$ = univeristy),

   and

   j indicates a lower-order unit within a collective unit
   ($j = 1$ = individual,
   $j = 2$ = department,
   $j = 3$ = division, and
   $j = 4$ = college).

For purposes of the university illustration, we would then have

$$u_{i,j} = (a_1 U_T + a_2 U_R + a_3 U_E)i,j$$

In short, every operating unit is expected to act to maximize the utility function. The components are relatively simple to explain. Initially, we must suggest that U_T, U_R, and U_E may be constant across all operating units, for they carry the generic utility values assigned at the strategic level (reflecting expectations about the relative importance of each of the three functions to the organization as a whole). In this way, the executives (strategists) of the organization can make their judgmental determinations take effect at the tactical (managerial) level. For the higher weighting of the preferred function means that a given utility index (point value) can be scored there with a lower performance rating (a smaller coefficient) than in one of the lower-weighted functional areas. It is hoped, then, that individual operating units may be gradually "nudged" into aligning themselves with the strategic priorities of the organization's executives. This implicit form of control may often be quite important, for there are sometimes distinct limits on the ability of higher management to directly control behavior of lower-level units. Therefore, the weighting of functions within the accountability framework is generally an exercise in suasion, and a legitimate control device when coercion or direct determinacy are either unavailable or impolitic.

In some instances, the accountability mechanism may operate on a regional basis, so that there will be several different macroentities under a central authority (*e.g.*, a state's department of higher education, the chancellor's office of a multicampus system). In such a case, it is possible for the different units to be assigned different functional weightings by the central authority. That is, the generic utility indexes may be determined exogenously. The preferred practice would be to set certain ceilings on some of the functions. For example, the central authorities may want a state college to concentrate on mass education. Therefore, they might set a ceiling value on U_R and U_E. This would not bar the state college from investments or research or external service, but it would *a priori* limit the point contribution associated with such functions. By the same token, a state university might be expected to be all things to all people; therefore, the central authority might restrict its ability to concentrate excessively on any single function. For example, the university might not be allowed to assign any single function a utility value greater than 0.5. The same thing may be true *within* an institution, for certain units may be especially concerned with one or another function. An evening college, for example, might be expected to concentrate rather fully on teaching; a graduate program, on the other hand, might be expected to emphasize research strongly. Therefore, we have to give executives the opportunity to impose certain floor and ceiling limits on the utilities associated with any major function, as follows:

$$\text{Teaching} \quad (t_1 \leqslant U_T \leqslant t_2)$$

$$\text{Research} \quad (r_1 \leqslant U_R \leqslant r_2)$$

$$\text{External service} \quad (e_1 \leqslant U_E \leqslant e_2)$$

where $U_T + U_R + U_E = 1$. This imposition of ranges on utility values may, however, not merely restrict latitude, but may protect the integrity of certain specialized units, which would suffer a real loss of effectiveness were all three functional dimensions weighted equally ($U_T = U_R = U_E = 0.333$).

The heart of the accountability process, given the assigned values or ranges for the generic functional utilities, is the matter of assigning specific quantitative values to the coefficients in the master equation: the *a*s. These will, as a rule, be utilities in their own right and should, therefore, range between 0 and 1.0. But from what we earlier suggested, we know that each coefficient will really be a productivity index, with two major components: quality (L) and some quantity measure (N).* Now, to allow some latitude to operating units, we may let these variables be indexed by subcoefficients, so that we get a formulation such as the following:

$$a_{i,j} = gl + kN$$

where $(g + k) = 1.0$. In short, the use of the g and k factors allows us to assign different weights to account for different levels of responsibility within any unit. For example, a graduate-level instructor may be responsible for fewer students, yet be expected to deliver high-quality education. Therefore, we might escalate the g value relative to k (which compensates for the inherently smaller classes that exist at the graduate level). Or a researcher, who is at work on a long-range project, might have little opportunity for publishing immediate (or intermediate) results; therefore, we might assign him a higher g value than we would someone whose research area permits a more favorable publication date. Of course, where no clear-cut predilection for quantity or quality exists, due to structural or contextual considerations, the g and k values may be removed from the formulation, or set as $g = k = 0.5$. At any rate, we must try to get a value for the coefficients themselves on both subdimensions (quality and quantity). In this respect, consider Table 4.

We may go through each of the components of the table very quickly. First, quantity indexes for all three functions are first of all matters of a raw count (*e.g.*, number of students taught for a certain number of hours, number of publications, number of external appearances). These are, however, subject to qualification on the basis of certain subfactors. For the teaching function, for example, we might be concerned about the number of different preparations the instructor has. The instructor who teaches four sections of the same course still has only one preparation, and would, therefore, have the expected capability to handle a larger student population. Some courses require a lot of student counseling (*e.g.*, professional seminars, laboratory courses, terminal or capstone courses); other courses—notably undergraduate survey offerings—require little counseling. Therefore, the teacher with a lower counseling load might be expected to handle a relatively higher number of students. Finally, the evaluation of students differs considerably from one course to the next. For example, it is relatively easy to grade mathematics homework, for the right answer is usually objectively determined and clearly accessible; essay or creative writing courses,

*These reflect the magnitude of achievements by a unit in one or another of the functional areas.

Table 4. Tactical evaluation criteria.

COEFFICIENT/FUNCTION	QUANTITY (N)		QUALITY (L)	
	BASE	QUALIFIERS	BASE	QUALIFIERS
a_1 (Teaching)	Student contact index = Courses × Enrollment × Credit hours	(a) Preparation schedule (b) Counseling imputations (c) Evaluation requirements, *etc.*	Student evaluation of instructor performance through questionnaire; relative enrollment, schedule; drop figures	(a) Subject area (b) Distribution of enrollment properties (c) Scheduling data
a_2 (Research)	Number of publications	(a) Book = x_1 (b) Monograph = x_2 (c) Article = x_3 (d) Book reviews = x_4 (e) Editorial = x_5	Data available on sales, reprint requests, citations, book reviews, *etc.*, essentially measuring impact and visibility	(a) Publisher/journal (b) Subject area (c) Progress reports
a_3 (External services)	Number of appearances	(a) Address (b) Lecture (c) Reading (d) Consultation	Data availabel on attendance, reviews, acceptance, *etc.*; return of contacts or requests for services, *etc.*	(a) Sponsoring organization (b) Impact

on the other hand, make great demands on the instructor and reduce the student population he can be expected to handle adequately.

As for teaching quality, several evaluation schemes can be implemented. Probably the most direct is asking the students to "grade" the instructor's performance. We might want to qualify this effectiveness index, however, by considering the subject to be taught or the nature of the student audience. For example, we may readily expect students to be more enthusiastic about an elective course than a required course. Moreover, if the author were looking for a handsome grade from students, he would generally prefer to teach something about sex or abnormal psychology than to teach integral calculus or general system theory. As for audience (enrollment properties), some classes will be filled by more enthusiastic students to begin with, especially where enrollment is restricted because of certain prerequisites or where there is a strict limit to class size, on a first-come, first-served basis. Finally, scheduling might affect students' evaluation of their instructors. For example, a class scheduled at 8 A.M. or at 9 P.M. might be expected to labor under inherent detriments that are no fault of the teacher. But there are also some relatively objective data that might be used to estimate quality of instruction. For example, in a free enrollment system, students will tend naturally to gravitate toward the best instructors in a field; therefore, under certain conditions, relative enrollment may reflect quality. Or, again assuming free enrollment, the best instructors may have their classes filled to the limit before less favorable instructors, on the basis of word-of-mouth advertising among students.* Finally, the number of drops in a course (relative to other sections of the same course) may be an indication of the instructor's quality. At any rate, these are just some of the criteria that might be employed in setting the performance coefficient on the teaching dimension.

As for the research function, the number of publications would be indexed by a point-value assigned the different types of publications one might produce. For example, a book would generally be expected to rate higher than an article, an article would imply more effort and prestige than a book review, and so on. As for research quality, we might employ many surrogates. With respect to a book, we might want to look at the quality of the reviews it received (and assign a qualitative value such as "excellent," "poor," *etc.*, with different points associated with each value). Or we might judge a book's quality by the volume of sales. A good surrogate for the imputed quality of an article or scholarly paper is the number of reprint requests, whether it is republished as part of a collection, and so forth. The number of times a publication is cited and praised by other authors is often an indication of quality. (As a qualifier, however, we

*Naturally, we would want to factor out "cinch" courses, and so forth.

would have to adjust for the possibility that works critical of established practices may be attacked by a majority of reviewers.) But there are also qualifications that might be raised to lend a subjective amplification to research quality. For example, members of a specific discipline might get together and rank the different journals of a field, so that some are ranked higher than others. The same is true of publishing houses. Thus, a publication in a more prestigious journal or by a "better" house would earn the author more points than publication by a lower-ranking journal or house. Moreover, some subjects are more open to publication than others. For example, geriatrics, racial studies, and studies of the "work ethic" are quite easy to publish at the current time. Inquiries into pure mathematics or other erudite studies are always difficult to publish. Finally, there may be an internal consensus about the expected impact of the study or investigation, perhaps in an effort to protect those who are working on long-range projects. Such consensus would presumably be made on the basis of progress reports submitted to a review committee, which might then be used to evaluate research performance where there are no publications. This would be especially important in the appointment of newly graduated faculty, who would probably not be published and could offer only a research plan or a prospectus.

Essentially the same investigatory logic holds true when we move to the external services dimension. For example, a major address to the American Association for the Advancement of Science would earn the author more points than a lecture given to the college French club or a luncheon speech to the local Rotary Club. Consultation for a major branch of government on a critical problem would count for more than a week's work for the local bakery or the occupation of an honorary position on the board of the local sewer authority. Coaching a football team with a winning season would earn the coach more support and affection than would a losing season. At any rate, when we move to the area of external service, we usually will have to rely most heavily on judgmental performance indexes—point assignments that are essentially subjective in origin.

We hope that the basic features of these tactical accountability criteria are reasonably clear, although they are offered here strictly to further our illustration and not as a set to be immediately introduced into any operating situation. But the major point is that, wherever possible, quantitative data are sought, supplemented where necessary (or desirable) by subjective data. These subjective data, which result in the assignment of points on the basis of opinion rather than direct measurement, are not to be looked at askance. For as this accountability system would be employed, the subjective assignments could be made by a specially designed, disciplined qualitative analysis. This would minimize the probability of "irrational" factors entering the calculus, *e.g.*, prejudice, personality, jealousy, internal politics. Moreover, subjective indices may be developed with significant precision. For example, recall that the "quality" of a publication is to be measured in part by the imputed quality of the publisher. Let us assume that we are interested in sociology. In this case, a committee of sociologists would be formed either in a single location or as part of a correspondence team (perhaps with members from outside the particular department or university). They would be given a list of all sociological journals and asked to rank them as to imputed prestige, with this ranking perhaps reflecting something about the rejection rate for manuscripts, exhaustiveness of the review process, legitimacy of the particular journal as a source of sociological opinion, and so on. Thus, the assignment of point values to other journals could be a very disciplined process indeed, and need not be casual or arbitrary. Indeed, as many sophisticated analysts well know, there are techniques available for injecting "objectivity" into subjective analyses [7].

We need not spend any more time on the calculative aspects of the model, as they are open to modification and imagination from many different directions. But the major point—that performance indices can be developed to lend substance to our accountability coefficients—should be beyond dispute. The question now is: what do we do with these indices after we have developed them? The answer, of course, is that they are the primary base for resource allocation decisions at the tactical level.

Particularly, we must note that, given an actual point score (utility) index for any unit of the organization, we may quickly develop a cost-effectiveness index. Recall that the utility index is the output of a performance audit conducted according to the following formulation:

$$u_{i,j} = (a_1 u_T + a_2 u_R + a_3 u_E)_{i,j}.$$

Now, we can usually identify the costs associated with the maintenance of any unit (*e.g.*, salary and benefits paid to an individual, budget and overload associated with a department or division). Therefore, we have at hand the following:

$$\text{Cost/benefit}_{i,j} = \$i_{,j}/u_{i,j}.$$

And, of course, cost-benefit ratios may be aggregated for any level of the organization. For example, the cost-benefit index associated with a department would be the aggregate of the indices for the members of that department. A division's cost-benefit index would be the aggregate of the indices of its departments; the aggregate cost-effectiveness index of a college might be arrived at by aggregating those of the divisions and departments under its aegis:

$$u_i = \Sigma\Sigma a_{n,j} U_n.$$

Given this, we can compute the aggregate cost-benefit index for any macrosystem (collectively), such as a university. While this would give the directors a reading of the overall effectiveness and efficiency of the organization, it could also be used for the rational allocation of resources among competing organizations within a regional educational system, (*e.g.*, between the state university and the several state colleges, or among several state colleges).

Thus, the three major allocation decisions of any system may be lent discipline by the result of the accountability process:

1. allocation of increases in x/y,
2. allocation of cuts associated with a decrease in x/y,
3. allocation of existing resources under the constant-sum game context in the hopes of maximizing G (the increase in unallocated overhead inputs between operating periods).

In Figure 9 several different units within some collectivity (i) are all competing for shares of some aggregate budget (x). These competing units (the $X_{i,j}$s) are arrayed according to their performance (utility) indices. Now, the optimum allocation schedule can be found in such a way that a "directional threshold" is established. Entities to the left of this threshold would receive proportionally larger allocations relative to demand than units to the right. In other instances, the resource allocations made to the units falling to the left of the threshold might be expanded, at the direct expense of the units to the right of the threshold (the constant-sum game context), using the relative utilities to weight the redistribution process. Finally, a release threshold might be established, so that units falling below some absolute performance level are automatically deprived of their allocations (*e.g.*, disbanded or retired). For selection and promotion purposes, we might establish definite utility thresholds above which an individual must rise if he or she is to become a serious candidate. If there are scarce positions or promotional dollars, these would be allocated to the candidates with the highest utilities. In short, the decision-maker with a fair command of standard cost-accounting and a rudimentary knowledge of basic optimization procedures should be able to *rationalize* resource allocations considerably throughout

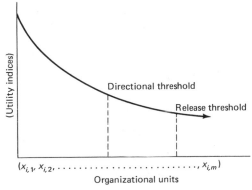

Figure 9. Tactical resource allocation curve.

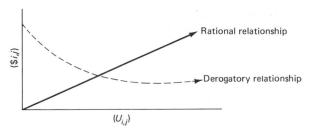

Figure 10. Utility/resource map.

the service organization or throughout some regional collection of organizations, given the output from an accountability process such as that we have described.

For purposes of collective bargaining and personnel compensation within service organizations—and, of course, service enterprises have been increasingly subject to strikes by, and recriminations from, their employees in recent years—the accountability model might also provide an answer. It is possible to develop a simple "map" of the relationships between costs (compensations or allocations) and performance, as shown in Figure 10.

The origin of the rational relationship is simple. We merely develop a scatter diagram of the various cost-performance ratios that emerge for each operating unit. To the extent that resource allocations (costs) completely reflect performance, we should get a positive and directly proportional relationship. Departures from the rationalized relationship might be indicated were a regression curve such as the nonnormative trajectory to develop. Here, as we can see, costs (resource allocations) are in a significantly inverse (but roughly proportional) relationship to performances. In short, through seniority, tenure, inertial budgeting, or some other device that insulates compensation from contribution, we have arrived at the situation where the greatest consumers of resources are the least productive users of those resources.

There are, of course, variations on the procedures and logics set out here were we to consider other types of public enterprise [8]. But we should see that the overall strategic objective of service organizations, their operational objective, and the tactical objective are all equivalent:

$$MAX(\$x/y) \equiv MAX \frac{(G)}{EVG} \equiv MAX(u_{n,i,j}).$$

In the short run, it is always possible to achieve the first objective without benefit of the third.* But if proper accountability processes were operating across the service sector, then we would expect the various funding sources to make

*Through the mechanisms that allow an organization to abrogate the relationship between growth and efficiency.

their aggregate allocations according to the utility criteria, and, thus, make the connection between effectiveness and efficiency that rationality demands. To the extent that organizational directors—and the resource-providing agencies themselves—do not demand accountability in service organizations, there is no way to guarantee that allocations at any level are related to productivity criteria.

NOTES AND REFERENCES

1. To some extent, business organizations have become more susceptible to exogenous factors (*e.g.*, environmental constraints, inquiries into marketing or political functions, class-action consumer suits). It is interesting to note, however, that these considerations may never be incorporated into the calculus of the line manager, but rather may be dealt with as a public relations problem. Hence, they pass from the realm of responsibility to the realm of appearances in which public relations people travel.
2. For more on this, see my *Managing Social Service Systems*, New York: Petrocelli Books, 1977.
3. Note that the entire decision-accountability process described here would be a case of overkill were we to try to apply it to, say, an elementary school or a high school. In these latter cases—as opposed to the context of higher education in which we shall be working—standardized tests enable us to get a more or less well-conceived ordinal measurement of educational effectiveness. When such quantitative referents are available, relatively straightforward optimization (*e.g.*, standard operations research) techniques are to be used, not the somewhat tortuous and comparatively expensive processes set out here.
4. In this case, if reductions in resources are proportional to increases in efficiency, the level of service is not revised upward, and gross effectiveness thus remains unaffected.
5. Both constant-sum and positive-sum games will concern us in this volume, although not in great detail. A good report on these two gaming contexts—and others—is given by Anatol Rapoport, *Two Person Game Theory: The Essential Ideas*, Ann Arbor, Mich.: University of Michigan Press, 1966.
6. The responsibilities of the tactical decision-maker within the context of most service organizations is really more complicated than is suggested here. For they must generally allocate resources not only on the basis of historical performance criteria, but also in a way that will deal with demand problems. For example, there may be a low inherent demand for a particular service, yet its maintenance at some level might be considered absolutely necessary (perhaps even legislated). Such necessary but unfavorable services become exogenous constraints on the tactical decision-maker, and might thus set a "floor" under the aggregate efficiency he might achieve. However, resources allocated to these *a priori* fixed programs or units may still be undertaken within the rationality framework developed here. Moreover, we can adjust tactical performance measures to reflect factors over which they have no control.
7. For example, see my paper "Attacking Indeterminacy: The Case for the Hypothetico-Deductive Method and Consensus Statistics," *The Journal of Technological Forecasting and Social Change* 6(1974).
8. For accountability concepts as applied to Social Service Systems, see Chapter 4 of *Managing Social Service Systems*, op. cit.

5

PPB and the Marketing Contribution: Implications for the Management of Public Enterprise

Stephen W. Brown, Lonnie L. Ostrom,
and John L. Schlacter
Arizona State University

A story is told of the return of the chief scout to the camp of Lewis and Clark's northwest expedition after an extended scouting trip. His report included some good news as well as some bad news. The good news was, he said, that the expedition was making excellent progress. The bad news was that they were lost. A similar scouting report could be filed concerning the current position or dilemma of some public enterprises. Although experiencing growth and development in recent decades, many public bodies find themselves plagued by financial crisis, demand for accountability, and a sizable credibility gap, all of which might well prompt one to question to what end all this progress is directed [1].

A partial explanation for this predicament rests in the limited exposure public administrators have had to contemporary marketing concepts. Marketing may be defined as the effective administration by an organization of the exchange relationships with its various markets. Although traditionally confined to private enterprise, modern marketing suggests that *all* organizations, public or private, operate for the purpose of satisfying their various publics (*e.g.*, markets).

Additionally, unlike business firms, public agencies to do not have a precise measure of performance. In the absence of profit criteria, these bodies have to rely on surrogate measures. One approach taken by a number of public institutions has been the adoption of the planning-programming-budgeting (PPB) approach. During Lyndon Johnson's administration, PPB was developed by the executive branch of the US Government to help establish a system that would be useful in determining priorities, formulating plans, choosing between programs, and measuring costs against meaningful performance yardsticks.

720

We contend that PPB, while becoming increasingly utilized by a variety of public agencies, is essentially an internal administrative process. PPB, therefore, suffers from an absence of inputs from relevant *external* environments or markets. This "outside" source of information is often critical in establishing appropriate objectives, plans, programs, and budgets. The addition of a marketing orientation to the PPB framework can help remedy this situation.

The purpose of this paper is to integrate marketing and PPB concepts in public agencies. We use the public university to provide a systemic illustration of the desired integration. The findings should, however, by equally applicable to other public entities.

AN OVERVIEW

One of the primary topics on the agenda of a recent educational management conference was "Marketing in Higher Education." The information brochure advertising the conference stated that "While most successful enterprises are customer- or market-oriented, higher education tends to be production- or research-oriented due to decades of operating in a sellers market [2] . . . . A careful analysis of the previous statement reveals that, at present, institutions of higher education are either in the process of, or on the verge of, going through a transition that the business world experienced during the late 1950s and throughout the 1960s—a transition period in which the managerial emphasis within the firm shifted to one of marketing. The individual firm can no longer afford to operate under the assumption that supply creates its own demand. Rather, the reverse logic that demand creates supply became the governing principle.

Robert Fenske, director of the Center for Higher Educational Administration at Arizona State University, suggests that one of the primary postulates underlying the theory of effective college and university administration is that "good business practice is good education practice" [3]. For a number of universities, 'good business practice" has meant the adoption of PPB processes. Thus, both PPB and marketing are receiving increasing attention from university administrations.

Figure 1 illustrates how public enterprises such as higher education institutions can utilize marketing and PPB processes. The two circles on the right side of the figure represent the external environments. The ultimate environment consists of the broad social, economic, technological, and political and legal forces that influence the institution's activities. The inner circle, termed the proximate environment, consists of the institution's markets.

The internal mechanism for generating feedback from the external environments is marketing intelligences. As shown in Figure 1, this intelligence is a major input to the institution's various PPB processes—objective setting, plan-

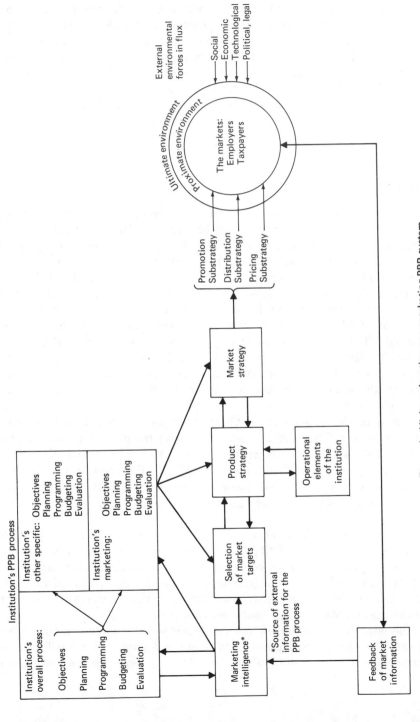

Figure 1. Higher education as a marketing PPB system.

ning, programming, budgeting, and evaluation. PPB determinants, along with marketing intelligence, assist in the selection of market targets or segments. These targets represent the specific markets (*e.g.*, employers interested in engineering graduates) to which the university elects to direct its efforts.

Market segmentation is a critical activity for any organization, whether public or private. Segmentation is the process of taking the heterogeneous whole and dividing it into operational segments based upon some common characteristic or characteristics. Far too often these characteristics are couched in purely economic terms. Although there is no denying the importance of economic criteria, such additional criteria as psychosocial variables and various demographic measures also merit serious attention. The segmentation process is completed with the selection of those segments (*i.e.*, selection of market targets) that the university wishes to attract. Selection is based upon both the potential of the various segments, as revealed by the marketing intelligence systems through an analysis of objectives, and the resource constraints of the university. Product strategy can then be developed in conformity with market needs.

Product strategy consists of developing educational offerings that will appeal to the university's chosen markets. These offerings are then presented to the markets *via* the institution's substrategies of promotion, distribution, and pricing.

These strategies are usually developed on the basis of comprehensive cost-benefit analyses. In effect what is required is the determination of elasticity measures for each of the elements so that marginal expenditures can be made to the point at which revenue for promotion just equals marginal cost, the same relationship also holding true for distribution and pricing. In equation form the complex of marketing substrategies is optimized at the point where:

$$\frac{\text{MR Promotion}}{\text{MC Promotion}} = \frac{\text{MR Distribution}}{\text{MC Distribution}} = \frac{\text{MR Price}}{\text{MC Price}} = 1$$

Realistically, the authors recognize that such precision may be impossible in most public agencies. Nevertheless, the concept does provide direction for marketing efforts.

This "model" of PPB and marketing serves as a framework for much of the balance of the article. In the succeeding three sections PPB and marketing are discussed in greater detail within the context of a university system. Given this basis, the article then demonstrates how the two concepts can be incorporated and together serve as a significant aid to decision-making in higher education.

PLANNING-PROGRAMMING-BUDGETING

Planning-programming-budgeting is a means through which a nonprofit organization can assign resources to accomplish its objectives more effectively and efficiently. As such, PPB is a means by which a higher educational institution's outputs, programs, plans, and alternatives are taken into account to achieve an integrated course of action for the organization as a whole. In general, PPB is an administrative concept designed to produce better planning and decision-making in public organizations. It attempts to help an organization achieve its objectives by identifying programs that most effectively employ the resources available to attain these objectives.

Background of PPB

Planning-programming-budgeting originated in the US Government. Antecedent forms of PPB were used to consider federal public works as early as 1902 [4]. The approach did not achieve any degree of sophistication, however, until the sharply increased demand for better advice on government problems was coupled with the increased capability of providing that advice.

The groundwork for modern PPB was laid by the Hoover Commission, the RAND Corporation, and certain welfare economists. In 1949 the Hoover Commission on Organization of the Executive Branch of the Government recommended that the government adopt a budget based on functions, activities, and projects, which it labeled a "performance budget" [5]. Five years later, researchers at the RAND Corporation presented a proposal showing how the new concept could be applied to military spending. David Novick, in a RAND study entitled, *Efficiency and Economy in Government Through New Budgeting Procedures*, recommended PPB for adoption by the Department of Defense. Further study continued at RAND, culminating in 1960 with two significant publications: *The Economics of Defense in the Nuclear Age* by Charles J. Hitch and Roland N. McKean; and *New Tools for Planners and Programmers* by David Novick [6]. At approximately the same time, two welfare economists published books evaluating the cost-benefit analysis undertaken by federal water resource agencies [7]. These two books, which furnish criteria for ascertaining the optimal allocation of public funds among competing uses, contain many of the major elements of PPB.

Joining the theory and practice of PPB took place with President Kennedy's appointment of Robert S. McNamara as Secretary of Defense in 1961 [4, p. xv]. McNamara had been involved in systems analysis during World War II and later at the Ford Motor Co. Charles Hitch, formerly with the RAND Corporation, was appointed Assistant Secretary under McNamara and brought a number of his RAND personnel to the Department of Defense. The RAND people offered new ways to approach defense problems, and they applied PPB methods on a departmentwide basis. The department's planning and budgeting, for example, were reorganized in terms of objectives (deterrence of nuclear attack, capability for limited war, *etc.*), rather than in terms of inputs used (personnel, equipment, *etc.*), or the often arbitrary classifications given by legislative or administrative tradition (Army, Marine Corps, *etc.*) [8].

The success of PPB thinking in the Department of Defense led President Johnson to apply the process to all civilian agencies of the government. On August 25, 1965, he informed the press that he had asked each member of the cabinet [9]:

> ... to immediately begin to introduce a very new and a very revolutionary system of planning and programming and budgeting throughout the vast Federal Government, so that through the tools of modern management the full promise of a finer life can be brought to every American at the lowest possible cost.

Predictably, the introduction of this new process in the federal government aroused interest in other areas, including academic circles. While several large educational institutions are using PPB processes, evidence exists to suggest that the actual implementation of the process is still in its elementary stages [10]. Nevertheless, university systems in California [11], Utah [12], and Pittsburgh [13], to name a few, have made major advances in using PPB. According to Charles J. Courey, assistant vice-president of planning for the California system, the process has aided in planning and resource allocation, particularly on the growing campuses. He also notes that PPB has intensified cost consciousness in all aspects of university operations [11].

Nature of PPB

As a normative method of decision-making, the PPB process may be delineated into a number of general procedures. The following procedures were synthesized from the works of a number of scholars of public administration:

1. Careful identification and examination of the objectives in the relevant areas of organizational functioning (objectives).
2. Formulation of objectives and programs extending beyond the immediate date of program submission (planning).
3. Analysis and management of the activities of a decision unit in terms of its programs, and how these programs contribute to the unit's and organization's objectives (programming) and financial requirements (budgeting).
4. Appraisal of objectives, programs, and budgets in the light of experience and a changing environment (evaluation).

As suggested above, the four procedures are not mutually exclusive. Planning activities, for example, will often need to take into account programming considerations. The following pages highlight each of the four procedures.

Objectives

Formal PPB begins with a careful identification of objectives in each major area of organizational activity. The concept attempts to force the organization and its units to reflect on the fundamental aims of their current and future programs. Although the definition of broad program objectives is vital, wherever possible objectives should be precisely stated. The expression of precise objectives does not mean that all objectives must be quantifiable. Instead, the program objectives are to be expressed in terms susceptible of translation into analytical assessment.

Establishing the objectives of organizational activity provides two values crucial to the success of PPB. First, they provide the foundation for demonstrating the relationship among programs. This foundation is necessary for structuring the PPB process. Second, they provide the foundation for program activity and the standards for determining whether a program is accomplishing its goals.

The PPB approach recognizes the likelihood of different objectives among various levels and units in the organization: long-term versus short-term. In a university, for example, the academic department will not have the same range of objectives as the college of liberal arts; nor will the college deal with as broad a spectrum as the university. Although PPB aims to have each decision-maker's objectives consistent with the institution's objectives, no attempt is made to have the objectives of each level identical. Instead, the approach strives to develop a harmony among objectives.

Planning

A second aspect of PPB is the projection of objectives and programs into the future. Since most programs cannot achieve their intended objectives in a month or even a single year, PPB seeks to relate current activities to longer range plans. Thus, the present activities of an organization are to be carried out within the framework of annual and multiyear plans.

In general, the common elements of the plan consist of a forecast of the environment in which the organization or unit will be functioning; a statement of the objectives the body intends to pursue; a discussion of how the unit intends to pursue those objectives; and, in all probability, the resources required to achieve the objectives. A listing of the elements of a plan leads to a brief discussion of guidelines for planning in a PPB framework. First, planning must be continuous. The process never stops; and, to some extent, planning is employed on a contingency basis. The conditional nature of some planning leads to a second guideline. Planning is initiated within a framework of factors relatively uncontrollable by the institution. According to Dror, the uncontrollable factors include basic external environmental factors that limit the alternatives to be considered in the planning process and influence general organizational objectives and values set prior to planning [14].

A most important aspect of planning in PPB is the imaginative search for all realistic means of accomplishing objectives at various decision levels. Thus, a decision-maker cannot be blindly committed to the existing manner of doing things. Since the best alternative cannot be selected unless it is considered, one must search critically for alternative means. In addition to searching for alternatives, PPB suggests that the alternatives be assessed by weighting the anticipated benefits to be gained against the projected costs that will be incurred.

Programming

The third procedure is termed "programming." A program is an identifiable activity that has inputs that can be related to outputs. The essence of programming (or program budgeting) is to relate inputs to outputs in terms of how the outputs of the program contribute to the institution's objectives.

Traditional planning and budgeting in public institutions is input-oriented. Within a PPB framework, however, the decision-maker's attention is turned toward outputs, along with program and institutional objectives, and away from detailed scrutiny of input categories, such as wages and equipment.

Although programming goes beyond the scope of typical budgeting in public organizations, it remains a theoretical exercise unless implemented through the budget. The PPB budget should be classified by programs rather than by inputs. The programs in turn have an output that should contribute to the objective of a given decision unit and the institution as a whole.

For the sake of clarity, different terms are generally used to indicate the level at which a program is being considered. Figure 2 shows that three levels are identified in programming. The first level of detail is termed "program categories," which are groupings of an organization's activities serving the same broad objective. Program subcategories are the second level of breakdown. The group activities are based on somewhat narrower objectives, but they contribute directly to the broad goals of the program category.

The final level of detail is the program element, which is a subdivision of program subcategories. The element is the basic building block of PPB. An example using these three terms may help to distinguish them. A program category of a university may relate to the broad objective of developing the fundamental knowledge of students. A program subcategory may be associated with the goal of developing the knowledge of graduate students, and a program element may be the establishment of a Ph.D. program in geography. As the basic building block, program elements generally consist of the existing and proposed departments of the university [15].

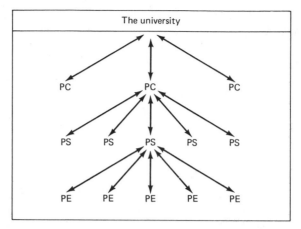

Figure 2. Program levels and their interdependency.

The output orientation of programming implies that the end products of programs are identifiable and measurable. In administration in the public economy, however, outputs are sometimes hard to identify and often unsusceptible to quantification. Although PPB cannot insist on precise output indicators, it does insist on the identification and attempted measurement of outputs.

Evaluation

Evaluation is another part of PPB. Assessment is made of objective or program accomplishment. PPB recommends the construction of indicators that will help measure how well an objective is being attained. Analysis of this nature can subject public programs to a rigor that will help determine whether more worthwhile objectives or programs should be considered in lieu of current objectives.

PPB evaluative techniques are in need of further development. Many of the techniques are treated on a conceptual (as opposed to quantitative) level. The ability to quantify the techniques is handicapped by the difficulties encountered in the measurement of benefits arising from a program's or organization's outputs [16].

Thus, the evaluative step in PPB falls short of pure scientific inquiry. Evaluation serves primarily to advise decision-makers through as rigorous an analysis as possible, given the limitations of output measurement and human judgment.

Interrelationship of decisions

A recognition of decision interrelationship is a final important aspect of PPB. The concept implicitly suggests that an organization is composed of units that relate to one another in such a way that if the program of one unit is modified other programs are affected. For example, the objective of a program element contributes to the objective of a program subcategory, whose objective is harmonious with those of its program category. In addition, two or more program elements are interrelated if they are associated with the same subcategory or the same category. In a like manner, two or more subcategories are interrelated if they are associated with the same category. Thus, a change in a program category, subcategory, or element will have ramifications outside the individual unit.

The interrelationship of program categories, subcategories, and elements sometimes cuts across traditional decision structures rather than coinciding with them. The reason for this possible occurrence is that PPB is an attempt at rational decision-making, whereas existing administrative structures are often a product of tradition, inertia, and intuitive action.

Investigation of the decision process

Prior to introducing PPB, a thorough research of the decision process in the organization or unit under study is recommended. PPB reflects a rational management process, but to apply the concept one must first comprehend the characteristics of the existing decision process. For example, the researcher may discover that in a given area no clear objectives have ever been developed. The existence or nonexistence of objectives in an area will determine in part the ease with which PPB can be applied.

Misconceptions About PPB

The attention that PPB has received has led to a number of misconceptions about the concept. Identifying these misconceptions should further clarify the nature of PPB. First, PPB is not a substitute for the experience and judgment of the decision-maker. On the contrary, its main role is to sharpen one's judgment by stating objectives, programs, and outputs more precisely, by uncovering new alternatives, and by making explicit comparisons among alternatives.

Second, PPB is not decision-making by computer, and it is not limited to cost accounting and narrow economic considerations. Wherever relevant, quantitative measures are encouraged, but PPB is more of an orientation than a body of quantitative techniques. As such, it does not attempt to assign numbers to all aspects of a problem. Often subjective evaluations of intangibles are made through the appropriate use of good judgment.

Third, cost-benefit analysis, cost-effectiveness analysis, and program budgeting, are not synonyms for PPB. The preceding terms are often used interchangeably with PPB, but each term is only a component of PPB. A term that can be closely identified with PPB is systems analysis. In fact, the application of systems analysis to a business firm is very similar to the application of PPB to a public or nonprofit institution. Although the two concepts are analogous, one major distinction is worth noting. In the public sector of the economy, systems analysis has been almost exclusively restricted to quantitative considerations. PPB recognizes the significance of quantitative measures, but also considers qualitative analysis. Thus, PPB encompasses systems analysis in the public economy.

PPB Myopia

The virtues of PPB have been stressed in nearly every piece of literature on the concept. Because of this orientation, a tendency exists to overlook a major limitation of the approach.

The PPB literature indicates that the process is primarily inward-looking. That is, it is essentially an administrative process that seeks to develop objectives and the plans and programs necessary to accomplish them. The plans and programs in turn are quantified in the form of budgets. There is relatively little in the literature, unfortunately, dealing with the information base upon which objectives, plans, programs, and budgets are established. Too often the objectives, plans, programs, and budgets are established on the basis of some modification of last year's budget, the resources available, the desires of administrators, or the perception of what the legislature, in the case of a state university system, may provide.

All of these considerations are important and provide valuable input into the PPB process. Further, the PPB concept can and should accommodate information input of this type. The PPB concept in theory, of course, simply requires information inputs to the planning process. *It does not specify the source of the information. Herein lies the potential weakness of the system.* Note that in the preceding discussion of the nature of PPB none of the sources of information related *demand in the ultimate marketplace to PPB.* More specifically, the product of the university system (supply) has not been effectively related to the desires of the marketplace (demand) for the output of the university system in the PPB process. Furthermore, while theoretically, the system adjusts to the situation, often this does not take place as efficiently as it might, given such barriers as the high capital outlay required to build insitutions of higher learning.

A potential solution to the dilemma described above is the application of the Marketing Concept to the PPB process. The Marketing Concept is primarily a consumer- or market-oriented philosophy that seeks to satisfy various markets at a profit (or satisfactory cost-benefit ratio, within the university system). The essential element in the concept, particularly as it applies to the position taken in this paper is that the focus is on the ultimate users of the output of the university system. The *primary* sources of information for the PPB process are these markets, and objectives, plans, programs, and budgets are generated with the purpose of satisfying the requirements (demand) of these publics. In short, while the PPB process itself remains the same, the basic input is dramatically altered, thereby moving the focus of the PPB process from an internal orientation to a recognition and appreciation of primary (external to the university system) markets.

The following section will develop the idea of the Marketing Concept as it relates to a university system.

MARKETING AND THE UNIVERSITY SETTING

Traditional definitions of marketing conceived of marketing activities as designed primarily to facilitate the flow of title, goods, and services from producer to consumer. In other words, "marketing" began only after the creation of a product, and was mainly directed toward distribution of that product. This concept of marketing was viable in a period when the demand for goods and services exceeded the available supply.

But, as productive capacity increased, bringing the supply of goods and services more in line with existing demand, new problems arose for the producer. Now, he had to adjust his production to demand. Interest in selling activities began to increase dramatically during this period, for it was the salesman who could facilitate the adjustment required. His function, however, was still primarily to locate acceptable markets for the company's products.

Our economy then entered a third state—one in which the potential supply of goods could far outstrip the demand. This created a whole new role for marketing. The logic is straightforward: since a producer cannot afford to produce in excess of demand, he should understand the nature and extent of demand for his product before he initiates production.

Today, therefore, marketing has a consumer orientation—that is, the process attempts to recognize and define the needs and desires of the consuming public and to adjust productive output to meet these needs and desires [17]. Philosophically, this concept is extremely important for marketers, because it recognizes that the market process must be initiated prior to production. Such a concept is also important to the consumer, for it considers his needs and wants as well as those of the producer.

Much of the criticism now being leveled at institutions of higher education has some validity in terms of the marketing philosophy just described. Many feel there has been inadequate, misdirected, and inefficient allocation of resources to needs in higher education. Going one step farther, certain critics suggest that neither higher education's "needs," nor even its "consuming publics," have been correctly identified. "It is the needs of the public and of the donor that the colleges must stress—not their own [18] . . . .

In the business world, there are several publics that today impinge on marketing and its activities.   These include government (federal, state, and local), society as a whole, special interest groups, and several other broadly defined publics.   Also included are those publics with which marketing interacts on virtually a daily basis—suppliers, competitors, and particularly customers.   Any marketing organization that does not recognize and monitor these publics is doomed to failure.

In a marketing sense, then, the consumers and potential consumers of graduates of institutions of higher education, as well as other affected publics, are not only questioning the quality of the "product" and the efficiency with which it is distributed, but also the very need for the product in a number of disciplines.

In a recent article, a legislator chastised the present educational system for wasting funds by educating students for jobs that do not exist [19] :

> There are great and continuing needs for trained professionals in many areas. There are others where university graduation is adding to the existing surplus. . . .

> While it would be impossible to match university admission and school training programs with societal requirements, effort should be made to bring them into greater balance.

Viewed in this light, the challenge ahead for higher education becomes the marketing of higher education in a buyer's market as opposed to the production of higher education in a seller's market [1] .

In essence, it is a position of this paper that the management emphasis in institutions of higher education must shift from one of production (internal orientation) to one of marketing; and that those institutions of higher education that fail to read accurately the "markets" they serve will be threatened with extinction or stagnation.

The Concept of a Marketing System

A helpful perspective, one that complements the PPB process, considers a marketing systemic approach to activities in the area of higher education. Figure 1 illustrated such a system [20] .

The ultimate environment, represented by the outer circle on the right-hand side of the model, shows the broad forces (*i.e.*, social, economic, technological, and political and legal) that impinge both directly and indirectly on the institution's activities.   The "proximate environment" includes those organizations, institutions, and individuals that receive day-to-day attention, such as employers and taxpayers.

If higher education is to respond effectively to its external environments, it must first be aware of them, and second, learn something about them. This requires a marketing intelligence system to gather and distil information from the environment. All of us use some "intelligence system," however informal, to acquire information. It is the contention here that higher education must *formally* and *systematically* consider and create those elements and processes within the institution that facilitate the efficient acquisition of necessary marketing data. This, in itself, becomes an objective within the PPB process of the university system.

As illustrated in Figure 1 the information generated by the "intelligence system" is used in the formulation of the institution's overall and marketing objectives, plans, programs, budgets, and evaluation process. The establishment of these guidelines, combined with knowledge of markets provided by the intelligence system, allows markets to be segmented into relatively homogeneous units exhibiting similar characteristics, patterns, and need structures. The "target markets" upon which the individual institution of higher education wishes to focus its attention (ordinarily those showing greatest potential) can then be selected from among those segments.

This additional knowledge of markets, combined with internal information concerning the operational capabilities of the institution, permits the formulation of specific product (program) strategies. Product strategy, in turn, leads to market strategies—those strategies designed to bring the product to its markets in the most efficient manner possible. Market strategies encompass promotion, pricing, and distribution dimensions. At this point, the marketing loop is closed.

The following sections of this paper will elaborate on selected elements in Figure 1; the last section will be devoted to an integration of the Marketing Concept with the PPB process.

Monitoring of Publics: The Marketing Intelligence System

In a buyer's market, the first priority of any institution of higher education is monitoring the needs and wants of its publics and developing strategies for satisfying them. While it is true that some institutions of higher education have already begun to monitor their consumer publics, the question is whether this evolution toward a marketing function in higher education will be a planned change or a chaotic evolution.

What higher education really needs is an effective intelligence system that will accurately monitor the marketplace, as well as other relevant publics. Such a system must provide the administrator with the external information he needs concerning the publics his institution serves; and it must be provided in the form he wants and on a timely basis.

In most instances an organization's traditional system definition is stated in vague and often ambiguous terminology. Before an intelligence system can be established, these statements must be refined and restated in explicit terms. This rigor will enable the organization to distinguish between relevant and irrelevant variables in its environment.

Obviously, some of the environmental information relates to variables that are totally beyond the control of the institution, but affect the survival and operations of the organization. These variables form part of what may be termed the 'ultimate environment" (see Figure 1). In other instances, the organization can exercise varying degrees of influence over the variables. These variables, with which the organization is in direct and frequent contact, form part of what may be termed the "proximate environment." In the case of a state university, for example, the administration may have no control over Congress' appropriations to the Office of Education, but these appropriations affect university operations. In acting through its board of regents, however, the administration may have some weight in determining state legislative appropriations for their institution.

Gathering intelligence

Intelligence varies in its availability. Information may be gathered from published sources (secondary information) or by the institution's own means (primary information). Secondary information serves as a base for all external information flows, and provides information on many subjects relevant to institutional management, such as population, economic conditions, and so forth. Primary information should be gathered only after external secondary information has been inventoried.

An intelligence system can gather primary information through a number of research techniques. Some of the more formal means include surveying, simulation, and experiments. Nevertheless, intelligence is not limited to sophisticated research methods. In addition to the techniques just mentioned, an organization can acquire valuable information from opinions, rumors, etc. For example, a university may receive informal intelligence from accrediting bodies, the state legislature, other institutions of higher learning, etc.

All units in the university should be involved in informal intelligence collection and processing. Much of the external information, however, should be gathered and processed centrally [21]. By centralizing much of the intelligence function, top-level administrators can perceive the whole pattern and report findings to individual units in the organization. Furthermore, an intelligence department can employ the services of research specialists and computer assistance, whereas each unit cannot support such decision aids. Parenthetically, centralizing the function is not to imply that individual university entities are discouraged from being attuned to their environments.

In addition to providing support for managing change, intelligence benefits an institution in other ways [22]. First, intelligence expands the planning horizons of the university. The systematic gathering and processing of data should greatly improve the quantity and quality of information available for PPB purposes. Second, intelligence helps evaluate the many uncertainties that enter the decision-making matrix. Anything that can potentially reduce these uncertainties will help a university to anticipate and cope with trends, problems, and opportunities. Third, the systematic collecting of external information often opens up new and superior sources of information.

The irony is that many educational institutions already possess the mechanisms for effectively monitoring the marketplace but, unfortunately, seldom utilize these mechanisms for the purpose. For example, the Career Services Placement Office at most institutions is usually so engrossed in selling what the institution wishes to produce that the other potentially more beneficial function it could perform, that of informing the institution concerning market demand, is seldom carried out.

Responsibility for monitoring publics for the purpose of gathering market intelligence must be shouldered by all of the functional areas in the institution. Integrated institutional marketing requires that the various functional areas in the institution (*i.e.*, the vice-president of academic affairs, and the vice-president of student affairs, as well as college and department heads) all recognize that the actions they take may have a profound effect upon the ability of the institution to serve its many publics effectively. For example, the establishment of a new program in the liberal arts college by the vice-president of academic affairs, the establishment of a new legal service for students by the vice-president of student affairs, or the implementation of a $20 tuition hike by the vice-president of business affairs should be undertaken only after careful market intelligence has been gathered to determine the impact of such decisions upon the institution's publics. Even though such decisions may appear attractive internally, they may be highly undesirable from the market point of view.

To summarize, one of the most important managerial or administrative activities in any institution has become the management of change. Since many changes are precipitated by developments outside the institution's inner operations, the accurate monitoring of external factors, as well as internal environments, is crucial to the management of change within higher education.

Segmentation and Selection of Markets

The current enrollment crisis being experienced by many institutions is proof positive that the market for higher education could tolerate closer scrutiny. The very fact that the publics of higher education are heterogeneous makes it imperative that institutions of higher education, operating in a buyer's market, identify the subgroups of their consumer publics. Or to state it in marketing terminology, the heterogeneous market has to be segmented into several smaller, homogeneous groups.

A marketing adage is that no organization can be all things to all people. Only through effective segmentation of markets can an institution determine the appropriateness and focus of individual programs [1, p. 94].

Through effective segmentation, the educational institution is, in effect, acknowledging that:

1. Each target population requires a particular approach.
2. Its product may not appeal to a broader consumer composite.
3. Individual market segment demand may not justify the addition of a contemplated program addition if one such program is already serving that segment.

An excellent example of effective market segmentation is the recent establishment of a center for criminal justice at a large southwestern university. The center was created to meet a growing demand for more formal educational training and research to combat crime and increase efficiency in the courts and legal system.

Another example of the benefits of effective monitoring, leading to market segmentation, is the establishment of a Center for Executive Development in the College of Business Administration at Arizona State University. The center was created in response to a growing need, expressed by several firms in the metropolitan Phoenix area, to provide middle-level management with a source of continuing education to improve their job skills.

Some institutions have reduced their program offerings because of market considerations. A midwestern university recently eliminated its engineering curriculum because the job market being serviced by the institution was glutted for the short term with qualified engineers, and other institutions in the area could adequately handle the demand [23].

There are, of course, also many examples of poor market segmentation resulting from lack of effective monitoring and intelligence activity. A classic example is an eastern university that recently made chemistry a requirement for undergraduate students—not because research had indicated a rising demand for chemistry graduates, but rather because enrollments in chemistry classes had *declined* so much that the chemistry department was threatened with extinction [23].

In another recent case, three closely related higher education administration Ph.D. programs have evolved within one state-wide system—a system that serves an immediate population of less than two million people. The end result of such need assessment and market definition quite possibly will be an oversupply of terminally qualified personnel and poor utilization of the state's limited education resources.

The problem with these schools as with many other institutions of higher learning is that their attention is riveted on a specific set of products or course offerings, instead of on trying to interpret and serve a set of evolving human needs through effective marketing intelligence and target marketing.

The segmentation and selection process is not an easy one. The potential long-term benefits are great, however, as are the potential losses for those who fail to recognize emerging new markets and the decline of the old.

The Product of Higher Education

The essential factor critical to the success of any business enterprise is the product it offers to the marketplace. The situation in higher education is no different, except that the product may be somewhat more difficult to define and may be almost impossible to measure [24]. Nevertheless, a discussion of higher education's product is necessary in applying a marketing systems framework to higher education.

The classic definition of the primary output or product of higher education is the educated student, with various employers representing the major market for the product. An alternative approach considers the curriculum or course offerings of higher education as the major "product" and the student as the primary market.

While one could define both perspectives taken in regard to "product," in this paper the "classic" definition is emphasized. Colleges and universities as social institutions exist to serve society's needs. Society, therefore, is the ultimate consumer of the product of higher education, the educated student. Viewed this way, the "uneducated" student represents "raw material" in the production process, which in turn is represented by the programs and disciplines in which the student becomes involved. Ultimately, the product (student) is purchased (employed) by the market (an organization in the private or public sector of the economy).

Universities create many different "products" by virtue of the variety of programs to which students are exposed. Standardization within product lines (*e.g.*, business, engineering, education, law, medicine, *etc.*) is achieved through the standardization of programs within disciplines and through the quality control imposed by administration on both faculty and students alike. The essential point, which must not be lost, is that the student-to-program match must be in response to a real market (social) need.

Integrated Marketing Strategies: Promotion, Distribution, and Pricing

Once the appropriate product has been created to conform to the needs of the target market, the remaining primary subsystems of marketing become important. They are promotion, pricing, and distribution.

Promotion

Higher education must accurately communicate to the public the direction its programs will take, as well as the existence of the programs themselves. And it must communicate this message efficiently and effectively through appropriate consumer-approved channels, just as in the case of a conventional product. The communication itself should become an effective part of the total product-service mixture.

Progressive institutions are just now coming to realize the potential and need for more dynamic career-service-placement functions. For example, many offices of career services today perform the function of bringing the graduates of the institutions to the attention of the marketplace—actively promoting and advertising their output.

Another example of positive communication concerns the university that recently began publicizing a "contract" that guaranteed junior college students full transfer credit for courses if a certain prescribed program of study was followed. Such a strategy helps to ensure the "source of supply," which the institution needs to meet its market obligation.

Distribution

Higher education must be aware, and is in fact so becoming, of the need to develop alternative delivery systems or channels of distribution to make the product available at the point of market need.

The advent of innovations such as educational television, the open university in England and the university without walls in the New York State System are excellent examples of progressive new methods of delivering higher education to the market.

The historical concept of a centralized campus to which hordes of students flock must of necessity be replaced or at least modified by new distribution techniques, such as those discussed above, in a buyer's market. The growth and development of the branch campus system and cooperative education programs between universities and community colleges to provide upper division courses at the community colleges are good examples of additional methods of distributing higher education—needed methods and techniques consistent with the development of a market-oriented philosophy in the management and administration of higher education.

Pricing

Higher education also must be aware of the potential role it plays in indirectly controlling the pricing mechanism in the marketplace. The primary tenet of economic theory, which states that price is determined by the interplay of supply and demand, is no less true with regard to the primary output of higher education—the student.

Effective monitoring and segmentation by the institution should provide the institution with an indication of the number of graduates needed in any given discipline. The institution violates its trust and runs the risk of extinction or stagnation when it produces an oversupply of people in any one field. If excess supply forces the market price for its product (the student) down, the result is dissatisfied graduates, and potential students who will seek alternatives more attractive than enrolling. Likewise, the institution misses great opportunities by not responding in educational areas where market demand is high, since the prevailing market price for graduates acts to attract potential students.

A good example of institutional myopia has occurred in colleges of education where administrators have allowed supply to far outstrip demand and, hence, create downward price distortions. Conversely, colleges of business have underestimated the demand for accountants. As a result, starting salaries in this field are as much as $14,000 a year for qualified graduates.

It should be clear that higher education is indirectly responsible for the prevailing pricing structure in the marketplace and that only through effective interaction of intelligence, segmentation, promotion, and distribution can higher education respond with an appropriate product at a fair market price.

Marketing Process Paradigm

The previous discussion has presented a model of the marketing system, the relationships of which will be further clarified and summarized in this section.

Basically, the marketing process within an academic setting proceeds as outlined in Figure 3.

Each step is predicated on the results of previous steps. The quality of decisions at any point is dependent upon the quality of decisions in previous stages.

Figure 3. The academic marketing process.

In the balance of this section, these stages are expressed as functional relationships and then briefly discussed.

$QMI = f$ (E, Data sources, QMI systems)

The quality of market intelligence is a function of the environments studied, the relevance of various data sources, and the quality of the market intelligence system within the university. These factors have been previously discussed, and are summarized here in terms of the broad and proximate environments from which useful data can be generated for intelligence usage:

Broad environments	*Proximate environments*
Social	Employers
Economic	Taxpayers
Technological	Legislature
Political and legal	Special interest
	Suppliers
	Internal groups

 Obviously, a variety of environments must be "tapped," and the intelligence system has at its disposal a variety of data sources and collection techniques.

$QMSA = f$ (QMI, MSS)

The quality of the university's market segmentation analysis is a function of the quality of market intelligence and the appropriateness of its choice of market segment selection factors.
   The university is faced with segmenting two major aggregate markets, the student market and the employer market. Each of these markets can be segmented three ways. Available segmentation variables, depending on the "market" might include:

Demographic dimensions

Age
Sex
Occupation
Education
SIC Code
Size

Geographic dimensions

World
Nation
Region
State
County
City

Psychographic dimensions

Life Style
Benefits sought
User status
Loyalty status
Readiness stage

Regardless of the approach followed, an explicit understanding of potential markets is necessary before selection of markets should take place and the "product" and special strategic appeals are developed.

$QMSS = f(QMSA)$

The quality of the market segment selected is a function of the quality of the segmentation analysis (*i.e.*, the quality of the selection criteria and the quality of the selection techniques employed).

Having segmented markets, the next task is to select for attention those markets that will prove most profitable from the university's point of view. For example, the working middle manager may be approached for a business college's new weekend MBA program. Likewise, data-processing firms might be contacted as a viable market for graduating majors in computer information systems.

Markets must be selected that are consistent with the aims and objectives of the university. A state university often feels it has an obligation to serve first the agencies and industry of the state. The target market, therefore, may be the state, and only secondarily regional and wider geographic markets.

Last, the techniques of market selection must be considered. However performed, some type of cost-benefit analysis that allows the ranking of market segments in terms of potential payoff is necessary.

$PD = f(MSS,$ Resources$)$

The "product" of the university system is a function of the desires of the markets segments selected and the resources of the university.

The marketing concept suggests that the organization create products to satisfy the needs of its various markets. It is no different within the university setting. Furthermore, the organization must be assured that it has the resource capability to satisfy the market need. These two factors combine to dictate the form of the "product" produced, whether the product in an academic context is engineers, teachers, lawyers, *etc.*

$$SPPD = f(PD, MSS)$$

Price, promotion, and distribution strategies are a function of the product produced by the university system and the market segments selected.

Price elasticity measurements have been implicitly built into the demand analysis that is an integral part of market selection. Nevertheless, specific attention to elasticity measurements can have a very favorable payoff. A center for executive development, for example, must be extremely sensitive to this factor in the pricing of its various seminars.

Promotional elasticities might also be considered, although measurement is more difficult. In addition, the various elements of the promotional mix should be given attention. What should be the balance in the mix among advertising, personal selling, sales promotion, publicity, and public relations ingredients? And how can the several offices and colleges of the university work together to combine promotional effort in order to achieve efficiencies and avoid redundancies?

Distribution strategy is the final marketing mix strategy. In an academic setting, distribution strategy is primarily location strategy, and may often, but not necessarily, involve creation of university structures, *e.g.*, branch campuses. Other alternatives exist, however, such as correspondence study and the use of the physical plant of other insitutions.

It is evident from the foregoing that the marketing process is not so simple and is extremely tedious. Close attention must be given at each step to relevant relationships and factors if a meaningful response to the marketplace is to be forthcoming.

SYNTHESIZATION OF THE MARKETING AND PPB CONCEPTS

The marketing concept and framework developed earlier have direct application to the PPB process [25]. Conceptually, the important point is that the *primary* source of information for the PPB process is the marketplace for the products and services of the university system. While information from other "publics" related to the university system, such as the state legislature, is considered, the significance lies in the relative emphasis given to each.

The marketing concept also has *practical* impact for PPB administrators. The

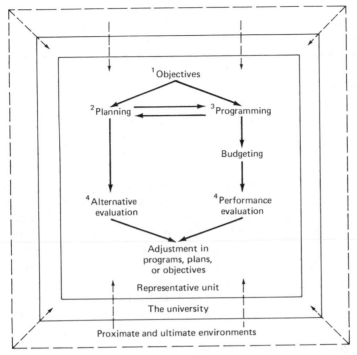

Figure 4. PPB activities of a representative unit.

marketing intelligence system should provide the data base for relating the university's markets to specific institutional objectives. Further, data generated by the intelligence system also provide the opportunity to segment markets and potential markets more clearly in order to select from among them those that require attention or may be exploited most effectively.

In the following paragraphs the contributions of intelligence to PPB are specifically examined. To avoid unnecessary complexity, the discussion will focus on a "representative unit" within the university. In practice, departmental, central administration, and governing board decision units would all observe these general guidelines. Intelligence gathered from the proximate and ultimate environments, should be of assistance to the unit in the objective, planning, programming, and evaluation procedures (see Figure 4).

The delineation of *objectives* is the key and guiding step for all other aspects of the process. Intelligence should be assigned the function of assessing the impact of external variables on a unit's objectives. If one were focusing on the university presidency as the representative unit, for example, one would note that the traditionally expressed objectives of student development, research, and public service are closely associated with factors outside the president's direct control. Although the objectives of the university will typically be more general at higher levels in the institution, the model stresses that all units in the university should express their objectives as precisely as possible.

Planning should seek to relate current and proposed programs to intermediate and longer range objectives. The process should be continuous. Some reasonable planning horizon, such as five years, should be established, and a forecast of objectives, outputs, and resource needs should be made in the base year for the five-year period. In each succeeding year, the plan is updated and advanced another year. Planning and intelligence go hand in hand, because current and future information is a necessary component of planning. Generally, a university unit wants to foresee the environment in which it operates, the alternative actions that will be available, and the manner in which the environment will react to various actions. External information, evaluated in a planning framework, is necessary to anticipate these events. Of the four basic **PPB** procedures, a unit's planning activities will probably make the most use of intelligence. If the board of regents, for example, desires a forecast of anticipated student enrollments in the university over five- and ten-year periods, the administration should have the research expertise to conduct such a study. Alternative appraisal is a by-product of the planning process. In planning, a unit must search for all realistic means of accomplishing objectives. In evaluating various means of reaching objectives, a body should weigh the anticipated benefits of a course of action against the anticipated cost.

Programming is the organization and management of the activities of a unit in terms of how the unit's inputs contribute to the unit's and the university's outputs and objectives. Thus, programming is the translation of objectives and plans into actual operations. Since the first two procedures are dependent on the external environment, programming should also note relevant intelligence. With this procedure, specific attention is given to the outputs of a unit's programs, and how these outputs contribute to the unit's and the university's objectives. For example, an academic department may consider the publication of scholarly research as one of its major outputs. In considering its available resources, the department should note how various inputs contribute to this output, and the university's outputs and objectives.

The *evaluation* procedure of PPB involves performance appraisal. Performance evaluation grows out of actual program activities, and acts as a control mechanism. With this type of appraisal, the decision-maker weighs actual benefits accruing against actual costs. The products of both evaluations will result either in a reinforcement of the existing programs, plans, or objectives of the unit, or a redefining of the same. Changes in environmental forces should be sensed because they are often the primary factors that steer programs away from intended goals.

To further emphasize the marketing implications for PPB, a specific illustration will be used in the balance of this section. Assume that our intelligence system has told us that there is a demand for architecture graduates as a result of the overall growth pattern in a given regional area and the resulting construction boom. Furthermore, suppose that a continuance of the growth pattern has been forecast to extend over the next two decades.

Given this information, it would be entirely reasonable to consider the creation or upgrading of an architecture curriculum within the university system serving that regional area. An objective would be established to reflect this desire. More specific objectives could deal with the variety of architectural skills required of various submarkets (*e.g.*, the regional planner, the commercial developer).

The market demand as reflected in the objectives would then dictate the nature of the *product* (architecture curriculum) that the university system would be asked to produce. The planning phase of the PPB process would be designed to insure that, in fact, such a "product" was forthcoming. Plans dealing with course additions, and hiring of qualified faculty, for example, might be necessary.

Next, programming of promotion, distribution, and price strategies would be required. Promotional issues could involve convincing the ultimate marketplace of the quality of the architecture graduate, appealing to the legislature for necessary funds to develop resources and facilities to accommodate new programs, or attracting students (the "raw material" for the system) to the college.

Cost and benefits of the system must be programmed. Can a student afford a five-year, undergraduate program leading to a degree in architecture? Can means be found within the university system to subsidize student enrollment (scholarships, loans, assistantships)? Will business contribute to support the program? Is the demand for graduates reflected in the starting salaries and advancement rate of graduates relative to the disciplines? In short, is the price the public (market) is willing to pay in terms of employment of graduates and support of programs reasonable given the costs to the system?

Finally, *distribution strategies* must be considered. Should branch campus programs be provided? Would internship programs provide effective contact with the ultimate market? What market area is our institution designed to serve? Can the institution attract employers to the campus to select its graduates?

In short, the concepts of market intelligence and segmentation, as well as product, promotion, price, and distribution strategies all have direct relevance to the establishment of the objectives, plans, and programs that constitute the heart of the PPB process. As a last step in that process, the plans and programs developed must be translated into a budget. The budget figures, of course, are those that reflect the resources necessary to accomplish the objective of satisfying market demand.

CONCLUSION

Public administrators have received minimal exposure to marketing concepts. This paper has taken a basic public adminstration process, PPB, and integrated it with marketing fundamentals within the setting of higher education. In doing so, it has drawn analogies between marketing-oriented firms in the private enterprise system, on the one hand, and public institutions (*e.g.*, higher education) on the other.

There is little question in the minds of the authors that the management and administration of most institutions of higher education, even those employing a sophisticated PPB system are not sensitive enough to evolving changes in the marketplace—changes in products, consumers, competition, and distribution channels. It takes little imagination to see that many institutions of higher education seem quite oblivious to the changes in the marketplace and seem, in fact, content to "sell" their traditional educational programs through traditional methods and channels. Just as some great firms of the past are no longer in existence because they adhered to a definition of their business and their products that was production- and sales-oriented, so many institutions of higher education may yet disappear for the same reason.

Conversely, institutions of higher education that move toward integrating marketing with a PPB approach through a series of carefully planned and organized changes will benefit both themselves and society. Perceiving themselves as institutions dedicated to sensing, serving, and satisfying evolving consumer needs frees institutions from a fixation with present products and structures. It helps them to recognize new opportunities and to avoid stagnation. It leads society's resources to move in the direction of social need, thereby bringing the interests of institutions of higher education and the interests of society together in an effective working partnership. More specifically, it provides the correct focus for the PPB process. Managing the University of California, the University of Maine, or the University of Kansas is every bit as challenging and demanding and dependent upon the development of an institutional marketing concept as is managing General Motors, Standard Oil, or Xerox.

It has been the intent of this paper to build a case both historically and conceptually for the necessity and importance of the development of marketing in higher education to complement the emerging PPB approach. In addition, an attempt has been made to create a basic framework from which the public administrator or academician can apply both PPB and marketing strategies to higher education in developing such a complement.

In short, the choice facing those who manage and administer institutions of higher education is not whether to market or not to market. The choice is whether to do it well or poorly, whether to create planned and controlled change or whether to let it evolve haphazardly. If higher education is truly interested in identifying and responding to the needs of its publics, then the relevant planning concepts discussed in this paper must assume a more influential role in the establishment of top-level institutional policy and administration.

NOTES AND REFERENCES

1. "Colleges Learn the Hard Sell." *Business Week* (February 14, 1977) 92.
2. "Institute for Educational Management, *Fifth Annual Program.*" June 16–July 26, 1974. Cambridge, Mass.: Harvard University Press, p. 10.
3. Fenske, Robert. Lecture, College of Education, Arizona State University, February 13, 1974.
4. Hovey, Harold A. *The Planning-Programming-Budgeting Approach to Government Decision Making.* New York: Praeger, 1968, p. xii.
5. Held, Virginia. "PPBS Comes to Washington." *The Public Interest* 4(1966): 103.
6. Novick, David. *Program Budgeting.* Cambridge, Mass.: Harvard University Press, 1967, p. xxi.
7. Eckstein, Otto. *Water Resource Development: The Economics of Project Evaluation.* Cambridge, Mass.: Harvard University Press, 1958; McKean, Roland. *Efficiency in Government through Systems Analysis with Emphasis on Water Resource Development.* New York: Wiley, 1958.
8. Olson, Mancur. "An Analytic Framework for Social Reporting and Policy Analysis." *The Annals of the American Academy of Political and Social Science* 388(1970): 117.
9. *New York Times*, August 25, 1965.
10. Andrew, Loyd D., and Leon Robertson. "PPB in Higher Education: A Case Study." *Educational Record* 54(1973): 60–67. Kershaw, Joseph A., and Alex M. Mood. "Resource Allocation in Higher Education." *American Economic Review* 40(1970): 341–346.
11. Courey, Charles J. "Resource Planning for Higher Education." *Managerial Planning* 23(1975): 17–20.
12. Andrew and Robertson, "PPB in Higher Education," cited above.
13. Smith, Stephen, and Arch Miller, Jr. "Getting Started in Program Budgeting." *College and University Business* 55(1973): 32–33.
14. Dror, Yehezkel. "The Planning Process: A Facet Design." *International Review of Administrative Science* 29(1963): 52.
15. Brown, Stephen W. "The PPB Approach Applied to a University Unit." *Managerial Planning* 22(1973): 27–31; Dyer, James S. "The Use of PPBS in a Public System of Higher Education: 'Is It Cost-Effective'?" *Academy of Management Journal* 13(1970): 293.
16. Rowen, Henry. Prepared statement before the Subcommittee on Economy in Government of the Joint Economic Committee, 90th Congress, 1st Session. Washington, D.C.: Government Printing Office, 1967, p. 187.
17. For a more detailed discussion of contemporary marketing, see: Robert F. Gwinner *et al., Marketing: An Environmental Perspective*, St. Paul: West Publishing, 1977; and Philip Kotler, *Marketing For Nonprofit Organizations*, Englewood Cliffs, N.J.: Prentice-Hall, 1975.
18. Hunter, Willard. "Colleges Must Stress Needs of Public Not Their Own." *Public Relations Journal* (July 1966): 24.
19. Laser, Marvin. "Towards a Sense of Community." *Journal of Higher Education* 37(1967): 66.

20. A model adapted from George D. Downing, *Basic Marketing, A Strategic Systems Approach*, Columbus, Ohio: Charles E. Merril Publishing, 1971, p. 61.

21. Kelley, William T. *Marketing Intelligence*. London: Staples Press, 1968, pp. 30–31.

22. Cox, Donald F., and Robert E. Good. "How to Build a Marketing Information System." *Harvard Business Review* 45(1967): 386–87; and William T. Kelley. *Marketing Intelligence*. London: Staples Press, 1968, pp. 25–26, 30.

23. Interview with Robert Fenske, director, Center for Higher Education, College of Education, Arizona State University.

24. Adams, Walter. "The State of Higher Education: Myths and Realities." *AALP Bulletin* (summer 1974): 124; and "Colleges Learn the Hard Sell." *Business Week* (February 14, 1977).

25. Brown, Stephen W., and Bruce J. Walker. "Two Approaches to Improved University Decision Making." *American Institute for Decision Sciences Proceedings* (October 1976): 354–356.

PART VI
Organizational and Human Relations Concerns

The "fuzziness" of operations and control problems in the public sector increases as we move into the realm of people-management concerns. The orientation of existing organizational and behavioral research to the business environment creates severe "technology transfer" problems for the public administrator. Noel Tichy and Richard Beckhard offer an authoritative survey of recent developments in applied behavioral science, with a human services orientation. Walter Baker, Raoul Elias, and David Griggs present a classical example of the inherent power of general systems theory to assist the administrator in his confrontation with grossly unstructured situations. Their study is a lucid demonstration of the possibility that other approaches to organizational and human behavior problems may be used alternately or mutually with applied behavioral science. Paul Selbst underscores the great variety exhibited by crises in the public sector. Through an exhaustive taxonomy of crisis types, certain clear-cut therapeutic strategies are offered to line-executives in the public sector. James Begin then sets guidelines for dealing with the situation where employee-employer relationships have been reduced to confrontation at the bargaining table. The multiplicity of groups affected in a public "confrontation" transforms such a situation into a potentially explosive and unmanageable process.

PART VI

Organizational and Human Relations Concerns

1

Managing Behavioral Factors in Human Service Organizations

Noel M. Tichy
Columbia University
and
Richard Beckhard
Massachusetts Institute for Technology

INTRODUCTION

The core problem of the executive manager in a complex organization is to make the best *choices* around whom to bring together, in which organizations, to make what happen, in whose interpretation of the public interest [22].

Managers of service institutions are caught up on the crest of a major wave of change that will extend through the next decade. Drucker poses a formidable challenge to service institutions in stating that [28, p. 166]:

What service institutions need is not to be more businesslike. They need to be subjected to performance tests. . . . Few service institutions today suffer from having too few administrators; most of them are over-administered and suffer from a surplus of procedures, organization charts and management techniques. What now has to be learned is to manage service institutions for performance. This may well be the biggest and most important management task in this century.

The applied behavioral sciences provide some of the conceptual and action tools for helping administrators manage this complexity. The more complex organizations become, the more relevant are the concepts and techniques discussed here. Human service organizations, those delivering health, social service, and educational services, represent some of the most complex organizational forms. This is primarily due to the nature of their missions, which in the case of health organizations, have a life-and-death component, as well as due to the complexity of managing multiple professional and nonprofessional groups, and to the environmental pressures that must be balanced and managed.

The behavioral sciences consist of knowledge embraced in the core disciplines of sociology, psychology, social psychology, and anthropology. Applied behavioral science is the technology of systematically employing the principles derived from the behavioral sciences to organizational and community settings. The subdisciplines of organization theory, organizational psychology, and sociology provide the bridge between the disciplines and the applied behavioral sciences.

Applied behavioral science is to the behavioral science disciplines as engineering is to physics. It is not a specific discipline, but an amalgamation of applied principles focusing on people in organizational and group settings, organizational characteristics, organizational processes, managerial style, managerial processes, and the management of change.

Our purpose here, then, is to provide a map of the applied behavioral sciences field as it relates to the work of human service administrators. We will discuss some of the problems faced by human service administrators for which there are implications for the applied behavioral sciences. This is followed by a discussion of the "state of the art," both in terms of current knowledge and current technologies. We will review the normative positions that guide applied behavioral scientists in working with organizations by stating the characteristics of a healthy organization. We will follow with a section on the management of change processes. Section II looks at several techniques and their specific application in human service settings.

I. MARRYING BEHAVIORAL SCIENCE APPLICATIONS TO HUMAN SERVICE MANAGEMENT PROBLEMS

In any one day a human service administrator is likely to find himself or herself juggling a variety of problems. At any hour the focus of action might be on dealing with a set of interface problems caused by conflicting external demands from interest groups and regulatory or funding sources. In the next hour it would not be unusual to find the human service manager attempting to put out "fires" within the organization created by conflict between units or, conflicts between professional groups such as nurses and physicians, social workers and psychologists, or teachers and guidance counselors. Finally, in the midst of juggling current problems the manager is supposed to be thinking about the future, developing and monitoring some sort of strategic plan for the organization.

Of all the problems faced by human service managers the following are the areas where the applied behavioral sciences can help:

1. *Understanding and specifying the mission of the organization:* In times of relative environmental stability and surplus resources it is possible for or-

ganizations to function quite effectively with nebulous and shifting goals and priorities, such as is often the case in human service organizations with teaching, research, and service interests. As the pressure mounts, so does the need for a clear statement of purpose and organizational mission to guide the organization in strategic decisions. The human service administrator will be called upon to guide the organization in establishing its core mission.

2. *Understanding and mapping environmental pressures on the organization:* Planning will take place within an increasingly turbulent and complex environment. Human service organizations will, therefore, need to develop managerial competence in identifying and predicting environmental pressures.

3. *Managing organizational planning processes:* In order to meet Drucker's challenge for performance—oriented organizations within the context of increasing complexity and increasing cost-cutting pressures, human service organizations will have to develop more sophisticated planning processes that can realistically engage the relevant interest groups.

4. *Setting strategies and operational objectives:* Having a clear mission does not insure that the organization will be subjected to performance tests. This requires the development of a strategic plan with operational objectives at multiple levels of the organization.

5. *Organizational designs to cope with changing tasks:* Organizational structure and design comprise one of the basic tools of management for carrying out its strategic plan. The human service administrator needs to be equipped with an array of organizational design models enabling him or her to cope with multiple and changing organizational tasks.

6. *Managing consensual decision-making:* Unlike industrial organizations, human service organizations have multiple bases of authority; therefore, clear lines of decision-making authority are blurred, making it imperative that human service administrators understand and be able to utilize consensual decision-making approaches.

7. *Managing multiple tasks:* It is often the case in human service organizations that individuals perform multiple and often very different tasks. This is most pronounced in some health organizations, which are divided into different functional areas, such as ambulatory care, internal medicine, pediatrics, and surgery, with varying mixtures of service, teaching, and research commitments. They also include individuals who divide themselves between tasks and wear multiple hats during any one day, *e.g.*, teacher-research-clinician. The management of multiple tasks and multiple task organization members requires special managerial skills.

8. *Coping with interunit and interorganizational conflict:* The role of human service administrator includes being coordinator and integrator dealing with the constant pressure of organizational conflicts that require explicit attention and management.

9. *Managing and motivating multiple professionals:* The outmoded "one best

way" approach to motivating performance is even less applicable in human service organizations where motivation and control vary not only because of differences between individuals, but because of differences between professional groups.

10. *Managing change in the organization:* A variety of change processes require managing:

changes in structure,
changes in the way work gets done,
changes in the reward systems,
changes in interactions with the environment,
changes in staff and management relationships,
changes in union and staff relationships,
changes in the utilization of teams,
changes in the management structure.

For each of the above problem areas, the administrator can expect guidance from existing science principles and methodologies, of which selected ones will be discussed later, following an overview of the field.

STATE OF THE ART

Applied behavioral science has its roots in a broad base of theory, research, and practice spanning over 40 years and several disciplines. One of the main roots, however, grew out of the work of Kurt Lewin and followers during and after World War II. Lewin, a social psychologist, was very much involved in research on group dynamics and leadership. His strong commitment to social change led him to do a great deal of what he termed "action research"—systematic research conducted in applied settings designed to lead to change in the setting. By the late 1940s a field called applied behavioral science emerged, primarily focused on group, interpersonal, and individual functioning. In 1947 the National Training Laboratories was created. It was a training and research institute aimed at applying Lewin's theories and developing the group-learning approach Lewin had been working with. This became the "laboratory method" or "T-group" training approach and has led to other forms of "awareness" training.

In the mid-1950s applied behavioral science practice was very much oriented toward group dynamics applications [16]. In the late 1950s application efforts tended to branch in two directions. One was an increased focus on interpersonal, personal, and humanistic psychology. The other was focused on organizations as systems, the change process, and work and structural arrangements in order to improve organizational effectiveness.

Our focus is primarily on the second branch as the one most useful for the administrator.

An Organizational Model

To help organize our thinking about systems, we will briefly look at some aspects of organizations. In the behavioral sciences there are many different approaches to diagnosing and understanding organizations. For the purpose of this paper we have selected a simple model of an organization to guide our discussion. This model is based on a view of an organization (Figure 1) [71]:

> ... social structures created by individuals to allow the collaborative pursuit of specified goals. Although the specific goals pursued may be highly diverse ... all organizations confront certain common problems or tasks. All must define (and redefine) objectives; all must induce participants to contribute services; all must control and coordinate contributions; resources must be garnered from the environment and products or services dispensed; participants must be selected and trained and replaced; and some sort of working accommodation achieved with the neighbors.

The model is a systems model that underscores the importance of conceiving of an organization as dynamic and in constant interaction with its environment—

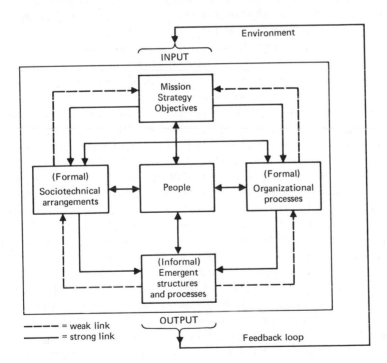

Figure 1. Organizational model.

taking in *inputs* and transforming them into *outputs*, which are exported to the external environment.

One of our assumptions is that organizations operate in an environment that provides opportunities as well as constraints. The problem for the manager is the choice among these constraints and opportunities. The criteria for the choice are developed from the perceptions of key organizational actors who often have a negotiated consensus as to the organization's purpose, its *raison d'etre*, its *mission* [24]. For example, there are important managerial and organizational consequences for academic medical centers based on management's definition of the core mission. Two cases are presented in Section II of this chapter of medical centers that defined their core missions differently. In one case, it was to do biomedical research, while in the other, to provide training for practitioner-oriented physicians.

The administrator in a complex organization must make choices among apparently equal priorities in order to develop criteria for an organizational strategy. Strategy is the process of setting goals and objectives in the context of the organization's mission. The goals and objectives provide a set of targets and controls necessary in order to achieve the mission. Every organization has a *mission*, *strategy*, and *objectives*. They may not be clear, and people may behave in ways that are inconsistent with them, but they exist nonetheless.

Accomplishing an organization's mission and implementing its strategy requires the use of technology, a social structure, and a set of organizational processes. The component labeled *sociotechnical arrangements* refers to the technology by which the work of the organization is carried out and to the related social structure necessary to operate the technology. By technology, we mean the machines, equipment, and, most importantly, the process whereby raw materials (either human, symbolic, or material) are transformed into desirable goods or services, such as being cured or attaining better "health." By social structure, we are referring to the arrangements of people in the organization, *e.g.*, authority relations, work interdependencies, communication linkages, *etc*.

Technology limits and constrains the way in which the organization gets structured, but should not totally determine the structures. People's needs are the other component of how work is done. Different structures result in different social psychological consequences for workers and clients. In industry throughout the world, traditional means of production are being reexamined in terms of human motivation and are being replaced by new work designs [21]. In health settings, such new work design programs are also beginning to take place. A notable example is now under way at a major metropolitan hospital as part of the University of Michigan's Quality of Working Life Program [63].

As Figure 1 implies, the particular sociotechnical arrangements flow in part from the mission, strategy, and objectives of the organization, but are also influenced by the other components. The core issue is how best to organize work so as to optimize human and technological effectiveness. For example, the school administrator is concerned with how best to organize the work in a school. This entails reexamining the work to look at alternatives for organizing teachers, guidance personnel, and paraprofessionals who interact with the technology of education in the school.

In addition to sociotechnical arrangements, the organization needs mechanisms that enable the sociotechnical system to perform its work, these are called *organizational processes*. These include communication processes, control processes, problem-solving and decision-making processes and conflict management processes.

Most importantly, organizations have *people* who operate within the sociotechnical arrangements and operate the organizational processes. People vary in terms of their motivation, their interpersonal styles, and their skills. These differences have managerial and organization design implications. For example, the administrator needs to determine how to have consistent and equitable incentive and control systems while at the same time allowing for vast individual differences.

The above discussion of sociotechnical arrangements and organizational processes implies that these arrangements are somehow totally and formally prescribed and rationally planned. As has been recognized for years [68], this is not so; systems have extensive informal structures and processes that emerge as a result of human interaction in the organization. Figure 1 focuses on both the formal prescribed arrangements and processes and the informal or emergent ones [83]. These emerge becasue individuals tend to: 1) formulate, reformulate, and interpret the mission, 2) understand, abide by, or change the prescribed sociotechnical arrangements and organizational processes, 3) use, abuse, and alter the technology, and 4) differentially respond to changing environmental conditions. As a result new, unplanned, and often unanticipated, structures and social patterns of work emerge in the organization. These new forms of structures and processes perforce affect the course of decision-making, problem-solving, leadership, power distribution, *etc*.

These unplanned structures and processes are needed to get the work done; this is especially true in human service organizations, which are so complex that blueprints or plans can never be developed for all contingencies. They emerge to get the work done. They are potentially double-edged, in that they may either facilitate or hinder the accomplishment of an organization's mission. For example, coalitions of professionals may form that work either toward helping the organization be more effective or toward helping conflicting special self-interests, as is often the case with interprofessional power struggles.

In addition to the dimensions of our model as outlined in Figure 1, we will focus on organizational change processes. That is, how to manage alterations in the components of the model.

SELECTED BEHAVIORAL SCIENCE RESEARCH OUTPUT AND RELATED APPLIED BEHAVIORAL SCIENCE TECHNOLOGIES

Behavioral and social science research is not without serious problems and limitations. First, because of the relative youth of many of these disciplines and the difficulty and complexity of research in fields such as sociology, social psychology, and anthropology, there is a lack of grand integrating theories of behavior. Rather there are a number of descriptive theories dealing with a variety of aspects of behavior. This has contributed to fragmented knowledge. Keeping this limitation in mind, we will highlight some of what is currently known from research as it relates to the use of the applied behavioral sciences in human service administration. The categories of our organization model are used to organize the research. Examples of applied behavioral science techniques will be presented in each category. In addition to categories of our model we present research and techniques in the area of teams and patient care. Table 1 summarizes this material. A few specific aspects from Table 1 are discussed in more detail below.

Organizations and Environments

As indicated in Table 1, there are a number of subcategories under this heading. The first area, characteristics of environments, includes recent theory and research, which indicates that there is an important relationship between environmental uncertainty and organizational design [49; 75]. For example, organizations attempting to function effectively in fast-changing, complex environments require more highly differentiated and flexible (more organic) strucures to perform effectively. A multidimensional approach to classifying organizational environments has been developed by Shortell [73].

Another subcategory of importance to the applied behavioral sciences is interfacing with other organizations. The trend is for human service institutions, government agencies, and, in the case of health, private third-party payers to become more interdependently linked, thus requiring greater interorganizational planning and coordination. Research by Levine and White [51], and Aiken et al. [1] sheds light on the dynamics of such relationships.

Public accountability is a relatively new pressure on many human service administrators. As Etzioni indicates [30], the concept is ambiguous and leads to dysfunctional organizational responses in many cases. An interesting and relevant health care case of a rather successful approach to this issue is found in the

Table 1. Behavioral science research and applications relevant to health administration.

FOCUS	EXAMPLES OF BEHAVIORAL SCIENCE RESEARCH	EXAMPLES OF APPLIED BEHAVIORAL SCIENCE INTERVENTION
Organizations and environment		
Characteristics of environments	Impact of environment on organizational structure and functioning [29; 49; 73]	Contingency organization design Open systems planning Organization set analysis Macrosystem interlocking
Interfacing	Interorganization relationships	Delphi method Confrontation meetings Third-party conflict intervention
Public accountability	Accountability in health administration [30]	Social accounting Surveys
Assessing needs— health planning	Social indicators [7]	
Mission strategy objectives	Integration of individual and organization goals [6] Organizational goals, and goal setting [31; 64]	MBO (management by objectives) Strategic planning—confrontation meeting
Sociotechnical arrangements	Impact of technology on organization design [91; 40] Structural design of organizations [73; 64]	Contingency design Sociotechnical system design
Organizational processes		
Central structure	Control structures for regulating organization performance [31; 47] Dysfunctions of control structures [13]	Data feedback Decision centers
Management systems	Managerial functions [60] Information Systems [4] Planning systems [17]	Management development Network analysis

Table 1. (*cont.*)

FOCUS	EXAMPLES OF BEHAVIORAL SCIENCE RESEARCH	EXAMPLES OF APPLIED BEHAVIORAL SCIENCE INTERVENTION
Communication	Communication networks [5]	Responsibility charting
Decision-making	Strategic planning and decision-making [61]	
People		
Leadership	Leadership functions: monitoring, forecasting, taking direct action, heading off problems, exploiting opportunities [58]	Managerial grid
	Contingency leadership [32; 87]	Contingency style training
Interdisciplinary collaboration	Integration of roles in task groups [44]	Interdisciplinary training
	Socialization research on professionals	Role conflict interventions for work settings— role negotiations
Work motivation and productivity	Relationship between varying worker needs and job design as related to satisfaction and productivity [37]	Job enrichment
		Flexible hours
Career planning	Research on career paths and development [39; 69]	Career assessment and planning workshops
		Life planning workshops
Emergent "informal" structure	Research on informal groups and networks in organizations [81]	Emergent network design and management principles
Teams		
Structure	Communication networks [5]	Designing autonomous work groups
	Task type [72]	
Process	Group use of discretionary stimuli to affect members in organizations [38]	T-groups
	The functioning of group behavioral norms [43]	Team development
	Individual versus group performance [54]	Process consultation
		Third-party interpersonal peacemaking

The Patient/client/student

Managing their own care/learning	Research on psychosocial causes of illness [59] Research on human motivation [62; 57; 2] Attitude and behavior change Learning theory and research [46; 74]	Healer-patient-relationship training Client-centered therapy Sensitivity training and self-help groups Social marketing Behavior modification-instrumented instructional material
Patient consumer advocacy	Conflict resolution [27]	Conflict resolution interventions
Family as basic unit for service delivery	Family structure and dynamics [36; 14]	Family therapy Network therapy Marriage enrichment programs

case study of one neighborhood health center, The Dr. Martin Luther King Health Center in the Bronx, New York [82; 83]

There is a growing body of behavioral science literature on the development and use of social indicators, for example, measures taken on the general population to indicate job and life satisfaction. Such indicators can be utilized to provide help in assessing needs and for guiding the human service planning process [7].

In order to help managers and organizations deal with the issues and concerns identified above, a number of applied behavioral science technologies are identified in Table 1. The open-systems-planning model, which is described in detail in the case portion of this chapter, provides one such technique for mapping environmental forces.

An approach for facilitating more effective interorganizational interfacing is "organization set analysis," which includes procedures for:

1. Identifying the significant other organizations with which an organization interacts.
2. Diagnosing the frequency and quality of the interorganizational linkages identified in step 1.
3. Developing plans for altering interorganizational linkages so as to foster more effective organizational performance.

Finally, there is a set of techniques, such as the Delphi technique, that use interactive questionnaires and feedback from a panel of "experts" to involve outside input into the organization's strategic information system [26].

Mission, Strategy, and Objectives

As stated in our brief model discussion, the mission is the organization's "reason for being." The strategy defines the constraints and the plan for carrying out the mission within a particular environment and includes specific measurable objectives.

The behavioral science literature does not use the term organizational "core missions." The distinction made by the management literature between core missions and objectives is generally combined under the heading of "organizational goals," which are defined as desired future states of affairs [31]. Organizational goals can serve the following functions:

1. focus energy and act as guidelines for what should be;
2. provide a source of legitimacy for people's activities and decisions;
3. serve as standards for how well individuals, subunits, and the total organization are performing; and
4. provide insight into the true character of the organization.

Perrow [64] provides a comprehensive categorization scheme of organizational goals that provides more goal distinctions than we are making here.

Although goals provide such opportunities as listed above, the reality is that organizational goal formulation is not a totally rational process. It is often characterized by highly political activities [24; 85], and, as a result, important organizational issues become: who determines the goals, how clear are they to organizational members, how have they changed over time, and do they really guide the work of the organization [76; 71]. One applied behavioral science technique appropriate for dealing with some of these issues is "goal confrontation," in which organization members engage in a series of structured activities to confront and resolve goal differences [9].

Closely related to the organization's mission is strategic decision-making and planning. Strategic decisions and strategy formulation refer to those decisions that have important total organization importance in terms of allocation of resources or precedents set. The literature provides many normative models and techniques for strategic decision-making, such as cost-benefit analysis, strategy planning models of the firm, *etc.*, but, as Mintzberg has recently pointed out, little empirical evidence that these models accurately describe the process [61]. Mintzberg's recent research on strategic decision-making indicates that the process is immensely complex and involves a mixture of rational and political dynamics that require new managerial techniques. An applied behavioral science response to this set of issues is dealt with through open-systems planning.

Sociotechnical Arrangements

Implicit in our organizational model and the way in which we approach the sociotechnical component of organizations is a view consistent with the recent "contingency" theories of organizational design. These "theories" are based on the realization that organizational effectiveness is largely a function of matching organization structure, leadership style, planning, and control systems to the demands of the organization's environment and task or technology [34]. This explains the emphasis on sociotechnical arrangements in our model. An important example of contingency thinking is related to technology and structure.

Perrow [65] proposes that as technology varies in terms of the number of exceptions from predetermined standards and the difficulty of problem search when exceptions occur, so does the type of people best able to perform successfully and the type of structure most supportive of the work. There should, therefore, be a "fit" between technology, structure, and people (those who do the work). An illustration of this matching is to fit technologies requiring few exceptions and having analyzable search procedures, such as routine medical laboratory tests and screening or filing requests for welfare benefits with a structure that is more mechanistic or bureaucratic and with people who are less interested in receiving achievement and fulfillment on the job than in receiving money. In contrast, more fluid and organic structures and individuals who desire achievement and fulfillment on the job are more consistent with technologies where many exceptions occur, such as are found in basic research departments and in the jobs of most health administrators.

An excellent review of the literature on environment, technology, and structure was done by Shortell [73]. Shortell's work develops a new scheme for classifying organizations dependent on combinations of organizational dimensions.

The applied behavioral science techniques associated with the sociotechnical category fall into three categories: 1) overall organization design; 2) unit design; and 3) job design.

The overall organization design approach is guided by an "information processing" model of organizations that attempts to design or redesign organizations according to the information needs of task and the interdependence of tasks with each other [34]. The approach involves:

1. In designing the tasks of a subunit, a) assessing the degree of environmental uncertainty, and b) assessing the complexity of the technology, both of which contribute to variations in the amount of information needed to accomplish the task.
2. Matching simple, mechanistic structure to stable environment and simple technology, and a complex, organic structure to an unstable environment and complex technology.
3. Determining the degree of interdependence with other units and developing appropriate integrating mechanisms (the more interdependence, the more elaborate the integrating mechanisms) [85].

The second level of applied behavioral science techniques is focused on unit design. Since the work of Eric Trist and Ken Banforth of the Tavistock Institute in the 1940s, the applied behavioral sciences have designed and implemented autonomous work groups as a sociotechnical approach to unit design. These groups are largely self-managed, generally rotate jobs, and often have "enriched" jobs. The growing importance of alternative forms of work is attested to by the recent NATO conference, and is included in *Personal Goals and Work Design* (1976), edited by Peter Warr.

The final set of applied behavioral science techniques comprises those related to the redesign of individual jobs. Recent theories of motivation have shown the important impact the design of jobs can have on performance and satisfaction. Recent job enrichment work indicates that tasks need to be designed to optimize: 1) worker feelings of personal responsibility for a meaningful portion of work; 2) providing outcomes that are intrinsically meaningful and otherwise experienced as worthwhile by individuals; and 3) providing feedback about what is accomplished. All too little work in this has been done in the human service field, which has many jobs, especially those of nonprofessionals that call for redesign.

Organizational Processes

Behavioral science research focuses attention on all the following issues, relative to each of the processes.

Communication

Small group research has indicated that information networks are important determinants of both problem-solving effectiveness and member satisfaction. The key contingency is task characteristics, simply routine problems being more efficiently solved with centralized networks, and more complex problems requiring more open structures [50]. At the organization level, research on formal organizational networks, including Management Information Systems indicate that the key problems for management entail developing communication procedures that minimize distortion and provide more timely information. Additional attention needs to be focused on whether the organization has sufficient openness to facilitate upward and downward communication.

Control

Organizations require control structures for regulating organizational performance [31;47]. Unfortunately, all too often control systems foster dysfunctional organizational behavior, and are known for encouraging playing the numbers game [13]. Some of the characteristics identified by research in this area of successful organizational control systems are: 1) establishing controls with participation of those being controlled by them; 2) making control measurements explicit and realistic; 3) identifying proper people for monitoring performance; 4) establishing procedures and responsibility for who and how performance is compared to standards; and 5) determining by whom and how corrective action is taken when performance does not match standards.

Problem-Solving and Decision-Making

A recent review of the research on problem-solving in organizations [55] presents a contingency theory for managerial strategies to deal with problems based on the degree of problem uncertainty, the amount of problem complexity, and the level of conflict among problem-solvers. For each type of problem, strategies ranging from computer modeling to Delphi methods are discussed. Such research implies that the applied behavioral sciences should locate decision-making at appropriate organizational levels where the best sources of data reside, involve those affected by the decision, and develop mechanisms for managing the political conflict that surrounds many organizational decisions.

Reward Systems

Research has clearly shown that what organizations want to reward is often not what they are rewarding. It is also clear that reward systems at all levels of the organization greatly affect behavior. The challenge to the applied behavioral sciences is to help organizations develop reward systems that reward behavior that enhances organizational objectives and recognizes differences between groups and individuals regarding what is rewarding [48]. The expectancy model of motivation discussed by Lawler and Nadler is a powerful tool for the applied behavioral sciences [47].

Conflict Management

The behavioral research on conflict has shown that it is an inevitable fact of personal, group, and organizational life that needs to be appropriately diagnosed and managed in order to avoid its dysfunctional consequences and to enhance the potential of obtaining some of its benefits [27; 88].

The organizational processes category includes the largest array of applied behavioral science techniques. As a result, we will highlight only two of those listed in Table 1.

Probably one of the most popular of management techniques for improving organizational accountability and control is management by objectives (MBO). It is often touted as a panacea for all organizational problems. As Huse recently pointed out [42], in practice it has fallen miserably short of meeting such expectations. Its beauty, however, is that it makes a great deal of simply intuitive sense. The basic premise is that people should be evaluated for what they accomplish, not for how they do it, and that if people participate in setting their own objectives, they will be more committed to them. MBO is a systematic procedure for joint goal-setting and follow-up evaluation by boss and subordinate. Where it works successfully, a number of conditions appear to be necessary. Thus, the successful application of MBO occurs when: 1) the goals are truly set collaboratively; 2) there is relatively high trust; and 3) communication is relatively open. MBO does not fix these problems and cannot work unless these other things are fixed, but when MBO works, it does improve control and communication.

Another applied behavioral science technique for improving organizational processes is called data feedback, based on an action research model. It is a procedure whereby members of the organization participate in the design, collection, and analysis of data about aspects of their functioning. The process is designed to stimulate open communication and confrontation around jointly defined problems. It aims to improve organizational communication and problem-solving [15; 63].

People

There are three areas of research that we consider in this area: 1) individual motivation; 2) interpersonal relationships and interdisciplinary collaboration; and 3) leadership.

The most central of these factors is individual motivation. Applied behavioral science is very much influenced by the recent research of behavioral scientists that indicates earlier theories of motivation—whether they be reinforcement theories, self-actualization theories [56] or social man theories [69]—are all too simplistic and are being supplanted by contingency theories such as represented in the Porter-Lawler expectancy model presented by Lawler and Nadler [47]. The contemporary view of motivation is that worker motivation is complex and that the relationship between worker needs and motivation, performance, and satisfaction is contingent on a variety of factors including the individual's need structure, the characteristics of the job, and the structure of the organization [37].

In addition to important motivational variations between organizational members, there are significant interpersonal style differences that affect the ability of individuals to work collaboratively. This is especially relevant with regard to team and group work. Research indicates that interpersonal relationships are affected by both individual style and the organization structure. Very often what appears to be an interpersonal problem is really a fault of the sociotechnical arrangement, such as when a nurse concerned with patient comfort confronts the housekeeping staff for waking up a sleeping patient while mopping the floor. The interpersonal problem experienced by both individuals is probably due to the structure of the situation, not to conflicting personal styles.

Finally, leadership style is part of the individual component of an organization. Traditionally, research was carried out in one of two camps: those trying to identify the characteristics of a great leader; and those trying to identify the characteristics of a good leadership role. More recent leadership research has taken a contingency point of view, arguing that effective leadership is a combination of the individual leadership style and the particular demands of the situation [32; 87]. The position taken by some is that the leadership style of an individual remains quite constant and that one must match leaders with the "right" situation [32]. Others argue that leaders are able to modify their styles to fit the situation [87].

Some of the applied behavioral science techniques listed in Table 1 are focused primarily on changing individual attitudes and behavior. These range from training to improve organizational skill to interpersonal human relations training.

Emergent Structures and Processes

As stated earlier, all organizations have emergent (informal) structures and processes. The importance of these structures and processes has long been recognized, but until recently they have not been systematically studied. Recent research on organizational decision-making attests to the importance of such emergent structures as coalitions and cliques as they operate in complex organizations. The applied behavioral sciences are just beginning to address the issue of developing techniques for designing organizations that promote the emergence of informal structures (networks, coalitions, and cliques) that are beneficial to both individual members and the performance of the organization [84; 41].

This area represents one of the leading edges of applied behavioral science technology in complex organizations. Only recently have techniques been developed. Hornstein and Tichy describe techniques for managing emergent structures and processes, including an organization design developed by Marvin Weisbord and Paul Lawrence, that combines a matrix and a functional structure in a medical center. The structure fostered open and direct negotiation between departments and informal interest groups for the allocation of resources.

Teams in Organizations

Since World War II, largely through the work sparked by Kurt Lewin and his students (Cartwright and Zander), a growing body of group dynamics research has emerged, which is being applied in organizational settings including human service settings. The research can be divided into two broad categories, structure and process. Group and team structure research has focused on such issues as the effects of group size, communication structure, and task type on group performance [25]. The process research has focused on how the group deals with information, group norms, individual versus group performance, and decision-making [46]. The results of 30 years of research have led to a contingency view of team functions, that is, team performance depends on a mixture of situational variables including the characteristics of the task, the size of the groups, the group norms, the time available to accomplish the task, the type of decision-making process used, and the characteristics of group members. The applied behavioral sciences have been actively involved in translating this research on groups and teams into action since the now-famous research project that led to the start of T-groups [16]. The most comprehensive applied behavioral science work in this area has been carried out by Rubin, Plovnick, and Fry [67], who have developed team-development procedures for interdisciplinary teams.

Change Processes

Research on the process of change, both at a macrosocietal level and an organizational level, is relevant to administrators. At the macro level, change research focuses on the impact of changing structure versus individual behavior on organizational performance and the evaluation of the impact of various intervention technologies [63]. Studies have also been conducted on the agents of planned change (including behavioral science and management consultants) comparing their theories and approaches [77].

Patient/Client/Student

The final area of relevant behavioral science research is related to factors affecting patient and client care and student learning. There are three relevant areas of research. First, the work in social psychology on attitudes and behavior change, learning theory, and the relationship between psychosocial factors and illness provides the groundwork for a variety of applied behavioral science interventions that can be used to facilitate patients, clients, and students taking more control of their own health or learning. Learning theory has led to the development of various behavior modification programs for dealing with such psychosocial issues as phobias, smoking, and overeating, as well as for dealing with skill acquisition.

Another area is patient or consumer advocacy. The work by Deutsch [27] and others on conflict resolution provides relevant behavioral science material for constructively managing the interface between consumer needs and demands and the service delivery system response.

Finally, the extensive anthropological, sociological, and psychological work on families provides a basis for understanding the impact of family structure and process on human services. A variety of family interventions exists to aid in treating the family as the basic unit of service delivery [14].

This brief overview of behavioral science research and related application has provided examples of how knowledge is being developed and employed to improve organizational effectiveness. Such a discussion of research and technology related to our model components provides a limited and incomplete view of how we propose that the applied behavioral sciences can be most useful for human service administration. Rather than dealing with each component separately, we advocate a more integrated total organization approach to using some of these techniques. Such an approach to applied behavioral science in organizational settings is generally referred to as organization development [9; 33; 42]. The remainder of this section will focus on the organization development process.

CHARACTERISTICS OF A HEALTHY ORGANIZATION

In shifting our focus to an organization development orientation, we draw upon Matthew B. Miles' four-level conceptualization of organizational functioning.* Managers have to be able to operate at all four levels. Table 2 looks at some of the managerial skills related to each level.

The first level is *steady-state operation*, that is, the ongoing regular routines of the organization. The administrator spends a certain percentage of his or her time doing steady-state operations, *e.g.*, attending regular meetings, filling out reports, monitoring the budget. Alas, all organizations break down and require *repair operations*. The administrator spends a certain percentage of time doing "crisis" management or putting out fires, *e.g.*, conflict between departments,

Table 2. Levels of organizational functioning.

LEVELS OF ORGANIZATIONAL FUNCTIONING	RELATED MANAGERIAL SKILLS
Steady-state operation	Organizational design (authority, decision-making, work process, rewards, communication staffing) Planning, organizing, directing controlling, and coordinating Management Information Systems Cost-benefit analysis
Repair operation	Conflict management (interpersonal, intragroup, intergroup) Unprogrammed, nonroutine decision-making Problem-solving methods (force field, Delphi method, group vs. individual) Contingency planning
Innovative operation	PERT and Critical Path Method for new programs Management innovations (MBO, participatory style) Organizational innovations (job redesign, team-building) Program innovations
Self-renewal operation	Open-system planning Organization development Organizational diagnosis and improvement strategies Data-feedback systems

*Relating Miles' concepts to the applied behavioral sciences was first introduced to one of the authors by Dr. Kenneth Pollock.

budget crises, union problems. Luckily most organizations also introduce innovations into their systems. Therefore, the administrator spends time at innovation, keeping up on new developments in the field or on how to manage more effectively and then works at implementing innovation, *e.g.*, new computer system, new MBO system. The final level of organizational functioning is *self-renewal*, that is, taking time out from levels 1, 2, and 3 and developing ways of doing levels 1, 2, and 3 better. It is analogous to preventive medicine for the organization. Self-renewal operation rarely occurs in organizations because of the seeming paradox of having to take time away from the other three levels to be able to make those levels function better. The applied behavioral sciences provide techniques for improving organizational functioning at the first three levels, but, as an overall integrated approach to improving organizational health, applied behavioral sciences are most related to level four, *self-renewal operation*.

We propose that part of the administrator's role should be to engage in self-renewal operation, and that not to do so leads to what John Gardner refers to as organizational "dry rot." Organization development is an approach to organization self-renewal.

We will briefly discuss the organization development process as applied to health organizations.

When talking about self-renewal and organizational effectiveness, it becomes necessary to define what is meant by an effective and healthy organization. Beckhard has developed normative criteria for a healthy organization based on a set of assumptions about individuals, groups, and organizations. These are all presented below [9].

Criteria of a Healthy Organization

1. It tends to be *purposeful* and *goal-directed*. The leadership of the organization, the heads of functions and programs, individual units, and people have, in addition to day-to-day interests, some relatively explicit goals and directions toward which they are working.
2. *Form* follows *function*. The organization chart, the ways work is organized and resources allocated, the location of decision points, are defined by the *work* requirements, not by the authority or power requirements. Power is widely dispersed and differentiated from (official) authority.
3. Decisions are based on locations of information rather than roles in the hierarchy.
4. The reward systems are related to the work to be done—attention is paid to intrinsic as well as extrinsic rewards, *e.g.*, the lower paid pediatrician's work is no less *valued* than the higher paid surgeon's work.
5. Communication is *relatively* open. The norms or ground rules of this system *reward* differences of opinion regarding ideas, solutions to problems, goals, *etc.*, regardless of the authority relationship of "differers."

6. *Inappropriate* competition is minimized; collaboration is rewarded where it is in the organization's best interests.
7. Conflict is *managed*, not suppressed or avoided. The management of conflicts over ideas, work, *etc.*, is seen as an essential part of everyone's job.
8. The organization is seen as an *open system*, embedded in complex environment, the parts of which are constantly making *demands*. The management of this complex of demands is a major part of the executive job.
9. There is a conscious effort on the part of management to support each individual's identity, integrity, and freedom. Work and rewards are organized to maintain these.
10. There is an "action research" mode of management. The organization sees itself as always "in process"—needing to have mechanisms for collecting information of the state of things and consciously planning improvements. There are built in "feedback mechanisms" (how are we doing?) at all levels.

These normative criteria are based on the following assumptions held by most applied behavioral scientists about individuals, groups, and organizations [42, pp. 23-24].

Assumptions about Individuals

1. Western peoples have needs for personal growth and development. These needs are most likely to be satisfied in a supportive and challenging environment.
2. Most workers are underutilized and are capable of taking on more responsibility for their own actions and of making a greater contribution to organizational© goals than is permitted in most organizational environments. Therefore, the job design, managerial assumptions, or other factors frequently "demotivate" individuals in formal organizations.

Assumptions about People in Groups

1. Groups are highly important to people, and most people satisfy their needs within groups, especially the work group. The work group includes both peers and the supervisor, and is highly influential on the individual within the group.
2. Work groups, as such, are essentially neutral. Depending on its nature; the group can be either helpful or harmful to the organization.
3. Work groups can greatly increase their effectiveness in attaining individual needs and organizational requirements by working together collaboratively. In order for a group to increase its effectiveness, the formal leader cannot exercise all of the leadership functions at all times and in all circumstances. Group members can become more effective in assisting one another.

Assumptions about People in Organizations

1. Since the organization is a system, changes in one subsystem (social, technological, or managerial) will affect other subsystems.
2. Most people have feelings and attitudes that affect their behavior, but the culture of the organization tends to suppress the expression of these feelings and attitudes. When feelings are suppressed, problem-solving, job satisfaction, and personal growth are adversely affected.
3. In most organizations, the level of interpersonal support, trust, and cooperation is much lower than is desirable and necessary.
4. Although "win-lose" strategies can be appropriate in some situations, many "win-lose" situations are dysfunctional to both employees and the organization.
5. Many "personality clashes" between individuals or groups are functions of organizational design rather than of the individuals involved.
6. When feelings are seen as important data, additional avenues for improved leadership, communications, goal-setting, intergroup collaboration, and job satisfaction are opened.
7. Shifting the emphasis of conflict resolution from "edicting" or "smoothing" to open discussion of ideas facilitates both personal growth and the accomplishment of organizational goals.
8. Organizational structure and the design of jobs can be modified to more effectively meet the needs of the individual, the group, and the organization.

The Process of Organization Development

In terms of large systems, Beckhard defines organization development as a 1) planned, 2) systemwide, 3) top-supported, 4) behavioral-science-knowledge-based effort to improve organizational health [9]. In order to accomplish these objectives the following conditions generally need to exist:

1. There is a planned program involving the whole system based on careful system diagnosis.
2. The top of the organization is aware of, and committed to, the program and the management.
3. It is related to the organization's mission (the applied behavioral science effort is not a program to improve effectiveness in the abstract; rather, it is an effort to improve effectiveness aimed specifically at creating organization conditions that will improve the organization's ability to achieve its mission goals).
4. It is a long-term effort. Usually two or three years are required for any large organizational change to take effect and be maintained.

In order to carry out successful organization development effort, specific aspects of the change process are critical. We have organized these under the headings of: diagnosing organizational health, planning improvement strategies, selecting intervention technologies, action plan and action, and evaluating applied behavioral science efforts.

It should be noted here that many organization development efforts involve the use of external behavioral science consultants who work with the organization in the planning and implementing phases. The role of the consultant is to work collaboratively with the organization rather than as an expert who directs the effort. Therefore, it should be kept in mind that the following discussion of the organization development process is one in which outside consultant help is generally required.

MANAGEMENT OF THE CHANGE PROCESS: SELF-RENEWAL OPERATION

All self-renewal operations involve organizational change. Here, we examine the phases of the change process.

Diagnosing Organizational Health

At the core of all organization development efforts is a careful diagnosis of current organizational conditions. As emphasized in earlier writings by Beckhard [9], "The development of a strategy for systematic improvement of an organization demands an examination of the present state of things."

In order to avoid the "little-boy-with-a-hammer problem,"[2] an organization model such as the one we presented is used for diagnosis. The model provides the guidelines for selecting diagnostic information and for arranging the collected information into meaningful patterns. This forms the basis for evaluating dysfunctional aspects of social systems. The organization model functions much like a physician's model of the human system. The physician conducts tests, collects certain vital information on the human system, and evaluates and interprets this information based on his model. Once the diagnosis is made, the model guides the selection of the appropriate medical intervention. The organizational model is used in a similar fashion, guiding the collection of information, its analysis, and the selection of an intervention strategy, which, in turn, is followed by selection of appropriate intervention techniques, as assessment of conditions for success, an evaluation, and an action plan.

The medical analogy must be made with great caution as the applied behavioral science approach to organizational health runs counter to many of the practices of traditional medical care. In traditional practice, the medical expert

[2]Kaplan compares scientists to "little boys with hammers" [45]. He states that "if you give a little boy a hammer he will find that everything needs pounding." Likewise, if you give a manager an applied behavioral science technique, he may find it improves everything.

prescribes to the patient, whereas in the organization development approach the patient is actively involved in his or her own diagnosis and prescription [82] .

Table 3 shows how one would proceed to diagnose a system using our organizational model. For each of the components of the model, examples of information being sought and methods for obtaining the information are presented.

Table 3. Diagnosing organizations using behavioral science criteria[a].

MODEL CATEGORY	INFORMATION SOUGHT	DATA-COLLECTION METHODS
Organization and environment	What are key environmental domains, properties, and demands? What linkages are present; what are population characteristics?	Open-system planning with management, personnel, and population interviews and demographics, *etc.*
Mission and objectives	What is the goal-set and how are goals-objectives established? Are the skills there?	Observations, interviews, and auditing actual processes and procedures
Sociotechnical properties	What is the task and flow schedule? What about exceptions; role definitions?	Interviews, observations, and structural analysis, *etc.*
Organizational and decision processes	What is the schedule of decision, authority, and skills on the management side?	Processual (functional) analysis; observation of decision behavior
Conflict management	What is the schedule of conflicts and mechanisms for resolution? Does reward system impose conflict?	Interviewing, observation, and third-party solicitation, *etc.*
Communication	How do communications channels graph; are they congruent with "mission?"	Observation and directed discussions; sociometric modeling
Emergent aspects	How do functional and personal relationships graph?	Sociometric analysis of organizational interchange
Individual and group interfaces	Are individual and group goals aligned; is career development system good?	Cross-sectional and longitudinal interviews, observation, and perceptual-diagnostic analysis.
Output	What are success-failure parameters? General performance properties? Individual satisfaction and behavioral records?	Mixed analysis of sociotechnical and economic (financial) data; interviews and directed observation; analysis of turnover, absenteeism, *etc.*

[a]Portions of this table were adapted from French and Bell [33] .

Note that not all organization development efforts start with a total system diagnosis, often a subsystem, such as a department, is the starting point. In either case, however, the first step is systematic diagnosis using a diagnostic model.

The diagnosis is conducted in a collaborative-action-research mode, that is, the manager, possibly with the help of an organization development consultant, actively collaborates with organization members in collecting and analyzing information for action planning.

Action research describes the process that provides the underpinning for the applied behavioral science self-renewal process. French and Bell define action research as [33, pp. 84–85]:

> the process of systematically collecting research data about an ongoing system relative to some objective, goal or need of the system; feeding this data back to the system based on the data and on hypotheses and evaluating the results of actions by collecting more data.

The long-term objective of organization development efforts is to create the conditions and skills for the organization to engage continually in the self-renewal, action-research process to enhance organizational effectiveness. Therefore, the phases are steps in a problem-solving process that must be continually reaccomplished [70; 89]. The implementation of the diagnostic phase involves meeting with key organization members: 1) to determine the system to be diagnosed, *i.e.*, total organization, management team, department; 2) to agree on the model for diagnosis, such as, our model; 3) to agree on how data is to be collected, by whom and when; and 4) how data will be used to develop a change strategy.

Data-Collection Procedures

There are five basic procedures for collecting diagnostic information, each with advantages and disadvantages. Table 4 summarizes the five approaches, including some of their advantages, disadvantages, and sources for further reading. The choice of diagnostic procedures is guided by an assessment of the trade-offs involved in any given situation, although it is generally desirable to use multiple diagnostic techniques [52]. Examples of diagnostic data collection approaches include:

1. A hospital administrator and his department heads decide to conduct a hospitalwide survey of the 1500 staff members by means of a structured questionnaire, the results of which are to be fed back to work groups throughout the hospital in order for them to seek ways to improve.
2. An ambulatory care unit decides to have a consultant interview each member, observe them at work, and hold a one-day feedback session in order to begin developing a strategy for improving the effectiveness of the unit.

Table 4. Procedures for collecting diagnostic data.

ROCEDURE	ADVANTAGE	DISADVANTAGE	FURTHER READING
tionnaire survey	Data from large number of people Standardization for measuring change over time Relatively inexpensive Quick	Measures attitudes not behavior Questionable validity Requires honesty on part of respondents	Price, *Handbook of Organization Measurements*
rvation	Rich behavioral data Deep understanding of an organization's culture Build relationships with members of the organization	Takes a great deal of time Sampling bias (may get biased view of system because everything can't be observed) Subjective, therefore measurement of change over time difficult Requires a great deal of trust to get accepted to make observations	Strauss, *Field Methods*
views	Combines some advantages of questionnaire with a chance to observe some member behavior and establish relationships with organizations	Limited data on actual organizational bahavior Time consuming Sampling problems in large systems	Cook *et al.*, *Research Methods in Social*
kshops gnostic meetings	Mobilizes organizational groups to take action Quick Makes data real for everyone involved Reinforces the "action research" process	Requires high commitment to take action May lead to superficial, biased diagnosis	Beckhard, *Organization Development*
uments and cords	Often readily available Provides good unobtrusive measures Provides data over time Inexpensive data source	Limited number of relevant diagnostic areas recorded in documents and records	Webb *et al.*, *Unobtrusive Measures*

3. The director of a neighborhood health center decides to have the 5 members of top management meet with 25 middle managers in a one-day diagnostic confrontation meeting at which a consultant aides in identifying issues that a) top management alone needs to work on, b) top management in collaboration with middle management can work on. The day ends by planning subsequent next steps.

Interpretation of Data

Once the information has been collected, the organization model provides the framework for its interpretation. The basic underlying approach to interpreting complex systems is what Nadler and Tushman describe as the "fit" hypothesis [73]:

> Other things being equal, the greater the total degree of consistency or fit between the various components, the more effective will be organizational behavior at multiple levels. Effective organizational behavior is defined as behavior which leads to higher levels of goal attainment, utilization of resources, and the adaptation.

In addition to the "fit" between the components of the organization model, is the fit between current organizational conditions and the criteria of a healthy organization listed previously.

The actual format for interpretation varies depending on the situation, but follows a general set of guidelines:

1. Recognition of diagnosis as an intervention—purpose of organizational diagnosis is not limited to providing a systematic understanding of current systems conditions, but, equally important, it is a collaborative process for energizing system members to want to work on jointly "felt needs." The orderly collection of data and its public feedback to system members results in mobilizing and releasing energies for change.
2. Opportunity for thorough processing of diagnostic data—it is important for organization members to feel "ownership" of the diagnostic data; therefore, meetings need to be held with organization members in which the data and their implications can be openly discussed and explored.
3. Identification of areas for organizational improvement—using the fit hypothesis and the applied behavioral science model, the organization members, often in collaboration with a consultant, identify organizational areas needing improvement. If possible, priorities are established regarding what needs to be improved first.

The next phase in the organization development effort is strategy formulation.

Planning Improvement Strategies

Once the diagnostic activities have resulted in identifying areas for improvement, the next step is to begin deciding on what to do in order to improve the current state of affairs. The tendency of most administrators is to jump quickly to solutions. This often results in immediately selecting an improvement technique without having worked out an improvement strategy. For example, if the problem is identified as conflict between teachers and administrators, jumping right to an intervention technique, such as sensitivity training, assumes that the appropriate strategy is to alter individual and interpersonal style, when in fact the real cause of the problem may be embedded in the sociotechnical arrangements, thus requiring an altogether different intervention. It is important to distinguish between an intervention *strategy*, which entails identifying the underlying change mechanisms, and an intervention *technology*, which is the specific set of procedures for carrying out the strategy. (See Table 5 for examples of strategy and technology.)

Strategy formulation entails the use of the organizational model to help in identifying levers for change and improvement. These levers emerge from an understanding of what happens when different categories of the model are altered. For example, it is necessary to know what happens when the sociotechnical arrangements are changed: how change will affect decision-making and communication and *vice versa*. Strategy formulation is based on the dynamic-systems view of organization, which assumes that change in any one component in the model will ultimately lead to first- and second-order changes elsewhere in the system.

As outlined in previous writing on strategy formulation, Beckhard [9] indicates that the final determination of a change strategy is arrived at through a complex sorting out of issues and trade-offs. The following issues need to be taken into account.

1. What is the change problem? Attitudes? Behaviors? Structural changes? Process changes? What are the interrelationships and the priorities?
2. What is the appropriate subsystem involved in the problem? Which individuals, groups, or units are involved and affected? This may or may not be related to the organizational chart.
3. What is the willingness and capability of the system to change? What are the competencies and environmental constraints? Is the person or persons who want to bring about change in the right location? What is his influence potential?
4. When a consultant is used, what are the motives and resources of the change agent? To what degree is he an advocate or a methodological

Table 5. Examples of change strategies and technologies.

MODEL CATEGORY	STRATEGIES	TECHNOLOGIES
Input	Change the environment Anticipate environmental changes Alter characteristics of input	Interorganizational linkages Coalition building Organizational set analysis Open-systems planning[a] Strategic planning
Transformation process mission & objectives	Clarify Change Build ongoing mechanism for re-examining and changing	Goal confrontation meeting Multilevel planning
Sociotechnical arrangements Prescribed Emergent	Technical change (work flow) Social structure change Explicitly examine emergent networks and change through new prescribed arrangements	Contingency theories of organization design, *e.g.*, differentiation and integration[a] Autonomous work groups Job enrichment Role analysis technique Sociometric network analysis
Organizational processes Communication	Change the flow Change the content Change the quality level of distortion	Redesign communication networks Data feedback[a]
Control	Establish collaboratively designed control system Clarify standards and corrective action mechanisms	Management by objectives[a] system Management information system
Problem-solving and decision-making	Develop routine and nonroutine procedures Alter decision-making structure levels, patterns of involvment	Data feedback-survey feedback[a] Responsibility analysis

Reward system	Deal with individual differences	Scanlan plan
	Relate to organizational objectives	Integrating mechanisms
Conflict management	Alter sociotechnical arrangements	Organizational mirroring
	Develop intergroup mechanism for handling	Confrontation meeting
	Develop interpersonal for handling conflict	Role negotiation
		Third-party consultation[a]
Individual-group component		
Individual style	Alter selection and placement of individuals	Life planning—career development[a]
		Assessment center
	Train individuals	Different selection criteria
	Develop individuals for future	Leadership training
		Education: technical skills
		Sensitivity training
		Coaching and counseling
Interpersonal	Increased interaction and communication	Sensitivity training
Group culture	Change the norms and values about work and how to behave in work settings	Team building[a]
		Process consultation[a]

[a]These techniques will be presented in more detail in Table 6.

Table 6. Modern OD techniques.[a]

OD TECHNIQUES	DEFINITION	FOCUS	BASIC ASSUMPTIONS	GOALS	ADVANTAGES	DISADVANTAGES
1. Differentiation and integration	A diagnostic approach that gathers information about the interdepartmental and intergroup differences of orientation with respect to time, interpersonal relations, goals, and structure. It also identifies the integrative mechanisms for dealing with those differences in order to achieve collaboration within the total organization.	Each group, department, or unit is studied in terms of its needs and methods of meeting those needs in order to best accomplish its task. Intergroup interfaces and methods of dealing with differences are also of major interest.	Different areas of assignment within an organization need to be structured differently in order to accomplish their purposes best. Integrative mechanisms must be designed to bridge the differences and provide effective collaboration.	Identify differentiation needs, integrative mechanisms, and methods of conflict resolution. Redesign to fit better the environmental demands upon the various groups.	Helps in identifying possible intergroup problems. Very effective as a diagnostic tool. Focuses on task, structure, goals, etc., rather than personality dimensions. Useful in identifying environmental demands. Takes into account system interdependencies. Adaptable in a consistent manner to local conditions and problems. Written diagnosis is usually provided.	Extensive complex diagnosis is necessary. Minimum focus on individual problems. Depends heavily on other techniques for implementation of change. Relatively less used now than other common approaches.
2. Life planning—career development	A process for identifying personal strengths and successes in order to establish a base for accomplishing personal, career, and organizational goals.	Personal development and increased contribution to organizational goals; Career opportunities. More creative use of individual and organizational resources.	Identifying strengths and providing relevant training does lead to a more productive use of individual resources. The organization exists for the benefit of all members. Individual fulfillment brings increased organizational effectiveness and optimizes use of member skills. Individual and organizational goals can complement each other.	Improve individual resources. Match tasks with individual strengths and resources and desires. Increase personal growth and fulfillment. Harmonize organizational and individual goals.	Career conflicts faced and resolved. Especially useful in mergers; rapid growth; acquisitions, etc. Actualization of potential of all members. Clarification of roles and expectations. Identification of personal goals and organizational goals. Team-building device for an already cohesive group. Happy, dedicated, contributing, self-actualizing employees.	May not survive change in top management. Dissatisfaction if work styles cannot be altered. Possible incongruency between reality and what one would like work to be. Conflicts between individuals' career goals. Requires great amount of flexibility on the part of management.
3. Management by objectives	A process whereby the superior and the subordinate members of an enterprise jointly analyze their assignments in terms of reason for existence and contribution to the mission of the organization. Mutually they identify expected results and establish measures as guides for	Primarily "end results," hence on "task." Key to success is when groups and individuals mesh goals and efforts to succeed in the "situation." It can apply to any manager or individual no matter what level of function, and to any organization, regardless of size	Organization and/or individuals have, or can be given, elements of "planning" and "control" as well as the function of "doing." Reasonable and normal control over activities and results is desirable. Theory Y beliefs about people, if maximum potential of MBO as OD tools is	Improved performance of organization and individuals. Coordination of resources. Increased ownership in decisions and goals. Improved measurement of results. Clarification of responsibilities and goals.	Focuses on measurable results. Contains in its processes the traditionally recognized management structure. Gives participant responsibility for decision-making. Does not limit methods—only end results.	Results focus tends to obscure process and climate issues. The tendency to "simulate" shared decision-making when in reality the decisions are unilateral. Diverse misconceptions about what MBO is or is not.

desired *results*, not on the methods of achieving the results.

	Description	Target	Assumptions	Uses	Limitations
4. Open-systems planning	A method of studying an organization by identifying its "mission" and analyzing all relevant variables *without* as well as *within* the organization.	All aspects of the internal and external environmental systems. The organizational processes that need to be modified in order to adapt best to environmental demands.	System has right and responsibility to make itself the way it wants to be. Organizations can to a great degree control their internal and external operations and environment. The complex organization is a set of interdependent parts that together make up a whole because each contributes something and receives something from the whole, which in turn is interdependent with some larger environment. Understanding organizations involves much more than understanding goals and the arrangements that are developed for their accomplishment. Organizations are affected by what comes into them in the form of input, by what transpires inside the organization, and by the nature of the environmental acceptance of the organization and its output.	Clarify organization's mission. Make explicit the demands from other systems. Look at present organizational response to demands. Redesign of system to be more active in meeting its environment and accomplishing its mission. Directly specifying those elements important for organizational analysis. Survival of the system.	Useful when major changes are to be made such as mergers, new top management, *etc.* Useful when things seem *too good.* Useful when ability to perform is impaired by other outside groups. Useful when a group is just forming or coming into existence. Useful at regular intervals of approximately 5 years. Especially useful for organizations with "service" type technologies. Useful when organization receives undue criticism. Useful to unite total organization to accomplish its mission. When well done, it resolves some of the organization's most difficult problems. Establishes a representative "core group."	A complex and demanding procedure that entails some risk of negative outcome. Typically requires much effort in follow-through. Requires careful planning, management, and commitment. Usually requires a fairly high time commitment especially on the part of top management. Relatively new and undeveloped at present.
5. Process consultation	PC is a set of activities on the part of the consultant that help the client to perceive, understand, and act upon process events that occur in the client's environment. This process consultant seeks to give the cli-	All interpersonal processes within the organization. All (or at least primary) relationships and procedures.	The process model starts with the assumption that the organization knows how to solve its particular problems or knows how to get help in solving them, but that it often does not know how to *use its own resources effec-*	The goal of the process consultant is to help the organization to solve its own problems by making it aware of organizational processes and of the consequences of these processes and the organization to learn from self-diagnosis and self-intervention. The ultimate concern	Goes hand in hand with team and interpersonal relations training. Conducted on the job in the normal work setting. Effective solution of interpersonal, individual, and intergroup problems. Intended to build the needed skill in the participants to	Does not afford the intensive involvement offered by various forms of interpersonal relations training or team building. Takes into account only the process issues. Requires sustained involvement over a 2- or 3-year period.

Table 6. (cont.).

OD TECHNIQUES	DEFINITION	FOCUS	BASIC ASSUMPTIONS	GOALS	ADVANTAGES	DISADVANTAGES
	ents "insight" into what is going on around them, within them, and between them and other people. The events to be observed and learned from are primarily the various human actions that occur in the normal flow of work, in the conduct of meetings, and in formal or informal encounters between members of the organization. Of particular relevance are the client's own actions and their impact on other people.		tively either in initial problem solution or in implementation of solutions. The process model further assumes that inadequate use of internal resources or ineffective implementation results from process problems, i.e., that people fail to communicate effectively with each other, or develop mistrust, or engage in destructive competition, or punish those they mean to reward and vice versa, or fail to give feedback, and so on.	of the process consultant is the organization's capacity to do for itself what he or she has done for it. Where the standard consultant is more concerned about passing on knowledge, the process consultant is concerned about passing on skills and values.	carry on, with little external contact. Participants assume full responsibility for change efforts. Change tends to be relatively permanent. Organic in nature. Contributes toward effective solutions in any and all areas involving beings.	
6. Survey-feedback-action planning	A process of gathering data usually by interview, observation, or questionnaire about important organizational or group concerns. The data are summarized and fed back to the group members and used as impetus for discussion of needed changes. Plans for action are then made and in most cases a resurvey is taken to provide a comparative measure of change before and after discussion.	Getting information flowing within the system. Work groups and their work-related concerns. Relevant issues as defined by consultant or client. Organizational climate and/or management.	Data alone will provide an impetus for discussion and solution of problems. Decision-makers will accept the implications of scientifically valid data. Data-gathering methods have no disagreeable significant intervention impact upon the organization.	Providing the necessary accurate information for proper decision-making to those responsible for decisions. Increasing the participation of a greater number of resource people in management decisions.	Can be adapted to any areas of interest or issue relevant to organization members. Can be organizationwide or used only by those groups most interested. Provides for easy measurement and comparison of before and after any chosen intervention. Validated, reliable questionnaires already available for use in several areas of concern. May be an effective way of changing hard data indicators as well as less objective measures.	Often requires computer for analysis of data. Ownership of data is often difficult to achieve. Requires extensive preparation for feedback sessions in order to ensure effectiveness. Time lag between data collection and feedback minimizes effectiveness.
7. Team and interpersonal relations	A method of learning and planning for change in which the participants are helped to diagnose and experience their own behavior,	Interpersonal and group skills. Group expectations and goals. Intensive problem solving.	The amount of work carried out by workers is determined not by their physical capacities but by their physical capacities; noneconomic re-	Increased trust, openness, and team work. Joint planning and commitment to action. Improved work climate. Improved individual and group	Cultural and environmental change. Improved conflict resolution skills. Improved data flow within organizations.	Payoffs sometimes individually rather than organizationally oriented. Possible tendencies toward extremism on the part of some participants.

	and planning are done in a specially designed environment.		as groups and not as individuals; the leader is not necessarily the person appointed to be in charge; informal leaders can develop who have more power; the effective supervisor is "employee-centered" and "job-centered"; that is, he or she regards his or her job of dealing with human beings as well as with the work; communication and participation in decision-making are some of the most significant rewards that can be offered to obtain the commitment of the individuals.		Provides opportunity for interpersonal feedback analysis of interpersonal processes. Provide opportunity for examination of the social impact and consequences of one's behavior. Builds democratic and participative norms.	Possible misuse as "therapy" for unstable or unproductive members in the organization.
8. Third-party consultation	A process of diagnosing recurrent conflict between persons or groups. Then on the basis of our understanding of the dynamics of interpersonal conflict episodes, performing a number of strategic functions that facilitate a constructive confrontation of the conflict.	"Interpersonal conflict in organizational settings," such as differences between fellow members of a governing committee, heads of interrelated departments, a manager, and his or her boss. Interpersonal conflict is defined broadly to include both 1) interpersonal disagreement over substantive issues, such as differences over organizational structures, policies, and practices, and 2) interpersonal antagonisms, that is, the more personal and emotional differences that arise between interdependent human beings.	The innumerable interdependencies inherent in organizations make interpersonal conflicts inevitable. Even if it were thought to be desirable, it would not be possible to create organizations free from interpersonal conflicts. The amount of emotional energy necessary to confront a conflict and resolve it is often less in the long run than the amount of energy necessary to suppress it. Indirect conflicts, have the longest life expectancy and have the most costs that cannot be charged back against the original conflict.	To develop the interpersonal skills and to create an open confrontive organizational climate conducive to effective conflict resolution. To develop capacities within or available to organizations that make it possible to resolve more of the interpersonal conflicts and lessen the costs of those that cannot readily be resolved. To increase the authenticity of the relationships and the personal integrity experienced in the relationships.	Useful on the job in the "real" work setting. Provides resolution of problems so that energies can be used for productive purposes rather than to protect or defend. Provides a balance of power for the disadvantaged. Provides a third ("objective") view of otherwise polarized issues. Provides for the "referee" function in interpersonal flict issues. Can provide a constructive amount of anxiety, *i.e.*, a certain pressure is sometimes necessary for resolution or confrontation of problems.	Deals with only one of many development areas. Requires a highly skilled consultant. If they are not well managed, confrontations can further polarize the individuals, increase the costs of the conflict, or discourage the principals from further efforts. As in all areas of possible high return, the risks can also be high if the proper precautions are not taken.

[a] From Fred Luthars, *Organizational Behavior*, New York: McGraw-Hill,

consultant? What is the desired change from the consultant's point of view? What resources does he have or not have for the problem?

5. What are the intermediate change goals and strategies? What should be done in the short run? In the long run? If, for example, it seems appropriate to start with team-building or goal-setting, where should it start? What is an intermediate strategy, *e.g.*, starting with the top team? What other approaches should be considered?

6. What are the initial entry points? What leverage does the change agent have within the system? What is the *readiness* of the system to change? What *accessibility* is there to the change manager? What is the linkage to the system? What approaches can balance the three (readiness, accessibility, and linkage) to provide an optimum effect?

Table 5 provides specific examples of strategies and how they relate to the model categories. Often multiple strategies are used in the same applied behavioral science effort; therefore, Table 5 can be misconstrued as an oversimplification. An example of how diagnosis can lead to strategy formulation is:

The diagnosis indicated that individuals in the laboratory were frustrated because of the boring, repetitive nature of their work, each being limited to narrow, highly specialized tasks resulting in high absenteeism and turnover. The problem was diagnosed as an individual/task incongruent fit. Two alternative strategies are to: 1) change the selection and training procedures to find people with lower needs for interesting work; or 2) to alter the task providing more variety and complexity. Once the preferred strategy is selected then the specific change technology can be determined, examples of which are found in Table 6.

Selecting Intervention Technologies

Each technique for organizational improvement works well only under a limited set of conditions. For example, job enrichment may not work well in a situation in which there is a high degree of worker-management mistrust; technical rearrangement may not be a successful intervention if no one has a "felt need" for change. Based on behavioral science experience and research, the consultant and organization members need to ascertain the conditions necessary for a particular technique to work. Some of the important conditions to consider are:

1. The extent to which a supportive external environment is required (legislation, government, community).
2. The extent to which there is a need for substantial agreement between individual and organization goals.

3. The extent to which the organization has highly trained and qualified staff.
4. The extent to which it is important for the system to be open enough for members to be willing to discuss problems.
5. The extent to which a moderate level of dissatisfaction is needed to energize people to work on improvement.
6. The extent to which the consultant needs access to various kinds of information in the system.
7. The amount of trust required between staff and the consultant working with them.

Once agreement is reached on what the necessary conditions are for the successful use of a technique, the current state of the system along these dimensions needs to be assessed. If the necessary conditions are lacking, the technique should not be tried; either a new one should be selected or the strategy should be reformulated.

An example of some of the pitfalls of not assessing conditions necessary for success can be found in the following case of a small county social service agency. The management group, made up of four members, was constantly involved in a series of very messy and dysfunctional conflicts, costing the agency a great deal of money and problems at multiple levels. A consultant was called in to try to help the situation. The consultant identified the causes of the conflict as poorly defined and conflicting organizational goals resulting in different administrators pulling in different directions. The consultant decided that the strategy for correcting the situation was to involve top management in clarifying organizational goals. As a result, the consultant initiated a collaborative goal-setting meeting with the four administrators. The meeting was a dismal failure. The four complained about each other bitterly, and finally decided to discontinue the services of the consultant whom they felt had made matters worse.

Had the consultant and the management group considered the conditions necessary for a successful collaborative, goal-setting meeting, the outcome might have been different. Such a meeting requires a moderate degree of trust between consultant and members, a willingness on the part of participants to deal openly and honestly with each other, and an ability to cope with conflict. None of these conditions was present; in fact, in the above case, the consultant was seen as the pawn of the director, and two of the department heads were not on speaking terms.

Even though the consultant's diagnosis was correct and the strategy for dealing with it was consistent with the diagnosis, the absence of certain necessary conditions should have shifted the focus to one of dealing more openly and honestly with each other and managing their conflict.

ACTION PLAN AND ACTION:
TRANSITION TO NEW ORGANIZATIONAL STATE

The diagnosis, strategy formulation, and technique selection must all be incorporated into a plan of action. The success or failure of an action plan is contingent on a critical assessment of such factors as: 1) who should participate in different activities, 2) who should be kept informed about different activities, 3) who is able to be responsible for following through, 4) what is the timetable, and 5) what special resources are needed to carry out an activity.

The transition to a new organizational state can occur in a variety of ways. Often it requires the use of temporary management and organization systems [9]. That is the task of management and organizational resources. The temporary task force is one of the most useful transition vehicles. Membership on the task force should be guided by concerns for 1) including needed skills and expertise, and 2) including representation from those to be most directly affected by the change, as well as insuring sufficient legitimacy and power to accomplish its mission. Several of the cases in Section II demonstrate the use of transition systems to manage the change.

EVALUATING APPLIED BEHAVIORAL SCIENCE EFFORTS:
MONITORING THE CHANGE PROCESS

The action research mode of operation discussed in the diagnosis phase is again relevant to this stage of an organization development effort. The long-term objective of such an effort is to create the conditions for constant self-renewal. This means that there is a need for ongoing evaluation and feedback of results. Although almost everyone agrees with this idea, only a few organizations actively attempt to evaluate success. There is little learning from mistakes, nor is there any clear-cut confirmation of success.

Evaluation is clearly an underdeveloped area as it relates to organization development efforts.

Before focusing on how evaluation processes can be integrated into organization development efforts, it should be noted that in recent years, we have begun to see more sophisticated methods of evaluation emerge. Rubin Harris has developed a process for evaluating the effectiveness of patient care; Beckhard and others have evaluated the intervention of change in managing at two nursing schools (Massachusetts General), at a number of community health centers, etc. Change measurement instruments are emerging and, although little has been done to date, it is possible to look systematically at the effects of organization development efforts. The University of Michigan Institute for Survey Research, Quality of Working Life Project is developing a package of new evaluation techniques.

Table 7. Twenty questions for evaluating organizational improvement efforts.[a]

FACTOR	QUESTION
Outcome	
Objectives	1. *What were the intended outcomes of the program and what were the actual outcomes?* It is necessary to determine why the program was initiated and its impact on "bottom line" outcomes, such as productivity, turnover, absenteeism, and satisfaction.
Context	
External Factors	
Labor market and characteristics of work force	2. *How tight was the labor market and what were the characteristics of the available labor pool?* Ascertain unemployment level and characteristics of work force when evaluating an organization improvement program.
Social and political trends	3. *Were these changes occurring in society affecting workers and the organization?* The success of a program may be affected by how consistent it is with certain societal trends.
Economy and market	4. *What was the general state of the economy at the time of the improvement program?* Certain programs may work only in favorable economic conditions.
Environmental stability	5. *How changing is the organization's immediate environment, and is the organization structure appropriately matched?* A program may be greatly affected by the degree of congruence between an organization's structure and the degree of environmental uncertainty that exists for the organization.
Internal Factors	
Product technology	6. *What is the product of the organization and the primary technology used to transform inputs into outputs?* Ascertain the match between technology, structure, and type of people, and whether the program is congruent or attempts to make technology, structure, and types of people congruent.
Structure	7. *Where on the mechanistic to organic structure continuum is the organization?* The program should be consistent with the organization's structure or explicitly attend to changing it.
Size	8. *How large is the organization and the plant, or division within which the program is taking place?* Size affects complexity of programs and the organizational resources available.

Table 7. (*cont.*).

FACTOR	QUESTION
Organizational climate	9. *What are the prevailing norms and values in the organization regarding involvement in organizational improvement efforts?* Programs require changed behavior, thus changed climate, which requires program attention to resistance.
Organizational Improvement Program Guiding Assumptions and model Model	10. *How explicit were the assumptions about organizations and change that guided the organization improvement program?* Being explicit about assumptions increases the chance that all parties understand the program and that the assumptions are more carefully examined and tested.
	11. *How comprehensive and consistent with current organizational theory were the guiding assumptions and models?* Success of a program can be influenced by internal logic as well as failure to incorporate what we know about organizations and improvement.
Program phases Initiation phase	12. *What was the reason for starting the program and who was initially involved?* Programs generally require a broadly shared "felt need" and involvement of affected people to succeed.
Entry and start-up phase	13. *What were the initial activities at the start of the program and who was involved?* The pitfall to avoid is premature implementation; moving into a program tends to inadequate diagnosis and resistance due to lack of understanding and support. Prescription without diagnosis leads to malpractice.
Diagnostic phase	14. *What were their explicit diagnostic activities?*
	15. *What aspects of the organization were diagnosed and how?* Pitfalls include the "elephant problem," *e.g.*, sending eight blind men out to touch organization and try to put pieces together, also the "expert" problem in which outsiders do fancy diagnosis that no one understands.
Strategy-planning phase	16. *How was the actual program planned and by whom?* The two dimensions to assess are 1) how available resources (internal and external consultants) used, and 2) how the diagnostic model and data were used.

Table 7. (*cont.*).

FACTOR	QUESTION
Implementation phase	17. *How explicit and detailed were the plans?* Lack of planning leads to seat-of-the-pants implementation of a program. 18. *What was actually done, how, when, and by whom?* Two pitfalls are incomplete, patchwork implementation and *intervention interruptus*, not carrying program through to completion.
Evaluation and corrective action phase	19. *Was there explicit evaluation and monitoring of the program, and if so, what was measured and how?* Political pressure often exists to cover advocate programs setting up forces against evaluation. Evaluation measures should be directly related to intended program outcomes. 20. *What was done with the evaluation; did it result in corrective action or modification of the program?* No corrective action may occur due to lack of top level organization commitment and/or due to *postimplementation letdown* and regression when novelty wears off.

[a]Based on N. Tichy [78].

There are two basic types of evaluation. The first is ongoing monitoring of key indicators and the second is a more in-depth evaluation of an effort to determine more conclusively whether it was successful and what the factors were that contributed to success or failure. Table 7 provides a framework for a deeper focus. These two levels of evaluation are not inconsistent with each other and, in fact, should be mutually reinforcing. They do, however, require different resources.

Ongoing monitoring is best accomplished by organization members developing key indicators that they will monitor themselves at predetermined points in time. For example, employee attitudes toward a new work flow might be monitored several times a year through an attitude survey, as well as by watching absenteeism, turnover, and production figures. Similar data would be used in a more in-depth analysis of this improvement effort, but in addition a more comprehensive model for evaluation would be used. (For such a model, see Table 7.)

In addition to the ongoing monitoring of key indicators and more in-depth evaluations, mechanisms to sustain the self-renewal process are needed.

The processes discussed in this section require administrators, as well as other organization members, to engage in complex planned activities often requiring people to behave in new ways, thus necessitating dealing with individual and group resistance to change. In order to continue such new behaviors on an ongoing, systematic basis, there needs to be explicit management and organization commitment to the goals of improving organizational health.

The success of such efforts in human service organizations is in large part related to the quality of the management of the efforts and the commitment of the top management of the organization to invest. In order to do this, the administrator and the organization need to engage in the action research mode of management, which entails regularly recycling through the organization development self-renewal process. Beckhard identified some feedback systems frequently used for monitoring and maintaining change [8]:

1. periodic team meetings to review where a team is and what its next goal priorities should be;
2. organization-sensing meetings—the top of an organization meets, on a systematic, planned basis, with a sample of employees from a variety of different organizational centers, in order to keep appraised of the state of the system;
3. periodic intergroup meetings between interdependent units of an organization;
4. Renewal conferences. For example, one company has an annual planning meeting with its top management. Three weeks prior to that meeting, the same management group and their spouses go to a retreat for two or three days to take a look at where they are, where their personal and company priorities are, what the new forces in the environment are, what they need to keep in mind in their upcoming planning, what has happened in the way they work and in their relationships that need review before the planning meeting;
5. performance review on a systematic goal directed basis; and
6. Periodic visits from outside consultants to keep the organization leaders thinking about the organization's renewal.

Conclusion to Section I

This section has presented an overview of the applied behavioral sciences as it relates to aspects of human service administration. The major thrust has been to identify the process by which behavioral sciences can be used in complex organizations; thus, the emphasis has been on having an organizational model, comprehensive diagnosis, strategy formulation, technique selection, action planning, and evaluation. This explicit focus on a comprehensive problem-solving application of the behavioral sciences represents our protest against the proliferation of panacea, all-purpose behavioral science techniques that contribute to the "little-boy-with-a-hammer problem" among managers. Such techniques as MBO, transactional analysis, sensitivity training, and job enrichment have all been misused in this way. It is our contention that all these techniques have their place, but are best employed within a broader context of fostering ongoing organizational health.

II. THE USE OF BEHAVIORAL SCIENCE APPLICATIONS IN HUMAN SERVICE ADMINISTRATION

This section moves from an overview of the field to specific cases dealing with: 1) defining organizational missions, 2) designing an organization to manage multiple tasks and multiple professionals, 3) managing interface problems, 4) managing the change process, and 5) team development. Each of the cases demonstrates the use of a particular applied behavioral science technology for carrying out an improvement strategy. For example, open-systems planning, a specific technology for helping organizations articulate their mission and develop a strategic plan, is dealt with in two cases that concern medical centers.

The cases are summarized in Table 8, and related to one of the managerial problems identified at the beginning of Section I. The table then goes on to identify the improvement strategy pursued and the particular intervention technology used in the case. This section ends with an assessment of the future leading edge of the applied behavioral sciences.

In each case, we will define the problem, look briefly at the technology and its application to the problem, describe a case or two that illustrates the applications, and examine some implications for the training of administrators.

Understanding and Specifying the Mission of the Organization: Open-Systems Planning

Most administrators in large organizations are used to planning their work against goals or objectives. When organizations become more complex and the demands of the external environment more differentiated, administrators in such complex organizations as medical centers, social service agencies, and schools constantly face developing program and budget allocations from competing demands for resources. The criteria for allocating these resources tend to be based either against organization objectives or personal priorities or tradition and past experience. The core mission of the organization was defined in Section I as its *reason to be*—"the nature of the beast." Objectives and goals are the place or condition to which one aspires. There is a significant difference between *reason to be* (mission) and *place you want to get to* (goals). Yet much administrative planning allocates resources based on objectives or goals without being clear around mission priorities.

In simple organizations, and those with "slack" resources, it is possible to have

Table 8. Case examples.

	MANAGERIAL PROBLEM	ORGANIZATIONAL IMPROVEMENT STRATEGY	TECHNOLOGY
Medical Centers *A* and *B* Hospital *X*	Understanding and specifying the mission of the organization	Organization mission	Open-systems planning
Neighborhood health center	Managing and motivating multiple health professionals	Sociotechnical arrangements	Matrix design
Quality of care for house staff	Coping with interunit conflict	Organizational processes	Responsibility charting
Social work	Managing change in the organization	Organizational processes	Transition organization
School curriculum change			Trading activities
Residency rotation	Managing change in the organization	Changes in the structure	Structural alterations

multiple "core missions" because they can all be achieved. In health delivery, social service agencies, and educational organizations, when costs were lower, research funding higher, and a balance of need and service fairly clear, the issue of whether the core mission was training, service, or research was not a major concern of administrators. Obviously, the mission was all of these. As long as one could keep the resources in some kind of balance, the problem could be managed.

With increased organizational complexity, changes in funding practices, escalating costs of service delivery, and increasing community pressure, this issue is much more difficult for an administrator. In fact, some part of the governance of the institution probably must make a conscious decision putting *priorities* against two different possible *core* missions.

The behavior of people in administrative or leadership positions is significantly *affected* by their *concept* of the mission of the institution. Therefore, if this is not clear, others in the organization get mixed signals.

The process of core mission development is for key people in an organization (or department or unit) to develop a consensus on a core mission statement. After examining the alternatives, and getting a first position around the core mission, it is then desirable to "map the environment." This process involves thinking through and identifying the various institutions, groups, value systems, *etc.* that are making demands on the administration of the institution or department. For example, in a hospital there might be community demands for more ambulatory care; there might be medical society demands for more access of community physicians; there might be demands in the medical school for more sophisticated equipment for specialty training; in a particular department there might be demands for more efficiency in filling beds; or a demand for limiting support staff.

Using this process, all of these competing demands are listed. They add up to what is called the *demand system* (Figure 2). This provides a way of looking at the core mission in the context of the *open system* of the organization and its environment. It is sometimes necessary to modify or revise the core mission statement after an analysis of the demands.

We will give two different types of illustrations of applications of the core mission concept. The first is a pair of cases, although the two institutions involved have no awareness of the activity engaged in by the other institution. The illustration is of an application of core mission planning by two academic medical schools.

Center A. This is a large, prestigious medical school and teaching hospital in the western half of the country. The school is well known for its scientific research and clinical excellence. The graduates represent a distinguished scientific and medical group including some Nobel laureates. The institution is also

Step 1

Identify the core mission of the organization. Ask the group to specify what it is the organization is in existence for (specify below).

Core mission:_____

_____

_____

Step 2

Specify the key environmental domains affecting the transformation process.

Step 3

Specify the demands or pressures that each domain puts on the focal organization in behavioral terms.

Example:
   We the customers demand X and Y of the organization.
   We the union demand X of the organization.

Step 4

Define what responses the system now makes to those demands.

Step 6

What response mechanisms must be developed to cope with the future demands and pressures effectively (this might include changing domains as well as internal mechanisms).

Step 7

Assess what resources are needed to carry out step 6 (time, money, *etc*.).

Step 5

Project five years into the future. What is the relevant environment likely to be then? Specify the demands and pressures of each domain.

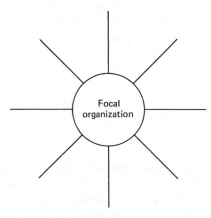

Figure 2. Steps in open-systems planning.

noted for the quality of its teaching in both undergraduate school and post-graduate residencies.   It has a high number of specialties in which it has made significant contributions to biomedical research and treatment. Practically all students specialize. It has not focused on training general practitioners. The institution is located in a community that is well served by private practice physicians.

As new legislation arose and new pressures appeared for training more primary care physicians in medical schools and teaching hospitals, the leaders of the school and hospitals examined their criteria for allocating resources. The facts were that research grants had been sharply reduced as in all medical institutions. There was an indication that, if medical schools were not going to prepare signif-icant numbers of students for primary care practice, capitation funding of tuition might be cut off. There was tremendous social pressure for more com-munity service. At the same time, there was a lot of pressure from the pres-tigious faculty not to destroy the "elegance" of the research and training of the institution.

A series of meetings between the university leadership, medical school leader-ship, the hospital leadership, *etc.* looked at these various demands. The leaders decided to conduct a core mission exercise to find out where the consensus was around the *basic mission* of that particular institution.   After a number of meetings the consensus emerged.   Briefly stated, it was: "We are basically a scientific institution engaged in inquiry and application of new knowledge. So research and its application is our core mission. To support this core mission, we wish to train qualified specialists to carry out the applications of this research and clinical practice. We are not here to train doctors in the broad sense. Nor are we here primarily to service the community in which we are located. There-fore, we will focus our resource allocation on protecting our research primacy and the quality of our clinical teaching. We see as a natural by-product high quality care for those persons who go through our system as patients."

The leadership group knew that the consequences of this decision might mean that capitation would be withheld or challenged; they knew it might mean diffi-culties from the community.   The executive management of the organization decided that these consequences would have to be accepted and managed.

Medical Center B.   In another part of the country, Medical Center *B* was also known for its quality of care, its good research and clinical practice, and its high quality teaching program in health sciences. The medical school and teaching hospitals were part of the university complex, but were located some distance from the main campus in a primarily rural state. Significant numbers of medical school graduates went into practice in the state, where there was a great need for practitioners and for more comprehensive preventive care, as well as for more ambulatory centers because of the geographical distance between treatment centers and patients.

When research funding slowed down, faculty recruitment became more difficult, and requirements for increased numbers of students were put on the institutions, the dean of the school, the hospital administrator, and the university's
leadership, as well as the key clinical and teaching heads and community representatives took a look at the core mission of the medical center.

From these deliberations came the position that: "From the possible primary
missions of research, teaching, and delivery of care to the community, we have
determined that the delivery of care to the community is our primary reason
to be. We see as part of that core mission, the training of medical practitioners
to provide such care. We see as *supportive*, the need for a good clinical teaching
program; in back of that good basic research, in order that the practitioners we
train can provide the kind of service needed."

From that decision, they recognized that some of the faculty, anticipating
smaller research allocations, would be disenchanted and perhaps leave. They
also realized that their faculty recruitment problems would be more difficult.
They realized, too, that they would probably have to increase facilities for ambulatory care in order to carry out the primary mission.

In both these cases, the managment of the institution, through the exercise of
a core mission process, arrived at a definitive statement of priorities, which then
produced specific actions and rather significant consequences in both cases. Let
us move on to the third case, which occurred within an institution.

Hospital X.   *X* is a large teaching hospital. In the medical department, a group
of residents and some faculty wanted to initiate a change in the care procedure
for longer staying medical patients. The standard practice, as in most such hospitals, was that, after the patient was admitted, an intern was assigned direct
responsibility for that patient. Interns would, therefore, have four, five, six, or
more patients for whom they were the primary contact. These patients might
be scattered at the far ends of long corridors because they were allocated as they
came into the hospital. Each area of the hospital had the normal complement of
nurses, nurse's aides, *etc.* assigned to a particular physical location or number of
rooms or beds.

A group of residents interested in change and a couple of members of the
medical staff interested in improving basic care proposed an experiment. They
would reallocate the primary responsibility for coordination of the care of the
patient to the nurses in the area; they would move all the beds of one intern's
patients into the same physical area, so that he or she could handle coordination
with the nurses in that area.

The director of the hospital, who was very interested in increasing the *quality*
of care, approved the experiment. The chairman and chief of medicine, who was
interested in improving educational opportunities for the house staff, thought it
was worth a try—purely as an experiment. The nurses on the ward were excited
at the possibility. Most of the medical department staff were opposed to this

"disruption," being primarily concerned with their own education. The administrative staff of the hospital saw it as a confusing, unnecessary process and actively opposed it.

In core mission terms, the *core* mission as perceived by the main actors was as follows: hospital director—quality of care at reasonable cost; chief of medicine—effective teaching of interns and residents; majority of house staff—learning everything possible from the faculty; minority of house staff—trying to improve care by changing the procedures; nursing group on the ward—improving care through better utilization of deliverers; administrative staff—maintaining a smooth-running, efficient organization. Given those unstated and unshared descriptions of the core mission, what happened is not a surprise. As interns were normally rotated on a monthly basis, all agreed to try this experiment for one month on one ward. Nurses and interns, as well as some residents, who were most enthusiastic about the opportunity, worked on the problem and trained themselves to handle the patient problems and the administrative problems. Approval was given by the chief of medicine and hospital director, and a date was set for starting.

On the starting date, it was not possible to get any support people to move the 20 beds necessary for the experiment, so the doctors—residents and interns—moved the beds themselves. This caused panic in the administrative organization. The reception and intake people complained to the director and administrator that their system was ruined; the telephone operators complained bitterly.

The difficulties grew so great that the hospital director had to be called in to mediate certain issues and to personally support the experiment once again.

At the end of one month when the rotation changed, the incoming residents immediately went back to the old system. It was just too much aggravation for them. It got in the way of teaching and learning.

This experiment was doomed to failure because the *core* missions were "different." Given that condition, the "establishment" or traditions will usually prevail.

Implications for Training Administrators

Human service administrators will be moving into positions in which the decisions about resource allocation will be both more complex and continuing. These decisions are not taken only at the director level, but are now much a part of the middle management of the organization. Therefore, it should be part of the available management tools for managers in human service institutions to be able to engage in a mission identification process. They should also be able to differentiate a mission developing process from an objective or goal setting process. Planning that includes both of these will be a primary skill needed in the future. It would also be desirable in training managers to expose them to *open-systems planning*, which includes establishing the core mission; mapping the environment through the development of the demand system previously mentioned; defining a response system by recording present responses to the various demands; and defining strategic priorities and desired states. This preplanning process can help considerably in developing strategic plans and priorities for objectives. We would suggest that this general concept be part of the curriculum in all management training.

Organizational Designs to Cope with Changing Tasks and Managing Multiple Professionals

The Problem

As organizational tasks become more differentiated, making different demands on different parts of the organization, it is often necessary to rethink the way the organization is structured; *i.e.*, whether it is structured in relation to the *tasks* to be performed. Historically, organization managers built their organizations on the basis of functional suborganizations based on such related technologies as medicine, surgery, a business department, a dietitians department, and so forth. People with like backgrounds and like tasks were put together.

As an organization becomes more complex, it is sometimes necessary to put together people from different technologies or disciplines who are organized around a *mission* in a program, such as community medicine or primary care. In this situation, the organization structure may be defined as *mission-* or *program-*oriented.

In the kinds of institutions in which administrators are operating, you will often find multitask professionals, which sometimes requires a matrix organization, where a particular person is part of more than one "home room"—reporting to more than one boss. He or she must decide how to allocate the job assignments, the rewards, *etc.* to the person who is "matrixed."

This is an increasingly common problem for administrators managing multitask professionals. An obvious and recurrent example is a doctor who is on staff of the hospital, has a private practice, and has a faculty appointment in the medical school.

We would like to discuss briefly a case where an organization *redesign* was necessary in order to get the form (structure of the organization) to fit the functions (tasks of the organization). The institution in question was a community health center serving a population of 45,000 people in an urban ghetto area. The center was a part of a large medical center and teaching hospital; it was well-funded by federal funds and had excellent physical facilities and a large staff. The organization structure consisted of a project or center director who was a department chief in the medical center, a medical director, a director of training, a director of community advocacy, and an administrator. Reporting to the medical director were chiefs of medicine, pediatrics, and nursing. Reporting also to the medical director were team leaders from eight delivery teams. All the health care was delivered to the community through interdisciplinary delivery teams composed of an internist, a pediatrician, a nurse practitioner who coordinated the team, and three family health workers—paraprofessionals with special clinical training. Each team had a geographic location in which its total patient panel was situated. In addition, the center had a medical records department, medical administrators, *etc.*

The reporting system was functional. All the pediatricians reported to the chief pediatrician. The family health workers had no direct functional line, but reported through their nurse coordinators.

With this structure, the work of the organization was pursued with some difficulty. There was poor communication and location of authority within the delivery teams because of the multiple reporting systems. There was poor use of support resources such as medical records, because they reported into different lines and had no way of influencing each other's work. There was difficulty in the development of people, particularly the family health workers, since they had no "home room" after they left their training "nest" in which they were located for the first six months. The coordination was very "loose" at the top.

The technology of organization design and redesign is a task-based approach that starts with looking at the work to be done, such as delivery of care, getting records of families, *etc.*—the best resource allocation to achieve it, and the best information flow and reporting system to support the resource allocation. Without detailing this case, which is fully detailed in Beckhard's "Organizational Issues in the Team Delivery of Health Care," the change was as follows: Starting with the issue of the stated mission—to deliver health care to 45,000 people in that community—the teams were reorganized to reflect that mission. More sharing of information about patient needs, community needs, and care technology was built into the team planning itself. Because of previous conflict between the formal organization (nurse in charge) and the practical way of working (doctors taking over), it was seen as necessary to have an administrative direction that facilitated the delivery—teams getting the kinds of support they needed—and to provide linkage between the teams and the rest of the organization. Team leaders who were administrators, not MDs, were created. They had responsibility for the effectiveness of the team. They could fire any team members, including the doctors, from the team, but not from the center. They were the access point to the support systems such as medical records and others. They reported directly to the director of health services. The former chiefs of the technologies or functions—pediatrics, nursing, *etc.*—became the *office of health services*. Their primary tasks changed from being decision-makers on day-to-day operations, which were now assigned to the teams, to becoming program developers, quality controllers, and educators. They were available as consultants to practitioners in their own and other disciplines; they produced and monitored quality standards of care; they developed protocols for providing treatments in that particular setting. For example, because of the availability of house visits through family health workers, monitoring of hypertension could be handled very differently than in a middle class private patient-physician situation.

The administrative support items such as medical records, which had reported to the administrator, were now brought into the health services area so that all the functions primarily concerned with care and patient contact were in the same "family."

Through this reallocation and training, the productivity of the center improved by several hundred percent with quality standards being maintained according to accepted quality measurements.

The Implications for Training Administrators

This case illustrates a situation where the organization and form appropriate to one set of tasks was moved to another set of tasks where it was less appropriate. The center was originally organized just like the hospital in which it was centered. In the hospital the chief of a service does the complicated procedures, and the juniors on the service do the less complicated ones. In a community health center, all the care is delivered by the people at the bottom of the professional ladder. The senior professionals supply support and provide guidance. (They also may serve as members of delivery teams). When the tasks differ, as they did in this case, the structure must also differ in order to get work done optimally. It is recommended that curricula of management training should contain sessions on *organization design*, which deals with concepts of how to assign tasks based on the particular set of functions and their relationship to the environment; content issues around integration between parts of an organization, and how to design the structure to do that; issues around functional, program-matrix structures, their utilitzation, and consequences; and issues around information systems.

Coping with Interunit Conflict—Conflict Management and Responsibility Charting

Much change and tension in an organization occur where functions, departments, or areas of work intersect or interface. Ambiguity about who should make what decisions, who should report to whom, who has power, *etc.* are common issues that administrators face at all levels in a complex organization. In the absence of other methodologies, these things are usually resolved on the basis of who has the most power or the most status in the organization.

Almost any new development or major change in an organization produces an interface problem. For example if one changes a program that was entirely under one department so that part of it is under the control of another department, an interface is created between two departments. The resources must be split; the people who used to be in one department now confront a situation where the new and the old departments are competing for their services. Somebody must make the decisions about "where Mr. Smith spends Friday."

A technology, called responsibility charting, has been developed to work such conflict issues. It assumes that much of the dysfunctional human behavior one sees in organizations and to which one ascribes the term "personality conflict" is, in fact, not a clash of personalities or characters, but is a clash of people caused by some organization malfunction or dysfunction.

A good place to start looking for the causes of such conflict is in the organizational allocation of responsibility or behavior. Typically and traditionally, when there is a conflict around who does what to whom, attempts to resolve it take the form of trying to get the roles clearer. This is done either by writing clearer job descriptions or by mediation from higher levels—the boss deciding what each role should be; or by some negotiation process between power centers. Reponsibility charting has been designed to change the way this conflict is managed to a problem-solving mode.   The task—the work that must be done—defines the behavior of all people who are connected to that set of tasks or work.

In this process, those involved come together around a particular issue or set of issues. They list those on one side of a grid or a chart, including the specific kinds of actions or decisions that need to be taken (Figure 3). To use a simple example: if we were talking about hiring a secretary, the actions that would be involved would include. recruiting, early interviews, final screening, decision to hire, assignment of work, *etc.* On the other axis of the grid, one identifies the "actors" who might have something to do with that particular decision. Using the same illustration, one might list the director, the immediate department head, the supervisor of the secretary, the personnel recruiter, the controller, the recruiter, the other secretaries in the area *etc.*

Having listed both the types of decisions and the people to involve in the process, we assign a behavior to each actor. There are four possible behaviors: 1) responsibility (this means the responsibility for seeing that action is taken); 2) approval, the right to veto (this means that on the particular action involved, this role has the right to veto and stop the action); 3) support (this means that this role must provide support and resources (has no choice) on the particular act; resources might be information or people; and 4) inform, which means must be informed, but by implication does not have veto power.

One important part of the technique is that only one R or *responsibility* can be assigned to one act. So, if we go back to our secretarial illustration, the R might be located in the immediate supervisor, in the personnel department, or in the recruiter. Those involved would have to decide where the R is located. If the participants themselves cannot decide, then there are three choices: 1) move the R up one level; 2) move the *decision* of where the R goes up one

Decisions	Actors															

Code: R – responsibility (initiates)
        A – approval (right to veto)
        S – support (put resources against)
        I – inform (to be informed)

Figure 3. Responsibility chart.

level; or 3) break the problem into parts. For example, it might be that hiring an executive secretary would be different from hiring a clerk typist.

Let us briefly illustrate a situation in which this process was applied.

Who is Responsible for Quality of Care of House Staff in the Teaching Hospital?

Given current legislation on peer review and other quality requirements, how would you allocate responsibility for the quality of care provided by residents and other practitioners in the hospital. Clearly the hospital administrator or director has some responsibility and accountability; clearly the board is accountable in some ways; clearly the head of professional service has responsibility; clearly the head of the particular discipline has some responsibility; clearly chief residents have some responsibility; clearly colleagues, such as nurses who work with the house staff, have some responsibility. A number of hospitals are beginning to use the process of responsibility charting for breaking this problem down into its specific behaviors. They then can assign role behaviors to the various people who are concerned about the problem. This has been found useful for getting some sense of order, direction, and action in a very complex problem.

Implications for Training Administrators

The curriculum of management education should include analysis of interface management issues, of the conflict resolution methods available, and specifically how to allocate behaviors to different roles under different circumstances. Responsibility charting as a technique should probably be included also.

Managing Change in the Organization

Most administrators today have to be simultaneously concerned with 1) managing day-to-day operations; 2) managing planning for the future; 3) managing interfaces with the outside environment; and 4) managing organization change. Frequently administrators see this fourth process—managing change—as a subpart of one of the first three. There is a rapidly increasing body of knowledge and experience that indicates that *managing change* is a separate though frequently interdependent process, as we indicated in the four levels or organizational functioning in Section I. Managing change refers to the self-renewal operation.

In the management of organization change we suggest that a systematic planning and control process can make a significant difference in the effectiveness of the change. Some of the factors affecting changing strategy are whether the change is purely technical, whether it has social implications, whether it defies traditions and values, *etc*.

A few illustrations of the kinds of frequently recurring situations that require planned change management are: introducing family practice department into a teaching hospital; introducing a primary care curriculum or rotation; enlarging or changing the ambulatory care system and facilities; working with a professional union such as a teachers union, a house staff union, a social workers union; and combining professional and technical resources within different subunits.

The areas of applied behavioral science that pertain directly to these kinds of problems include: 1) the change process, resistance to change, analyzing the forces in a change situation; 2) developing a change strategy; 3) developing methods for managing the transition between the old state and the new state; 4) developing a plan for getting commitment of key people to the change; and 5) planning and managing the stabilization or maintenance of the new state. We now present two cases where a conscious change strategy was applied to manage a major change effort.

The Case of the Nursing School

A large, undergraduate nursing school decided to change its curriculum from the traditional discipline-based subject areas to a programmatic curriculum based on type of setting—health care, community, social service agency. The faculty agreed to the change in concept, and the appropriate administrative bodies approved it. The dean appointed some committees to pursue curriculum development. These committees were *ad hoc*, reporting to her.

If we examine the processes at this point, we see a traditional model for managing the change; set up a committee of people who are interested and have them do the job. Give them space and a reporting line. This method produced an almost predictable result. In the first place these committees were composed of members who reported to functional or discipline units and the chairmen of these units had major control over the activities of the members of the committees in terms of time available for work, tasks, and priorities. The stresses on the committee members—who were mostly enthusiastic junior faculty—were tremendous. Secondly, the implicit resistance of many heads of traditional disciplines could be mobilized and could keep any change from being more than cosmetic. Third, conflict in the system was considerably increased, particularly as the deadlines for new courses approached.

A group of us at the Sloan School at MIT, who were studying the process of change in organizations, offered to provide some analysis and a few interventions.

The analysis showed that the forces in the situation included: 1) sharp resistance among some traditional faculty for losing control of any major part of the curriculum; 2) strong differences between some tenured, discipline-oriented faculty and some junior action-oriented faculty; 3) the sense that no new unit or committee had any real power or could have any real power; 4) a generally shared feeling that the dean would have to control most of the change, if it were to happen; and 5) a wide split as to whether the change was to be cosmetic or fundamental.

From this brief analysis (or at least briefly described), it was decided that a first condition—given the resistance to change that existed—would be some kind of "unfreezing" process, in which the entire faculty could become aware of the organizational conditions as well as the situation regarding the curriculum change. The target of such an activity was to get real commitment on the part of the total faculty to the *fact* of the change, to build a managment system for managing it, and to make the faculty recognize that there were three states or conditions in the change process—the *old condition*, meaning the currently conducted curriculum, the *new condition*, when the curriculum would have changed from discipline-oriented to setting-oriented, and the *transition* period, when there would be some programs in both modes, and when people would be teaching in both programs and would, therefore, experience conflict around priorities. Another goal was to provide the awareness that it was necessary to develop a management system for this transition state. It would not necessarily be the same as the management of the *new* state. It would *definitely* not be the same as the management of the old state.

Following this diagnosis, a one-day meeting of the entire faculty was convened by the dean. Consultants presented some behavioral science concepts about the change process in organizations. A case had been developed. The entire faculty was broken into two groups and given the case, which looked strangely like their own institution. They were given the "situation" and asked to prepare an organization diagnosis and a consultation with the "dean" (an actor) on how best to manage the change.

In these subgroups, which were composed of senior and junior faculty, and across disciplines, participants were required to come up with some solution. Representatives presented their recommendations to the "dean" (the real one was present).

As a result of this exercise, it became evident to all that a transition management system was needed, that collaboration and cooperation from the disciplines was essential, that *planning* the new curriculum had to be separated or differentiated from *teaching* the new curriculum, and that different types of decision-making and information exchange were appropriate in each of these situations.

As a result, the dean appointed three full-time coordinators—one for health, one for community, and one for the social service agency setting. They were to be released from other responsibilities, and to have full-time responsibilities for managing and developing the curriculum, and for jointly "managing" the change process.

To link the present state, and to create a management team for this prupose, the curriculum coordinator, who was the number two person in the hierarchy, became the chairman of this coordinator's group. The group reported to the dean. This became the change management mechanism.

The coordinators then recruited faculty from the various disciplines in collaboration with the discipline department heads, and developed planning teams. These teams each underwent a brief development session in order to get clear on their charter and their ways of work, their ways of managing the conflict of time between their regular or previous assignments and this new assignment. They worked for a period of time, linking back to the discipline groups, until the curricula were developed. They then worked with the discipline department heads on recruiting and assigning faculty to teach the various courses and to assign evaluation units to maintain them. The curriculum coordinators retained their role as program evaluators, and managers of program improvement, for a year *after* the new curriculum was introduced.

Another part of the diagnosis had indicated that, although there would be enthusiasm after the initial activity, and probably maximum cooperation during the early stages of the curriculum planning, as the situation came down to the wire and courses were about to be given, some of the old resistance from the disciplines would reoccur. Mechanisms were needed for continuing the dialogue between the parts of the system.

Based on a number of experiences using education interventions as a strategy for facilitating change, the MIT group conducted a six-session course in "basics in management." It was voluntary for all faculty; credit could be received. A significant number of the faculty attended this program, which covered a number of issues such as interface management, decision-making, communications, and goal setting, all of which were relevant to the situation at hand, and provided a basis for the faculty to use their own organizational condition as material for testing the principles and for learning how to function better in the change situation.

Changing the Residency Rotation

The X hospital had a department of medicine, which had a traditional rotation of residents, including the normal intern rotation and a fair amount of specialization in the next two years of residency. The curriculum rotations were almost entirely managed in the hospital, with the exception of the usual emergency room rotations.

In the light of the increasing emphasis on training general practitioners, and as a result of a survey of graduates in general practice, the chief of medicine felt strongly that it would be necessary to modify the curriculum for residents to include an extended rotation in an ambulatory setting. The great majority of the residents in the hospital had chosen their residence there because of the specialties available, and at this point in their career were clearly not considering general practice as their major career. Statistics had shown, however, that significant numbers of their "older brothers" ended up in general practice within five years.

The chief decided that the first year of residency after internship would have a one-month rotation in an ambulatory setting, and that the second year would have a one-month rotation. In order for this to occur, and to maintain what was seen as essential time for other learning needs, the first-year residents would have to give up the one month of free time that had been called individual study, and the second-year residents would have to give up some part of their chief residency. The medical center had a social medicine department in medicine, which was composed of a small group of house staff whose focus of interest was ambulatory care, and who had already developed a rotation system that had been in use for several years.

The chief of medicine knew, from his diagnosis, that attitudes regarding the change was as follows: 1) the social medicine house staff was actively for the change since it meant reinforcement of its existing practice; 2) the faculty in social medicine was actively for the change; 3) some of the people conducting ambulatory care activities in the hospital complex were for the change. Others were against having to take on additional teaching or preceptorships. The majority of the faculty of medicine was quite against the change, considering it a threat to their time for training in specialties. Most residents were actively against the change, since they saw it as cutting into private time or their own time and being tangential to their learning needs.

Given this analysis, the chairman felt that a persuasion strategy would not in any way achieve what had to be done. He felt that organizationally he had to legitimize the primary care aspect of the curriculum. His methods of doing this included: 1) making two faculty appointments on his staff in primary care; 2) appointing a group of people from ambulatory delivery situations and from the chief residency group in social medicine to serve as preceptors for these rotations; 3) revising his own personal program to include one afternoon a week in an ambulatory care setting as a preceptor; 4) creating a change management mechanism composed of the chief residents, two senior faculty, the primary care faculty, the director of social medicine, and some representatives of the delivery sites. This group, chaired by him, had the responsibility of developing a specific curriculum around primary care for that setting, building in an evaluation mechanism, and dealing with the change and the resistance to change among the house staff.

This latter process—the management mechanism—was initiated only after the first rotation was conducted. It had been a mild disaster in the sense that most of the residents had resisted and resented the program. Before the second program was given for new first-year residents, and a first program for the group that now comprised second-year residents, further analysis was done, opinions were collected, people were asked how to improve the program, and a large involvement process was undertaken. It had a significant effect on the second set of courses, and the process continues to be developed at this point.

In this case, too, developing a specific strategy and a way of testing the strategy made this otherwise very distasteful change more palatable and certainly viable.

Implications for Training Administrators

Unquestionably the subject of change in large organizations should be included in administrator training. Issues pertinent to the dynamics of change, the change process, change strategies, evaluation of change, maintaining change, *etc.* should be included.

Team Development

Team development is perhaps one of the most misunderstood and misused applications of behavioral sciences in the whole organization field. We hope to provide here a few clarifying definitions.

The *team*, as we will use it here, is a group of people who *must* have each other's resources in order for some particular set of tasks to be done. Thus, an interdisciplinary service team is a team by definition of the task. A task force, such as has been described in the last two cases, is a team in the sense that the job requires the various resources brought together. An organizational hierarchy, such as a director and his assistants, is *not* necessarily a team except for certain tasks. The administrator has on the chart a number of functions reporting to him including, let us say, medical services, nursing, dietitian, engineer, *etc.* These are not a team as regards day-to-day operations. The very reason for creating different functional departments is so the work can be done within those departments. On some issues affecting the entire organization, however, that group must have *all of* the resources of the different disciplines or functions in order for the tasks to be accomplished. In such situations, they are functioning as a *team*.

Teams are any groups of people engaged in any set of work or even play tasks. Teams, as a class of social system, have dynamics processes, which are often necessary to improve in order that the tasks can be done more effectively. For example, if team members are spending a great deal of time worrying about who makes what decisions, that energy is not available for delivering care or doing whatever the proper task is. Contrary to much public opinion, the healthy or effective team spends *little* time discussing group dynamics and most of its time working on its *tasks*. The *less* effective team spends a great deal of time worrying about its working, the power distribution, *etc.*, and this takes time away from doing the work for which the team exists.

There is a fairly well-developed technology that has been applied in hundreds of team settings for helping teams in organizations work on improving their effectiveness. This process of team development is relevant only when there is a strategy for the team owning its own development and seeing the improvement of its internal workings as being a significant aspect of improving its effectiveness.

Implications for Training Administrators

Unquestionably more and more work in health delivery, education, and social service institutions will be done in teams (using the definition above). The applied behavioral science contribution is to find ways of making that work as efficiently and effectively as possible. Conscious attention to process factors affecting meetings, factors affecting openness of communication, factors affecting conflict management, and factors affecting role clarity will significantly improve the effectiveness of the team in whatever tasks it is doing. Any administrator of any organization today needs techniques: understanding the dynamics of groups; the characteristics of groups that affect effectiveness; and awareness of the kinds of programs and activities that can be undertaken by groups to increase their operational effectiveness.

The Future Leading Edge

Interest in applying behavioral science knowledge to the management of human service institutions has increased systematically in the last few years. The types of behavioral science applications that seem to be moving more into the forefront suggest that there will be continued work in the applications of open-systems concepts—the organization and its environment. This is an increasingly central problem for administrators, and they seem to have greater need for systematic knowledge to help them. At the same time, knowledge is being developed in this area.

There will be a continuing thrust in the area of structural organization—organization design. The concept "form follows function," rather than the traditional hierarchy, seems to be becoming more central. *Planning*, both strategic and tactical, will certainly receive more attention in the years ahead as the complexity of organizations increases.

The management of *system* change will be, we believe, a central part of the skills required of administrators.

The improvement of the organization of work, both quantitatively and qualitatively, will require the attention of administrators.

The development of more effective interpersonal competence and skills in working with groups will be a continuing need and perhaps a growing one in the near future.

Other trends include:

1. More interdisciplinary focus. Gradually the applied behavioral sciences are joining other disciplines, including political science and economics. Only a handful of people are involved in such discipline spanning efforts, yet it is clear that the need is there [29].
2. Greater emphasis on contingency models of arrangement and organization:

    a. not always good to have a participatory management style,
    b. not always functional to push decision-making to lower levels,
    c. bureaucratic organization can allow individuals to achieve sense of competence and growth if they are properly designed to fit their environment,
    d. not always good to work toward groups in an organization sharing their viewpoints and reaching understanding,
    e. team work many times less efficient and functional than individual effort.

3. Increased emphasis on evaluating "bottom line" effectiveness of applied behavioral science efforts for the organization. It is no longer just a "good" thing to do; hard-nosed questions of organizational payoff are more prevalent.
4. Increased efforts to make applied behavioral science a legitimate function of line managers. Less reliance on both external and internal consultants except as providers of supportive assistance to line managers.

It is clear that the traditional distance between the human service professions and human service management, and the behavioral sciences is being reduced, and probably will be eliminated in the years ahead. The increasing knowledge on both sides of the need for each other's resources and the possible usefulness of this body of knowledge to the practice of human service administration should lead to further collaboration, further joint inquiry, and further synergy.

NOTES AND REFERENCES

1. Aiken, M., R. Dewar, N. DiTomaso, J. Hage, and G. Zeitz. *Coordinating Human Services*. San Francisco: Jossey-Bass, 1975.
2. Alderfer, C. P. *Existence, Relatedness and Growth: Human Needs in Organizational Settings*. New York: Free Press, 1972.
3. Allison *et al.* "The Role of Health Services Administrators and Implications for Education." In *Selected Papers of the Commission on Education for Health Administration*, vol. 2. Ann Arbor, Mich.: Health Administration Press, 1975.
4. Argyris, C. "Management Information Systems: The Challenge to Rationality." *Management Science* 17(1971): 275–292.
5. Barelas, A. and D. Barrett. "An Experimental Approach to Organizational Communication." *Personnel* 27(1951): 367–371.
6. Barrett, J. H. *Individual Goals and Organizational Objectives: A Study of Integration Mechanisms*. Ann Arbor: Institute for Social Research, University of Michigan, 1970.
7. Bauer, R., ed. *Social Indicators*. Cambridge: MIT Press, 1966.
8. Beckhard, R. "Organization Development in Large Systems." In *The Laboratory Method of Changing and Learning*. Edited by Benne, Bradford, Gibb, and Lippitt. Palo Alto, Calif.: Science and Behavior Books, 1975.
9. Beckhard, R. *Organizational Development: Strategies and Models*. Reading, Mass.: Addison-Wesley, 1969.
10. Beckhard, Richard. "Organizational Issues in the Team Delivery of Comprehensive Health Care. *Millbank Memorial Fund Quarterly* (July 1, 1972): 287–316.
11. Beckhard, Richard. *Large System Change*. Reading, Mass.: Addison-Wesley, forthcoming.
12. Bergin, A. E. "Some Implications of Psychotherapy Research for Therapeutic Practice." *Journal of Abnormal Psychology* 71(1966): 225–46.
13. Blau, P. *The Dynamics of Bureaucracy*. Chicago: University of Chicago Press, 1955.
14. Bott, E. *Family and Social Network*. New York: Free Press, 1971.
15. Bowers, D. "OD Techniques and Their Results in 23 Organizations: The Michigan ICL Study." *Journal of Applied Behavioral Science* 9(1973): 21–43.
16. Bradford, L., J. Gibb, and K. Benne. *T-Group Theory and Method*. New York: Wiley, 1964.
17. Braybrooke, D., and C. E. Lindblom. *A Strategy of Decision*. New York: Free Press, 1963.
18. Burke, W., and H. Hornstein. *The Social Technology of Organization Development*. National Training Laboratories–Learning Resources, 1972.
19. Burns, T., and G. M. Stalker. *The Management of Innovation*. London: Tavistock, 1965.
20. Chapple, E. D., and L. R. Sayles. *The Measure of Management*. New York: Macmillan, 1961.

21. Cherns, A. "Perspectives on the quality of working life." *Journal of Occupational Psychology* 48(1975): 155–167.
22. Cleveland, H. *The Future Executive*. New York: Harper and Row, 1972.
23. Commission on Education for Health Administration. *Selected Papers*, vol. 1. Ann Arbor, Mich.: Health Administration Press, 1975.
24. Cyert, R. M., and J. G. March. *A Behavioral Theory of the Firm*. Englewood Cliffs, N.J.: Prentice-Hall, 1963.
25. Davis, J. *Group Performance*. Reading, Mass.: Addison-Wesley, 1969.
26. Delbecq, A. L., A. Vandeven, and D. Gustafson. *Group Techniques for Program Planning*. Glenview, Ill.: Scott Foresman, 1975.
27. Deutsch, M. *The Resolution of Conflict*. New Haven: Yale University Press, 1973.
28. Drucker, P. *Management*. New York: Harper and Row, 1973.
29. Emery, F., and E. Trist. "The Causal Texture of Organizational Environments." *Human Relations* 18(1965): 21–32.
30. Etzioni, A. "Accountability in Health Administration." In *Education for Health Administration, vol. 2*. Ann Arbor: Health Administration Press, 1975.
31. Etzioni, A. *An Analysis of Complex Organizations*, 2nd ed. New York: Free Press, 1975.
32. Fiedler, F. E. *Leadership*. New York: General Learning Press, 1971.
33. French, W., and C. Bell. *Organization Development*. Englewood Cliffs, N.J.: Prentice-Hall, 1973.
34. Galbraith, J. *Designing Complex Organizations*. Reading, Mass.: Addison-Wesley, 1971.
35. Gardner, John. *Self-Renewal*. New York: Harper and Row, 1963.
36. Goode, W. *The Family*. Englewood Cliffs, N.J.: Prentice-Hall, 1964.
37. Hackman, J. R., and E. E. Lawler. "Employee Reactions to Job Characteristics." *Journal of Applied Psychology* 55(1971): 259–286.
38. Hackman, R. "Group Influences on Individuals in Organizations." In *Handbook of Industrial and Organizational Psychology*. Edited by M. D. Dunnette. Chicago: Rand McNally, 1976.
39. Hall, D., B. Schneider, and A. T. Nygren. "Personal factors in organizational identification." *Administrative Science Quarterly* 15(1970): 176–190.
40. Hickson, D. J. "A Convergence in Organization Theory." *Administrative Science Quarterly* 11(1966): 110–121.
41. Hornstein, H. A., and N. Tichy. "Developing Organizational Development for Multinational Corporations." *Columbia Journal of World Business* (summer, 1976).
42. Huse, E. *Organization Development and Change*. New York: West Publishing, 1975.
43. Jackson, J. "Structural Characteristics of Norms." In *Current Studies in Social Psychology*. Edited by I. D. Steiner and M. Fishbein. New York: Holt, Rinehart and Winston, 1965.
44. Kahn, R., D. Wolfe, R. D. Quinn, J. D. Snoek, and P. F. Rosenthal. *Organizational Stress: Studies in Role Conflict and Ambiguity*. New York: Wiley, 1964.
45. Kaplan, A. *The Conduct of Inquiry*. San Francisco, Calif.: Chandler Publishing, 1964.
46. Kelley, H., and J. Thibaut. "Group Problem Solving." In *Handbook of Social Psychology*. Edited by G. Lindsey and E. Aronson. Reading, Mass.: Addison-Wesley, 1968.
47. Lawler, E. E., and D. Nadler. "Organizational Psychology." AUPHA chapter, 1976.
48. Lawler, E. E. *Pay and Organizational Performance: A Psychological View*. New York: McGraw-Hill, 1971.
49. Lawrence, P. R., and J. W. Lorsch. *Organization and Environment*. Boston: Harvard Business School, Division of Research, 1967.

50. Leavitt, H. "Some Effects of Certain Communication Patterns on Group Performance." *Journal of Abnormal Social Psychology* 46(1951): 38-50.
51. Levine, S., and P. White. "Exchange and Interorganizational Relationships." *Administrative Science Quarterly* 5(1961).
52. Levinson, H. *Organizational Diagnosis*. Cambridge, Mass.: Harvard University Press, 1972.
53. Likert, R. *New Patterns of Management*. New York: McGraw-Hill, 1961.
54. Lorge, I., and H. Solomon. "Two Models of Group Behavior in The Solution of Eureka-Type Problems. *Psychometrika* 20(1955): 139-148.
55. MacCrimmon, D., and D. Taylor. "Decision-making and Problem Solving." In *Handbook of Industrial and Organizational Psychology*. Edited by M. D. Dunette. Chicago: Rand McNally, 1976.
56. Maslow, A. *Motivation and Personality*. New York: Harper and Row, 1954.
57. McClelland, D. "Toward a Theory of Motive Acquisition." *American Psychologist* 20(1965): 321-333.
58. McGrath, J. E. "Leadership Behavior." Office of Career Development, US Civil Service Commission, 1962.
59. Mechanic, D. "Social Psychological Factors Affecting the Presentation of Bodily Complaints." *New England Journal of Medicine* 286(1972): 1132-1139.
60. Mintzberg, H. *The Nature of Managerial Work*. New York: Harper and Row, 1973.
61. Mintzberg, H. "The Structure of Unstructured Decision Processes." *Administrative Science Quarterly* 21(1976).
62. Murray, H. *Explorations in Personality*. New York: Oxford University Press, 1938.
63. Nadler, D., and M. Tushman. "A Diagnostic Model for Organizational Behavior." Research Paper No. 103, Graduate School of Business, Columbia University, 1976.
64. Perrow, C. *Complex Organizations: A Critical Essay*. Glenview, Ill.: Scott, Foresman, 1972.
65. Perrow, C. "A Framework for Comparative Organizational Analysis." *American Sociological Review* 32(1969): 194-208.
66. Porter, L., E. E. Lawler, and R. Hackman. *Behavior in Organizations*. New York: McGraw-Hill, 1975.
67. Rubin, I. M., M. S. Plovinick, and R. E. Fry. *Improving the Coordination of Care: A Program for Health Team Development*. Cambridge, Mass.: Ballinger, 1975.
68. Sayles, L. R. *Behavior of Industrial Work Groups*. New York: Wiley, 1958.
69. Schein, E. *Organizational Psychology*, 2nd ed. Englewood Cliffs, N.J.: Prentice-Hall, 1970.
70. Schein, E. "Organizational Socialization and the Profession of Management." *Industrial Management Review* 9(1968): 1-16.
71. Scott, W. "Organization Theory." 1976.
72. Shaw, M. D. "Communication Networks." In *Advances in Experimental Social Psychology*. Edited by L. Berkowitz. New York: Academic Press, 1964.
73. Shortell, S. "The Role of Environment In a Configurational Theory of Organizations." *Human Relations* 30(1977).
74. Skinner, B. F. "What is the Experimental Analysis of Behavior?" *Journal of Experimental Analysis of Behavior* 9(1966): 213-18.
75. Starbuck, W. "Organizations and Their Environment." In *Handbook of Industrial and Organizational Psychology*. Edited by M. D. Dunnette. Chicago: Rand McNally, 1976.
76. Thompson, J. D. *Organizations in Action*. New York: McGraw-Hill, 1967.

77. Tichy, N. "Agents of Planned Social Change: Congruence of Values, Cognitions, and Actions." *Administrative Science Quarterly* (June 1974): 164–182.
78. Tichy, N. "Evaluating Organizational Innovations: Work Restructuring at Volvo and General Motors." *Organizational Dynamics* (Summer 1976).
79. Tichy, N. "How Different Types of Change Agents Diagnose Organizations." *Human Relations* 28(1975): 771–799.
80. Tichy, N. "Organizational Innovations in Sweden." *Columbia Journal of World Business* (Summer 1974): 18–28.
81. Tichy, N. "Organizational Networks, Coalitions and Cliques." In *Handbook of Organization Design.* Edited by W. Starbuck. New York: Elsevier Press, 1978.
82. Tichy, N., H. A. Hornstein, and J. Nisberg. "Participative Organization Diagnosis and Intervention Strategies." *Academy of Management Review* 1(1976).
83. Tichy, Noel. "Community Control of Health Services: Dr. Martin Luther King, Jr. Health Center's Community Management System." *Health Education Monographs* 4(1976).
84. Tichy, Noel. *Organization Design for Primary Health Care.* New York: Praeger, 1977.
85. Tushman, Michael, and David Nadler. "Organization Structure and Design: A Review and Interpretation." Columbia University Business School Working Paper, 1976.
86. Tushman, M. "A Political Approach to Organizations: A Review, Rationale, and Some Implications." *Academy of Management Review* (in press).
87. Vroom, V. H., and D. W. Yetton. *Leadership and Decision-Making.* Pittsburgh: University of Pittsburgh Press, 1973.
88. Walton, R. *Interpersonal Peacemaking: Confrontation and Third Party Consultation.* Reading, Mass.: Addison-Wesley, 1969.
89. Weick, K. *The Social Psychology of Organizing.* Reading, Mass.: Addison-Wesley, 1969.
90. Wise, H., R. Beckhard, I. Rubin, and A. Kyte. *Making Health Teams Work.* Cambridge, Mass.: Ballinger, 1974.
91. Woodward, J. *Industrial Organization: Theory and Practice.* London: Oxford University Press, 1965.
92. Zald, M. *Power in Organizations.* Nashville, Tenn.: Vanderbilt University Press, 1972.

2

Managerial Involvement in the Design of Adaptive Systems

Walter Baker, Raoul Elias, and David Griggs
Fisheries and Marine Service, Government of Canada

INTRODUCTION

The Fisheries and Marine Service (F&MS) of Environment Canada was established in January 1973. The organizational structure shown in Figure 1 was implemented during the spring and summer of 1974.

The reorganization brought together in somewhat uneasy relationship the long established Fisheries Service, itself comprising the two distinct arms of Fisheries Research and Development and Fisheries Operations, a Marine Sciences Directorate from Energy, Mines, and Resources, and a Small Craft Harbors unit from the Department of Public Works.

The activities of the operational arm of the Fisheries Service were oriented primarily to improving the well-being of Canadian fisherman. It has been described, not unkindly, as being staffed in the main with those "born with fish in their hands," contrasting sharply, therefore, with the scientists who predominate in the Marine Sciences Directorate (renamed Ocean and Aquatic Affairs in the reorganization). Moreover, the marine scientists judged their clientele to be worldwide, and were not at all comfortable with the idea that they might be merged with one particular client, the Fisheries Service. Finally, Small Craft Harbors was concerned with the construction and maintenance of marine harbors, in part in the service of commercial fishing, but also in the service of growing recreational demands.

The consequence was that, despite a structural repackaging within a single unit, what continued to exist into 1974 was a complex of four distinct solitudes, two of a research nature and two operationally oriented. Stafford Beer, whose theoretical work was later to play an important role in the further reorganization

SADM
F&MS

MANAGEMENT SERVICES	INTERNATIONAL BRANCH	INFORMATION SERVICES	PROVINCIAL FEDERAL AFFAIRS	AQUATIC CONTAMINANTS
	ADM FISHERIES MANAGEMENT		ADM OCEAN & AQUATIC AFFAIRS	

ADM FISHERIES MANAGEMENT

Headquarters
Small Craft Harbors
Industrial Development

Resource Management
Inspection

Social Science Research
Office of the Editor

Research & Development Programming

Marketing

Recreational Fisheries

Commercial Fisheries Secretariat

Five regions
Pacific

Central

Quebec

Maritimes

Newfoundland

ADM OCEAN & AQUATIC AFFAIRS

Headquarters
Administration

Ships

Hydrography
Oceanography

Three regions
Pacific

Central

Atlantic

Figure 1. Organization chart, 1974.

of F&MS, has stated that one of the most interesting facets of reorganization is that, in many cases, structural entities "live on" in barely changed form, despite efforts to combine them, and this was certainly the case with F&MS in 1974.

Heading F&MS was a young and extremely vigorous Senior Assistant Deputy Minister, Ken Lucas. A former engineer, knowledgeable in the systems area, he saw strongly the need to develop a rational and viable approach to integrating more carefully the four entities he had inherited and for which he was accountable. Modest forays toward integration in 1973 and early 1974 had led to the structure shown in Figure 1. He saw this as an interim step only, however, and he recognized that the split into two main divisions, Fisheries and Ocean and Aquatic Affairs, each with its separate regional structure, merited much more careful study to determine if a merger or significant transfers were warranted. Accordingly, he initiated a comprehensive formal study to assist in deciding upon the best way to organize and manage F&MS.

By the time the study was finally launched, in mid-1974, there were three key areas identified upon which it was to focus:

1. As a preliminary concern, and to inform the subsequent analysis, the study was to reveal the type of work F&MS was actually performing, the specific services it was rendering, the different clients it served and its external contacts more generally, and the various functions performed at the different levels of the service.

2. Of a more creative and forward-looking nature, the study was to review and recommend upon each of three points: the *role* of the F&MS (its most appropriate and propitious niche within the Department of the Environment, the Government of Canada, and in relation to its clientele); its existing management philosophy and style of managing, and whether changes were warranted; and the diagnosis of existing managerial capacity and ways to enhance it.

3. On the basis of the first two steps, the study was to address six specific organizational issues:

    • the possible merger of the two divisions: Fisheries Management, and Ocean and Aquatic Affairs;
    • integration of the two F&MS functions: research activity and activities of an operational nature;
    • a possible reduction in the number of responsibility centers;
    • the clarification of jurisdictional boundaries between headquarters and regional offices;
    • the establishment of cooperative planning processes and the coordination of programs: regionally, at headquarters, and across F&MS as a whole; and
    • the identification and establishment of common services.

ORIGINS OF MIDAS

Although Ken Lucas was convinced a major study was in order, he was not at all decided, initially, on how to proceed with it. Accordingly, he delegated to the Acting Director of the F&MS Management Services Branch, Roy Bartlett, the task of recommending an approach to the study itself. The only direction he gave Bartlett was that it should be capable of addressing the three key areas with reasonable dispatch (he didn't want a prolonged study, as F&MS had already been in a "holding" pattern for close to eighteen months), and that it should rest solidly on a base of self-analysis by the managers themselves, rather than depending heavily upon the insights of external consultants. In the discussions of approach Bartlett himself identified a third condition, based in part on his understanding of the background and managerial "bent" of Ken Lucas; namely, that it should be an approach very much at the frontier of modern systems and organizational analysis.

Concerning the commitment to self-analysis, it should be pointed out that F&MS is an extremely decentralized agency, with over 95% of its personnel in the regions. Moreover, the issues of merger and integration, with their implications for loss of autonomy and shifts in power, had surfaced sufficiently clearly to convince Ken Lucas that any *imposed* plan of management or overall structure, instituted by a distant top management group to resolve a set of issues in which so many officers of the F&MS had already developed a genuine career and emotional stake, would have most important negative consequences in terms of morale and level of commitment. Further, and complementing the belief in the values of participation for morale and commitment reasons, Lucas recognized that a viable structure could be evolved only upon information drawn from a wide base, and upon judgments reflecting all significant F&MS perspectives, rather than only the perspective of senior management.

Roy Bartlett's assignment was not an easy one. He was not, himself, an expert in organizational analysis, and very few of the members of his unit had had experience in this area. Casting around somewhat pressingly for an approach he could recommend, he contacted the Organization Division of the Treasury Board Secretariat, and hence encountered Don Dunlop of that division. Dunlop was a committed disciple of Stafford Beer, and recommended the Beer approach as the preferred one for F&MS.

Roy Barlett saw in the Beer approach a "near-perfect match" to his understanding of what Ken Lucas wanted; before recommending it, however, he judged it prudent to investigate it further. He relied heavily, in the process, upon the Coordinator of his Program Analysis Group, David Griggs, who, though at the time totally unfamiliar with Beer's work, *was* well-grounded in program analysis methodologies. The net result was that both Bartlett and Griggs became very familiar with Beer's writings, particularly *The Brain of the Firm*, and enthusiastic over the potential of the model. Accordingly, they went together to Ken Lucas and recommended it as the preferred approach.

Roy Bartlett had assessed the reaction of Ken Lucas accurately; he did, indeed, see its potential readily, accepted their recommendation, and authorized them to establish a preliminary study team to prepare a formal proposal to F&MS management. The team comprised three members: Roy Bartlett, Don Dunlop, and David Griggs.

The team stressed three key strengths of the Beer model in their formal presentation. First, they saw it as meeting the need for a standard model able to unify the language, perceptions, and communications of the 200 managers it was hoped would participate—and they judged such a standard model an essential prerequisite to a participative exercise. (A preliminary study, allowing participants to use their own models, had produced such a diversity of answers that integration and communication of results were judged impossible to achieve.) Moreover, in support of a standard model, team members adopted the position that "order and simplification are the first steps toward the mastery of any subject"; to analyze the complex behavior of an organization of 5000 people, it was necessary to reduce the complexity to manageable proportions. Secondly, the Beer model seemed exceptionally appropriate for the initial nondirective, nonnormative self-analysis; by seeking to meet the analytical criteria of the model, "personalities" and "empires" would be de-emphasized. Finally, not only was it judged necessary to find a theoretically sound model; the model chosen had to be acceptable to practicing managers, many of whom had little patience with theoretical analysis—and the team judged they would have little difficulty in selling the Beer model to F&MS scientists: the model was analogous to human neurophysiology, and biology was the dominant professional background in F&MS. Once the Beer model was decided upon as the appropriate one, the question remained of how actually to apply it as the basis of the study; while managers would carry out the great bulk of the analysis, they would need initial instruction and expert guidance. Moreover, technical forms and procedures had to be developed. Accordingly, the team recommended the use of outside expertise, and two management consultants were subsequently hired, working under contract.

F&MS management accepted the team's recommendations, David Griggs was appointed Project Director, and Project MIDAS was developed in conformity with the proposed methodology. Since the methodology is comparatively new, its fundamental concepts are outlined below.

Methodology: The Adapted Beer Model

The most useful facet of the Beer Model is its representation of the communication and control aspects of an organization. The basic building block of the model is the "homeostat," a device to maintain equilibrium through feedback. An example of homeostasis is the normal household thermostat, which maintains the temperature of the house at a given level.

Applied in an organizational setting Claude Shannon's communication model, used by Beer within his own more comprehensive model, describes the information flow necessary to achieve a state of homeostasis (equilibrium) in managerial communications. In the model, a message originates from an information source (1), which codes and transmits the message through a transmitter (2). The transmitter relays the message to a receiver (4), although in the process "noise sources" in the communication channel (3) may change the message during transmission. The receiver acts as an inverse transmitter, turning the transmitted signal back into a message and handing it on to the destination (5). Even simple communications, therefore, involve five identifiable elements, malfunction in any one of which can lead to distortions in the message being sent.

This case study is itself a communication process, of course. The writers' brains are the information source, their writing the coding device (also known as a transducer), and the communication channel, transmitting the message, is the book the reader is holding. The decoding device (also a transducer) is the actual reading process, and the final destination the reader's brain. As for "noise sources," a little reflection will show how the writers might not have captured fully, in writing, what they wanted to convey, and how easily what they actually wrote could be transformed into different messages as individual readers receive it from their different perspectives. This specific example is a *one-way communication process* (unless the reader communicates his feedback to the writers) as can be judged from Figure 2. In a managerial situation the communication is normally a two-way information flow with *attenuation* (*i.e.*, reduction, aggre-

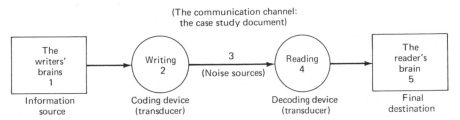

Figure 2. Claude Shannon's communication model.

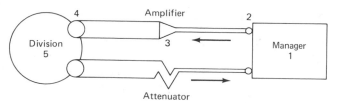

Figure 3. Attenuation and amplification.

gation, or simplification) and *amplification* (*i.e.*, expansion) relays. Figure 3 reflects the attenuation/amplification factors in the example to be discussed in the following paragraphs.

A manager approves a project during a divisional meeting. The project involves the full-time work of five people for a month. The information originating from this meeting has been amplified several times through the work of five man-months. The results of the project are then *attenuated* through the use of a report or a brief oral presentation to the manager. If the amplification and attenuation mechanisms function well, the manager will have gained insights equivalent to five man-months in a matter of hours. This attenuation and amplification is also essential if control is to be exercised by the manager and equilibrium maintained. In virtually all organizational situations those whose activities have to be controlled outnumber the managers who are charged with such control. In cybernetic language, the controlled dispose more "variety," defined as the number of distinct states they can adopt.

The concept of variety was explored by cybernetician Ross Ashby, who postulated the "Law of Requisite Variety"—only variety can absorb variety. In a well-known example, if society wanted to control its criminal element *perfectly*, it should have at least as many policemen as there are criminals. Yet this is patently infeasible. Accordingly, society seeks ways to reduce the "variety," on the criminal side, and increase the range of a single policeman's impact through the use of radio, police cars, computers, international link-ups and so on (the intrinsic "variety" on the criminal side of the equation always outweighs the "variety" on the policeman's side).

In organizational terms, in order for homeostasis to be maintained, the intrinsic variety of the manager must be amplified (through delegated authority, power to issue instructions and general rules of behavior, ability to confer rewards and punishments, *etc.*), and the intrinsic variety of the subordinates must be attenuated (through formal reporting structures, aggregation and distillation of information, screening mechanisms such as the manager's secretary, *etc.*). If there is an imbalance in realized variety in the manager's favor, overcontrol results; if in the subordinate's favor, anarchy.

When the communication process is optimal, such that the manager receives the information he needs and can usefully use, and, in turn, his organization receives the guidelines it needs from the manager, the system is said to be in equilibrium or in a state of homeostasis. Four criteria have to be met, then, in order for an organizational unit to be in equilibrium. These are as follows:

1. Information flowing from the unit to its management has to be reduced to manageable size—this, in the terminology of the model, is *attenuation*. The reverse is also necessary. Information received from management has to be fleshed out, or *amplified* (Ashby's law of requisite variety).
2. The channel capacity must permit an optimal flow of information, without distortion or noise generation.
3. The transmitter and receivers (transducers) need to be capable of handling information without distorting it.
4. The three points above, applying as stated to the internal operations of a unit, apply also to communication with the external environment. Operational units, in contact with the environment, must pay special attention to the quality of communications.

As noted earlier, Stafford Beer incorporates this relatively simple communication model into a much more inclusive organizational one. According to Beer an organization, as a "viable system," is a hierarchy of units interacting with each other and the environment to produce outputs in the service of overall objectives, with the interactions obeying the rules of requisite variety and homeostasis. His model is proposed as a structured way of displaying and analyzing these formal organizational arrangements. It is built around the concept that an organization can be viewed as comprising five identifiable control systems (Systems One through Five), each representing a major control function common to all viable organizations.[1] These five systems are as follows:

System One (S1): Operational Control

The most fundamental element in the Beer model was defined, for the purpose of the F&MS exercise, as the control of an operational unit rendering a discrete service or services to the external world. It represents a direct point of interface between the external world and the internal world of the organization, and only units with such an external contact are S1s. Each S1 consists of a control element in the form of its management (M), and an operation.

The Inspection Branch of F&MS can be thought of as an S1 (at one level),

---

[1] The term "control" is used throughout Stafford Beer's work and this case study with value-neutral scientific, rather than the traditional organizational connotations of a negative nature. It is concerned with the positive control required to ensure appropriate outputs, rather than with merely the control of inputs.

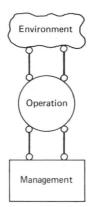

Figure 4A. The building block of the Beer model, System One (S1).

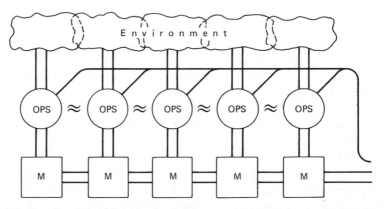

Figure 4B. The elements of System One of an organization with several operations.   S1 comprises the full set of operations.

because is renders a specific service to the external world (inspecting fish). The Administration Branch is *not* an S1 (at any level), since it renders services only to other F&MS units. Beer has special symbols to represent each of his systems. How he represents S1s is shown in Figure 4A and expanded somewhat in Figure 4B. Transducers, amplifiers, and attenuators are not shown in Figure 4A in order not to overcrowd the model. The lines joining the three units of the figure are meant to represent, nevertheless, the Shannon communication model in total, and to obey the rules of requisite variety and homeostasis. Figure 4B shows two types of informal communication; in the environments, which overlap, and between S1s, the wavy lines depicting technical exchange.

System Two (S2): The Regulatory Function

Organizations are made up of a number of S1s, with varying degrees of autonomy. Each S1 manager (M) thinks differently, is subject to different working constraints, and wants to optimize his own unit's operations. This situation, if not controlled by coordinating regulatory systems, could result in unduly large "oscillations" threatening the integration and stability of the larger organization of which they are part, and hence needing to be kept within tolerable bounds. Such regulatory (and basically inhibitory) systems together comprise System Two (S2). Thus, in Beer's terms, S2 is a "coordinator and not a dictator." (It should be kept in mind that Beer is offering an ideal model, to be used to analyze and map real-world organizations. In a particular organization some regulatory units may follow a dictatorial, rather than a coordinative approach).

The key characteristic of an S2 unit is that it works *automatically* as a dampening regulator, reducing the autonomy of the individual S1 only when the S1 is provoking unacceptable degrees of oscillation.

S2s in the Beer model are represented by a network of triangles (see Figure 5). Examples of elements of the S2 function are the accounting system, the personnel system, the budgeting system, and all laws and regulations, whether formal or informal.

The concept of an S2 function is an elusive one, not easily identified in a com-

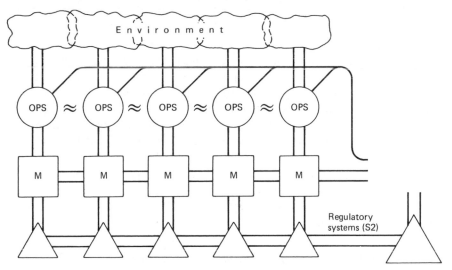

Figure 5. System Two, an organization with several coordinated operations, regulating System One by means of automatic regulatory information systems.

plex organization. Accordingly, in the F&MS exercise, S2 was judged to comprise only ongoing routine information-dissemination functions having as their primary purpose the coordination and regulation of S1 units. It should be stressed, however, that managers understood that this degree of oversimplification was resorted to only to meet time and other modelling constraints.

System Three (S3): The Operational Management Function

However useful S2 can be for "antioscillation" purposes, it cannot control or make unprogrammed decisions affecting the organization as a whole. This is the role of corporate management.

The first level of corporate management in the Beer model is the function responsible for ongoing operational activities, and he designates this System Three (S3).

S3 is responsible for the day-to-day decisions concerning the delivery of the product on time and at the appropriate place, under certain conditions and constraints. In industry, the S3 function is carried out by the vice-president of operations and the administrative mechanisms he evolves and oversees. S3 does not have to be linked to a single manager in the line hierarchy, however; *as a function* it comprises whatever exists to ensure that ongoing operational activities are well managed. In the model S3 is a "black box"; what is in the box will vary from organization to organization (unit to unit).

There are three kinds of communication channels converging on S3, as can be seen from Figure 6. The first is to and from S2, comprising systematic, programmed information. The second channel is depicted by the management line; this is the formal authority line, normally reflected in the organization chart. This channel transmits general instructions and resource allocations downward and receives requests for action and reports on performance upward. The third channel is one of direct access to an S1 unit, bypassing the unit's management. This is the link that allows corporate management to audit the operations and get first-hand exposure to internal information otherwise not available to it.

Systems One, Two, and Three together comprise the internal autonomic control system of the organization. They are able to regulate internal functions and basic productive capability, but react only to those direct external stimuli involved in S1 and, hence, cannot evolve or, having no view of the future, adapt to changing circumstances.

System Four (S4): The Corporate Development Function

The organization, as described to this stage, is balanced insofar as the ongoing production operations of the system are concerned; what goes on in the individual operational unit (S1) is coordinated by routine integrative antioscillation

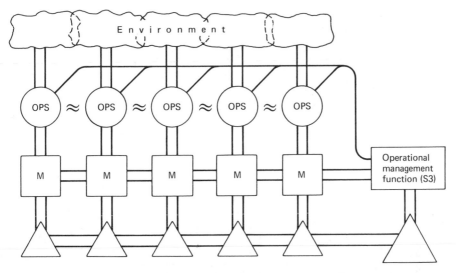

Figure 6. System Three, the operational management function in an autonomic organization (in conjunction with Systems One and Two).

systems (S2), and managed from a corporate perspective (S3). In the long run, however, organizational health and even survival require both a concern with growth and development, and a concern with the future in relation to environmental changes. Such activities comprise the corporate development function, a second key aspect of corporate management, which Beer designates System Four (S4) (illustrated in Figure 7 as part of the overall model).

The S4 activities, then, are all related to *new developments* or to the *improvement of existing aspects of the organization*. They include, for example, corporate planning, market research, operations research, research and development, and public relations. Such activities are more often than not handled on a project basis (MIDAS was itself an S4 function, since it dealt with the development of a new organizational and managerial framework), and are usually handled by Headquarters staff when the project concerns the whole organization.

S4 functions are outward and future-oriented, as distinct from the inward and present and past orientations of the autonomic system. To draw an analogy with human neurology, S4 functions are "sensory" rather than "motor" functions (a point which will be expanded later).

Concerning S4 activities, Beer notes the communication difficulties between them and the S1-S3 functions, which are normally line functions, problems originating in part because of the management culture and the different educational and experience backgrounds of S4 and S3 personnel. He stresses that even though S4 is depicted in the model as being on the main management line, this does not imply the authority of S4 over S3. Each system, S1 through S4, de-

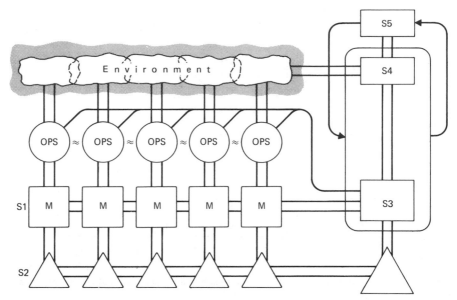

Figure 7. The Stafford Beer "viable systems" organizational model, covering all five control systems.

picts a control function; no single control system is dominant; each has the capability to override the others on occasion.

System Five (S5): "The Boss"

At the corporate level, the problem of finding a correct balance between S3 and S4 is one of the biggest problems facing modern institutions. Typically, corporate managers form a group composed of line and staff to decide on the appropriate balance. Whether this is done by committee, by a decision of the board of directors, or by the president as chief executive officer, these decisions are ultimate ones for the corporation, and comprise the System Five function (S5).

System Five, then, is the final decision-maker, "the boss." Its basic responsibility is to monitor S3 and S4 relationships to achieve an optimal balance between "corporate development" and "ongoing operations."

Beer believes that what happens in practice in most organizations is that S4 is either isolated from its S3–S1 counterparts, or does not exist formally. Whenever this happens it leads to the lack of sensory and developmental functions, and S5 becomes in reality S3 (day-to-day corporate operational management) or, even worse, involves itself directly in S1 functions (basic operational control at the lowest level).

The identification of these five control systems was originally derived from the study of human neurology. In the original analogy, S1 functions relate to the control of local musculature and organic functions in the arms, legs, heart, *etc.*; S2 corresponds to the sympathetic nervous system, which rations, and makes short-term productions of, oxygen intake, energy consumption, *etc.*; S3 is the autonomic controller that maintains bodily functions without conscious intervention, *e.g.*, respiration, heartbeat, *etc.*, and incorporates both the central and the parasympathetic nervous systems; S4 comprises the sensory functions, *e.g.*, sight, hearing, touch, and so on, acquiring the external data required to adjust and improve existing activities and calculating future requirements; finally, S5 is the cerebral cortex and the ultimate decision-maker, and can at any time override the autonomic system and demand more information on an individual function.

An example used by the MIDAS study team illustrates the function and interrelationship of these control functions.

I decide to run to catch a bus (an S5 decision based on S4 estimates of distance, probable time available, likely obstacles, *etc.*, and an S3 report on internal capability and present fitness). Overall instructions are issued (S5) and are amplified (S3) into specific muscular output requirements to be implemented under precise operational control by my S1s. I start to run, with overall coordination of internal functions being controlled (despite the sudden change in required output levels) by S3. S2 monitors and controls oxygen intake and distribution, hormonal functions, *etc.* S4 offers information on midcourse corrections (direction, speed) as required. At any time the direct access channel to S3 may give warning of an internal crisis (impending heart attack, pulled muscle) and I may stop running. My S4 may arrive at an estimate that I am unlikely to catch the bus, so I may curtail my effort. I may catch the bus, in which case everything has worked well and I can use the information collected in future assessments of desire and capability. There is a further possibility: in the course of chasing the bus, my sensory apparatus may draw my S5 attention to a pretty girl walking in the other direction and be urging a change of plan. Here is a clear conflict between developmental planning and the execution of ongoing operations—an S5 decision.

Levels of Recursion

Beer's S1 through S5 control systems have, to this point, been outlined in relation to an organization. He sees the model applying equally well to a single unit or individual person.

To summarize Beer's five systems before moving further with the concept of recursion, they exist as a set of five interlocking systems, each responsible for a key organizational control function and together comprising, for Beer, *all* key control functions:

S1, which is the system of basic operational control; the operational *raison d'être* of the organization, providing on its behalf goods and services to its clients.

S2, the next-level regulatory system dealing with the simple reality that, left to themselves, S1 units tend to diverge from overall organizational objectives. It is distinguished from S3 in that it provides *automatic, programmed, systematic* coordination across S1 unit lines, in the service of organizational goals.

S3, the corporate operational management system. It, also, is concerned with coordinating operational activities, but within the broader context of managing ongoing operations and taking day-to-day decisions of a *less systematic* and *unprogrammed* nature (in contrast to the automatic, programmed nature of the S2 systems).

S4, the corporate innovation and development function. Where the S3 system focuses on the day-to-day managing of ongoing operations, the S4 system develops new operations or works to improve the old, functioning from a futures' stance and with knowledge of the external environment.

S5, responsible for bringing together and balancing the S3 and S4 systems, and, hence, for managing the organization overall.

Relating these five systems to the concept of recursion, which is an important aspect of the model, each S1 unit can be isolated for study as an "S1 through S5." It is itself, then, a complete system within the larger system. Its managers deal with a number of discrete activity outputs (S1), regulate these and arrange for their systematic and programmed coordination in the interests of unit objectives (S2), coordinate and manage the ongoing activities of an unprogrammed, day-to-day basis (S3), give time to development and future concerns (S4), and balance operational and future activities in managing the unit overall (S5). In the same way each discrete activity producing an output itself contains all five control systems, mapped at the next lower level of recursion of the model, and so on.

Without anticipating too much of the results of the analysis in Fisheries and Marine Service, the concept of recursion can be illustrated by reference to the organization of the F&MS. In the organization (corporate level), all five control systems clearly exist in some form, with the S1 operational controls being first exercised at the ADM level, *e.g.* Fisheries Management. Within Fisheries Management, however, all control systems are again present, with S1 functions being exercised by the various regional offices. If we next consider a region, we again find that the Stafford Beer viable systems model is an appropriate means of describing control, and here the S1s are district offices. Within the district office it is possible that the S1 functions are handled by individual officers, and of course each individual maintains within himself (or herself) the five control systems, since it was from the human neurophysiological analogy that the model was first derived; it is the lowest level of recursion of the model.

Thus, the F&MS can be described with five levels of recursion (in this simplified example), and the viable systems model is seen to be an appropriate way of describing and analyzing control functions at each level.

PROJECT MIDAS IN ACTION

Once the original three-man team had decided upon the Beer model as appropriate for its purpose, it adapted and simplified it to conform to F&MS practices and terminology; for example, believing that managers would too readily confuse the managerial line with the normal hierarchy, the Beer model was somewhat simplified and laid on its side. A formal presentation was then made to senior management, advocating its use. The presentation formed one aspect only of a more comprehensive plan covering the total MIDAS project. As initially presented to and formally approved by senior management, the MIDAS plan incorporated seven major steps:

1. The establishment of a corporate steering committee and a network of regional and headquarters steering committees, supported by a working national study team and a network of regional and headquarters project teams.
2. The development and use of a training program to introduce managers to the adapted Beer model, and of the forms and procedures required to implement the model and other aspects of MIDAS.
3. The holding of an inaugural meeting of directors-general to brief them on Project MIDAS and seek their commitment to it.
4. The application of the Beer model, nationally and in the regions, the development and use of complementary models, and the analysis of findings.
5. The presentation and discussion of findings.
6. The synthesis and roll-up of the results of the entire exercise to produce a National Study Team Report.
7. Review of the National Study Team Report and related material by senior management, followed by the required action decisions and the institution of appropriate follow-up action.

We shall now explore these seven steps more fully in the implementation of Project MIDAS.

1. *The establishment of a national and regional network of steering committees and working project teams.* To give overall guidance to MIDAS a corporate steering committee was established, composed of the senior assistant deputy minister and his two assistant deputy ministers. This committee deliberately adopted a listening stance during the early phases of the project, in the hope that all F&MS managers and staff would be encouraged to express themselves

freely on any MIDAS issue. Indeed, one of the concerns noted about Project MIDAS is that, throughout the project, top management resolutely refused to indicate how it felt about different recommendations or concerns, as these emerged. In the minds of some managers, it was nondirective to a fault, and, hence, *not* a steering committee in any real sense. It reversed this stance at the conclusion of the project, however, as discussed below, and this, too, caused problems for some managers.

To head MIDAS in an operational sense a national study team was appointed. This consisted of the original three-man team, two full-time consultants, and five subject-matter specialists, taken from various F&MS programs in order to combine headquarters and regional representation.

The national study team was responsible for the following functions:

- To develop the initial plans of action to guide Project MIDAS.
- To develop the methodology, procedures, formats, and training methodology.
- To advise and assist the various managers and regional and headquarters steering committees during the application and analysis phase.
- To answer requests from the various project teams regarding any forms, documents, or facilities.
- To act as a catalyst, and coordinate the work done by the various project teams.
- At the conclusion of the project, to make a synthesis of all material prepared by the various project teams, and make formal recommendations to the corporate steering committee.

In complement to the national units, each of the eight directors-general selected a regional steering committee and a related project team for their respective regions. Headquarters steering committees and associated project teams were also established for the two major sectors of the F&MS: Fisheries Management; and Ocean and Aquatic Affairs. The project teams then selected their respective project managers. Team members were selected to allow for maximum branch or divisional representation. Project managers were involved almost full time for the duration of the exercise, while project team members were usually called in as the need arose. It should be emphasized that the national study team did not seek in any way to influence the composition of the regional and headquarters steering committees, nor the selection of project managers. Indeed, the nondirective posture extended as far as not seeking to ensure that the different steering committees contained at least one representative from or in direct network contact with the national study team.

The following list enumerates the managerial levels involved and hence the levels of recursion. Each level comprises both a steering committee and a project team (the national study team being, in effect, the national project team).

Level	Code	Organization
1	L1	The Fisheries and Marine Service
2	L2F	Fisheries Management
	L2O	Ocean and Aquatic Affairs
3	L3F1	Fisheries—Headquarters
	L3F2	Fisheries—Newfoundland
	L3F3	Fisheries—Maritimes
	L3F4	Fisheries—Quebec
	L3F5	Fisheries—Atlantic Research and Development
	L3F6	Fisheries—Central
	L3F7	Fisheries—Pacific
3	L3O1	Ocean and Aquatic—Headquarters
	L3O2	Ocean and Aquatic—Atlantic
	L3O3	Ocean and Aquatic—Central
	L3O4	Ocean and Aquatic—Pacific

In total, therefore, 14 sets of steering committees and project teams were formed (plus an additional project team covering the staff branches reporting directly to the senior ADM), with quite loose coordination among them being the responsibility of the corporate steering committee and the national study team. In this way, the basic framework was established for managerial self-analysis.

2. *The development of a training program, forms and procedures.* The national study team split into training groups, each including, where possible, a member of the original three-man group, a consultant, and a representative from the area receiving the training. These groups visited the regions and headquarters directorates and trained local project teams in the use of cybernetics and related modeling techniques. A slide presentation and printed material formed the basis for the training.

This was an important step. Very few F&MS personnel had had any prior exposure to Stafford Beer's work or experience in rigorous organizational analysis. Yet it was believed by F&MS's top management that the quality of the final output in each region, and, hence, overall, would depend to a high degree upon the successful use of the adapted Beer model; *not* by external, highly-trained consultants, but by the managers themselves. Happily, many F&MS personnel took readily to the Beer model, in light of their biological backgrounds, although the nonscientists in the operational line had somewhat more difficulty with it. Age, too, had a bearing, younger managers tending on balance to take to the model more readily than older ones.

The national study team, in consultation with the various project teams, also developed and explained the use of four sets of forms to be used in the application and analysis phase, and explained the use of modeling. The first two sets of forms related directly to the adapted Beer model. These sets insured the standardization of perception, language, and modeling procedures. Using them, the project teams could map the location and function of each organizational unit at each recursion level, and make an assessment, based on data provided directly by the managers and officers in each unit, of the load carried by the various communication channels and of the effectiveness of the amplifiers, attenuators, and transducers in each channel.

The third set of forms was used to model the relevant external environment of F&MS. Its purpose was to identify the type of work performed, and the interactions taking place between the service and the external world. This set was an original design for Project MIDAS, developed primarily by Raoul Elias, one of the external consultants. (Elias had worked with Stafford Beer on several projects, the most recent being for the Government of Alberta.) The fourth set of forms dealt with the future of the F&MS, in contrast to the other sets that dealt primarily with what actually existed.

3. *The inaugural meeting of directors-general.*   The purpose of this meeting was to brief directors-general on the project, in the hope of developing an informed consensus and gaining their backing. The meeting lasted a day-and-a-half, involved top managers across the regions and headquarters, and was judged by those involved to have generated the hoped-for level of managerial commitment.

Two days later managerial support had been sought and obtained, and some 60 headquarters staff were given the training session to be used in each region, including the slide presentation. Some minor modifications were made to the presentation as a result of this session.

4. *Application of the Beer model, the development and use of complementary models, and the analysis of findings.* Preceding steps had prepared the ground for the actual application of the Beer model by F&MS managers. Equipped with the specially designed forms and procedures, the 15 project teams proceeded to work with their respective units in such application.

The MIDAS methodology was believed capable of identifying and documenting potential organizational improvements arising either from the manager's experience or as the result of insights from applying the Beer model—and in a standard, easily understood and retrievable manner. Some recommended improvements of a purely local nature were acted upon immediately.

This step was the most important and time-consuming of the exercise. The final outcome consisted of 15 studies, one for each of the levels involved, presented and documented in a standard format. Each included, among other things, the following:

a. A self-diagnosis of organizational structure and communications, using the adapted Beer model.
b. A model of the external interactions with the outside world.
c. An identification of the services rendered and their costs.
d. A client distribution correlated with cost.
e. A work distribution correlated with cost.
f. A statement of problems, opportunities, and recommendations.
g. A critique, based on the modeling, of communication with higher recursion levels.

In addition to these standard analyses, some project teams applied other techniques for gaining further insights into particular aspects of their respective organizations. One region used input-output analysis, another analyzed formal and informal communication flows and developed a computer program to calculate the interfaces among its various divisions, a third one used colored Gantt charts to represent the cost per activity structure. Several teams attempted quantified information flow diagramming as an input to the cybernetic modeling.

To seek a measure of coordination of activities during the analysis phase of Project MIDAS, the national study team members traveled across the country, visiting each region on three or four occasions. During these visits study team members assisted the local project teams, and as a result cross-fertilization from team to team took place. The four Atlantic regional offices (Quebec, Newfoundland, Atlantic, and Maritimes) formed an Atlantic steering committee to solve particular problems of interface, and to evaluate the reports produced by the project team on Atlantic Fisheries Research and Development.

It would extend the scope of this case study too widely if an attempt were to be made to capture in any depth the richness of this phase. It was compressed into less than four months, generated in some parts of the F&MS an impressively high level of activity and expectations, but differed widely from region to region in commitment, quality, and results. On the positive side, one region identified 13 S1 units (by definition, interacting directly with the F&MS external environment), was able after analysis to consolidate these into only 9 operational units (hence, dispensing with 4 director-level positions), and in the course of the analysis discovered one operation that could be discarded completely because it made no independent contribution whatsoever to F&MS objectives! Less positively, one region devoted the entire exercise to examining its relationships with headquarters, avoiding internal analysis virtually completely. What *is* clear, in retrospect, is that the commitment to nondirective self-analysis released in some areas a high level of analytical effort and enthusiasm; it also left the overall project very much at the mercy of any manager who decided *not* to collaborate.

5. *The presentation and discussion of findings in selected centers.* At the conclusion of the analysis stage there were meetings in Ottawa, Toronto, Halifax, and Vancouver. These four meetings allowed the regions to present their final results in the presence of senior executives and headquarters representatives, and *vice versa.* All senior personnel, regional as well as headquarters, attended all four meetings, to hear and discuss in succession the various presentations.

The meetings lasted on average a day-and-a-half. Presentations included audio-visual presentations, and each presentation was followed by a free-wheeling discussion session in which major findings and recommendations were reviewed and compared with the analyses in other areas. Top management of F&MS attended these discussions, but deliberately avoided being drawn into them for fear that their views would dominate as conclusions were reached.

These regional meetings were judged, overall, a decided plus. They provided a sounding board and forum for examining results, and their general tenor was an atmosphere of free-flowing discussion. Yet in the judgment of some managers, the sessions were somewhat weakened by the low level of top-management involvement. Managers had come to the sessions with well-documented formal presentations; they hoped for and, indeed, expected immediate and direct feedback, not only from their peers but from those they knew would make the ultimate decisions. They received the feedback from peers, in healthy abundance, but left the meetings somewhat troubled by a perceived lack of guidance from top management. Yet as noted these four meetings took place sequentially, and top management was aware that all the evidence would not be in until the end of the final meeting of the series. They also knew how even chance remarks of a judgmental nature could influence subsequent presentations, and, hence, disciplined themselves to ask questions only where they saw the need for clarification. And even though they sat somewhat apart from the round-table discussions, they did remain throughout every meeting, and most managers appeared to understand why they bent over backwards *not* to dominate the discussions.

Although the presentations from the various steering committees differed considerably from each other in terms of the completeness of the data presented and of the quality of analysis, there was a high degree of commonality in the major problems and opportunities identified. In particular, there appeared to be agreement that universal weaknesses existed in relation to Systems Two and Four, that there was widespread confusion as to the proper role of some DOE and F&MS headquarters branches, and that extensive duplication was apparent in relation to some services provided to clients and gaps in others.

The information transfer and communications were subsequently judged by participants to have been impressive, while F&MS senior managers stated that they were "extremely pleased by the hard work of their staff and the results achieved." There was general consensus that the modeling techniques adopted had aided and standardized the analysis in a most useful manner.

6. *Synthesis and roll-up.* The national study team retreated for three consecutive weeks to a hotel in Ottawa. The original team was supplemented by the addition of representatives from some of the regional project teams and the establishment of an internal review group consisting of middle-level managers from headquarters. Secretarial assistance was also allocated. Fifteen team members worked to aggregate the results of the main reports and some 250 regional and headquarters recommendations.

The first tasks were to standardize the models and data displays for the organizational levels surveyed, and to summarize the statements of problems and opportunities developed by the various steering committees and project teams. Once these onerous and time-consuming tasks were completed, the expanded study team split into subgroups dealing with the following subjects:

the articulation of the role of the F&MS;
modeling its role in its relations with other agencies;
modeling its interactions with its total environment and clients;
the improvement of Systems Two and Four;
organizational alternatives at each recursion level;
development of appropriate and consistent managerial philosophy;
the role of central DOE directorates; and
the role of headquarters branches.

As positions were developed in each of these areas, they were discussed in "committees of the whole," usually convened in the evenings, and also presented to the internal review group whenever suitable arrangements could be made. The senior executive made several visits to the retreat and participated in informal discussion sessions with the study team.

The whole of the material developed was finally combined into a draft report of the national study team and submitted to the Corporate Steering Committee. This report was accompanied by a critique prepared by the national study team's internal review group, which had maintained an independent stance throughout the retreat period.

One striking aspect of Project MIDAS was that, from start to finish, the data-gathering and analysis lasted *less than five months.* In major part this was the result of the expectations of top management and in particular Ken Lucas, who was anxious to proceed with a reorganization he anticipated could be of major proportions. At no stage in the project, however, were the time constraints more apparent than during the three-week retreat.

The Project Director, David Griggs, has stated that the pressures were quite incredibly high, with the days and evenings running together regularly into 16-hour work periods, broken only by brief meals and coffee. What appeared to be happening was that the enriched national study team became the lightning rod, the touchstone, the focal point for insights running the gamut from the well-developed to last minute hasty formulations. F&MS personnel wanted to be sure their views were fully considered in the formulation of the final proposals. As noted earlier, Project MIDAS had succeeded in stirring the imaginations and engaging the analytical propensities of close to 200 managers, and the result was a formidable range of ideas to review and positions to consider. To quote David Griggs, "The Team went absolutely flat out," even over weekends.

7. *Senior management review, action decisions, and follow-up.* The final stage of MIDAS was to review what turned out, even in predigested form, to be a most comprehensive body of information and recommendations, and to take whatever action decisions were indicated.

All action decisions of a regional nature were made by regional management and implemented locally. Those of a national nature were made by the corporate steering committee, after consultation with regional and headquarters management. Overall, decisions were taken on the role of the F&MS, the services it should provide (or, in business parlance, "the businesses it should be in"), organizational changes in headquarters and the regions, and general considerations of F&MS management.

The national study team, as noted earlier, hammered out its report within three weeks, under very considerable pressure. Some degree of "let-down" was experienced by the team, therefore, when top management took six weeks to formulate its response; this was by no means a lengthy period in which to develop key decisions, but it appeared so to the waiting, highly committed team. The forum for announcing top-management decisions was a national meeting, held in Toronto. There, the decisions were announced, an indication was given of what would be required in the way of new systems and procedures, and the review and approval process for further adjustments to the detail of local organizational structures was outlined.

It is worth remarking that Project MIDAS departed markedly, at this point, from its original participative hallmark. In the first place, the national study team's final report was not circulated among the 200 managers who had contributed to it, although the augmentation of the national study team had resulted in a considerable degree of informal dissemination of its contents.

In the second place, the Toronto meeting was intended to be a *briefing* session rather than a discussion forum. Top management had taken its decisions before Toronto, wanted to move with dispatch upon them, and judged any further discussion inappropriate. The meeting *did* develop into a discussion session, however, as managers were too involved *not* to question decisions. The participative approach of Project MIDAS had developed a head of steam, as Ken Lucas had hoped it would; he could take a real measure of satisfaction from this while concerned, nevertheless, to move ahead with decisions.

A revised organization chart was formally reviewed by the deputy minister, and subsequently implemented. A new task force was appointed to develop regulatory and coordination systems (System Two) for the total F&MS. New information systems were to include an operations room (a favorite control mechanism of Stafford Beer's), telecommunication facilities, the development of appropriate data bases, and information storage and retrieval systems. Work was subsequently begun on program planning and review processes and a project management and cost accounting system, both designed to effect improved operational coordination in ongoing activities and research projects, while administrative and financial services for Fisheries Management and Ocean and Aquatic Affairs were amalgamated into a single unit (thus changing System Three at the first recursion level).

The whole planning and developmental capability of F&MS was also strengthened (System Four) by the implementation of program and policy analysis groups in Ocean and Aquatic Affairs and Fisheries Management, and in regional offices. From this new emphasis on planning and development in F&MS have subsequently come "powerful responses" to statements of governmental priorities (incorporating many of the role concepts developed in MIDAS), a proposal for a new program/activity structure for the F&MS, and, most recently, the development of new operational objectives for use in program review and evaluation. These last-named relate to statements of services to clients (businesses), which were developed following the submission of the Project MIDAS results.

One big issue identified in advance of the study was the possible integration of fisheries research and operational fisheries activities, through the merger of Fisheries Management and Fisheries Research into a single unit. The decision was taken to proceed with this, as the analysis had demonstrated strong functional links between the two areas.

The more comprehensive merger of Fisheries Management with Ocean and Aquatic Affairs, examined at one point in the analysis, was rejected on the basis of clearly differentiable work structures and client groupings. A most intriguing concept, the "Aquatic Corporation," was developed and diagrammed during the project, demonstrating to the satisfaction of top management that aquatic concerns of the federal government extended well beyond Fisheries, and that Ocean and Aquatic Affairs had, indeed, been correct in its original assertion that Fisheries was only one of its clients and that it should not be merged with it.

There seems a consensus among members of the corporate steering committee, shared by the national study team, that MIDAS led to discernible changes in the quality of managerial communications and in managerial philosophy and style. These changes were judged to be in the direction of a continuation of the openness and collaboration required in the MIDAS project and, hence, fostered by it, although there also seems to be some modest offsetting degree of conviction that the shift *away* from openness and participation during the vital concluding stage of the project caused a negative reaction in some managers. There appears, too, in the judgment of the committee, to be a greater degree of rigor in systems thinking, concepts, and language among headquarters and regional managers, although not universally.

As for the overall judgment of the corporate steering committee, which in effect "commissioned" the study, this seems to be strongly positive. Perhaps the best way to indicate it is to quote at some length, by way of conclusion, the chairman's own statement of his impressions of Project MIDAS, made a year after its completion. Adding weight to his comments, of course, is the fact that the chairman was the senior assistant deputy minister and, in effect, therefore, in a Department that gives very considerable decision power to a senior ADM, the final decision-maker in most areas:

A cybernetic analysis such as the one involved in the project is, in my opinion, useful for any organization. However, it is particularly necessary for complex ones—and by complex I mean along the following dimensions:

- —Size, in terms of output and number of employees;
- —Services rendered: number; diversity; overlaps;
- —Environment: dynamic; rapidly changing; uncertain;
- —Structure: several layers of management; elaborate decision-making processes;
- —Interactions among organizational units: high dependency of information between units; sequential work processes;
- —External influences: regulations by external agencies; extensive interactions with other agencies; number and complexities of external demands;
- —Crisis management: lack of adaptation to the environment; little or no planning;
- —Communication problems: lack of formal information systems; isolated organization units; overlaps in services.

Yet however complex an organization is, if the managers are not open-minded and willing to adopt a new way of thinking, a cybernetic exercise, in the manner it was applied at F&MS, has in my judgement no chance of succeeding. The full support of managers at all levels of the organization is a prime condition for success, if our experience is any guide.

From the beginning of the exercise, we insisted on getting the full participation of managers across the service. The National Study Team was only to act as an advisory body. As a result, the managerial involvement at F&MS was very considerable.

It exposed as many people as possible to the use of cybernetics, allowed them to take part in the diagnosis of their own units and regions and made it easier for them to implement whatever decisions were later made. It put the onus of making regional decisions on the regional steering committees as well as on ourselves for service-wide concerns. Conflicts of interest were solved at the proper time and in the appropriate place. It improved the morale across the service and gave the various groups the feeling they were part of the same family. It also increased communication to a level never achieved before.

In thinking particularly about our decision to adapt the Beer model to our purposes, I think this was a right one. It provided us with a standard diagnostic tool, but also proved a most useful vehicle for not only *allowing* but encouraging managers to participate in the design of their own organization. We saw its use in an analogy with medicine. The cybernetic models were like x-rays; they helped locate problems but did not presume to cure them. Helping in diagnosis was the territory of cybernetics; cure rested squarely with the managers.

As to the problems we encountered in MIDAS, and there were a number, one has to keep in mind the innovative nature of the approach and the fact that this was the first time cybernetic theory had been applied by us in this manner, Among other difficulties the following were the more serious ones:

a) Some confusion about the precise nature of Beer's classification (Systems One through Five).

b) Some confusion between the functional character of the model and the organization chart; some managers found it difficult to accept that SYSTEM THREE was not a one-to-one reflection of the managerial hierarchy. This was mainly due, I believe, to the general hang-up on power and positions, which is by no means peculiar to F&MS.

c) Some units went into an extremely-detailed breakdown of dollars and man-years, while others did not provide enough information.

d) The project teams were better prepared to deal with cybernetic systems than their respective steering committees, perhaps because we prepared them better, and this created communication problems.

e) Some project teams became too large to be operational, and in some instances the number of participants had to be cut down.

f) Some managers filtered the recommendations of their subordinates far too rigorously prior to their dissemination to the rest of the organization.

g) Representation from the regions and headquarters on the National Study Team presented a conflict of interest at the time of final recommendations; it would have been too much to expect that the project would succeed in breaking down completely a phenomenon that is endemic to large decentralized organizations. Conflicts emerged, particularly when centralization-decentralization issues were discussed.

h) Models were not always interpreted in the same manner. Deviations from the instructions were common. However, this did not affect the general understanding of the objectives.

i) It was suggested to the Committee that a few managers went through the whole of the study simply to justify their request for additional resources; that such managers never gave the *informed* commitment we needed. This may well have been the case, but we never had the feeling that the numbers in this category came anywhere close to invalidating the exercise.

j) Finally, I am aware that some concern exists that we moved too quickly at the conclusion of the project. The fact is that even though the major stages of the project spanned only five months, we had been considering reorganization for over 18 months, before the project began; and pressures were mounting across the Service for decisions. We weighed our commitment to participation against this very real competing pressure, and opted for moving with dispatch. Our hope was that over the five months of the project we *had* succeeded in demonstrating our commitment to self-diagnosis and participation, and that F&MS personnel would therefore respect our judgements on timing, and our prerogatives in such top-level decision-making.

3

The Containment and Control of Organizational Crises

Paul L. Selbst
Columbia University

CRISIS AS A POINT OF DEPARTURE

Organizations experience disruptive crises at various points in their existences, which represent serious threats to their effectiveness or viability. A number of different types of crisis may be identified, which can be observed at some time in all complex organizations: business, government, or voluntary. Classification, and understanding their characteristics, can help us to predict the likelihood of various crises occurring, fathom the actual and potential behavior of organizational members, and avoid or cope, as appropriate, in the essential maintenance of organizational stability. Stability is emphasized here, rather than adaptation to external pressures or internal innovation, although it is recognized that crisis often stimulates some favorable changes so that an organization can adapt to its environment. Those are fringe benefits, however; crisis, not change, is the problem. Crisis may occur once, in multiples, or recur periodically. These all have qualitatively similar effects on an organization, although different in degree, and jeopardize its survival or, if it survives, impair its function. Regrettably, both recurring and multiple crises are no strangers, especially to public organizations. Although one may find much literature on the management of change and of conflict, there seems to be little on the management of crisis, and that is the ultimate concern of this discussion. We find that there are generally misconceptions about the nature of crisis and responses to it. *First*, from reading the literature of organization theory, one may infer that crisis is an internal matter in a public organization, perhaps arising from management incompetence, structural obsolescence, or conflict. Yet public administrators know empirically that many crises arise from outside their agencies, for reasons germane to the political

843

environments in which they work. *Second*, crisis as a phenomenon tends to be oversimplified. We know an organization may have an internal emergency, but we do not know its characteristics. There are a variety of crises, ranging from developmental stresses of organization growth, through dysfunctions of processes, interpersonal relationships, or leadership, to environmental constraints that impinge on the resources or control systems of the organization; or to crises that are provoked as instruments of deliberate strategy, aimed at achieving some desired organizational or political objectives. In the following classification scheme, different crises are identified. These are frequent throughout all industries, and prevalent in society at large. *Third*, there has been little guidance for public managers in formulating responses to these kinds of crisis situations, beyond exhortations for avoidance or, perhaps, exploitation in order to effect changes or diagnose weaknesses in the organization. There is nothing wrong with such advice, but it is inherently limited. There is a great deal that can be done to prevent, contain, or cope with crisis. This is not to deny the sad consequences of many uncontrollable crises that cannot be managed or even survived, but many are amenable to preventive and tactical managerial actions.

Why choose the local public hospital as the frame of reference for this analysis? In general, hospitals are particular organizations whose makeup and social purposes predispose them to a variety of crises. But the local public hospital adds its complexities to this, and may be the epitome of a crisis-ridden public organization. Publicly owned and operated community hospitals reflect the vulnerabilities and conflicts of public (and therefore political) organizations, while retaining all of the conflicts and ambiguities in hospitals generally, as professionalized service institutions. Representing the extreme, therefore, the hospital provides a rich lode for analysis and examples. Like other agencies, public hospitals are vehicles through which major social policies (in this case, medical care) are channeled and satisfied. So the effects of multiple crises on a public hospital must also be viewed beyond the narrow administrative questions of a single agency's performance efficiency or decision-making processes, to the broader public welfare purposes it serves. Crises can create an institutional incapacity to perform, and provoke not only dysfunction but paralysis. These influence alteration in hospital resource choices or priorities, which forces revision of the hospital's policies, resulting in program and goal compromises. It is in this context that positive understanding and management of crisis is discussed, relating to the ultimate social outcome of the work of public administrators. These dynamics should be applicable to all kinds of public organizations.

GENERAL ORGANIZATIONAL CHARACTERISTICS OF HOSPITALS

Hospitals, regardless of their ownership, contain basically similar characteristics of functional organization, management practices, social stratification among their professional and nonprofessional staffs, and uneasy environmental relationships.

In behavioral terms the hospital has been described as a composite of systems [1]:

1. complex, work-performing and problem-solving systems, responding in appropriate manner and intensity to somewhat unpredictable client demands on them,
2. social systems of highly structural, informational, and sociopsychological complexity, and
3. task-oriented, sociotechnical systems, rationally organized and based on hierarchical authority principles, bureaucratic rules, impersonal controls, and formal work roles. These are shaped by the processes and pressures of clinical decision-making. Within this context salient organization features are informed by:

   a. the hospital's major objective of personalized patient care,
   b. unpredictable work load and constant readiness. This overtly imposes functional and moral responsibility on the institution and its members,
   c. the unpredictability of work demands, which is subject to exploitation by the medical staff in strengthening their organization and share of resources, on the grounds of "emergency,"
   d. little effective control by the hospital over the medical staff, while they in turn exert tremendous influence on the work performance, strategic functions, and resources of the hospital,
   e. exacting performance expectations imposed on staff members, contributing to role inflexibilities,
   f. people with extremely different skills, basic abilities, and backgrounds, who are in constant interaction, within a tight framework of functional interdependence and close cooperation (this is why the impact of errors or institutional difficulties can quickly generalize throughout the hospital),
   g. many sources of stress and misunderstandings because of this staff diversity, with some containment of conflict resting on member adjustment and voluntary cooperation more than on formal authority,
   h. expectations that members will relate with one another according to their shared tasks and on an impersonal basis. This leads to some subordination of personal interests, unsatisfied social needs, and fragmented relationships,
   i. multiple lines of authority involving planning, delivery of services, and management that are duplicated, overlapped, or ambiguous among medical staff, other professional staff, governing authority, management staff, and unions,
   j. an unclear and troublesome character of the work force because of rising professional aspirations and role conflicts among many hospital occupations, continuing proliferation of specialized medical auxiliary oc-

cupations, part-time workers, and some shortages of technical specialists,
k. continually expanding training needs, to keep pace with the diversity of
occupations, while trying to maintain the currency of member skills,
l. a shift in a basic locus of hospital coordination; this has significantly
shifted from the nursing staff as nurses have become more specialized
and professional.

We may add other characteristics that act as antecedents to crisis in the prototypical hospital. Despite the stated primacy of patient care, the actual mission
of the hospital is not clear-cut. It is often difficult for the objectives of patient
care, teaching, research, and community health to be reconciled in one institution, especially as these functions may all be discharged by one person at a clinical departmental level. As it often happens, a hospital will contain several multi-
functional persons in highly responsible administrative-therapeutic-educational
positions, such as medical chiefs of service, and there are unclear coordinative
mechanisms for balancing priorities among these functions or these individuals.
This creates goal conflicts and leads to the dominance of strong personal whims
[2; 3]. Further, hospital studies have shown that internal differences among
administrative units, along lines of structure, goal outcomes, time-oriented
processes, and interpersonal relationships, contribute more significantly to performance (efficiency of administrative services, as distinct from quality of
patient care services) than do formalized mechanisms for integrative activity [4].
So there are vastly different tactical approaches and management techniques
in the same organization.

Interwoven within these dynamics is a very great potential for conflict in the
hospital, arising from its professional character. There is, first, the usual problem of the professional versus the administrator, and the sense of competence
(authority of knowledge) that results from a professional's unwillingness to
accept orders, follow rules, accept institutional goals, or yield status. A second
form of conflict develops among professionals who encounter resistance and
counterclaims of competence, in the same jurisdiction, from other professionals.
With continuing specialization of work in the hospital, task boundaries are often
obscured. A third type of conflict, internal to a work group, occurs when
professionals inwardly resist professional values, orienting themselves to their
clients almost exclusively [5]. These lead to continual clashes, the development of defensive coalitions, and references to sources of authority or the behavior of counterpart groups in neighboring hospitals, for support in upholding
their positions.

Overall, to maintain the system, personnel are enmeshed in a complex nego-
tiative process. This is needed in order to accomplish their individual purposes
within an established and interdependent division of labor, toward both clear
and vague institutional objectives (*i.e.*, clear, operate an emergency room;
vague, promote community health). The social order is built upon a combina-

tion of rules, policies, agreements, understanding, and contracts. Any changes impinging on this order (new staff member, a breach of contract, a disrupting event, a new technology) will require reappraisal or renegotiation [6]. Considering all of these various elements, we may conclude that attention both to internal structure and bargaining are fundamental skills for top-level administrators, with the entire system highly sensitive to a delicate state of interpersonal and political balance. But the system is not a unitary (single) one. There are multiple power centers. Division occurs by program (patient care versus teaching), by status (professional versus nonprofessional), and by function (governance, management, delivery of services.) All managers are not equally skilled.

This all takes place in an environment from which there is increasing social control over hospitals through lawsuits and economic regulation; where community expectations and vocal demands for health care services are rising; where relationships with clients are subject to increasing friction; where hospitals must compete with each other for professional staff and funds for program operation and training; where (expensive and disruptive) outside technical and social innovations must be continuously assimilated; and where labor unions are getting stronger and are pressing for more inflexible definition of tasks and a greater share of resources. Given these conditions, under ordinary circumstances, the maintenance of the system is a major continuing problem, even while the hospital is simultaneously adapting to necessary changes. *Maintenance* refers to the preservation of an organization's identity in the face of constant change, threat, and disruption. It is instrumental in the long-run continuity and integrity of the hospital, permitting consistent responses to both its continuing and future problems. Maintenance permits regularity in the hospital's performance, which is prerequisite for its mobility, growth, and ultimate degree of effectiveness [1, p. 29]. Perhaps this helps to explain the hospital's peculiar bureaucratic (closed system) character, at a time when many organizations are loosening their hierarchy and broadening their decision-making. Its federative nature (multiple power centers), high differentiation, disparate goals, and integrative machinery require a high degree of basic structure.

LOCAL PUBLIC HOSPITALS

Local public hospitals are owned and operated by a local unit of government, usually a county or city. They serve prescribed neighborhoods or districts, providing general short-term services, are partially supported by local taxes, and are regarded by their users as local community resources. Traditionally their charters have required that they serve the needy poor (exclusively until the advent of medicare and medicaid in 1966), constitute clinical training sites for medical education, and provide emergency medical and ambulance services [7].

There are three equally valid ways in which one may view a local public hospital.   One view is of such a hospital as an archetypal hospital, possessing the characteristics and problems of all hospitals.   Another view is of the public institution as a special category of hospital, with programs and obligations to the poor community it typically serves, and somewhat unusual among hospitals in its structure and values.   The third view regards the public hospital as an archetypal public bureaucratic agency, exemplifying characteristics of all public agencies.   As these three dimensions are indeed all present, and as hospitals generally have been considered among the more complex of organizations, the local public hospital thus emerges as one of the most complicated species in the entire genus of *organization*.

As a public agency, the public hospital is created by a higher controlling body of government, such as a city council.   It may be a mayor's responsibility.   It has continued dependency on one or both bodies for its duration of life, such as annual approval for operating authority or appropriations, or for periodic major changes in structure, programs, and facilities.   At times the higher authority may intervene directly in organization structure or operating procedures [8].   For example, it can grant or withhold funds or authority, create new organizational structure or work units, or prevent change.   It can further intrude by demanding designation of accountability, public hearings, or the imposition of deadlines.   Political power within the hospital is fragmented through checks and balances arising from operating departments that depend on other line and overhead government agencies (*e.g.*, purchasing, public works, personnel).   Civil service, in addition to unions, creates manpower and organizational inflexibilities.   Survival and effectiveness depend on collaboration with this controlling environment and appropriate alliances with health organizations, regulatory agencies of the city or state, clientele groups, and constituents, as does any comparable public agency.

To fulfill their special social role, local public hospitals care for patients who— for reasons of medical condition, financial indigency, poor transportation, or social undesirability—are not accepted for care in the nonpublic sector, and have few alternative choices.   They also serve as primary sites for education of various types of medical, nursing, and health manpower [9].   They generally differ from nonpublic hospitals in several respects [10] :

1. a mandated obligation as community hospitals of "last resort" for needy citizens,
2. the magnitude of medical teaching programs,
3. the employment of salaried rather than voluntary medical staff,
4. financial support or subsidy through taxes,
5. governance through elected officials or politically appointed boards,
6. socially-oriented policies and programs,
7. planning and capitalization, as conducted and regulated through the public capital budgeting process,

8. the prevalence of acute crisis conditions.

In the prototypical public hospital one may observe an antiquated physical plant, a central and possibly difficult-to-reach inner-city location, extensive outpatient and emergency services, shoddy upkeep of the premises, and a huge number of young medical house officers. In discussion with personnel one finds complaints of inflexible personnel procedures, underfunding for supplies and maintenance, rigid purchasing and construction procedures, concern over a poor image of the overall quality of care provided, and awareness of a growing disparity between public and nonpublic hospitals, related to rigid operation and worsening public finances [11]. In 1974 there were 1730 public community hospitals in the US, which amounted to about 10% of all hospitals and 75% of all public hospitals [12].

OTHER FACTORS PREDISPOSING TO CRISIS IN THE LOCAL PUBLIC HOSPITAL

The malaise of local public hospitals may very well be typified by the report of a commission constituted to study the New York City municipal hospital system as of 1968 [13]. Their findings:

1. treatment for acute illness or injury is compromised for lack of an adequate setting for modern medical care,
2. ambulatory care services are inadequate,
3. long-term care services are too limited in availability and uncertain in quality,
4. there is a serious inability to supply supporting staff, supplies, equipment, and instruments, and to maintain the physical plant,
5. resources are wasted through declining patient utilization and physical deterioration,
6. the mission of the hospitals is fragmented, their administrative structures are archaic, and authority is dissipated by the checks and balances of overhead agencies and state and city law.

As visible resources of local government, public hospitals reflect its image, and are subject to its constraints. They are targets for criticism and hostility from the disadvantaged inner-city residents they serve. At the same time their members typically have strong commitments to the higher social roles they have accepted, and are frustrated by their inability to alter substantially the conditions under which they labor. This creates strain. As the hospitals are often located in slums, they are themselves affected by problems of the slums, such as transit, safety hazards, personal danger from crime, theft, and consequent recruitment difficulties. The hospitals are exploited or harassed by politicians for reelection purposes, as they play roles of budget-cutter, antibureaucratic reformer, or neighborhood savior, demanding specific programs. Hospitals are also forced to assume some social roles that conflict with those that engage their primary attention, such as employment and training of slum residents. They are subject to tactics of confrontation politics by consumers, workers, and even professional staff, as these tactics have proven successful over conventional means of achieving progress [14]. One means for trying to develop stronger political support from within the community has been through the mandated creation of community advisory boards as allied hospital interest groups. This has generally not been successful, and has occasionally been counterproductive, as the boards themselves may become politicized, splintering in their goals or attacking the hospital or its staff [15].

As the hospital is a public agency, the observations of Sayre and Kaufman may be pertinent as well. They point out that local public agencies are aggregates of employee groups that are splintered along functional, professional, and union lines. These are galvanized to action by a relatively narrow range of self-interest issues. They reportedly tend toward preservation of the *status quo*, a norm of political hesitancy, incentives for delay, and resulting frustrated leadership [16]. Further, in view of the many problems of the public hospital, in the context of its political existence, there are often efforts to improve it through traditional political reform methods such as replacement of the leadership. Not only does this create administrative discontinuity, which of itself may predispose to crisis, but it may result in an incompetent leader and it tends to harden the wariness of employees. They dread frequent change. Each new administrator tries to assert control and project his personal image through change, then usually adapts to the contours of the institution. "Reform" connotes a personally inspired, impetuous, dubious, and probably ephemeral approach that they feel is best disregarded [8, p. 43].

Because of their political visibility, and perhaps because they really provide the only medical resource in a poor community, local public hospitals are subject to more demands for services than they can accommodate. As a result, continuous responsibilities are generated in the hospitals, with each additional one bringing new problems. Very often not enough time or resources can be focused on any one problem to solve it, or to do more than acknowledge it and hope that it will go away, be superseded by one commanding greater attention, or that someone else will solve it.

Other Antecedents

Some further reasons for organizational fragility have been advanced by Greiner [17]. He traces development of an organization through five distinguishable phases, each of which contains a relatively calm period of growth ending with a management crisis. The phases embrace:

1. organization establishment,
2. growth and formalization,
3. decentralization,
4. administrative reorganization, and
5. reconstitution under new work units.

These "life-cycle" dynamics can be seen in the local public hospital. Crozier describes other prerequisites for crisis that also seem applicable [18]. That is, crisis may arise from organization stalemates within a rigid structure, such as may appear between physicians and nurses in a surgical suite. Or it may arise from the accumulation of changes that are needed in an organization, over time, but not provided because of cost, union, or political pressures, on a piecemeal basis. Changes are often expediently "lumped" for accomplishment at one time, but before this happens the organization becomes susceptible to visible dysfunction, and the change it sought may no longer be enough to restore it to its former tranquility. Dalton describes other pertinent organization conflicts concerning strains arising from economic and labor pressures, promotion impediments, and internal political contracts [19]. Finally, any of the constraining features characterizing the public hospital or hospitals in general, if carried to extremes, can tip the balance of stability.

Conflict and Crisis

Conflicts swirl in and around the local public hospital. There are resource problems, power struggles, boundary disputes, and the usual panoply of organizational strains over roles, values, and personal compatibilities. Although conflict and crisis are different phenomena, one can lead to the other. That is, unresolved conflict can produce dysfuntions of severe stress resulting in crisis, or crisis—arising from other causes—can produce conflict as a by-product. It may be helpful, therefore, to take a brief look at organization behavior relevant to conflict, and the nature of conflict as a final prelude to considering crisis alone.

In a general sense, and as described in psychology, conflict represents incompatible demands. Analagously, in organizations, conflict arises when two or more parties are in opposition or battle over some perceived relative deprivation. These may involve win-lose situations, competition over resources or technology, status incongruencies, or value differences [20]. Power relationships, and the one-sided dependencies inherent in these, among competing parties, are a common element that contributes to these adversarial conditions of conflict [21]. Power, and ensuing organizational dominance, usually adhere to individuals or groups who perform the most difficult or critical tasks, such as

1. those that sustain the basic functioning of the organization,
2. those that affect development of the organization, or

3. those that define its identity and relate to the outside environment of the organization [22].

Such parties usually constitute a dominant coalition in the organization. But other coalitions exist in carrying forward other goals, technologies, and decisions. These several groups attain mutual adjustments and agreements on objectives through bargaining and an acceptable internal structure of authority, rules, and communications channels. These fluctuate according to environmental changes [23]. Those critical aspects of the environment that affect internal technology, structure, and power relationships of organizations include [24]:

1. the sentiments of supporters or antagonists concerning the social value of the organization and its modes of operation.
2. how external governing bodies define goals for the organization, and its priority for their attention,
3. whether goals are too ambiguous, or tasks too complex for outsiders to scrutinize. Control would then pass inward to the key coalitions,
4. the relationship with the controlling political leadership and the degree of organizational autonomy allowed,
5. whether lack of unity of goals may result in internal splintering of interests and external politicization, and
6. whether services can be manipulated to serve those clients whose support can be valuable.

Collectively these external factors, together with those susceptible to conflict in the organization, create pressures that may convert a public organization from its routine to controversy and crisis.

How do individuals respond to conflict? Many react negatively, exhibiting such signs of maladjustment as psychological discomfort, cognitive inefficiency, disturbances of body functioning, and deviation in behavior. Continued or severe conflict may lead to psychopathologies such as ego-defense mechanisms, neuroses, psychoses, and character disorders [25]. For the group it may lead to similar behavior manifested in avoidance of conflict, irrational decisions, paralysis of functions, retreat behind rules and hierarchical structure, or redefinition of priorities toward surveillance of problems and insulation from them.

That these dysfunctional responses to conflict exist can be seen in organizations where serious conflict exists. Despite this, a number of benefits have also been perceived in relation to conflict:

1. elimination of the *status quo*, permitting individual mobility that might previously have been blocked,
2. serving as a signal of danger in terms of organizational weaknesses,
3. it leads to search and innovation,
4. it energizes people to activity and zest,
5. it changes the power relationships, perhaps for the better,

6. it provides opportunities for educating the parties about critical organizational and environmental issues,
7. it enables the organization to avoid ritualism and stagnation,
8. it can lead to increased cohesion of the group, and
9. it serves to establish and maintain identities and boundary lines [20, pp. 179-180; 26]. It is understandable, then, that conflict is often referred to as "constructive."

In relating conflict to crisis, it is important to comprehend these various dynamics of conflict. Although conflict, as an underlying causal condition, contributes directly to few of the total types of crises, those are qualitatively important types, affecting the viability of the organization. Also, conflict may be an outcome of crisis, and subject to control in minimizing its potential for aggravating crisis or instigating the recurrence of crisis. Conflict resolution is not synonymous with crisis management, and is subject to other strategies and methods for mitigation or channeling into constructive purposes. In short, there is indeed a relationship between conflict and crisis. Both should be understood on their own terms. Both require skillful management for confinement within tolerable limits.

A STATE OF CRISIS

Almost daily the public is reminded that serious problems exist in their local public hospital. Dramatic headlines jolt them into awareness that employees are going on strike over inadequate wages and working conditions; that nurses and physicians accuse the administrators, or their political superiors, of insensitivity to appalling conditions, which—they charge—result in patient deaths; that accrediting agencies threaten withdrawal of accreditation for failures to meet minimum standards of staffing and professional practice; that health department officials threaten closure for violation of physical safety codes; that crusading politicians blitz through the corridors with photographers, and proclaim inadequacies in personnel, supplies, and facilities; that budgets are being cut, resulting in layoffs and curtailment of vital services; that workers and patients alike are frustrated and handicapped by inefficiencies and impeded by obsolete buildings [27]. There is often a surging public accusation of blame among mayors, hospital governing boards, administrators, legislators, and employee unions. There may be official investigations of a hospital by various agencies. The depth of a crisis may even be roughly gauged by the number of such studies occurring concurrently [28]. Following these dramatic events and revelations there are too typically cries of citizen concern, followed quickly by responsive action. Voters and taxpayers are reassured. Promises are publicly made. Money is pumped in for critical safety improvements and publicly visible patient programs. Some reorganization may occur [29]. But while all this is going on, hospital staff must still function. They must still deal with the routine diabetic as well as with matters of life, death, and suffering. Around them crisis seems to descend, intractable, and often incomprehensible.

THE NATURE OF CRISIS

The hospital is organized to respond to other people's crises in the performance of its normal task functions. Personal illness and community disaster comprise its expected demand, and are smoothly managed. Within the hospital the patient's emergency becomes the professional's routine. It is a different matter though when the crisis is intrinsic to the identity, viability, or survival of the institution itself.

Crisis has been technically defined as "a condition of instability, perhaps as a stage in a sequence of events, representing a turning point which determines the trend of future events, and leading to a decisive change" [30]. This definition may be operationally amended as it applies to the local public hospital. Crisis is usually worse than this definition implies. It is regarded as destructive by those it affects, and it does not necessarily result in a noticeable change. This failure to change has its own corrosive effect, which can lead to chronic crisis and performance pathologies in those it affects, such as loss of competence or loss of confidence. Conditions may continue to decline. For example, layoffs in a hospital dietary department may represent a hospitalwide crisis in terms of the meal-preparing and patient-feeding processes. The nursing staff must then play a greater role in setting up and distributing patient meals, which diverts them from other critical patient care tasks. Thus, one crisis begets another. Nor need a crisis be part of a sequence of events. A sudden unexpected attack by a city councilman sponsoring a new zoning law can trigger a crisis. So, in a working definition, "crisis" can be conceived as *any action or failure to act that significantly interferes with a hospital's ongoing functions, the acceptable attainment of its objectives, its viability or survival, or that has a detrimental personal effect as perceived by the majority of its employees, clients, or constituents.* Although they could be either, these conditions are held to be the effects of crisis, rather than the causes, for the purpose of this discussion. Devastating effects include the disintegration of the organization's technical, interpersonal, or resource structures or its social order, or its individual ways of life, security, and opportunity for the members. There is usually a combination of these effects [31]. It is also helpful to remember that crisis may be, to a degree, subject to interpretation by the party affected; a crisis in one situation may not be in another, *e.g.*, union organization, or community demands for representation on a hospital governing board.

TYPOLOGY OF CRISES

Several categories of crisis can be classified and illustrated within the local public hospital. Though these seem distinct, it should be understood that local public hospitals experience multiple crises simultaneously, with some precipitating, reinforcing, or temporarily obscuring others, according to their seriousness and priority impact on functions, staff, or patients.

Intensity of Crisis

There are two levels of intensity, for which personnel apprehensions and responses differ.

The Perceived Threat

This is the expectation that something will or will not happen, which primes personnel for a crisis.

The Occurrence

It happens, requiring a response.

Conditions of Crisis

Developmental Crises

These are associated with organizational upheavals at different stages in its life [17]. They may be observed comparably in all complex organizations over a period of time. Following relatively stable periods of growth and incremental change, there are pressures of technology, social change, or lack of revision in the work organization that expose dysfunctions in which the organization is out of step with its needs.

Leadership Crisis. The style of management, perhaps charismatic or entrepreneurial, that was appropriate to the establishment and dynamic growth of a small organization is no longer appropriate. Informal leadership, with direct involvement in all details of operation, is ineffectual.

Autonomy Crisis. The organization has grown and become formalized. Hierarchy is now inflexible, as centralization creates dysfunctions. Labor matters, expenditures, supply approvals, and hiring of personnel are carried out at a top-management level. Middle managers are frustrated and handicapped by a lack of authority. Decentralized decision-making is vital for performance.

Control Crisis. There has been decentralization, and delegation is now out of control. Middle-management levels have too much authority and evolve individualistic systems of budgeting, reporting, handling personnel, and interpreting policies. Coordination of planning, resource allocation, or technology suffer.

Red-Tape Crisis. Administrative reorganization has resulted in red tape. Work rules proliferate. Hierarchical levels are added. Information is filtered. Decisions take a long time. Systems are too formal and rigid. Work units lack flexible coordination. This potential for developmental problems is further underscored by Ernest Dale who describes the needs of enterprises at various stages of their growth. Those with 10 employees require formalized delegation and interpersonal accomodation. Those with 50 to 100 employees require delegation of more management functions and defined span of control. From 100 to 400 employees, functionalization and staff specialization are needed. From 100 to 500 employees, coordination of management functions and group decision-making are vital. Over 500 employees, decentralization is critical [32].

Localized Crisis

This is found in specific departments, or among occupational groups or work units in the organization. It does not directly affect the whole, although it seriously disrupts the parties involved. For example, social workers in a hospital, with tremendous record-keeping needs, have been informed that their secretarial staff will be cut by two-thirds.

Managerial Crises

These are associated either with the actions of management or the success of the entire organization as a reflection of the management. The ability of management, its tactical proficiency, or its credibility, contribute to the instability.

Executive Competency Crisis. This results from executive incompetence or its serious neglect of operations or the adequacy of facilities. For example, a hospital administrator may decide to allocate capital funds to a department, based on its political usefulness in supporting his incumbency, rather than to the seriously antiquated emergency service from which many problems arise daily and the hospital reputation declines. Instability also arises from management's failure to establish a definite sense of purpose and direction, and from poor rules, poor organization, poor coordination, and poor communication. The results: confusion of objectives and lack of unity of purpose.

Innovation Crisis. Organizational stability is best preserved if change takes place gradually, in moderate increments, with accommodation to existing norms, social relationships of members, and work practices. Continuity, predictability, and conflict avoidance are primary. Innovations that are introduced rapidly, affecting routine matters, aimed at the major mission or systems of the organization, and radically different cause fear in personnel. The social order is threatened, as are individual modes of operation, security, and perhaps, personal opportunity. Crisis is triggered. In the hospital, for example, suddenly introducing an ombudsman has a corrosive effect on patient care staff [33].

Failure Crisis. An organization having a prescribed and visible mission, from which success is expected by its controlling and constituent environments, fails to accomplish its fundamental goals. The outraged controlling authorities demand change. Resources are reallocated, leadership is removed, members are replaced, outside surveillance is intensified, the locus of decisions is shifted outside. The mid-1970s failure of New York City to solve its financial problems is an example of this. In the hospital it is exemplified by the laboratory, which begins to exhibit a pattern of errors in clinical chemistry reports.

Continuity Crisis. This may manifest itself in two ways: 1) Especially in the public sector there is a frequent turnover of administrative leadership as a consequence of the political appointment process or the voluntary departure of administrators from the frustrations of public life. This is inevitably accompanied by reorganization, internal struggles for power, shifts in priorities, and other forms of instability. If it happens often enough the organization is in crisis [33, p. 38]; 2) Where there is stable cadre of top management personnel, who are at a comparable older age and nearing retirement, younger members will struggle for succession. That struggle may focus on present power over policies and resources. It can seriously lead to instability or vulnerability from other weaknesses, which result in crisis [34].

Structural Crises

These are associated with clarity in the distribution of authority, functional domains (territorial responsibilities), or decision-making rules.

Rules Crisis. Organization members are unable to act in response to a major problem because of unclear or nonexistent procedures or rules. For example, a physician who is caught stealing medical instruments may not be suspended or discharged from the medical staff because the medical staff by-laws have no provision for dealing with felonious behavior.

Factional Crisis. This is marked by dissension over jurisdictional disputes between competing specialized groups. It might appear in a struggle for expanded authority, such as conflict between medical and surgical clinical departments concerning supervision of the Emergency Service. Or it might appear as unwillingness to accept additional responsibility. For example, the hospital nursing and dietary departments may both decide that the other one should be responsible for delivering meal trays to patients, in the interest of good patient care. One of the features of this crisis condition, impeding its swift resolution before it reaches crisis strength, is the fact that such contending professional groups lean heavily on ideological arguments to support their contentions.

Strategic Crises

These affect the organization's reasons for existence or the carefully defined existing boundaries of its domain.

Allegiance Crisis. Essential organizational members, or constituents, either abandon the organization or stop supporting it. For example, a large number of the medical staff may abandon a hospital because of a dispute over a jurisdiction, such as an intensive care unit. Their presence is critical for the hospital's financial solvency and social legitimacy.

Resource Crisis. The budget may be summarily cut, prices of services may be arbitrarily frozen, or vital staff may become unavailable. For example, New York City, in the height of its fiscal crisis, forced each municipal hospital to sustain a 10% reduction in its already inadequate budget and personnel.

Domain Crisis. The organization's basic mission, and objectives are seriously placed into question by actions of other agencies. This occurs when a local government permits its health department to provide prenatal care in competition with the nearby local public hospital.

Role Crisis. Polarization occurs within the organization over the question of, or propriety of, its role in the face of social change. This would affect a hospital that was organized and designed to provide short-term general care services. As the community has changed and is now primarily elderly and non-English speaking, it is difficult to respond adequately to their needs, without reorganization, different services, and alteration of the physical facilities. Still, the hospital's prestige and political strength come from its reputation for acute care and medical teaching programs.

Status Crisis. The organization's reputation, and, accordingly, its volume of business and constituent support, suffer because of criticism and adverse decisions of regulatory agencies. For example, the Joint Commission on Hospital Accreditation has threatened disaccreditation of a hospital for inadequate medical records and an unsanitary surgical suite.

Technical Crisis

This concerns swift external changes in the core technology of the organization that cannot be introduced rapidly into it. In other words, essential innovation is blocked. For example, the New York health code requires that an isolation hood and air conditioning be installed in a laboratory that processes tuberculosis specimens. But space for the bulky hood and electrical power for the air conditioning are unavailable. Sputum cannot be sent elsewhere without loss of patients, which would affect occupancy and reimbursement, and laboratory staff threaten to quit unless the area is protected. The other personnel see the present situation as bad faith on the part of management.

Manipulated Crises

These are crises manufactured as means to gaining some otherwise less attainable ends.

Competitive Crisis. A crisis may be maliciously provoked by a rival organization for the purpose of inflicting injury and, therefore, increasing its own domain or volume of business. For example, the director of medical affairs, at a neighboring hospital, informs the newspapers *sub rosa* that this hospital's postoperative wound infection rate is suspiciously high. The community is in a furor. Important donors sever their relationships.

Instrumental Crisis. The organization is used as an unwilling instrument in the struggle between two superior forces. For example, the State Health Department threatens closure of the local public hospital, as a means to assert its dominance over the local government's health establishment.

Beneficial Crisis. Crisis may be instigated by the leadership of the organization, as a desperate strategy to stimulate some benefits. It is recognized that crisis often serves to bring about change; it may, perhaps, strengthen the personal position of the management against adversaries or increase the cohesiveness of the members against a common threat. For example, a hospital administrator confidentially discloses to a newspaper reporter that deplorable hospital conditions, such as broken equipment and a shortage of nurses on the night shift, has led to patient deaths. Despite the clear risks of loss of control or backlash in this approach, such instigated crises are not uncommon. Proposed changes that may have been previously unacceptable for functional or ideological reasons (*e.g.*, affiliation with another hospital and regionalization of services) may quickly become acceptable in achieving the more compelling goal of survival. This approach is also used to force another public agency to assume an obligation it has ignored, such as the assumption of the costs of mental health care from the local public hospital by the state.

Perceptual Crises

These are not necessarily crises at all, in the usual sense. That is, both internal and external conditions are placid, and the organization would not be operationally in jeopardy except for perceptions of members or constituents who stir up a crisis based on their erroneous beliefs. Such perceptions are neither correct nor malicious, but they still catapult the organization into real disarray.

Success Crisis. An organization succeeds admirably with its goals, and raises further expectations among its members or clients that it is then unable to satisfy. In a local public hospital this is illustrated in the establishment of a special program through explicit federal funding, such as a screening clinic for lead poisoning in urban children. Neighborhood groups, not aware of the limitations of such funding, want an extension of services, which they think is logical, into related screening for sickle cell anemia and hypertension. But there are no funds for this without the sacrifice of other important services. Local groups do not understand and become angry. They petition the political leadership. An investigation is launched and the hospital is threatened.

Phantom Crisis. No crisis may exist, but one is thought to be present by members, due to misunderstanding of a situation, who then respond as if it were real. In thus responding they actually create the instability and conflict. For example an interpersonal dispute may arise between a white medical house officer (high status) and a minority-group dietary employee (low status). The incident is interpreted by the other employees as racial bias, without knowing the facts. The entire staff of the hospital immediately divides over the issue and other incidents begin to erupt.

Patterns of Crisis

In considering the ways in which crisis may be manifested, four patterns are identified.

Long-Lead Erosion

This encompasses a variety of operational and interpersonal problems and conflicts, at a minimum crisis threshold; they gradually build into a critical mass over a period of time. Eventually the effectiveness of the leadership or the organization is eroded, along with morale, until an acute crisis condition erupts.

Acute

Crisis erupts, with little or no warning. Although some signs of vulnerability may have been discerned in the organization or the environment, the occurrence is largely unanticipated. For example: racial conflict, a transit strike, a power emergency, or a change in the state health code that mandates alterations the hospital cannot make.

Chronic

This pertains to crisis that persists for months or years. It may be marked by a number of crises at low levels of intensity that singly, or collectively are not sufficient to destroy an organization. These may exist all together at once, or in succession, or both. This is often characteristic of local public hospitals. This pattern is frequently referred to as "management by crisis."

Recurring

Some major threats or actual disruptions occur on a periodic basis, and are even predictable, as when, for example, a new political administration takes office and forces staff turnover in key positions, or threatens drastic change in existing priorities and programs. Another instance: the local public hospital may anticipate each year that political budget-gamesmanship will threaten its necessary supply of operating funds.

Further Dynamics That Influence Crisis

Escalation

Where the nature of the crisis is such that massive disruptive effects can be contained until the crisis subsides, there is yet a danger of escalation and prolongation. This may occur through inappropriate local responses, such as a counterattack against another public agency, a defensive publicity barrage, or recriminatory name-calling among the victims or against the political leadership. From another standpoint, crisis may be prolonged by some distortion of values of those in power, who prefer to maintain the *status quo* in order to perpetuate their rule. Subordinates within the organization are suppressed, in advancement or authority, who would otherwise become a force for reform of past practices. They are replaced or superseded by persons from outside the organization who accept the present values of the leadership, and are chosen for their compatability.

Macropolitics

Crisis, in an organization like a local public hospital, once it is visible to the public, is a phenomenon that is irresistable to politicians and the news media. They concentrate on the issue, exploiting it for their own purposes. Its relative importance may be magnified in the process. This is an external form of escalation, which can complicate a crisis or precipitate other crises of resources, domain, or discontinuity. This can be even more insidious if a developmental crisis, which is a natural and predictable result of organization growth and development, is made to appear as a failure of leadership, policy, or priority. The organization may thus die aborning.

Manipulation

Although there are believed to be some positive benefits arising from crisis situations, such as diagnosis of organization weaknesses, organization renewal, cohesion of employees, new leadership, strengthened leadership, forced assumption of obligations, *etc.*, there are also grave dangers. Matters of resources, authority, group cohesion, and institutional role, which are often at the root of a manipulated crisis, may be correctable without one, through rational planning, sound management practices, political sensitivity, and the replacement of incompetent personnel. Reliance on a crisis for improvement is problematical, as it may unleash other problems and can easily get out of control. It often leaves a residue of bitterness, and can unseat the person who instigates it. The dilemma of the public hospital admininstrator, unhappily, is that rationality is often a luxury. Resources and program definition are often controlled by others, and his authority is limited in other ways (*e.g.*, appointment of key personnel). No progress may in fact be made in solving many problems *unless* there is a crisis to awaken and force the hands of higher authorities.

Behavioral Impact of Crisis

Crisis, or the threat of it, is a profound force for motivating organization members. It threatens their security, social order, work practices, and opportunities. And if these are not significantly disturbed, a person still may not like his reputation associated with a crisis-ridden organization that has been publicly criticized or even condemned. Warwick has correlated several types of motivational appeal and responsive organizational behavior [8, p. 103]. These are listed here as customary behavior (a) with our elaboration relevant to crisis (b).

Primary motivation appeal

1. Fear
    a. Punishment for failure to meet standards (intrinsic to employee)
    b. Loss of job, prestige, social group identification, *etc.* (extrinsic to the employee)

    a. Minimum compliance with performance standards, risk-taking, high turnover, strong pressure for rules.

    b. Strong compliance with performance standards, greater risk-taking, pressure for rules will vary by degree of discretionary authority possessed, high turnover.

Note: depending on whether an organization member's fear arises from his own inadequacy or factors beyond his control, his responses may differ, even be completely opposite.

2. Security
    Salary, benefits, tenure, advancement, stability

    a. Dependability, occasional risk-taking in extraordinary circumstances. Performance may be beyond minimal standards.

    b. If crisis provokes greater loyalty, responses are likely to be more tenacious.

3. Group identification
    Esprit de corps, loyalty to tradition of elite cadre

    a. Conformity to traditions of the group, risk-taking if rewarded by the group, pressure to advance elite interests, interunit conflicts.

    b. If crisis is localized, the group affected is likely to become more cohesive; if widespread, loyalty to the organization will transcend that of the group.

Note: Group identification will vary according to conditions of normality, local crisis, or systemwide crisis. In normality, occupational status and recognition are always at stake. In local crisis, discretionary authority, latitude of means, and task-accomplishment are also at stake. In systemwide crisis, survival itself is the issue, as well as reputation reflected from the overall organization's status. When pressure subsides, initial personal and group interests will again be asserted.

4. Power
    Individual advancement, influence over policy decisions, broader jurisdictional rights

    a. Competition is intense, risk-taking is high, alliances are developed to extend influence, low dependability.

b. In crisis, power-seeking depends on the tactical values of the crisis. If it helps in gaining power, the fact of the crisis will be used to justify extraordinary methods. If power will be lost unless the crisis is checked, all efforts will be united toward preserving the organization, with coalitions in a state of truce.

Note: Ordinarily in an organization, the more uncertainty there is, the more bases of power exist. In crisis, however, though uncertainty is vast, centralization of power is usually required.

5. Internalization
Incorporation of organizational goals into one's own value system and concept of self

a. High risk-taking and innovation, low emphasis on rules and hierarchy, moderate to high competition between individuals and work units.

b. Internalization is valuable in a crisis, but at the same time, hierarchy and rules are likely to increase, to permit control, coordination, and consistency by the leadership. These means should be acceptable for the duration of the emergency, although resented if continued beyond it.

In general, behavior of individuals and groups, or at least the motivational forces influencing their perceptions and values, are likely to shift from higher objectives of recognition and self-fulfillment to more basic ones of survival and security, heavily overlaid with fear. Natural defense responses may be brought into play at such times, such as rigidifying the social system, apathetic hesitancy before acting, aggression, or distortions of reality [33, pp. 172-188]. These tendencies can be overcome by channeling them into support for the organization and its leadership. Improving the quality, scope, and dissemination of information to reduce ambiguities, together with the necessary temporary restructuring of the organization during the emergency, and clear direction of efforts, to the degree that these are feasible, can neutralize defensive behavior. But by and large it is still a problem to be reckoned with. We will discuss this further below.

Other ways of looking at behavioral effects of crises may be drawn out of the concepts in Tables 1 and 2. There are different overall organizational behaviors noted in response to the duration and intensity of crisis. In a *short-term crisis*, an *anticipated threat* will evoke anxiety and produce some organizationwide planning to blunt its attack, providing that the organization knows the boundaries and conditions of the crisis. Once the acute crisis erupts the members are likely to *mobilize* their efforts and resources to resist the *occurrence*. This is for episodic crisis. In the *long-term* situation, the preconditions for crisis exist as a constant gnawing presence; this is typical of the local public hospital. Staff resistance may be lowered by internalization of the problems over time. The *threat* of an acute episode may then evoke an attitude of *resigned indifference* and some calculation as to whom it is likely to affect adversely and how badly. On *occurrence*, those who mobilize are probably those whom the situation most affects. Other members may *disperse*, that is, go about their businesses.

As shown in Table 2, behaviors are shaped by the pattern of the crisis condition and the level of its impact. Within the *overall organization* an *acute* crisis, especially the type that affects authority, role, or domain, may set off a survival response. Members will pull together to save the organization. If the crisis develops gradually, members may divide their opinions, questioning the premises of the likely result of the crisis, and *polarizing* in their responses. Some may react ideologically in one way, others in another way. A chronic crisis is ingrained within the fabric of the organization. Neither mobilization nor polarization seems helpful. *Stasis* results. This is a condition of quiescence or stagnation. It can lead to loss of confidence and an *ad hoc* approach to day-to-day problems, aptly called "crisis management," often observed in local public agencies. On the subunit level, *acute* crisis spurs *persons or groups* to defend their integrity.

Table 1. Effects of crises over time.

| | INTENSITY OF CRISIS | |
DURATION OF CRISIS	THREAT	OCCURRENCE
Short-term	Anticipation	Mobilization
Long-term	Resignation	Dispersion

Table 2. Organizational and individual reponses to crises.

| | SITE OF CRISIS | |
PATTERN OF CRISIS	OVERALL ORGANIZATION	GROUPS AND INDIVIDUALS
Acute	Survival	Survival/social system
Gradual	Polarization	Politicization
Chronic	Stasis	Demoralization

They fight for group or personal *survival* and, since the fight is local, engage in alliances with other persons or groups, using the political resources of the *social system*. In the case of *gradual* escalation there is enough time for this political process to harden, and *politicization* may occur as they seek alliances both within and outside the organization. For a *chronic* condition, the personal equivalent of stasis is a state of *demoralization*.

As there are different types of crises, the behavior of organization members will vary commensurately. Warwick aptly describes reaction to crisis along lines that can be empirically observed in a local public hospital as well [8, pp. 20, 192]: paralysis of activity, increased employee turnover, amplified gossip and rumors, attitudes of caution and conformity, wariness and suspicion of changes, resistance to change, and decline in voluntary coordination. Where staff are personally threatened, less openness and trust, interpersonal withdrawal, increased dependency on superiors, and minimal risk-taking or assumption of responsibility may follow. Further, complexity, uncertainty, and threat create pressures for extensive reporting, increased information handling, reliance on written communication, and demands for accountability and centralization. In the short run, and under positive conditions of staff motivation, crisis may serve to unify and mobilize the staff: perhaps to resist; perhaps to endure; perhaps to realign in new social patterns and group alliances; perhaps to polarize, politicize, or function under new work norms. Negative effects on the organization, however, force its aim to shift to survival more than to good performance or creative development. Especially in the local public hospital it can be observed that the goal of maintenance may displace other functional or even basic social goals (*e.g.*, supervisory training, productivity, patient health education, preventive medicine). Organization structure tends to become more rigid. The leadership discharges its highest priorities and becomes preoccupied with frustration. It may suffer from a "siege" mentality. There is great emphasis on hierarchy and procedures. Visibility of performance may assume political importance, competition for resources becomes more cutthroat, and tolerance of change diminishes. Priorities shift to conserve resources, to become less ambiguous, or to present a "good face." For example, evaluation of performance will shift, from less tangible outcome measures to process, which is more tangible, and finally to structure and inputs, which are most visible and clearly understood (*e.g.*, from helping inpatients to recover personal independence, to days of inpatient care, to hours of nursing care per inpatient [35]. After a while, administrators, too, succumb. There comes a point when they worry about their effectiveness, currency of professional skills, and reputation. Public hospital administrators often demonstrate amazing resilience in the face of limited authority and repeated crisis, but they do become brittle if pressures are unrelenting.

Coping with Crisis

It is unrealistic to imagine that many crisis situations can be rationalized, pre- vented, or managed, especially those that unremittingly involve external controls and issues of resources, domain, and authority. But, conversely, it is not useful to take an attitude that not much can be done about it or that "better managers" or "less conflict" are what the doctor would order. We can consider preventive measures when feasible, the institution of an early warning system, and a cal- culated defensive strategy. Of course this assumes that the formal leadership has enough control, and is not itself the root cause of the emergency, so that it can deal with the situation. There are some preconditions: *First*, and pertaining particularly to public hospitals, public hospital administrators need a clear conception of themselves as public administrators, rather than more generically as hospital administrators. Their major focus should be raised from too much fixation with hospital internal organization, medical staff, and demands of per- sonnel and neighborhood groups, to the political considerations of outside agen- cies, constituents, and strategic bureaucratic practices. This identity issue is less of a problem for other public agencies. *Second*, solutions to crisis, or amelioration of their predisposing conditions, must not conflict with important value systems of organization members. This is tricky in complex and diverse organizations. In a medical center with strong teaching programs, for example, it would be folly to propose abolishing medical residents and hiring full-time salaried physicians to replace them. *Third*, perspective is critical. After enough struggle with crisis, a view of reality may give way to fantasies of wish-fulfillment. *Fourth*, information must be developed and understood equally by the parties involved in the crisis. This is imperative. Unless there is agreement on the ac- tuality and severity of a crisis, it may be denied by organization members or even considered a self-aggrandizing ruse by the leadership, who may meet ef- forts to resist it with skeptical antagonism. Understandable information about the status of the crisis and prospects for organization resistance must come from a reliable source that is credible to the entire organization and its allies. Redundancy of information, from duplicative sources, should also be considered as a way of avoiding distortion or withholding (even misinterpreting) unpleas- ant information. If the full impact of a crisis is upon the organization, the most appropriate actions are those that will preserve viability, starting from the most fundamental levels. For example, if your house is on fire the most important action to take is evacuation (survival). Next, shelter, food, and clothing must be provided (sustenance). Another dwelling, furnishings, and personal effects should be arranged for (security and continuity), and so on. In an organization ordinary activities, routine information processing, and desirable amenities are superseded by those directed at survival and life-support. It is not uncommon to find physicians mopping floors and administrators running elevators when hospital employees are on strike.

There are four spheres of additional administrative action that serve both as early resistance and crisis-management approaches, and we now discuss them.

Strategic Sphere

This deals with the mission of the organization, its legitimacy, its leadership, and the coherence of its members.

1. If the organization is threatened with shrinkage or extinction, new functions for it may be found, justified, and vigorously promoted. For example, an abortion clinic may shift to provide care to high-risk pregnant teenagers [34, p. 22].
2. The organization should appear to be realizing an important central value of society. This should further its autonomy over means and resources, while assuring its legitimacy. Under attack, it can gain support and assure its survival, despite changes. For example, demonstrate that no other hospital in the area can provide services for the elderly [24, p. 41].
3. The organization's technical core can be protected and insulated from external political and economic contingencies that would disrupt task accomplishment. This is done by maintaining consistent levels and standardizing input and output flows, forecasting fluctuations, and scheduling adjustments. Examples: preventive maintenance; training technical personnel within; developing contingency planning; introducing new capabilities, i.e., legal, facilities planning; or diversifying economically, e.g., buying real estate, developing income-producing units [24, p. 66].
4. Sacrifice part of the organization if the remainder will live. (Example: eliminate the cafeteria). Seek alternatives to crisis-prone elements. (Example: contract for some services).
5. Seek formal and visible means to legitimate the leadership, e.g., by higher title or reaffirmation of authority from external sources.
6. Renegotiate the domain of the organization, toward preservation of stability and most major functions. (Example: health department screens well babies, hospital gets prenatal care).
7. Create patience and a sense of endurance among constituents, e.g., by means of a timetable showing likely progress of the crisis, and some forecast of possibly beneficial effects.
8. Assure that there is a clarity of written and informal norms relating to assigned authority, status, and tasks throughout the organization [31, p. 242].
9. Further, cultivate a sense of common purpose and loyalty to the organization among the members, e.g., rituals, rewards, training indoctrination, and continued reminders of higher-purpose goals [5, pp. 723–724, 745].
10. Consider how, and to whom, blame should be assigned if the need arises.

This may involve an individual, or group, but might also be some structural feature of the organization, *e.g.*, a department, a committee, an approval process for capital purchases [31, p. 245].

11. Managers tend to place their greatest confidence in people like themselves. This normal reliance would intensify in a crisis emergency, but it may be poor strategy. Subordinate strengths and weaknesses must be considered.

Political Sphere

1. Management's basic professional competency in administration should be visibly demonstrated so that its image of proficiency can bolster confidence, strengthen its position, and help to give it additional leverage. For example, restructuring the budgetary procedures, dealing with regulatory agencies, setting up an information-processing system.

2. The skills of persuasion, influence, and negotiation should be mastered and practiced by the leadership (before the crisis) [35, pp. 125–131].

3. Diagnostic political sensitivity should be cultivated in perceiving the motives, susceptibilities, and predictable behavior of points who affect the organization or with whom it should deal. Choices will be made (or engineered) often on political grounds, rather than the classical ones of economy or efficiency. Many managers are uncomfortable in this role. If so, they should appoint a counselor to help them.

4. Aspects of bureaucratic politics are essential, especially those that relate to political courtship and collaboration of important groups that provide support and linkages to key public bodies and higher political officials. These include business, educational, media, consumer, and union groups.

5. Direct lines of communication with local political leaders may be mutually rewarding.

6. Remember that politics can be an avoidance of, as well as a seeking after, power.

Structural Sphere

1. It is presumed that the basics of good organization have been carried out, at least as much as feasible (this is not always the case in a local public hospital), and that this is not a major factor *per se* in the crisis situation, *i.e.*, reasonable departmentalization, clear boundaries of responsibility, competent supervisors, clear lines of authority, sufficiently unambiguous goals, and reasonable performance measures. If the crisis is exacerbated because these elements are absent or dysfunctional, these need correction. It depends, of course, on the nature of the crisis, but if these are incapable of correction, then the crisis may not be manageable.

2. Creation of a special office, or work unit, to monitor the environment may help in identifying significant danger and relate it to points of organizational vulnerability. In so doing, it must take care not to attract politi-

cal or public attention and subsequent controversy or suspicion of the organization's motives. While this function might also be realized by decentralization to local units, which are technically skilled to carry out search and resistance, as they are the specialized work-performing units, decentralization is not a preferred structural form in crisis management.

3. In a federative organization, where there are disparate and highly specialized work units with differing goals, and multiple sources of authority, it is less likely to pull toward overriding common objectives, quickly, with efficient coordination, and smooth information processing as required by a crisis. Unification seems warranted, and unitary leadership. Yet, and perhaps seemingly contradictory, needs exist for local decision-making. But this is significant for operations, on a day-to-day basis, whereas the organization must centralize strategic planning, allocation of resources, and overall responses to the environment. The types and levels of discretionary decision-making should, therefore, be defined, and deliberately linked through coordinative mechanisms (committee, crisis specialist) to attain necessary integration.

4. Consider reconstituting major elements of the organization into a temporary organization; *i.e.*, converting departments into programs, with different administrative identities and leadership. This may permit the integration of warring factions, while it submerges their multiple goals into a smaller number that they can agree upon. For example, medical and surgical chiefs of service each have functional authority for patient care and educational activities in their respective specialties. This extends over both inpatient and outpatient care. In a crisis, temporary inpatient and outpatient councils may be established and separately conducted, with administrators as chairmen.

5. There are further considerations for more hierarchical differentiation, routinized standard operating procedures, and rules.

   a. Crisis generates additional communication: to assess status, report progress, plan, direct, advise, and receive advice on conditions and resources, and feedback on perceptions from and about the environment. Messages must be transmitted rapidly, free from distortion, to the right parties. Important information must supersede lower priority information temporarily. Information is often redundant (from several sources) and this may be desirable, as a means of assuring that it is not withheld or distorted. Care must be taken to prevent too much information from overwhelming the higher command levels of the leadership. Additional work units and hierarchical levels to process information, and procedures to deal with the work, may be warranted. This can help, too, in controlling undesirable access to the information. Those who have access to and control communications can react before others and have a powerful impact in defining situations [24, p. 72; 8, p. 97].

   b. In crisis there is a need for more coordination than usual, and for more control over schedules, resources, and work outcomes. This can lead to more administrative intervention, requiring proportionately greater hierarchy and more rules.

c. Variation in the external environment (either the source of danger or a source of support) requires rules to cover shifting contingencies. This is especially true in a novel situation in which rules evolved from prior experience may not be applicable [8, pp. 192-193; 36].

d. It has been demonstrated that certain types of coordination have a desired impact on efficiency and quality of work, whereas others do not. Four types have been described: 1) corrective, to rectify an error or correct a dysfunction; 2) preventive, to prevent occurrence of anticipated problems; 3) regulatory, to maintain existing arrangements; and 4) promotive, to improve existing organizational arrangements generally. Especially in the hospital, the preventive and promotive modes have proved most useful in their relationships to efficiency and quality of care. As a matter for deliberate administrative intervention and control in a crisis, and to maintain consistency over time, hierarchical structure and rules seem the preferred way.

6. The physical setting may also be considered, in terms of its effect on the accomplishment of tasks, on organizational arrangements, coordination, supervision, communication, and general work efficiency. Physical redesign of facilities may be an important element for promoting cohesion of members and neutralizing distance as a political factor.

7. The value of using outsiders should be reviewed. These may be consultants, contractors to whom certain responsibilities are delegated, or some higher authority (*e.g.*, New York City, in its fiscal crisis used the Emergency Financial Control Board). This can provide greater backbone to the organization to resist crisis. For example, consultants may offer authoritative and objective recommendations about improvements needed or potential harm from proposed policy changes, which can cause higher officials to stop and weigh their own tactical options. Or, contracting services out may link the organization with a strong ally. For example, a hospital may contract with a university and then utilize its strengths of resources and political influence to help in time of crisis. One risk here is that if crisis still occurs, there are fewer work units in the organization among which the effects can be distributed. These may fall disproportionately on a smaller number of members.

In general, structure aims to remove ambiguity and conflict as much as possible, while its differentiation and integrational effects permit better division of labor, coordination, leadership control, communication, and responses to contingencies. Further, it is used to minimize dependencies, maneuvering, and compromises. This hints at potential causes for rigidity that may create future adaptation problems. In like manner, rules that are too inflexible may predispose the organization to future instability. Structure is thus an ally and an impediment. It permits the *internalization* of crisis through anticipation and *reduction* to organization and procedure. It is an impediment in that it makes roles too prominent and fixes authority, channels of communication, and, ways of doing things. Consolidative behavior is promoted. This is a dilemma of which we must be aware. Perhaps, some rigidity is still preferable to life-threatening instability and crisis, if those are our only options, and if we are sensible enough to modify these conditions later [37].

Institutional Sphere

This refers to operational strategies and tactics that result in administrative practices. It aims at institutionalizing methods for enabling organization members to submit themselves to the basic survival goals of the organization, to withstand crisis by being ready for it, and to draw upon the organization's prior experiences as a means of promoting current stability.

1. Through various means, such as good supervision, fair treatment, pertinent participation, rewards, rituals, training, and group identification, loyalty may be developed in organization members. In those instances in which loyalty is not unswerving, especially at midmanagement or professional levels, members may respond to evidence of their self-interest being furthered by the organization's interest. This may be reinforced by appealing to their ideologies or by subtle forms of bargaining and agreement. Wildansky regards the budget in the latter light [38]. He sees it as a contract, imposing a set of mutual obligations and controls on the contracting parties. The leadership obligates itself to support the requests. The subordinates support the leadership. Points of vulnerability may be defined for each party, as well as sanctions for misconduct.

2. There is also a negative dimension to the business of motivating organization members to defend the organization during crisis. It is observed, although not generally advocated here, that organizations do this by exploiting the fears of personnel. Some also assure conformity in otherwise antagonistic or disinterested members, by imposing cause-and-effect sanctions widely, creating pressures on dissidents from their fellow members. An emergency would have to be quite drastic to resort to these methods, as they do tend to encourage hatred of the leadership over time. If employed, they should be abandoned as soon as possible. It has been noted, however, that a combination of rewards and punishment does soften resistance to change, and acceptance of organizational objectives [39].

3. Aim to assure that decision-making is carried out in reasonably nonthreatening and nondisruptive ways. For example: seek satisfactory rather than optimum solutions to problems; apply the principle of remediality, *i.e.*, we don't know what will work, but we know what won't work, so we can eliminate certain policies and practices; assume that minor problems will

arise during the operation of a plan, and anticipate them so that they can be dealt with; work incrementally, *i.e.*, concentrate attention on the familiar experiences of members and reduce the number of alternatives to understand [40].

4. Routines are well-defined procedures that focus attention on a limited number of considerations in a given situation, and simplify possibly complex decisions. They contribute to stability by making decisions predictable under most conditions [41]. Through anticipation of the more devastating crisis contingencies likely to occur within a two-year period, it is possible to develop plans for response to a good many of them. This is likely to be done already for predictably recurring crises, such as annual threatened curtailment of the budget. Thus, procedures can be specified and practiced. Allison has shown how crisis situations can be institutionalized and routinized, and that organization action is often shaped by this. Standard operating procedures are marked out in detail for various aspects of contingencies, and groups of such procedures then constitute repertoires for responding to the contingencies. These are rehearsed. The result is that the contingency plans influence the nature and intensity of the organization's conception of the problems, define the responsive actions, and provide information and options for organization members. They, in turn, are programmed by drill to perform efficiently in executing such plans [42]. Hospitals do this now for such contingencies as civil disaster or disorder, fire emergencies, power failures, strikes, heavy snow, or cardiac arrests.

5. Another institutional device for adapting and reacting to crisis is the "memory" of the organization. As previous crises have been experienced, and precedents established, some safeguards and patterns become permanently internalized. These help to ameliorate uncertainty and quickly guide action, without the need to develop novel solutions or negotiate new organizational power arrangements.

Examples are [43]:
a. The organizational structure itself, reflecting scope and jurisdiction of authority, responsibility for outcomes, and reporting relationships. (It is understood that the abilities and limitations of individuals are taken into account in placing them in particular roles within the organization).
b. Committees, *i.e.*, the fact of their existence, the makeup of their membership, and formats for their reports of business conducted (such as minutes).
c. By-laws, expressing purposes and methods (especially for voluntary organizations).
d. The nature of enabling and modifying legislation (for public agencies).
e. Outside regulation of the industry, by agencies of government.
f. Customary work practices among professionals or work groups.

Table 3. Types of crises and coping responses.

TYPES OF CRISIS	PATTERNS OF CRISIS			COPING RESPONSES			
	ACUTE	RECURRING	CHRONIC	STRATEGIC	POLITICAL	STRUCTURAL	INSTITUTIONAL
Developmental							
Leadership	X			S	LF	P	T
Autonomy	X			S	LF	P	S
Control		X		S	LF	P	P
Red-Tape			X	S	LF	P	P
Localized	X			P	P	S	S
Managerial							
Executive competency			X	P	P	S	LF
Innovation		X		P	P	P	S
Failure	X			P	P	S	S
Continuity		X		T	P	P	P
Structural							
Rules			X	S	T	P	P
Factional			X	LF	P	P	S
Strategic							
Allegiance	X			P	P	T	S
Resource		X		P	P	P	S
Domain		X		P	P	S	T
Role	X			P	P	T	LF
Status		X		P	S	S	LF
Technical	X			P	S	P	P
Manipulated							
Competitive	X			S	P	S	P
Instrumental	X			P	P	S	P
Beneficial	X			P	P	S	P
Perceptual							
Success	X			T	P	T	P
Phantom	X			T	P	T	P

X = frequent manifestation.   P = primary emphasis.   S = secondary emphasis.   T = tertiary emphasis.   LF = less of a factor.

g. Labor unions contracts.

h. Routines and budgets, as previously discussed.

TYPES OF CRISES AND COPING RESPONSES: A RECAPITULATION

Table 3 graphically portrays the various types of crises, the important patterns in which crises appear, and levels of the four major approaches to dealing with them.

We have tried to suggest the most likely manifestation of each crisis and the relative importance of the responses to it. It should be understood, however, that this is a generalized and overly simplified view. It is offered primarily as a means to bring order; to distinguish and show some relationships among a great variety of crises, manifestations, and responses.   Any actual crisis will vary according to its own circumstances.

CONCLUSION

Returning to the local public hospital, if it is well-led and viable, *i.e.*, having a will to resist, it should have enough vitality to manage a variety of crises. To do this as well as is feasible requires strategic planning and organization. (It should be understood that if the hospital is no longer viable, then none of this discussion obtains.) Within the spectrum of crisis situations, some have more or less virulent effects through impact on services, disruption of the organization, or impact on the personal lives of key staff. Such situations deserve prioritization and, to some extent, this depends on the perceptions of the people involved. Occasionally they have the power to define when a problem becomes a crisis. Given such recognition, perhaps administrators can pick among some of their crises for those that can contribute directly or indirectly to policy, for example, using a revolt of voluntary physicians as leverage for employment of salaried physicians in emergency rooms.   Indirectly, the tactical handling of crises, through a process of involving constituents may lead to their bringing pressure on legislators, resulting in the hospital getting more autonomy in policy priorities and hospital operations. But neither staff nor constituents can endure situations of uncertainty, stress, struggle, and harm for long. So, from a critical maintenance standpoint, it is sensible to calculate the likelihood of crisis and institutionalize, routinize, and contain the effects of crisis. It may be asked whether local public hospital administrators deserve low marks if they fare poorly in controlling their institutions so that they become prone to crisis, and then often demonstrate a short-range and "fire-fighting" attitude in handling crisis. The major weaknesses lie not in its administrative leadership, but in the system itself, as public community hospitals are too complex and changing too rapidly to exist effectively under the labyrinthine constraints of the public bureaucracy. They may be eventually liberated under some other form of governance, more closely resembling that of the nonpublic sector, but as long as they are public, they remain under outside control, and this is one sizable political and crisis-producing problem that hampers the operating effectiveness of public hospital administrators. If they identify too closely with hospitals in general, and do not regard themselves consciously as public administrators, their hospitals cannot compete as effectively with other public agencies, such as police, housing, highways, and parks. As they are fighting for freedom of action and resources, public hospital administrators are obliged to understand the uses of administrative politics or their hospitals will fall short of meeting the public's needs and fulfilling their social purposes. Administrators will also personally suffer from stigmatized reputations and the prolonged effects of frustration and failure.

By adapting to crisis, by recognizing its reality and incorporating it as a condition of existence, rather than as a perpetual harassment or threat, perhaps the psyches of administrators can be calmed, relatively more rational day-to-day decisions made, and institutional policies subverted less.

The local hospital, as a public agency, draws crises as a lightning rod draws energy. Thus, we must reconsider the traditional management wisdom of "anticipate and avoid crisis." This is transmuted in the local public hospital, and perhaps other local agencies as applicable, to "anticipate, routinize, and manage crisis." In the public sector this is more pertinent wisdom.

NOTES AND REFERENCES

1. Georgopoulos, Basil, ed. *Organization Research On Health Institutions.* Ann Arbor: Institute For Social Research, The University of Michigan, 1972, pp. 9–48.
2. Weisbrod, Marvin. "Why Organization Development Hasn't Work (So Far) in Medical Centers." *Health Care Management Review* 1(1976): 20–21.
3. Schulz, Rockwell, and Alton Johnson. *Management of Hospitals.* New York: McGraw-Hill, 1976, pp. 223–228.
4. Baldwin, L. Eugene. "An Empirical Study: The Effect of Organizational Differentiation and Integration on Hospital Performance." *Hospital Administration* 17(1972): 69; Kaluzny, Arnold, James Veney, David Smith, and William Elliot. "Predicting Two Types of Hospital Innovation." *Hospital Administration* 21(1976): 24–38.
5. Gross, Edward. "When Occupations Meet: Professions in Trouble." *Hospital Administration* 12(1967): 44–49.
6. Strauss, Anselm, Leonard Schatzman, Darvita Ehrlich, Rue Bucher, and Melvin Sabshin. "The Hospital and its Negotiated Order." In *The Hospital in Modern Society.* Edited by Eliot Freidson. New York: The Free Press, 1963, p. 165.
7. Hamilton, James. *Patterns of Hospital Ownership and Control.* Minneapolis: University of Minnesota Press, 1959, p. 23.
8. Warwick, Donald. *A Theory of Public Bureaucracy.* Cambridge: Harvard University Press, 1975, p. 59.

9. The Council of Urban Health Providers. *Report of the Airlie House Conference on Public Hospitals, October 9-11, 1972.* Washington, D.C.: The Council of Urban Health Providers, 1973, pp. 6-7.

10. Tetelman, Alice. "Public Hospital–Critical or Recovering?" *Health Services Reports* (April 1973): 295-304.

11. Health Policy Advisory Center. "Turning Point For Public Hospitals." *Health/PAC Bulletin*, No. 51. April, 1973, p. 2.

12. American Hospital Association. *1974 Statistical Profile of Public General Hospitals.* Chicago: AHA, 1976.

13. *Comprehensive Community Health Services For New York City.* New York: Report of Commission on the Delivery of Personal Health Services, 1969, pp. 6-7.

14. Johnson, Everett. "Goodbye, Tight Little Island." *Administrative Briefs* 9(1975).

15. Lipsky, Michael, and Morris Lounds. "Citizen Participation and Health Care: Problems of Government Induced Participation." *Journal of Health Politics, Policy and Law* 1(1976): 85-111.

16. Sayre, Wallace, and Herbert Kaufman. *Governing New York City.* New York: Russell Sage Foundation, 1960, pp. 713-720.

17. Greiner, Larry. "Evolution and Revolution as Organizations Grow." *Harvard Business Review* (July-August 1972): 40-44.

18. Crozier, Michel. *The Bureaucratic Phenomenon.* Chicago: The University of Chicago Press, 1964, p. 226.

19. Dalton, Melville. *Men Who Manage.* New York: Wiley, 1959, p. 4.

20. Litterer, Joseph. "Conflict in Organization: A Re-Examination." *Academy of Management Journal* 9(1966): 178-186.

21. Dalton, Gene W., Louis B. Barnes, and Abraham Zaleznik. *The Distribution of Authority in Formal Organizations.* Cambridge: MIT Press, 1968, pp. 173-174.

22. Perrow, Charles. "Goals and Power Structures." In *The Hospital in Modern Society.* Edited by Eliot Freidson. New York: Free Press, 1963, p. 113.

23. Cyert, Richard M., and James G. March. *A Behavioral Theory of the Firm.* Englewood Cliffs, N.J.: Prentice-Hall, 1963, pp. 27-29.

24. Wamsley, Gary L., and Mayer N. Zald. *The Political Economy of Public Organizations.* Lexington, Mass.: Lexington Books, 1973, pp. 15-65.

25. Lazarus, Richard. *Personality and Adjustment.* Englewood Cliffs, N.J.: Prentice-Hall, 1963, pp. 14, 20-23.

26. Coser, Lewis A. "Some Social Functions of Violence." In *Patterns of Violence.* The Annals of the American Academy of Political & Social Science, Philadelphia, March 1966, pp. 12-13; Haas, J. Eugene, and Thomas E. Drabek. *Complex Organizations: A Sociological Perspective.* New York: Macmillan, 1973, pp. 57-59.

27. Cooney, James. "Public Hospitals: We Must Love Them or Leave Them, Study Says." *Modern Hospital* (May 1972): 87-92.

28. Health Services Research Center, Institute For Interdisciplinary Studies. *Public General Hospitals in Transition: A Summary of Issues and View Points.* Minneapolis: American Rehabilitation Foundation, 1969.

29. Derzon, Robert. "A Changing Role For the Public Hospital." In *Evolving Health Care Patterns and Issues.* St. Louis, Mo.: Catholic Hospital Association, 1969, pp. 77-88; City Hospital Visiting Committee. *Summary-Special Interim Reports on Municipal Hospitals–July, 1972-February, 1973.* New York: United Hospital Fund, 1973, pp. ii–vii.

30. *Random House Dictionary of the English Language.* New York: Random House, 1969.

31. Haas, J. Eugene, and Thomas E. Drabek. *Complex Organizations: A Sociological Perspective*. New York: Macmillan, 1973, p. 119.
32. Cited by Bertram M. Gross, *The Managing of Organizations: The Administrative Struggle*, New York: Free Press, 1964, p. 681.
33. Gawthrop, Louis C. *Bureaucratic Behavior in The Executive Branch*. New York: Free Press, 1969, pp. 181–185, 240.
34. Downs, Anthony. *Inside Bureaucracy*. Boston: Little, Brown, 1967, p. 21.
35. Thompson, James D. *Organizations in Action*. New York: McGraw-Hill, 1967, pp. 87–92.
36. McKean, Roland N. "Collective Choice." In *Social Responsibility and the Business Predicament*. Washington, D.C.: The Brookings Institute, 1974, pp. 109–134.
37. Simon, Herbert A. "The Birth of an Organization: The Economic Cooperation Administration." Cited in Cyert and March, note 23 above, p. 33.
38. Wildansky, Aaron. *The Politics of the Budgetary Process*. Boston: Little, Brown, 1974, pp. 2–3.
39. Johns, E. A. *The Sociology of Organizational Change*. Oxford: Pergamon Press, 1973, p. 32.
40. Rehfuss, John. *Public Administration as Political Process*. New York: Scribner's, 1973, p. 163.
41. Sharkansky, Ira. *The Routines of Politics*. New York: Van Nostrand Reinhold, 1970, p. 3.
42. Allison, Graham T. *Essence of Decision*. Boston: Little, Brown, 1971, p. 89.
43. Items a through d were drawn from the author's experience as a public administrator; items e through g were drawn from Herbert Kaufman, *The Limits of Organizational Change*, Alabama: University of Alabama Press, 1971.

4

Multilateral Bargaining in the Public Sector: Causes, Effects, and Accommodations

James P. Begin
Rutgers University

INTRODUCTION

The rapid emergence of collective bargaining in the public sector has been one of the most important developments in collective bargaining in recent years. Since the early 1960s large numbers of federal, state, and local employees have been unionized. In fact, the percentage of public sector employees unionized has surpassed by far the percentage of private sector employees organized over a much longer period [1].

Accompanying this rapid growth of public sector bargaining has come a vast literature describing the problems of developing a collective bargaining system appropriate to the public sector [2]. This chapter deals with aspects of public sector bargaining that many authors have identified as among the most difficult the parties have confronted, that is, the extent to which the complex organizational and bargaining structures of the public sector interact with political factors to complicate the bargaining process [3]. Few public unions and public employers would argue that operating a collective bargaining system in the public sector is not a complex task. Consider the following examples.

In New Jersey, negotiators from the Office of Employee Relations, in negotiating for 1977 salary increases for employees in units representing state employees, had held steadfastly to a state proposal that would have provided a 5% across-the-board salary increase in each of two years. There were to be *no* increments, indicating that increases within the civil service pay ranges were being abandoned, at least for the two-year period of the agreement. As the primary elections neared, the legislature voted to provide money for the increments, thus negating the many months of tough negotiating by the state negotiators. The state employees ended up with the 5% across-the-board increases plus increments in each of two years. Several leaders of state employee unions were present when the bill providing the funds was signed by the governor, a democrat working hard for renomination and reelection.

In another instance, when the New Jersey legislature agreed to reduce the state contribution to the pension plan covering the large portion of higher education employees, the faculty unions from the several bargaining units joined forces with higher education administrators to protest the change. Their efforts, to date, have been unsuccessful, but, in another instance, joint union-employer efforts, spurred by the American Association of University Professors representing the Rutgers University faculty and the Rutgers administration, were successful in changing the tax status of the faculty pension system.

The faculty at the four university centers (Albany, Buffalo, Binghamton, and Stony Brook) of the State University of New York (SUNY) petitioned for a separate collective bargaining unit for those four campuses. They were displeased with their representation under a statewide bargaining unit that encompassed large numbers of nonteaching professionals and 20 institutions with widely varying missions.

In several New York and New Jersey institutions of higher education, college or university presidents have negotiated informally with local faculty union groups to solve problems at the institutional level. These "local" negotiations were not sanctioned by state authorities and usually these authorities were not aware of local settlements until much later, if at all.

In college and university faculty negotiations around the country, students have often sought participation in negotiations. Indeed, in Montana student participation on the employer bargaining team is statutorily mandated. In most instances, student participation has been less direct, involving primarily an opportunity to review bargaining demands and, in some instances, to sit at the bargaining table [4]. In Florida, a "sunshine" law requires that all negotiating activities of public employees take place in public.

DEFINITION OF MULTILATERAL BARGAINING

The situations discussed above represent examples of what has been defined as multilateral bargaining. According to Moskow and McLennan, who are given credit for developing the word *multilateral*, "by definition bargaining is multilateral when more than two groups are involved in the bargaining process. It is possible for the additional parties to participate in the negotiating sessions, but typically the third-party groups operate on the fringe of the bargaining. In order for these groups to influence bargaining, they must be in a position to impose a cost (economic, political, or otherwise) on the parties to the agreement" [5].

This definition referred to the participation of third-party interest groups in negotiations, for example, parent or other community groups in school district negotiations [5, p. 228]. In the subsequent literature, however, the term has been broadened to include other types of public sector bargaining activities. Juris and Feuille added a dimension to the definition of multilateral when they included the effect of "non-labor relations city officials" in the bargaining process [6]. These officials often become involved in the bargaining process when the unions end-run to a higher level of management than is represented at the bargaining table.

Begin defined multilateral bargaining as including all bargaining activities that violate the relationships comprising bilateral contract negotiations. Bilateral contract negotiations in turn were defined, drawing on Walton and McKersie's behavioral theory of negotiations, as including the negotiations between the employee and employer bargaining agents *at the bargaining table* and the *internal* bargaining activities that occur between the union negotiators and the members of the bargaining unit and between the union negotiators and other employer levels not represented at the table [7]. Walton and McKersie label these internal bargaining activities "intraorganization bargaining" [8]. As an illustration of this type of bargaining, Kochan described how one city negotiator found it necessary to threaten to coalesce with the city council so that the mayor would overrule a department head who was blocking settlement. This negotiator was utilizing intraorganizational bargaining tactics to achieve a consensus on *his* side of the table [9].

Kochan points out additional assumptions underlying the bilateral bargaining process: "all interactions between management officials and the employee organization are channeled through the formally designated negotiators. In addition, the negotiators are assumed to serve as the public spokesmen for the parties on bargaining issues" [9, p. 144].

Table 1 illustrates the various interactions that can occur among the union negotiating team, union members, employer negotiating team, and other levels of the employer not at the bargaining table. Two basic types of multilateral bargaining could emerge: 1) union *leadership* coalitions, with employer authority at, above, or below the level of employer authority at the bargaining table, that bypass bilateral negotiations. If the union leadership coalitions are with employers above or below the level of employer at the bargaining table, then the coalitions are with employer *factions*; 2) union *faction* (union membership other than the leadership) coalitions with employer authority at, above, or below the level of employer authority at the bargaining table. Again, if the union faction coalitions are with employers above or below the level of employer at the bargaining table, then the coalitions are with employer *factions*. In all types of multilateral bargaining, the use of the word *coalition* indicates that there is *joint* agreement between the parties to the coalition to engage in bar-

Table 1. Classification of union and employer interactions.

	UNION REPRESENTATIVES AT TABLE	UNION MEMBERS	EMPLOYER REPRESENTATIVES AT TABLE	OTHER LEVELS OF SAME EMPLOYER
Union representatives at table		Bilateral: intra-organizational bargaining	Bilateral or multilateral union-employer coalitions	Multilateral: union-employer faction coalitions
Unions members			Multilateral union faction–employer coalitions	Multilateral: union faction–employer faction coalitions
Employer representatives at table				Bilateral: intra-organizational bargaining
Other levels of same employer				

gaining activities that bypass the bilateral bargaining relationship. In other words, if the union leadership of bargaining units containing state employees end-runs to the governor of a state to put pressure on negotiations, this is not considered to be multilateral bargaining unless the governor *agrees* to pursue union objectives.

In addition to the multilateral bargaining activities developing out of the relationships of the direct union and employer participants, a third general category of multilateral bargaining emerges from the desire of the parties to the negotiations to bring other influences to bear on negotiations. For example, students and parent groups often attempt to influence the process and outcomes of negotiations. These third parties usually do not have a *legal* status in the bargaining relationship since bargaining laws do not usually give them a bargaining status, but they do have the potential to inflict a *cost* on the parties [10]. Unions or employers often form coalitions with these other groups, although the groups can also act in their own interest as independent third parties.

There is a range of other strategies the parties to negotiation can utilize to attempt to influence the course of negotiations; these can arguably be defined as multilateral bargaining since they involve the use of groups who are not direct parties to the negotiations. As one example, the utilization of the services of the courts or administration agencies such as the New York Public Employment Relations Board to process unfair labor practices or resolve negotiating impasses represents an attempt to enhance relative power at the bargaining table. As another example, unions and employers often form associations with other unions and employers from other political jurisdictions for the purpose of exchanging information or forming common bargaining strategies.

The parties' use of legal procedures to enhance their respective bargaining power will not be treated here, primarily because any differences in their usage between the public and private sector are less interesting than the public and private sector differences in the other types of multilateral bargaining. In summary, the following four types of multilateral bargaining have been identified for discussion:

1. Union leadership-employer coalitions and union leadership-employer faction coalitions;
2. Union faction-employer coalitions and union faction-employer faction coalitions;
3. Multiple organization union coalitions and multiple organization employer coalitions;
4. Third-party participation by groups directly affected by the negotiations who are able to exert a cost on the parties in negotiations, usually the immediate users of the services or products provided by the organization in which negotiations are taking place.

CAUSES OF MULTILATERAL BARGAINING: AN OVERVIEW

The greater development of multilateral bargaining in the public sector is likely linked to a number of interacting factors that differentially affect bargaining systems in the public and private sectors.

It is not argued here that multilateral bargaining does not occur in the private sector. As numerous authors commenting on private sector experiences over the years have pointed out, unions will always seek out the source of authority if it appears that the level of employer authority at the table is insufficient or does not have the consensus of the employer officials [11]. This discussion below will provide examples of multilateral bargaining in the private sector. Still, there are differences between public and private organizations that create greater opportunities for multilateral bargaining activities in the public sector. For example: 1) the concept of the separation of power in government organization (legislative, administrative, and judicial) creates a complex diffusion of power in governmental agencies; 2) the election by popular vote of many governmental legislators and administrators adds a political element to the basic economic market context of the private sector; 3) many government agencies provide essentially monopolistic services to communities; 4) many government agencies process people, not products, for example, prisons, welfare agencies, and schools; 5) reflecting the centralization of authority on many issues in governmental agencies, the bargaining units in the public sector tend to be broader, particularly at the state and federal levels; and 6) many conditions of employment for public employees prior to unionization were statutorily determined, for example, civil service and education statutes [12]. All of these interacting forces, as will be discussed below, operate to provide opportunities for multilateral bargaining.

The general framework setting out the basic relationships is depicted in Figure 1 [13]. Generally, it is postulated that multilateral bargaining is generated by breakdowns in the operation of the bilateral bargaining process that cause the parties to seek to enhance their relative *power* by bypassing the bilateral bargaining process either to put pressure on the bilateral process (see dotted line, Figure 1) or to negotiate settlements outside of the bilateral process. *The basic proposition of this framework is that the greater the internal conflict within union or employer organizations, the greater the degree of factionalism, and, thus, the greater the degree of multilateral bargaining* [14].

Union or employer internal conflict is likely the product of a variety of environmental, union, and organizational factors, but it will be argued here that organizational structure and authority are the basic determinants of the internal conflict that produces multilateral bargaining activities.

The more important of these factors are believed to be the following:

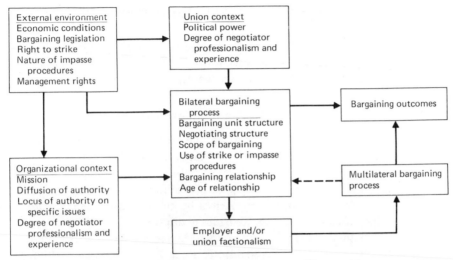

Figure 1. Multilateral bargaining: the general framework.

1. *Extent of diffusion of employer authority*; that is, the more diffuse the authority, the greater the likelihood that employer factions will develop and that multilateral bargaining will occur (see Figure 2).
2. *The locus of employer authority on issues of interest to unions in relation to the level of employer authority at the bargaining table*; that is, the greater the inability of the employer negotiator at the table to solve problems, the greater the likelihood of multilateral bargaining.
3. *The composition of bargaining units*; that is, the more heterogeneous the units, the greater the likelihood that union factions will develop and that multilateral bargaining will occur (see Figure 2).
4. *The mission of the organization*; that is, multilateral bargaining activities will be greater if the organization A) processes people (for example, students), B) provides an essentially monopolistic service to the community; or

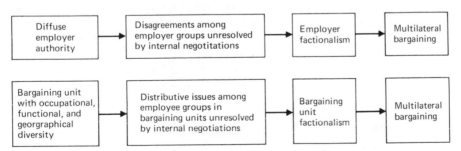

Figure 2. Basic structural causes of employer and union factionalism.

C) has labor and product market characteristics similar to other organizations.

These factors will be specified to a greater degree and related to specific types of multilateral bargaining in the discussion below. A discussion of other factors moderating the development of multilateral bargaining activities will follow.

Union Leadership Coalitions With Employer or Employer Factions

Agreements arrived at by union leadership and employer groups at, above, or below the level of employer authority at the bargaining table that bypass the bilateral bargaining process constitute one form of multilateral bargaining. Unions can approach these levels of employer singly or in coalition with other unions when the level of employer authority approached by the coalition is the *common* employer of the different unions on the issues in dispute.

The basic structural cause of most of these bypassing activities is employer factionalism. Bargaining unit factionalism is not a consideration here, although the formation of coalitions among unions for the purposes of negotiations could be an indication in some instances that a proliferation of bargaining units has created a need for them to join together to get meaningful negotiations. On some issues in the public sector, particularly the economic issues, high-level coalitions may always emerge. In other instances the coalitions indicate that, at least in terms of the issues that join them, the level of authority to reach settlement does not exist at the bilateral bargaining table.

A primary cause of employer factionalism is diffusion of employer authority. A broad diffusion of employer authority increases the probability that the employer intraorganizational bargaining process will break down, leading to bargaining at different levels of the employer as the employee organizations seek out the optimum settlement.

The forms that union leadership-employer coalitions can take are varied and tend to depend on the extent of diffusion of employer authority, the level of that authority at the bargaining table (negotiating structure), the composition of the bargaining units, and the locus of employer authority on the issues in dispute.

Attempts by unions to form coalitions with employers who are not at the table can take place at any level of the organization. Figure 3 illustrates the forms of multilateral bargaining deriving from employer factionalism.

Union Coalitions With Higher Level Employers

If the level of employer authority at the table is perceived to be insufficient in respect to certain issues, then end-runs by unions to higher levels of employers

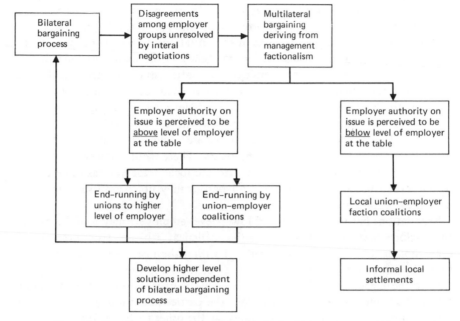

Figure 3. Employer factionalism and union leadership-employer coalitions.

can be expected. Employee bargaining agents will usually attempt to bargain with employers other than those at the negotiating table whenever a lack of consensus over policy or jurisdiction is perceived to exist among employer levels. The motivations for the separate negotiations are to exert pressure or leverage on the employer representatives at the table by going to the source of authority on certain issues. Alternatively, the end-running activities might lead to policy changes independent of the bilateral bargaining process. For example, in many states employee benefits, such as pensions and insurance, are set by statute. Accordingly, the proper level of negotiations over those issues in the eyes of the unions is not at the bargaining table, but through lobbying activities with the legislature. Unions representing federal employees have lobbied with the federal legislature for years to obtain employee benefits. In fact, the continuing nonnegotiability of salaries in the federal service provides continuing impetus to lobbying activities.

Union Coalitions With Lower Level Employers

Union leadership-employer coalitions may also involve agreements with lower level employers. This is likely to happen when both the union and the lower level employer (for example, the head of a single agency involved in multiagency negotiations) view levels of employers external to the agency (for example, a state office of employee relations) as outsiders who are interfering in local affairs.

Multilateral bargaining is done in these situations to avoid the purview of higher employers or to protect the local agency's autonomy. As indicated in Figure 3, the union and lower employer can settle issues directly, establishing either local rules that do not appear in the agreement or local deviations to circumvent the broader formal contract. The parties may also engage in grievance negotiations so that higher level authorities will not be involved in decision-making. This would occur particularly where higher levels of the grievance procedure involved higher levels of employers. These tactics, however, are likely to be effective in the long run only where the local employer has some degree of autonomy because the circumvented parties may not permit such activities once they become aware of them.

Negotiations between a union and lower level employers may lead the parties to conclude that the problem has to be settled at a higher level of employer even though they initially thought it fell within the lower employer's jurisdiction. In this case the parties may form a coalition and present their joint position to the higher level of employer who may or may not be at the bargaining table. To avoid the charge of collusion, the parties might lobby separately, or simply form a tacit coalition by not opposing the other party's efforts.

Union Coalitions With Common Employer

The activities described above can also be engaged in by more than one union, for whenever a particular level of employer is the common employer of employees represented in several different bargaining units, then multilateral bargaining is likely to occur between this level of the employer and coalitions that form among the bargaining units. The coalitions form around issues and problems that the different bargaining units perceive they have in common and issues for which a particular level of employer has formulated a uniform policy for all the employees in the coalition. The coalitions are attempts to enhance the power of the unions, and coalitions accomplish this in part by improving communications among the different employee groups, thereby minimizing employer whipsawing attempts [15].

In a diffuse organizational structure, coalition formation is likely to occur on several levels. At the lowest level, employee groups from a single agency or geographical location might form a coalition with the local employer to deal with a problem relevant only to that location. For example, the various unions representing the employees of Rutgers University have formed a formal coalition organization. The organization evolved out of an attempt of the administration to change parking fees and the method for paying employee salaries. The unions also communicate about progress in negotiations.

At a higher level, coalitions may form when a level of employer is common to many different unions. For example, a state department of higher education may be receptive to meeting with unions representing several institutions that bargain locally with their unions. At the highest level, coalitions may form between employee groups in higher education and unions representing other types of state employees. These unions may coalesce against a state office of employee relations or the state legislature. Statewide coalitions have developed in a number of states around common bargaining issues, usually economic ones, for example, Connecticut, Oregon, New York, New Jersey, and Nebraska. At the federal level, the several post office unions have often formed coalitions for lobbying purposes.

Coalitions have also formed at state and local levels to lobby legislatures into passing collective bargaining legislation. At the national level, the Coalition of American Public Employees, comprising several public employee unions such as American Federation of State, County, and Municipal Employees (AFSCME), International Association of Firefighters (IAFF), National Education Association (NEA), and National Association of Social Workers (NASW), have lobbied for some time for federal legislation to regulate public employee bargaining at the state and local levels. In essence, wherever a legislature, state or federal, has the authority to change policies affecting employee relations, then the legislature becomes the common employer for all employees affected by the policy in question.

It could be expected that coalitions of unions would be unstable in the long run due to the competitive nature of unions and the fact that issues that are distributive among the bargaining units would tend to weaken or break up the coalitions. For example, the membership of the New Jersey coalition of state employees has varied considerably over the years as various issues have split the coalition. On the other hand, coalition formation could lead to a more permanent tie among certain groups by establishing a precedent for a permanent coalition, such as the one that emerged in New York on pension issues, or, ultimately, to a permanent redefinition of a bargaining unit. Such a decision, formalizing a *de facto* coalition among separate bargaining units at each of the state colleges, has been made for the New Jersey state colleges. An informal coalition between the separate faculty units at Rutgers University, the College of Medicine and Dentistry of New Jersey, and the New Jersey Institute of Technology also produced a joint fact-finding effort on economic issues for these three institutions.

Union Faction Coalitions With Employer and Employer Factions

Agreements by bargaining unit factions other than union leadership at the bargaining table and employers at, below, or above the level of employer authority at the table represent multilateral negotiations because the union bargaining team leadership and sometimes the employer team leadership have been by-passed in achieving an agreement.

A faction, such as that indicated by the SUNY example, may arise within a bargaining unit whenever members of a unit have dissimilar interests. For example, there may be differences between geographical locations, junior and senior employees, males and females, minority groups, or different occupations or skills. A bargaining unit with broad occupational diversity is particularly susceptible to factionalism because of the varying needs often differentiating the dissimilar occupations.

Unit factionalism is not peculiar to the public sector by any means. In the automobile industry, the United Automobile Workers (UAW) union has had persisting problems over the years between the craft employees and the less skilled workers. Nevertheless, the tendency in the public sector to formulate broad units, particularly at the state and federal level, creates possibilities that unit factionalism will occur. In several states (for example, Alaska, Hawaii, and Wisconsin) several occupationally defined bargaining units, cutting across several state departments, were established by legislation. The Wisconsin statute for state employees provides for six occupational units: clerical and related employees, blue-collar and nonbuilding trades, building trades and craft, security and public safety, technical, and professional (the professional category is broken into nine units) [16]. In other states, such as New York, Pennsylvania, and New Jersey, the statewide units were determined by administrative decision.

These broad units were felt to be desirable for a number of reasons [17]. First, it is believed that more economical negotiations are possible since a proliferation of bargaining units would require complex administrative arrangements. Second, many conditions of employment are established to cover all employees. So if meaningful negotiations are to take place, the bargaining units must be large. In addition, it was felt that large units would encourage union stability and prevent the whipsawing that would occur with many units.

Despite these advantages, broad units complicate considerably the task of the union leadership in achieving consensus within their unions because it is difficult for them to respond to the varying needs [18]. The executive director of the SUNY faculty union, for example, indicated that it was an impossible task to serve the needs of the best brain surgeon in the country as well as the employee who shovels cow manure on the farm. Martin's findings reinforced this point. After studying whether broad occupational bargaining units or departmental units were more appropriate for state employees, he concluded that departmental units might be responsive to labor and managment needs. He found significant differences among the four Illinois state departments he studied regarding the employee's feel for bargaining, seniority, and faculty size, and among geographical areas by job satisfaction, seniority, and faculty size [19].

Generally, unions are able to resolve many differences through internal negotiating processes. When this intraorganizational bargaining process breaks down,
however, one can expect employer negotiators to be approached by unit factions
for a resolution of their problems.

Figure 4 illustrates the development of three forms of union faction-employer
coalitions. As indicated, bargaining unit factionalism is the primary cause of this
type of multilateral bargaining, but employer factionalism interacts with bargaining unit factionalism to create one type of coalition.

In its simplest form, issues of concern to a particular group may be driven off
the bargaining table as the faction seeks some differential advantage by bargaining informally with the employer negotiators *at the table*. The outcome desired
may be an informal, off-the-record agreement or an agreement from the employer to adopt the faction's position in the contract settlement.

In a second form, where the level of employer at the bargaining table is *above
local agency management*, for example, where a state office of employee relations official is leading the negotiations for a unit covering similar occupations in
several state departments, union-management coalitions may develop at the department level. In other words, bargaining unit factionalism, in combination with
management factionalism, creates opportunities for multilateral bargaining at the
subbargaining unit organizational level. For example, the administrator of one
state department of several included in an occupational unit may agree to negotiate informally with unit members over local issues, creating rule changes that deviate from statewide agreements. In the administration of the grievance process,

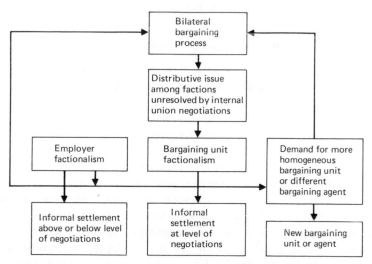

Figure 4. Bargaining unit factionalism, employer factionalism, and union faction-employer
coalitions.

the local parties may agree to local settlements rather than have their "dirty linen" aired at higher levels. As noted previously, the motivation for engaging in these local coalitions is to avoid the purview of higher employer authority, to protect the local agency's autonomy, or both.

Where the local parties agree that a higher level of employer is needed to re-solve the problem, the parties may form a coalition to present their positions, jointly or separately, to the higher level of employer. The primary purpose here would be to affect the outcome of bilateral negotiations. For example, the ad-ministration of a city department that is part of a city-wide bargaining unit may agree to support the local union leadership's position that an overtime allocation system negotiated citywide is inappropriate for that department's special needs.

In a third form, where informal multilateral negotiations are consistently unable to resolve the problems presented by a particular faction, a request for unit redefinition may develop, such as the unsuccessful attempt by the faculty at SUNY in the example noted previously. Most efforts at unit realignment have a low probability of success, however. In some instances, internal factionalism may lead to efforts by the faction to turn over the existing bargaining agent. At the New Jersey state colleges factions consisting of administrators, librarians, and teacher training faculty versus liberal arts faculty were determinative in a close race in turning out the NEA affiliate for an AFT affilate (the AFT received exactly the number of votes needed to win, 50% plus 1 of the unit members voting). In each instance, the factions involved had been dissatisfied with NEA representation. The *primary* effect of demands to change the unit or agent would be to feed back on the primary bargaining process by creating pressure on the bilateral negotiators to meet the faction's demands.

Multiple Organization Union and Employer Coalitions

In the process of attempting to enhance bargaining power, unions or employers may form informal coalitions that cut across the boundaries of several employers. The employers could be separate entities within the same political jurisdiction negotiating with different bargaining units, or unions or employers from differ-ent political jurisdictions joining together to develop common bargaining strate-gies. It should be emphasized that it is the informal union or employer activities that comprise multilateral bargaining in this instance, since the formalization of multiemployer relationships constitutes a redefinition of the bargaining structure to expand the bilateral negotiations to several employers. What was previously an attempt by either unions or employers to affect bilateral negotiations of individual units by developing common bargaining strategies becomes intraor-ganizational bargaining as the individual units are combined. As an example, the formation of a negotiator's organization in New Jersey's two-year public colleges, comprising the chief negotiators from the separate bargaining units at each college, represents a *de facto* expansion of the employer bargaining team beyond the bilateral negotiations at individual institutions. The unions at the colleges have similar statewide organizations that have the same purposes. If the two-year colleges were later combined into a single statewide unit, then the employer interactions combined with other employers and union interactions with other unions (or other locals of same union) would then represent intraorganizational bargaining.

In essence what the parties are indicating when they attempt to expand the bargaining structure, informally or formally, across several employers is that the decision-making authority (bargaining power) of the smaller units on many issues is insufficient. They are attempting to create pressure on the bilateral negotiations. The major difference between this type of multilateral bargaining and the other types is that the respective sides attempt to change the membership of their respective bargaining teams at a *common* level of employer. In the other forms the parties, usually the unions, attempt to change the *other* side's bargaining team by going to *different levels* of unions or employers in the same organization.

The development of informal multiemployer relationships in the public sector have been quite common. Kornbluh reported on such activity in Michigan school districts [20], and Feuille *et al.* reported on cooperation across municipal employers [21]. The author's study of the New Jersey higher education experience also turned up several examples of multiemployer relationships.

These informal relationships in time may lead to a broadening of the bargaining unit to encompass the cooperating groups. Despite the popularity of multiemployer bargaining in the private sector [22], it has been very slow to emerge in the public sector, even though there are a number of apparent advantages to employers of such arrangements. Pegnetter noted the advantages of multiemployer relationships as: 1) protection against whipsawing; 2) avoidance of costly duplication; 3) greater expertise at the bargaining table; and 4) flexibility of bargaining structure, that is, the arrangements can be abandoned or altered when their usefulness has dissipated [23].

At the federal level some multiunit negotiations have emerged. In addition to coalescing for the advantages noted above, Pegnetter felt the fact that one union was involved in each of the multiunit arrangements reduced internal union problems. Also, the narrow scope of negotiations limited the possibilities for internal bargaining differences for both the unions and the employers [23, p. 13].

The experience at the state and local level has been extremely limited. Kornbluh reported a few examples from school bargaining in Michigan [20, p. 522]. Still, he indicated that the reluctance of the boards to enter such arrangements has led to attempts by the Michigan Education Association to coordinate the bargaining of contracts with similar provisions with individual boards [20, p. 523]. The different associations hold formal representation elections tying the districts together on the union side, but the prime functions of the organization are to provide trained negotiators and to coordinate negotiations across districts.

The findings of Fueille *et al.* provide insight into why more state and local units do not engage in multilateral bargaining [24]. They identified several environmental factors that created greater opportunities for multiemployer bargaining: 1) highly competitive product markets and undifferentiated products; 2) operations in the same labor markets; 3) close geographical proximity; and 4) the same union dealing with many small employers [24, p. 132]. In the public sector, the labor markets may be similar, but public employers often enjoy a product market monopoly, and each employer operated in an independent political jurisdiction.   For these reasons, they found no permanent multiemployer bargaining in the 225 municipal employers studied [24, p. 134]. They concluded that the public employers in their study were not ready to trade highly desired autonomy for the advantages of multiemployer bargaining. They did find a degree of information-sharing across the political jurisdictions, so eventually this type of activity may evolve into more formal arrangements [24, pp. 135-136]. They concluded, "While multiemployer bargaining among local governments has been touted as a very worthwhile phenomenon, our study indicates that it is a phenomenon whose time has not yet come" [24, pp. 135-136].   In the meantime, informal interactions between unions or employers that cross employer boundaries will continue to be used in an attempt to affect bilateral negotiations of each employer, a form of multilateral bargaining that may eventually produce changes in bilateral relationships.

Third-Party Participation

In the public sector the greater visibility of governmental activities to the public, and the predominance of service activities, particularly those of the people-processing type, create opportunities for the users of public services (communities and the people being processed) to become involved in collective bargaining negotiations [25]. In fact, the term multilateral bargaining was originally developed to refer to this type of third-party activities in bargaining [5].   The parties to negotiations may seek to encourage the participation of these groups to enhance their respective power at the bargaining table; also, these groups may often become involved in order to protect their own perceived interests. The effect of their involvement would be to influence the outcomes of negotiations. The participation of community groups in multilateral bargaining activities is more likely to occur where the missions of the public agencies bring them into close contact with the local communities.

To date, the bulk of this type of multilateral bargaining has developed in educational institutions—students in higher education and community groups in elementary and secondary districts, particularly in urban areas.

Cheng argues for more student and community involvement in teacher negotiations because he feels that one of the major effects of teacher bargaining has been to exclude parents and other groups from educational policy-making due to the way in which bargaining has centralized decision-making. He recommends the following alternative solutions [26] :

> First, encouraging unions and boards to seek community input during the formation of bargaining demands; second, establishing multilevel bargaining whereby supplementary agreements to the master contract are negotiated with regional and/or local school boards; third, permitting citizens to view negotiations in open bargaining sessions; fourth, granting observer status to community groups and allowing observers to report to the public; and, fifth, introducing multiparty negotiations in which a third force would be formally recognized at the bargaining table.

Cheng also indicated that [26, p. 155] :

> It is my position that citizen involvement may be appropriate in any negotiations, public or private, where community interests are at stake. For example, there is every reason to consider citizen participation in contract negotiations in the automobile, steel, and communications industries. . . . Certainly the consumer movement, while it lacks a sharp political focus, illustrates the desire of citizens to have a say in processes whose outcomes affect the quality and price of critical consumer goods.

While Cheng's research indicated that examples of each of the alternative forms of participation could be cited, at this point in time community or student participation in negotiations in school districts is not pervasive, and it occurs primarily where there are community problems, particularly in urban areas, that carry over into the operation of the schools [26, p. 171] .

Although students in school districts have rarely been involved in teacher negotiations, students in higher education institutions have been involved to a greater, yet still limited, degree. Indeed, student lobbies in Oregon and Montana have succeeded in having statutes passed mandating student participation, in Montana on the employer side of the table. As pointed out by Shark, Brouder, and associates, student participation has ranged from consultation on bargaining issues outside of the bargaining room to varying degrees of participation in the bargaining room, from observer status (Long Island University) to some participation (Massachusetts state colleges), to direct third-party negotiation (Massachusetts state colleges on student issues) [27] . Most negotiations still proceed, however, without student involvement, particularly in the two-year colleges.

Some participation of client groups has occurred in other types of public organizations, but experience in this area has not been extensive, or at least it has been widely reported [28].

OTHER CONTRIBUTING FACTORS

In addition to the organizational context and bargaining process variables discussed above, there are a number of other variables indicated in Figure 1 that likely have differential effects on the incidence of multilateral bargaining. Except for a study by Kochan [29], there has been little empirical testing of these variables. Most appear to be relevant because they tend to effect the power balance of the parties. Some of these factors have been touched upon in the above discussion.

External Environment

Economic Conditions

When the employer is forced to hold the line on economic increases, it could be expected that unions would try to exhaust all procedural alternatives to increase the economic package. The state union coalition to the New Jersey legislature and governor, in the example cited in the introduction, was partially motivated by a difficult economic climate in the state of New Jersey.

Bargaining Legislation

It might also be expected that the more comprehensive the bargaining legislation, the less apt unions will be to use multilateral bargaining tactics. The basic argument here is that the more public sector bargaining develops into a private sector model, the less likely multilateral bargaining tactics will be needed by public unions. For example, it would be expected that where public employees have the right to strike, they would be much less interested in end-running activities or forming coalitions with other groups if they can use whatever power they have to withhold services at the level of bargaining. Of course, the factors normally affecting the bargaining power of the employees would come into play, and it could be expected that the weaker bargaining units would continue to enhance their power in any way open to them. Alternatively, perhaps the unions would exhaust all multilateral opportunities before using the ultimate weapon. With the limited right to strike or compulsory arbitration available in some states, a more extensive empirical test of this hypothesis is now possible. In the one study testing the impact of the bargaining law, no relationship between the nature of the law and the incidence of multilateral bargaining was found [29, p. 156].

Organizational Contexts

Degree of Professionalism and Experience of Employer Negotiators

It could be expected that the greater the training and experience of the employer negotiators, the greater the likelihood that the employer negotiators, through intraorganizational bargaining tactics, can minimize the incidence of multilateral bargaining. Again, the only test of this relationship found no correlation [29, p. 156].

Size

In larger organizations, it might be expected that larger labor relations staffs and more difficult communications patterns would lead to a greater formalization of the bargaining process and, thus less multilateral bargaining. Little evidence was found to support this assumption [29, p. 157]. Size is also likely correlated with a greater diffusion of employer authority, however, and, as argued above, it is expected that more diffusion creates more multilateral bargaining opportunities.

Union Context

Degree of Professionalism and Experience of Union Negotiators

As with employer negotiators, it would be expected that more highly trained and seasoned union negotiators would be able to achieve their ends without multilateral bargaining tactics because 1) they can better achieve internal consensus through the use of intraorganizational tactics, thus, minimizing factionalism, and 2) they can extract what they want from the bilateral process without resorting to multilateral bargaining. On the other hand, experienced union negotiators will 1) be quicker to sense internal management disagreements that they can use to their advantage or 2) be more aware of where the real power lies on certain issues and, thus, be less likely to waste much time with the bilateral process.

Union Political Power

It could be expected that the greater the union's political power, the greater the likelihood that the union will engage in multilateral bargaining. An impending election may serve to enhance a union's political power, particularly if a democratic incumbent is running hard for reelection and needs union support. Kochan's study supported the hypothesis in the expected direction [29, p. 153]. Feuille also confirmed this hypothesis with the following examples [25, p. 162]:

The Detroit Police Officer's Association had improved access to the mayor's offices because of its endorsement of former Wayne County Sheriff Roman Gribbs for mayor. In 1969 the Seattle Police Guild endorsed and made a contribution to mayoral candidate Wes Uhlman; within two months of his election Uhlman signed a police union contract with [which] both union and management interviewees were characterized as generous. In 1970, a midwestern city council approved a generous police contract; interview comments portrayed the reluctant approval as an exchange for the union's assistance in securing passage of state legislation enabling the city to levy a sales tax. . . .

Homogeneity of Union Representation Across Bargaining Units

Union coalitions are notoriously unstable (for example, the NEA-AFT merger in New York state), so they are more likely to develop across several bargaining units or employers where the same union represents all units. Pegnetter pointed this out as one of the important determinants of the multiunit coalitions in the federal service [30]. In the private sector, as well, the most stable union alliances have involved various locals of the same international union, such as the UAW in the automobile industry and the United Steelworkers of America (USW) in the steel industry [31].

Bargaining Process

Scope of Bargaining

The scope of negotiations could be expected to have an affect on the incidence of multilateral bargaining. As pointed out by Pegnetter in his analysis of the federal sector, a narrow scope encourages multiunit bargaining because it minimizes the issues over which disagreement can arise within the union or management hierarchy: that is, the internal decision-making process of each side is facilitated [30]. A narrow scope also means that much of the real decision-making power resides elsewhere in the organization, for example, in the legislature, so multilateral bargaining is necessary to reach the source of power. Coalition bargaining of New York state employees emerged when pensions were statutorily removed from the scope of negotiations. Thus, the more the legislature gets involved in setting conditions of employment, the more intense the lobbying activities with which it is going to be confronted from both sides of the table. In fact, one danger is that under collective bargaining public employers and unions will attempt to legislate changes that they cannot get at the bargaining table. The bargaining statute and its relationship to existing statutes on employee working conditions is key here. That is, which takes precedence, the bargaining statute or the existing statutes on employee working conditions?

Nature of Bargaining Relationship

Local informal negotiations are unlikely to develop where the relationship is a contentious one. As pointed out by Walton and McKersie, a high-conflict, adversary relationship is certain to interfere with the "number of matters" with which the parties deal informally in "active consultation" outside the contract [8, p. 202]. Unions will also likely resort to end-running tactics more often in such situations. Any number of factors could contribute to adversary relationships from both sides of the table, but Kochan hypothesized that "the weaker the commitment of management decision-makers to collective bargaining, the more likely that multilateral bargaining will occur" [29, p. 145]. However, his data did not support his hypothesis [29, p. 155]. The age of the bargaining relationship may also minimize multilateral bargaining as the relationship formalizes, although Kochan found no such relationship [29, p. 155].

Use of Impasse Procedures or Threat to Strike

The more visible the ongoing negotiations to the political leaders and the public, the more likely that multilateral bargaining will occur. Moskow and McLennan predicted, for example, that third-party interest in negotiations would particularly accelerate as a strike deadline neared [5, pp. 230–231]. In a recent New Jersey two-year college strike, for example, shortly before the strike the students threatened to get an injunction to stop it. Moskow and McLennan predicted that the mission of the organization would moderate third-party interest, that interest being highest in public education and social welfare strikes, and lower in police and garbage strikes [5]. Kochan found a positive relationship between the use of impasse procedures and the incidence of multilateral bargaining between unions and city leaders (union leadership-employer faction coalitions) [29, p. 153].

Bargaining Outcomes

The more divergent the terms and conditions of employment of a bargaining unit from other similar units, the more likely it is that the union will engage in multilateral bargaining. In other words, the historical output of bargaining can stimulate the use of multilateral tactics where the unit members perceive themselves to be in inferior positions. In Newark, New Jersey, for example [32]:

> Ignoring by Mayor Kenneth A. Gibson of the plight of city employees who receive only half the pay of their counterparts in Essex County employment has prompted leaders of Essex Council No. 1, New Jersey Civil Service Association, to talk of reviving the city-wide coalition of public employees.

EFFECTS OF MULTILATERAL BARGAINING

The organizational impact of multilateral bargaining is varied, depending on the specific type employed.

Union leadership or union faction coalitions with levels of employer above the bargaining table reinforces the centralization of authority, which is one product of collective bargaining generally. As seen in examples cited in previous discussions, union coalitions formed against a common employer or across political jurisdictions sometimes lead to formal redefinitions of bargaining units, multi-employer negotiations, or both. Union mergers can be another consequence.

On the one hand, the development of broader informal or formal bargaining structures represents an adaptation to the power needs of employers and unions as they seek out the proper locus of decision-making in public organizations, particularly on economic issues where politics plays an important role. One effect of centralization, of course, is to relieve lower level employers of the flexibility they should have to respond to and resolve local employee problems, particularly on issues where uniformity of policy across all departments, one advantage of centralized negotiations, is not appropriate for widely varying working conditions. Additionally, the centralization of decision-making to the highest level may also mean that public sector bargaining becomes more politicized than it needs to be. Finally, if the politicians end up making most of the major decisions, it will be difficult over the long run to develop highly professional labor relations staffs. If the threat of undermining by end-running is persistent, then it is likely that morale will suffer. The dilemma is summarized quite nicely by Kornbluh [20, p. 527] :

> Collective bargaining structures are often a trade-off between increased power, efficiency, and equitable effects of uniformity, on the one hand, and the benefits of more localized decision-making on the other. . . .

On the other hand, the development of union leadership and union faction coalitions with lower levels of employers represents an adaptation to the high level of decision-making under collective bargaining in large organizations as the parties seek to protect local autonomy. When conducted on an informal basis, these negotiations have the opposite effect of end-runs in the upper direction, that is, local policies emerge that are inconsistent across departments. Thus, the bargaining efficiency advantages of large units is reduced somewhat. One effect of these local negotiations was noted by Pegnetter. A multiple employer coalition between the International Association of Firefighters (IAFF) and Minnesota's Twin Cities failed because disagreements at the multiemployer table "soon were 'supplemented' by clandestine, separate deals with individual locals. The multiemployer negotiations were soon dissolved and were abandoned" [30, p. 14] .

Another effect of informal local negotiations is the institutionalization of this activity into formal local bargaining over local issues, such as occurred at the New Jersey state colleges. State officials had strongly opposed local negotiations initially, but subsequently agreed to formalize the substantial amount of local negotiating that was taking place. The signal here is that local negotiations should not be viewed with alarm. Rather, they should be viewed as natural adaptations to the needs of local employers and employees to respond to local problems.

It can be argued that third-party bargaining by students or the public democratizes bargaining along the lines suggested by Cheng, so that the parties of direct interest have an input to changes in employer working conditions that may affect them, an input that has decreased under the decentralizing effects of collective bargaining [26, pp. 153-174]. On the other hand, Summers argues that the employer negotiating team "represents the summarized and consolidated interest of the groups opposing the employees' interest [33]. He notes at another point, "They [public employees] are not one interest group among many in multilateral bargaining, but rather stand alone confronting the combined opposition of all the other interest groups" [33]. He would likely argue that third-party presence at the bargaining table would provide the public with two bites of the apple, one by representatives of elected officials, the other by the public doing the voting. Since experience with third-party negotiations is not widespread, and research reports on the effects of third-party bargaining are even less frequent, it is not possible at this point to draw generalizations about third-party negotiations. Some union and employer negotiators, however, after initial misgivings about third-party participation have not found the consequences all unfavorable [34].

ACCOMMODATIONS TO MULTILATERAL BARGAINING

Shaw and Clark have a negative perspective on one type of multilateral bargaining: "If collective bargaining is going to work in the public sector, it is necessary that the 'end run' be eliminated" [35]. But it has been the thesis here that the various types of multilateral bargaining that develop in collective bargaining, public or private, are not aberrations. Rather, these activities represent natural adaptations to organizational structure and authority distribution, bargaining structure, and, of course, the derivative issue of bargaining power [36]. As such, these activities should provide signals as to how organizations should accommodate to the pressures that create multilateral bargaining. Thus, the question is not how can multilateral bargaining be eliminated, but how can it be minimized by 1) institutionalizing and, thus, controlling some of its forms, and 2) improving the intraorganizational bargaining expertise of the parties to minimize factions.

Experience indicates that in broad units local negotiations are likely to take place even in the absence of formal provisions for such activity. Experience also produces the generalization that decisions on some issues, particularly economic issues, are centralized, usually in a political governing body. Given these ground rules, it is apparent that accommodations to multilateral bargaining will necessarily require a multiple-tiered approach. If bargaining units are to be very broad, a master contract should be negotiated, and provision should be made for local negotiations. The number of levels of local negotiations should be related to the complexity of the organization and the locus of authority on various issues. The institutionalization of local negotiations preserves local employer authority and provides some control over the development of inconsistent policies. Local negotiations also tend to reduce union factionalism and permit the parties to concentrate on local problems. As Summers pointed out, factionalism makes it difficult for a union to meet diverse needs. Thus, in a heterogeneous bargaining unit, the employer may be confronted with large numbers of demands because the union is unable to assign priorities to the demands of its various constituencies [37].

One disadvantage of local negotiations under a master contract was pointed out by Chernish from the UAW experience; local strikes over local issues can disrupt company operations [38]. But local strikes over local issues would seem to be preferred to companywide strikes over local issues. The same conclusion would be true in the public sector, where a local strike of state employees would have less impact than a statewide strike.

An alternative bargaining structure would consist of smaller, more homogeneous bargaining units, linked together where necessary by pattern bargaining or union coalitions. In fact, Martin argues that the development of pattern bargaining for state employees eliminates the need for statewide occupational units [19, p. 11]. Examples of institutionalized coalitions are evolving in several states. In New York, the removal of pensions from negotiations has led to the formation of two union coalitions for the purpose of providing input on this issue, one coalition for police and fire pensions, and another for all other public employees [39]. In Oregon, the state had set up six coalitions combining 82 separate bargaining units, but the Oregon Employment Relations Board objected to those coalitions not including like classifications, and to a coalition of coalitions proposed by the state for negotiating changes in state personnel rules. The board also rejected the state's suggestion that the issue under discussion should dictate the bargaining unit composition of the joint sessions [40]. Based on the discussions in this chapter, the board's findings seem ill-founded, since the state's proposals seemed to be an innovative accommodation to local and statewide concerns.

An alternative to statewide coalitions or pattern bargaining would be the use of "lump sum" budgeting for economic issues. In other words, the total dollars to be included in a budget for employee salary or benefit increases could be determined by the legislative body, in consultation perhaps with a union coalition through a legislative bargaining committee [41]. The allocation of the monies to different benefits could then be accomplished across the table with the different bargaining units. A union representing state highway workers may want all the funds in an across-the-board increase. Faculty and university administrators may want to use a portion of the money for merit increases or to provide a greater salary increase to junior faculty. State police may desire an improved uniform allowance, or fewer working hours. Smaller political units, such as school districts, already utilize such procedures, and some centralized state bargaining authorities, such as the New York Office of Employee Relations, also try to shape the increases to meet unique unit needs. Yet smaller bargaining units with economic negotiations at the agency level may be more responsive to organizational needs. Local economic negotiations would also deal with one problem of dual-level negotiations; the negotiations of primarily economic issues at one level and primarily noneconomic issues at another level prevent trade-offs between the two in negotiations. A higher education negotiator in Minnesota felt that this was a major problem of centralized bargaining on state issues [42].

Another desirable change is related to the scope of negotiations. Prior to collective bargaining, employee groups, such as state education associations, proposed and lobbied for legislation aimed at improving the working conditions of public employees. Now, under collective bargaining, some of the legislation sought by employee groups has placed practical and often legal limitations on the scope of negotiations. Indeed, both unions and employers continue to seek statutory changes in employee working conditions, sometimes because of an ability to achieve the desired objectives at the bargaining table. To minimize this type of multilateral bargaining, it is suggested that consideration be given by legislatures or governing bodies to 1) resist legislating or 2) remove from legislative control matters that can be more appropriately dealt with in other forums. Economic decisions will likely always be centralized, but the decentralization of other issues would have the potential for reducing employer factionalism and would return the responsibility for dealing with employee problems to professional managers.

Various accommodations to third-party participation in negotiations already have been outlined elsewhere. The major point to be made here is that if there is serious and persistent pressure from student groups or the public to get involved in negotiations, then arrangements that institutionalize this involvement are likely preferable to uncontrolled activities that are disruptive to negotiations.

Finally, improvements in intraorganizational bargaining expertise by both union and employer officials would facilitate the development of consensus within their respective organizations. The complex structure of public organizations will not permit the derivative factions to be elminated, but the failure to deal with the diverse needs intraorganizationally lays the groundwork for multilateral bargaining.

As Shaw and Clark point out, basic to effective bilateral negotiations is a properly organized, trained, and staffed labor relations function [35]. Extending training to all employer personnel, including governing bodies, would also sensitize them concerning the need to develop a cohesive bargaining strategy.

Unions, as well, should take steps to monitor, and be sensitive to, the needs of its diverse membership to minimize the development of union faction-employer coalitions. The failure to do so can be costly; the unresolved problems of factions within the New Jersey state college faculty unit, as noted previously, eventually cost the NEA the bargaining unit. It should be noted, however, that the diverse units typical of the public sector complicate the unions' intraorganizational problems.

CONCLUSION

It was the purpose of this paper to describe and analyze one of the more complex issues related to the development of public sector bargaining systems: multilateral bargaining. Though the framework set out was derived from existing partial theories and empirical studies, much work remains to be accomplished before the relationships among all factors are fully understood. Nevertheless, the current state of knowledge on multilateral bargaining provides us with some guidelines for practical policy development.

The important point was made that multilateral bargaining activities in both the private and public sectors should be viewed not as aberrations to be eliminated in any way possible, but rather as adaptations to the stresses and strains inherent in complex organizations, as the parties seek to enhance relative bargaining power on specific issues in dispute. The emergence of multilateral bargaining, in fact, provides important signals for ways to minimize its more undesirable consequences. By institutionalizing and, thus, controlling some of the forms of multilateral bargaining, and by improving intraorganizational bargaining tactics, the needs of both union and employer factions can be more easily accommodated.

Finally, structural factors and organizational functions appear to be primary determinants of the various multilateral bargaining activities. Still, such other factors as the availability of the right to strike, the scope of negotiations, the nature of the bargaining relationship, and the level of union and employer expertise also likely affect the incidence of multilateral bargaining. A sensitivity to the presence or absence of these factors in particular bargaining relationships will facilitate the development of useful accommodations to multilateral bargaining.

NOTES AND REFERENCES

1. For example, recent information on the extent of organization of federal employees indicates that 58% are in exclusive bargaining units, 83% of the wage board employees, and 51% of the general service employees. US Civil Service Commission, *Union Recognition in the Federal Government*, Washington, D.C.: Office of Labor-Management Relations, US Civil Service Commission, November 1976, p. 21.
2. Ayres, Richard M., and Thomas L. Wheelen, eds. *Collective Bargaining in the Public Sector—Selected Readings in Law Enforcement.* Gaithersburg, Md.: International Association of Chiefs of Police, 1977. Cresswell, Anthony M., and Michael J. Murphy. *Education and Collective Bargaining.* Berkeley, Calif.: McCutchan Publishing, 1976. Gerwin, Donald, ed. *The Employment of Teachers.* Berkeley, Calif.: McCutchan Publishing, 1974. Nesbitt, Murray B. *Labor Relations in the Federal Government Service.* Washington, D.C.: Bureau of National Affairs, 1976. Smith, Russell A., Harry T. Edwards, and R. Theodore Clark, Jr. *Labor Relations Law in the Public Sector.* Indianapolis, Ind.: Bobbs-Merrill, 1974.
3. These complications have led some authors to suggest that collective bargaining is not appropriate in the public sector. See Harry H. Wellington and Ralph K. Winter, Jr., *The Unions and the Cities*, Washington, D.C.: Brookings Institution, 1971, particularly ch. 1, pp. 7–24.
4. Shark, Alan R., Kathleen Brouder, and associates. *Students and Collective Bargaining.* Washington, D.C.: National Student Educational Fund, 1976.
5. McLennan, Kenneth, and Michael H. Moskow. "Multilateral Bargaining in the Public Sector." *Collective Bargaining in Government.* Englewood Cliffs, N.J.: Prentice-Hall, 1972, pp. 227–228.
6. Juris, Hervey A., and Peter Feuille. *Police Unionism.* Lexington, Mass.: D. C. Heath, 1973, pp. 45–50.
7. Begin, James P. *Faculty Bargaining: A Conceptual Discussion.* New Brunswick, N.J.: Institute of Management and Labor Relations, Rutgers Univeristy, 1973, p. 51.
8. Walton, Richard E., and Robert B. McKersie. *A Behavioral Theory of Labor Negotiations.* New York: McGraw-Hill, 1965, p. 5.
9. Kochan, Thomas A. "Resolving Internal Management Conflicts for Labor Negotiations." In *Public Sector Labor Relations.* Edited by David Lewin, Peter Feuille, and Thomas A. Kochan. New Jersey: Thomas Horton and Daughters, 1977, p. 127.
10. As noted previously, a Montana statute gave students a legal status as members of the employer bargaining team. Sunshine bargaining laws also give the public a right to observe negotiations.
11. Commons, John R. "Labor and Administration." In *Collective Bargaining in City X: Government Labor Relations in Transition.* Edited by James A. Belasco. Personnel Report, No. 662. Chicago: Public Personnel Association, 1966.
12. See, for example, Kochan, "A Theory of Multilateral Collective Bargaining in City Governments," Peter Feuille, "Police Labor Relations and Multilateralism," and Clyde W. Summers, "Public Employee Bargaining: A Political Perspective," in *Public Sector Labor Relations*, edited by Lewin *et al.*

13. A number of the concepts used to generate the framework were deduced from available partial theories, while others were grounded in empirical research conducted by the author in faculty collective bargaining.

14. It is not argued here that multilateral bargaining occurs only in the context of formalized bargaining relationships. There are many examples of prebargaining multilateral bargaining activities, for example, the lobbying of federal employee groups.

15. Cooperative efforts among unions are not new to the American labor movement. The coordinated bargaining activities of the unions at General Electric illustrate one such example. See William N. Chernish, *Coalition Bargaining: A Study of Union Tactics and Public Policy*, Philadelphia, Pa.: University of Pennsylvania, 1969, p. 253.

16. Subchapter V of Chapter III, enacted by Chapter 612, 1966L., as amended by A.B. 475, 1971L, Wisconsin.

17. See, for example, Lee C. Shaw and Theodore R. Clark, "The Practical Differences between Public and Private Sector Collective Bargaining," in *Public Sector Labor Relations,* edited by Lewin *et al.*, pp. 112–124; and Summers, "Public Employee Bargaining," pp. 44–52.

18. Gilroy, Thomas P., and Anthony C. Russo. *Bargaining Unit Issues: Problems, Criteria, Tactics.* Public Employment Relations Library, 43. Chicago, Ill.: International Personnel Management Association, 1973. Martin, James E. "Appropriate Bargaining Units for State Employees." Paper presented at the Thirty-Seventh Annual Meeting of the Academy of Management, Kissimmee, Florida, August 15, 1977. Pegnetter, Richard. *Multiemployer Bargaining in the Public Sector: Purposes and Experiences.* Public Employment Relations Library, 52. Chicago, Ill.: International Personnel Management Assn. Rock, Eli. "Bargaining Units in the Public Service: The Problem of Proliferation." In *Collective Bargaining in Government.* Edited by J. Joseph Loewenberg and Michael H. Moskow. Englewood Cliffs, N.J.: Prentice-Hall, 1972, pp. 117–126.

19. Martin. "Appropriate Bargaining Units for State Employees." As cited above, p. 10.

20. Kornbluh, Hy. "Public Schools–Multi-Unit Common Bargaining Agents: A Next Phase in Teacher-School Board Bargaining in Michigan?" In *Proceedings of the 1976 Annual Spring Meeting.* Madison, Wis.: Industrial Relations Research Assn., 1976, p. 521.

21. Feuille, Peter, *et al.* "Multiemployer Negotiations Among Local Governments." In *Public Sector Labor Relations.* Edited by Lewin *et al.* Pp. 135–136.

22. Chernish. *Coalition Bargaining.* Pp. 254–255. As noted by Chernish, there have been numerous examples of multiemployer bargaining in the private sector, for example, in the steel, construction, and metals industries.

23. Pegnetter. *Multiemployer Bargaining.* Pp. 21–26.

24. Feuille *et al.* "Multiemployer Negotiations Among Local Governments." Pp. 131–137.

25. Feuille. "Police Labor Relations." P. 161.

26. Cheng, Charles W. "Community Representation in Teacher Collective Bargaining: Problems and Prospects." *Harvard Educational Review* 46(1976): 167.

27. See Shark and Brouder, *Students and Collective Bargaining*, pp. 29–38. Also see Donald E. Walters, "Do Students Have A Place in Collective Bargaining?" Pp. 97–101; Alan Shark, "Do Students Have Any Place in Collective Bargaining?" pp. 102–105; Norman Swenson, "Do Students Have Any Place in Collective Bargaining?" pp. 106–110, in *Collective Bargaining in Higher Education Proceedings, Second Annual Conference*, New York: National Center for the Study of Collective Bargaining in Higher Education, Baruch College-CUNY, 1974.

28. As reported by Tia Schneider Denenberg, prisoner bargaining could possibly affect the negotiated rights of prison guards. See her "The Application of Labor-Management Dispute Settlement Procedures to Prison Inmate Grievances," in *Proceedings of the Twenty-Ninth Annual Winter Meeting*, Madison, Wis.: Industrial Relations Research Assn., 1977, pp. 170–176.

29. Kochan, "A Theory of Multilateral Bargaining," pp. 142–159.

30. Pegnetter. *Multiemployer Bargaining*. P. 13.

31. Lahne, Herbert J. "Coalition Bargaining and the Future of Union Structure." *Labor Law Journal* 17(1967).

32. "Ignored Newark Workers May Restore Coalition." *The Shield Civil Service News* (Sept. 18, 1976): 1, 8.

33. Summers. "Public Employee Bargaining." P. 48.

34. For example, see Walters, "Do Students Have a Place?" pp. 97–101; and Swenson, "Do Students Have Any Place?" pp. 106–110.

35. See Shaw and Clark, "The Practical Differences between Public and Private Sector Collective Bargaining," p. 114.

36. George H. Hildebrand has hypothesized that private sector union coalition bargaining derives from bargaining power deficiencies of the unions; in Chernish, *Coalition Bargaining*, p. 258. Kochan's finding also supports this statement for the public sector; Kochan, "A Theory of Multilateral Bargaining," p. 157.

37. Summers, "Public Employee Bargaining."

38. Chernish. *Coalition Bargaining*. P. 267.

39. "PERB Recommended to Administer Two Statewide Pension Coalitions." *PERB News* 7(1974): 1.

40. "Oregon Board Rules on Union Security, Coalition Bargaining at State Level." *Government Employee Relations Report*, No. 702. April 4, 1977, p. 16.

41. Derber, Milton, Peter Pashler, and Mary Beth Ryan. *Collective Bargaining by State Governments in the Twelve Midwestern States*. Urbana-Champaign, Ill.: Institute of Labor and Industrial Relations, University of Illinois, 1974, p. 76. The state of Wisconsin is reported to have a legislative committee of this type.

42. Begin, James P., Theodore C. Settle, and Laurie Berke-Weiss. *Community College Collective Bargaining in New Jersey*. New Brunswick, N.J.: Department of Research, Institute of Management and Labor Relations, Rutgers, The State University, 1977, p. 55.

Index

Abstract relational categories, 6
Academic freedom, 80
Accountability, 608–748
 differentiated from accounting, 651
 of hospital administrators, 804
 improved technology in, 660–661
 organizational, 651–653, 696, 766
 origins of, 689
 in public enterprise, 689–719
 and public funds, 656
 scientific, 83–84
 in service organizations, 719
 stages of, 653–659
 standard practices of, 79
 systems, 92–93
 in universities, 693
Accounting, 455
 and accountability, 651
 costs, 687
 definition of, 467
Accreditation, 658
Adaptation, as feedback, 10
Adaptive controller, 51–52, 56
Adaptive planning, 432
Administrative sciences, 81
Administrators, 302, 643, 644, 646,
 651, 653, 656, 892
 accountability of, 804
 audits, 658–659
 choices of, 756
 concerns of, 805
 and conflict, 779
 and control, 850
 in education, 733, 757, 903
 and evaluation, 629
 governmental, 884
 in hospitals, 853, 859, 862, 866, 867,
 875, 876
 human service, 751, 752, 753, 799
 ideologic responsibilities of, 179

Administrators (*cont.*)
 and long-range plans, 644
 mission of, 795
 and negotiators, 891
 and policy-making, 433, 476–477
 and PPB, 742
 problems of, 475, 657, 754, 800, 811
 public. *See* Public administrators
 role of, 89, 650, 771
 and steady-state operations, 770
 and strategic manager, 94
 systems, 85
 and teams, 801, 810
 training of, 86, 793, 802, 805, 809, 810
 values of, 228, 246
Advisory board, 107
AEC, 91
Affluence, 217–219
Algorithms
 contrasted with Gestalt-Systemic
 approach, 87, 88
 and static systems, 77
Ambiguous world, 334–361
 and costly procedures, 344
 and policy-makers, 341–342, 360–361
 and shared learning, 347
 and specific procedures, 349–359
 understanding of, 348
Amortization, 79
Amplification strategy, 18
Amplificatory trend, 9
Analysis
 of constraints, 8, 9, fig. 2
 static methods of, 79
 in system dynamics, 108
Anonymous method. *See* Delphi method
Anthropological theory, 5
Anthropology, 758
 and scientific management, 80
Anti-Semitism, 167